AN INTRODUCTION TO
DERIVATIVES
FOURTH EDITION

Don M. Chance
Virginia Tech

THE DRYDEN PRESS
Harcourt Brace College Publishers
Fort Worth   Philadelphia   San Diego   New York   Orlando   Austin   San Antonio
Toronto   Montreal   London   Sydney   Tokyo

Publisher	George Provol
Executive Editor	Mike Reynolds
Product Manager	Craig Johnson
Developmental Editor	Terri House
Project Editor	Jim Patterson
Art Director	Bill Brammer
Production Manager	Carlyn Hauser

Cover Photography: Stephen Green-Armytage

ISBN: 0-03-024483-8
Library of Congress Catalog Card Number: 97-67526

Address for orders: The Dryden Press, 6277 Sea Harbor Drive, Orlando, FL 32887-6777, 1-800-782-4479

Address for editorial correspondence: The Dryden Press, 301 Commerce Street, Suite 3700, Fort Worth, TX 76102

Web site address: http://www.hbcollege.com

The Dryden Press, Dryden, and the Dryden Press logo are registered trademarks of Harcourt Brace & Company.

Printed in the United States of America

7 8 9 0 1 2 3 4 5 6   039   9 8 7 6 5 4 3 2

The Dryden Press
Harcourt Brace College Publishers

The Dryden Press Series in Finance

Amling and Droms
Investment Fundamentals

Berry and Young
Managing Investments: A Case Approach

Boone, Kurtz, and Hearth
Planning Your Financial Future

Brigham
Brigham's Interactive Guide to Finance
CD-ROM

Brigham and Houston
Fundamentals of Financial Management
Eighth Edition

Brigham, Aberwald, and Gapenski
Finance with Lotus 1-2-3
Second Edition

Brigham, Gapenski, and Klein
1998 Cases in Financial Management: Dryden Request

Brigham and Gapenski
Financial Management: Theory and Practice
Eighth Edition

Brigham and Gapenski
Intermediate Financial Management
Fifth Edition

Brigham and Houston
Fundamentals of Financial Management: The Concise Edition

Chance
An Introduction to Derivatives
Fourth Edition

Clark, Gerlach, and Olson
Restructuring Corporate America

Cooley
Advances in Business Financial Management: A Collection of Readings
Second Edition

Dickerson, Campsey, and Brigham
Introduction to Financial Management
Fourth Edition

Eaker, Fabozzi, and Grant
International Corporate Finance

Fama and Miller
The Theory of Finance

Gardner and Mills
Managing Financial Institutions: An Asset/Liability Approach
Third Edition

Gitman and Joehnk
Personal Financial Planning
Seventh Edition

Greenbaum and Thakor
Contemporary Financial Intermediation

Harrington and Eades
Case Studies in Financial Decision Making
Third Edition

Hayes and Meerschwam
Financial Institutions: Contemporary Cases in the Financial Services Industry

Hearth and Zaima
Contemporary Investments: Security and Portfolio Analysis
Second Edition

Johnson
Issues and Readings in Managerial Finance
Fourth Edition

Kidwell, Peterson, and Blackwell
Financial Institutions, Markets, and Money
Sixth Edition

Koch
Bank Management
Third Edition

Leahigh
Pocket Guide to Finance

Maisel
Real Estate Finance
Second Edition

Maness and Zietlow
Short-Term Financial Management

Martin, Cox, and MacMinn
The Theory of Finance: Evidence and Applications

Mayes and Shank
Advanced Financial Analysis with Microsoft Excel

Mayes and Shank
*Financial Analysis with Lotus
1-2-3 for Windows*

Mayes and Shank
*Financial Analysis with
Microsoft Excel*

Mayo
*Financial Institutions,
Investments, and Management:
An Introduction*
Sixth Edition

Mayo
Investments: An Introduction
Fifth Edition

**Osteryoung, Newman, and
Davies**
*Small Firm Finance: An
Entrepreneurial Analysis*

Reilly and Brown
*Investment Analysis and
Portfolio Management*
Fifth Edition

Reilly and Norton
Investments
Fourth Edition

Sears and Trennepohl
Investment Management

Seitz and Ellison
*Capital Budgeting and Long-
Term Financing Decisions*
Second Edition

Siegel and Siegel
Futures Markets

Smith and Spudeck
*Interest Rates: Principles and
Applications*

Stickney
*Financial Reporting and
Statement Analysis: A Strategic
Perspective*
Third Edition

Weston, Besley, and Brigham
Essentials of Managerial Finance
Eleventh Edition

Reflecting the continuous evolution of the derivatives industry, this Fourth Edition introduces a number of new topics as well as many new, and hopefully, useful and interesting features.

For example, the following new topics are covered:

- The binomial term structure model of Ho and Lee
- The local expectations hypothesis
- An appendix on Monte Carlo simulation
- Mortgage securities
- Structured notes
- Basis swaps
- Managing market risk with delta, gamma, and vega
- Managing credit risk
- VaR (Value at Risk)
- The risk management function and industry, including some examples of bad risk management

Coverage is expanded for the following topics:

- Interest rate derivative pricing
- Swaptions and forward swaps
- Path-dependent options

Instructors will note that these topics reflect the growing emphasis on interest-rate derivatives and the importance of using derivatives in a comprehensive risk management function. From the time of the First Edition, which was then titled *An Introduction to Options and Futures,* this book has evolved to reflect the changes in this industry. Yet, instructors who used the First Edition will find that the basic material on options and futures remains in its place with a modicum of core changes, but numerous extensions and improvements. The primary additions have come near the end of the book, most notably the expanded coverage in Chapter 14 of interest-rate derivatives, a modification of Chapter 15 from advanced equity derivatives and strategies to just advanced derivatives and strategies that includes some advanced interest rate derivatives, and a new Chapter 16 on risk management. One interesting feature of this new chapter is a set of stories

about four widely publicized cases of bad-risk management, which led to large financial losses.

Instructors and students should hopefully appreciate the supplements, which include Microsoft PowerPoint Presentation slides, Version 7.0 for Windows 95, available to adopters. These contain most of the significant highlights of the book and can either be used as an outline that guides instructors from topic to topic or can constitute most of the details of the material presented in class. In addition to the PowerPoint files, adopters will also have access to Adobe Acrobat files containing the solutions to all end-of-chapter problems. Instructors can then provide them to students to avoid the burdensome process of obtaining copyright permission for the *Instructor's Manual* and then copying the solutions from the manual and placing them on reserve at libraries or copy centers. This feature should save instructors and students a great deal of time and will, of course, save the students money.

The Fourth Edition contains several new pedagogical features. First, each chapter has completely new beginning-of-chapter quotes. They have been chosen to provide a contemporary relevance to the topics that follow. Also, each chapter begins with a list of chapter objectives and ends with a list of key terms.

The Fourth Edition software diskette has been entirely rewritten in Microsoft Excel, Version 7.0 for Windows 95, which will generally also work in Excel 5.0 in Windows 3.1 and is included with each copy of the book. This change reflects the dominance of Excel as the preferred spreadsheet in the business world. For those who prefer Lotus 1-2-3, the spreadsheets from the Third Edition are available, but these have not been updated and will not be further supported.

An important new feature "Software Demonstrations," contains explanations, views of the spreadsheets, and examples near the topics for which the software is designed to address. In addition, I have now built the binomial option pricing model into the Black-Scholes spreadsheet so that either or both can be calculated from the same screen. This greatly facilitates the comparison of European option prices with American option prices.

Since the publication of the Third Edition, one of the most significant changes in the world has been the growth of the Internet. This book reflects those changes by incorporating a home page and E-mail addresses for various organizations, regulatory agencies, and futures and options exchanges. In addition, I shall maintain a home page for this book at the address http://www.cob.vt.edu/finance/faculty/dmc/InDrv4e.htm. This home page will contain postings of corrections and will be an easy link for instructors and students to contact me. I invite comments, criticisms, and corrections and will acknowledge the person, with his or her consent, on the home page.

Organization of the Book

Chapter 1 provides a general introduction to the subject of derivatives and a brief treatment of the basic concepts of risk, return, arbitrage, and efficient markets. It also contains information about the derivatives industry, including, where available, home page and Internet addresses of publications, organizations, agencies, and exchanges, as well as sites maintained by individuals and organizations containing extensive links to derivatives information on the Internet.

Part I covers options. It begins with Chapter 2, which presents institutional information about the options markets. Chapter 3 discusses and illustrates the theoretical foundations of option pricing and establishes the rational principles that must be mastered to understand how options are priced. Chapter 4 deals with option pricing models, specifically the binomial and Black-Scholes models. Chapter 5 covers the basic strategies of buying and selling stock, calls, and puts. Chapter 6 presents advanced trading strategies, which combine previously covered option strategies.

Part II covers forward and futures markets and the structure parallels that of Part I. Chapter 7 provides the institutional background on forward and futures markets. Chapter 8 deals with the basic principles of pricing spot instruments. Chapter 9 discusses and illustrates the principles of futures and forward pricing. Chapter 10 demonstrates how futures can be used in hedging situations. Chapter 11 presents advanced futures strategies including spread and arbitrage trading.

Part III is called Advanced Topics and includes material on many different types of derivatives. Chapter 12 covers options on futures. Chapter 13 explores foreign currency derivatives, including forwards, futures, options, and swaps. Chapter 14 covers interest rate derivatives, specifically interest rate swaps, forward rate agreements, and options. Chapter 15 deals with advanced derivatives and strategies such as equity swaps, equity-linked debt, basis swaps, structured notes, mortgage-backed securities, and exotic options. The book concludes with Chapter 16 on risk management, covering such topics as the need for risk management, the structure of the risk management industry and its participants, managing market risk, Value at Risk, managing credit risk, organizational issues in developing a risk management function, the Group of 30 Recommendations for best practices in risk management, and lessons in bad risk management from the stories of Metallgesellschaft, Orange County, Barings, and Procter & Gamble.

Use of the Book

The typical use of this book is in a one-semester course in options, options and futures, or derivatives at the advanced undergraduate or MBA level. It is almost impossible to cover the entire book in one semester but the book is sufficiently flexible to allow skipping of numerous topics and chapters.

My own one-semester course consists of Chapters 1–10, a small part of Chapter 11, Chapter 14, a part of Chapter 15, and most of Chapter 16. We are contemplating a two-semester course, however, that would allow time for coverage of the entire book. Given the growing emphasis on derivatives in the financial world, student demand, and the increasing complexity of the subject, a two-semester course is highly recommended.

Acknowledgments

Many individuals contributed greatly to this project. I would like to thank the following colleagues for participating in a survey for the Fourth Edition: Robert Brooks, Charles Cao, Gordon H. Dash, Jr., Michael L. Hemler, Riaz Hussain, Davinder K. Malhotra, Thomas W. Miller, Jr., Majed R. Muhtaseb, John Polonchek, Arlyn R. Rubash, John D. Schatzberg, Leonard J. Schneck, Garland Simmons, Elizabeth Tashjian, Alan M. Weatherford, Jill Wetmore, and Shee Q. Wong.

I would also like to thank the Dryden team led by Mike Reynolds, the finance executive editor. Terri House, the senior developmental editor, and Jim Patterson, the senior project editor, did an outstanding job reviewing the project from manuscript to bound book and were a pleasure to work with. Bill Brammer, the art director, created an appealing design for the Fourth Edition. Carlyn Hauser, the production manager, kept the project on schedule. Shirley Webster, art and literary rights editor, attended to the permissions needs, and Craig Johnson, product manager, secured our market position.

Despite our best efforts, some errors will surely remain and I accept full responsibility. I encourage you to send me your corrections and suggestions. Each new edition benefits greatly from the comments of instructors and students.

Finally, I wish to thank my wife, Jan, and my children, Kim and Ashley, for their support in my life and especially throughout the four editions of this book.

Don M. Chance
First Union Professor of Financial Risk Management
Department of Finance
Virginia Tech
Blacksburg, VA 24061-0221
dmc@vt.edu; www.cob.vt.edu/finance/faculty/dmc
September 1997

Contents

We must avoid the temptation to demonise derivatives, which are a vital tool in modern financial markets. They are so useful in managing risk that if they didn't exist, we would surely have to invent them.

ARTHUR LEVITT, Chairman, U.S. Securities and Exchange Commission
Risk/Emerging Markets Investor, April 1996

CHAPTER 1

Introduction

Derivative products have undoubtedly allowed management to achieve significant gains in the efficiency of their business, so much so that the successful use of derivatives has become an essential component of product management.

"Risk Management: Laying Firm Foundations"
Controlling Risk: Risk Magazine Special Supplement, June 1995

Chapter Objectives

■ To introduce derivatives and their markets and to explain how they relate to the markets for financial assets, real assets, and services as well as the international financial system

■ To provide brief introductions to the different types of derivatives: options, forward contracts, futures contracts, options on futures, and swaps

■ To reacquaint you with the concepts of risk preference, short selling, the risk-return relationship, and market efficiency

■ To define the important concept of theoretical fair value, which will be used throughout the book

■ To explain the relationship between spot and derivative markets through the mechanisms of arbitrage, storage, and delivery

■ To identify the role that derivative markets play through its four main advantages

■ To address some criticisms of derivatives

Few subjects command as much interest as that of making money. One way people make money is through their investments. Many people outside of the financial industry seem to know—or at least profess to know—something about stocks and bonds. Investing in stocks and bonds is a common topic at social gatherings, yet the investment world is much broader than the stock and bond markets. For example, real estate, gold, and foreign currencies also represent outlets for investing one's money.

Stocks, bonds, real estate, and such, however, are only some of the ways in which people can structure their investments. Another way is through the use of **derivatives.** Derivatives are instruments whose returns are derived from those of other instruments. That is, their performance depends on how another asset performed.

Although derivative markets have been around in some form for centuries, their growth has accelerated rapidly in the last 10 years. They are now used widely by professional investors and many individuals. They have been enthusiastically embraced by corporations and government units, who use derivatives to manage their diverse risks. The benefits of derivatives are numerous, and derivatives play an important but frequently misunderstood role in the financial world. The cost of not knowing what derivatives are is quite high. By deciding to take a course and/or read this book, you have taken the first step in an important and exciting journey that will lead you to the cutting edge of financial techniques. This book explores the characteristics of derivatives and their relationship to stocks,

bonds, and other assets. It also explains how to determine their prices and how to use them in investment and financial management strategies.

This chapter presents some introductory concepts that will bring the role of derivative markets into focus and lay the foundation for investigating these instruments. We begin by examining the structure of the economic and financial system used in modern, capitalist societies.

An Overview of the Economic/Financial System

The economic/financial system can be characterized in many ways. One way is to organize it into two types of markets: the market for real assets and services and the market for financial assets.

The Market for Real Assets and Services

Real assets are tangibles; **services** are intangibles. There are markets for tangibles, such as food, clothing, and shelter, and markets for intangibles, such as haircuts, auto repairs, and financial advice. These assets are derived from the economy's natural and human resources. Individuals organize their creativity and channel their labor into the production of goods and services that society demands.

A price system governs the operations of the market for real assets and services. Society expresses its needs by its willingness to pay a price to obtain a product or service. If that good or service can be produced and sold to earn a profit, society's needs will be met.

Most of the products and services that we purchase in these markets are offered to us through business units. However, business units require capital—the financial resource needed to acquire the labor, machinery, and managerial talent necessary for supplying society's needs. Thousands of small businesses obtain capital from a variety of sources, including local banks, relatives, and their owners' pockets. A viable economy, however, could not exist without money and capital markets, that is, the market for financial assets.

The Market for Financial Assets

A **financial asset** is a claim on an economic unit, such as a business or an individual. For example, you might borrow money from a relative by giving a promissory note. That note is a financial asset that your relative, the lender, holds and that represents a claim on you, the borrower. From your perspective, the note is a financial liability or simply a liability, since nearly all liabilities are financial.

Many financial assets, such as the stocks and bonds issued by businesses and the bonds issued by government units, trade in organized markets. After a company issues stock, the stock can, in turn, be sold by one

individual to another. An active stock market makes it easier for a company to raise equity capital by assuring investors that shares purchased from the company can be sold to other investors if necessary. The purchase of shares directly from the company takes place in the primary market, while the trading of shares among investors occurs in the secondary market.

The financial markets usually are broken down into two submarkets—money markets and capital markets. The money market is the market for short-term debt instruments. The capital market is the market for long-term debt instruments and stock issued by companies.

International Market Integration

An important phenomenon of recent years has been the tremendous growth in international markets. Fueled by advances in communications technology and the breakdown of communism, we have seen economic systems change and new financial markets develop in nearly all countries of the world. The continued growth of large multinational corporations, particularly financial institutions, has brought down barriers between countries, making it much easier to trade real and financial assets across country lines. For example, a corporation can borrow dollars from a bank in New York City or dollars from a bank in London (called Eurodollars) or yen from a bank in Tokyo and convert the yen to dollars. It can even guarantee the amount of dollars that it will have to pay back to the Japanese bank. In fact it is likely to be overwhelmed with the number of different ways it can structure a transaction utilizing the vast economic resources of the entire world.

This phenomenon whereby markets in various countries behave in a competitive and unified manner is called **international market integration.** It creates challenges and opportunities for today's financial and investment managers. It is no longer sufficient to study a country's markets in isolation. We must be fully cognizant of the interactions among markets of different countries. As Eastern Europe develops its market economies, Western Europe moves toward a unified economic/financial system, rapid growth continues in the Pacific Rim, and Japan adjusts to the pressures caused by its enormous economic power, the challenges of operating in a global market become greater indeed.

In the markets we have been describing so far, purchases and sales require that the underlying good or security be delivered either immediately or shortly thereafter. Payment usually is made immediately, although credit arrangements are sometimes used. Because of these characteristics, we refer to these markets as **cash markets** or **spot markets.** The sale is made, the payment is remitted, and the good or security is delivered.

In other situations, the good or security is to be delivered at a later date. Still other types of arrangements let the buyer or seller choose whether or not to go through with the sale. These types of arrangements are conducted in derivative markets.

Derivative Markets

In contrast to the market for financial assets, derivative markets are markets for contractual instruments whose performance is determined by how another instrument or asset performs. Notice that we referred to derivatives as contracts. Like all contracts, they are agreements between two parties—a buyer and a seller—in which each party does something for the other. These contracts have a price, and buyers try to buy as cheaply as possible while sellers try to sell as dearly as possible. This section briefly introduces the various types of derivative contracts: options, forward contracts, futures contracts, and swaps and related derivatives.

Options

An **option** is a contract between two parties—a buyer and a seller—that gives the buyer the right, but not the obligation, to purchase or sell something at a later date at a price agreed upon today.

The option buyer pays the seller a sum of money called the price or premium. The option seller stands ready to sell or buy according to the contract terms if and when the buyer so desires. An option to buy something is referred to as a **call;** an option to sell something is called a **put.** Options trade in organized markets, much like the stock market that you may already be familiar with. However, a large amount of option trading is conducted privately between two parties who find that contracting with each other may be preferable to a public transaction on the exchange. This type of market, called an over-the-counter market, was actually the first type of options market. The creation of an organized options exchange in 1973 reduced the interest in over-the-counter option markets. In recent years, however, the over-the-counter market has been revived and is now very large and widely used, mostly by corporations and financial institutions.

Most of the options that we shall focus on trade on organized options exchanges. However, the principles of pricing and using options are pretty much the same, regardless of where the option trades. Most of the options of our interest are for the purchase or sale of financial assets such as stocks or bonds. However, there are also options on futures contracts, metals, and foreign currencies. Many other types of financial arrangements, such as lines of credit, loan guaranties, and insurance, are forms of options. Moreover, stock itself is equivalent to an option on the firm's assets.

Forward Contracts

A **forward contract** is an agreement between two parties—a buyer and a seller—to purchase or sell something at a later date at a price agreed upon today. A forward contract sounds a lot like an option. However, an option carries the right, not the obligation, to go through with the transaction. If the price of the underlying good changes, the option holder may decide to forgo buying or selling at the fixed price. On the other hand, the two parties in a forward contract incur the obligation to ultimately buy and sell the good.

Although forward markets have existed in this country for a long time, they are somewhat less familiar. Unlike options markets, they have no physical facilities for trading; there is no building or formal corporate body organized as the market. They trade strictly in an over-the-counter market consisting of direct communications among major financial institutions.

Forward markets for foreign exchange have existed for many years. However, not many other instruments were traded in the forward markets. With the rapid growth of derivative markets, we have seen an explosion of growth in forward markets for other instruments. It is now just as easy to enter into forward contracts for a stock index or oil as it was formerly to trade foreign currencies. Forward contracts are also extremely useful in that they facilitate the understanding of futures contracts.

Futures Contracts

A **futures contract** is an agreement between two parties—a buyer and a seller—to buy or sell something at a future date. The contract trades on a futures exchange and is subject to a daily settlement procedure. Futures contracts evolved out of forward contracts and possess many of the same characteristics. In essence, they are like liquid forward contracts. Unlike forward contracts, however, futures contracts trade on organized exchanges, called **futures markets.** For example, the buyer of a futures contract, who has the obligation to buy the good at the later date, can sell the contract in the futures market, which relieves him or her of the obligation to purchase the good. Likewise, the seller of the futures contract, who is obligated to sell the good at the later date, can buy the contract back in the futures market, relieving him or her of the obligation to sell the good.

Futures contracts also differ from forward contracts in that they are subject to a daily settlement procedure. In the daily settlement, investors who incur losses pay them every day to investors who make profits. We shall learn more about this in Chapter 7.

Futures prices fluctuate from day to day, and contract buyers and sellers attempt to profit from these price changes and to lower the risk of transacting in the underlying goods.

Options on Futures

Options on futures, sometimes called commodity options or futures options, are an important synthesis of futures and options markets. An option on a futures contract gives the buyer the right to buy or sell a futures contract at a later date at a price agreed upon today. Options on futures trade on futures exchanges and are a rare case where the derivative contract and the instrument on which it is derived trade side by side in an open market. Although options on futures are quite similar to options on spot assets, there are a few important differences. We shall cover options on futures in more depth in Chapter 12.

Swaps and Other Derivatives

Although options, forwards, and futures compose the set of basic instruments in derivative markets, there are many more combinations and variations. One of the most popular is called a **swap.** A swap is a contract in which two parties agree to exchange cash flows. For example, one party is currently receiving cash from one investment but would prefer another type of investment in which the cash flows are different. The party goes to a swap dealer, a firm operating in the over-the-counter market, who takes the opposite side of the transaction. The firm and the dealer, in effect, swap cash flow streams. Depending on what later happens to prices or interest rates, one party might gain at the expense of the other. In another type of arrangement, a firm might elect to tie the payments it makes on the swap contract to the price of a commodity, called a commodity swap, while in a different deal, a firm might buy an option to enter into a swap, called a **swaption.** As we shall show later, swaps can be viewed as a combination of forward contracts, and swaptions are quite similar to options.

The size of the swap market is almost beyond comprehension. But swaps are only one of many types of contracts that combine elements of forwards, futures, and options. For example, a firm that borrows money at a floating rate is susceptible to rising interest rates. However, it can reduce that risk by buying a cap, which is essentially an option that pays off whenever interest rates rise above a threshold. Another firm may choose to purchase an option whose performance depends not on how one asset performs but rather on the better or worse performing of two or even more than two assets, called an alternative option.

Some of these types of contract are referred to as **hybrids** because they combine the elements of several other types of contracts. All of them are indications of the ingenuity of participants in today's financial markets, who are constantly creating new and useful products to meet the diverse needs of investors. This process of creating new financial products is sometimes referred to as **financial engineering.** These hybrid instruments represent the effects of progress in our financial system. They are examples of

change and innovation that have led to improved opportunities for risk management. Swaps, caps, and many other hybrid instruments are covered in Chapters 14 and 15.

Some Important Concepts in Financial and Derivative Markets

Before undertaking any further study of derivative markets, let us review some introductory concepts pertaining to investment opportunities and investors. Many of these ideas may already be familiar and usually are applied in the context of trading in stocks and bonds. These concepts also apply with slight modifications to trading in derivatives.

Risk Preference

Suppose you were faced with two equally likely outcomes. If the first outcome occurs, you receive $5. If the second outcome occurs, you pay $2. From elementary statistics, you know that the expected outcome is $5(.5) − $2(.5) = $1.50, which is the amount you would expect to receive on average after playing the game many times. How much would you be willing to pay to take this risk? If you say $1.50, you are not recognizing the risk inherent in the situation. You are simply saying that a fair trade would be for you to give up $1.50 for the chance to make $1.50 on average. You would be described as **risk neutral,** meaning that you are indifferent to the risk. Most individuals, however, would not find this a fair trade. They recognize that the $1.50 you pay is given up for certain, while the $1.50 you expect to receive is earned only on average. The uncertainty of possibly losing $2 on some occasions would probably bother you.

Thus, we say that most individuals have **risk aversion.** They would pay less than $1.50 to take this risk. How much less depends on how risk averse they are. People differ in their degrees of risk aversion. But let us say you would pay $1.35. Then the difference between $1.50 and $1.35 is considered the **risk premium.** This is the additional return you expect to earn to justify taking the risk.

Although most individuals are indeed risk averse, it may surprise you to find that in the world of derivative markets, we can actually pretend that most people are risk neutral. No, we are not making some heroic but unrealistic assumption. It turns out that we obtain the same results in a world of risk aversion as we do in a world of risk neutrality. Although this is a useful point in understanding derivative markets, we shall not explore it in much depth at the level of this book. Yet without realizing it, you will probably grow to accept and understand derivative models and the hidden implication of risk neutrality.

Short Selling

If you have already taken an investments course, you probably have been exposed to the idea of short selling. Nonetheless, the concept is not too straightforward and a little review will be beneficial.

A typical transaction in the stock market involves one party buying stock from another party. It is possible, however, that the party selling the stock does not actually own the stock. That party could borrow the stock from a broker. That person is said to be **selling short** and sometimes shorting. He or she is doing so in the anticipation of the price falling, at which time the short seller would then buy back the stock at a lower price, capturing a profit and repaying the shares to the broker. You may have heard the expression, "Don't sell yourself short," which simply means not to view yourself as being less talented or less correct than someone else. Similarly, a short seller views the stock as being worth less than the market price.

Establishing a short position creates a liability. The short seller is obligated to someday buy back the stock and return it to the broker. Unlike an ordinary loan in which a borrower knows exactly how much he or she must pay back the lender, the short seller does not know how much he or she will have to pay to buy back the shares. This makes it a rather risky type of borrowing. Indeed short selling is a very daring investment strategy.

However, short selling can be quite beneficial in that the risk of short positions can be useful in offsetting the risk of long positions. The short selling of derivatives is particularly helpful. Short selling of stocks can be quite complex and expensive relative to buying stocks, whereas short selling of derivatives is as simple as buying derivatives. Thus, it is common to find an investor holding a stock and protecting it by selling short a derivative.

We should note that anyone who has an obligation to purchase something at a later date has the equivalent of a short sale. It is not necessary to have borrowed stock from a broker. In either case an increase in the price will be harmful.

Return and Risk

Return is the quantitative measure of investment performance. It represents the percentage increase in the investor's wealth that results from making the investment. In the case of stocks, the return is the percentage change in price plus the dividend yield. The concept of return also applies to options, but, as we shall see later, the definition of the return on a futures or forward contract is somewhat unclear.

One fundamental characteristic of investors is their desire to increase their wealth. This translates into obtaining the highest return possible— but higher returns are accompanied by greater risk. **Risk** is the uncertainty of future returns. As we noted earlier, investors generally dislike risk, and they demonstrate this by avoiding risky situations when riskless ones

that offer equivalent expected returns exist; however, they cannot always avoid uncertainty. Fortunately, the competitive nature of financial and derivative markets enables investors to identify investments by their degrees of risk.

For example, the stock of a company that specializes in drilling wildcat oil wells will, all other things being equal, sell for less than the stock of a company that supplies health care.[1] That is because the drilling company is engaged in a more uncertain line of business. Risk, of course, runs the spectrum from zero risk to high risk. The prices of securities will reflect the differences in the companies' risk levels. The additional return one expects to earn from assuming risk is the risk premium, which we mentioned earlier.

What other factors influence a company's stock price and expected return? Consider a hypothetical company with no risk. Will people be willing to invest money in this company if they expect no return? Certainly not. They will require a minimum return, one sufficient to compensate them for giving up the opportunity to spend their money today. This return is called the **risk-free rate** and is the investment's opportunity cost.[2]

The return investors expect is composed of the risk-free rate and a risk premium. This relationship is illustrated in Figure 1.1, where $E(r_s)$ is the expected return on the spot asset, r is the risk-free rate, and $E(\phi)$ is the risk premium—the excess of expected return over the risk-free rate.

Note that we have not identified how risk is measured. You might recall risk measures such as standard deviation and beta. At this point, we need not be concerned with the specific measure of risk. The important point is the positive relationship between risk and return known as the **risk-return trade-off.** The risk-return trade-off arises because all investors seek to maximize return subject to a minimum level of risk. If a stock moves up the line into a higher risk level, some investors will find it too risky and will sell the stock, which will drive down its price. New investors in the stock will expect to earn higher returns by virtue of paying a lower price for it.

The financial markets are very effective at discriminating among firms with different risk levels. Firms with low risk will find capital plentiful and inexpensive. Firms with high risk may have trouble raising capital and will

---

[1]In this context, "all other things being equal" means that the comparisons have not been distorted by differences in the number of shares outstanding or the amount of leverage.

[2]The concept of the risk-free rate and opportunity cost is nicely illustrated by the parable about the wealthy man who entrusted three servants to manage some of his money. Two of the servants earned 100 percent returns, while the third buried the money and returned only the principal sum. The man was infuriated that the third servant had not even earned the risk-free interest rate by putting the money in the bank, whereupon he reallocated the funds to one of the other servants' portfolios. The third servant, who was summarily discharged, evidently was not destined for a career as an investment manager.

FIGURE 1.1	Risk-Return Trade-off

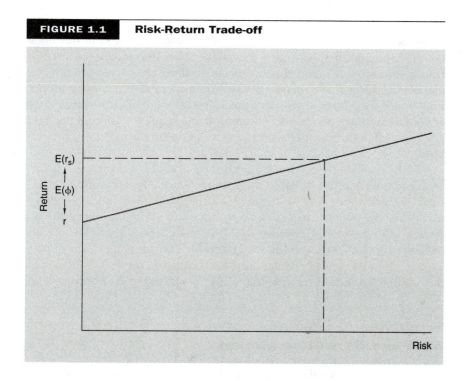

pay dearly. Markets that do a good job of pricing the instruments trading therein are said to be efficient and the assets are said to be priced at their **theoretical fair values.**

Market Efficiency and Theoretical Fair Value

Market efficiency is the characteristic of a market in which the prices of the instruments trading therein reflect their true economic values to investors. In an efficient market, prices fluctuate randomly and investors cannot consistently earn returns above those that would compensate them for the level of risk they assume.

The idea that an asset has a "true economic value" is a particularly appealing concept. It suggests that somewhere out there is the *real* value of the asset. If we could determine the real value, we could perhaps make lots of money buying when the asset is priced too low and selling when it is priced too high. But finding the true economic value requires a model of how the asset is priced.

In this book we shall call the true economic value of the asset its *theoretical fair value.* There are many models that give the theoretical fair values of assets. You have probably already heard of the Capital Asset Pricing

An efficient market is one in which the price of an asset equals its true economic value, which is called the **theoretical fair value.** Spot and derivative markets are normally quite efficient.

Model and perhaps the Arbitrage Pricing Theory. Derivatives also have theoretical fair values and a great deal of emphasis is placed in this book on determining the theoretical fair value of a derivative contract. Of course, these models and their respective values are correct only if the market is efficient. Fortunately, there is considerable statistical evidence supporting the notion that our markets are efficient. This is not surprising. Market efficiency is such a natural consequence of rational and knowledgeable investor behavior that we should be surprised if it did not hold.

Thus, as we weave our way through the world of derivatives, we should keep in mind that by and large these markets are efficient. Although this book presents numerous strategies for using derivatives, all of them assume that the investor has already developed expectations about the direction of the market. Derivative strategies show how to profit if those expectations prove correct and how to minimize the risk of loss if they prove wrong. These strategies are methods for managing the level of risk and thus should be considered essential tools for survival in efficient markets.

Fundamental Linkages between Spot and Derivative Markets

So far we have not established a formal connection between spot and derivative markets. Instruments such as options, forwards, and futures are available for the purchase and sale of spot market assets, such as stocks and bonds. The prices of the derivatives are related to those of the underlying spot market instruments through several important mechanisms. Chapters 3, 4, 8, and 9 examine these linkages in detail; nevertheless, a general overview of the process here will be beneficial.

Arbitrage and the Law of One Price

Arbitrage is a type of transaction in which an investor seeks to profit when the same good sells for two different prices. The individual engaging in the arbitrage, called the arbitrageur, buys the good at the lower price and immediately sells it at the higher price. Arbitrage is an attractive strategy for investors. Thousands of individuals devote their time to looking for arbitrage opportunities. If a stock sells on one exchange at one price and on another at a different price, arbitrageurs will go to work buying at the low price and selling at the high price. The low price will be driven up and the high price driven down until the two prices are equal.

In your day-to-day life, you make many purchases and sales. Sometimes you encounter the same good selling for two different prices; for example, a PC from a mail-order discount house may cost less than the same PC at a local computer store. Why is there a difference? The store may

offer longer warranties, localized service, and other conveniences not available through the discounter. Likewise, a pair of running shoes purchased at a local discounter may be cheaper than the same one purchased at a sporting goods store, where you pay extra for service and product knowledge. Where real differences exist between identical goods, the prices will differ.

But sometimes the differences appear real when they actually are not. For example, suppose there are two possible outcomes that might occur. We call these states of the world. Look at the outcomes illustrated in Figure 1.2 for two securities, S1 and S2. If state 1 occurs, stock S1 will be worth $100, while if state 2 occurs, it will be worth $80. In state 1 stock S2 will be worth $50, and in state 2 it will be worth $40. It should be obvious that stock S1 is equivalent to two shares of stock S2. Or in other words, by buying two shares of stock S2, you could obtain the same outcomes as by buying one share of stock S1.

Now suppose stock S1 is selling for $85. What should be the price of S2? Suppose it is $39. Then you could buy two shares of S2, paying $78, and sell short one share of S1 by borrowing the share from your broker. The short sale of S1 means you will receive its price, $85, up front. Then

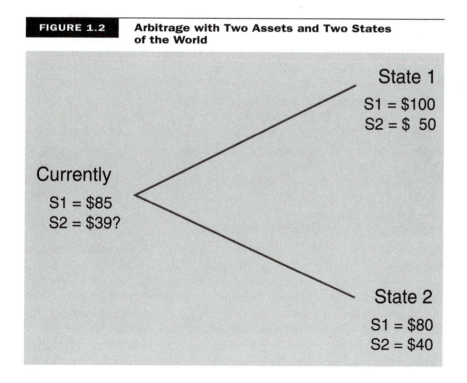

FIGURE 1.2   **Arbitrage with Two Assets and Two States of the World**

State 1
S1 = $100
S2 = $ 50

Currently
S1 = $85
S2 = $39?

State 2
S1 = $80
S2 = $40

when the state of the world is revealed, you can sell your two shares of S2 and generate exactly the amount of cash needed to buy the one share of S1 you will need to pay back your broker. Thus, there is no risk to this transaction and yet you received a net cash flow of $7 up front. This is like a loan in which you borrow $7 and do not have to pay back anything. Obviously everyone would do this, which would push up the price of S2 and push down the price of S1 until the price of S1 was exactly equal to two times the price of S2.

The rule that states that these prices must be driven into line in this manner is called the **law of one price.** The law of one price does not mean that the price of S2 must equal the price of S1. Rather it states that equivalent combinations of financial instruments must have a single price. Here the combination of two units of S2 must have the same price as one unit of S1.

Markets ruled by the law of one price have the following four characteristics:

The *law of one price* requires that equivalent combinations of assets, meaning those that offer the same outcomes, must sell for a single price or else there would be an opportunity for profitable arbitrage that would quickly eliminate the price differential.

- Investors always prefer more wealth to less.

- Given two investment opportunities, investors will always prefer one that performs at least as well as the other in all states and better in at least one state.

- If two investment opportunities offer equivalent outcomes, they must have equivalent prices.

- An investment opportunity that produces the same return in all states is risk-free and must earn the risk-free rate.

In later chapters, we shall see these rules in action.

In an efficient market, violations of the law of one price should never occur. But occasionally prices get out of line, perhaps through momentary oversight. Arbitrage is the mechanism that keeps prices in line. To make intelligent investment decisions, we need to learn how arbitrage transactions are made, which we shall do in later chapters.

The Storage Mechanism:
Spreading Consumption across Time

Storage is an important linkage between spot and derivative markets. Many types of assets can be purchased and stored. Holding a stock is a form of storage. One can also buy a commodity, such as wheat or corn, and store it in a grain elevator. Storage is a form of investment in which the investor defers selling the item in the hope of obtaining a higher price for it at a later date. It is also a way to spread consumption across time.

Because prices constantly fluctuate, storage entails risk. Derivatives can be used to reduce that risk by providing a means of establishing today

the item's future sale price. This suggests that the risk entailed in storing the item can be removed. In that case, the overall investment should offer the risk-free rate. Therefore, it is not surprising that the prices of the storable item, the derivative contract, and the risk-free rate will all be related.

Delivery and Settlement

Another important linkage between spot and derivative markets is delivery and settlement. At expiration, a forward or futures contract calls for either immediate delivery of the item or a cash payment of the same value. Thus, an expiring forward or futures contract is equivalent to a spot transaction. The price of the expiring contract, therefore, must equal the spot price. Though options differ somewhat from forwards and futures at expiration, these instruments have an unambiguous value at expiration that is determined by the spot price.

Few derivative traders hold their positions until the contracts expire.[3] They use the market's liquidity to enter into offsetting transactions. Nonetheless, the fact that delivery or an equivalent cash payment will occur on positions open at expiration is an important consideration in pricing the spot and derivative instruments.

The foregoing properties play an important role in these markets' performance. Derivative and spot markets are inextricably linked. Nonetheless, we have not yet determined what role derivative markets play in the operations of spot markets.

The Role of Derivative Markets

Risk Management

Because derivative prices are related to the prices of the underlying spot market goods, they can be used to reduce or increase the risk of owning the spot items. For example, buying the spot item and selling a futures contract or call option reduces the investor's risk. If the good's price falls, the price of the futures or option contract will also fall. The investor can then repurchase the contract at the lower price, effecting a gain that can at least partially offset the loss on the spot item. This type of transaction is known as a hedge.

As we noted earlier, investors have different risk preferences. Some are more tolerant of risk than others. All investors, however, want to keep their investments at an acceptable risk level. Derivative markets enable those wishing to reduce their risk to transfer it to those wishing to increase

---

[3]On derivative contracts that do not call for delivery at expiration, but specify that an economically equivalent cash payment be made, positions are more likely to be held to expiration.

it, whom we call speculators. Because these markets are so effective at re-allocating risk among investors, no one need assume an uncomfortable level of risk. Consequently, investors are willing to supply more funds to the financial markets. This benefits the economy, because it enables more firms to raise capital and keeps the cost of that capital as low as possible.

As noted, on the other side of hedging is speculation. Unless a hedger can find another hedger with opposite needs, the hedger's risk must be assumed by a speculator. Derivative markets provide an alternative and efficient means of speculating. Instead of trading the underlying stocks or bonds, an investor can trade a derivative contract. Many investors prefer to speculate with derivatives rather than with the underlying securities. The ease with which speculation can be done using derivatives in turn makes it easier and less costly for hedgers.

We would be remiss, however, if we left it at that. Speculation is controversial. Derivative markets have taken much criticism from outsiders, including accusations that their activities are tantamount to legalized gambling. We shall look at this point in a later section.

Price Discovery

Futures and forward markets are an important means of obtaining information about investors' expectations of future prices. In fact, many people believe that the price of a futures or forward contract is the expected future spot price. Although this issue is controversial, the consensus is that futures and forward prices do contain at least some valuable information about future spot prices.

Information about the future normally is not cheap, nor is it necessarily accurate. Forecasting future prices is a multimillion-dollar industry. Futures and forward markets, however, offer forecasts of future prices at virtually no cost to the general public. There is considerable evidence that these forecasts are nearly as accurate as the more expensive ones.

Options markets do not directly provide forecasts of future spot prices. They do, however, provide valuable information about the volatility and hence the risk of the underlying spot asset.

Operational Advantages

Derivative markets offer several operational advantages. First, they entail lower transaction costs. This means that commissions and other trading costs are lower for traders in these markets. This makes it easy and attractive to use these markets either in lieu of spot market investments or as a complement to spot positions.

Second, derivative markets, particularly the futures and options exchanges, have greater liquidity than the spot markets. Although stock and bond markets generally are quite liquid for the securities of major com-

panies, they cannot always absorb some of the large dollar transactions without substantial price changes. In some cases, investors can obtain the same levels of expected return and risk by using derivative markets, which can more easily accommodate high-volume trades. The reason for this higher liquidity is at least partly due to the smaller amount of capital required for participation in derivative markets. Returns and risks can be adjusted to any level desired, but since less capital is required, these markets can absorb more trading.

Third, as noted earlier, derivative markets allow investors to sell short more easily. Securities markets impose several restrictions designed to limit or discourage short selling that are not applied to derivative transactions. Consequently, many investors sell short in these markets in lieu of selling short the underlying securities.

Market Efficiency

Stock and bond markets probably would be efficient even if there were no derivative markets. However, a few profitable arbitrage opportunities exist even in markets that are usually efficient. The presence of these opportunities means that the prices of some assets are temporarily out of line with what they should be. Investors can earn returns that exceed what the market deems fair for the given risk level.

As noted earlier, there are important linkages among spot and derivative prices. The ease and low cost of transacting in these markets facilitate the arbitrage trading and rapid price adjustments that quickly eradicate these profit opportunities. Society benefits because the prices of the underlying goods more accurately reflect the goods' true economic values.

Criticisms of Derivative Markets

As noted earlier, derivative markets allow the transfer of risk from those wanting to remove or decrease it to those wanting to assume or increase it. These markets require the presence of speculators willing to assume risk to accommodate the hedgers wishing to reduce it. Most speculators do not actually deal in the underlying goods and sometimes are alleged to know nothing about them. Consequently, these speculators have been characterized as little more than gamblers.

This view is a bit one sided and ignores the many benefits of derivative markets. More important, it suggests that these markets siphon capital into wildly speculative schemes. However, nothing could be further from the truth. Unlike financial markets, derivative markets neither create nor destroy wealth—they merely transfer it.

For example, stock markets can create wealth. Consider a firm with a new idea that offers stock to the public. Investors buy the stock, and the

firm uses the capital to develop and market the idea. Customers then buy the product or service, the firm earns a profit, the stock price increases, and everyone is better off. In contrast, in derivative markets one investor's gains are another's losses. These markets put no additional risk into the economy; they merely allow risk to be passed from one investor to another. More important, they allow the risk of transacting in real goods to be transferred from those not wanting it to those willing to accept it.

An important distinction between derivative markets and gambling is in the benefits provided to society. Gambling benefits only the participants and perhaps a few others who profit indirectly. The benefits of derivatives, however, extend far beyond the market participants. Derivatives help financial markets become more efficient and provide better opportunities for managing risk. These benefits spill over into society as a whole.

Misuses of Derivatives

In recent years derivatives have taken much criticism for having been the source of large losses by some corporations, investment funds, state and local governments, and nonprofit investors. Are derivatives really at fault? Is electricity to be faulted when someone with little knowledge of it mishandles it? Is fire to be blamed when someone using it becomes careless?

There is little question that derivatives are powerful instruments. They typically are charged with a high degree of leverage, meaning that small price changes can lead to large gains and losses. Though this would appear to be an undesirable feature of derivatives, it actually is what makes them most useful in providing the benefits discussed earlier. These are points we shall study later. At this time, however, you should recognize that to use derivatives without having the requisite knowledge is dangerous. That is all the more reason why you should be glad you have chosen to study the subject.

Having acquired that knowledge, however, does not free you of the responsibility to act sensibly. To use derivatives in inappropriate situations is dangerous. The temptation to speculate when one should be hedging is a risk that even the knowledgeable often take. Having excessive confidence in one's ability to forecast prices or interest rates and then acting on those forecasts by using derivatives can be extremely risky. You should never forget what we said about efficient markets. Regrettably in recent years many individuals have led their firms down the path of danger and destruction by forgetting these points, with the consequence that derivatives are often blamed.

Fortunately derivatives are normally used by knowledgeable persons in situations where they serve an appropriate purpose. We hear far too little about the firms and investors who saved money, avoided losses, and restructured their risks successfully.

Derivatives and Your Career

It is tempting to believe that derivatives are but an interesting subject for study. You might feel that you would someday want to buy an option for your personal investment portfolio. You might think that you are unlikely to encounter derivatives in your career in business. That is simply not true.

As we noted earlier, the primary use of derivatives is in risk management. Businesses, by their very nature, face risks. Some of those risks are acceptable; indeed a business must assume some type of risk or there is no reason to be in business. But other types of risks are unacceptable and should be managed, if not eliminated. For example, a small furniture manufacturer may borrow money from a bank at a rate that will be adjusted periodically to reflect current interest rates. The furniture manufacturer is in the business of making money off the furniture market. It is not particularly suited to forecasting interest rates. Yet interest rate increases could severely hamper its ability to make a profit from its furniture business. If that firm sells its products in foreign countries, even in our nearby neighbors Canada and Mexico, it may face significant foreign exchange risk. If the raw materials it purchases and the energy it consumes are subject to uncertain future prices, as they surely are, the firm faces additional risks, all having the potential to undermine its success in its main line of business.

It was but a few years ago that a small firm would not be expected to use derivatives to manage its interest rate or foreign exchange risk, nor would it be able to do so if it wanted. The minimum sizes of transactions were too large. Times have changed now and smaller firms are more able to use derivatives.

If your career takes you into investment management, you will surely encounter derivatives. Those in public service who manage the assets of governments are finding numerous applications of derivatives. Those responsible for the commodities and energy purchased by firms will encounter situations where derivatives are or can be used. In short, derivatives are becoming commonplace and are likely to be even more so for the foreseeable future.

By taking a course and/or reading this book on derivatives, you are making the first step toward obtaining the tools necessary to understand the nature and management of risk, a subject that lies at the very heart of a business.

Summary

This chapter began with a general overview of the economic/financial system. It illustrated the role that derivative markets play in the economy and outlined their advantages and critical linkages with spot markets. This material establishes a foundation for the theme of this book: the study of derivatives.

Chapters 2 through 6 discuss options markets, and Chapters 7 through 11 cover forward and futures markets. Parts One and Two take a parallel approach. Chapters 2 and 7 discuss the characteristics of these markets; Chapters 3, 4, 8, and 9 are devoted to pricing principles; and Chapters 5, 6, 10, and 11 illustrate popular trading strategies.

Part Three contains four chapters that deal with advanced topics in derivatives. Chapter 12 covers options on futures. Chapter 13 focuses on foreign currency derivatives. Chapter 14 examines swaps and other interest rate derivatives. Chapter 15 covers advanced derivatives and strategies. Chapter 16 concludes the book with the subject of risk management.

Key Terms

Before continuing to Chapter 2, you should be able to give brief definitions of the following terms.

- derivative
- real asset
- financial asset
- international market integration
- cash market/spot market
- option
- call
- put
- forward contract
- futures contract
- option on futures
- swap
- swaption
- hybrid
- financial engineering
- risk neutrality
- risk aversion
- risk premium
- selling short
- return
- risk
- risk-free rate
- risk-return trade-off
- theoretical fair value
- market efficiency
- arbitrage
- law of one price

Questions and Problems

1. Distinguish between real assets and financial assets.

2. The price system works in the markets for real assets/services and financial assets. Is it likely to work in derivative markets as well? Why or why not?

3. Why do you think international markets are said to be integrated?

4. What is the difference between primary and secondary markets?

5. What is the difference between securities and contracts such as derivatives?

6. What is the difference between an investor who is risk neutral and one who is risk averse?

7. Explain the concept of a risk-return trade-off.

8. What are the components of the expected return?

9. What is an efficient market? Why do efficient markets benefit society?

10. Define arbitrage and the law of one price. What role do they play in our market system? What do we call the "one price" of an asset?

11.   Suppose you are shopping for a new automobile. You find the same car at two dealers but at different prices. Is the law of one price being violated? Why or why not?

12.   What is storage? Why is it risky? What role does it play in the economy?

13.   Why is delivery important if so few futures contracts end in delivery?

14.   What are the major functions of derivative markets in the U.S. economy?

15.   Why is speculation controversial? How does it differ from gambling?

16.   What are the three ways in which derivatives can be misused?

17.   Assume you have an opportunity to visit a civilization in outer space. Its society is at roughly the same stage of development as the U.S. society is now. Its economic system is virtually identical to that of the United States, but derivative trading is illegal. Compare and contrast this economy with the U.S. economy, emphasizing the differences due to the presence of derivative markets in the latter.

APPENDIX 1
Sources of Information on Derivatives

The derivative markets have become so visible in today's financial system that virtually any publication that covers the stock and bond markets contains some coverage of derivatives. *The Wall Street Journal,* published by Dow Jones and Co. and the nation's leading financial newspaper, covers derivatives in its column "Commodities Corner," which is devoted primarily to commodity futures. However, its coverage of all financial markets results in its usually giving some mention to derivatives. It occasionally contains articles specifically about derivatives, and it provides extensive coverage of exchange prices and trading volume. Its sister publication, *Barron's,* is published weekly and includes a column called "The Striking Price," devoted exclusively to options and futures, and another column called "Commodities," devoted to commodity futures.

More detailed information about derivative markets is provided in numerous other publications listed below. The address, phone number, and, where available, e-mail address are for subscriptions. Some publications have World Wide Web sites, some of which provide information on published and forthcoming articles.

Specialized Trade Publications

These publications, targeted toward practitioners, provide the most current and practical information about the derivative markets.

Risk: 104-112 Marylebone Lane, London W1M 5FU, U.K.; 44-0-171-487-5326

Futures and Options World: 1-800-METAL-25; webmaster@fow.com; http://www.fow.com

Futures: 250 South Wacker Drive, Suite 1150, Chicago, IL 60606; 312-977-0999; http://www.futuresmag.com/

Derivatives Strategy: 153 Waverly Place, New York, NY 10014; 212-366-9578

Futures Industry: Pennsylvania Ave., Suite 600, Washington, DC 20006-1807; 202-466-5460

Derivatives Week: 488 Madison Avenue, 14th Floor, New York, NY 10022; 212-224-3300

Swaps Monitor: 648 Broadway, Suite 705, New York, NY 10012; 212-254-9500

General Finance Academic Journals

Academic journals provide the results of research conducted primarily by academics but sometimes by practitioners. Most are subject to high standards, and the articles are usually quite technical. Each issue typically contains one or two articles on derivatives.

The Journal of Finance: Professor Michael Keenan, Stern School of Business, New York University, 44 Fourth West Street, Suite 9-190, New York, NY 10012; 212-998-0370; http://www.cob.ohio-state.edu/dept/fin/journal

Journal of Financial Economics: Elsevier Science, P.O. Box 945, New York, NY 10159-0945; 212-633-3730; http://jfe.rochester.edu

Review of Financial Studies: Oxford University Press, Journals Subscriptions Department, 2001 Evans Road, Cary, NC 27513; 800-852-7323

The Journal of Business: Graduate School of Business, The University of Chicago, 1101 E. 58th Street, Chicago, IL 60637; 312-702-7743; http://www.journals.uchicago.edu/JB

Journal of Financial and Quantitative Analysis: School of Business Administration, The University of Washington, Box 353200, Seattle, WA 98195-3200; 206-543-4598; http://weber.u.washington.edu/~jfqa/

Academic-Practitioner Finance Journals

These journals focus on articles written with clarity and practicality but which meet generally high standards of analytical rigor.

Financial Analysts Journal: AIMR, FAJ Subscriptions, P.O. Box 3668, 5 Boar's Head Lane, Charlottesville, VA 22903; 804-977-3668; http://www.aimr.com/aimr/pubs/faj/fajhome.html

The Journal of Portfolio Management: Institutional Investor, 488 Madison Ave., New York, NY 10022; 212-303-3300

The Journal of Fixed Income: Institutional Investor, 488 Madison Ave., New York, NY 10022; 212-303-3300

Specialized Derivatives Journals

The specialized derivatives journals are generally of high academic quality but appeal to academics as well as to practitioners.

The Journal of Derivatives: Institutional Investor, 488 Madison Ave., New York, NY 10022; 212-303-3300

The Journal of Financial Engineering: International Association of Financial Engineers, Administrative Office, 646-16 Main Street, Port Jefferson, NY 11777-2230; 516-331-8069; http://www.iafe.org/iafe2.html/Journal

Review of Futures Markets: Education and Marketing Services Department, Chicago Board of Trade, 141 W. Jackson Blvd., Chicago, IL 60604-2994; 312-435-7218

The Journal of Futures Markets: John Wiley and Sons, 605 Third Avenue, New York, NY 10158; 212-850-6645; subinfo@jwiley.com

Derivatives Quarterly: Institutional Investor, 488 Madison Ave., New York, NY 10022; 212-303-3300

Review of Derivatives Research: Kluwer Academic Publishers, 101 Philip Drive, Assinippi Park, Norwell, MA 02061

Advances in Futures and Options Research: JAI Press, 55 Old Post Road, No. 2, P.O. Box 1678, Greenwich, CT 06836-1678; 203-661-7602

World Wide Web and Internet Sites

With the rapidly expanding Internet, derivatives information is widely available on the World Wide Web. Given the speed with which information is updated, it is impossible to provide current information in print. Listed here are several excellent sites maintained by individuals and institutions that provide links to derivatives resources on the Internet.

Gibbon's Burkes' Hot Links for Traders: http://www.io.com/~gibbonsb/wahoo.html

Layer Eight Systems, Inc.: http://www.eight.com/websites.html

Finance Wat.ch: http://Finance.Wat.ch/

INO: http://www.ino.com/

Numa Web Internet Resource Center for Derivatives:
http://www.numa.com/index.htm

Waldemar's List: http://www.netservers.com/~waldemar/list.shtml

Applied Derivatives Trading: http://www.adtrading.com

Contingency Analysis:
http://www.contingencyanalysis.com/index.htm

The author of this book will maintain and update this list on his home page
at http://www.cob.vt.edu/finance/faculty/dmc/derivs/drvsites.htm

In addition, the *Financial Economics Network* provides an electronic service for delivery of abstracts of working papers and forthcoming articles in various fields of the social sciences. A series in derivatives is available:

1831 West 18th Street
P.O. Box 1210
Boca Grande, FL 33921-1210
206-364-0636
Sandy_Barnes@SSRN.com
http://www.ssrn.com/FEN

The two usenet groups misc.invest.options and misc.invest.futures are also useful resources.

Other Sources

The following organizations provide information, much of it free, on derivatives. In addition, the futures and options exchanges, whose addresses are given in Chapters 2 and 7, as well as brokerage firms are excellent and inexpensive sources of information.

Commodity Futures Trading Commission, 3 Lafayette Centre, 1155 21st St., NW, Washington, DC 20581; 202-418-5498; http://www.cftc.gov

Federal Reserve Board, 20th Street and Constitution Avenue, NW, Washington, DC 20551; 202-452-3000; http://www.bog.frb.fed.us/

Futures Industry Association, 2001 Pennsylvania Avenue, NW, Suite 600, Washington, DC 20006-1807; 202-466-5460

Global Association of Risk Professionals, 98 North Broadway, Suite 292, Tarrytown, NY 10591; 914-654-7803; http://www.chadmarc.net/garp

International Association of Financial Engineers, Administrative Office, 646-16 Main Street, Port Jefferson, NY 11777-2230; 516-331-8069; main@iafe.org; http://www.iafe.org

International Organization of Securities Commissions, 800 Square Victoria, P.O. Box 171, Tour de la Bourse, Montreal, Quebec H4Z 1C8 Canada; 514-875-8278

International Swaps and Derivatives Association, Inc., 600 5th Avenue, 27th Floor, Rockefeller Center, New York, NY 10020; 212-332-1200; http://www.isda.org

Managed Futures Association, P.O. Box 761, Palo Alto, CA 94302; 415-325-4500; http://www.mfahome.com

National Futures Association, 200 W. Madison Street, Suite 1600, Chicago, IL 60606-3447; 312-781-1300; http://www.nfa.futures.org

National Options and Futures Society, Exchange Block Building, 369 Pine Street, Suite 720, San Francisco, CA 94104; 415-398-7790

Securities and Exchange Commission, 450 Fifth Street, NW, Washington, DC 20549; 202-942-4144; http://www.sec.gov

CHAPTER 2

The Structure of Options Markets

After I'd gotten my seat on the exchange, one of the guys I'd just finessed came up out of the pit and congratulated me. It's that sort of crazy business. "You've got a great future in options," he predicted. "You can scream loud, jump high, think fast and count without using your fingers."

LAURA PEDERSEN, options trader, American Stock Exchange
Play Money, 1991

Chapter Objectives

■ To define and provide examples of call and put options

■ To describe the institutional characteristics of options markets, including both the exchange and over-the-counter markets

■ To provide information on the options available for trading and the volume of trading on exchanges

■ To describe the process of placing an order to trade an option on an exchange

■ To illustrate the role of the clearinghouse in exchange-listed options trading

■ To show how option prices are quoted in *The Wall Street Journal*

■ To present information on the magnitude and effects of transaction costs in option trading

■ To discuss the regulatory structure of options markets

■ To illustrate how margins and taxes affect options transactions

In Chapter 1 we introduced the concept of an option, a contract between two parties—a buyer and a seller, or writer—in which the buyer purchases from the writer the right to buy or sell an asset at a fixed price. As in any contract, each party grants something to the other. The buyer pays the seller a fee called the **premium,** which is the option's price. The writer grants the buyer the right to buy or sell the asset at a fixed price.

An option to buy an asset is a **call option.** An option to sell an asset is a **put option.** The fixed price at which the option buyer can either buy or sell the asset is called the **exercise price** or **strike price,** or sometimes **striking price.** In addition, the option has a definite life. The right to buy or sell the asset at a fixed price exists up to a specified **expiration date.**

Options are often encountered in everyday life. For example, a rain check offered by a store to allow you to return and purchase a sale item that is temporarily out of stock is an option. You return to the store and buy the item, if it is really worth it. Or you can throw the rain check away. You could even give (or sell) it to someone else. A coupon clipped from the newspaper that allows you to buy an item for a special price any time up to an expiration date is also an option. Suppose you plan to purchase a deeply discounted airline ticket. However, you are afraid your plans

might change and the airline says the ticket at that price is nonrefundable. However, for just $75 more, you can obtain the right to cancel the ticket at the last minute. If you pay the extra $75 for the right to cancel, you have just purchased an option. Finally, there is a good chance you are taking a college course right now, and you probably hold a valuable option: your right to drop the course up to a specific date. That right is paid for automatically with your tuition payment. On a certain date later in the term, you will decide whether to continue with the course or drop it. This is certainly a valuable option, but one we hope you will not use, at least not in this course.

In each example, you hold the right to do something, if it turns out to be worth it to you. While that is the essence of an option, options on securities and other assets do have a few more complicating features. But first let us take a look at how options markets developed.

The Development of Options Markets

There are plenty of examples of options in everyday life. Historians and archaeologists have even discovered primitive options. Though these arrangements may resemble modern options, the current system of options markets traces its origins to the nineteenth century, when puts and calls were offered on shares of stock. Little is known about the options world of the 1800s other than that it was fraught with corruption.

Then, in the early 1900s, a group of firms calling itself the Put and Call Brokers and Dealers Association created an options market. If someone wanted to buy an option, a member of the association would find a seller willing to write it. If the member firm could not find a writer, it would write the option itself. Thus, a member firm could be either a broker—one who matches buyer and seller—or a dealer—one who actually takes a position in the transaction.

Although this over-the-counter options market was viable, it suffered from several deficiencies. First, it did not provide the option holder the opportunity to sell the option to someone else before it expired. Options were designed to be held all the way to expiration, whereupon they were either exercised or allowed to expire. Thus, an option contract had little or no liquidity. Second, the writer's performance was guaranteed only by the broker-dealer firm. If the writer or the Put and Call Brokers and Dealers Association member firm went bankrupt, the option holder was simply out of luck.[1] Third, the cost of transacting was relatively high, due partly to the first two problems.

---

[1]The individual or firm could, of course, pursue costly legal remedies.

In 1973, a revolutionary change occurred in the options world. The Chicago Board of Trade, the world's oldest and largest exchange for the trading of commodity futures contracts, organized an exchange exclusively for trading options on stocks. The exchange was named the Chicago Board Options Exchange (CBOE). It opened its doors for call option trading on April 26, 1973, and the first puts were added in June 1977.

The CBOE created a central marketplace for options. By standardizing the terms and conditions of option contracts, it added liquidity. In other words, an investor who had previously bought or sold an option could go back into the market prior to its expiration and sell or buy the option, thus, offsetting the original position. Most importantly, however, the CBOE added a clearinghouse that guaranteed to the buyer that the writer would fulfill his or her end of the contract. Thus, unlike in the over-the-counter market, option buyers no longer had to worry about the credit risk of the writer. This made options more attractive to the general public.

Since that time, several stock exchanges and almost all commodity futures exchanges have begun trading options. Fueled by the public's taste for options, the industry grew tremendously until the great stock market crash of 1987. Hit by the shock of the crash, many individual investors who had formerly used options have stayed away and volume has not recovered to its 1987 level.

Although institutional trading on the options exchanges remained fairly strong after the crash, a concurrent trend forced the exchanges to address a new competitive threat: the revival of the over-the-counter options markets. In the early 1980s, many corporations began to use currency and interest rate swaps to manage their risk. These contracts, which we briefly mentioned in Chapter 1 and shall cover in more detail in later chapters, are private transactions that are tailored to the specific needs of the two parties. They are subject to credit risk in that a party could default, leaving the opposite party holding a claim that had to be pursued in bankruptcy courts. As it turned out, however, these claims were few and far between and the market functioned exceptionally well. Soon thereafter, firms began to create other types of over-the-counter contracts, such as forwards, and, as expected, options began to be used as well. Because of the large minimum size of each transaction, however, the general public is unable to participate in this new, revived over-the-counter market. The growth in this institutional over-the-counter market has placed severe pressures on the options exchanges. By the early 1990s the exchanges were trying to become more innovative to win back institutional trading and to stimulate the public's interest in options. These trends, however, should not suggest that options are fading in popularity; in fact they are more popular than ever with corporations and financial institutions, but the growth is concentrated in the over-the-counter market.

Call Options

A call option is an option to buy an asset at a fixed price—the exercise price. Options are available on many types of assets, but for now we shall concentrate on options on stock.[2] Consider the following example.

On July 15, 1997, the Chicago Board Options Exchange offered options on the stock of Hewlett-Packard. One particular call option had an exercise price of $70 and an expiration date of August 16. The Hewlett-Packard stock had a price of $68.25. The buyer of this option received the right to buy the stock any time up through August 16 at $70 per share. The writer of that option therefore was obligated to sell the stock at $70 per share through August 16 whenever the buyer wanted it. For this privilege, the buyer paid the writer the premium, or price, of $2.75.

Why would either party have entered into the call option contract? The buyer would not have done so to immediately exercise the option, because the stock could be bought in the market for $68.25, which was less than the exercise price of $70. The buyer must have anticipated that the stock's price would rise above $70 before the option expired. Conversely, the writer expected that the stock price would not get above $70 before the option expired. The buyer and writer negotiated the premium of $2.75, which can be viewed as the buyer's wager on the stock's price going above $70 by August 16. Alternatively, either the buyer or writer may have been using the option to protect a position in the stock—a strategy we mentioned in Chapter 1 called hedging.

Suppose that immediately after a call is purchased, the stock price increases. Because the exercise price is constant, the call option is now more valuable. New call options with the same terms will sell for higher premiums. Therefore, older call options with the same expiration date and exercise price must also sell for higher premiums. Similarly, if the stock price falls, the call's price also will decline. Clearly the buyer of a call option has bullish expectations about the stock.

A call in which the stock price exceeds the exercise price is said to be **in-the-money.** However, as we shall see in Chapter 3, in-the-money calls should not necessarily be exercised prior to expiration. If the stock price is less than the exercise price, the call option is said to be **out-of-the-money.** Out-of-the-money calls should never be exercised. We shall explore these points more thoroughly in Chapter 3. If the stock price equals the exercise price, the option is **at-the-money.**

---

[2]Options that trade on commodity futures exchanges are actually options on futures contracts and are covered in Chapter 12. Since a futures contract is not an asset, an option need not be an "option on an asset," although we shall continue to use that expression until Chapter 12.

Put Options

A put option is an option to sell an asset, such as a stock. Consider the put option on Hewlett-Packard stock on July 15, 1997, with an exercise price of $70 per share and an expiration date of August 16. It allowed the put holder to sell the stock at $70 per share any time up through August 16. The stock currently was selling for $68.25. Therefore, the put holder could have elected to exercise the option, selling the stock to the writer for $70 per share. However, the put holder may have preferred to wait and see if the stock price fell further below the exercise price. The put buyer expected the stock price to fall, while the writer expected it to remain the same or rise.

The buyer and writer negotiated a premium of $4, which the buyer paid to the writer. The premium can be viewed as the buyer's wager that the stock price would not rise above $70 per share by August 16. The writer accepted the premium because it was deemed to be fair compensation for the willingness to buy the stock for $70 any time up through August 16. As in the case of calls, either the buyer or the writer might have been using the put to hedge a position in the stock.

Since the put allows the holder to sell the stock for a fixed price, a decrease in the stock price will make the put more valuable. Conversely, if the stock price increases, the put will be less valuable. It should be apparent that the buyer of a put has bearish expectations for the stock.

If the stock price is less than the exercise price, the put is said to be **in-the-money.** In Chapter 3, we shall see that it is sometimes, but not always, optimal to exercise an in-the-money put prior to expiration. If the stock price is more than the exercise price, the put is **out-of-the-money.** An out-of-the-money put should never be exercised. When the stock price equals the exercise price, the put is **at-the-money.**

The Over-the-Counter Options Market

As noted earlier, there is now a rather large over-the-counter options market dominated by institutional investors. Chicago is no longer the center of the options industry. The scope of this market is worldwide. An option bought by an American corporation in Minnesota from the New York office of a Japanese bank, who in turn buys an offsetting option from the London office of a Swiss bank, would not at all be unusual. These contracts are entered into privately by large corporations, financial institutions, and sometimes even governments in which the option buyer is either familiar with the creditworthiness of the writer or has had the credit risk reduced by some type of collateral guarantee or other credit enhancement. Nonetheless, there is nearly always some credit risk faced by

the buyers of these options. However, there are several main advantages of this type of option.

The first advantage is that the terms and conditions of the options can be tailored to the specific needs of the two parties. For example, suppose the manager of a pension fund would like to protect the profit in the fund's portfolio against a general decline in the market. As we shall discuss in great detail in Chapter 5, the purchase of a put in which the holder of the portfolio can sell it to the option writer for a specific value on a certain date can assure the manager of a minimum return. Unfortunately, this type of transaction cannot always be accomplished on the options exchange. First, the options available on the exchange are based on certain stocks or stock indexes. The manager would need an option on the specific portfolio, which might not match the indexes on which options were available.[3] Second, the options on the exchange expire at specific dates, which might not match the manager's investment horizon. Third, even if options were available, there might not be enough liquidity to handle the large trades necessary to protect the entire portfolio. In the over-the-counter market, the manager can specify precisely which combination of stocks the option should be written on and when it should be exercised.[4] Although unusually large transactions could take some time to arrange, it is likely that most pension fund managers could get the desired transactions accomplished.

A second advantage is that the over-the-counter market is a private market in which neither the general public nor other investors, including competitors, need know that the transactions were completed. This does not mean that the transactions are illegal or suspicious. On the options exchange, a large order to buy puts could send a signal to the market that someone might have some bad news. This could send the market reeling as it worries about what impending information might soon come out.

Another advantage is that over-the-counter trading is essentially unregulated. Its rules are those of commonsense business honesty and courtesy. Institutions that do not conform would find themselves unable to find counterparties with which to trade. This largely unregulated environment means that government approval is not needed to offer new types of options. The contracts are simply created by parties that see mutual gain in doing business with each other. There are no costly constraints or bureaucratic red tape to cut through.

Clearly there are some disadvantages to over-the-counter trading, the primary one of which is that credit risk exists and excludes many

---

[3]It would be wasteful to purchase an option on each security, even if they were available, because that would protect the portfolio against risk that is already eliminated by its diversification.

[4]Because the specific combination of stocks is called a *basket*, these types of options are called *basket options*.

customers who are unable to establish their creditworthiness in this market. The credit risk problem is an important and highly visible contemporary issue in the swaps market and we shall discuss it more in Chapter 16. In addition to the credit risk problem, the sizes of the transactions in the over-the-counter market are larger than many investors can handle. It is not clear that over-the-counter trading is any more or less costly than trading on the exchange.

The over-the-counter market is quite large, but because of the private nature of the transactions, gauging its size is difficult. The International Swaps and Derivatives Association (ISDA) conducts semiannual surveys that attempt to provide some data. These surveys, however, take a long time to complete and are published with a considerable lag. The surveys measure the notional principal, which is essentially the face value of the instrument underlying the option, but not the size of the option premiums or the number of transactions. The ISDA's latest survey estimated that in mid-1996, the notional principal of interest rate options, which are the most widely used over-the-counter options, was about 4 trillion dollars.

Most of the options created on the over-the-counter market are not the traditional case of an option on an individual common stock. They tend to be options on bonds, interest rates, commodities, swaps, and foreign currencies and include many variations that combine options with other instruments. However, as noted earlier, a significant number are created on equities, meaning stock portfolios or indexes. Many are on foreign stock indexes. The principles behind pricing and using options, however, are pretty much the same, whether the option is created on the CBOE or in the over-the-counter market. There are obvious variations to accommodate the different types of options. We shall cover many of these in later chapters. Most of the material on options, which comprises Chapters 2 through 6, however, will use examples that come from the organized markets. Now let us take a look at how the organized options markets operate.

Organized Options Trading

An exchange is a legal corporate entity organized for the trading of securities, options, or futures. It provides a physical facility and stipulates rules and regulations governing the transactions in the instruments trading thereon. In the options markets, organized exchanges evolved in response to the lack of standardization and liquidity of over-the-counter options. Over-the-counter options were written for specific buyers by particular sellers. The terms and conditions of the contracts, such as the exercise price and expiration date, were tailored for the parties involved. Organized exchanges filled the need for standardized option contracts wherein the ex-

change would specify the contracts' terms and conditions. Consequently, a secondary market for the contracts was made possible. This made options more accessible and attractive to the general public.

By providing a physical trading floor, specifying rules and regulations, and standardizing contracts, options became as marketable as stocks. If an option holder wanted to sell the option before the expiration date or an option writer wished to get out of the obligation to buy or sell the stock, a closing transaction could be arranged at the options exchange. We shall examine these procedures in more detail in a later section.

The Chicago Board Options Exchange, the first organized options exchange, established the procedures that made options marketable. In addition, it paved the way for the American, Philadelphia, Pacific, and New York Stock Exchanges to begin option trading. The next several sections examine the CBOE's contract specifications.

Listing Requirements

The options exchange specifies the assets on which option trading is allowed. For stock options, the exchange's listing requirements prescribe the eligible stocks on which options can be traded. At one time, these requirements limited options listings to stocks of large firms, but these requirements have been relaxed, and more small firms' options are available for trading. The exchange also specifies minimum requirements that a stock must meet to maintain the listing of options on it. These requirements are similar to but slightly less stringent than those for the initial listing. In all cases, however, the exchange has the authority to make exceptions to the listing and delisting requirements.

All options of a particular type—call or put—on a given stock are referred to as an option **class.** For example, the Hewlett-Packard calls are one option class and the Hewlett-Packard puts are another. An option **series** is all the options of a given class with the same exercise price and expiration. For example, the Hewlett-Packard August 70 calls are a particular series, as are the Hewlett-Packard September 65 puts.

In recent years many options have become listed on more than one exchange. In any case, however, it should be remembered that it is the options exchanges that determine whether options of a particular stock will be listed. The company itself has no influence. One firm, Golden Nugget, opposed the listing of options on its stock and even took legal action to try to prevent option trading on its stock. After more than two years in court, Golden Nugget lost its case.

Contract Size

A standard exchange-traded option contract consists of 100 individual options. Thus, if an investor purchases one contract, it actually represents

options to buy 100 shares of stock. An exception to the standard contract size occurs when either a stock splits or the company declares a stock dividend. In that case, the number of shares represented by a standard contract is adjusted to reflect the change in the company's capitalization. For example, if a company declares a 15 percent stock dividend, the number of shares represented by an outstanding contract changes from 100 to 115. In addition, the exercise price is adjusted to $1/1.15 = .8696$, rounded to the nearest eighth—.875—of its former value. If a stock split or stock dividend results in the new number of shares being an even multiple of 100, holders of outstanding contracts are credited with additional contracts. For example, if the stock splits two for one, buyers and writers are credited with two contracts for every one formerly held. In addition, the exercise price is reduced to half of its previous value.

Contract sizes for options on indexes and certain other instruments are specified as a multiple. For example, an option on the S&P 100 has a multiple of 100; an investor who buys one contract actually buys 100 options.

Exercise Prices

On options exchanges the exercise prices are standardized. The exchange prescribes the exercise prices at which options can be written. Investors must be willing to trade options with the specified exercise prices. Of course, over-the-counter transactions can have any exercise price the two participants agree on.

The exchange's objective in establishing the exercise prices is to provide options that will attract trading volume. Most option trading is concentrated in options in which the stock price is close to the exercise price. Accordingly, exchange officials tend to list options in which the exercise prices surround but are close to the current stock price. They must use their judgment as to whether an exercise price is too far above or below the stock price to generate sufficient trading volume. If the stock price moves up or down, new exercise prices close to the stock price are added.

In establishing exercise prices of stock options, the exchange generally follows the rule that the exercise prices are in $2.50 intervals if the stock price is less than $25, in $5 intervals if the stock price is between $25 and $200, and in $10 intervals if the stock price is above $200. For index options, exercise prices are in $5 intervals. However, the exchange will waive these rules if it believes that it must to attract sufficient trading volume.

In 1993 the CBOE launched the FLEX (for flexible) option, a new type of option that represented a dramatic departure from the standardization of organized options markets. FLEX options can have any exercise price. In addition there are other variations that we shall mention when we discuss expirations. FLEX options are available with a minimum face value of $10 million.

When a stock pays a dividend, the stock price falls by the amount of the dividend on the ex-dividend day, which is the day after the last day on which the purchaser of the stock is entitled to receive the upcoming dividend. Because call option holders do not receive dividends and benefit from increases in the stock price and put option holders benefit from stock price decreases, the ex-dividend decrease in the stock price would arbitrarily hurt call holders and help put holders. In the old over-the-counter options market, options were said to be dividend-protected. If the company declared a $1 dividend, the exercise price was reduced by $1. Since over-the-counter options were not meant to be traded, the frequent dividend adjustments caused no problems. For exchange-listed options, however, such dividend adjustments would have generated many nonstandard exercise prices. Thus, the exchanges elected not to adjust the exercise price when a cash dividend was paid. This is also true in the current over-the-counter market.

Expiration Dates

Expiration dates of over-the-counter options are tailored to the buyers' and writers' needs. On the options exchanges, each stock is classified into a particular expiration cycle. The expiration cycles are (1) January, April, July, and October; (2) February, May, August, and November; and (3) March, June, September, and December. These were called the *January, February,* and *March cycles.* The available expirations are the current month, the next month, and the next two months within the January, February, or March cycle to which the stock is assigned. For example, in early June, IBM, which is assigned to the January cycle, will have options expiring in June and July plus the next two months in the January cycle: October and the following January. When the June options expire, the August options will be added; when the July options expire, the September options will be added; and when the August options expire, the April options will be added. Index options typically have expirations of the current and next two months.

The maturities of options on individual stocks go out about nine months with a few exceptions. LEAPS (Long-Term Equity Anticipation Shares) are options on certain stocks and indices that have expirations of up to three years. LEAPS have proven to be very popular with more than 3.5 million contracts traded on the CBOE in 1996.[5] Although LEAPS are available on index options, most of the trading volume is in LEAPS on individual stocks.

As noted above, FLEX options are available on stocks and indices and permit the investor to specify any exercise price. FLEX options can also

---

[5]CBOE, *Market Statistics,* 1996.

have any desired expiration up to five years. FLEX options are a response on the part of the options exchanges to the growing over-the-counter market in which options have tailored exercise prices and expirations.

The expiration day of an exchange-traded option is the Saturday following the third Friday of the month. The last day on which the option trades is the third Friday of the month. In addition, because many portfolio managers are evaluated at the end of each quarter, there are index options that expire on the last day of each quarter.

Position and Exercise Limits

The Securities and Exchange Commission forces the options exchanges to impose **position limits** that define the maximum number of options an investor can hold on one side of the market. For example, because they are both bullish strategies, a long call and a short put on the same stock are transactions on the same side of the market. Likewise, a short call and a long put are both bearish strategies and thus are considered to be on the same side of the market. The options exchange publishes the position limit for each stock, which varies from 4,500 to 25,000, depending on the stock's trading volume and number of outstanding shares. Position limits are higher for index options. For the S&P 500, the limit is 100,000 contracts but certain investors qualify for limits as high as 350,000. In addition, market makers have certain exemptions from these position limits.

Exercise limits are similar to position limits. An **exercise limit** is the maximum number of options that can be exercised on any five consecutive business days by any individual or group of individuals acting together. The figure for the exercise limit is the same as that for the position limit.

The purpose of position and exercise limits is to prevent a single individual or group from having a significant effect on the market. It is not clear, however, that such restrictions are necessary. They do, however, prevent many large investors from using exchange-traded options, and they reduce liquidity. They have probably hurt the options exchanges by forcing institutional investors to take their business to the over-the-counter markets.

Exchanges on Which Options Trade

Options trading currently exists on several U.S. and many foreign exchanges. The CBOE is the only U.S. exchange devoted solely to options trading; the other exchanges trade stocks as well as options. Table 2.1 lists the exchanges and the addresses and telephone numbers of the U.S. exchanges.

Options trading is not confined to these exchanges. Chapter 12 covers options on futures, which trade on virtually every commodity futures exchange in the country. We shall defer discussing those contracts and exchanges until Chapters 7 and 12.

TABLE 2.1	Exchanges on Which Options on Spot Assets Trade, July 1997

U.S. Exchanges

Chicago Board Options Exchange
(CBOE)
400 S. LaSalle St.
Chicago, IL 60605
312-786-5000; 800-678-4667
http://www.cboe.com
Options on: stocks, stock indices

Philadelphia Stock Exchange
(PHLX)
1900 Market St.
Philadelphia, PA 19103
215-496-5000; 800-843-7459
http://www.phlx.com
Options on: stocks, stock indices, currencies

American Stock Exchange
(AMEX)
86 Trinity Place
New York, NY 10006
212-306-1000
http://www.amex.com
Options on: stocks, stock indices; also warrants on stock indices, currencies

Pacific Stock Exchange
(PSE)
301 Pine St.
San Francisco, CA 94104
415-393-4000
Options on: stocks, stock indices

Foreign Exchanges

Australian Stock Exchange (Sydney)
Austrian Futures and Options
  Exchange (Vienna)
Belgian Futures and Options Exchange
  (Brussels)
Bolsa de Mercadorias & Futuros
  (São Paulo)
Montreal Exchange
Toronto Stock Exchange
Vancouver Stock Exchange
Santiago Stock Exchange
Copenhagen Stock Exchange
Finnish Options Exchange (Helsinki)
Finnish Securities and Derivatives
  Exchange (Helsinki)
South African Futures Exchange
  (Johannesburg)
Meff Renta Variables (Madrid)
OM Stockholm AB
Swiss Options and Financial Futures
  Exchange (Zurich)

London International Financial
  Futures and Options Exchange
London Securities and Derivatives
  Exchange
Marché à Terme International de
  France (Paris)
Marché des Options Negociables de
  Paris
Deutsche Terminboerse (Frankfurt)
Hong Kong Futures Exchange
Stock Exchange of Hong Kong
Tel Aviv Stock Exchange
Italian Stock Exchange (Milan)
Nagoya Stock Exchange
Osaka Securities Exchange
Tokyo Stock Exchange
Amsterdam Exchange
New Zealand Futures and Options
  Exchange (Auckland)
Oslo Stock Exchange

Note: Exchanges on which options on futures trade are covered in Chapter 7.

Figure 2.1 shows the volume of option trading on the five U.S. exchanges on which options trade. This figure includes volume on the New York Stock Exchange, which has since merged with the Chicago Board Options Exchange. Growth in option trading had been quite phenomenal until 1987. The market crash of 1987 resulted in a reduction in volume of about 35 percent in 1988 from 1987 as many individual investors shied away from the markets. Volume in 1996 is still slightly below the 1987 peak. The

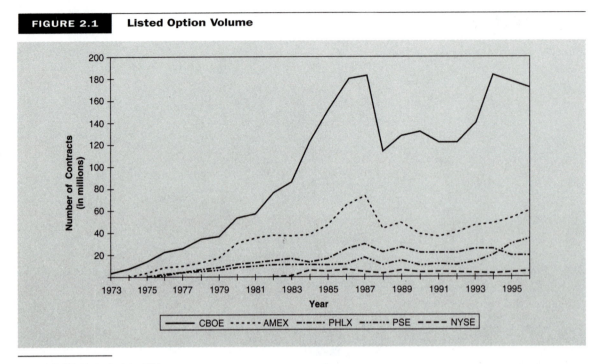

FIGURE 2.1   **Listed Option Volume**

Source: CBOE, *Market Statistics,* 1996

crash had an even greater impact on index option volume, which is still well below its pre-crash level. Some of this loss of volume, however, is not a result of the crash, but of the growing use of over-the-counter options and related contracts by institutional investors.

The CBOE's share of stock option volume has declined over the years from about 66 percent in 1976, the first full year in which options were traded on the AMEX, to the 44 percent share it captured in 1996. However, when index, foreign currency, and bond options are included, the CBOE's share, as shown in Figure 2.2, is about 60 percent. This is because of the CBOE's share of the index option market of over 92 percent.

Option Traders

In the over-the-counter market, certain institutions, which may be banks or brokerage firms, stand ready to make markets in options. Exchange-listed options, of course, are created on an exchange, which is a legal corporate entity whose members are individuals or firms. Each membership is referred to as a **seat.** Although the organizational structures of the various exchanges differ somewhat, membership generally entitles one to

FIGURE 2.2	Share of Option Volume

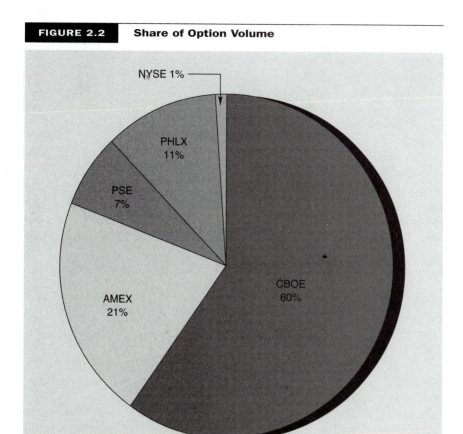

Source: CBOE, *Market Statistics*, 1996

physically go onto the trading floor and trade options. The following sections discuss the types of traders who operate both on and off the exchange floor. This system of traders is based on the market maker system used by the CBOE and the Pacific Stock Exchange.

The Market Maker

An individual who has purchased a seat on the CBOE can apply to be either a market maker or a floor broker.[6] The **market maker** is responsible

---

[6]Exchange rules allow an individual to be both a market maker *and* a floor broker, but not on the same day. The practice of being both a market maker and a floor trader is called **dual trading** and is a controversial issue in the futures markets.

for meeting the public's demand for options. When someone from the public wishes to buy (sell) an option and no other member of the public is willing to sell (buy) it, the market maker completes the trade. This type of system ensures that if a private investor wishes to buy a particular option, there will be a seller willing to make an offer, and if one buys an option and later wants to sell it, there will be a buyer available. The market maker offers the public the convenience of immediate execution of trades.

The market maker is essentially an entrepreneur. To survive, the market maker must profit by buying at one price and selling at a higher price. One way this is done is by quoting a bid price and an ask price. The **bid price** is the maximum price the market maker will pay for the option. The **ask price** is the minimum price the market maker will accept for the option. The ask price is set higher than the bid price. The exchange imposes upper limits on the difference between the ask and bid prices, called the **bid-ask spread,** which tends to vary from 1/4 point to 1 full point.

The bid-ask spread is a significant transaction cost for those who must trade with a market maker. To the market maker, however, it represents the reward for the willingness to buy when the public is selling and sell when the public is buying. Bid-ask spreads are discussed further in the section on transaction costs.

Market makers use a variety of techniques to trade options intelligently and profitably. Many look at fundamentals, such as interest rates, economic conditions, and company performance. Others rely on technical analysis, which purports to find signals of the direction of future stock prices in the behavior of past stock prices. Still others rely simply on intuition and experience. In addition, market makers tend to employ different trading styles. Some are **scalpers,** who try to buy at the bid and sell at the ask before the price moves downward or after the price moves just slightly upward. Scalpers seldom hold positions for more than a few minutes. In contrast, **position traders** have somewhat longer holding periods. Many option traders, including some scalpers and position traders, are also **spreaders,** who buy one option and sell another in the hope of earning small profits at low risk. Option spreading strategies are covered in more detail in Chapter 6.

The Floor Broker

The **floor broker** is another type of trader on the exchange. The floor broker executes trades for members of the public. If someone wishes to buy or sell an option, that individual must first establish an account with a brokerage firm. That firm must either employ a floor broker or have an arrangement whereby it contracts with either an independent floor broker or a floor broker of a competing firm.

The floor broker executes orders for nonmembers and earns either a flat salary or a commission on each order executed. The floor broker generally need not be concerned about whether the price is expected to go up or down; however, a good broker will work diligently to obtain the best price for the customer.

The Order Book Official

A third type of trader at the CBOE is the **order book official (OBO)** or **board broker,** an employee of the exchange. To see how an OBO works, suppose you place a **limit order**—an order specifying a maximum price to be paid on a purchase or a minimum acceptable price on a sale—to buy a call option at a maximum price of $3. The floor broker handling your order determines that the best quote offered by a market maker is 2 3/4 bid and 3 1/4 ask. This means that the lowest price at which a market maker will sell the call is 3 1/4. If your floor broker has other orders to execute, the OBO takes your limit order and enters it into the computer along with all the other public limit orders. The market makers are informed of the best public limit orders. If conditions change such that at least one market maker is willing to quote an ask price of $3 or lower, the OBO will execute your limit order.

Public limit orders are always executed before market maker orders; however, the market makers, being aware of the best public limit orders, know the maximum and minimum prices at which they can trade. For example, if your limit order to buy at 3 is the highest bid and the market maker is quoting an ask price of 3 1/4, the market maker chooses between accepting your bid and selling the call at 3 or holding out for an offer of 3 1/8 or higher. If no one bids 3 1/8 within a reasonable time period, the market maker might choose to take your bid of 3.

The options exchanges also have brought the benefits of modern technology to their order-processing operations. This increased use of technology has resulted in proposals to extend option trading to hours after the exchange is closed. As we shall see in Chapter 7, the futures industry has moved more quickly than the securities and options industry toward 24-hour trading, but the securities and options exchanges are beginning to catch up in that regard.

Other Option Trading Systems

The CBOE and the Pacific Stock Exchange use the system of competing market makers. The American and Philadelphia Stock Exchanges use a slightly different system. Here an individual called a **specialist** is responsible for making bids and offers on options. The specialist maintains and attempts to fill public limit orders but does not disclose them to others. In addition to the specialist are individuals called **registered option traders**

(ROTs), who buy and sell options for themselves or act as brokers for others. Unlike the CBOE market makers, ROTs are not obligated to make a market in the options; market making is the specialist's task.

Clerks, runners, and exchange officials are also present on the exchange floor. Other than the traders on the floor, the most important participants in the options industry are the individuals and institutions that trade off the floor.

Off-Floor Option Traders

The financial world consists of a vast number of institutions of all sizes, many of which participate in option trading. Some of these institutions are brokerage firms that execute orders for the public. Most brokerage firms employ individuals responsible for recommending profitable option trades to their brokers. Many, however, have specialized option-trading departments that search for mispriced options, trade in them, and in so doing contribute to their firms' profitability. Many large institutional investors, such as pension funds, trusts, and mutual funds, also trade options. In most cases, these types of investors write options on the stocks held in their portfolios. A growing contingent of foreign institutions also trade options. In addition to the large institutional investors, there are, of course, numerous individuals—some wealthy and some not—who trade options. Among those who trade options themselves, there are many wealthy people who turn over their financial affairs to specialized managers and thus participate in the options market without being personally involved. The dollar amounts required for trading exchange-listed options are so small that virtually anyone can afford to participate.

Cost and Profitability of Exchange Membership

An individual who decides to purchase a seat on an exchange that has option trading can take one of several routes. The most obvious is to purchase a seat from an existing member. Figure 2.3 shows the history of the price of a seat on the CBOE.

At around $500,000, the cost of obtaining membership would seem prohibitive to most individuals. However, there are other ways to gain membership. Some seat owners lease their seats to others; rental rates run about .50 to .75 percent of the seat's price per month. Also, some members allow "trainees" to trade with their seats and charge them a percentage of the trading profits.

The CBOE has 931 members and there are 340 members of the Chicago Board of Trade who have option-trading privileges at the CBOE. The AMEX has 661 full members, who primarily trade its stocks, and 203 options members. The Philadelphia Stock Exchange has 505 members with option-trading privileges, and the Pacific Stock Exchange has 551 members.

FIGURE 2.3   **CBOE Quarterly Seat Prices**

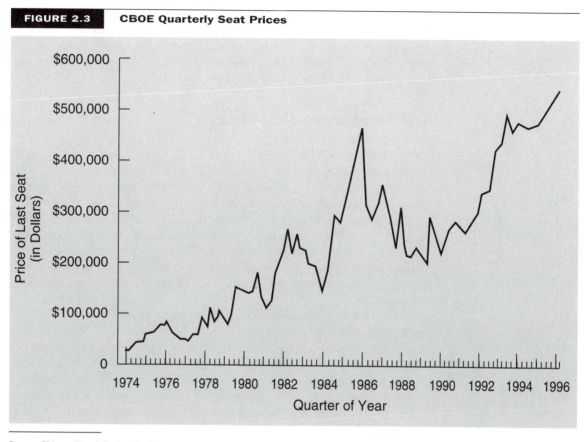

Source: Chicago Board Options Exchange

These prices are not the full cost of trading. They provide only access to the floor. Capital must be available to cover losses and a member must arrange for a firm to guarantee his or her creditworthiness. The minimum amount of capital is about $50,000. Members must also undergo training and pass an examination verifying that they know the rules and procedures, and they must agree to conform to all exchange and SEC regulations. There are additional start-up costs and monthly expenses.

It is difficult to determine how profitable option memberships are. An SEC study in 1978 showed that the average market maker earned a respectable but not unusually large amount of money. However, that study is outdated since the options markets have changed much since that time, particularly after the crash of 1987. Anecdotal evidence suggests that options market making is a relatively high-risk profession characterized by

extreme pressure. The temptation to take undue risks in the hope of making large profits is quite great. Many new market makers end up out of the business rather quickly. Those that are successful generally have pursued conservative strategies. Due to the stress, the typical market maker is a young person in his or her 20s or early 30s.

The Mechanics of Trading

Placing an Opening Order

An individual who wants to trade options must first open an account with a brokerage firm. The individual then instructs the broker to buy or sell a particular option. The broker sends the order to the firm's floor broker on the exchange on which the option trades. All orders must be executed during the normal trading hours that vary by product from 8:30 A.M. to either 3:02 P.M. or 3:15 P.M. central time. Trading is performed within the trading pit designated for the particular option. The trading pit is a multilevel, octagonally shaped area within which the market makers and floor brokers stand.

An investor can place several types of orders. A **market order** instructs the floor broker to obtain the best price. A **limit order,** as indicated earlier, specifies a maximum price to pay if buying or a minimum price to accept if selling. Limit orders may be either good-till-canceled or day orders. A **good-till-canceled order** remains in effect until canceled. A **day order** stays in effect for the remainder of the day. Finally, an investor holding a particular option might place a **stop order** at a price lower than the current price. If the market price falls to the specified price, the broker is instructed to sell the option at the best available price. There are a number of other types of orders designed to handle different contingencies.

In addition to specifying the option the investor wishes to buy or sell, the order must indicate the number of contracts desired. The order might be a request to purchase 10 contracts at the best possible price. The market maker's quote, however, need apply to only one contract. Therefore, if multiple contracts are needed, the market maker may offer a less favorable price. In that case, the order might be only partially filled. To avoid a partial fill, the investor can place an all or none or an all or none, same price order. An **all or none order** allows the broker to fill part of the order at one price and part at another. An **all or none, same price order** requires the broker to either fill the whole order at the same price or not fill the order at all. In 1996, the CBOE reported that the average number of contracts per trade was 14.3.[7]

---

[7]CBOE, *Market Statistics,* 1996.

The Role of the Clearinghouse

After the trade is consummated, the clearinghouse enters the process. The **clearinghouse,** formally known as the **Options Clearing Corporation (OCC),** is an independent corporation that guarantees the writer's performance. The OCC is the intermediary in each transaction. A buyer exercising an option looks not to the writer but to the clearinghouse. A writer exercising an option makes payment for or delivery of the stock to the clearinghouse.

Each OCC member, known as a **clearing firm,** has an account with the OCC. Each market maker must clear all trades through a member firm, as must every brokerage firm, although in some cases a brokerage firm is also a clearing firm.

Figure 2.4 illustrates the flow of money and information as an option transaction is consummated and cleared. We shall illustrate how the clearinghouse operates by assuming that you bought the Hewlett-Packard August 70 call we described earlier. You contacted your broker, who, through either his or her firm's floor broker or an independent floor broker, found a seller. You bought 10 contracts at a price of $2.75 per option, which totals $2,750. The seller, whose identity you do not know, has an account with another brokerage firm.

Your brokerage firm clears its trades through XYZ Trading Company, a clearing firm that is a member of the OCC. The seller's broker clears through ABC Options, another member of the OCC. You pay your broker the $2,750, and your broker pays XYZ Trading Company. XYZ pools the transactions of all its customers and, through a predetermined formula, deposits a sum of money with the OCC.

Let us also assume that the seller does not already own the stock, so he or she will have to deposit some additional money, called **margin,** with ABC. The amount of margin required is discussed in Appendix 2A; for now, however, just assume that the amount is 20 percent of the value of the stock, which comes to $13,650. The seller gives the $13,650 to the broker, who deposits it with ABC Options, which also keeps the $2,750 premium. ABC, in turn, is required to deposit with the OCC an amount of money determined according to a formula that takes its outstanding contracts into account.

The OCC guarantees the performance of ABC, the seller's clearing firm. Thus, you, the buyer, need not worry about whether the shares will be there if you decide to exercise your option. If the shares are not delivered by the seller, the OCC will look to ABC who will look to the seller's brokerage firm, which will look to the seller's personal broker, who will look to the seller for payment or delivery of the shares.

The total number of option contracts outstanding at any given time is called the **open interest.** The open interest figure indicates the number of closing transactions that might be made before the option expires. In July

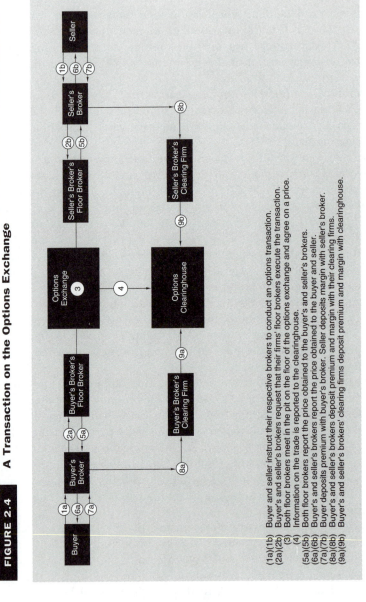

FIGURE 2.4   A Transaction on the Options Exchange

(1a)(1b)   Buyer and seller instruct their respective brokers to conduct an options transaction.
(2a)(2b)   Buyer's and seller's brokers request that their firms' floor brokers execute the transaction.
   (3)   Both floor brokers meet in the pit on the floor of the options exchange and agree on a price.
   (4)   Information on the trade is reported to the clearinghouse.
(5a)(5b)   Both floor brokers report the price obtained to the buyer's and seller's brokers.
(6a)(6b)   Buyer's and seller's brokers report the price obtained to the buyer and seller.
(7a)(7b)   Buyer deposits premium with buyer's broker. Seller deposits margin with seller's broker.
(8a)(8b)   Buyer's and seller's brokers deposit premium and margin with their clearing firms.
(9a)(9b)   Buyer's and seller's brokers' clearing firms deposit premium and margin with clearinghouse.

Note: Either buyer or seller (or both) could be a floor trader, eliminating the broker and floor broker.

1997, open interest in stock and index options on all exchanges was over 37 million contracts.[8]

The OCC thus fulfills the important responsibility of guaranteeing option writers' performances. A call buyer need not examine the writer's credit; in fact, in the case of individuals and firms off the floor, the buyers do not even know the writers' identities.

Because the member clearing firms assume some risk, the OCC imposes minimum capital requirements on them. The OCC has a claim on their securities and margin deposits in the event of their default. As a further safeguard, the OCC maintains a special fund supported by its members. If that fund is depleted, the OCC can assess its other members to ensure its survival as well as that of the options market in general.

Of course, in the over-the-counter market there is no clearinghouse, and the buyer is exposed to credit risk on the part of the writer.

Placing an Offsetting Order

Suppose an investor holds a call option. The stock price recently has been increasing, and the call's price is now much higher than the original purchase price. The liquidity of the options market makes it possible for the investor to take the profit by selling the option in the market. This is called an **offsetting order** or simply an **offset.** The order is executed in the same manner as an opening order. Continuing with our example in which you bought 10 contracts of the Hewlett-Packard August 70 calls, suppose the price of the calls is now $3.125. You instruct your broker to sell the calls. Your broker orders his firm's floor broker to sell the calls. The floor broker finds a buyer who agrees to the price of $3.125. The buyer pays $3,125 to her broker, who passes the funds through to the company's clearing firm, which passes the funds through to the OCC. The OCC then credits the $3,125 to the account of your broker's clearing firm, XYZ Trading Company, which credits your broker's firm, which in turn credits your account. You now have $3,125 and no outstanding position in this option. The individual who bought these options from you may have been offsetting a previously established short position in the calls or may be establishing a new, long position in them.

In 1996, the CBOE reported that about 57 percent of all opening stock option transactions were closed in this manner.[9] In some cases, however, option traders may wish to exercise the option.

In the over-the-counter markets, there is no facility for selling back an option previously bought or buying back an option previously sold. These

---

[8]*The Wall Street Journal,* July 16, 1997.

[9]CBOE, *Market Statistics,* 1996.

contracts are created with the objective of being held to expiration. As circumstances change, however, many holders or writers of over-the-counter options find that they need to reverse their positions. This can be done by simply entering the market and attempting to construct an offsetting position. In other words, if you had previously bought an October 3900 call on London's Financial Times 100 index and now would like to reverse the transaction before expiration, you simply call a dealer and offer to sell the same option. In the over-the-counter market, however, there is not likely to be someone trying to do the exact offsetting trade at the same time. A dealer takes the opposite position, but there are many dealers willing to do the trade. The most important difference between offsetting in the over-the-counter market and offsetting in the exchange-listed market is that in the latter the contracts cancel any obligations of the writer. In the former both contracts remain on the books so they are both subject to default risk.[10]

Exercising an Option

An American option can be exercised on any day up through the expiration date. European options, which have nothing to do with Europe, can be exercised only on the expiration date. Suppose you elect to **exercise** the Hewlett-Packard August 70 calls, which, like all options on stocks in the United States, are American options. You notify your brokerage firm, which in turn notifies the clearing firm through which the trade originally was cleared. The clearing firm then places an exercise order with the OCC, which randomly selects a clearing firm through which someone has written the same option. The clearing firm, using a procedure established and made known to its customers in advance, selects someone who has written that option.[11] The chosen writer is said to be **assigned.**

If the option is a call option on an individual stock, the writer must deliver the stock. You then pay the exercise price, which is passed on to the writer. If the option had been a put option on an individual stock, you would have to deliver the stock. The writer pays the exercise price, which is passed on to you. For either type of option, however, the writer who originally wrote the contract might not be the one who is assigned the exercise.

Because an index represents a portfolio of stocks, exercise of the option ordinarily would require the delivery of the stocks weighted in the same proportions as they are in the index. This would be quite difficult

---

[10]In some cases, a reversing trade with the same dealer with whom one did the original contract can be structured as an offset, thereby terminating both contracts.

[11]Procedures such as first-in, first-out or random selection are commonly used.

and inconvenient. Instead, an alternative exercise procedure called **cash settlement** is used. With this method, if an index call option is exercised, the writer pays the buyer the contract multiple times the difference between the index level and the exercise price. For example, assume you buy one index call option that has a multiple of 100. The index is at 900, and the exercise price is at 895. If you exercise the option, the assigned writer pays you $100(900 - 895) = 500 in cash. No stock changes hands. A put option is exercised by the writer paying the buyer the multiple times the difference between the exercise price and the index level.

An order to exercise an index option during the day is executed after the close of trading. The index value *at the end of the day,* rather than the index value when the exercise was ordered, is used to determine the amount of the settlement. Thus, an investor is well advised to wait until the end of the day to order an exercise of an index option. In addition certain index options settle based on the index value at the opening of the next day.

On expiration day, if you find that the stock price is less than the exercise price or, for a put, that the stock price is greater than the exercise price, you allow the option to expire by doing nothing. When the expiration day passes, the option contract is removed from the records of the clearing firm and the OCC.

In 1996, about 14 percent of calls and 12 percent of puts on the CBOE were exercised and about 28 percent of the calls and 39 percent of the puts expired.[12] In some cases, options that should have been exercised at expiration were not, due to customer ignorance or oversight. Some brokerage firms have a policy of exercising options automatically when doing so is to the customer's advantage. Such a policy usually is stated in the agreement that the customer signs when opening the account. The OCC automatically exercises options that are at least slightly in-the-money at expiration.

Option Price Quotations

Option prices are available daily in *The Wall Street Journal* and in many daily newspapers in larger cities. Figure 2.5 illustrates how *The Wall Street Journal* reports options on individual stocks. *The Wall Street Journal* shows only the most active short-term options on stocks and the most active LEAPS on stocks.

Consider the options on American Express stock (abbreviated AmExpr). On the first line in the first of the seven columns is the name of

---

[12]CBOE, *Market Statistics,* 1996. These figures are for options on stocks only.

FIGURE 2.5 **Stock Option Quotations in *The Wall Street Journal,* Trading Day of July 15, 1997**

Tuesday, July 15, 1997

Composite volume and close for actively traded equity and LEAPS, or long-term options, with results for the corresponding put or call contract. Volume figures are unofficial. Open interest is total outstanding for all exchanges and reflects previous trading day. Close when possible is shown for the underlying stock on primary market. **CB**-Chicago Board Options Exchange. **AM**-American Stock Exchange. **PB**-Philadelphia Stock Exchange. **PC**-Pacific Stock Exchange. **NY**-New York Stock Exchange. **XC**-Composite. **p**-Put.

MOST ACTIVE CONTRACTS

Option/Strike				Vol	Exch	Last	Net Chg	a-Close	Open Int
Intel	Jul	80		21,444	AM	3	+ 1 5/8	80 29/32	43,574
Intel	Jul	82 1/2		15,918	AM	1 7/8	+ 1 5/16	80 29/32	27,878
Intel	Jul	75	p	14,774	AM	9/16	− 3/16	80 29/32	35,551
Intel	Jul	85		13,591	AM	1	+ 11/16	80 29/32	24,077
Intel	Jul	80	p	11,579	AM	2 1/4	− 1/2	80 29/32	27,877
TelBrasl	Aug	150	p	10,595	XC	17 1/2	+ 8 1/4	135	10,941
Intel	Jul	77 1/2		9,834	AM	4 3/8	+ 1 7/8	80 29/32	39,485
MicrTc	Jul	42 1/2		9,025	XC	6 1/8	+ 1 3/8	48 5/8	16,213
Intel	Jul	77 1/2	p	8,992	AM	1 1/8	− 3/8	80 29/32	22,056
Intel	Jul	75		8,575	AM	5 7/8	+ 1 5/8	80 29/32	50,522
Intel	Aug	80		8,305	AM	4 1/2	+ 1 1/8	80 29/32	14,243
3Com	Jul	45		8,094	PC	12 3/4	+ 2 5/8	57 23/32	17,519
Hewlet	Aug	60		8,040	CB	9 3/8	+ 3 1/4	68 1/4	12,851
3Com	Aug	55		7,873	PC	5 1/8	+ 1 3/8	57 23/32	7,131
TelMex	Aug	50		7,393	XC	2 1/2	− 1 1/2	50 3/4	20,545
TelBrasl	Aug	140		7,375	XC	6 1/2	− 5 3/8	135	3,255
TelBrasl	Jul	140		6,790	XC	1 5/8	− 5 3/4	135	3,786
Intel	Jul	72 1/2	p	6,751	AM	1/4	− 3/16	80 29/32	.47,314
MicrTc	Jul	47 1/2		6,661	XC	1 5/8	+ 13/16	48 5/8	3,407
OfceDp	Jul	17 1/2		6,607	AM	3/8	+ 5/16	17 1/2	35,217

Option/Strike				Vol	Exch	Last	Net Chg	a-Close	Open Int
3Com	Jul	55		6,571	PC	3 1/8	+ 1 5/8	57 23/32	15,069
Intel	Aug	85		6,376	AM	2 3/8	...	80 29/32	3,580
M C I	Aug	35	p	6,331	CB	2 3/8	+ 1/2	35 15/16	2,593
3Com	Aug	45		6,036	PC	12 3/4	+ 2 1/4	57 23/32	2,124
AscendC	Jul	55		5,706	XC	1 3/8	+ 1/8	53 7/8	8,394
TelBrasl	Aug	150		5,621	XC	3	− 3 3/4	135	10,841
Micsft	Jul	140		5,335	PC	2	+ 1 1/16	138 15/32	5,371
TelMex	Aug	45		5,222	XC	6 3/8	− 1 3/4	50 3/4	8,251
M C I	Aug	32 1/2	p	5,160	CB	1 3/4	+ 1/2	35 15/16	5,165
Intel	Jul	90		5,155	AM	5/16	+ 1/4	80 29/32	19,917
TelMex	Jul	50		4,961	XC	1 1/4	− 1 1/2	50 3/4	14,602
Micsft	Jul	135		4,950	PC	4 5/8	+ 1 5/8	138 15/32	8,698
TelBrasl	Jul	30		4,942	XC	6 7/8	− 13 3/4	135	4,398
Oracle	Aug	55		4,869	CB	3 5/8	+ 1 5/8	56 15/32	3,509
MicrTc	Aug	50		4,659	XC	2 3/8	...	48 5/8	1,638
Dig Eq	Jul	40		4,504	XC	11/16	− 1/16	40 1/8	16,806
Intel	Aug	75		4,502	AM	7 1/2	+ 1 3/8	80 29/32	13,088
Motorola	Oct	80		4,430	AM	10 1/2	+ 1 1/2	87 1/8	5,809
I B M	Jul	95		4,278	XC	1 13/16	+ 7/16	96	12,862
GnMotr	Jan 98	70		4,250	CB	7/16	+ 1/16	54 1/4	4,958

wsj.com Complete equity option listings and data are available in The Wall Street Journal Interactive Edition at **http://wsj.com** on the Internet's World Wide Web.

Option/Strike		Exp.	Call Vol.	Call Last	Put Vol.	Put Last
AES Cp	75	Aug	1566	5 7/8	40	2 1/4
79 1/4	80	Aug	726	2 7/8	30	4 3/8
A M R	90	Jul	2055	4 1/4	200	1/8
95 1/16	95	Jul	1171	1 1/4	10	2 3/16
95 1/16	100	Jul	310	3/16	5	5 1/8
AT&T o	35	Jul	582	7/16	298	3/8
35	35	Aug	581	1 1/4	308	1
35	40	Aug	294	3/16	...	...
35	40	Jan	130	1	1000	5 1/8
Aames	20	Jul	299	11/16	30	1/2
Abbt L	65	Aug	432	1 7/8	27	2 3/4
Adaptc	40	Jul	567	3 3/8	79	1/4
43 15/32	42 1/2	Jul	299	1 5/16	29	1/2
A M D	35	Jul	170	4	498	1/8
38 11/16	37 1/2	Jul	77	1 3/4	990	3/8
38 11/16	40	Jul	659	3/8	724	1 3/8
38 11/16	40	Aug	290	2	14	2 7/8
AdvTis	12 1/2	Jul	293	1 5/8	350	3/16
AdvanB	35	Jul	97	1	270	1 5/8
34 3/8	35	Aug	510	3 1/4	5	2 7/8
34 3/8	40	Aug	550	1 3/8	...	...
Agourn	80	Jul	314	3	310	7/8
AlnSemi	10	Jul	1489	1/2	...	...
9 3/4	10	Aug	342	15/16	...	...
Allste	75	Jan	5	6 3/8	1350	4
76 13/16	80	Jan	2405	4 1/2	...	...
AlphaBta	7 1/2	Aug	847	1 5/16	589	1 1/2
7 9/16	10	Aug	702	3/4	...	...
7 9/16	12 1/2	Aug	749	9/16	...	...
Altera	55	Jul	641	5 5/8	140	5/16
60 1/2	60	Jul	482	1 7/8	40	1 3/16
60 1/2	60	Aug	355	4 1/4	119	3 5/8
Alcoa	75	Jul	1033	4 5/8	...	...
79 5/8	75	Aug	1000	5 7/8	...	...
Amdahl	10	Nov	405	1 7/8	...	...
AmerOn	60	Aug	10	14 5/8	423	1/2
73	70	Jul	351	4	213	5/16
73	70	Aug	138	6 5/8	484	2 15/16
AmExpr	80	Jul	972	1 7/16	50	1 1/4
80 3/16	80	Aug	298	4 1/2	30	3 3/4
80 3/16	85	Jul	1209	3/8	...	...
80 3/16	85	Aug	866	2 3/4	...	...
Amgen	50	Jul	28	5 3/4	500	1/4
57 1/4	55	Jul	965	2 1/2	495	1/2
57 1/4	55	Aug	610	3 7/8	189	1 1/2
57 1/4	60	Jul	1042	1/4	197	3
57 1/4	60	Aug	648	1 1/4	9	3 3/4
57 1/4	60	Oct	363	3 1/8	27	5 1/8
Analog	30	Jul	621	2 5/8	3	3/8
32 13/16	30	Aug	104	3 1/2	320	7/8
Anheusr	50	Dec	400	1	...	...
AnnTay	17 1/2	Aug	...	...	1000	15/16
19	20	Jul	...	...	1000	1 7/16
AppleC	12 1/2	Jul	40	3 1/2	675	3/16
15 15/16	15	Jul	446	1 3/16	861	7/16
15 15/16	17 1/2	Aug	1766	3/4	10	2 3/8
Aplbee	30	Nov	312	2	...	...
ApplMg	25	Jul	1222	6 3/8	1065	1/16
31 3/16	25	Oct	556	8 1/2	424	1 5/8
31 3/16	30	Jul	1849	1 9/16	889	3/8
31 3/16	30	Aug	3920	3 5/8	432	1 3/4
31 3/16	30	Oct	3386	5 3/8	2779	3 7/8
31 3/16	35	Jul	294	1/8	2	3 1/4
31 3/16	35	Aug	751	1 5/16	30	4 7/8
31 3/16	35	Oct	360	3 5/8	18	6 3/8
31 3/16	35	Jan	264	5 1/8	50	8 1/2
31 3/16	40	Oct	257	2 3/16	4	10 3/8
AplMat	55	Jul	28	27 1/4	395	1/16
81 13/16	70	Jul	165	12 1/8	620	1/16
81 13/16	75	Jul	286	6 7/8	390	1/8
81 13/16	80	Jul	2905	2 7/8	428	1
AscendC	45	Jul	913	8 5/8	1088	3/16
53 7/8	45	Sep	168	11	254	2
53 7/8	50	Jul	3695	4 1/2	2545	1/2
53 7/8	50	Aug	1175	6 3/8	716	2 3/16
53 7/8	50	Sep	677	7 7/8	120	3 1/2
53 7/8	55	Jul	5706	1 3/8	1451	2 3/4
53 7/8	55	Aug	2431	4	181	4 1/2
53 7/8	55	Sep	1038	5 3/4	32	6
53 7/8	60	Jul	1658	7/16	...	...
53 7/8	60	Sep	666	3 3/4	41	9 1/2
53 7/8	65	Sep	2873	2 3/8	...	...
53 7/8	80	Sep	341	9/16	...	...
Atl R	75	Jul	515	1/16	...	...
Atmel	22 1/2	Nov	211	12 1/2	302	3/8
34 3/8	25	Aug	265	9 1/4	15	1/8
34 3/8	30	Aug	504	4 7/8	62	1/2
34 3/8	30	Nov	124	6 5/8	355	1 13/16
34 3/8	32 1/2	Aug	295	3 1/8	53	1 1/8
34 3/8	35	Aug	596	1 5/8	41	2 1/16
34 3/8	35	Nov	314	4	...	...
34 3/8	37 1/2	Aug	424	11/16	10	4 1/2
SoNatCp	40	Jul	790	7 3/8	...	...
47 1/2	45	Jul	790	2 3/8	...	...
Baan	60	Jul	300	17 3/4	...	...
77 5/8	65	Aug	703	13 1/8	4	3/4
BakrHu	35	Jul	1004	10	...	...
44 3/4	37 1/2	Jul	1012	7 1/2	...	...
44 3/4	40	Aug	2283	5 1/2	10	11/16
44 3/4	40	Oct	17	6 1/8	3015	1 1/8
44 3/4	42 1/2	Oct	4043	5	2	2 1/8
44 3/4	45	Oct	535	3 1/2	1	3 5/8
BancOne	47 1/2	Jul	23	11/16	506	5/16
BankAm	67 1/2	Jul	312	5/8	40	1 1/16
Bard	35	Jul	1000	1 3/4	150	5/16
BarickG	25	Jan	565	7/8	...	...
BayNwk	25	Jul	844	2 9/16	...	...
27 5/8	25	Aug	776	3 1/2	8	15/16
27 5/8	27 1/2	Jul	346	9/16	35	5/8
27 5/8	30	Aug	559	1	10	3 1/2
BellAtl	55	Jul	761	16 7/8	...	...
Beth S	10	Jul	335	7/16	...	...
BioPhar	25	Aug	511	1 3/16	10	2 1/4
Biogen	30	Aug	458	7 1/4	...	...
36 15/32	35	Jul	291	1 3/8	35	7/16
36 15/32	40	Aug	329	15/16	...	...
Boeing	42 1/2	Jul	325	14 3/4	...	...
58 1/16	52 1/2	Aug	268	6 1/4	6	7/16
58 1/16	55	Jul	830	3	113	1/8
58 1/16	55	Aug	588	3 7/8	80	7/8
58 1/16	57 1/2	Aug	264	2 3/8	21	1 9/16
58 1/16	60	Aug	462	1 3/8	23	2 7/8
58 1/16	60	Nov	359	3 5/8	15	4 3/4
Borland	5	Jan	261	2 5/8	5	7/16
7 1/4	7 1/2	Jul	341	1/8	10	1/2
7 1/4	7 1/2	Jan	755	1 1/16	...	...
BostChkn	10	Aug	276	2 7/16	181	3/8
12 5/16	10	Jan	14	3 3/4	880	1 1/2
12 5/16	12 1/2	Jan	510	2 5/8	15	2 11/16
12 5/16	17 1/2	Aug	...	...	2168	5 1/4
12 5/16	17 1/2	Jan	1015	1 1/8	...	...
12 5/16	20	Jul	...	...	2161	7 5/8
BostSc	60	Jul	1280	10 3/4	...	...
70 7/8	65	Aug	1250	7 1/2	...	...
70 7/8	70	Jul	300	1 1/4	83	5/8
BrMSq	67 1/2	Sep	400	19 1/2	...	...
87 3/16	70	Sep	600	17 1/8	60	1/4
C-CUBE	15	Aug	721	5 7/8	...	...
20 3/8	17 1/2	Aug	36	3 1/2	366	7/8
20 3/8	20	Jul	548	3/4	403	5/8
20 3/8	20	Aug	727	1 15/16	82	1 11/16
20 3/8	22 1/2	Nov	51	2 3/4	327	5
Cabltrn	30	Jul	273	2 3/4	40	1/8
32 15/16	35	Jul	90	1/8	1035	2 1/8
32 15/16	35	Aug	214	1 1/4	1000	3 3/8
Cabot	30	Aug	...	...	396	2 5/8
Cadence	40	Aug	355	2 7/8	...	...
CartWl	20	Jul	335	3/16	...	...
CascCm	35	Jul	447	3	2230	9/16
...	40	Jul	414	9/16	...	...
Caterp	55	Jul	616	7/8	60	11/16
55 1/2	55	Aug	677	2 7/16	33	1 5/8
ChamIn	50	Jul	500	10 3/4	...	...
Chase n	95	Jul	433	8	...	...
102 9/16	95	Aug	480	9	...	...
102 9/16	100	Jul	378	3	310	1/2
102 9/16	100	Aug	492	5 1/4	160	2
102 9/16	105	Jul	656	3/8	10	2 1/2
102 9/16	105	Aug	485	2 1/2	...	...
ChesEng	7 1/2	Aug	37	1 1/8	540	5/8
Chevrn	70	Jul	328	5 7/8	...	...
76 5/8	75	Sep	339	3 1/8	20	1 7/8
ChipsTc	12 1/2	Jul	687	7/8	61	3/16
Chiron	20	Jul	1640	15/16	...	...
20 15/16	22 1/2	Jul	506	1/16	...	...
Chryslr	30	Jul	263	5 1/4	...	...
35 5/8	35	Jul	481	3/4	315	1/4
35 5/8	35	Jan	47	2 3/4	510	2 5/16
Cirrus	15	Sep	256	3/8	8	3 3/8
Cisco	60	Jul	195	18 1/8	406	1/16
77 21/32	65	Jul	370	12 3/4	104	1/16
77 21/32	65	Oct	469	15 1/4	49	1 3/4
77 21/32	70	Jul	1141	7 7/8	96	1/16

Source: *The Wall Street Journal,* July 16, 1997

the stock. In that same column below the first line is the closing New York Stock Exchange price of the stock. Note that if more than two options are shown, the closing stock price is repeated to fill the space. For some inactive options, such as those on Amdahl, there is only one line and the closing stock price is not shown. The second column contains the exercise price and the third column contains the month of expiration. Thus, each line is a separate combination of exercise price and expiration. The next column is the number of call contracts that traded that day and the following column is the closing call price. The next two columns are the put volume and closing put price. Thus, for example, the American Express call options expiring in August with an exercise price of 80 closed at 4 1/2 or $4.50. Two hundred ninety-eight contracts traded that day. The August 80 puts closed at 3 3/4 or $3.75 and 30 contracts traded. Ellipses (...) are used to fill in spaces left by option series that did not trade that day.

At the very top of the page is a list of the most active option contracts for that day. Each line also shows the volume, the exchange where it was traded, the closing price, the net change from the previous day, the stock closing price, and the open interest, which is the number of contracts currently outstanding. If the option is a put, it is indicated with a lowercase "p." Not shown here but appearing at the end of the listings is a summary of the volume and open interest by exchange.

A glance over the option pages usually reveals some options in which the stock name is followed by an *o*. With those options, the terms and conditions of the contract have been modified to reflect stock splits or stock dividends.

Figure 2.6 shows a *Wall Street Journal* listing for index options. These are grouped by exchange (e.g., CHICAGO stands for Chicago Board Options Exchange). For each index, the ticker symbol appears beside the name. Each row contains one option series, as indicated by the expiration month, the exercise price, and the letter "c" or "p" indicating call or put. The next column contains the volume in contracts and the next column contains the closing price. The next column contains the price change over the previous day and the final column contains the open interest. The large box in the center contains information on the values of the underlying indices.

The price quotations provided in *The Wall Street Journal* are useful measures of the approximate prices at which options are bought and sold. By the time they reach the public, however, those prices are already old. In addition, they are not necessarily synchronized with one another and with the stock price. The closing price of each option and of the stock reflect only the price of the last transaction. The last transaction of the day may have taken place at any time during that day. Therefore, when the last option transaction was made, the stock price may well have been something else.

FIGURE 2.6 **Index Option Quotations in *The Wall Street Journal*, Trading Day of July 15, 1997**

INDEX OPTIONS TRADING

Tuesday, July 15, 1997

Volume, last, net change and open interest for all contracts. Volume figures are unofficial. Open interest reflects previous trading day. p-Put c-Call

CHICAGO

Strike		Vol.	Last	Net Chg.	Open Int.
CB MEXICO INDEX(MEX)					
Oct	90 c	2	30	− 7	105
Jul	105 c	5	13¼	− ⅜	33
Aug	110 c	40	9¾	− 3⅞	556
Aug	110 p	5	1 9/16	+ 15/16	...
Jul	115 c	20	2 9/16	− 6 1/16	35
Jul	115 p	70	⅜	− 3/16	80
Sep	115 c	22	9	− 3⅞	129
Jul	120 c	40	⅝	− 2⅛	14
Jul	120 p	30	3	+ 2⅜	50
Oct	120 c	15	9¼	− 2¼	72
Aug	125 c	420	1⅝	− 2⅛	35
Sep	125 c	80	3⅞	− 2¾	192
Aug	130 p	25	11⅛	+ 3¼	35
Aug	135 c	200	⅜	− 13/16	40
Sep	135 c	200	1½	− 1 7/16	2
Call Vol.		1,044	Open Int.		3,073
Put Vol.		130	Open Int.		1,451
CB TECHNOLOGY(TXX)					
Aug	200 p	5	½	− 2¾	5
Jul	210 c	2	37	+ 9⅝	110
Aug	220 p	2	2 3/16	− 13/16	33
Aug	235 p	8	4⅝	− 3¼	3
Jul	240 p	5	1 3/16	− 1¾	5
Aug	240 c	3	13⅜	+ 3⅛	100
Jul	245 c	2	5⅛	+ 3 5/16	2
Jul	245 p	40	2 3/16	...	...
Aug	245 c	100	11	...	...
Call Vol.		107	Open Int.		848
Put Vol.		65	Open Int.		1,058
GS TECH COMPOSITE(GTC)					
Sep	150 c	6	10⅜	+ 1½	16
Sep	170 c	6	2⅛	...	...
Call Vol.		14	Open Int.		21
Put Vol.		0	Open Int.		361
MS MULTINATIONAL(NFT)					
Jul	490 c	500	30	+ 5	875
Sep	495 p	1	9⅞	...	...
Jul	510 c	4,000	5¾	− 1¼	7,480
Jul	510 p	5	2⅞	− 2⅝	9
Sep	510 c	2	24	− ⅝	21
Jul	515 p	4	2⅛	− 1¾	14
Sep	515 c	3	20¾	− ¼	13
Jul	520 p	2	6⅛	− 17	10
Aug	520 c	1,600	11½	+ 4⅜	325
Sep	520 c	1	18¼	...	...
Aug	540 c	1,125	4½	+ ⅜	500
Call Vol.		7,231	Open Int.		29,950
Put Vol.		12	Open Int.		8,699

RANGES FOR UNDERLYING INDEXES

Tuesday, July 15, 1997

	High	Low	Close	Net Chg.	From Dec. 31	% Chg.
S&P 100 (OEX)	904.95	891.94	904.20	+ 7.67	+ 184.22	+ 25.6
S&P 500 -A.M.(SPX)	926.15	914.52	925.76	+ 7.38	+ 185.02	+ 25.0
CB-Tech (TXX)	249.26	242.61	248.39	+ 5.78	+ 48.51	+ 24.3
CB-Mexico (MEX)	122.20	116.75	117.33	− 4.87	+ 35.37	+ 43.2
CB-Lps Mex (VEX)	12.22	11.68	11.73	− 0.49	+ 3.53	+ 43.1
MS Multintl (NFT)	520.58	512.61	520.22	+ 5.60	+ 121.77	+ 30.6
GSTI Comp (GTC)	155.88	152.17	155.52	+ 3.35	+ 39.07	+ 33.6
Nasdaq 100 (NDX)	1063.04	1041.88	1059.01	+ 17.13	+ 237.65	+ 28.9
NYSE (NYA)	480.99	476.39	480.99	+ 2.88	+ 88.69	+ 22.6
Russell 2000 (RUT)	406.41	403.85	406.39	+ 2.54	+ 43.78	+ 12.1
Lps S&P 100 (OEX)	90.50	89.19	90.42	+ 0.77	+ 18.42	+ 25.6
Lps S&P 500 (SPX)	92.62	91.45	92.58	+ 0.74	+ 18.51	+ 25.0
S&P Midcap (MID)	302.87	300.87	302.85	+ 1.98	+ 47.27	+ 18.5
Major Mkt (XMI)	819.56	809.78	819.56	+ 2.71	+ 151.77	+ 22.7
Leaps MMkt (XLT)	81.96	80.98	81.96	+ 0.27	+ 15.18	+ 22.7
Hong Kong (HKO)			308.57	+ 2.04	+ 35.32	+ 12.9
Leaps HK (HKL)			30.86	+ 0.21	+ 3.54	+ 13.0
IW Internet (IIX)	278.43	272.47	277.40	+ 4.93	+ 33.32	+ 13.7
AM-Mexico (MXY)	133.44	127.77	128.35	− 5.09	+ 38.63	+ 43.1
Institut'l -A.M.(XII)	1015.81	1001.37	1015.26	+ 8.24	+ 222.58	+ 28.1
Japan (JPN)			204.77	− 1.61	+ 7.68	+ 3.9
MS Cyclical (CYC)	503.36	498.04	502.79	+ 2.46	+ 114.23	+ 29.4
MS Consumr (CMR)	422.13	417.54	422.11	+ 3.27	+ 86.16	+ 25.7
MS Hi Tech (MSH)	491.48	480.78	490.33	+ 9.55	+ 107.29	+ 28.0
Pharma (DRG)	504.07	497.52	503.46	+ 1.29	+ 144.00	+ 40.1
Biotech (BTK)	142.33	139.91	142.33	+ 2.15	− 1.97	− 1.4
Comp Tech (XCI)	476.95	462.90	474.80	+ 11.90	+ 134.88	+ 39.7
Gold/Silver (XAU)	91.65	89.58	89.91	− 1.07	− 26.84	− 23.0
OTC (XOC)	752.43	739.44	749.88	+ 10.44	+ 167.01	+ 28.7
Utility (UTY)	258.94	256.77	258.92	+ 1.52	+ 2.36	+ 0.9
Value Line (VLE)	815.98	811.79	815.97	+ 3.25	+ 133.35	+ 19.5
Bank (BKX)	661.59	653.65	658.58	− 1.30	+ 120.90	+ 22.5
Semicond (SOX)	362.41	348.34	360.49	+ 12.15	+ 120.19	+ 50.0
Top 100 (TPX)	870.01	857.79	869.50	+ 7.94	+ 190.42	+ 28.0
PSE Tech (PSE)	317.02	313.84	316.53	+ 3.34	+ 74.34	+ 30.7

Strike		Vol.	Last	Net Chg.	Open Int.
Aug	875 p	238	9⅝	− 4	790

Strike		Vol.	Last	Net Chg.	Open Int.
Aug	960 p	1	40½	− 9	256

PHILADELPHIA

Strike		Vol.	Last	Net Chg.	Open Int.
GOLD/SILVER(XAU)					
Aug	80 c	15	11¼	− 1½	44
Aug	80 p	2	⅝	+ 3/16	46
Jul	85 c	16	6½	− 1⅝	128
Aug	85 c	7	7¼	− 1¾	62
Aug	85 p	125	1 5/16	+ 1/16	166
Sep	85 c	1	9¾	...	18
Sep	85 p	1	3	+ ½	3,038
Jul	90 p	270	1¼	+ 11/16	1,044
Aug	90 c	35	3¾	− 2½	2,491
Aug	90 p	90	3⅛	+ ⅛	679
Sep	90 c	11	5⅞	− 1½	195
Sep	90 p	11	4⅞	+ ⅞	447
Jul	95 c	45	¼	− ¼	2,221
Jul	95 p	31	4½	+ 1 9/16	365
Aug	95 c	20	2½	− ¼	616
Aug	95 p	2	6¾	+ 2⅛	129
Sep	95 c	10	3⅜	− 1⅞	192
Sep	95 p	3	8¼	+ 2	187
Jul	100 c	500	1/16	− 3/16	1,145
Jul	100 p	20	9½	+ 1¾	349
Aug	100 c	7	1 5/16	− 1/16	2,421
Aug	100 p	31	10⅛	+ 2	877
Aug	110 c	5	½	− ¼	375
Aug	115 c	7	¼	− 1/16	108
Sep	115 c	5	7/16	− 9/16	145
Sep	125 c	5	3/16	− 7/16	107
Call Vol.		748	Open Int.		31,327
Put Vol.		616	Open Int.		15,321
OTC INDEX(XOC)					
Aug	700 c	5	54¾	+ 24⅛	5
Jul	720 c	5	32	+ 13	36
Aug	720 c	16	45⅝	+ 23⅝	16
Aug	730 p	10	16⅞	...	...
Jul	740 c	5	16¼	+ 6¾	13
Jul	750 c	11	11¼	+ 9¼	34
Jul	750 p	10	12⅞	...	...
Call Vol.		42	Open Int.		605
Put Vol.		20	Open Int.		1,749
PHLX KBW BANK(BKX)					
Aug	600 p	10	4⅞	− 3	202
Aug	615 p	25	5½	...	...
Jul	650 c	1	10	− 7	211
Jul	650 p	87	4⅛	+ ⅝	373
Aug	650 p	26	15	...	...
Jul	655 c	46	7¼	− 4	62
Jul	655 p	30	4½	− 1	37
Aug	655 c	100	22½	− 2¾	117
Jul	660 c	39	5	+ ¾	447
Jul	660 p	97	5⅞	− 1½	33
Aug	660 p	1	19⅝	+ 3	27
Jul	665 c	100	3⅜	− 3⅛	90
Jul	665 p	31	7¼	− 2⅛	201
Jul	670 c	10	⅝	− 2⅞	94
Aug	670 c	20	13	− 1⅜	113

Source: *The Wall Street Journal*, July 16, 1997

Another problem with prices reported in a newspaper is that they reflect only the price of the last trade and do not indicate whether that price was a market maker's bid or ask price. For example, suppose the market maker is quoting a bid of 1 3/4 and an ask of 2. If the last trade of the day is a public order to buy, the order is filled at 2; if it is a public order to sell, the order is filled at 1 3/4. Thus, the closing price shown in the newspaper could be either 1 3/4 or 2.

Most serious option traders and certainly all institutional option traders require immediate access to bid and ask prices as well as to online market price information. These data are available from many commercial price-reporting services, although the costs are somewhat high for individuals. With the growing use of personal computers, however, many individuals are finding that they can access option price quotes from their homes by subscribing to computerized telecommunication services.

Types of Options

Stock Options

Options on individual stocks are often called **equity options.** As of August 1996, the CBOE had 913, the AMEX 705, the Philadelphia Stock Exchange about 557, the Pacific Stock Exchange about 583, and the New York Stock Exchange about 264, though in 1997 it sold its options business to the CBOE. Of course, many stocks' options are listed on more than one exchange. On the CBOE, the most active options in 1996 were (in order) IBM, Cisco Systems, Micron Technology, Hewlett-Packard, Texas Instruments, Bay Networks, Iomega, Oracle, Coca-Cola, and Merck.[13]

Index Options

The construction of stock indices is discussed in some detail in Chapter 8. For now, however, let us simply consider a stock index as a measure of the overall value of a group of stocks.

An **index option** is an option on an index of stocks. The first index option, the CBOE 100—since renamed the S&P 100—was launched on March 11, 1983. The S&P 100, commonly known by its ticker symbol, OEX, had an opening-day volume of 4,575 contracts. Soon afterward other exchanges added index options, and the success of these contracts has been phenomenal. On all exchanges combined, index option volume is approximately 31 percent of the total volume of all options; however,

---

[13]Ibid.

TABLE 2.2	Index Options Trading on U.S. Exchanges, July 1997

Chicago Board Options Exchange	**Philadelphia Stock Exchange**
Standard & Poor's 100 Index	Gold/Silver Stock Exchange
Standard & Poor's 500 Index	Over-the-Counter Stock Index
Goldman Sachs Technology Composite	KBW Bank Index
NASDAQ 100 Index	Semiconductor Stock Index
Mexico Index	Top 100 Index
Russell 2000	Utility Stock Index
Morgan Stanley Multinational	Value Line Index
New York Stock Exchange Index	
Nikkei 300 Index	
Israel Index	
Technology Industry Index	
American Stock Exchange	
Mexico Index	
Computer Technology Stock Index	
Hong Kong Index	
Institutional Index	
Internet Stock Index	
Japan Index	
Major Market Index	
Morgan Stanley Consumer Stock Index	
Morgan Stanley Cyclical Stock Index	
Morgan Stanley HiTech 35 Stock Index	
Pharmaceutical Index	
Standard & Poor's Midcap 400 Index	

These offerings of index options change frequently as exchanges experiment with different indices and terms of the contracts. For the latest information, contact the exchanges directly. Some of these options are available with long expirations and with flexible (nonstandard) terms. Some of these options are European style and some are American style.

at the CBOE, index option volume is over 49 percent of its total volume.[14]

Table 2.2 lists the current index options. The most active index option is the CBOE's S&P 100 followed by the CBOE's S&P 500.

Index options have been popular for two reasons. First, the cash settlement feature enables investors to trade options without having to take or make delivery of stock. Cash settlement has, however, been both a blessing and a curse. Many institutional investors hold large portfolios of stocks that purport to replicate the index. They then write call options or sell fu-

---

[14]Ibid.

tures against these portfolios. At other times, these investors sell short the stocks and buy call options or futures. When the options approach the expiration date, the institutional investors, not wanting to hold the stocks after the options expire, attempt to unwind their stock positions. Holders of stock sell the stock, and short sellers buy it back. As a result, many large stock transactions are made near expiration and are accompanied by increased volatility. The cash settlement feature of index options and futures has been blamed for this volatility, although it is not clear that it is truly the cause.

The second reason for the popularity of index options is the fact that they are options on the market as a whole. Because there are so many stocks on which options trade, few investors have the time to screen that many opportunities. Many prefer to analyze the market as a whole and use index options (and futures) to act on their forecasts.

Other Types of Options

The options exchanges have experimented with a number of different types of options, including options on bonds, though these have attracted little interest. However, options on bonds and related options called *interest rate options* are extremely popular in the over-the-counter markets. We shall explore these in Chapter 14. In addition, options on foreign currencies are quite popular, especially in the over-the-counter markets. In the exchange market, they trade on the Philadelphia Stock Exchange. We shall cover foreign currency options in Chapter 13, when we look at foreign currency derivatives.

Many financial institutions now offer deposits on which they pay interest based on a minimum value plus the performance of the stock market above a specific level. This is like a call option plus a bond. Other innovative options include some that pay off based on how the price of a commodity, like oil, does in the over-the-counter markets. It is possible to trade an option that pays off based on which stock index, say the S&P 500 or London's Financial Times 100, performs better. There are also options that expire if the stock price falls to a certain level; options that are based on the average, maximum, or minimum stock price during the life of the option; and an option that allows you to decide, after buying it but before it expires, whether to make it a put or a call. These options, often called **exotics,** are but a sampling of the tremendous number of innovations that have developed in the over-the-counter markets in recent years. We shall take a look at some of these kinds of instruments in Chapter 15.

A number of other common instruments are practically identical to options. For example, many corporations issue warrants, which are long-term options to buy the companies' stock. Warrants often are issued in conjunction with a public offering of debt or equity. Many corporations

issue convertible bonds, which allow the holder to convert the bond into a certain number of shares of stock. The right to convert is itself a call option. Callable bonds, which give the issuing firm the right to repay the bonds early, contain an option-like component. Stock itself is equivalent to a call option on the firm's assets written by the bondholders with an exercise price equal to the amount due on the debt. Executive stock options, which are call options written by a corporation and given to their executives, are used extensively as compensation and to give executives an incentive to engage in activities that maximize shareholder wealth.

Indices of Options Market Activity

The stock market is widely covered by various indices. Everyone has heard of the Dow Jones Industrial Average, and most are familiar with the S&P 500. Indices of options market activity are less known, because it is difficult to construct an option index. If an option were included in an index, the index's composition would change as the option approached expiration. For example, an index consisting primarily of six-month calls would consist of three-month calls three months later. As we shall see in later chapters, the behavior of three-month calls differs substantially from that of six-month calls. Moreover, the options contained in the index eventually would expire and have to be replaced by other options. Thus, the composition of the index would constantly change.

Despite these problems, options indices have been developed by Galai (1979), Gastineau (1977), and Eckerdt and Williams (1984) and by some private firms, such as *Value Line Options*, a weekly publication of Arnold Bernhard Company. The CBOE has also constructed two indices, one for puts and one for calls. The CBOE indices measure the average premium on six-month calls and puts in which the stock price is close to the exercise price. However, options indices are not followed by most investors.

Transaction Costs in Option Trading

Option trading entails certain transaction costs. The costs depend on whether the trader is a member of the exchange, a nonmember institutional investor, or a member of the public who is trading through a broker. This section discusses the different types of transaction costs.

Floor Trading and Clearing Fees

Floor trading and clearing fees are the minimum charges assessed by the exchange, the clearing corporation, and the clearing firms for handling a transaction. For trades that go through a broker, these fees are included in the broker's commission, discussed in the next section. For market makers, the fees are collected by the market maker's clearing firm.

The clearing firm enters into a contractual arrangement with a market maker to clear trades for a fee usually stated on a per contract basis. The amount is subject to negotiation and typically is lower the larger the number of contracts cleared. The nature of the clearing business is highly competitive, and market makers often find that lower fees are available by switching to a different clearing firm. Phillips and Smith (1980) report that these fees range from $.50 to $1 per contract; however, large-volume traders often obtain smaller fees.

For over-the-counter options, these types of costs are not incurred, but comparable, if not higher, costs are associated with processing the paperwork.

Commissions

One of the main advantages of owning a seat on an exchange is that it lets one avoid paying commissions on each trade. The market maker pays indirectly via the opportunity cost associated with the funds tied up in the seat price, the labor involved in trading, and forgoing the earnings that would be realized in another line of work. The savings in commissions, however, are quite substantial.

Table 2.3 is a sample commission schedule for a major discount brokerage house. Discount brokers offer the lowest commission rates, but frequent or large trades sometimes are necessary to take advantage of their prices. A discount brokerage firm does not provide the advice and research available from full-service brokers charging higher commission rates. However, one should not automatically assume that a full-service broker is more costly.

As an example of how commission charges are determined, consider the following orders using the schedule presented in Table 2.3:

1. *One contract of an option priced at 3 1/4.* The commission would be $4.50, but the minimum commission is $35, so the commission would be $35.

TABLE 2.3	Sample Option Commission Schedule		
Option Price	**1st–10th Contracts**	**11th–30th Contracts**	**31st + Contracts**
<$2.00	$3.00	$2.00	$1.50
$2–3 7/8	$4.50	$2.50	$2.00
$4–7 7/8	$6.50	$3.50	$3.00
$8+	$8.00	$6.00	$5.00

Minimum Commission = $35.00

2.   *Twenty contracts of an option priced at 2 3/4.* The commission would be $4.50 per contract for the first 10 contracts and $2.50 per contract for the next 10 contracts, for a total of 10($4.50) + 10($2.50) = $70. This exceeds the minimum of $35, so the commission would be $70.

Other brokers may charge based on the total dollar size of the transaction, but almost all use a sliding scale so that the cost per contract declines the more contracts traded.

When exercising a stock option, the investor must pay the commission for buying or selling the stock. (Stock commissions are discussed in a later section.) If an investor exercises a cash settlement option, the transaction entails only a bookkeeping entry. Some brokerage firms do not charge to exercise a cash settlement option. When any type of option expires unexercised, there normally is no commission.

Individuals pay commission rates such as those shown in Table 2.3. All commissions are subject to negotiation between the investor and the broker. Many large institutional investors trade in sufficiently large volume that they can negotiate lower commission rates from their brokers. However, they would be unable to get lower overall transaction costs than market makers, because the latter pay no commissions at all.

For over-the-counter options, commissions are not generally incurred, because the option buyer or seller usually trades directly with the opposite party.

Bid-Ask Spread

The market maker's spread is a significant transaction cost. Suppose the market maker is quoting a bid price of 3 and an ask price of 3 1/4 on a call. An investor who buys the call immediately incurs a "cost" of the bid-ask spread, or 1/4 point; that is, if the investor immediately sold the call, it would fetch only $3, the bid price, and the investor would immediately incur a 1/4 point, or $25, loss. However, this does not mean that the investor cannot make a profit. The call price may well increase before the option is sold, but if the spread is constant, the bid price must increase by at least the amount of the bid-ask spread before a profit can be made.

The bid-ask spread is the cost of immediacy—the assurance that market makers are willing and able to buy and sell the options on demand. The cost is not explicitly observed, and the investor will not see it on the monthly statement from the broker. It is, however, a real cost and can be quite substantial. Phillips and Smith (1980) estimate that the median bid-ask spread is 4.23 percent on calls and 3.39 percent on puts.

It may appear that market makers can avoid the bid-ask spread transaction cost. This is true in some cases. However, if the market maker must

buy or sell an option, there may be no public orders of the opposite position. In that case, the market maker would have to trade with another market maker and thus would incur the cost of the bid-ask spread.

In the over-the-counter market, the buyer or seller trades directly with the opposite party. In many cases, one of the parties is a financial institution that makes markets in whatever options its clients want. Thus, the client will probably face a bid-ask spread that could be quite significant, but of course, the client is free to shop around.

Other Transaction Costs

Option traders incur several other types of transaction costs. Some of these costs, such as margins and taxes, are discussed in Appendixes 2A and 2B, respectively. Most option traders also trade stocks. Thus, the transaction costs of stock trades are a factor in option trading costs.

Stock trading commissions vary widely among brokerage firms. However, 1 percent to 2 percent of the stock's value for a single purchase or sale transaction is a reasonable estimate. Market makers normally obtain more favorable rates from their clearing firms. Also, large institutional investors usually can negotiate volume discounts from their brokers.

All of the transaction costs discussed here are for single transactions. If the option or stock is subsequently purchased or sold in the market, the transaction cost is incurred again.

The Regulation of Options Markets

The exchange-traded options industry is regulated at several levels. While federal and state regulations predominate, the industry also regulates itself according to rules and standards established by the exchanges and the Options Clearing Corporation.

The Securities and Exchange Commission (SEC) is the primary regulator of the options market. The SEC is a federal regulatory agency created in 1934 to oversee the securities industry, which includes stocks, bonds, options, and mutual funds. The SEC's general purpose is to ensure full disclosure of all pertinent information on publicly offered investments. It has the authority to establish certain rules and procedures and to investigate possible violations of federal securities laws. If the SEC observes a violation it may seek injunctive relief, recommend that the Justice Department press charges, or impose some sanctions itself. For more information on the SEC, see its excellent website at http://www.sec.gov.

The exchanges establish rules and procedures that apply to all members as well as to individuals and firms participating in options transactions. Rule violations may be punishable by fines and/or suspensions. The

Options Clearing Corporation also regulates its members to help ensure that all activities in the options markets are proper and do not pose a risk to the market's viability.

The regulatory authority of an individual state extends to any securities or options trading occurring within that state. States with significant option trading, such as Illinois and New York, actively enforce their own laws on the propriety of transactions conducted therein. Many important issues in the options industry as a whole are settled in state courts in Illinois and New York.

Other levels of regulation are imposed by the Federal Reserve System, which regulates the extension of margin credit; the Securities Investor Protection Corporation, which provides insurance against the failure of brokerage firms; and the National Association of Securities Dealers (NASD), of which most firms involved in options trading are members. In addition, several regional and national organizations, such as the Association for Investment Management and Research, indirectly regulate the industry by prescribing ethical standards for their members.

Many new exchange-traded option products were introduced in the 1980s, including options on stock indices, options on foreign currencies, and options on futures. These products created some confusion as to whether the SEC or the Commodity Futures Trading Commission (CFTC) had regulatory purview. The options on futures instrument caused the greatest confusion, because it is like an option and a futures. In an important step in resolving the matter, the then chairmen of these agencies—John Shad of the SEC and Phillip McBryde Johnson of the CFTC—reached an agreement. In what has come to be known as the **Johnson-Shad agreement** or **CFTC-SEC accord,** it was decided that the SEC would regulate options on stocks, stock indices, and foreign currencies while the CFTC would govern options on all futures contracts. Also, a CFTC-regulated contract cannot permit delivery of instruments regulated by the SEC. Although the Johnson-Shad agreement was a milestone in regulatory cooperation, continued disputes between the SEC and the CFTC characterized the regulatory environment of the early 1990s. We shall learn more about these issues when we cover futures.

The primary purpose of the exchange-traded regulatory system is to protect the public. Over the years, many controversial issues have been raised and discussed. In an industry as large as the options industry, some abuses are certain to occur. In recent years, the options industry has been subjected to criticisms that it has manipulated the stock market and abused the public's trust by charging exorbitant prices for options. However, there is no evidence that any of these charges are true. There have even been a few defaults by writers, but, thanks to the clearinghouse, in no case has any buyer lost money because of a writer's failure to perform. The options industry works hard to maintain the public's trust by operating in

an environment of self-regulation. By policing itself and punishing wrong-doers, some of the cost of having federal regulation is offset for taxpayers.

As noted earlier in the chapter, the over-the-counter market is an un-regulated market, bound loosely by customs and accepted procedures. The firms that participate, however, are often regulated by the NASD, the Federal Reserve, or the Comptroller of the Currency. Of course, commercial laws always apply. The SEC and the CFTC, however, have no direct regulatory authority over the over-the-counter options market.

Summary

This chapter provided the foundation for an understanding of the types of options, individuals, and institutions involved in the options markets. It examined contract specifications, mechanics of trading, transaction costs, and regulations. This information is a prerequisite to the study of option trading strategies and the pricing of options.

Chapters 3 and 4 focus on the principles and models that determine option prices. Chapters 5 and 6 concentrate on applying this knowledge to the implementation of option trading strategies.

Key Terms

Before continuing to Chapter 3, you should be able to give brief definitions of the following terms.

- call option
- put option
- exercise price/strike price/ striking price
- expiration date
- in-/out-of-/at-the-money
- position limit
- exercise limit
- market maker
- floor broker
- board broker/order book official

- bid price
- ask price
- bid-ask spread
- clearinghouse
- margin
- open interest
- offsetting order/offset
- exercise
- cash settlement
- equity option
- index option

Questions and Problems

1. Determine whether each of the following arrangements is an option. If so, decide whether it is a call or a put and identify the premium.
    a. You purchase homeowner's insurance for your house.
    b. You are a high school senior evaluating possible college choices. One school promises that if you enroll, it will guarantee your tuition rate for the next four years.
    c. You enter into a noncancellable, long-term apartment lease.

2. Explain the difference between an American option and a European option. What do they have in common?

3. Explain each of the terms in the following description of an option: AT&T January 65 call.

4. What adjustments to the contract terms of CBOE options would be made in the following situations?
   a. An option has an exercise price of 60. The company declares a 10 percent stock dividend.
   b. An option has an exercise price of 25. The company declares a two-for-one stock split.
   c. An option has an exercise price of 85. The company declares a four-for-three stock split.
   d. An option has an exercise price of 50. The company declares a cash dividend of $.75.

5. Consider the January, February, and March stock option exercise cycles discussed in the chapter. For each of the following dates, indicate which expirations in each cycle would be listed for trading in stock options.
   a. February 1
   b. July 1
   c. December 1

6. Why are short puts and long calls grouped together when considering position limits?

7. Compare and contrast the roles of market maker and floor broker. Why do you think an individual cannot be both?

8. Explain how the CBOE's order book official (OBO) handles public limit orders.

9. Contrast the market maker system of the CBOE and Pacific Stock Exchange with the specialist system of the AMEX and Philadelphia Stock Exchange. What advantages and disadvantages do you see in each system?

10. Suppose you are an individual investor with an options account at a brokerage firm. You purchase 20 call contracts at a price of $2.25 each. Explain how your premium ends up at the clearinghouse.

11. Compare and contrast the exercise procedure for stock options with that for index options. What major advantage does exercising an index option have over exercising a stock option?

12. Discuss the limitations of prices obtained from newspapers such as *The Wall Street Journal*.

13. Discuss the three possible ways in which an open option position can be terminated. Is your answer different if the option is created in the over-the-counter market?

14. Name and briefly describe at least two other instruments that are very similar to options.

15. Identify and briefly discuss the various types of option transaction costs. How do these costs differ for market makers, floor brokers, and firms trading in the over-the-counter market?

16. Using the commission schedule in Table 2.3, determine the commissions on the following option transactions:
    a. One contract at a price of 2 7/8
    b. Five contracts at a price of 8 1/2
    c. Twenty contracts at a price of 4 3/4

17. Explain the major difference between the regulation of exchange-traded options and over-the-counter options.

APPENDIX 2A
Margin Requirements

Margin is the amount of money an individual puts down when entering into an investment. The remainder is borrowed from the brokerage firm. The objective of a margin trade is to earn a higher return by virtue of investing less of one's own funds. However, this advantage is accompanied by increased risk. If the stock price does not move sufficiently in the desired direction, the profit from the investment may not be enough to pay off the loan.

Regulation T of the Federal Reserve Act authorizes the Federal Reserve to regulate the extension of credit in the United States. This authority extends to the regulation of margin credit on transactions in stocks and options.

The **initial margin** is the minimum amount of funds the investor supplies on the day of the transaction. The **maintenance margin** is the minimum amount of funds required each day thereafter. However, on any day on which a trade is executed, the initial margin requirement must be met.

The rules presented here apply to public investors. Specialists and market makers have more lenient margin requirements. Clearing firm margins deposited with the OCC are calculated differently based on a netting out of certain identical long and short positions and an additional amount based on the probabilities of customer defaults.

Margin Requirements on Stock Transactions

The minimum initial margin for stock purchases and short sales is 50 percent. The minimum maintenance margin is 25 percent. Many brokerage firms add an additional 5 percent or more to these requirements.

Margin Requirements on Option Purchases

All option purchases must be fully margined; that is, the investor must pay the option premium in full. This rule exists because options already

contain a substantial leverage component. The additional use of margin would add leverage and thus greatly increase the risk of the investor's position.

Margin Requirements on the Uncovered Sale of Options

An **uncovered call** is a transaction in which an investor writes a call on stock not already owned. If the option is exercised, the writer must buy the stock in the market at the current price, which has no upper limit. Thus, the risk is quite high. Many brokerage firms do not allow their customers to write uncovered calls. Those that do usually restrict such trades to wealthy investors who can afford large losses; yet even these must meet the minimum margin requirements.

For an uncovered call, the investor must deposit the premium plus 20 percent of the stock's value. If the call is out-of-the-money, the requirement is reduced by the amount by which the call is out-of-the-money. The margin must be at least 10 percent of the value of the stock. Consider an investor who writes one call contract at an exercise price of $30 on a stock priced at $33 for a premium of $4.50. The required margin is .2($3,300) + $450 = $1,110. If the stock is priced at $28 and the call is at $.50, the margin is .2($2,800) + $50 − $200 = $410. These amounts are greater than 10 percent of the value of the stock. The amount by which the call is out-of-the-money reduces the required margin.

The same rules apply for puts. If a put is written at an exercise price of $30 when the stock price is $33 and the put price is $2.375, the required margin is .2($3,300) + $237.50 − $300 = $597.50. If the stock price is $29 and the put price is $3.25, the margin is .2($2,900) + $325 = $905. These amounts are greater than 10 percent of the value of the stock.

Index options are somewhat less volatile than options on individual stocks and, appropriately, have lower margin requirements. The required margin is 15 percent, instead of 20 percent, of the stock's value.

Margin Requirements on Covered Calls

A **covered call** is a transaction in which an investor writes an option against a stock already owned. If the option's exercise price is at least equal to the stock price, the investor need not deposit any additional margin beyond that required on the stock. Also, the premium on the option can be used to reduce the margin required on the stock. If, however, the exercise price is less than the stock price, the maximum amount the investor can borrow on the stock is based on the call's exercise price rather than on the stock

price. For example, if the stock price is $40 and the exercise price is $35, the investor can borrow only .5($3,500) = $1,750, not .5($4,000) = $2,000, on the purchase of the stock.

Although it is possible to hold a portfolio of stocks that is identical to the index, current margin requirements do not recognize covered index call writing. Therefore, all short positions in index options must be margined according to the rules that apply to uncovered writing.

There are exceptions to many of these rules, particularly when spreads, straddles, and more complex option transactions are used. In these cases, the margin requirements often are complicated. Investors should consult a broker or some of the trade-oriented publications for additional information on margin requirements for the more complex transactions.

Questions and Problems

1. Suppose a stock is currently priced at $50. The margin requirement is 20 percent on uncovered calls and 50 percent on stocks. Calculate the required margin, in dollars, for each of the following trades:
    a. Write 10 call contracts with an exercise price of 45 and a premium of 7.
    b. Write 10 call contracts with an exercise price of 55 and a premium of 3.
    c. Write 10 put contracts with an exercise price of 45 and a premium of 3.
    d. Write 10 put contracts with an exercise price of 55 and a premium of 7.
    e. Buy 1,000 shares of stock and write 10 call contracts with an exercise price of 45 and a premium of 7.
    f. Buy 20 put contracts with an exercise price of 50 and a premium of 5.

APPENDIX 2B
Taxation of Option Transactions

Determining the applicable taxation of many investment transactions is a complex process that requires the advice of highly trained specialists. The rules covered in this appendix outline most of the basic option transactions. However, there are many exceptions and loopholes, and the laws change frequently. In all cases, one should secure competent professional advice.

The ordinary income of most individuals is taxed at either 28 percent or 31 percent. Long-term capital gains, defined as profits from positions held more than 18 months, are taxed at a maximum of 20 percent. Although there are some exceptions noted herein, most options profits are short-term.

In these examples, we ignore brokerage commissions; however, they are tax deductible. The commission on the purchase of the asset is added

to the purchase price; the commission on its sale is subtracted from the sale price.

The deductibility of any losses is determined by offsetting them against other investment gains. If the losses exceed the gains, any excess up to $3,000 per year is deductible against the investor's ordinary income.

These rules apply to individual investors. Corporations and other institutions trading options, especially over-the-counter options, may be subject to different tax rules and interpretations.

Taxation of Long Call Transactions

If an investor purchases a call and sells it back at a later date at a higher price, there is a capital gain, which is either long- or short-term, usually short-term. Thus, it is taxed at the ordinary income rate. If the investor sells the call at a loss or allows it to expire, the loss is deductible as previously described.

Consider an investor in the 28 percent tax bracket who purchases a call at $3.50 on a stock priced at $36 with an exercise price of $35. Less than 18 months later but before expiration, the investor sells the call at $4.75. The profit of $1.25 is taxed at 28 percent for a tax of $1.25(.28) = $.35. If the call were sold at a loss, the loss would be deductible as described earlier.

If the investor exercised the call, the call price plus the exercise price would be treated as the stock's purchase price and subsequently used to determine the taxable gain on the stock. For example, if the above call were exercised when the stock price was $38, the purchase price of the stock would be considered as the $35 exercise price plus the $3.50 call price for a total of $38.50. If the investor later sold the stock for $40, the taxable gain would be $1.50 and the tax $1.50(.28) = $.42. A tax liability or deduction arises only when the stock is subsequently sold.

Taxation of Short Call Transactions

If an investor sells a call and later repurchases it or allows it to expire, any profit is a short-term capital gain and taxed at the ordinary income rate. If the call is exercised, the exercise price plus the call price is treated as the price at which the stock is sold. Then the difference between the price at which the stock is sold and the price at which it is purchased is the taxable gain.

For example, if the above investor writes the call at a price of $5.25 and subsequently buys it at $3.50 before expiration, the profit of $1.75 will be taxed at 28 percent for a tax of $1.75(.28) = $.49. A loss would be de-

ductible as previously described. If the call were exercised, the writer would deliver the stock. Suppose the stock price were $38 and the writer did not already own the stock. Then the writer would purchase the stock for $38 and sell it to the buyer for $35. The sum of the exercise price plus the premium, $35 + $5.25 = $40.25, would be treated as the stock's sale price. The taxable gain to the writer would be $2.25 and the tax $2.25(.28) = $0.63. Had the writer purchased the stock at an earlier date at $30, the taxable gain would be $10.25 and the tax $10.25(.28) = $2.87.

Taxation of Long Put Transactions

If an investor purchases a put and sells it or allows it to expire less than 18 months later, the profit is a short-term capital gain and is taxed at the ordinary income rate. If the put is exercised, the exercise price minus the premium is treated as the stock's sale price. Then the profit from the stock is taxed at the ordinary income rate.

Consider an investor in the 28 percent tax bracket who purchases a put at $3 on a stock priced at $52 with an exercise price of $50. Later the investor sells the put for $4.25. The gain of $1.25 is taxed at 28 percent for a tax of $1.25(.28) = $.35. If the put is sold at a loss, the loss is deductible as previously described.

Suppose the investor exercises the put when the stock price is $46. The law would treat this as the sale of stock at $50 less the premium of $3 for a net gain of $47. If the investor purchases the stock at $46 and exercises the put, the taxable gain is $1 and the tax is $1(.28) = $.28. If the investor had previously purchased the stock at $40, the taxable gain would be $7 and the tax $7(.28) = $1.96. Had the investor purchased the stock at a price higher than $47, the loss would be deductible as described earlier.

Another possibility is that the investor uses the exercise of the put to sell short the stock. Recall from Chapter 1 that a short sale occurs when an investor borrows stock from the broker and sells it. If the stock price falls, the investor can buy back the stock at a lower price, repay the broker the shares, and capture a profit. A short sale is made in order to profit in a falling market. In our example, the stock is sold short at $47. When the investor later repurchases the stock, any gain on the stock is taxable or any loss is deductible.

Taxation of Short Put Transactions

If an investor writes a put and subsequently buys it back before expiration, any gain is considered a short-term capital gain and is taxed at the ordinary income rate and any loss is deductible. If the put is exercised, the

put's exercise price minus the premium is considered to be the stock's purchase price. The taxable gain or loss on the stock is determined by the difference between the purchase and sale prices of the stock.

Consider the put with an exercise price of $50 written at $3 when the stock price is $52. Suppose the stock price goes to $46 and the put is exercised. The put writer is considered to have purchased the stock for $50 − $3, or $47. If the investor later sells the stock for $55, the taxable gain is $8 and the tax is $8(.28) = $2.24.

Taxation of Non-Equity Options

Index options, debt options, and foreign currency options have a special tax status. At the end of the calendar year, all realized *and unrealized* gains are taxable. All losses are deductible as previously described. The profits are taxed at a blended rate in which 60 percent are taxed at the long-term capital gains rate and 40 percent are taxed at the short-term capital gains rate, which is the ordinary income rate. For an investor in the 31 percent bracket, this is an effective rate of .6(.20) + .4(.31) = .244.

For example, assume that during the year an investor in the 31 percent bracket had $1,250 of net profits (profits minus losses) on index options. At the end of the year, the investor holds 1,000 index options worth $2.25 that previously had been purchased for $1.75. The unrealized profit is thus $500. The total taxable profits are $1,250 + $500 = $1,750. The tax is $1,750(.6)(.20) + $1,750(.4)(.31) = $427.

The Wash Sale Rule: A Special Consideration

Option traders should be aware of an important tax condition called the **wash sale rule.** A wash sale is a transaction in which an investor sells a security at a loss and replaces it with essentially the same security shortly thereafter. Tax laws disallow the deduction of the loss on the sale of the original security. The purpose of the wash sale rule is to prevent investors from taking losses at the end of a calendar year and then immediately replacing the securities. The time period within which the purchase of the security cannot occur is the 61-day period from 30 days before the sale of the stock through 30 days after.

Although, as with many tax laws, there is some murkiness, the wash sale rule usually treats a call option as being the same security as the stock. Thereafter, if the investor sells the stock at a loss and buys a call within the applicable 61-day period, the loss on the stock is not deductible.

Questions and Problems

1. Suppose a stock is priced at $30 and an eight-month call on the stock with an exercise price of $25 is priced at $6. Compute the taxable gain and tax due for each of the following cases assuming your tax bracket is 28 percent. Assume 100 shares and 100 calls.

   a. You buy the call. Four months later, the stock is at $28 and the call is at $4.50. You then sell the call.

   b. You buy the call. Three months later, the stock is at $31 and the call is at $6.50. You then sell the call.

   c. You buy the call. At expiration, the stock is at $32. You exercise the call and sell the stock a month later for $35.

   d. You buy the stock and write the call. You hold the position until expiration, whereupon the stock is at $28.

   e. You write the call. Two months later, the stock is at $28 and the call is at $3.50. You buy back the call.

2. Consider an index option. The index is at 425.48, and a two-month call with an exercise price of 425 is priced at $15. You are in the 31 percent tax bracket. Compute the after-tax profit for the following cases. Assume 100 calls.

   a. You buy the call. One month later, the index is at 428 and the call is at $12. You sell the call.

   b. You buy the call and hold it until expiration, whereupon the index is at 441.35. You exercise the call.

   c. You hold the call until expiration, when the index is at 417.15.

   d. How will your answers in parts a and b be affected if the option positions are not closed out by the end of the year?

3. Which of the following would be a wash sale? Explain.

   a. You buy a stock at $30. Three weeks later, you sell the stock at $26. Two weeks later, you buy a call on the stock.

   b. You buy a stock at $40. One month later, you buy a call on the stock. One week later, you sell the stock for $38.

   c. You buy a stock for $40. Three months later, you sell the stock for $42 and buy a call on the stock.

CHAPTER 3

Principles of Option Pricing

Order and simplification are the first steps toward mastery of a subject—the actual enemy is the unknown.

THOMAS MANN
The Magic Mountain, 1924

This chapter identifies and shows why certain factors affect an option's price. It examines option boundary conditions—rules that characterize rational option prices. Then it explores the relationship between options that differ by exercise price alone and those that differ only by time to expiration. Finally, the chapter discusses how put and call prices are related as well as several other important principles. An overriding point throughout this chapter, and indeed throughout this entire book, is that arbitrage opportunities are quickly eliminated by investors.

Suppose an individual offers you the following proposition. You can play a game called Game I in which you draw a ball from a hat known to contain three red balls and three blue balls. If you draw a red ball, you receive nothing; if you draw a blue ball, you receive $10. Will you play? Because the individual did not mention an entry fee, of course you will play. You incur no cash outlay up front and have the opportunity to earn $10. Of course, this opportunity is too good to be true and only an irrational person would make such an offer without charging an entry fee.

Now suppose a fair fee to play this game is $4. Now consider a new game called Game II. The person offers to pay you $20 if you draw a blue ball and nothing if you draw a red ball. Will the entry fee be higher or lower? If you draw a red ball, you receive the same payoff as in Game I; if you draw a blue ball, you receive a higher payoff than in Game I. You should be willing to pay more to play Game II because these payoffs dominate those of Game I.

From these simple games and opportunities, it is easy to see some of the basic principles of how rational people behave when faced with risky

situations. The collective behavior of rational investors operates in an identical manner to determine the fundamental principles of option pricing. As you read the various examples in this chapter in which arbitrage is used to establish fundamental rules about option pricing, keep in mind the similarity of the investment situation to the games just described. In so doing, the rational result should become clear to you.

In this chapter, we do not derive the exact price of an option; rather, we confine the discussion to identifying upper and lower limits and factors that influence an option's price. Chapter 4 explains how the exact option price is determined.

Basic Notation and Terminology

The following symbols are used throughout the book:

S = stock price today
E = exercise price
T = time to expiration as defined below
r = risk-free rate as defined below
S_T = stock price at option's expiration, i.e., after the passage of a period of time of length T
$C(S,T,E)$ = price of a call option in which the stock price is S, the time to expiration is T, and the exercise price is E
$P(S,T,E)$ = price of a put option in which the stock price is S, the time to expiration is T, and the exercise price is E

In some situations, we may need to distinguish an American call from a European call. If so, the call price will be denoted as either $C_a(S,T,E)$ or $C_e(S,T,E)$ for the American and European calls, respectively. If there is no a or e subscript, the call can be either an American or a European call. In the case where two options differ only by exercise price, the notations $C(S,T,E_1)$ and $C(S,T,E_2)$ will identify the prices of the calls with E_1 less than E_2. A good way to remember this is to keep in mind that the subscript of the lower exercise price is smaller than that of the higher exercise price. In the case where two options differ only by time to expiration, the times to expiration will be T_1 and T_2, where $T_1 < T_2$. The options' prices will be $C(S,T_1,E)$ and $C(S,T_2,E)$. Identical adjustments will be made for put option prices.

For most of the examples we shall assume that the stock pays no dividends. If, during the life of the option, the stock pays dividends of D_1, D_2, . . . , etc., then we can make a simple adjustment and obtain similar results. To do so, we simply subtract the present value of the dividends, $\sum_{j=1}^{N} D_j(1 + r)^{-t_j}$ where there are N dividends and t_j is the time to each ex-dividend day, from the stock price. We assume the dividends are known ahead of time.

The time to expiration is expressed as a decimal fraction of a year. For example, if the current date is April 9 and the option's expiration date is July 18, we simply count the number of days between these two dates. That would be 21 days remaining in April, 31 in May, 30 in June, and 18 in July for a total of 100 days. The time to expiration therefore would be $100/365 = .274$.

The risk-free rate, r, is the rate earned on a riskless investment. An example of such an investment is a U.S. Treasury bill, or T-bill. A Treasury bill is a security issued by the U.S. government for purchase by investors. Bills with original maturities of 91 and 182 days are auctioned by the Federal Reserve each week; bills with maturities of 365 days are auctioned every four weeks. All bills mature on a Thursday.[1] Because most options expire on Fridays, there is always a Treasury bill maturing the day before expiration. The rate of return on that Treasury bill would be a proxy for the risk-free rate.

Treasury bills pay interest not through coupons but by selling at a discount. The bill is purchased at less than face value. The difference between the purchase price and the face value is called the discount. If the investor holds the bill to maturity, it is redeemed at face value. Therefore, the discount is the profit earned by the bill holder.

Bid and ask discounts for several T-bills for the business day of June 12 of a particular year are as follows:

Maturity	Bid	Ask
6/18	4.75	4.56
7/16	5.16	5.10
10/15	5.63	5.59

The bid and ask figures are the discounts quoted by dealers trading in Treasury bills. The bid is the discount if one is selling to the dealer, and the ask is the discount if one is buying from the dealer. Bid and ask quotes are reported daily in *The Wall Street Journal*.

Options expire on the third Friday of the month. In the preceding example, the third Friday of June was June 19. To find an estimate of the T-bill rate, we use the average of the bid and ask discounts, which is $(4.75 + 4.56)/2 = 4.66$. Then we find the discount from par value as $4.66(7/360) = .0906$, which reflects the fact that the bill has 7 days until maturity. Thus, the price is

$$100 - .0906 = 99.9094.$$

---

[1] If Thursday is a holiday, such as Thanksgiving, the Treasury bill matures on Wednesday of that week.

Note that the price is determined by assuming a 360-day year. This is a long-standing tradition in the financial community, originating from the days before calculators, when bank loans often were for 60, 90, or 180 days. A banker could more easily calculate the discount using the fraction 60/360, 90/360, or 180/360. This tradition survives today.

The yield on our T-bill is based on the assumption of buying it at 99.9094 and holding it for 7 days, at which time it will be worth 100.[2] This is a return of $(100 - 99.9094)/99.9094 = .00091$. If we repeated this transaction every seven days for a full year, the return would be

$$(1.00091)^{365/7} - 1 = .0484,$$

where 1.00091 is simply 100/99.9094, or one plus the seven-day return. Note that when we annualize the return, we use the full 365-day year. Thus, we would use 4.84 percent as our proxy for the risk-free rate for options expiring on June 19.

To illustrate the principles of option pricing with real-life options, Table 3.1 presents some prices of Digital Equipment options on June 12 of a particular year. The June option expires on June 19, the July expires on July 17, and the October expires on October 16. Following the same procedure described for the June T-bill and using the Treasury bill data from the previous example gives us risk-free rates of 5.35 and 5.91 for the July and October expirations, respectively. The times to expiration are .0192 (7 days) for the June options, .0959 (35 days) for the July options, and .3452 (126 days) for the October options.

TABLE 3.1	Digital Equipment Option Data, June 12					
	Calls			Puts		
Exercise Price	Jun	Jul	Oct	Jun	Jul	Oct
160	4 5/8	8 5/8	15 1/4	13/16	3 7/8	8 1/8
165	1 7/8	5 3/4	13 1/4	2 15/16	6	9 3/4
170	1/2	3 3/4	10 3/4	6 1/2	8 1/2	NA
175	1/16	2 3/8	8 1/2	NA	NA	NA

Current stock price: 164
Expirations: June 19, July 17, October 16

---

[2]Actually the the number of days is counted from the settlement day, which is the second business day after the purchase day. We shall disregard this point in the calculations in this book.

Principles of Call Option Pricing

In this section we formulate rules that enable us to better understand how call options are priced. It is important to keep in mind that our objective is to determine the price of a call option *prior* to its expiration day.

The Minimum Value of a Call

Because a call option need not be exercised, its minimum value is zero.

A call option is an instrument with limited liability. If the call holder sees that it is advantageous to exercise it, the call will be exercised. If exercising it will decrease the call holder's wealth, the holder will not exercise it. The option cannot have negative value, because the holder cannot be forced to exercise it. Therefore,

$$C(S,T,E) \geq 0.$$

For an American call, the statement that a call option has a minimum value of zero is dominated by a much stronger statement:

$$C_a(S,T,E) \geq Max(0, S - E).$$

The expression $Max(0, S - E)$ means "Take the maximum value of the two arguments, zero or $S - E$."

The intrinsic value of an American call is the greater of zero or the difference between the stock price and the exercise price.

The minimum value of an option is called its **intrinsic value,** sometimes referred to as **parity value, parity,** or **exercise value.** Intrinsic value, which is positive for in-the-money calls and zero for out-of-the-money calls, is the value the call holder receives from exercising the option and the value the call writer gives up when the option is exercised. Note that we are not concerned about the appropriateness of immediately exercising the option; we note only that one could do so if a profit opportunity were available.

To prove the intrinsic value rule, consider the Digital Equipment July 160 call. The stock price is $164, and the exercise price is $160. Evaluating the expression gives $Max(0, 164 - 160) = 4$. Now consider what would happen if the call were priced at less than $4—say, $3. An option trader could buy the call for $3, exercise it—which would entail purchasing the stock for $160—and then sell the stock for $164. This arbitrage transaction would net an immediate riskless profit of $1 on each share.[3] All investors would do this, which would drive up the option's price. When the price of the option reached $4, the transaction would no longer be profitable. Thus, $4 is the minimum price of the call.

---

[3]Actually, it would not be necessary to sell the stock. In the absence of transaction costs, it is immaterial whether one holds the stock—an asset valued at $164—or converts it to another asset—cash—worth $164.

What if the exercise price exceeds the stock price, as do the options with an exercise price of $165? Then Max(0, 164 − 165) = 0, and the minimum value will be zero.

Now look at all of the Digital Equipment calls. Those with an exercise price of $160 have a minimum value of Max(0, 164 − 160) = 4. All three calls with an exercise price of $160 indeed have prices of no less than $4. The calls with an exercise price of $165 have minimum values of Max(0, 164 − 165) = 0. The calls with an exercise price of 170 have minimum values of Max(0, 164 − 170) = 0. All of those options obviously have nonnegative values. Thus, all of the Digital Equipment call options conform to the intrinsic value rule. In fact, extensive empirical testing has revealed that options in general conform quite closely to the rule.

The intrinsic value concept applies only to an American call, because a European call can be exercised only on the expiration day. If the price of a European call were less than Max(0, S − E), the inability to exercise it would prevent traders from engaging in the aforementioned arbitrage that would drive up the call's price.

The price of an American call normally exceeds its intrinsic value. The difference between the price and the intrinsic value is called the **time value** or **speculative value** of the call, which is defined as $C_a(S,T,E) -$ Max(0, S − E). The time value reflects what traders are willing to pay for the uncertainty of the underlying stock. Table 3.2 presents the intrinsic values and time values of the Digital Equipment calls. Note that the time values increase with the time to expiration.

The time value of an American call is the difference between the call price and the intrinsic value.

Figure 3.1 illustrates what we have established so far. The call price lies in the shaded area. Note how the American call price lies in a smaller area. This does not mean that the American call price is less than the European call price but only that its range of possible values is narrower.

TABLE 3.2	Intrinsic Values and Time Values of Digital Equipment Calls			
			Time Value	
Exercise Price	**Intrinsic Value**	**Jun**	**Jul**	**Oct**
160	4.000	0.625	4.625	11.250
165	0.000	1.875	5.750	13.250
170	0.000	0.500	3.750	10.750

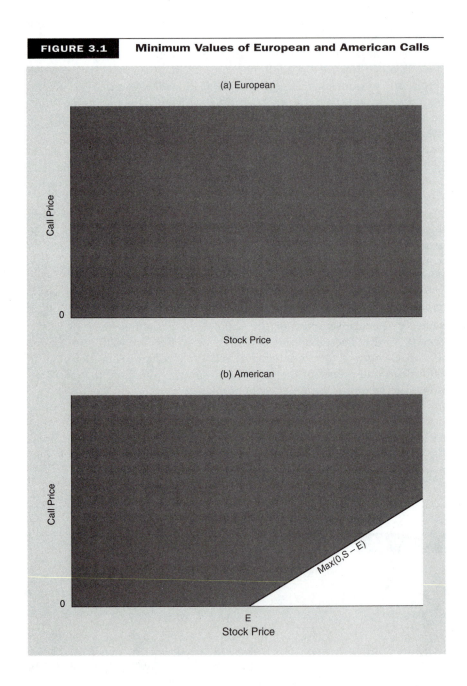

FIGURE 3.1   **Minimum Values of European and American Calls**

(a) European

Call Price

0

Stock Price

(b) American

Call Price

Max(0, S − E)

0

E

Stock Price

The Maximum Value of a Call

A call option also has a maximum value:

$$C(S,T,E) \leq S.$$

The call is a conduit through which an investor can obtain the stock. The most one can expect to gain from the call is the stock's value less the exercise price. Even if the exercise price were zero, no one would pay more for the call than for the stock. However, one call that is worth the stock price is one with an infinite maturity. It is obvious that all of the Digital Equipment calls are worth no more than the value of the stock.

The maximum value of a call is the price of the stock.

Figure 3.2 adds the maximum value rule to Figure 3.1. Notice that the maximum value rule has significantly reduced the range of possible option values.

The Value of a Call at Expiration

The price of a call at expiration is given as

$$C(S_T,0,E) = \mathrm{Max}(0, S_T - E).$$

Because no time remains in the option's life, the call price contains no time value. The prospect of future stock price increases is irrelevant to the price of the expiring option, which will be simply its intrinsic value.[4]

At expiration, a call option is worth the intrinsic value.

At expiration, an American option and a European option are identical instruments. Therefore, this rule holds for both types of options.

Figure 3.3 illustrates the value of the call at expiration. This is one situation in which the value of the call is unambiguous. But do not confuse this with our ultimate objective, which is to find the value of the call *prior to* expiration.

The Effect of Time to Expiration

Consider two American calls that differ only in their times to expiration. One has a time to expiration of T_1 and a price of $C_a(S,T_1,E)$; the other has a time to expiration of T_2 and a price of $C_a(S,T_2,E)$. Remember that T_2 is greater than T_1. Which of these two options will have the greater value?

Suppose today is the expiration day of the shorter-lived option. The stock price is S_{T_1}. The value of the expiring option is $\mathrm{Max}(0, S_{T_1} - E)$. The second option has a time to expiration of $T_2 - T_1$. Its minimum value is

---

[4]Because of the transaction cost of exercising the option, it could be worth slightly less than the intrinsic value.

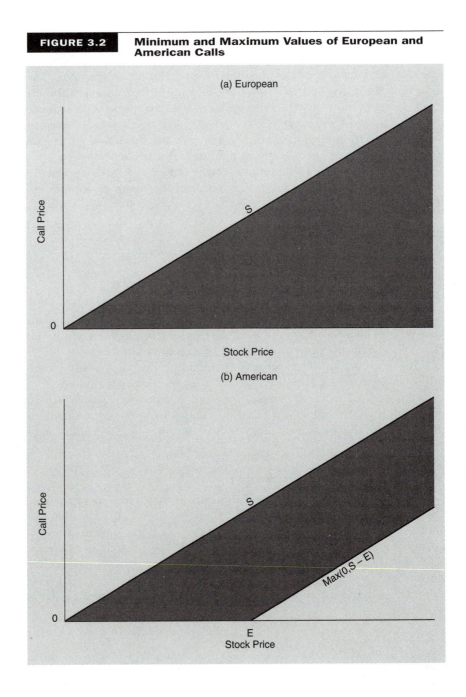

FIGURE 3.2　**Minimum and Maximum Values of European and American Calls**

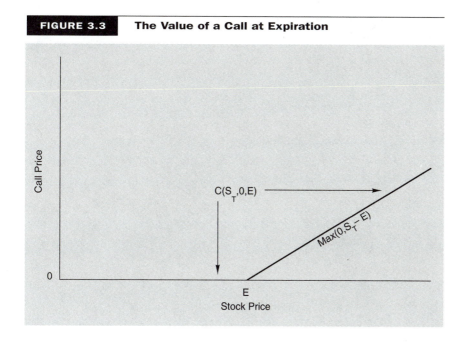

FIGURE 3.3   **The Value of a Call at Expiration**

Call Price

$C(S_T,0,E)$

$Max(0,S_T - E)$

0

E
Stock Price

$Max(0, S_{T_1} - E)$. Thus, when the shorter-lived option expires, its value is the minimum value of the longer-lived option. Therefore,

$$C_a(S,T_2,E) \geq C_a(S,T_1,E).$$

Normally the longer-lived call is worth more, but if it carries no time value when the shorter-lived option expires, the two options will have the same price. This can occur if the stock price is either very high or very low. Looking at the prices of the Digital Equipment calls, we can see that this is the case. The longer the time to expiration, the greater the call's value.

The time value of a call option varies with the time to expiration and the proximity of the stock price to the exercise price. Investors pay for the time value of the call based on the uncertainty of the future stock price. If the stock price is very high, the call is said to be **deep-in-the-money** and the time value will be low. If the stock price is very low, the call is said to be **deep-out-of-the-money** and the time value likewise will be low. The time value will be low because at these extremes, the uncertainty about the call expiring in- or out-of-the-money is lower. The uncertainty is greater when the stock price is near the exercise price, and it is at this point that the time value is higher.

A simple analogy is useful for understanding why time value is highest when the stock price is close to the exercise price. Suppose you were

A longer-lived American call must always be worth at least as much as a shorter-lived American call with the same terms.

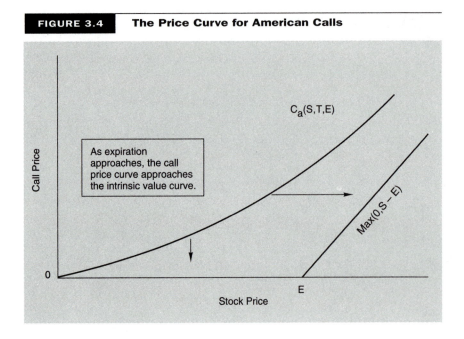

FIGURE 3.4   **The Price Curve for American Calls**

$C_a(S,T,E)$

As expiration approaches, the call price curve approaches the intrinsic value curve.

$\text{Max}(0, S - E)$

Call Price

0

E

Stock Price

watching an important basketball game between the Charlotte Hornets and the Atlanta Hawks. Let us assume that you enjoy a good game but have no sentimental attachment to either team. It is now halftime. Suppose Charlotte is ahead 65–38. How interesting is the game now? How probable is it that Charlotte will win? Are you likely to keep watching if there is something more interesting to do with your time? But suppose, instead, that the score is tied at 55–55. Isn't the game much more interesting now? Aren't you more likely to watch the second half?

An option with the stock price near the exercise price is like a close game. A deep-in- or out-of-the-money option is like a game with one team well ahead. A close game and an option nearly at-the-money are situations to which people are more willing to allocate scarce resources, for example, time to watch the game or money to buy the option.

These properties of the time value and our previous results enable us to get a general idea of what the call price looks like relative to the stock price. Figure 3.4 illustrates this point for American calls. The curved line is the price of the call, which lies above the intrinsic value, $\text{Max}(0, S - E)$. As expiration approaches, the call price loses its time value, a process called **time value decay,** and the curve moves gradually toward the intrinsic value. At expiration, the call price curve collapses onto the intrinsic value and the curve looks exactly like Figure 3.3.

The time value effect is evident in the Digital Equipment calls. Note that in Table 3.2, for a given exercise price the time values increase with the time to expiration. For a given time to expiration, the time values are highest for the calls with an exercise price of 165, the exercise price closest to the stock price.

The relationship between time to expiration and option price also holds for European calls. Nevertheless, we cannot yet formally accept this as fact, because we have not yet established a minimum value for a European call. That will come a bit later.

The Effect of Exercise Price

THE EFFECT ON OPTION VALUE   Consider two European calls that are identical in all respects except that the exercise price of one is E_1 and that of the other is E_2. Recall that E_2 is greater than E_1. We want to know which price is greater—$C_e(S,T,E_1)$ or $C_e(S,T,E_2)$.

Now consider two portfolios, A and B. Portfolio A consists of a long position in the call with the exercise price of E_1 and a short position in the call with the exercise price of E_2. This type of portfolio is called a money spread and is discussed further in Chapter 6. Because we pay $C_e(S,T,E_1)$ and receive $C_e(S,T,E_2)$, this portfolio will have an initial value of $C_e(S,T,E_1) - C_e(S,T,E_2)$. We do not yet know whether the initial value is positive or negative; that will depend on which option price is higher.

Portfolio B consists simply of risk-free bonds with a face value of $E_2 - E_1$. These bonds should be considered as pure discount instruments, like Treasury bills, and as maturing at the options' expiration. Thus, the value of this portfolio is the present value of the bonds' face value, or simply $(E_2 - E_1)(1 + r)^{-T}$.

For the time being, we shall concentrate on portfolio A. First, we need to determine the portfolio's value at expiration. The value of any portfolio will be its cash flow or payoff when the options expire contingent on the stock price at expiration, S_T. The stock price at expiration has three possible ranges: (1) $S_T < E_1$; (2) $E_1 \leq S_T < E_2$; or (3) $E_1 < E_2 \leq S_T$. Table 3.3 illustrates the values of portfolios A and B at expiration.

When S_T is greater than E_1, the call option with exercise price E_1 will be worth $S_T - E_1$. If S_T exceeds E_2, the call option with exercise price E_2 will be worth $S_T - E_2$. However, we are short the option with exercise price E_2. Because the buyer receives a payoff of $S_T - E_2$ when this option expires in-the-money, the writer has a payoff of $-S_T + E_2$. Adding the payoffs from the two options shows that portfolio A will always produce a payoff of no less than zero and, in some cases, more than zero. Therefore,

$$C_e(S,T,E_1) \geq C_e(S,T,E_2).$$

| | | **TABLE 3.3** | **The Effect of Exercise Price on Call Value: Payoffs at Expiration of Portfolios A and B** |

Portfolio	Current Value	Payoffs from Portfolio Given Stock Price at Expiration		
		$S_T < E_1$	$E_1 \le S_T < E_2$	$E_1 < E_2 \le S_T$
A	$+C_e(S,T,E_1)$	0	$S_T - E_1$	$S_T - E_1$
	$-C_e(S,T,E_2)$	0	0	$-S_T + E_2$
		0	$S_T - E_1 \ge 0$	$E_2 - E_1 > 0$
B	$(E_2 - E_1)(1 + r)^{-T}$	$E_2 - E_1 > 0$	$E_2 - E_1 > 0$	$E_2 - E_1 > 0$

The price of a European call must be at least as high as the price of an otherwise identical European call with a higher exercise price.

The price of an American call must be at least as high as the price of another otherwise identical American call with a higher exercise price.

Why is this so? The best way to understand this rule is to look at the contradiction. Suppose $C_e(S,T,E_1) < C_e(S,T,E_2)$. Since we pay $C_e(S,T,E_1)$ for the option bought and receive $C_e(S,T,E_2)$ for the option sold, we will have a net cash inflow at the beginning of the transaction. The payoffs at expiration were shown to be nonnegative. Anyone would jump at the opportunity to construct a portfolio with a positive cash inflow up front and no possibility of a cash outflow at expiration. There would be no way to lose money. Everyone would try to execute this transaction, which would drive up the price of the call with exercise price E_1 and drive down the price of the call with exercise price E_2. When the call with the lower exercise price is worth at least as much as the call with the higher exercise price, the portfolio will no longer offer a positive cash flow up front.

We have proven this result only for European calls. With American calls the long call need not be exercised, so we need only consider what would happen if the short call were exercised early.

Suppose the stock price prior to expiration is S_t and exceeds E_2. For whatever reason, the short call is exercised. This produces a negative cash flow, $-(S_t - E_2)$. The trader then exercises the long call, which produces a positive cash flow of $S_t - E_1$. The sum of these two cash flows is $E_2 - E_1$, which is positive because $E_2 > E_1$. Thus, early exercise will not generate a negative cash flow. Portfolio A therefore will never produce a negative cash flow at expiration even if the options are American calls. Thus, our result holds for American calls as well as for European calls.

Note that this result shows that the price of the call with the lower exercise price cannot be less than that of the call with the higher exercise price. However, the two call prices conceivably could be equal. That could occur if the stock price were very low, in which case both calls would be deep-out-of-the-money. Neither would be expected to expire in-the-money,

and both would have an intrinsic value of zero. Therefore, both prices could be approximately zero. However, with a very high stock price, the call with the lower exercise price would carry a greater intrinsic value, and thus its price would be higher than that of the call with the higher exercise price.

The prices of the Digital Equipment calls adhere to the predicted relationships. The lower the exercise price, the higher the call option price.

LIMITS ON THE DIFFERENCE IN PREMIUMS   Now compare the results of portfolio A with those of portfolio B. Note that in Table 3.3, portfolio B's return is never less than portfolio A's. Therefore, investors would not pay less for portfolio B than for portfolio A. The price of portfolio A is $C_e(S,T,E_1) - C_e(S,T,E_2)$, the price of the option purchased minus the price of the option sold. The price of portfolio B is $(E_2 - E_1)(1 + r)^{-T}$, the present value of the bond's face value. Thus,

The difference in the prices of two European calls that differ only by exercise price cannot exceed the present value of the difference in their exercise prices.

$$(E_2 - E_1)(1 + r)^{-T} \geq C_e(S,T,E_1) - C_e(S,T,E_2).$$

A related and useful statement is

$$E_2 - E_1 \geq C_e(S,T,E_1) - C_e(S,T,E_2).$$

This follows because the difference in the exercise prices is greater than the present value of the difference in the exercise prices. For two options differing only in exercise price, the difference in the premiums cannot exceed the difference in the exercise prices.

The intuition behind this result is simple: The advantage of buying an option with a lower exercise price over one with a higher exercise price will not be more than the difference in the exercise prices. For example, if you own the Digital Equipment July 165 call and are considering replacing it with the July 160 call, the most you can gain by the switch is $5. Therefore, you would not pay more than an additional $5 for the 160 over the 165. This result will be useful in Chapter 6, where we discuss spread strategies.

For American calls, the call with the lower exercise price is worth at least as much as the call with the higher exercise price. However, the statement that the difference in premiums cannot exceed the present value of the difference in exercise prices does not hold for the American call. If both calls are exercised at time t before expiration and the payoff of $E_2 - E_1$ is invested in risk-free bonds, portfolio A's return will be $(E_2 - E_1)(1 + r)^{(T - t)}$, which will exceed portfolio B's return of $E_2 - E_1$. Thus, portfolio B will not always outperform or match portfolio A.

If, however, the bonds purchased for portfolio B have a face value of $(E_2 - E_1)(1 + r)^T$, and thus a present value of $E_2 - E_1$, portfolio B will

The difference in the prices of two American calls that differ only by exercise price cannot exceed the difference in their exercise prices.

always outperform portfolio A. In that case, the current value of portfolio A cannot exceed that of portfolio B. Accordingly, we can state that for American calls

$$E_2 - E_1 \geq C_a(S,T,E_1) - C_a(S,T,E_2).$$

Table 3.4 presents the appropriate calculations for examining these properties on the Digital Equipment calls. Consider the June 160 and 165 calls. The difference in their premiums is 2.75.

The present value of the difference in exercise prices is $5(1.0484)^{-.0192} = 4.996$. The remaining combinations are calculated similarly using the appropriate risk-free rates and times to expiration for those options. Since these are American calls, the difference in their prices must be no greater than the difference in their exercise prices. As Table 3.4 shows, all of the calls conform to this condition. In addition, all of the differences in the call prices are less than the present value of the difference between the exercise prices. Remember that this result need not hold for American calls because they can be exercised early.

The Lower Bound of a European Call

We know that for an American call,

$$C_a(S,T,E) \geq Max(0, S - E).$$

TABLE 3.4	**The Relationship between Exercise Price and Call Price: Digital Equipment Calls**			
		Difference between Call Prices (Present Value of Difference between Exercise Prices in Parentheses)		
Exercise Price	Exercise Price Difference	Jun	Jul	Oct
160,165	5	2.750 (4.996)	2.875 (4.975)	2.000 (4.902)
160,170	10	4.125 (9.991)	4.875 (9.950)	4.500 (9.804)
165,170	5	1.375 (4.996)	2.000 (4.975)	2.500 (4.902)

Note: Risk-free rates are .0484 (Jun); .0535 (Jul); .0591 (Oct). Times to expiration are .0192 (Jun); .0959 (Jul); .3452 (Oct).

Because of the requirement that immediate exercise be possible, we were unable to make such a statement for a European call. We can, however, develop a lower bound for a European call that will be higher than the intrinsic value of an American call.

Again consider two portfolios, A and B. Portfolio A consists of a single share of stock currently priced at S, while portfolio B contains a European call priced at $C_e(S,T,E)$ and risk-free bonds with a face value of E and, therefore, a present value of $E(1 + r)^{-T}$. The current value of this portfolio thus is $C_e(S,T,E) + E(1 + r)^{-T}$. The payoffs from these two portfolios are shown in Table 3.5.

As the table shows, the return on portfolio B is always at least as large as that of portfolio A and sometimes larger. Investors will recognize this fact and price portfolio B at a value at least as great as portfolio A's; that is,

$$C_e(S,T,E) + E(1 + r)^{-T} \geq S.$$

Rearranging this expression gives

$$C_e(S,T,E) \geq S - E(1 + r)^{-T}.$$

If $S - E(1 + r)^{-T}$ is negative, we invoke the rule that the minimum value of a call is zero. Combining these results gives

$$C_e(S,T,E) \geq Max[0, S - E(1 + r)^{-T}].$$

The price of a European call must at least equal the greater of zero or the stock price minus the present value of the exercise price.

If the call price is less than the stock price minus the present value of the exercise price, we can construct an arbitrage portfolio. We buy the call and risk-free bonds and sell short the stock. This portfolio has a positive initial cash flow, because the call price plus the bond price is less than the stock price. At expiration, the payoff is $E - S_T$ if $E > S_T$ and zero otherwise. The portfolio has a positive cash flow today and either

TABLE 3.5	The Lower Bound of a European Call: Payoffs at Expiration of Portfolios A and B		
		Payoffs from Portfolio Given Stock Price at Expiration	
Portfolio	Current Value	$S_T \leq E$	$S_T > E$
A	S	S_T	S_T
B	$C_e(S,T,E) + E(1 + r)^{-T}$	E	$(S_T - E) + E = S_T$

a zero or positive cash flow at expiration. Again there is no way to lose money.

Figure 3.5 shows this result for European calls. The curved line is the call price, which must lie above the lower bound. As expiration approaches, T becomes smaller such that the lower bound moves to the right with the call price following it. At expiration, the lower bound and price curves converge with the Max$(0, S - E)$ curve.

When we showed that the intrinsic value of an American call is Max$(0, S - E)$, we noted that the inability to exercise early prevents this result from holding for a European call. Now we can see that this limitation is of no consequence. Because the present value of the exercise price is less than the exercise price itself, the lower bound of a European call is greater than the intrinsic value of an American call.

In the earlier description of how time to expiration affects the price of an American call, we could not draw the same relationship for a European call. Now we can. Consider two European calls that differ by their times to expiration, T_1 and T_2. Their prices are $C_e(S,T_1,E)$ and $C_e(S,T_2,E)$, respectively. At time T_1, the shorter-lived option expires and is worth Max$(0, S_{T_1} - E)$. The minimum value of the longer-lived option is Max$(0, S_{T_1} - E(1 + r)^{-(T_2 - T_1)})$. Thus, the value of the shorter-lived option is less than the lower bound of the longer-lived option. Therefore, the longer-lived call must be priced at least as high as the shorter-lived call.

For European calls, a longer-lived call will always be worth at least as much as a shorter-lived call with the same terms.

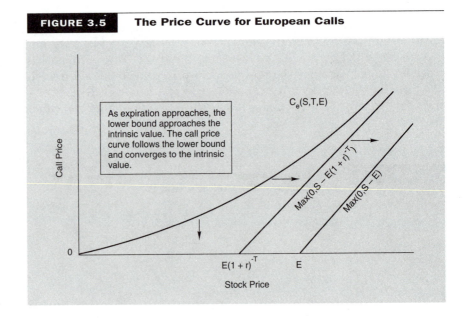

| **FIGURE 3.5** | **The Price Curve for European Calls** |

As expiration approaches, the lower bound approaches the intrinsic value. The call price curve follows the lower bound and converges to the intrinsic value.

$C_e(S,T,E)$

Max$(0, S - E(1 + r)^{-T})$

Max$(0, S - E)$

Call Price

$E(1 + r)^{-T}$ E

Stock Price

Finally we should note that if the stock pays dividends such that the stock price minus the present value of the dividends is $S' = S - \sum_{j=1}^{N} D_j (1+r)^{-t_j}$ then the lower bound is restated as

$$C_e(S,T,E) \geq Max \ [0, \ S' - E(1+r)^{-T}].$$

American Call versus European Call

Many of the results presented so far apply only to European calls. For example, we restricted the derivation of the lower bound to European calls. That is because an early exercise of an American call can negate the cash flows expected from the portfolio at expiration.

In many cases, however, American calls behave exactly like European calls. In fact, an American call can be viewed as a European call with the added feature that it can be exercised early. Since exercising an option is never mandatory,

An American call will be at least as valuable as a European call with the same terms.

$$C_a(S,T,E) \geq C_e(S,T,E).$$

We already proved that the minimum value of an American call is $Max(0, S - E)$ while the lower bound of a European call is $Max[0, S - E(1+r)^{-T}]$. Because $S - E(1+r)^{-T}$ is greater than $S - E$, as shown in Figure 3.5, the lower bound value of the American call must also be $Max[0, S - E(1+r)^{-T}]$.

Let us now examine the Digital Equipment options to determine whether their prices exceed the lower boundary. Table 3.6 presents the lower bound of each Digital Equipment call. To see how the computations are performed, take the June 160 call. The time to expiration is .0192, and the risk-free rate is .0484. Thus,

$$Max[0, \ S - E(1+r)^{-T}] = Max[0, \ 164 - 160(1.0484)^{-.0192}] = 4.144.$$

TABLE 3.6   **Lower Bounds of Digital Equipment Calls**

Exercise Price	Expiration Date		
	Jun	**Jul**	**Oct**
160	4.144	4.800	7.130
165	0.000	0.000	2.230
170	0.000	0.000	0.000

Note: Risk-free rates are .0484 (Jun); .0535 (Jul); .0591 (Oct). Times to expiration are .0192 (Jun); .0959 (Jul); .3452 (Oct).

An American call on a non-dividend-paying stock will never be exercised early, and we can treat such a call as if it were European.

From Table 3.1, the price of the call is \$4.625. Thus, this option does meet the boundary condition. Using Tables 3.1 and 3.6 reveals that the remaining calls also conform to the lower boundary. In general, studies show that call prices conform closely to the lower bound rule.

With the lower bound of an American call established, we can now examine whether an American call should ever be exercised early. If the stock price is S, exercising the call produces a cash flow of $S - E$.[5] The call's price, however, must be at least $S - E(1 + r)^{-T}$. Since the cash flow from exercising, $S - E$, can never exceed the call's lower bound, $S - E(1 + r)^{-T}$, it will always be better to sell the call in the market. When the transaction cost of exercising is compared to the transaction cost of selling the call, the argument that a call should not be exercised early is strengthened. Thus, if the stock pays no dividends, Figure 3.5 is also the call price curve for American calls.

Although many people find it difficult to believe that an American option on a non-dividend-paying stock would never be exercised early, it is really quite easy to see by analogy. Have you ever subscribed to a magazine and, shortly afterward, received a renewal notice mentioning the attractive rate they could offer you? You have barely begun receiving the magazine, perhaps have not yet decided if you like it, and already you are granted an option to renew. Do you immediately renew? Hardly any rational person would do so. Not only would you be giving the magazine company the interest on your money, you would also be giving up the right to decide later if you want to renew. It is almost always the case that you would still have the right to renew much later at the same rate. Likewise, exercising a call option early not only gives the writer the interest on your money, but also throws away the right to decide later if you want to own the stock.

If that argument is not convincing, simply consider this. The urge to exercise a deep-in-the-money call simply because you think the stock has gone as far up as you think it will should be suppressed. If your views on the stock are correct, you will not be any more pleased to own a stock that is not increasing than you would to be holding the call option. The story changes, however, if the stock pays dividends.

The Early Exercise of American Calls on Dividend-Paying Stocks

When a company declares a dividend, it specifies that the dividend is payable to all stockholders as of a certain date, called the holder-of-record date. Four business days before that date is the ex-dividend date. To be the stockholder of record by the holder-of-record date, one must buy the stock by the ex-dividend date. The stock price tends to fall by the amount of the dividend on the ex-dividend date.

---

[5]We are assuming that the option is in-the-money, because no one would consider exercising it if it were out-of-the-money.

When a stock goes ex-dividend, the call price drops along with it. The amount by which the call price falls cannot be determined at this point in our understanding of option pricing. Since the call is a means of obtaining the stock, however, its price could never change by more than the stock price change. Thus, the call price will fall by no more than the dividend. An investor could avoid this loss in value by exercising the option immediately before the stock goes ex-dividend. This is the only time the call should be exercised early.

Another way to see that early exercise could occur is to recall that we stated that the lower bound of a European call on a dividend-paying stock is $\text{Max}[0, S' - E(1 + r)^{-T}]$ where S' is the stock price minus the present value of the dividends. To keep things simple, assume only one dividend of the amount D, and the stock will go ex-dividend in the next instant. Then S' is approximately equal to $S - D$ (since the present value of D is almost D). Since we would consider exercising only in-the-money calls, assume that S exceeds E. Then it is easy to see that $S - E$ could exceed S' minus the present value of E. By exercising the option, the call holder obtains the value $S - E$. Suppose you were holding a European call whose value was only slightly above the lower bound. Then you might wish it were an American call because an American call could be exercised to capture the value $S - E$. If you were holding a European call and wished it were an American call for at least that instant, then it should be obvious that the right to exercise early would have value. So an American call could be worth more than a European call. Note that this does not mean that exercise will definitely occur at the ex-dividend instant. It means only that exercise *could* occur. The value of the right to exercise early is what distinguishes an American call from a European call. That right is worth something only when there are dividends on the stock.

It may be optimal to exercise an American call early if the stock is about to go ex-dividend.

There is one other situation in which you can determine that the right to exercise early has no value. If the present value of all of the dividends over the life of the option is less than $E(1 - (1 + r)^{-T})$, then the option would never be exercised early because the dividends are not large enough to offset the loss of interest from paying out the exercise price early.

In Chapter 4 we shall learn about a model that will give us the exact price of the option. We will then be able to see the early exercise value more explicitly.

The Effect of Interest Rates

The price of a call is directly related to interest rates.

Interest rates affect a call option's price. Although the effect of interest rates is somewhat complex, an easy way to see it is to think of a call as a way to purchase stock by paying an amount of money less than the face value of the stock. By paying the call premium, you save the difference between the call price and the exercise price, the price you are willing to pay for the stock. The higher the interest rate, the more interest you can earn

The price of a call is directly related to the volatility of the underlying stock.

on the money you saved by buying the call. Thus, when interest rates are higher, calls are more attractive than buying stock.[6]

The Effect of Stock Volatility

One of the basic principles of investor behavior is that individuals prefer less risk to more. For holders of stocks, higher risk means lower value. But higher risk in a stock translates into greater value for a call option on it. This is because greater volatility increases the gains on the call if the stock price increases, because the stock price can then exceed the exercise price by a larger amount. On the other hand, greater volatility means that if the stock price goes down, it can be much lower than the exercise price. To a call holder, however, this does not matter because the potential loss is limited; it is said to be truncated at the exercise price. For example, consider the Digital Equipment July 165 call. Suppose the stock price is equally likely to be at 150, 160, 170, or 180 at expiration. The call, then, is equally likely to be worth 0, 0, 5, and 15 at expiration. Now suppose the stock's volatility increases so that it has an equal chance of being at 140, 160, 170, or 190. From a stockholder's point of view, the stock is far riskier, which is less desirable. From the option holder's perspective, the equally possible option prices at expiration are 0, 0, 5, and 25, which is more desirable. In fact, the option holder will not care how low the stock can go. If the possibility of lower stock prices is accompanied by the possibility of higher stock prices, the option holder will benefit, and the option will be priced higher when the volatility is higher.

Another way to understand the effect of volatility on the call price is to consider the extreme case of zero volatility. If the stock price is less than the exercise price, the absence of volatility guarantees that the option will expire out-of-the-money. No one would pay anything for this option. If the stock price exceeds the exercise price and has zero volatility, it will expire in-the-money and will be worth S − E at expiration, where S is the current stock price. In this case, the call will then be worth the present value of S − E and thus will simply be a risk-free asset. High stock volatility is what makes call options attractive, and investors are willing to pay higher premiums on options with greater volatility.

Principles of Put Option Pricing

Many of the rules applicable to call options apply in a straightforward manner to put options. However, there are some significant differences.

---

[6]The exact relationship between interest rates and call prices is slightly more involved than this, however. The purchase of a call is actually more than just an option to defer purchase of the stock. Holding the call instead of the stock limits your loss to much less than if you had bought the stock. A call is said to have insurance value. Interest rates affect the insurance value of the call in a negative manner, but the overall effect on the call price is still positive.

The Minimum Value of a Put

A put is an option to sell a stock. A put holder is not obligated to exercise it and will not do so if exercising will decrease wealth. Thus, a put can never have a negative value:

Because a put option need not be exercised, its minimum value is zero.

$$P(S,T,E) \geq 0.$$

An American put can be exercised early. Therefore,

$$P_a(S,T,E) \geq Max(0, E - S).$$

Suppose that the Digital Equipment July 170 put sells for less than $E - S$. Let the put sell for $5. Then it would be worthwhile to buy the stock for $164, buy the put for $5, and exercise the put. This would net an immediate risk-free profit of $1. The combined actions of all investors conducting this arbitrage would force the put price up to at least $6, the difference between the exercise price and the stock price.

Figure 3.6 illustrates these points for puts. The European put price lies somewhere in the shaded area of graph (a). The American put price lies somewhere in the shaded area of graph (b).

The value, $Max(0, E - S)$, is called the put's **intrinsic value.** An in-the-money put has a positive intrinsic value, while an out-of-the-money put has an intrinsic value of zero. The difference between the put price and the intrinsic value is the **time value** or **speculative value.** The time value is defined as $P_a(S,T,E) - Max(0, E - S)$. As with calls, the time value reflects what an investor is willing to pay for the uncertainty of the final outcome.

The intrinsic value of an American put is the greater of zero or the difference between the exercise price and the stock price.

Table 3.7 presents the intrinsic values and time values of the Digital Equipment puts. Note how the time values increase with the time to expiration.

The intrinsic value specification, $Max(0, E - S)$, does not hold for European puts. That is because the option must be exercisable for an investor to execute the arbitrage transaction previously described. European puts indeed can sell for less than the intrinsic value. Later this will help us understand the early exercise of American puts.

The time value of an American put is the difference between the put price and the intrinsic value.

The Maximum Value of a Put

At expiration, the payoff from a European put is $Max(0, E - S)$. The best outcome that a put holder can expect is for the company to go bankrupt. In that case, the stock will be worthless $(S = 0)$ and the put holder will be able to sell the shares to the put writer for E dollars.

The maximum value of a European put is the present value of the exercise price. The maximum value of an American put is the exercise price.

Thus, the present value of the exercise price is the European put's maximum possible value. Since an American put can be exercised at any time, its maximum value is the exercise price.

$$P_e(S,T,E) \leq E(1 + r)^{-T},$$
$$P_a(S,T,E) \leq E.$$

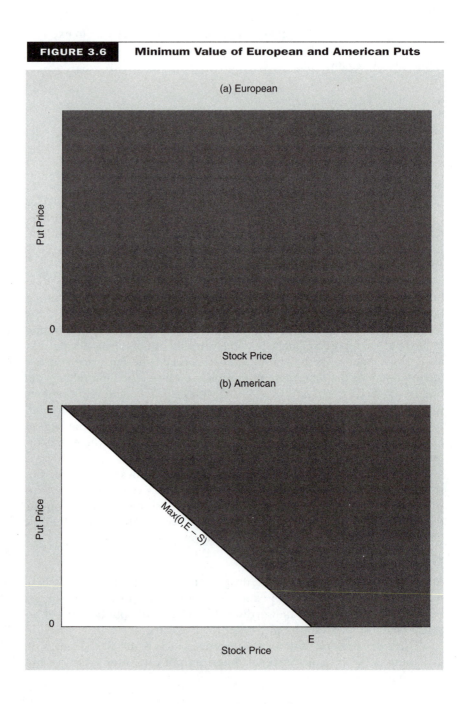

FIGURE 3.6   Minimum Value of European and American Puts

| TABLE 3.7 | Intrinsic Values and Time Values of Digital Equipment Puts | | | |

Exercise Price	Intrinsic Value	Time Value		
		Jun	Jul	Oct
160	0.000	0.8125	3.8750	8.1250
165	1.000	1.9375	5.0000	8.7500
170	6.000	0.5000	2.5000	NA

Figure 3.7 adds the maximum value rule to Figure 3.6. While the range of possible values is reduced somewhat, there is still a broad range of possible values.

The Value of a Put at Expiration

On the put's expiration date, no time value will remain. Expiring American puts therefore are the same as European puts. The value of either type of put must be the intrinsic value. Thus,

$$P(S_T, 0, E) = \text{Max}(0, E - S_T).$$

 At expiration, a put option is worth the intrinsic value.

If $E > S_T$ and the put price is less than $E - S_T$, investors can buy the put and the stock and exercise the put for an immediate risk-free profit. If the put expires out-of-the-money ($E < S_T$), it will be worthless. Figure 3.8 illustrates the value of the put at expiration.

The Effect of Time to Expiration

Consider two American puts, one with a time to expiration of T_1 and the other with a time to expiration of T_2, where $T_2 > T_1$. Now assume today is the expiration date of the shorter-lived put. The stock price is S_{T_1}. The expiring put is worth $\text{Max}(0, E - S_{T_1})$. The other put, which has a remaining time to expiration of $T_2 - T_1$, is worth at least $\text{Max}(0, E - S_{T_1})$. Thus,

$$P_a(S, T_2, E) \geq P_a(S, T_1, E).$$

 A longer-lived American put must always be worth at least as much as a shorter-lived American put with the same terms.

Note that the two puts could be worth the same; however, this would occur only if both puts were very deep-in- or out-of-the-money. Even then, the longer-lived put would likely be worth a little more than the shorter-lived put. The longer-lived put can do everything the shorter-lived put can do and has an additional period of time in which to increase in value.

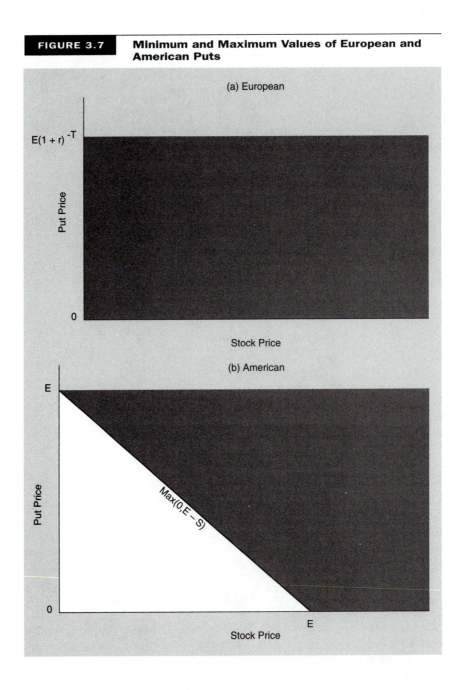

FIGURE 3.7   **Minimum and Maximum Values of European and American Puts**

FIGURE 3.8   **The Value of a Put at Expiration**

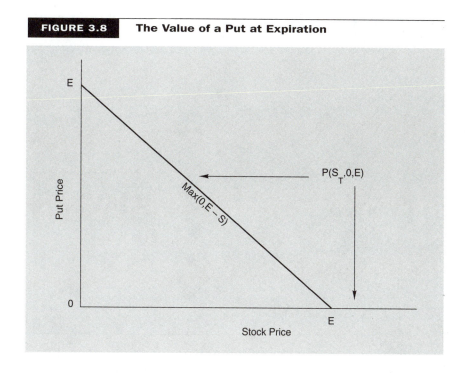

The principles that underlie the time value of a put are the same as those that underlie the time value of a call. The time value is largest when the stock price is near the exercise price and smallest when the stock price is either very high or very low relative to the exercise price. With these points in mind, we can now see that the American put price would look like Figure 3.9. As expiration approaches, the put price curve approaches the intrinsic value, which is due to the time value decay. At expiration the put price equals the intrinsic value, as in Figure 3.8.

The relationship between time to expiration and put price is more complex for European puts. Think of buying a put as deferring the sale of stock at the exercise price, E. The further into the future the expiration date, the longer the put holder must wait to sell the stock and receive E dollars. This can make the longer-lived European put less valuable than the shorter-lived one. This does not hold for an American put, because the holder can always exercise it and receive E dollars today. For a European put, the longer time to expiration is both an advantage—the greater time value—and a disadvantage—the longer wait to receive the exercise price. The time value effect tends to dominate, however, and in most cases longer-lived puts will be more valuable than shorter-lived puts.

Because the Digital Equipment puts are American options, the longer-term puts should be expected to show higher prices. A check of their premiums, shown in Table 3.1, confirms this point.

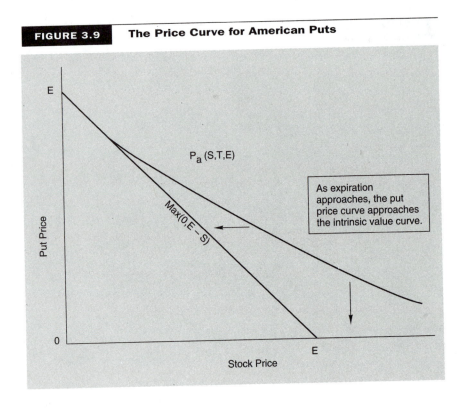

FIGURE 3.9 | **The Price Curve for American Puts**

P_a(S,T,E)

Max(0,E − S)

As expiration approaches, the put price curve approaches the intrinsic value curve.

Put Price

Stock Price

E

0

E

The Effect of Exercise Price

THE EFFECT ON OPTION VALUE   Consider two European puts identical in all respects except exercise price. One put has an exercise price of E_1 and a premium of $P_e(S,T,E_1)$; the other has an exercise price of E_2 and a premium of $P_e(S,T,E_2)$. As before, $E_2 > E_1$. Which put will be more valuable?

Consider two portfolios. Portfolio A consists of a long position in the put priced at $P_e(S,T,E_2)$ and a short position in the put priced at $P_e(S,T,E_1)$. Portfolio B consists of a long position in risk-free bonds with a face value of $E_2 - E_1$ and a present value of $(E_2 - E_1)(1 + r)^{-T}$. Table 3.8 presents these portfolios' payoffs at expiration.

For portfolio A, all outcomes are nonnegative. Because this portfolio cannot produce a cash outflow for the holder, the price of the put purchased must be no less than the price of the put sold; that is,

The price of a European put must be at least as high as the price of an otherwise identical European put with a lower exercise price.

$$P_e(S,T,E_2) \geq P_e(S,T,E_1).$$

| TABLE 3.8 | The Effect of Exercise Price on Put Value: Payoffs at Expiration of Portfolios A and B | | | |

Portfolio	Current Value	$S_T < E_1$	$E_1 \le S_T < E_2$	$E_1 < E_2 \le S_T$
		Payoffs from Portfolio Given Stock Price at Expiration		
A	$-P_e(S,T,E_1)$	$-E_1 + S_T$	0	0
	$+P_e(S,T,E_2)$	$E_2 - S_T$	$E_2 - S_T$	0
		$E_2 - E_1 > 0$	$E_2 - S_T > 0$	0
B	$(E_2 - E_1)(1 + r)^{-T}$	$E_2 - E_1 > 0$	$E_2 - E_1 > 0$	$E_2 - E_1 > 0$

To understand why this is so, consider what would happen if it were not. Suppose the price of the put sold were greater than the price of the put purchased. Then an investor would receive more for the put sold than would be paid for the put purchased. That would produce a net positive cash flow up front, and, from Table 3.8, there would be no possibility of having to pay out any cash at expiration. This transaction would be like a loan that need not be paid back. Obviously, this portfolio would be very attractive and would draw the attention of other investors, who would buy the put with the higher exercise price and sell the put with the lower exercise price. This would tend to drive up the price of the former and drive down the price of the latter. The transaction would cease to be attractive when the put with the higher exercise price became at least as valuable as the put with the lower exercise price.

The intuition behind why a put with a higher exercise price is worth more than one with a lower exercise price is quite simple. A put is an option to sell stock at a fixed price. The higher the price at which the put holder can sell the stock, the more attractive the put.

Suppose these were American puts. In that case, the put with the lower exercise price could be exercised early. For example, let the stock price at time t prior to expiration be S_t, where $S_t < E_1$. Let the option with exercise price E_1 be exercised. Then the investor simply exercises the option with exercise price E_2. The cash flow from these two transactions is $-(E_1 - S_t) + (E_2 - S_t) = E_2 - E_1$, which is positive. Early exercise will not generate a negative cash flow. Thus, our result holds for American puts as well as for European puts.

The price of an American put must be at least as high as the price of an otherwise identical American put with a lower exercise price.

LIMITS ON THE DIFFERENCE IN PREMIUMS   Now let us compare the outcomes of portfolios A and B. We see that portfolio B's outcomes are never

less than portfolio A's. Therefore, no one would pay more for portfolio A than for portfolio B; that is,

$$(E_2 - E_1)(1 + r)^{-T} \geq P_e(S,T,E_2) - P_e(S,T,E_1).$$

The difference in the prices of two European puts that differ only by exercise price cannot exceed the present value of the difference in their exercise prices.

However, this result does not hold for American puts. If the puts were American and both were exercised, the investor would receive $E_2 - E_1$ dollars. This amount would be invested in risk-free bonds and would earn interest over the options' remaining lives. At expiration, the investor would have more than $E_2 - E_1$, the payoff from portfolio B.

Since the difference in exercise prices is greater than the present value of the difference in exercise prices, we can state that for European puts,

$$E_2 - E_1 \geq P_e(S,T,E_2) - P_e(S,T,E_1).$$

This means that the difference in premiums cannot exceed the difference in exercise prices. This result holds for American as well as European puts. To see this, let portfolio B's bonds have a face value of $(E_2 - E_1)(1 + r)^T$ and a present value of $E_2 - E_1$. If early exercise occurred at time t, the most the holder of portfolio A would have at expiration is $(E_2 - E_1)(1 + r)^{T-t}$. The holder of portfolio B would have a larger amount, $(E_2 - E_1)(1 + r)^T$. So again portfolio A would never pay more at expiration than would portfolio B. Therefore, the current value of portfolio A, $P_a(S,T,E_2) - P_a(S,T,E_1)$, could not exceed the current value of portfolio B, $E_2 - E_1$. Thus,

$$E_2 - E_1 \geq P_a(S,T,E_2) - P_a(S,T,E_1).$$

The difference in the prices of two American puts that differ only by exercise price cannot exceed the difference in their exercise prices.

Table 3.9 shows the differences between the put premiums and exercise prices for the Digital Equipment puts. Since these are American puts, we would expect only that the difference in their put premiums will not exceed the difference in their exercise prices—which indeed is the case. In addition, the differences in premiums do not exceed the present values of the differences in exercise prices.

The Lower Bound of a European Put

We showed that the minimum value of an American put is $Max(0, E - S)$. This statement does not hold for a European put, because it cannot be exercised early. However, it is possible to derive a positive lower bound for a European put.

Again consider two portfolios, A and B. Portfolio A consists of a single share of stock. Portfolio B consists of a short position in a European put

| TABLE 3.9 | The Relationship between Exercise Price and Put Price: Digital Equipment Puts |

Exercise Price	Exercise Price Difference	Difference between Put Prices (Present Value of Difference between Exercise Prices in Parentheses)		
		Jun	Jul	Oct
160, 165	5	2.125	2.125	1.625
		(4.996)	(4.975)	(4.902)
160, 170	10	5.688	4.625	NA
		(9.991)	(9.950)	(9.804)
165, 170	5	3.563	4.625	NA
		(4.996)	(4.975)	(4.902)

Note: Risk-free rates are .0484 (Jun); .0535 (Jul); .0591 (Oct). Times to expiration are .0192 (Jun); .0959 (Jul); .3452 (Oct).

priced at $P_e(S,T,E)$ and a long position in risk-free bonds with a face value of E and a present value of $E(1 + r)^{-T}$. The payoffs at expiration from these portfolios are shown in Table 3.10.

Portfolio A's outcome is always at least as favorable as portfolio B's. Therefore, no one would be willing to pay more for portfolio B than for portfolio A. Portfolio A's current value must be no less than portfolio B's; that is,

$$S \geq E(1 + r)^{-T} - P_e(S,T,E).$$

Rearranging this statement gives

$$P_e(S,T,E) \geq E(1 + r)^{-T} - S.$$

| TABLE 3.10 | Lower Bound of a European Put: Payoffs at Expiration of Portfolios A and B |

Portfolio	Current Value	Payoffs from Portfolio Given Stock Price at Expiration	
		$S_T < E$	$S_T \geq E$
A	S	S_T	S_T
B	$E(1 + r)^{-T} - P_e(S,T,E)$	$E - (E - S_T) = S_T$	E

If the present value of the exercise price is less than the stock price, this lower bound will be negative. Since we know that a put cannot be worth less than zero, we can say that

$$P_e(S,T,E) \geq \text{Max}[0, E(1 + r)^{-T} - S].$$

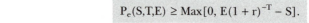

The price of a European put must at least equal the greater of zero or the present value of the exercise price minus the stock price.

Figure 3.10 illustrates these results. The curved line is the European put price, which must lie above the lower bound. As expiration approaches, T gets smaller so the lower bound moves to the right, with the put price curve following it. However, as time goes by, the put price gradually declines. At expiration, the put price and the lower bound converge to $\text{Max}(0, E - S)$, as in Figure 3.8.

Now let us compare the minimum price of the American put, its intrinsic value of $\text{Max}(0, E - S)$, with the lower bound of the European put, $\text{Max}[0, E(1 + r)^{-T} - S]$. Since $E - S$ is greater than $E(1 + r)^{-T} - S$, the American put's intrinsic value is higher than the European put's lower bound. Therefore, the European put's lower bound is irrelevant to the American put price because it is a lower minimum as seen in Figure 3.10. However, $\text{Max}[0, E(1 + r)^{-T} - S]$ is relevant to the European put's price.

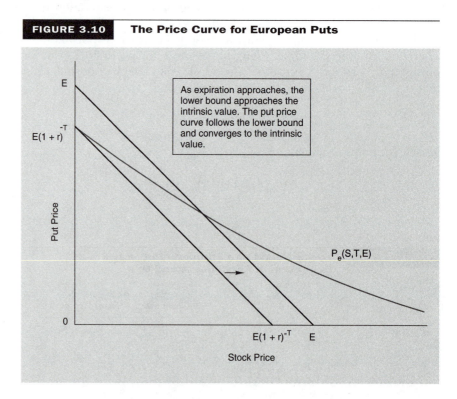

FIGURE 3.10   The Price Curve for European Puts

As expiration approaches, the lower bound approaches the intrinsic value. The put price curve follows the lower bound and converges to the intrinsic value.

E

$E(1 + r)^{-T}$

Put Price

$P_e(S,T,E)$

0

$E(1 + r)^{-T}$ E

Stock Price

Finally, we can use the lower bound of a European put to examine the effect of time to expiration on the option. Earlier we stated that the direction of this effect is uncertain. Consider two puts with times to expiration of T_1 and T_2, where $T_2 > T_1$. Suppose we are at time T_1, the stock price is S_{T_1}, and the shorter-lived put is expiring and worth $\text{Max}(0, E - S_{T_1})$. The longer-lived put has a remaining life of $T_2 - T_1$ and a lower bound of $\text{Max}[0, E(1 + r)^{-(T_2-T_1)} - S_{T_1}]$. Although the lower bound of the longer-lived put is less than the shorter-lived put's intrinsic value, the value of the additional time on the former during which the stock price can move can more than make up the difference. Therefore, we cannot unambiguously tell whether a longer- or shorter-lived European put will be worth more.

If the stock pays dividends such that $S' = S - \sum_{j=1}^{N} = D_j(1 + r)^{-t_j}$, that is, the stock price minus the present value of the dividends, the rule becomes

$$P_e(S,T,E) \geq \text{Max } [0, E(1 + r)^{-T} - S'].$$

American Put versus European Put

Everything that can be done with a European put can be done with an American put. In addition, an American put can be exercised at any time prior to expiration. Therefore, the American put price must at least equal the European put price; that is,

An American put will be at least as valuable as a European put with the same terms.

$$P_a(S,T,E) \geq P_e(S,T,E).$$

The Early Exercise of American Puts

Recall that it might be advisable to exercise an American call if the stock is about to go ex-dividend. If the stock does not pay dividends, then the call will not be exercised early and an American call will have the same value as a European call. The same cannot be said for American puts.

Let us suppose there are no dividends. Suppose you hold an American put and the stock goes bankrupt, meaning that the stock price goes to zero. You are holding an option to sell it for E dollars. There is no reason to wait until expiration to exercise it and obtain your E dollars. You might as well exercise it now. Thus, bankruptcy is one obvious situation in which an American put would be exercised early. However, *bankruptcy is not required to justify early exercise*. Look back at Figure 3.10. Note that the curved line representing the European put price crosses the straight line representing the intrinsic value of the American put. That means that at that stock price, the holder of the European put would prefer to have had an American put and would be willing to pay more to have one. This particular stock price, however, is not the one that would trigger early exercise of

If the stock price falls to a critical level, an American put might be exercised early. The likelihood of early exercise is reduced if the stock pays dividends.

Put-call parity is the relationship among the call price, the put price, the stock price, the exercise price, the risk-free rate, and the time to expiration.

the American put because if the put were American, it would be optimal to hold it until the stock price dropped a little more.

If the stock pays dividends, it might still be worthwhile to exercise it early, but since dividends drive the stock price down, they make American puts less likely to be exercised early. In fact, if the dividends are sufficiently large, it can sometimes be shown that the put would never be exercised early, thus making it effectively a European put.

At this point in our material the exact situation at which an American put would be exercised early cannot be specified. We shall cover this topic again in more detail, however, in Chapter 4.

Put-Call Parity

The prices of European puts and calls on the same stock with identical exercise prices and expiration dates have a special relationship. The put price, call price, stock price, exercise price, time to expiration, and risk-free rate are all related by a formula called **put-call parity.** Let us see how this formula is derived.

Imagine a portfolio, called portfolio A, consisting of one share of stock and a European put. This portfolio will require an investment of $S + P_e(S,T,E)$. Now consider a second portfolio, called portfolio B, consisting of a European call with the same exercise price and risk-free pure discount bonds with a face value of E. That portfolio will require an investment of $C_e(S,T,E) + E(1 + r)^{-T}$. Now let us look at what happens at the expiration. Table 3.11 presents the outcomes.

The stock is worth S_T regardless of whether S_T is more or less than E. Likewise the risk-free bonds are worth E regardless of the outcome. If S_T exceeds E, the call expires in-the-money and is worth $S_T - E$ and the put expires worthless. If S_T is less than or equal to E, the put expires in-the-money worth $E - S_T$ and the call expires worthless. The total values of portfolios A and B are equal. Recalling our Law of One Price, the current values of the two portfolios must be equal. Thus, we require that

$$S + P_e(S,T,E) = C_e(S,T,E) + E(1 + r)^{-T}.$$

This statement is referred to as put-call parity and it is probably one of the most important results in understanding options. It says that a share of stock plus a put is equivalent to a call plus risk-free bonds. It shows the relationship between the call and put prices, the stock price, the time to expiration, the risk-free rate, and the exercise price.

Suppose the combination of the put and the stock is worth less than the combination of the call and the bonds. Then you could buy the put and the stock and sell short the call and the bonds. Selling short the call just means to write the call and selling short the bonds simply means to

TABLE 3.11	Put-Call Parity			
			Payoffs from Portfolio Given Stock Price at Expiration	
Payoff From	**Current Value**		$S_T \leq E$	$S_T > E$
A Stock	S		S_T	S_T
Put	$P_e(S,T,E)$		$\dfrac{E - S_T}{E}$	$\dfrac{0}{S_T}$
B Call	$C_e(S,T,E)$		0	$S_T - E$
Bonds	$E(1 + r)^{-T}$		$\dfrac{E}{E}$	$\dfrac{E}{S_T}$

borrow the present value of E and promise to pay back E at the options' expiration. The cash inflow of the value of the call and the bonds would exceed the cash outflow for the put and the stock. At expiration, there would be no cash inflow or outflow because you would have stock worth S_T and owe the principal on the bonds of E, but you would also have a put worth $E - S_T$ and a call worth zero or a call worth $-(S_T - E)$ and a put worth zero. All of this adds up to zero (check it). In other words, you would get some money up front but not have to pay any out at expiration. Since everyone would start doing this transaction, the prices would be forced back in line with the put-call parity equation.

By observing the signs in front of each term, we can easily determine which combinations replicate others. If the sign is positive, we should buy the option, stock, or bond. If it is negative, we should sell. For example, suppose we isolate the call price,

$$C_e(S,T,E) = P_e(S,T,E) + S - E(1 + r)^{-T}.$$

Then owning a call is equivalent to owning a put, owning the stock, and selling short the bonds (borrowing). If we isolate the put price,

$$P_e(S,T,E) = C_e(S,T,E) - S + E(1 + r)^{-T}.$$

This means that owning a put is equivalent to owning a call, selling short the stock, and buying the bonds. Likewise, we could isolate the stock or the bonds.

To convince yourself that these combinations on the right-hand side of the equation are equivalent to the combinations on the left-hand side, it would be helpful to set up a table like Table 3.11. Analyze the outcomes

at expiration and you will see that the various combinations on the right-hand side do indeed replicate the positions taken on the left-hand side.

If the stock pays dividends, once again, we simply insert S′, which is the stock price minus the present value of the dividends, for the stock price S.

While put-call parity is an extremely important and useful result, it does not hold so neatly if the options are American. The put-call parity rule for American options must be stated as inequalities,

$$C_a(S',T,E) + E + \sum_{j=1}^{N} D_j(1+r)^{-t_j} \geq S + P_a(S',T,E) \geq C_a(S',T,E) + E(1+r)^{-T},$$

where S′ is, again, the stock price minus the present value of the dividends. Although we shall skip the formal proof of this statement, it is, nonetheless, easy to make the calculations to determine if the rule is violated.

Now let us take a look at whether put-call parity holds for the Digital Equipment options. Since the stock does not pay dividends, the Digital Equipment calls are effectively European calls. However, the puts are strictly American. But first let us apply the European put-call parity rule. Panel A of Table 3.12 shows the appropriate calculations. Each cell represents a combination of exercise price and expiration and contains two figures. The upper figure is the value of the stock plus the put while the lower is the value of the call plus the bonds. If put-call parity holds, these two figures should be identical. Of course, we might not expect it to hold perfectly, because transaction costs may prevent some arbitrage opportunities from being worth exploiting. In most of the cases, the figures are very close. The October 165, however, is noticeably different.

Now we apply the correct American put-call parity rule. Panel B contains three figures for each cell. Recalling that there are no dividends, the top figure is $C_a(S,T,E) + E$, the middle figure is $S + P_a(S,T,E)$, and the bottom figure is $C_a(S,T,E) + E(1+r)^{-T}$. These figures should line up in descending order, that is, the top figure should be no lower than the middle figure, which should be no lower than the bottom figure in each cell. This is not the case for the June 160 and 165, the October 165, and the July 170 options.

Put-call parity is the linkage between the call, put, stock, and risk-free bond. Figure 3.11 illustrates these relationships. Throughout the book, we shall further develop this figure to show other important relationships between derivative contracts, the underlying asset, and the risk-free bond market.

The Effect of Interest Rates

The price of a put is inversely related to interest rates.

In contrast to call option prices, which vary directly with interest rates, put option prices vary inversely with interest rates. Purchasing a put is like de-

TABLE 3.12	**Put-Call Parity for Digital Equipment Options**

A European Put-Call Parity

Top row of cell: $S + P_e(S,T,E)$
Bottom row of cell: $C_e(S,T,E) + E(1 + r)^{-T}$

	June	July	October
160	164.81	167.88	172.13
	164.48	167.83	172.11
165	166.94	170.00	173.75
	166.73	169.93	175.01
170	170.50	172.50	*
	170.35	172.90	*

B American Put-Call Parity

Top row of cell: $C_a(S,T,E) + E$ (note no dividends so $S' = S$)
Middle row of cell: $S + P_a(S,T,E)$
Bottom row of cell: $C_a(S,T,E) + E(1 + r)^{-T}$

	June	July	October
160	164.63	168.63	175.25
	164.81	167.88	172.13
	164.48	167.83	172.11
165	166.88	170.75	178.25
	166.94	170.00	173.75
	166.73	169.93	175.01
170	170.50	173.75	*
	170.50	172.50	*
	170.35	172.90	*

*Not computed due to no price on October 170 put.

ferring the sale of stock. When you finally sell the stock by exercising the put, you receive E dollars. If interest rates increase, the E dollars will have a lower present value. Thus, a put holder forgoes higher interest while waiting to exercise the option and receive the exercise price. Higher interest rates make puts less attractive to investors.

The Effect of Stock Volatility

The effect of volatility on a put's price is the same as that for a call: Higher volatility increases the possible gains for a put holder. For example, in our discussion of the effect of volatility on a call, we considered four equally likely stock prices at expiration for Digital Equipment: 150, 160, 170, and

---

FIGURE 3.11   **The Linkage between Calls, Puts, Stock, and Risk-Free Bonds**

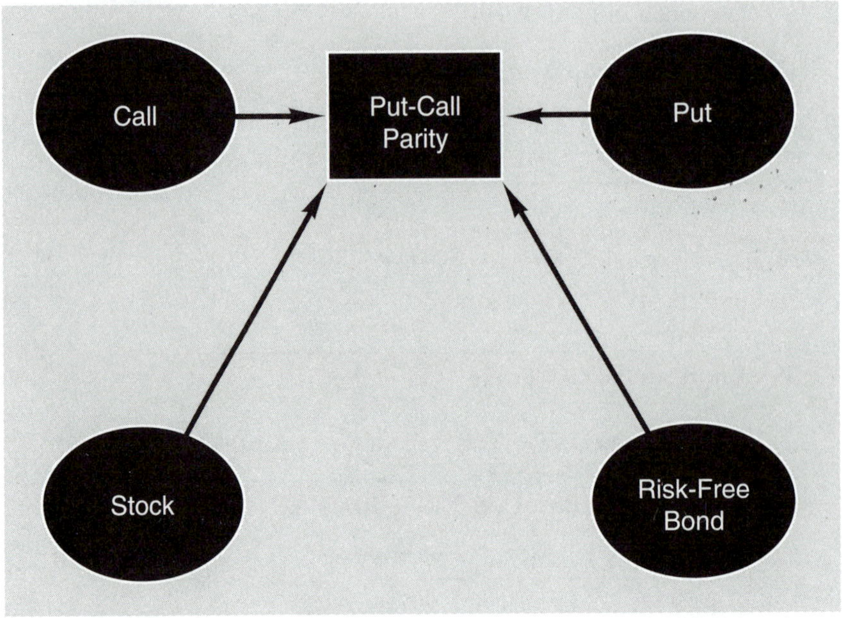

Call → Put-Call Parity ← Put

Stock ↗ Put-Call Parity ↖ Risk-Free Bond

180. The four possible put prices at expiration for a 165 put are 15, 5, 0, and 0. If the volatility increases so that the four possible stock prices at expiration are 140, 160, 170, and 190, the four possible put prices at expiration are 25, 5, 0, and 0. For the holder of a put, this increase in volatility is desirable because the put price now can rise much higher. It does not matter that the put can be even deeper out-of-the-money when it expires, because its lowest possible value is still zero. The put holder's loss thus is truncated. Therefore, the put will have a higher price if the volatility is higher.

The price of a put is directly related to the volatility of the underlying stock.

Another approach to understanding the volatility effect is to consider a European put on a stock with zero volatility. If the put is currently in-the-money, it will be worth the present value of E − S, because no further changes in the stock price will be expected. If the put is out-of-the-money, it will be worthless, because it will have no chance of expiring in-the-money. Either of these cases would be like a risk-free asset and would have no use for either hedgers or speculators.

Summary

This chapter examined the basic principles of option pricing. It identified rules that impose upper and lower limits on put and call prices and examined the vari-

ables that affect an option's price. In addition, it demonstrated how put and call prices are related to each other by the put-call parity rule. Finally, the chapter examined the conditions that can induce an option trader to exercise an option prior to expiration.

We learned a number of principles that apply in some cases to European options only, in others to American options only, and in still others to both. Table 3.13 summarizes these principles.

An often confusing principle is the establishment of a minimum price. We started off by establishing a low minimum and then worked our way up until we could establish the highest possible minimum. First, we developed the absolute minimum price of any call, which is zero. For American calls, the intrinsic value will provide a higher minimum if the option is in-the-money. Thus, it dominates the minimum of zero. However, it does not apply to European calls, because they cannot be exercised early. Nonetheless, there is a lower bound for European calls, which is the maximum of zero or the stock price minus the present value of the exercise price. This is at least as high as the intrinsic value of the American call. Because American calls must be worth at least as much as European calls, this lower bound applies to American calls as well. Thus, the ultimate minimum for both European and American calls on non-dividend-paying stocks is the lower bound we established for European calls.

Both American and European puts have an absolute minimum value of zero. American puts have an intrinsic value, which is the maximum of zero or the exercise

---

TABLE 3.13   **Summary of the Principles of Option Pricing**

	European Calls	American Calls	European Puts	American Puts
Assuming no dividends:				
Minimum value	≥ 0	≥ 0	≥ 0	≥ 0
Intrinsic value (IV)	NA	$\text{Max}(0, S-E)$	NA	$\text{Max}(0, E-S)$
Time value	$C_e(S,T,E) - \text{Max}(0, S-E)$	$C_a(S,T,E) - IV$	$P_e(S,T,E) - \text{Max}(0, E-S)$	$P_a(S,T,E) - IV$
Maximum value	S	S	$E(1+r)^{-T}$	E
Effect of time to expiration	$C_e(S,T_2,E)$ $\geq C_e(S,T_1,E)$	$C_a(S,T_2,E)$ $\geq C_a(S,T_1,E)$	$P_e(S,T_2,E)$ $\geqq P_e(S,T_1,E)$	$P_a(S,T_2,E)$ $\geq P_a(S,T_1,E)$
Effect of exercise price	$C_e(S,T,E_1)$ $\geq C_e(S,T,E_2)$	$C_a(S,T,E_1)$ $\geq C_a(S,T,E_2)$	$P_e(S,T,E_2)$ $\geq P_e(S,T,E_1)$	$P_a(S,T,E_2)$ $\geq P_a(S,T,E_1)$
Maximum difference in premiums	$(E_2 - E_1)(1+r)^{-T}$	$E_2 - E_1$	$(E_2 - E_1)(1+r)^{-T}$	$E_2 - E_1$
Lower bound	$\text{Max}[0, S - E(1+r)^{-T}]$	$\text{Max}[0, S - E(1+r)^{-T}]$	$\text{Max}[0, E(1+r)^{-T} - S]$	$\text{Max}(0, E-S)$
Other results:				
American versus European option prices	$C_a(S,T,E) \geq C_e(S,T,E)$ $P_a(S,T,E) \geq P_e(S,T,E)$			
Put-call parity	$P_e(S,T,E) = C_e(S,T,E) - S + E(1+r)^{-T}$ (European) $C_a(S,T,E) + E \geq S + P_a(S,T,E) \geq C_a(S,T,E) + E(1+r)^{-T}$ (American)			
Effect of dividends	Replace S with $S' = S - \sum_{j=1}^{N} D_j(1+r)^{-t_j}$ and for American put-call parity add $\sum_{j=1}^{N} D_j(1+r)^{-t_j}$ to the left-hand term.			

Derivatives in Action

Some Sage Advice on Put-Call Parity

From the days of Plato and Aristotle, the lending of money at interest has sometimes been viewed as immoral. Not until the Middle Ages was it considered acceptable to profit off of lending money, but even so, a maximum permissable interest rate was established. Lending at an interest rate above the maximum was called "usury" and was illegal. Even to this day, maximum interest rates are specified on certain types of transactions.

Russell Sage was a famous nineteenth-century financier. A clever man with a sharp mathematical mind, Sage was an active dealer in puts and calls. In fact he was truly one of the first option traders in the

United States and he understood the famous put-call parity relationship:

$$P_e(S,T,E) + S = C_e(S,T,E) + E(1 + r)^{-T}.$$

Now turn this equation around to isolate the risk-free bonds:

$$E(1 + r)^{-T} = P_e(S,T,E) + S - C_e(S,T,E).$$

The left-hand side says that the holder of a loan, in which the borrower receives the present value of E and promises to pay back E after a period of time T, is equivalent to owning a put and the stock and sell-

price minus the stock price. This minimum does not apply to European puts, because they cannot be exercised early. European puts have a lower bound that is the maximum of zero or the present value of the exercise price minus the stock price. Because this lower bound is never greater than the intrinsic value of the American put, it does not help us raise the minimum for American puts. Thus, the lower bound is the minimum for European puts and the intrinsic value is the minimum for American puts (on non-dividend-paying stocks).

While we have identified the factors relevant to determining an option's price, we have not yet discussed how to determine the exact price. Although put-call parity appears to be a method of pricing options, it is only a relative option pricing model. To price the put, we need to know the call's price; to price the call, we must know the put's price. Therefore, we cannot use put-call parity to price one instrument without either accepting the market price of the other as correct or having a model that first gives us the price of the other.

In short, we need an option pricing model—a formula that gives the option's price as a function of the variables that should affect it. If the option pricing model is correct, it should give option prices that conform to these boundary conditions. Most important, it should establish the theoretically correct option price. If the market price is out of line with the model price, arbitrage should force it to move toward the model price. We are now ready to look at option pricing models.

ing a call. Sage used put-call parity to create a synthetic loan with an interest rate that exceeded the statutory limit. This was accomplished by buying the stock and a put from his customer and then selling the customer a call. From the above formula, this is equivalent to holding a risk-free bond or loan paying off E at expiration. Sage specified the put and call prices such that the interest rate implied on the loan was greater than permitted by law.

For example, the statutory maximum in the 1860s was about 7 percent. A customer comes to Sage with stock worth $45 but needs cash and asks for a one-year loan of $50. Sage buys the stock for $45 and a put for $30 and sells the call for $25, all transac-

tions done with the customer. The exercise price is $70. The customer receives $50 ($45 + $30 − $25 = $50). But one year later, the customer would end up buying the stock for $70 (either by exercising the call or having Sage exercise the put). The customer has borrowed $50 and, one year later, paid back $70, an interest rate of 40 percent! Of course, if the customer or the authorities had understood put-call parity, the transaction would not have occurred.

_____

Source: This material is drawn from Paul Sarnoff, *Russell Sage: The Money King* (New York: Ivan Obolensky, 1965).

Key Terms

Before continuing to Chapter 4, you should be able to give brief definitions of the following terms.

- intrinsic value/parity value/ parity/exercise value
- time value/speculative value
- deep-in-the-money/deep-out-of-the- money
- time value decay
- put-call parity

Questions and Problems

1. Consider an option that expires in 68 days. The bid and ask discounts on the Treasury bill maturing in 67 days are 8.20 and 8.24, respectively. Find the approximate risk-free rate.

2. What would happen in the options market if the price of an American call were less than the value Max$(0, S − E)$? Would your answer differ if the option were European?

3. In this chapter, we did not learn how to obtain the exact price of a call without knowing the price of the put and using put-call parity. In one special case, however, we can obtain an exact price for a call. Assume the option has an infinite maturity. Then use the maximum and minimum values we learned in this chapter to obtain the prices of European and American calls.

4. Why might two calls or puts alike in all respects but time to expiration have approximately the same price?

5. Why might two calls or puts alike in all respects but exercise price have approximately the same price?

6. Suppose you observe a European call option that is priced at less than the value $Max[0, S - E(1 + r)^{-T}]$. What type of transaction should you execute to achieve the maximum benefit?

7. Explain why an option's time value is greatest when the stock price is near the exercise price and why it nearly disappears when the option is deep-in- or out-of-the-money.

8. Critique the following statement, made by an options investor: "My call option is very deep-in-the-money. I don't see how it can go any higher. I think I should exercise it."

9. Call prices are directly related to the stock's volatility, yet higher volatility means that the stock price can go lower. How would you resolve this apparent paradox?

10. The value $Max[0, E(1 + r)^{-T} - S]$ was shown to be the lowest possible value of a European put. Why is this value irrelevant for an American put?

11. Why do higher interest rates lead to higher call option prices but lower put option prices?

12. Suppose a European put price exceeds the value predicted by put-call parity. How could an investor profit?

13. Why does the justification for exercising an American call early not hold up when considering an American put?

The following option prices were observed for a stock on July 6 of a particular year. Use this information to solve problems 14 through 19. Unless otherwise indicated, ignore dividends on the stock. The stock is priced at 165 1/8. The expirations are July 17, August 21, and October 16. The risk-free rates are .0516, .0550, and .0588, respectively.

	Calls			**Puts**		
Strike	**Jul**	**Aug**	**Oct**	**Jul**	**Aug**	**Oct**
155	10.5	11.75	14	.1875	1.25	2.75
160	6	8.125	11.125	.75	2.75	4.5
165	2.6875	5.25	8.125	2.375	4.75	6.75
170	.8125	3.25	6	5.75	7.5	9

14. Compute the intrinsic values, time values, and lower bounds of the following calls. Identify any profit opportunities that may exist.
    a. July 160
    b. October 155
    c. August 170

15. Compute the intrinsic values, time values, and lower bounds of the following puts. Identify any profit opportunities that may exist.
    a. July 165
    b. August 160
    c. October 170

16. Check the following combinations of puts and calls, and determine whether they conform to the put-call parity rule for European options. If you see any violations, suggest a strategy.
    a. July 155
    b. August 160
    c. October 170

17. Repeat Question 16 using American put-call parity, but do not suggest a strategy.

18. Examine the following pairs of calls, which differ only by exercise price. Determine whether any violate the rules regarding relationships between American options that differ only by exercise price.
    a. August 155 and 160
    b. October 160 and 165

19. Examine the following pairs of puts, which differ only by exercise price. Determine if any violate the rules regarding relationships between American options that differ only by exercise price.
    a. August 155 and 160
    b. October 160 and 170

20. (Concept Problem) Put-call parity is a powerful formula that can be used to create equivalent combinations of options, risk-free bonds, and stock. Suppose there are options available on the number of points Shaquille O'Neal will score in his next game. For example, a call option with an exercise price of 32 would pay off $\text{Max}(0, S - 32)$, where S is the number of points Shaq has recorded by the end of the game. Thus, if he scores 35, call holders receive $3 for each call. If he scores less than 32, call holders receive nothing. A put with an exercise price of 32 would pay off $\text{Max}(0, 32 - S)$. If Shaq scores more than 32, put holders receive nothing. If he scores 28, put holders receive $4 for each put. Obviously there is no way to actually buy a position in the underlying asset, a point. However, put-call parity shows that the underlying asset can be re-created from a combination of puts, calls, and risk-free bonds. Show how this would be done, and give the formula for the price of a point.

21. (Concept Question) Suppose Congress decides that investors should not profit when stock prices go down so it outlaws short selling. Congress has not figured out options, however, so there are no restrictions on option trading. Explain how to accomplish the equivalent of a short sale by using options.

CHAPTER 4

Option Pricing Models

Mathematics is being applied to finance—breaking down the whole into its fundamental building blocks which determines and explains its characteristics.

RON DEMBO
The Wall Street Journal, October 18, 1991

This chapter examines option pricing models. A **model** is a simplified representation of reality that uses certain inputs to produce an output, or result. An **option pricing model** is a mathematical formula that uses the factors determining the option's price as inputs. The output is the theoretical fair value of the option. If the model performs as it should, the option's market price will equal the theoretical fair value.

In Chapter 3, we examined some basic concepts on determining option prices. However, we saw only how to price options relative to other options; for example, put-call parity demonstrates that given the price of a call, one can determine the price of a put. We also discovered relationships among the prices of options that differ by exercise prices and examined the upper and lower bounds on call and put prices. We did not, however, learn how to determine the exact option price directly from the factors that influence it.

A large body of academic literature on option pricing exists. Much of it goes far beyond the intended level of this book. The models range from the relatively simple to the extremely complex. All of the models have much in common, and it is necessary to understand the basic models before moving on to the more complex but more realistic ones.

We begin this chapter with a simple model called the **binomial option pricing model.** After taking the binomial model through several stages, we move on to the **Black-Scholes option pricing model.** Later we examine several simple modifications of the Black-Scholes model that improve its performance.

114

The One-Period Binomial Model

First, consider what we mean by a one-period world. An option has a defined life, typically expressed in days. Assume the option's life is one unit of time. This time period can be as short or as long as necessary. If the time period is one day and the option has more than one day remaining, we will need a multiperiod model, which we shall examine later. For now, we will assume the option's life is a single time period.

The model is called a **binomial** model. It allows the stock price to go up or down, possibly at different rates. A binomial probability distribution is a distribution in which there are two outcomes or states. The probability of an up or down movement is governed by the binomial probability distribution. Because of this, the model is also called a **two-state** model.

In applying the binomial model to the stock market, however, it is immediately obvious that the range of possible outcomes is greater than the two states the binomial distribution can accommodate. However, that makes the model no less worthwhile. Its virtues are its simplicity and its ability to present the fundamental concepts of option pricing models clearly and concisely. In so doing, it establishes a foundation that facilitates an understanding of the Black-Scholes model.

Consider a world in which there is a stock priced at S on which call options are available.[1] The call has one period remaining before it expires. When the call expires, the stock can take on one of two values: It can go up at a rate of u or down at a rate of d. If it goes up the stock price will be S_u, which equals $S(1 + u)$. If it goes down it will be S_d, which equals $S(1 + d)$.

For example, suppose the stock price is currently $50 and can go either up by 10 percent or down by 8 percent. Thus, $u = .10$ and $d = -.08$. The variables u and d, therefore, are the rates of return on the stock. When the call expires, the stock will be either $50(1.10) = 55$ or $50(.92) = 46$.

Consider a call option on the stock with an exercise price of E and a current price of C. When the option expires, it will be worth either C_u or C_d. Because at expiration the call price is its intrinsic value,

$$C_u = Max[0, S(1 + u) - E]$$
$$C_d = Max[0, S(1 + d) - E].$$

Figure 4.1 illustrates the paths of both the stock and the call prices. This tree diagram is simple, but it will become more complex when we introduce the two-period model.

---

[1]The model can also price put options. We shall see how this is done in a later section and in an end-of-chapter problem.

FIGURE 4.1   **The One-Period Binomial Tree**

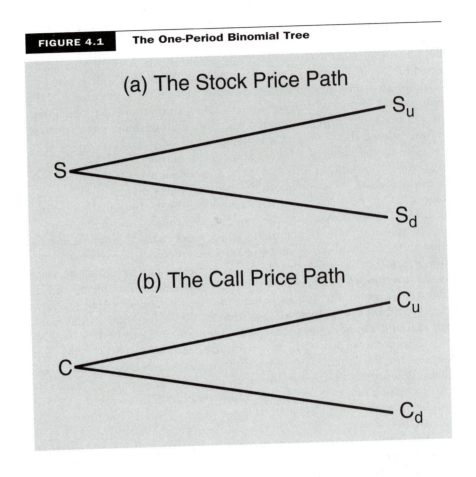

(a) The Stock Price Path

S_u

S

S_d

(b) The Call Price Path

C_u

C

C_d

If both stock prices resulted in the option expiring in-the-money, the option would not be very speculative; however, it would still be correctly priced by the model. The writer would receive a premium compensating for the future cash outflow expected upon exercising the option. To make things more interesting, however, we shall define our variables such that the option has a chance of expiring out-of-the-money. Assume $S(1 + d)$ is less than E; that is, if the stock price goes down, the option will expire out-of-the-money. Also assume $S(1 + u)$ is greater than E such that if the stock price goes up, the option will expire in-the-money.

As in previous chapters, let the risk-free rate be identified by the symbol r. The risk-free rate is the interest earned on a riskless investment over a time period equal to the option's remaining life. The risk-free rate falls between the rate of return if the stock goes up and the rate of return if the

stock goes down. Thus, $d < r < u$.[2] We shall assume all investors can borrow or lend at the risk-free rate.

The objective of this model is to derive a formula for the theoretical fair value of the option, the variable C. The theoretical fair value is then compared against the actual price and reveals whether the option is overpriced, underpriced, or correctly priced. The formula for C is developed by constructing a riskless portfolio of stock and options. A riskless portfolio should earn the risk-free rate. Given the stock's values and the riskless return on the portfolio, the call's value can be inferred from the other variables.

This riskless portfolio is called a **hedge portfolio** and consists of h shares of stock and a single written call. The model provides the **hedge ratio,** h. The current value of the portfolio is the value of the h shares minus the value of the short call. We subtract the call's value from the value of the h shares because the shares are assets and the short call is a liability. Thus, the portfolio value is assets minus liabilities, or simply net worth. The current portfolio value is denoted as V, where $V = hS - C$.

At expiration, the portfolio value will be either V_u if the stock goes up or V_d if the stock goes down. Using the previously defined terms,

$$V_u = hS_u - C_u = hS(1 + u) - C_u$$
$$V_d = hS_d - C_d = hS(1 + d) - C_d.$$

If the same outcome is achieved regardless of what the stock price does, the position is riskless. We can choose a value of h that will make this happen. We simply set $V_u = V_d$ so that

$$hS(1 + u) - C_u = hS(1 + d) - C_d.$$

Solving for h,

$$h = \frac{C_u - C_d}{S(1 + u) - S(1 + d)} = \frac{C_u - C_d}{S_u - S_d}.$$

Since we know the values of S, u, and d, we can determine C_u, C_d, and h.

A riskless investment must earn a return equal to the risk-free rate. Thus, the portfolio's value one period later should equal its current value compounded for one period at the risk-free rate. If it does not, the portfolio will be incorrectly valued and represent a potential arbitrage opportunity. Later we shall see how the arbitrage would be executed.

---

[2]This requirement is necessary or there would be arbitrage opportunities.

If the portfolio's current value grows at the risk-free rate, its value at the option's expiration will be $(hS - C)(1 + r)$. The two values of the portfolio at expiration, V_u and V_d, are equal, so we can select either one. Choosing V_u and setting it equal to the original value of the portfolio compounded at the risk-free rate gives

$$V(1 + r) = V_u$$
$$(hS - C)(1 + r) = hS(1 + u) - C_u.$$

The one-period binomial option pricing formula provides the option price as a weighted average of the two possible option prices at expiration, discounted at the risk-free rate.

Substituting the formula for h and solving this equation for C gives the option pricing formula,

$$C = \frac{pC_u + (1 - p)C_d}{1 + r},$$

where p is defined as $(r - d)/(u - d)$. The formula gives the call option's price as a function of the variables C_u, C_d, p, and r. However, C_u and C_d are determined by the variables S, u, d, and E. Thus, the variables affecting the call option price are the current stock price, S, the exercise price, E, the risk-free rate, r, and the parameters, u and d, which define the possible future stock prices at expiration. Notice how the call price is a weighted average of the two possible call prices the next period, discounted at the risk-free rate. Notice also that we never specified the probabilities of the two stock price movements; they do not enter into the model. The option is priced relative to the stock. Therefore, given the stock price, one can obtain the option price. The stock, however, is priced independently of the option, and thus the probabilities of the stock price movements would be a factor in pricing the stock. But pricing the stock is not our concern. We already have the stock price, S.

In Chapter 1, we introduced the concept of risk neutrality and noted that we would be using it to price derivatives. The investor's feelings about risk play an important role in the pricing of securities, but in the risk-neutral option pricing framework, investors' sensitivities to risk are of no consequence. This does not mean, however, that the model assumes investors are risk neutral. The stock price is determined by how investors feel about risk. If investors are risk neutral and determine that a stock is worth $20, the model will use $20 and take no account of investors' feelings about risk. If investors are risk averse and determine that a stock is worth $20, the model will use $20 and disregard investors' feelings about risk. This does not mean that the stock will be priced equally by risk-averse and risk-neutral investors; rather, the model will accept the stock price as given and pay no attention to how risk was used to obtain the stock price.

An Illustrative Example

Consider a stock currently priced at $60. One period later it can go up to $69, an increase of 15 percent, or down to $48, a decrease of 20 percent. Assume a call option with an exercise price of $50. The risk-free rate is 10 percent. The inputs are summarized as follows:

$$S = 60 \qquad d = -.20$$
$$E = 50 \qquad r = .10$$
$$u = .15$$

First, find the values of C_u and C_d:

$$C_u = \text{Max } [0, S(1 + u) - E]$$
$$= \text{Max } [0, 60(1.15) - 50]$$
$$= 19$$
$$C_d = \text{Max } [0, S(1 + d) - E]$$
$$= \text{Max } [0, 60(.80) - 50]$$
$$= 0.$$

The hedge ratio, h, is

$$h = \frac{19 - 0}{69 - 48} = .905.$$

The hedge requires .905 shares of stock for each call.[3] The value of p is

$$p = \frac{r - d}{u - d} = \frac{.10 - (-.20)}{.15 - (-.20)} = .857.$$

Then

$$1 - p = 1 - .857 = .143.$$

Plugging into the formula for C gives

$$C = \frac{19(.857) + 0(.143)}{1.10} = 14.80.$$

Thus, the theoretical fair value of the call is $14.80.

A Hedged Portfolio

Consider a hedged portfolio consisting of a short position in 1,000 calls and a long position in 905 shares of stock. The number of shares is

---

[3]We assume odd lots of stock can be purchased.

determined by the hedge ratio of .905 shares per written call. The current value of this portfolio is

$$905(60) - 1,000(14.80) = 39,500.$$

Thus, you buy 905 shares at $60 per share and write 1,000 calls at $14.80. This requires a payment of $905($60) = $54,300$ for the stock and takes in $1,000($14.80) = $14,800$ for the calls. The net cash outlay is $54,300 – $14,800 = $39,500. This total represents the assets (the stock) minus the liabilities (the calls) and thus is the net worth, or the amount the investor must commit to the transaction. Figure 4.2 illustrates the process.

If the stock goes up to $69, the call will be exercised for a value of $69 – $50 = $19. The stock will be worth $905($69) = $62,445$. Thus, the portfolio will be worth $905($69) - 1,000($69 - $50) = $43,445$. If the stock goes down to $48, the call will expire out-of-the-money. The portfolio will be worth $905($48) = $43,440$. These two values of the portfolio at expiration are essentially equal, because the $5 difference is due only to the rounding off of the hedge ratio and the initial call price. The return on this hedged portfolio is

$$r_h = \left(\frac{\$43,445}{\$39,500}\right) - 1 \approx .10,$$

FIGURE 4.2   **One-Period Binomial Example**

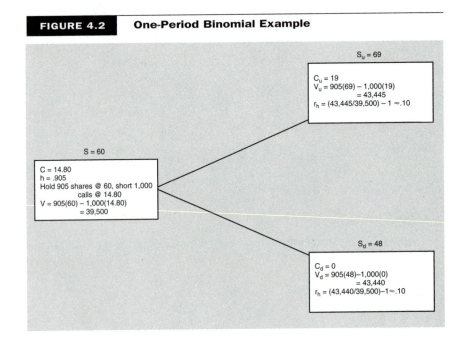

which is the risk-free rate. The original investment of $39,500 will have grown to $43,445—a return of about 10 percent, the risk-free rate.

If the call price were not $14.80, an arbitrage opportunity would exist. First we will consider the case where the call is overpriced.

An Overpriced Call

If the call were overpriced, a riskless hedge could generate a riskless return in excess of the risk-free rate. Suppose the market price of the call is $15.50. If you buy 905 shares and write 1,000 calls, the value of the investment today is

$$905(\$60) - 1,000(\$15.50) = \$38,800.$$

If the stock goes up to $69, at expiration the call will be priced at $19 and the portfolio will be worth $905(\$69) - 1,000(\$19) = \$43,445$. If the stock goes down to $48, the call will be worth nothing and the portfolio will be worth $905(\$48) = \$43,440$. In either case, the portfolio will be worth the same, the difference of $5 being due to rounding. The initial investment of $38,800 will have grown to $43,445, a return of

$$r_h = \left(\frac{\$43,445}{\$38,800}\right) - 1 \approx .12,$$

which is considerably higher than the risk-free rate.

A riskless portfolio that will earn more than the risk-free rate obviously is very attractive. All investors will recognize this opportunity and hurry to execute the transaction. This will increase the demand for the stock and the supply of the option. Consequently, the stock price will tend to increase and the option price to decrease until the option is correctly priced. For illustrative purposes, assume that the stock price stays at $60. Then the option price must fall from $15.50 to $14.80. Only at an option price of $14.80 will this risk-free portfolio offer a return equal to the risk-free rate.

Now consider what happens if the option is underpriced.

An Underpriced Call

If the option is underpriced, it is necessary to buy it. To hedge a long option position, you must sell the stock short. Suppose the call is priced at $14. Then you sell short 905 shares at $60, which generates a cash inflow of $905(\$60) = \$54,300$. Now you buy 1,000 calls at $14 each for a cost of $14,000. This produces a net cash inflow of $40,300.

If the stock goes to $69, you buy it back at $905(\$69) = \$62,445$. You exercise the calls for a gain of $1,000(\$69 - \$50) = \$19,000$. The net cash flow is $-\$62,445 + \$19,000 = -\$43,445$. If the stock goes down to $48, you buy

it back, paying 905($48) = $43,440 while the calls expire worthless. The $5 difference is due solely to rounding.

In both outcomes, the returns are essentially equivalent. The overall transaction is like a loan in which you receive $40,300 up front and pay back $43,440 later. This is equivalent to an interest rate of ($43,440/ $40,300) − 1 = .078. Because this transaction is the same as borrowing at a rate of 7.8 percent and the risk-free rate is 10 percent, it is an attractive borrowing opportunity. All investors will recognize this and execute the transaction. This will tend to drive up the call price, or possibly drive down the stock price, until equilibrium is reached. If the price of the stock stays at $60, equilibrium will be reached when the call price rises to $14.80.

This model considered only a single period. In the next section, we extend the model to a two-period world.

The Two-Period Binomial Model

In the single-period world, the stock price goes either up or down. Thus, there are only two possible future stock prices. To increase the degree of realism, we will now add another period. This will increase the number of possible outcomes at expiration.

Suppose that at the end of the first period the stock price has risen to $S(1 + u)$. During the second period it could go either up or down, in which case it would end up at either $S_{u^2} = S(1 + u)^2$ or $S_{ud} = S(1 + u)(1 + d)$. If the stock price has gone down in the first period to $S(1 + d)$, during the second period it will either go down again or go back up, in which case it will end up at either $S_{d^2} = S(1 + d)^2$ or $S_{du} = S(1 + d)(1 + u)$.

Figure 4.3 illustrates the paths of the stock price and the corresponding call prices. The option prices at expiration are

$$C_{u^2} = Max[0, S(1 + u)^2 − E]$$
$$C_{ud} = Max[0, S(1 + u)(1 + d) − E]$$
$$C_{d^2} = Max[0, S(1 + d)^2 − E].$$

The possible option prices at the end of the first period, C_u and C_d, initially are unknown; however, they can be found.

Suppose that in the first period the stock price increases to S_u. Because there will be only one period remaining with two possible outcomes, the one-period binomial model is appropriate for finding the option price, C_u. If at the end of the first period the stock price decreases to S_d, we will again find ourselves facing a single-period world with two possible outcomes. Here we can again use the one-period binomial model to obtain the value of C_d. Using the one-period model, the option prices C_u and C_d are

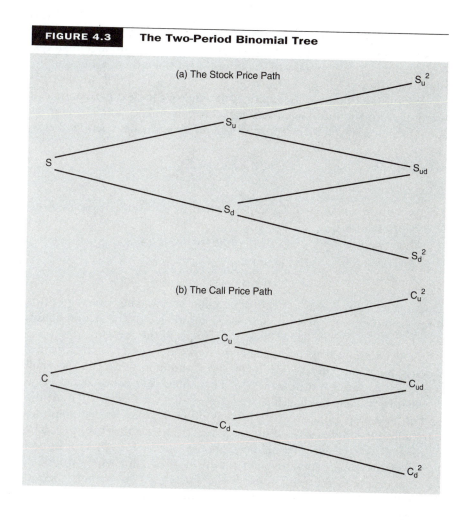

FIGURE 4.3   The Two-Period Binomial Tree

(a) The Stock Price Path

S

S_u

S_d

S_u^2

S_{ud}

S_d^2

(b) The Call Price Path

C

C_u

C_d

C_u^2

C_{ud}

C_d^2

$$C_u = \frac{pC_{u^2} + (1-p)C_{ud}}{1+r}$$

and

$$C_d = \frac{pC_{ud} + (1-p)C_{d^2}}{1+r}.$$

In a single-period world, a call option's value is a weighted average of the option's two possible values at the end of the next period. The call's value if the stock goes up in the next period is weighted by the factor p; its value if the stock goes down in the next period is weighted by the factor $1 - p$. To obtain the call price at the start of the period, we discount the

weighted average of the two possible future call prices at the risk-free rate for one period. The single-period binomial model is, thus, a general formula that can be used in any multiperiod world when there is but one period remaining.

Even if the call does not expire at the end of the next period, we can use the formula to find the current call price, the theoretical fair value, as a weighted average of the two possible call prices in the next period; that is,

$$C = \frac{pC_u + (1 - p)C_d}{1 + r}.$$

The two-period binomial option pricing formula provides the option price as a weighted average of the two possible option prices the next period, discounted at the risk-free rate. The two future option prices are obtained from the one-period binomial model.

First, we find the values of C_u and C_d; then we substitute these into the above formula for C.

Those who prefer a more direct approach can use

$$C = \frac{p^2 C_{u^2} + 2p(1 - p)C_{ud} + (1 - p)^2 C_{d^2}}{(1 + r)^2}.$$

This formula illustrates that the call's value is a weighted average of its three possible values at expiration two periods later. The denominator, $(1 + r)^2$, discounts this figure back two periods to the present.

Notice that we have not actually derived the formula by constructing a hedge portfolio. This is possible, however, and in a later section we shall see how the hedge portfolio works. First, note that the hedge is constructed by initially holding h shares of stock for each call written. At the end of the first period, the stock price is either S_u or S_d. At that point, we must adjust the hedge ratio. If the stock is at S_u, let the new hedge ratio be designated as h_u; if at S_d, let the new ratio be h_d. The formulas for h_u and h_d are of the same general type as that of h in the single-period model. The numerator is the call's value if the stock goes up the next period minus the call's value if the stock goes down the next period. The denominator is the price of the stock if it goes up the next period minus its price if it goes down the next period. In equation form,

$$h = \frac{C_u - C_d}{S_u - S_d}, \; h_u = \frac{C_{u^2} - C_{ud}}{S_{u^2} - S_{ud}}, \text{ and } h_d = \frac{C_{ud} - C_{d^2}}{S_{ud} - S_{d^2}}.$$

An Illustrative Example

Consider the example in a two-period world from the previous section. All input values remain the same. The possible stock prices at expiration are

$$S(1 + u)^2 = 60(1.15)^2$$
$$= 79.35$$
$$S(1 + u)(1 + d) = 60(1.15)(.80)$$
$$= 55.20$$

$$S(1 + d)^2 = 60(.80)^2$$
$$= 38.40.$$

The call prices at expiration are

$$C_u^2 = Max[0, S(1 + u)^2 - E]$$
$$= Max(0, 79.35 - 50)$$
$$= 29.35$$
$$C_{ud} = Max[0, S(1 + u)(1 + d) - E]$$
$$= Max(0, 55.20 - 50)$$
$$= 5.20$$
$$C_d^2 = Max[0, S(1 + d)^2 - E]$$
$$= Max(0, 38.40 - 50)$$
$$= 0.$$

The value of p is the same regardless of the number of periods in the model.

We can find the call's value by either of the two methods discussed in the previous section. Let us first compute the values of C_u and C_d:

$$C_u = \frac{(.857)(29.35) + (.143)(5.20)}{1.10} = 23.54$$

$$C_d = \frac{(.857)(5.20) + (.143)(0)}{1.10} = 4.05.$$

The value of the call today is a weighted average of the two possible call values one period later:

$$C = \frac{(.857)(23.54) + (.143)(4.05)}{1.10} = \$18.87.$$

Note that the same call analyzed in the one-period world is worth more in the two-period world. Why? Recall from Chapter 3 that a call option with a longer maturity is never worth less than one with a shorter maturity and usually is worth more. If this principle did not hold here, something would have been wrong with the model.

A Hedged Portfolio

Now consider a hedged portfolio. Figure 4.4 illustrates this process. It would be very helpful to keep an eye on the figure as we move through the example. Let the call be trading in the market at its theoretical fair value of $18.87. The hedge will consist of 1,000 short calls. The number of shares purchased is given by the formula for h,

FIGURE 4.4   **Two-Period Binomial Example**

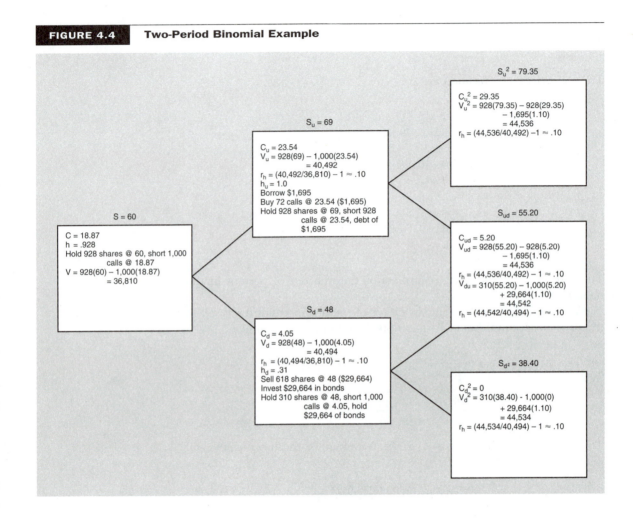

$$h = \frac{23.54 - 4.05}{69 - 48} = .928.$$

Thus, we buy 928 shares of stock and write 1,000 calls. The transaction can be summarized as follows:

Buy 928 shares at $60 = $55,680 (assets);
write 1,000 calls at $18.87 = −$18,870 (liabilities);
net investment = $36,810 (net worth).

STOCK GOES TO 69   The portfolio consists of 928 shares at $69 and 1,000 calls at $23.54. The value of the portfolio is 928($69) − 1,000($23.54) =

$40,492. Our investment has grown from $36,810 to $40,492. You should be able to verify that this is a 10 percent return, the risk-free rate. To maintain a hedge through the next period, we need to revise the hedge ratio. The new hedge ratio, h_u, is

$$h_u = \frac{29.35 - 5.20}{79.35 - 55.20} = 1.$$

The new hedge ratio will be one share of stock for each call. In fact, if the call has one period remaining and there is no possibility of it expiring out-of-the-money, the hedge ratio will always be 1.[4]

To establish the new hedge ratio, we need either 928 calls or 1,000 shares of stock. We can either buy back 72 calls, leaving us with 928, or buy 72 shares, giving us 1,000 shares. Since it is less expensive to buy the calls, let us buy back 72 calls at $23.54 each for a total cost of $1,695. To avoid putting out more of our own funds, we borrow the money at the risk-free rate.

STOCK GOES TO 48   The portfolio consists of 928 shares valued at $48 and 1,000 calls valued at $4.05. The portfolio value is 928($48) − 1,000($4.05) = $40,494, which differs from the outcome at a stock price of $69 only by a round-off error. Since the return is the same regardless of the change in the stock price, the portfolio is riskless. To maintain the hedge through the next period, we adjust the hedge ratio to

$$h_d = \frac{5.20 - 0}{55.20 - 38.40} = .31.$$

Thus, we need 310 shares of stock for the 1,000 calls. We currently hold 928 shares, so we can sell off 618 shares at $48 and receive $29,664. Then we invest this money in riskless bonds paying the risk-free rate. At the end of the second period, the bonds will pay off $29,664 plus 10 percent interest.

STOCK GOES FROM 69 TO 79.35   We sell the 928 shares at $79.35, the calls are exercised at $29.35 each, and we repay the loan of $1,695 plus 10 percent interest. The value of the portfolio is 928($79.35) − 928($29.35) − $1,695(1.10) = $44,536, a return of 10 percent from the previous period.

STOCK GOES FROM 69 TO 55.20   We have 928 shares valued at $55.20, 928 calls exercised at $5.20, and the repayment of the loan of $1,695 plus interest for a total portfolio value of 928($55.20) − 928($5.20) − $1,695(1.10) = $44,536, a return of 10 percent from the previous period.

---

[4]This statement can easily be verified by substituting $S(1 + u)^2 - E$ for C_{u^2} and $S(1 + u)(1 + d) - E$ for C_{ud} in the formula for h_u.

Stock Goes from 48 to 55.20   The portfolio consists of 310 shares valued at $55.20, 1,000 calls exercised at $5.20, and bonds worth $29,664 plus 10 percent interest. The total value of the portfolio is 310($55.20) − 1,000($5.20) + $29,664(1.10) = $44,542, a 10 percent return from the previous period.

Stock Goes from 48 to 38.40   We have 310 shares at $38.40, 1,000 calls expiring worthless, and principal and interest on the risk-free bonds. The value of this portfolio is 310($38.40) + $29,664(1.10) = $44,534. This is essentially the same amount received as in the other cases; the difference is due only to a round-off error. Thus, regardless of which path the stock takes, the hedge will produce an increase in wealth of 10 percent in each period.

Now let us consider what happens if the call is mispriced.

A Mispriced Call in the Two-Period World

If the call is mispriced at the outset, an arbitrage opportunity exists. If the call is underpriced, we should purchase it and sell short h shares of stock. If the call is overpriced, we should write it and purchase h shares of stock. Whether we earn the arbitrage return over the first period, the second period, or both periods, however, will depend on whether the call price adjusts to its theoretical fair value at the end of the first period. If it does not, we may not earn a return in excess of the risk-free rate over the first period. However, the call must be correctly priced at the end of the second period, because it expires at that time.

The two-period return will be the geometric average of the two one-period returns; that is, if 8 percent is the first-period return and 12 percent is the second-period return, the two-period return will be $\sqrt{(1.08)(1.12)} - 1 = .0998$. If one of the two returns equals the risk-free rate and the other exceeds it, the two-period return will exceed the risk-free rate. If one of the two returns is less than the risk-free rate and the other is greater, the overall return can still exceed the risk-free rate. The return earned over the full two periods will exceed the risk-free rate if the option is mispriced at the outset, the proper long or short position is taken, and the correct hedge ratio is maintained.

There are many possible outcomes of such a hedge, and it would take an entire chapter to illustrate them. We therefore shall discuss the possibilities only in general terms. In each case, we will assume the proper hedge ratio is maintained and the investor buys calls only when they are underpriced or correctly priced and sells calls only when they are overpriced or correctly priced.

Suppose the call originally was overpriced and is still overpriced at the end of the first period. Since the call has not fallen sufficiently to be cor-

rectly priced, the return over the first period actually can be less than the risk-free rate. However, because the call must be correctly priced at the end of the second period, the return earned over the second period will more than make up for it. Overall, the return earned over the two periods will exceed the risk-free rate.

If the call originally is overpriced and becomes correctly priced at the end of the first period, the return earned over that period must exceed the risk-free rate. The return earned over the second period will equal the risk-free rate, because the call was correctly priced at the beginning of the second period and is correctly priced at the end of it. Thus, the full two-period return will exceed the risk-free rate.

If the call is overpriced at the start and becomes underpriced at the end of the first period, the return earned over that period will exceed the risk-free rate. This is because the call will have fallen in price more than is justified and now is worth considerably less than it should be. At this point, we should close out the hedge and initiate a new hedge for the second period consisting of a long position in the underpriced call and a short position in the stock. We can invest the excess proceeds in risk-free bonds. The second-period return will far exceed the risk-free rate. The overall two-period return obviously will be above the risk-free rate.

Table 4.1 summarizes these results. Similar conclusions apply for an underpriced call, although the interpretation differs somewhat because the hedge portfolio is short.

It should be apparent that the binomial model can easily be extended to a three-period world. At some point, however, its usefulness would succumb to monotony and tedium. Fortunately, there is a general pricing formula for the case of n periods. This is discussed in Appendix 4A. The binomial model is easily programmed on a computer. This book includes binomial model software, which is illustrated in a later section.

TABLE 4.1	**Hedge Results in the Two-Period Binomial Model**		
	Return from Hedge Compared to Risk-Free Rate		
	Period 1	Period 2	Two-Period
Options Overpriced at Start of Period 1			
Status of option at start of period 2			
Overpriced	indeterminate	better	better
Correctly priced	better	equal	better
Underpriced	better	better	better

Some Useful Extensions of the Binomial Model

Pricing Put Options

We can use the binomial model to price put options just as we can for call options. We use the same formulas, but instead of specifying the call payoffs at expiration, we use the put payoffs at expiration. To see the difference, look at Figure 4.3 on page 123. Then we simply replace every C with a P; likewise, we substitute P for C in each formula; and the rest is easy. A concept problem at the end of the chapter asks you to perform some binomial put option pricing calculations.

American Options and Early Exercise

Binomial models are particularly useful in capturing the effect of early exercise. For call options on stocks without dividends, there will, of course, never be an early exercise. For put options, with or without dividends, early exercise is quite possible. The concept problem on the binomial put option pricing model will ask you to evaluate the early exercise effect on the American put. For now, let us consider how early exercise will affect American calls in the binomial model.

There are a number of ways to incorporate dividends into the model. The simplest is to assume a constant yield of δ percent per period. Thus, each time the stock price moves to a new value, it immediately declines by δ percent as it goes ex-dividend. We then use the ex-dividend stock prices in the binomial formulas. At any point, if the intrinsic value of the call exceeds the value of the call given by the binomial formula, the call should be exercised. Then the intrinsic value replaces the formula value.

Consider the same two-period problem we worked earlier in the chapter. Because we want to see a case where the call is exercised early, let us assume a fairly high dividend yield—say, 8 percent—and, of course, let the call be American. The ex-dividend stock prices become

The binomial model can accommodate early exercise by simply replacing the computed value with the intrinsic value if the latter is greater.

$$S_u = 60(1.15)(1 - .08) = 63.48$$
$$S_d = 60(.8)(1 - .08) = 44.16$$
$$S_{u^2} = 63.48(1.15)(1 - .08) = 67.16$$
$$S_{ud} = S_{du} = 63.48(.8)(1 - .08) = 46.72$$
$$S_{d^2} = 44.16(.8)(1 - .08) = 32.50.$$

The corresponding call prices at expiration are

$$C_{u^2} = \text{Max}(0, 67.16 - 50) = 17.16$$
$$C_{ud} = C_{du} = \text{Max}(0, 46.72 - 50) = 0$$
$$C_{d^2} = \text{Max}(0, 32.50 - 50) = 0.$$

The call prices after one period are

$$C_u = \frac{(.857)(17.16) + (.143)(0)}{1.10} = 13.37$$
$$C_d = \frac{(.857)(0) + (.143)(0)}{1.10} = 0.$$

Note, however, that when the stock price is at $S_u = 63.48$, the intrinsic value of the call is $Max(0, 63.48 - 50) = 13.48$. This is slightly higher than the value of the call given by the formula, 13.37. Thus, the call is exercised and we redefine C_u to be 13.48. Then the current value of the call is

$$C = \frac{(.857)(13.48) + (.143)(0)}{1.10} = 10.50.$$

We also have to check and see if the call should be exercised immediately. Its intrinsic value is $Max(0, 60 - 50) = 10$. This is less than 10.50, so it should not be exercised now, and its value is, thus, 10.50. The value of the option if it were a European call would be 10.42.

Suppose that instead of assuming a constant yield, we assume that the stock pays a discrete dividend of $5 at time 1. Provided that we define u and d to represent the movement of *the stock price minus the present value of the dividends,* the problem is very easily solved. Let S be the stock price and S′ be the stock price minus the present value of the dividends. So, we let the values of u and d apply to S′ instead of S. However, the exercise decision is based on the value of S relative to E. If the stock goes ex-dividend at time 1, the present value of the dividend today is $5/1.10 = 4.55$. Thus, while S′ is 60, S is $60 + 4.55 = 64.55$.

Now let us say the stock goes up the next period. While S′ will go up to 69, S will go to $69 + 5 = 74$ for an instant and then fall, while remaining at the same point in the tree, to 69. Note that now the present value of the dividend is 5. When the stock goes ex-dividend, S′ falls to 69 and becomes equivalent to S (there are no other dividends before the option expires). With a stock price of 69, we already know the call value will be 23.54. For that brief instant before the stock goes ex-dividend, it is at 74, and the call is in-the-money by $24 and could be exercised for a value of 24, which is more than what it would be worth as soon as the stock goes ex-dividend. Thus, we would replace the value of C_u of 23.54 with 24.

Had the stock gone down, S′ would go from 60 to 48. S would have gone from 64.55 to $48 + 5 = 53$. Then for the instant while the stock is at 53, the call could be exercised for a value of 3. An instant later, the stock will fall to 48 where the call will be worth 4.05. Obviously, it is not worth exercising in this case. Note that the call moved from in-the-money to out-of-the-money and yet it was still not worth exercising.

Thus, the value of the call today is a weighted average of 24 and 4.05,

$$C = \frac{(.857)24 + (.143)4.05}{1.10} = 19.22.$$

Had the option been European with the $5 dividend, its value would have been the same 18.87 that we previously calculated. This seems to raise an interesting question. When we worked the problem for a European option without a dividend, we obtained 18.87. Adding the dividend to the problem gave us the same European option value. This suggests that dividends do not affect the value of the European option, which seems counterintuitive. Dividends paid by a company reduce the growth potential, which should hurt call option holders.

The key distinction here is that we were forced to let u and d represent the movements from a value of 60 in both cases. To avoid some rather complex pricing problems, option pricing models typically allow the stock price minus the present value of the dividends to follow the process described by u and d. A European option's price is, thus, determined with respect to S′ and u and d are applied to S′. If we took the dividends out of the problem, the option would be priced with respect to the same value of the stock price, in this case 60. If we tried to let u and d apply to the full value of the stock price, that is, to include the present value of the dividends, the nice convenient binomial tree "explodes," which means that it grows extremely large very rapidly and imposes some severe computational problems. Thus, it is best to allow the stock price minus the present value of the dividends to follow the process described by u and d.

The binomial option pricing model is not necessarily meant to be realistic. The number of possible stock prices at expiration is unlimited in reality. Although the binomial model must impose some finite limits, it becomes more realistic as the number of periods increases. The model's importance, however, is not in its ability to explain real-world option prices but in its usefulness for explicating the process by which an option's price is determined.

So far we have seen that an option's price is determined by the stock price, exercise price, time to expiration, risk-free rate, and parameters defining the volatility of the stock price. The option must be priced according to the formula, or investors will engage in the type of riskless arbitrage illustrated in earlier sections. These traders' combined actions will force the option price to equal the model price. The option's price is determined without accounting for the expected future stock price or investors' feelings about risk. These particular characteristics of the manner in which option prices are determined will continue to hold as we move into our examination of a more realistic model for pricing options.

The Black-Scholes Option Pricing Model

The year 1973 was an important one in the history of options. In that year, the Chicago Board Options Exchange was founded and became the first organized facility for options trading. Also, two professors at the Massachusetts Institute of Technology, Fischer Black and Myron Scholes, published an article in the *Journal of Political Economy* that presented a formula for pricing an option. The formula, which became known as the **Black-Scholes option pricing model,** was one of the most significant developments in the pricing of financial instruments. It has generated a long line of subsequent research attempting to test the model and improve on it. A new industry of option pricing products based on the Black-Scholes model also has developed. Even if one does not agree with everything the model says, knowing something about it is important for surviving in the options markets.

Although the Black-Scholes model did not evolve directly from the binomial model, it is a mathematical extension of it. Recall that the binomial model can be extended to any number of time periods. Suppose we let n equal infinity so that each time period is very small. The interest rate, r, is the risk-free rate over each time period. As you can imagine, the number of stock prices at expiration will be very large—in fact, infinite. Although the algebra is somewhat complex, the equation for the binomial model becomes the equation for the Black-Scholes model. Later in this chapter, we shall illustrate how the binomial price converges to the Black-Scholes price.

However, Black and Scholes did not derive their model by extending the binomial model to an infinite number of periods. The binomial model had not even been discovered when they began examining some early research on option pricing models. They supplied the intuition that an option can be priced by forming a riskless hedge portfolio consisting of stock and options. Black and Scholes applied what was to finance a new branch of mathematics called stochastic calculus. The mathematics of their derivation is quite complex. Interested readers can find it in the original paper, Black and Scholes (1973), and the books by Hull (1997) and Shimko (1992).

We shall omit the math here, but it is important to review the model's assumptions:

1. The rate of return on the stock follows a **lognormal distribution.** This means that the logarithm of 1 plus the rate of return follows the normal, or bell-shaped, curve. The lognormal distribution is a convenient and realistic characterization of stock returns because it reflects stockholders' limited liability.

2. The risk-free rate and variance of the return on the stock are constant throughout the option's life.

3. There are no taxes or transaction costs.

4. The stock pays no dividends. (We shall relax this assumption later.)

5. The calls are European. As we saw in Chapter 3, this assumption is not necessary for preventing early exercise if assumption 4 holds.

Black and Scholes derived a formula for pricing an option:

The Black-Scholes call option pricing formula gives the call price in terms of the stock price, exercise price, risk-free rate, time to expiration, and variance of the stock return.

$$C = SN(d_1) - Ee^{-r_cT}N(d_2),$$

where

$$d_1 = \frac{\ln(S/E) + (r_c + \sigma^2/2)T}{\sigma\sqrt{T}}$$

$$d_2 = d_1 - \sigma\sqrt{T}$$

$N(d_1), N(d_2)$ = cumulative normal probabilities

σ^2 = annualized variance of the continuously compounded return on the stock

r_c = continuously compounded risk-free rate

All other variables are the same ones previously used.

The Normal Distribution

Since the Black-Scholes model requires the normal probability distribution, it will probably be helpful to review this concept. Figure 4.5 illustrates the normal, or bell-shaped, curve. Recall that the curve is symmetric and everything we need to know about it is contained in the expected value, or mean, and the variance. Approximately 68 percent of the observations in a sample drawn from a normal distribution will occur within one standard deviation of the expected value. About 95 percent of the observations will lie within two standard deviations and about 99 percent within three standard deviations.

A standard normal random variable is called a **z statistic.** One can take any normally distributed random variable, convert it to a standard normal or z statistic, and use a table to determine the probability that an observed value of the random variable will be less than or equal to the value of interest.

Table 4.2 gives the cumulative probabilities of the standard normal distribution. Suppose we want to know the probability of observing a value of z less than or equal to 1.57. We go to the table and look down the first column for 1.5, then move over to the right under the column labeled 0.07; that is, the 1.5 and 0.07 add up to the z value, 1.57. The entry in the 1.5 row/0.07 column is .9418, the probability in a normal distribution of observing a value of z less than or equal to 1.57.

FIGURE 4.5   The Normal Probability Distribution

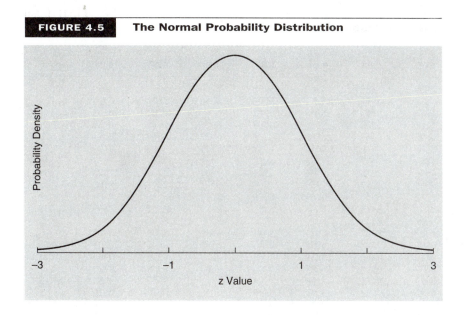

Suppose the value of z is less than zero—say, −1.12. We look for the appropriate value for a positive 1.12. In the 1.1 row/0.02 column is the value .8686. Then we subtract this number from 1. The answer is .1314. Because the table is symmetric, it is not necessary to show negative values. The probability of observing a value less than or equal to −1.12 is the same as that of observing a value greater than or equal to 1.12. The probability of observing a value greater than or equal to 1.12 is 1 minus the probability of observing a value less than or equal to 1.12. Note that we overlapped with the probability of observing a value exactly equal to 1.12. The probability of observing any single value is zero. This is so because we can observe an infinite number of possible values.

Instead of using tables, the normal probability can be accurately approximated with a polynomial equation. There are several formulas that give good approximations for the normal probability. In addition, the mathematical functions NORMSDIST in Excel and @NORMAL in Lotus 1-2-3 are easy to use. Keep in mind, however, that Black-Scholes option values are highly sensitive to the normal probability calculation and can be off by several cents depending on which method is used.

A Numerical Example

Let us use the Black-Scholes model to price the Digital Equipment July 165 call. Recall that the inputs are a stock price of $164, an exercise price of $165, and a time to expiration of .0959. We gave the risk-free rate of 5.35 percent as

TABLE 4.2		Standard Normal Probabilities							

z	0.00	0.01	0.02	0.03	0.04	0.05	0.06	0.07	0.08	0.09
0.0	.5000	.5040	.5080	.5120	.5160	.5199	.5239	.5279	.5319	.5359
0.1	.5398	.5438	.5478	.5517	.5557	.5596	.5636	.5675	.5714	.5753
0.2	.5793	.5832	.5871	.5910	.5948	.5987	.6026	.6064	.6103	.6141
0.3	.6179	.6217	.6255	.6293	.6331	.6368	.6406	.6443	.6480	.6517
0.4	.6554	.6591	.6628	.6664	.6700	.6736	.6772	.6808	.6844	.6879
0.5	.6915	.6950	.6985	.7019	.7054	.7088	.7123	.7157	.7190	.7224
0.6	.7257	.7291	.7324	.7357	.7389	.7422	.7454	.7486	.7517	.7549
0.7	.7580	.7611	.7642	.7673	.7704	.7734	.7764	.7794	.7823	.7852
0.8	.7881	.7910	.7939	.7967	.7995	.8023	.8051	.8078	.8106	.8133
0.9	.8159	.8186	.8212	.8238	.8264	.8289	.8315	.8340	.8365	.8389
1.0	.8413	.8438	.8461	.8485	.8508	.8531	.8554	.8577	.8599	.8621
1.1	.8643	.8665	.8686	.8708	.8729	.8749	.8770	.8790	.8810	.8830
1.2	.8849	.8860	.8888	.8907	.8925	.8943	.8962	.8980	.8997	.9015
1.3	.9032	.9049	.9066	.9082	.9099	.9115	.9131	.9147	.9162	.9177
1.4	.9192	.9207	.9222	.9236	.9251	.9265	.9279	.9292	.9306	.9319
1.5	.9332	.9345	.9357	.9370	.9382	.9394	.9406	.9418	.9429	.9441
1.6	.9452	.9463	.9474	.9484	.9495	.9505	.9515	.9525	.9535	.9545
1.7	.9554	.9564	.9573	.9582	.9591	.9599	.9608	.9616	.9625	.9633
1.8	.9641	.9649	.9656	.9664	.9671	.9678	.9686	.9693	.9699	.9706
1.9	.9713	.9719	.9726	.9732	.9738	.9744	.9750	.9756	.9761	.9767
2.0	.9772	.9778	.9783	.9788	.9793	.9798	.9803	.9808	.9812	.9817
2.1	.9821	.9826	.9830	.9834	.9838	.9842	.9846	.9850	.9854	.9857
2.2	.9861	.9864	.9868	.9871	.9875	.9878	.9881	.9884	.9887	.9890
2.3	.9893	.9896	.9898	.9901	.9904	.9906	.9909	.9911	.9913	.9916
2.4	.9918	.9920	.9922	.9925	.9927	.9929	.9931	.9932	.9934	.9936
2.5	.9938	.9940	.9941	.9943	.9945	.9946	.9948	.9949	.9951	.9952
2.6	.9953	.9955	.9956	.9957	.9959	.9960	.9961	.9962	.9963	.9964
2.7	.9965	.9966	.9967	.9968	.9969	.9970	.9971	.9972	.9973	.9974
2.8	.9974	.9975	.9976	.9977	.9977	.9978	.9979	.9979	.9980	.9981
2.9	.9981	.9982	.9982	.9983	.9984	.9984	.9985	.9985	.9986	.9986
3.0	.9987	.9987	.9987	.9988	.9988	.9989	.9989	.9989	.9990	.9990

the Treasury bill yield that corresponds to the option's expiration. In the Black-Scholes model, however, the risk-free rate must be expressed as a continuously compounded yield. The continuously compounded equivalent of 5.35 percent is $\ln(1.0535) = .0521$. Later in this chapter, we shall take a closer look at the basis for this transformation and at how the variance or standard deviation can be determined. For now we will use .29 as the standard deviation, which corresponds to a variance of .0841.

The computation of the Black-Scholes price is a five-step process that is presented in Table 4.3. You first calculate the values of d_1 and d_2. Then you look up $N(d_1)$ and $N(d_2)$ in the normal probability table. Then you plug the values into the formula for C.

Here, the theoretical fair value for the July 165 call is $5.803. The call's actual market price is $5.75. This suggests that the call is slightly un-

---

TABLE 4.3   Calculating the Black-Scholes Price

1. $S = 164$ $E = 165$ $r_c = .0521$ $\sigma^2 = .0841$ $T = .0959$
   Compute d_1

$$d_1 = \frac{\ln(164/165) + (.0521 + .0841/2).0959}{.29\sqrt{.0959}} = .0328$$

2. Compute d_2

$$d_2 = .0328 - .29\sqrt{.0959} = -.0570$$

3. Look up $N(d_1)$

$$N(.03) = .5120$$

4. Look up $N(d_2)$

$$N(-.06) = .4761$$

5. Plug into formula for C

$$C = 164(.5120) - 165e^{-(.0521)(.0959)}(.4761) = 5.803$$

---

derpriced. Assuming no transaction costs, an investor should buy the call. The number of calls to buy to form a riskless hedge portfolio that will outperform the risk-free rate is discussed in a later section.

The accompanying Excel spreadsheet bsbin1.xls calculates the Black-Scholes price, as well as the binomial price. Software Demonstration 4.1 illustrates how to use bsbin1.xls to obtain the Black-Scholes price. For those who prefer not to use spreadsheets, Appendix 4C demonstrates the Windows program bsbwin2.exe.

SOFTWARE DEMONSTRATION 4.1   Calculating the Black-Scholes Price with the Excel Spreadsheet bsbin1.xls

The Excel spreadsheet bsbin1.xls, which operates in Windows 3.1 or Windows 95 and requires Excel 5.0 or higher, calculates both the Black-Scholes and binomial option pricing models. For the Black-Scholes model, bsbin1.xls provides European and American call and put prices, as well as the delta, gamma, theta, vega, and rho. No installation is necessary; simply place the file in whatever directory you prefer or access it directly from the 3.5-inch diskette provided with this book. To use the software, do the following:

1. Make sure you are in Windows 3.1 or Windows 95.
2. Run Excel 5.0 or higher.
3. Open the file bsbin1.xls.

Now let us calculate an option price. Assume that you wish to find the Black-Scholes price of the option illustrated in the book, the Digital Equipment July 165. The DEC stock is at 164, the exercise price is 165, the continuously compounded risk-free rate is .0521, the standard deviation is .29, and the option expires in 35 days, meaning that its time to expiration is 35/365 = .0959. There are no dividends on the stock.

Observe on the spreadsheet a section labeled **Inputs:** Each cell that will accept input has a double-line border and the values are in blue. Output cells have a single-line border. Enter the stock price of 164 beside the words "Asset Price (S)" and enter the remaining inputs in the appropriate cells below. Leave the dividend yield and the discrete dividends blank or enter zeros. The risk-free rate and volatility can be entered as either percentages or decimals. For example, you can enter either ".0521" or "5.21" for the risk-free rate.

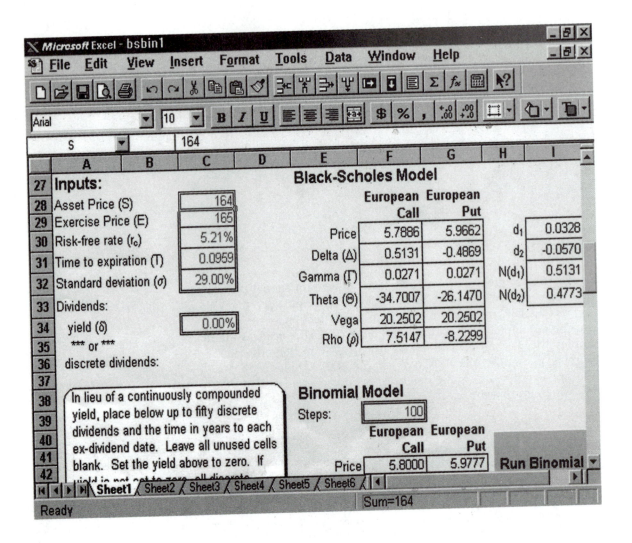

The time to expiration should be expressed in years. In our example, the option has 35 days until expiration, which means that the time to expiration is 35/365 = .0959. You can enter either ".0959" or the Excel formula "=35/365". If you know only that, for example, the current date is June 12, 1997, and the expiration date is July 17, 1997, you can calculate the time to expiration directly in Excel. Simply click on one of the blank spreadsheet tabs at the bottom. This takes you to a new spreadsheet. Enter 6/12/97 in one cell and 7/17/97 in another. Then in a third cell enter the formula "=(XX − YY)/365" where XX is the cell where you entered 7/17/97 and YY is the cell where you entered 6/12/97. Excel will then calculate the time in years. Then use this value in your calculations.

To observe the result, see the section labeled **Black-Scholes Model.** Note that we obtain a slightly different value for the call option than we found when working the problem by hand in Table 4.3. This is because the spreadsheet calculates values more precisely, carrying them out to a greater number of decimal places. We have not yet covered the concepts of delta, gamma, theta, vega, and rho nor have we covered the Black-Scholes model for puts, but these will come later in this chapter.

For those who prefer Lotus 1-2-3, the diskette also contains the spreadsheet bsm3.wk3 and its format file bsm3.fm3. This spreadsheet is from the previous edition of this book and does not contain all of the features of the Excel spreadsheet, but it will provide Black-Scholes prices. For those who prefer not to use a spreadsheet, Appendix 4C demonstrates how to use the Windows program bsbwin2.exe, which provides Black-Scholes and binomial prices in a standard Windows environment.

The Variables in the Black-Scholes Model

The Black-Scholes formula tells us that five variables affect the option's price: (1) the stock price, (2) the exercise price, (3) the risk-free rate, (4) the time to expiration, and (5) the variance or standard deviation. Chapter 3 explained the effect of each variable on the option's price. With the Black-Scholes model, we can see these effects more directly.

The Stock Price

A higher stock price should lead to a higher call price. Suppose the stock price is $168 instead of $164. Then the values of d_1 and d_2 are .3012 and .2114. This gives values of $N(.30)$ and $N(.21)$ of .6179 and .5832. Plugging into the formula gives a value of C of $8.059, which is higher than the previously obtained value, $5.803.

The value of our Digital Equipment call for a broad range of stock prices is illustrated in Figure 4.6. Note that this graph is similar to Figure 3.5, where we showed what a European call price curve should look like.

The relationship between the stock price and the call price is often expressed as a single value, referred to as its **delta.** The delta is obtained from the calculus procedure of differentiating the call price with respect to the stock price. The mathematical details of the procedure are a bit technical but the end result is quite simple:

$$\text{Call } Delta = N(d_1).$$

Since $N(d_1)$ is a probability, the delta must range from zero to one.

Because of the assumptions behind the calculus, the delta is the change in the call price for a *very small* change in the stock price. Here our delta is .5120. This is somewhat loosely defined to mean that the option price moves 51.2 percent of the move in the stock price. Technically this is correct only for a very small move in the stock price. For example, we noted above that if the stock price were $168, a $4 move, the call price would be $8.059, a move of $2.26, which is about 56 percent of the stock price move. Thus, while delta is a very important measure of the option's sensitivity to the stock price, it is precise only if the stock price makes a very small move.

Recall from our discussion of the binomial model how we bought h shares of stock and sold one call. As long as we adjusted the number of options per share according to the formula for h, we maintained a risk-free hedge. In the Black-Scholes world, this is called a **delta hedge** and must be done continuously. A delta-hedged position is said to be **delta neutral.** For example, suppose the stock price is $164. Recall that the delta is .512 so we construct a delta hedge by buying 512 shares and selling 1,000 calls. If the stock price falls by a small amount, say .01, we shall lose .01(512) = 5.12 on the stock. However, the option price will fall by approximately .01(.512) or .00512. Since we have 1,000 calls, the options collectively will fall by

Derivatives in Action

The Scientific Evolution of Option Pricing

While the Black-Scholes option pricing formula looks somewhat complex, it is actually fairly easy to compute. However, beneath the surface of the model are many years of research that evolved from an understanding of the mathematics and physics of how heat is conducted. It all started in the 1820s when a Scottish scientist, Robert Brown, observed the motion of pollen dust suspended in water. Brown noticed that the movements followed no distinct pattern, moving essentially randomly, independent of any current in the water. This phenomenon came to be known as Brownian motion. Similar versions of Brownian motion were subsequently discovered by other scientists using other natural phenomena.

Albert Einstein is widely regarded as one of the most intelligent human beings ever to live. In the early years of the twentieth century, Einstein, working on the foundations of his theories of relativity, utilized the principles of Brownian motion to explain movements of molecules. This work eventually led to several research papers that went on to earn Einstein the Nobel Prize and world renown. By that time a fairly well-developed branch of mathematics, often attributed to the mathematician Norbert Wiener, proved useful for explaining the movements of random particles. Other contributions to the mathematics were made by the Japanese mathematician Kiyoshi Itô, who

in 1951 developed an extremely important result, called Itô's Lemma, that 20 years later made it possible to find an option's price. Keep in mind, however, that these scientists were working on complex theoretical problems in physics and mathematics, not economics and finance.

The mathematics that was used to model random movements had now evolved into its own subdiscipline, which came to be known as stochastic calculus. While ordinary calculus defined the rates of change of known functions, stochastic calculus defined the rates of change of functions in which one or more terms were unknown but behaved according to well-defined rules of probability.

In the late 1960s, Fischer Black finished his doctorate in mathematics at Harvard, but, passing up a career as a mathematician, went to work for Arthur Little, a management consulting firm in Boston. Black met a young MIT professor named Myron Scholes and the two began a mutual interchange of ideas on how capital markets worked. Soon Black joined the MIT finance faculty, where he made many contributions to our understanding of how assets other than options were priced. Black and Scholes began studying options, which were then traded only on the over-the-counter market. They studied the attempts of previous researchers to find the elusive option pricing formula. Black and Scholes took two approaches to finding the

.00512(1,000) = 5.12. Since we are short the options, we gain 5.12, which offsets the loss on the stock. A similar result is obtained if the price goes up. However, once the price changes or time elapses, which it does continuously, the delta changes and a new hedge ratio must be constructed. If this is done properly, then a risk-free return is earned, provided the call was correctly priced at the onset. Of course, in practice it is impossible to do a perfect delta hedge because one cannot trade continuously.

An additional risk in delta hedging is that the stock price will not change by a very small amount. For example, suppose the stock went up to 168 and the call went to 8.059, as in our example. Then our 512 shares of stock would have gained 4(512) = 2,048. Our 1,000 calls would have

price. One was by assuming that all assets were priced according to the Capital Asset Pricing Theory. The other approach was by utilizing the mathematics of stochastic calculus, which led them to a differential equation, for which they did not know the solution. Fortunately, Black found out that the differential equation was the same one that described the movement of heat as it travels across an object. There was a solution already known and Black and Scholes simply looked up the answer, worked through the algebraic details, and then wrote their paper. Strangely enough the paper was rejected by two academic journals before being published and going on to become one of the most important discoveries in twentieth-century finance and economics.

In all fairness, however, credit must also be given to Paul Samuelson and Robert Merton. Samuelson, one of the most famous economists of all time, had previously brought a high level of mathematical sophistication to economics. He was also fascinated by options, but his efforts to find the formula had been unsuccessful. However, one of Samuelson's graduate students, Robert Merton, had a strong background in mathematics. Working independently but in the same department as Black and Scholes, Merton found the same formula and many other useful results about options. Merton's modesty, however, compelled him to ask a journal editor that his paper not be published

before that of Black and Scholes. As it turned out, both papers were published in separate journals but at about the same time. Thus, the Black-Scholes model should probably be known as the Black-Scholes-Merton formula, but unfortunately, Merton has never received his full credit.

Fischer Black remained an academic until 1983, when he left to join Goldman Sachs where he quickly became a partner. He continued to publish numerous articles until his death in August 1995 at the age of 57. Scholes retains his academic ties to Stanford University but is now actively involved in an investment management business. Merton has remained an academic but was lured from MIT by the Harvard Business School. He, too, has become a part-time practitioner.

In conclusion, the option pricing formula you study in this chapter would likely never have been possible had it not been for the pioneering work of Brown, Einstein, Wiener, Itô, and others who worked on problems far removed from options and who never profited from trading them.

Source: This material is drawn from Peter L. Bernstein, "The Universal Financial Device," Chapter 11, in *Capital Ideas: The Improbable Origins of Modern Wall Street* (New York: The Free Press, 1992) and Fischer Black, "How We Came Up With the Option Formula," *Journal of Portfolio Management*, Vol. 15 (Winter 1989), pp. 4–8, as well as hearsay on how the science of option pricing evolved.

gone up by $(8.059 - 5.803)(1,000) = 2,256$. Since we are short the calls, the overall position would have suffered a loss.

This type of risk is captured by the option's **gamma.** The gamma is the change in the delta for a very small change in the stock price. The formula for gamma is

$$\text{Call } Gamma = \frac{e^{-d_1^2/2}}{S\sigma\sqrt{2\pi T}}.$$

In our example with the stock at 164, the gamma is calculated as $e^{-(.0328)^2/2}/(164(.29)\sqrt{2(3.14159)(.0959)}) = .0271$. This suggests that if

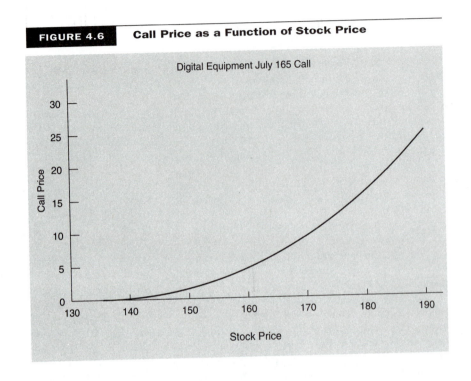

FIGURE 4.6 **Call Price as a Function of Stock Price**

Digital Equipment July 165 Call

the stock increased to 168, the delta would go from .512 to .512 + (168 − 164)(.0271) = .6204. The actual delta if the stock goes to 168 is .6179. Of course, the gamma provides only an estimate of the change in the delta, but in this case the estimate is a good one.

The larger is the gamma, the more sensitive is the delta to a stock price change and the harder it is to maintain a delta neutral position. The gamma is always positive and is largest when the stock price is near the exercise price. When the stock price is large relative to the exercise price, the delta is close to one and the gamma is near zero. When the stock price is low relative to the exercise price, the delta is close to zero and the gamma is near zero. Of course, both the delta and the gamma change as the option approaches expiration. The delta of an in-the-money call approaches one and its gamma approaches zero. The delta of an out-of-the-money call approaches zero and its gamma approaches zero. However, if the option is at-the-money, the uncertainty of whether it will finish in- or out-of-the-money causes the gamma to increase dramatically as expiration approaches.

To maintain a portfolio that is insulated from gamma risk requires that an additional instrument, such as another option, be added to the position. Then it would be possible to set both delta and gamma to zero. This is an advanced topic, which we cover in Chapter 16.

The Exercise Price

Now let us change the exercise price to $170, which should decrease the call's value. Specifically, let us examine the July 170 call. We retain all of the other original values, including the stock price of $164. The values of d_1 and d_2 are $-.2996$ and $-.3894$. The normal probabilities are .3821 and .3483 and the resulting call price is $3.749, which is less than the original $5.803.

The change in the call price for a very small change in the exercise price is negative and is given by the formula $-e^{-r_cT}N(d_2)$. However, the exercise price of a given option does not change so this concept is meaningful only in considering how much more or less a call with a different exercise price would be worth.[5] In that case, the difference in the exercise price would probably be too large to apply the formula above, which, as noted above, holds only when E changes by a very small amount.

The Risk-Free Rate

Chapter 3 showed how to identify the risk-free rate for the purpose of examining an option's boundary conditions. Within the Black-Scholes framework, the risk-free rate must be expressed as a continuously compounded rate.

A simple or discrete risk-free rate assumes only annual compounding. A continuously compounded rate assumes interest compounds continuously. A simple rate can be converted to a continuously compounded rate by taking the natural logarithm of 1 plus the simple rate. For example, if the simple rate is 6 percent, $100 invested at 6 percent for one year becomes $106. The equivalent continuously compounded rate is $\ln(1.06) = .0583$. Thus, $100 invested at 5.83 percent compounded continuously grows to $106 in one year. The continuously compounded rate is always less than the simple rate. To convert a continuously compounded rate to a simple rate, use the exponential function, the inverse of the logarithmic function, that is, $e^{.0583} - 1 = .06$.

In our previous problem, the risk-free rate was 5.21 percent. We obtained this as $\ln(1.0535)$, where .0535 was the simple rate that we obtained in Chapter 3. The Black-Scholes formula requires the use of the continuously compounded rate so we specify the rate as r_c where it appears in two places in the formula. Note that in the equation for C, we compute Ee^{-r_cT}, which is the present value of the exercise price when the interest rate is continuously compounded. The same value would have been obtained had we used $E(1 + r)^{-T}$, where r is the discrete rate.

The value of our Digital Equipment call for a range of continuously compounded risk-free rates is illustrated in Figure 4.7. The call price is nearly linear in the risk-free rate and does not change much over a very broad range

---

[5]It is possible to create an option in which the exercise price changes randomly, but we shall not cover these at this level.

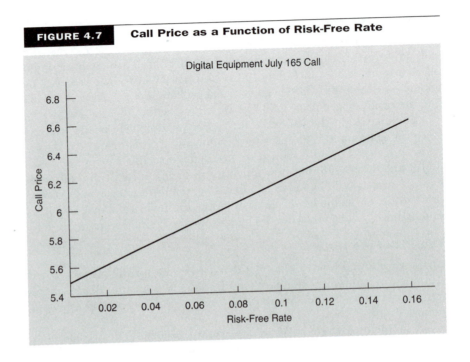

FIGURE 4.7   **Call Price as a Function of Risk-Free Rate**

Digital Equipment July 165 Call

of risk-free rates. For example, at a risk-free rate of 5.21 percent, we obtained a call price of 5.803. If we raised the risk-free rate to 12 percent, a rather large change, the call price would increase to only 6.313. The sensitivity of the call price to the risk-free rate is called its **rho** and is given by the formula,

$$\text{Call } Rho = TEe^{-r_cT}N(d_2).$$

In our original problem, with the risk-free rate of 5.21 percent, the rho would be $(.0959)165e^{-.0521(.0959)}(.4761) = 7.49$. If we let the risk-free rate go from .0521 to .12, the rho would predict a change in the call price of $(.12 - .0521)(7.49) = .51$. The actual change was $6.313 - 5.803 = .51$. The nearly linear relationship between the option price and the risk-free rate makes the rho a fairly accurate measure of the option's sensitivity to interest rate changes. One should keep in mind, however, that the Black-Scholes model assumes that interest rates do not change during the life of the option. More sophisticated models are required to accurately capture the effects of changing interest rates. We cover this topic in Chapter 14.

The Variance or Standard Deviation

The variance or standard deviation is a critical variable in the Black-Scholes model. Sometimes this variable is referred to as the **volatility,** which is the term we shall use in this text. We shall let volatility refer to the stan-

| FIGURE 4.8 | **Call Price as a Function of Volatility** |

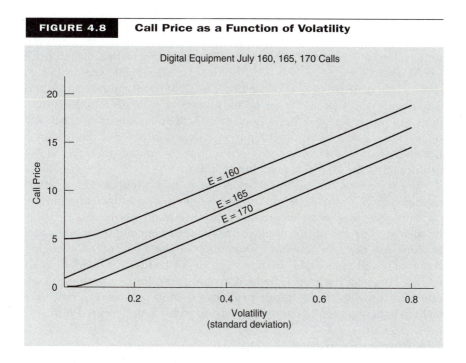

Digital Equipment July 160, 165, 170 Calls

dard deviation. This is the standard deviation of the continuously compounded return on the stock. Since this is the only unobservable variable, we devote an entire section later in the chapter to estimating its value.

Figure 4.8 shows the option price for a range of standard deviations. Because in-, at-, and out-of-the-money calls behave somewhat differently with respect to volatility, we show the graph for options with exercise prices of 160, 165, and 170. Recall that our 165 call had a price of 5.803 when its volatility was .29. If we raise that volatility to .35, the call price is about 7. If we lower it to .2, the call price is about 3.97. These are fairly large changes in the call price over a fairly small range of volatilities.

The sensitivity of the call price to a *very small* change in volatility is called its **vega** and is given as[6]

$$\text{Call } Vega = \frac{S\sqrt{T}e^{-d_1^2/2}}{\sqrt{2\pi}}.$$

In our original problem the vega is $164\sqrt{.0959}e^{-(.0328)^2/2}/\sqrt{2(3.14159)} = 20.25$. This suggests that if volatility changes by a very small amount, say,

---

[6]It is also sometimes called its **kappa** or **lambda**.

.01, the call price would change by 20.25(.01) = .20. The actual call price change if volatility went to .30, an increase of .01, would be .19. However, if the volatility increased by .11 to .40, the vega predicts that the call price would increase by 20.25(.11) = 2.23, when the actual call price would go to 8.015, an increase of 8.015 − 5.803 = 2.21. This is still quite accurate and is due to the fact that, as Figure 4.8 illustrates, the volatility and the option price are nearly linear if the option is nearly at-the-money. This result will be useful in a later section. As Figure 4.8 shows, however, if the option is not at-the-money, the relationship is not quite linear and the vega will not capture all of the risk of a changing volatility.

Regardless of the option's "moneyness" and whether the volatility change is large or small, the option is still quite sensitive to changes in the volatility. The Black-Scholes model does not actually permit the volatility to change while the option is alive. There are more complex models that account for this phenomenon. Nonetheless, the concept of changing volatility is still considered by option traders who use the Black-Scholes model. This vega risk can be hedged by using an offsetting position in another instrument, such as another call, based on its relative vega risk. Like gamma hedging, vega hedging is an advanced topic not covered here.

The Time to Expiration

To examine the time to expiration, let us use the October option, which has a longer time to expiration of 126 days where T = .3452. For the October option, the discrete risk-free rate was 5.91 percent so the continuously compounded risk-free rate would be $\ln(1.0591) = .0574$. The price of the call would be 12.217. Now suppose we were about one month down the road so that the October option now has only 100 days left and T = 100/365 = .274. Then the price of the call would be 10.685. As expected, the shorter time to expiration decreases the call price.

The relationship between the option price and the time to expiration is illustrated in Figure 4.9. We present the results for the October 160, 165, and 170 calls. The decrease in the value of the call as time elapses is the time value decay, as we discussed in Chapter 3. The rate of time value decay is measured by the option's **theta,** which is given as

$$\text{Call } \textit{Theta} = -\frac{S\sigma e^{-d_1^2/2}}{2\sqrt{2\pi T}} - r_c E e^{-r_c T} N(d_2).$$

For the October 165, d_1 is .1658, $N(d_2)$ is .4982, and theta is $-164(.29)e^{-(.1658)^2/2}/(2\sqrt{2}(3.14159)(.3452) - (.0574)165e^{-(.0574)(.3452)}(.4982) = -21.00$. Thus, if the time to expiration goes from .3452 to .274, the option price would be predicted to change by $(.3452 - .274)(-21.00) = -1.49$. The actual price changes by $(10.685 - 12.217) = -1.53$. Of course,

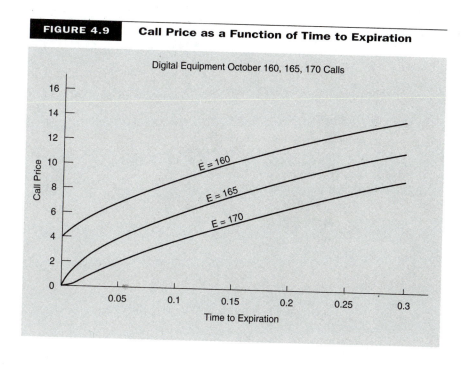

FIGURE 4.9   Call Price as a Function of Time to Expiration

Digital Equipment October 160, 165, 170 Calls

the theta is most accurate only for a very small change in time, but the predicted price change is still very close to the actual price change. Since time itself is not a source of risk, however, it makes no sense to worry about it, but, of course, that does not mean that we do not need to know the rate of time value decay.

We should note that the delta, gamma, rho, vega, and theta of a combination of options is simply a weighted average of those values for the component options where the weights are equal to the values of the options relative to the full value of the option portfolio. Of course, the portfolio can contain stock as well so we should note that the gamma, rho, vega, and theta of stock are assumed to be zero while the delta is one.

The Excel spreadsheet bsbin1.xls, illustrated in Software Demonstration 4.1, provides the values of delta, gamma, rho, vega, and theta.

The Black-Scholes Model in the Presence of Dividends

The Black-Scholes model in the form we have seen so far applies to stocks that do not pay dividends, such as Digital Equipment. As we saw in Chapter

TABLE 4.4	**Calculating the Black-Scholes Price When There Are Known Discrete Dividends**

$S = 164$ $E = 165$ $r_c = .0521$ $\sigma^2 = .0841$ $T = .0959$
One dividend of 2, ex-dividend in 33 days

1.   Determine the amounts of the dividends
$$D_t = 2.$$

2.   Determine the times to the ex-dividend dates
33 days so $t = 33/365 = .0904$.

3.   Subtract the present value of the dividends from the stock price to obtain S'
$$S' = 164 - 2e^{-(.0521)(.0904)} = 162.01.$$

4.   Compute d_1, using S' in place of S
$$d_1 = \frac{\ln(162.01/165) + (.0521 + .0841/2).0959}{.29\sqrt{.0959}} = -.1031.$$

5.   Compute d_2
$$d_2 = -.1031 - .29\sqrt{.0959} = -.1929.$$

6.   Look up $N(d_1)$
$$N(-.10) = .4602.$$

7.   Look up $N(d_2)$
$$N(-.19) = .4247.$$

8.   Plug into formula for C, using S' in place of S
$$C = 162.01(.4602) - 165e^{-(.0521)(.0959)}(.4247) = 4.831.$$

3, dividends tend to reduce the call option's price and may induce early exercise. Incorporating dividends into the Black-Scholes model for European options is not difficult. There are several suggested approaches, none of which have proven superior to the others. We shall discuss two here.

Known Discrete Dividends

Suppose a stock pays a dividend of D_t at some time during the option's life. This dividend is payable after a time period t, which is defined by the ex-dividend date. The dividend is assumed to be known with certainty. If we make a small adjustment to the stock price, the Black-Scholes model will remain applicable to the pricing of this option.

The adjustment is one we have done several times before. We subtract the present value of the dividend from the stock price and use the adjusted stock price in the formula. Let the stock price in the Black-Scholes formula be S', defined as $S' = S - D_t e^{-r_c t}$. If there were other dividends during the life of the option, their present values would be subtracted as well.

As noted earlier, the Digital Equipment stock does not pay a dividend. For illustrative purposes, however, we will now assume that it pays a $2 dividend and has an ex-dividend date of July 15. All other variables are the same. The procedure for calculating the Black-Scholes price is laid out in Table 4.4. Note that now the call price is lower as we would expect.

The Excel spreadsheet bsbin1.xls, illustrated in Software Demonstration 4.1, permits you to enter up to 50 known discrete dividends. You sim-

The Black-Scholes model can be adjusted to account for dividends by lowering the stock price by the present value of the dividends.

ply enter the dividend amount and the time in years to the ex-dividend date. Be sure that you do not enter a yield or the software will ignore the discrete dividends and use the yield.

Continuous Dividend Yield

Another approach to the problem of adjusting the Black-Scholes formula for dividends on the stock is to assume the dividend is paid continuously at a known yield. This method assumes the dividend accrues continuously, which means that a dividend is constantly being paid. We express the annual rate as a percentage, δ. For example, let the Digital Equipment stock have an annual dividend yield of $\delta = .04$. Given the current stock price of $164, the annual dividend is $164(.04) = \$6.56$. This dividend is not paid in four quarterly installments of $1.64 each; rather, it accrues continuously in very small increments that are reinvested and accumulate over the year to $6.56. Because the stock price fluctuates throughout the year, the actual dividend can change but the yield will remain constant. Thus, this model does not require the assumption that the dividend is known or is constant; it requires only that the dividend being paid at that instant be a constant percentage of the stock price.

The adjustment procedure requires substituting the value S' for S in the Black-Scholes model, where $S' = Se^{-\delta T}$. The expression $S(1 - e^{-\delta T})$ is the present value of the dividends. Subtracting this from S gives S' as given above. The adjustment removes the present value of the dividends during the option's life from the stock price. Table 4.5 illustrates the computation of the option price. Again we see that the effect of dividends is to lower the option's price under what it would be if there were no dividends. There is, of course, no assurance that the discrete and continuous dividend adjustments will give equivalent option prices. Because the Digital Equipment stock does not pay dividends, the dividend amount and the yield are merely assumptions made for illustration purposes and are not intended to be equivalent.

The assumption of a continuous dividend is unrealistic for most options on stocks; however, the convenience of using a single yield figure in lieu of obtaining the precise dividends could justify its use. For options on stocks, however, only a few dividends are paid over the option's life; thus the discrete dividend adjustment is not especially difficult. For index options, however, the use of a yield may be preferable. The dividends on the component stocks in the index would be paid more or less continuously, and thus it would be difficult to obtain an accurate day-by-day figure for the dividends.[7]

---

[7]Dividends and ex-dividend dates are available in *Moody's Dividend Record* (New York: Moody's Investor Services). However, the adjustment procedure for an index option will depend on how the index is constructed. Standard and Poor's does produce a daily dividend series for its indices.

TABLE 4.5	Calculating the Black-Scholes Price When There Are Continuous Dividends

$$S = 164 \quad E = 165 \quad r_c = .0521 \quad \sigma^2 = .0841 \quad T = .0959 \quad \delta = .04$$

1. Compute the stock price minus the present value of the dividends as $S' = Se^{-\delta T}$
$$S' = 164e^{-.04(.0959)} = 163.37.$$

2. Compute d_1, using S' in place of S
$$d_1 = \frac{\ln(163.37/165) + (.0521 + .0841/2).0959}{.29\sqrt{.0959}} = -.01.$$

3. Compute d_2
$$d_2 = -.01 - .29\sqrt{.0959} = -.0998.$$

4. Look up $N(d_1)$
$$N(-.01) = .4960.$$

5. Look up $N(d_2)$
$$N(-.10) = .4602.$$

6. Plug into formula for C, using S' in place of S
$$C = 163.37(.4960) - 165e^{-(.0521)(.0959)}(.4602) = 5.477.$$

The Excel spreadsheet bsbin1.xls, illustrated in Software Demonstration 4.1, permits you to enter a continuous dividend yield when calculating an option price.

American Options

None of the adjustments here make the Black-Scholes model capable of pricing American options. However, now having seen the Black-Scholes model, we can use it to gain a greater understanding of why call options might be exercised early.

Consider our Digital Equipment options. Let us take an option that is well in-the-money, the July 160. Using the Black-Scholes model, we would find this option to be worth 8.50. Let us change things around a little. Suppose the stock is going to go ex-dividend in another instant. How large of a dividend would it take to justify exercising it before it goes ex-dividend? Let us assume that this is the last dividend that the stock will pay during the option's life, so after the stock has gone ex-dividend, we can safely use the Black-Scholes model.

In Table 4.6 we try dividend levels of \$1–\$10. When the stock goes ex-dividend, it will fall by the amount of the dividend and we then can re-compute the option value using the Black-Scholes model, remembering that once the stock goes ex-dividend, the Black-Scholes model will correctly price the call because there are no more dividends during the option's remaining life. The value obtained if you exercise the option just before the stock goes ex-dividend is always the intrinsic value, here \$4. The

| TABLE 4.6 | The Early Exercise Decision |

| | $S = 164$ | $E = 160$ | $r_c = .0521$ | $\sigma^2 = .0841$ | $T = .0959$ | |

Dividend	Value if Exercised[1]	Value When Stock Goes Ex-Dividend[2]	Exercise?
0	4	8.50	No
1	4	7.87	No
2	4	7.26	No
3	4	6.68	No
4	4	6.12	No
5	4	5.60	No
6	4	5.10	No
7	4	4.63	No
8	4	4.18	No
9	4	3.77	Yes
10	4	3.38	Yes

[1]The intrinsic value before the stock goes ex-dividend.
[2]Computed using the Black-Scholes model, using the ex-dividend stock price, 164 – dividend.

stock will then go ex-dividend and fall by the amount of the dividend. The third column shows the ex-dividend price of the call. You would exercise the option if the intrinsic value exceeds the ex-dividend option value. Here it would take a dividend of a little more than $8 to justify early exercise.

Note that we never calculated the value of the option at any time before it went ex-dividend. This would require an American option pricing model. At that instant before the stock goes ex-dividend, if the dividend is not large enough to justify early exercise, the American call price would sell for the European call price. If the dividend is large enough to justify early exercise, the American call price would be $4, the intrinsic value. However, well before the ex-dividend instant, it is much more difficult to price the option because the stock price at the ex-dividend instant is unknown. Thus, we would require an American option pricing model. In addition if there were more than one dividend, we would need an American option pricing model to account for the remaining dividends. American option pricing models are generally beyond the scope of this book. However, recall that we covered the binomial model and demonstrated how it can be used to price American options. This is the preferred method used by professional option traders. Your Excel spreadsheet bsbin1.xls will calculate American call prices using the binomial model, as will the Windows program bsbwin2.exe, both of which are demonstrated later in this chapter.

Estimating the Volatility (Standard Deviation)

Obtaining a reliable estimate of the volatility is difficult. Moreover, the model is extremely sensitive to that estimate. There are two approaches to estimating the volatility: the historical volatility and the implied volatility.

Historical Volatility

The **historical volatility** estimate is based on the assumption that the volatility that prevailed over the recent past will continue to hold in the future. First, we take a sample of returns on the stock over a recent period. We convert these returns to continuously compounded returns. Then we compute the standard deviation of the continuously compounded returns.

The returns can be daily, weekly, monthly, or any desired time interval. If we use daily returns, the result will be a daily standard deviation. To obtain the annualized standard deviation the model requires, we must multiply either the variance by the number of trading days in a year, which is about 250, or the standard deviation by $\sqrt{250}$. If we use monthly returns, the result will be a monthly variance (or standard deviation) and must be multiplied by either 12 (or $\sqrt{12}$) to obtain an annualized figure.

There is no minimum number of observations; a sample size of about 60 will be adequate in most cases. The trade-off in selecting a sample size is that the more observations one uses, the further back in time one must go. The further back one goes, the more likely the volatility will change. In the example used here we do not use many historical observations, but this is primarily to keep the computations brief.

Assume we have a series of J continuously compounded returns, where each return is identified as r_t^c, which equals $\ln(1 + r_t)$ and t goes from 1 to J. First, we calculate the mean return as

The historical volatility is estimated from a sample of recent continuously compounded returns on the stock.

$$\bar{r}^c = \sum_{t=1}^{J} r_t^c / J.$$

Then the variance is

$$\sigma^2 = \frac{\sum_{t=1}^{J} (r_t^c - \bar{r}^c)^2}{J - 1}$$

$$= \frac{\sum_{t=1}^{J} (r_t^c)^2 - \left(\sum_{t=1}^{J} r_t^c\right)^2 / J}{J - 1}.$$

Note that we divide the sum of the squared deviations around the mean by J − 1. This is the appropriate divisor if the observations are a sample taken from a larger population. This adjustment is necessary for the estimate of the sample variance to be an unbiased estimate of the population variance.

| TABLE 4.7 | Estimating Historical Volatility (Digital Equipment: Weekly Data, 12/12–6/12) | | | |

Week	Price	r_t	r_t^c	$(r_t^c - \bar{r}^c)^2$
12/12	106.125	—	—	—
12/19	106.375	.0024	.0024	.0002
12/26	106.750	.0035	.0035	.0002
1/2	105.750	−.0094	−.0094	.0007
1/9	113.750	.0757	.0729	.0032
1/16	138.000	.2132	.1933	.0312
1/23	143.000	.0362	.0356	.0004
1/30	145.125	.0149	.0148	.0000
2/6	152.500	.0508	.0496	.0011
2/13	151.500	−.0066	−.0066	.0005
2/20	153.875	.0157	.0156	.0000
2/27	153.250	−.0041	−.0041	.0004
3/6	169.125	.1036	.0986	.0067
3/13	163.750	−.0318	−.0323	.0024
3/20	166.500	.0168	.0167	.0000
3/27	161.125	−.0323	−.0328	.0025
4/3	169.125	.0497	.0485	.0010
4/10	166.125	−.0177	−.0179	.0012
4/16	157.000	−.0549	−.0565	.0054
4/24	162.125	.0326	.0321	.0002
5/1	172.500	.0640	.0620	.0021
5/8	167.125	−.0312	−.0317	.0023
5/15	159.500	−.0456	−.0467	.0040
5/22	155.000	−.0282	−.0286	.0021
5/29	157.375	.0153	.0152	.0000
6/5	162.000	.0294	.0290	.0001
6/12	164.000	.0123	.0123	.0000
Totals			0.4352	0.0678

$\bar{r}^c = \dfrac{0.4352}{26} = .0167.$

$\sigma^2 = \dfrac{.0678}{25} = .0027.$

Annualized $\sigma^2 = .0027(52) = .1410.$

Annualized $\sigma = \sqrt{.1410} = .3755.$

Table 4.7 illustrates this procedure for the Digital Equipment stock using weekly closing prices. The simple return, r_t, is computed and converted to a continuously compounded return, r_t^c. Then the mean and variance of the series of continuously compounded returns are calculated. The resulting variance is a weekly variance, so it must be multiplied by 52 to be converted to an annual variance. The annualized standard deviation, or volatility, thus is .3755.

The accompanying Excel spreadsheet hisv.xls calculates the historical volatility. Software Demonstration 4.2 illustrates how to use hisv.xls.

SOFTWARE DEMONSTRATION 4.2   **Calculating the Historical Volatility with the Excel Spreadsheet hisv.xls**

	A	B	C	D	E	F	G	H	
42	**Inputs:**				**Results:**				
43	Enter the data frequency:						Periodic	Annualized	
44		w				Variance	0.001699	0.088351	
45	(d = daily, w = weekly, m = monthly,				Standard Deviation		4.12%	29.72%	
46	y = yearly; upper or lower case)				Mean		0.16%	8.54%	
47									
48					Continuously				
49					Compounded				
50			Asset	Simple	Rate	Squared			
51	Obs.	Date	Price	of Return	of Return	Deviation			
52	1	6-Jul	44.7500	NA	NA	NA			
53	2	13-Jul	44.8750	0.28%	0.28%	0.000001			
54	3	20-Jul	47.3750	5.57%	5.42%	0.002764			
55	4	27-Jul	45.6250	-3.69%	-3.76%	0.001543			
56	5	3-Aug	43.6250	-4.38%	-4.48%	0.002159			
57	6	10-Aug	43.7500	0.29%	0.29%	0.000001			
58	7	17-Aug	42.0000	-4.00%	-4.08%	0.001803			

The Excel spreadsheet hisv.xls, which operates in Windows 3.1 or Windows 95 and requires Excel 5.0 or higher, calculates the historical volatility (standard deviation) for a sample of stock prices. No installation is necessary; simply place the file in whatever directory you prefer or access it directly from the 3.5-inch diskette provided with this book. To use the software, do the following:

1.   Make sure you are in Windows 3.1 or Windows 95.
2.   Run Excel 5.0 or higher.
3.   Open the file hisv.xls.

Now let us assume that you wish to calculate a historical volatility. In the accompanying example, already entered into the cells is a set of 26 weekly prices for a stock. Each cell that will accept input has a double-line border and the values are in blue.

Output cells have a single-line border. In the section called **Inputs:,** you should enter the data frequency. In other words, if your data are daily prices, enter a "d"; if they are weekly prices, enter a "w"; if they are monthly prices, enter an "m"; or, if they are yearly prices, enter a "y" (either an uppercase or lowercase letter is acceptable). Directly below is a set of cells containing your data observations. It is not necessary to enter the observation number or the date but it may be useful. Enter the prices in the column labeled "Asset Price."

To obtain the results, hit the F9 (manual recalculation) key. The output is shown in the section labeled **Results:** The output consists of the variance, standard deviation, and the mean return. The column labeled "Periodic" provides the results in terms of the data frequency you entered. In the example shown, you have a standard deviation of 4.12%, which is for weekly data; thus, 4.12% is the weekly standard deviation. The column labeled "Annualized" provides the figures annualized by multiplying by an appropriate factor. The variance and mean are annualized by multiplying by 250, the approximate number of trading days in a year, 52, 12, or 1, depending on your data frequency. The annualized standard deviation is then the square root of the annualized variance.

In this example, there are 26 prices, which leads to 25 returns. Obviously you may wish to use this spreadsheet for a different number of prices. The spreadsheet is set on protected status so unprotect it by choosing Tools/Protection/Unprotect Sheet from Excel's main menu. Then enter or remove lines at the bottom by using the familiar Windows commands for adding rows and copying formulas or deleting rows. Always leave the double lines, however, as the overall formulas look for those lines to determine the end of the data. You should probably return the spreadsheet to protected status by choosing Tools/Protection/Protect Sheet, which will prompt you for a password. You can simply hit the Enter key or give it a password if desired.

If you prefer, you can calculate statistics such as these by building your own spreadsheet and using Excel's statistical functions AVERAGE, VAR, and STDEV.

For those who prefer Lotus 1-2-3, the diskette also contains the spreadsheet hisv.wk3 and its format file hisv.fm3. This spreadsheet is from the previous edition of this book and does not contain all of the features of the Excel spreadsheet, but it will provide the historical volatility following essentially the same procedure.

Implied Volatility

The second approach to estimating the volatility is called the **implied volatility,** which we shall denote as $\hat{\sigma}$. This procedure assumes the option's market price reflects the stock's current volatility. The Black-Scholes or any other acceptable option pricing model is used to infer a standard deviation. The implied volatility is the standard deviation that makes the Black-Scholes price equal the option's current market price.

The implied volatility approach would be simple if the Black-Scholes equation could be solved for the standard deviation. Since that cannot be done, we obtain the solution by plugging in values of σ until we find the one that makes the Black-Scholes price equal the market price. The procedure is illustrated in Figure 4.10. Because it requires a trial-and-error search, it can be quite laborious, and it is helpful to use a computer to do the calculations.[8]

Let us estimate the implied volatility for the Digital Equipment July 165 call. The input values are S = 164, E = 165, r_c = .0521, and T = .0959. The market price of the call is 5.75. We need to find the value of σ that

The implied volatility is obtained by finding the standard deviation that when used in the Black-Scholes model makes the model price equal the market price of the option.

---

[8]A shortcut method is presented in Appendix 4B.

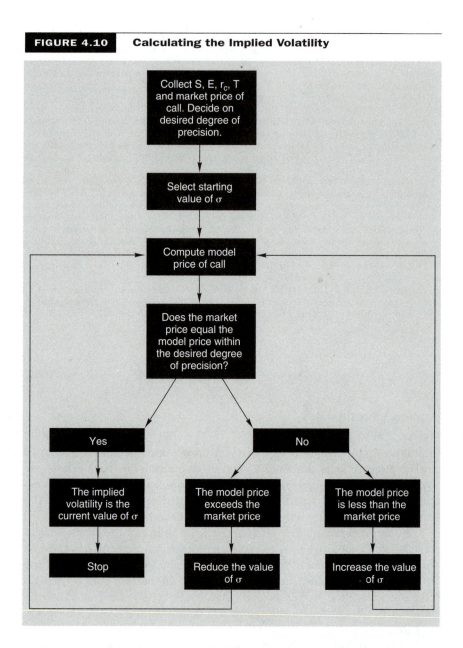

FIGURE 4.10   **Calculating the Implied Volatility**

will make the Black-Scholes value come to 5.75. We must also be prepared to specify a certain degree of precision in our answer; that is, how close should the model price come to the market price or how many decimal places to the right of zero do we require in our implied volatility? For illustrative purposes, we shall use two decimal places in the implied volatil-

ity and stop the trial-and-error process when we determine that the true implied volatility is within .01 of our answer.

Deriving the implied volatility will involve repetitive Black-Scholes calculations. This is an excellent opportunity to use the Excel spreadsheet bsbin1.xls. Load bsbin1.xls and insert the appropriate values for the asset (stock) price, exercise price, risk-free rate, and time to expiration. Let us start with a σ of .5. We see that the Black-Scholes call price is 10.04. Obviously this is too high, so let us try a σ of .2. The Black-Scholes call price is 3.97, which is too low. At a σ of .4, we get 8.02; a σ of .3 gives 5.99; a σ of .29 gives 5.79; and a σ of .28 gives 5.59. Thus, our answer is between .28 and .29. We shall use .29 as the implied standard deviation and $(.29)^2 =$ .0841 as the implied variance.

Because σ is the stock's volatility, all options on a given stock with the same expiration should give the same implied volatility. For various reasons, including the possibility that the Black-Scholes model is deficient, different options on the same stock sometimes produce different implied volatilities.

Table 4.8 presents the implied standard deviations obtained for the two options whose exercise prices surround the stock price. The implied standard deviations range from .21 to .32. This forces us to choose a single value for the overall implied standard deviation.

Several methods have been suggested. Some involve taking a simple arithmetic average of the various implied volatilities. Others recommend using a weighted average. Still others simply select the implied standard deviation of the option whose exercise price is closest to the current stock price.

Recall from Figure 4.8 that we noticed that the call is nearly linear in the volatility if the call is at-the-money. Brenner and Subrahmanyam (1988) exploited this fact and showed that an at-the-money call price is approximately given as

$$C \approx (0.398)S\sigma \sqrt{T},$$

TABLE 4.8	Implied Standard Deviations of Digital Equipment Calls		
		Expiration	
Exercise Price	**June**	**July**	**October**
160	.21	.30	.30
165	.25	.29	.32

where they define at-the-money as when the stock price equals the present value of the exercise price, $S = Ee^{-r_cT}$. The implied volatility of an at-the-money call can then be obtained as

$$\hat{\sigma} \approx \frac{C}{(0.398)S \sqrt{T}}$$

where C is the market price of the call.[9] For example, our Digital Equipment July 165 has C = 5.75, S = 164, and T = .0959. Thus,

$$\hat{\sigma} \approx \frac{5.75}{(0.398)164 \sqrt{.0959}} = .2845.$$

Because this particular call is very close to at-the-money (S = 164, E = $165e^{-.0521(.0959)}$ = 164.18), the answer is very close to its actual implied volatility, which we obtained earlier by trial and error.

Implied volatility is widely used in practice. In fact, many option traders prefer to think in terms of whether the implied volatility is more or less than a reasonable estimate of the actual volatility than whether the model price is more or less than the theoretical fair value. A commonly observed condition is that a graph of the implied volatility against the exercise price produces a u-shaped plot, more commonly known as the **volatility smile.** In other words, the implied volatility tends to be increasingly higher the more out-of-the-money the option is and the more in-the-money the option is. This phenomenon is puzzling because, as noted earlier, the implied volatility should reflect the volatility of the stock; clearly there can be only one true volatility of the stock. Consequently, the concept of implied volatility seems somehow flawed. The reason for the volatility smile is not clear, but obviously the Black-Scholes model is not a perfect representation of reality. Unfortunately, no other model has been found to work better for European options without sacrificing so much in simplicity. Most option traders, therefore, use the Black-Scholes model, keeping in mind the bias as indicated by the presence of the volatility smile.

The uncertainty of the correct value for the volatility is one of the reasons why options attract so much speculative interest. If everyone agreed on the volatility estimate, the option would always be correctly priced and there would be no reason to buy or sell. It is the ambiguity of the volatility estimation that leads to disagreement among traders. This disagree-

---

[9]For the curious, 0.398 is $\frac{1}{\sqrt{2\pi}}$, which is used to calculate the normal probability.

ment, in turn, leads to trading among those who believe the option is incorrectly priced.[10]

The Binomial Model and the Black-Scholes Model

Earlier in the chapter, we briefly mentioned that the binomial model price will converge to the Black-Scholes price when n is large. Now we shall see how that is accomplished. Again let us take the Digital Equipment July 165 call. In the binomial example, we looked at a one-period call and then a two-period call. The two cases were options with different expirations. Now we compute the value of a single option when its life is divided into a greater number of periods. When we increase the number of periods, the length of each period decreases.

We start off with the inputs used in the Black-Scholes model, $S = 164$, $E = 165$, $r_c = .0521$, $T = .0959$, and $\sigma = .29$. To convert to the binomial framework, we must change the continuously compounded risk-free rate to a discrete rate (r) as we described earlier. Thus, $e^{.0521} - 1 = .0535$, which is our risk-free rate. Now let n equal the number of periods used. For a given n, the inputs in the binomial model are

Risk-free rate $\qquad = (1 + r)^{T/n} - 1.$

Up parameter (u) $\quad = e^{\sigma \sqrt{T/n}} - 1.$

Down parameter (d) $= \left[\dfrac{1}{1 + u}\right] - 1.$

For n = 1, we have a risk-free rate of[11]

$$(1.0535)^{.0959/1} - 1 = .0050,$$

an up parameter of

$$u = e^{.29\sqrt{.0959/1}} - 1 = .094,$$

and a down parameter of

$$\left(\frac{1}{1.094}\right) - 1 = -.0859.$$

---

[10]Mark Twain in *Pudd'nhead Wilson* (1894) expressed this point succinctly by saying, "It were not best that we should think alike; it is difference of opinion that makes horse races."

[11]If there is a continuous dividend yield of δ, convert it the same way as the continuous risk-free rate.

SOFTWARE DEMONSTRATION 4.3   **Calculating the Binomial Price with the Excel Spreadsheet bsbin1.xls**

X *Microsoft* Excel - bsbin1

| File | Edit | View | Insert | Format | Tools | Data | Window | Help |

Arial | 10 | **B** *I* U | $ % |

| nsteps | 100 |

	A	B	C	D	E	F	G	H	I
38	In lieu of a continuously compounded yield, place below up to fifty discrete dividends and the time in years to each ex-dividend date. Leave all unused cells blank. Set the yield above to zero. If yield is not set to zero, all discrete dividends are disregarded.				**Binomial Model**				
39					Steps:		100		
40						**European**	**European**		
41						**Call**	**Put**		
42					Price	5.8000	5.9777	**Run Binomial**	
43					Delta (Δ)	0.5137	-0.4863	**Option Pricing**	
44					Gamma (Γ)	0.0269	0.0269	**Model**	
45					Theta (Θ)	-34.6418	-26.0881		
46	Dividend #	Dividend	Time to ex date	Present Value					
47	1	0.0000	0.0000	0.0000					
48	2	0.0000	0.0000	0.0000		**American**	**American**		
49	3	0.0000	0.0000	0.0000		**Call**	**Put**		
50	4			0.0000	Price	5.8000	6.0451		
51	5			0.0000	Delta (Δ)	0.5137	-0.4938		
52	6			0.0000	Gamma (Γ)	0.0269	0.0276		
53	7			0.0000	Theta (Θ)	-34.6418	-26.8247		
54	8			0.0000					

| ◄ ► Sheet1 / Sheet2 / Sheet3 / Sheet4 / Sheet5 / Sheet6 |

Ready | Sum=100 |

The Excel spreadsheet bsbin1.xls, which operates in Windows 3.1 or Windows 95 and requires Excel 5.0 or higher, calculates both the Black-Scholes and binomial option pricing models. For the binomial model, bsbin1.xls provides European and American call and put prices as well as the delta, gamma, and theta. No installation is necessary; simply place the file in whatever directory you prefer or access it directly from the 3.5-inch diskette provided with this book. To use the software, do the following:

1. Make sure you are in Windows 3.1 or Windows 95.
2. Run Excel 5.0 or higher.
3. Open the file bsbin1.xls.

Now let us calculate an option price. Assume that you wish to find the binomial price of the option illustrated in the book, the Digital Equipment July 165. The DEC stock is at 164, the exercise price is 165, the continuously compounded risk-free rate is .0521, the standard deviation is .29, and the option expires in 35 days, meaning that its time to expiration is 35/365 = .0959. There are no dividends on the stock.

Observe on the accompanying spreadsheet a section labeled **Inputs:** Each cell that will accept input has a double-line border and the values are in blue. Output cells have a single-line border. Enter the stock price of 164 in the cell beside the words "Asset Price (S)" and enter the remaining inputs in the appropriate cells below the same way you entered them to calculate the Black-Scholes price as illustrated in Software Demonstration 4.1. Leave the dividend yield and the discrete dividends blank or enter zeros.

Note the section labeled **Binomial Model.** Enter the number of time steps. The program will handle up to 1,000. Since the binomial calculation can be time consuming, the spreadsheet does not automatically calculate the binomial value. You must move your cursor over the button labeled **Run Binomial Option Pricing Model** and click. While the program is running, Excel's status bar will count down by showing the line "Iterating through binomial tree at time step # xxx" where xxx is the number of the time step the program is on. This gives you an idea of how much longer you will have to wait. Of course, the length of the wait depends on the speed of your computer. Try it with 100 time steps. Your answer for our example option should correspond very closely to the appropriate value in Table 4.9.

For those who prefer not to use a spreadsheet, Appendix 4C demonstrates how to use the Windows program bsbwin2.exe, which provides Black-Scholes and binomial prices in a standard Windows environment. The DOS program binom3.exe is also provided from previous editions of the book.

Plugging into the binomial model gives us a call price of 7.25. This is not particularly close to the Black-Scholes value of 5.803, but we should not expect it to be just yet. However, in Table 4.9 and Figure 4.11, notice what happens as we increase the number of time periods, n. Of course, when n is large, these calculations must be done on a computer. The binomial price with n = 50 is almost 5.80, the Black-Scholes price. Note that the binomial estimates bounce around the Black-Scholes price until settling down to a value close to that price.

The binomial model price converges to the Black-Scholes model price as the number of time periods increases.

| TABLE 4.9 | Convergence of the Binomial Price to the Black-Scholes Price |

S = 164, E = 165, r = .0535 (discrete), σ = .29, T = .0959
Black-Scholes price = 5.803

n	u	d	r	C
1	.0940	−.0859	.0050	7.247
2	.0656	−.0615	.0025	5.357
5	.0410	−.0394	.0010	6.071
10	.0289	−.0280	.0005	5.753
25	.0181	−.0178	.0002	5.834
50	.0128	−.0126	.0001	5.802
100	.0090	−.0089	.0001	5.800

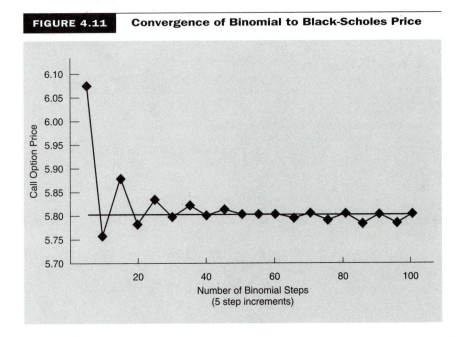

FIGURE 4.11   **Convergence of Binomial to Black-Scholes Price**

The Excel spreadsheet bsbin1.xls, which we previously illustrated for the Black-Scholes model, also provides binomial option prices for up to 1,000 time steps. Software Demonstration 4.3 illustrates how to obtain binomial option prices with bsbin1.xls. For those who prefer not to use spreadsheets, Appendix 4C demonstrates the Windows program bsbwin2.exe. Both programs will calculate American option prices as well as European option prices.

Option pricing models have been developed primarily for call options. We now turn our attention to the pricing of put options.

Put Option Pricing Models

Recall that the put-call parity formula gives the relationship between a put price and a call price. Expressing the put price as a function of the call price, we have

$$P_e(S,T,E) = C_e(S,T,E) - S + E(1 + r)^{-T}.$$

In the Black-Scholes world, it is necessary to use continuous compounding and discounting. Restating put-call parity so that the present value of the exercise price is computed using continuous discounting gives

The Black-Scholes call option pricing model can be turned into a put option pricing model by inserting it into put-call parity.

$$P_e(S,T,E) = C_e(S,T,E) - S + Ee^{-r_cT},$$

where, as discussed earlier, r_c is the continuously compounded rate. Then we can substitute the Black-Scholes value for the call price. Letting P stand for $P_e(S,T,E)$ gives the Black-Scholes European put option pricing model:

$$P = Ee^{-r_cT}\,[1 - N(d_2)] - S\,[1 - N(d_1)],$$

where d_1 and d_2 are the same as in the call option pricing model.

In the example of the July 165 call, the values of $N(d_1)$ and $N(d_2)$ were .5120 and .4761, respectively. Plugging into the formula, we get

$$P = 165e^{-(.0521)(.0959)}(1 - .4761) - 164(1 - .5120)$$
$$= 5.981.$$

The actual market price of the July 165 put was 6. Because this price must also include a premium for the additional benefit of early exercise, the difference between the market and model prices could be the effect of early exercise. In other words, if the put option pricing model reflected the early exercise premium, it would produce a higher theoretical price.

The same variables that affect the call's price affect the put's price, although in some cases in a different manner. The problems of delta hedging, gamma risk, and such also apply to puts. Table 4.10 summarizes these important concepts for puts.

The Excel spreadsheet bsbin1.xls, illustrated in Software Demonstrations 4.1 and 4.3, provides the Black-Scholes and binomial calculations for puts as well as calls.

Early Exercise of an American Put

In Chapter 3 we saw how an American put might be exercised early. We noted that if the stock price fell to zero, the holder of an American put would obviously exercise it and receive the E dollars immediately. While it is not necessary for the stock price to fall to zero to justify exercising the put early, it is impossible to determine exactly when the put should be exercised unless you have an option pricing model that will handle American puts. Fortunately, the binomial model will do so. As noted previously in this chapter, to handle an American option, you simply need to calculate the value of the European option at each point in the binomial tree. Then you calculate the intrinsic value. If the intrinsic value exceeds the value of the European option, you replace the value of the European option with the intrinsic value. Since the calculations start at the right and work backwards, the value of exercising early will properly show up in a higher price today, the leftmost point in the tree. A concept problem asks you to try this yourself. Your Excel spreadsheet bsbin1.xls will do this for

---

TABLE 4.10	**The Effects of Variables on the Black-Scholes Put Option Price**

The results for put options are obtained by using the put-call parity relationship, $P = C - S + Ee^{-r_cT}$.

Stock Price

The relationship between the stock price and the put price is called the put **delta.**

$$\text{Put } Delta = N(d_1) - 1.$$

Since $N(d_1)$ is between 0 and 1, the put delta is negative. This simply means that a put option moves in an opposite direction to the stock. A delta neutral position with stock and puts will require long positions in both stock and puts. The relationship between the put delta and the stock price is called the put **gamma.**

$$\text{Put } Gamma = \frac{e^{-d_1^2/2}}{S\sigma\sqrt{2\pi T}}.$$

Notice that the put gamma is the same as the call gamma. The gamma is highest when the put is at-the-money.

Exercise Price

For a difference in the exercise price, the put price will change by $e^{-r_cT}[1 - N(d_2)]$. Because both of the terms are positive, the overall expression is positive.

Risk-Free Rate

The relationship between the put price and the risk-free rate is called the put **rho.**

you as will the Windows program bsbwin2.exe, as presented in Appendix 4C. Use either of these methods and calculate the European and American put prices for the Digital Equipment July 165 puts. Note the higher price for the American put.

For a given time to expiration, there is a stock price, below the exercise price, at which the price of the American put will exactly equal the intrinsic value. If the actual stock price is at or below this critical stock price, then the put should be exercised. Finding this critical stock price requires inserting various stock prices into the binomial model until the American put price equals the intrinsic value.

The critical stock price moves upward as expiration approaches. At expiration, the critical stock price is, quite naturally, the exercise price. Table

TABLE 4.10   *(continued)*

$$\text{Put } Rho = -TEe^{-r_cT}\left[1 - N(d_2)\right].$$

This expression is always negative meaning that the put price moves inversely to interest rates.

Volatility

The relationship between the put price and the volatility is called the **vega**.

$$\text{Put } Vega = \frac{S\sqrt{T}\,e^{-d_1^2/2}}{\sqrt{2\pi}}.$$

This is the same expression as the vega for a call. Like a call, a put is highly sensitive to the volatility.

Time to Expiration

The relationship between the put price and the time to expiration is called the **theta**.

$$\text{Put } Theta = -\frac{S\sigma e^{-d_1^2/2}}{2\sqrt{2\pi T}} + r_c Ee^{-r_cT}\left(1 - N(d_2)\right).$$

This expression can be positive or negative, a point we have covered in Chapter 3. A European put can either increase or decrease with time. The tendency to increase occurs because there is more time for the stock to move favorably. The tendency to decrease occurs because the additional time means waiting longer to receive the exercise price at expiration.

4.11 shows these results for our Digital Equipment October 170 put. The first line indicates that on June 12 there were 126 days remaining, which is a time to expiration of .3452. With the stock price at 164, the European put price is 12.63 while the American put price is 13.06. This is a rather significant difference. The critical stock price is 134.7. In other words, if the stock price were at 134.7, the American put should be exercised immediately. Its intrinsic value would be 170 − 134.7 = 35.3 and the American put price would also be 35.3. Of course, the actual stock price is 164, which is not low enough to justify immediate exercise. Nonetheless, the American put price exceeds the European put price because there is a possibility that the stock price will fall below the critical stock price sometime during the life of the option.

TABLE 4.11	American and European Put Prices and Critical Stock Price for Early Exercise of Digital Equipment October 170 Put

$S = 164$ $E = 170$ $r_c = .0574$ $\sigma^2 = .0841$

Date	Days Remaining	Time Remaining	P_e	P_a	Critical Stock Price
6/12	126	.3452	12.63	13.06	134.7
6/19	119	.3260	12.42	12.82	135.2
6/26	112	.3068	12.20	12.57	135.9
7/3	105	.2877	11.96	12.32	136.5
7/10	98	.2685	11.72	12.05	137.2
7/17	91	.2493	11.46	11.77	137.8
7/24	84	.2301	11.19	11.48	138.5
7/31	77	.2110	10.90	11.18	139.3
8/7	70	.1918	10.60	10.86	140.1
8/14	63	.1726	10.30	10.54	141.1
8/21	56	.1534	9.99	10.20	142.1
8/28	49	.1342	9.65	9.83	143.3
9/4	42	.1151	9.28	9.43	144.7
9/11	35	.0959	8.86	8.99	146.2
9/18	28	.0767	8.39	8.50	147.9
9/25	21	.0575	8.17	8.27	148.7
10/2	14	.0384	7.25	7.31	152.6
10/9	7	.0192	6.53	6.57	156.6
10/16	0	.0000	6.00	6.00	170.0

The table also shows the results moving forward one week in time and Figure 4.12 shows the critical stock price along with the current stock price and the exercise price. Notice how the critical stock price rises through time, somewhat slowly but then rapidly approaching the exercise price at the end of the option's life. If, at any time, the actual stock price hits the critical stock price, the put would be exercised immediately.

FIGURE 4.12   **Critical Stock Price for Early Exercise of Digital Equipment October 170 Put**

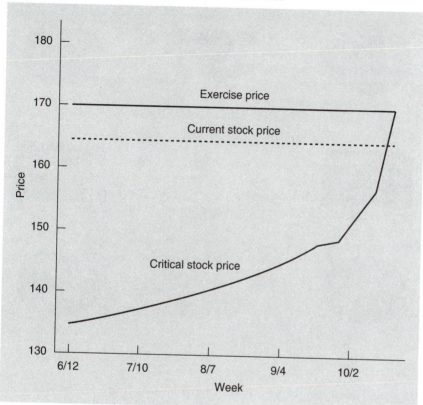

Summary

This chapter examined option pricing models. Starting with the simple one-period binomial option pricing model, it developed the formula and illustrated why investors' actions would force the model to hold. Then it extended the one-period model to a two-period world. Here the model was shown to be only slightly more complex but more realistic.

One reason for presenting the binomial model was to provide a foundation for the Black-Scholes model. One can avoid the mathematics necessary for deriving the Black-Scholes model if one can grasp the intuition behind the binomial model. In addition, the binomial model can be extended to converge to the Black-Scholes model, and it can provide American option prices as well.

The Black-Scholes model was shown to be a practical method for obtaining the theoretical fair value for a call option. The chapter reviewed the effects of changing the various inputs and observed the difficulty of obtaining certain inputs, such as the volatility of the underlying stock. The volatility was shown to be

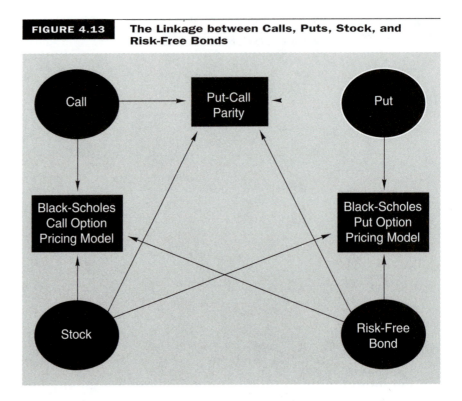

FIGURE 4.13   **The Linkage between Calls, Puts, Stock, and Risk-Free Bonds**

the most critical item because it must be estimated. Moreover, the model was found to be highly sensitive to the volatility. By using put-call parity, the Black-Scholes model can also be applied to European puts.

In Chapter 3 we used put-call parity to find relative option prices. A put, call, and stock could be priced in relation to each other. But we had to have two of the three prices already. Now we have an absolute option pricing model, the Black-Scholes model. Figure 4.13 shows how the Black-Scholes models link the call and put with the stock and risk-free bond.

Chapters 3 and 4 examined option pricing theory and the economic rationale behind the pricing of options. Chapters 5 and 6 examine some of the popular practical option trading strategies. However, we should not lose sight of the theoretical underpinnings of options. In fact, the basic principles of pricing options will remain with us for the next two chapters and will help us understand and evaluate trading strategies.

Key Terms

Before continuing to Chapter 5, you should be able to give brief definitions of the following terms.

- option pricing model
- binomial option pricing model
- Black-Scholes option pricing model
- hedge portfolio

- hedge ratio
- delta/delta hedge/delta neutral
- gamma
- rho

- vega
- theta
- historical volatility
- implied volatility

Questions and Problems

1. Explain the similarities and differences between pricing an option by its boundary conditions and using an exact option pricing formula.

2. Explain how an n-period binomial option pricing model is similar to the Black-Scholes model.

3. What is the principal benefit of a binomial option pricing model?

4. Compare the variables in the binomial model with those in the Black-Scholes model. Note any differences and explain.

5. What is the most critical variable in the Black-Scholes model? Explain.

6. Consider the various versions of the Black-Scholes model presented here that allow for the inclusion of dividends. Why are these models not strictly appropriate for pricing most exchange-listed options?

7. Explain each of the following concepts as they relate to call options.
    a. Delta
    b. Gamma
    c. Rho
    d. Vega
    e. Theta

8. Suppose you are planning to use the Black-Scholes model to price a call option. Unfortunately, you have no access to any information on Treasury bill yields. You elect to substitute the yield on high-grade commercial paper. Assess the likely implications of this substitution.

9. Suppose you subscribe to a service that gives you estimates of the theoretically correct standard deviations of stocks. You note that the implied standard deviation of a particular option is substantially higher than the theoretical standard deviation. What action should you take?

10. Consider a two-period, two-state world. Let the current stock price be 45 and the risk-free rate be 5 percent. Each period the stock price can go either up by 10 percent or down by 10 percent. A call option expiring at the end of the second period has an exercise price of 40.
    a. Find the stock price sequence.
    b. Determine the possible prices of the call at expiration.
    c. Find the possible prices of the call at the end of the first period.
    d. What is the current price of the call?
    e. What is the initial hedge ratio?
    f. What are the two possible hedge ratios at the end of the first period?
    g. Construct an example showing that the hedge works. Make sure the example illustrates how the hedge portfolio earns the risk-free rate over both periods.
    h. What would an investor do if the call were overpriced? If it were underpriced?

11.   Consider the following binomial option pricing problem involving an American call. This call has two periods to go before expiring. Its stock price is 30, and its exercise price is 25. The risk-free rate is .05. The value of u is .15, and the value of d is −.1. The dividend yield is .06. Find the value of the call.

The following option prices were observed for calls and puts on a stock for the trading day of July 6 of a particular year. Use this information in problems 12 through 20. The stock was priced at 165 1/8. The expirations were July 17, August 21, and October 16. The continuously compounded risk-free rates associated with the three expirations were .0503, .0535, and .0571, respectively. Unless otherwise indicated, assume the options are European.

	Calls			**Puts**		
Strike	**Jul**	**Aug**	**Oct**	**Jul**	**Aug**	**Oct**
155	10.5	11.75	14	.1875	1.25	2.75
160	6	8.125	11.125	.75	2.75	4.5
165	2.6875	5.25	8.125	2.375	4.75	6.75
170	.8125	3.25	6	5.750	7.5	9

12.   Let the standard deviation of the continuously compounded return on the stock be .21. Ignore dividends. Answer the following:

a.   What is the theoretical fair value of the October 165 call? Calculate this answer by hand and then recalculate it using either bsbin1.xls or bsbwin2.exe.

b.   Based on your answer in part a, recommend a riskless strategy.

c.   If the stock price decreases by $1, how will the option position offset the loss on the stock?

13.   Use the Black-Scholes European put option pricing formula for the October 165 put option. Repeat parts a, b, and c of question 12 with respect to the put.

14.   Suppose the stock pays a $1.10 dividend with an ex-dividend date of September 10. Rework part a of problem 12 using an appropriate dividend-adjusted procedure. Calculate this answer by hand and then recalculate it using either bsbin1.xls or bsbwin2.exe.

15.   On July 6, the dividend yield on the stock is 2.7 percent. Rework part a of problem 12 using the yield-based dividend adjustment procedure. Calculate this answer by hand and then recalculate it using either the bsbin1.xls or the bsbwin2.exe software program.

16.   Suppose on July 7 the stock will go ex-dividend with a dividend of $2. If the options were American, determine whether the July 160 call would be exercised.

17.   Following is the sequence of daily prices on the stock for the preceding month of June:

Date	Price	Date	Price
6/1	159.875	6/16	162.000
6/2	157.250	6/17	161.375
6/3	160.250	6/18	160.875
6/4	161.375	6/19	161.375
6/5	160.000	6/22	163.250
6/8	161.250	6/23	164.875
6/9	159.875	6/24	166.125
6/10	157.750	6/25	167.875
6/11	157.625	6/26	166.500
6/12	156.625	6/29	165.375
6/15	159.625	6/30	162.500

Estimate the historical standard deviation of the stock for use in the Black-Scholes model. (Ignore dividends on the stock.)

18. Estimate the implied volatility of the August 165 call. Compare your answer with that obtained in problem 17. Use trial and error. Stop when your answer is within .01 of the true implied volatility. Use the Excel spreadsheet bsbin1.xls or the Windows program bsbwin2.exe.

19. Repeat problem 18 using the approximation for an at-the-money call. Compare your answer with the one you obtained in problem 18. Is the approximation a good one?

20. In problem 12, you estimated the value of the October 165 call using the Black-Scholes model. Now estimate the value of that option using the binomial model for 1, 5, 10, 25, and 50 time periods. Use the Excel spreadsheet bsbin1.xls or the Windows program bsbwin2.exe.

21. (Concept Problem) Find the value of an American put option using the binomial option pricing model. The parameters are $S = 62$, $E = 70$, $r = .08$, $u = .1$, and $d = -.05$. There are no dividends. Use $n = 2$ periods.

22. (Concept Problem) Find the value of a European call option using the Black-Scholes option pricing model. The parameters are $S = 80$, $E = 80$, $r_c = .05$, $\sigma = .35$, and $T = .25$. Determine the delta and estimate the change in the call price if the stock goes to the following prices: 70, 75, 78, 79, 81, 82, 85, 90. Then compute the Black-Scholes values for each of these new stock prices. Compare your estimates with the actual prices, and comment on the differences. Use the Excel spreadsheet bsbin1.xls or the Windows program bsbwin2.exe.

APPENDIX 4A
THE N-PERIOD BINOMIAL MODEL

With n periods remaining until the option expires, the call price is given by the formula:

$$C = \frac{\sum_{j=0}^{n} \frac{n!}{j!(n-j)!} p^j (1-p)^{n-j} \text{Max}[0, S(1+u)^j(1+d)^{n-j} - E]}{(1+r)^n}.$$

This seemingly difficult formula actually is not nearly as complex as it appears. It simply captures all of the possible stock price paths over the n periods until the option expires. Consider the example from the text in a three-period world where j will go from 0 to 3. First, we find the summation of the following terms.

For j = 0,

$$\frac{3!}{0!3!}(.857)^0(.143)^3\text{Max}[0,60(1.15)^0(.80)^3 - 50] = 0.$$

For j = 1,

$$\frac{3!}{1!2!}(.857)^1(.143)^2\text{Max}[0,60(1.15)^1(.80)^2 - 50] = 0.$$

For j = 2,

$$\frac{3!}{2!1!}(.857)^2(.143)^1\text{Max}[0,60(1.15)^2(.80)^1 - 50] = 4.2473.$$

For j = 3,

$$\frac{3!}{3!0!}(.857)^3(.143)^0\text{Max}[0,60(1.15)^3(.80)^0 - 50] = 25.9653.$$

Adding these and dividing by $(1.10)^3$ gives

$$\frac{0 + 0 + 4.2473 + 25.9653}{(1.10)^3} = 22.70.$$

The value of the call is higher in the three-period world than in the two-period world. This reflects the effect of a longer time to expiration.

The n-period binomial formula works because the factorial term, $n!/j!(n-j)!$, counts the number of ways a stock price could end up at a

certain level. For example, when n = 3, the stock price at the end of the third period could be either S_{d^3}, S_{ud^2}, S_{u^2d}, or S_{u^3}. There is only one path the stock could have taken for it to end up at S_{d^3}: to go down three straight periods. There is only one path it could have taken for it to end up at S_{u^3}: to go up three straight periods. For the stock price to end up at S_{ud^2}, there are three possible routes: (1) up, down, down; (2) down, down, up; or (3) down, up, down. For the stock to end up at S_{u^2d}, there are three paths: (1) up, down, up; (2) down, up, up; and (3) up, up, down. The factorial expression enumerates the routes that a stock can take to reach a certain level. The remaining terms in the formula then apply exactly as we have seen in the one- and two-period cases.

APPENDIX 4B
A Shortcut to the Calculation of Implied Volatility

Solving for the implied volatility can be a tedious trial-and-error process. However, Manaster and Koehler (1982) provide a shortcut that can quickly lead to the solution. The technique employs a Newton-Raphson search procedure.

Suppose that for a given standard deviation, σ^*, the Black-Scholes formula gives the call price as $C(\sigma^*)$. The true market price, however, is $C(\sigma)$, where σ is the true volatility. Manaster and Koehler recommend an initial guess of σ_1^*, where

$$\sigma_1^* = \sqrt{\left| \ln\left(\frac{S}{E}\right) + r_c T \right| \left(\frac{2}{T}\right)}.$$

Then compute the value of $C(\sigma_1^*)$ and compare it to the market price, $C(\sigma)$. If this is not close enough, the next guess should be

$$\sigma_2^* = \sigma_1^* - \frac{\left[C\left(\sigma_1^*\right) - C\left(\sigma\right)\right] e^{d_1^2/2} \sqrt{2\pi}}{S\sqrt{T}},$$

where d_1 is computed using σ_1^*. Then compute the value $C(\sigma_2^*)$ and compare it to the market price, $C(\sigma)$. If it is not close enough, the next guess should be

$$\sigma_3^* = \sigma_2^* - \frac{\left[C\left(\sigma_2^*\right) - C\left(\sigma\right)\right] e^{d_1^2/2} \sqrt{2\pi}}{S\sqrt{T}},$$

with d_1 computed using σ_2^*. Repeat the process until the model price is sufficiently close to the market price. In other words, given the ith guess of the implied volatility, the $(i + 1)$th guess should be

$$\sigma_{i+1}^* = \sigma_i^* - \frac{\left[C\left(\sigma_i^*\right) - C\left(\sigma\right)\right]e^{d_1^2/2}\sqrt{2\pi}}{S\sqrt{T}},$$

where d_1 is computed using σ_i^*.

Let us apply this procedure to the problem in the text. We have $S = 164$, $E = 165$, $T = .0959$, $r_c = .0521$, and $C(\sigma) = 5.75$. The initial guess for the implied volatility is

$$\sigma_1^* = \sqrt{\left|\ln\left(\frac{164}{165}\right) + .0521(.0959)\right|\left(\frac{2}{.0959}\right)} = .1503.$$

At a volatility of .1503, the Black-Scholes value is 2.959. The next guess should be

$$\sigma_2^* = .1503 - \frac{[2.959 - 5.75]e^{(.000012)^2/2}(2.5066)}{164\sqrt{.0959}} = .2881,$$

where .000012 is the value of d_1 computed from the Black-Scholes model using .1503 as the standard deviation. The value 2.5066 is $\sqrt{2\pi}$. The Black-Scholes price using .2881 as the volatility is 5.75.

Thus, we have found the solution in only two steps. In the chapter we noted that the implied volatility was .29, with the slight difference being due to rounding off our answer.

APPENDIX 4C
The BSBWIN2 Windows Software

For those who prefer not to use a spreadsheet to calculate option prices but are comfortable with Windows 3.1 or Windows 95, the software program bsbwin2.exe calculates Black-Scholes and binomial option prices along with deltas, gammas, and thetas. This Windows-based program offers many attractive features. In addition, the binomial program runs considerably faster than the Excel spreadsheet bsbin1.xls. and, thus, may be preferred if many time steps are required.

To run the program, you will need Windows 3.1 or Windows 95 and the file VBRUN300.DLL. This program is included in most versions of Windows. Your software diskette includes a copy of the program. If VBRUN300.DLL is already on your hard disk, it will probably be found in the \windows\system subdirectory or folder. If it is not there, copy the file from the diskette to your hard drive. To run bsbwin2.exe, use any of the standard Windows 3.1 or Windows 95 methods for running an executable

program, such as double-clicking on the program in file manager (**My Computer** or **Windows Explorer** in Windows 95) or using the **File Run** command available in Windows 3.1 (**Run** in Windows 95). You may wish to set up an icon in a window in 3.1 (or a shortcut in Windows 95). In any case, follow the instructions for any of the numerous ways to run an executable file as demonstrated in your Windows manual.

When you run the program, you will see the window shown below: From the main screen choose either the Black-Scholes or Binomial model. You will then be taken to either a Black-Scholes or Binomial window, both of which are shown on the following pages:
At the top of each window is a bar you can click on to receive instructions for that window. Although bsbwin2.exe does not contain traditional Win-

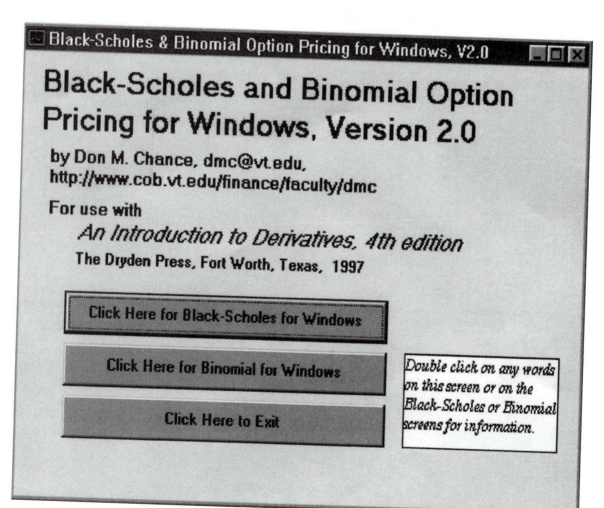

Black-Scholes for Windows

Click here for Instructions

Time Calculator (optional)

	First date	Second date
Month (1-12)		
Day (1-31)		
Year (yyyy)		

Time in Years

Asset Price   164

Exercise Price   165

Risk-Free Rate   .0521

Time to Expiration   .0959

Standard Deviation   .29

Dividends (click one)

⦿ **None**

○ **Continuous Yield**

○ **Discrete**

Amount   **Time to Ex-Dividend Day**

	Call	Put
Price	5.8228	6.0004
Delta	.5132	-.4868
Gamma	.0271	.0271
Theta	-34.6998	-26.1461
Vega	20.2502	20.2502
Rho	7.5131	-8.2315

Compute   **Return**

dows Help files, you can double-click on most of the key words or phrases on the main window and on the Black-Scholes and Binomial windows and see a box containing information. Try this feature out by double-clicking on any words you see on either the main window or the Black-Scholes or Binomial windows.

The program contains many error checkers, such as entering a negative asset price or dividend or forgetting to specify any time steps in the binomial model. You can, however, have a zero risk-free rate or a zero time to expiration. In the latter case, any value you insert for the standard deviation or risk-free rate is ignored. Up to three dividends can be accommodated, but any dividend you enter that occurs after the option's life triggers a warning that deletes the dividend.

A useful feature is the Time Calculator, which enables you to enter two dates and obtain the time in years between those two dates. If you double-click on the "Time to Expiration" cell or any of the "Time to Ex-Dividend Day" cells, the Time Calculator is automatically invoked and you can insert the time into the appropriate cell as soon as you enter the dates and click on the "Time in Years" cell. When entering the year, you should use the format yyyy, but for any years less than 2000, the short format yy will work.

You can terminate the program the same way you close any Windows program, using the icons in the upper left- and right-hand corners or the pull down menu in the upper left-hand corner. Alternatively you can close it by clicking on the appropriate buttons in the window itself. You can mini-mize the window, drag it, and resize it, as with any Windows program.

CHAPTER 5

Basic Option Strategies

A bird in the hand is an apt way to describe the strategy of today's options investor. Taking the immediate income of writing a covered call, the battle-tested investor is strategically managing market risk.

LAWRENCE SEVERN

Futures and Options World, October 1995

Chapter Objectives

■ To introduce the three-way procedure for examining the risk and return of an option strategy: by equation, by graph, and by numerical example

■ To examine the basic strategies of buying and selling stock, calls, and puts

■ To examine the combination strategies of covered calls, protective puts, conversions, and reversals

■ To explain how the choice of exercise price affects the possible outcomes of a strategy

■ To explain how the length of the chosen holding period affects the outcomes of a strategy

■ To illustrate the accompanying software for analyzing option strategies

One of the most interesting characteristics of an option is that it can be combined with stock or other options to produce a wide variety of alternative strategies. The profit possibilities are so diverse that virtually any investor can find an option strategy to suit his or her risk preference and market forecast.

In a world without options, the available strategies would be quite limited. If the market were expected to go up, one would buy stock; if it were expected to go down, one would sell short stock. As noted in Chapter 1, however, selling short stock requires an investor to meet certain requirements, such as having a minimum amount of capital to risk, selling short on an uptick or zero-plus tick, and maintaining minimum margins. Options make it simple to convert a forecast into a plan of action that will pay off if correct. Of course, any strategy will penalize if the forecast is wrong. With the judicious use of options, however, the penalties can be relatively small and known in advance.

This and the next chapter examine some of the more popular option strategies. It is not possible to cover all the strategies option traders could use. The ones we examine here should provide a basic understanding of the process of analyzing option strategies. Further study and analysis of the more advanced and complex strategies can be done using the framework presented here.

This chapter presents the basic option strategies. These strategies are the easiest to understand and involve the fewest transactions. Specifically, we

shall cover the strategies of calls, puts, and stock and combining calls with stock and puts with stock. We shall see how calls and stock can be combined to form puts and how puts and stock can be combined to form calls. Chapter 6 will look at spread strategies, which involve one short option and one long option, and combination strategies, which entail both puts and calls.

The approach we use here to analyze option strategies is to determine the profit a strategy will produce for a broad range of stock prices when the position is closed. This methodology is simple yet powerful enough to demonstrate its strengths. One attractive feature is that there are actually three ways to present the strategy. Because reinforcement enhances learning, we shall utilize all three presentations.

The first method is to determine an equation that gives the profit from the strategy as a function of the stock price when the position is closed. You will find that the equations are quite simple and build on skills covered in Chapters 3 and 4. The second method is a graphical analysis that uses the equations to construct graphs of the profit as a function of the stock price when the position is closed. The third approach is to use a specific numerical example to illustrate how the equations and graphs apply to real-world options. We continue with the same Digital Equipment options previously examined.

Keep in mind that there are options on other types of assets, such as commodities and bonds, and there are also options on futures contracts and interest rates, which we shall encounter in later chapters. The basic principles covered in this chapter apply in a fairly straightforward manner to those cases.

As with our earlier analyses of options, we require several symbols. For convenience and because there are a few new notations, the following section presents the complete set of symbols.

Terminology and Notation

C = current call price
P = current put price
S = current stock price
T = time to expiration as a fraction of a year
E = exercise price
S_T = stock price at option's expiration
Π = profit from the strategy

The following symbols indicate the number of calls, puts, or shares of stock:

N_C = number of calls
N_P = number of puts
N_S = number of shares of stock

As indicated in Chapter 2, the standard number of calls, puts, and shares is 100. For our purposes, it will not matter if we use a simple number such as 1 or 2. When working with the numerical examples, however, we shall assume a standard contract of options or block of stock, which, of course, means 100 options or shares.

The Profit Equations

One of the powerful features of the N_C, N_P, and N_S notation is that these numbers' signs indicate whether the position is long or short. For example,

> If $N_C > (<)$ 0, the investor is buying (writing) calls.
> If $N_P > (<)$ 0, the investor is buying (writing) puts.
> If $N_S > (<)$ 0, the investor is buying (selling short) stock.

To determine the profit from a particular strategy, we need only know how many calls, puts, and shares of stock are involved, whether the position is long or short, the prices at which the options or stock were purchased or written, and the prices at which the positions were closed. With calls held to the expiration date, we already know that the call will be worth its intrinsic value at expiration. Thus, the profit can be written as

$$\Pi = N_C[\text{Max}(0, S_T - E) - C].$$

Notice how the sign of N_C allows the equation to give the profit for both the call buyer and the call writer. For example, a buyer with one call, $N_C = 1$, has a profit of

$$\Pi = \text{Max}(0, S_T - E) - C.$$

For the writer with one call, $N_C = -1$, profit is

$$\Pi = -\text{Max}(0, S_T - E) + C.$$

For a put option, the profit can be written as

$$\Pi = N_P[\text{Max}(0, E - S_T) - P].$$

For a buyer with one put, $N_P = 1$,

$$\Pi = \text{Max}(0, E - S_T) - P.$$

For a writer with one put, $N_P = -1$,

$$\Pi = -\text{Max}(0, E - S_T) + P.$$

For a transaction involving only stock, the profit equation is simply

$$\Pi = N_S(S_T - S).$$

For a buyer of one share of stock, $N_S = 1$, profit is

$$\Pi = S_T - S.$$

For a short seller of one share of stock, $N_S = -1$, profit is

$$\Pi = -S_T + S.$$

These profit equations make it simple to determine the profit from any transaction. Take, for example, the equations for the call buyer and the put buyer. In both cases, the profit is simply the dollar amount received from exercising the option minus the dollar amount paid for the option. This figure is then multiplied by the number of options. For the call writer and put writer, the profit is the amount received as the premium minus the amount paid out from exercising the option. This figure is then multiplied by the number of options written. Similarly, the profit for a stock buyer is simply the price at which the stock is sold minus the price paid for the stock. This figure is then multiplied by the number of shares. For the short seller, the profit is the price received from the short sale minus the price paid for repurchasing the stock. This figure is then multiplied by the number of shares sold short. To keep the analysis as simple as possible, we shall ignore the interest foregone or implicitly earned on a long or short position in options or stock.

Finally, we shall often find ourselves using the terms **bull** and **bear,** which are part of the lingo of financial markets. A bull market is one in which the price goes up. A bear market is one in which the price goes down. A bullish investor believes a bull market is coming, and a bearish investor believes a bear market is coming.

Different Holding Periods

The cases described in the previous section are strategies in which the position is held until the option expires. Because the option has no time value remaining and sells for its intrinsic value, the profit is easy to determine. It is not necessary, however, that an option trader hold the position open until the option expires. The length of the investor's holding period can be any time interval desired. In the case of a position closed out prior to the option's expiration, it is necessary to determine at what price the option would sell. How would we go about doing this?

Remember that the available information would be the exercise price and the time remaining on the option. We would want to know at what

price the option would sell given a certain stock price. If the risk-free rate and an estimate of the variance of the return on the stock were available, we could use the Black-Scholes model. Here we shall assume this information is available, and we shall use the model to estimate the option's remaining time value to determine the profit from the strategy.

For illustrative purposes, we define three points in time: T_1, T_2, and T. We allow the investor to hold the position until either T_1, T_2, or all the way to expiration, T. The holding period from today until T_1 is the shortest. If an investor closes out the position at time T_1, the option will have a remaining time to expiration of $T - T_1$. The holding period from today until T_2 is of intermediate length. The investor who chooses it closes the option position with a remaining time to expiration of $T - T_2$. If the investor holds the position until expiration, the remaining time is $T - T = 0$.

Thus, the profit from a call position, if terminated at time T_1 before expiration and when the stock price is S_{T_1}, is written as

$$\Pi = N_C[C(S_{T_1}, T - T_1, E) - C],$$

where $C(S_{T_1}, T - T_1, E)$ is the value obtained from the Black-Scholes or any other appropriate call option pricing model using a stock price of S_{T_1} and a time to expiration of $T - T_1$. C is, of course, the original price of the call. The expression for puts is the same except that we use a P instead of a C and employ the Black-Scholes or any other appropriate put option pricing model to calculate $P(S_{T_1}, T - T_1, E)$. Similar expressions obviously apply when the position is closed at T_2.

Although the examples in this chapter use exchange-traded options, they are equally applicable to over-the-counter options. Although there is no specific market for liquidating over-the-counter options before expiration, the equivalent result can be obtained by simply creating a new option that offsets the old option. This procedure, of course, assumes that the writer does not default.

Assumptions

Several important assumptions underlie the analysis of option strategies.

First, we assume the stock pays no dividends. As we saw in Chapters 3 and 4, dividends can complicate option decisions. While including them here would not be especially difficult, we will intentionally omit them to keep the analysis simple. Where it is especially important, we will discuss the effect of dividends.

Second, we assume no taxes or transaction costs. These already have been covered and certainly are a consideration in option decisions, but they would add little to the analysis here. Where there are special tax and transaction cost factors, we provide an interpretation of their effects.

| TABLE 5.1 | Digital Equipment Option Data, June 12 | | | | | | |

Exercise Price	Calls			Puts			
	Jun	Jul	Oct	Jun	Jul	Oct
160	4 5/8	8 5/8	15 1/4	13/16	3 7/8	8 1/8
165	1 7/8	5 3/4	13 1/4	2 15/16	6	8 1/8
170	1/2	3 3/4	10 3/4	6 1/2	8 1/2	9 3/4
175	1/16	2 3/8	8 1/2	NA	NA	NA

Current stock price: 164
Expirations: June 19, July 17, October 16
Risk-free rates: .0473 (Jun); .0521 (Jul); .0574 (Oct)

Recall that we have been analyzing the Digital Equipment options in previous chapters. For convenience, Table 5.1 repeats those data.

Now let us move on to analyzing the strategies. The first group of strategies we shall examine are transactions involving stock.

Stock Transactions

Because combining stocks with options is sometimes an attractive strategy, it is important that we first establish the framework for stocks.

Buy Stock

The simplest transaction is the purchase of stock. The profit equation is

$$\Pi = N_S(S_T - S) \text{ given that } N_S > 0.$$

For illustrative purposes, let $N_S = 100$, a single round lot of stock. Figure 5.1 shows how the profit from this transaction varies with the stock price when the position is closed. The transaction is profitable if the Digital Equipment stock ultimately is sold at a price higher than $164, the price paid for the stock. Dividends would lower this breakeven by the amount of the dividends, while transaction costs would raise it by the amount of those costs.

Sell Short Stock

The short sale of stock is the mirror image of the purchase of stock. The profit equation is

$$\Pi = N_S(S_T - S) \text{ given that } N_S < 0.$$

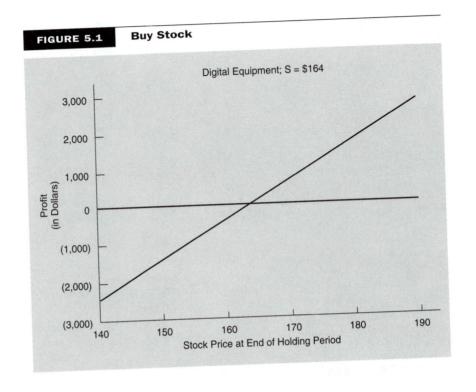

FIGURE 5.1   **Buy Stock**

Digital Equipment; S = $164

In this example, let $N_S = -100$, which means that 100 shares have been sold short. Figure 5.2 shows how the profit from the short sale varies with the price of the Digital Equipment stock at the end of the investor's holding period. Short selling is a strategy undertaken in anticipation of a bear market. The investor borrows the stock from the broker, sells it at $164, and repurchases at—hopefully—a lower price.[1] If the shares are repurchased at less than $164, the transaction earns a profit. As Figure 5.2 shows, selling short has the potential for unlimited losses if the investor guesses wrong and the stock price rises.

Now we turn to the first of the option strategies—the call transactions.

Call Option Transactions

There are two types of call option transactions. We first examine the strategy of buying a call.

---

[1] Any dividends paid while the stock is sold short go to whoever purchased the stock from the short seller. In addition, the short seller must pay the broker the amount of the dividends.

FIGURE 5.2   **Sell Short Stock**

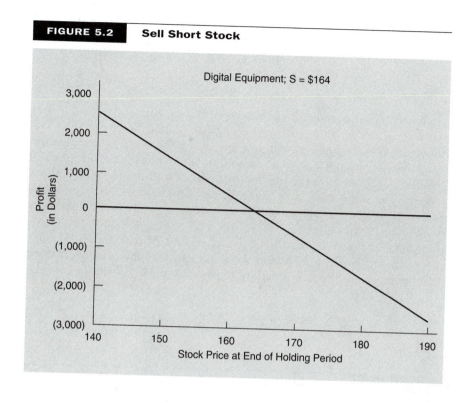

Digital Equipment; S = $164

Buy a Call

The profit from a call option purchase is

$$\Pi = N_C[\text{Max}(0, S_T - E) - C] \text{ given that } N_C > 0.$$

Consider the case where the number of calls purchased is simply 1 ($N_C = 1$). Suppose the stock price at expiration is less than or equal to the exercise price so that the option expires out-of-the-money. What is the profit from the call? Since the call expires unexercised, the profit is simply $-C$. The call buyer incurs a loss equal to the premium paid for the call.

Suppose the call option ends up in-the-money. Then the call buyer will exercise the call, buying the stock for E and selling it for S_T, which will net a profit of $S_T - E - C.$[2] These results are summarized as follows:

---

[2]The stock need not be sold for this result to hold. The call buyer can retain the stock worth S_T or convert it to cash. An even better strategy would be to sell the call an instant before it expires. At that time it should have little, if any, time value left. This would avoid the high transaction cost of taking delivery of the stock.

$$\Pi = S_T - E - C \qquad \text{if } S_T > E$$

$$\Pi = - C \qquad \text{if } S_T \leq E.$$

Figure 5.3 illustrates this transaction for the Digital Equipment July 165 call, which sells for $5.75. The call has limited downside risk. The maximum possible loss for a single contract is $575, which is the premium times 100. At any stock price at expiration less than the exercise price of 165, the call buyer loses the maximum amount. If the stock price is above 165, the loss will be less than $575. Losses, however, are incurred if the stock price is below a critical stock price, which we shall call the **breakeven stock price** at expiration.

Notice in Figure 5.3 that the breakeven stock price is above the exercise price and between $170 and $175. We can find the breakeven stock price at expiration by simply setting to zero the profit for the case where

| FIGURE 5.3 | Buy Call |

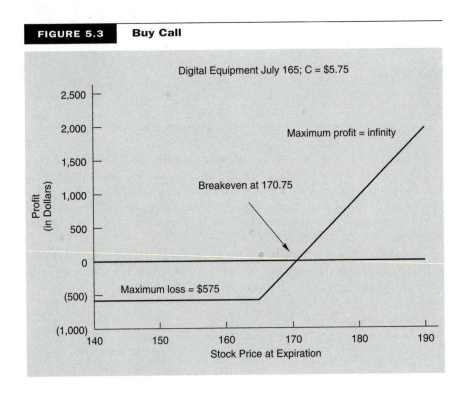

stock price exceeds exercise price. We then solve for the breakeven stock price, S_T^*. Thus,

$$\Pi = S_T^* - E - C = 0.$$

Solving for S_T^* gives

$$S_T^* = E + C.$$

The breakeven stock price at expiration, then, is the exercise price plus the call price. The call premium, C, is the amount already paid for the call. To break even, the call buyer must exercise the option at a price high enough to recover the option's cost. For every dollar by which the stock price at expiration exceeds the exercise price, the call buyer gains a dollar. Therefore, the stock price must exceed the exercise price by C dollars for the call buyer to recover the cost of the option. In this problem, the breakeven stock price at expiration is $165 + $5.75 = $170.75.

Buying a call is a bullish strategy that has a limited loss (the call premium) and an unlimited potential gain.

Notice how the call option offers the buyer a potentially unlimited profit while restricting the loss to the amount paid for the option. Although the likelihood of abnormally large profits is minimal, it is comforting to know that the potential loss is small. This makes the purchase of a call a particularly attractive strategy for those with limited budgets who wish to "play the market" while limiting their losses to a level that will not wipe them out.

THE CHOICE OF EXERCISE PRICE   Usually several options with the same expirations but different strike prices are available. Which option should we buy? There is no unambiguous answer.

Figure 5.4 compares the profit graphs for the three Digital Equipment July calls with strike prices of 160, 165, and 170. There are advantages and disadvantages to each. First, compare the 165, which we previously examined, with the 170. If we choose a higher strike price, the gain if the stock price rises will be less. However, because the call with the higher exercise price commands a lower premium, the loss if the stock price falls will be smaller. The breakeven for the 170 is E + C = 170 + 3.75 = 173.75, which is higher than that for the 165.

Buying a call with a lower exercise price has a greater maximum loss but greater upside gains.

If we choose the 160 over the 165, we have the potential for a greater profit if the stock price at expiration is higher. Also, the breakeven is E + C = 160 + 8.625 = 168.625. If the market is down, however, the loss will be greater. The potential loss is the full premium of $862.50. This is because the call with the lower exercise price will command a greater premium.

Thus, the choice of which option to purchase is not easy and depends on how confident the call buyer is about the market outlook. If one feels

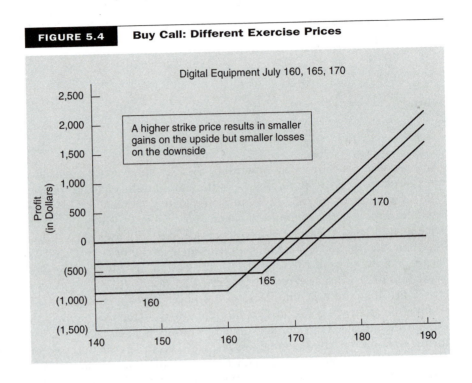

FIGURE 5.4   **Buy Call: Different Exercise Prices**

Digital Equipment July 160, 165, 170

A higher strike price results in smaller gains on the upside but smaller losses on the downside

strongly that the stock price will increase, the call with the lowest exercise price is preferable. Otherwise, a higher exercise price will minimize the potential loss.

THE CHOICE OF HOLDING PERIOD   The strategies previously examined assume the investor holds the option until the expiration date. Alternatively, the call buyer could sell the option prior to expiration. Let us look at what happens if a shorter holding period is chosen.

Recall that we plan to examine three holding periods. The shortest holding period involves the sale of the call at time T_1. The intermediate-length holding period is that in which the call is sold at time T_2. The longest holding period is that in which the option is held until expiration. If the option is sold at time T_1, the profit is the call price at the time of the sale minus the price originally paid for it. We can use the Black-Scholes model with a time to expiration of $T - T_1$ to estimate the price of the call for a broad range of possible stock prices and, thereby, determine the profit graph. Using the October 165 call, the three holding periods are (1) sell the call on July 24, T_1; (2) sell the call on September 4, T_2; and (3) hold the call until it expires on October 16, T.

For the shortest holding period, in which the position is closed on July 24, the time remaining is 84 days; that is, there are 84 days between July 24 and October 16. Thus, the call price will be based on a remaining time to expiration of $84/365 = .2301$. The call's time to expiration is $T - T_1 = .2301$. For the intermediate-length holding period, in which the position is held until September 4, the time remaining to expiration is 42 days. Thus, the time to expiration is $42/365 = .1151$ and $T - T_2 = .1151$. For the longest holding period, the time remaining is, of course, zero. The parameters used in the model are $E = 165$, $\sigma = .29$, and $r_c = .0574$.

The results are shown in Table 5.2. As an example, note that on July 24, at a stock price of $145, the call would have a Black-Scholes value of $2.4160. Since the investor paid $13.25 for the call, the profit per contract is $100(\$2.4160 - \$13.25) = -\$1,083.40$. If the stock price were $150, the call would be worth $3.7210 and the profit would be $100(\$3.7210 - \$13.25) = -\$952.90$. On September 4, at a stock price of $145, the call would be worth $.7728 and the profit would be $100(\$.7728 - \$13.25) = -\$1,247.72$. The remaining entries are computed in the same manner.

In Figure 5.5, the profit per contract is graphed as the dependent variable and the stock price at the end of the holding period is graphed as the independent variable. The graph indicates that the shortest holding period provides a higher profit for all stock prices at expiration. It would appear that the shorter the holding period, the greater the potential profit. This is because with a shorter holding period, the call can be sold to recover some of its remaining time value. The longer the call is held, the greater is the time value lost.

TABLE 5.2	Estimation of Black-Scholes Prices and Profits for Digital Equipment October 165 Call			
Position Closed at:	7/24		9/4	
Time to Expiration:	.2301		.1151	
Stock Price at End of Holding Period	Black-Scholes Call Price	Profit per Contract	Black-Scholes Call Price	Profit per Contract
140	$1.4788	-$1,177.12	$0.3438	-$1,290.62
145	2.4160	-1,083.40	0.7728	-1,247.72
150	3.7210	-952.90	1.5437	-1,170.63
155	5.4417	-780.83	2.7823	-1,046.77
160	7.6045	-564.55	4.5881	-866.19
165	10.2129	-303.71	7.0102	-623.98
170	13.2485	-.15	10.0380	-321.20
175	16.6756	342.56	13.6091	35.91
180	20.4470	719.70	17.6282	437.82
185	24.5100	1,126.00	21.9893	873.93
190	28.8113	1,556.13	26.5937	1,334.37

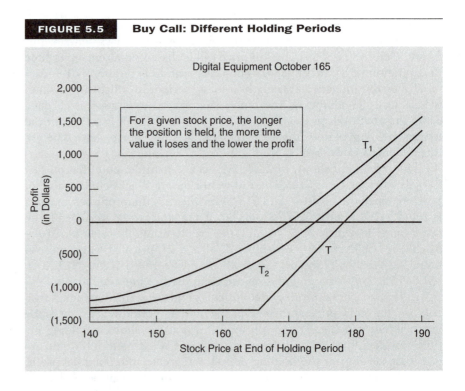

FIGURE 5.5   **Buy Call: Different Holding Periods**

Digital Equipment October 165

For a given stock price, the longer the position is held, the more time value it loses and the lower the profit

Profit (in Dollars)

Stock Price at End of Holding Period

For a given stock price, the longer a call is held, the more time value it loses and the lower the profit.

This seems to present a paradox: It suggests that to maximize profits, one should hold the option for the shortest time possible. Obviously option traders do not always use such short holding periods. What is missing from the explanation?

The answer is that the shorter holding period provides superior profits *for a given stock price.* The profit graph does not indicate the likelihood that the stock price will end up high or low. In fact, with a shorter holding period, the possible range of stock prices is much lower because there is less time for the stock price to move. The longer holding period, on the other hand, gives the stock price more time to increase.

This completes our discussion of the strategy of buying a call. We now turn to the strategy of writing a call.

Write a Call

An option trader who writes a call without concurrently owning the stock is said to be writing an **uncovered** or **naked call.** The reason for this nomenclature is that the position is a high-risk strategy, one with the potential for unlimited losses. The uncovered call writer undertakes the

obligation to sell stock not currently owned to the call buyer at the latter's request. The writer therefore may have to buy the stock at an unfavorable price. As a result, writing an uncovered call is a privilege restricted to those few traders with sufficient capital to risk. Since the brokerage firm must make up losses to the clearinghouse, it too is at risk. Therefore, a trader's broker must agree to handle the transaction—and that is likely to be done only for the best and wealthiest customers. Of course, traders owning seats on the exchange or low credit-risk institutions in the over-the-counter market are less restricted and can more easily write uncovered calls, but because of the high risk even they do so infrequently. Moreover, with stocks that pay dividends, the writer faces the risk of early exercise if the calls are American, as discussed in Chapter 3.

If writing an uncovered call is such a risky strategy, why should we examine it? The reason is that writing an uncovered call can be combined with other strategies, such as buying stock or another option, to produce a strategy with very low risk. Therefore, it is necessary to establish the results for the short call before combining it with other strategies.

Because the buyer's and writer's profits are the mirror images of each other, the profit equations and graphs are already familiar. The writer's profit is

$$\Pi = N_C[\text{Max}(0, S_T - E) - C] \text{ given that } N_C < 0.$$

Assume one call, $N_C = -1$. Then the profit is

$$\Pi = C \qquad\qquad \text{if } S_T \leq E$$
$$\Pi = -S_T + E + C \qquad \text{if } S_T > E.$$

Figure 5.6 illustrates the profit graph for the writer of 100 Digital Equipment July 165 calls at a price of $5.75. Note that the breakeven stock price for the writer must be the breakeven stock price for the buyer, $E + C = $170.75. The maximum loss for the buyer is also the maximum gain for the writer, $575. If the stock price ends up above the exercise price, the loss to the writer can be substantial—and, as is obvious from the graph, there is no limit to the possible loss in a bull market.

Selling a call is a bearish strategy that has a limited gain (the premium) and an unlimited loss.

THE CHOICE OF EXERCISE PRICE   Figure 5.7 compares the strategy of writing calls at different strike prices by showing the 160, 165, and 170 calls. Figure 5.7 is the mirror image of Figure 5.4. The greatest profit potential is in the 160, which has the highest premium, $862.50, but is accompanied by the greatest loss potential and the lowest breakeven, $E + C = 160 + 8.625 = 168.625$. This would be the highest-risk strategy. The 170 would have the lowest risk of the three with the highest breakeven, $E + C = 170 + 3.75 = 173.75$, but also the lowest profit potential, the $375 premium.

Selling a call with a lower exercise price has a greater maximum gain but greater upside losses.

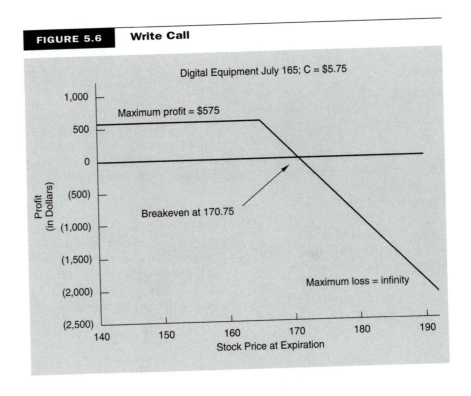

FIGURE 5.6   **Write Call**

Digital Equipment July 165; C = $5.75

Maximum profit = $575

Breakeven at 170.75

Maximum loss = infinity

Profit (in Dollars)

Stock Price at Expiration

For a given stock price, the longer a short call is maintained, the more time value it loses and the greater the profit.

THE CHOICE OF HOLDING PERIOD   Figure 5.8 illustrates the profit for the three possible holding periods previously described. These are the October 165 calls in which the holding period T_1 involves the repurchase of the call on July 24; T_2 assumes the call is repurchased on September 4; and T allows the call to be held until expiration, when it either is exercised or expires out-of-the-money.

Figure 5.8 is the mirror image of Figure 5.5. A writer repurchasing the call prior to expiration will have to pay for some of the remaining time value. Therefore, for the call writer, the profit is lowest with the shortest holding period *for a given stock price*. This is because the time value repurchased is greater with the shorter holding period. However, with a shorter holding period, the stock price is less likely to move substantially; thus, the range of possible profits is far smaller. If the investor holds the position until expiration, the profit may be greater but the stock will have had more time to move—perhaps unfavorably.

This completes our discussion of call buying and writing, which we see are mirror images of each other. We next turn to put option transactions.

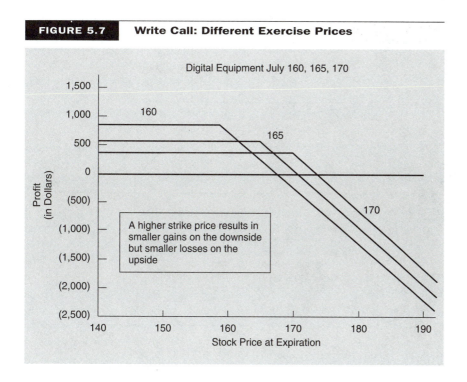

FIGURE 5.7   **Write Call: Different Exercise Prices**

Digital Equipment July 160, 165, 170

Put Option Transactions

Buy a Put

Buying a put is a strategy for a bear market. The potential loss is limited to the premium paid. The gain is also limited but can still be quite substantial. The profit from the purchase of a put is given by the equation

$$\Pi = N_P[\text{Max}(0, E - S_T) - P] \text{ given that } N_P > 0.$$

As in the example for calls, assume the purchase of a single put, $N_P = 1$. If the stock price at expiration ends up less than the exercise price, the put is in-the-money and is exercised. If the stock price at expiration is greater than or equal to the exercise price, the put ends up out-of-the-money. The profits are

$$\Pi = E - S_T - P \qquad \text{if } S_T < E$$
$$\Pi = -P \qquad\qquad\;\; \text{if } S_T \geq E.$$

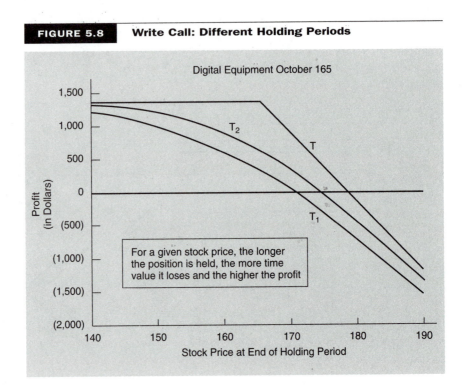

FIGURE 5.8   **Write Call: Different Holding Periods**

Digital Equipment October 165

Figure 5.9 illustrates the profits from the put-buying strategy for the Digital Equipment July 165 put with a premium of $6. The potential loss is limited to the premium paid, which in this case is $600. The profit is also limited, because there is a limit to how low the stock price can fall. The best outcome for a put buyer is for the company to go bankrupt. In that case, the stock would be worthless, $S_T = 0$, and the profit would be $E - P$. In this example, that would be $100(165 - 6) = 15,900$.

Notice that the breakeven occurs where the stock price is below the exercise price. Setting the profit equation for this case equal to zero gives

$$\Pi = E - S_T^* - P = 0.$$

Solving for the breakeven stock price, S_T^*, at expiration reveals that

$$S_T^* = E - P.$$

The put buyer must recover enough from the option's exercise to cover the premium already paid. For every dollar by which the option is in-the-money, the put buyer gains a dollar. Therefore, the stock price must fall

FIGURE 5.9   **Buy Put**

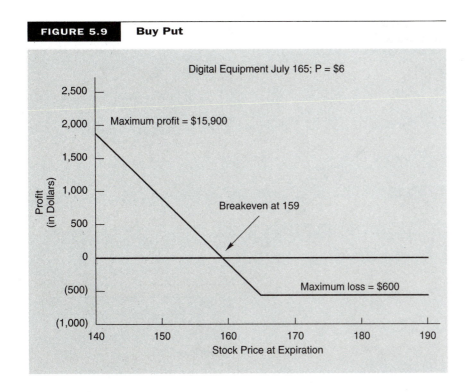

Digital Equipment July 165; P = $6

Maximum profit = $15,900

Breakeven at 159

Maximum loss = $600

below the exercise price by the amount of the premium. In this instance, this is $165 - 6 = 159$. For the investor to profit from this put, the stock price must fall to $159 or less by the expiration date.

Buying a put is an appropriate strategy when anticipating a bear market. The loss is limited to the premium paid, and the potential gain is quite high. Moreover, it is easier to execute a put transaction than a short sale. Puts need not be bought when the stock is on an uptick or zero-plus tick, and the amount paid for the put is far less than the margin on a short sale. More important, a put limits the loss while a short sale has an unlimited loss.

Buying a put is a bearish strategy that has a limited loss (the put premium) and a large, but limited, potential gain.

THE CHOICE OF EXERCISE PRICE   Figure 5.10 compares the profit graphs for puts with different strike prices using the July 160, 165, and 170 puts. The highest exercise price, the 170, has the highest premium; thus, the potential loss is greatest—in this case, $850. Its profit potential is highest, however, with a maximum possible profit of $100(170 - 8.50) = 16,150$ if the stock price at expiration is zero. The breakeven is $170 - 8.50 = 161.50$. The 160 has the lowest potential profit, $100(160 - 3.875) = 15,612.50$, and the lowest breakeven stock price, $160 - 3.875 = 156.125$. However, it also

Buying a put with a higher exercise price has a greater maximum loss but a greater downside gain.

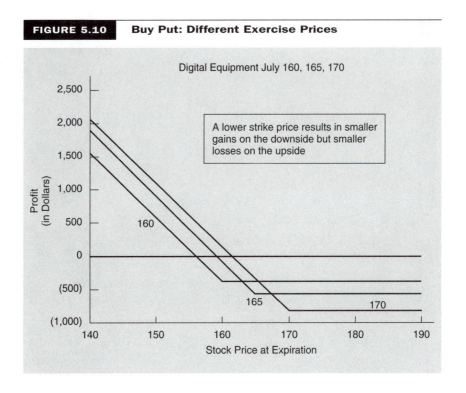

FIGURE 5.10   Buy Put: Different Exercise Prices

Digital Equipment July 160, 165, 170

A lower strike price results in smaller gains on the downside but smaller losses on the upside

has the lowest loss potential, its premium of $387.50. The put chosen will be determined by the risk the option trader is willing to take. The more aggressive trader will go for the maximum profit potential and choose the highest exercise price. The more conservative trader will choose a lower exercise price to limit the potential loss.

For a given stock price, the longer a put is held, the more time value it loses and the lower the profit. For European puts, this effect is reversed when the stock price is low.

THE CHOICE OF HOLDING PERIOD   Figure 5.11 compares the profit potential of the three holding periods for the October 165 put. The Black-Scholes option pricing model for European puts was used to estimate the put prices for the shorter holding periods.

By electing a shorter holding period—say, T_1—the put buyer can sell the put back for some of the time value originally purchased. If the put buyer holds until T_2, less time value will be recovered. If held until expiration, no remaining time value will be recaptured. As with the case for calls, the shorter holding periods show greater potential profit *for a given stock price*. However, they allow less time for the stock price to go down. Therefore, shorter holding periods are not necessarily inferior or superior to longer ones. The choice depends on the trader's forecast for the stock

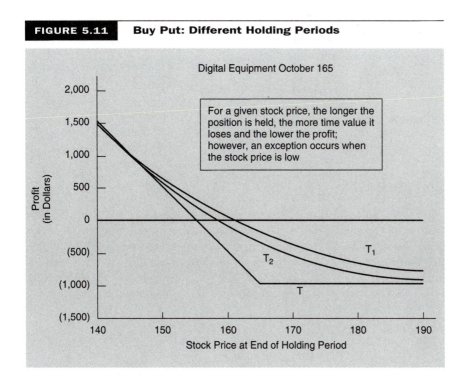

FIGURE 5.11   Buy Put: Different Holding Periods

Digital Equipment October 165

For a given stock price, the longer the position is held, the more time value it loses and the lower the profit; however, an exception occurs when the stock price is low

price, specifically how much it is expected to move, the direction, and in how much time.

An exception to the pattern of time value decay occurs at very low stock prices. Recall that it is possible that a European put can increase in value with a decrease in time. This point shows up in Figure 5.11 when the stock price is low and the profit curves cross over. Although the Digital Equipment option is actually American, we treated it as if it were European when we used the Black-Scholes model to estimate its value at the end of the holding period.

With an understanding of the put buyer's profit potential, it should be simple to examine the case for the put writer. As you probably expect, the put writer's position is the mirror image of the put buyer's.

Write a Put

The put writer is obligated to buy the stock from the put buyer at the exercise price. The put writer profits if the stock price goes up and the put therefore is not exercised, in which case the writer keeps the premium. If the stock price falls such that the put is exercised, the put writer is forced

to buy the stock at a price greater than its market value. For an American put this can, of course, occur prior to as well as at expiration.

The profit equation for the put writer is

$$\Pi = N_P[\text{Max}(0, E - S_T) - P] \text{ given that } N_P < 0.$$

Assume the simple case of a single short put, $N_P = -1$. The writer's profits are the mirror images of the buyer's:

$$\Pi = -E + S_T + P \qquad \text{if } S_T < E$$
$$\Pi = P \qquad\qquad\quad \text{if } S_T \geq E.$$

Selling a put is a bullish strategy that has a limited gain (the premium) and a large, but limited, potential loss.

Figure 5.12 illustrates the put writer's profits using the July 165 put written at a premium of $6. The writer's maximum potential profit is the buyer's maximum potential loss—the amount of the premium, $600. The maximum potential loss for the writer is limited, but like the buyer's maximum potential gain, it is a very large amount—here, $15,900. The breakeven stock price at expiration is the same as that for the buyer—E – P, or $159.

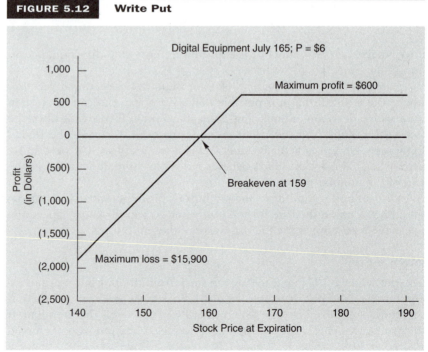

FIGURE 5.12   **Write Put**

Digital Equipment July 165; P = $6

THE CHOICE OF EXERCISE PRICE   Figure 5.13 compares the put writer's profits for different strike prices using the July puts. The highest strike price, 170, offers the greatest premium income and therefore the greatest profit potential. The maximum profit is $850, and the breakeven is 170 − 8.50 = 161.50. The risk, however, is greatest, since any losses will be larger in a bear market. The lowest strike price offers the lowest maximum profit—the premium income of $387.50—but also has the lowest breakeven—160 − 3.875 = 156.125—and the lowest loss if the market is down. Once again the range of exercise prices offers the put writer several choices for assuming various degrees of risk and expected reward.

Selling a put with a higher exercise price has a greater maximum gain but a greater downside loss.

THE CHOICE OF HOLDING PERIOD   Figure 5.14 compares the put writer's profits for different holding periods. Like the call writer, the put writer who chooses a shorter holding period makes a smaller profit or incurs a greater loss *for a given stock price.* This is because the writer buying back the put before expiration must pay for some of the remaining time value. The advantage to the writer, however, is that with a short holding period there is a much smaller probability of a large, unfavorable stock price move. Again the choice of holding period depends on the forecast

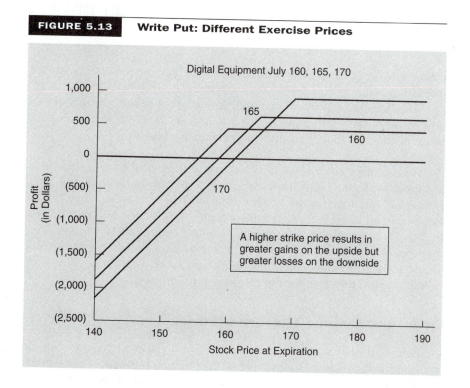

FIGURE 5.13   **Write Put: Different Exercise Prices**

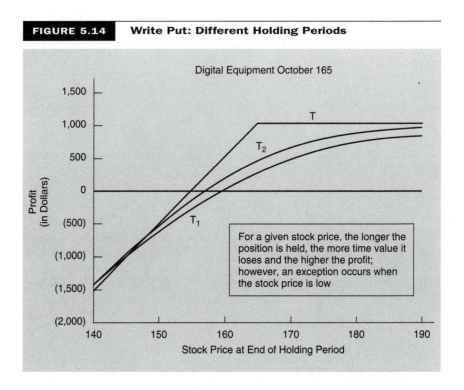

FIGURE 5.14   **Write Put: Different Holding Periods**

Digital Equipment October 165

For a given stock price, the longer the position is held, the more time value it loses and the higher the profit; however, an exception occurs when the stock price is low

For a given stock price, the longer a short put is maintained, the more time value it loses and the greater the profit. For European puts, this effect is reversed when the stock price is low.

for the market price and the time frame over which the writer expects that forecast to hold.

With European puts, we see that at low stock prices, the pattern of time value decay reverses itself. With American puts, the writer must be aware of the possibility that they will be exercised early.

We now have covered all of the simple strategies of buying stock, selling short stock, buying calls, writing calls, buying puts, and writing puts. Figure 5.15 summarizes the profit graphs of these strategies. They can be viewed as building blocks that are combined to produce other strategies. In fact, all of the remaining strategies are but combinations of these simple ones. The remainder of this chapter examines the strategies of combining calls with stock, combining puts with stock, replicating puts with calls and stock, and replicating calls with puts and stock.

Calls and Stock: The Covered Call

Chapter 4 showed that it is possible to form a riskless hedge by buying stock and writing calls. The number of calls written must exceed the number of shares, and the appropriate hedge ratio must be maintained

FIGURE 5.15   **Summary of Profit Graphs for Positions Held to Expiration**

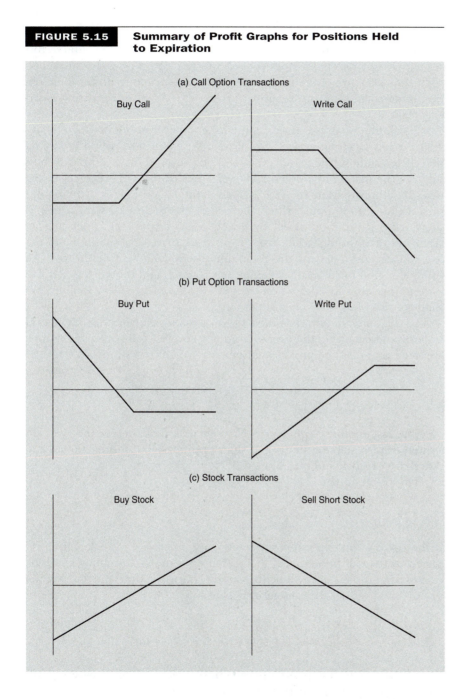

throughout the holding period. A simpler but nevertheless low-risk strategy involves writing one call for each share of stock owned. Although this strategy is not riskless, it does reduce the risk of holding the stock outright. It is also one of the most popular strategies among professional option traders. An investor executing this strategy is said to be writing a **covered call.**

Recall that we previously examined the uncovered call in which the investor writes a call on a stock not owned. We found the risk to be unlimited. If the option trader owns the stock, however, there is no risk of buying it in the market at a potentially high price. If the call is exercised, the investor simply delivers the stock. From another point of view, the holder of stock with no options written thereon is exposed to substantial risk of the stock price moving down. By writing a call against that stock, the investor reduces the downside risk. If the stock price falls substantially, the loss will be cushioned by the premium received for writing the call. Although in a bull market the call may be exercised and the stockholder will have to give up the stock, there are ways to minimize this possibility. We shall consider how to do this later.

Because we already examined the strategies of buying stock and writing calls, determining the profits from the covered call strategy is simple: We need only add the profit equations from these two strategies. Thus,

$$\Pi = N_S(S_T - S) + N_C[\text{Max}(0, S_T - E) - C]$$
$$\text{given that } N_S > 0, N_C < 0, \text{ and } N_S = -N_C.$$

The last requirement, $N_S = -N_C$, specifies that the number of calls written must equal the number of shares purchased. Consider the case of one share of stock and one short call, $N_S = 1$, $N_C = -1$.

The profit equation is

$$\Pi = S_T - S - \text{Max}[0, S_T - E] + C.$$

If the option ends up out-of-the-money, the loss on the stock will be reduced by the call premium. If the option ends up in-the-money, it will be exercised and the stock will be delivered. This will reduce the gain on the stock. These results are summarized as follows:

$$\Pi = S_T - S + C \qquad\qquad \text{if } S_T \leq E.$$
$$\Pi = S_T - S - S_T + E + C = E - S + C \qquad \text{if } S_T > E.$$

Notice that in the case where the call ends up out-of-the-money, the profit increases for every dollar by which the stock price at expiration exceeds the original stock price. In the case where the call ends up in-the-money, the profit is unaffected by the stock price at expiration.

These results are illustrated in Figure 5.16 for the Digital Equipment July 165 call written at a premium of $5.75. The dashed line is the profit from simply holding the stock. Notice that the covered call has a smaller loss on the downside but relinquishes the upside gain and has a lower breakeven. The maximum profit occurs when the stock price exceeds the exercise price; this profit is E − S + C, which in this example is 100(165 − 164 + 5.75) = 675. The maximum loss occurs if the stock price at expiration goes to zero. In that case, the profit will simply be −S + C, which is 100(−164 + 5.75) = −15,825.

A covered call reduces downside losses on the stock at the expense of upside gains.

The breakeven stock price occurs where the profit is zero. This happens when the call ends up out-of-the-money. Setting the profit equal to zero for the case where the call is out-of-the-money,

$$\Pi = S_T^* - S + C = 0,$$

and solving for S_T^* gives a breakeven of

$$S_T^* = S - C.$$

FIGURE 5.16   Covered Call

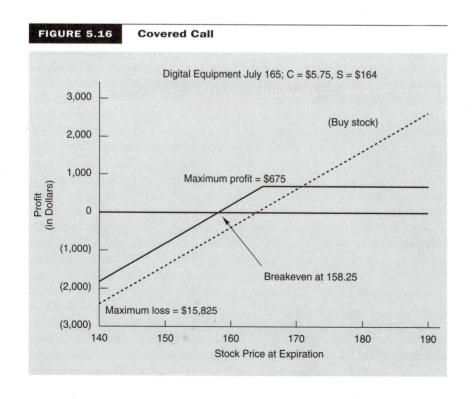

Digital Equipment July 165; C = $5.75, S = $164

(Buy stock)

Maximum profit = $675

Breakeven at 158.25

Maximum loss = $15,825

Profit (in Dollars)

Stock Price at Expiration

A covered call with a lower exercise price provides greater downside protection but a lower maximum gain on the upside.

Here the breakeven is 164 − 5.75 = 158.25. At any stock price above $158.25, this covered call is profitable. Another way to view this is that the covered call provides a profit at any stock price at expiration down to $158.25. Ownership of the stock without the protection of the call provides a profit only at a stock price above $164, the current stock price.

THE CHOICE OF EXERCISE PRICE   The covered call writer has a choice of calls at different strike prices. Figure 5.17 illustrates the profit graphs for the covered call using the Digital Equipment July calls with strike prices of 160, 165, and 170. Because the highest strike price, the 170, has the lowest premium with which to cushion a stock price decrease, it offers the least amount of protection for the covered call writer. It offers the maximum profit potential, however, because the high strike price allows the writer to receive a greater amount for the stock if the call is exercised. In this example, the 170 call has a maximum profit of $100(170 − 164 + 3.75) = 975$. The breakeven is 164 − 3.75 = 160.25. The minimum profit, which occurs if the stock price at expiration is zero, is $100(−164 + 3.75) = −16,025$.

In contrast, the lowest exercise price, the 160, offers the most protection. Because it has the highest premium, the cushion on the downside is

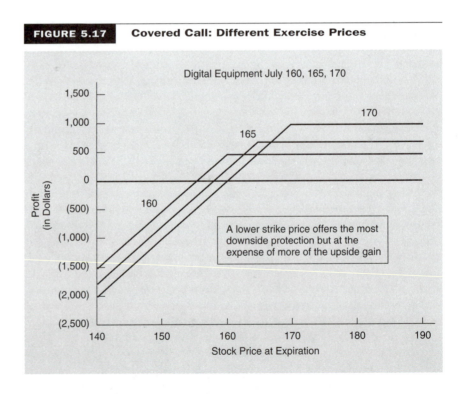

FIGURE 5.17   **Covered Call: Different Exercise Prices**

Digital Equipment July 160, 165, 170

A lower strike price offers the most downside protection but at the expense of more of the upside gain

greater. However, if the stock moves up and the call is exercised, the writer will receive a lower price for the stock. The maximum profit is $100(160 - 164 + 8.625) = 462.50$. The breakeven stock price is $164 - 8.625 = 155.375$. The minimum profit, which occurs at a stock price at expiration of zero, is $100(-164 + 8.625) = -15,537.50$.

Writing a covered call at the lowest exercise price is the most conservative choice, because the loss on the downside is lower; however, the gain on the upside is also lower. Writing a covered call at the highest exercise price is a riskier strategy, because the upside profit potential is greater but the downside protection is less. Regardless of the exercise price chosen, writing a covered call is far less risky than owning the stock outright. The premium on the call, no matter how large or small, cushions the stockholder against a loss on the stock in a falling market.

THE CHOICE OF HOLDING PERIOD   Figure 5.18 illustrates the October 165 covered call in which the position is closed out prior to expiration. Again the Black-Scholes model was used to estimate the call's value in the manner described earlier in the chapter. The shortest holding period, T_1, which corresponds to closing out the position on July 24, gives the smallest

For a given stock price, the longer a covered call is maintained, the more time value is lost and the greater the profit.

FIGURE 5.18   Covered Call: Different Holding Periods

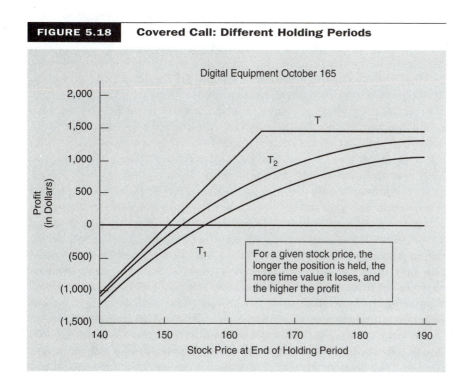

Digital Equipment October 165

For a given stock price, the longer the position is held, the more time value it loses, and the higher the profit

profit *for a given stock price.* This is because the writer closes out the position by buying back the call. If there is time remaining, the writer must buy back some of the remaining time value. If a longer holding period is used, the remaining time value, which must be bought back, is less. If held to expiration, there is no time value remaining for repurchase.

Does this suggest that covered call writers should use short holding periods? Not necessarily. Again it depends on the covered call writer's forecast for the stock price and the time frame over which it applies. The investor might earn a larger profit by holding the position until expiration, but such a long holding period will also give the stock price more time to move down. A shorter holding period increases the likelihood that the stock price will not move much, and this could be more profitable for the covered call writer.

Some General Considerations with Covered Calls

As indicated earlier, covered call writing is a very popular strategy among professional option traders. This is because it is a low-risk strategy—much less risky than buying stock or options outright. There are also studies that showed that covered call writing is more profitable then simply buying options. This should make one wonder why everyone does not simply write covered calls. Obviously, if that occurred the prices of the calls would fall so low that the strategy would no longer be attractive. This superior performance of covered call writing is most likely attributable to the fact that the studies covered years in which listed options were new. Veterans of those early years widely agree that the public avidly purchased these new instruments as a cheap and exciting way to play the market. Little regard was paid to whether the calls were fairly priced. In fact, option pricing theory itself was in its infancy, and little was known about pricing options. Public demand, coupled with ignorance, most likely kept call prices artificially high and led to substantial profits for clever call writers in those years. Although there have been no similar studies recently, it seems unlikely that such superior performance could be sustained.

It is commonly believed that writing covered calls is a way to pick up extra income from a stock. However, writing a call imposes on the stockholder the possibility of having to sell the stock at an inconvenient or unsuitable time. If the stock price goes up, the covered call writer will be unable to participate in the resulting gains and the stock will likely be called away by exercise. If, however, the call is exercised early, the writer will be no worse off from a financial perspective. The profit will still be $E - S + C$, the maximum expected profit at expiration. In fact, the writer actually will be better off, because this amount will be available before expiration.

Suppose the covered writer does not want to lose the stock by exercise. One way to minimize the likelihood of exercise is to write calls at a high exercise price so that the call is deep-out-of-the-money. This reduces the

chance of the call ending up in-the-money. Suppose the stock price starts upward and it appears that the out-of-the-money call will move in-the-money and thus increase the chance of exercise. The writer can then buy the call back and write a new call at a higher exercise price, a strategy called *rolling up*. If the stock price continues to rise, the writer can buy back the new call and write another one at an even higher exercise price. In this manner, the covered call writer establishes a position in which the exercise price will always stay well ahead of the stock price. The purpose of this strategy is to avoid exercise and keep the stock in the portfolio. This may be important to someone who likes to hold on to certain stocks for various reasons. The disadvantage of this strategy is that the high exercise price means a lower premium and less downside protection. Also, transaction costs from the frequent rollovers will be higher. These factors can be weighed against the inconvenience of exercise and the investor's willingness to give up the stock.

Many institutional investors also use a covered call writing strategy. Those holding large portfolios of stocks that are expected to gain little value often believe that their portfolios' performances will improve if they write calls against the stock they own. But covered call writing—or any other strategy—cannot be the gate to unlimited wealth. In fact, it is more likely to *reduce* the portfolio's return, because it decreases its risk. It therefore should be viewed as a risk-reducing rather than return-enhancing strategy.

As one might imagine, the opposite of a long-stock–short-call position is to buy a call to protect a short-stock position. The results obtained from this strategy are the mirror image of the covered call results. We explore this strategy in an end-of-chapter problem.

Another option strategy that can be used to reduce the risk of holding stock is the protective put—the topic of the next section.

Puts and Stock: The Protective Put

As discussed in the previous section, a stockholder who wants protection against falling stock prices may elect to write a call. In a strong bull market, the stock is likely to be called away by exercise. One way to obtain protection against a bear market and still be able to participate in a bull market is to buy a **protective put;** that is, the investor simply buys stock and buys a put. The put provides a minimum selling price for the stock.

The profit equation for the protective put is found by simply adding the profit equations for the strategies of buying stock and buying a put. From this we get

$$\Pi = N_S(S_T - S) + N_P[Max(0, E - S_T) - P]$$
$$\text{given that } N_S > 0, N_P > 0, \text{ and } N_S = N_P.$$

As in previous examples, assume one share of stock and one put, $N_S = 1$, $N_P = 1$. If the stock price ends up above the exercise price, the put will expire out-of-the-money. If the stock price ends up less than the exercise price, the put will be exercised. The results are as follows:

$$\Pi = S_T - S - P \qquad\qquad\qquad\qquad\qquad \text{if } S_T \geq E$$
$$\Pi = S_T - S + E - S_T - P = E - S - P \qquad \text{if } S_T < E.$$

The protective put works like an insurance policy. When you buy insurance for an asset such as a house, you pay a premium that assures you that in the event of a loss, the insurance policy will cover at least some of the loss. If the loss does not occur during the policy's life, you simply lose the premium. Similarly, the protective put is insurance for a stock. In a bear market, a loss on the stock is somewhat offset by the put's exercise. This is like filing a claim on the insurance policy. In a bull market, the insurance is not needed and the gain on the upside is reduced by the premium paid.

From the above equations, it is clear that the profit in a bull market varies directly with the stock price at expiration. The higher S_T is, the higher is the profit, Π. In a bear market, the profit is not affected by the stock price at expiration. Whatever losses are incurred on the stock are offset by gains on the put. The profit graph for a protective put is illustrated in Figure 5.19 for the Digital Equipment July 165 put purchased at a premium of $6. The dashed line is the profit from simply holding the stock. Notice that the protective put has a smaller downside loss and smaller upside gain as well as a higher breakeven.

A protective put sets a maximum downside loss at the expense of some of the upside gain. It is equivalent to an insurance policy on the asset.

The maximum loss on a protective put is found as the profit if the stock price at expiration ends up below the exercise price. Since the profit equation shows that this is $E - S - P$, the Digital Equipment protective put has a minimum profit of $100(165 - 164 - 6) = -500$. Clearly there is no maximum gain, because the investor profits dollar for dollar with the excess of the stock price over the exercise price. Notice how the graph of the protective put is the same shape as that of a long call. This is due to put-call parity.

The breakeven stock price at expiration occurs when the stock price at expiration exceeds the exercise price. Setting this profit to zero and solving for the breakeven stock price, S_T^*, gives

$$\Pi = S_T^* - S - P = 0$$
$$S_T^* = P + S.$$

Thus, breakeven occurs at a stock price at expiration equal to the original stock price plus the premium. This should be apparent, since the stock price must rise above the original stock price by an amount sufficient to

FIGURE 5.19   Protective Put

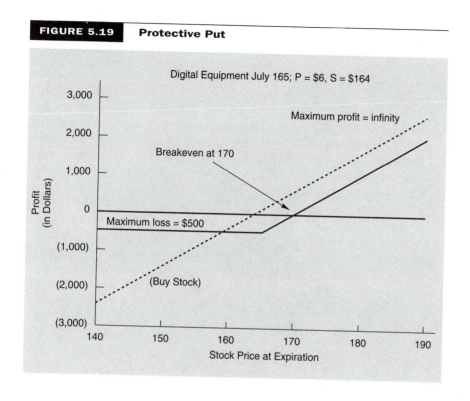

Digital Equipment July 165; P = $6, S = $164

Maximum profit = infinity

Breakeven at 170

Maximum loss = $500

(Buy Stock)

Profit (in Dollars) — vertical axis: 3,000; 2,000; 1,000; 0; (1,000); (2,000); (3,000)

Stock Price at Expiration — horizontal axis: 140, 150, 160, 170, 180, 190

cover the premium paid for the put. In this example, the breakeven stock price at expiration is 6 + 164 = 170.

THE CHOICE OF EXERCISE PRICE: THE DEDUCTIBLE DECISION   The amount of coverage the protective put provides is affected by the chosen exercise price. This is equivalent to the insurance problem of deciding on the deductible. A higher deductible means that the insured bears more of the risk and thus pays a lower premium. With a lower deductible, the insurer bears more of the risk and charges a higher premium. With a protective put, a higher exercise price is equivalent to a lower deductible.

Figure 5.20 illustrates the comparative performances of Digital Equipment protective puts at different exercise prices. The 170 put gives the stockholder the right to sell the stock at $170 per share. The breakeven on this strategy is 164 + 8.5 = 172.5. This will be the most expensive insurance but will provide the greatest coverage, with a minimum profit of 100(170 − 164 − 8.5) = −250. If the stock price rises and the put is not needed, the gain from the stock will be lower than it would be with a lower exercise price. This is because the more expensive premium was paid but the insurance was not needed.

A protective put with a higher exercise price provides greater downside protection, but lower upside gains.

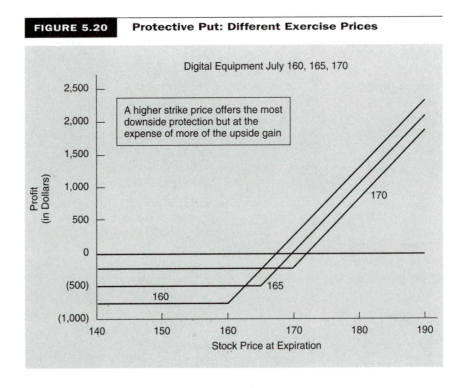

FIGURE 5.20   **Protective Put: Different Exercise Prices**

Digital Equipment July 160, 165, 170

A higher strike price offers the most downside protection but at the expense of more of the upside gain

Profit (in Dollars)

Stock Price at Expiration

The lowest exercise price, the 160, provides the least coverage. The breakeven is $164 + 3.875 = 167.875$. The minimum profit is $100(160 - 164 - 3.875) = -787.50$. If the market rises, the less expensive insurance will reduce the gain by a smaller amount.

As you can see, selecting an exercise price is like choosing a deductible: The investor must balance the willingness to assume some of the risk against the ability to pay for the coverage.

THE CHOICE OF HOLDING PERIOD   Figure 5.21 illustrates the profit for different holding periods for the Digital Equipment October 165 protective put. The shorter holding period provides more coverage *for a given stock price.* This is because with a shorter holding period, the investor can sell back the put before expiration and recover some of the time value previously purchased. With a longer holding period, there will be less time value to recover. Again, however, we see an exception to this rule when the stock price is low. By holding all the way to expiration, there will be no time value to recover.

The choice of holding period depends on the investor's view of the probable stock price moves and the period over which they are likely to

For a given stock price, the longer a protective put is held, the more time value is lost and the lower the profit. For European puts, this effect is reversed when the stock price is low.

FIGURE 5.21   **Protective Put: Different Holding Periods**

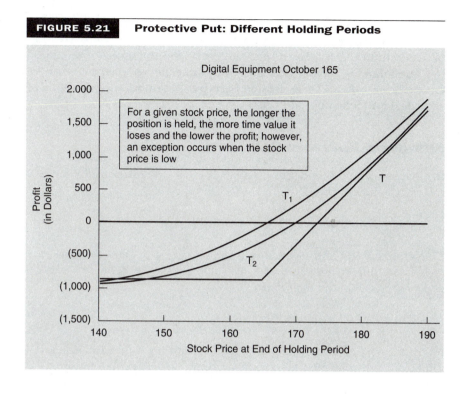

Digital Equipment October 165

For a given stock price, the longer the position is held, the more time value it loses and the lower the profit; however, an exception occurs when the stock price is low

occur. If a large stock price move is needed to provide a profit, a longer holding period will allow more time for the stock price to move. A shorter holding period is preferable if the stock price is not expected to move much. However, the stock price must increase by at least the amount of the premium for the investor to break even. Therefore, the investor must weigh the likelihood of this occurring over the holding period.

The protective put strategy can also be turned around so that a short sale of stock is protected by a short put, or vice versa. The results would be the mirror image of those presented here. We examine this strategy as an end-of-chapter problem.

We have seen that investors holding stock can use both the covered call and the protective put to reduce risk. Which strategy is preferable? The answer depends on the investor's outlook for the market. If a bull market is believed more likely to occur, the protective put will allow the investor to participate in it. However, the protective put will be more expensive, because the investor must pay for it. The covered call writer actually receives money for writing the call. Thus, there are advantages and disadvantages to each strategy that one must carefully weigh before making a decision.

The role of put options in providing insurance is explored more thoroughly in Chapter 15. That material will show how puts, calls, Treasury bills, and futures can be used to create portfolio insurance.

The following section examines some strategies in which puts can be created from calls and calls created from puts. For obvious reasons, these are called **synthetic puts** and **calls.**

Synthetic Puts and Calls

In Chapters 3 and 4 we discussed put-call parity, the relationship between call prices and put prices:

$$P + S = C + Ee^{-r_cT}.$$

The left-hand side of the equation is the value of a put and the stock; the right-hand side is the value of a call and a risk-free bond. We can rearrange put-call parity such that

$$P = C - S + Ee^{-r_cT},$$

where the left-hand side is the value of a put and the right-hand side is the value of a portfolio that behaves like a put. That portfolio consists of a long call, a short sale of stock, and the purchase of a pure discount bond, or making of a loan, with a face value equal to the exercise price. Note that the signs in front of the prices in the equations indicate whether we are long or short in puts, calls, or stocks. Long positions are represented by plus (+) signs and short positions by minus (−) signs.

We actually need not buy a bond to replicate a put. The term representing the present value of the exercise price is simply a constant value that does not affect the shape of the profit graph. For example, consider a **synthetic put,** which consists of long calls and the short sale of an equal number of shares of stock. The profit is simply

$$\Pi = N_C[\text{Max}(0, S_T - E) - C] + N_S(S_T - S)$$
$$\text{given that } N_C > 0, N_S < 0, \text{ and } N_C = -N_S.$$

Letting the number of shares and the number of calls both be 1, the profits for the two possible ranges of stock prices at expiration are

$$\Pi = -C - S_T + S \qquad\qquad \text{if } S_T \leq E$$
$$\Pi = S_T - E - C - S_T + S = S - E - C \qquad \text{if } S_T > E.$$

If the stock price at expiration is equal to or below the exercise price, the profit will vary inversely with the stock price at expiration. If the stock

price at expiration is above the exercise price, the profit will not be affected by the stock price at expiration. This is the same general outcome provided by a put, hence the name synthetic put.

We can see the difference between the actual put and the synthetic put from the put-call parity formula. In put-call parity, one replicates the put by buying a call, selling short a stock, and buying a pure discount bond with a face value equal to the exercise price. To replicate a put precisely, we need to buy that pure discount bond. In practice, however, most traders simply buy the call and sell short the stock.

Figure 5.22 compares the synthetic put and its actual counterpart using the Digital Equipment October 165 options. The synthetic put has a profit of

$$-C - S_T + S \quad \text{if} \ S_T \leq E$$
$$S - E - C \quad \text{if} \ S_T > E.$$

The actual put has a profit of

$$E - S_T - P \quad \text{if} \ S_T \leq E$$
$$-P \quad \text{if} \ S_T > E.$$

FIGURE 5.22 **Synthetic and Actual Put**

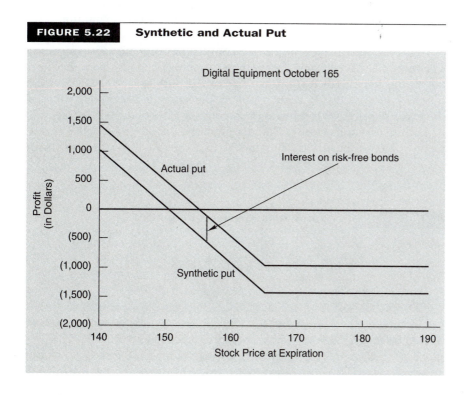

The difference is the profit of the actual put minus the profit of the synthetic put, E − P + C − S, in either case. From put-call parity, we can substitute C − S + Ee$^{-r_cT}$ for P. The difference is then

$$E(1 - e^{-r_cT}),$$

which is the interest lost by not buying the pure discount bond.

There are two reasons why someone would want to use a synthetic put. First, there once were restrictions on the listing of puts on the exchanges; puts were phased in slowly. There was also a moratorium on new option listings that started soon after the first few puts were listed in 1977. This prevented more puts from being listed until the moratorium was lifted in 1980. During the period, an investor could have created a synthetic put to use in lieu of the actual put.

Second, one can use a synthetic put to take advantage of mispricing in the relationship between puts and calls. For example, the difference between the actual put price, P, and the value of the synthetic put, C − S, should be Ee$^{-r_cT}$; however, if P − (C − S) is greater than Ee$^{-r_cT}$, either the actual put is overpriced or the synthetic put is underpriced. The investor should sell the actual put and buy the synthetic put by purchasing the call and selling short the stock. This strategy often is called a **reverse conversion** or simply **reversal.** It will generate a cash outflow at expiration of E, as shown in Table 5.3.

This property makes the reverse conversion resemble a risk-free loan. The money received when the position is opened is (1) S (from the short sale of the stock), (2) P (from the sale of the put), and (3) −C (from the purchase of the call). If, as we assumed, this exceeds the present value of the exercise price, we can invest the amount S + P − C at the risk-free rate, r_c, until the options expire. The accumulated future value of this investment will then exceed E. This means that we can repay the loan with

---

TABLE 5.3	Payoffs from Reverse Conversion

Position	*Payoffs from Portfolio Given Stock Price at Expiration*	
	$S_T \leq E$	$S_T > E$
Long call	0	$S_T - E$
Short stock	$-S_T$	$-S_T$
Short put	$-E + S_T$	0
	$-E$	$-E$

money left over.[3] Of course, investing this money at the risk-free rate is equivalent to buying the risk-free bonds.

We can also create **synthetic calls** by buying stock and an equal number of puts. It should be apparent that this strategy is like a call, because it is nothing more than a protective put. The graph for the protective put is, as we saw earlier, the same type of graph as that for a call.

Many investors buy the synthetic call and write the actual call when the latter is overpriced. This strategy is called a **conversion** and is used to exploit mispricing in the relationship between put and call prices.

Synthetic puts and calls can be constructed from options and stock.

The accompanying Excel spreadsheet stratlyz1.xls calculates and graphs the profits from any combination of positions in the asset and up to six different options on the same asset. Positions can be held to expiration or closed out prior to expiration.

Summary

This chapter examined the basic option strategies. Designing the profit equations and graphs is a simple extension of material learned in previous chapters. For positions held to expiration, it is necessary only to determine the intrinsic values of puts and calls. If we elect not to hold the options until expiration, we can use the Black-Scholes model to estimate their prices. The material in this chapter, however, is basic. Option investors should always be aware of the factors that lead to early exercise, as well as tax and dividend implications. Moreover, transaction costs will lower profits, increase losses, and make breakevens higher for bullish strategies and lower for bearish strategies. The more options and stocks employed, the greater will be the transaction costs. Understanding how option transactions produce payoffs is only the first step toward using options. Unfortunately, there are no simple or even complex formulas for predicting the future. We have seen, however, that options can be used to modify risk—to increase or decrease it as needed.

The strategies examined here form the building blocks for exploring more exotic strategies. Chapter 6 looks at these advanced strategies, which combine many of the strategies discussed here to produce a much more diverse set of opportunities.

---

[3]If the options are American and the short put is exercised early, however, we will have to pay out E dollars prior to expiration. Thus, it is possible that the interest earned on the cash inflow will be insufficient to make the required payout.

SOFTWARE DEMONSTRATION 5.1   **Examining the Outcomes of Option Strategies Using the Excel Spreadsheet stratlyz1.xls**

The Excel spreadsheet stratlyz1.xls, which operates in Windows 3.1 or Windows 95 and requires Excel 5.0 or higher, calculates and graphs the profits from option strategies with up to six options and positions in the underlying asset. No installation is

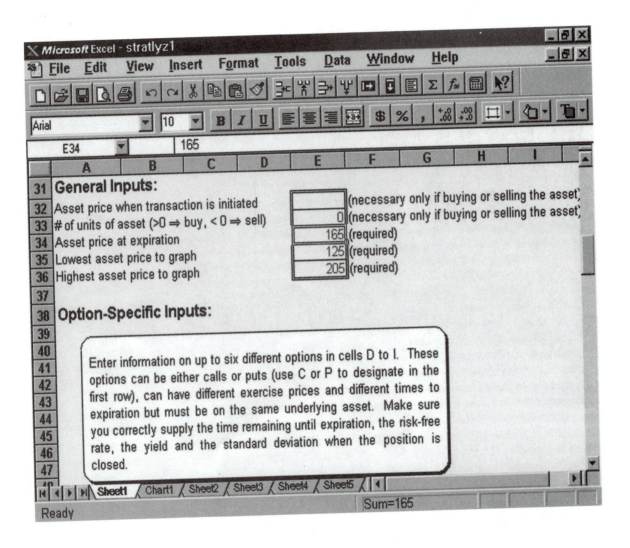

necessary; simply place the file in whatever directory you prefer or access it directly from the 3.5-inch diskette provided in this book. To use the software, do the following:

1. Make sure you are in Windows 3.1 or Windows 95.

2. Run Excel 5.0 or higher.

3. Open the file stratlyz1.xls.

Now let us do an example. Assume you wish to find the results for a simple strategy of buying one Digital Equipment July 165 call. The call is priced at $5.75. The DEC stock is at 164. First let us examine the strategy of holding the position until expiration and then we shall close the position prior to expiration.

Observe the section labeled **General Inputs** in the accompanying figure : It requests five pieces of information. Each cell that will accept input has a double-line border and the values are in blue. The first input item is the asset price when the transaction is initiated, but this is required only if your strategy includes buying or selling short the asset. Insert a blank for our ex-

ample. The next input is the number of units of the asset, with a positive number for buying and a negative number for selling. Insert a zero or leave it blank. The next input is the asset price at expiration. This information is required in order to center the graph. Although you obviously do not know where the asset will be at expiration, you can choose any price. Let us choose the exercise price of 165. The graph will be centered around this price and the overall profit of the strategy for this particular price will be calculated and shown in the section below. The next two required inputs are the lowest and highest asset prices to graph. This simply defines a range over which the graph will be drawn. Let us arbitrarily choose a range of $40 on either side so the minimum is 125 and the maximum is 205.

The next section is called **Option-Specific Inputs:** Here you can enter information on up to six options that differ by either time to expiration or exercise price and can be either calls or puts. Insert blanks or zeros for options not used. All options must be on the same underlying asset. In the first row of the cell, designate the type of option with either a "C" or a "P" for call or put. We should insert a "C" for our call purchase strategy. The next row should contain the exercise price, 165 in our case. The next row should contain the original option price. This is the price at which the option is either purchased or sold when the transaction is initiated, which is $5.75 in this example. The next line contains the number of options with a positive number for buying and a negative number for selling. Let us insert "100" for a standard long contract. The next four input

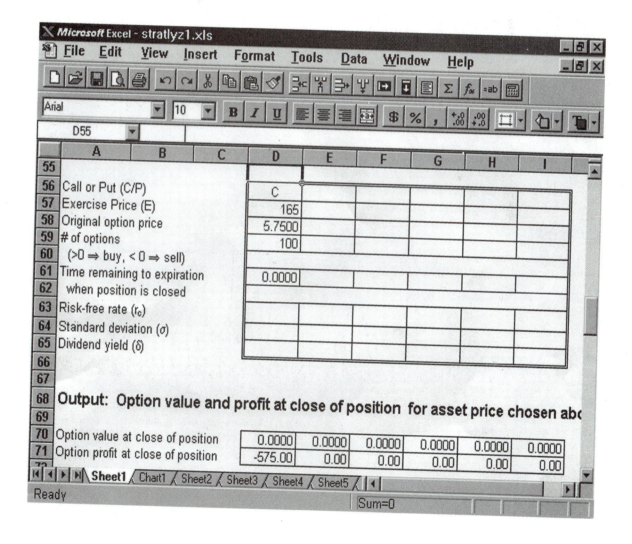

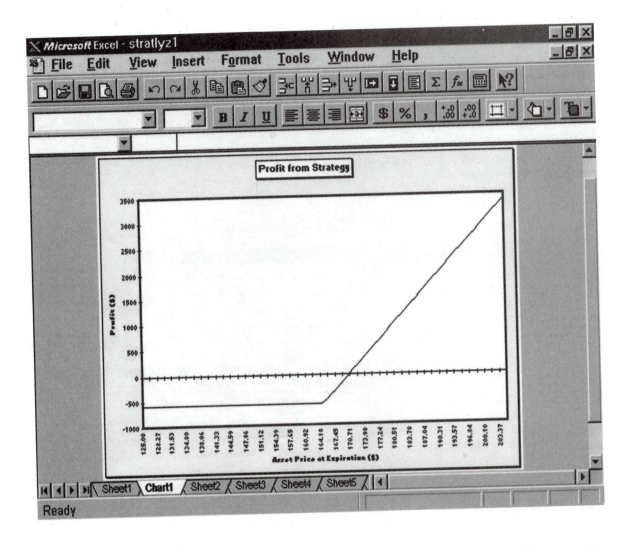

cells contain information that is necessary only if the position is closed prior to expiration. If the position is held to expiration, the "Time remaining to expiration when position is closed" will be zero and the last three lines can be left blank. Insert a zero for our example. If the position is closed prior to expiration, insert the remaining time in years and then insert the risk-free rate, volatility, and dividend yield in the next three cells below. This permits the program to use the Black-Scholes model to calculate the option's value when the position is terminated for a given asset price. We shall leave this information blank. Hit the F9 (manual recalculation) key.

The section labeled **Output: Option value and profit at close of position for asset price chosen above** shows for each option the value of the option at the close of the position, the profit on the option transaction, and the overall profit on the transaction, which includes option(s) and potential positions in the asset, for the asset price you specified above. Note that output cells have a single-line border. These answers, of course, represent only one point on the profit graph. In our example the profit is −$575 because we specified an asset price at expiration of 165, which is the exercise price. The next section, **Data Table for Graphic Results,** shows the overall profit for the strategy for 50 possible asset prices at the end of the holding period, running from the minimum to the maximum price you specified, centered around the asset price at expiration you specified. The graph is provided on a different spreadsheet, which you can access by clicking on the tab labeled **Chart 1** near the bottom of your screen.

As noted above, for positions closed out prior to expiration, the program automatically calculates Black-Scholes prices for the options for each possible asset price in the range speci-fied, provided you supply it with the necessary information on the time remaining, the volatility, the interest rate, and the dividend yield, if any. For example, if there are 15 days remaining until expiration (time = 15/365 = .0411), the risk-free rate is 5.2 percent, the volatility is .33, and the dividend yield is zero, the call value is 4.5764 and the profit is −117.36.

While stratlyz1.xls will correctly graph any strategy you choose, it is possible that the graph will not look exactly as you ex-pect it. The various possible combinations of inputs and outputs, along with the fixed parameters used to generate the graph, such as 50 asset prices, will not always produce visually appealing graphs the first time. This is often due to the fact that the graph's tick marks are not located on the exercise price(s). If anything looks unusual, experiment with different maximum and minimum asset prices until your graph looks as expected.

Key Terms

Before continuing to Chapter 6, you should be able to give brief definitions of the following terms.
- breakeven stock price
- uncovered/naked call
- covered call
- protective put
- synthetic put/call

Questions and Problems

1. Explain the advantages and disadvantages to a call buyer of closing out a po-sition prior to expiration rather than holding all the way until expiration.

2. Suppose one is considering buying a call at a particular exercise price. What reasons could be given for the alternative of buying a call at a higher exer-cise price? At a lower exercise price?

3. Explain how a protective put is like purchasing insurance on a stock.

4. Why is the choice of exercise price on a protective put like the decision on which deductible to take on an insurance policy?

5. Discuss and compare the two bullish strategies of buying a call and writing a put. Why would one strategy be preferable to the other?

6. Suppose you wish to buy stock and protect yourself against a downside move-ment in its price. You consider both a covered call and a protective put. What factors will affect your decision?

7. You have inherited some stock from a rich relative. The stock has had poor performance recently, and analysts believe it has little growth potential. You would like to write calls against the stock; however, the will stipulates that you must agree not to sell it unless you need the funds for a personal finan-cial emergency. How can you write covered calls and minimize the likeli-hood of exercise?

8. We briefly mentioned the synthetic call, which consists of stock and an equal number of puts. Assume the combined value of the puts and stock exceeds the value of the actual call by less than the present value of the exercise price. Show how an arbitrage profit can be made. Note: Do not use the data from the chap-ter. Show your point as it was illustrated in the text for the synthetic put.

9. A short position in stock can be protected by holding a call option. Deter-mine the profit equations for this position, and identify the breakeven stock price at expiration and maximum and minimum profits.

10. A short stock can be protected by selling a put. Determine the profit equations for this position, and identify the breakeven stock price at expiration and maximum and minimum profits.

11. Explain the advantages and disadvantages to a covered call writer of closing out the position prior to expiration.

12. Explain the considerations facing a covered call writer regarding the choice of exercise prices.

The following option prices were observed for a stock for July 6 of a particular year. Use this information in problems 13 through 18. Ignore dividends on the stock. The stock is priced at 165 1/8. The expirations are July 17, August 21, and October 16. The continuously compounded risk-free rates are .0503, .0535, and .0571, respectively. The standard deviation is .21. Assume the options are European.

	Calls			**Puts**		
Strike	**Jul**	**Aug**	**Oct**	**Jul**	**Aug**	**Oct**
165	2 11/16	5 1/4	8 1/8	2 3/8	4 3/4	6 3/4
170	13/16	3 1/4	6	5 3/4	7 1/2	9

In problems 13 through 18, determine the profits for possible stock prices of 150, 155, 160, 165, 170, 175, and 180. Answer any other questions as requested. Note: Your Excel spreadsheet stratlyz1.xls will be useful here for obtaining graphs as requested, but it does not allow you to calculate the profits for several user-specified asset prices. It permits you to specify one asset price and a maximum and minimum. Use stratlyz1.xls to produce the graph for the range of prices from 150 to 180 but determine the profits for the prices of 150, 160, . . . , 180 by hand for positions held to expiration. For positions closed prior to expiration, use the spreadsheet bsbin1.xls or the Windows program bsbwin2.exe to determine the option price when the position is closed; then calculate the profit by hand.

13. Buy one August 165 call contract. Hold until the options expire. Determine the profits and graph the results. Then identify the breakeven stock price at expiration. What is the maximum possible loss on this transaction?

14. Repeat problem 13, but close the position on August 1. Calculate the profit by hand when the stock price on August 1 is 155. Then use the spreadsheet or calculate by hand to find the profits for the possible stock prices on August 1. Generate a graph and use it to identify the approximate breakeven stock price.

15. Buy one October 165 put contract. Hold until the options expire. Determine the profits and graph the results. Identify the breakeven stock price at expiration. What are the maximum possible gain and loss on this transaction?

16. Buy 100 shares of stock and write one October 170 call contract. Hold the position until expiration. Determine the profits and graph the results. Identify the breakeven stock price at expiration, the maximum profit, and the maximum loss.

17. Repeat problem 16, but close the position on September 1. Calculate the profit by hand when the stock price on September 1 is 155. Then use the spreadsheet or calculate by hand to find the profits for the possible stock

prices on September 1. Generate a graph and use it to approximate the breakeven stock price.

18. Buy 100 shares of stock and buy one August 165 put contract. Hold the position until expiration. Determine the profits and graph the results. Determine the breakeven stock price at expiration, the maximum profit, and the maximum loss.

19. (Concept Problem) In each case examined in the chapter and in the preceding problems, we did not account for the interest on funds invested. One useful way to observe the effect of interest is to look at a conversion or a reverse conversion. Evaluate the August 165 puts and calls, and recommend a conversion or a reverse conversion. Determine the profit from the transaction if the options are held to expiration. Make sure the profit properly accounts for the interest that accrues over the holding period.

20. (Concept Problem) Another consideration in evaluating option strategies is the effect of transaction costs. Suppose purchases and sales of an option incur a brokerage commission of 1 percent of the option's value. Purchases and sales of a share of stock incur a brokerage commission of .5 percent of the stock's value. If the option is exercised, there is a transaction cost on the purchase or sale of the stock. Determine the profit equations for the following strategies assuming the options are held to expiration and exercised if in-the-money rather than sold back. Assume that one option and/or share is used and that any shares left in the portfolio are sold.
   a. Long call
   b. Long put
   c. Covered call
   d. Protective put

CHAPTER 6

Advanced Option Strategies

You can get as fancy as you want with your option strategies, but in this business, there's no substitute for being right. There's never been a guarantee for incremental returns.

GENE BRODY
Risk, June 1995

Chapter Objectives

■ To present and analyze the option spread strategies, including money spread strategies, including money spread, calendar spreads, and ratio spreads

■ To present and analyze the option combination strategies, including straddles/straps/strips and box spreads

Chapter 5 provided a foundation for the basic option strategies. We can now move on to some of the more advanced strategies. As often noted, options can be combined in some interesting and unusual ways. In this chapter, we look at two types of advanced option strategies: spreads and combinations.

Option Spreads: Basic Concepts

A **spread** is the purchase of one option and the sale of another. There are two general types of spreads. One is the **vertical, strike,** or **money spread.** This strategy involves the purchase of an option with a particular exercise price and the sale of another option differing only by exercise price. For example, one might purchase an option on UAL expiring in October with an exercise price of 150 and sell an option on UAL also expiring in October but with an exercise price of 155; hence the terms *strike* and *money spread*. Because exercise prices were formerly arranged vertically in the option pages of newspapers, this also became known as a *vertical spread*.

Another type of spread is a **horizontal, time,** or **calendar spread.** In this spread, the investor purchases an option with an expiration of a given month and sells an otherwise identical option with a different expiration month. For example, one might purchase a UAL October 150 call and sell

a UAL January 150 call.[1] The term *horizontal spread* is due to the horizontal arrangement of expiration months in newspaper option pages, a practice since discontinued.

Sometimes spreads are identified by a special notation. The aforementioned UAL money spread is referred to as the October 150/155 spread. The month is given first; the exercise price before the slash (/) is the option purchased; and the exercise price after the slash is the option sold. If the investor buys the October 155 and sells the October 150, the result is an October 155/150 spread. The calendar spread described in the previous paragraph is identified as the October/January 150 spread. The month preceding the slash is the option purchased, while the month following the slash identifies the option sold.

Spreads can be executed using either calls or puts. An October 150/155 call spread is a net long position. This is because the 150 call costs more than the 155 call; that is, the cash outflow from buying the 150 exceeds the inflow received for selling the 155. This transaction is called **buying the spread** and is sometimes referred to as a **debit spread** for the type of accounting entry associated with it. In the October 150/155 put spread, the cash inflow received from selling the 155 put is more than the cash outflow paid in buying the 150 put. This transaction is known as **selling the spread** or a **credit spread** and results in a net short position.

For calendar spreads, the October/January 150 call spread would be net short and selling the spread, because an investor would receive more for the January call than he or she would pay for the October call. The January/October 150 call spread would be net long and buying the spread, because the January call would cost more than the October call. The terms *debit* and *credit spread* are also used here. With calendar spreads the terminology is similar for both calls and puts, because the premiums for both are greater the longer the time to expiration.

Why Investors Use Option Spreads

Spreads offer the potential for a small profit while limiting the risk. They are not, of course, the sure route to riches; we already have seen that no such strategy is. But spreads can be very useful in modifying risk while allowing profits if market forecasts prove accurate.

Risk reduction is achieved by being long in one option and short in another. If the stock price decreases, the loss on a long call will be somewhat offset by a gain on a short call. Whether the gain outweighs the loss depends on the volatility of each call. We shall illustrate this effect later. For now, consider a money spread held to expiration. Assume we buy the

---

[1]We assume the January call is the one following the October call rather than the one preceding it.

call with the low strike price and sell the call with the high strike price. In a bull market we will make money, because the low-exercise-price call will bring a higher payoff at expiration than will the high-exercise-price call. In a bear market, both calls will probably expire worthless and we will lose money. For that reason, the spread involving the purchase of the low-exercise-price call is referred to as a **bull spread.** Similarly, in a bear market we make money if we are long the high-exercise-price call and short the low-exercise-price call. This is called a **bear spread.** Opposite rules apply for puts: A position of long (short) the low-exercise-price put and short (long) the high-exercise-price put is a bull (bear) spread. In general, a bull spread should profit in a bull market and a bear spread should profit in a bear market.

Time spreads are not classified into bull and bear spreads. They profit by either increased or decreased volatility. We shall reserve further discussion of time spreads for a later section.

Transaction costs are an important practical consideration in spread trading. These costs can represent a significant portion of invested funds, especially for small traders. Spreads involve several option positions, and the transaction costs can quickly become prohibitive for all but floor traders and large institutional investors. As in Chapter 5, we will not build transaction costs directly into the analyses here but will discuss their special relevance where appropriate.

Notation

The notation here is the same as that used in previous chapters. However, we must add some distinguishing symbols for the spreads' different strike prices and expirations. For a money spread, we will use subscripts to distinguish options differing by strike price. For example,

$$E_1, E_2, E_3 = \text{exercise prices of calls where } E_1 < E_2 < E_3$$
$$C_1, C_2, C_3 = \text{prices of calls with exercise prices } E_1, E_2, E_3$$
$$N_1, N_2, N_3 = \text{quantity held of each option.}$$

The N notation indicates the number of options where a positive N is a long position and a negative N is a short position.

In time spreads,

$$T_1, T_2 = \text{times to expiration where } T_1 < T_2$$
$$C_1, C_2 = \text{prices of calls with times to expiration of } T_1, T_2$$
$$N_1, N_2 = \text{quantity held of each option.}$$

The numerical illustrations will use the Digital Equipment options presented in earlier chapters. For convenience, Table 6.1 repeats the data. Unless otherwise stated, assume 100 options are employed.

TABLE 6.1	Digital Equipment Option Data, June 12					
	Calls			Puts		
Exercise Price	Jun	Jul	Oct	Jun	Jul	Oct
160	4 5/8	8 5/8	15 1/4	13/16	3 7/8	8 1/8
165	1 7/8	5 3/4	13 1/4	2 15/16	6	9 3/4
170	1/2	3 3/4	10 3/4	6 1/2	8 1/2	NA
175	1/16	2 3/8	8 1/2	NA	NA	NA

Current stock price: 164
Expirations: June 19, July 17, October 16
Risk-free rates: .0473 (Jun); .0521 (Jul); .0574 (Oct)

Because the analyses of call and put spreads are so similar, we shall spend little time on put spreads. We will cover any important considerations but reserve treatment of put spreads mainly for end-of-chapter problems. This will give readers an opportunity to determine whether they understand the concepts well enough to apply them to slightly different situations.

Your Excel spreadsheet opstrat1.xls can be very useful for analyzing spreads and, indeed, all the transactions in this chapter.

Money Spreads

As indicated earlier, money spreads can be designed to profit in either a bull market or a bear market. The former is called a bull spread.

Bull Spreads

Consider two call options differing only by exercise price, E_1 and E_2, where $E_1 < E_2$. Their premiums are C_1 and C_2, and we know that $C_1 > C_2$. A bull spread consists of the purchase of the option with the lower exercise price and the sale of the option with the higher exercise price. Assuming one option of each, $N_1 = 1$ and $N_2 = -1$, the profit equations are

$$\Pi = \text{Max}(0, S_T - E_1) - C_1 - \text{Max}(0, S_T - E_2) + C_2.$$

The stock price at expiration can fall in one of three ranges: less than or equal to E_1, greater than E_1 but less than or equal to E_2, or greater than E_2. The profits for these three ranges are as follows:

$$\Pi = -C_1 + C_2 \qquad\qquad \text{if } S_T \leq E_1 < E_2$$
$$\Pi = S_T - E_1 - C_1 + C_2 \qquad \text{if } E_1 < S_T \leq E_2$$
$$\Pi = S_T - E_1 - C_1 - S_T + E_2 + C_2$$
$$\quad = E_2 - E_1 - C_1 + C_2 \qquad \text{if } E_1 < E_2 < S_T.$$

In the case where the stock price ends up equal to or below the lower exercise price, both options expire out-of-the-money. The spreader loses the premium on the long call and retains the premium on the short call. The profit is the same regardless of how far below the lower exercise price the stock price is. However, because the premium on the long call is greater than the premium on the short call, this profit is actually a loss.

In the third case, where both options end up in-the-money, the short call is exercised on the spreader, who exercises the long call and then delivers the stock. The effect of the stock price cancels and the profit is constant for any stock price above the higher exercise price. Is this profit positive? The profit is $(E_2 - E_1) - (C_1 - C_2)$, or the difference between the exercise prices minus the difference between the premiums. Recall from Chapter 3 that the difference in premiums cannot exceed the difference in exercise prices. The spreader paid a premium of C_1, received a premium of C_2, and thus obtained the spread for a net investment of $C_1 - C_2$. The maximum payoff from the spread is $E_2 - E_1$. No one would pay more than the maximum payoff from an investment. Therefore, the profit is positive.

Only in the second case, where the long call ends up in-the-money and the short call is out-of-the-money, is there any uncertainty. The equation shows that the profit increases dollar for dollar with the stock price at expiration.

Figure 6.1 illustrates the profits from the bull spread strategy for the Digital Equipment July 165 and 170 calls with premiums of $5.75 and $3.75, respectively. The dashed line is the profit graph had we simply purchased the 165 call. The maximum loss is the net premium of $575 – $375, or $200, which occurs at any stock price at expiration at or below 165. The maximum gain is the difference in strike prices minus the difference in premiums, $100(170 - 165 - 2) = 300$, which occurs at any stock price at expiration above 170.

From the graph, it is apparent that the breakeven stock price at expiration is between the two exercise prices. To find this breakeven—call it S_T^*—take the profit equation for the second case, where the stock price is between both exercise prices, and set it equal to zero:

A call bull spread has a limited gain, which occurs in a bull market, and a limited loss, which occurs in a bear market.

$$\Pi = S_T^* - E_1 - C_1 + C_2 = 0.$$

Then solve for S_T^*:

$$S_T^* = E_1 + C_1 - C_2.$$

FIGURE 6.1   Call Bull Spread

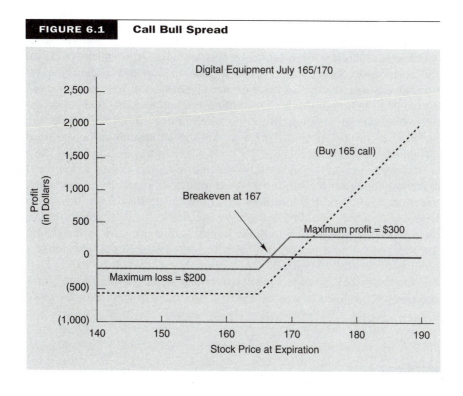

Digital Equipment July 165/170

The stock price must exceed the lower exercise price by the difference in the premiums. This makes sense. The spreader exercises the call with exercise price E_1. The higher the stock price, the greater the amount received from the exercise. To break even, the spreader must receive enough to recover the net premium, $C_1 - C_2$. In this problem, the breakeven stock price at expiration is $165 + 5.75 - 3.75 = 167$.

Note that in comparison to simply buying the 165 call, the spreader reduces the maximum loss by the premium on the short 170 call and lowers the breakeven, but gives up the chance for large gains if the stock moves up substantially.

Early exercise poses no problem with the bull spread. Suppose the stock price prior to expiration is S_t. If the short call is exercised, the stock price must be greater than E_2. This means that the stock price is also greater than E_1, and the long call can be exercised for a net payoff of $(S_t - E_1) - (S_t - E_2) = E_2 - E_1$. This is the best outcome one could obtain by holding the spread all the way to expiration.

THE CHOICE OF HOLDING PERIOD   As with any option strategy, it is possible to hold the position for a period shorter than the option's entire life.

Recall that in Chapter 5 we made assumptions about closing out the option positions prior to expiration. We used short holding periods of T_1, which meant closing the position on July 24, and T_2, in which we closed the position on September 4. When a position is closed prior to expiration, we estimate the option price for a range of stock prices and use those estimates to generate the profit graph. We illustrated the general procedure in Chapter 5. Using the same methodology here, we obtain the graph in Figure 6.2, the bull spread under the assumption of three different holding periods.

Recall that T_1 is the shortest holding period, T_2 is slightly longer, and T represents holding all the way to expiration. The graph indicates that the short holding period has the lowest range of profits. If the stock price is low, the shortest holding period produces the smallest loss while the longest holding period produces the largest loss. If the stock price is high, the shortest holding period produces the smallest gain and the longest holding period the largest gain.

The logic behind these results is simple. First, recall that the low-exercise-price call will always be worth more than the high-exercise-price

For a given stock price, the profit of a call bull spread increases as expiration approaches if the stock price is on the high side and decreases if the stock price is on the low side.

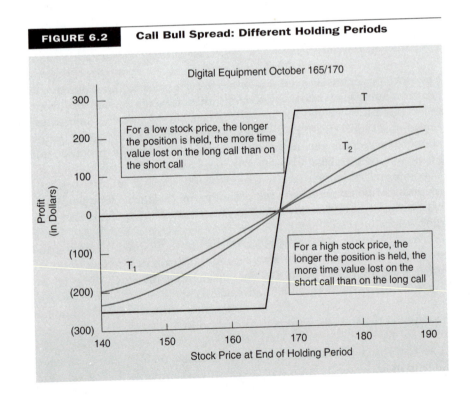

FIGURE 6.2   **Call Bull Spread: Different Holding Periods**

Digital Equipment October 165/170

For a low stock price, the longer the position is held, the more time value lost on the long call than on the short call

For a high stock price, the longer the position is held, the more time value lost on the short call than on the long call

Profit (in Dollars)

Stock Price at End of Holding Period

call; however, their relative time values will differ. An option's time value is greatest when the stock price is near the exercise price. Therefore, when stock prices are high, the high-exercise-price call will have the greater time value and when they are low, the low-exercise-price call will have the greater time value.

When we close out the spread prior to expiration, we can always expect the long call to sell for more than the short call because the long call has the lower exercise price. However, the excess of the long call's price over the short call's price will decrease at high stock prices. This is because the time value will be greater on the short call, because the stock price is closer to the exercise price. The long call will still sell for a higher price because it has more intrinsic value, but the difference will be smaller at high stock prices. Conversely, at low stock prices the long call will have a greater time value because its exercise price is closer to the stock price.

The result of all this is that when we close the bull spread well before expiration, the profit will be lower at high stock prices and higher at low stock prices than if we did so closer to expiration. If we hold the position longer but not all the way to expiration, we will obtain the same effect, but the impact will be smaller because the time value will be less.

Which holding period should an investor choose? There is no consistently right or wrong answer. An investor who is strongly bullish should realize that the longer the position is held, the greater the profit that can be made if the forecast is correct. In addition, a long holding period allows more time for the stock price to move upward. If the forecast proves incorrect, the loss will be lower the shorter the holding period. With short holding periods, however, there is less time for a large stock price change.

The following section examines a call bear spread. We shall see that a bear spread is, in many respects, the opposite of a bull spread but carries the risk of early exercise.

Bear Spreads

A bear spread is the mirror image of a bull spread: The trader is long the high-exercise-price call and short the low-exercise-price call. Since $N_1 = -1$ and $N_2 = 1$, the profit equation is simply

A call bear spread has a limited gain, which occurs in a bear market, and a limited loss, which occurs in a bull market.

$$\Pi = -\text{Max}(0, S_T - E_1) + C_1 + \text{Max}(0, S_T - E_2) - C_2.$$

The outcomes are as follows:

$$\Pi = C_1 - C_2 \qquad \text{if } S_T \le E_1 < E_2$$
$$\Pi = -S_T + E_1 + C_1 - C_2 \qquad \text{if } E_1 < S_T \le E_2$$
$$\Pi = -S_T + E_1 + C_1 + S_T - E_2 - C_2$$
$$\quad = E_1 - E_2 + C_1 - C_2 \qquad \text{if } E_1 < E_2 < S_T$$

Figure 6.3 illustrates the bear spread with the Digital Equipment July 165 and 170 calls. The dashed line is a naked short position in the 165 call. The spread is profitable if the stock price is low and loses money if the stock price is high. Because a bear spread is the opposite of a bull spread, the formula for the breakeven stock price is still $E_1 + C_1 - C_2$. In this example, the breakeven stock price is $165 + 5.75 - 3.75 = 167$. The maximum and minimum profits are

Maximum: $C_1 - C_2 = 100(5.75 - 3.75) = 200$
Minimum: $E_1 - E_2 + C_1 - C_2 = 100(165 - 170 + 5.75 - 3.75) = -300$.

Relative to the naked short call, the bear spread has a lower maximum profit by the amount of the premium of the purchased call, a lower breakeven, and a lower loss on the upside, which is limited to $300.

The risk of early exercise for bear spreads is a special problem. The short call can be sufficiently in-the-money to justify early exercise while the long call is still out-of-the-money. Even if the long call is in-the-money, the cash flow from early exercise will be negative.

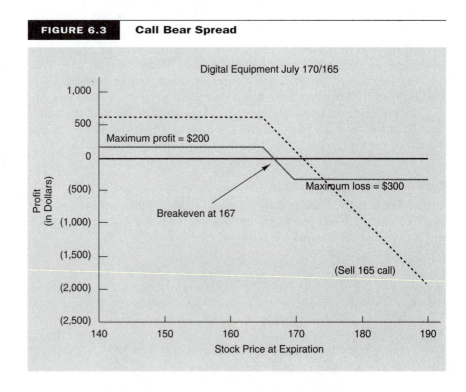

FIGURE 6.3   **Call Bear Spread**

Digital Equipment July 170/165

Maximum profit = $200

Breakeven at 167

Maximum loss = $300

(Sell 165 call)

Profit (in Dollars)

Stock Price at Expiration

For example, suppose S_t is the stock price prior to expiration. The cash flow from the exercise of the short call is $-(S_t - E_1)$, while the cash flow from the exercise of the long call is $S_t - E_2$. This gives a total cash flow of $E_1 - E_2$, which is negative. Early exercise ensures that the bear spreader will incur a cash outflow. Because the loss occurs prior to expiration, it is greater in present value terms than if it had occurred at expiration. Thus, the call bear spread entails a risk not associated with the bull spread. To profit in a bear market, it may be better to execute a put spread, which we briefly discuss in a later section.

THE CHOICE OF HOLDING PERIOD   Figure 6.4 illustrates a bear spread when different holding periods are used. The longer holding period produces higher profits in a bear market and larger losses in a bull market. Again this is because of the time value effect. The spread trader closing the position prior to expiration buys back the time value of the short call and sells the long call's remaining time value. For high stock prices, there will be more time value on the high-exercise-price call than on the low-exercise-price call. That means that more time value can be captured on

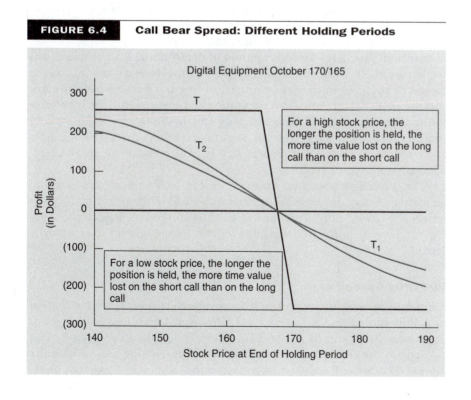

FIGURE 6.4   **Call Bear Spread: Different Holding Periods**

Digital Equipment October 170/165

For a high stock price, the longer the position is held, the more time value lost on the long call than on the short call

For a low stock price, the longer the position is held, the more time value lost on the short call than on the long call

the resale of the long call than must be paid for on the repurchase of the short call. However, both calls are in-the-money; thus, the short call has more intrinsic value to be repurchased. Therefore, the short holding period produces a loss at high stock prices. This loss increases with longer holding periods, because the long call's time value advantage is diminished. With low stock prices, the opposite effect prevails: The profit is greater for longer holding periods and is maximized when holding all the way to expiration.

For a given stock price, the profit of a call bear spread increases as expiration approaches if the stock price is on the low side and decreases if the stock price is on the high side.

We should repeat, however, that these statements do not advocate a short or long holding period, because the length of the holding period affects the range of possible stock prices.

A Word about Put Money Spreads

As we have seen, it is possible to design a call money spread that will profit in a bull market or another that will profit in a bear market. It is also possible to construct put money spreads. Like a call spread, a put spread is considered a bull spread if designed to make money in a bull market and a bear spread if designed to make money in a bear market.

Given that both bull and bear spreads can be constructed from calls, put spreads would seem unnecessary. For illustrative purposes, this is probably true. As a practical matter, however, put spreads occasionally offer opportunities unavailable with call spreads. As we saw in Chapter 4, the Black-Scholes model provides a method of determining if an option is correctly priced. If a put is incorrectly priced, the investor can execute a spread to profit from the mispricing. Also, the put bear spread does not run the same risk of early exercise as the call bear spread. This is because the put bear spread will have the long put in-the-money whenever the short put is in-the-money. If the short put is exercised, the long put can be exercised for an overall cash flow of $E_2 - E_1$, which is the maximum payoff obtainable if held to expiration.

For illustrative purposes, however, we can analyze put spreads in the same manner as call spreads. We need only change the intrinsic values to reflect the use of puts. This we will leave as an end-of-chapter problem. For now, we will turn to a variation of the money spread: the butterfly spread.

Butterfly Spreads

A **butterfly spread,** sometimes called a **sandwich spread,** is a combination of a bull spread and a bear spread. However, this transaction involves three exercise prices: E_1, E_2, and E_3, where E_2 is halfway between E_1 and E_3. Suppose we construct a call bull spread by purchasing the call with the low exercise price, E_1, and writing the call with the middle exercise price, E_2. Then we also construct a call bear spread by purchasing the call with

the high exercise price, E_3, and writing the call with the middle exercise price, E_2. Combining these positions shows that we are long one each of the low- and high-exercise-price options and short two middle-exercise-price options. Since $N_1 = 1$, $N_2 = -2$, and $N_3 = 1$, the profit equation is

$$\Pi = \text{Max}(0, S_T - E_1) - C_1 - 2\text{Max}(0, S_T - E_2) + 2C_2 + \text{Max}(0, S_T - E_3) - C_3.$$

To analyze the behavior of the profit equation, we must examine four ranges of the stock price at expiration:

$$
\begin{aligned}
&\Pi = -C_1 + 2C_2 - C_3 && \text{if } S_T \leq E_1 < E_2 < E_3 \\
&\Pi = S_T - E_1 - C_1 + 2C_2 - C_3 && \text{if } E_1 < S_T \leq E_2 < E_3 \\
&\Pi = S_T - E_1 - C_1 - 2S_T + 2E_2 + 2C_2 - C_3 \\
&\quad = -S_T + 2E_2 - E_1 - C_1 + 2C_2 - C_3 && \text{if } E_1 < E_2 < S_T \leq E_3 \\
&\Pi = S_T - E_1 - C_1 - 2S_T + 2E_2 + 2C_2 + S_T - E_3 - C_3 \\
&\quad = -E_1 + 2E_2 - E_3 - C_1 + 2C_2 - C_3 && \text{if } E_1 < E_2 < E_3 < S_T.
\end{aligned}
$$

Now look at the first profit equation, $-C_1 + 2C_2 - C_3$. This can be separated into $-C_1 + C_2$ and $C_2 - C_3$. We already know that a low-exercise-price call is worth more than a high-exercise-price call. Thus, the first pair of terms is negative and the second pair is positive. Which pair will be greater in an absolute sense? The first pair will. The advantage of a low-exercise-price call over a high-exercise-price call is smaller at higher exercise prices, because there the likelihood of both calls expiring out-of-the-money is greater. If that happens, neither call will be of any value to the trader. Because $-C_1 + C_2$ is larger in an absolute sense than $C_2 - C_3$, the profit for the lowest range of stock prices at expiration is negative.

For the second range, the profit is $S_T - E_1 - C_1 + 2C_2 - C_3$. The last three terms, $-C_1 + 2C_2 - C_3$, represent the net price paid for the butterfly spread. Because the stock price at expiration has a direct effect on the profit, a graph would show the profit varying dollar for dollar and in a positive manner with the stock price at expiration. However, the profit in this range of stock prices can be either positive or negative. This implies that there is a breakeven stock price at expiration. To find that stock price, S_T^*, set this profit equal to zero:

$$S_T^* - E_1 - C_1 + 2C_2 - C_3 = 0.$$

Solving for S_T^* gives

$$S_T^* = E_1 + C_1 - 2C_2 + C_3.$$

The breakeven equation indicates that a butterfly spread is profitable if the stock price at expiration exceeds the low exercise price by an amount large enough to cover the net price paid for the spread.

Now look at the third profit equation. Since the profit varies inversely dollar for dollar with the stock price at expiration, a graph would show the profit decreasing one for one with the stock price at expiration. The profit can be either positive or negative; hence, there is a second breakeven stock price. To find it, set the profit equal to zero:

$$-S_T^* + 2E_2 - E_1 - C_1 + 2C_2 - C_3 = 0.$$

Solving for S_T^* gives

$$S_T^* = 2E_2 - E_1 - C_1 + 2C_2 - C_3.$$

Recall that in this range of stock prices, the profit declines with higher stock prices. Profit will disappear completely if the stock price is so high that it exceeds the cash flow received from the exercise of the middle-exercise-price call, $2E_2$, minus the cash flow paid for the exercise of the low-exercise-price call, E_1, minus the net premiums on the calls.

In the final range of the stock price at expiration, profit is the net premiums paid plus the difference in the exercise prices. Since E_2 is halfway between E_1 and E_3, then $E_2 - E_1$ is the same as $E_3 - E_2$. Therefore, $-E_1 + 2E_2 - E_3 = 0$. This means that the profit in this range is the same as that in the first range and is simply the difference in the premiums.

A butterfly spread has a limited loss, which occurs on large stock price moves, either up or down, and a limited gain, which occurs if the stock price ends up at the middle exercise price.

Now we have a good idea of what a butterfly spread looks like. Figure 6.5 illustrates the butterfly spread for the Digital Equipment July 160, 165, and 170 calls. The worst outcome is simply the net premiums, or $100[-8.625 + 2(5.75) - 3.75] = -87.50$. This is obtained for any stock price less than \$160 or greater than \$170. The maximum profit is obtained when the stock price at expiration is at the middle exercise price. Using the second profit equation and letting $S_T = E_2$, the maximum profit is

$$\Pi = E_2 - E_1 - C_1 + 2C_2 - C_3,$$

which in this example is $100[165 - 160 - 8.625 + 2(5.75) - 3.75] = 412.50$. The lower breakeven is $E_1 + C_1 - 2C_2 + C_3$, which in this case is $160 + 8.625 - 2(5.75) + 3.75 = 160.875$. The upper breakeven is $2E_2 - E_1 - C_1 + 2C_2 - C_3$, which in this example is $2(165) - 160 - 8.625 + 2(5.75) - 3.75 = 169.125$.

The butterfly spread strategy assumes the stock price will fluctuate very little. In this example, the trader is betting that the stock price will stay within the range of \$160.875 to \$169.125. However, if this prediction of low stock price volatility proves incorrect, the potential loss will be limited—in this case, to \$87.50. Thus, the butterfly spread is a low-risk transaction.

A trader who believes the stock price will be extremely volatile and will fall outside of the two breakeven stock prices might want to write a but-

| FIGURE 6.5 | Call Butterfly Spread |

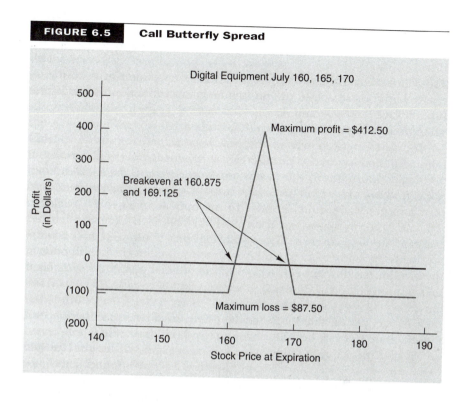

terfly spread. This will involve one short position in each of the E_1 and E_3 calls and two long positions in the E_2 call. We shall leave it as an end-of-chapter problem to explore the short butterfly spread.

Early exercise can pose a problem for holders of butterfly spreads. Suppose the stock price prior to expiration is S_t, where S_t is greater than or equal to E_2 and less than or equal to E_3. Assume the short calls are exercised shortly before the stock goes ex-dividend. The spreader then exercises the long call with exercise price E_1. The cash flow from the short calls is $-(2S_t - 2E_2)$, and the cash flow from the long call is $S_t - E_1$. This gives a total cash flow of $-S_t + E_2 + E_2 - E_1$. The minimum value of this expression is $-E_3 + E_2 + E_2 - E_1$, which occurs if $S_t = E_3$. Since the exercise prices are equally spaced, this equals zero. The maximum value occurs when $S_t = E_2$ and is $-E_2 + E_2 + E_2 - E_1 = E_2 - E_1$, which is positive. If S_t exceeds E_3 and the two short calls are exercised, they will be offset by the exercise of both long calls, and the overall cash flow will be zero.

Thus, early exercise does not result in a cash outflow, but that does not mean that it poses no risk. If the options are exercised early, there is no possibility of achieving the maximum profit obtainable at expiration when $S_T = E_2$. If the spread were reversed and the E_1 and E_3 calls were sold

while two of the E_2 calls were bought, early exercise could generate a negative cash flow.

THE CHOICE OF HOLDING PERIOD   As with any option strategy, the investor might wish to close the position prior to expiration. Consider the July 160, 165, and 170 calls. Let holding period T_1 involve closing the position on July 1 and holding period T_2 on July 10.[2]

In this example, a plot of the results would reveal that the shortest holding period would not profit at any stock price. That would create an arbitrage opportunity. If the transaction were reversed, the shortest holding period would have no loss at any stock price. Thus, the general results of this example are quite sensitive to the options' prices. The reason is that the butterfly spread involves more options than most of the other strategies we have covered. That means that the strategy is sensitive to the possibility of option mispricing. Also, the short holding periods imply that the investor has little time to recapture the original cost of the options. If that cost is incorrectly estimated, the results will be greatly affected. To remove this bias, let us use the three calls' Black-Scholes prices instead of their market prices. The Black-Scholes prices are 8.5 for the 160, 5.79 for the 165, and 3.74 for the 170. The graph is shown in Figure 6.6.

For a given stock price, the profit of a butterfly spread increases as expiration approaches if the stock price is near the middle exercise price and decreases if the stock price is on the low or high side.

At high stock prices, time value will be greatest on the call with the highest exercise price. Since we are long that call, we gain the advantage of being able to sell it back early and recapture some of the time value. This advantage, however, erodes with a longer holding period because the time value decreases.

At low stock prices, the time value will be greatest on the call with the lowest exercise price. Since we are also long that call, we can sell it back early and recapture some of its remaining time value. However, this advantage also decreases as we hold the position longer and time value decays.

In the middle range of stock prices, the time value will be very high on the two short calls. For short holding periods, this is a disadvantage because we have to buy back these calls, which means that we must pay for the remaining time value. However, this disadvantage turns to an advantage as the holding period lengthens and time value begins to disappear. At expiration, no time value remains; thus, profit is maximized in this range.

The breakeven stock prices are substantially further away with shorter holding periods and are highest with the shortest. This is advantageous, because it will then take a much larger stock price change to produce a loss.

---

[2]The holding period was changed in this example because the time value decay does not show up as clearly for the holding periods we have previously used.

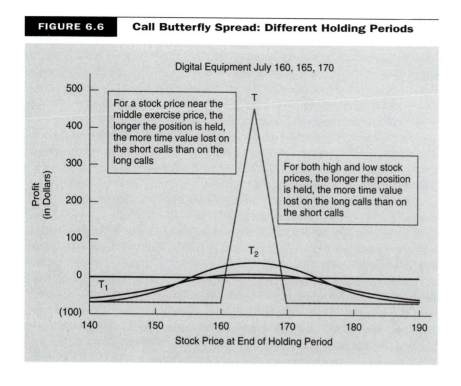

FIGURE 6.6 **Call Butterfly Spread: Different Holding Periods**

Digital Equipment July 160, 165, 170

For a stock price near the middle exercise price, the longer the position is held, the more time value lost on the short calls than on the long calls

For both high and low stock prices, the longer the position is held, the more time value lost on the long calls than on the short calls

As always, we cannot specifically identify an optimal holding period. Because the butterfly spread is one in which the trader expects the stock price to stay within a narrow range, profit is maximized with a long holding period. The disadvantage of a long holding period, however, is that it gives the stock price more time to move outside of the profitable range.

All of the above spreads are money spreads. We now turn to an examination of calendar spreads.

Calendar Spreads

A calendar spread, also known as a time or horizontal spread, involves the purchase of an option with one expiration date and the sale of an otherwise identical option with a different expiration date. Because it is not possible to hold both options until expiration, analyzing a calendar spread is more complicated than analyzing a money spread. Since one option expires before the other, the longest possible holding period would be to hold the position until the shorter-maturity option's expiration. Then the other option would have some remaining time value that must be estimated.

Because both options have the same exercise prices, they will have the same intrinsic values; thus, the profitability of the calendar spread will be determined solely by the difference in their time values. The longer-term call will have more time value. However, this does not necessarily mean that one should always buy the longer-term call and sell the shorter-term call. As with most option strategies, which option is purchased and which one is sold depends on the investor's outlook for the stock.

To best understand the calendar spread, we will again illustrate with the Digital Equipment calls. This spread consists of the purchase of the October 160 call at $15.25 and the sale of the July 160 call at $8.625. This position is net long, because you pay more for the October than you receive for the July. Consider two possible holding periods. One, T_1, will involve the spread's termination on July 1; the other, T_2, will have the spread held until July 17, the date of the July call's expiration. Using the Black-Scholes model to estimate the remaining time values produced the graph in Figure 6.7.

For a given stock price, a long calendar spread gains as expiration approaches if the stock price is near the exercise price and loses if the stock price is on the low or high side.

Like the butterfly spread, the calendar spread is one in which the stock's volatility is the major factor in its performance. The investor obtains the greatest profit if the stock has low volatility and thus trades within a narrow range. If the stock price moves substantially, the investor will likely incur a loss.

How does the calendar spread work? Recall that we are short the July call and long the October call. When closing out the position, we buy back the July call and sell the October call. If the stock price is around the exercise price, both calls will have more time value remaining than if the stock price were at the extremes. However, the July call will always have less time value than the October call on any given date. Thus, when we close out the position, the time value repurchased on the July call will be low relative to the remaining time value received from the sale of the October call. As we hold the position closer and closer to the July call's expiration, the remaining time value we must repurchase on that option will get lower and lower.

If the stock price is at the high or low extreme, the time values of both options will be low. If the stock price is high enough or low enough, there may be little, if any, time value on either option. Thus, when closing out the position there may be little time value to recover from the October option. Since the October call is more expensive, we will end up losing money on the overall transaction.

The breakeven stock prices can be obtained only by visual examination.[3] In this example, the shortest holding period has a tighter range between its two breakeven stock prices, about $154 and $170. For the longer

---

[3]However, it is possible to use a computer search routine with the Black-Scholes model to find the precise breakeven.

FIGURE 6.7   **Call Calendar Spread**

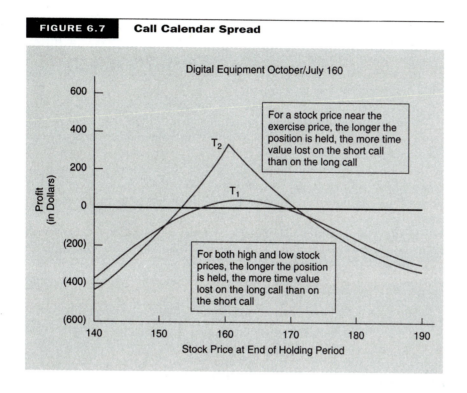

Digital Equipment October/July 160

For a stock price near the exercise price, the longer the position is held, the more time value lost on the short call than on the long call

For both high and low stock prices, the longer the position is held, the more time value lost on the long call than on the short call

Profit (in Dollars)

Stock Price at End of Holding Period

holding period, the lower breakeven is about $152 and the higher breakeven is around $171.

An investor who expected the stock price to move into the extremes could execute a reverse calendar spread. This would require purchasing the July call and selling the October call. If the stock price became extremely low or high, there would be little time value remaining to be repurchased on the October call. Since the spreader received more money from the sale of the October call than was paid for the purchase of the July call, a profit would be made. However, if the stock price ended up around the exercise price, the trader could incur a potentially large loss. This is because the October call would possibly have a large time value that would have to be repurchased.

THE TIME VALUE DECAY   Because a calendar spread is completely influenced by the behavior of the two calls' time value decay, it provides a good opportunity to examine how time values decay. Using the Black-Scholes model, we can compute the week-by-week time values for each call during the spread's life, holding the stock price constant at $164. Keep in mind, of course, that time values will change if the stock price changes. Because time values are greatest for at-the-money options, we use the July and

October 165 calls. The pattern of time values at various points during the options' lives is presented in Table 6.2. The table also presents the thetas, which we learned from Chapter 4 are the changes in the option prices for a very small change in time. Negative thetas imply that the option price will fall as we move forward in time.

Notice what happens as expiration approaches. Because of the July call's earlier expiration its theta is more negative, and its time value decays more rapidly than does that of the October call. Since we are long the October call and short the July call, the spread's time value—the time value of the long call minus the time value of the short call—increases, as is indicated by its positive theta. Once the July call expires, however, we are left with a long position in the October call, which leaves us with a negative theta. Time value will then begin decaying.

Figure 6.8 illustrates the pattern of time value decay. As expiration approaches, the time value of the July call rapidly decreases and the overall time value of the spread increases. At expiration of the July call, the spread's time value is composed entirely of the October call's time value.

The time value decay would appear to make it easy to profit with a time spread. One would simply buy the longer-term option and write the shorter-term option. As the time values decayed, the spread would gain value. In reality, however, it seldom works out like this. The pattern of time value decay illustrated here was obtained by holding the stock price constant. In the real world, the stock price probably will not remain constant. Thus, there is indeed risk to a calendar spread. However, this risk is mitigated somewhat by the fact that the investor is long one option and short the other. Nonetheless, the calendar spread, in which one buys the long-

Time value decays more rapidly as expiration approaches.

TABLE 6.2			Time Value Decay, July and October 165 and Calendar Spread					
		July 165			*October 165*		*Spread*	
Date	Time	Time Value	Theta	Time	Time Value	Theta	Time Value	Theta
June 12	.0959	5.79	−34.70	.3452	12.21	−20.55	6.42	14.15
June 19	.0767	5.09	−38.30	.3260	11.81	−21.03	6.72	17.27
June 26	.0575	4.31	−43.56	.3068	11.41	−21.55	7.10	22.01
July 3	.0384	3.40	−52.34	.2877	10.99	−22.12	7.59	30.22
July 10	.0192	2.24	−71.91	.2685	10.56	−22.75	8.32	49.16
July 17	.0000	0.00	—	.2493	10.11	−23.45	10.11	−23.45

$\sigma = .29$, $S = 164$, r_c(July) $= .0521$, r_c(October) $= .0574$
The spread time value and theta equal the time value and theta on the long October call minus the time value and theta on the short July call.

term option and writes the short-term option, is a good strategy if one expects the stock price to remain fairly stable.

The degree of risk of early exercise on a calendar spread depends on which call is bought and which is sold. Since both calls have the same exercise price, the extent to which they are in-the-money is the same. However, as discussed in Chapter 3, the time to expiration is a factor in encouraging early exercise. We saw that if everything else is equal, the shorter-term option is the one more likely to be exercised early. Thus, if we write the shorter-term option, it could be exercised early. However, we always have the choice of exercising the longer-term option early. It will certainly be in-the-money if the shorter-term option is in-the-money. If S_t is the stock price prior to expiration and the shorter-term call is exercised, the cash flow will be $-(S_t - E)$ while the cash flow from exercising the longer-term option will be $S_t - E$. Thus, the total cash flow will be zero. This means that in the event of early exercise there will be no negative cash flow. However, it does not mean that there will be no overall loss on the transaction. The longer-term call is more expensive than the shorter-term call. This means that early exercise would ensure a loss by preventing us from waiting to capture the time value decay.

FIGURE 6.8   **Time Value Decay**

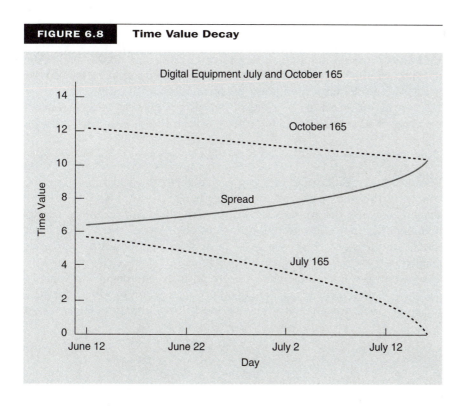

Digital Equipment July and October 165

Calendar spreads can also be constructed with puts. By using the Black-Scholes model to determine the time value on the puts, similar results can be obtained. Like money spreads, put calendar spreads should not be overlooked. The puts could be mispriced, in which case a spread might offer the most profitable opportunity.

The butterfly spread and calendar spread are two of several transactions called **volatility strategies.** We shall look at the others later in this chapter. For now, however, note that all the strategies covered so far are risky. Some option traders prefer riskless strategies because if the options are mispriced, it may be possible to construct a riskless portfolio that will earn a return in excess of the risk-free rate.

Ratio Spreads

Chapter 4 examined the Black-Scholes model. It showed that when an option is mispriced, an investor can construct a riskless hedge by buying an underpriced call and selling short the stock or by buying stock and selling an overpriced call. Because of margin requirements and the uptick rule, selling short stock can be complicated. By using spreads, however, the investor can buy an underpriced call and sell an overpriced or correctly priced call, producing a ratio of one call to the other that creates a riskless position. This transaction is called a **ratio spread.**

The ratio spread can be either a money spread or a calendar spread. Consider two calls priced at C_1 and C_2. Initially we need not be concerned with which one is purchased and which one is sold, nor do we need to determine whether the two calls differ by time to expiration or by exercise price. The model presented here can accommodate all cases.

Let the investor hold N_1 units of the call priced at C_1 and N_2 units of the call priced at C_2. The value of the portfolio is

$$V = N_1 C_1 + N_2 C_2.$$

Recall that the delta of a call is the change in the call price over the change in the stock price, assuming the change in the stock price is very small. Let us use the symbols Δ_1 and Δ_2 as the deltas of the two calls. Remember that the deltas are the values of $N(d_1)$ from the Black-Scholes model. If the stock price changes, the first call generates a total price change of $N_1 \Delta_1$ and the second call generates a total price change of $N_2 \Delta_2$. Thus, when the stock price changes, the portfolio will change in value by the sum of these two values. A hedged position is one in which the portfolio value will not change when the stock price changes. Thus, we set $N_1 \Delta_1 + N_2 \Delta_2$ to zero and solve for the ratio N_1/N_2:

$$\frac{N_1}{N_2} = -\frac{\Delta_2}{\Delta_1}.$$

Thus, a riskless position is established if the ratio of the quantity of the first call to the quantity of the second call equals minus the inverse ratio of their deltas. The transaction would then be delta neutral.

Consider an example using the Digital Equipment July 160 and July 165 calls. Using S = 164, r_c = .0521, and T = .0959 in the Black-Scholes model gives a value of $N(d_1)$ of .646 for the July 160 and .513 for the July 165. Thus, the ratio of the number of July 160s to July 165s should be −(.513/.646) = −.794. Hence, the investor would buy 794 of the July 160s and sell 1,000 of the July 165s.

A ratio spread is a risk-free transaction involving two options weighted according to their deltas.

Note that the investor could have purchased 1,000 of the July 165s and sold 794 of the July 160s. The minus sign in the formula is a reminder to be long one option and short the other. An investor should, of course, always buy underpriced or correctly priced calls and sell overpriced or correctly priced calls.

If the stock price decreases by $1, the July 160 should decrease by .646 and the July 165 by .513. The investor is long 794 of the July 160s and therefore loses .646(794) ≈ 513. Likewise, the investor is short 1,000 of the July 165s and thus gains .513(1,000) ≈ 513. The gain on one call offsets the loss on the other.

The ratio spread, of course, does not remain riskless unless the ratio is continuously adjusted. Because this is somewhat impractical, no truly riskless hedge can be constructed. Moreover, the values of $N(d_1)$ are simply approximations of the change in the call price for a change in the stock price. They apply for only very small changes in the stock price. For larger changes in the stock price, the hedger would need to consider the gamma, which we discussed in Chapter 4. Nonetheless, spreads of this type are frequently done by option traders attempting to replicate riskless positions. Although the positions may not always be exactly riskless, they will come very close to being so as long as the ratio does not deviate too far from the optimum.

This completes our coverage of option spread strategies. The next group of strategies are called **combinations,** because they involve combined positions in puts and calls. We previously covered some combination strategies, namely conversions and reversals, which we used to illustrate put-call parity. The strategies covered in the remainder of this chapter are straddles, straps, strips, and box spreads. We will use the same approach as before; the notation should be quite familiar by now.

Straddles, Straps, and Strips

Straddles, straps, and strips, like calendar and butterfly spreads, are volatility strategies because they are based on the expectation of high or low volatility rather than the direction of the stock.

A **straddle** is the purchase of a call and a put that have the same exercise price and expiration date. By holding both a call and a put, the trader can capitalize on stock price movements in either direction.

Consider the purchase of a straddle with the call and put having an exercise price of E and an expiration of T. Then $N_C = 1$ and $N_P = 1$, and the profit from this transaction if held to expiration is

$$\Pi = \text{Max}(0, S_T - E) - C + \text{Max}(0, E - S_T) - P.$$

Since there is only one exercise price involved, there are only two ranges of the stock price at expiration. The profits are as follows:

$$\Pi = S_T - E - C - P \text{ if } S_T \geq E$$
$$\Pi = E - S_T - C - P \text{ if } S_T < E.$$

For the first case, in which the stock price equals or exceeds the exercise price, the call expires in-the-money.[4] It is exercised for a gain of $S_T - E$, while the put expires out-of-the-money. The profit is the gain on the call minus the premiums paid on the call and the put. For the second case, in which the stock price is less than the exercise price, the put expires in-the-money and is exercised for a gain of $E - S_T$. The profit is the gain on the put minus the premiums paid for the put and the call.

For the range of stock prices above the exercise price, the profit increases dollar for dollar with the stock price at expiration. For the range of stock prices below the exercise price, the profit decreases dollar for dollar with the stock price at expiration. When the options expire with the stock price at the exercise price, both options are at-the-money and essentially expire worthless. The profit then equals the premiums paid, which, of course, makes it a loss. These results suggest that the graph is V-shaped. Figure 6.9 illustrates the straddle for the Digital Equipment July 165 options. The dashed lines are the strategies of buying the call and the put separately.

As noted, the straddle is designed to capitalize on high stock price volatility. To create a profit, the stock price must move substantially in either direction. It is not necessary to know which way the stock will go; it is necessary only that it make a significant move. How much must it move? Look at the two breakeven points.

For the case in which the stock price exceeds the exercise price, set the profit equal to zero:

$$S_T^* - E - C - P = 0.$$

---

[4]The case in which $S_T = E$ is included in this range. Even though $S_T = E$ means that the call is at-the-money, it can still be exercised for a gain of $S_T - E = 0$.

FIGURE 6.9   **Straddle**

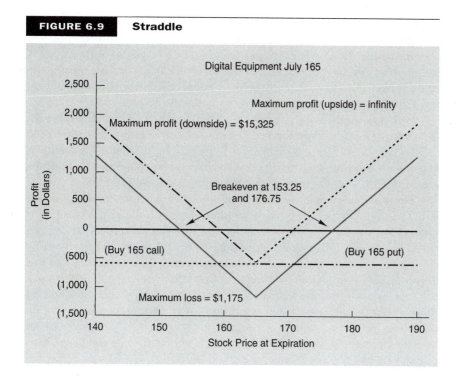

Solving for S_T^* gives a breakeven of

$$S_T^* = E + C + P.$$

The upside breakeven is simply the exercise price plus the premiums paid for the options.

For the case in which the stock price is below the exercise price, set the profit equal to zero:

$$E - S_T^* - C - P = 0.$$

Solving for S_T^* gives a breakeven of

$$S_T^* = E - C - P.$$

The downside breakeven is the exercise price minus the premiums paid on the options.

Thus, the breakeven stock prices are simply the exercise price plus or minus the premiums paid for the call and the put. This makes sense. On the upside, the call is exercised for a gain equal to the difference between the stock price and the exercise price. For the investor to profit, the stock

A straddle is a strategy designed to profit if there is a large up or down move in the stock.

price must exceed the exercise price by enough that the gain from exercising the call will cover the premiums paid for the call and the put. On the downside, the put is exercised for a gain equal to the difference between the exercise price and the stock price. To generate a profit, the stock price must be sufficiently below the exercise price that the gain on the put will cover the premiums on the call and the put.

In this example, the premiums are $5.75 for the call and $6 for the put for a total of $11.75. Thus, the breakeven stock prices at expiration are $165 plus or minus $11.75, or $153.25 and $176.75. The stock price currently is at $164. To generate a profit, the stock price must increase by $12.75 or decrease by $10.75 in the remaining 35 days until the options expire.

The worst-case outcome for a straddle is for the stock price to end up equal to the exercise price where neither the call nor the put can be exercised for a gain.[5] The option trader will lose the premiums on the call and the put, which in this example total $100(5.75 + 6) = 1,175$.

The profit potential on a straddle is unlimited. The stock price can rise infinitely, and the straddle will earn profits dollar for dollar with the stock price in excess of the exercise price. On the downside, the profit is limited simply because the stock price can go no lower than zero. The downside maximum profit is found by setting the stock price at expiration equal to zero for the case in which the stock price is below the exercise price. This gives a profit of $E - C - P$, which here is $100(165 - 5.75 - 6) = 15,325$.

The potentially large profits on a straddle can be a temptation too hard to resist. One should be aware that the straddle normally requires a fairly large stock price move to be profitable. Even to a novice investor stock prices always seem highly volatile, but that volatility may be misleading.

For example, consider a two-month straddle on a market index. A reasonable estimate of the market's annualized standard deviation would be about .14. For a two-month holding period, the standard deviation would be about $\sqrt{(2/12)(.14)^2} = .0572$. Assuming a normal distribution of returns, the stock price would be expected to fluctuate within 5.72 percent up or down about two-thirds of the time. This is a fairly small stock price change and would result in a loss in many straddle transactions. In this example, it would require about an 8 percent increase or a 7 percent decrease in the stock price to make a profit. An investor considering a straddle is advised to carefully assess the probability that the stock price will move into the profitable range.

Because both the call and the put are owned, the problem of early exercise does not exist with a straddle. The early-exercise decision is up to the straddle holder. However, transaction costs need to be considered.

---

[5]Either the put, the call, or both could be exercised, but the gain on either would be zero. Transaction costs associated with exercise would suggest that neither the call nor the put would be exercised when $S_T = E$.

When the straddle is established, there is a commission on both the call and the put. At exercise there will be a commission only on either the call or the put, whichever is in-the-money. Suppose the stock price ends up slightly higher than the exercise price. Because of the commission on the exercise of the call, it might be inadvisable to exercise the call even though it is in-the-money. A similar argument can be made for the case against exercising the put when the stock price ends up slightly less than the exercise price. This means that, as with any option strategy, the maximum loss is slightly more than the analysis indicates because of the commission. Moreover, the stock price at which such a loss occurs is actually a range around the exercise price.

THE CHOICE OF HOLDING PERIOD   Now consider what happens upon closing the position prior to expiration. Figure 6.10 illustrates the outcomes for the Digital Equipment October 165 straddle using the same three holding periods employed in examining the other strategies;[6] that

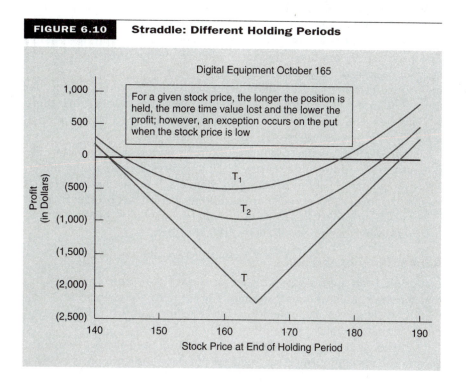

FIGURE 6.10   Straddle: Different Holding Periods

Digital Equipment October 165

For a given stock price, the longer the position is held, the more time value lost and the lower the profit; however, an exception occurs on the put when the stock price is low

[6]Specifically, the holding period T_1 means that the remaining maturity is .2301 based on 84 days remaining, T_2 means that the remaining maturity is .1151 based on 42 days remaining, and $T = 0$ assumes holding all the way to expiration.

is, the shortest holding period involves closing the position on July 24, the intermediate-length holding period on September 4, and the long holding period at expiration. The profit graphs are curves that collapse onto the straight line for the case in which the position is held to expiration. The highest curve is the shortest holding period.

We should keep in mind that this graph does not imply that the shortest holding period is the best strategy. For a given stock price, the shortest holding period indeed provides the highest profit. The uncertainty of the stock price at expiration prevents the short holding period from dominating the longer holding periods. Because a straddle is designed to permit profiting from large stock price fluctuations, the short holding period leaves less time for the stock price to make a significant move.

When the straddle is closed out prior to expiration, both the call and the put will contain some remaining time value. If the stock price is extremely high or low, neither option will have much time value, but either the call or the put will have a high intrinsic value. If the stock price is close to the exercise price, both options will have a fair amount of time value. When closing out the position, the investor sells the options back and recovers this time value. As the holding period is extended closer to the expiration date, there is less time value to recover and the profit declines. The profit curve gradually decreases until at expiration it becomes the curve for the case in which the straddle is held to expiration. Thus, the higher profits from shorter holding periods come from recapturing the time value of the put and the call. Notice, once again, however, that there is a slight exception to the time value decay pattern when the stock price is low. This is because we treated the put as European.

For a given stock price, a straddle, being long two options, loses value as expiration approaches.

Figure 6.10 shows that the shorter holding period leads to a lower upside and higher downside breakeven. This reduces the risk to the trader, because the range of stock prices in which a loss can be incurred is smaller. In this example, the shortest holding period has breakeven stock prices of about $145 and $177 and the intermediate-term holding period has breakeven stock prices of about $143 and $185.

Applications of Straddles

A straddle is an appropriate strategy for situations in which one suspects that the stock price will move substantially but does not know in which direction it will go. An example of this occurs when a major bank or corporation is about to fail.

Suppose a failing bank applies for a bailout from the government.[7] During the period in which the request is under consideration, a straddle

---

[7] Bailouts frequently take the form of loan guaranties but can also involve sale of unproductive assets, or sale of new equity or hybrid securities.

will be a potentially profitable strategy. If the request is denied, the bank probably will fail and the stock will become worthless. If the bailout is granted, the bank may be able to turn itself around, in which case the stock price will rise substantially.

A similar scenario exists when a major corporation applies for federal loan guaranties. A straddle is also an appropriate strategy for situations in which important news is about to be released and it is expected that it will be either very favorable or very unfavorable. The weekly money supply announcements present opportunities that possibly could be exploited with index options. Corporate earnings announcements are other examples of situations in which uncertain information will be released on a specific date.

The straddle certainly is not without risk, however. If investors already know or expect the information, the stock price may move very little when the announcement is made. If this happens, the investor might be tempted to hold on to the straddle in the faint hope that some other, unanticipated news will be released before the options expire. In all likelihood, however, the stock price will move very little and the straddle will produce a loss. The trader might wish to cut the loss quickly by closing the position if the expected move does not materialize.

The most important thing to remember when evaluating a straddle is to note that the greater uncertainty associated with the examples described here is known by everyone. Thus, the options would be priced according to a higher stock volatility, making the straddle more expensive. The most attractive straddles will be those in which the investor is confident that the stock will be more volatile than everyone else believes.

A Short Straddle

An investor who expects the market to stay within a narrow trading range might consider writing a straddle. This would involve the sale of a put and a call with the same exercise price and expiration date. From the previous analysis, it should be obvious that the profit graph would be an inverted V. A short straddle would be a high-risk strategy because of the potential for large losses if the stock price moved substantially, particularly upward. Also, there would be the risk of early exercise of either the put or the call.

There are two popular variations of the straddle: the strap and the strip.

Straps

A **strap** can be more easily understood by comparing it to a straddle. Suppose an investor expects the stock price to make a large move but does not know the direction. If the stock is as likely to increase as it is to decrease, a straddle will be appropriate because it has a symmetric payoff. Large

stock price increases are as profitable as equivalent stock price decreases. A straddle can be viewed as a wager in which the trader places equal bets on a bull and bear market.

Now suppose an investor is feeling slightly more bullish than bearish. He or she expects a large stock price movement, but feels it is more likely that the stock price will increase than decrease. It would make sense to increase the number of calls relative to the number of puts. The more calls used, the more bullish is the investor. A strap, then, is the special case in which two calls are purchased for each put.

In a strap, $N_C = 2$ and $N_P = 1$. The profit is

$$\Pi = 2\text{Max}(0, S_T - E) - 2C + \text{Max}(0, E - S_T) - P.$$

The profits for the two ranges of stock price at expiration are as follows:

$$\Pi = 2S_T - 2E - 2C - P \text{ if } S_T \geq E$$
$$\Pi = -2C + E - S_T - P \text{ if } S_T < E.$$

For the case in which the stock price equals or exceeds the exercise price, the strap's profit is greater than the straddle's by the amount $S_T - E - C$. For the case in which the stock price is less than the exercise price, the strap's profit is lower than the straddle's by the amount C, the premium on the additional call. The second call was purchased, but with this outcome it expires worthless.

A strap is a slightly bullish variation of a straddle, involving two calls and one put.

Figure 6.11 illustrates the strap overlaid with the straddle for the Digital Equipment July 165 options. Notice how the maximum loss still occurs if the stock price ends up at the exercise price of 165. In this case, neither the two calls nor the one put end up in-the-money. The strap is a slightly "tilted" version of the straddle. The upside profit of a strap can be greater than the straddle's if the stock price is sufficiently high. On the downside, however, the strap will always do worse than the straddle. This is because of the lost premium on the second call if the stock price ends up below the exercise price.

The two breakeven stock prices at expiration are found by setting the two profit equations to zero and solving for the stock price at expiration, S_T^*. For the case in which the stock price exceeds the exercise price,

$$2S_T^* - 2E - 2C - P = 0.$$

Solving for S_T^* gives

$$S_T^* = E + C + \frac{P}{2}.$$

FIGURE 6.11   **Strap**

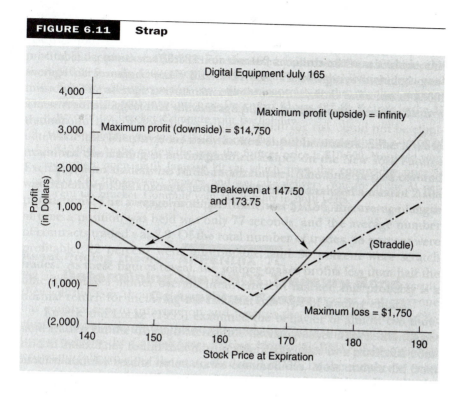

For the case in which the stock price is less than the exercise price,

$$-2C + E - S_T^* - P = 0.$$

Solving for S_T^* gives

$$S_T^* = E - P - 2C.$$

The upside breakeven stock price is lower by one-half of the put premium. The downside breakeven is lower by the call premium. This means that the upside breakeven stock price is easier to reach and the downside breakeven stock price is harder. This is the price one pays with such a strategy. By increasing the "bet" on a bull market, the payoff in a bull market is higher but the payoff in a bear market is lower.

In this example, the upside breakeven is $165 + 5.75 + 6/2 = 173.75$ as opposed to $176.75 for the straddle. The downside breakeven is $165 - 6 - 2(5.75) = 147.50$ as opposed to $153.25 for the straddle. The maximum profit is infinity on the upside and $100(-2C + E - P) = 100[-2(5.75)$

+ 165 − 6] = 14,750 on the downside. The worst outcome is the profit at a stock price at expiration equal to the exercise price. This is $100[−2(5.75) − 6] = −1,750$. In the straddle, the worst outcome is a loss of $1,175.

Strips

A **strip** is simply a long position in two puts and one call. Compared to the straddle, the strip involves increasing one's bet that the market will go down. The investor is still uncertain which way the market will go but is feeling slightly more bearish than bullish. If the market goes down, there will be two puts to exercise. If the market goes up, the cost of the second put will cut into the profit.

In a strip, $N_C = 1$ and $N_P = 2$. The profit equation is

$$\Pi = \text{Max}(0, S_T − E) − C + 2\text{Max}(0, E − S_T) − 2P.$$

The profit equations for the two possible ranges of stock price at expiration are as follows:

$$\Pi = S_T − E − C − 2P \qquad \text{if } S_T \geq E$$
$$\Pi = −C + 2E − 2S_T − 2P \quad \text{if } S_T < E.$$

When the stock price at expiration is below the exercise price, the extra put adds the amount $E − S_T − P$ to the profit. If the stock price ends up above the exercise price, the profit from the strip falls below the profit from a straddle by the amount of the second put premium.

Figure 6.12 illustrates the strip overlaid with the straddle for the Digital Equipment July 165 options. The strip "tilts" the straddle up from the left. The worst case is still when the stock price ends up at the exercise price, because with that outcome neither the puts nor the call is worth anything. The profit in this case is $−C − 2P$, which here equals $100[−5.75 − 2(6)] = −1,775$.

The upside breakeven is found by setting to zero the profit for the case in which the stock price at expiration exceeds the exercise price:

$$S_T^* − E − C − 2P = 0.$$

Solving for S_T^* gives

$$S_T^* = E + C + 2P.$$

The downside breakeven is found by setting to zero the profit for the case in which the stock price at expiration is less than the exercise price:

$$−C + 2E − 2S_T^* − 2P = 0.$$

A strip is a slightly bearish variation of a straddle, involving two puts and one call.

FIGURE 6.12	**Strip**

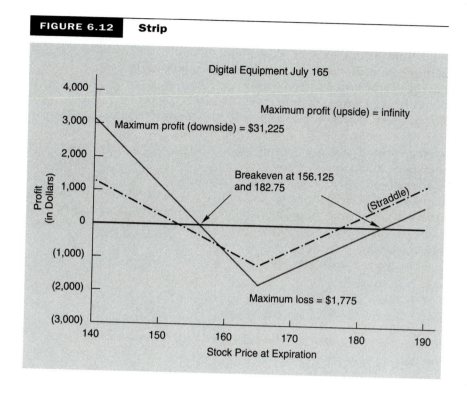

Solving for S_T^* gives

$$S_T^* = E - P - \left(\frac{C}{2}\right).$$

The upside breakeven reflects the fact that the stock price must exceed the exercise price by the premiums on the one call and the two puts. On the downside, the breakeven is reduced by one-half of the premium on the call. In this example, the upside breakeven is $165 + 5.75 + 2(6) = 182.75$ and the downside breakeven is $165 - 6 - 5.75/2 = 156.125$. Recall that for the straddle the breakevens were \$153.25 and \$176.75. The downside breakeven on the strip is higher, meaning that the stock price need not fall as much to create a profit. On the upside, however, the stock price must increase more with the strip than with the straddle to generate a profit. The maximum profit is still infinity on the upside and $100(-C + 2E - 2P) = 100[-5.75 + 2(165) - 2(6)] = 31,225$ on the downside. The worst outcome is the loss of the premiums paid out, $100[-2(6) - 5.75] = -1,775$.

Box Spreads

A **box spread** is a combination of a bull call money spread and a bear put money spread. In contrast to the volatility strategies, the box spread is a low-risk—in fact, riskless—strategy.

Consider a group of options with two exercise prices, E_1 and E_2, and the same expiration. A bull call spread would involve the purchase of the call with exercise price E_1 at a premium of C_1 and the sale of the call with exercise price E_2 at a premium of C_2. A bear put spread would require the purchase of the put with exercise price E_2 at a premium of P_2 and the sale of the put with exercise price E_1 at a premium of P_1. Under the rules for the effect of exercise price on put and call prices, both the call and put spread would involve an initial cash outflow, because $C_1 > C_2$ and $P_2 > P_1$. Thus, the box spread would have a net cash outflow at the initiation of the strategy.

The profit at expiration is

$$\Pi = \text{Max}(0, S_T - E_1) - C_1 - \text{Max}(0, S_T - E_2) + C_2$$
$$+ \text{Max}(0, E_2 - S_T) - P_2 - \text{Max}(0, E_1 - S_T) + P_1.$$

Because there are two exercise prices, we must examine three ranges of the stock price at expiration. The profits are

$$\begin{aligned}
\Pi &= -C_1 + C_2 + E_2 - S_T - P_2 - E_1 + S_T + P_1 \\
&= E_2 - E_1 - C_1 + C_2 - P_2 + P_1 && \text{if } S_T \le E_1 < E_2 \\
\Pi &= S_T - E_1 - C_1 + C_2 + E_2 - S_T - P_2 + P_1 \\
&= E_2 - E_1 - C_1 + C_2 - P_2 + P_1 && \text{if } E_1 < S_T \le E_2 \\
\Pi &= S_T - E_1 - C_1 + E_2 - S_T + C_2 - P_2 + P_1 \\
&= E_2 - E_1 - C_1 + C_2 - P_2 + P_1 && \text{if } E_1 < E_2 < S_T.
\end{aligned}$$

Notice that the profit is the same in each case: The box spread will be worth $E_2 - E_1$ at expiration, and the profit will be $E_2 - E_1$ minus the premiums paid, $C_1 - C_2 + P_2 - P_1$. The box spread is thus a riskless strategy. Why would anyone want to execute a box spread if one can more easily earn the risk-free rate by purchasing Treasury bills? The reason is that the box spread may prove to be incorrectly priced, as a valuation analysis can reveal.

Because the box spread is a riskless transaction that pays off the difference in the exercise prices at expiration, it should be easy to determine whether it is correctly priced. The payoff can be discounted at the risk-free rate. The present value of this amount is then compared to the cost of obtaining the box spread, which is the net premiums paid. This procedure is like analyzing a capital budgeting problem. The present value of the payoff at expiration minus the net premiums is a net present value (NPV). Since the objective of any investment decision is to maximize NPV, an investor should undertake all box spreads in which the NPV is positive. On

those spreads with a negative NPV, one should execute a reverse box spread.

The net present value of a box spread is

$$NPV = (E_2 - E_1)(1 + r)^{-T} - C_1 + C_2 - P_2 + P_1,$$

where r is the risk-free rate and T is the time to expiration.[8] If NPV is positive, the present value of the payoff at expiration will exceed the net premiums paid. If NPV is negative, the total amount of the premiums paid will exceed the present value of the payoff at expiration. The process is illustrated in Figure 6.13.

An alternative way to view the box spread is as the difference between two put-call parities. For example, for the options with exercise price E_1, put-call parity is

$$P_1 = C_1 - S + E_1 (1 + r)^{-T},$$

and for the options with exercise price E_2, put-call parity is

$$P_2 = C_2 - S + E_2 (1 + r)^{-T}.$$

Rearranging both equations to isolate the stock price gives

$$S = C_1 - P_1 + E_1(1 + r)^{-T}$$
$$S = C_2 - P_2 + E_2(1 + r)^{-T}.$$

FIGURE 6.13 **The Box Spread**

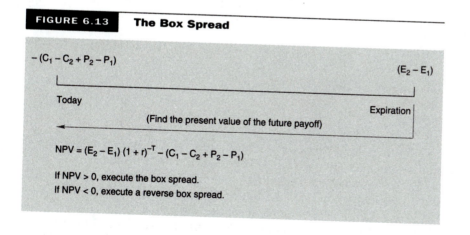

$- (C_1 - C_2 + P_2 - P_1)$

$(E_2 - E_1)$

Today

Expiration

(Find the present value of the future payoff)

$NPV = (E_2 - E_1)(1 + r)^{-T} - (C_1 - C_2 + P_2 - P_1)$

If NPV > 0, execute the box spread.

If NPV < 0, execute a reverse box spread.

---

[8]Alternatively, one could compute the present value of $E_2 - E_1$ as $(E_2 - E_1)e^{-r_c T}$ and obtain the same result.

Derivatives in Action

Options Sur le Super Bowl

Société Générale (SG), a large French bank, decided to have a little fun and teach something about options using the 1992 Super Bowl between the Washington Redskins and the Buffalo Bills. SG held a large Super Bowl party and allowed participants to create puts and calls on the game. Everyone was given 200 dollars of play money with which to trade the options. The biggest winner took home a trip to Paris. Here's how it worked.

Let W = Washington's score, B = Buffalo's score. An option (call or put) can be created with any exercise price, E. Calls pay off at the end of the game according to whether the team on whom the option is written won and the spread exceeded the exercise price. For example, consider a call on Washington. Its value at the end of the game is $Max(0, (W - B) - E)$. A call on Buffalo is worth $Max(0, (B - W) - E)$ when the game is over. In other words, a call on a given team pays off only if the team wins and the point spread exceeds the exercise price. Calls can be purchased or sold. In addition it is possible to trade puts and to con-struct straddles, spreads, and other combination strategies. Trading begins 20 minutes before game time and is prohibited during commercials.

During the game the option prices rise and fall with the activity of the game. Of course, they are European and, thus, cannot be exercised until the game is over. There is not much time (60 official minutes) in their lives but a considerable amount of information is packed into that time.

Let C^W and C^B be the prices before the game is over of the calls on Washington and Buffalo. Here's how the game went. The time to expiration is the time remaining in the game. We cannot determine exactly what the options would sell for but we know any option would have a minimum value of the amount by which it is in the money, adjusting for the present value of the exercise price. Since the option's life is so short we need not worry about the present value ad-justment.

In this example, we shall assume an exercise price of 10. Thus, a call on a team pays off at the end of the game if the team wins by at least 10 points.

Since the left-hand sides are equal, the right-hand sides must also be equal; therefore,

$$C_1 - P_1 + E_1(1 + r)^{-T} = C_2 - P_2 + E_2(1 + r)^{-T}.$$

Rearranging this equation gives

$$0 = (E_2 - E_1)(1 + r)^{-T} - C_1 + C_2 - P_2 + P_1.$$

This is our put-call parity equation when the NPV is zero, which results if all puts and calls are correctly priced relative to one another.

Let us examine the Digital Equipment July box spread using the 165 and 170 options. Consider the following transaction: Buy the 165 call at $5.75, buy the 170 put at $8.50, write the 170 call at $3.75, and write the 165 put at $6.00. The premiums paid for the 165 call and 170 put minus the premiums received for the 170 call and 165 put net out to $4.50. Thus, it will cost $450 to buy the box spread.

Quarter	Scoring	Score W	Score B	Time to Expiration	Minimum Values C^W	Minimum Values C^B
2	Washington field goal	3	0	43:02	0	0
	Washington touchdown	10	0	39:54	0	0
	Washington touchdown	17	0	37:17	7	0
3	Washington touchdown	24	0	29:44	14	0
	Buffalo field goal	24	3	26:59	11	0
	Buffalo touchdown	24	10	20:58	4	0
	Washington touchdown	31	10	16:24	11	0
4	Washington field goal	34	10	14:54	14	0
	Washington field goal	37	10	11:36	17	0
	Buffalo touchdown	37	17	5:37	10	0
	Buffalo touchdown	37	24	3:55	3	0

As the game progresses and it appears that Washington is playing well, the value of its calls would have to rise as the options traders anticipate a rout. However, with each Buffalo score the Washington calls begin to decline and the Buffalo calls begin to rise. In the end the Washington calls paid off 3 points because Washington won by 13 points.

Although SG's efforts to educate people on the use of options in some way make them appear to be gambling, they do illustrate nicely how options work and how their prices rise and fall with the uncertainty about the final outcome.

Source: This material is drawn from Robert J. McCartney, "'Skins Up by 10? You Make the Call: Punt or Put?" *Washington Post,* January 26, 1992, p. H1.

The payoff at expiration is $E_2 - E_1$. The net present value is

$$NPV = 100[(170 - 165)(1.0535)^{-.0959} - 4.50] = \$47.51,$$

where .0535 is the discrete risk-free rate for July as determined in Chapter 3 and .0959 is the time to expiration from June 12 to July 17. Thus, the spread is underpriced and should be purchased. Had the NPV been negative, the box spread would have been overpriced and should be sold. In that case, an investor would buy the 170 call and 165 put and sell the 165 call and 170 put. This would generate a positive cash flow up front that exceeded the present value of the cash outflow of $E_2 - E_1$ at expiration.

If the investor is holding a long box spread, the risk of early exercise is unimportant. Suppose the short call is exercised. Because the short call is in-the-money, the long call will be even deeper in-the-money. The investor can then exercise the long call. If the short put is exercised, the investor can in turn exercise the long put, which will be even deeper in-the-money than the short put. The net effect is a cash inflow of $E_2 - E_1$, the

A box spread is a risk-free transaction in which the value can be easily calculated as the present value of a future payoff minus the initial outlay.

maximum payoff at expiration. For the short box spread, however, early exercise will result in a cash outflow of $E_2 - E_1$. Thus, the early exercise problem is an important consideration for short box spreads.

Transaction costs on a box spread will be high because four options are involved. However, at least two of the four options will expire out-of-the-money. Nonetheless, the high transaction costs will make the box spread costly to execute for all but those who own seats on the exchange.

Summary

This chapter showed how some of the basic option strategies introduced in Chapter 5 can be combined to produce more complex strategies such as spreads and combinations. Spreads were shown to be relatively low-risk strategies. Money spreads can be designed to profit in a bull or a bear market. Calendar spreads and butterfly spreads are used to profit in either the presence or absence of high volatility. Straddles, straps, and strips were also shown to be attractive in periods of high or low volatility. Straps and strips are variations of the straddle in which a trader can increase a bet on the direction of the market. Finally, the chapter introduced the box spread, a riskless transaction that lends itself to a variation of a standard capital budgeting analysis with the end result being a net present value, a concept often encountered elsewhere in finance.

The strategies covered in this and the preceding chapter are but a few of the many possible option strategies. Those interested in furthering their knowledge of option strategies can explore the many excellent books cited in the references. The framework developed here should be sufficient to get you started. At this point, you should be capable of assessing the risks and rewards of a few simple option strategies. This book is an introduction and hopefully will encourage you to explore option strategies in more depth.

At one time, options, forward, and futures markets existed almost independently of each other. Now it is sometimes difficult to tell where one market ends and the other begins. Although we shall leave the world of options for awhile, we will return to it in Chapter 11.

Key Terms

Before continuing to Chapter 7, you should be able to give brief definitions of the following terms.

- spread
- vertical/strike/money spread
- horizontal/time/calendar spread
- buying the spread/debit spread
- selling the spread/credit spread
- bull spread
- bear spread
- butterfly spread/sandwich spread
- volatility strategy
- ratio spread
- combination
- straddle/strap/strip
- box spread

Questions and Problems

1. Explain why option traders often use spreads instead of simple long or short options and combined positions of options and stock.

2. Suppose an option trader has a call bull spread. The stock price has risen substantially, and the trader is considering closing the position early. What factors should the trader consider with regard to closing the transaction before the options expire?

3. Suppose you are following the stock of a firm that has been experiencing severe problems. Failure is imminent unless the firm is granted government-guaranteed loans. If the firm fails, its stock will, of course, fall substantially. If the loans are granted, it is expected that the stock will rise substantially. Identify two strategies that would be appropriate for this situation. Justify your answers.

4. Explain why in some situations a put bear spread could offer an advantage over a similar call bear spread.

5. Derive the profit equations for a put bull spread. Determine the maximum and minimum profits and the breakeven stock price at expiration.

6. Explain the process by which the profit of a short straddle closed out prior to expiration is influenced by the time values of the put and call.

7. Explain why selecting a strap over a straddle implies a slightly more bullish outlook.

8. The chapter showed how analyzing a box spread is like a capital budgeting problem using the net present value approach. Consider the internal rate of return method of examining capital budgeting problems and analyze the box spread in that context.

The following option prices were observed for calls and puts on a stock on July 6 of a particular year. Use this information for problems 9 through 21. The stock was priced at 165 1/8. The expirations are July 17, August 21, and October 16. The continuously compounded risk-free rates associated with the three expirations are .0503, .0535, and .0571, respectively. The standard deviation is .21.

Strike	Calls			Puts		
	Jul	Aug	Oct	Jul	Aug	Oct
160	6	8 1/8	11 1/8	3/4	2 3/4	4 1/2
165	2 11/16	5 1/4	8 1/8	2 3/8	4 3/4	6 3/4
170	13/16	3 1/4	6	5 3/4	7 1/2	9

For problems 9 through 12 and 15 through 18, determine the profits for the holding period indicated for possible stock prices of 150, 155, 160, 165, 170, 175, and 180 at the end of the holding period. Answer any other questions as indicated. Note: Your Excel spreadsheet stratlyz1.xls will be useful here for obtaining graphs as requested but it does not allow you to calculate the profits for several user-specified asset prices. It permits you to specify one asset price and a maximum and minimum. Use stratlyz1.xls to produce the graph for the range of prices from 150 to 180 but determine the profits for the prices of 150, 155, . . . , 180 by hand for positions held to expiration. For positions closed prior to expiration, use the spreadsheet bsbin1.xls or the Windows program bsbwin2.exe to determine the option price when the position is closed; then calculate the profit by hand.

9. Construct a bear money spread using the October 165 and 170 calls. Hold until the options expire. Determine the profits and graph the results. Identify the breakeven stock price at expiration and the maximum and minimum profits.

10. Repeat problem 9, but close the position on September 20. Calculate the profit by hand when the stock price on September 20 is 155. Then use the spreadsheet or calculate by hand to find the profits for the possible stock prices on September 20. Generate a graph and use it to identify the approximate breakeven stock price.

11. Suppose you are expecting the stock price to move substantially over the next three months. You are considering a butterfly spread. Construct an appropriate butterfly spread using the October 160, 165, and 170 calls. Hold the position until expiration. Determine the profits and graph the results. Identify the two breakeven stock prices and the maximum and minimum profits.

12. Construct a calendar spread using the August and October 170 calls that will profit from high volatility. Close the position on August 1. Calculate the profit by hand when the stock price on August 1 is 155. Then use the spreadsheet or calculate by hand to find the profits for the possible stock prices on August 1. Generate a graph and use it to estimate the maximum and minimum profits and the breakeven stock prices.

13. Using the Black-Scholes model, compute and graph the time value decay of the October 165 call on the following dates: July 15, July 31, August 15, August 31, September 15, September 30, and October 16. Assume the stock price remains constant. Calculate the time value on July 15 by hand and then use the spreadsheet or calculate by hand to find the time value in all of the cases.

14. Consider a riskless spread with a long position in the August 160 call and a short position in the October 160 call. Determine the appropriate hedge ratio. Then show how a $1 stock price increase would have a neutral effect on the spread value. Discuss any limitations of this procedure.

15. Construct a long straddle using the October 165 options. Hold until the options expire. Determine the profits and graph the results. Identify the breakeven stock prices at expiration and the minimum profit.

16. Repeat problem 15, but close the positions on September 20. Calculate the profit by hand when the stock price on September 20 is 155. Then use the spreadsheet or calculate by hand to find the profits for the possible stock prices on September 20. Generate a graph and use it to identify the approximate breakeven stock prices.

17. Construct a long strap using the October 165 options. Hold the position until expiration. Determine the profits and graph the results. Identify the breakeven stock prices at expiration and the minimum profit. Compare the results with the October 165 straddle.

18. Construct a short strip using the August 170 options. Hold the position until the options expire. Determine the profits and graph the results. Identify the breakeven stock prices at expiration and the minimum profit.

19. Analyze the August 160/170 box spread. Determine whether a profit opportunity exists and, if so, how one should exploit it.

20. (Concept Problem) The chapter presented two variations of the straddle: straps and strips. Another variation of the straddle is called a *strangle*. A strangle is the purchase of a call with a higher exercise price and a put with a lower exercise price. Evaluate the strangle strategy by examining the purchase of the August 165 put and 170 call. As in the problems above, determine the profits for stock prices of 150, 155, 160, 165, 170, 175, and 180. Hold the position until expiration and graph the results. Find the breakeven stock prices at expiration. Explain why one would want to use a strangle.

21. (Concept Problem) Many option traders use a combination of a money spread and a calendar spread called a *diagonal spread*. This transaction involves the purchase of a call with a lower exercise price and longer time to expiration and the sale of a call with a higher exercise price and shorter time to expiration. Evaluate the diagonal spread that involves the purchase of the October 165 call and the sale of the August 170 call. Determine the profits for the same stock prices you previously examined under the assumption that the position is closed on August 1. Calculate the profit by hand when the stock price on August 1 is 155. Then use the spreadsheet or calculate by hand to find the profits for the possible stock prices on August 1. Generate a graph and use it to estimate the breakeven stock price at the end of the holding period.

PART TWO

Forwards and Futures

CHAPTER 7

The Structure of Forward and Futures Markets

Futures markets are designed to permit trading among strangers, as against other markets which permit only trading among friends.

TERENCE MARTELL
The Wall Street Journal, March 2, 1995

Chapter Objectives

■ To define and provide examples of forward contracts and futures contracts

■ To describe the institutional characteristics of forward and futures markets, especially the daily settlement procedure in futures markets and the delivery process

■ To provide information on the futures contracts available for trading, including the price quotation conventions of Treasury bills, Eurodollars, Treasury notes and bonds, and stock index futures

■ To explain the conversion factor system used in Treasury bond and note futures

■ To describe the process of placing an order to trade a futures contract

■ To illustrate the role of the clearinghouse in futures trading

■ To show how futures prices are quoted in *The Wall Street Journal*

■ To present information on the magnitude and effects of transaction costs in futures trading

■ To discuss the regulatory structure of futures and forward markets

■ To illustrate how taxes affect futures transactions

■ To illustrate the accompanying software for calculating the Treasury

Part One explored the world of options markets. The next five chapters look at forward and futures markets. A **forward contract** is an agreement between two parties, a buyer and a seller, that calls for the delivery of a commodity at a future point in time with a price agreed upon today. A **futures contract** is a forward contract that has standardized terms, is traded on an organized exchange, and follows a daily settlement procedure in which the losses of one party to the contract are paid to the other party.

Forward and futures contracts have many of the characteristics of option contracts. Both provide for the sale and delivery of a commodity on a later date at a price agreed upon today. An option—more specifically, a call option—gives the holder the right to forgo the future purchase of the good. This is done, as we have seen, if the good's price is below the exercise price. A forward or futures contract does not offer the right to forgo purchase of the good. However, like an exchange-listed option, a futures contract can be sold in the market prior to expiration. Like an over-the-counter option, a forward contract can be offset by creating a new forward contract.

Forward contracts, sometimes called **forward commitments,** are very common in everyday life. For example, an apartment lease is a series of forward contracts. The current month's use of the apartment is a spot transaction, but the two parties also have agreed to usage of the apartment for future months at a rate agreed upon today. A magazine subscription renewed for several years locks in the rate for not only the current year (a

spot transaction) but for future years (a forward transaction). Of course, some deals permit you to cancel the subscription, thus turning the forward contract into something much closer to an option. A nonrefundable airline ticket is a forward contract. As we noted in Chapter 2, however, some airline tickets permit cancellation if you are willing to pay a higher price for the ticket, which makes the agreement an option. Near and dear to the hearts of most college students (and many others) is your basic pizza delivery order, which is also a forward contract. The customer and the restaurant agree that the customer will buy the pizza at a specific price at a future point in time ("30 minutes or less"). Upon delivery, the customer must accept and pay for the pizza, even though in the interim the customer might have noticed an ad or a coupon that would make an identical pizza cost less.

Any type of contractual arrangement calling for the delivery of a good or service at a future date at a price agreed upon today is a forward contract. Neither party can legally get out of the commitment. However, either party can enter into a new, offsetting forward contract with someone else. For example, suppose after ordering the pizza, you decide that you would prefer Chinese food. You know, however, that your neighbor next door is practically addicted to pizza so you offer to sell the pizza to your neighbor when it is delivered. You might even be able to negotiate a better price, depending on how hungry your neighbor is. In that case, you contracted to deliver the pizza to your neighbor and you agreed upon a price. You are long a forward contract with the restaurant and short a forward contract with your neighbor. In the case of the apartment lease, subleasing your apartment is a way of offsetting your forward contract with the landlord.

Of course, all of these transactions are subject to a degree of uncertainty about whether a party will perform as promised. For example, suppose the pizza delivery person shows up at your door and finds no one there because you changed your mind and went out for Chinese food. Alternatively, perhaps you accepted delivery of your pizza, but your neighbor refused to accept the pizza because he changed his mind. Likewise, a landlord may find that the tenant skipped town. This potential for default is quite similar to that of the over-the-counter options market. There the buyer faced the potential default of the writer. In a forward contract, however, each party is subject to the default of the other. The pizza restaurant faces the potential that you will default. Do you face the potential that the restaurant will default by not delivering your pizza? The risk is slight but still there. Here the pizza delivery order is an example of a forward contract between an extremely creditworthy customer, the restaurant, and one with lower credit quality, yourself.

These examples are but small-scale, familiar cases of forward contracting. If we substitute agricultural products, precious metals, securities,

or currencies for pizza, apartments, magazines, and airline tickets, we have the real world of big-time forward contracting. To mitigate the risk of default, many forward markets evolved into futures markets. Futures markets permit organized trading in standardized versions of these forward contracts. To reduce the risk of default, futures contracts require a daily settling of gains and losses. As we move through the chapter, we shall look at these characteristics in more detail. But first, let us see how these markets evolved.

The Development of Forward and Futures Markets

As noted above, forward contracts are common in everyday life. Quite naturally such contracts go back to the beginnings of commerce. For example, in medieval trade fairs merchants often contracted for deferred delivery of goods at a price agreed to in advance. Over the next few hundred years, organized spot markets for commodities began to develop in major European cities. Meanwhile, a similar market for rice developed in Japan. The characteristics of these markets were not too unlike those of today's futures markets. Modern futures markets, however, generally trace back to the formation of the Chicago Board of Trade in 1848.

Chicago Futures Markets

In the 1840s, Chicago was rapidly becoming the transportation and distribution center of the Midwest. Farmers shipped their grain from the farm belt to Chicago for sale and subsequent distribution eastward along rail lines and the Great Lakes. However, due to the seasonal nature of grain production, large quantities of grain were shipped to Chicago in the late summer and fall. The city's storage facilities were inadequate for accommodating this temporary increase in supply. Prices fell drastically at harvest time as supplies increased and then rose steadily as supplies were consumed.

In 1848, a group of businessmen took the first step toward alleviating this problem by forming the Chicago Board of Trade (CBOT). The CBOT initially was organized for the purpose of standardizing the quantities and qualities of the grains. A few years later, the first forward contract was developed. Called a to-arrive contract, it provided that a farmer could agree to deliver the grain at a future date at a price determined in advance. This meant that the farmer would not ship the grain to Chicago at harvest time but could fix the price and the date at which the grain subsequently would be sold.

These to-arrive contracts proved to be a curious instrument. Speculators soon found that rather than buy and sell the grain itself they could buy and sell the contracts. In that way, they could speculate on the price

of grain to be delivered at a future date and not have to worry about taking delivery of and storing the grain. Soon thereafter, the exchange established a set of rules and regulations for governing these transactions. In the 1920s, the Clearinghouse was established. By that time, most of the essential ingredients of futures contracts were in place.

In 1874, the Chicago Produce Exchange was formed and later became the Chicago Butter and Egg Board. In 1898, it was reorganized as the Chicago Mercantile Exchange, which is now the world's second largest futures exchange. Over the years many new exchanges were formed, including the New York Futures Exchange, started in 1979 as a subsidiary of the New York Stock Exchange.

The Development of Financial Futures

For the first 120 years, futures exchanges offered trading in contracts on commodities such as agricultural goods and metals. Then, in 1971, the major Western economies began to allow their currency exchange rates to fluctuate. This opened the way for the formation in 1972 of the International Monetary Market (IMM), a subsidiary of the Chicago Mercantile Exchange that specializes in the trading of futures contracts on foreign currencies. These were the first futures contracts that could be called **financial futures.** The first interest rate futures contract appeared in 1975, when the Chicago Board of Trade originated its GNMA futures, a contract on Government National Mortgage Association pass-through certificates, whose yields reflect mortgage interest rates.

In 1976, the International Monetary Market introduced the first futures contract on a government security and a short-term financial instrument—90-day U.S. Treasury bills. This contract was actively traded for many years, but its popularity has declined somewhat, at least partly due to the remarkable success of a competing contract, the Eurodollar futures, which was launched in 1981.

In 1977, the Chicago Board of Trade started what became the most successful contract of all time—U.S. Treasury bond futures. In just a few years, this instrument became the most actively traded contract, surpassing many grain futures that had traded for more than 100 years.

The 1980s brought the highly successful stock index futures contract. This instrument, sometimes referred to as "pin-stripe pork bellies," has helped bridge the long-standing gap between New York's stock traders and Chicago's futures traders. Interestingly, however, the first stock index futures contract appeared not in New York or Chicago but in Kansas City. The Kansas City Board of Trade completed the formal registration process ahead of its New York and Chicago counterparts and on February 16, 1982, launched the Value Line Index futures. The Index and Option Market, a division of the Chicago Mercantile Exchange, followed on April 21 with its S&P 500 futures contract. The

New York Futures Exchange entered the game on May 6 with its New York Stock Exchange Index futures.

The ensuing years saw a tremendous degree of competition between the futures exchanges to introduce new contracts that would generate significant trading volume. Barely a month passed without at least one new futures contract being introduced. A few of these contracts, such as municipal bond futures, were moderately successful. Some, such as oil futures, were highly successful. Most of the contracts, like inflation futures, commercial paper futures, and corporate bond index futures, failed to attract much trading volume. Even the original GNMA futures contract died and attempts to modify and revive it failed. You should note, however, that such failures are not a sign of weakness but rather of a healthy and highly competitive business in which only those contracts that truly meet a need will survive.

The Parallel Development of Over-the-Counter Markets

The most active early forward market was the market for foreign exchange, called the **interbank market.** This market grew tremendously in response to the floating of currencies in the early 1970s, as mentioned above. It consists of hundreds of banks worldwide who make forward and spot commitments with each other, representing either themselves or their clients. The market is quite large, though the exact size is difficult to estimate, since the transactions are essentially private and unregulated. The transaction sizes are quite large as well and it would be unusual for individual investors to be able to participate in this market. We shall discuss this market in more detail in Chapter 13, when we cover foreign currency derivatives.

Forward markets for various financial instruments and commodities have also developed in recent years. The decade of the 1980s saw a tremendous jump in the level of understanding and appreciation for derivative instruments. While futures and options markets were growing, forward markets began to grow as well. The primary stimulant for forward market growth was the development of swaps. A swap is an agreement between two parties to exchange payments. There are quite a few variations on this basic theme, but in general swaps are similar to forward contracts. We shall cover swaps in considerably more detail in Chapter 14. For now, however, let us note that the growing acceptance of swaps stimulated the development of other over-the-counter transactions, such as options as noted in Chapter 2, and a variety of other forward contracts. For example, one can enter into a forward contract, called a forward rate agreement or FRA, that is simply an arrangement for one party to pay a certain fixed amount of cash while the other party pays an amount of cash determined by the interest rate at a predetermined future date. This contract can be used to hedge or speculate on interest rates. It does not actually require delivery of a security or commodity as it is settled by simply exchanging

cash. It is also possible to arrange for forward delivery of almost any security or commodity at a price agreed upon today. The forward market is a large and healthy one that competes and, yet, complements the futures market.

The Over-the-Counter Forward Market

In Chapter 2 we discussed how over-the-counter options differ from exchange-traded options. Now we shall do the same for forward and futures contracts. The forward market is large and worldwide. Its participants are banks, corporations, and governments. The two parties to a forward contract must agree to do business with each other, which means that each party accepts credit risk from the other. That is, unlike in options markets where the writer does not assume any credit risk from the buyer, in forward markets each party accepts the credit risk of the other. In spite of the credit risk, however, forward contracts offer many advantages.

The primary advantage is that the terms and conditions are tailored to the specific needs of the two parties. Suppose a firm would like to secure the future purchase price of 400,000 bushels of sorghum, a grain similar in use to corn. As we shall see later, the futures markets permit trading only in contracts on specific commodities and with certain expiration dates. There is no sorghum futures contract that would permit the company to lock in the future purchase price of the sorghum. If the firm could substitute corn, however, there is a corn futures contract on the Chicago Board of Trade, though its expiration might not match the horizon date of the firm. Moreover, it might permit the seller of the futures to deliver any of several grades of corn at any of several locations. The firm would perhaps prefer to arrange a specific contract with the terms tailored to meet its needs. Similar arguments can be made with respect to financial contracts. A portfolio manager might wish to lock in the market value of a specific portfolio on a certain date. If the futures market does not have such a contract, the manager might look to the forward market.

As noted about the over-the-counter options market, the forward market also has the advantage of being a private market in which the general public does not know that the transaction was done. This prevents other traders from interpreting the size of various trades as perhaps false signals of information.

The over-the-counter market is also an unregulated market. Although there is now much debate about whether this market should be regulated, the government currently views these contracts as private arrangements. This gives investors considerably more flexibility, saves money, and allows the market to quickly respond to changing needs and circumstances by developing new variations of old contracts.

Of course, all of this comes at the expense of assuming credit risk and the requirement that the transactions be of a rather large size, several million dollars or more. It is not clear which is more costly, forwards or futures, but since the markets coexist, they must be serving their clientele in an efficient manner.

How large is the market? Since the transactions are private, it is difficult to tell. A 1996 survey taken by the International Swaps and Derivatives Association estimates the size of the over-the-counter derivatives market at over $21 trillion of face value. That survey, however, did not cover the huge foreign currency market and much of this volume is in swaps and options. It is difficult to determine the amount represented by forward contracts.

Organized Futures Trading

Futures trading is organized around the concept of a futures exchange. The exchange is probably the most important component of a futures market and distinguishes it from forward markets.

A **futures exchange** is a corporate entity comprised of members. Although some exchanges allow corporate memberships, most members are individuals. The members elect a board of directors, which in turn selects individuals to manage the exchange. The exchange has a corporate hierarchy consisting of officers, employees, and committees. The exchange establishes rules for its members and may impose sanctions on violators.

Contract Development

One of the exchange's important ongoing activities is identifying new and useful futures contracts. Most exchanges maintain research staffs that continuously examine the feasibility of new contracts. When the exchange determines that a contract is likely to be successful, it writes a proposal specifying the terms and conditions and applies to the Commodity Futures Trading Commission (CFTC), the regulatory authority, for permission to initiate trading.[1]

It is becoming increasingly difficult to determine the characteristics of an asset that make it a likely candidate for a successful futures contract. At one time, it was thought that the asset had to be storable, but there is a contract on an index of ocean freight rates, which are certainly not storable. What does seem to be a common thread is the existence of an identifiable, volatile spot price and a group of investors who face risk of loss if

---

[1]The CFTC's responsibility is discussed later in the chapter.

prices move in a certain direction. It is not necessary that the spot price be the price of an asset that one can actually buy and hold.

Thus, it is conceivable that virtually anything can have a futures contract traded on it. Whether the contract will be actively traded will depend on whether it fills the needs of hedgers and whether speculators are interested enough to take risks in it.

Contract Terms and Conditions

The contract's terms and conditions are determined by the exchange subject to CFTC approval. The specifications for each contract are the size, quotation unit, minimum price fluctuation, grade, and trading hours. In addition, the contract specifies delivery terms and daily price limits as well as delivery procedures, which are discussed in separate sections. Complete contract terms on selected financial futures contracts are provided in Appendix 7A.

Contract size means that one contract covers a specific number of units of the commodity. This might be a designated number of bushels of a grain or dollars of face value of a financial instrument. Contract size is an important decision. If too small, speculators will find it more costly to trade because there is a cost for trading each contract. The contracts are not divisible; thus, if they are too large, hedgers may be unable to get a matching number of contracts. For example, if the Chicago Board of Trade established $1 million as the Treasury bond contract, a hedger with $500,000 of bonds to hedge probably would be unable to use it.[2]

The quotation unit is simply the unit in which the price is specified. For example, corn is quoted in fourths of a cent and Treasury bonds in percentage points and thirty-seconds of a point of par value. In most cases, the spot market quotation unit is used.

Closely related to the quotation unit is the minimum price fluctuation. This is usually the smallest unit of quotation. For example, Treasury bonds are quoted in a minimum unit of thirty-seconds. Thus, the minimum price change on a Treasury bond futures contract is 1/32 of 1 percent of the contract price, or .0003125. Since the contract has a face value (contract size) of $100,000, the minimum price change is .0003125 × ($100,000) = $31.25.

The exchange also establishes the contract grade. In the case of agricultural commodities there may be numerous grades, each of which would command a quality price differential in the spot market. The contract must specify the grades that are acceptable for delivery. Financial futures

---

[2]We say *probably* because if the bonds being hedged were twice as volatile as the futures contract, one contract would be the correct number. Chapter 10 explains this point.

contracts must indicate exactly which financial instrument or instruments are eligible for delivery. If multiple instruments are deliverable, the seller of the contract holds a potentially valuable option, which we shall discuss in Chapter 11.

The exchange also specifies the hours during which the contract trades. Most agricultural futures trade for four to five hours during the day. Most financial futures trade for about six hours. The Chicago Board of Trade ran a night session for its highly active Treasury bond futures contract, but discontinued it in 1997 in favor of after-hours trading, using an electronic system.

Delivery Terms

The contract must also indicate a specific delivery date or dates, the delivery procedure, and a set of expiration months. In the case of harvestable commodities, the exchange usually establishes expiration months to correspond with harvest months. In nonharvestable commodities, such as financial futures, the exchange usually has followed the pattern of allowing expirations in March, June, September, and December. There are some exceptions, however.

The exchange also decides how far into the future the expiration dates will be set. For some contracts, the expirations extend only a year or two, while the Eurodollar contract extends about 10 years.

Once the expiration month has been set, the exchange determines a final trading day. This may be any day in the month, but the most common ones are the third Friday of the month and the business day prior to the last business day of the month. The first delivery day also must be set. Most contracts allow delivery on any day of the month following a particular day. Usually the first eligible delivery day is the first business day of the month, but for certain contracts other days may be specified. In the case of stock index futures and other cash-settled contracts, the settlement occurs on the last trading day or on the day after the last trading day.

For non-cash-settled contracts, the delivery procedure must be specified. The deliverable spot commodity must be sent to any of several eligible locations. Financial adjustments to the price received upon delivery are required when an acceptable but lower-grade commodity is delivered. We shall say more about the delivery procedure later.

Daily Price Limits and Trading Halts

During the course of a trading day prices fluctuate continuously, but many contracts have limits on the maximum daily price change. If a contract price hits the upper limit, the market is said to be **limit up.** If the price moves to the lower limit, the market is said to be **limit down.** Any such move, up or down, is called a **limit move.** Normally no transactions

above or below the limit price are allowed. Some contracts have limits only during the opening minutes; others have limits that can be expanded according to prescribed rules if prices remain at the limits for extended periods.

In conjunction with price limits, some futures contracts—notably stock index futures—contain built-in trading halts sometimes called **circuit breakers.** When prices move rapidly, trading can be stopped for predetermined periods. These halts can be accompanied by similar halts in the spot market. Such cessations of trading were installed after the stock market crash of 1987 in response to concern that extremely volatile markets might need a cooling-off period. While it is not clear that trading halts are necessarily effective, it seems likely that they will continue to be used in futures markets.

Other Exchange Responsibilities

The exchange also specifies that members meet minimum financial responsibility requirements. In some contracts it may establish position limits, which, like those in options markets, restrict the number of contracts that an individual trader can hold. The exchange establishes rules governing activities on the trading floor and maintains a department responsible for monitoring trading to determine whether anyone is attempting to manipulate the market. In some extreme cases, the exchange may elect to suspend trading if unusual events occur.[3]

Futures Exchanges

Futures trading takes place on eight futures exchanges in the United States and on several electronic systems. Table 7.1 lists the exchanges and provides pertinent information about each.

Table 7.1 also shows the many futures exchanges in other countries. The number has grown rapidly, and today almost every large country—and even a few small ones—has a futures exchange. Some of the more active futures exchanges are in Sydney, Hong Kong, Tokyo, Osaka, Paris, London, Singapore, and Toronto. Several of the foreign futures exchanges are fully automated, meaning that there is no trading floor with buyers and sellers calling out bids and offers; rather, everyone trades through computers.

One should not underestimate the size of foreign futures markets. Futures are as actively traded and sometimes more so in Japan and England

---

[3] The 1980 grain embargo against the Soviet Union and the 1987 stock market crash were two such cases.

TABLE 7.1	Exchanges on Which Futures Trade, January 1997

U.S. Exchanges

Chicago Board of Trade
141 W. Jackson Blvd.
Chicago, IL 60604-2994
312-435-3500
http://www.cbot.com
futures on: grains and oilseeds, metals,
 financials

Chicago Mercantile Exchange
30 S. Wacker Drive
Chicago, IL 60606
312-930-1000
http://www.cme.com
Divisions: International Monetary Market,
 Index and Option Market
futures on: livestock, meat, financials

Coffee, Sugar and Cocoa Exchange
4 World Trade Center
New York, NY 10048
800-433-4348
http://www.csce.com/
futures on: food and fiber

Kansas City Board of Trade
4800 Main St., Suite 303
Kansas City, MO 64112
800-821-5228
http://www.kcbt.com
futures on: grains and oilseeds, financials,
 energy

MidAmerica Commodity Exchange
 (an affiliate of the Chicago Board
 of Trade)
141 W. Jackson Blvd.
Chicago, IL 60604
312-341-3000
http://www.midam.com
futures on: grains and oilseeds, live
 stock and meat, metals, energy,
 financials

Minneapolis Grain Exchange
400 S. Fourth St.
Minneapolis, MN 55415
612-338-6212
http://www.mgex.com
futures on: grains and oilseeds,
 seafood

New York Cotton Exchange
4 World Trade Center
New York, NY 10048
212-742-5050
http://www.nyce.com
Divisions: Citrus Associates,
 Financial Instruments Exchange,
 New York Futures Exchange
futures on: food and fiber, financials

New York Mercantile Exchange
#1 North End Ave.
World Financial Center
New York, NY 10282-1101
212-299-2000
Divisions: NYMEX, COMEX
http://www.nymex.com
futures on: metals, energy, financials

as in the United States. There are an increasing number of futures exchanges in former communist countries.

One advantage of such global futures trading, particularly when it is fully automated, is the potential it offers for linkages between exchanges. For example, the Chicago Mercantile Exchange and the Singapore International Monetary Exchange (SIMEX) are linked so that a trader opening a position in Eurodollars or certain foreign currencies on one exchange can close the position on the other.

TABLE 7.1   *(continued)*

Foreign Exchanges

Sydney Futures Exchange	Tokyo Commodity Exchange
Austrian Futures & Options Exchange (Vienna)	Tokyo Grain Exchange
Belgian Futures and Options Exchange (Brussels)	Tokyo International Financial Futures Exchange
Bolsa de Mercadorias & Futuros (São Paulo)	Tokyo Stock Exchange
Montreal Exchange	Kuala Lumpur Commodity Exchange
Toronto Futures Exchange	European Options Exchange (Amsterdam)
Winnipeg Commodity Exchange	Financiele Termijnmarkt (Amsterdam)
Santiago Stock Exchange	New Zealand Futures & Options Exchange (Auckland)
Beijing Commodity Exchange	Oslo Stock Exchange
Copenhagen Stock Exchange	Manila International Futures Exchange
Finnish Options Exchange (Helsinki)	Singapore Commodity Exchange
Finnish Securities and Derivatives Exchange (Helsinki)	Singapore International Monetary Exchange
Marché à Terme International de France (Paris)	South African Futures Exchange
Deutsche Terminboerse (Frankfurt)	MEFF Renta FIJA (Barcelona)
Hong Kong Futures Exchange	MEFF Renta Variable (Madrid)
Budapest Commodity Exchange	OM Stockholm AB
Budapest Stock Exchange	Swiss Options & Financial Futures Exchange (Zurich)
Irish Futures & Options Exchange (Dublin)	International Petroleum Exchange (London)
Tel Aviv Stock Exchange	London International Financial Futures and Options Exchange
Italian Stock Exchange (Milan)	London Metal Exchange
Chubu Commodity Exchange (Nagoya)	London Securities & Derivatives Exchange
Kansai Agricultural Commodities Exchange (Osaka)	
Kobe Rubber Exchange	
Kobe Raw Silk Exchange	
Osaka Securities Exchange	
Osaka Textile Exchange	

In addition, some of the foreign futures exchanges trade contracts on assets primarily from outside their countries. For example, the London International Financial Futures Exchange (LIFFE) began trading a contract on the German government bond well before Germany even had a futures market.

The trading of futures on foreign products and the opportunities to open a contract in one market and offset it in another move the markets toward near 24-hour trading. For example, the U.S. Treasury bond futures

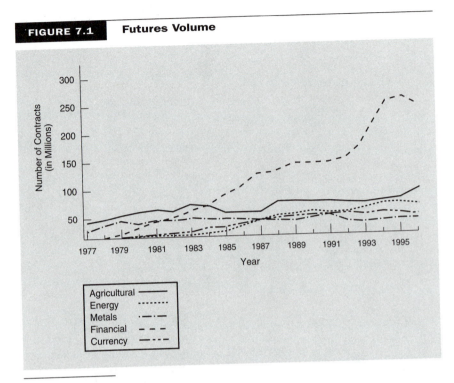

FIGURE 7.1   **Futures Volume**

Source: CFTC *Annual Report 1996*

contract trades on the Chicago Board of Trade in London, in Tokyo, and in Australia. The exchanges are not necessarily linked and the contracts are not necessarily identical but one can at least trade the basic instrument, Treasury bond futures, in several time zones.

A growing trend in futures trading worldwide is the use of electronic trading systems. For a fee, computer terminals are placed in trading rooms of institutions and individuals. These terminals permit traders to submit bids and offers and to consummate trades by simply moving the computer's mouse over the bid or offer the trader wishes to accept and then clicking. Alternative systems match up bids and offers automatically. The Chicago Mercantile Exchange (CME) began the process with a system called GLOBEX, which eventually included access to trading not only in the CME's contracts but also in contracts of certain other exchanges. Several U.S. and several foreign exchanges have developed their own electronic trading systems. The German futures exchange, the Deutsche Terminboerse, became the first foreign exchange to locate terminals in the United States that provided access to its contracts. Some foreign exchanges, such as the Swiss Options & Financial Futures Exchange

(SOFFEX), have moved away from partial pit trading–partial electronic to a fully electronic system.

It should be noted that some of these electronic systems are after-hours systems. Because trading in the pits is a popular tradition in most futures exchanges, the electronic systems are operated to complement and not compete with pit trading. The global trend, however, appears to be that electronic systems may supplant pit trading, though it is doubtful that pit trading will ever cease on U.S. exchanges.

Figure 7.1 illustrates the volume of trading in futures contracts on U.S. futures exchanges since 1977. As can be seen, the growth of trading volume has been quite phenomenal. Most of the growth has come from financial futures contracts. Many futures traders who formerly traded in porkbellies and corn have switched to various financial contracts. In addition, the remarkable success of stock index futures has brought many investors and institutions that formerly traded only in stocks and bonds to the arena of futures trading. It is also particularly noteworthy that energy futures are rapidly growing in popularity, a reflection of the crucial role of oil in the world's economy.

The Chicago Board of Trade remains the largest U.S. futures exchange. Table 7.2 indicates that the CBOT's 1996 market share was about 43 percent. The Chicago Mercantile Exchange is the second-largest exchange, capturing about 36 percent of the market. The New York Mercantile

TABLE 7.2	Trading Volume by Exchange, CFTC Fiscal Year 1996
Exchange	**Number of Contracts**
Chicago Board of Trade	169,378,503
Chicago Mercantile Exchange	141,141,225
New York Mercantile Exchange	47,523,299
Commodity Exchange*	15,868,065
Coffee, Sugar and Cocoa Exchange	8,982,678
New York Cotton Exchange	3,956,976
MidAmerica Commodity Exchange	3,250,036
Kansas City Board of Trade	2,137,063
Minneapolis Grain Exchange	1,000,542
New York Futures Exchange*	897,510
Philadelphia Board of Trade*	46,525
Total	394,182,422

*Commodity Exchange has since merged with New York Mercantile Exchange; New York Futures Exchange has since merged with New York Cotton Exchange; Philadelphia Board of Trade no longer operates.

Source: CFTC *Annual Report 1996*

Exchange ranks third, a result of its increasingly popular energy futures contracts. It has since merged with the Commodity Exchange and their combined volumes represent about 16 percent of the market. Volume figures can be deceptive, however, as they are greatly influenced by the size of the contract, which is specified by the exchange when it first proposes to offer the contract. Nonetheless, the CBOT and the CME clearly are the industry leaders, with the other exchanges dividing among themselves the remainder of a very large pie.

Futures Traders

The members of the exchange are individuals who physically go on the exchange floor and trade futures contracts. There are several ways to characterize these futures traders.

General Classes of Futures Traders

All traders on the floor of the futures exchange are either commission brokers or locals.

Commission brokers simply execute transactions for other people. A commission broker can be an independent businessperson who executes trades for individuals or institutions or a representative of a major brokerage firm. In the futures industry, these brokerage firms are called **futures commission merchants (FCM).** The commission broker simply executes trades for the FCM's customers. Commission brokers make their money by charging a commission for each trade.

Locals are individuals in business for themselves who trade from their own accounts. They attempt to profit by buying contracts at a given price and selling them at a higher price. Their trading provides liquidity for the public. Locals assume the risk and reap the rewards from their skill at futures trading. It has been said that locals represent the purest form of capitalism and entrepreneurship.

Because a futures trader can be a local or an FCM, a conflict occasionally arises between traders' loyalty to themselves and their customers' interests. For example, some traders engage in **dual trading,** in which they trade for themselves and also trade as brokers for someone else. Dual trading has become very controversial in recent years. To illustrate the conflict that might arise, suppose a trader holds a set of orders that includes a large order for a customer. Knowing that the price may move substantially when the customer's order is placed, the trader executes a purchase for his or her own account prior to placing the customer's order. There are a number of other ways in which dual trading can be profitable to the trader at the expense of the customer. However, for this to occur the trader must act unscrupulously. The exchanges argue that abuses of dual trading are

rare. Moreover, they claim that dual trading provides liquidity to the market. Some limitations on dual trading have been enacted.

Classification by Trading Strategy

Futures traders can be further classified by the strategies they employ.

Recall that in Chapter 1 we briefly discussed hedging. A **hedger** holds a position in the spot market. This might involve owning a commodity, or it may simply mean that the individual plans or is committed to the future purchase or sale of the commodity. Taking a futures contract that is opposite to the position in the spot market reduces the risk. For example, if you hold a portfolio of stocks, you can hedge that portfolio's value by selling a stock index futures contract. If the stocks' prices fall, the portfolio will lose value, but the price of the futures contract is also likely to fall. Since you are short the futures contract, you can repurchase it at a lower price, thus making a profit. The gain from the futures position will at least partially offset the loss on the portfolio.

Hedging is an important activity in any futures or derivatives market. This section has given only a cursory overview of it. Chapter 10 is devoted exclusively to hedging.

Speculators attempt to profit from guessing the direction of the market. Speculators include locals as well as the thousands of individuals and institutions off the exchange floor. They play an important role in the market by providing the liquidity that makes hedging possible and assuming the risk that hedgers are trying to eliminate. Speculating is discussed in more detail in Chapter 11.

Spreaders use futures spreads to speculate at a low level of risk. Like an option spread, a futures spread involves a long position in one contract and a short position in another. Spreads may be intracommodity or intercommodity. An intracommodity spread is like a time spread in options. The spreader buys a contract with one expiration month and sells an otherwise identical contract with a different expiration month. An intercommodity spread, which normally is not used in options, consists of a long position in a futures contract on one commodity and a short position in a contract on another. In some cases, the two commodities even trade on different exchanges. The rationale for this type of spread rests on a perceived "normal" difference between the prices of the two futures contracts. When the prices move out of line, traders employ intercommodity spreads to take advantage of the expected price realignment.

Futures spreads work much like option time spreads in that the long position in one contract is somewhat offset by the short position in the other. There actually is no real difference between this type of spread and a hedge. For example, suppose the contract is on Treasury bills, the current month is October, and the available futures expirations are December, March, and June. A hedger holds Treasury bills and sells a December

contract. A spreader holds a December contract and sells a March contract. Each holds a long position in a spot or nearby futures contract and a short position in a deferred futures contract. Each is attempting to profit from one position while expecting a loss on the other. Neither knows which position will make a profit and which will create a loss.

Arbitrageurs attempt to profit from differences in the prices of otherwise identical spot and futures positions. An analogous type of arbitrage that we already covered is the execution of conversions and reversals to take advantage of option prices that fail to conform to put-call parity. In futures markets there are some important theoretical relationships, which we shall study in Chapters 9 and 11. When prices get out of line with these theoretical predictions, arbitrageurs enter the market and execute trades that bring prices back in line. Because arbitrage is designed to be riskless, it resembles hedging and spreading. In many cases, however, it is difficult to determine whether a given strategy is arbitrage, hedging, or spreading.

Classification by Trading Style

Futures traders can also be classified by the style of trading they practice. There are three distinct trading styles: scalping, day trading, and position trading.

Scalpers attempt to profit from small changes in the contract price. Scalpers seldom hold their positions for more than a few minutes. They trade by using their skill at sensing the market's short-term direction and by buying from the public at the bid price and selling to the public at the ask price. They are constantly alert for large inflows of orders and short-term trends. Because they operate with very low transaction costs, they can profit from small moves in contract prices. The practice of making a large number of quick, small profits is referred to as scalping.

Day traders hold their positions for no longer than the duration of the trading day. Like scalpers, they attempt to profit from short-term market movements; however, they hold their positions much longer than do scalpers. Nonetheless, they are unwilling to assume the risk of adverse news that might occur overnight or on weekends.

Position traders hold their transactions open for much longer periods than do scalpers and day traders. Position traders believe they can make profits by waiting for a major market movement. This may take as much as several weeks or may not come at all.

Scalpers, day traders, and position traders are not mutually exclusive. A speculator may employ any or all of these techniques in transactions.

In addition to those who trade on the floor of the exchange, there are many individuals who trade off the exchange floor and employ some of the same techniques.

Off-Floor Futures Traders

Participants in the futures markets also include thousands of individuals and institutions. Institutions include banks and financial intermediaries, investment banking firms, mutual funds, pension funds, and other corporations. In addition, some farmers and numerous individuals actively trade futures contracts. As noted earlier, foreign institutions are becoming increasingly active in U.S. futures markets. The extent of this off-floor participation in futures markets has greatly increased in recent years, due in part to the popularity of stock index futures but also to the contracts on U.S. Treasury securities, foreign currencies, and Eurodollars.

In addition to those who directly participate in trading, federal law recognizes and regulates certain other participants. An **introducing broker (IB)** is an individual who solicits orders from public customers to trade futures contracts. IBs do not execute orders themselves, nor do their firms; rather, they subcontract with FCMs to do this. The IB and the FCM divide the commission.

A **commodity trading advisor (CTA)** is an individual or firm that analyzes futures markets and issues reports, gives advice, and makes recommendations on the purchase and sale of contracts. CTAs earn fees for their services but do not necessarily trade contracts themselves.

A **commodity pool operator (CPO)** is an individual or firm that solicits funds from the public, pools them, and uses them to trade futures contracts. The CPO profits by collecting a percentage of the assets in the fund and sometimes through sales commissions. A CPO essentially is the operator of a futures fund, a topic discussed later in this chapter. However, some commodity pools are privately operated and not open for public participation.

An **associated person (AP)** is an individual associated with any of the above individuals or institutions or any other firm engaged in the futures business. APs include directors, partners, officers, and employees but not clerical personnel.

The Cost and Profitability of Exchange Membership

Most futures exchanges have a limited number of full memberships, called **seats.** There usually is a market for seats, with the highest and lowest bids publicly reported. Seat prices tend to fluctuate with the amount of trading activity in the market and the number of new contracts introduced. Figure 7.2 illustrates the history of seat prices since 1974 for a full membership on the Chicago Board of Trade and the Chicago Mercantile Exchange. The price has been almost $1,000,000 and as low as about $70,000.

Seats can also be leased, and some exchanges have different levels of membership. For example, the Chicago Board of Trade has 1,402 full members and a lesser number of Associate Members; Government Instrument Market Membership Interests; Index, Debt, and Energy Membership

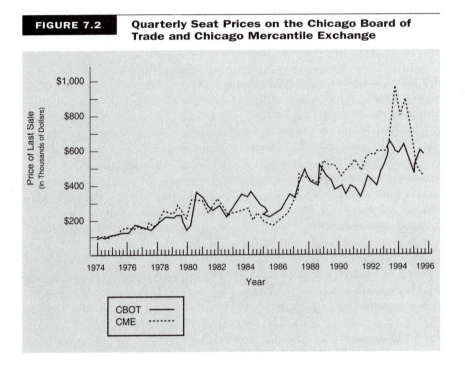

FIGURE 7.2   **Quarterly Seat Prices on the Chicago Board of Trade and Chicago Mercantile Exchange**

Interests; and Commodity Options Membership Interests. Associate Members can trade in all markets except agricultural futures. Government Instrument Market Memberships allow trading in futures contracts on government securities. Index, Debt, and Energy Membership Interests allow trading in futures on stock indices, bonds, and any energy-related contracts as well as options on those futures. Commodity option memberships allow trading in any options on futures contracts; these are covered in Chapter 12.

Like options markets, futures markets do not create or destroy wealth. Therefore, one trader's gains are another's losses subject to some slippage due to commissions and taxes. It has been said, however, that the vast majority of futures traders lose money. It is not surprising that a small number of individuals probably earn large profits while assuming high risks. Some are lucky and, of course, some are unlucky. There have been several studies of speculators' performances. Unfortunately, most of those studies are somewhat dated, but we shall look at three of them here.

Hieronymous (1977) examined all trades executed in 1969 by an unnamed futures commission merchant.[4] A total of 462 accounts were ex-

---

[4]This and several other similar studies are discussed in Teweles and Jones (1987).

amined, of which 164 earned a profit and 298 incurred a loss. The average profit for profitable accounts was $2,819, while the average loss for unprofitable accounts was $3,783. For the 462 accounts taken as a whole, the average performance was a loss of $1,439. These figures included commissions. The average performance before commissions was a loss of $560. These results suggest that the average public trader does poorly in futures trading.

While the Hieronymous study looked at public traders, Silber (1984) examined the trading of an unidentified scalper on the New York Futures Exchange who traded the NYSE Index futures. The time period covered was December 1982 through January 1983. Silber analyzed a total of 2,106 transactions. The average profit per trade was $10.56, the average length of time a position was held was only 77 seconds, and the average number of contracts traded was 2.9. Of the total number of trades, 48 percent were profitable, 22 percent were unprofitable, and 30 percent were scratch trades.[5] As these figures reveal, the scalper makes profits less than half the time but makes money overall. In an efficient market, this probably is a normal return for incurring the risk that this type of trading entails.

Kuserk and Locke (1993) examined the behavior of almost two thousand traders on the Chicago Mercantile Exchange over a three-month period in 1990. They found that most scalpers specialize in a particular commodity, and the results varied across commodities. Most traders did from 30 to 40 trades a day, with each trade made up of about three contracts on average, although Eurodollar trades averaged 14 contracts. Median income ranged from $270 a day in Live Cattle to $1,038 a day in the British Pound. The top fourth of the traders in all markets earned at least $1,000 a day. Scalping, thus, appears to be highly profitable, but the authors also found that profitability was directly related to the volatility of profits. Thus, the risk-return trade-off, discussed in Chapter 1, is alive and well on the floor of the futures exchange.

Forward Market Traders

The forward market is dominated by large institutions, such as banks and corporations. A typical forward market trader is an individual sitting at a desk with a telephone and a computer terminal. Using the computer or telephone, the trader finds out the current prices available in the market. The trader can then agree upon a price with another trader at another firm. The trader may represent his or her own firm or may execute a trade

---

[5]A *scratch trade* essentially is a breakeven trade. For example, suppose a trader wants to buy two contracts but gets an offer for four contracts. The trader might take the offer, buy the four contracts, and immediately sell two of the contracts at the same price at which they were purchased.

for a client. The trade may be a hedge, a spread, or an arbitrage. In fact, it is the thousands of traders off the floor whose arbitrage activities play a crucial role in making the market so efficient.

It would be remiss to suggest that the forward and futures markets are not linked. In a formal sense, forward contracts cannot be reversed by futures contracts. It is common, however, that a trader will do a forward contract and then immediately do a futures contract to hedge or offset the forward market risk. In fact, the trader might even combine these positions with an option or a swap. Why a trader might do this is a subject we shall get into later when we look at relationships between the prices in these markets.

The Mechanics of Futures Trading

Before placing an order to trade futures contracts, an individual must open an account with a broker. Because the risk of futures trading can be quite high, the individual must make a minimum deposit—usually at least $5,000—and sign a disclosure statement acknowledging the possible risks.

Placing an Order

One can place several types of orders. These are essentially the same as the option orders covered in Chapter 2. Stop orders and limit orders are used as well as good-till-canceled and day orders.

When an investor places an order, the broker phones the firm's trading desk on the exchange floor and relays the order to the firm's floor broker. The floor broker goes to the pit in which the contract trades. The pit is an octagonal- or polygonal-shaped ring with steps descending to the center. Hand signals and a considerable amount of verbal activity are used to place bids and make offers. This process is called **open outcry.** When the order is filled, the information is relayed back, ultimately to the broker's office, whereupon the broker telephones the customer to confirm the trade.

The process of placing and executing an order through the open-outcry system is a 140-year tradition. However, it may become a thing of the past. As noted earlier, several new futures exchanges in foreign countries are fully automated so that bids and offers are submitted through a computer and trades are executed off the floor. Some systems will even match buyer and seller. As we noted in Chapter 2, the CBOE has made some progress in automating its option orders, but it too remains essentially an open-outcry market. This primarily reflects the desire of the exchange members to preserve the open-outcry system, in which they participate and indeed enjoy each day.

As noted earlier, various exchanges have developed electronic trading systems, which are used only during hours when the exchanges are closed. A few foreign exchanges use exclusively electronic systems.

The Role of the Clearinghouse

At this point in the process, the clearinghouse intervenes. Each futures exchange operates its own independent clearinghouse. The clearinghouse in futures markets works like that in options markets, so its basic operations should be familiar to you from Chapter 2.

The concept of a clearinghouse as an intermediary and guarantor to every trade is not nearly as old as the futures markets themselves. The first such clearinghouse was organized in 1925 at the Chicago Board of Trade. The clearinghouse is an independent corporation, and its stockholders are its member clearing firms. Each firm maintains a margin account with the clearinghouse and must meet minimum standards of financial responsibility.

For each transaction, obviously, there is both a buyer, usually called the **long,** and a seller, typically called the **short.** In the absence of a clearinghouse, each party would be responsible to the other. If one party defaulted, the other would be left with a worthless claim. The clearinghouse assumes the role of intermediary to each transaction. It guarantees the buyer that the seller will perform and guarantees the seller that the buyer will perform. The clearinghouse's financial accounts contain separate records of contracts owned and the respective clearing firms and contracts sold and the respective clearing firms. Note that the clearinghouse keeps track only of its member firms. The clearing firms, in turn, monitor the long and short positions of individual traders and firms. All parties to futures transactions must have an account with a clearing firm or with a firm that has an account with a clearing firm.

Figure 7.3 illustrates the flow of money and information as a futures transaction is consummated and cleared. Let us illustrate how the clearinghouse operates by assuming you sell a U.S. Treasury bond futures contract at a price of 97 27/32, which is $97,843.75. You have contacted your broker, who either is a futures commission merchant (FCM) or contracts with an FCM, whose commission broker finds a buyer in the U.S. Treasury bond futures pit of the Chicago Board of Trade. The buyer might be a local or a commission broker, representing a customer off the floor.

Your brokerage firm clears its trades through ABC Futures, a member firm of the Chicago Board of Trade Clearing Corporation (BOTCC). The buyer's FCM clears through ACME Trading Company, a clearing firm that is also a member of the BOTCC. The required margin changes often on these contracts; we shall assume it is $2,500. You deposit this amount with ABC. ABC pools the transactions of all of its customers and deposits an amount required in its account with the BOTCC. The buyer deposits the same amount with ACME, which also deposits a sum of money, based on its customers' open positions, with the BOTCC.

The BOTCC guarantees the performance of you and the buyer. Thus, neither of you has to worry about whether the other will be able to make

FIGURE 7.3   **A Transaction on the Futures Exchange**

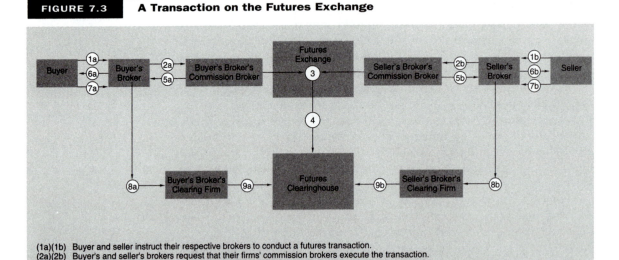

(1a)(1b) Buyer and seller instruct their respective brokers to conduct a futures transaction.
(2a)(2b) Buyer's and seller's brokers request that their firms' commission brokers execute the transaction.
   (3)   Both commission brokers meet in the pit on the floor of the futures exchange and agree on a price.
   (4)   Information on the trade is reported to the clearinghouse.
(5a)(5b) Both commission brokers report the price obtained to the buyer's and seller's brokers.
(6a)(6b) Buyer's and seller's brokers report the price obtained to the buyer and seller.
(7a)(7b) Buyer and seller deposit margin with their brokers.
(8a)(8b) Buyer's and seller's brokers deposit margin with their clearing firms.
(9a)(9b) Buyer's and seller's brokers' clearing firms deposit margin with clearinghouse.

Note: Either buyer or seller (or both) could be a floor trader, eliminating the broker and the commission broker.

up the losses. The BOTCC will look to the clearing firms, ABC and ACME, for payment, and they in turn will look to you and the buyer.

Of course the forward market is an over-the-counter market. The parties to the contract deal directly with each other. There is currently no clearinghouse to guarantee to each party that the other will perform, although there are plans under way to begin a type of clearinghouse for certain over-the-counter transactions.

Daily Settlement

One way in which the clearinghouse helps ensure its survival is by using margins and the daily settlement of accounts. For each contract there is both an **initial margin,** the amount that must be deposited on the day the transaction is opened, and a **maintenance margin,** the amount that must be maintained every day thereafter. There are also initial and maintenance margins for spread and hedge transactions, which usually are lower than those for purely speculative positions.

The margin deposit is not quite like the margin on a stock trade. In stock trading, the investor deposits margin money and borrows the re-

mainder of the stock price from the broker. In futures trading, not only is the margin requirement much smaller, but the remainder of the funds are not borrowed. The margin deposit is more like a good-faith security deposit. In fact some prefer to call them **performance bonds** rather than margins so that the distinction is clear. In any case, some large and actively trading investors are able to deposit Treasury bills for margins. Others are required to deposit cash.

At the end of each day, a committee composed of clearinghouse officials establishes a **settlement price.** This usually is an average of the prices of the last few trades of the day. Using the settlement price, each account is **marked to market.** The difference in the current settlement price and the previous day's settlement price is determined. If the difference is positive because the settlement price increased, the dollar amount is credited to the margin accounts of those holding long positions. Where does the money come from? It is charged to the accounts of those holding short positions. If the difference is negative because the settlement price decreased, the dollar amount is credited to the holders of short positions and charged to those holding long positions.

This process, sometimes called the **daily settlement,** is an important feature of futures markets and a major difference between futures and forward markets. In forward markets, the gains and losses are normally incurred at the end of the contract's life, when delivery is made. Futures markets credit and charge the price changes on a daily basis. This helps ensure the markets' integrity, because large losses are covered a little at a time rather than all at the end, by which time the holder of the losing position may be unable to cover the loss.

To illustrate the daily settlement procedure, let us consider the transaction we previously described. We assume it was initiated on Friday, August 1. You sold one Treasury bond futures contract on the Chicago Board of Trade at that day's opening price of 97 27/32. One such contract is for a face value of $100,000, so the price is .9784375($100,000) = $97,843.75. We shall assume that the initial margin requirement was $2,500, and the maintenance margin requirement was $2,000. You maintain the position until repurchasing the contract on August 18 at the opening price of 100 16/32, or $100,500. Table 7.3 illustrates the transactions to the account while the position was open.

Note that the account is first marked to market on the day of the trade and you made a profit of $437.50 on the first day. Each day thereafter, you must maintain $2,000 in the account so that on any given day when the balance is greater than $2,000, the excess over the initial margin can be withdrawn. However, we shall assume you do not withdraw the excess. If the balance falls below the $2,000 maintenance margin requirement, you receive a margin call and must deposit enough funds to bring the balance back up to the initial margin requirement. The additional funds deposited

TABLE 7.3	Daily Settlement Example

Assume that on Friday, August 1, you sell one Chicago Board of Trade September Treasury bond futures contract at the opening price of 97 27/32 ($97,843.75). The initial margin requirement is $2,500, and the maintenance margin requirement is $2,000. You maintain your position every day through Friday, August 15, and then buy back the contract at the opening price on Monday, August 18. The example below illustrates the daily price changes and the flows in and out of the margin account.

Date	Settlement Price	Settlement Price ($)	Mark-to-Market	Other Entries	Account Balance	Explanation
8/1	97-13	$97,406.25	+ $437.50	+ $2,500	+ $ 2,937.50	Initial margin deposit of $2,500. Price fell by 14/32 leaving profit by day-end of $437.50.
8/4	97-25	97,781.25	− 375.00		2,562.50	Price rose by 12/32 giving loss of $375. Balance exceeds maintenance requirement.
8/5	96-18	96,562.50	+ 1,218.75		3,781.25	Price fell by 1 7/32 giving profit of $1,218.75. Balance well above maintenance requirement.
8/6	96-07	96,218.75	+ 343.75		4,125.00	Price fell by 11/32 giving profit of $343.75. Balance well above maintenance requirement.
8/7	97-05	97,156.25	− 937.50		3,187.50	Price rose by 30/32 giving loss of $937.50. Balance still above maintenance requirement.
8/8	99-03	99,093.75	− 1,937.50		1,250.00	Price rose by 1 30/32 giving loss of $1,937.50. Balance short by $750.
8/11	101-01	101,031.25	− 1,937.50	+ 1,250.00	562.50	$1,250.00 deposited. Price rose 1 30/32 giving loss of $1,937.50. Balance short by $1,437.50.
8/12	99-25	99,781.25	+ 1,250.00	+ 1,937.50	3,750.00	$1,937.50 deposited. Price fell 1 8/32 giving profit of $1,250. Balance well above maintenance requirement.
8/13	101-01	101,031.25	− 1,250.00		2,500.00	Price rose by 1 8/32 giving loss of $1,250. Balance still above maintenance requirement.
8/14	100-25	100,781.25	+ 250.00		2,750.00	Price fell by 8/32 giving profit of $250. Balance still above maintenance requirement.
8/15	100-25	100,781.25	0.00		2,750.00	Price did not change.
8/18	100-16	100,500.00	+ 281.25	− 3,031.25	0.00	Bought contract back at gain of 9/32 or $281.25. Withdrew remaining balance.

are called the **variation margin.** They are officially due within a few days but usually are required to be deposited immediately; we shall assume the money is deposited before trading begins on the day you receive the margin call. By the end of the day on Friday, August 8, the account shows a balance of $1,250. On Monday morning you receive a margin call for $1,250, which is immediately deposited. Another margin call, for $1,937.50, follows the next morning. Undaunted and still confident of ultimately turning things around, you make the deposit on August 12. When

you finally buy back the contract on August 18, the account balance withdrawn is $3,031.25. In all, you have made deposits of $2,500, $1,250, and $1,937.50 for a total of $5,687.50. Thus, the overall loss on the trade is $2,656.25.

The preceding example is not at all unusual. It was selected at random. You, the seller of this contract, quickly incurred a substantial loss. However, for every dollar lost, there is a dollar gained by someone else. Traders who were bullish on Treasury bond futures from August 1 to 18 did quite well. Nonetheless, the large dollar flows from day to day serve as a stern reminder of the substantial leverage component that futures contracts offer.

It is also important to note that with futures contracts it is possible to lose more money than one has invested. For example, assume the market makes a substantial move against the investor. The account balance is depleted, and the broker asks the investor to deposit additional funds. If the investor does not have the funds, the broker will attempt to close out the position. Now assume the market moves quickly before the contracts can be closed. Ultimately the contracts are sold out, but not before the investor has incurred additional losses. Those losses must be covered in cash. In the limit, a long position can ultimately lose the full price of the contract. This would occur if the price went to zero. On a short position, however, there is no upper limit on the price. Therefore, the loss theoretically is infinite.

One method futures exchanges use to limit the losses incurred on any given day is the daily price limit, which we briefly discussed earlier. Also the clearinghouse can request that additional margin funds be deposited during a trading session rather than waiting until the end of the day.

Of course in forward markets, there is no clearinghouse, price limits, or daily settlement. There may or may not be margins required; this would depend on the creditworthiness of the party. In many cases credit is established by posting a letter of credit provided by a bank, who, in effect, stands ready to lend money to cover losses.[6]

The total number of futures contracts outstanding at any one time is called the **open interest.** The concept is the same as it is for options markets. Each contract has both a long and a short position and counts as one contract of open interest. As an example of the potential size of open interest, the average month-ending open interest in the CFTC's 1996 fiscal year was about 6.7 million contracts, with financial and currency futures contracts accounting for about two-thirds of the total.[7]

---

[6]Some swaps and other over-the-counter contracts have begun periodically settling gains and losses but to date this is the exception and not the rule.

[7]CFTC *Annual Report 1996.*

The clearinghouse has fulfilled quite well its mission to protect the market. In March 1985, Volume Investors, a clearing firm, failed to meet a margin call due to a default by several of its customers who were carrying large short positions in options on gold futures. The potential damage to the market never materialized, as the clearinghouse handled the affair with a barely discernible ripple.

Most futures traders do not hold their positions to expiration; rather, they simply reenter the market and execute an offsetting transaction. In other words, if one held a long position in a contract, one might elect to simply sell that contract in the market. The clearinghouse would properly note that the trader's positions were offsetting. If the position were not offset before the expiration month, delivery would become likely.

Delivery and Cash Settlement

All contracts eventually expire. As noted earlier, each contract has a delivery month. The delivery procedure varies among contracts. Some contracts can be delivered on any business day of the delivery month. Others permit delivery only after the contract has traded for the last day—a day that also varies from contract to contract. Still others are cash settled; thus, there is no delivery at all.

Most non-cash-settled financial futures contracts permit delivery any business day of the delivery month. Delivery usually is a three-day sequence beginning two business days prior to the first possible delivery day. The clearing member firms report to the clearinghouse those of their customers who hold long positions. Two business days before the intended delivery day, the holder of a short position who intends to make delivery notifies the clearinghouse of its desire to deliver. This day is called the **position day.** On the next business day, called the **notice of intention day,** the exchange selects the holder of the oldest long position to receive delivery. On the third day, the **delivery day,** delivery takes place and the long pays the short. For most financial futures, delivery is consummated by wire transfer.

Most futures contracts allow for more than one deliverable instrument. The contract usually specifies that the price paid by the long to the short be adjusted to reflect a difference in the quality of the deliverable good. We shall look at this more closely in Chapter 11.

On cash-settled contracts, such as stock index futures, the settlement price on the last trading day is fixed at the closing spot price of the underlying instrument, such as the stock index. All contracts are marked to market on that day, and the positions are deemed to be closed. One exception to this procedure is the S&P 500 futures contract, which closes trading on the Thursday before the third Friday of the expiration month but bases the final settlement price on the opening stock price on Friday morning. This procedure was installed to avoid some problems created

when a contract settles at the closing prices, a point we shall discuss in Chapter 11.

The fact that all futures contracts can be delivered or cash settled is critical to their pricing. However, most contracts are not delivered. In the CFTC's fiscal year 1996, 394 million contracts were traded, but only 2.9 million—fewer than 1 percent—ended in delivery; this figure includes cash-settled contracts.[8] Thus, delivery, albeit an important feature of futures contracts, seldom takes place. Most traders close out their positions prior to expiration, a process called **offsetting.** The futures market is not the best route to acquiring a commodity, because the long contract holder is at the mercy of the short contract holder. The short can deliver on any of several delivery days and can choose to deliver any of several related but slightly different commodities. The long must accept whatever the short offers. Thus, the long usually closes out the position early. Therefore, if one needs the commodity, one often will do better to purchase it in the spot market.

Despite the flexibility sellers have in determining the delivery terms, some contracts actually are delivered through a process called **exchange for physicals (EFP),** also known as **against actuals** or **versus cash.** This is, in fact, the only type of permissible futures transaction that occurs off the floor of the exchange. In an EFP transaction, the holders of long and short positions get together and agree on a cash transaction that would close out their futures positions. For example, farmer A holds a short position in a wheat contract and firm B holds a long position in the same contract. Firm B wants to buy farmer A's wheat, but either the wheat is not one of the grades acceptable for delivery on the contract or the farmer would find it prohibitively expensive to deliver at Chicago or Toledo as the contract requires. In either case, farmer A and firm B could arrange for A to deliver the wheat at some other acceptable location and B to pay A for the wheat at an agreed-upon price. Then A and B would be permitted to report this transaction to the CBOT as though each had offset its futures contract with a trade with the other party. Thus, the EFP market simply gives the parties additional flexibility in making delivery, choosing the terms, and conducting such business when the exchanges are closed. EFPs can also be used in cash settlement contracts. EFPs are used in several futures markets and compose almost 100 percent of deliveries made in oil futures markets.

Because forward contracts do not have standard terms and conditions like futures contracts, it is not as simple to offset them the way one can with futures. If an institution has purchased a forward contract obligating

---

[8]Ibid.

it to purchase a commodity at a future date, however, it can generally sell a new forward contract obligating it to deliver the commodity on that date. Of course, the price negotiated may lead to a profit or a loss. While this type of transaction is basically an offsetting transaction, the liquidity of the forward market may be such that it might be somewhat more difficult to find someone to do the precise transaction the institution wants. In addition, the new transaction also entails some credit risk. In the futures markets, at least in the most liquid markets such as grains, T-bonds, Eurodollars, and the S&P 500, offsetting is a fairly simple procedure, as noted above, and is subject to essentially no credit risk. In some cases, however, a forward contract can be offset by entering into the opposite transaction with the same party in which one contracted originally. By mutual agreement, the parties can treat the contracts as offsetting, thereby terminating both contracts and eliminating the credit risk.

When a forward contract is written, the intention is generally to hold it to the expiration day and take delivery. Some contracts, however, do stipulate a cash settlement. Thus, an expiring forward contract works pretty much like an expiring futures contract.

Futures Price Quotations

The best source of daily futures prices is *The Wall Street Journal*. Figure 7.4 illustrates how *The Wall Street Journal* reports futures prices. Contracts are grouped into categories: grains and oilseeds, livestock and meat, food and fiber, metals and petroleum, interest rate, currency and index.

At the top of the column are headings. Above the heading for the grains and oilseeds, we have the day's open, high, low, and settlement prices, followed by the change in the settlement price from the previous day. The next two columns give the high and low over the contract's life. The final column is the open interest.

The first line indicates the name of the commodity and the abbreviation for the exchange, followed by the contract size and the units of quotation. For example, the corn contract is traded at the Chicago Board of Trade, which is abbreviated here as CBT. One contract is for 5,000 bushels, and the prices are in cents per bushel.

Each line in the quotes indicates a particular contract. For corn we see the September 97 contract, followed by the December 97, March 98, May, July, September, and December contracts. The September 97 contract had a settlement price of 247 1/4 cents, or $2.4725, per bushel.

At the end of each contract's quotes are estimates of that day's volume (here 50,000 contracts), volume the previous day (53,840), total open interest (266,367)—which is the total as of the beginning of the trading session—and the change in open interest from the previous day (+2,369).

FIGURE 7.4 **Futures Quotations in *The Wall Street Journal*, Trading Day of July 23, 1997**

Wednesday, July 23, 1997

Open Interest Reflects Previous Trading Day.

GRAINS AND OILSEEDS

CORN (CBT) 5,000 bu.; cents per bu.

	Open	High	Low	Settle	Change	Lifetime High	Lifetime Low	Open Interest
Sept	247½	250¼	245½	247¼	− ¼	335	227½	64,860
Dec	249½	251	245¾	247¾	− ¾	310	227½	150,920
Mr98	256¼	259	253¾	255¾	− ½	305	236	28,542
May	262	263½	259	261¼	....	303	241¾	5,926
July	265¼	266¾	262¾	264½	+ ¼	315½	245	9,072
Sept	257¾	258¾	256½	257¼	+ ¾	262	244	1,133
Dec	262½	262½	259½	261½	+ ¾	293	247	5,224

Est vol 50,000; vol Tue 53,840; open int 266,367, +2,369.

OATS (CBT) 5,000 bu.; cents per bu.

	Open	High	Low	Settle	Change	Lifetime High	Lifetime Low	Open Interest
Sept	156½	158	153½	153¾	− 2	185	144	2,125
Dec	154	156	152¾	153½	+ ¼	183	143	4,978
Mr98	156½	160	156½	157½	+ 1	174½	148¼	612

Est vol 1,100; vol Tue 853; open int 7,756, −4.

SOYBEANS (CBT) 5,000 bu.; cents per bu.

	Open	High	Low	Settle	Change	Lifetime High	Lifetime Low	Open Interest
Aug	736¼	741½	728	739	+ 3¾	869½	663	25,170
Sept	646	652	643	647½	+ 2¾	803¾	605	13,904
Nov	601½	610	597½	603	+ 2	750	577	73,661
Ja98	606	613½	601½	606¼	+ 3¾	752	583	15,185
Mar	616½	620½	610	615	+ 1¾	749	593	4,980
May	623½	628½	617	622½	+ 3½	745	601	3,362
July	630	635	624½	629¼	+ 3¼	751	611½	2,087
Nov	614	617	612	615¾	+ 4¾	702	597	877

Est vol 40,000; vol Tue 39,203; open int 139,802, −954.

LIVESTOCK AND MEAT

CATTLE-FEEDER (CME) 50,000 lbs.; cents per lb.

	Open	High	Low	Settle	Change	Lifetime High	Lifetime Low	Open Interest
Aug	82.05	83.20	81.62	82.67	+ .60	83.40	64.05	10,536
Sept	81.60	82.75	81.25	82.47	+ .57	82.95	65.60	3,168
Oct	81.60	82.95	81.40	82.45	+ .55	83.15	66.10	4,636
Nov	83.00	84.05	82.60	83.65	+ .30	84.30	67.95	3,377
Ja98	83.25	84.00	83.10	83.72	-.15	84.95	76.25	1,745
Mar	83.10	83.70	82.85	83.37	+ .12	84.50	76.00	839
Apr	82.75	83.35	82.70	83.20	+ .15	84.45	77.75	191
May		....	....	83.30	+ .27	84.25	78.25	129

Est vol 4,335; vol Tu 3,868; open int 24,621, +241.

CATTLE-LIVE (CME) 40,000 lbs.; cents per lb.

	Open	High	Low	Settle	Change	Lifetime High	Lifetime Low	Open Interest
Aug	65.75	66.85	65.55	66.70	+ .92	66.90	62.00	30,721
Oct	68.70	69.70	68.65	69.60	+ .90	69.70	64.55	36,563
Dec	71.00	71.70	70.97	71.67	+ .57	72.10	65.25	16,280
Fb98	73.00	73.47	72.80	73.42	+ .32	73.77	67.50	9,014
Apr	74.87	75.32	74.65	75.30	+ .35	75.55	72.00	3,529
June	71.50	71.85	71.35	71.60	+ .10	72.37	68.50	2,611
Aug	71.50	71.72	71.25	71.45	− .15	72.15	68.80	204

Est vol 16,725; vol Tu 13,282; open int 98,922, +2,153.

HOGS (CME) 40,000 lbs.; cents per lb.

	Open	High	Low	Settle	Change	Lifetime High	Lifetime Low	Open Interest
Aug	79.95	80.72	79.75	79.95	− .40	84.45	66.00	12,534
Oct	72.10	72.85	72.00	72.42	− .02	77.00	60.60	12,279
Dec	69.10	69.60	68.95	69.12	− .17	73.90	60.10	5,433
Fb98	67.60	67.85	67.35	67.60	− .10	71.90	61.75	1,940
Apr	63.60	63.70	63.25	63.35	+ .10	68.15	57.00	1,302
June	66.80	66.80	66.40	66.66	− .02	73.70	62.50	748
July	64.80	65.00	64.80	64.80	− .20	71.75	63.60	479
Oct	59.00	59.00	58.62	58.80	− .02	66.00	58.00	118

Est vol 7,829; vol Tu 5,302; open int 34,929, −8.

PORK BELLIES (CME) 40,000 lbs.; cents per lb.

	Open	High	Low	Settle	Change	Lifetime High	Lifetime Low	Open Interest
July	84.30	84.70	82.80	82.80	− 3.00	94.95	63.00	380
Aug	81.70	82.25	80.60	81.10	− 2.17	93.85	65.45	4,310
Fb98	70.00	70.60	69.80	70.10	− 0.27	81.02	66.90	1,142

Est vol 2,044; vol Tu 2,450; open int 5,870, +169.

INTEREST RATE

TREASURY BONDS (CBT)-$100,000; pts. 32nds of 100%

	Open	High	Low	Settle	Change	Lifetime High	Lifetime Low	Open Interest
Sept	115-10	115-23	115-07	115-12	+ 4	117-21	100-18	498,219
Dec	114-28	115-13	114-27	115-00	+ 4	118-08	100-08	36,428
Mr98	114-29	115-00	114-21	114-23	+ 4	116-26	104-21	16,186
June	114-19	114-19	114-11	114-11	+ 3	116-14	104-03	661
Sept	....	....	....	114-00	+ 2	111-28	103-22	816

Est vol 505,000; vol Tue 423,128; open int 552,601, +23,150.

TREASURY BONDS (MCE)-$50,000; pts. 32nds of 100%

	Open	High	Low	Settle	Change	Lifetime High	Lifetime Low	Open Interest
Sept	115-20	115-23	115-07	115-08	− 8	115-23	105-31	17,194

Est vol 5,650; vol Tue 8,771; open int 17,209, +40.

TREASURY NOTES (CBT)-$100,000; pts. 32nds of 100%

	Open	High	Low	Settle	Change	Lifetime High	Lifetime Low	Open Interest
Sept	110-04	110-12	110-03	110-05	+ 2	110-15	104-21	358,492
Dec	109-31	110-03	109-27	109-27	+ 2	110-05	104-10	11,827

Est vol 88,888; vol Tue 66,948; open int 370,547, +6,905.

5 YR TREAS NOTES (CBT)-$100,000; pts. 32nds of 100%

	Open	High	Low	Settle	Change	Lifetime High	Lifetime Low	Open Interest
Sept	07-125	07-165	107-12	07-125	+ 1.0	07-165	103-21	227,558
Dec	07-065	07-075	07-045	07-045	+ 1.0	07-075	04-005	2,549

Est vol 46,000; vol Tue 50,369; open int 230,107, +619.

2 YR TREAS NOTES (CBT)-$200,000, pts. 32nds of 100%

	Open	High	Low	Settle	Change	Lifetime High	Lifetime Low	Open Interest
Sept	03-157	03-182	03-158	03-165	+ .3	03-182	01-305	35,975

Est vol 2,500; vol Tue 2,861; open int 36,038, +613.

30-DAY FEDERAL FUNDS (CBT)-$5 million; pts. of 100%

	Open	High	Low	Settle	Change	Lifetime High	Lifetime Low	Open Interest
July	94.500	94.500	94.495	94.500	+ .005	94.640	93.800	12,313
Aug	94.49	94.49	94.49	94.49	+ .01	94.57	94.09	19,594
Sept	94.46	94.47	94.46	94.47	....	94.53	94.00	6,073
Oct	94.45	94.46	94.45	94.45	+ .01	94.46	93.90	2,191
Nov	94.41	94.42	94.40	94.41	+ .03	94.42	93.88	976
Dec	94.33	94.36	94.33	94.35	+ .04	94.36	93.78	395

Est vol 2,222; vol Tue 2,475; open int 41,732, −427.

MUNI BOND INDEX (CBT)-$1,000; times Bond Buyer MBI

	Open	High	Low	Settle	Change	Lifetime High	Lifetime Low	Open Interest
Sept	121-13	121-17	121-04	121-06	+ 2	121-17	109-28	20,348

Est vol 3,700; vol Tue 4,802; open int 20,376, −265.
The index: Close 122-04; Yield 5.45.

TREASURY BILLS (CME)-$1 mil.; pts. of 100%

	Open	High	Low	Settle	Chg	Discount Settle	Discount Chg	Open Interest
Sept	94.92	94.93	94.92	94.92	+ .02	5.08	− .02	7,831
Dec	94.81	94.83	94.81	94.83	+ .03	5.18	− .03	646

Est vol 266; vol Tue 2,619; open int 8,513, −10.

LIBOR-1 MO. (CME)-$3,000,000; points of 100%

	Open	High	Low	Settle	Chg	Discount Settle	Discount Chg	Open Interest
Aug	94.36	94.38	94.36	94.36	+ .01	5.64	− .01	23,328
Sept	94.36	94.37	94.35	94.36	+ .01	5.64	− .01	9,434
Oct	94.33	94.34	94.33	94.33	+ .01	5.67	− .01	3,944
Nov	94.30	94.30	94.29	94.30	+ .02	5.71	− .02	1,956
Dec	94.11	94.11	94.10	94.11	+ .02	5.89	− .02	1,082
Mr98	94.20	94.21	94.19	94.19	+ .02	5.82	− .02	205

Est vol 5,064; vol Tue 3,358; open int 40,826, −691.

EURODOLLAR (CME)-$1 million; pts of 100%

	Open	High	Low	Settle	Chg	Yield Settle	Yield Chg	Open Interest
Aug	94.29	94.29	94.28	94.29	+ .01	5.71	− .01	23,529
Sept	94.26	94.28	94.26	94.28	+ .02	5.72	− .02	529,594
Dec	94.13	94.15	94.12	94.14	+ .02	5.86	− .02	467,173
Mr98	94.09	94.12	94.08	94.10	+ .02	5.90	− .02	328,164
June	94.00	94.03	93.99	94.01	+ .02	5.99	− .02	267,059
Sept	93.92	93.93	93.90	93.91	+ .01	6.09	− .01	206,348
Dec	93.81	93.83	93.79	93.81	+ .02	6.19	− .02	159,881
Mr99	93.78	93.80	93.77	93.79	+ .02	6.21	− .02	123,753
June	93.76	93.76	93.74	93.75	+ .02	6.25	− .02	93,190
Sept	93.72	93.74	93.71	93.72	+ .02	6.28	− .02	77,940
Dec	93.65	93.67	93.64	93.65	+ .02	6.35	− .02	69,775
Mr00	93.65	93.66	93.63	93.65	+ .03	6.35	− .03	60,955
June	93.61	93.63	93.60	93.62	+ .03	6.38	− .03	46,172
Sept	93.59	93.61	93.58	93.59	+ .03	6.41	− .03	40,576

INDEX

S&P 500 INDEX (CME) $500 times index

	Open	High	Low	Settle	Chg	High	Low	Open Interest
Sept	942.35	949.25	940.00	941.25	− 1.00	949.25	707.50	176,788
Dec	953.25	959.00	950.50	951.40	− .95	959.00	753.00	5,424
Mr98		....	....	961.40	− .85	934.30	762.20	1,917
June		....	....	971.85	− .60	976.50	873.00	619

Est vol 65,238; vol Tu 84,205; open int 184,801, −6,653.
Indx prelim High 941.80; Low 933.98; Close 936.56 + 2.58

S&P MIDCAP 400 (CME) $500 times index

	Open	High	Low	Settle	Chg	High	Low	Open Interest
Sept	308.00	309.30	307.90	309.30	+ 2.50	309.40	248.80	11,259

Est vol 297; vol Tu 372; open int 11,283, +13.
The index: High 307.10; Low 305.12; Close 307.10 + 1.98

NIKKEI 225 STOCK AVERAGE (CME)-$5 times index

	Open	High	Low	Settle	Chg	High	Low	Open Interest
Sept	20240.	20300.	20175.	20295.	− 50	22000.	17300.	17,508

Est vol 541; vol Tu 495; open int 17,540, +153.
The index: High 20324.03; Low 19999.80; Close 20130.51 − 26.51

NASDAQ 100 (CME)-$100 times index

	Open	High	Low	Settle	Chg	High	Low	Open Interest
Sept	110900	111995	109600	109850	− 3.00	112500	803.00	1,804
Dec	111500	113000	111300	111300	− 3.00	113000	811.35	479
Mr98	113200	113800	112700	112700	− 3.00	114750	99250	103

Est vol 3,702; vol Tu 2,771; open int 6,386, −91.
The index: High 1106.70; Low 1087.15; Close 1092.06 + 11.20

GSCI (CME)-$250 times nearby index

	Open	High	Low	Settle	Chg	High	Low	Open Interest
Aug	184.30	185.80	184.30	185.60	+ 1.50	199.0	181.00	21,813
Sept	185.50	185.50	185.30	185.40	+ 1.40	198.00	181.50	313

Est vol 316; vol Tu 387; open int '22,128, +9.
The index: High 185.87; Low 184.32; Close 185.70 + 1.74

Source: *The Wall Street Journal*, July 23, 1997

The total open interest figure normally equals the total of the open interest figures for each contract; however, the markets move so quickly that sometimes this information is not completely accurate.

The second column of quotations contains some interest rate futures. The headings vary slightly. Look at the Treasury bond futures prices. The contract is at the CBT, is for $100,000 face value, and is quoted in points and thirty-seconds of 100 percent. Thus, we can interpret the settlement price of the September 97 contract as 115 12/32 (115.3750) or $115,375.00. The change in the settlement price is an increase of 4/32. The next two columns give the lifetime high and low, and the final column gives the open interest. Summary figures for volume and open interest appear at the end of the list of contracts.

The quotes for the Eurodollar and Treasury bill contracts differ slightly, but that is due primarily to the manner in which their prices are quoted. We shall take a closer look at those contracts later in this chapter.

In the third column are the stock index futures prices. The headings are the same as those for the grains and oilseeds. Below the volume and open interest figures are information on the spot index.

As you might expect, these prices will be dated by the time you read them. Futures markets move very quickly, and serious traders will wish to acquire real-time quotes from a commercial vendor.

Types of Futures Contracts

Almost 100 types of futures contracts trade on U.S. futures exchanges. Some of these contracts are essentially the same underlying commodity. Many of those listed are not actively traded; some have not been traded at all for some time. Table 7.4 lists all registered contracts on U.S. futures exchanges covered in *The Wall Street Journal* on July 25, 1997, the exchanges that list them, and contract sizes. Keep in mind that new contracts are frequently introduced and old contracts are sometimes delisted. A brief discussion of some of the characteristics of each major group of contracts follows. A more detailed discussion is provided for the contracts we focus on for the remainder of the book.

Grains and Oilseeds

Grains and oilseeds compose the oldest category of futures contracts. For many years, these contracts were the most actively traded futures; however, in recent years their volume has been surpassed by the financials. The primary trading interest comes from speculative activity and hedging by farmers, food processors, grain storage firms, exporters, and an increasing number of foreign countries that import grain. These futures prices are heavily influenced by agricultural production, weather, government farm policies, and international trade, among other factors.

TABLE 7.4   **Registered Futures Contracts on U.S. Futures Exchanges Covered in *The Wall Street Journal* (as of July 25, 1997)**

Exchange symbols:

Chicago Board of Trade (CBOT)
Chicago Mercantile Exchange (CME)
COMEX division of New York Mercantile Exchange (COMEX)
FINEX division of New York Cotton Exchange (FINEX)
Index and Option Market division of Chicago Mercantile Exchange (IOM)
International Monetary Market division of Chicago Mercantile Exchange (IMM)

Kansas City Board of Trade (KCBT)
MidAmerica Commodity Exchange (MCE)
Minneapolis Grain Exchange (MGE)
New York Cotton Exchange (NYCTN)
New York Futures Exchange division of New York Cotton Exchange (NYFE)
New York Mercantile Exchange (NYMEX)

Contract	Exchange	Contract Size
Grains and Oilseeds		
Corn	CBOT	5,000 bu.
Corn	MCE	1,000 bu.
Oats	CBOT	5,000 bu.
Soybeans	CBOT	5,000 bu.
Soybeans	MCE	1,000 bu.
Soybean meal	CBOT	100 tons
Soybean oil	CBOT	60,000 lbs.
Rough rice	CBOT	2,000 cwt.
Wheat	CBOT	5,000 bu.
Wheat	KCBT	5,000 bu.
Wheat	MCE	1,000 bu.
Wheat	MGE	5,000 bu.
Livestock and Meat		
Feeder cattle	CME	50,000 lbs.
Hogs	CME	40,000 lbs.
Live cattle	CME	40,000 lbs.
Pork bellies	CME	40,000 lbs.
Food and Fiber		
Cocoa	CSCE	10 metric tons
Coffee	CSCE	37,500 lbs.
Cotton	NYCTN	50,000 lbs.
Domestic sugar	CSCE	112,000 lbs.
Orange juice	NYCTN	15,000 lbs.
World sugar	CSCE	112,000 lbs.
Metals and Energy		
Copper	COMEX	25,000 lbs.
Crude oil	NYMEX	1,000 bbls.
Gold	COMEX	100 troy ozs.
Heating oil—no. 2	NYMEX	42,000 gals.
Natural gas	NYMEX	10,000 million BTUs

(continued)

Livestock and Meat

In the livestock and meat category of futures contracts are the celebrated pork bellies, so often acclaimed as the quintessential speculative instrument. In reality, however, pork bellies are no more speculative than most

TABLE 7.4   (continued)

Western Natural Gas	KCBT	10,000 million BTUs
Electricity	NYMEX	736 megawatts
Palladium	NYMEX	100 troy ozs.
Platinum	NYMEX	50 troy ozs.
Propane	NYMEX	42,000 gals.
Silver	COMEX	5,000 troy ozs.
Silver	CBOT	1,000 troy ozs.
Unleaded gasoline	NYMEX	42,000 gals.
Miscellaneous		
Lumber	CME	80,000 board ft
Foreign Currency/Eurodollar		
Australian dollar	IMM	100,000 $A
British pound	IMM	62,500 £
Canadian dollar	IMM	100,000 CD
German mark	IMM	125,000 DM
Eurodollar—90-day	IMM	1,000,000 $
Eurodollar—30-day	IMM	3,000,000 $
Euroyen	IMM	100 million ¥
Mexican peso	IMM	500,000 pesos
Brazilian real	IMM	100,000 reals
British pound/German mark cross rate	FINEX	125,000 £
German mark/French franc cross rate	FINEX	500,000 DM
German mark/Japanese yen cross rate	FINEX	125,000 DM
French franc	IMM	500,000 FF
Japanese yen	IMM	12,500,000 ¥
Swiss franc	IMM	125,000 SFr
Economic Indices		
Commodity Research Bureau Index	NYFE	$500 × Index
Goldman Sachs Commodity Index	IOM	$250 × Index
Stock Indices		
Eurotop 100 Index	IOM	$500 × Index
Nikkei 225 Index	IOM	$5 × Index
NASDAQ 100	IOM	$100 × Index
New York Stock Exchange Index	NYFE	$500 × Index
Russell 2000 Index	IOM	$500 × Index
S&P 500 Index	IOM	$500 × Index
S&P 400 Midcap Index	IOM	$500 × Index
Interest Rates		
Municipal Bond Index	CBOT	$1,000 × Index
30-day Federal Funds	CBOT	$5,000,000
Treasury bills	IMM	$1,000,000
Treasury bonds	CBOT	$100,000
Treasury bonds	MCE	$50,000
Treasury notes (6 1/2–10 yr.)	CBOT	$100,000
Treasury notes (5 yr.)	CBOT	$100,000
Treasury notes (2 yr.)	CBOT	$200,000

other futures contracts; neither are hogs, live cattle, or feeder cattle, the other contracts in this category. Prices of livestock and meat futures are influenced not only by the obvious—domestic and worldwide demand for meat—but by the not so obvious—prices of grains used as feed, as well as

government policies, demographic trends, and international trade. Traders in this category include farmers, slaughterhouses, meat packers, and major users of beef and pork, such as fast-food restaurant chains.

Food and Fiber

Food and fiber is a diverse category that includes coffee, cocoa, cotton, orange juice, and sugar. Prices are influenced by many of the same factors cited for the previous categories. Other factors include weather in central Florida (orange juice), Africa (cocoa and coffee), and Central and South America (coffee). Because most of these commodities are imported, international economic and political conditions also are major considerations.

Metals and Energy

The metal and energy category includes metals used in jewelry and industry and in energy-related products. Each of these commodities is considered a nonrenewable natural resource. Many are produced in politically unstable foreign countries. A considerable volume of spot and futures trading in these commodities takes place in foreign cities such as London, Paris, Amsterdam, and Zurich. Without question, international economic and political factors are critical influences in these markets. The risks, particularly political, are quite high, as are the stakes.

Miscellaneous

This is a relatively small group. It includes a lumber futures contract, and has formerly included futures on fertilizers. These contracts have not been very actively traded.

Foreign Currency

Foreign currency futures were introduced in 1972 and were the forerunners of the pure interest rate futures contracts. Over the years their popularity has increased, but trading has concentrated in British pounds, Japanese yen, Swiss francs, German marks, and French francs. These contracts are covered in more detail in Chapter 13.

Treasury Bills and Eurodollars

Treasury bill and Eurodollar contracts trade on the International Monetary Market of the Chicago Mercantile Exchange. They are the most actively traded futures contracts on short-term money market instruments. Because we shall use them many times in later chapters, we shall take a detailed look at them now.

TREASURY BILLS   We introduced T-bills in Chapter 3 when we needed a return to use as the risk-free rate. T-bills are auctioned each week and normally mature in 91 days. T-bills are pure-discount instruments, and the discount is quoted on a 360-day basis.

Although generally 91-day bills are delivered, the futures contract allows delivery of a 90-, 91-, or 92-day bill. To augment the supply of deliverable bills, the futures contract expiration is timed to correspond to the date on which the U.S. Treasury's 365-day bill, which is auctioned every four weeks, has 90, 91, or 92 days remaining. However, the contract price is always quoted based on a 90-day bill. For example, suppose a T-bill futures contract is priced such that the discount is 8.25. The IMM quotes the bill price as $100 - 8.25 = 91.75$. This is called the **IMM Index.** Therefore, when you observe the futures price, it will be 91.75. However, that is not the actual price at which you trade the contract and thus is not the real futures price. The actual futures price per $100 is given by the formula

$$f = 100 - (100 - \text{IMM Index})(90/360).$$

For example, if the IMM Index is 91.75,

$$f = 100 - (100 - 91.75)(90/360) = 97.9375.$$

The standard size of a single contract is $1 million face value of T-bills; thus, the futures price is $979,375.

The purpose of assuming a 90-day bill in the formula is that it implies that a one-point move in the IMM Index converts to a $25 change in the futures price. For example, if the IMM Index goes up to 91.76, the futures price will be $979,400. Thus, followers of the contract can quickly assess the dollar impact of a change in the IMM Index. If the holder of the short position elects to make delivery of a 90- or 92-day bill, the formula is adjusted on the delivery day so that 90 or 92 is used instead of 90 in calculating the final price.

The contract expiration months are March, June, September, and December, going out about two years. The last trading day is the business day prior to the date of issue of T-bills in the third week of the month. Delivery can take place on the business day after the last trading day and any day thereafter during the expiration month.

EURODOLLARS   The Eurodollar contract is the most successful of the several short-term interest rate futures contracts. A **Eurodollar** is a dollar deposited in a foreign bank or foreign branch of a U.S. bank. The deposit is denominated in dollars rather than in the country's currency. Eurodollars avoid U.S. reserve requirements and many other regulations, and in recent years their use by U.S. corporations and banks has greatly increased.

The primary Eurodollar interest rate, called **LIBOR** for **London Interbank Offer Rate,** is considered one of the best indicators of the cost of short-term borrowing. The Eurodollar futures contract has achieved great success, quickly surpassing in volume the Treasury bill futures contract, the first short-term interest rate futures contract. The Eurodollar contract's success is at least partly due to its cash settlement feature.

A major difference between T-bills and Eurodollars is the manner in which their rates are interpreted. The T-bill is a discount instrument, and the Eurodollar is an add-on instrument. For example, although we noted that T-bills and Eurodollars would not have equivalent rates, suppose we assume the quoted rate is 10 percent for both 90-day T-bills and Eurodollars. Then we know that the T-bill price per $100 face value would be $100 - 10(90/360) = 97.5$ and that the yield would be $(100/97.5)^{365/90} - 1 = .1081$. Thus, the investor puts down $97.50 today and receives $100 in 90 days. For a Eurodollar deposit of $97.50, the interest would be figured as $97.50(.10)(90/360) = \$2.44$, thus the investor would get back $97.50 + \$2.44 = \$99.94$ at expiration. The return would be $(99.94/97.50)^{365/90} - 1 = .1054$. T-bills will not, however, yield more than Eurodollars in general because T-bills have no credit risk while Eurodollar borrowers could default. The Eurodollar rate would simply be quoted higher.

The Eurodollar futures contract is based on a three-month Eurodollar time deposit, which is a loan made by one bank to another. The contract is for $1 million face value and is quoted by the IMM Index method—the same procedure used for T-bills. However, the Eurodollar contract is settled in cash. The settlement price on the last day of trading is the LIBOR rate as determined by the CME clearinghouse. Contract expirations are March, June, September, and December and extend out 10 years. The last trading day is the second London business day before the third Wednesday of the month. There is also a contract on the rate on 30-day Eurodollar deposits.

The Eurodollar contract is very actively traded and is much more liquid than the T-bill contract. It is considered an excellent contract for hedging or speculating on short-term interest rates and is widely used for hedging by institutions who take positions as dealers in interest rate swaps and other over-the-counter interest rate derivatives, as we discuss in Chapter 14.

Treasury Notes and Bonds

Treasury note and bond contracts, which are traded on the Chicago Board of Trade, are virtually identical except that there are three T-note contracts that are based on 2-year, 5-year, and 10-year maturities while the T-bond contract is based on Treasury bonds with maturities of at least 15

years that are not callable for at least 15 years. Thus, the T-note contracts are intermediate-term interest rate futures contracts and the T-bond contract is a long-term interest rate futures contract. The T-note contracts are traded quite actively, but the T-bond contract is one of the most active of all futures contracts. Other than the difference in maturity of the underlying instruments and the margin requirements, the contract terms are essentially identical. We shall, therefore, discuss only the T-bond contract.

The T-bond contract is based on the assumption that the underlying bond has an 8 percent coupon and, as mentioned, a maturity or call date of not less than 15 years. The 8 percent coupon requirement is not restrictive, however. The CBOT permits delivery of bonds with coupons other than 8 percent, with an appropriate adjustment made to the price received for the bonds. There can easily be 30 or more different bond issues eligible for delivery on a given contract.

T-bond futures prices are quoted in dollars and thirty-seconds of par value of $100. For example, a futures price of 93-14 is 93 14/32, or 93.4375. The face value of T-bonds underlying the contract is $100,000; therefore, a price of 93.4375 is actually $93,437.50. Expiration months are March, June, September, and December, extending out about two years. The last trading day is the business day prior to the last seven days of the expiration month. The first delivery day is the first business day of the month.

As with most other futures contracts, delivery seldom takes place, but the possibility of delivery is what keeps the contract price in line with conditions in the spot market. Let us examine how the price the holder of the long position receives for the bond upon delivery is determined.

Suppose you are short the December 1996 contract. As the holder of the short position, you have the choice of which day during the delivery month to make delivery and which bond from among the eligible bonds you will deliver. Let us assume you have decided to deliver the bonds with a coupon of 9 7/8 percent and maturing on November 15, 2015. Delivery will be made on Wednesday, December 4, 1996.

Since the contract assumes delivery of a bond with an 8 percent coupon, the delivery of the 9 7/8s requires an adjustment to the price paid by the long to the short. The adjustment is based on the CBOT's conversion factor system. The **conversion factor, CF,** is defined for each eligible bond for a given contract. The CF is the price of a bond with a face value of $1, coupon and maturity equal to that of the deliverable bond, and yield of 8 percent. The maturity is defined as the maturity of the bond on the first day of the delivery month. If the bond is callable, the call date is substituted for the maturity date. The CF for the 9 7/8s of 2015 would be the price of a bond with a face value of $1, coupon of 9 7/8 percent, maturity equal to the time remaining from December 2, 1996, the first business day of the month, to November 15, 2015, the maturity date of the

bond, and yield of 8 percent. That same bond delivered on the March 1997 contract would have a different CF because it would have a different maturity in March 1997 than in December 1996. A different bond delivered on the December 1996 contract would have a different conversion factor.

The conversion factor system is designed to place all bonds on an equivalent basis for delivery purposes. If the holder of the short position delivers a bond with a coupon greater than 8 percent, the CF will be greater than 1. The short will then receive more than the futures price in payment for the bond. If the coupon is less than 8 percent, the CF will be less than 1 and the short will receive less than the futures price in payment for the bond.

Tables of conversion factors are available, and there is a specific formula for determining the conversion factor, which is provided in Appendix 7C. Your software includes the Excel spreadsheet cf.xls that calculates the conversion factor and it is explained in the appendix. In this problem, the CF for the 9 7/8s of 2015 delivered on the December 1996 contract would be 1.1803. To determine the invoice price—the amount the long pays to the short for the bond—multiply the CF by the settlement price on the position day. Then the accrued interest from the last coupon payment date until the delivery date is added:[9]

Invoice price = (Settlement price on position day) (Conversion factor) + Accrued interest.

In this problem, assume the settlement price on Monday, December 2, the position day, was 112-16, or $112,500. The bond has coupon payment dates of May 15 and November 15. Thus, the last coupon payment date was November 15, 1996. The number of days from November 15 to December 4 is 19, and the number of days between coupon payment dates of November 15, 1996, and May 15, 1997, is 181. Thus, the accrued interest is

$$\$100,000(.09875/2)(19/181) = \$518.$$

---

[9]The accrued interest is the amount of interest that has built up since the last coupon date. Most bonds pay interest semiannually on the maturity day and six months hence. Thus a bond maturing on November 15, 2015, would pay interest every year on November 15 and May 15. The accrued interest is the semiannual coupon times the number of days since the last coupon date divided by the number of days between the last coupon date and the next coupon date. It is simply a proration of the next coupon. The buyer of a bond will receive the full next coupon, but, because he is not entitled to all of it, must pay the seller the accrued interest. The actual correct bond price will accurately include the accrued interest in it, though the quoted price will not.

The invoice price therefore is

$$\$112,500(1.1803) + \$518 = \$133,302.$$

On the notice of intention day, Tuesday, December 3, the holder of the long position receives an invoice of $133,302 and must pay this amount and accept the bond on the delivery day.

Table 7.5 presents CFs and invoice prices for other bonds deliverable on the December 1996 contract. Note how the CFs vary directly with the level of the coupon.

TABLE 7.5	Conversion Factors and Invoice Prices for Deliverable Bonds (December 1996, T-Bond Futures Contract)

Contract price: 112.50 ($112,500)
Delivery date: December 4, 1996

Coupon	Maturity Date	CF	Accrued Interest	Invoice Price
11 1/4	2/15/15	1.3073	$3,393	$150,460
10 5/8	8/15/15	1.2512	3,205	143,970
9 7/8	11/15/15	1.1803	518	133,300
9 1/4	2/15/16	1.1210	2,790	128,908
7 1/4	5/15/16	0.9268	381	104,644
7 1/2	11/15/16	0.9506	394	107,335
8 3/4	5/15/17	1.0744	459	121,328
8 7/8	8/15/17	1.0875	2,677	125,017
9 1/8	5/15/18	1.1138	479	125,787
9	11/15/18	1.1021	472	124,457
8 7/8	2/15/19	1.0899	2,677	125,291
8 1/8	8/15/19	1.0130	2,451	116,408
8 1/2	2/15/20	1.0522	2,564	120,938
8 3/4	5/15/20	1.0784	459	121,780
8 3/4	8/15/20	1.0789	2,639	124,017
7 7/8	2/15/21	0.9868	2,375	113,385
8 1/8	5/15/21	1.0131	427	114,400
8 1/8	8/15/21	1.0133	2,451	116,451
8	11/15/21	0.9998	420	112,898
7 1/4	8/15/22	0.9189	2,187	105,567
7 5/8	11/15/22	0.9592	400	108,305
7 1/8	2/15/23	0.9049	2,149	103,945
6 1/4	8/15/23	0.8086	1,885	92,854
7 1/2	11/15/24	0.9444	394	106,639
7 5/8	2/15/25	0.9583	2,300	110,113
6 7/8	8/15/25	0.8744	2,074	100,445
6	2/15/26	0.7757	1,810	89,077
6 3/4	8/15/26	0.8592	2,036	98,696

Other interest rate contracts include a municipal bond index futures, which is a contract based on an index of municipal bonds, and a 30-day federal funds rate futures, which is a contract based on the rate banks charge when they lend to each other. These contracts have been moderately successful.

Economic Indices

The first economic index futures contract, the Consumer Price Index futures, was launched with much fanfare in June 1985. Although promoted as a means of hedging the uncertainty of inflation, the contract never generated much trading volume. Exchange officials attributed this to the relatively low and stable inflation rate since the contract's initiation, although the lack of a clearly defined spot market and the unavailability of continuous information on the true spot price probably were more serious impediments.

This category includes the Commodity Research Bureau Index and the Goldman Sachs Commodity Index, both contracts based on indices of other futures. Neither has attracted much trading volume.

Stock Indices

Stock index futures have been one of the spectacular success stories of the financial markets in recent years. These cash-settled contracts are indices of combinations of stocks. Investors use them to hedge positions in stock, speculate on the direction of the stock market in general, and arbitrage the contracts against comparable combinations of stocks.

Stock index futures contracts are based on indices of common stocks. The most widely traded contract is the S&P 500 futures at the Index and Option Market of the Chicago Mercantile Exchange. In Chapter 8, we shall see how this index and others are actually computed.

The futures price is quoted in the same manner as the index. The futures contract, however, has an implicit multiplier of $500. Thus, if the futures price is 925, the actual price is 925($500) = $462,500. At expiration, the settlement price is set at the price of the S&P 500 index and the contract is settled in cash. The expirations are March, June, September, and December. The last trading day is the Thursday before the third Friday of the expiration month.

Table 7.6 lists the most active futures contracts. As can be seen, financial futures contracts are among the most popular. Appendix 7A provides a detailed list of contract specifications for the actively traded financial futures contracts.

TABLE 7.6	Most Active Futures Contracts, 1996
Contract (Exchange)	Volume (Number of Contracts)
Eurodollars (CME)	89,987,368
Treasury Bonds (CBOT)	82,732,197
Crude Oil (NYMEX)	23,363,334
Ten-Year Treasury Notes (CBOT)	21,507,470
Corn (CBOT)	20,335,842
S&P 500 (CME)	19,700,597
Soybeans (CBOT)	13,711,569
Five-Year Treasury Notes (CBOT)	11,536,031
Gold (COMEX)*	8,868,206
Natural Gas (NYMEX)	8,682,127

*COMEX has subsequently merged with NYMEX.

Source: CFTC *Annual Report 1996*

Managed Futures

Recent years have witnessed the development of the **managed futures** industry. Managed futures is simply a term that refers to the arrangement by which an investor hires a professional futures trader to conduct transactions on his or her behalf. The futures manager is a commodity trading advisor (CTA), which we discussed earlier. Managed futures can exist in one of three forms: futures funds, private pools, or a specialized contract with one or more CTAs.

Futures funds, sometimes called **commodity funds,** are essentially mutual funds that pool investors' money and trade futures. Most funds invest only about 20 percent of their money in margin positions. The remainder is kept in interest-earning assets. Futures funds offer the public a way of participating in the futures market with a very low financial commitment. Oftentimes, a fund will accept deposits of $1,000 or less. In some cases, the organizers of a fund guarantee that the investor will not lose more than the original investment.

In spite of the apparent attractiveness of funds, they have been quite controversial and with just cause. Their performance has been highly volatile and their costs are quite high, often running to 20 percent of the value of the fund in a given year.

Commodity pools, mentioned earlier in the context of the pool operator or CPO, are private arrangements that operate much like futures funds. The latter, however, are open to the general public while pools normally solicit funds from specific investors. When the fund reaches a certain size, the pool is closed to other investors. They generally require at

least a $10,000 investment. Pools, like funds, have suffered some of the same problems, namely inconsistent performance and heavy costs.

An increasingly popular form of managed futures is the private contractual arrangement with one or more CTAs. A typical one would involve a large institutional investor agreeing to allocate a portion of its funds to a group of CTAs. In some cases, the CTAs are supervised by a consultant or introducing broker. Since these arrangements are negotiated between the institutional investor and the introducing broker and the CTAs, the costs are usually significantly lower. Often a rather large number of CTAs, sometimes 20 to 30, is used, leading to diversified and somewhat stable performance. These arrangements are growing in popularity, particularly among pension funds.

The primary reason for using managed futures is the belief that the returns from managed futures trading have a fairly low correlation with the returns on the more traditional portfolios of stocks and bonds, leading to a greater degree of diversification, a point we shall address again in Chapter 8. Studies have generally supported this belief. Overall, the managed futures industry is responsible for over $16 billion of investors' funds.

Indices of Futures Market Activity

In Chapter 2, we noted that indices of options market activity are relatively rare and difficult to construct. This is also true of futures market indices. There are so many diverse futures contracts with different expirations and quotations in different units that futures indices never have attracted much attention. The best-known index is the aforementioned Goldman Sachs Commodity Index, which is an average of the prices of a number of futures contracts. The prices are weighted by world production of the commodity. As a result, the index is highly influenced by oil. In general, however, few investors pay much attention to futures indices since they mostly reflect the spot market, which is well covered with indices.

Transaction Costs in Forward and Futures Trading

In Chapter 2, we discussed the different types of option trading costs that the public and professional traders incur. In this section, we shall do the same for forwards and futures. However, there is less material available on the trading costs in these markets. One reason is that futures markets have very low trading costs—indeed, that is one of their major advantages. In addition, the costs of trading futures contracts are less documented than the cost of trading options and stocks. Also, forward markets are private and the costs are less publicized; however, forward contracting, being tailored to the specific needs of the parties, can be quite costly.

Commissions

Commissions paid by the public to brokers are assessed on the basis of a dollar charge per contract. The commission is paid at the order's initiation and includes both the opening and closing commissions; that is, a round-trip commission is charged regardless of whether the trader ultimately closes out the contract, makes or takes delivery, or makes a cash settlement. There is no typical commission rate. Investors can negotiate with brokers for whatever deals they can get. Many brokerage firms advertise specials for new customers, offering rates as low as $10 per contract. Some even do a few contracts free. Active traders can trade at the CBOT for about $12.

All traders, whether on or off the exchange floor, incur a minimum charge that is paid to the clearing firm and includes the exchange fee and a fee assessed by the National Futures Association, an organization we shall discuss in a later section. For floor traders, a typical charge might be about $0.50–$0.75 per contract. As in options trading, this fee is negotiable between trader and clearing firm. For public traders who pay commissions, this figure usually is included in the commission.

In the forward market, transactions are usually conducted directly with dealers so there is typically no commission. There are, however, significant costs associated with processing the paperwork.

Bid-Ask Spread

A second type of trading cost is the bid-ask spread. Chapter 2 explained the concept of the spread for options. Unlike for options and stock markets, however, there is no real market maker. Many floor traders, particularly spreaders and scalpers, quote prices at which they are willing to simultaneously buy at the bid price and sell at the ask price. The bid-ask spread is the cost to the public of liquidity—the ability to buy and sell quickly without a large price concession. Because the spread is not captured and reported electronically, there is little statistical evidence on its size. The spread usually is the value of a minimum price fluctuation, called a **tick,** but occasionally equals a few more ticks for less liquid markets.

In the forward markets, bid-ask spreads are set by dealers in much the same way as they are on the exchange floor. These spreads can be quite large, depending on how eager the dealer and its competitors are to make a trade.

Delivery Costs

A futures trader who holds a position to delivery faces the potential for incurring a substantial delivery cost. In the case of most financial instruments, this cost is rather small. For commodities, however, it is necessary to arrange for the commodity's physical transportation, delivery, and stor-

age. While the proverbial story of the careless futures trader who woke up to find thousands of pounds of pork bellies dumped on the front lawn certainly is an exaggeration, anyone holding a long position in the delivery month must be aware of the delivery possibility. This no doubt explains part of the popularity of cash settlement contracts.

In forward markets, transactions are tailored to the needs of the parties. Consequently, the terms are usually set to keep delivery costs at a minimum. Cash settlement is frequently used.

The Regulation of Futures Markets

As noted previously, forward markets are largely unregulated. Futures markets, however, have been heavily regulated. Many regulators and legislators have taken a dim view of futures trading, likening it to gambling. In the nineteenth century, there were numerous attempts to outlaw futures trading. Most of the early regulation was at the state and local levels.

Early Federal Regulation

The first attempt at federal regulation was the 1914 Cotton Futures Act, which was a relatively weak law. It was followed in 1922 by the Grain Futures Act, but that too was weak and prohibited only "excessive speculation," which was difficult to define. In 1936 the Commodity Exchange Act created the Commodity Exchange Authority (CEA), a division of the Department of Agriculture. The first federal futures regulatory agency, the CEA was authorized to regulate specific futures contracts. As new contracts were added, various amendments expanded the CEA's coverage. With the introduction of currency futures and the anticipated birth of financial futures, Congress decided that a major new law was needed. It passed the Commodity Futures Trading Commission Act of 1974, which created the Commodity Futures Trading Commission.

The Commodity Futures Trading Commission

The Commodity Futures Trading Commission (CFTC) is a federal agency that regulates futures markets. The CFTC is responsible for licensing futures exchanges and contracts. It approves all terms and conditions of each proposed contract as well as modifications of the terms of existing contracts. To be approved by the CFTC, a contract must have an economic purpose and not be contrary to the "public interest." An "economic purpose" generally is construed to mean that it can be used for hedging.

The CFTC is responsible for ensuring that the exchanges make price information available to the public. It also establishes requirements for **reportable positions,** stipulating that futures traders report their outstanding positions if they exceed certain levels, which vary from contract to

contract. The CFTC also establishes **position limits,** the maximum number of contracts a trader can have at any one time.

The commission is responsible for the authorization or licensing of individuals offering their services to the public. This includes floor brokers, FCMs, APs, CTAs, and CPOs as discussed earlier. These individuals must meet minimum capital requirements, and their backgrounds must be investigated.

The CFTC has the authority to require exchanges to establish and enforce disciplinary actions against members found to be in violation of the exchange's rules. The CFTC can also seek court injunctions and impose certain disciplinary actions itself.

The CFTC is also authorized to establish a system of addressing complaints brought by the public against brokers, traders, and other licensed futures professionals. As we shall see shortly, much of this authority has been turned over to the National Futures Association.

One of the CFTC's primary responsibilities is market surveillance. Federal law makes it a felony to attempt to manipulate the futures market. The CFTC monitors trading for indications of possible manipulation.

As part of the requirements of the 1974 law, the CFTC was formally reviewed and reauthorized in 1978 and again in 1982, when several changes were instituted into law. The CFTC's registration requirements for individuals were expanded, and authority was granted for a test program in agricultural options, which until that time had been banned. The 1982 amendment also confirmed the Johnson-Shad agreement, discussed in Chapter 2, which helped establish the lines of regulatory authority over options and options on futures.

In 1986 Congress passed the Futures Trading Act, which reauthorized the CFTC for three more years. The act extended the agency's powers to include regulation of any futures transaction, whether conducted on or off an exchange.

The latest CFTC reauthorization took several years longer than anticipated. When it was finally completed in the fall of 1992, a number of important changes were made in the way futures markets are regulated. As you should recall, the period of the late 1980s through 1992 was one characterized by rapid growth of the over-the-counter markets. These markets, being unregulated, had shown a tremendous propensity to innovate by developing new types of contracts such as swaps. Many members of Congress argued that the over-the-counter market should be regulated and the futures exchanges, who compete with the over-the-counter markets, supported that position. The final act, however, simply granted the CFTC the authority to exempt swaps and other related financial contracts from its own regulation. It exercised that authority a few months later by declaring those instruments free of CFTC, and, therefore, all government regulation. The reauthorization bill also granted the Federal Reserve the authority to oversee the setting of margin requirements on stock index fu-

tures. These are set by the futures clearinghouses. The Federal Reserve already had margin-setting authority in the stock market. It does not appear at this time, however, that the Fed will actively exercise this authority in the futures markets.

The reauthorization act also placed new restrictions on dual trading by forcing the exchanges to prohibit it or introduce audit procedures that would catch abuses. Recall that dual trading is when a floor trader executes trades for his or her own account as well as for customers. In addition to the restrictions on dual trading, the CFTC also introduced tough new rulings on trading futures based on inside information.

More information on the CFTC can be obtained at its excellent web site: http://www.cftc.gov.

Over the years, the states have been restricted from regulating futures trading. That too changed in 1982, when the states were given some limited regulatory authority. Also, individuals were allowed to pursue private lawsuits against brokers and firms involved in futures trading. However, the most significant regulatory development of that year was the establishment of the National Futures Association.

The National Futures Association

The National Futures Association (NFA) is an organization of individuals and firms that participate in the futures industry. The NFA is an industry self-regulatory agency. The 1974 law had encouraged the development of such an organization, and in 1982 the NFA was formally chartered.

All FCMs, CPOs, IBs, APs, and CTAs are required to join the NFA, and no NFA member may accept a transaction from anyone other than an NFA member. Floor traders, floor brokers, and exchanges are not required to join; they are regulated solely by the CFTC.

The NFA's objective is to prevent fraud and manipulation, protect the public interest, and encourage free markets. The NFA requires registration of its members, who must meet strict requirements and pass an examination. Like the CFTC, the NFA is authorized to monitor trading and identify rule violations as well as impose disciplinary action. Thus, it relieves the CFTC of some of this responsibility and turns the regulatory authority over to the market participants themselves.

The NFA has established a system of arbitrating disputes between individuals and registered futures markets participants. The system is designed so that individuals can obtain faster, more efficient claim settlements than would be possible with the CFTC or through the legal system.

The NFA's web site is http://www.nfa.futures.org.

Summary

This chapter provided the descriptive material necessary for understanding how the forward and futures markets operate. We learned what a futures contract is, which contracts trade in U.S. markets, the characteristics of the markets and

traders, the role of the exchange, and the mechanics of trading. We also examined the nature of transaction costs and the structure of regulation. We learned what forward contracts are and how they differ from futures contracts.

The next four chapters deal with specific aspects of futures and forward trading. Chapters 8 and 9 explain the concepts of pricing spot transactions and the related contracts. Chapter 10 examines hedging strategies and provides illustrations of hedge transactions. Chapter 11 looks at some advanced strategies, including arbitrage, speculation, and spread transactions.

Key Terms

Before continuing to Chapter 8, you should be able to give brief definitions of the following terms.

- forward contract
- futures contract
- interbank market
- limit move
- circuit breaker
- futures commission merchant (FCM)
- local
- dual trading
- hedger
- speculator
- spreader
- arbitrageur
- scalper
- day trader
- position trader

- open outcry
- initial margin
- maintenance margin
- settlement price
- daily settlement/marking to market
- variation margin
- offsetting
- Eurodollar
- LIBOR
- conversion factor (CF)
- managed futures
- futures fund
- commodity pool
- tick

Questions and Problems

1. Explain the difference between a forward contract and an option.

2. What factors distinguish a forward contract from a futures contract? What do forward and futures contracts have in common? What advantages does each have over the other?

3. Identify the most actively traded contract from each of the following groups of futures contracts: (a) financial futures, (b) non-agricultural commodity futures, and (c) agricultural commodity futures.

4. The open interest in a futures contract changes from day to day. Suppose investors holding long positions are divided into two groups: A is an individual investor and OL represents other investors. Investors holding short positions are denoted as S. Currently A holds 1,000 contracts and OL holds 4,200; thus, S is short 5,200 contracts. Determine the holdings of A, OL, and S after each of the following transactions.
   a. A sells 500 contracts, OL buys 500 contracts.
   b. A buys 700 contracts, OL sells 700 contracts.
   c. A buys 200 contracts, S sells 200 contracts.
   d. A sells 800 contracts, S buys 800 contracts.

   What determines whether volume increases or decreases open interest?

5. List and briefly explain the important contributions provided by futures exchanges.

6. How do locals differ from commission brokers? How do the latter differ from futures commission merchants?

7. Explain the basic differences between open outcry and electronic trading systems.

8. One of the more controversial floor trading practices is dual trading. Explain what dual trading is, and give an example of how a dual trader could profit at the expense of a customer. (Hint: Consider the types of orders public customers can place. These are briefly mentioned in this chapter and discussed in more detail in Chapter 2.) What benefit is associated with dual trading?

9. What factors would determine whether a particular strategy is a hedge or a speculative strategy?

10. How are spread and arbitrage strategies forms of speculation? How can they be interpreted as hedges?

11. What are the differences among scalpers, day traders, and position traders?

12. What are the various ways in which an individual may obtain the right to go on to the floor of an exchange and trade futures?

13. What are daily price limits, and why are they used?

14. What are circuit breakers? What are their advantages and disadvantages?

15. Explain how the clearinghouse operates to protect the futures market.

16. Explain the differences among the three means of terminating a futures contract: an offsetting trade, cash settlement, and delivery. How is a forward contract terminated?

17. Suppose you buy a stock index futures contract at the opening price of 452.25 on July 1. The multiplier on the contract is 500, so the price is $500 (452.25) = $226,125. You hold the position open until selling it on July 16 at the opening price of 435.50. The initial margin requirement is $9,000, and the maintenance margin requirement is $6,000. Assume you deposit the initial margin and do not withdraw the excess on any given day. Construct a table showing the charges and credits to the margin account. The daily prices on the intervening days are as follows:

Day	Settlement Price
7/1	453.95
7/2	454.50
7/3	452.00
7/7	443.55
7/8	441.65
7/9	442.85
7/10	444.15
7/11	442.25
7/14	438.30
7/15	435.05
7/16	435.50

18. Explain in general terms the responsibility of the CFTC.

19. What role does the National Futures Association play in regulating the futures industry?

20. Following are prices for IMM T-bill and Eurodollar futures contracts. The quotes are based on the IMM Index. Determine the actual contract prices.

   a. T-bills: 89.72

   b. Eurodollars: 87.24

21. For each of the following bonds, determine whether the bond is eligible for delivery on the March 1998 T-bond futures contract. (Assume all bonds mature on the fifteenth.)
   a.   9 3/8s of February 2006
   b.   8 7/8s of February 2019
   c.   10 3/4s of August 2005
   d.   7 1/2s of November 2024
   e.   11 3/4s of November 2014, callable in November 2009

22. On March 13, you are short the March T-bond futures contract. You plan to deliver a Treasury bond that has a coupon of 11 1/4 percent payable semiannually on May 15 and November 15 and a conversion factor of 1.3661. The delivery date is Friday, March 15. The settlement price on March 13 is 69 6/32. Determine the invoice price, and describe the three-day sequence leading to delivery.

APPENDIX 7A
Selected Financial Futures Contract Specifications

Contract	Exchange	Trading Hours	Delivery Months	Contract Size	Minimum Price Change	Daily Price Limits	Last Trading Day	First Delivery Day	Margin
U.S. Treasury bonds	CBOT	7:20–2:00 (M–F)	M,J,S,D	$100,000	1/32 = $31.25	96/32 = $3,000	Business day prior to last seven business days	First business day of month	$ 2,700 (I) $ 2,000 (M)
U.S. Treasury notes (5 year)	CBOT	7:20–2:00 (M–F)	M,J,S,D	$100,000	1/64 = $15.625	96/32 = $3,000	Business day prior to last seven business days	First business day of month	$ 1,215 (I) $ 900 (M)
U.S. Treasury notes (6 1/2–10 year)	CBOT	7:20–2:00 (M–F)	M,J,S,D	$100,000	1/32 = $31.25	96/32 = $3,000	Business day prior to last seven business days	First business day of month	$ 1,755 (I) $ 1,300 (M)
Eurodollars (90-day)	CME (IMM)	7:20–2:00	M,J,S,D	$1,000,000	.01 = $25	None	2nd London business day before 3rd Wednesday	Cash settled on last trading day	$473–540 (I) $350–400 (M)
U.S. Treasury bills	CME (IMM)	7:20–2:00	M,J,S,D	$1,000,000	.01 = $25	None	Business day prior to issue date	First business day of month	$ 270 (I) $ 200 (M)
S&P 500 Index	CME (IOM)	8:30–3:15	M,J,S,D	$500 × Index	.05 = $25	Varies (contact exchange)	Thursday prior to third Friday	Cash settled on Friday after last trade date	$ 21,000 (I) $ 17,500 (M)

Notes: All times are local. All trading days are Monday through Friday unless otherwise indicated. Evening trading hours vary during DST. Margins shown are initial (I) and maintenance (M). These are for speculators. Hedge and spread margins are usually lower. This material is believed to be current as of January 1997. Contract specifications sometimes change and margins and price limits often change. Investors should consult the exchanges for the latest information. Currency contract specifications are provided in Appendix 13A.

Source: The exchanges

APPENDIX 7B
Taxation of Futures Transactions

Investors and traders' profits from futures contracts, as well as index options, are considered to be 60 percent capital gains and 40 percent ordinary income. Capital gains are taxed at the ordinary income rate, but subject to a maximum of 20 percent. Thus, an investor in the 31 percent tax bracket would have futures profits taxed at a blended rate of .6(.20) + .4(.31) = .244.

In addition, all futures and index options profits are subject to a mark-to-market rule in which accumulated profits are taxable in the current year even if the contract has not been closed out. For example, assume you bought a futures contract on October 15 at a price of $1,000. Your account was, of course, marked to market daily. At the end of the year, the accumulated profit in the account was $400, meaning that the futures price at the end of the year was $1,400. Then you would have to pay the tax that year on $400 even though you had not closed out the contract. In other words, realized and unrealized profits are taxed and losses are recognized.

These rules apply only to speculative transactions. Taxation of hedge transactions is more complex and will be examined in Chapter 10.

Consider the following example. Suppose an investor in the 31 percent tax bracket purchases a futures contract at $1,000 on October 15 and ultimately sells it at $1,300 on January 20 of the next year. Assume the contract price was $1,400 at the end of the year. The first year the tax liability is on $400, so the tax is $400(.6)(.20) + $400(.4)(.31) = $97.60, an effective rate of 24.4 percent. In the second year, there is a taxable loss of $1,400 − $1,300 = $100. This can be used to offset taxable gains; thus, it will save the trader .244($100) = $24.40 in taxes on profitable futures trades in that year. Losses can be used to offset gains, but not more than the total amount of taxable gains. Any losses not used can be carried back to offset prior trading profits for up to three years.

Suppose the contract expired in February and the investor took delivery of the commodity. Let the price at expiration be $1,500. Then it would be assumed that the commodity was purchased at $1,500. The investor would have paid tax on the $400 profit at the end of the year in which the contract was bought; the investor would owe tax on the $100 profit that accrued between the end of the year and the expiration.

Although recent tax laws have greatly simplified the taxation of futures contracts, many complexities remain. Competent tax advice is necessary to keep up with the many changes and ensure compliance with the various rules.

Questions and Problems

1. On October 1, you purchase one March stock index futures contract at the opening price of 410.30. The contract multiplier is $500, so the price of 410.30 is really $500(410.30) = $205,150. You hold the position open until February 20, whereupon you sell the contract at the opening price of 427.30. The settlement price on December 31 was 422.40. You are in the 31 percent tax bracket. Compute your tax liability.

2. In November you buy a futures contract on a commodity at a price of $10,000. At the end of the year, the futures price is $10,500. You hold your position open until January 20, at which time the commodity price is $11,200, the contract expires, and you take delivery. You are in the 31 percent tax bracket. Compute your tax liability in both years.

APPENDIX 7C
Determining the CBOT Treasury Bond Conversion Factor

Step 1   Determine the maturity of the bond in years, months, and days as of the first day of the expiration month. If the bond is callable, use the first call date instead of the maturity date. Let YRS be the number of years and MOS the number of months. Ignore the number of days. Let c be the coupon rate on the bond.

Step 2   Round the number of months down to 0, 3, 6, or 9. Call this MOS*.

Step 3   If MOS* = 0,

$$CF_0 = \frac{c}{2}\left[\frac{1 - (1.04)^{-2*\text{YRS}}}{.04}\right] + (1.04)^{-2*\text{YRS}}.$$

If MOS* = 3,

$$CF_3 = (CF_0 + c/2)(1.04)^{-.5} - c/4.$$

If MOS* = 6,

$$CF_6 = \frac{c}{2}\left[\frac{1 - (1.04)^{-(2*\text{YRS} + 1)}}{.04}\right] + (1.04)^{-(2*\text{YRS} + 1)}.$$

If MOS* = 9,

$$CF_9 = (CF_6 + c/2)(1.04)^{-.5} - c/4.$$

Example: Determine the CF for delivery of the 9 7/8s of November 15, 2015, on the December 1996 T-bond futures contract.

On December 1, 1996, the bond's remaining life is 18 years, 11 months, and 14 days. Thus, YRS = 18 and MOS = 11. Rounding down gives MOS* = 9. First, we must find CF_6:

$$CF_6 = \frac{.09875}{2}\left[\frac{1-(1.04)^{-(2(18)+1)}}{.04}\right]+(1.04)^{-(2(18)+1)},$$
$$= 1.1795$$

Then we find CF_9 as

$$CF_9 = (1.1795+.09875/2)(1.04)^{-.5}-.09875/4 = 1.1803$$

which is shown in Table 7.5 in the chapter.

The Excel spreadsheet cf.xls will automatically calculate the conversion factor for you. Software Demonstration 7.1 illustrates how to use cf.xls.

SOFTWARE DEMONSTRATION 7.1   **Calculating the Treasury Bond Futures Conversion Factor with the Excel Spreadsheet cf.xls**

The Excel spreadsheet cf.xls, which operates in Windows 3.1 or Windows 95 and requires Excel 5.0 or higher, calculates the conversion factor for a bond delivery on the Chicago Board of Trade's Treasury bond futures contract. These conversion factors are also valid for the various Treasury note contracts at the CBOT. No installation is necessary; simply place the file in whatever directory you prefer or access it directly from the 3.5-inch diskette provided in the book. To use the software, do the following:

1. Make sure you are in Windows 3.1 or Windows 95.
2. Run Excel 5.0 or higher.
3. Open the file cf.xls.

Now let us assume that you wish to calculate a conversion factor. In the example in the book, we wish to deliver the 9 7/8s maturing on November 15, 2015, on the December 1996 contract. Each cell that will accept input has a double-line border and the values are in blue. In the section labeled **Inputs:** you should enter the delivery date. This will always be simply a month and year. Enter it in the form mm/yyyy. Thus, you should insert "12/1996" in the cell. Several rows below you should enter the coupon rate and maturity date. Enter the coupon rate as a percentage or decimal. For example, our bond's coupon is 9.875, so enter "9.875" or ".09875". Enter the maturity date in the format mm/dd/yyyy. Thus, in this case you would enter "11/15/2015". The spreadsheet displays both of these dates in Excel's date format. Hit F9 (manual recalculation).

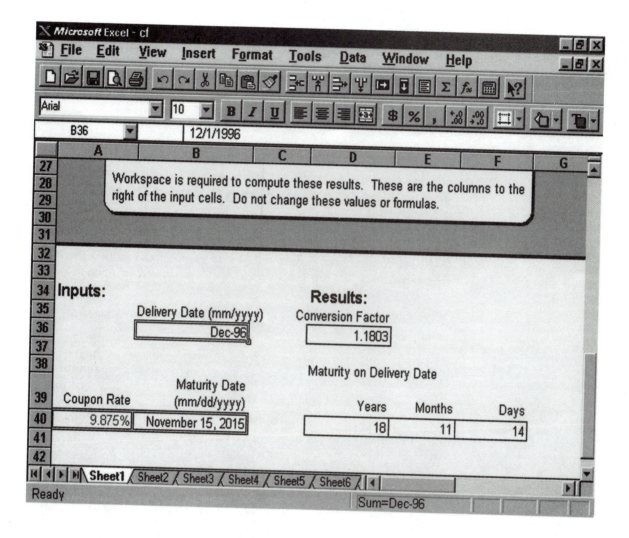

The results are automatically calculated and appear in the section labeled **Results:** Output values have a single-line border. The conversion factor here is 1.1803. The spreadsheet also shows the maturity in years (here, 18), months (here, 11) and days (here, 14). This enables you to see if the bond has a sufficiently long maturity to be eligible for delivery on the bond or note contracts.

For those who prefer Lotus 1-2-3, the diskette also contains the spreadsheet cf.wk3 and its format file cf.fm3. This spreadsheet is from the previous edition of this book and does not contain all of the features of the Excel spreadsheet, but it will provide the conversion factor following essentially the same procedure.

CHAPTER 8

Principles of Spot Pricing

The simple fact of the matter is that no one knows the future with any certainty at all. Refusal to admit that explains why so many people lose money investing in commodities.

MARK RITCHIE

God in the Pits: Confessions of a Commodities Trader, 1990

Chapter Objectives

■ To review the concept of the term structure of interest rates and to clearly distinguish between spot and forward rates

■ To review the principles of the pricing of bonds, the relationship between bond price volatility and yield changes, the effects of the coupon and maturity, and duration

■ To demonstrate how the term structure can be constructed from the futures market

■ To review the principles of asset pricing theory, especially the concepts of diversification and beta

■ To introduce the important concept of the cost of carry and the role it plays in the pricing of assets under conditions of certainty, uncertainty and risk neutrality, and uncertainty and risk aversion

■ To illustrate the accompanying software for calculating duration and beta

A sound foundation in the principles of pricing the underlying spot instruments is important to understanding how forward and futures contracts are priced. Since this book is devoted primarily to financial derivatives, we need to understand how stocks and bonds are priced. Accordingly, in this chapter we deal with the basic principles of pricing these instruments. In addition, we look at a simple approach to pricing all risky instruments. We will use these models in Chapter 9, when we examine the pricing of forward and futures contracts.

Principles and Pricing of Fixed-Income Securities

Fixed-income securities, commonly known as **bonds,** are priced according to the size and timing of the cash flows promised by the issuer and the interest rates available in the market. The market-determined interest rates are defined by the term structure of interest rates. The **term structure of interest rates,** sometimes called simply the **term structure,** is the relationship among interest rates on bonds of different maturities. To understand the term structure, we must first examine the difference between spot and forward rates.

The Concept of Spot and Forward Rates

The interest rate on a loan made immediately is called the **spot rate** or, in the parlance of derivative markets, the **cash rate.** Sometimes, however, a

loan is to be made at a future point in time but the terms and conditions, such as the rate and maturity, are established today. This type of transaction is a forward loan, and the agreement is a forward contract or forward rate commitment, as discussed in Chapter 7. The agreed-upon interest rate is called the **forward rate.**

A spot rate is the rate on a bond or loan that begins today. A forward rate is the rate, agreed upon today, on a bond or loan that begins at a future date.

Let us consider some notation for spot and forward rates. Let $r(a,b)$ be the interest rate on a loan made at time a and paid back at time b. The loan has a maturity of $b - a$. It is a **pure-discount loan,** meaning that the interest is taken out in advance. If $a = 0$, $r(0,b)$ is a spot rate; if $a > 0$, $r(a,b)$ is a forward rate. Note that b must always exceed a.[1]

Suppose that today you take out a $1,000 loan with the promise to pay it back in one year at a rate of 10 percent. Then $r(0,1) = .10$. The price of the loan, which is the amount of money you receive today, is $1,000(1.10)^{-1} = 909.09$. Now suppose you actually do not need the money until one year from now. You ask the lender what the rate would be if you borrowed one year from now. The lender quotes you a rate of 12 percent. Then $r(1,2) = .12$. The forward price is $1,000(1.12)^{-1} = 892.86$. This is the amount you will receive in one year. A year after that, or two years from today, you will pay back $1,000.

The Relationship between Spot and Forward Rates

Assume all loans are free of default risk. Then we can examine the relationship between spot and forward rates by observing the term structure. The term structure defines the spot rates for various maturities. Although the forward rates are not explicitly defined by the term structure, they can be inferred.

Consider the following term structure:

$$r(0,1) = .06 \qquad r(0,2) = .08 \qquad r(0,3) = .09 \qquad r(0,4) = .10.$$

These are annual rates on loans of one to four years. As you can see, the rates increase with maturity. The term structure thus is said to be increasing, or upward sloping.

For a given set of Z spot rates, there are $Z(Z - 1)/2$ forward rates. For example, the rates $r(1,2)$, $r(1,3)$, $r(1,4)$, $r(2,3)$, $r(2,4)$, and $r(3,4)$ are six forward rates that can be derived from these four spot rates; that is, $4(4 - 1)/2 = 6$.[2] Figure 8.1 indicates the spot and forward rates for this term structure. Each rate is positioned in the time interval to which it

---

[1]After all, a loan cannot be paid off before it is taken out.

[2]Actually, there are an infinite number of forward rates. For example, $r(1,2.5)$, $r(2,3.7)$, and so forth are forward rates. When we say there are $Z(Z - 1)/2$ forward rates, we are considering only integer time points.

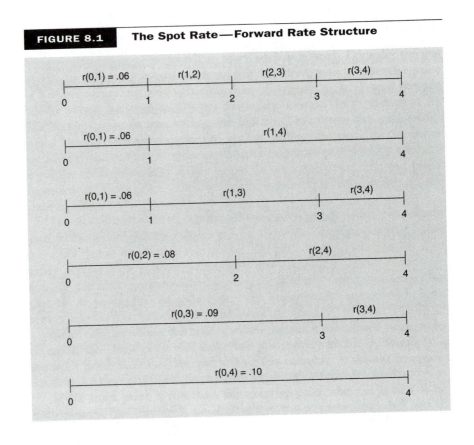

FIGURE 8.1   **The Spot Rate—Forward Rate Structure**

applies. We know the value of each spot rate, so we can derive the values of the forward rates.

Assume you need to borrow \$1 today for two years, after which you will pay back $[1 + r(0,2)]^2$ dollars. Alternatively, you take out a one-year loan today and simultaneously enter into a forward contract with a lender that will let you borrow one year from now at the rate $r(1,2)$, with that loan to be repaid a year later. In other words, you make a one-year loan, followed by a one-year loan; however, the rate on the second loan is agreed upon today. At the end of the first year, you will owe $[1 + r(0,1)]$. You then take out the second loan. At the end of the second year, you will owe $[1 + r(0,1)][1 + r(1,2)]$. Assuming you and the lender are indifferent between the one two-year loan and the two one-year loans, the amount ultimately paid back under the two arrangements should be equal; that is,

$$[1 + r(0,2)]^2 = [1 + r(0,1)][1 + r(1,2)].$$

Knowing the values r(0,2) and r(0,1), you can solve for r(1,2):

$$r(1,2) = \frac{[1 + r(0,2)]^2}{[1 + r(0,1)]} - 1.$$

In this example,

$$r(1,2) = \frac{(1.08)^2}{1.06} - 1 = .1004.$$

We can derive any forward rate from our knowledge of two overlapping spot rates. Look again at Figure 8.1. We can derive r(1,4) by equating the payoff from a spot four-year loan with the payoff from a spot one-year loan plus a forward loan taken out at the end of year 1 and paid back at the end of year 4:

Forward rates can be obtained from the relationship among overlapping spot rates.

$$[1 + r(0,4)]^4 = [1 + r(0, 1)][1 + r(1, 4)]^3.$$

Note that 1 + r(1,4) is raised to the third power because it is a three-year loan. The implied forward rate is

$$r(1,4) = \left[\frac{[1 + r(0,4)]^4}{1 + r(0,1)} \right]^{1/3} - 1.$$

Because the rate r(1,4) is a three-year rate, the third root of the term in brackets is taken. This converts the three-year rate to an annual rate, which is the conventional method of quoting interest rates. The answer is r(1,4) = .1137. You should now be able to derive all the other forward rates. The answers are r(2,3) = .1103, r(3,4) = .1306, r(2,4) = .1204, and r(1,3) = .1053.

Now suppose the above relationships did not hold. For example, consider the two-year spot rate of .08 and the one-year spot rate of .06. Suppose a lender offered a forward rate, r(1,2), of .098 instead of the implied forward rate of .1004. Borrowers would besiege the lender for one-year spot loans at 6 percent and one-year forward loans at 9.8 percent. These borrowers would then become lenders themselves by using the proceeds of their loans to make two-year spot loans at 8 percent. At the end of two years, they would owe (1.06)(1.098) = 1.1639 for every dollar borrowed but would receive (1.08)² = 1.1664 for every dollar lent. Because the transaction would be riskless, this type of arbitrage would be attractive and would increase the demand for one-year spot loans and one-year forward loans and the supply of two-year spot loans. This would force a realignment of rates until the forward and spot rates offered no further arbitrage opportunities.

Theories of the Term Structure

If we plotted the relationship between interest rate and maturity for a set of bonds of a given level of risk, we might get any of the three general types of curves shown in Figure 8.2. Although some term structures are humped, in general the curves tend to be upward sloping, downward sloping, or approximately flat. Why the term structure takes on the shape it does has been a subject of much conjecture for most of this century. Economists have posited three possible explanations: expectations, liquidity preference, and market segmentation. In addition there is a fourth theory, the local expectations theory, that looks at the term structure in a different way.

THE EXPECTATIONS THEORY   The **expectations theory** assumes there are no transaction costs and either there is no uncertainty or investors are risk neutral. Under these conditions, forward rates will be the market's expectations of future spot rates.

Let the borrower take out a one-year loan. One year later, the borrower takes out another one-year loan. Under the expectations theory, borrowers and lenders would be indifferent between this arrangement and a one-year loan plus a one-year forward loan. This means the implied forward rate represents the investor's expectation of the future spot rate.

FIGURE 8.2   **Term Structures**

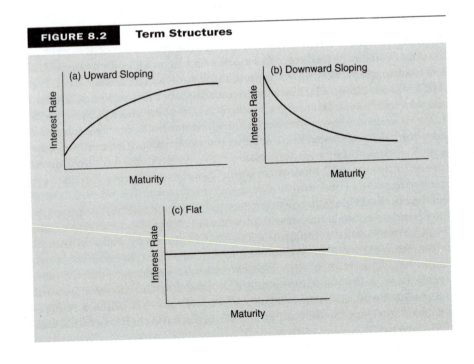

Thus, in the example in which r(1,2) = .1004, both borrower and lender believe that in one year the spot rate on one-year loans will be 10.04 percent. Because of their risk neutrality, they are willing to engage in the transaction without considering that the actual rate one year from now may turn out to be something other than 10.04 percent.

Recall that the formula for r(1,2) is

$$r(1,2) = \frac{[1 + r(0,2)]^2}{[1 + r(0,1)]} - 1.$$

An upward-sloping term structure would be one in which the two-year rate, r(0,2), was greater than the one-year rate, r(0,1). The above formula implies that if r(0,2) > r(0,1), then r(1,2) > r(0,1). Likewise, r(0,2) < r(0,1) as r(1,2) < r(0,1). In other words, an upward-sloping term structure implies that the one-year forward rate on one-year loans exceeds the spot rate on one-year loans. Since the one-year forward rate on one-year loans is the market's expectation of the future spot rate on one-year loans, the market is forecasting that spot rates on one-year loans will increase. Similarly, a downward-sloping term structure suggests a market forecast of declining spot rates on one-year loans. A flat term structure is a forecast of no change in spot rates.

The expectations theory assumes that forward rates are the market's expectations of future spot rates and thus implies that the shape of the term structure indicates the expected direction of future interest rates.

THE LIQUIDITY PREFERENCE THEORY   The **liquidity preference theory** states that lenders prefer to maintain liquidity and thus have a preference for short-term loans. To justify long-term loans, lenders must expect a higher return in the form of a liquidity premium. Thus, long-term rates should naturally be above short-term rates. This would explain an upward-sloping term structure. If this theory is correct, the forward rate will systematically overestimate the expected future spot rate.

For example, assume the expectations theory holds and investors believe there will be no change in interest rates. Let the one-year rate be 6 percent. This means the two-year rate will be 6 percent and the implied forward rate will be 6 percent. Now let us propose that investors suddenly recognize that making two-year loans means giving up some liquidity. Lenders decide they do not particularly want to make two-year loans, so they start charging 7 percent for them. Now the forward rate will be $(1.07)^2/(1.06) - 1 = .0801$. Although the implied forward rate is 8.01 percent, investors still expect one-year rates in one year to be 6 percent. Because it contains the liquidity premium, the forward rate will consistently overestimate the future spot rate. Thus, forward rates are **biased** estimates of future spot rates.

The liquidity preference theory assumes that long-term rates must exceed short-term rates to induce lenders to give up their liquidity and make long-term loans. Thus, it implies that forward rates will be biased expectations of future spot rates.

THE MARKET SEGMENTATION THEORY   The **market segmentation theory,** sometimes called the **preferred habitat theory,** argues that long- and

short-term markets are separate. Long-term borrowers and lenders transact only in long-term markets, while short-term borrowers and lenders deal only in short-term markets. Because of this, the arbitrage transactions necessary for forcing a mathematical relationship between long- and short-term rates are not executed. Instead, supply and demand conditions in the respective markets define the term structure. An upward-sloping term structure is caused by tighter monetary conditions in long-term markets than in short-term markets.

The market segmentation theory assumes that short-term and long-term markets are completely separate and that supply and demand conditions in the two markets determine their respective rates.

To see the market segmentation theory at work, consider a market in which the expectations theory holds. Now suppose a new, totalitarian government passes a law that defines three distinct types of lenders. One lender can make only one-year loans, one only ten-year loans, and one only nine-year forward loans that will start in one year. As one of the few freedoms left, each lender can charge whatever rate it wants. The first lender offers the one-year loans at 6 percent, the second offers the ten-year loans at 10 percent, and the third offers the nine-year forward loans at 10.25 percent. A simple calculation reveals that a 6 percent one-year rate and a 10 percent ten-year rate produce an implied forward rate of not 10.25 percent but 10.45 percent. Obviously, an arbitrage transaction is possible, but wait—we said there were only three types of lenders and each lender could make only one type of loan. To execute the arbitrage, someone would have to make one of the other types of loans. Depending on the government's law enforcement and judicial policies, this could land the arbitraging lender in jail or worse! Thus, the arbitrage would not be made, and short- and long-term rates would bear no necessary relationship to each other as they would if the expectations (or liquidity preference) theory held. Of course, in practice the laws are not that restrictive, but often lenders stick to particular maturity ranges.

The local expectations theory assumes that only one-period-ahead forward rates equal expected future spot rates and then only using risk neutral probabilities. It is consistent with the principle that no arbitrage opportunities exist across the term structure.

THE LOCAL EXPECTATIONS THEORY   The **local expectations theory** is a variation of the expectations theory, but it does not impose the stringent requirement that everybody be risk neutral and it does not assume away uncertainty. Under the expectations theory, any forward rate is an unbiased estimate of the expected future spot rate. For example, suppose today I am interested in the forward rate r(10,15), which is the forward rate for a loan starting 10 years from now and maturing 15 years from now. Under the expectations theory, this forward rate is an unbiased predictor of the expected future spot rate, or, in other words, the spot rate on a five-year loan 10 years from now. It is difficult to believe that forward rates could have such predictive power over the entire term structure, which is limitless. The local expectations theory preserves some of the simplicity of the expectations theory while imposing less stringent predictive power on borrowers and lenders. It simply says that the one-period-ahead forward

rate is a predictor of the expected future spot rate. In other words, all forward rates r(1,b), where b can be any maturity in the future, are unbiased predictors of future spot rates for only one period ahead. This gives forward rates some predictive power but not a lot. Beyond one period, forward rates will be biased predictors of future spot rates. Although a formal proof is beyond the scope of this book, it can also be shown that the local expectations theory is consistent with the principle that bonds are priced across the term structure such that no arbitrage opportunities exist. This is equivalent to the risk neutrality approach to pricing options that we previously discussed. In fact, when the one-period-ahead forward rate equals the expected spot rate, the latter is determined using the risk neutral probabilities, not the true probabilities. But, as we noted in Chapters 3 and 4, this does not mean that investors are risk neutral. It means only that the pricing techniques we use would be the same whether investors were risk neutral or risk averse.

WHICH THEORY IS CORRECT?   The current view of scholars and professional traders clearly favors the local expectations theory. It admits no arbitrage opportunities, a principle we have repeatedly encountered, and permits forward rates to have limited predictive power, at least in a risk neutral sense. It forms the core of much of the advanced theory of pricing bonds and their derivatives. For our purposes at this beginning level, we do not have to specifically espouse a particular view, but it is important to be aware of the various explanations of the shape of the term structure. In particular, it is important not to attribute too much predictive power to forward rates, something of which, regrettably, scholars and textbooks have been quite guilty over the past 30 years.

The Pricing of Bonds

Consider an investor holding a portfolio of four pure-discount bonds. One bond matures at the end of one year; the others mature at the end of two, three, and four years, respectively. The first three bonds have face values of $80 and the fourth a face value of $1,080. Let the term structure be defined as in the previous example: $r(0,1) = .06$, $r(0,2) = .08$, $r(0,3) = .09$, and $r(0,4) = .10$. The prices of the four bonds are

$$
\begin{array}{lll}
\text{Bond 1:} & 80(1.06)^{-1} = & 75.47 \\
\text{Bond 2:} & 80(1.08)^{-2} = & 68.59 \\
\text{Bond 3:} & 80(1.09)^{-3} = & 61.77 \\
\text{Bond 4:} & 1{,}080(1.10)^{-4} = & 737.65.
\end{array}
$$

The total value of the investor's portfolio of bonds is $75.47 + $68.59 + $61.77 + $737.65 = $943.48.

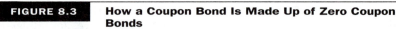

FIGURE 8.3	How a Coupon Bond Is Made Up of Zero Coupon Bonds

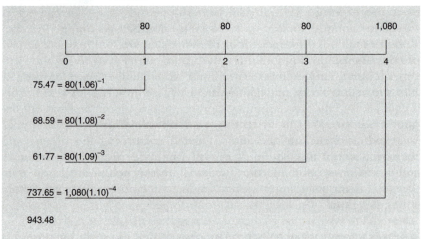

A coupon bond can be decomposed into a portfolio of zero coupon bonds.

Now consider a second investor who holds a four-year, $1,000-face-value bond paying coupons of 8 percent annually.[3] Figure 8.3 illustrates the time pattern of this bond's cash flows. We see that the two investors will receive identical cash flows; thus, their portfolios' values must be the same. This means the four-year bond must be worth $943.48. This value can, of course, be found as the present value of each coupon and the final principal payment, with each cash flow discounted by the respective spot rate given by the term structure:

$$B = \sum_{t=1}^{T} CI_t[1 + r(0,t)]^{-t} + FV[1 + r(0,T)]^{-T}$$
$$= 80(1.06)^{-1} + 80(1.08)^{-2} + 80(1.09)^{-3} + 80(1.10)^{-4} + 1,000(1.10)^{-4}$$
$$= 943.48,$$

where

$$CI_t = \text{coupon interest at time t}$$
$$FV = \text{principal repayment at time T}$$
$$T = \text{time to maturity.}$$

The yield on a bond is the discount rate that equates the present value of the bond's coupons and face value to its price.

THE BOND YIELD   The **yield to maturity,** or simply **yield,** is the single discount rate that when applied to the bond's coupons and face value

[3]Most bonds pay interest semiannually, but we shall use annual interest at this point. Later, and in the chapters in which we begin working with actual bonds, we shall use semiannual interest.

gives a present value equal to the actual market price. The formula for the price is

$$B = \sum_{t=1}^{T} CP_t(1 + y)^{-t},$$

where y is the yield and CP_t is the cash payment, the coupon or principal, at time t. Assuming the coupons are fixed, we can express them as a series of equivalent values, CI, followed by the principal repayment of FV. Then the formula can be expressed as

$$B = CI \left[\sum_{t=1}^{T} (1 + y)^{-t} \right] + FV(1 + y)^{-T}.$$

The term in brackets is the compound factor for an annuity and has a known formula. Using that formula, the price of the bond can be expressed as

$$B = CI \left[\frac{1 - (1 + y)^{-T}}{y} \right] + FV(1 + y)^{-T}.$$

Normally we would know the price and would have to solve for the yield. This is a tedious task best left to computers and financial calculators. In this problem, the yield that equates the present value of a four-year, 8 percent coupon bond to a price of $943.48 is approximately 9.77 percent. The reader can verify this answer by plugging .0977 into the above formula for B where CI = 80, FV = 1,000, T = 4, and B = 943.48.

TREASURY BOND PRICE QUOTATIONS   To apply the principles of bond pricing to actual bonds, we must first examine how bond prices are quoted. Consider the set of U.S. Treasury bond and note price quotes taken from *The Wall Street Journal* shown in Figure 8.4.

Note the first bond listed. In the first column is the annual coupon rate of 5 1/2 percent, paid in semiannual installments of $27.50 for a $1,000-par-value bond. The next two columns give the maturity year and month, July 1997.[4] Most government bonds mature on the fifteenth of the month. A few mature on the last business day of the month, which is apparently the case here. The interest payment days are the maturity day and the day exactly six months prior (or hence). Some bonds, including this one, have an *n* beside the year, which indicates a Treasury note.[5] Some bonds have two maturity dates indicating that the bond is callable

---

[4] In the language of financial markets, the bonds are said to be the 5 1/2s of July 97.

[5] Treasury notes have initial maturities of from 2 to 10 years; Treasury bonds have initial maturities of 10 years or more.

FIGURE 8.4 **Treasury Bond Quotations in *The Wall Street Journal,* Trading Day of July 23, 1997**

TREASURY BONDS, NOTES & BILLS

Wednesday, July 23, 1997

Representative and Indicative Over-the-Counter quotations based on $1 million or more.

Treasury bond, note and bill quotes are as of mid-afternoon. Colons in bond and note bid-and-asked quotes represent 32nds; 101:01 means 101 1/32. Net changes in 32nds. Treasury bill quotes in hundredths, quoted in terms of a rate discount. Days to maturity calculated from settlement date. All yields are based on a one-day settlement and calculated on the offer quote. Current 13-week and 26-week bills are boldfaced. For bonds callable prior to maturity, yields are computed to the earliest call date for issues quoted above par and to the maturity date for issues quoted below par. n-Treasury note. i-Inflation-indexed. wi-When issued. iw-Inflation-indexed when issued; daily change is expressed in basis points.

Source: Dow Jones/Cantor Fitzgerald.

U.S. Treasury strips as of 3 p.m. Eastern time, also based on transactions of $1 million or more. Colons in bid-and-asked quotes represent 32nds; 99:01 means 99 1/32. Net changes in 32nds. Yields calculated on the asked quotation. ci-stripped coupon interest. bp-Treasury bond, stripped principal. np-Treasury note, stripped principal. For bonds callable prior to maturity, yields are computed to the earliest call date for issues quoted above par and to the maturity date for issues below par.

Source: Bear, Stearns & Co. via Street Software Technology Inc.

GOVT. BONDS & NOTES

Rate	Maturity Mo/Yr	Bid	Asked	Chg.	Ask Yld.
5 1/2	Jul 97n	99:30	100:00	....	5.36
5 7/8	Jul 97n	99:30	100:00	....	5.71
6 1/2	Aug 97n	100:00	100:02	....	5.32
8 5/8	Aug 97n	100:04	100:06	− 1	5.33
5 5/8	Aug 97n	99:31	100:01	....	5.21
6	Aug 97n	100:00	100:02	....	5.27
5 1/2	Sep 97n	99:31	100:01	....	5.24
5 3/4	Sep 97n	100:00	100:02	....	5.31
8 3/4	Oct 97n	100:22	100:24	....	5.28
5 5/8	Oct 97n	100:00	100:02	....	5.32
5 3/4	Oct 97n	100:01	100:03	....	5.33
7 3/8	Nov 97n	100:16	100:18	....	5.45
8 7/8	Nov 97n	100:31	101:01	....	5.40
5 3/8	Nov 97n	99:29	99:31	....	5.42
6	Nov 97n	100:04	100:06	....	5.41
5 1/4	Dec 97n	99:28	99:30	+ 1	5.38
6	Dec 97n	100:06	100:08	....	5.39
7 7/8	Jan 98n	101:02	101:04	....	5.44
5	Jan 98n	99:21	99:23	....	5.55
5 5/8	Jan 98n	100:00	100:02	+ 1	5.50
7 1/4	Feb 98n	100:27	100:29	....	5.58
8 1/8	Feb 98n	101:11	101:13	+ 1	5.53
5 1/8	Feb 98n	99:22	99:24	....	5.54
5 1/8	Mar 98n	99:22	99:24	....	5.49
6 1/8	Mar 98n	100:11	100:13	....	5.50
7 7/8	Apr 98n	101:19	101:21	+ 1	5.50
5 1/8	Apr 98n	99:20	99:22	....	5.53
5 7/8	Apr 98n	100:06	100:08	+ 1	5.53
6 1/8	May 98n	100:12	100:14	+ 1	5.55
9	May 98n	102:20	102:22	+ 1	5.54
5 3/8	May 98n	99:25	99:27	+ 1	5.56
6	May 98n	100:09	100:11	+ 1	5.57
5 1/8	Jun 98n	99:18	99:20	+ 1	5.54
6 1/4	Jun 98n	100:18	100:20	+ 1	5.55
8 1/4	Jul 98n	102:13	102:15	+ 1	5.61
5 1/4	Jul 98n	99:19	99:21	+ 1	5.60
6 1/4	Jul 98n	100:17	100:19	....	5.64
5 7/8	Aug 98n	100:04	100:06	+ 1	5.69
9 1/4	Aug 98n	103:18	103:20	+ 1	5.67
4 3/4	Aug 98n	98:31	99:01	+ 1	5.66
6 1/8	Aug 98n	100:13	100:15	+ 1	5.67
4 3/4	Sep 98n	98:28	98:30	+ 1	5.68
6	Sep 98n	100:09	100:11	....	5.69
7 1/8	Oct 98n	101:19	101:21	+ 1	5.70
4 3/4	Oct 98n	98:24	98:26	+ 1	5.73
5 7/8	Oct 98n	100:03	100:05	+ 1	5.74
3 1/2	Nov 98	98:30	99:30	....	3.55
5 1/2	Nov 98n	99:20	99:22	+ 1	5.74
8 7/8	Nov 98n	103:27	103:29	+ 1	5.72
5 1/8	Nov 98n	99:05	99:07	+ 1	5.73
5 5/8	Nov 98n	99:25	99:27	+ 1	5.74
5 1/8	Dec 98n	99:04	99:06	+ 1	5.72
5 3/4	Dec 98n	99:31	100:01	+ 1	5.72

Rate	Maturity Mo./Yr.	Bid	Asked	Chg.	Ask Yld.
5 3/4	Aug 03n	98:10	98:12	+ 6	6.07
11 1/8	Aug 03	125:00	125:06	+ 7	6.09
11 7/8	Nov 03	129:20	129:26	+ 7	6.11
5 7/8	Feb 04n	98:25	98:27	+ 7	6.09
7 1/4	May 04n	106:07	106:09	+ 6	6.11
12 3/8	May 04	134:05	134:11	+ 8	6.13
7 1/4	Aug 04n	106:11	106:13	+ 17	6.12
13 3/4	Aug 04	142:30	143:04	+ 9	6.13
7 7/8	Nov 04n	110:00	110:04	+ 7	6.13
11 5/8	Nov 04	131:22	131:28	+ 9	6.14
7 1/2	Feb 05n	108:02	108:04	+ 8	6.14
6 1/2	May 05n	102:02	102:04	+ 8	6.15
8 1/4	May 00-05	105:13	105:16	+ 3	6.08
12	May 05	135:16	135:22	+ 8	6.17
6 1/2	Aug 05n	102:02	102:04	+ 8	6.16
10 3/4	Aug 05	128:16	128:22	+ 8	6.18
5 7/8	Nov 05n	98:02	98:04	+ 8	6.17
5 5/8	Feb 06n	96:10	96:12	+ 7	6.18
9 3/8	Feb 06	121:01	121:07	+ 9	6.15
6 7/8	May 06n	104:19	104:21	+ 8	6.18
7	Jul 06n	105:18	105:20	+ 10	6.17
6 1/2	Oct 06n	102:08	102:12	+ 14	6.16
3 3/8	Jan 07i	97:19	97:21	− 4	3.67
6 1/4	Feb 07n	100:19	100:22	+ 24	6.15
7 5/8	Feb 02-07	105:14	105:17	+ 4	6.21
6 5/8	May 07n	103:16	103:17	+ 24	6.14
7 7/8	Nov 02-07	108:02	108:05	+ 6	6.05
8 3/8	Aug 03-08	111:10	111:14	+ 7	6.09
8 3/4	Nov 03-08	112:24	112:28	+ 6	6.25
9 1/8	May 04-09	115:20	115:24	+ 7	6.25
10 3/8	Nov 04-09	123:24	123:30	+ 8	6.24
11 3/4	Feb 05-10	132:22	132:28	+ 7	6.23
10	May 05-10	122:23	122:29	+ 9	6.25
12 3/4	Nov 05-10	141:14	141:20	+ 8	6.25
13 7/8	May 06-11	150:25	150:31	+ 9	6.26
14	Nov 06-11	153:25	153:31	+ 10	6.26
10 3/8	Nov 07-12	130:04	130:10	+ 9	6.33
12	Aug 08-13	144:10	144:16	+ 11	6.34
13 1/4	May 09-14	156:13	156:19	+ 12	6.36
12 1/2	Aug 09-14	150:28	151:02	+ 12	6.37
11 3/4	Nov 09-14	145:12	145:18	+ 12	6.36
11 1/4	Feb 15	150:13	150:19	+ 15	6.41
10 5/8	Aug 15	144:03	144:09	+ 16	6.44
9 7/8	Nov 15	136:08	136:14	+ 14	6.45
9 1/4	Feb 16	129:24	129:30	+ 13	6.46
7 1/4	May 16	108:15	108:17	+ 11	6.46
7 1/2	Nov 16	111:03	111:07	+ 12	6.47
8 3/4	May 17	124:31	125:05	+ 13	6.48
8 7/8	Aug 17	126:16	126:22	+ 13	6.48
9 1/8	May 18	129:25	129:31	+ 15	6.48
9	Nov 18	128:18	128:24	+ 13	6.49
8 7/8	Feb 19	127:08	127:14	+ 12	6.49
8 1/8	Aug 19	118:26	118:30	+ 13	6.50
8 1/2	Feb 20	123:10	123:16	+ 12	6.50

Mat.	Type	Bid	Asked	Chg.	Ask Yld.
Aug 05	np	61:04	61:09	+ 3	6.17
Nov 05	ci	60:01	60:05	+ 2	6.21
Nov 05	bp	60:06	60:11	+ 3	6.18
Feb 06	ci	58:30	59:03	+ 3	6.24
Feb 06	bp	59:06	59:11	+ 3	6.19
May 06	ci	57:31	58:04	+ 3	6.26
Aug 06	ci	57:01	57:06	+ 3	6.26
Nov 06	ci	56:05	56:10	+ 3	6.27
Feb 07	ci	55:05	55:10	+ 3	6.29
May 07	ci	54:08	54:13	+ 3	6.30
Aug 07	ci	53:13	53:18	+ 3	6.30
Nov 07	ci	52:17	52:22	+ 3	6.32
Feb 08	ci	51:18	51:23	+ 2	6.34
May 08	ci	50:22	50:27	+ 2	6.36
Aug 08	ci	49:28	50:01	+ 2	6.36
Nov 08	ci	49:00	49:05	+ 2	6.38
Feb 09	ci	48:05	48:10	+ 2	6.39
May 09	ci	47:11	47:17	+ 2	6.40
Aug 09	ci	46:19	46:24	+ 2	6.41
Nov 09	ci	45:26	45:31	+ 2	6.42
Nov 09	bp	45:13	45:18	+ 2	6.49
Feb 10	ci	45:01	45:06	+ 2	6.43
May 10	ci	44:08	44:14	+ 2	6.44
Aug 10	ci	43:16	43:21	+ 2	6.45
Nov 10	ci	42:24	42:30	+ 2	6.46
Feb 11	ci	42:01	42:06	+ 3	6.47
May 11	ci	41:10	41:16	+ 3	6.47
Aug 11	ci	40:20	40:25	+ 3	6.48
Nov 11	ci	39:30	40:03	+ 3	6.49
Feb 12	ci	39:09	39:14	+ 3	6.49
May 12	ci	38:19	38:25	+ 3	6.50
Aug 12	ci	37:30	38:04	+ 3	6.51
Nov 12	ci	37:10	37:15	+ 3	6.52
Feb 13	ci	36:21	36:27	+ 3	6.52
May 13	ci	36:02	36:07	+ 3	6.53
Aug 13	ci	35:14	35:19	+ 3	6.54
Nov 13	ci	34:27	35:00	+ 3	6.54
Feb 14	ci	34:08	34:13	+ 3	6.55
May 14	ci	33:21	33:26	+ 3	6.55
Aug 14	ci	33:03	33:08	+ 3	6.56
Nov 14	ci	32:17	32:22	+ 3	6.56
Feb 15	ci	32:00	32:05	+ 3	6.57
Feb 15	bp	32:13	32:18	+ 3	6.49
May 15	ci	31:15	31:20	+ 3	6.57
Aug 15	ci	30:29	31:03	+ 3	6.58
Aug 15	bp	30:31	31:04	+ 2	6.57
Nov 15	ci	30:13	30:18	+ 3	6.58
Nov 15	bp	30:14	30:19	+ 2	6.58
Feb 16	ci	29:28	30:01	+ 3	6.59
Feb 16	bp	29:29	30:02	+ 2	6.58
May 16	ci	29:12	29:17	+ 3	6.59
May 16	bp	29:20	29:25	+ 3	6.54
Aug 16	ci	28:29	29:02	+ 3	6.59
Nov 16	ci	28:14	28:19	+ 3	6.59
Nov 16	bp	28:17	28:22	+ 3	6.57
Feb 17	ci	27:30	28:03	+ 3	6.60
May 17	ci	27:15	27:20	+ 2	6.60
May 17	bp	27:16	27:21	+ 2	6.59
Aug 17	ci	27:00	27:05	+ 2	6.60
Aug 17	bp	27:01	27:06	+ 2	6.60
Nov 17	ci	26:18	26:23	+ 2	6.60
Feb 18	ci	26:03	26:08	+ 2	6.61
May 18	ci	25:21	25:26	+ 2	6.61
May 18	bp	25:22	25:27	+ 2	6.61
Aug 18	ci	25:08	25:13	+ 2	6.61
Nov 18	ci	24:27	25:00	+ 2	6.61
Nov 18	bp	24:28	25:01	+ 2	6.61
Feb 19	ci	24:14	24:18	+ 2	6.62
Feb 19	bp	24:14	24:19	+ 2	6.61
May 19	ci	24:01	24:06	+ 2	6.62
Aug 19	ci	23:20	23:25	+ 2	6.62
Aug 19	bp	23:22	23:27	+ 2	6.61
Nov 19	ci	23:09	23:14	+ 2	6.61
Feb 20	ci	22:28	23:01	+ 2	6.62
Feb 20	bp	22:29	23:01	+ 2	6.61
May 20	ci	22:16	22:21	+ 2	6.62
May 20	bp	22:17	22:22	+ 2	6.61

Source: *The Wall Street Journal,* July 24, 1997

beginning on the first date and matures on the second. The next two columns give the bid and ask prices in units of par value of 100 and thirty-seconds. Here the bid price is 99 30/32 and the ask price is 100. The next column is the bid change in thirty-seconds. The final column is the yield based on the ask price.

Of course a bond price is the present value of all future cash payments made on the bond. Owing to a tradition in the bond market, the actual quoted price does not include the interest that has accrued since the last coupon payment. We briefly mentioned this point in Chapter 7 when we looked at the invoice price on a Treasury bond futures. This accumulated interest, called the accrued interest, is a figure that represents the pro-rated fraction of the next coupon payment that the buyer of a bond pays to the seller. The buyer receives the entire next coupon but is entitled only to a fraction of it. That fraction is based on the number of days in the current interest payment period on which the buyer held the bond. Since interest is paid semiannually there are anywhere from 181 to 184 days in each interest payment period. If the upcoming interest payment date is 183 days since the last interest payment date and the buyer purchases the bond with 36 days remaining until the next interest payment date, the buyer would be entitled to only 36/183 of the next coupon. The prices you see in *The Wall Street Journal* do not include this accrued interest. Thus, when taking a bond price from *The Wall Street Journal* you must also calculate and add the accrued interest. This will cause some minor complications in certain calculations we will encounter in future chapters.[6]

The final column in Figure 8.4 is a portion of a listing of a group of bonds called **stripped treasuries.** These are actually zero coupon Treasury bonds. This is an arrangement in which firms that have bought coupon Treasury securities sell claims on the underlying coupons and principal. The notation *np* or *bp* means that it is either Treasury note or bond principal; *ci* indicates that the bond is a claim on coupon interest. Recall that earlier we saw how a coupon bond can be shown to consist of an equivalent combination of zero coupon bonds. Firms that strip these Treasury bonds apply that result to create these long-term zero coupon bonds.

The Relationship between Bond Prices and Yields

There are several important mathematical relationships between bond prices and yields. The discussion in this book is limited to those that are useful for understanding futures markets. The other important bond

---

[6]In practice, all calculations in the bond market are based on the settlement date. Thus, when a bond is purchased on a given day, it is not actually paid for until the second business day after the trade day. Thus, the settlement day is the actual day from which interest begins accruing. It is also the day on which the yield calculation is based.

pricing principles are presented in most investments texts.

First, let us introduce the concept of a basis point. A **basis point** is one one-hundredth of a percent. It is used to measure a yield or yield change. For example, a yield that increases from 9 percent to 9.5 percent is a change of 50 basis points.

BOND PRICE AND YIELD CHANGES   The first important principle is the inverse relationship between bond prices and yields.

Consider a 10-year bond with an 11.75 percent coupon and annual interest payments. Its price at a yield of 11.75 percent is

$$B = 117.50 \left[\frac{1 - (1.1175)^{-10}}{.1175} \right] + 1,000(1.1175)^{-10} = 1,000.$$

When the coupon equals the yield, the price equals the par value. Such a bond is said to be **selling at par.**

Now suppose the yield increases 25 basis points to 12 percent. Then the price will decrease to

$$B = 117.50 \left[\frac{1 - (1.12)^{-10}}{.12} \right] + 1,000(1.12)^{-10} = 985.87.$$

When the yield exceeds the coupon, the price will be less than par. That bond is said to be **selling at a discount.**

Now let the yield be 11 percent. Then the price will increase to

$$B = 117.50 \left[\frac{1 - (1.11)^{-10}}{.11} \right] + 1,000(1.11)^{-10} = 1,044.17.$$

When the coupon exceeds the yield, the price will be greater than par. Such a bond is said to be **selling at a premium.**

Figure 8.5 illustrates this relationship for this example.

BOND PRICE VOLATILITY AND MATURITY   The second important principle is that for a given change in yields, the bond price changes by a percentage that varies inversely with the bond's maturity. For illustrative purposes, we shall refer to the percentage price change as the volatility.

Consider a bond with a coupon of 10 percent and an original yield of 10 percent. Both a 10- and a 20-year bond will have a price of $1,000. Suppose the yield increases by 100 basis points to 11 percent. The price of the 10-year bond will be

$$B = 100 \left[\frac{1 - (1.11)^{-10}}{.11} \right] + 1,000(1.11)^{-10} = 941.11,$$

Bond prices and yields move inversely.

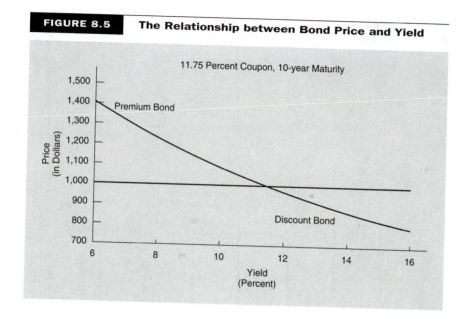

FIGURE 8.5   **The Relationship between Bond Price and Yield**

11.75 Percent Coupon, 10-year Maturity

a decrease of about 5.9 percent. The price of the 20-year bond will be

$$B = 100 \left[\frac{1 - (1.11)^{-20}}{.11} \right] + 1,000(1.11)^{-20} = 920.37,$$

a decrease of almost 8 percent. Had the yield decreased, the 20-year bond would have experienced the greater percentage increase.

Figure 8.6 illustrates the relationship between maturity and volatility for a broad range of maturities for bonds with a coupon of 10 percent and a yield change of from 10 percent to 11 percent. As you can see, longer-maturity bonds experience greater percentage decreases in their prices. However, this relationship flattens out at a maturity of around 40 years.

Holding everything else constant, the longer the maturity, the greater the percentage change in the bond price for a given basis point change in the yield.

BOND PRICE VOLATILITY AND COUPON   The third important principle deals with the relationship between the bond price volatility and the coupon. Consider two bonds alike in all respects except coupon. We know that if the yield decreases, both bonds will have price increases, but which one will experience the greater percentage increase? It will be the one with the lower coupon.

Consider two bonds, each with a maturity of five years. Let the yield be 11 percent. One bond has a coupon of 11 percent and the other a coupon of 10 percent. The 11 percent coupon bond will have a price of $1,000 (coupon = yield). The 10 percent bond will have a price of

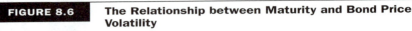

FIGURE 8.6   **The Relationship between Maturity and Bond Price Volatility**

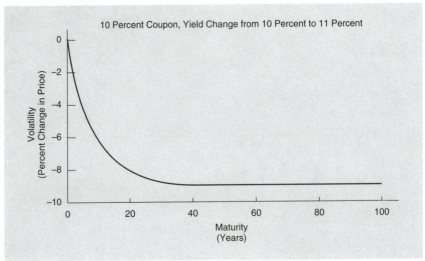

$$B = 100 \left[\frac{1 - (1.11)^{-5}}{.11} \right] + 1{,}000(1.11)^{-5} = 963.04.$$

If the yield moves down 100 basis points to 10 percent, the bond with the 11 percent coupon will have a price of

$$B = 110 \left[\frac{1 - (1.10)^{-5}}{.10} \right] + 1{,}000(1.10)^{-5} = 1{,}037.91.$$

Holding everything else constant, the greater the coupon, the lower the percentage change in the bond price for a given basis point change in the yield.

We know that the bond with the 10 percent coupon will now be priced at $1,000. The percentage change of the 11 percent coupon bond is 3.79 percent (from $1,000 to $1,037.91); the percentage change of the 10 percent coupon bond is 3.84 percent. Had the yield increased, the lower-coupon bond again would have had the greater percentage price decrease.

Figure 8.7 illustrates the percentage price change for five-year bonds of various coupons when the yield goes from 11 to 10 percent.

Putting our last two results together, we would expect that the most volatile bonds would be those with longer maturities and lower coupons. Figure 8.8 demonstrates this result. The three lines represent bonds with 8 percent, 10 percent, and 12 percent coupons, with their maturities varied from zero to 50 years. The yield has been changed from 10 percent to 11 percent. For very short and very long maturity bonds, there is little dif-

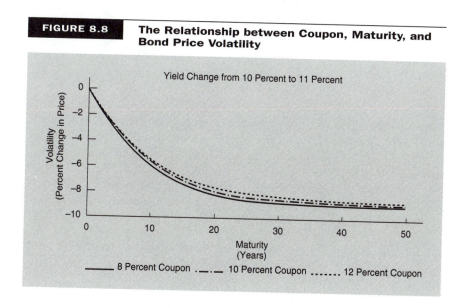

FIGURE 8.7   **The Relationship between Coupon and Bond Price Volatility**

5-Year Maturity, Yield Change from 11 Percent to 10 Percent

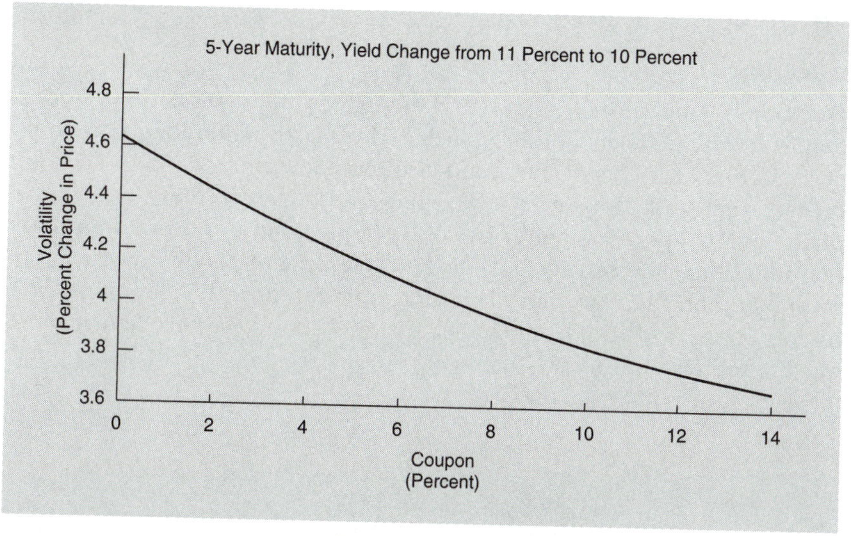

FIGURE 8.8   **The Relationship between Coupon, Maturity, and Bond Price Volatility**

Yield Change from 10 Percent to 11 Percent

—— 8 Percent Coupon   .—.—. 10 Percent Coupon   .... 12 Percent Coupon

ference in their volatilities. Over the range of five to 40 years, the volatilities line up in inverse order with their coupons. Consider, however, the 22-year, 8 percent bond. Its price declined by 8.47 percent. Yet a 30-year bond with 12 percent coupon had a nearly equivalent price decline of 8.55 percent. Which is the more powerful effect, coupon or maturity? It should be

apparent that either effect can dominate. To tell which is the more powerful, we turn to a one-dimensional measure called duration.

Duration

Duration is a measure of the size and timing of a bond's cash flows. For example, a long-maturity bond requires its holder to wait a long time to receive all the payments. If that bond also has a low coupon, the holder will receive small cash flows over a long time period. In contrast, a short-maturity, high-coupon bond gives its holder large cash flows over a short time period. Clearly the second bond is less volatile and pays its return more promptly than the first bond. Duration thus captures the magnitude and timing of the cash flows and indicates which bond pays its return more quickly and which is more volatile.

Duration is given by the formula

$$
DUR = \frac{\displaystyle\sum_{t=1}^{T} tCP_t(1+y)^{-t}}{B},
$$

where B is the bond price and CP_t is the cash payment, the coupon or principal, at time t. To better understand this formula, let us rewrite it as

$$
DUR = \sum_{t=1}^{T} t\left[\frac{CP_t(1+y)^{-t}}{B}\right].
$$

Note that the value of t is weighted (multiplied) by the term in brackets, which is the present value of the cash flow received at time t divided by the total present value (price) of the bond. Thus, the values of t are multiplied by a set of weights. The sum of the weights is 1. Therefore, the formula for duration takes a weighted average of the numbers t = 1, 2, . . . , T.

Consider a four-year bond with a coupon of 8 percent and a yield of 10 percent. The price would be 936.60. The duration would be

$$
DUR = \frac{(1)(80)(1.10)^{-1} + (2)(80)(1.10)^{-2} + (3)(80)(1.10)^{-3} + (4)(1,080)(1.10)^{-4}}{936.60}
$$

$$
= 3.56.
$$

Duration is the weighted-average maturity of a bond.

For this bond, duration is a weighted average of the numbers 1, 2, 3, and 4. Note how the average tilts toward 4 because of the large principal repayment.

If the bond's life has many years remaining, adding up all the terms could be tedious. Fortunately, the duration formula has been simplified considerably. Caks, Lane, Greenleaf, and Joules (1985) showed that the formula reduces to

$$DUR = \frac{CI(1 + y)[(1 + y)^T - 1] + Ty(FVy - CI)}{CIy[(1 + y)^T - 1] + FVy^2}.$$

In our example,

$$DUR = \frac{80(1.10)[(1.10)^4 - 1] + 4(.10)[1,000(.10) - 80]}{80(.10)[(1.10)^4 - 1] + 1,000(.10)^2} = 3.56.$$

The article also presents alternative versions of the formula for cases in which the bond is at par or the price and duration are calculated between coupon payment dates.

In the examples shown so far, the bond's time to maturity has been easily expressed as a whole number of years. In nearly all real-world situations one has to price the bond and find its duration between interest payment dates. Fortunately the formulas presented here can be adapted to that situation but the computations are best done on a financial calculator or a computer. Software Demonstration 8.1 presents the Excel spreadsheet bpd3.xls, which calculates the bond price and duration when the current date can be between coupon dates.

Table 8.1 presents some durations for a representative range of coupons and maturities at a yield of 10 percent. Note how for a given level of maturity, duration decreases as the coupon increases. For a given coupon, duration generally increases as maturity increases; however, there are some exceptions to that rule for low coupons. For discount coupon bonds, duration increases with maturity to a point and then starts to decrease. Given that most bonds have original maturities of no more than 30 years, we can say that duration normally increases with maturity. Note also that as maturity lengthens, duration increases, but at a decreasing rate.[7] For that reason, durations of more than 13 years would be somewhat rare.

Because duration is a measure of coupon and maturity, it should also be a measure of volatility. In fact, duration is related to volatility by the following approximation:[8]

$$\frac{\Delta B}{B} \approx -DUR\left(\frac{\Delta y}{1 + y}\right),$$

where $\Delta B/B$ is the percentage price change for a yield change of Δy. For example, the 4-year, 8 percent coupon bond with a 10 percent yield has a

Duration provides a reasonable means of approximating the new bond price when the yield changes.

---

[7]Although not shown here, there is also a yield effect: The higher the yield, the lower the duration.

[8]If the bond pays coupons semiannually, Δy should be divided by $1 + (y/2)$ instead of $1 + y$.

SOFTWARE DEMONSTRATION 8.1   **Calculating the Duration of a Bond with the Spreadsheet bpd3.xls**

The Excel spreadsheet bpd3.xls, which operates in Windows 3.1 or Windows 95 and requires Excel 5.0 or higher, calculates the price and duration of a bond based on a current date and maturity date. No installation is necessary; simply place the file in whatever directory you prefer or access it directly from the 3.5-inch diskette provided in the book. To use the software, do the following:

1. Make sure you are in Windows 3.1 or Windows 95.
2. Run Excel 5.0 or higher.
3. Open the file bpd3.xls.

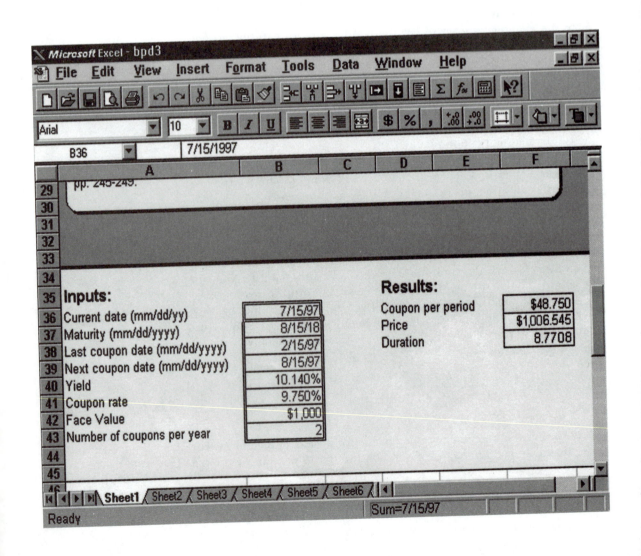

Inputs:		Results:	
Current date (mm/dd/yy)	7/15/97	Coupon per period	$48.750
Maturity (mm/dd/yyyy)	8/15/18	Price	$1,006.545
Last coupon date (mm/dd/yyyy)	2/15/97	Duration	8.7708
Next coupon date (mm/dd/yyyy)	8/15/97		
Yield	10.140%		
Coupon rate	9.750%		
Face Value	$1,000		
Number of coupons per year	2		

Now let us assume that you wish to calculate the price and duration of a bond on July 15, 1997. The bond has a yield of 10.14 percent, a coupon of 9.75 percent, and matures on August 15, 2018. Its face value is $1,000, it pays two coupons per year, and its last coupon was on February 15, 1997. Its next coupon will be on August 15, 1997. Insert these values in the highlighted cells in the **Inputs:** section. Cells that will accept input have a double-line border and the values are in blue. Insert all dates in the format mm/dd/yyyy. Enter the yield in the form "10.14" or ".1014" and use the same format for the coupon rate.

The results are automatically calculated and appear in the section labeled **Results:** Output cells have a single-line border. The coupon per period is $48.75. The price is $1,006.545 and the duration is 8.7708 years.

The algorithm used is from the article "A Simple Formula for Duration," by J. Caks, W. R. Lane, R. W. Greenleaf, and R. G. Joules in *The Journal of Financial Research* 8 (Fall 1985): 245–249.

For those who prefer Lotus 1-2-3, the diskette also contains the spreadsheet bpd2.wk3 and its format file bpd2.fm3. This spreadsheet is from the previous edition of this textbook and does not contain all of the features of the Excel spreadsheet, but it will provide the price and duration following essentially the same procedure.

duration of 3.56. That means that if the yield increases by 100 basis points to 11 percent, the approximate percentage price change will be

$$\frac{\Delta B}{B} \approx -3.56\left(\frac{.01}{1.10}\right) = -.0324.$$

This equation suggests that there is a linear relationship between duration and volatility. Figure 8.9 illustrates that point. Notice that the line is straight. This makes duration a particularly simple and useful tool for assessing interest rate risk. Duration, however, should not be used without regard to its limitations. The most obvious one is that duration is but an approximation of the effect of an interest rate change on the bond price. The equation above is obtained from the calculus and is correct only for very small changes in the yield. In our example, the predicted percentage price change was −3.24 percent. If we simply inserted the new yield of 11

TABLE 8.1	Durations for Various Coupons and Maturities (10 Percent Yield)							

Maturity (Years)		Coupon (%)							
	0	2	4	6	8	10	12	14	16
5	5	4.76	4.57	4.41	4.28	4.17	4.07	3.99	3.92
10	10	8.73	7.95	7.42	7.04	6.76	6.54	6.36	6.21
15	15	11.61	10.12	9.28	8.74	8.37	8.09	7.88	7.71
20	20	13.33	11.30	10.32	9.75	9.36	9.09	8.89	8.74
25	25	14.03	11.81	10.86	10.32	9.98	9.75	9.58	9.45
30	30	14.03	11.92	11.09	10.65	10.37	10.18	10.04	9.94
35	35	13.64	11.84	11.17	10.82	10.61	10.46	10.36	10.28
40	40	13.13	11.70	11.18	10.92	10.76	10.65	10.57	10.51
50	50	12.19	11.40	11.40	10.99	10.91	10.85	10.81	10.78
100	100	11.02	11.01	11.00	11.00	11.00	11.00	11.00	11.00

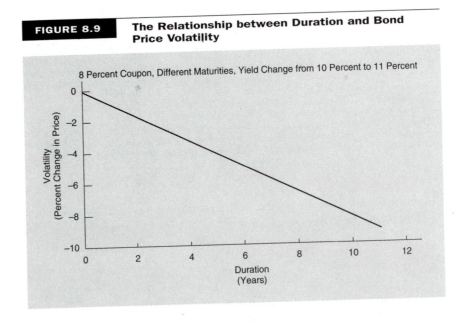

FIGURE 8.9   **The Relationship between Duration and Bond Price Volatility**

percent into the formula for the bond price and recomputed, we would find that it actually falls to 906.93, a decrease of 3.17 percent. In this case, duration makes a fairly accurate prediction but that is because we did not allow the yield to change by much.

Figure 8.10 shows the relationship between the bond price and the yield along with a dashed line tangent to the curve at a yield of 10 percent and a price of 936.60. If we inject a yield change, the actual new bond price is obtained from the solid line. The predicted new bond price is read from the dashed line. As you can see, if we stray too far away from the yield of 10 percent, the solid and dashed lines diverge and duration would make a far less accurate prediction.

The difference in the solid and dashed lines is due to the **convexity** of the solid line. The solid line is the relationship between the bond's price and its yield. This relationship is not linear. Rather, it is convex. A convex curve is one in which a straight line drawn from any two points on the curve would lie above the curve. Ordinary bonds, i.e., those not callable or convertible, have convexity. The reason this is important for us is that duration is frequently used as a measure of how sensitive a bond price is to a yield change. This becomes a critical input into constructing the best futures hedge. Duration will serve well as a measure of bond price volatility provided that interest rates do not change by much over a short period of time. When this is not the case, it will be necessary to account for the bond's convexity. It turns out that hedging the duration effect is roughly

The accuracy of duration as a measure of volatility is limited to the case of small yield changes. For large yield changes, the convexity of the bond price-yield curve makes duration a less accurate means of predicting the new bond price.

FIGURE 8.10   **Duration, Convexity, and Bond Price**

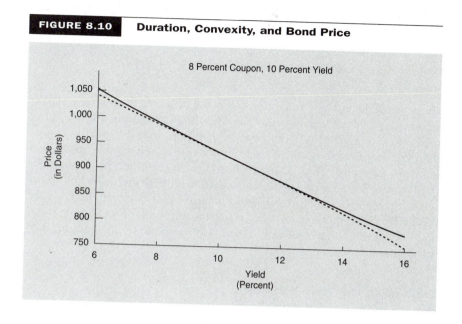

8 Percent Coupon, 10 Percent Yield

equivalent to taking into account the delta in options, while hedging the convexity effect is like taking into account the gamma.

In addition to being a measure of bond price volatility, duration is an important portfolio management concept. Under certain assumptions, we know that bonds whose holding period equals the duration are protected against losses resulting from interest rate changes. This strategy, called immunization, has been very popular, particularly during periods of high and volatile interest rates.

The Term Structure and the Yield Curve

The term structure is the relationship between the rates on pure-discount bonds and their maturities. The yield curve is the relationship between yields on coupon bonds and their maturities. The two curves are similar, but there are some differences. For example, let the term structure be defined as follows:

$$r(0,1) = .16 \qquad r(0,2) = .14 \qquad r(0,3) = .12 \qquad r(0,4) = .10.$$

A four-year bond with an 8 percent coupon would be priced as

$$B = 80(1.16)^{-1} + 80(1.14)^{-2} + 80(1.12)^{-3} + 1{,}080(1.10)^{-4}$$
$$= 925.12.$$

The yield would be the value of y that solves the equation

$$925.12 = 80 \left[\frac{1 - (1 + y)^{-4}}{y} \right] + 1{,}000(1 + y)^{-4},$$

and y would be .1038. Notice that the term structure is quoting a rate of 10 percent on four-year investments, while the yield implied by the price of the four-year bond is 10.38 percent. Note too that the yield is greater than the four-year spot rate. This will always be true for a downward-sloping term structure. Thus, if the term structure is downward sloping, the yield on any T-year bond will be more than the T-year spot rate. For an upward-sloping term structure, the yield on any T-year bond will be less than the T-year spot rate. Only for a flat term structure will the yield on a T-year bond equal the T-year spot rate. These relationships are illustrated in Figure 8.11.

Estimating the Term Structure

Figure 8.12 illustrates a recent actual term structure constructed from U.S. Treasury strips. This is a fairly common upward-sloping term structure. It turns slightly down, however, at the long end.

There are a number of ways to construct the term structure, in addition to just taking the yields on Treasury strips. Of particular interest to us is the fact that the futures market will reveal the term structure.

TERM STRUCTURE CONSTRUCTED WITH FUTURES   The Treasury bill futures contract at the International Monetary Market of the Chicago Mercantile Exchange calls for delivery of a 91-day Treasury bill. The contract expirations are March, June, September, and December, with maturities extending out about two years. Consider the prices on November 15 of a particular year.

The December contract is quoted at a price of 96.84, which is interpreted as a discount of $100 - 96.84 = 3.16$. Using the convention of the Treasury bill spot market, the price per \$100 of par value is

$$100 - 3.16(91/360) = 99.2012.$$

Although the actual futures price is based on a 90-day bill, we have computed it here as a 91-day T-bill price. That is because we are using the T-bill futures market to derive an implied forward price for 91-day T-bills. From Chapter 3, the yield on the purchase of a 91-day T-bill at 99.2012 is

$$(100/99.2012)^{(365/91)} - 1 = .0327.$$

FIGURE 8.11   **The Term Structure and the Yield Curve**

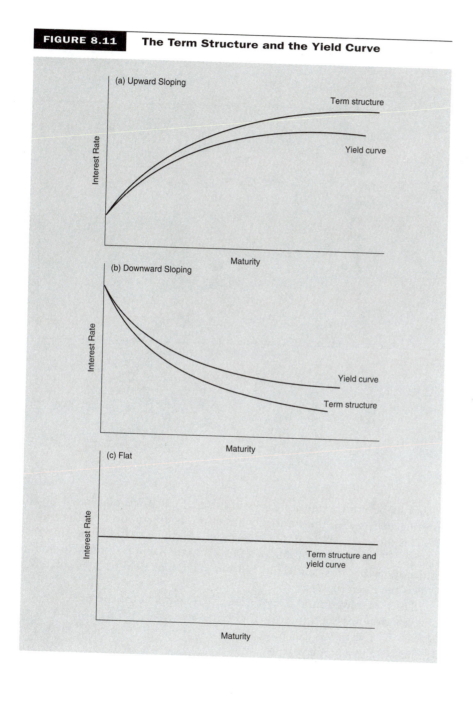

FIGURE 8.12   **The Term Structure of Interest Rates**

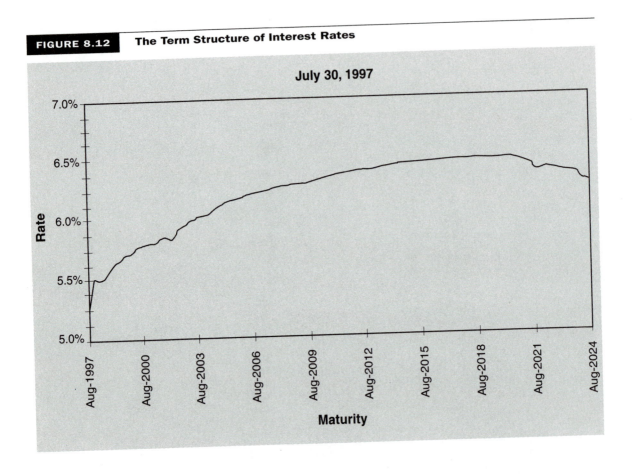

This can be interpreted as the yield on a 91-day T-bill purchased by accepting delivery on the futures contract on its expiration day, December 17. It is the rate r(32,123). On November 15, the spot T-bill maturing December 17 has a discount rate of 2.96. Using the same procedure as above and noting that this is a 32-day bill, we get a spot yield of 3.05 percent.[9] This is the rate r(0,32).

Thus, we have found a spot rate of 3.05 percent for the next 32/365 of a year, followed by a futures (forward) rate of 3.27 percent for the next 91/365 of a year. We can now derive a spot rate for the next 32/365 + 91/365 = 123/365 of a year as

---

[9]This is found as

$$100 - 2.96(32/360) = 99.7369.$$
$$(100/99.7369)^{(365/32)} - 1 = .0305.$$

$$[(1.0305)^{32/365}(1.0327)^{(91/365)}]^{(365/123)} - 1 = r(0,123) = .0321.$$

So now we know that the annualized spot rate for 32 days is 3.05 percent and the annualized spot rate for 123 days is 3.21 percent. The latter is the rate $r(0,123)$.

There are also futures contracts expiring in later months that can be used to extend the term structure out further. The March contract has a price of 96.69, implying a discount rate of 3.31. The contract expiration is March 18, which is 91 days after the December contract expiration. Now we can extend the term structure out $123 + 91 = 214$ days. The futures price for a discount of 3.31 is

$$100 - 3.31(91/360) = 99.1633,$$

which implies a yield of

$$(100/99.1633)^{(365/91)} - 1 = .0343.$$

Thus, a bill purchased by accepting delivery on the March contract would have a yield of 3.43 percent. This is the rate $r(123,214)$. So far we know that the rate $r(0,123)$ is 3.21 and the rate $r(123,214) = 3.43$. Thus, we can find the rate $r(0,214)$ as follows:

$$[(1.0321)^{(123/365)}(1.0343)^{(91/365)}]^{(365/214)} - 1 = .0330.$$

Thus, the 214-day rate is 3.30 percent. We can extend this 91 days further by using the June contract. Its price is quoted at 96.45 and it expires on June 17. With a 91-day bill delivered on June 17, we can extend the term structure out 91 days past June 17 to September 16. As a good exercise, work out this part of the problem on your own. You should find that the June T-bill implied yield would be 3.68 percent, which is $r(214,305)$. The 305-day spot rate, $r(0,305)$, is 3.41 percent.

Figure 8.13 summarizes what we have just done. We want to find the spot rates for maturities as far out as the futures market will reveal. The spot rate for the first 32 days is revealed by the spot T-bill maturing on December 17. The forward rate for the period December 17 to March 18 is revealed by the implied rate on the December futures contract, which calls for delivery of a bill maturing March 18. That rate is 3.27 percent. Linking the December spot rate of 3.05 percent to the December futures rate of 3.27 percent gives a March spot rate of 3.21 percent. In a similar manner, the March futures, calling for delivery of a bill maturing June 17, reveals the forward rate from March 18 to June 17 as 3.43 percent. Linking this rate to the previously determined March spot rate of 3.21 percent gives the June spot rate of 3.30 percent. Linking this rate with the June futures,

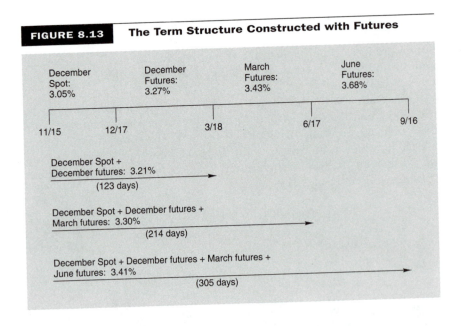

FIGURE 8.13   **The Term Structure Constructed with Futures**

The term structure of spot rates can be constructed by linking the nearby spot rate with the forward rates implied by the futures market.

which calls for delivery of a bill maturing September 16 with an implied yield of 3.68 percent, gives the September spot rate of 3.41 percent.

So now we have pieced together at least part of the term structure. Why did we do this? We have to defer a full answer until a later chapter but we can get a peek right now. Suppose an actual spot T-bill maturing in March were yielding more or less than the March spot rate of 3.21 percent. Then something would be out of line, and we could make an arbitrage profit. In this case, however, the actual spot March 17 T-bill was yielding 3.22 percent, practically the same rate. Markets being pretty efficient, arbitrage opportunities are indeed quite rare, but making the calculations and verifying that there is no arbitrage possibility is as important as finding that there is one.

In this chapter, we examined a number of principles of pricing fixed-income securities. Because of their widespread use in the design of futures contracts, we have focused on U.S. Treasury securities. Corporate and municipal bonds play a lesser role in the futures markets, and an understanding of those bonds requires attention to factors such as default risk and taxes. Also, we have ignored a number of other factors that might be associated with a bond, such as the ability of the bondholder to convert the bond to stock and the ability of the issuing firm or government to call the bond and retire it early. These issues are important but are beyond the scope of this book.

This completes our discussion of the pricing of fixed-income securities. We will use these principles frequently in later chapters. For now, we turn to the pricing of equity securities.

Principles and Pricing of Equity Securities

We said a great deal about equity securities in Part One. We have not, however, dealt with the pricing of equities. That is because option pricing theory takes the price of the stock as given. This allowed us to price the option without regard for how the stock is priced or even whether it is priced correctly. To some extent, that is also true of futures. However, we shall need to understand some of the methods of equity pricing to fully appreciate the utility of stock index futures and, in particular, to apply hedging techniques.

In general terms, a stock is priced by discounting its expected future dividends. The appropriate discount rate is the stockholders' required rate of return. Where does the required rate come from? In Chapter 1, we alluded to the idea that investors require returns consisting of a risk-free rate plus a risk premium, the latter being the additional return expected for bearing risk. In the next section, we shall look at where these risk premiums come from. For this we will appeal to a branch of investment analysis called **portfolio theory.**

Portfolio Theory

Portfolio theory is the study of the relationship between the expected return and the risk of securities and portfolios. Starting with the assumption that investors like return and dislike risk, it proceeds to derive several important properties about the way in which people invest their money. One of the key results is that investors should diversify their portfolios.

Diversification simply means not putting all your eggs in one basket. If an investor holds a broadly diversified portfolio, the performance of the overall portfolio will be relatively insensitive to the ups and downs of the individual securities. While some securities will go up, others will go down. To at least some extent, these ups and downs will be offsetting.

Unsystematic risk is the risk associated with the uncertainty of individual securities. Holding the optimal number of securities in a portfolio provides the diversification capable of eliminating unsystematic risk. For obvious reasons, unsystematic risk is also called **diversifiable risk.** What remains is **systematic** or **nondiversifiable risk.**

Systematic risk is the risk associated with broad market movements resulting from uncertainty about the economy as a whole. In contrast, the uncertainty associated with an individual firm is unsystematic risk. An

Investors tend to hold broadly diversified portfolios, leaving only systematic risk.

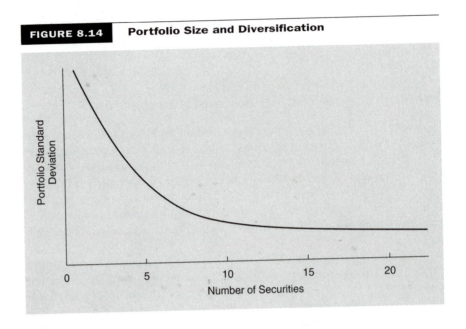

FIGURE 8.14   **Portfolio Size and Diversification**

example of unsystematic risk would be the recall of a potentially danger-ous product. Because this risk would not be associated with firms in gen-eral, it would not be systematic.[10] However, a major change in Federal Re-serve monetary policy would have an impact on the entire economy and thus would be a source of systematic risk.

Earlier we noted that holding enough securities in a portfolio will eliminate unsystematic risk. Portfolio theory has provided mathematical algorithms for determining how to do this. It turns out, however, that we need not hold very many securities or combine them in any prescribed manner to see the effects of diversification. Figure 8.14 depicts the rela-tionship between a portfolio's standard deviation and the number of se-curities in the portfolio. Studies have revealed that it takes surprisingly few securities to reach a point where the portfolio standard deviation will de-cline very little with the addition of more securities.[11] The graph shows that somewhere between 10 and 20 securities are all one needs to achieve diversification.

---

[10]If consumers fear similar defects in competing products, some of the effects might carry over to other firms in the industry. This would be a type of industry effect, a risk associated with firms in an industry but not with the economy as a whole.

[11]John Evans and Stephen H. Archer, "Diversification and the Reduction of Dispersion: An Empirical Analysis," *The Journal of Finance* 23 (December 1968): 761–767; and Wayne Wagner and Sheila Lau, "The Effect of Diversification on Risk," *Financial Analysts Journal* 27 (November–December 1971): 48–53.

The reduction in standard deviation as we add more securities reflects the diversification effect. The minimum level of risk remaining is the systematic risk, which cannot be eliminated by further diversification. Although investors can modify their portfolios' risk levels by investing a portion of their funds in low-risk or risk-free assets such as Treasury bills, the systematic risk associated with their security holdings will remain. Before the introduction of stock index futures, systematic risk could not be eliminated. In later chapters, we shall see how these contracts can be used to modify or eliminate systematic risk.

To understand how to measure systematic risk, we need a model that will explain how risk is reflected in the market prices of securities. Asset pricing theory, an outgrowth of portfolio theory, will give us some of these answers.

Asset Pricing Theory

Previously we assumed investors like return and dislike risk. As a result, they will diversify their holdings. If we add the assumption that everyone has equal access to information and reaches the same assessments of securities' expected returns, variances, and the correlations among securities, we obtain the **Capital Asset Pricing Model (CAPM).**[12] The model is written as follows:

$$E(r_S) = r + [E(r_M) - r]\,\beta,$$

where

$$E(r_S) = \text{expected return on the asset}$$
$$r = \text{risk-free rate}$$
$$E(r_M) = \text{expected return on the market}$$
$$\beta = \text{beta, or systematic risk.}$$

If the market is efficient, the expected rate equals the required rate.

The security's **beta** is its measure of risk and is defined as

$$\beta = \frac{\sigma_{SM}}{\sigma_M^2}.$$

[12]Three authors are credited with developing the model: William F. Sharpe, "Capital Asset Prices: A Theory of Market Equilibrium under Conditions of Risk," *The Journal of Finance* 19 (September 1964): 425–442; John Lintner, "The Valuation of Risk Assets and the Selection of Risky Investments in Stock Portfolios and Capital Budgets," *Review of Economics and Statistics* 47 (February 1965): 13–37; and Jan Mossin, "Equilibrium in a Capital Asset Market," *Econometrica* 34 (October 1966): 768–783.

The Capital Asset Pricing Model explains how the expected return on an asset is made up of the risk-free rate and a risk premium, with the latter determined by the covariance between the asset's return and the return on the market portfolio.

The numerator is the covariance between the returns on the security and the market. It measures the extent to which the security and the market move together. The relationship between security and market, as reflected in the covariance, captures the systematic risk. The denominator is the variance of the return on the market.

Note that the security's variance, which reflects both its systematic and unsystematic risk, is not a factor in the equation. The market defines risk as systematic risk. Because unsystematic risk can be eliminated by diversification, investors cannot expect to earn a return by assuming it. In the absence of systematic risk, $\beta = 0$ and $E(r_S) = r$, meaning that the expected return is the risk-free rate. The amount $[E(r_M) - r]\beta$ is the risk premium: the additional return investors expect as a result of the stock's risk.

The market portfolio has a special role in the model: Its beta is 1. All individual stocks' betas can be regarded as measures of the securities' risk relative to the market beta. Securities with betas greater than 1 are considered to be of above-average risk and securities with betas less than 1 of below-average risk. The market portfolio, therefore, defines the average level of risk.

The CAPM is illustrated in Figure 8.15. Two stocks, X and Y, are shown. The beta of X is less than the market beta of 1; thus, its expected return is less than the expected return on the market. The beta of Y is greater than the market beta; hence, its expected return is greater than the expected return on the market.

Primarily because of its simplicity, the CAPM has been a very popular model. In recent years, however, it has been criticized for its dependence

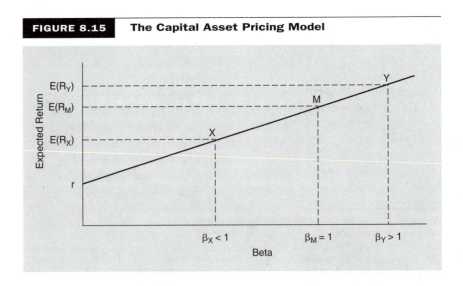

FIGURE 8.15   The Capital Asset Pricing Model

on the market portfolio of all risky assets. The next major revolution in asset pricing theory seems to be the Arbitrage Pricing Theory, or APT.[13] The APT allows security returns to be generated by a larger number of factors than simply the market portfolio. In fact, the market portfolio need not even be a determinant of security returns. Although most experts agree that general market movements will always play a role in the pricing of securities, the APT goes beyond that assumption to allow various other factors to determine security prices.

Although the CAPM has lost some of its luster in recent years, the concept of systematic risk remains on firm ground, even in the APT framework. We next turn to the problem of measuring systematic risk.

Measuring Systematic Risk

Since beta is a measure of systematic risk, we can attempt to measure it by estimating the covariance between a security's return and the market's return and the variance of the market's return. Table 8.2 presents some data for estimating the beta of Gannett Communications stock. We shall use the S&P 500 return as a proxy for the market. The data are weekly prices from the period of January 10 through June 26 of a recent year.

Recall that we performed similar calculations to obtain a historical estimate of the standard deviation for the Black-Scholes model in Chapter 4. That example used logarithmic (continuously compounded) returns. This example uses only simple returns, primarily because the results will differ only slightly. The simple returns are given in columns 5 and 8 of Table 8.2.

Column 9 gives the cross product, which is the return on the stock multiplied by the return on the market. Column 10 gives the squared return on the market. The summations of Columns 5, 8, 9, and 10 are used in the calculations for beta.

Covariance is estimated as follows:

$$\sigma_{SM} = \frac{\sum\limits_{t=1}^{J} r_{St} r_{Mt} - \left(\sum\limits_{t=1}^{J} r_{St} \sum\limits_{t=1}^{J} r_{Mt} \right)/J}{J-1},$$

where r_{St} and r_{Mt} are the returns at time t for the stock and market, respectively, and J is the number of returns. The variance of the market is estimated by the formula

---

[13]For an excellent treatment of Arbitrage Pricing Theory, see Richard Roll and Stephen A. Ross, "The Arbitrage Pricing Theory Approach to Strategic Portfolio Planning," *Financial Analysts Journal* 40 (May–June 1984): 14–26.

TABLE 8.2				Estimation of Beta for Gannett Communications (GCI) Using the S&P 500					
Obs.	Date	GCI Price	GCI Dividend	R_{GCI}	S&P	S&P Dividend	$R_{S\&P}$	$R_{GCI}R_{S\&P}$	$R_{S\&P}{}^2$
(1)	(2)	(3)	(4)	(5)	(6)	(7)	(8)	(9)	(10)
1	Jan 10	59.250			598.48				
2	Jan 17	61.375	0.000	0.0359	606.37	0.086	0.0133	0.0005	0.0002
3	Jan 24	63.125	0.000	0.0285	619.96	0.093	0.0226	0.0006	0.0005
4	Jan 31	63.500	0.000	0.0059	636.02	0.264	0.0263	0.0002	0.0007
5	Feb 7	65.750	0.000	0.0354	649.93	0.328	0.0224	0.0008	0.0005
6	Feb 14	67.125	0.000	0.0209	655.58	0.482	0.0094	0.0002	0.0001
7	Feb 21	67.500	0.000	0.0056	648.10	0.327	-0.0109	-0.0001	0.0001
8	Feb 28	68.250	0.000	0.0111	644.75	0.317	-0.0047	-0.0001	0.0000
9	Mar 6	67.750	0.000	-0.0073	652.00	0.437	0.0119	-0.0001	0.0001
10	Mar 13	68.625	0.000	0.0129	638.55	0.378	-0.0200	-0.0003	0.0004
11	Mar 20	70.750	0.000	0.0310	649.98	0.084	0.0180	0.0006	0.0003
12	Mar 27	67.000	0.000	-0.0530	648.91	0.240	-0.0013	0.0001	0.0000
13	Apr 3	67.375	0.350	0.0108	655.88	0.163	0.0110	0.0001	0.0001
14	Apr 10	65.375	0.000	-0.0297	633.50	0.311	-0.0336	0.0010	0.0011
15	Apr 17	65.375	0.000	0.0000	641.61	0.147	0.0130	0.0000	0.0002
16	Apr 24	68.500	0.000	0.0478	650.17	0.056	0.0134	0.0006	0.0002
17	May 1	68.875	0.000	0.0055	654.58	0.253	0.0072	0.0000	0.0001
18	May 8	65.875	0.000	-0.0436	644.78	0.630	-0.0140	0.0006	0.0002
19	May 15	67.500	0.000	0.0247	665.42	0.577	0.0329	0.0008	0.0011
20	May 22	68.125	0.000	0.0093	678.42	0.508	0.0203	0.0002	0.0004
21	May 29	69.000	0.000	0.0128	667.93	0.200	-0.0152	-0.0002	0.0002
22	Jun 5	71.250	0.000	0.0326	678.44	0.376	0.0163	0.0005	0.0003
23	Jun 12	71.625	0.000	0.0053	669.04	0.460	-0.0132	-0.0001	0.0002
24	Jun 19	69.375	0.000	-0.0314	661.96	0.092	-0.0104	0.0003	0.0001
25	Jun 26	68.875	0.000	-0.0072	664.39	0.252	0.0041	0.0000	0.0000
Sum				0.1638			0.1188	0.0064	0.0071

$$\sigma_M^2 = \frac{\displaystyle\sum_{t=1}^{J} r_{Mt}^2 - \left(\sum_{t=1}^{J} r_{Mt}\right)^2 / J}{J-1}.$$

The beta estimate is the ratio of the covariance over the variance. Note that the $J-1$ in both denominators cancels. Referring to Table 8.2, we obtain the summed terms and compute the beta as follows:

$$\beta = \frac{0.0064 - (0.1638)(0.1188)/24}{0.0071 - (0.1188)^2/24} = 0.86.$$

Beta can be estimated by regressing the stock return on the market return.

In this example, Gannett Communications' beta is 0.86. Since it is less than 1, it is considered less volatile than the market.

This procedure is a simple linear regression of the stock's return on the market return. The computed beta is an estimate obtained by an optimal statistical technique. Nonetheless, the estimate may vary from one time period to the next. For illustrative purposes, however, we shall take our regression estimates of betas as being accurate. Still, we should keep in mind that these estimates can be suspect at times, a point that will become apparent in some of the strategies illustrated in later chapters.

Software Demonstration 8.2 presents the Excel spreadsheet beta.xls, which calculates the beta for a stock.

SOFTWARE DEMONSTRATION 8.2   **Calculating a Stock's Beta with the Excel Spreadsheet beta.xls**

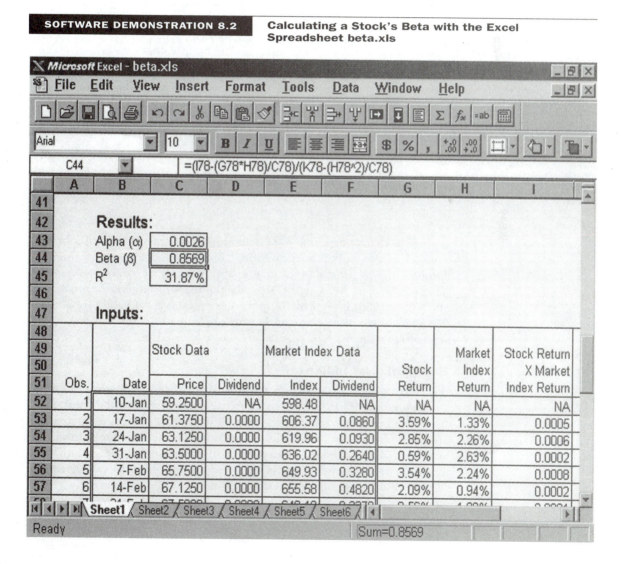

The Excel spreadsheet beta.xls, which operates in Windows 3.1 or Windows 95 and requires Excel 5.0 or higher, calculates the beta of a stock. No installation is necessary; simply place the file in whatever directory you prefer or access it directly from the 3.5-inch diskette provided in this textbook. To use the software, do the following:

1.   Make sure you are in Windows 3.1 or Windows 95.
2.   Run Excel 5.0 or higher.
3.   Open the file beta.xls.

Now assume that you wish to calculate a beta for the Gannett Communications example in the book. You should collect the prices for the stock and a market index. Dividends, which are part of the return calculation, can be collected and used, but they do not tend to affect the beta estimate very much. On the spreadsheet is a large array labeled **Inputs:** containing the input data and associated calculations. Cells that will accept input have a double-line border and the values are in blue. The observation date is optional but recommended. You should insert the stock prices and the stock's dividends and the market index and its dividends in the cells so labeled in columns C, D, E, and F. The spreadsheet is set on manual recalculation, so hit the F9 key to recalculate. The results appear in the section labeled **Results:**, which appears before the input section. Output cells have a single-line border. In our example, Gannett Communications' beta is 0.8569. Its alpha, which is the intercept from the regression, is 0.0026. The R^2, which is not used at this point in the book, is 31.87 percent. This is the percentage of the variation in Gannett Communications' stock that is explained by the market index. It serves as a measure of how well the regression fits the data. In this case, the regression is about what would be expected for a typical stock.

   To change the number of observations, add or delete rows above the double line at the bottom. Copy the formulas in columns G, H, I, J, and K of the last row of data onto any new rows you add. Make sure you do not erase the double line on the row between your last observation and the totals. The formulas use this line to determine the end of the data. Also, be sure there are no additional rows between the double line and the totals. The spreadsheet is on protected status. To insert or delete rows, you will need to remove the protection. Choose Tools/Protection/Unprotect Sheet from the main menu. To protect the spreadsheet, choose Tools/Protection/Protect Sheet.

   For those who prefer Lotus 1-2-3, the diskette also contains the spreadsheet beta.wk3 and its format file beta.fm3. This spreadsheet is from the previous edition of this book and does not contain all of the features of the Excel spreadsheet, but it will provide the beta following essentially the same procedure.

   We have now seen that beta is an appropriate measure of risk for a security. It is also a good measure of risk for a portfolio. The beta of a portfolio is simply a weighted average of the betas of the component stocks. The weight of a given security's beta is the market value of the stock held in the portfolio divided by the portfolio's total market value. In Chapter 10, we shall see in more detail how to compute and apply the concept of a portfolio beta.

Equity Market Indices

There are over 1,500 stocks on the New York Stock Exchange, and several thousand more trade on various other exchanges and over the counter. To assess the overall performance of the equity market, indices often are constructed. One of the most widely cited indices is the Dow Jones Industrial Average (DJIA). The DJIA is an average of the prices of 30 large industrial stocks. It originally was constructed by adding up the prices of the stocks and dividing by the number of stocks. However, when there are stock splits or stock dividends, the average will be distorted if adjustments are not made. Thus, the divisor is changed to leave the average unaltered by the split or dividend.

While the DJIA is the most widely cited average, it suffers from two major deficiencies. First, it consists of only 30 stocks, and thus may not be representative of the market as a whole. Second, its performance tends to be influenced more strongly by higher-priced stocks. Dow Jones and Company had prohibited the trading of exchange-listed derivatives on its index. As a result, the Chicago Board of Trade and the American Stock Exchange created the Major Market Index (MMI), which consists of 20 industrial stocks, 15 of which are in the DJIA. The MMI is constructed like the DJIA. Though volume is small, the CME trades futures on the MMI, and the AMEX trades options on it. In 1997, however, Dow Jones approved the trading of futures and options on its average.

One market average that does not suffer from the criticisms of the Dow Jones Industrial Average is the Standard and Poor's 500 (S&P 500), which is a market-value-weighted average index of 500 large stocks. It is influenced more strongly by stocks of firms that have the largest market value of their equity, not just the highest prices. Such firms are referred to as large capitalization, or large cap, firms. Let us illustrate the computation of the S&P 500 index with an example of three stocks. We shall call this the S&P 3. Their prices and number of shares for two days are shown below.

| Stock | Day1 | | Day 2 | |
	Price	Number of Shares	Price	Number of Shares
A	19	5,700	18	5,700
B	36	4,100	17.5	8,200
C	71	2,300	73	2,300

One day 1, we compute the market value of the three stocks:

$$19(5,700) + 36(4,100) + 71(2,300) = 419,200.$$

On the first day, the index is given an arbitrary starting value; we shall use 10. Thus, the S&P 3 on day 1 is at 10. On day 2, we take the market value of the stocks on day 2, divide by the market value of the stocks on day 1, and multiply the result by the base value of 10. Thus, the S&P 3 on day 2 is

$$\text{S\&P } 3_2 = 10 \left[\frac{18(5,700) + 17.5(8,200) + 73(2,300)}{419,200} \right] = 9.88.$$

Note that we need not make any adjustments as a result of the stock split. Since both the shares and the price adjust, the index is not biased by the split.

TABLE 8.3	World Stock Indices (F indicates futures available; O indicates options available)

Index	Market	
All-Ordinaries Share Price Index	Sydney Futures Exchange	F
Austrian Traded Index	Austrian Futures and Options Exchange	F,O
BEL 20 Index	Belgian Futures & Options Exchange	F,O
IBOVESPA Stock Index	Bolsa Mercadorias & Futuros	F
Toronto 35 Stock Index	Toronto Futures Exchange	F
TSE 100 Stock Index	Toronto Futures Exchange	F
Toronto 35 Index	Toronto Stock Exchange	O
TSE 100 Stock Index	Toronto Stock Exchange	O
IPSA Index	Santiago Stock Exchange	F
KFX Stock Index	Copenhagen Stock Exchange	F,O
Finnish Options Index	Finnish Securities & Derivatives Exchange	F,O
CAC 40 Stock Index	Marché à Terme International de France	F
CAC 40 Stock Index	Marché des Options Negociables de Paris	O
DAX	Deutsche Terminboerse	F,O
Hang Seng Stock Index	Hong Kong Futures Exchange	F,O
MAOF-25 Index	Tel Aviv Stock Exchange	F,O
MIB 30 Index	Italian Stock Exchange	F,O
Option 25 Index	Nagoya Stock Exchange	O
Nikkei 225 Stock Index	Osaka Securities Exchange	F,O
Nikkei 300 Stock Index	Osaka Securities Exchange	F,O
Tokyo Stock Price Index	Tokyo Stock Exchange	F,O
Dutch Top 5 Index	European Options Exchange	F,O
Eurotop 100 Index	European Options Exchange	F,O
Dutch Top 5 Index	Financiele Termijnmarkt Amsterdam	F
EOE Dutch Stock Index	Financiele Termijnmarkt Amsterdam	F
NZSE-10 Capital Share Price Index	New Zealand Futures & Options Exchange	F
OBX Index	Oslo Stock Exchange	F,O
Nikkei 225 Stock Index	Singapore International Monetary Exchange	F
Nikkei 300 Stock Index	Singapore International Monetary Exchange	F
SIMEX MSCI Hong Kong Index	Singapore International Monetary Exchange	F
All Share Index	South African Futures Exchange	F,O
All Gold Index	South African Futures Exchange	F,O

In the real world, the S&P index consists of 500 stocks and has a base value of 10 established over the 1941–1943 period. Each day the S&P 500 is constructed by determining the market value of the 500 stocks divided by the market value of the same stocks averaged over the 1941–1943 period and multiplied by the base value.

In Part One we said a great deal about stock index options and in Part Two, we shall cover stock index futures. These instruments have proven to be so popular that nearly every major country has stock indices and most have index futures and options. Table 8.3 provides a list of the various indices around the world on which futures and options exist.

In the final section of this chapter, we shall take a break from stocks and bonds and simply discuss a generic commodity. By this we mean any

TABLE 8.3   *(continued)*

Index	Market	
JSE Industrial Index	South African Futures Exchange	F,O
Financial Industrial Index	South African Futures Exchange	F,O
IBEX-35 Stock Index	MEFF Renta Variable	F,O
Swedish OMX Stock Index	OM Stockholm	F,O
Swiss Market Index	Swiss Options & Financial Futures Exchange	F,O
FT-SE 100 Index	London International Financial Futures Exchange	F
FT-SE Mid 250 Index	London International Financial Futures Exchange	F
OMX Index	London Securities & Derivatives Exchange	F,O
Nikkei 225 Stock Index	Chicago Mercantile Exchange	F
S&P 500 Stock Index	Chicago Mercantile Exchange	F
S&P MidCap 400 Stock Index	Chicago Mercantile Exchange	F
S&P 500/BARRA Growth Index	Chicago Mercantile Exchange	F
S&P 500/BARRA Value Index	Chicago Mercantile Exchange	F
FT-SE 100 Stock Index	Chicago Mercantile Exchange	F
Russell 200 Stock Index	Chicago Mercantile Exchange	F
Major Market Index	Chicago Mercantile Exchange	F
Value Line Index	Kansas City Board of Trade	F
S&P 100 Stock Index	Chicago Board Options Exchange	O
S&P 500 Stock Index	Chicago Board Options Exchange	O
NASDAQ 100 Stock Index	Chicago Board Options Exchange	O
S&P SmallCap 600 Stock Index	Chicago Board Options Exchange	O
Russell 2000 Stock Index	Chicago Board Options Exchange	O
CBOE Mexico Stock Index	Chicago Board Options Exchange	O
Latin 15 Index	Chicago Board Options Exchange	O
Nikkei 300 Stock Index	Chicago Board Options Exchange	O
CBOE Israel Stock Index	Chicago Board Options Exchange	O
CBOE Technology Index	Chicago Board Options Exchange	O
Morgan Stanley Multinational	Chicago Board Options Exchange	O
NYSE Composite Index	FINEX (New York Cotton Exchange)	F
PSE Technology Index	FINEX (New York Cotton Exchange)	F
Eurotop 100 Stock Index	COMEX (New York Mercantile Exchange)	F
NYSE Stock Index	New York Stock Exchange	O

Source: *Futures 1997 Source Book*

kind of asset that one could hold. Our goal is to develop a simple framework for determining the commodity's spot price.

The Formation of Spot Prices

In the first part of this chapter, we examined some basic concepts for pricing bonds and stocks. These principles will serve us well, and we will retain them throughout. In this section, we shall look at a simple model for determining spot prices. For convenience, we will assume the asset is a commodity such as corn or oil though it could just as easily be a stock or a bond. In some cases, it will be important to point out the differences

among the various types of commodities. We start our discussion of the model in a world of certainty.

The Spot Pricing Model under Certainty

Consider a commodity that is consumed at a constant, known rate. There is an initial supply that steadily decreases until replenished. This would be the case for an agricultural commodity that has a constant demand and a supply that increases at a harvest date. At that point, the crop is immediately harvested and its size is known. These assumptions mean that we are operating in a world of certainty. Figure 8.16 illustrates the model.

In panel a, the supply of the good is shown on the vertical axis and time on the horizontal axis. Supply follows a saw-toothed pattern, falling at a steady rate from a high of Q_2 immediately after the harvest to a low of Q_1 immediately before the next harvest. The times T_1, T_2, T_3, and T_4 are the harvest dates.

Panel b shows the evolution of the commodity price. When the supply is highest (at Q_2), the price is lowest (S_1). Then the price steadily increases as the supply decreases. Immediately before the next harvest, when the supply is lowest (Q_1), the price is highest (S_2).

Under certainty, today's spot price equals the future spot price minus the cost of storage and the interest forgone.

Now imagine a person who purchases the commodity at the lowest price, S_1, at T_1 and stores it until time T_2 an instant before the harvest. Then the person sells the commodity at price S_2. During the time the commodity is stored, costs are incurred, which include the interest forgone on funds tied up. Storage will be profitable as long as the profit from the sale of the commodity exceeds the cost. However, if that is true, there will be an incentive to buy the good and store it. This will place upward pressure on the good's spot price and the price of storage. The additional storage will also tend to increase the future supply of the good, leading to a lower future spot price. If buying the good and storing it is unprofitable, this fact will discourage storage and encourage immediate consumption. This will drive down the spot price and the price of storage. It follows that today's spot price must equal the future spot price minus the cost of storage and the interest forgone.

The Spot Pricing Model under Uncertainty

Now let us remove the certainty assumption and suppose that future demand and supply are uncertain. For the present, however, let us assume individuals are indifferent to risk; that is, they are risk neutral.

UNCERTAINTY AND RISK NEUTRALITY   If there is uncertainty, the future spot price is unknown. Therefore, let us define investors' expectation of the spot price at a future time T as $E(S_T)$. This value is found by weighting each possible spot price at T by the probability of its occurrence. The

FIGURE 8.16   **A Simple Spot Pricing Model under Certainty**

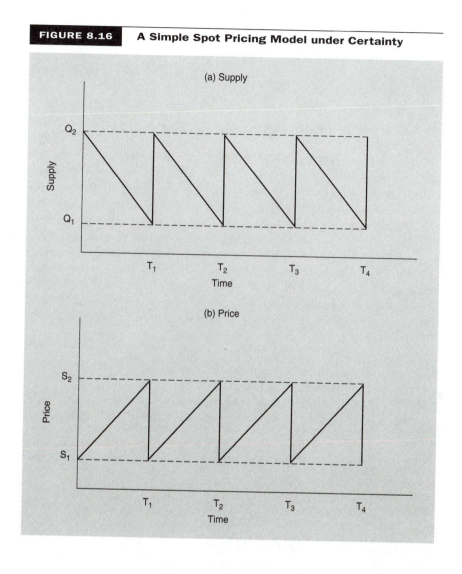

current spot price is S. Then we should expect to be able to buy the good at S, store and incur costs of s, forgo interest of i on the funds tied up, and sell the good at a price of $E(S_T)$[14] The market will price the good and the storage service such that there will be an incentive to store some of the good; that is,

---

[14]The actual amount of interest forgone must be determined jointly with the spot price since the interest will depend on the magnitude of the spot price.

$$S + s + i = E(S_T),$$

or

$$S = E(S_T) - s - i.$$

Under uncertainty and risk neutrality, today's spot price equals the expected future spot price minus the cost of storage and the interest forgone.

Inefficient storers—those whose costs are higher than s—will be driven out of business.

The inappropriateness of the risk neutrality assumption is seen by noting that because the future spot price is uncertain, no rational person would be willing to undertake storage without expecting a risk premium. It may seem inconsistent to argue against assuming investors are risk neutral. We discussed the risk neutral approach to pricing options earlier in this book and even promoted this view earlier in this chapter when discussing the local expectations theory. In those instances the risk neutrality approach was supported by the existence of several assets or derivatives that could be combined to form perfect substitutes for one another. In pricing a single spot asset as in this material, we do not have that luxury. Thus, it is necessary and important to introduce the concept of risk aversion and a risk premium.

UNCERTAINTY AND RISK AVERSION   So now we assume that individuals are not indifferent to risk. To induce someone to buy the good, store it, and sell it at an uncertain future price will require a risk premium. We denote this risk premium as $E(\phi)$. The relationship among the variables is

$$S + s + i + E(\phi) = E(S_T),$$

or

$$S = E(S_T) - s - i - E(\phi).$$

Under uncertainty and risk aversion, today's spot price equals the expected future spot price minus the cost of storage, the interest forgone, and the risk premium.

Thus, to offer a risk premium, the expected spot price must exceed the current spot price by a greater amount. Individuals who are unable to keep storage costs at or below s and whose risk aversion is so high as to make $E(\phi)$ an unacceptable risk premium will not engage in storage.

Recall from our earlier discussion that the Capital Asset Pricing Model also gives a risk premium, which we identified as $[E(r_M) - r]\beta$. This equation is entirely consistent with the above risk premium expression. When we used the CAPM, we expressed things in terms of percentages; in this section, we express things in terms of dollars. Suppose we rewrite the preceding equation as follows:

$$E(S_T) - S = s + i + E(\phi).$$

Now we divide everything by S. We can then write $[E(S_T) - S]/S$ as $E(r_S)$:

$$\frac{E(S_T) - S}{S} = E(r_s) = \left(\frac{s+i}{S}\right) + \left(\frac{E(\phi)}{S}\right).$$

The first expression on the right, $(s + i)/S$, is the percentage opportunity cost of storing or investing in the asset. The interest forgone as a percentage of the price, i/S, is equivalent to the risk-free rate. The overall percentage opportunity cost differs only from the risk-free rate in that here we have included a storage cost, s. In the CAPM, we traditionally omit the storage cost because we tend to apply the CAPM to securities, which have no storage costs. If we applied the CAPM to commodities that are costly to store, we would have to include a storage cost with the risk-free rate. Thus, the expected return on such an asset would reflect the risk-free rate plus the storage cost expressed as a percentage of the asset's price.

The second term on the right is the expected risk premium expressed as a percentage of the spot price, $E(\phi)/S$. This is equivalent to the term $[E(r_M) - r]\beta$ in the CAPM. The CAPM simply provides a more explicit statement of the source of the risk premium, which is the systematic risk. Thus, we see that the equation developed in this section is a more general statement of the risk-return relationship. It is true regardless of whether or not the CAPM is valid.

Figure 8.17 summarizes what we have learned in this section. The spot market assesses the expected future spot price from the probability distribution of the spot price at T. It also determines the cost of storage from the storage market, the interest forgone from the bond market, and its own feelings about risk. These factors then combine to produce the spot price.

A Further Word on Storage

The physical process of storage incurs costs that we have defined as s. For some goods, such as agricultural commodities, these costs can be substantial. They include the direct costs of the storage facility, plus insurance and a factor that reflects spoilage and obsolescence. For other goods, such as stocks and bonds, the direct costs of storage are insignificant. In addition, some securities even offer a return from storage in the form of dividends or coupon interest.

Let us now define the important concept of the **cost of carry** as the cost of storage, s, plus the interest forgone, i. The cost of carry is positive if storage creates a net cash outflow and negative if dividends or coupon interest are large enough to offset the cost of storage and the interest forgone. Sometimes, however, this concept is referred to as simply the **carry.** The carry is the coupon interest or dividends earned minus the cost of

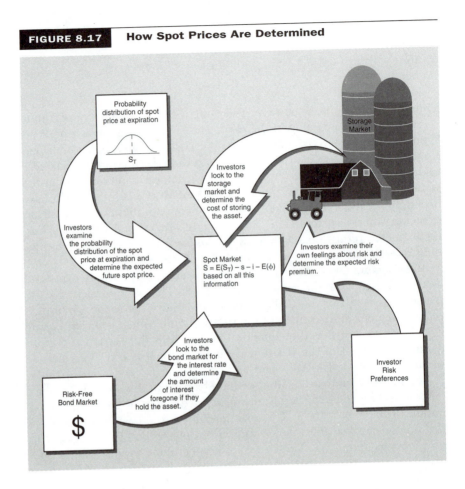

FIGURE 8.17   **How Spot Prices Are Determined**

storage and the interest forgone. Thus, assets that offer dividends or coupon interest in excess of the costs of storing and the forgone interest are said to have a positive carry. In this text, we shall prefer to use the concept of the *cost of carry*.

While the cost of carry is an important concept in spot market pricing, it is even more vital in defining the relationship among the spot price, expected future spot price, and the forward or futures price. We shall have much more to say about the cost of carry in Chapter 9. Now let us consider two extreme cases: goods that are nonstorable and goods that are indefinitely storable.

For a nonstorable good, such as electricity, there would not necessarily be a relationship between today's spot price and the expected future spot price. Supply and demand conditions today and in the future

would be independent. The risk of uncertain future supplies could not be reduced by storing some of the good currently owned. Large price fluctuations likely would occur. The cost of carry would be a meaningless concept.

At the other extreme, a commodity might be indefinitely storable. Some financial assets, metals, and natural resources such as oil are examples. Their spot prices would be set in accordance with current supply and demand conditions, the cost of carry, investors' expected risk premia, and expected future supply and demand conditions.

For many agricultural commodities, limited storability is the rule. Grains have a fairly long storage life, while frozen concentrated orange juice has a more limited one. In the financial markets Treasury bills, which mature in less than a year, have a short storage life. Treasury bonds, with their longer maturities, have a much longer storage life.

For any storable commodity, the spot price is related to the expected future spot price by the cost of carry and the expected risk premium. This important relationship will carry through to Chapter 9, where we introduce forward and futures markets into the model.

Summary

To understand how forward and futures prices are determined, we must first look at how spot prices are calculated. In this chapter, we examined basic principles of the spot pricing of stocks, bonds, and commodities. We saw how a bond is priced as the present value of the future coupon and principal payments. We considered the role of the discount rate by examining the term structure of interest rates and the behavior of bond prices in response to yield changes. We looked at the concept of duration and how the yield curve and the term structure are related. We learned how the futures market can reveal information about the term structure.

Next, we turned to equities and noted how they too are priced as the present value of future cash flows. We briefly examined the principles of portfolio theory and developed the concepts of diversification and the Capital Asset Pricing Model. We illustrated a simple regression technique for estimating systematic risk.

Finally, we looked at a simple model of the pricing of a commodity in the spot market. We developed the concept first under a world of certainty, then under a world of uncertainty and risk neutrality, and finally in a world of uncertainty with risk-averse investors. We found that spot prices are formed by taking into account the cost of storage, the interest forgone on the money tied up, the expected risk premium, and the expected future spot price. This model can apply to any commodity that is storable for at least a limited time period. This would include most agricultural commodities as well as financial instruments.

In Chapter 9, we shall introduce forward and futures contracts into the model. We shall see how forward or futures prices, spot prices, the cost of carry, the risk premium, and expected future spot prices are related. In addition, we shall see how futures prices are related to other futures prices and to the prices of forward contracts.

Key Terms

Before continuing to Chapter 9, you should be able to give brief definitions of the following terms.

- bonds
- term structure of interest rates
- spot rate/cash rate
- forward rate
- pure-discount loan
- yield

- basis point
- duration
- diversification
- systematic risk
- Capital Asset Pricing Model
- cost of carry

Questions and Problems

1. Explain and distinguish between the concepts of spot and forward rates.

2. To which of the theories of the term structure do each of the following statements refer? Explain your answers.

    a. Long-term rates are higher than short-term rates because the U.S. Treasury currently is shifting the average maturity of its debt by borrowing more heavily with Treasury bonds than with Treasury bills.

    b. The current structure of interest rates is the market's way of saying that interest rates are expected to increase in the future.

    c. The term structure is upward sloping because lenders are reluctant to make long-term loans.

    d. No arbitrage opportunities across the term structure are possible.

3. Use the following term structure to derive the requested forward rates:

$$r(0,1) = .08 \qquad r(0,2) = .085 \qquad r(0,3) = .09.$$

    a. $r(1,2)$
    b. $r(1,3)$
    c. $r(2,3)$

4. Find the price of a 9 percent coupon bond with annual coupons, a three-year maturity, $1,000-face-value, and a yield of 8.94 percent.

5. Verify that if the price of the bond in problem 4 is $898, the yield is 13.35 percent.

6. Consider a three-year $1,000-face-value bond with coupons of 6 percent, paid annually, and a yield of 8 percent. Show how the bond is made up of zero coupon bonds and find the value of a portfolio of the zero coupon bonds. Assume the term structure is flat.

7. Find the price and duration of a bond with a coupon of 12 percent, payable annually, a yield of 14 percent, a face value of $1,000, and a maturity of five years. Use both formulas to calculate duration.

8. Consider two $1,000-face-value bonds with 10 percent coupons, paid annually, and 10 percent yields. One bond has a maturity of 8 years and the other a maturity of 12 years. Show that the 12-year bond is more volatile for a given yield change.

9. Consider two $1,000-face-value bonds each with an eight-year maturity and a 10 percent yield. One bond has an 8 percent coupon and the other a 10 percent coupon. Show that the 8 percent coupon bond is more volatile for a given yield change. Both bonds pay coupons annually.

10. Use the Excel spreadsheet bpd3.xls and determine the price and duration of the following bonds. Let the current date be August 6, 1997. Let the bonds have a face value of $1,000 and pay coupons semiannually, once on the month and day corresponding to the maturity month and day, and once six months later.

   a. A bond that matures on March 15, 2011, has a coupon of 12.5 percent, and a yield of 9.875 percent.

   b. A bond that matures on November 15, 1999, has a coupon of 6.25 percent, and a yield of 7.125 percent.

   c. A bond that matures on February 15, 2005, has a coupon of 7.5 percent, and a yield of 8.875 percent.

   d. A bond that matures on August 15, 2025, has a coupon of 9.625 percent, and a yield of 9.5 percent.

11. On March 15, the spot discount rate on 97-day T-bills is 8.48. This rate is based on a 360-day year. The following rates are discount rates on that day for the 90-day T-bill futures contracts expiring on the dates indicated. Derive the futures term structure.

Contract	Rate	Expiration
June	9.22	June 20
September	9.74	September 19
December	10.06	December 19

12. Carefully explain the distinction between systematic and unsystematic risk. Then identify whether each of the following is a source of systematic or unsystematic risk:

   a. A strike by employees of a firm whose stock you own

   b. A change in the Federal Reserve discount rate

   c. A major recall of a product owned by a firm whose stock you do not own; however, you do own a competitor's stock

13. Write out the equation for the Capital Asset Pricing Model. Explain what each term means. Then discuss why investors earn returns only for assuming systematic risk.

14. The following prices for Microsoft stock and the S&P 500 index are given at weekly intervals at the dates indicated. Estimate the beta for Microsoft. Ignore dividends.

Date	Microsoft	S&P 500
6/5	120.875	678.44
6/12	125.000	669.04
6/19	121.750	661.96
6/26	120.500	664.39
7/3	121.125	672.40
7/10	119.500	656.06
7/17	117.125	634.07
7/24	114.750	626.65
7/31	117.875	639.95
8/7	124.750	664.16
8/14	124.875	662.05
8/21	123.500	665.07
8/28	125.625	664.81

15. Suppose you are interested in constructing market indices using three component stocks. The index is begun on day 1 and computed every day thereafter. The data for day 1 and day 2 are as follows:

	Day 1		Day 2	
Stock	Number of Shares	Price	Number of Shares	Price
X	100	$21.50	100	$22.00
Y	225	11.00	225	12.75
Z	80	32.00	240	11.00

Construct an index like the S&P 500, and determine its value on day 2 assuming a base value of 100 on day 1.

16. Consider a stock priced at $80. An investor plans to buy the stock and hold it for one year. During that time, the investor will forgo $4 of interest on the money invested. There are no storage costs involved in holding the stock. Determine the expected future stock price under the conditions described in parts a, b, and c. Then answer part d.

   a. The investor lives in a world of certainty.
   b. The investor lives in a world of uncertainty but is considered risk neutral.
   c. The investor lives in a world of uncertainty but is considered risk averse. The expected risk premium for holding this stock for one year is deemed to be $12.
   d. Now suppose the investor determines that the expected return on the market is .22. If the CAPM describes expected returns, determine the beta of the stock.

17. Explain how storage costs enter into the determination of the current spot price and expected return. How is your answer affected if the asset is perishable?

18. (Concept Problem) In the text and in problem 16, we determined the expected future spot price based on the current spot price plus other parameters. Why, in reality, is this perhaps like putting the cart before the horse?

CHAPTER 9

Principles of Forward and Futures Pricing

Different investors place different prices on risk. If you are able, as it were, to buy risk from one investor cheaply and sell it to another investor dearly, you can make money without taking any risk at all.

MICHAEL LEWIS
Liar's Poker, 1989

In Chapter 8, we examined some basic principles of the pricing of the underlying spot market instruments. We saw how the term structure of interest rates determines bond prices and how the Capital Asset Pricing Model and the beta are viewed as fundamental determinants of the relationship between return and risk. Expectations of the future price, the opportunity cost of money, and the risk premium combine to produce the current price.

We are now ready to move directly into the pricing of forward and futures contracts. The very nature of the word *futures* suggests that futures prices concern expectations of prices in the future. The word *forward* suggests a looking ahead. In this chapter, we shall see how futures prices, forward prices, spot prices, expectations, and the cost of carry are interrelated. As with options, our objective is to link the price of the futures or forward contract to the price of the underlying instrument and to identify factors that influence the relationship between these prices.

In the early part of this chapter, we shall treat forward and futures contracts as though they were entirely separate instruments. Recall that a forward contract is an agreement between two parties to exchange an asset for a fixed price at a future date. No money changes hands, and the agreement is binding. In order to reverse the transaction, it is necessary to find someone willing to take the opposite side of a new, offsetting forward

Chapter Objectives

■ To introduce the basic concepts of price and value for futures and forward contracts

■ To show the conditions under which futures and forward prices are equivalent and when they are different

■ To present the cost of carry formula for the theoretical fair price of futures and forward contracts

■ To introduce the concepts of contango, backwardation, and convenience yield

■ To present the two opposing views to the question of whether futures prices reward speculators with a risk premium

■ To illustrate how intermediate cash flows such as dividends affect the cost of carry model

■ To show how futures spreads are priced

contract calling for delivery of the asset at the same time as the original contract. A forward contract is created in the over-the-counter market and is subject to default risk. A futures contract is also an agreement between two parties to exchange an asset for a fixed price at a future date. However, the agreement is made on a futures exchange and is regulated by that exchange. The contract requires that the parties make margin deposits, and their accounts are marked to market every day. The contracts are standardized and can be bought and sold during regular trading hours. These differences between forward and futures contracts, particularly the marking to market, create some differences in their prices and values. As we shall see later, these differences may prove quite minor; for now, we shall proceed as though forward and futures contracts were entirely different instruments.

Some Properties of Forward and Futures Prices

The Concept of Price versus Value

In Chapter 1, we discussed how an efficient market means that the price of an asset equals its true economic value. The holder of an asset has money tied up in the asset. If the holder is willing to retain the asset, the asset must have a value at least equal to its price. If the asset's value were less than its price, the owner would sell it. The value is the present value of the future cash flows, with the discount rate reflecting the opportunity cost of money and a premium for the risk assumed.

While this line of reasoning is sound in securities markets, it can get one into trouble in forward and futures markets. A forward or futures contract is not an asset. You can buy a futures contract, but do you actually pay for it? A futures requires a small margin deposit, but is this really the price? You can buy 100 shares of a $20 stock by placing $1,000 in a margin account and borrowing $1,000 from a broker. Does that make the stock worth $10 per share? Certainly not. The stock is worth $20 per share: You have $10 per share invested and $10 per share borrowed.

The margin requirement on a futures contract is not really a margin in the same sense as the margin on a stock. You might deposit 3 percent to 5 percent of the price of the futures contract in a margin account, but you do not borrow the remainder. The margin is only a type of security deposit. Thus, the buyer of a futures contract does not actually "pay" for it, and, of course, the seller really receives no money for it. As long as the price does not change, neither party can execute an offsetting trade that would generate a profit.

As noted previously, a forward contract may or may not require a margin deposit or some type of credit enhancement, but if it does, the principle is still the same: The forward price is not the margin.

When dealing with futures contracts, we must be careful to distinguish between **price** and **value.** The futures price is an observable number. The value is less obvious. However, the contract's initial value is zero. This is because neither party pays anything and neither party receives anything of monetary value. That does not imply, however, that neither party will pay or receive money at a later date. This point is equally applicable to forward contracts. The values of futures and forward contracts during their lives, however, are not necessarily equal either to each other or to zero.

The value of a futures contract when written is zero.

The Value of a Forward Contract

In this section we shall determine how forward contracts are valued. We shall use an upper-case V to represent the value of the forward contract. A subscript will denote the time at which the valuation is taken. We use a capital F for the forward price, with a subscript denoting the point in time at which the contract is originally written. When we move to futures contracts, we shall use lower-case letters.

The value of a forward contract when written is zero.

THE FORWARD PRICE AT EXPIRATION   The first and most important principle is that the price of a forward contract that is created at expiration must be the spot price. Such a contract will call for delivery, an instant later, of the asset. Thus, the contract is equivalent to a spot transaction, and its price must, therefore, equal the spot price. Thus, we can say

$$F_T = S_T.$$

If this statement were not true, it would be possible to make an immediate arbitrage profit by either buying the asset and selling an expiring forward contract or selling the asset and buying an expiring forward contract.

The price of a forward contract that expires immediately is the spot price.

THE VALUE OF A FORWARD CONTRACT AT EXPIRATION   At expiration, the value of a forward contract is easily found. Ignoring delivery costs, the value of a forward contract at expiration, V_T, is the profit on the forward contract. The profit is the spot price minus the original forward price. Thus,

$$V_T = S_T - F.$$

When you enter into a long forward contract with a price of F, you agree to buy the asset at T, paying the price F. Thus, your profit will be $S_T - F$. This is the value of owning the forward contract. At the time the contract was written, the contract had zero value. At expiration, however, anyone owning a contract permitting him or her to buy an asset worth S_T by paying a price F has a guaranteed profit of $S_T - F$. Thus, the contract has a

The value of a forward contract at expiration is the spot price minus the original forward price.

value of $S_T - F$. Of course, this value can be either positive or negative. The value to the holder of the short position is simply minus one times the value to the holder of the long position.

THE VALUE OF A FORWARD CONTRACT PRIOR TO EXPIRATION   To explain how a forward contract can have value during its life but prior to expiration, let us introduce the following notation for forward contracts expiring at T:

F = price of a forward contract written today calling for delivery at T of the underlying asset

F_t = price of a new forward contract written at time t (prior to expiration) calling for delivery of the same underlying asset at T

V_t = value at time t (prior to expiration) of the forward contract written today

V_T = value at time T (expiration) of the forward contract written today. We already know that this equals $S_T - F$.

Note that we have two distinct forward contracts, one written today that we shall call the "old" contract, and a new one written at t that we shall call the "new" contract. We wish to determine what the value of the old contract will be at t, which is during its life. When we find its value, we will know what it would be worth to an investor to own it.

Before we begin, however, let us take note of why it is important to place a value on the forward contract. If a firm enters into a forward contract, it does not initially appear on the balance sheet. Although it may appear in a footnote, the contract is not an asset or liability. During the life of the forward contract, however, value may be created or destroyed as a result of changing market conditions. For example, we already saw that the forward contract has a value at expiration of $S_T - F$, which may be positive or negative. To give a fair assessment of the assets and liabilities of the company, it would be important to determine the value of the contract before expiration. If that value is positive, the contract can be properly viewed and recorded as an asset; if it is negative, the contract should be viewed and recorded as a liability. Investors should be informed about the values of forward contracts and, indeed, all derivatives so that they can make informed decisions about the impact of derivative transactions on the overall value of the firm.

The value of a forward contract prior to expiration is the present value of the difference between the prices of a newly written forward contract calling for delivery of the same asset at the same expiration and the original forward contract.

Table 9.1 illustrates how we determine the value. Today we simply enter into a long forward contract. At t we enter into a new short forward contract. At expiration we shall end up buying the asset using the old long forward contract and delivering the asset using the new short forward contract, thus guaranteeing a cash flow of $F_t - F$ at expiration. This amount is known at t so its present value can be found by discounting it at the risk-free rate over the period $T - t$. This present value should equal the value of the position at t. At t, the value of the position consists solely of the

TABLE 9.1	Valuing a Forward Contract Prior to Expiration

The time line

```
|_____|_____|
Today      t     T (expiration)
```

Time	Situation	Action	Value
Today	Forward contract calling for delivery of asset at T has price of F.	Enter into long forward contract.	0
t	New forward contract calling for delivery of asset at T has price of F_t.	Sell new forward contract. Hold on to old long forward contract.	–0 V_t
		Total value at t	V_t
T	Spot price is S_T.	Accept delivery of asset on old long forward contract, paying F. Make delivery of asset on new short forward contract, receiving F_t.	$S_T - F$ $-(S_T - F_t)$
		Total value at T	$F_t - F$

Conclusion: At time t, the investor's position (long a forward contract, obligating purchase of the asset at T at a price F and short a forward contract, obligating delivery of the asset at T for a price F_t) guarantees a value of $F_t - F$ at the expiration. Thus, the value of the investor's position at t (V_t) is the present value of $F_t - F$. Since $F_t - F$ is a known amount at t, the risk-free rate can be used to find the present value. Thus,

$$V_t = (F_t - F)(1 + r)^{-(T - t)}.$$

Because the value of the new forward contract at t is zero, the value of the position at t consists solely of the value of the old forward contract. Thus, the value of the old forward contract at t is given by the above formula.

value of the old long forward contract as the value of the new short forward contract is zero. Thus, the value of the old long forward contract at t is the present value of the difference between the new forward contract price and the old forward contract price:

$$V_t = (F_t - F)(1 + r)^{-(T - t)}.$$

You should note that this value can be negative.

A NUMERICAL EXAMPLE   Suppose you buy a forward contract today at a price of $100. The contract expires in 45 days. The risk-free rate is 10 percent.

The forward contract is an agreement to buy the asset at a price of $100 in 45 days. Now, 20 days later, new forward contracts expiring at the same time—in 25 days—are being written at a price of $104. The value of your forward contract is

$$(104 - 100)(1.10)^{-25/365} = 3.974.$$

Why is your contract worth $3.974? You cannot liquidate the contract, but you can sell a new forward contract at the new price of $104. When both contracts expire in 25 days, you will buy the asset at $100 using your first contract and sell it at $104 using your second contract. Your total payoff will be $4. At 25 days before expiration, you know you will receive $4 at expiration. The present value of $4 at the risk-free rate is $3.974. To the seller, the first forward contract has a value at t of −$3.974.

The Value of a Futures Contract

In this section, we shall look at the valuation of futures contracts. As noted previously, we shall use a lower-case f for the futures price and a lower-case v for the value of a futures. Let us recall that a futures contract is marked to market each day. We have already noted that the value of a futures contract when originally written is zero.

THE FUTURES PRICE AT EXPIRATION   At the instant at which a futures contract is expiring, its price must be the spot price. In other words, if you enter into a long futures contract that will expire an instant later, you have agreed to buy the asset an instant later, paying the futures price. This is the same as a spot transaction. Thus,

$$f_T = S_T.$$

The price of a futures contract that expires immediately is the spot price.

If this statement were not true, buying the spot and selling the futures or selling the spot and buying the futures would generate an arbitrage profit.

THE VALUE OF A FUTURES CONTRACT DURING THE TRADING DAY BUT BEFORE BEING MARKED TO MARKET   When we looked at forward contracts, the second result we obtained was the value of a forward contract at expiration. In the case of futures contracts, it is more useful to look next at how one values a futures contract before it is marked to market. In other words, what is a futures contract worth during the trading day?

Suppose we arbitrarily let the time period between today and time t be one day. Suppose you purchase a futures contract today, when the futures price is f. Let us assume that this is the opening price of the day and that it equals the settlement price the previous day. Now let us say we are at the end of the day, but the market is not yet closed. The price is f_t. What is the

value of the contract? If you sell the contract, it generates a gain of $f_t - f$. Thus, we can say that the value of the futures contract is

$$v_t = f_t - f \text{ before the contract is marked to market.}$$

In fact, if we let f_t represent the price at any time (not just at the end of the trading day), the value of the futures contract is simply the price change since the time the contract was opened or, if it was opened on a previous day, the last price change since marking to market. Note, of course, that the value could be negative. If we were considering the value of the futures to the holder of the short position, we would simply change the sign.

THE VALUE OF A FUTURES CONTRACT IMMEDIATELY AFTER BEING MARKED TO MARKET

When a futures contract is marked to market, the price change since the last marking to market or, if the contract was opened during the day, the price change since it was opened is distributed to the party in whose favor the price moved and charged to the party to whom the price moved against. This, of course, is the mark-to-market procedure. As soon as the contract is marked to market, the value of the contract goes back to zero. Thus,

$$v_t = 0 \text{ as soon as the contract is marked to market.}$$

If the futures price was still at the last settlement price and the futures trader then tried to sell the contract to capture its value, it would generate no profit, which is consistent with its zero value.

Thus, to summarize these two results, we find that the value of a long futures contract at any point in time is the profit that would be generated if the contract were sold. Because of the daily marking to market, the value of a futures contract reverts back to zero as soon as it is marked to market. The value for the holder of a short futures contract is minus one times the value for the holder of the long futures contract. For a long futures contract, value is created by positive price changes; for a short futures contract, value is created by negative price changes.

In this section we have seen how the price and the value of futures and forward contracts are two entirely different concepts. For most assets we think that price equals value in an efficient market. For forward and futures contracts, no cash is paid out up front so the contracts have zero value when first written. The confusion over price and value could perhaps be avoided if we thought of the forward or futures price as a concept more akin to the exercise price of an option. We know that the exercise price does not equal an option's value. It simply represents the figure that the two parties agreed would be the price paid by the call buyer or

The value of a futures contract during a trading day but before it is marked to market is the amount by which the price changed since the contract was opened or last marked to market, whichever comes later.

As soon as a futures contract is marked to market, its value goes back to zero.

received by the put buyer if the option is ultimately exercised. In a similar sense, the futures or forward price is simply the figure that the two parties agreed will be paid by the buyer to the seller at expiration in exchange for the underlying asset. While we could call the forward price or the futures price the "exercise price" of the contract, the use of the terms "forward price" and "futures price" is so traditional that it would be unwise not to use them.

Forward versus Futures Prices

At expiration, forward and futures prices equal the spot price. Are they equal at any other time? Do forward and futures contracts accomplish the same result? In this section we shall see. We shall examine two cases: (1) one day prior to expiration (time t) and (2) two days or more prior to expiration.

ONE DAY PRIOR TO EXPIRATION Table 9.2 illustrates how we examine the difference between forward and futures prices one day prior to expiration. At time t, we go long a forward contract and short a futures contract. Such a transaction has zero initial value. At expiration, we end up buying the asset with the forward contract and selling it with the futures contract. Since we put up no money and this transaction is risk-free, the forward price would have to equal the futures price or we would make a guaranteed profit at no cost.[1] Thus,

$$f_t = F_t \text{ one day prior to expiration.}$$

Provided that there is no default risk, forward and futures prices are equal one day prior to expiration.

An important assumption here is that there is no default risk. We can reasonably assume this holds on the futures contract. Forward contracts are clearly subject to some default risk. However, with one day remaining the default risk should be fairly small.

Now let us back up one day.

TWO DAYS OR MORE PRIOR TO EXPIRATION Now we are forced to make an important assumption: The interest rate on both days is r; that is, r does not change.[2] The futures price is f and the forward price is F. We are currently at the time denoted as "Today." One day later, we shall be at time t. One day after that we shall be at expiration. Table 9.3 demonstrates that we should construct a portfolio consisting of a long forward contract

---

[1]If the forward price were larger than the futures price, we would initially do the opposite transaction—go short the forward contract and long the futures contract. If the futures price were higher, we would initially do the transaction as indicated in Table 9.2.

[2]Technically, the interest rate can change as long as we know what it will change to.

TABLE 9.2	**The Difference between Forward and Futures Prices One Day Prior to Expiration**

The time line

```
———————————— 1 day ————————————
|                                          |
t                                          T (expiration)
```

Time	Situation	Action	Value
t	Forward contract calling for delivery of asset at T has price of F_t.	Enter into long forward contract.	0
	Futures contract calling for delivery of asset at T has price of f_t.	Enter into short futures contract.	-0
		Total value at t	0
T	Spot price is S_T.	Accept delivery of asset on long forward contract, paying F_t.	$S_T - F_t$
		Make delivery of asset on short futures contract, receiving f_t.	$-(S_T - f_t)$
		Total value at T	$f_t - F_t$

Conclusion: At time t, the investor's position (long a forward contract, obligating purchase of the asset at T at a price F_t, and short a futures contract, obligating delivery of the asset at T for a price f_t) guarantees a value of $f_t - F_t$ at the expiration. Thus, the value of the investor's position at t, which is zero, must equal the present value of $f_t - F_t$. The only way this can hold is that

$$f_t = F_t.$$

So the futures price must equal the forward price when there is one day remaining.

and $(1 + r)^{-1/365}$ short futures contracts. The reason we use such a seemingly strange number of futures contracts $((1 + r)^{-1/365})$ is to adjust for the marking to market that will occur once before expiration. If there were three days before expiration, we would use 2/365 in the exponent.

One day later, at t, the futures account is marked to market. If there is a profit we take the cash and reinvest it for one day at the risk-free rate, r. If there is a loss, we replace the funds in the margin account by borrowing the necessary amount for one day at the risk-free rate, r. We close out the $(1 + r)^{-1/365}$ futures contracts by buying them back and sell one new futures contract.[3]

---

[3]This procedure of closing out contracts and buying a new one can be done by buying back the $(1 + r)^{-1/365}$ contracts an instant before the close of the day and then selling one new contract or by selling $1 - (1 + r)^{-1/365}$ additional contracts at the close.

TABLE 9.3	The Difference between Forward and Futures Prices Two Days Prior to Expiration

The time line

—————— 1 day —————— —————— 1 day ——————

Today   t   T (expiration)

Time	Situation	Action	Value
Today	Forward contract calling for delivery of asset at T has price of F.	Enter into long forward contract.	0
	Futures contract calling for delivery of asset at T has price of f.	Enter into $(1 + r)^{-1/365}$ short futures contracts.	-0
		Total value Today	0
t	The futures price is f_t. The futures position is marked to market for a cash flow of $-(1 + r)^{-1/365}(f_t - f)$.	Buy back the $(1 + r)^{-1/365}$ futures contracts.	0
		Invest the mark-to-market profit of $-(1 + r)^{-1/365}(f_t - f)$ in risk-free bonds. (If this amount is negative, borrow it at the risk-free rate.)	$-(1 + r)^{-1/365}(f_t - f)$
		Sell one new futures contract.	-0
		Total value at t	$-(1 + r)^{-1/365}(f_t - f)$
T	Spot price is S_T. Futures price, f_T, converges to spot price, S_T. Bonds (or loan) matures for a value of $-(1 + r)^{-1/365}(f_t - f)$ $(1 + r)^{1/365} = -(f_t - f)$.	Accept delivery of asset on long forward contract, paying F.	$S_T - F$
		Make delivery of asset on short futures contract, receiving f_t.	$-(S_T - f_t)$
		Redeem bonds (or pay off loan).	$-(f_t - f)$
		Total value at T	$f - F$

Conclusion: The investor's position today (long a forward contract, obligating purchase of the asset at T at a price F, and short $(1 + r)^{-1/365}$ futures contracts, obligating delivery of the asset at T for a price f) guarantees a value of $f - F$ at the expiration. Thus, the value of the investor's position today, which is zero, must equal the present value of $f - F$. The only way this can happen is if

$$f = F.$$

So the futures price must equal the forward price when there are two days remaining.

One day later at T, both contracts expire. We accept delivery on the forward contract and make delivery on the futures contract. If we had reinvested a mark-to-market profit or borrowed to cover a mark-to-market loss at t, it would now be worth $-(f_t - f)$. The overall cash flow at expiration is $f - F$, the difference in the original futures and forward prices. Since this transaction never required that we pay out or receive any funds, $f - F$ must be zero. Otherwise, we could generate an arbitrage profit by doing the transaction or doing the opposite if necessary. This argument can be repeatedly applied so as to show that forward and futures prices are equivalent at any time prior to expiration. Thus, in general,

$$f = F.$$

It is important, however, to remember two key assumptions. We already mentioned the assumption that there is no default risk. If the contracts have many days remaining, the assumption of no default risk is less plausible. As we have noted many times, forward contracts are clearly subject to default risk that can be quite large if traders of somewhat lower quality engage in such contracts. Another key assumption is that interest rates are constant or at least known in advance. We shall cover this point one section later. But first let us take a look at an example.

If interest rates are known and constant and there is no default risk, forward prices will equal futures prices at any time prior to expiration.

A NUMERICAL EXAMPLE   Consider a September S&P 500 futures contract. On September 18, two days prior to expiration, the contract was priced at 932.15. There are no forward markets for the S&P 500, but assume one can buy a forward contract at 930. Thus, the futures price exceeds the forward price by 2.15. The interest rate is 6 percent and will not change for two days. An arbitrageur would observe that the futures price is too high and/or the forward price too low. Suppose the arbitrageur has sufficient capital to undertake a transaction of 10,000 forward contracts. Thus, the arbitrageur will attempt to capture a risk-free profit of $10,000(\$2.15) = \$21,500$ by selling futures contracts and buying forward contracts. The number of futures contracts is $10,000 \times (1.06)^{-1/365} = 9,998$, and the number of forward contracts is 10,000.

The next day, the futures price is 933.25. The arbitrageur has incurred a loss on the futures contracts of $9,998(933.25 - 932.15) = 10,998$. The loss must be made up, so the arbitrageur borrows $10,998 for one day at 6 percent. The futures contracts are closed out, and a new position of 10,000 short futures is opened.

At expiration, the loan is due and the arbitrageur owes $10,998(1.06)^{1/365} = 11,000$. Let the S&P spot index be 934 on the expiration day. To keep things simple we will assume the S&P forward contract is cash settled, so the arbitrageur settles the forward contract by receiving a payment equal to the spot price at expiration minus the original forward

Derivatives in Action

A Hill of Beans

The relationship between the futures price and the spot price is based on the idea that at expiration, a futures contract can be settled by delivering the underlying asset. The futures price converges to the spot price, and holders of long positions will be forced to accept delivery made by holders of short positions. If the market works properly, prices will behave normally and holders of the short contracts should have no difficulty buying up a sufficient quantity of the asset to deliver. We should not expect sharp price changes at expiration. Nearly all of the time this is precisely what happens. But on rare occasions, some investors attempt to buy up the deliverable supply of the asset, while simultaneously holding a large number of long futures positions. Then as the contract approaches expiration, the holders of the short positions are forced to buy the asset from this person or firm, who exacts an inflated price. This is called a "short squeeze." It can have severe impacts on holders of short positions, which often includes farmers and processors. In July 1989, just such an occurrence happened at the Chicago Board of Trade. Ferruzzi Finanziaria S.p.A. is an Italian conglomerate with annual sales of about $30 billion and international activities in the financial and commodities markets. Its efforts to control the delivery of soybeans on the July futures sent the Chicago Board of Trade and the Commodity Futures Trading Commission on a controversial course of actions.

First let us take a look at how exchanges attempt to prevent such actions. As we noted in Chapter 7, there are position limits, which represent the maximum number of contracts that can be held by one trader. However, businesses that deal in the underlying commodity often require exceptions to these limits in order to hedge a large quantity of the underlying commodity. The limit for speculators in soybean futures, called the speculative limit, is 3 million bushels. Businesses that can demonstrate a genuine hedging need routinely apply for and are granted exceptions to the limit.

In 1988 a severe drought damaged much of the corn and soybean crops. Supplies of soybeans that could be carried over to meet delivery requirements in 1989 were quite low. In the spring of 1989, the CBOT and CFTC began to notice that Ferruzzi was accumulating an unusually large number of contracts in the May futures which, it contended, had been authorized by the CFTC on the basis of Ferruzzi's expressed need for large supplies of soybeans for its American subsidiary, Central Soya, a soybean processor. It argued that it was simply hedging the purchase of these soybeans. With one day remaining before the May contract expired, the CFTC revoked Ferruzzi's position limit exemption and ordered it to immediately

price times the number of contracts, or $10,000(934 - 930) = 40,000$. The futures is settled in cash, so the arbitrageur makes a payment of $10,000(934 - 933.25) = 7,500$. Thus, the net cash flow to the arbitrageur on the expiration day is $-11,000 + 40,000 - 7,500 = 21,500$. This is the original amount the arbitrageur set out to capture with this riskless hedge. The combined effects of numerous arbitrageurs buying forward contracts and selling futures contracts will drive the forward and the futures prices together.

WHY FORWARD AND FUTURES PRICES MAY NOT BE EQUAL Under the assumptions of known or constant interest rates and no default risk, we see that forward and futures prices should be equal. Let us now consider what

liquidate all contracts in excess of the speculative limit of 3 million bushels. Ferruzzi sold the May futures but immediately purchased the July futures, setting the stage for a showdown in midsummer.

Ferruzzi was also accumulating supplies of soybeans. By early July, Ferruzzi owned 85 percent of the deliverable supply of soybeans and 53 percent of the outstanding long futures contracts. As July approached, the CBOT and CFTC began worrying that Ferruzzi was attempting a short squeeze. Ferruzzi argued that it was simply hedging its anticipated purchase of soybeans. If that were the case, however, Ferruzzi would be bidding competitively in the various spot markets that were located near its processor. Instead it placed bids well below the spot price, clearly indicating that hedging was not its intention. Simple computations showed that Ferruzzi's intent to take delivery would result in it paying far more for the soybeans than it would have to have paid had it done what hedgers typically do. Of course, such calculations assume a competitive market. If Ferruzzi had executed a short squeeze, it could have hiked the price of soybeans and exacted a stiff premium from holders of short positions.

Over a period of about six weeks the CFTC and CBOT, in a series of increasingly stronger statements, advised Ferruzzi to begin liquidating its 22 million bushel position. Ferruzzi made little effort to comply.

On July 11, nine days before expiration, the CBOT invoked an emergency provision in its rules and ordered Ferruzzi to liquidate its contracts down to the 3 million speculative limit by July 18 and down to 1 million by July 20. In addition the CBOT ordered all holders of long positions to do likewise. Many traders criticized the CBOT for, in effect, intervening in the free-market process.

What subsequently happened? The soybeans held by Ferruzzi as of fall 1989 had not yet been entered into production, suggesting that it never actually needed the beans. In September 1989, its three principal traders resigned. Ferruzzi filed a complaint and a lawsuit against the CBOT, which in turn fined Ferruzzi $2 million plus $1 million in legal costs and demanded that Ferruzzi turn over its membership on the CBOT to its subsidiary, Central Soya. Ferruzzi, while not admitting guilt, paid the fines.

While the potential for extreme price movements was clearly quite real, a study showed that there were practically no price effects from the incident. Attempts to squeeze the shorts are quite rare and fraught with risk. Fortunately, the futures markets have proven to have an effective mechanism for detecting and dealing with such attempts to manipulate the market as the contracts expire.

happens when we relax the interest rate assumption. Note that we sold $(1 + r)^{-1/365}$ futures contracts for every forward contract. If $f_t > f$, we covered the loss by borrowing additional funds. The amount of interest paid on the loan was completely offset by the fact that we had only $(1 + r)^{-1/365}$ contracts for every forward contract. We borrowed $(1 + r)^{-1/365} (f_t - f)$ times the number of forward contracts and the next day paid back $(1 + r)^{-1/365} (f_t - f)(1 + r)^{1/365} = (f_t - f)$ times the number of forward contracts. If $f_t < f$, the interest earned on the reinvested profit was offset by having only $(1 + r)^{-1/365}$ futures contracts for every forward contract.

When short-term interest rates are known in advance, forward prices will equal futures prices. When short-term interest rates are uncertain, arbitrageurs will not know how many futures contracts to trade to ensure a

risk-free profit. Then futures and forward prices may differ. With a little intuition, we can see which would be greater.

Suppose the futures price increases over the contract's life. Then holders of long futures contracts will receive positive cash flows from marking to market. If, during the same time, interest rates increase, the daily reinvestment of the profits will earn more interest. If futures prices decrease, the holder of a long position will incur losses. If those losses occur during a period of falling interest rates, they can be covered by borrowing at increasingly lower rates. Thus, if interest rates and futures prices are positively correlated, futures contracts will offer an advantage over forward contracts and will be priced higher.

If futures prices and interest rates move in opposite directions, profits from rising futures prices will be reinvested in a falling interest rate environment. Losses from falling futures prices will be covered by borrowing in a rising interest rate environment. This will create a preference for forward contracts and will cause forward prices to exceed futures prices. Table 9.4 summarizes these points.

The effect of default risk on futures and forward prices is a controversial subject that is currently being studied by many academics, practitioners, and regulators. It is difficult to determine which would be higher—the futures or forward price—in the presence of default risk. Suppose the two parties to a contract consist of one risk-free party and the other, a party who might default. The risk-free party wants to go long and the risky party wants to go short. If the two parties traded a forward contract, they should be able to negotiate a deal that would permit the higher-risk party to compensate the lower-risk party. This could be done by having them agree to a lower forward price than would be the case if they were both risk-free. Thus, the risk-free counterparty would be committing to paying less for the asset as compensation for the possibility that the risky counterparty might not fulfill his or her end of the deal. If the risk-free party wanted to go short, the forward price should be higher. So for an individual contract, it is possible to identify whether there would be a higher or lower forward price, depending on the credit risks of the two parties and the sides of the contract they desire. It is impossible to make any comments about what would happen in the market as a whole since that would depend on the composition of participants in terms of credit quality and their preferences for long or short positions. Thus, it is impossible to say whether forward prices would be higher than futures prices. For the sake of comparison, however, let us assume that the forward price on this transaction is discounted to compensate for the credit risk of the risky counterparty. Now let us compare what would happen with that same contract if it were created on a futures exchange.

In order for any party to trade futures, it must qualify by having a minimum acceptable level of credit quality. All qualifying parties, however, are

Ignoring default risk, futures prices will exceed forward prices when futures prices and interest rates are positively correlated. Forward prices will exceed futures prices when futures prices and interest rates are negatively correlated.

TABLE 9.4	Why Futures Prices Can Differ from Forward Prices with More than One Day Remaining	
Condition	**When**	**Why**
Futures price > Forward price	The correlation between futures prices and interest rates is positive.	Long futures contracts are preferred over long forward contracts because profits will occur when interest rates are rising and losses will occur when interest rates are falling. Thus, the marking to market of futures contracts benefits the holder of a long futures contract.
Futures price < Forward price	The correlation between futures prices and interest rates is negative.	Long forward contracts are preferred over long futures contracts because profits will occur when interest rates are falling and losses will occur when interest rates are rising. Thus, realizing all gains and losses at the end of the life of the contract benefits the holder of a long forward contract.

Note: The default risks of the two parties can raise or lower forward prices above or below futures prices.

not of equivalent credit risk. Our risk-free party obviously qualifies. Let us assume our risky party does also and so the parties decide to trade on the futures exchange. On the surface it might appear that both parties benefit because the clearinghouse guarantees the risky party. However, it does so at a cost, which is reflected in the required margins, trading costs, and price limits. Since it imposes the same cost on all participants, the risk-free firm pays an excessive cost to trade. Its unimpeachable credit quality is further enhanced at a cost. If the risky party is of lower risk than average, its credit is enhanced at a bargain price. In other words, each party is treated as if it were of average credit quality. Thus, the risk-free firm would find futures somewhat less attractive and it would prefer forward contracts. The risky counterparty, assuming its risk were greater than average, would prefer futures contracts. Since this party is selling, the futures price would tend to be lower. Thus, both parties would agree that a forward contract would carry a higher price.

Of course, we can make such a statement only about a specific transaction, given the characteristics of the two parties. On another trade the risk-free firm might prefer to be selling. Then its preference for forward

Default risk can affect the forward-futures price differential but the direction of the effect is unclear.

contracts would tend to make the forward price higher. If both counter-parties were risk-free, they would both prefer forward contracts and the forward price should be equivalent to what it would have been had the contract been created in the futures market. If both parties were of lower than average credit risk, they would both prefer futures contracts and we would likely see only a small difference between the price of the futures contract and the price that would exist had the contract been created on the forward market.

There may yet be other reasons for a forward-futures price differential, such as liquidity and transaction cost differences. So in the market as a whole, it is impossible to say how default risk affects the difference between futures and forward prices. We can, however, look at an empirical example.

A COMPARISON OF FORWARD AND FUTURES PRICES   Are forward and futures prices equal? Let us examine some forward and futures prices of Treasury bills.

On January 6, the spot price of a Treasury bill expiring on March 20 is quoted at a discount of 7.01. From Chapter 3, we know the price is calculated as

$$100 - 7.01(73/360) = 98.5785,$$

which reflects the fact that 73 days remain until expiration. The annualized yield is

$$(100/98.5785)^{365/73} - 1 = .0742.$$

The T-bill maturing on June 19, 164 days from now, has a discount of 7.09. Its price is

$$100 - 7.09(164/360) = 96.7701,$$

which implies a yield of

$$(100/96.7701)^{365/164} - 1 = .0758.$$

We can now derive a forward rate for the period of March 20 to June 19, which is 91 days. Using the relationship between spot and forward rates covered in Chapter 8, the forward rate is derived as

$$(1.0758)^{164/365} = (1.0742)^{73/365} [1 + r (73,164)]^{91/365}.$$

This statement says that the return for a 164-day investment equals the returns from a 73-day investment followed by a 91-day investment at the rate

r(73,164). Solving this equation for r(73,164) gives 7.71 percent, the implied forward rate. The forward price is the value of F in the equation

$$(100/F)^{365/91} - 1 = .0771.$$

Solving for F gives 98.1653. The forward price of a 91-day bill of 98.1653 gives an implied forward rate of 7.71 percent.

On the same day, the price of the March futures contract is 98.2659. In this instance, the futures price was higher than the forward price. Figure 9.1 shows the forward and futures prices over the next 10 weeks. With the exception of one week, the futures price is above the forward price.

Ignoring for the moment the credit risk, T-bill futures prices should not exceed forward prices. The futures price is definitely negatively correlated with interest rates. Holders of long futures positions will earn profits when interest rates are falling and incur losses when interest rates are rising. The observed preference for futures over forwards, as indicated in the higher price of the former, is puzzling, at least with regard to the interest rate effect. The explanation may involve the credit risk. It would be preferable if we had prices of actual forward contracts on T-bills. Such

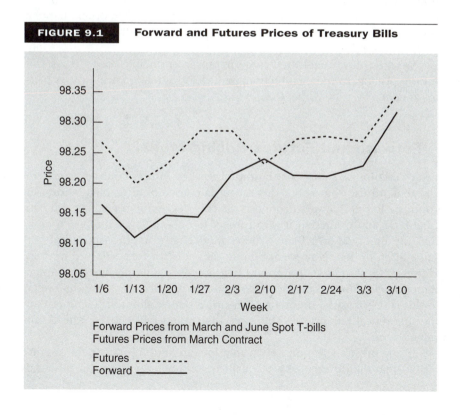

FIGURE 9.1   **Forward and Futures Prices of Treasury Bills**

Forward Prices from March and June Spot T-bills
Futures Prices from March Contract

Futures ----------
Forward ————

data do not exist because the contracts are created privately and the prices are not reported to the public. So in computing the implied forward rates, we are acting as though a counterparty, who could sell short a shorter-term T-bill and buy a longer-term T-bill, had entered into a long forward contract with the government. The counterparty could default when buying back the T-bill to cover the short sale, but the government is risk-free. The actual market for forward contracts involves direct rather than implied forward contracts. One party typically commits to buying the T-bill at a future time while the other party commits to selling it. Neither party is the government. Thus, the credit risk in a direct forward contract may differ substantially from that in an implied forward contract, where one party is implicitly the government.

Our look at the forward-futures price differential has left us with no clear explanation for what to expect. Fortunately, empirical studies have shown that the differential is actually quite small and can usually be ignored. In many of the remaining examples of this book, we shall ignore the marking to market of futures contracts and assume that the entire payoff is received at the end. We shall, however, look at some examples of forward contracts, primarily for the purpose of underscoring the fact that some types of specialized situations require contracts that do not exist on futures exchanges. For all intents and purposes, however, most of what we cover in the remainder of this chapter and the examples in other chapters will treat the contracts as economically equivalent, which means that their prices are the same.

We have now established some important principles of forward and futures pricing. In the next section, we develop a forward and futures pricing model.

A Forward and Futures Pricing Model

In this section we shall learn how a forward or futures contract is priced. In other words, what is the theoretical fair price of a forward or futures contract? Recall that we introduced the concept of theoretical fair value in Chapter 1 and examined it with respect to options in Chapter 4. We saw that the binomial and Black-Scholes models give us the theoretical fair value of an option. Now we are doing the same for forwards and futures. However, we should keep in mind that, as covered earlier in the chapter, the value of a futures contract is not equal to its price. Thus, we shall refer to this concept as the theoretical fair price, but we should remember that the theoretical fair price is the price that would imply a theoretical fair value of zero.

In the previous section we saw that forward and futures prices can differ but that the differences are usually quite small. To make things sound

The theoretical fair price of a futures or forward contract is the price that would imply a theoretical fair value of zero.

a little smoother, we shall stop referring to these contracts as both forward and futures contracts and shall simply refer to them as futures contracts. We shall assume that marking to market is done only on the expiration day, thus making a futures contract be essentially a forward contract.

We initially assume that the margin requirement is zero. First let us recall from Chapter 8 the relationship between today's spot price and the expected future spot price,

$$S = E(S_T) - \theta - E(\phi),$$

where θ is the cost of carry and equals the storage cost (s) plus the opportunity cost of money (i) and $E(\phi)$ is the expected risk premium, the reward for assuming risk.

The Theoretical Fair Price

Consider the following transaction: Buy the spot asset at a price of S, and sell a futures contract at a price of f. At expiration, the spot price is S_T and the futures price is f_T, which equals S_T. At expiration, you deliver the asset. The profit on the transaction is $f - S$ minus the storage costs incurred and the opportunity cost of the funds tied up:

$$\Pi = f - S - s - i = f - S - \theta.$$

Since the expression $f - S$ involves no unknown terms, the profit is riskless, meaning the transaction should not generate a risk premium. The amount invested is S, the original price of the spot asset. The profit from the transaction is $f - S - \theta$, which should equal zero. Thus,

$$f = S + \theta.$$

The futures price equals the spot price plus the cost of carry. The cost of carry therefore is the difference between the futures price and the spot price and is sometimes referred to as the basis.[4] We shall say much more about the basis in Chapter 10.

In equilibrium, the futures price equals the spot price plus the cost of carry.

An alternative interpretation of this transaction is seen in Figure 9.2. The value of the position when initiated is S; the value at expiration is $f - \theta$. Since $f - \theta$ is known when the transaction is initiated, the transaction is risk-free. So S should equal the present value of $f - \theta$, using the risk-free rate. But the present value adjustment has already been made since θ includes the interest lost on S over the holding period. Thus, $f = S + \theta$.

---

[4]The basis usually is defined as the spot price minus the futures price, and we shall use this definition in Chapter 10.

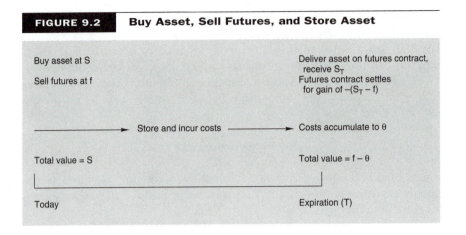

FIGURE 9.2   **Buy Asset, Sell Futures, and Store Asset**

Buy asset at S

Sell futures at f

Store and incur costs

Total value = S

Today

Deliver asset on futures contract, receive S_T

Futures contract settles for gain of $-(S_T - f)$

Costs accumulate to θ

Total value = $f - \theta$

Expiration (T)

What makes this relationship hold? Assume the futures price is higher than the spot price plus the cost of carry:

$$f > S + \theta.$$

Arbitrageurs will then buy the spot asset and sell the futures contract. This will generate a positive profit equal to $f - S - \theta$. Many arbitrageurs will execute the same transaction, which will put downward pressure on the futures price. When $f = S + \theta$, the opportunity to earn this profit will be gone.

Now suppose the futures price is less than the spot price plus the cost of carry; that is,

$$f < S + \theta.$$

First, let us assume the asset is a financial instrument. Then arbitrageurs will sell short the asset and buy the futures. When the instrument is sold short, the short seller will not incur the storage costs. Instead of incurring the opportunity cost of funds tied up in the asset, the short seller can earn interest on the funds received from the short sale.

Thus, the cost of carry is not paid but received. The profit thus is $S + \theta - f$, which is positive. The combined actions of arbitrageurs will put downward pressure on the spot price and upward pressure on the futures price until the profit is eradicated. At that point, $f = S + \theta$.

Short selling may not actually be necessary for inducing the arbitrage activity. Consider an investor who holds the asset unhedged. That person could sell the asset and buy a futures contract. While the asset is not owned, the arbitrageur avoids the storage costs and earns interest on the funds received from its sale. At expiration, the arbitrageur takes delivery and again owns the asset unhedged. The profit from the trans-

action is $S + \theta - f$, which is positive. Thus, the transaction temporarily removes the asset from the investor's total assets, earns a risk-free profit, and then replaces the asset into the investor's total assets. Because many arbitrageurs will do this, it will force the spot price down and the futures price up until no further opportunities exist. This transaction is called **quasi arbitrage.**

There has been some confusion even among experts over whether futures prices reflect expectations about future spot prices. Some have said that futures prices provide expectations about future spot prices, while others have argued that futures prices reflect only the cost of carry. Still others have said that part of the time futures reveal expectations and part of the time they reveal the cost of carry. We shall more fully address the issue of whether futures prices reveal expectations in a later section; here we should note that both positions are correct. Because the futures price equals the spot price plus the cost of carry, the futures price definitely reflects the cost of carry. The spot price, however, reflects expectations. This is a fundamental tenet of spot pricing that we examined in Chapter 8. Because the futures price will include the spot price, it too reflects expectations; however, it does so indirectly through the spot price. The overall process is illustrated in Figure 9.3.

So far we have been ignoring the fact that a small margin requirement is imposed on futures traders. Suppose in the transaction involving the purchase of the asset at S and sale of the futures at f, the trader was required to deposit M dollars in a margin account. Let us assume that the M dollars will earn interest at the risk-free rate. Then at expiration the trader will have delivered the asset and received an effective price of f and have incurred the cost of carry of θ. In addition, the trader will be able to release the margin deposit of M dollars plus the interest on it. Since the total value at expiration, $f - \theta + M +$ interest on M, is known in advance, the overall transaction remains risk-free. On the front end, however, the trader put up S dollars to buy the asset and M dollars for the margin account. The present value of the total value at expiration should, therefore, equal $S + M$. Obviously the present value of M plus the interest on M equals M. This means that S must still equal $f - \theta$, giving us our **cost of carry model,** $f = S + \theta$. If, however, interest is not paid on the margin deposit, the futures price can be affected by the loss of interest on the margin account. How the futures price is affected is not clear, because the trader who does the reverse arbitrage, selling or selling short the asset and buying the futures, also faces the same margin requirement. Does it really matter? Probably not. Large traders typically are able to deposit interest-bearing securities. The price we observe is almost surely being determined by large traders. So it seems reasonable to assume that the margin deposit is irrelevant to the pricing of futures.

For storable assets, as well as for securities that do not pay interest or dividends, the cost of carry normally is positive. This would cause the

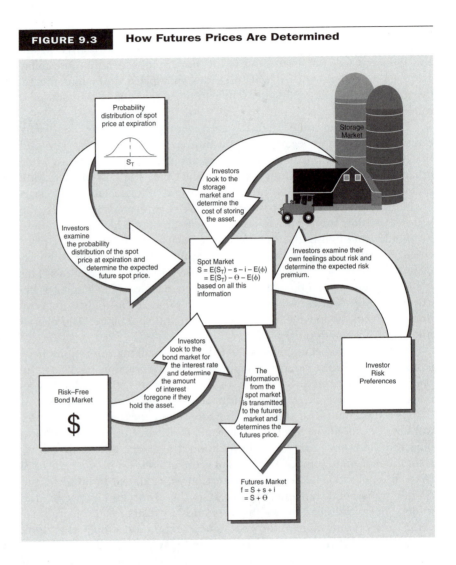

FIGURE 9.3　**How Futures Prices Are Determined**

In a contango market, the futures price exceeds the spot price.

futures price to lie above the current spot price. A market of this type is referred to as a **contango.**

Table 9.5 presents some spot and futures prices from a contango market. The example is for cotton traded on the New York Cotton Exchange. The cost of carry implied for the October contract is $41.60 - 36.75 = 4.85$. Remember that this figure includes the interest forgone on the investment of $36.75¢$ for a pound of cotton and the actual physical costs of storing the cotton from late September until the contract's expiration in October.

It would be convenient if fact always conformed to theory. If that were the case, we would never observe the spot price in excess of the futures

TABLE 9.5	A Contango Market: Cotton, September 26

Expiration	Settlement Price (Cents per Pound)
Spot	36.75
October	41.60
December	42.05
March	42.77
May	43.50
July	43.80
October	45.20
December	45.85

price. In reality, spot prices sometimes exceed futures prices. A possible explanation is the convenience yield.

THE CONVENIENCE YIELD   We are seeking an explanation for the case in which the futures price is less than the spot price. If $f = S + \theta$ and $f < S$, then $\theta < 0$. What type of market condition might produce a negative cost of carry?

Suppose the commodity is in short supply; current consumption is unusually high relative to supplies of the good. This is producing an abnormally high spot price. The current tight market conditions discourage individuals from storing the commodity. If the situation is severe enough, the current spot price could be above the expected future spot price. If the spot price is sufficiently high, the futures price may lie below it. The relationship between the futures price and the spot price is then given as

$$f = S + \theta - \chi,$$

where χ is simply a positive value that accounts for the difference between f and $S + \theta$. If χ is sufficiently large, the futures price will lie below the spot price. This need not be the case, however, since χ can be small.

The value χ often is referred to as the **convenience yield.** It is the premium earned by those who hold inventories of a commodity that is in short supply. By holding inventories of a good in short supply, one could earn an additional return, the convenience yield. Note that we are not saying that the commodity is stored for future sale or consumption. Indeed, when the spot price is sufficiently high, the return from storage is negative. There is no incentive to store the good. In fact, there is an incentive to borrow as much of the good as possible and sell short.

For some assets a convenience yield can be viewed as a type of non-pecuniary return. For example, consider a person who owns a house, which usually offers some potential for price appreciation but the expected gain

The convenience yield is the additional return earned by holding a commodity in short supply or a non-pecuniary gain from an asset.

is rarely sufficient to compensate for the risk involved. In some cases, the expected gain may be no more or even less than the risk-free rate. The house, however, provides a non-pecuniary yield, which is the utility from living in the house. The buyer of the house is normally willing to pay more, thereby reducing the expected return, for the right to live in the house.

When the commodity has a convenience yield, the futures price may be less than the spot price plus the cost of carry. In that case, the futures is said to be at **less than full carry.**

A market in which the futures price lies below the current spot price is referred to as **backwardation** or sometimes an **inverted market.** An example of a backwardation market is presented in Table 9.6. Notice how the October futures price is lower than the spot price. In fact 9 out of 10 futures prices are lower than the spot price. If a commodities dealer bought the soybean meal on September 10 at 198.10 and sold a futures contract expiring in October at 195, it would be guaranteeing a loss of 3.10 over a period of about one month. Soybeans are harvested in the months of September to October. Meal is produced as a residual after soybean oil is extracted from the raw soybeans. At this point in time, the supply of soybeans is undoubtedly somewhat low since it is just before the harvest. Buying the soybean meal, storing it, and bringing it to the market at a time when the harvest will bring a large supply onto the market is not an economically attractive thing to do. The spot price is high, however, because at least for a few weeks, soybean meal is in short supply. Thus, someone who holds soybeans, knowing that its price is likely to fall, would be doing so to avoid the costs of not having the commodity on hand when customers want it.

In a backwardation market, the spot price exceeds the futures price.

TABLE 9.6	A Backwardation Market: Soybean Meal, September 10
Expiration	**Price ($ per ton)**
Spot	198.10
October	195.00
December	194.30
January	194.60
March	196.10
May	196.80
July	198.70
August	198.00
September	197.50
October	198.00
December	197.00

It is not uncommon to see characteristics of both backwardation and contango in a market at the same time. For example, suppose the commodities dealer went long the January contract and short the March contract. The dealer would be committing to buying the soybean meal at 194.60 and selling it for 196.10. This would imply a contango market with a cost of carry from January to March of 1.50. Note as you go down the list of futures prices, you see some that are higher than the previous one and some that are lower. This occurs because the futures market reflects expectations as well as the cost of carry. It does so because any futures contract is priced off of the spot price and the cost of carry. The former will always reflect the expected future spot price, which will be influenced by what people feel about the likely success of the next harvest. In some cases the expectations effect will dominate the cost of carry effect.

Another factor that can produce backwardation in commodity markets is the inability to sell the commodity short and the reluctance on the part of holders of the commodity to sell it when its price is higher than it should be and replace it with an underpriced long futures contract. In the previous section we referred to this as quasi arbitrage. If quasi arbitrage is not executed in sufficient volume to bring the futures price to its theoretical fair price, then we could see backwardation. The spot price becomes too high and there is no one willing to sell the asset and replace it with a futures or no one able to sell short the asset.

Of course for financial assets, the cost of storage is negligible, and supply of the commodity is fairly constant. Yet we still often observe an inverted market. For interest-sensitive assets like Treasury bills and bonds, either backwardation or contango can be observed depending on which of the three explanations of the term structure that we discussed in Chapter 8 holds. Later in this chapter we shall look at some other reasons why financial futures prices can be below spot prices.

With these concepts in mind, we now turn to an important and highly controversial issue in futures markets: Do futures prices contain a risk premium?

Futures Prices and Risk Premia

We already discussed the concept of a risk premium in spot prices. No one would hold the spot commodity unless a risk premium were expected. Although investors do not always earn a risk premium, they must do so on average. Is there a risk premium in futures prices? Are speculators in futures contracts rewarded, on average, with a risk premium? There are two schools of thought on the subject.

THE NO RISK PREMIUM HYPOTHESIS   Consider a simple futures market in which there are only speculators. The underlying commodity is the total

number of points scored by all National Football League teams in a given week. Each contract trades every day for a week. On Tuesday morning, the contracts are cash settled. During the week, individuals can buy or sell contracts at whatever price they agree on.

For example, suppose two individuals make a contract at a price of 420. If the total number of points is above 420 at expiration, the trader holding the short position pays the holder of the long position a sum equal to the total number of points minus 420. Because no one can "hold" the commodity, there is no hedging or arbitrage.

Now suppose that after a period of several weeks, it is obvious that the longs are consistently beating the shorts. The shorts conclude that it is a very good year for the offense. Determined to improve their lot, those individuals who have been going short begin to go long. Of course, those who have been going long have no desire to go short. Now everyone wants to go long, and no one will go short. This drives up the futures price to a level at which someone finds it so high that it looks good to go short. Now suppose the price has been driven up so high that the opposite occurs: The shorts begin to consistently beat the longs. This causes the longs to turn around and go short. Ultimately an equilibrium must be reached in which neither the longs nor the shorts consistently beat the other side. In such a market, there is no risk premium. Neither side wins at the expense of the other.

In futures markets, this argument means that on average the futures price today equals the expected price of the futures contract at expiration; that is, $f = E(f_T)$. Because the expected futures price at expiration equals the expected spot price at expiration, $E(f_T) = E(S_T)$, we obtain the following result:

$$f = E(S_T).$$

If the futures price does not contain a risk premium, then speculators are not rewarded for taking on risk. Futures prices will then be unbiased expectations of future spot prices.

This is an extremely important and powerful statement. It says that *the futures price is the market's expectation of the future spot price.* If one wishes to obtain a forecast of the future spot price, one need only observe the futures price. In the language of economists, *futures prices are unbiased expectations of future spot prices.*

As an example, on September 26 of a particular year the spot price of silver was $5.58 per troy ounce. The December futures price was $5.64 per troy ounce. If futures prices contain no risk premium, the market is forecasting that the spot price of silver in December will be $5.64. Futures traders who buy the contract at $5.64 expect to sell it at $5.64.

Figure 9.4 illustrates a situation that is reasonably consistent with this view. The May wheat futures contract is shown along with the spot price for a period of 20 weeks prior to expiration. Both prices fluctuate, and the

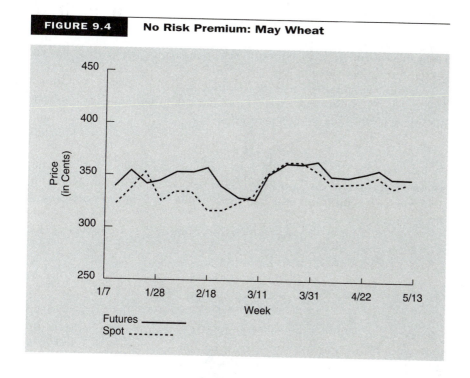

FIGURE 9.4   **No Risk Premium: May Wheat**

Futures ——————
Spot - - - - - - - -

spot price exhibits a small risk premium as suggested by the slight upward trend.[5] The futures price, however, follows no apparent trend.

We must caution, of course, that this is just an isolated case. The question of whether futures prices contain a risk premium must be answered by empirical studies. First, however, let us turn to the arguments supporting the view that futures prices do contain a risk premium.

THE RISK PREMIUM HYPOTHESIS   If a risk premium were observed, we would see that

$$E(f_T) > f.$$

The futures price would be expected to increase. Buyers of futures contracts at price f would expect to sell them at $E(f_T)$. Since futures and spot prices should converge at expiration, $E(f_T) = E(S_T)$,

---

[5]The upward drift could also be due to the risk-free rate or possibly the storage costs.

$$E(f_T) = E(S_T) > f.$$

From this we conclude that the futures price is a low estimate of the expected future spot price.

Consider a contango market in which the cost of carry is positive. Holders of the commodity expect to earn a risk premium, $E(\phi)$, given by the following formula from Chapter 8:

$$E(S_T) = S + \theta + E(\phi),$$

where θ is the cost of carry and $E(\phi)$ is the risk premium. Because $f = S + \theta$, then $S = f - \theta$. Substituting for S in the formula for $E(S_T)$, we get

$$E(S_T) = f - \theta + \theta + E(\phi),$$

or simply,

$$E(S_T) = f + E(\phi) = E(f_T).$$

The expected futures price at expiration is higher than the current futures price by the amount of the risk premium. This means that buyers of futures contracts expect to earn a risk premium. However, they do not earn a risk premium because the futures contract is risky. They earn the risk premium that existed in the spot market; it was merely transferred to the futures market.

Now consider the silver example in the previous section. The spot price is $5.58, and the December futures price is $5.64. The interest lost on $5.58 for two months is about $.05. Let us assume that the cost of storing silver for two months is $.01. Let us also suppose that buyers of silver expect to earn a $.02 risk premium. Thus, the variables are

$$S = 5.58$$
$$f = 5.64$$
$$\theta = .05 + .01 = .06$$
$$E(\phi) = .02.$$

The expected spot price of silver in December is

$$E(S_T) = S + \theta + E(\phi) = 5.58 + .06 + .02 = 5.66.$$

Because the expected spot price of silver in December equals the expected futures price in December, $E(f_T) = 5.66$. This can also be found as

$$E(f_T) = f + E(\phi) = 5.64 + .02 = 5.66.$$

Futures traders who buy the contract at 5.64 expect to sell it at 5.66 and earn a risk premium of .02. The futures price of 5.64 is an understatement of the expected spot price in December by the amount of the risk premium.

The process is illustrated as follow:

Spot:	Buy silver $5.58	Store and incur costs + $0.06	Expected risk premium + $0.02	Expected selling price = $5.66
Futures:	Buy silver futures $5.64		Expected risk premium + $0.02	Expected selling price = $5.66

The idea that futures prices contain a risk premium was proposed by two famous economists, Keynes (1930) and Hicks (1939). They argued that futures and spot markets are dominated by individuals who hold long positions in the underlying commodities. These individuals desire the protection afforded by selling futures contracts. That means they need traders who are willing to take long positions in futures. To induce speculators to take long positions in futures, the futures price must be below the expected price of the contract at expiration, which is the expected future spot price. Therefore, Keynes and Hicks argued, *futures prices are biased expectations of future spot prices,* with the bias attributable to the risk premium. The risk premium in futures prices exists only because it is transferred from the spot market.

If the futures price contains a risk premium, then speculators are rewarded for taking on risk. Futures prices will then be biased expectations of future spot prices.

An example of such a case is shown in Figure 9.5, which illustrates a June S&P 500 futures contract. Both the spot and futures prices exhibit an upward trend.[6] Again, however, we must caution that this is only an isolated case.

How can we explain the existence of a risk premium when we argued earlier that neither longs nor shorts would consistently win at the expense of the other side? The major difference in the two examples is the nature of the spot market. In the first example, in which the futures contract was on the point total of NFL teams, there was no opportunity to take a "position" in the spot market. In fact, there was no spot market; futures traders were simply competing with one another in a pure gambling situation. When we allow for a spot market, we introduce individuals who hold speculative long positions in commodities. If the positions are unhedged, these individuals expect to earn a risk premium. If they are unwilling to accept the risk, they sell futures contracts. They are, in effect, purchasing insurance

---

[6]Again the upward drift in the spot price could be due to the risk-free rate.

FIGURE 9.5   **The Spot Rate—Forward Rate Structure**

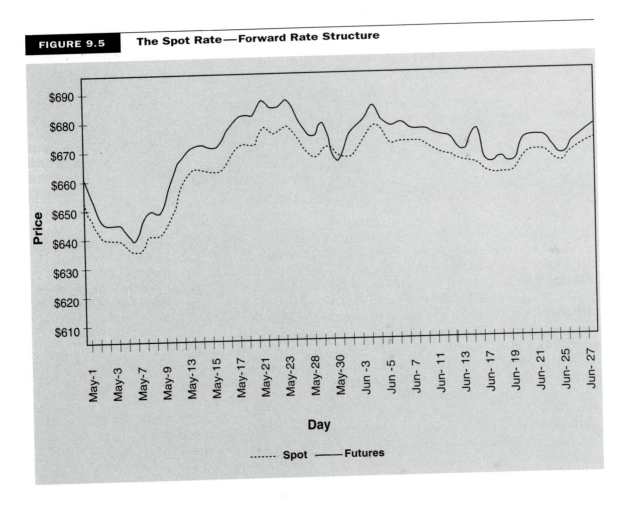

from the futures traders, and in so doing they transfer the risk and the risk premium to the futures markets.

   This explanation is useful in seeing why futures markets should not be viewed as a form of legalized gambling. There are probably no greater risk takers in our society than farmers. They risk nearly all of their wealth on the output of their farms, which are subject to the uncertainties of weather, government interference, and foreign competition, not to mention the normal fluctuations of supply and demand. Farmers can lay off some or all of that risk by hedging in the futures markets. In so doing, they transfer the risk to parties willing to bear it. Yet no one would call farming legalized gambling. Nor would anyone criticize pension fund portfolio managers for gambling. Futures markets, and indeed all derivative markets, serve a purpose in facilitating risk transfer from parties not wanting it to parties willing to take it—for a price.

What about situations in which the hedgers buy futures? This would occur if hedgers were predominantly short the commodity. This would drive up futures prices, and futures prices would, on average, exhibit a downward trend as contracts approached expiration. Futures prices would overestimate future spot prices. Speculators who sold futures would earn a risk premium.

A market in which the futures price is below the expected future spot price is called **normal backwardation,** and one in which the futures price is above the expected future spot price is called **normal contango.** The choice of names for these markets is a bit confusing, and they must be distinguished from simply contango and backwardation.

$$\text{Contango: } S < f$$
$$\text{Backwardation: } f < S$$
$$\text{Normal contango: } E(S_T) < f$$
$$\text{Normal backwardation: } f < E(S_T)$$

Because the spot price can lie below the futures price, which in turn can lie below the expected future spot price, we can have contango and normal backwardation simultaneously; indeed, this is the more typical occurrence. We can also have backwardation and normal contango simultaneously, although this is less likely.

Which view on the existence of a risk premium is correct? Since there is almost certainly a risk premium in spot prices, the existence of hedgers who hold spot positions means that the risk premium is transferred to futures traders. Thus, there would seem to be a risk premium in futures prices. However, if there are not enough spot positions being hedged or if most hedging is being done by investors who are short in the spot market, there may be no observable risk premium in futures prices. Empirical studies have given us no clear-cut answer and suggest that the issue is still unresolved.

The Effect of Intermediate Cash Flows

Until now we have avoided any consideration of how intermediate cash flows, such as interest and dividends, affect the futures price. We did note in Chapter 8 that these cash payments would have an effect on the cost of carry, possibly making it negative. Now we shall look more closely at how they affect futures prices.

The contracts in which these factors apply are stock index and bond futures. We shall concentrate on stock index futures, although the general principles are the same in both cases.

For simplicity, assume there is only one stock in the index, which pays a sure dividend of D_T on the expiration date. Now suppose an investor buys the stock at a spot price of S and sells a futures contract at a price of f.

At expiration, the stock is sold at S_T, the dividend D_T is collected, and the futures contract generates a cash flow of $-(f_T - f)$, which equals $-(S_T - f)$. Thus, the total cash flow at expiration is $D_T + f$. This amount is known in advance; therefore, the current value of the portfolio must equal the present value of $D_T + f$. The current portfolio value is simply the amount paid for the stock, S. Putting these results together gives

$$S = (f + D_T)(1 + r)^{-T}$$

or

$$f = S(1 + r)^T - D_T.$$

Here we see that the futures price is the spot price compounded at the risk-free rate minus the dividend. A sufficiently large dividend could obviously bring the futures price down below the spot price.

To take our model one step closer to reality, let us assume the stock pays several dividends. In fact, our stock could actually be a portfolio of stocks that is identical to an index such as the S&P 500. Suppose N dividends will be paid during the life of the futures. Each dividend is denoted as D_j and is paid t_j years from today. Now suppose we buy the stock and sell the futures. During the life of the futures, we collect each dividend and reinvest it in risk-free bonds earning the rate r. Thus, dividend D_1 will grow to a value of $D_1(1 + r)^{T - t_1}$ at expiration. By the expiration day, the dividends will have grown to a value of

$$\sum_{j=1}^{N} D_j(1 + r)^{T - t_j},$$

which we shall write compactly as D_T. Thus, now we let D_T be the accumulated value at T of all dividends over the life of the futures plus the interest earned on them. In the previous example, we had only one dividend but D_T was still the same concept, the accumulated future value of the dividends. At expiration the stock is sold for S_T, and the futures is settled and generates a cash flow of $-(f_T - f)$, which equals $-(S_T - f)$. Thus, the total cash flow at expiration is

$$S_T - (S_T - f) + D_T$$

or

$$f + D_T.$$

This amount is also known in advance, so its present value, discounted at the risk-free rate, must equal the current value of the portfolio, which is the value of the stock, S. Setting these terms equal and solving for f gives

$$f = S(1 + r)^T - D_T.$$

Thus, the futures price is the spot price compounded at the risk-free rate minus the compound future value of the dividends. The entire process of buying the stock, selling a futures, collecting and reinvesting dividends to produce a risk-free transaction is illustrated in Figure 9.6 for a stock that pays two dividends during the life of the futures. The total value accumulated at expiration is set equal to the total value today.

It might appear that our futures pricing model is inconsistent with the cost of carry equation we previously developed, in which $f = S + \theta$. We can show, however, that the formulas are identical and that the cost of carry will reflect the interest minus any offsetting dividends. Suppose we add and subtract S on the right-hand side of the above equation:

$$f = S + S(1 + r)^T - S - D_T.$$

Then rearranging terms gives

$$f = S + \{S[(1 + r)^T - 1] - D_T\}.$$

The term in braces is θ, the cost of carry. Within the braces, the first term, $S[(1 + r)^T - 1]$, is the interest forgone on an investment of S dollars for a

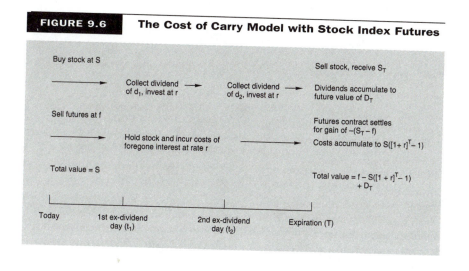

FIGURE 9.6   The Cost of Carry Model with Stock Index Futures

Buy stock at S

Collect dividend of d_1, invest at r → Collect dividend of d_2, invest at r → Sell stock, receive S_T

Dividends accumulate to future value of D_T

Sell futures at f

Hold stock and incur costs of foregone interest at rate r

Futures contract settles for gain of $-(S_T - f)$

Costs accumulate to $S([1 + r]^T - 1)$

Total value = S

Total value = $f - S([1 + r]^T - 1) + D_T$

Today   1st ex-dividend day (t_1)   2nd ex-dividend day (t_2)   Expiration (T)

period of T years. The second term represents the compound future value of the dividends earned. Thus, the entire term added to S is the cost of carry.

A stock index is a weighted combination of securities, most of which pay dividends. In reality, the dividend flow is more or less continuous, although not of a constant amount. However, as we did with options, we can fairly safely assume a continuous flow of dividends at a constant yield, δ. Using r_c as the continuously compounded risk-free rate and S as the spot price of the index, the model is written as

$$f = Se^{(r_c - \delta)T}.$$

A stock index futures price is the stock price compounded at the risk-free rate minus the future value of the dividends. Alternatively it can be viewed as the dividend-adjusted stock price compounded at the risk-free rate.

It is worth noting that this formula is precisely what one would obtain if all of the assumptions of the Black-Scholes model were applied to futures.

This format makes an interpretation somewhat easier. Suppose an investor is considering speculating on the stock market. There are two ways to do this: buy the stock index portfolio or buy the futures contract. If the portfolio is purchased, the investor receives dividends at a rate of δ. If the futures contract is purchased, the investor receives no dividends. The dividend yield enters the model as the factor $e^{-\delta T}$, which is less than 1. Thus, the effect of dividends is to make the futures price lower than it would be without them. Note that the futures price will exceed (be less than) the spot price if the risk-free rate is higher (lower) than the dividend yield. Alternatively, the formula can be written as $f = (Se^{-\delta T})e^{r_c T}$, which is simply the dividend-adjusted stock price compounded at the risk-free rate.

The futures pricing equation for the case of continuous dividends is also consistent with our simple cost of carry equation, $f = S + \theta$. To see this, we add and subtract S to the right-hand side, giving

$$f = Se^{(r_c - \delta)T} + S - S,$$

which we can then express as

$$f = S + \{S[e^{(r_c - \delta)T} - 1]\}.$$

The term in braces on the right-hand side is the cost of carry, θ. The exponential function determines the compound future value of S growing at the rate of $r_c - \delta$. Subtracting the 1 removes the original value of S, leaving the interest minus the dividends that accumulate over the life of the futures.

A Numerical Example   Consider the following problem. A stock index is at 50, the continuously compounded risk-free rate is 8 percent, the con-

tinuously compounded dividend yield is 6 percent, and the time to expiration is 60 days, so T is $60/365 = .164$. Then the futures price is

$$f = 50e^{(.08 - .06)(.164)} = 50.16.$$

If the risk-free rate were 5 percent, the futures price would be

$$f = 50e^{(.05 - .06)(.164)} = 49.92.$$

The stock index futures pricing model is used extensively by traders and institutions to evaluate stock index futures contracts. If the futures price does not conform to the model, an opportunity to earn a riskless profit in excess of the risk-free rate is possible. Empirical research tends to support the pricing model, but we shall defer further discussion and illustration of this issue until Chapter 11. For now, let us look at how futures contracts of different expirations are related.

Prices of Futures Contracts of Different Expirations

Earlier we presented the important relationship

$$f = S + \theta,$$

which, with no dividend or interest payments or a shortage of the good, means that the futures price is above the spot price. Now consider two futures contracts on the same commodity but with different expirations. Let those two expirations be T_1 and T_2, where $T_2 > T_1$. We shall use the notation 1 and 2 to denote the respective time points. Thus,

$$f_1, f_2 = \text{futures prices}$$
$$\theta_1, \theta_2 = \text{cost of carry on each contract, respectively.}$$

Because it costs more to carry a commodity longer, the cost of carry for the contract expiring at T_2 is greater than that for the contract expiring at T_1. The futures–spot price relationships for the two contracts are

$$f_1 = S + \theta_1$$
$$f_2 = S + \theta_2.$$

Solving each of these for the spot price, S, gives

$$S = f_1 - \theta_1$$
$$S = f_2 - \theta_2.$$

We then can set these equal to each other and solve for $f_2 - f_1$:

The spread between the prices of two futures contracts is the difference in their costs of carry and represents the cost of carry over the period starting at the expiration of the nearby contract and ending at the expiration of the deferred contract.

$$f_2 - f_1 = \theta_2 - \theta_1.$$

This equation defines the spread between futures prices. The spread between the nearby and deferred contracts is the difference in their respective costs of carry. The term $\theta_2 - \theta_1$ is the cost of carry for the time interval between T_1 and T_2.

As an example, consider the following soybean oil contract. On September 26 of a particular year, the December contract was priced at 14.64 cents per pound and the January contract at 14.75 cents per pound. The difference of .11 cents per pound is the cost of carry of soybean oil from December to January.

It is helpful to examine the behavior of the spread through time. Figures 9.7 and 9.8 illustrate these relationships for June and September Eurodollar contracts. Figure 9.7 is the spread—the June futures price minus the September futures price—starting at about 60 trading days prior to the June expiration. Figure 9.8 presents the June and September futures prices and the spot price. Note that the September contract price is less than the June contract price. As the two contracts approach the June expiration, the spread narrows. This reflects the fact that the cost of carry of

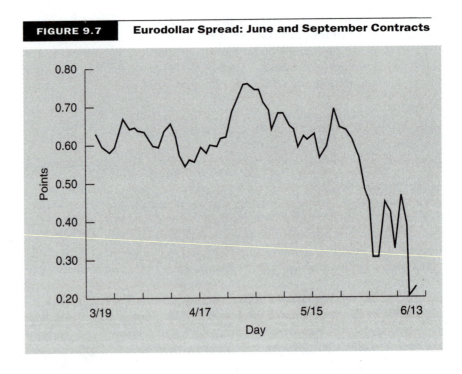

FIGURE 9.7   Eurodollar Spread: June and September Contracts

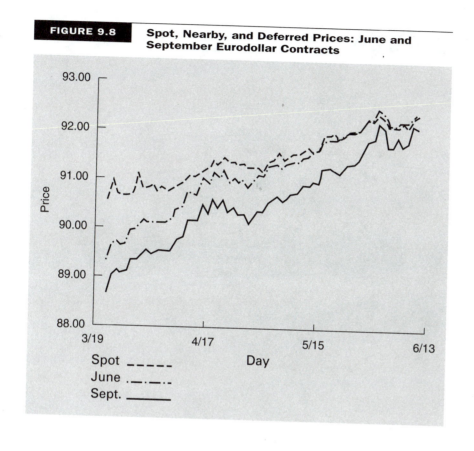

FIGURE 9.8   **Spot, Nearby, and Deferred Prices: June and September Eurodollar Contracts**

Spot _ _ _ _ _
June ._._._..
Sept. _____

the June contract is approaching zero. The June contract is beginning to behave like the spot Eurodollar. The cost of carry of the September contract also declines, but less rapidly than that of the June contract. The spread obviously does not change in a perfectly predictable manner, which is one reason spread trading is so popular among futures traders. As we shall see in Chapter 11, there are strategies to take advantage of changes in the spread.

Summary

This chapter introduced several approaches to understanding the pricing of forward and futures contracts. It developed the concept of cost of carry and examined the relationship between futures and spot prices. It also addressed the joint issues of whether futures prices are unbiased estimators of future spot prices and whether futures prices offer risk premiums to speculators. The chapter examined the relationship between forward and futures prices. We saw that if future interest rates are uncertain, forward prices need not equal futures

FIGURE 9.9	The Linkage between Forwards (or Futures), Stock, and Risk-Free Bonds

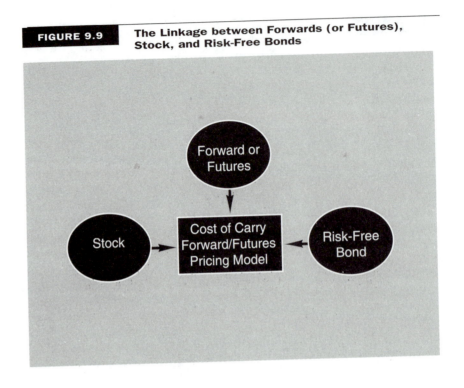

prices. We also saw that credit risk can affect the relationship between futures and forward prices.

So far in this book we have endeavored to understand the relationship between derivative prices and the prices of their underlying assets. We saw how put-call parity and the Black-Scholes model explain these relationships for options. The cost of carry model explains this relationship for forwards and futures. With our primary asset of interest being stock, Figure 9.9 illustrates this linkage.

As we move into Chapter 10, we should keep a few points in mind. We can reasonably accept the fact that forward and futures prices and spot prices are described by the cost of carry relationship. We do not know whether forward and futures prices are unbiased, but it seems logical to believe that holders of spot positions expect to earn a risk premium. When they hedge, they transfer the risk to forward and futures traders. Therefore, it is reasonable to expect forward and futures traders to demand a risk premium. Finally, although we have good reason to believe that forward prices are not precisely equal to futures prices, we see little reason to give much weight to the effect of marking to market on the performance of trading strategies. Accordingly, we shall ignore its effects in Chapter 10, which covers hedging strategies, and Chapter 11, which presents advanced strategies.

Key Terms

Before continuing to Chapter 10, you should be able to give brief definitions of the following terms.

- cost of carry model
- contango
- convenience yield
- backwardation

Questions and Problems

1. Assume there is a forward market for a commodity. The forward price of the commodity is $45. The contract expires in one year. The risk-free rate is 10 percent. Now, six months later, new forward contracts are being written at a price of $54. What is the original forward contract worth at this time? Explain why this is the correct value of the forward contract in six months by showing how the contract holder can capture that value even though the original contract does not have a liquid market like a futures contract.

2. Why is the value of a futures contract at the time it is purchased equal to zero? Contrast this with the value of the corresponding spot commodity.

3. On a particular day, the S&P 500 futures settlement price was 899.30. You buy one contract at around the close of the market at the settlement price. The next day, the contract opens at 899.70 and the settlement price at the close of the day is 899.10. Determine the value of the futures contract at the opening, an instant before the close, and after the close. Remember that the S&P futures contract has a $500 multiplier.

4. A particular stock index futures expires on March 15. On March 13, the contract is selling at 353.625. Assume that there is a forward contract that also expires on March 15. The current forward price is 353. The risk-free rate is 5 percent per year, and you can assume that this rate will remain in effect for the next two days. Answer the following questions:
    a. Identify the existence of an arbitrage opportunity. What transactions should be executed on March 13?
    b. On March 14 the futures price is 353.35, and on March 15 the futures expires at 350.125. Show that the arbitrage works.
    c. Given your answer in part b, what effect will this have on market prices?

5. Identify and explain five conditions under which forward and futures prices would be equal.

6. On June 28, the price of the September Treasury bill futures is 92.95. The spot price of 91-day Treasury bills is quoted at a discount of 7.06, while the spot price of 182-day Treasury bills is 7.24. Estimate the forward rate on 91-day Treasury bills, and compare it to the rate implied by the futures market.

7. Construct an arbitrage example involving an asset that can be sold short, and use it to explain the cost of carry model for pricing futures.

8. Comment on the following statement made by a futures trader: "Futures prices are determined by either expectations or the cost of carry."

9. If futures prices are less than spot prices, the explanation usually given is the convenience yield. Explain what the convenience yield is. Then identify certain

assets on which convenience yields are more likely to exist and other assets on which they are not likely to be found.

10. Suppose there is an asset on which you know there is no convenience yield, yet the futures price is below the spot price. Can you think of an explanation for this?

11. What is a contango market? How do we interpret the cost of carry in a contango market? What is a backwardation market? How do we explain the cost of carry in a backwardation market?

12. On September 26, the spot price of wheat was $3.5225 per bushel and the price of a December wheat futures was $3.64 per bushel. How do you interpret the futures price if there is no risk premium in the futures market?

13. Reconsider the wheat example in problem 12. The interest forgone on money tied up in a bushel until expiration is .03, and the cost of storing the wheat is .0875 per bushel. The risk premium is .035 per bushel.
    a. What is the expected price of wheat on the spot market in December?
    b. Show how the futures price is related to the spot price.
    c. Show how the expected spot price at expiration, your answer in part a, is related to the futures price today.
    d. Show how the expected futures price at expiration is related to the futures price today.
    e. Explain who earns the risk premium and why.

14. On a particular day, the September S&P 500 stock index futures was priced at 960.50. The S&P 500 index was at 956.49. The contract expires 73 days later. The risk-free rate is 5.96 percent, and the dividend yield on the index is 2.75 percent. Is the futures overpriced or underpriced?

15. How do you interpret the difference between the January frozen concentrated orange juice futures price of $1.077 per pound and the March futures price of $1.0785? The prices are as of the previous September. Explain why these values differ.

16. Suppose there is a commodity in which the expected future spot price is $60. To induce investors to buy futures contracts, a risk premium of $4 is required. To store the commodity for the life of the futures contract would cost $5.50. Find the futures price.

17. On July 10, a farmer observes that the spot price of corn is $2.735 per bushel and the September futures price is $2.76. The farmer would like a prediction of the spot price in September but believes the market is dominated by hedgers holding long positions in corn. Explain how the farmer would use this information in a forecast of the future price of corn.

18. Suppose the futures contract with the earliest expiration is priced higher than the one with the next earliest expiration. What explanation can you give for this condition?

19. The cost of carry futures pricing equation may appear slightly flawed to some people. To derive it, we equated a payoff at expiration with the initial outlay for the asset. Since these cash flows occur at different points in time, the time value of money seems to have been omitted. Explain why this interpretation is not correct.

20. (Concept Problem) Suppose there is a futures contract on a portfolio of stocks that currently are worth $100. The futures has a life of 90 days, and during that time the stocks will pay dividends of $0.75 in 30 days, $0.85 in 60 days, and $0.90 in 90 days. The simple interest rate is 12 percent.

   a. Find the price of the futures contract assuming no arbitrage opportunities are present.

   b. Find the value of θ, the cost of carry in dollars.

21. (Concept Problem) Suppose a futures margin account pays interest but at a rate that is less than the risk-free rate. Consider a trader who buys the asset and sells a futures to form a risk-free hedge. Would the trader believe the futures price should be lower or higher than if the margin account paid interest at the risk-free rate?

CHAPTER 10

Futures Hedging Strategies

I think the theoretical problems in risk management do not pose major difficulties to firms. Keep in mind that we have seen substantial volatility in the last few years and that, by and large, firms that wanted to be hedged experienced low revenue volatility.

JACOB GOLDFIELD

Controlling Risk: Risk Magazine Special Supplement, June 1995

Chapter Objectives

- To explain why firms hedge
- To present the basic concepts associated with hedging, such as the basis, short and long hedging, and the risks of hedging
- To identify the factors that are involved in deciding to undertake a hedge
- To illustrate the different methods (price sensitivity, minimum variance) of determining the number of futures contracts to use in a hedge
- To illustrate examples of short-term interest rate futures hedges, intermediate- and long-term interest rate futures hedges, and stock index futures hedges

Hedging is a transaction designed to reduce or, in some cases, eliminate risk. Our material on options presented numerous examples of hedges, the most obvious being the covered call and protective put. Now we shall find that it is also possible, in some cases preferable, to use forwards or futures to hedge.

Until now we have emphasized that there are many similarities and differences between forward and futures contracts. Both can be used for hedging. When choosing a forward or futures hedge over an option hedge, the hedger agrees to give up future gains and losses. No up-front cost is incurred. In contrast, an option hedge such as a protective put preserves future gains but at the expense of an up-front cost, the option premium. Forward contracting, as we previously noted, involves some credit risk and is generally available only in very large transaction sizes. We shall eventually study a number of types of forward hedges, but we defer that discussion until a later chapter, after which we have introduced swaps, a more popular type of forward hedge. In this chapter our focus is on the use of futures in hedging.

Why Hedge?

Before we begin with the technical aspects of hedging, it is worthwhile to ask two questions: (1) why do firms hedge? and (2) should they hedge?

Hedging is done to reduce risk, but is this desirable? If everyone hedged, would we not simply end up with an economy in which no one takes risks? This would surely lead to economic stagnancy. Moreover, we must wonder whether hedging can actually increase shareholder wealth.[1]

If the famous Modigliani-Miller propositions are correct, then the value of the firm is independent of any financial decisions, which include hedging. Hedging, however, may be desired by the shareholders simply to find a more acceptable combination of return and risk. It can be argued, however, that firms need not hedge since shareholders, if they wanted hedging, could do it themselves. But this ignores several important points. It assumes that shareholders can correctly assess all the firm's hedgeable risks. If a company is exposed to the risk associated with volatile raw materials prices, can the shareholders properly determine the degree of risk? Can they determine the periods over which that risk is greatest? Can they determine the correct number of futures contracts necessary to hedge their share of the total risk? Do they even qualify to open a futures brokerage account? Will their transaction costs be equal to or less than their proportional share of the transaction costs incurred if the firm did the hedging? The answer to each of these questions is "maybe not." It should be obvious that hedging is not something that shareholders can always do as effectively as firms.

In addition, there may be other reasons why firms hedge, such as tax advantages. Low-income firms, for example those that are below the highest corporate tax rate, can particularly benefit from the interaction between hedging and the progressive corporate income tax structure. Hedging also reduces the probability of bankruptcy. This is not necessarily valuable to the shareholders except that it can reduce the expected costs that are incurred if the firm does go bankrupt. Finally, a firm may choose to hedge because its managers' livelihoods may be heavily tied to the performance of the firm. The managers may then benefit from reducing the firm's risk. This may not be in the shareholders' best interests, but it can at least explain why some firms hedge. Finally, hedging may send a signal to potential creditors that the firm is making a concerted effort to protect the value of the underlying assets. This can result in more favorable credit terms and less costly, restrictive covenants.

Many firms, such as financial institutions, are constantly trading over-the-counter financial products like swaps and forwards on behalf of their

---

[1]The material in this section draws heavily from C. W. Smith and R. M. Stulz, "The Determinants of Firms' Hedging Policies," *Journal of Financial and Quantitative Analysis* 20 (1985): 391–405; D. Duffie, "Corporate Risk Management 101: Why Hedge?" *Corporate Risk Management* 3 (May 1991): 22–25; and D. R. Nance, C. W. Smith Jr., and C. W. Smithson, "On the Determinants of Corporate Hedging," *The Journal of Finance* 48 (March 1993): 267–284.

Firms hedge to save taxes, reduce bankruptcy costs, and, in some cases, because managers want to reduce the risk of their own wealth, which is tied to their firms' performance. Hedging is also done in the course of offering risk management services for clients and possibly because shareholders cannot hedge as effectively as firms.

A short hedge means to hedge by going short in the futures market. A long hedge means to hedge by going long in the futures market.

clients. They offer these services to help their clients manage their risks. These financial institutions then turn around and hedge the risk they have assumed on behalf of their clients. How do they make money? They quote rates and prices to their clients that reflect a spread sufficient to cover their hedging costs and include a profit. In this manner, they become retailers of hedging services.

So we see that there are many reasons why firms hedge. Now let us look at some important hedging concepts.

Hedging Concepts

Before we can understand why a certain hedge is placed or how it works, we must become acquainted with a few basic hedging concepts. We have mentioned some of these points before but have not specifically applied them to hedging strategies.

Short Hedge and Long Hedge

The terms **short hedge** and **long hedge** distinguish hedges that involve short and long positions in the futures contract, respectively. A hedger who holds the commodity and is concerned about a decrease in its price might consider hedging it with a short position in futures. If the spot price and futures price move together, the hedge will reduce some of the risk. For example, if the spot price decreases, the futures price also will decrease. Since the hedger is short the futures contract, the futures transaction produces a profit that at least partially offsets the loss on the spot position. This is called a *short hedge* because the hedger is short futures.

Another type of short hedge can be used in anticipation of the future sale of an asset. An example of this occurs when a firm decides that it will need to borrow money at a later date. Borrowing money is equivalent to issuing or selling a bond or promissory note. If interest rates increase before the money is borrowed, the loan will be more expensive. A similar risk exists if a firm has issued a floating rate liability. Since the rate is periodically reset, the firm has contracted for a series of future loans at unknown rates. To hedge this risk, the firm might short an interest rate futures contract. If rates increase, the futures transaction will generate a profit that will at least partially offset the higher interest rate on the loan. Because it is taken out in anticipation of a future transaction in the spot market, this type of hedge is known as an **anticipatory hedge.**

Another type of anticipatory hedge involves an individual who plans to purchase a commodity at a later date. Fearing an increase in the commodity's price, the investor might buy a futures contract. Then, if the price of the commodity increases, the futures price also will increase and

produce a profit on the futures position. That profit will at least partially offset the higher cost of purchasing the commodity. This is a *long hedge*, because the hedger is long in the futures market.

Another type of long hedge might be placed when one is short an asset. Although this hedge is less common, it would be appropriate for someone who has sold short a stock and is concerned that the market will go up. Rather than close out the short position, one might buy a futures and earn a profit on the long position in futures that will at least partially offset the loss on the short position in the stock.

In each of these cases, the hedger held a position in the spot market that was subject to risk. The futures transaction served as a temporary substitute for a spot transaction. Thus, when one holds the spot commodity and is concerned about a price decrease but does not want to sell it, one can execute a short futures trade. Selling the futures contract would substitute for selling the commodity. Table 10.1 summarizes these various hedging situations.

The Basis

The **basis** is one of the most important concepts in futures markets. The basis usually is defined as the spot price minus the futures price. However, some books and articles define it as the futures price minus the spot price. In this book, we shall use the former definition:

$$\text{Basis} = \text{Spot price} - \text{Futures price.}$$

The basis is the difference between the spot price and the futures price.

HEDGING AND THE BASIS   The basis plays an important role in understanding the process of hedging. Here we will look at the concept of hedging and how the basis affects the performance of a hedge. Ultimately we shall need to understand the factors that influence the basis.

TABLE 10.1   Summary of Hedging Situations

Condition Today	Risk	Appropriate Hedge
Hold asset	Asset price may fall	Short hedge
Plan to buy asset	Asset price may rise	Long hedge
Sold short asset	Asset price may rise	Long hedge
Issued floating-rate liability	Interest rates may rise	Short hedge
Plan to issue liability	Interest rates may rise	Short hedge

Note: Short hedge means long spot, short futures; long hedge means short spot, long futures.

Derivatives in Action

Hedging: It's the Law

There are many good reasons for hedging and occasionally good reasons for not hedging. Rarely does a firm have to worry about whether failing to hedge is breaking the law. In Indiana, it just might be. Take the case of *Brane v. Roth* (590 NE 2nd, 587).

Farmers Cooperative is a grain elevator co-op engaged in the business of buying, storing, and selling grain. The co-op's profits had been declining steadily over the period of 1977–1979. In 1979 its accountant recommended to its board of directors that the co-op begin hedging in the futures market. The board did authorize the co-op's manager to begin hedging, but a total of only about $20,000 of grain was hedged, during a period in which its grain sales were over $7 million. The co-op experienced substantial operating losses. Shareholders determined that a hedge would have saved them significant amounts of money and sued the board of directors. The plaintiffs argued that the board breached its duty by using a manager inexperienced in hedging and by failing to supervise the manager. The plaintiffs also argued that the board members failed to learn enough about hedging to protect the shareholders' interests. The Superior Court of Miami County, Indiana, agreed and ordered the directors to pay over $400,000 to the plaintiffs. The case was appealed to the

Let us define the following terms:

T = time to expiration
t = a time point prior to expiration
S = spot price today
f = futures price today
S_T = spot price at expiration
f_T = futures price at expiration
S_t = spot price at time t prior to expiration
f_t = futures price at time t prior to expiration
Π = profit from the strategy

For the time being, we shall ignore marking to market, any costs of storing the asset, and other transaction costs.

The concept of a hedge is not new. When we looked at options, we constructed several types of hedges, some of which were riskless. By taking a position in a stock and an opposite position in an option, gains (losses) on the stock are offset by losses (gains) on the option. We can do the same thing with futures: hold a long (short) position in the spot market and a short (long) position in the futures market. For a long position in the spot market, the profit from a hedge held to expiration is

$$\Pi \text{ (short hedge)} = S_T - S \text{ (from the spot market)} - (f_T - f)$$
$$\text{(from the futures market)}.$$

For a short position in the spot market and a long position in the futures market, the sign of each term in the above equation is reversed; that is,

Indiana Court of Appeals, which upheld the judgment in April 1992. The Appeals court stated that the losses were caused by a failure to hedge and that the directors had made no effort to learn about hedging.

Of course, after the fact it is always easy to say that losses could have been avoided had hedging been done. Consider the counterargument, however. Suppose the co-op had made money before accounting for any hedging activities. Now suppose it had been fully hedged. Then it would have made little if any money. Could the shareholders then have sued it for hedging? It seems that where the directors erred was in failing to be properly informed about the advan-

tages and disadvantages of hedging while authorizing, but not supervising, a modest hedging program. Had they made the effort to learn about the futures market, they might well have easily justified the small hedging program as experimental, with an eye toward gathering more information about the costs and benefits of hedging before launching into a more comprehensive hedging program.

Is failing to hedge illegal in general? Probably not, at least not yet. But it is clear that boards of directors, and probably management, are vulnerable to the charge that they failed to learn how derivative markets can help them run a business.

$$\Pi \text{ (long hedge)} = -S_T + S \text{ (from the spot market)} + (f_T - f)$$
$$\text{(from the futures market)}.$$

In some cases, we might wish to close out the position at time t, that is, before expiration. Then the profit from the hedge that is long in the spot market is

$$\Pi \text{ (short hedge)} = S_t - S - (f_t - f).$$

At expiration, a person buying a futures contract can expect to receive immediate delivery of the good. Thus, an expiring futures contract is the same as the purchase of the spot commodity; therefore, $S_T = f_T$. Thus, the profit if the hedge is held to expiration is simply $f - S$. That means that the hedge is equivalent to buying the asset at price S and immediately guaranteeing a sale price of f.

As an example, suppose you buy an asset for $100 and sell a futures contract on the asset at $103. At expiration, the spot and futures prices are both $97. You sell the asset for $97, taking a $3 loss, and close your futures contract at $97, making a $6 gain, for a net profit of $3. Alternatively, you could deliver the asset on your futures contract, receiving $97, and collect the $6 that has accumulated in your futures account, making the effective sale price of the asset $103. In either case, the transaction is equivalent to selling the asset for $103, the original futures price.

Since the basis is defined as the spot price minus the futures price, we can write it as a variable, b, where

$$b = S - f \text{ (initial basis)}$$
$$b_t = S_t - f_t \text{ (basis at time t)}$$
$$b_T = S_T - f_T \text{ (basis at expiration)}.$$

Thus, for a position closed out at time t,

$$\Pi \text{ (short hedge)} = S_t - f_t - (S - f),$$
$$= b_t - b.$$

Hedging entails the assumption of basis risk, the uncertainty of the basis over the hedge period. The hedge profit is the change in the basis.

The profit from the hedge is simply the change in the basis. The uncertainty regarding how the basis will change is called **basis risk.** A hedge substitutes the change in the basis for the change in the spot price. The basis change is far less variable than the spot price change; hence, the hedged position is less risky than the unhedged position. Because basis risk results from the uncertainty over the change in the basis, hedging is a speculative activity but produces a risk level much lower than that of an unhedged position.

Hedging can also be viewed as a transaction that attempts to establish the expected future sale price of an asset (or purchase price, if a long hedge). For example, the equation for the profit on a short hedge can be written as $f + (S_t - f_t) - S$. Since the hedger paid S dollars to purchase the asset, then the effective sale price of the asset can be viewed as $f + (S_t - f_t)$, which can be written as $f + b_t$. In other words, a short hedge establishes the future sale price of the asset as the current futures price plus the basis. Since f is known, the effective future sale price is uncertain only to the extent that the basis is uncertain. If the hedge is held to expiration, the effective sale price becomes $f + b_T$, which is simply f since the basis at expiration is zero. Thus, the sale price of the asset is established as f when the transaction is initiated. The hedger would be absolutely certain that he or she would be able to effectively sell the asset for the futures price. This is called a perfect hedge. Most hedges are imperfect for a variety of reasons but often because the hedger does not typically hold the position to expiration.

If the spot price increases by more than the futures price, the basis will increase. This is said to be a strengthening basis, and it improves the performance of the short hedge. If the futures price increases by more than the spot price, the basis will decrease, reducing the performance on the hedge. In that case, the basis is said to be weakening.

For a long hedger, however, everything is reversed. The profit equation is $-(S_t - S) + (f_t - f) = -b_t + b$. Now a weakening basis improves the performance and a strengthening basis reduces the performance. These relationships between hedging profitability and the basis are summarized in Table 10.2.

As noted above, if a hedge is held all the way to expiration, the basis goes to zero. In that case, the profit is simply $-b$ from a short hedge and $+b$ from a long hedge.

TABLE 10.2	Hedging Profitability and the Basis	
Type of Hedge	**Benefits from**	**Which Occurs if**
Short hedge	Strengthening basis	Spot price rises more than futures price rises
		or
		Spot price falls less than futures price falls
		or
		Spot price rises and futures price falls
Long hedge	Weakening basis	Spot price rises less than futures price rises
		or
		Spot price falls more than futures price falls
		or
		Spot price falls and futures price rises

Note: Short hedge means long spot, short futures; long hedge means short spot, long futures.

Finally, we should remember that hedging incurs costs, such as the transaction costs of the futures. In addition, if the asset is held, it will incur costs of storage. These will reduce the profit but their effects are generally known in advance and, thus, do not impose any additional risk.

A HEDGING EXAMPLE   Let us consider an example using gold. On March 30, the price of a gold futures expiring in June was $388.60 per troy ounce. The spot price of gold was $387.15. Suppose a gold dealer held 100 troy ounces of gold worth $100(387.15) - 38,715$. To protect against a decrease in the price of gold, the dealer might sell one futures contract on 100 troy ounces. In our notation,

$$S = 387.15$$
$$f = 388.60$$
$$b = 387.15 - 388.60 = -1.45.$$

If the hedge is held to expiration, the basis should converge to zero. However, it might not go precisely to zero, and we shall see why later. If it does, the profit should be −1 times the original basis times the number of ounces:

$$\Pi = -1(-1.45)(100) = 145.$$

Suppose that at expiration the spot price of gold is $408.50. Then the dealer sells the gold in the spot market for a profit of $100(408.50 - 387.15) = 2,135$. The short futures contract is offset by purchasing it in the futures market for a profit of $-100(408.50 - 388.60) = -1,990$. The overall profit therefore is $-1,990 + 2,135 = 145$, as we predicted.

Now suppose we close the position prior to expiration. For example, on May 5 the spot price of gold was $377.52 and the June futures price was $378.63. In our notation, $S_t = 377.52$ and $f_t = 378.63$. If the gold is sold in the spot market, the profit is $100(377.52 - 387.15) = -963$. The futures contract is bought back at 378.63 for a profit of $-100(378.63 - 388.60) = 997$. The net gain is $-963 + 997 = 34$. As we said earlier, this should equal the change in the basis, $b_t - b$. The original basis was -1.45. The basis when the position is closed is $S_t - f_t$, or $377.52 - 378.63 = -1.11$. The profit therefore is

$$-1.11 - (-1.45) = .34,$$

which is the gain on the hedge per ounce of gold.

THE BEHAVIOR OF THE BASIS   Figure 10.1 shows the basis on a June Eurodollar contract for a period of 60 days prior to expiration. Notice how

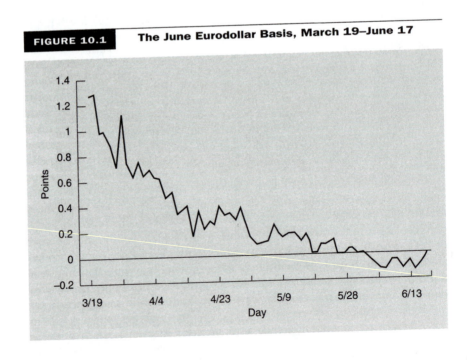

FIGURE 10.1   **The June Eurodollar Basis, March 19–June 17**

the basis starts off at about 1.3 and then gradually decreases as expiration nears. At around two weeks before expiration, the basis actually becomes negative. Because the Eurodollar contract is settled in cash, the basis on the expiration day automatically is zero.

In some cases, however, the basis does not converge exactly to zero. In the case of gold, for example, an investor who purchased gold on the spot market and immediately sold a futures contract that is about to expire would have to deliver the gold. There is a potentially significant delivery cost that could leave the futures price slightly above the spot price. For some commodities, there are several acceptable grades that can be delivered, so there are multiple spot prices. The short has control over the delivery and will choose to deliver the most economical grade. The futures price will tend to converge to the spot price of the commodity that is most likely to be delivered.

Some Risks of Hedging

Sometimes the commodity being hedged and the commodity underlying the futures contract differ. A typical example, which we shall illustrate later, is the hedging of a corporate bond with a Treasury bond futures contract. This is referred to as a **cross hedge** and is a type of basis risk much greater than that encountered by hedging government bonds with Treasury bond futures. Corporate and government bond prices tend to move together, but the relationship is weaker than that of two government bonds. In addition, bonds with higher ratings would be more highly correlated with government bonds. Thus, lower-quality corporate bonds would carry some additional basis risk, and hedges would tend to be less effective.

Cross hedging involves an additional source of basis risk arising from the fact that the asset being hedged is not the same as the asset underlying the futures.

In some cases, the price of the commodity being hedged and that of the futures contract move in opposite directions. Then a hedge will produce either a profit or a loss on both the spot and the futures positions. If one chooses the correct futures contract, this is unlikely to occur. If it occurs frequently, the hedger should find a different contract.

Hedging also entails another form of risk called **quantity risk.** As an example, suppose a farmer wishes to lock in the price at which an as yet unharvested crop will be sold. The farmer might sell a futures contract and thereby establish the future selling price of the crop. Yet what the farmer does not know and cannot hedge is the uncertainty over the size of the crop. This is the farmer's quantity risk. The farmer's total revenue is the product of the crop's price and its size. In a highly competitive market, the farmer's crop is too small to influence the price, but there are systematic factors, such as weather, that could influence everyone's crop. Thus, the crop size could be small when prices are high and large when prices are low. This situation creates its own natural hedge. When the

farmer hedges, the price volatility no longer offsets the uncertainty of the crop size. Thus, the hedge actually can *increase* the overall risk.

Quantity uncertainty is common in farming but is by no means restricted to it. Many corporations and financial institutions do not know the size of future cash flows and thus must contend with quantity risk.

Contract Choice

The choice of futures contract actually consists of four decisions: (1) which futures commodity, (2) which expiration month, (3) whether to be long or short, and (4) the number of contracts. The number of contracts is so important that we defer it to the next main section.

The futures contract used for hedging should be liquid and should be on an asset that is highly correlated with the asset being hedged.

WHICH FUTURES COMMODITY?   From the previous section, we can see that it is important to select a futures contract on a commodity that is highly correlated with the underlying commodity being hedged. In many cases the choice is obvious, but in some it is not.

For example, suppose one wishes to hedge the rate on bank CDs, which are short-term money market instruments issued by commercial banks. There is no bank CD futures contract so the hedger must choose from among some other similar contracts. Liquidity is important, because the hedger must be able to close the contract easily. If the futures contract lacks the necessary liquidity, the hedger should select a contract that has sufficient liquidity and is highly correlated with the spot commodity being hedged. Since both Treasury bills and Eurodollars are short-term money market instruments, their futures contracts, which are quite liquid, would seem appropriate for hedging bank CD rates. Of course, if the hedger wanted the hedging instrument to be identical to the underlying spot asset, he or she could go to the over-the-counter market and request a forward contract, but, as we have previously emphasized, that would entail some other considerations.

Another factor one should consider is whether the contract is correctly priced. A short hedger will be selling futures contracts and therefore should look for contracts that are overpriced or, in the worst case, correctly priced. A long hedger should hedge by buying underpriced contracts or, in the worst case, correctly priced contracts.

Sometimes the best hedge can be obtained by using more than one futures commodity. For example, a hedge of a corporate bond position might be more effective if both Treasury bond futures *and* municipal bond futures are used.

WHICH EXPIRATION?   Once one has selected the futures commodity, one must decide on the expiration month. As we know, only certain expiration months trade at a given time. For example, in September the Trea-

sury bond futures contract has expirations of December of the current year, March, June, September, and December of the following year, and March, June, and September of the year after that. If the Treasury bond futures contract is the appropriate hedging vehicle, the contract used must come from this group of expirations.

In most cases, there will be a time horizon over which the hedge remains in effect. To obtain the maximum reduction in basis risk, a hedger should hold the futures position until as close as possible to expiration. Thus, an appropriate contract expiration would be one that corresponded as closely as possible to the expiration date. However, the general rule of thumb is to avoid holding a futures position in the expiration month. This is because unusual price movements sometimes are observed in the expiration month, and this would pose an additional risk to hedgers. Thus, the hedger should choose an expiration month that is as close as possible to but after the month in which the hedge is terminated.[2]

Table 10.3 lists possible hedge termination dates for a Treasury bond futures hedge and the appropriate contracts for use. Consider, however, that *the longer the time to expiration, the less liquid the contract.* Therefore, the selection of a contract according to this criterion may need to be overruled by the necessity of using a liquid contract. If this happens, one should use a contract with a shorter expiration. When the contract moves into its expiration month, the futures position is closed out and a new position is opened in the next expiration month. This process, called *rolling the hedge forward,* generates some additional risk but can still be quite effective.

Of course, the time horizon problem can be handled perfectly by using a forward contract from the over-the-counter market. In fact some hedgers have horizons of longer than 10 years, which can be hedged only by using forward contracts.

LONG OR SHORT?   After selecting the futures commodity and expiration month, the hedger must decide whether to be long or short. This decision is critical and there is absolutely no room for a mistake here. If a hedger goes long (or short) when he should have been short (or long), he has doubled the risk. The end result will be a gain or loss twice the amount of the gain or loss of the unhedged position.

The decision of whether to go long or short requires a determination of which type of market move will result in a loss in the spot market. It then requires establishing a futures position that will be profitable while

The hedger should choose a contract that expires as close as possible to but after the hedge termination date.

---

[2]Not all contracts exhibit unusual price behavior in the expiration month. Thus, this rule need not always be strictly followed.

TABLE 10.3	Contract Expirations for Planned Hedge Termination Dates (Treasury Bond Futures Hedge Initiated on September 30, 1997)
Hedge Termination Date	**Appropriate Contract**
10/1/97–11/30/97	Dec 97
12/1/97–2/28/98	Mar 98
3/1/98–5/31/98	Jun 98
6/1/98–8/31/98	Sep 98
9/1/98–11/30/98	Dec 98
12/1/98–2/28/99	Mar 99
3/1/99–5/31/99	Jun 99
6/1/99–8/31/99	Sep 99
9/1/99–11/30/99	Dec 99

Note: The appropriate contract is based on the rule that the expiration date should be as soon as possible after the hedge termination date subject to no contract being held in its expiration month. Liquidity considerations may make some more distant contracts inappropriate.

The decision of whether to go long or short futures is critical and can be made by determining whether a spot market move will help or hurt the spot position and how the futures market can be used to offset that risk.

the spot position is losing. Table 10.4 summarizes three methods that will correctly identify the appropriate futures transaction. The first method requires that the hedger identify the worst case scenario and then establish a futures position that will profit if the worst case does occur. The second method requires taking a futures position that is opposite to the current spot position. This is a simple method, but in some cases it is difficult to identify the current spot position. The third method identifies the spot transaction that will be conducted when the hedge is terminated. The futures transaction that will be conducted when the hedge is terminated should be the opposite of this spot transaction. The futures transaction that should be done today should be the opposite of the futures transaction that should be done at the termination of the hedge.

Margin Requirements and Marking to Market

Two other considerations in hedging are the margin requirement and the effect of marking to market. We discussed these factors earlier, but now we need to consider their implications for hedging.

Margin requirements, as we know, are very small and virtually insignificant in relation to the size of the position being hedged. Moreover, margin requirements for hedges are even smaller than speculative margins. In addition, margins can sometimes be posted with Treasury bills; thus, interest on the money can still be earned. Therefore, the initial amount of margin posted is really not a major factor in hedging.

What is important, however, is the effect of marking to market and the potential for margin calls. Remember that the profit on a futures transac-

---

TABLE 10.4   **How to Determine Whether to Buy or Sell Futures When Hedging**

Worst Case Scenario Method

---

1. Assuming that the spot and futures markets move together, determine whether long and short positions in futures would be profitable if the market goes up or down.
2. What is the worst that could happen in the spot market?
   a. The spot market goes up.
   b. The spot market goes down.
3. Given your answer in 2, assume that the worst that *can* happen *will* happen.
4. Given your answer in 3, and using your answer in 1, take a futures position that will be profitable.

Current Spot Position Method

---

1. Determine whether your current position in the spot market is long or short.
   a. If you own or plan to sell an asset, your current position is long.
   b. If you are short an asset, your current position is short.
   c. If you are committed to buying an asset in the future, your current position is short.
   d. If you have issued a floating rate liability, your current position is long.
   e. If you plan to issue a liability, your current position is long.
2. Take a futures position that is opposite the position given by your answer in 1.

Anticipated Future Spot Transaction Method

---

1. Determine what type of spot transaction you will be making when the hedge is terminated.
   a. Sell an asset.
   b. Buy an asset.
   c. Issue (sell) a liability (this includes a liability with a floating rate reset).
2. Given your answer in 1, you will need to terminate a futures position at the horizon date by doing the opposite transaction to the one in 1, e.g., if your answer in 1 is "sell," your answer here is "buy a futures."
3. Given your answer in 2, you will need to open a futures contract today by doing the opposite, e.g., if your answer in 2 is "buy a futures," your answer here should be "sell a futures."

---

tion is supposed to offset the loss on the spot commodity. At least part of the time, there will be profits on the spot commodity and losses on the futures contract. On a given day when the futures contract generates a loss, the hedger must deposit additional margin money to cover that loss. Even if the spot position has generated a profit in excess of the loss on the futures contract, it may be impossible, or at least inconvenient, to withdraw the profit on the spot position to cover the loss on the futures.

This is one of the major obstacles to more widespread use of futures. Because futures profits and losses are realized immediately and spot profits and losses do not occur until the hedge is terminated, many potential

hedgers tend to weigh the losses on the futures position more heavily than the gains on the spot. They also tend to think of hedges on an ex post rather than ex ante basis. If the hedge produced a profit on the spot position and a loss on the futures position, it would be apparent *after the fact* that the hedge should not have been done. But this would not be known *before the fact*.

Thus, a hedger must be aware that hedging will produce both gains and losses on futures transactions and will require periodic margin calls. The alternative to not meeting a margin call is closing the futures position. It is tempting to do this after a streak of losses and margin calls. If the futures position is closed, however, the hedge will no longer be in effect and the individual or firm will be exposed to the risk in the spot market, which is greater than the risk of the hedge.

In Chapter 9, we examined the effect of marking to market on the futures price. We concluded that the impact is fairly small. If, however, the interest earned or paid on the variation margin is not insignificant, it is possible to take it into account when establishing the optimal number of contracts. We shall cover this topic in a later section.

These are several of the most important factors one must consider before initiating a hedge. As we noted earlier, another important consideration is the correct number of futures contracts, or the hedge ratio.

Determination of the Hedge Ratio

The hedge ratio is the number of futures contracts needed to offset the spot market risk.

The **hedge ratio** is the number of futures contracts one should use to hedge a particular exposure in the spot market.[3] The hedge ratio should be the one in which the futures profit or loss matches the spot profit or loss. There is no exact method of determining the hedge ratio before performing the hedge. However, there are several ways to estimate it.

The most elementary method is to take a position in the futures market equivalent in size to the position in the spot market. For example, if you hold $10 million of the commodity, you should hold futures contracts covering $10 million. If each futures contract has a price of $80,000, you should sell $10,000,000/$80,000 = 125 contracts. This approach is relatively naive, because it fails to consider that the futures and spot prices might not change in the same proportions. In some cases, however, particularly when the commodity being hedged is the same as the commodity underlying the futures contract, such a hedge ratio will be appropriate.

---

[3]Technically the hedge ratio is the dollar value of the futures position relative to the dollar value of the spot position. It is then used to determine the number of futures contracts necessary. In this book we shall let the hedge ratio refer to the number of futures contracts.

Nevertheless, in most other cases the futures and spot prices will change by different percentages. Suppose we write the profit from a hedge as follows:

$$\Pi = \Delta S + \Delta f N_f,$$

where the symbol Δ means *change in*. Thus, the profit is the change in the spot price (ΔS) plus the change in the futures price (Δf) multiplied by the number of futures contracts (N_f). A positive N_f means a long position and a negative N_f means a short position. For the futures profit or loss to completely offset the spot loss or profit, we set $\Pi = 0$ and find the value of N_f as

$$N_f = -\frac{\Delta S}{\Delta f}.$$

Because we assume futures and spot prices will move in the same direction, ΔS and Δf have the same sign; thus, N_f is negative. This example therefore is a short hedge, but the concept is equally applicable to a long hedge, where $\Pi = -\Delta S + \Delta f N_f$ and N_f would be positive.

Now we need to know the ratio $\Delta S/\Delta f$. There are several approaches to estimating this value.

Minimum Variance Hedge Ratio

The objective of a hedge—indeed, of any investment decision—is to maximize the investor's expected utility. In this book, however, we do not develop the principles of expected utility maximization. Therefore, we shall take a much simpler approach to the hedging problem and focus on risk minimization. The model used here comes from the work of Johnson (1960) and Stein (1961).

The profit from the short hedge is[4]

$$\Pi = \Delta S + \Delta f N_f.$$

The variance of the profit is

$$\sigma_\Pi^2 = \sigma_{\Delta S}^2 + \sigma_{\Delta f}^2 N_f^2 + 2\sigma_{\Delta S \Delta f} N_f,$$

where

σ_Π^2 = variance of hedged profit
$\sigma_{\Delta S}^2$ = variance of change in the spot price

The minimum variance hedge ratio gives the optimal number of futures when the objective is to minimize risk.

---

[4]The problem as formulated here is in terms of the profit. An alternative, and in some ways preferable, formulation is in terms of the rate of return on the hedger's wealth. We shall use the profit formulation here because it is more frequently seen in the literature.

$\sigma_{\Delta f}^2$ = variance of change in the futures price

$\sigma_{\Delta S \Delta f}$ = covariance of change in the spot price and change in the futures price.

The objective is to find the value of N_f that gives the minimum value of σ_Π^2. Appendix 10A presents the procedure. The formula for N_f is

$$N_f = -\frac{\sigma_{\Delta S \Delta f}}{\sigma_{\Delta f}^2}.$$

This formula gives the number of futures contracts that will produce the lowest possible variance. The negative sign means that the hedger should sell futures. If the problem were formulated as a long hedge, the sign would be positive.

You may recognize that the formula for N_f is very similar to that for β from a regression, which we covered in Chapter 8. In fact, we can estimate N_f by running a regression with ΔS as the dependent variable and Δf as the independent variable. Of course, this can give us the correct value of N_f only for a historical set of data. We cannot know the actual value of N_f over an upcoming period. Extrapolating the future from the past is risky, but at least it is a starting point.

The effectiveness of the minimum variance hedge can be determined by examining the percentage of the risk reduced. Suppose we define hedging effectiveness as

$$e^* = \frac{\text{Risk of unhedged position} - \text{Risk of hedged position}}{\text{Risk of unhedged position.}}.$$

This can be written as

$$e^* = \frac{\sigma_{\Delta S}^2 - \sigma_\Pi^2}{\sigma_{\Delta S}^2}.$$

Thus, e^* gives the percentage of the unhedged risk that the hedge eliminates. By substituting the formulas for σ_Π^2 and N_f in the formula for e^* and rearranging terms, we get

$$e^* = \frac{N_f^2 \sigma_{\Delta f}^2}{\sigma_{\Delta S}^2}.$$

This happens to be the formula for the coefficient of determination for the regression. This is the square of the correlation coefficient. It indicates the percentage of the variance in the dependent variable, ΔS, that is explained by the independent variable, Δf.

Price Sensitivity Hedge Ratio

The price sensitivity hedge ratio comes from the work of Kolb and Chiang (1981). The objective here is to determine the value of N_f that will result in no change in the portfolio's value. Because the strategy is designed to be used with interest rate futures, we will illustrate it with reference to a bond and a bond futures contract.

Suppose changes in interest rates on all bonds are caused by a change in a single interest rate, r, which can be viewed as a default-free government bond rate. Thus, when r changes, all other bond yields change. Let S be the price of the bond held in the spot market and y_S be its yield. We will assume the bond futures contract is based on a single government bond. The futures contract has a price of f. Based upon that price, the remaining life of the deliverable bond at the expiration of the futures, and the coupon of the deliverable bond, we can infer that the deliverable bond at expiration would have a yield of y_f and a duration of DUR_f. We shall refer to these as the **implied yield** and the **implied duration** of the futures.

The profit from a hedge is the change in value of the hedger's position as a result of a change in the rate, r. If we are hedged, this change in value is zero. Details of the solution are presented in Appendix 10A. The formula for N_f is

$$N_f = -\left(\frac{\Delta S}{\Delta f}\right)\left(\frac{\Delta y_f}{\Delta y_S}\right).$$

This expression can be considerably simplified. From a formula in Chapter 8 we can express duration as[5]

$$DUR_S \approx -\left(\frac{\Delta S}{S}\right)\left(\frac{1 + y_S}{\Delta y_S}\right).$$

The duration of a futures contract can be expressed in a similar manner as

$$DUR_f \approx -\left(\frac{\Delta f}{f}\right)\left(\frac{1 + y_f}{\Delta y_f}\right).$$

Letting $\Delta y_f = \Delta y_S$ and substituting in the expression for N_f gives

The price sensitivity hedge ratio gives the optimal number of futures to hedge against interest rate changes.

---

[5]The formula in Chapter 8 was expressed as

$$\frac{\Delta S}{S} \approx -DUR_S\left(\frac{\Delta y_S}{1 + y_S}\right).$$

$$N_f = -\left(\frac{DUR_S}{DUR_f}\right)\left(\frac{S}{f}\right)\left(\frac{1 + y_f}{1 + y_S}\right).$$

There is yet another version of the price sensitivity hedge ratio that is often used in practice. It is given as

$$N_f = -(\text{Yield beta})\frac{PVBP_S}{PVBP_f},$$

where $PVBP_S$ is the present value of a basis point change for the spot and is specifically defined as $\Delta S/\Delta y_S$, which we know is $-DUR_S S/(1 + y_S)$. $PVBP_f$ is the present value of a basis point change for the futures and is defined as $\Delta f/\Delta y_f$, which is $-DUR_f f/(1 + y_f)$. These variables are, in effect, the change in the price of the spot or futures for a change in the yield of Δy_S or Δy_f.

The **yield beta** is the coefficient from a regression of the spot yield on the implied yield of the futures. In the price sensitivity formula, we assumed the spot yield changes one for one with the implied yield on the futures. This makes the yield beta 1. Then, the preceding equation becomes

$$N_f = -\left(\frac{DUR_S}{DUR_f}\right)\left(\frac{S}{f}\right)\left(\frac{1 + y_f}{1 + y_S}\right),$$

which is the price sensitivity formula. However, if the hedger does not believe the spot and futures prices will change in a one-to-one ratio, the yield beta actually should be estimated. In the examples used in this chapter, we shall assume the yield beta is 1.

The price sensitivity formula takes into account the volatility of the spot and futures prices. Thus, it incorporates information from current prices rather than regressing past spot prices on past futures prices. There are merits to both approaches, and in practice one approach sometimes may be more practical than the other. We shall illustrate both methods in some hedging examples later in the chapter.

Stock Index Futures Hedging

Because the price sensitivity hedge is not applicable to stock index futures, the minimum variance hedge usually is employed. Suppose we define ΔS as Sr_S, where r_S is the return on the stock, which is the percentage change in price. Then we define Δf as fr_f, where r_f is the percentage change in the price of the futures contract. Note that this is not the return on the futures contract. Because there is no initial outlay, there is no return on a fu-

tures contract. If we substitute Sr_S and fr_f for ΔS and Δf in the minimum variance formula for N_f, we get

$$N_f = -\frac{S\sigma_{Sf}}{f\sigma_f^2},$$

where σ_{Sf} is the covariance between r_S and r_f and σ_f^2 is the variance of r_f. If we run a regression of the percentage change in the spot price on the percentage change in the futures price, we obtain a regression coefficient we can call β_S. Is this the beta from the Capital Asset Pricing Model? Not exactly, but since the futures contract is based on a market index, the beta will be very close—probably close enough for our purposes. In that case,

The minimum variance hedge ratio for stock index futures takes into account the stock portfolio's beta.

$$N_f = -\beta_S\left(\frac{S}{f}\right)$$

is the minimum variance hedge ratio for a stock index futures contract where β_S is the beta of the stock portfolio.

This hedge ratio is widely used in practice even though it ignores a few problems. For one, it disregards dividends on the portfolio of stocks. Also, it assumes the futures contract behaves exactly like the market portfolio or the underlying stock index. In other words, it assumes that the beta of the futures is 1. This will not be precisely the case. Thus, there is some basis risk that can impair the hedge's effectiveness. For our purposes, however, we shall stay with the above formula so we can concentrate on the essential concepts underlying the stock index futures hedge.

Tailing the Hedge

In Chapter 9, we discussed the impact of marking to market on futures prices. We saw that the effect is likely to be small, so we can treat forward contracts as though they were futures contracts and permit the profit from the contract to be earned entirely at expiration. In reality, there are some cases where the interest earned on daily profits and losses from futures positions can be significant enough to require consideration in the design of hedging models. In that case, we should make an adjustment to the optimal hedge ratio. This is called **tailing the hedge.**

Suppose we set up a hedge consisting of a long position in the spot asset priced at S and a short position in the futures priced at f. We shall hold the position until the futures expires at T. During the interim at times T_1 and T_2, the futures will be marked to market. This implies that from today until T_1 is one day, from T_1 until T_2 is one day, and from T_2 to T is one day. We shall assume the interest rate applied to settlement gains and losses is the risk-free rate, r, and this rate is constant until expiration.

When marking-to-market is an important factor, the hedge ratio should be adjusted to reflect the effect of the interest on the marking-to-market. This process is called tailing the hedge.

Table 10.5 illustrates the procedure for tailing the hedge. When the hedge is set up, it is necessary to sell, not one futures, but rather $(1 + r)^{-(T - T_1)}$ futures. Note that this is the present value factor for the period spanned from the end of the current day until expiration. This number will be slightly less than one. At T_1, the futures will be marked to market. The amount credited to the margin account should be invested in risk-free bonds until expiration. If the amount is negative, it should be financed by borrowing (issuing risk-free bonds) until expiration. When expiration arrives, this mark-to-market cash flow will have grown to a value of $-(f_{T_1} - f)$. Note how the number of futures contracts we set up, $(1 + r)^{-(T - T_1)}$, exactly offsets the compound interest factor, $(1 + r)^{(T - T_1)}$, so that the futures price change at T_1 is realized at expiration. Then at T_1 the number of futures must be adjusted to reflect the interest factor, $(1 + r)^{-(T - T_2)}$, for the remaining time until expiration. The same procedure is followed until expiration, at which time there will be f dollars remaining. Had this adjustment to the hedge ratio not been made, then the hedge would not have been risk free. Of course, if future interest rates were uncertain, then it would be impossible to correctly tail the hedge.

Consider the following simple example. Let S be 100 and f be 105. The interest rate, r, is .10. Without tailing the hedge, the hedger would buy 1 unit of the spot at 100 and sell 1 unit of the futures at 105. With the tail, however, the hedger should sell $(1.10)^{-(2/365)}$ futures when there are three days to go and $T - T_1$ is 2/365. This amounts to 0.9995 contracts. Thus, if the investor held 10,000 units of the spot, the hedge ratio would be 0.9995(10,000) futures, or 9,995 contracts. At time T_1, the hedge ratio would be changed to $(1.10)^{-(1/365)}$ or .9997, or 9,997 contracts. At time T_2, the hedge ratio would change to 1, or 10,000 contracts.

These adjustments to the hedge ratio may seem insignificant, but that is primarily because we let the hedge begin three days before expiration. Had we extended our example to, say, 100 days before expiration, and assuming marking to market daily, the hedge ratio would have been $(1.10)^{-(99/365)}$ or 9,745 contracts. Each day this ratio would change by incrementing the exponent by 1/365 until the day before expiration, when it would become 365/365, or 1. In practice, many professional hedgers do not necessarily adjust the hedge ratio daily; they do so only periodically and achieve results quite close to those of a daily adjustment. To keep our hedge examples fairly basic, we shall not use this tailing procedure; nevertheless, you should keep it in mind for situations you may encounter in the real world.

Hedging Strategies

So far we have examined some basic principles underlying the practice of hedging. The next step is to illustrate how these hedges are executed. We

TABLE 10.5   Tailing the Hedge

The time line

|————— 1 day —————| |————— 1 day —————| |————— 1 day —————|
| Today | T_1 | T_2 | T (Expiration) |

Time	Situation	Action	Value
Today	Asset is worth S. Futures contract on asset is selling for f.	Buy asset in spot market. Sell $(1 + r)^{-(T - T_1)}$ futures contracts.	S –0
		Total value Today	S
T_1	Futures price is f_{T_1}. Futures position is marked to market for a cash flow of $-(1 + r)^{-(T - T_1)}(f_{T_1} - f)$.	Buy back the $(1 + r)^{-(T - T_1)}$ futures contracts. Invest mark-to-market profit of $-(1 + r)^{-(T - T_1)}(f_{T_1} - f)$ in risk-free bonds, which will grow to a value of $-(f_{T_1} - f)$ at T. (If this amount is negative, borrow it at the risk-free rate.) Sell $(1 + r)^{-(T - T_2)}$ new futures contracts.	$-(1 + r)^{-(T - T_1)}(f_{T_1} - f)$ $+ (1 + r)^{-(T - T_1)}(f_{T_1} - f)$ –0
		Total value at T_1	0
T_2	Futures price is f_{T_2}. Futures position is marked to market for a cash flow of $-(1 + r)^{-(T - T_2)}(f_{T_2} - f_{T_1})$.	Buy back the $(1 + r)^{-(T - T_2)}$ futures contracts. Invest mark-to-market profit of $-(1 + r)^{-(T - T_2)}(f_{T_2} - f_{T_1})$ in risk-free bonds, which will grow to a value of $-(f_{T_2} - f_{T_1})$ at T. (If this amount is negative, borrow it at the risk-free rate.) Sell one new futures contract.	$-(1 + r)^{-(T - T_2)}(f_{T_2} - f_{T_1})$ $+(1 + r)^{-(T - T_2)}(f_{T_2} - f_{T_1})$ –0
		Total value at T_2	0
T	Spot asset is worth S_T. Futures price, f_T, converges to S_T. Futures account is marked to market for a cash flow of $-(S_T - f_{T_2})$.	Deliver spot asset on short futures and receive f_T, which equals S_T. Redeem (or pay off) bonds established at times T_1 and T_2.	$S_T - (S_T - f_{T_2})$ $-(f_{T_1} - f) - (f_{T_2} - f_{T_1})$
		Total value at T	f

shall look at some examples developed from a variety of economic and financial environments that illustrate several hedging principles.

The examples are divided into three groups: short-term interest rate hedges, intermediate- and long-term interest rate hedges, and stock hedges. We begin with short-term interest rate hedges.

Short-Term Interest Rate Hedges

HEDGING THE FUTURE PURCHASE OF A TREASURY BILL   Consider the following scenario. On February 15, a corporate treasurer learns that $1 million will be available on May 17. The funds will be needed for long-term investment later in the year, but meanwhile they should be invested in liquid, interest-earning securities. The treasurer decides to purchase 91-day Treasury bills at the weekly auction on May 17.

T-bills are currently offered at a discount of 8.20. The treasurer would like to lock in this rate, but knows that the forward rate would be a more accurate reflection of the rate he would expect to receive when he buys the T-bills. That rate is 8.94. The treasurer knows that there is an active futures contract on Treasury bills that has expirations of March, June, September, and December. The treasurer knows that the risk is that interest rates will fall. Thus, using the worst case scenario method, the treasurer assumes that interest rates will fall. If that happens, Treasury bill futures prices will rise. Thus, he knows that he needs to buy futures so that he will profit in the futures market if interest rates fall.

Table 10.6 presents the hedge. The treasurer wants to lock in the yield of 9.6 percent given by the forward price of T-bills. With a $1 million position and the futures contract covering $1 million of T-bills, the treasurer knows that he needs one contract.[6]

When the hedge is over, the treasurer is glad he did hedge. The T-bills he bought on May 17 yielded only 8.19 percent, but the futures transaction generated a profit of $3,050. This amount effectively reduces the $980,561 he paid for the T-bills, so the effective yield now becomes 9.55 percent.

This hedge worked because the spot and futures T-bill prices moved in the same direction. In this case, rates declined. Had rates risen, the T-bills would have been less expensive, thus offering a higher yield. The futures position would have produced a loss, however, and this would have offset some or all of the gain made in the spot market. In that case, the hedge

---

[6]Recall that the optimal hedge ratio requires the durations and yields of the spot and futures contracts. Since we are hedging 91-day T-bills with 90-day T-bill futures, the durations are essentially the same: .25. The yield implied by the futures price of 97.83 is 9.31 percent and the yield on the forward T-bill is 9.60 percent. Using the price sensitivity formula gives a value of N_f of one contract. In other examples in this chapter, we shall illustrate how differences in these factors affect the hedge ratio.

TABLE 10.6	**Anticipatory Hedge of a Future Purchase of a Treasury Bill**

Scenario: On February 15, a corporate treasurer learns that $1 million will become available on May 17. The treasurer plans to purchase 91-day U.S. Treasury bills at the weekly auction.

Date	Spot Market	Futures Market
February 15	The implied forward price of 91-day T-bills implies a discount of 8.94. Price per $100 face value: $100 - 8.94(91/360) = 97.74$. Proceeds from $1,000,000 face value: $977,400. Implied yield: $(100/97.74)^{365/91} - 1 = .0960$	June T-bill IMM Index is at 91.32. Price per $100 face value: $100 - (100 - 91.32)(90/360)$ $= 97.83$. Price per contract: $978,300. **Buy one contract**
May 17	91-day T-bills are selling for a discount of 7.69. Price per $100 face value: $100 - 7.69(91/360) = 98.0561$. Proceeds from $1,000,000 face value: $980,561. Implied yield: $(100/98.0561)^{365/91} - 1 = .0819$.	June T-bill IMM Index is at 92.54. Price per $100 face value: $100 - (100 - 92.54)(90/360)$ $= 98.135$. Price per contract: $981,350. **Sell one contract**

Analysis: When the $1,000,000 face value T-bills are purchased on May 17, the treasurer will pay $980,561, which implies a yield of 8.19 percent, which is much lower than the 9.60 percent implied forward rate in effect at the time the hedge was initiated.

The profit on the futures transaction is

$$\begin{array}{r} \$981,350 \text{ (sale price of futures)} \\ - \underline{\$978,300} \text{ (purchase price of futures)} \\ \$3,050 \text{ (profit on futures)} \end{array}$$

The profit on the futures can be considered as a reduction in the effective price of the T-bills. This makes the T-bills effectively cost $980,561 - $3,050 = $977,511.

Thus, the treasurer effectively paid $977,511 for $1,000,000 face value of T-bills. This implies a return of

$$(\$1,000,000/\$977,511)^{365/91} - 1 = .0955.$$

Thus, the effective return on the T-bills after accounting for the hedge is 9.55 percent, which is quite close to the 9.60 percent implied forward rate.

would have been effective, but the treasurer would have wished that the hedge had not been done. The price one pays for hedging is that it will occasionally produce losses on the futures position that will absorb gains made in the spot market.

The above hedge is just one of many types of long hedges one can execute with interest rate futures contracts on short-term instruments. Many types of firms and some individuals determine that they will be investing funds in money market instruments at a later date. As long as the decision to invest the funds is unlikely to be reversed, a hedge is appropriate. This does not mean, however, that one should always hedge. If the hedger believes rates are abnormally low and likely to rise, the hedge will lock in the low rate while money market rates might increase. Thus, the hedger should not blindly hedge in all interest rate environments. Although in an efficient market the hedger should be unable to effectively time the interest rate cycle, it would still be inappropriate for the hedger to ignore his or her own expectations. This will be true for all of the remaining cases.

Hedging a Future Commercial Paper Issue Corporations continuously borrow funds in short-term markets. These funds supply working capital used to finance inventory and accounts receivable and provide liquidity with which to meet interest payments on loans. Large, creditworthy corporations frequently borrow by issuing commercial paper, a short-term promissory note.

Suppose that on April 6 a corporate treasurer determines that on July 20, the firm will need to issue $10 million of commercial paper with a maturity of 180 days. Commercial paper rates are quoted on a 360-day basis, and the paper is discounted.[7] Thus, commercial paper is like Treasury bills, and the calculations for determining the purchase price and effective yield are the same.

The treasurer's worst case scenario is for rates to rise. He knows that if rates rise, interest rate futures prices will fall. So to profit from an increase in interest rates, the treasurer knows to take a short position in futures. Unfortunately there is no commercial paper futures contract, so the treasurer decides to use Eurodollar futures. Recall that Eurodollar futures are quoted like Treasury bill futures and have expirations of March, June, September, and December. The treasurer decides to use the September contract.

The hedge is presented in Table 10.7. The treasurer knows that the rate he would like to lock in is not the spot rate but the forward rate, which is 10.37 percent. If the paper were issued at that rate, it would bring

---

[7]We assume the firm can get by with slightly less than $10 million in cash. Otherwise, it would need to issue more than $10 million of face value of commercial paper.

TABLE 10.7	**Anticipatory Hedge of a Future Commercial Paper Issue**

Scenario: On April 6, a corporate treasurer learns that on July 20 the firm will have to issue $10 million face value of 180-day commercial paper.

Date	Spot Market	Futures Market
April 6	The implied forward rate on 180-day commercial paper is 10.37 percent. Proceeds per $100 face value: $100 - 10.37(180/360) = 94.815$. Proceeds from $10,000,000 face value: $9,481,500. Implied rate: $(100/94.815)^{365/180} - 1 = .1140$.	September Eurodollar futures IMM Index is at 88.23. Price per $100 face value: $100 - (100 - 88.23)(90/360)$ $= 97.0575$. Price per contract: $970,575. Implied yield: $(100/97.0575)^{365/90} - 1 = .1288$. Appropriate number of contracts: $$N_f = -\left(\frac{180/365}{90/365}\right)\left(\frac{9,481,500}{970,575}\right)\left(\frac{1.1288}{1.1140}\right)$$ $= -19.80$. **Sell 20 contracts**
July 20	Issue 180-day commercial paper at current spot rate of 11.34. Proceeds per $100 face value: $100 - 11.34(180/360) = 94.33$. Proceeds from $10,000,000 face value: $9,433,000. Implied rate: $(100/94.33)^{365/180} - 1 = .1257$.	September Eurodollar futures IMM Index is at 87.47. Price per $100 face value: $100 - (100 - 87.47)(90/360)$ $= 96.8675$. Price per contract: $968,675. **Buy 20 contracts**

Analysis: When the $10,000,000 face value of commercial paper is issued on July 20, the firm will receive $9,433,000, which implies a rate of 12.57 percent, which is much higher than the 11.40 percent implied forward rate in effect at the time the hedge was initiated.

The profit on the futures transaction is

$$
\begin{aligned}
20(\$970,575) & \quad \text{(sale price of futures)} \\
- 20(\$968,675) & \quad \text{(purchase price of futures)} \\
\hline
\$38,000 & \quad \text{(profit on futures)}
\end{aligned}
$$

The profit on the futures can be considered as an increase in the proceeds received from issuing the paper. This effectively changes the proceeds to $9,433,000 + $38,000 = $9,471,000.

Thus, the firm effectively received $9,471,000 for $10,000,000 face value of commercial paper. This implies a rate of

$$(\$10,000,000/\$9,471,000)^{365/180} - 1 = .1165.$$

Thus, the effective rate paid on the commercial paper after accounting for the hedge is 11.65 percent, which is reasonably close to the 11.40 percent implied forward rate.

proceeds of $9,481,500, which would mean that its yield would be 11.40 percent. The treasurer uses the price sensitivity hedge ratio, which is necessary here because the spot and futures instruments have different durations and yields. Also the futures contract covers $1 million of Eurodollars while the treasurer's exposure is almost $10 million. Using the formula as indicated in the table results in the treasurer selling 20 contracts.

When the hedge is terminated, the treasurer ends up issuing the paper at an effective yield of 12.57 percent. However, the futures transaction earned $38,000, which can be added to the proceeds from the paper so that the effective cost of the paper is 11.65 percent, which is reasonably close to the target of 11.40 percent, especially given that the hedge instrument, Eurodollar futures, is not the same as the underlying spot instrument, commercial paper. This example illustrates the importance of properly determining the hedge ratio. Had the hedger simply noted that a $10 million spot position hedged by a $1 million futures contract should require 10 contracts, the hedge would have been far less effective.

The hedge worked because Eurodollar and commercial paper rates moved in the same direction—in this case, upward. Had rates moved downward, there would have been a loss on the futures transaction and the loan would have been less expensive without the hedge. However, the firm would not have known that rates would decrease; thus, it bought the protection of the hedge at the risk of a decrease in interest rates.

What we have just seen is a short hedge. The example is applicable to a wide variety of similar situations. For example, the firm could take out a bank loan rather than issue commercial paper. A bank could plan to borrow funds by issuing CDs. Any type of firm that anticipated borrowing money at a future time would be able to reduce the uncertainty of the rate at which it would borrow by selling futures contracts.

HEDGING A FLOATING RATE LOAN   In addition to using interest rate futures, there are other ways to hedge the risk of changing interest rates. For example, a bank might require that the interest rate on a loan float with market interest rates. If interest rates increase, the rate the bank charges on the loan will go up and at least partially cover the additional cost to the bank of borrowing the money. Thus, the bank will pass on the interest rate risk to its loan customers.

This will place the burden of hedging on the borrower. If the loan rate is tied to a floating market rate, the borrower must get into a position to profit when interest rates increase. It can do this by selling interest rate futures contracts.

Consider the following situation. On February 3, a firm decides to take out a three-month, $10 million loan from a bank. The rate on the loan will be set on the first Friday of the month and will equal that day's 90-day LIBOR plus 100 basis points. For simplicity, we shall assume the

monthly rate will be one-twelfth of the annual rate. We shall also assume a flat term structure for 90 days so that the current spot rate is also the forward rate. The firm can repay any part or all of the loan at any time.

The current LIBOR is 9.68 so the rate for the first interest payment is already fixed at 10.68 percent. The firm knows it is exposed to rising interest rates, specifically the LIBOR on March 2 and April 6, the first Fridays of March and April. So the firm is exposed to two distinct risk events and it must hedge those risks separately. To hedge the first event, the rate reset on March 2, the firm must sell a certain number of futures contracts as determined by the price sensitivity formula. The optimal number is based on a spot exposure of $10 million, the initial loan balance. The second risk event is the rate reset on April 6. The optimal number of contracts to hedge this risk is based on the price sensitivity formula using a different amount of spot exposure, specifically the loan balance on March 2. This amount will be $10,000,000(1 + .1068/12) = $10,089,000, reflecting the interest over the first period at the rate of 10.68 percent. If there were any later rate resets, the loan balance would be calculated on the assumption that the hedge works perfectly to lock in the initial loan rate or, if the term structure were not flat, the forward rates. In this case, with the term structure flat, the rate the firm is trying to lock in is 10.68 percent each period. With the firm paying one-twelfth of 10.68 percent per month, the effective annual rate is $[1 + (.1068/12)]^{12} - 1 = .1122$.

Table 10.8 presents the results of this hedge. Using the price sensitivity hedge ratio, the risk associated with each reset date requires a position of three futures contracts to hedge. Note that on the first reset date, March 2, the firm buys back three of the contracts. Since rates rose from February 3 to March 2, those contracts were profitable and the gains were used to reduce the loan balance on March 2. This helped offset the higher rate to be paid on April 6, based on the balance on March 2. The same thing happens on April 6. Rates are even higher, but the second group of three futures contracts generated a profit that is used to lower the loan balance on April 6 so as to help offset the higher rate paid on May 4 based on the April 6 balance.

Ultimately, the loan ended up costing the firm 11.44 percent. This is reasonably close to the target of 11.22 percent and much better than the 11.78 percent it would have paid had it not hedged and simply accepted the risk of rising interest rates. Of course, had rates decreased the hedge would have cost the firm some or all of the savings it would have otherwise generated.

Floating-rate loans are very common in our financial system. They are but one means of passing on the interest rate risk to the borrower. Some banks prefer to offer their customers fixed-rate loans, but the rates on the CDs they issue float with market interest rates. The bank can then hedge its floating-rate financing and offer its loan customers a fixed rate. Since

---

TABLE 10.8   **Hedging a Floating Rate Loan with Eurodollars**

Scenario: On February 3 a firm decides to take out a three-month, $10 million loan from a bank. The rate for a given month will be set on the first Friday of the month and will equal that day's 90-day LIBOR plus 100 basis points. The monthly rate will be 1/12 of the annual rate. The firm can repay any or all of the loan at any time.

Date	Spot Market	Futures Market
February 3	The term structure is flat at 9.68 percent. Adding 100 basis points gives an effective rate of $[1 + (.1068/12)]^{12} - 1 = .1122$. This is the rate the firm is trying to lock in. The rate in effect for the first month is 10.68 percent. The spot position is $10,000,000 and the duration is 1/12 (one month).	The June Eurodollar IMM Index is at 90.75. This implies a price of $(100 - (100 - 90.75)(90/360)) =$ 97.6875 per $100, or $976,875 per contract. This implies a Eurodollar rate of $(100/97.6875)^{(365/90)} - 1$ $= .0995$. The duration is approximately 1/4 year. Appropriate number of contracts to hedge the first rate reset: $$N_f = -\left(\frac{1/12}{1/4}\right)\left(\frac{10,000,000}{976,875}\right)\left(\frac{1.0995}{1.1122}\right)$$ $= -3.37$. Appropriate number of contracts to hedge the second rate reset: $$N_f = -\left(\frac{1/12}{1/4}\right)\left(\frac{\$10,089,000}{976,875}\right)\left(\frac{1.0995}{1.1122}\right)$$ $= -3.40$. So the firm needs to sell three contracts to hedge the first rate reset and three more to hedge the second. **Sell six contracts**
March 2	Accumulated principal and interest: $10,000,000[1 + (.1068/12)] =$ $10,089,000. LIBOR is 10.09 so the rate is reset to 11.09. This is the rate that is in effect for the second month.	June Eurodollar IMM Index is at 90.47. This implies a price of $(100 - (100 - 90.47)(90/360)) =$ 97.6175 per $100, or $976,175 per contract. The profit on each futures contract is $976,875 - $976,175 = $700. **Buy back three contracts**

banks are probably more knowledgeable about the benefits of hedging, this type of arrangement should be common. Unfortunately, it is not always the case. Many banks do not use interest rate futures as much as one would think given their central position in the financial system and the risk exposure they face. Fortunately, however, the use of interest rate futures by banks is on the increase.

The type of hedge described in this section is called a **strip hedge** or simply a **strip.** It can also be used as an arbitrage strategy whereby the investor effectively creates a synthetic 90-day (or longer) fixed rate security. The return on this security can be compared against the return from ac-

TABLE 10.8	*(continued)*

		Futures profit = 3($700) = $2,100. Apply futures profit to loan balance reducing it to $10,089,000 − $2,100 = $10,086,900. Three short futures contracts are left.
April 6	Accumulated principal and interest: $10,086,900[1 + (.1109/12)] = $10,180,120. LIBOR is 10.79 so the rate is reset to 11.79. This is the rate that is in effect for the third month.	June Eurodollar IMM Index is at 89.99. This implies a price of $(100 − (100 − 89.99)(90/360)) =$ 97.4975 per $100, or $974,975 per contract. The profit on each futures contract is $976,875 − $974,975 = $1,900. **Buy back three contracts** Futures profit = 3($1,900) = $5,700. Apply futures profit to loan balance reducing it to $10,180,120 − $5,700 = $10,174,420. No futures contracts are left.
May 4	Accumulated principal and interest: $10,174,420[1 + (.1179/12)] = $10,274,384. Pay back this amount.	

Analysis: The firm borrowed $10,000,000 and paid back $10,274,384 for an effective rate of

$$(10,274,384/10,000,000)^4 − 1 = .1144.$$

This rate is only slightly higher than the 11.22 percent rate the firm was attempting to lock in. Had the firm not hedged, its rate would have been

$$\{[1 + (.1068/12)][1 + (.1109/12)][1 + (.1179/12)]\}^4 − 1 = .1178.$$

tual 90-day securities. A variation of the strip hedge is called a **rolling strip hedge,** in which the hedger attempts to extend the effective maturity further out than the availability of the futures contracts permits. In that case, the hedger simply rolls forward the expiring contracts into new contracts as they become available. When the liquidity of contracts with longer maturities raises concerns about using them, the hedger might wish to use a larger quantity of the shorter-term futures and gradually roll over into the longer-term futures as their expirations become shorter and they become more liquid. This transaction is referred to as a **stack hedge.** Of course, all the strategies involving rolling over into new contracts will entail some additional basis risk. Finally we should note that this type of problem is particularly appropriate for the use of forward rate agreements, interest rate options, and swaps, topics we shall cover in Chapter 14.

Intermediate- and Long-Term Interest Rate Hedges

HEDGING A LONG POSITION IN A GOVERNMENT BOND   Portfolio managers constantly face decisions about when to buy and sell securities. In some cases, such decisions are automatic. Securities are sold at certain times to generate cash for meeting obligations such as pension payments. Consider the following example.

On February 25, a portfolio manager holds $1 million face value of government bonds with a coupon of 11 7/8 percent and maturing in about 25 years. The bond currently is priced at 101 per $100 par value, and the yield is 11.74 percent. The duration is 7.83 years. The bond must be sold on March 28.[8]

The portfolio manager is concerned that interest rates will increase, resulting in a lower bond price and the possibility that the proceeds from the bond's sale will be inadequate for meeting the pension obligation. The manager knows that if interest rates increase, a short futures position will yield a profit that can offset at least part of any decrease in the bond's value. Since this is a government bond, the Treasury bond futures contract should be used.[9]

Table 10.9 presents the results of the hedge. The manager will use the June T-bond futures contract. Using the price sensitivity hedge ratio, the manager determines that he should sell 16 contracts. When the bonds were sold on March 28 they generated a loss of over $53,000. The futures transaction produced a profit of over $60,000. Thus, the hedge eliminated all of the loss and even produced a gain. Had bond prices moved up, the futures price would have increased and the futures transaction would have generated a loss that would have reduced or perhaps eliminated all of the increase in the value of the bonds.

This short hedge represents one of the most common hedging applications, and we shall see a slight variation of it later when we examine stock index futures hedging. This hedge is applicable to many firms and institutions, such as banks, insurance companies, pension funds, and mutual funds.

ANTICIPATORY HEDGE OF A FUTURE PURCHASE OF A TREASURY NOTE   Previously we saw how one could hedge the future purchase of a Treasury bill. In this example, we do the same with a Treasury note. We also take a slightly different approach to determining the hedge ratio.

---

[8]In actual situations a portfolio manager would hold a diversified portfolio of bonds. If the intention were to hedge the entire portfolio, the hedge ratio would be based on the overall portfolio value, yield, and duration. We assume the manager needs approximately $1 million of cash on March 28 and will sell only this bond to generate the cash.

[9]Technically, the accrued interest would be included here, but it is not subject to any uncertainty so we leave it out of the hedging examples.

TABLE 10.9	Hedging a Long Position in a Government Bond

Scenario: On February 25, a portfolio manager holds $1 million face value of a government bond, the 11 7/8s, which mature in about 25 years. The bond is currently priced at 101, has a duration of 7.83, and has a yield of 11.74 percent. The manager will sell the bond on March 28.

Date	Spot Market	Futures Market
February 25	The current price of the bonds is 101. Value of position: $1,010,000. The short end of the term structure is flat so this is the forward price of the bonds in March.	June T-bond futures is at 70 16/32. Price per contract: $70,500. The futures price and the characteristics of the deliverable bond imply a duration of 7.20 and a yield of 14.92 percent. Appropriate number of contracts:

$$N_f = -\left(\frac{7.83}{7.20}\right)\left(\frac{1,010,000}{70,500}\right)\left(\frac{1.1492}{1.1174}\right)$$
$$= -16.02.$$

Date	Spot Market	Futures Market
March 28	The bonds are sold at their current price of 95 22/32. This is a price of $956.875 per bond. Value of position: $956,875.	**Sell 16 contracts** June T-bond futures is at 66 23/32. Price per contract: $66,718.75. **Buy 16 contracts**

Analysis: When the $1 million face value bonds are sold on March 28, they are worth $956,875, a loss in value of $1,010,000 − $956,875 = $53,125.

The profit on the futures transaction is

$$\begin{array}{ll} 16(\$70,500) & \text{(sale price of futures)} \\ -\ 16(\$66,718.75) & \text{(purchase price of futures)} \\ \hline \$60,500 & \text{(profit on futures)} \end{array}$$

Thus, the hedge eliminated the entire loss in value and resulted in an overall gain in value of $60,500 − $53,125 = $7,375.

Suppose that on March 29, a portfolio manager determines that approximately $1 million will be available on July 15. The manager decides to purchase the 11 5/8 Treasury notes maturing in about nine years. The forward price of the notes is 97 28/32, or $978,750, for $1 million face value. The forward yield is 12.02 percent. If yields decline, the notes' price will increase and the manager may be unable to make the purchase. If this happens, a profit could have been made by purchasing futures contracts. Because the Treasury note futures contract is quite liquid, the manager decides to buy T-note futures. Because the hedge is to be terminated on July 15, the September contract is appropriate.

The manager has been gathering statistics on the relationship between the T-note spot and futures markets. He has run a regression of the spot price changes on the futures price changes and obtained a coefficient of 10.5. So he decides to use 11 futures contracts. The results are presented in Table 10.10.

When the bonds are ultimately purchased, they end up costing over $97,000 more but the futures transaction generated a profit of over $82,000. Thus, the effective purchase price is actually about $15,000 higher and gives an effective yield of 11.75 percent, which is reasonably close to the target forward yield of 12.02 percent.

Had bond prices moved down, the hedger would have regretted doing the hedge. The notes would have cost less, but this would have been offset

---

TABLE 10.10   **Anticipatory Hedge of a Future Purchase of a Treasury Note**

Scenario: On March 29, a portfolio manager determines that approximately $1 million will be available for investment on July 15. The manager plans to purchase the 11 5/8s Treasury notes maturing in about nine years.

Date	Spot Market	Futures Market
March 29	The forward price of the notes is 97 28/32.	September T-note futures are at 78 21/32.
	Current forward value of notes: $978,750.	Price per contract: $78,656.25.
	This implies a yield of 12.02 percent.	A regression of the change in the note price on the change in the futures price gave a regression coefficient of 10.5.
		Buy 11 contracts
July 15	The notes are purchased at their current price of 107 19/32.	September T-note futures is at 86 6/32.
	This is a price of $1,075.9375 per note.	Price per contract: $86,187.50.
	Value of position: $1,075,937.50.	**Sell 11 contracts**

Analysis: When the $1 million face value notes are purchased on July 15, they cost $1,075,937.50, an increased cost of $1,075,937.50 − $978,750 = $97,187.50. The yield at this price is 10.31 percent.

The profit on the futures transaction is

$$
\begin{aligned}
&11(\$86,187.50) \quad \text{(sale price of futures)} \\
-&11(\$78,656.25) \quad \text{(purchase price of futures)} \\
\hline
&\$82,843.75 \quad \text{(profit on futures)}
\end{aligned}
$$

Thus, the hedge offset about 85 percent of the increased cost. The effective purchase price of the notes is $1,075,937.50 − $82,843.75 = $993,093.75, which is an effective yield of 11.75 percent.

by a loss on the futures contract. Once again, this is the price of hedging—forgoing gains to limit losses.

HEDGING A CORPORATE BOND ISSUE   One interesting application of an interest rate futures hedge occurs when a firm decides to issue bonds at a future date. There is an interim period during which the firm prepares the necessary paperwork and works out an underwriting arrangement for distributing the bonds. During that period, interest rates could increase so that when the bonds ultimately are issued, they will command a higher yield. This will be more costly to the issuer.

Consider the following example. On February 24, a corporation decides to issue $5 million face value of bonds on May 24. As a standard of comparison, the firm currently has a bond issue outstanding with a coupon of 9 3/8 percent, a yield of 13.76 percent, and a maturity of about 21 years. Any new bonds issued will require a similar yield. Thus, the firm expects that when the bonds are issued in May, the coupon would be set at 13.76 percent, so the bonds would go out at par.

If rates increase, the firm will have to discount the bonds or adjust the coupon upward to the new market yield. We shall assume that the coupon is fixed so that the price will decrease. In either case, the firm will incur a loss. The firm realizes that if rates increase, it can make a profit from a short transaction in futures. Thus, it decides to hedge the issue by selling futures contracts.

There is no corporate bond futures contract, so the hedger chooses the Treasury bond futures contract. Because the hedge will be closed on May 24, the June contract is chosen.

The hedge is illustrated in Table 10.11. Using the price sensitivity hedge ratio, the firm sells 67 futures contracts. When the bonds are ultimately issued, the yield is 15.25 percent. This results in a loss of over $460,000 on the bonds, but the futures transaction made over $500,000. The firm made a net gain of about $44,000. The futures profit can be added to the proceeds from the bond of about $4.5 million so as to infer an effective issue price of slightly more than $5 million. This sets the effective yield on the bonds at 13.63 percent, which is quite close to the target of 13.76 percent.

Had interest rates declined, the firm would have obtained a higher price for the bonds; however, this would have been at least partially offset by a loss on the futures transaction. By executing the hedge, the firm was able to protect itself against an interest rate change while preparing the issue. In a similar vein, investment bankers might do this type of hedge. An investment banker purchases the bonds from the firm and then resells them to investors. Between the time the bonds are purchased and resold, the investment banker is exposed to the risk that bond yields will

---

TABLE 10.11	Hedging a Corporate Bond Issue

Scenario: On February 24, a corporation decides to issue $5 million of bonds on May 24. The firm currently has outstanding comparable bonds with a coupon of 9 3/8, a yield of 13.76 percent, and a maturity of about 21 years. The firm anticipates that if conditions do not change, the bonds when issued in May will go out with a 13.76 percent coupon and be priced at par with a 20-year maturity and a duration of 7.22.

Date	Spot Market	Futures Market
February 24	If issued in May, it is expected that the bonds would offer a coupon of 13.76 percent and be priced at par with a duration of 7.22. Value of position: $5,000,000.	June T-bond futures are at 68 11/32. Price per contract: $68,343.75. The futures price and the characteristics of the deliverable bond imply a duration of 7.83 and a yield of 13.60 percent. Appropriate number of contracts: $$N_f = -\left(\frac{7.22}{7.83}\right)\left(\frac{5,000,000}{68,343.75}\right)\left(\frac{1.1360}{1.1376}\right)$$ $$= -67.4.$$
May 24	The yield on comparable bonds is 15.25 percent. The bonds are issued with a 13.76 percent coupon at a price of 90.74638. Price per bond: $907.46. Value of bonds: $4,537,319.	**Sell 67 contracts** June T-bond futures is at 60 25/32. Price per contract: $60,781.25. **Buy 67 contracts**

Analysis: When the $5 million face value bonds are issued on May 24, they are worth $4,537,319, a loss in value of $5,000,000 − $4,537,319 = $462,681. The yield at this price is 15.25 percent. (Note: Alternatively, if the bonds actually were issued at par with the coupon set at the yield on May 24 of 15.25 percent, the firm would receive the full $5,000,000 but the present value of its increased interest cost would be $462,681.)

The profit on the futures transaction is

$$
\begin{array}{ll}
67(\$68,343.75) & \text{(sale price of futures)} \\
-\,67(\$60,781.25) & \text{(purchase price of futures)} \\
\hline
\$506,687.50 & \text{(profit on futures)}
\end{array}
$$

Thus, the hedge offset more than all of the increased cost and left a net gain of $506,687.50 − $462,681 = $44,006.50. The effective issue price of the bonds is $4,537,319 + $506,687.50 = $5,044,006.50, which is an effective yield of 13.63 percent.

increase.[10] Therefore, a short hedge such as this would be appropriate. Many investment banking firms have been able to protect themselves against large losses by hedging with interest rate futures.

Stock Index Futures Hedges

Several of the hedging examples illustrated with T-note and T-bond futures are similar to stock index futures hedges where a firm attempts to hedge a long position in a security or portfolio. The first example we shall look at is the hedge of a stock portfolio.

STOCK PORTFOLIO HEDGE   A central tenet of modern investment theory is that diversification eliminates unsystematic risk, leaving only systematic risk. Until the creation of stock index futures, investors had to accept the fact that systematic risk could not be eliminated. Now investors can use stock index futures to hedge the systematic risk. But should they do that? If all systematic and unsystematic risk is eliminated, the portfolio can expect to earn only the risk-free return. Why not just buy T-bills? The answer is that investors occasionally wish to change or eliminate systematic risk for brief periods. During times of unusual volatility in the market, they can use stock index futures to adjust or eliminate the systematic risk. This is much easier and less costly than adjusting the relative proportions invested in each stock. Later the portfolio manager can close out the futures position, and the portfolio systematic risk will be back at its original level.

Consider a portfolio manager who on March 31 is concerned about the market over the period ending July 27. The portfolio has accumulated an impressive profit, and the manager would like to protect the portfolio value over this time period. The manager knows that the portfolio is exposed to a loss in value resulting from a decline in the market as a whole, the systematic risk effect, as well as losses resulting from the unsystematic risk of the individual stocks. Although the portfolio contains only eight stocks, the manager is not particularly worried about the unsystematic risk. The manager knows that the systematic risk can be hedged by using S&P 500 stock index futures, specifically the September contract.

The results are shown in Table 10.12. The portfolio beta is a weighted average of the betas of the component stocks, where each weight of a given stock is the market value of that stock divided by the total market value of the portfolio. This gives a portfolio beta of 1.06. Using the minimum

---

[10]Investment bankers do employ other means of minimizing their risk exposure. The use of a syndicate, in which a large number of investment bankers individually take a small portion of the issue, spreads out the risk. Many issues are taken on a "best efforts" basis. This allows the investment banker to return the securities to the issuing firm if market conditions make the sale of the securities impossible without substantial price concessions.

TABLE 10.12   **Stock Portfolio Hedge**

Scenario: On March 31, a portfolio manager is concerned about the market over the next four months. The portfolio has accumulated an impressive profit, which the manager wishes to protect over the period ending July 27. The prices, number of shares, and betas are given below:

Stock	Price (3/31)	Number of Shares	Market Value	Weight	Beta
Federal Mogul	18.875	18,000	$ 339,750	.044	1.00
Martin Marietta	73.500	16,000	1,176,000	.152	0.80
IBM	50.875	7,000	356,125	.046	0.50
US West	43.625	10,800	471,150	.061	0.70
Bausch & Lomb	54.250	21,000	1,139,250	.147	1.10
First Union	47.750	28,800	1,375,200	.178	1.10
Walt Disney	44.500	25,000	1,112,500	.144	1.40
Delta Air Lines	52.875	33,200	1,755,450	.227	1.20
			$7,725,425		

Portfolio beta:
  .044(1.00) + .152(0.80) + .046(0.50) + .061(0.70)
  + .147(1.10) + .178(1.10) + .144(1.40) + .227(1.20)
  = 1.06.
S&P 500 September futures contract:
  Price on March 31: 652.50
  Multiplier: $500
  Price of one contract: $500(652.50) = $326,250
Optimal number of futures contracts:

$$ N_f = -1.06 \left(\frac{7,725,425}{326,250} \right) = -25.10. $$

Sell 25 contracts

---

variance hedge ratio results in the sale of 25 contracts. On July 27, the portfolio has declined in value by over $200,000, a loss of 2.68 percent. However, the futures transaction generated a profit of $60,000, which reduced the effective loss to only 1.90 percent.

The objective of the hedge was to eliminate systematic risk. Clearly systematic risk was reduced but not eliminated. The stock portfolio value declined about 2.68 percent while the futures price decreased a little over 1 percent. The hedge certainly helped but was far from perfect. There are several possible explanations for this result. One is that the betas are only an estimate taken from a popular investment advisory service. Beta estimates over the recent past have not necessarily been stable. It is also possible that the portfolio was not sufficiently diversified and some unsystematic risk contributed to the loss. Some of the stocks may have paid dividends during the hedge period. We did not account for these divi-

TABLE 10.12 (continued)		
Stock	**Price (7/27)**	**Market Value**
Federal Mogul	21.625	$ 389,250
Martin Marietta	81.500	1,304,000
IBM	43.875	307,125
US West	47.125	508,950
Bausch & Lomb	45.875	963,375
First Union	48.125	1,386,000
Walt Disney	40.000	1,000,000
Delta Air Lines	50.000	1,660,000
		$7,518,700

Results: The values of the stocks on July 27 are shown below:

S&P 500 September futures contract:

Price on July 27: 647.70

Multiplier: $500

Price of one contract: $500(647.70) = $323,850

Buy 25 contracts

Analysis: The market value of the stocks declined by $7,725,425 − $7,518,700 = $206,725, a loss of 2.68 percent.

The futures profit was

$$
\begin{array}{rl}
25(\$326,250) & \text{(sale price of futures)} \\
-\ 25(\$323,850) & \text{(purchase price of futures)} \\
\hline
\$60,000 & \text{(profit on futures)}
\end{array}
$$

Thus, the overall loss on the stocks was effectively reduced to $206,725 − $60,000 = $146,725, a loss of 1.90 percent.

dends in illustrating the hedge results. Dividends would have reduced the loss on the portfolio and made the hedge more effective.

Had the market moved up, the portfolio would have shown a profit, but this would have been at least partially offset by a loss on the futures transaction. In either outcome, however, the portfolio manager would have been reasonably successful in capturing at least some of the accumulated profit on the portfolio.

ANTICIPATORY HEDGE OF A TAKEOVER   The exciting world of mergers and takeovers offers an excellent opportunity to apply hedging concepts. The acquiring firm identifies a target firm and intends to make a bid for the latter's stock. Typically the acquiring firm plans to purchase enough stock to obtain control. Because of the large amount of stock usually involved and the speed with which takeover rumors travel, the acquiring firm frequently makes a series of smaller purchases until it has accumulated

sufficient shares to obtain control. During the period in which the acquiring firm is slowly and quietly buying the stock, it is exposed to the risk that stock prices in general will increase. This means that either the shares will cost more or fewer shares can be purchased.

Consider the following situation. On July 15, a firm has identified Helix Technology Corporation as a potential acquisition.[11] Helix stock currently is selling for $26.50 and has a beta of 1.80. The acquiring firm plans to buy 100,000 shares, so it will cost $2.65 million. The purchase will be made on August 15. This could be viewed as one purchase in a series of purchases designed to ultimately acquire controlling interest in the target firm. The acquiring firm realizes that if stock prices as a whole increase, the shares will be more expensive. However, if the firm purchases stock index futures, any general increase in stock prices will lead to a profit in the futures market.

Because the hedge will be terminated on August 15, the acquiring firm chooses to buy September S&P 500 futures. Table 10.13 shows the results of the hedge.

On August 15, the Helix stock price is $28.75. The shares thus cost an additional $225,000.[12] However, the profit on the futures transaction was $250,125. Thus, the effective cost of the shares is $26.25.

The hedge was successful in reducing some of the additional cost of the shares; however, the unsystematic risk cannot be hedged. In takeover situations, the unsystematic risk is likely to be very high. For example, if word leaks out that someone is buying up the stock, the price will tend to rise substantially. This can occur even if the market as a whole is going down. Also, federal regulations require that certain takeover attempts be announced beforehand. If there were options on the target firm's stock, however, the acquiring firm could use these to hedge the unsystematic risk.

The takeover game is intense and exciting, with high risk and the potential for large profits. Stock index futures can play an important role, but the extent to which futures are used to hedge this kind of risk is not known, because much of this kind of activity is done with a minimum of publicity.

The takeover example is but one type of situation wherein a firm can use a long hedge with stock index futures. Any time someone is considering buying a stock, there is the risk that the stock price will increase before the purchase is made. Stock index futures cannot hedge the risk that factors specific to the company will drive up the stock price, but they can be used to protect against increases in the market as a whole.

---

[11]The choice of Helix is merely for illustrative purposes. Helix is not known to be a takeover target as of this writing.

[12]It is unlikely that all of the 100,000 shares could have been purchased at the same price. Therefore, we should treat $28.75 as the average price at which the shares were acquired.

TABLE 10.13	Anticipatory Hedge of a Takeover

Scenario: On July 15, a firm has decided to begin buying up shares of Helix Technology Corporation with the ultimate objective of obtaining controlling interest. The acquisition will be made by purchasing lots of about 100,000 shares until sufficient control is obtained. The first purchase of 100,000 shares will take place on August 15. The stock is currently worth $26.50 and has a beta of 1.80.

Date	Spot Market	Futures Market
July 15	Current price of the stock is 26.50. Current cost of shares: 100,000($26.50) = $2,650,000. The beta is 1.80.	September S&P 500 futures is at 630.25. Price per contract: $315,125. Approximate number of contracts: $$N_f = -1.80 \left(\frac{2,650,000}{315,125} \right)$$ $$= -15.14.$$ Since it should buy futures, ignore the negative sign. **Buy 15 contracts**
August 15	The stock is purchased at its current price of 28.75. Cost of shares: 100,000($28.75) = $2,875,000.	September S&P 500 futures is at 663.60. Price per contract: $331,800. **Sell 15 contracts**

Analysis: When the 100,000 shares are purchased on August 15, they cost $2,875,000, an additional $225,000.

The profit on the futures transaction is

$$
\begin{array}{ll}
15(\$331,800) & \text{(sale price of futures)} \\
- \ 15(\$315,125) & \text{(purchase price of futures)} \\
\hline
\$250,125 & \text{(profit on futures)}
\end{array}
$$

Thus, the hedge eliminated all of the additional cost and left a small gain. The shares end up effectively costing ($2,875,000 − $250,125)/100,000 = 26.25.

Summary

This chapter looked at hedging with interest rate and stock index futures. It began by examining some basic concepts necessary for understanding and formulating hedge strategies. It explored the concepts of long and short hedging and basis risk and identified rules that help determine which contract to select, including the choice of commodity, expiration month, and whether to be long or short. The chapter also examined techniques for determining the optimal number of futures contracts for providing the volatility needed to offset the spot market risk.

The hedge examples were grouped by type of contract—short-term interest rate futures hedges, intermediate- and long-term interest rate futures hedges, and stock index futures hedges. While these examples span a broad range of

applications, there are numerous similar situations in which virtually the same type of hedge would apply. The emphasis was on understanding the concept of hedging by observing it in practical situations.

Chapter 11 continues our look at futures strategies by examining arbitrage, speculative, and spread strategies. These strategies are somewhat more complex and require more frequent reference to concepts developed in previous chapters. The reader may wish to review Chapters 8 and 9 before reading Chapter 11.

Key Terms

Before continuing to Chapter 11, you should be able to give brief definitions of the following terms.

- short hedge/long hedge
- anticipatory hedge
- basis/basis risk
- cross hedge
- quantity risk
- hedge ratio
- implied yield

- implied duration
- yield beta
- tailing the hedge
- strip hedge
- rolling strip hedge
- stack hedge

Questions and Problems

1. Explain the difference between a short hedge and a long hedge.

2. What is the basis? How is the basis expected to change over the life of a futures contract?

3. Explain why a strengthening basis benefits a short hedge and hurts a long hedge.

4. Suppose you are a dealer in sugar. It is September 26, and you hold 112,000 pounds of sugar worth $0.0479 per pound. The price of a futures contract expiring in January is $0.0550 per pound. Each contract is for 112,000 pounds. Determine the original basis. Then calculate the profit from a hedge if it is held to expiration and the basis converges to zero. Show how the profit is explained by movements in the basis alone.

5. Rework problem 4, but assume the hedge is closed on December 10, when the spot price is $0.0574 and the January futures price is $0.0590.

6. What factors must one consider in deciding on the appropriate futures commodity for a hedge?

7. For each of the following hedge termination dates, identify the appropriate contract expiration. Assume the available expiration months are March, June, September, and December.
   a. August 10
   b. December 15
   c. February 20
   d. June 14

8. State and explain two reasons why firms hedge.

9. What is the minimum variance hedge ratio and the measure of hedging effectiveness? What do these two values tell us?

10. What is the price sensitivity hedge ratio? How are the price sensitivity and minimum variance hedge ratios alike? How do they differ?

11. Suppose you are an oil dealer and hold a position of 1 million barrels of crude oil. You hedge by trading futures each of which is on 10,000 barrels. However, you consider the effects of marking to market to be sufficient to justify tailing the hedge. The hedge will be on for 60 days. The interest rate is 8.5 percent. You plan to hold the hedge all the way to the expiration date. Determine the number of contracts you should sell at the beginning of the hedge. Then determine the number of contracts you should be holding when the hedge has 20 days to go.

12. For each of the following situations, determine whether a long or short hedge is appropriate. Justify your answers.
   a. A firm anticipates issuing stock in three months.
   b. An investor plans to buy a bond in 30 days.
   c. A bank holds a floating rate security issued by another bank.
   d. A firm plans to borrow money in two months.

13. On October 26, a bank is considering making a $20 million, three-month, fixed-rate loan to a corporation. The loan will be taken out immediately and repaid on January 25. The bank knows it will have to finance the loan by issuing one-month CDs that will pay interest at the LIBOR. The CDs will mature on the last Friday of the month and will be repaid by issuing a new CD at the new rate.

   The forward LIBOR is 10.16 percent. The bank must keep its cost of financing as low as possible and will lose money on the loan if that cost exceeds 11 percent. December Eurodollar futures currently are at 89.33. March Eurodollar futures are at 88.89. Both figures are IMM Index values. The dates on which the CDs will be rolled over are November 30 and December 28.
   a. What should the firm do on October 26?
   b. On November 30, the December Eurodollar futures is at 90.54. The March contract is at 89.93. The LIBOR is 9.10 percent. Describe what happens on this day.
   c. On December 28, the March contract is at 90.56. The LIBOR is 8.63 percent. Describe what happens on this day.
   d. On January 25, the fixed-rate loan is repaid. The March contract is at 91.28. Determine the overall outcome of the hedge. Be sure to determine whether the firm met its objective of keeping the rate below 11 percent.

14. On July 6, a firm learns that it will have approximately $10 million available for short-term investment on November 30. It believes that the best use of the funds is to make a Eurodollar deposit. The forward rate on 90-day Eurodollar deposits is 12.25 percent. The firm is concerned that Eurodollar rates will decrease over the next few months. The December Eurodollar IMM Index is 86.30.

    a.   Describe the transaction the firm should execute to hedge the risk of a decrease in Eurodollar rates. What is the yield on Eurodollar deposits on July 6?

    b.   On November 30, the December Eurodollar IMM Index is at 90.54. The three-month Eurodollar deposit rate is 9.10 percent. Determine the outcome of the hedge. Calculate the effective yield on the Eurodollar deposit.

15.   On February 15, a firm learns that it will need to borrow $10 million on August 15 for 90 days. The loan will be at a fixed rate equal to the prime rate, which currently is 11 percent. The loan will be discounted and the rate stated on a 360-day basis. The company is concerned about rising interest rates and is considering hedging that risk. However, it is uncertain whether the T-bill or Eurodollar contract is a better hedge. The prime rate is administered by the bank and is not necessarily highly correlated with market rates. Lacking any specific knowledge of how to handle this problem, the firm decides to assume the prime rate changes 1 point for every 1-point change in T-bill and Eurodollar rates. The firm elects to use T-bill futures for the hedge but, for future reference, to track the performance of a Eurodollar hedge.

      The September T-bill IMM Index is 90.25, and the September Eurodollar IMM Index is 89.06. For each of the following questions, work out the results for both a T-bill and a Eurodollar hedge.

    a.   Determine the transaction the firm would make on February 15 to set up the hedge. Use the price sensitivity hedge ratio. Identify the effective rate if the loan were taken out today.

    b.   On August 15, the prime rate is at 13 percent. The September T-bill IMM Index is at 89.84, and the Eurodollar IMM Index is at 88.14. Determine the outcome of the hedge. What is the effective cost of borrowing?

16.   On January 31, a firm learns that it will have $5 million available on May 31. It will use the funds to purchase the APCO 9 1/2 percent bonds maturing in about 21 years. Interest is paid semiannually on March 1 and September 1. The bonds are rated A2 by Moody's and are selling for 78 7/8 per 100 and yielding 12.32 percent. The duration is 7.81.

      The firm is considering hedging the anticipated purchase with September T-bond futures. The futures price is 71 8/32. The firm believes the futures contract is tracking the Treasury bond with a coupon of 12 3/4 percent and maturing in about 25 years. It has determined that the implied yield on the futures contract is 11.40 percent and the duration of the contract is 8.32.

      The firm believes the APCO bond yield will change 1 point for every 1-point change in the yield on the bond underlying the futures contract.

    a.   Determine the transaction the firm should conduct on January 31 to set up the hedge.

    b.   On May 31, the APCO bonds were priced at 82 3/4. The September futures price was 76 14/32. Determine the outcome of the hedge.

17.   On July 1, a portfolio manager holds $1 million face value of Treasury bonds, the 11 1/4s maturing in about 29 years. The price is 107 14/32. The

bond will need to be sold on August 30. The manager is concerned about rising interest rates and believes a hedge would be appropriate. The September T-bond futures price is 77 15/32.

The manager decides to compute the minimum variance hedge ratio by regressing the daily change in the portfolio value on the change in the September futures price. The regression gives a coefficient of 13 and explains 95 percent of the variation.

a. What transaction should the firm make on July 1?

b. On August 30, the bond was selling for 101 12/32 and the futures price was 77 5/32. Determine the outcome of the hedge.

18. You are the manager of a stock portfolio. On October 1, your holdings consist of the eight stocks listed in the following table, which you intend to sell on December 31. You are concerned about a market decline over the next three months. The number of shares, their prices, and the betas are shown, as well as the prices on December 31.

Stock	Number of Shares	Beta	10/1 Price	12/31 Price
R. R. Donnelley	10,000	1.00	19 5/8	27 3/8
B. F. Goodrich	6,200	1.05	31 3/8	32 7/8
Raytheon	15,800	1.15	49 3/8	53 5/8
Maytag	8,900	.90	55 3/8	77 7/8
Kroger	11,000	.85	42 1/8	47 7/8
Comdisco	14,500	1.45	19 3/8	28 5/8
Cessna	9,900	1.20	29 3/4	30 1/8
Foxboro	4,500	.95	24 3/4	26

On October 1, you decide to execute a hedge using a stock index futures contract, which has a $500 multiplier. The March contract price is 376.20. On December 31, the March contract price is 424.90. Determine the outcome of the hedge.

19. On March 1, a securities analyst recommended General Cinema stock as a good purchase in the early summer. The portfolio manager plans to buy 20,000 shares of the stock on June 1 but is concerned that the market as a whole will be bullish over the next three months. General Cinema's stock currently is at 32 7/8, and the beta is 1.10.

Construct a hedge that will protect against movements in the stock market as a whole. Use the September stock index futures, which is priced at 375.30 on March 1 and which has a $500 multiplier. Evaluate the outcome of the hedge if on June 1 the futures price is 387.30 and General Cinema's stock price is 38 5/8.

20. (Concept Problem) As we discussed in the chapter, futures can be used to eliminate systematic risk in a stock portfolio, leaving it essentially a risk-free portfolio. However, a portfolio manager can achieve the same result by selling the stocks and replacing them with T-bills. Consider the following stock portfolio.

Stock	Number of Shares	Price	Beta
Northrop Grumman	14,870	18.125	1.10
H. J. Heinz	8,755	36.125	1.05
Washington Post	1,245	264	1.05
Disney	8,750	134.5	1.25
Wang Labs	33,995	4.25	1.20
Wisconsin Energy	12,480	29	0.65
General Motors	14,750	48.75	0.95
Union Pacific	12,900	71.5	1.20
Royal Dutch Shell	7,500	78.75	0.75
Illinois Power	3,550	15.5	0.60

Suppose the portfolio manager wishes to convert this portfolio to a risk-less portfolio for a period of one month. The price of a stock index futures with a $500 multiplier is 369.45. To sell each share would cost $20 per order plus $0.03 per share. Each company's shares would constitute a separate order. The futures contract would entail a cost of $27.50 per contract, round-trip. T-bill purchases cost $25 per trade for any number of T-bills. Determine the most cost-effective way to accomplish the manager's goal of converting the portfolio to a risk-free position for one month and then converting it back.

21. (Concept Problem) On January 2, a bank learns it will have about $10 million to invest in T-bills on November 28. The current T-bill discount rate is 7.11 percent. The bank believes T-bill rates will fall over the next nine months. It would like to hedge in the T-bill futures market but believes that only the nearby contract is sufficiently liquid to justify a hedge. Thus, it will use the March contract until February 28, the June contract from February 28 to May 30, the September contract from May 30 to August 29, and the December contract from August 29 to November 28. When it rolls out of one contract and into the next, it will take its futures gain (loss) and reinvest (borrow) at the market rates for the time remaining until November 28. These rates are, of course, unknown when the hedge is begun. The reinvestment (borrowing) rates turned out to be 8 percent from February 28 to November 28, 6.875 percent from May 30 to November 28, and 5.6875 percent from August 29 to November 28. Whatever amount is invested on the given date earns the rate indicated for the time remaining until November 28; however, these are annual rates, so adjust accordingly. The prices of the T-bill futures on the appropriate dates were as follows:

March contract: January 2 (93.18), February 28 (93.10)
June contract: February 28 (93.39), May 30 (93.71)
September contract: May 30 (93.77), August 29 (94.94)
December contract: August 29 (95.06), November 28 (94.71)

On November 28, the discount spot rate on 91-day T-bills was 5.41 percent. Determine the rate the bank would earn on the purchase of the spot T-bills on November 28 both with and without the hedge. Remember to account for the reinvestment of futures profits and losses as the hedge is rolled forward on the given dates.

APPENDIX 10A
Derivation of the Hedge Ratio[*]

Minimum Variance Hedge Ratio

The variance of the profit from the hedge is

$$\sigma_\Pi^2 = \sigma_{\Delta S}^2 + \sigma_{\Delta f}^2 N_f^2 + 2\sigma_{\Delta S \Delta f} N_f.$$

The value of N_f that minimizes σ_Π^2 is found by differentiating σ_Π^2 with respect to N_f.

$$\frac{\partial \sigma_\Pi^2}{\partial N_f} = 2\sigma_{\Delta f}^2 N_f + 2\sigma_{\Delta S \Delta f}.$$

Setting this equal to zero and solving for N_f gives

$$N_f = -\frac{\sigma_{\Delta S \Delta f}}{\sigma_{\Delta f}^2}.$$

A check of the second derivative verifies that this is a minimum.

Price Sensitivity Hedge Ratio

The value of the position can be specified as

$$V = S + V^f N_f,$$

where V^f is the value of the futures contract. Now we wish to find the effect of a change in r on V. Since $\partial V^f / \partial r = \partial f / \partial r$,

$$\frac{\partial V}{\partial r} = \frac{\partial S}{\partial r} + \frac{\partial f}{\partial r} N_f.$$

The optimal value of N_f is the one that makes this derivative equal to zero. We do not know the derivatives $\partial S / \partial r$ and $\partial f / \partial r$, but we can use the chain rule to express the equation as

$$\frac{\partial V}{\partial r} = \frac{\partial S}{\partial y_S} \frac{\partial y_S}{\partial r} + \frac{\partial f}{\partial y_f} \frac{\partial y_f}{\partial r} N_f = 0.$$

This procedure introduces the yield changes, ∂y_S and ∂y_f, into the problem. Usually it is assumed that $\partial y_S / \partial r = \partial y_f / \partial r$. Substituting and solving for N_f gives

[*]This appendix requires the use of calculus.

$$N_f = -\frac{(\partial S / \partial y_S)}{(\partial f / \partial y_f)}.$$

This is approximated as

$$N_f = -\frac{(\Delta S / \Delta y_S)}{(\Delta f / \Delta y_f)}$$

$$= -\left(\frac{\Delta S}{\Delta f}\right)\left(\frac{\Delta y_f}{\Delta y_S}\right).$$

APPENDIX 10B
Taxation of Hedging

The tax treatment of hedging was originally established in a 1936 IRS ruling that stated that using futures contracts to reduce business risk generates ordinary income or loss. The ruling was reaffirmed in a 1955 Supreme Court case involving a firm called Corn Products Refining Company. Corn Products had purchased futures contracts to hedge the future purchase of corn it expected to need. The futures price went up and Corn Products reported the profits as capital gains, which at that time were treated more favorably for tax purposes. The IRS disagreed and the case ultimately ended up in the Supreme Court, which ruled that the purchase of the corn futures was related to the everyday operations of the firm and, thus, should be considered ordinary income for tax purposes. From that point on, the taxation of futures hedges was determined by what came to be known as the *business motive test*. Put simply, was the hedge designed to reduce the firm's business risk? If so, then any profits or losses would be treated as ordinary income.

This interpretation held for 33 years until a shocking ruling occurred on a case that had nothing to do with hedging. Arkansas Best, a holding company, sold shares of the National Bank of Commerce of Dallas at a substantial loss, which it reported as an ordinary loss. Ordinary losses are more attractive to the taxpaying entity because capital losses are limited to the total of capital gains. So capital losses can potentially be unusable as tax credits while ordinary losses are fully deductible against ordinary income. In 1988 the Supreme Court ruled that the losses were capital. It argued that the shares did not constitute a sufficient exception to the established definition of a capital asset. In other words, the shares were not part of Arkansas Best's inventory. Since Best was a holding company, it felt that the shares were a part of its inventory.

The IRS then began using the Arkansas Best case to argue that certain futures hedges could be treated as capital transactions, thus calling into

question the millions of routine hedging transactions executed by businesses. It used the case to argue that the Federal National Mortgage Association (FNMA), a firm that buys and sells mortgages, must treat over $120 million in interest rate futures and options losses as capital. Furthermore, it ruled that while long futures and options to purchase (calls) could be viewed as substitutes for inventory positions and, thus, taxable as ordinary income, short positions and put options could never be used as substitutes for inventory because they represent contracts to sell.

The implications of such an interpretation are far reaching. They effectively mean that a business holding an inventory could not reduce its risk by agreeing to sell some of the inventory in advance, at least not without potentially serious tax consequences. In other words, the IRS ruling discourages conservative business practices. The implications for the futures markets and for businesses that had routinely hedged for years were far reaching. The futures markets could be effectively shut down and millions of back taxes might be owed.

The futures exchanges and many businesses lobbied Treasury Secretary Lloyd Bentsen. Finally on October 18, 1993, the IRS reversed its ruling on the FNMA case. The IRS did argue that hedgers would need to be able to prove that futures and options transactions to protect inventory were indeed hedges. In addition, the taxation of liability hedges, such as selling futures in anticipation of issuing liabilities in the future, of hedges to protect the cost of raw materials purchases, and of many over-the-counter market hedges, such as by using swaps, is still unclear.

Advanced Futures Strategies

Fund managers who aren't using futures and options are dealing with an incomplete set of resources.

PAUL DOLEY

Portfolio Managers Talk Futures and Risk Management
Chicago Mercantile Exchange Videotape, 1995

Chapter Objectives

■ To illustrate the futures spread and arbitrage strategies using short-term interest rate futures, intermediate- and long-term interest rate futures, and stock index futures

■ To demonstrate the accompanying software to identify the cheapest-to-deliver bond on the Treasury bond futures contract

This chapter looks at some advanced futures trading strategies. Some of these strategies are spreads and some are arbitrage strategies. Let us start out by defining these terms.

A **spread** is a strategy involving a long or short position in one futures contract and an opposite position in another. The concept of a spread certainly should not be new to you. We already covered time spreads in options, and we discussed **futures spreads** briefly in Chapter 9. A spread is a relatively low-risk strategy with several objectives. However, to regard a spread as a nonspeculative strategy is misleading. A spread involves an element of speculation, but the risk is much lower than that in an outright long or short position.

We discussed arbitrage frequently in previous chapters. Arbitrage is the mechanism that links derivative prices to spot prices. Without arbitrage, the markets would be far less efficient. However, derivative and spot prices do not always conform to their theoretical relationships. When this happens, arbitrageurs step in and execute profitable transactions that quickly drive prices back to their theoretical levels. This chapter illustrates some of the arbitrage transactions important to the proper functioning and efficiency of the futures markets. It should be noted that while we sometimes ignore transaction costs in these examples, in practice any arbitrage opportunities must be evaluated by considering whether the profits cover the transaction costs.

Our approach here is to examine three groups of contracts: short-term interest rate futures contracts, intermediate- and long-term interest

rate futures contracts, and stock index futures contracts. Within each group of contracts, we shall examine several popular trading strategies.

Short-Term Interest Rate Futures Strategies

In the category of short-term interest rate futures, we shall look at Treasury bill and Eurodollar futures strategies. The reader may first wish to review the contract specifications and hedging examples in Chapters 7 and 10.

Treasury Bill Cash-and-Carry/Implied Repo

In Chapter 9, we saw that the futures price is determined by the spot price and the cost of carry. The basic arbitrage transaction that determines this relationship often is referred to as a **cash-and-carry.** The investor purchases the security in the spot market and sells a futures contract. If the futures contract is held to expiration, the security's sale price is guaranteed.[1] Since the transaction is riskless, it should offer a return sufficient to cover the cost of carry. Because there is no risk, the investor will not earn a risk premium.

Another way to approach this problem is to focus on the rate at which the security's purchase can be financed. Often the financing is obtained by means of a repurchase agreement. A **repurchase agreement,** or **repo,** is an arrangement with a financial institution in which the owner of a security sells that security to the financial institution with an agreement to buy it back, usually a day later. This transaction is referred to as an overnight repo. The repo thus is a form of a secured loan. The investor obtains the use of the funds to buy the security by pledging it as collateral. The interest charged on a repo is usually quoted and calculated as if there were 360 days in a year, but here we shall use the assumption of a full 365-day year.

Repurchase agreements are frequently used in transactions involving government securities. Overnight repos are more common, but longer-term arrangements, called term repos, of up to two weeks are sometimes employed. In cash-and-carry transactions, the security is considered as being financed by using a repo. If the return from the transaction is greater than the repo rate, the arbitrage will be profitable.

From Chapter 9, the futures–spot price relationship is

$$f = S + \theta.$$

---

[1] Recall that this is true because the spot price at expiration equals the futures price at expiration. The profit on the spot transaction is $S_T - S$, and the profit on the futures transaction is $-(f_T - f)$. The total profit is $f - S$. Thus, f is the effective sale price of the underlying asset.

Since we are focusing on securities here, there is no significant storage cost; thus, the cost of carry, θ, is strictly the interest, i. Now let us define the implicit interest cost as

$$\theta = f - S.$$

The implied repo rate is the return implied by the cost-of-carry relationship between spot and futures prices and reflects the return to a cash-and-carry position.

Thus, θ is the implied cost of financing expressed in dollars. Suppose we express it as a percentage of the spot price, θ/S, and define this as $\hat{r}$. Then $\hat{r}$ is the **implied repo rate.** If the cost of financing the position—the actual repo rate—is less than the implied repo rate, the arbitrage will be profitable.

Readers familiar with the concept of internal rate of return will find that it is analogous to the implied repo rate. If the arbitrage brings no profit, the cost of financing is the implied repo rate. In a capital budgeting problem, a zero net present value defines the internal rate of return. If the opportunity cost is less than the IRR, the project is attractive and produces a positive NPV. Likewise, an arbitrage is profitable if it can be financed at a rate lower than the implied repo rate.

For example, suppose there is a security that matures at time T and an otherwise identical security that matures at an earlier time, t. There is also a futures contract that matures at time t. You buy the longer-term security at a price of S, finance it at the rate r (an annualized rate), and sell a futures contract. At time t, the futures expires and you deliver the security. You have effectively sold the security at t for a price of f. The profit from the transaction is

$$\Pi = f - S(1 + r)^{t}.$$

The term $S(1 + r)^{t}$ reflects what you paid for the security, factored up by the cost of financing over period t. The implied repo rate, $\hat{r}$, is the cost of financing that produces no arbitrage profit; therefore, with $\Pi = 0$,

$$\hat{r} = \left(\frac{f}{S}\right)^{(1/t)} - 1.$$

There is yet another approach to understanding the basic cash-and-carry arbitrage. Suppose we buy the security that matures at time T and simultaneously sell the futures contract that expires at time t (t < T). When the futures contract expires we deliver the security, which has a remaining maturity of T − t. The net effect is that we have taken a security that matures at T and shortened its maturity to t. Thus, we have created a synthetic t-period instrument. If the return from the synthetic t-period instrument is greater than the return from an actual security maturing at t, prices are out of line and an arbitrage profit is possible.

An example of this strategy is to buy a six-month T-bill and sell a futures contract expiring in three months. This transaction creates a synthetic three-month T-bill, with a return that should equal the return on an actual three-month T-bill. If it does not, investors will be attracted to the strategy and their transactions will drive up the price of the six-month T-bill and drive down the futures price, or vice versa, until the synthetic T-bill and the actual T-bill have the same returns.

AN EXAMPLE   Table 11.1 illustrates the cash-and-carry transaction with Treasury bills. This is an example of a situation in which buying a longer-term T-bill, selling a futures that expires before the T-bill matures, and delivering the T-bill when the futures expires creates a synthetic shorter-term T-bill. The return on this synthetic T-bill is 50 basis points higher than the return on an actual T-bill with the same maturity.

There are, however, some limitations to the effectiveness of this strategy. These prices were closing prices from *The Wall Street Journal*. As we acknowledged when studying options, the prices may not necessarily be synchronized. A professional arbitrageur would, of course, have access to current synchronized prices, but even in that case the prices might change before the transaction is completed.

Another limitation to the cash-and-carry arbitrage is that the repo rate is not fixed for the full time period. As noted earlier, some term repos for up to two weeks are available, but most repo financing is overnight. In either case, the financing rate on the T-bill is unknown when the arbitrage is executed. Each time a repo matures, new financing must be arranged, and the rate may well be much higher than originally expected. A number of other limitations, such as transaction costs, come into play when determining the implied repo rate from other futures instruments.

Eurodollar Arbitrage

As described in Chapter 8, the Eurodollar market is a large market in which foreign banks and foreign branches of U.S. banks issue dollar-denominated deposits and often commit to forward and futures transactions. Although the Eurodollar market is highly efficient, there may be occasional arbitrage opportunities resulting from violations of the cost-of-carry relationship between spot and futures or forward prices.

AN EXAMPLE   Table 11.2 illustrates a situation in which a London bank, needing to issue a 180-day Eurodollar time deposit, finds that it can get a better rate by issuing a 90-day time deposit and selling a futures expiring in 90 days. By stringing the 90-day time deposit to the futures contract, the bank creates a synthetic 180-day time deposit with a better rate.

It might appear that the result was contingent on the rate on the time deposit issued on December 16—a rate that was not known back in

---

TABLE 11.1	**Treasury Bill Cash-and-Carry Arbitrage**

Scenario: On September 26, the T-bill maturing on December 18, 83 days later, has a discount rate of 5.19. The T-bill maturing March 19, 174 days later, has a discount rate of 5.35. The December T-bill futures is priced at the IMM Index of 94.80. An arbitrage opportunity is available.

Date	Spot Market	Futures Market
September 26	The March 19 T-bill has a discount of 5.35. Price per $100 face value: $100 - 5.35(174/360) = 97.4142$.	December T-bill IMM Index is at 94.80. Price per $100 face value: $100 - (100 - 94.80)(90/360) = 98.70$.
December 18	**Buy one T-bill** The March T-bill still has 91 days remaining but the current spot price of the T-bill is irrelevant.	**Sell one contract** Deliver the March T-bill and receive an effective price of 98.70 based on the futures price at the time the contract was initiated. This closes out the futures position.

Analysis:
The T-bill was bought on September 26 at 97.4142. It was delivered on December 18 to close out the futures contract. There are 83 days between September 26 and December 18. Thus, the annualized rate of return on a security bought at 97.4142 and sold at 98.70 where the holding period is 83 days is

$$\left(\frac{98.70}{97.4142}\right)^{365/83} - 1 = .0594.$$

This can be compared to the return from buying an actual 83-day T-bill. Its price, based on the 5.19 discount in effect on September 26 for a T-bill maturing on December 18, is

$$100 - 5.19(83/360) = 98.8034.$$

If this bill were purchased and held until maturity on December 18, it would return its full face value of 100 for an overall return of

$$\left(\frac{100}{98.8034}\right)^{365/83} - 1 = .0544,$$

which is a full 50 basis points lower.

September. In fact, the result of this transaction was known when it was executed. The 90-day time deposit was issued at a rate of $.0825(90/360) = .020625$ for the 90 days. The Eurodollar futures was sold at a rate of $.0863(90/360) = .021575$. Thus, if the bank issued a 90-day time deposit at .020625 and followed that with a 90-day time deposit at .021575, the overall rate for 180 days would be

$$(1.020625)(1.021575) - 1 = .042645.$$

TABLE 11.2   **Eurodollar Arbitrage**

Scenario: On September 16, a London bank needs to issue $10 million of 180-day Eurodollar time deposits. The current rate on such time deposits is 8.75. The bank is considering the alternative of issuing a 90-day time deposit at its current rate of 8.25 and selling a Eurodollar futures contract. If the 180-day time deposit is issued, the bank will have to pay back

$$\$10,000,000[1 + .0875(180/360)] = \$10,437,500,$$

which is a rate of

$$\left(\frac{\$10,437,500}{\$10,000,000}\right)^{365/180} - 1 = .0907.$$

The rates available in the spot and futures markets are such that the bank can obtain a better rate by doing the following.

Date	Spot Market	Futures Market
September 16	The 90-day time deposit rate is 8.25.	December Eurodollar IMM Index is at 91.37. Price per $100 face value: $100 - (100 - 91.37)(90/360) = 97.8425$.
	Issue 90-day time deposit for $10,000,000	Price per contract: $978,425. **Sell 10 contracts**
December 16	The 90-day time deposit matures and the bank owes $10,000,000 $1 + .0825(90/360) = \$10,206,250$. The rate on new 90-day time deposits is 7.96.	December Eurodollar IMM Index is at 92.04. Price per $100 face value: $100 - (100 - 92.04)(90/360) = 98.01$. Price per contract: $980,100.
	Issue new 90-day time deposit for $10,223,000	**Buy 10 contracts**

Analysis: On September 16, the bank received $10,000,000 from the newly issued 90-day time deposits. On December 16, it bought back its ten futures contracts at a loss of 10($980,100 − $978,425) = $16,750. It issued $10,223,000 of new time deposits, using $16,750 to cover the loss in the futures account and the remaining $10,206,250 to pay off the maturing 90-day time deposit.

On March 16 it paid off the new time deposit, owing

$$\$10,223,000[1 + .0796(90/360)] = \$10,426,438.$$

Thus, on September 16, it received $10,000,000 and on March 16, it paid out $10,426,438. It had no other cash flows in the interim. Thus, its effective borrowing cost for 180 days was

$$\left(\frac{\$10,426,438}{\$10,000,000}\right)^{365/180} - 1 = .0884,$$

which is 23 basis points less than the cost of a 180-day Eurodollar time deposit.

Annualizing this rate gives

$$(1.042645)^{(365/180)} - 1 = .0884,$$

which is the rate obtained by the bank.

Intermediate- and Long-Term Interest Rate Futures Strategies

Intermediate- and long-term interest rate futures include Treasury note and Treasury bond futures. As we noted in earlier chapters, these instruments are virtually identical. Here we shall concentrate on the Treasury bond contract.

Determining the Cheapest-to-Deliver Bond on the Treasury Bond Futures Contract

As previously explained, the specifications on the Treasury bond contract allow delivery of many different bonds, subject to the minimum 15-year maturity or call date. At any given time prior to expiration, it is impossible to determine which bond will be delivered. It is, however, possible to identify the bond that is most likely to be delivered. That bond is referred to as the **cheapest to deliver** or **CTD.**

Suppose it is September 12, 1996, and you are interested in determining the bond that is most likely to be delivered on the upcoming December contract. The procedure involves a series of calculations that we shall illustrate for one particular bond—the 8 7/8s that mature on August 15, 2017.

If the holder of a long position in this bond also holds a short position in the T-bond futures contract, that trader can elect to maintain the position until expiration and deliver this particular bond. Even if another bond would be cheaper to deliver, the trader always has the option to deliver the bond already held. The cost of delivering the particular bond is the net profit or loss from buying the bond, selling a futures, holding the position until expiration, and then delivering the bond. Thus, the trader incurs the cost of carry on the bond held. Remember that this cost is somewhat offset by the coupons received on the bond.

For evaluating at time t the best bond to deliver at time T, the general expression for the cost of delivering a bond is

$$f(CF) + AI_T - [(B + AI_t)(1 + r)^{(T - t)} - FV \text{ of coupons at } T],$$

where AI_T is the accrued interest on the bond at T, the delivery date; AI_t is the accrued interest on the bond at t, today, and r is the risk-free rate

that represents the interest lost on the funds invested in the bond. The term inside the brackets is the spot price of the bond (quoted price plus accrued interest) factored up by the cost of carry and reduced by the compound future value of any coupons received while the position is held. These coupons, of course, help offset the cost of carry, and by subtracting them we are simply reflecting the net cost of carry. The bracketed term is, thus, the forward price of the bond. The first two terms are the amount the trader would receive from delivering the bond. This is the invoice price, which we covered in Chapter 7.

The futures price is 107 8/32 or 107.25 and the conversion factor for our bond is 1.0875. The accrued interest on September 12 is 0.68, and the accrued interest on December 2, the day we shall assume delivery, is 2.63. The price quoted for the bond is 117 19/32 or 117.59375. The repo rate is .051. There are 81 days between September 12 and December 2. The invoice price for the futures is

$$107.25(1.0875) + 2.63 = 119.26.$$

Since the coupons are paid on August 15 and February 15, no coupons are paid during the time the bond is held. Thus, the forward price of the bond, which is the spot price factored up by the cost of carry, is

$$(117.59375 + 0.68)(1.051)^{(81/365)} = 119.59.$$

Hence, the bond would cost .33 more than it would return.

This conclusion by itself does not enable us to make a decision. We can only compare this figure for one bond to that for another. Let us consider a second bond, the 9 1/8s maturing on May 15, 2018. Its conversion factor is 1.1138, and its price is 120 17/32 or 120.53125. In this case, however, the bond will make coupon payments on May 15 and November 15, so there will be a coupon payment while the bond is held. The accrued interest is 2.98 on September 12 and 0.43 on December 2. The coupon of 4.5625 received on November 15 is reinvested at 5.1 percent for 17 days and grows to a value of

$$4.5625(1.051)^{(17/365)} = 4.57.$$

Thus, the forward price of the bond is

$$(120.53125 + 2.98)(1.051)^{(81/365)} - 4.57 = 120.31.$$

The invoice price is

$$107.25(1.1138) + 0.43 = 119.89.$$

The cheapest bond to deliver is the bond for which the difference between the revenue received from delivery of the bond and the cost incurred to buy and hold the bond is maximized.

Thus, the difference between the amount received and the amount paid is $119.89 - 120.31 = -0.42$.

Therefore, it is clear that the 8 7/8 percent bond is better to deliver than the 9 1/8 percent bond. Of course, this calculation should be done for all bonds that are eligible for delivery. The bond for which the difference between the amount received and the amount paid is the maximum is the cheapest bond to deliver.

Table 11.3 presents these calculations for the December 1996 contract evaluated on September 12. Twenty-eight eligible bonds are calculated. The category labeled "Difference" is the difference between the invoice

TABLE 11.3	The Cheapest-to-Deliver Bond on the Treasury Bond Futures Contract

Current date: September 12, 1996
Delivery date: December 2, 1996
Repo rate: 5.1 percent
Futures price: 107 8/32

Coupon	Maturity	Ask Price	Forward Price	Invoice Price	Difference	Accrued Interest at t	Accrued Interest at T	Future Value of Coupon	CF
11.25	February 15, 2015	141 11/32	143.7781	143.5358	−0.2423	0.8560	3.3322	0.0000	1.3073
10.625	August 15, 2015	135 7/32	137.5370	137.3432	−0.1938	0.8084	3.1471	0.0000	1.2512
9.875	November 15, 2015	127 18/32	127.2853	127.0494	−0.2359	3.2201	0.4637	4.9490	1.1803
9.25	February 15, 2016	121 5/32	123.2127	122.9723	−0.2403	0.7038	2.7398	0.0000	1.1210
7.25	May 15, 2016	100 11/32	100.2145	99.7379	−0.4766	2.3641	0.3405	3.6334	0.9268
7.5	November 15, 2016	102 29/32	102.7626	102.3032	−0.4594	2.4457	0.3522	3.7587	0.9506
8.75	May 15, 2017	116 6/32	115.9769	115.6390	−0.3380	2.8533	0.4109	4.3851	1.0744
8.875	August 15, 2017	117 19/32	119.5818	119.2599	−0.3219	0.6753	2.6287	0.0000	1.0875
9.125	May 15, 2018	120 17/32	120.3046	119.8885	−0.4161	2.9755	0.4285	4.5731	1.1138
9	November 15, 2018	119 11/32	119.1254	118.6210	−0.5043	2.9348	0.4227	4.5104	1.1021
8.875	February 15, 2019	118 1/32	120.0241	119.5206	−0.5035	0.6753	2.6287	0.0000	1.0899
8.125	August 15, 2019	109 26/32	111.6565	111.0455	−0.6110	0.6182	2.4066	0.0000	1.0130
8.5	February 15, 2020	114 3/32	116.0141	115.3674	−0.6467	0.6467	2.5177	0.0000	1.0522
8.75	May 15, 2020	116 30/32	116.7353	116.0696	−0.6657	2.8533	0.4109	4.3851	1.0784
8.75	August 15, 2020	117 1/32	119.0034	118.3049	−0.6985	0.6658	2.5917	0.0000	1.0789
7.875	February 15, 2021	107 6/32	108.9831	108.1618	−0.8213	0.5992	2.3325	0.0000	0.9868
8.125	May 15, 2021	110 2/32	109.8911	109.0359	−0.8552	2.6495	0.3816	4.0719	1.0131
8.125	August 15, 2021	110 4/32	111.9724	111.0871	−0.8853	0.6182	2.4066	0.0000	1.0133
8	November 15, 2021	108 23/32	108.5539	107.6047	−0.9492	2.6087	0.3757	4.0093	0.9998
7.25	August 15, 2022	100 6/32	101.8573	100.7031	−1.1542	0.5516	2.1474	0.0000	0.9189
7.625	November 15, 2022	104 20/32	104.4790	103.2277	−1.2513	2.4864	0.3581	3.8213	0.9592
7.125	February 15, 2023	98 27/32	100.4890	99.1560	−1.3330	2.5421	2.1104	0.0000	0.9049
6.25	August 15, 2023	88 20/32	90.0895	88.5751	−1.5145	0.4755	1.8512	0.0000	0.8086
7.5	November 15, 2024	103 20/32	103.4893	101.6396	−1.8498	2.4457	0.3522	3.7587	0.9444
7.625	February 15, 2025	105 10/32	106.8586	104.8330	−2.0255	0.3730	2.0513	0.0000	0.9583
6.875	August 15, 2025	96 18/32	98.1632	95.8170	−2.3462	0.5231	2.0363	0.0000	0.8744
6	February 15, 2026	86 9/32	87.7005	84.9715	−2.7291	0.4565	1.7772	0.0000	0.7757
6.75	August 15, 2026	96 1/32	97.6165	94.1482	−3.4682	0.5136	1.9993	0.0000	0.8592

price and the forward price. All of these values are negative as they should be; otherwise one could earn an easy arbitrage profit. The cheapest bond to deliver is the one in which Difference is the closest to zero. In this case it is the 10 5/8 of August 15, 2015.

The Excel spreadsheet ctd.xls will automatically do these calculations for you. Software Demonstration 11.1 illustrates how to use ctd.xls.

The cheapest bond to deliver is important for several reasons. Any futures contract must reflect the behavior of the spot price. In the case of Treasury bond and note futures, the so-called "spot price" is not easy to determine. The cheapest bond to deliver is the bond that represents the spot instrument that the futures contract is tracking. Therefore, the cost of carry model examined in Chapter 9 would apply only to the cheapest bond to deliver. Also, the optimal hedge ratio would require knowledge of the cheapest bond to deliver.

Delivery Options

The characteristics of the Treasury bond futures contract create some interesting opportunities for alert investors. Specifically, the contract contains several imbedded options. While these **delivery options** are not formally traded in the same way stock options are, they have many of the characteristics of the options we studied in earlier chapters. We shall examine some of these options here.

THE WILD CARD OPTION   The **wild card option** results from a difference in the closing times of the spot and futures markets. The Treasury bond futures contract stops trading at 3:00 P.M. eastern time. However, the spot market for Treasury bonds operates until 5:00 P.M. eastern time. During the delivery month, the holder of a short position knows the settlement price for that day at 3:00 P.M. Multiplying the settlement price by the conversion factor gives the invoice price the holder would receive if a given bond were delivered. This figure is locked in until the next day's trading starts.

During the two-hour period after the futures market closes, the spot market continues to trade. If the spot price declines during those two hours, the holder of a short futures position may find it attractive to buy a bond and deliver it. Because the futures market is closed and the invoice price is fixed, the futures market is unable to react to the new information that drove the spot price down. Moreover, the short has until 9:00 P.M. to make the decision to deliver.

Let us use the following symbols:

f_3 = futures price at 3:00 P.M.
S_3 = spot price at 3:00 P.M.
CF = conversion factor of bond under consideration

SOFTWARE DEMONSTRATION 11.1   **Identifying the Cheapest-to-Deliver Bond with the Excel Spreadsheet ctd.xls**

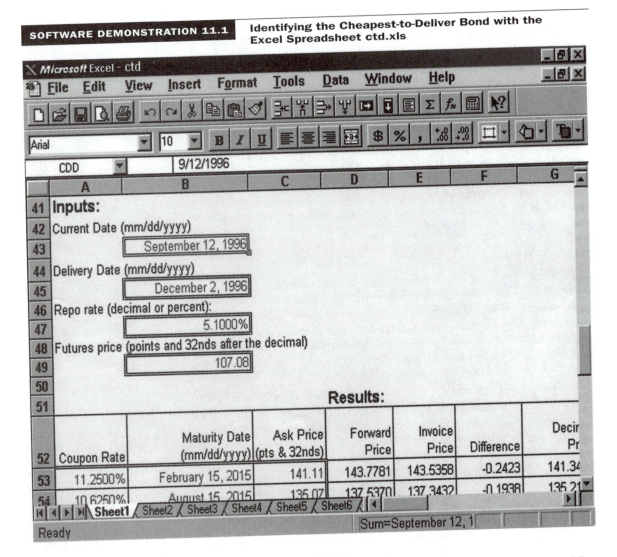

The Excel spreadsheet ctd.xls, which operates in Windows 3.1 or Windows 95 and requires Excel 5.0 or higher, identifies the cheapest-to-deliver bond from among a set of bonds for the Chicago Board of Trade bond futures contract. No installation is necessary; simply place the file in whatever directory you prefer or access it directly from the 3.5-inch diskette provided with this book. To use the software, first do the following:

1. Make sure you are in Windows 3.1 or Windows 95.
2. Run Excel 5.0 or higher.
3. Open the file ctd.xls.

Now let us work an example. Consider the problem in the text in which on September 12, 1996, you wish to identify the cheapest-to-deliver bond on the December 1996 contract. The current repo rate is 5.1 percent and the futures price is 107 8/32. You have identified 28 bonds that meet the 15-year maturity or callability requirement and are eligible for delivery.

Observe on the spreadsheet a section labeled **Inputs:** Each cell that will accept inputs has a double-line border and the values are in blue. Enter the current date in the form mm/dd/yyyy. Insert "9/12/1996" in the appropriate box. Then enter the delivery date "12/2/1996" in its box. The repo rate can be entered as either "5.1" or ".051" in the appropriate box. The futures price should be entered as points and thirty-seconds. Thus, 107 8/32 should be entered as "107.08." The trailing zero can be omitted for values like "103.2" for 103 20/32. A value like 103 5/32 should be entered as "103.05." List the individual bonds in the section below. Consider the first bond. Let it have a coupon rate of 11.25 percent, a maturity date of February 15, 2015, and an ask price of 141 11/32. For the coupon rate enter ".1125" or "11.25." Enter the maturity date as "2/15/2015." Enter the ask price the same way you did the futures price. Thus, 141 11/32 is entered as "141.11." Hit F9 to recalculate and the values will appear for each bond in the section labeled **Results:** Output cells have a single-line border.

The calculations shown are the forward price, the invoice price, the difference between the invoice price and forward price, the decimal price, which is simply the ask price converted from thirty-seconds to decimals, the accrued interest on the current date, the accrued interest on the delivery date, and the value of the coupons at delivery. The last figure is the value of the coupons paid between the current date and the delivery date plus any interest paid on their reinvestment. To the right of each row are additional columns used to perform the calculations. These columns include the conversion factor and various other figures used in the calculations. The category labeled "Difference" is the value that you are looking for. The bond with the largest difference, which should be the one with the least negative value, is the cheapest bond to deliver.

The number of bonds you wish to analyze will differ. To add rows, you will first need to unprotect the spreadsheet. From the Excel menu, choose Tools/Protection/Unprotect Sheet. Then on a new row, copy all of the formulas from columns D through AE. You should probably protect the spreadsheet by choosing Tools/Protection/Protect Sheet from the Excel menu.

For those who prefer Lotus 1-2-3, the diskette also contains the spreadsheet ctd.wk3 and its format file ctd.fm3. This Lotus spreadsheet is from the previous edition of this book and does not contain all of the features of the Excel spreadsheet, but it will provide the information following essentially the same procedure.

You hold a short position in the futures contract that is expiring during the current month. Assume you own $1/CF$ bonds. Why this unusual amount? If you do not own any bonds, your position will be quite risky. Also, the bond under consideration should be the cheapest bond to deliver. That way your risk is quite low. Unexpected changes in the futures price will be approximately matched by changes in the value of the $1/CF$ bonds. We require the case that $CF > 1.0$.

If you make delivery that day, you will be required to deliver one bond per contract. You own only $1/CF$ bonds, so you will have to buy $1 - 1/CF$ additional bonds. If the bonds' spot price declines sufficiently between 3:00 and 5:00, you may be able to buy the additional bonds at a price low enough to make a profit. These additional bonds are called the *tail*.

Now suppose that at 5:00 P.M. the bond price is S_5. If you buy the additional $1 - 1/CF$ bonds at the price of S_5, and deliver them, your profit will be

$$\Pi = f_3(CF) - \left[\left(\frac{1}{CF}\right)S_5 + \left(1 - \frac{1}{CF}\right)S_5\right] = f_3(CF) - S_5.$$

The first term, $f_3(CF)$, is the invoice price. This is simply the 3:00 P.M. settlement price on the futures contract times the conversion factor on the bond. The invoice price is the amount you receive upon delivery. The terms in brackets denote values of the bonds you are delivering. The first term, $(1/CF)S_5$, is the 5:00 P.M. value of the $1/CF$ bonds. The second term is the cost of the $1 - 1/CF$ bonds bought at the 5:00 P.M. price. As indicated above, the expression simplifies to $f_3(CF) - S_5$. Note that the 3:00 P.M. bond price does not enter into the decision to deliver because the

delivery decision is made at 5:00 P.M. By that time, the 1/CF bonds are worth $(1/CF)S_5$ and can be sold for that amount.

If the transaction is profitable, $\Pi > 0$. This requires that

$$S_5 < f_3(CF).$$

The wild card option is the opportunity the holder of the short futures contract has to lock in the invoice price at 3:00 P.M. and make delivery if the spot price falls below the established invoice price between 3:00 and 5:00 P.M. The option exists only during the delivery month.

A trader can observe the spot price at 5:00. If the price is sufficiently low, the trader should buy the remaining $1 - 1/CF$ bonds and make delivery. The wild card option thus will be profitable if the spot price at 5:00 P.M. falls below the invoice price established at 3:00 P.M.

As an example, suppose that on March 2 the March futures contract has a settlement price at 3:00 P.M. of 101.8125. The cheapest bonds to deliver were the 12 1/2s maturing in about 22 years, which have a conversion factor of 1.464. We do not have the 3:00 P.M. spot price, but let us assume it is 149.65. Suppose we are short 100 contracts, which obligates us to deliver bonds with a face value of $100(\$100,000) = \$10,000,000$. Assume each bond has a face value of $1,000. Thus, we will have to deliver 10,000 bonds. To begin this strategy, we must have a position in the spot T-bonds; otherwise, our risk will be quite high. We weight that position by the conversion factor; that is, we hold bonds with a face value of $\$10,000,000(1/1.464) = \$6,830,601$, in other words, about 6,831 bonds. To make delivery, we will need to buy 3,169 bonds. For us to make a profit, the 5:00 P.M. price must decline to

$$S_5 < 101.8125(1.464) = 149.05$$

or less. Thus, if the spot price declined by at least .60 by 5:00 P.M., it would pay to buy the remaining 3,169 bonds and make delivery.

The alternative to delivery is holding the position until the next day. In fact, that will always be the better choice if the conversion factor is less than 1.0. Note that if CF < 1.0, the hedged position will include 1/CF bonds, which exceeds 1.0. Thus, the hedger will hold more bonds than futures and there will be no tail, or additional bonds, to purchase at the lower 5:00 P.M. price. In that case, the wild card option is worthless. Moreover, if the price does not fall sufficiently by 5:00 P.M., holding the position is preferred over delivery. Of course, it is possible that the wild card option will never be worth exercising, meaning simply that it ends up, like many other options, out of the money.

THE QUALITY OPTION   The holder of the short position has the right to deliver any of a number of acceptable bonds. Sometimes the holder of the short position will be holding a bond that is not the best to deliver. A profit is sometimes possible by switching to another bond. This is called

the **quality option,** because the deliverable bonds are considered to be of different quality; it is also sometimes called the switching option.

The value of this option arises because of changes in the term structure of interest rates. You may be holding a hedged position in Treasury bonds and futures, anticipating that you will make delivery of the bond that you hold on the futures contract. Then if the term structure changes, another bond may become the cheapest to deliver. Although you could always deliver the bond you hold, the right to switch to a more favorably priced bond has value.

The quality option exists, not only in Treasury bond and note markets, but also in the markets for many commodity futures. For example, the Chicago Board of Trade's wheat futures contract specifies that the holder of the short position can deliver any of four different grades of wheat. Other agricultural contracts have similar options. In fact, agricultural contracts usually grant the right to deliver at one of several locations. This feature, called the location option, has essentially the same economic effect as the quality option.

In any case, however, the quality option conveys a right to the holder of the short position. Since this right has value, the futures price will tend to be lower by the value of this option. In other words, the seller of a futures receives a lower price that reflects the fact that a valuable option is attached to the contract. Likewise, the buyer pays a lower price for granting the seller this valuable right.

The quality option is the opportunity the holder of the short futures contract has to switch to another deliverable bond if it becomes more favorably priced. The option exists on any futures contract that permits delivery of one of several underlying assets, with the decision made by the holder of the short position.

THE END-OF-THE-MONTH OPTION   The last day for trading a T-bond futures contract is the eighth-to-last business day of the delivery month. Delivery can take place during the remaining business days. The invoice price during those final delivery days is based on the settlement price on the last trading day. Thus, during the last seven delivery days, the holder of the short position has full knowledge of the price that would be received for delivery of the bonds. This gives the holder of the short position the opportunity to watch the spot market for a fall in bond prices. The trader can continue to wait for spot prices to fall until the second-to-last business day, because delivery must occur by the last business day.

The **end-of-the-month option,** thus, is similar to the wild card option. There is a period during which spot prices can change while the delivery price is fixed. It is also related to the quality option, for the holder of the short position can also switch to another bond.

The end-of-the-month option is the opportunity the holder of the short futures contract has to deliver during the final business days of the month. The futures contract no longer trades so the invoice price is locked in, and the option can be profitable if the spot price falls during the last few trading days of the month.

THE TIMING OPTION   Since the short is often permitted to make delivery on any day during the delivery month, he or she holds another valuable option. Suppose the Treasury bond pays a coupon that exceeds the cost of

Derivatives in Action

The Dangers of Delivery

The following talk was given by Tom Kelly, member of the Chicago Board of Trade.

All of the advantages belong to the long cash/short futures positions. I would like to point out some of the fetters that the delivery process imposes on the short futures position.

Cash securities, i.e., U.S. Treasury bills, notes, or bonds, trade for next-day settlement (I buy them today, I pay for them tomorrow). At the time of the trade, other settlement dates can be arranged. However, although I have purchased securities for settlement tomorrow, I have no idea at what time the securities will be presented for payment. A valid delivery in the government market need only be made during the time that the Fed wire is open.

While normal hours are from 9:00 A.M. to 1:30 P.M., many times the close of the wire is extended to 3:00, 4:00, and even 5:00 P.M. In addition, recognized primary dealers in government securities get an additional 15 minutes of "dealer time" during which primary dealers may deliver to one another.

As a customer of the dealers, I can expect to receive the security very close to the time of the wire closing. My back office must be very quick to turn the securities around to the firm that I intend to deliver. If I cannot redeliver the securities in "good time," I am forced to eat a financing loss. Worse, if I have purchased a block of $1 million and $4 million pieces and have arranged to deliver a $5 million piece, and only the $4 million block arrives, I must sit on that piece until the smaller piece arrives.

Delivery on settlement does not mean a lot to securities firms. If the delivery is straightforward (no redeliveries or pieces) and the securities do not show up, I have lost nothing; indeed, I can make money by not having the securities arrive. At the very least, my clearing bank will pay me analysis on my cash position.

Contrast this to the Chicago Board of Trade (CBOT®) delivery process.

If I am short the futures contract I must inform the CBOT two business days before delivery that I intend to deliver futures contracts. On the next day, before 3:00 P.M., I must inform the CBOT as to what I am delivering, the appropriate monies, and my delivery agent. On the delivery day, my securities must be on the Fed wire by 9:00 A.M.

If I do not comply with the CBOT rules, I am subject to as much as a $7,000 per contract fine.

That potential fine is greater than all the potential option profits.

In addition, if I truly err, my CBOT firm that is carrying the short futures contracts can be closed by the CBOT Clearing Corporation. Obviously, such draconian penalties must be avoided.

The timing option is the opportunity the holder of the short futures contract has to deliver at any time during the expiration month. Early delivery is made if the cost of financing exceeds the coupon on the bond and later delivery is made if the coupon exceeds the cost of financing.

financing the position, which is the repo rate. Then the short should hold the long bond–short futures position as long as possible because it pays more than it costs. If the repo rate exceeds the bond coupon, then the position costs more to hold than it yields; thus, an early delivery is advised. Ignoring all other delivery options, this **timing option** would suggest that all deliveries would occur early or late in the month. As we have already noted, however, there are many other options that are in effect and early delivery would preclude the right to take advantage of some of these other options.

Determining the values of these delivery options is very difficult. Most contracts contain more than one option and, as noted above, the Treasury bond futures contract contains several delivery options. Thus, it is difficult to isolate them and observe their separate effects. There have been nu-

The short futures/long cash position must bank finance two business days in advance of the promised delivery date the securities that may be delivered. If the securities appear to be difficult to get in appropriate position, I must arrange to set up even earlier. Bank financing will cost a minimum of one half a percent over normal financing rates, and failure to retrieve securities that are out on repurchase agreement can and has occurred despite attempting to bank finance five business days before delivery. I can recall one time a few years ago that I asked Goldman, Sachs to please return my position that I financed with them. The securities did not show up the first day. The CBOT Office of Investigations and Audits (OIA) called up to remind me of the delivery procedures and what would happen to my firm if I did not comply. I told the OIA representative that Goldman, Sachs, a member clearing firm of the CBOT, was failing to me. "Tough." The securities did not show up.

I threatened to "buy-in" the securities. Goldman, Sachs said that they were sorry, but that they could not return the securities to me because Salomon Brothers was not delivering the securities to them. Can you imagine to whom I was to make delivery of the futures contracts? It was Plaza Clearing, Salomon Brothers' wholly owned futures clearing firm.

On the day before delivery was to be made, the OIA phoned again with the litany of possible punishments for noncompliance with the CBOT delivery rules. My clearing firm was very worried and pointed out with great explicitness that the small amount of money I had intended to make on delivery of 400 futures contracts was going to be more than offset by the $2,800,000 fine—did I have any idea how I was to pay the fine?

At 9:30 A.M. on the delivery day, no securities had appeared. An employee of Plaza Clearing phoned and asked where my securities were. I told them that he was failing to Goldman, Sachs and that they were failing to me. He also said, "Tough."

About a minute later, a block of one million bonds came in from Goldman, Sachs, who had arranged to borrow them from the New York Fed. I delivered the securities to Plaza who immediately returned them to Goldman, Sachs, who immediately delivered to me, who . . .

The entire delivery was finished by 10:00 A.M. No fines were engendered. But, I learned small profits are never offset by enormous losses.

Source: Reprinted with permission from *Review of Futures Markets*, Vol. 11, No. 2, published by the Chicago Board of Trade, pp. 162–164.

merous studies, which are reviewed in Chance and Hemler (1993). Most of them found that the value of delivery options is fairly small. That does not mean they should be dismissed as insignificant. To the holder of one or more of these options, the value may at times be quite large. For our purposes, however, we can safely conclude that the economic effects are minor in comparison to the more important factors that determine the futures price.

Implied Repo/Cost of Carry

Earlier in this chapter, we examined the concept of the implied repo rate in the context of the cost of carry model for Treasury bill futures. Although slightly more complex, the concept is equally applicable to Treasury bond futures.

First, we must identify the cheapest bond to deliver. If we buy that bond, we pay the spot price plus the accrued interest. The sale of a repo finances the bond's purchase. This means that we borrow the funds by selling the bond and agreeing to buy it back at a specified later date. We simultaneously sell a futures contract expiring at T. We hold the position until expiration, deliver the bond, and effectively receive f(CF), the futures price times the conversion factor, plus accrued interest for it. In an efficient market, there should be no arbitrage profit. Therefore, the amount we receive for the bond must equal the amount we paid for it plus the cost of carry:

$$f(CF) + AI_T = (S + AI)(1 + \hat{r})^T,$$

where AI_T is the accrued interest on the bond at expiration, AI is the accrued interest when the bond originally is bought, and $\hat{r}$ is the implied repo rate. The left-hand side of the formula is the amount we receive upon delivery. The right-hand side is the amount paid for the bond, S + AI, factored up by the cost of financing over the holding period, T. Solving for $\hat{r}$,

$$\hat{r} = \left[\frac{f(CF) + AI_T}{S + AI} \right]^{(1/T)} - 1.$$

If the bond can be financed in the repo market at a rate of less than $\hat{r}$, profitable arbitrage is possible.

AN EXAMPLE   On September 26 of a particular year, the cheapest bond to deliver on the December contract is the 12 1/2s maturing in about 23 years. The spot price is 141 16/32, the accrued interest is 1.43, the conversion factor is 1.4662, and the futures price is 95.65625. The accrued interest on December 1 is 3.669. From September 26 to December 1 is 66 days, so T = 66/365 = .1808.

The implied repo rate is

$$\hat{r} = \left[\frac{95.65625(1.4662) + 3.669}{141.5 + 1.43} \right]^{(1/.1808)} - 1 = .0389.$$

If the bond can be financed in the repo market for less than 3.89 percent, the arbitrage will be profitable. At that time the government was borrowing at 5 percent to 6 percent on T-bills, so it would not be possible to borrow at a rate that low. Thus, no arbitrage opportunity exists.

If a coupon is paid during the life of this cash-and-carry arbitrage, we must make a minor adjustment: The amount AI_T must reflect the accrual of any coupons and any interest earned from reinvesting the coupons. For

example, suppose a position was held for 50 days. After 32 days, the bond paid a coupon of $4.50 per $100 of face value. In that case, the coupon was received on day 32 and reinvested for 18 days. We must assume a reinvestment rate, so let us use 5.3 percent. There are 181 days between the bond's coupon payment dates. The forthcoming coupon accrues for 18 days, so the total for AI_T is

$$4.50(1.053)^{(18/365)} + 4.50(18/181) = 4.96.$$

A Treasury Bond Futures Spread

Treasury bond futures traders frequently use spreads. Suppose a trader takes a long position in a futures contract. If this is the only transaction, the risk is quite high. One way to modify the risk is to sell short a Treasury bond, but short selling requires that the trader execute a transaction in the spot market. In addition, there are large margin requirements on short sales. An alternative that is easy to execute is to simply sell another Treasury bond futures contract. That transaction could be executed within the same trading pit. In addition, the margin requirement on a spread is much lower than the margin requirement on either a long or a short position.

Table 11.4 presents an example of a simple spread taken in anticipation of changes in interest rates in the T-bond market. The trader goes short the September contract and long the December in the hope that a small gain will be made. If the trader's forecast is wrong, the loss is not likely to be large. This example involves a simple position of one contract long and one contract short. In practice many traders use weighted positions, taking more of either the long or short contract so as to balance their different volatilities. The proper number of each contract to provide a risk-free position is obtained by using their durations in the same manner that we did in Chapter 10 when we constructed long spot and short futures positions. In this example, the trader's expectations were not at all realized. Rates fell and bond futures prices rose. The September contract was not profitable, but the long December contract was profitable and the overall loss was negligible.

Treasury Bond Spread/Implied Repo Rate

The concept of an implied repo rate also applies to Treasury bond spreads. The implied repo rate can be used to help determine if the spread is correctly priced.

Suppose there is a futures contract expiring at time t and another expiring at time T with t coming before T. Suppose we sell the longer-term contract and buy the shorter-term contract. At time t, the shorter-term contract expires. We take delivery of the bond, financing it at the repo

---

TABLE 11.4	A Treasury Bond Futures Spread

Scenario: It is July 6. Interest rates have steadily risen over the last six months. The yield on long-term government bonds is 13.54 percent. You anticipate that rates will continue upward; however, the economy remains healthy and there are no indications that the Fed will tighten the money supply, which would drive rates further upward. Thus, while you are bearish you are encouraged by other economic factors. You want to take a speculative short position in T-bond futures but are concerned that rates will fall, generating a potentially large loss. You believe that if rates have not changed by late August, they will not change at all. Thus, you short the September contract and buy the December contract.

Date	Futures Market
July 6	The September T-bond futures price is 60 22/32 or 60.6875. Price per contract: $60,687.50 **Sell one contract** The December T-bond futures price is 60 2/32 or 60.0625. Price per contract: $60,062.50 **Buy one contract**
August 31	The September T-bond futures price is 65 27/32 or 65.84375. Price per contract: $65,843.75 **Buy one contract** The December T-bond futures price is 65 5/32 or 65.15625. Price per contract: $65,156.25 **Sell one contract**

Analysis:
The profit on the September contract was

$$\$60{,}687.50 - \$65{,}843.75 = -\$5{,}156.25.$$

The profit on the December contract was

$$\$65{,}156.25 - \$60{,}062.50 = \$5{,}093.75.$$

Thus, the overall profit was

$$-\$5{,}156.25 + \$5{,}093.75 = -\$62.50.$$

rate, r, and hold it until time T, when the longer-term contract expires. Because we are short that contract, we simply deliver the bond. Assume we can identify today the cheapest bond to be delivered on the shorter-term contract.

Consider the following notation:

$$CF^t = \text{conversion factor for bond delivered at t}$$
$$CF^T = \text{conversion factor for same bond delivered at T}$$

f^t = today's futures price for contract expiring at t
f^T = today's futures price for contract expiring at T
AI^t = accrued interest on bond as of time t
AI^T = accrued interest on bond as of time T

At time t, we take delivery of the bond and pay the invoice price,

$$f^t(CF^t) + AI_t.$$

To finance the acceptance and holding of this bond, we borrow this sum at the rate r. Then, at time T, we deliver the bond and receive the invoice price,

$$f^T(CF^T) + AI_T.$$

Since this transaction is riskless, the profit from it should be zero. Therefore,

$$[f^t(CF^t) + AI_t](1 + \hat{r})^{T-t} = f^T(CF^T) + AI_T.$$

The bracketed term on the left-hand side is the amount we paid for the bond at t. Since we borrowed this amount, we must factor it up by the interest rate compounded over the period T − t. The right-hand side is the amount received from delivering the bond at T. We can now solve for $\hat{r}$, the implied repo rate:

The implied repo rate on a spread is the implied cost of establishing a cash-and-carry position at the expiration of the earlier futures contract of the spread.

$$\hat{r} = \left[\frac{f^T(CF^T) + AI_T}{f^t(CF^t) + AI_t}\right]^{1/(T-t)} - 1.$$

The numerator is the amount received for the bond, and the denominator is the amount paid for it. Dividing these two numbers gives the rate of return over the period T − t. Raising this term to the power $1/(T-t)$ annualizes the rate. The implied repo thus is the return we could earn over the period T − t. If the bond can be financed at less than this rate, the transaction will be profitable.

AN EXAMPLE   Assume that on September 26, the cheapest bond to deliver was the 12 1/2s maturing on August 15 in about 29 years. Let us examine the December–March Treasury bond futures spread. The December contract is priced at 95.65625, and the conversion factor is 1.4662. The March futures price is 94.6875. The conversion factor for the 12 1/2s delivered on the March contract is 1.464. The accrued interest on the bond on December 1, the assumed delivery date, is 3.67, and the accrued

interest on March 1 is approximately 6.74. This reflects the payment of the coupon on February 15.[2]

Since the time from December 1 to March 1 is 90 days, the implied repo rate is

$$\hat{r} = \left[\frac{94.6875 \ (1.464) + 6.74}{95.65625 \ (1.4662) + 3.67} \right]^{365/90} - 1 = .0412.$$

The implied repo rate thus is 4.12 percent. Note that this is a forward rate, because it reflects the repo rate over the period from December 1 to March 1. If the bond can be financed at a rate of less than 4.12 percent from December 1 to March 1, the transaction will be profitable.

One way traders determine if the implied repo rate on the spread is attractive is to evaluate what is called a turtle trade. The implied repo rate of 4.12 percent is an implied forward rate. It can be compared to the implied rate in the T-bill futures market. If the T-bill futures rate is lower, the trader sells the T-bill futures and buys the T-bond spread. This creates a risk-free position and earns the difference between the implied repo rate on the T-bond spread and the implied rate on the T-bill futures. If the implied rate on the T-bill futures is higher, the investor reverses the T-bond spread and buys the T-bill futures.

In this problem, the T-bill futures price was the IMM Index of 94.80, which implies a discount of 5.20. This produces a futures price of $100 - 5.20(90/360) = 98.70$, which implies a rate of $(100/98.70)^{(365/90)} - 1 = .0545$. Thus, if the investor reversed the T-bond spread—sold the December contract and bought the March contract—the transaction would be equivalent to borrowing forward at a rate of 4.12 percent. By buying the T-bill futures, the investor would be lending forward at a rate of 5.45 percent. Thus, the turtle trade would lock in a return of 1.33 percent. As with many arbitrage transactions, however, there are a number of impediments to executing a successful trade, and the return might not be truly risk free.

Intermarket Spreads

We have discussed two forms of intramarket spreads. There are also a number of **intermarket spreads** or intercommodity spreads. These are transactions in which the two futures contracts are on different underlying instruments. For example, many traders execute what is called the NOB, or notes

---

[2]This was found by assuming a reinvestment rate on the coupon paid on February 15. It earns 14 days of interest until March 1. The next coupon accrues 14 days until March 1. Thus,

$$AI_T = 6.25(1.053)^{14/365} + 6.25(14/181) = 6.74,$$

where .053 is the reinvestment rate.

over bonds, spread. This spread involves a long (short) position in T-note futures and a short (long) position in T-bond futures. This trade would be used to capitalize on shifts in the yield curve. For example, if a trader believes that rates on the 7-to-10-year range of the yield curve will fall and rates on the 15-plus-year range will either rise or fall by less, a long position in the NOB spread might be warranted. If the investor's expectations prove correct, a profit could be made as T-note futures will rise and T-bond futures will either fall or rise by a smaller amount. Of course, if yields on the long-term end of the market fall, the trader could end up losing money because long-term bond prices will be expected to rise by a greater amount for a given yield change. Thus, the trader might prefer to take a weighted position in which the ratio of T-note to T-bond futures is something other than one-to-one. Thus, the NOB spread is designed to capitalize on changes in the relationship between Treasury note and Treasury bond futures prices.

Another intermarket spread is the MOB, or municipals over bonds, spread. This spread involves a long (short) position in the municipal bond futures contract and a short (long) position in the T-bond futures contract. There is no specific arbitrage relationship that defines the MOB spread, simply because T-bonds and municipals are not perfect substitutes; however, a perceived historical relationship has prevailed. Traders often watch that relationship for signs of abnormal behavior that might signal profit opportunities.

Bond Market Timing with Futures

In Chapter 10, we showed how hedge ratios can be constructed using futures. The procedure essentially combines futures so that the overall investment is insensitive to interest rate changes. In effect, this changes the duration to zero. Suppose a market timer believes that interest rates will move in one direction or the other but a duration of zero may not be appropriate. If interest rates are expected to fall, the timer may wish to increase the duration; if rates are expected to rise, the timer may wish to decrease the duration but not necessarily reduce it to zero.

Suppose a portfolio of bonds has a face value of S and a duration of DUR_S. The futures contract has a duration of DUR_f and a price of f. The timer wishes to change the spot duration to DUR_T, which we shall call the **target duration.** One way to do this is to put more money in high-duration bonds and less money in low-duration bonds. However, this would incur transaction costs on the purchase and sale of at least two bonds. Futures can be used to adjust the duration easily and at lower transaction costs.

The number of futures needed to change the duration to DUR_T is

$$N_f = -\left(\frac{DUR_S - DUR_T}{DUR_f}\right)\left(\frac{S}{f}\right)\left(\frac{1 + y_f}{1 + y_s}\right),$$

Buying or selling futures provides a simple way of increasing or decreasing a bond's duration.

where y_f is the yield implied by the futures price and y_S is the yield on the spot portfolio. Appendix 11A presents the derivation of this formula.

Notice how similar this formula is to the one given in Chapter 10. That formula was

$$N_f = -\left(\frac{DUR_S}{DUR_f}\right)\left(\frac{S}{f}\right)\left(\frac{1 + y_f}{1 + y_S}\right),$$

which reduces the interest sensitivity and duration to zero.[3] If the target duration were zero in our new formula, we would obtain the old formula. Thus, the new formula is a much more general restatement of the optimal hedge ratio, because it permits the duration to be adjusted to any chosen value. If the investor expected falling interest rates and wished to increase the duration, DUR_T would be larger than DUR_S. Then N_f would be positive and futures would be bought. This makes sense because adding futures to a long spot position should increase the risk. If the trader were bearish and wished to reduce the duration, DUR_T would be less than DUR_S and N_f would be negative, meaning that futures would be sold. This is so because an opposite position in futures should be required to reduce the risk.

AN EXAMPLE   Let us rework the T-bond hedging example that appeared in Table 10.9 in Chapter 10. In that problem, on February 25 the portfolio manager held $1 million face value of the 11 7/8s bond maturing in about 25 years. The bond price is 101, and the bond will be sold on March 28. In Chapter 10, we feared an increase in interest rates and lowered the duration to zero by selling 16 futures contracts. Suppose, however, that we wanted to lower the duration from its present level of 7.83 to 4. This would make the portfolio less sensitive to interest rates, but not completely unaffected by them. In that way, if the forecast proved incorrect, the positive duration would still leave room to profit.

The example is presented in Table 11.5. The bond ends up losing 2.26 percent. To determine how close the outcome was to the desired outcome, we need to know the change in the yield on the bonds. On February 25, the yield on the spot bond was 11.74 percent; on March 28, the yield that corresponded to a price of 95 22/32 was 12.50 percent. Recall from Chapter 8 that the following formula expresses the relationship between the change in the yield and the percentage change in the bond price:

$$\frac{\Delta B}{B} \approx -DUR\left(\frac{\Delta y}{1 + y}\right),$$

---

[3] We should note that strictly speaking, both of these formulas apply only to extremely short holding periods. Any increment of time or change in yield will require recalculation of the number of futures contracts, so the number of contracts will need adjustment throughout the holding period.

TABLE 11.5	Bond Market Timing with Futures

Scenario: On February 25, a portfolio manager holds $1 million face value of a government bond, the 11 7/8s, which matures in about 25 years. The bond is currently priced at 101, has a duration of 7.83, and has a yield of 11.74 percent. The manager plans to sell the bond on March 28. The manager is worried about rising interest rates and would like to reduce the bond's sensitivity to interest rates by lowering its duration to 4. This would reduce its interest sensitivity, which would help if rates increase, but would not eliminate the possibility of gains from falling rates.

Date	Spot Market	Futures Market
February 25	The current price of the bonds is 101. Value of position: $1,010,000. The short end of the term structure is flat, so this is the expected sale price of the bonds in March.	June T-bond futures is at 70 16/32. Price per contract: $70,500. The futures price and the characteristics of the deliverable bond imply a duration of 7.20 and a yield of 14.92 percent. Appropriate number of contracts:
		$$N_f = -\left(\frac{7.83 - 4}{7.20}\right)\left(\frac{1,010,000}{70,500}\right)\left(\frac{1.1492}{1.1174}\right)$$
		$$= -7.84.$$
		Sell 8 contracts
March 28	The bonds are sold at their current price of 95 22/32. This is a price of $956.875 per bond. Value of position: $956,875.	June T-bond futures is at 66 23/32. Price per contract: $66,718.75
		Buy 8 contracts

Analysis:

When the $1 million face value bonds are sold on March 28, they are worth $956,875, a loss in value of $1,010,000 − $956,875 = $53,125.

The profit on the futures transaction is

$$
\begin{array}{ll}
8(\$70,500) & \text{(sale price of futures)} \\
-8(\$66,718.75) & \text{(purchase price of futures)} \\
\hline
\$30,250 & \text{(profit on futures).}
\end{array}
$$

Thus, the overall transaction resulted in a loss in value of $53,125 − $30,250 = $22,875, which is a 2.26 percent decline in overall value.

where B represents the bond price. With a duration reset to 4, the formula predicts that for a yield change of .1250 − .1174 = .0076, the percentage price change would be

$$\frac{\Delta B}{B} \approx -4\left(\frac{.0076}{1.1174}\right) = -.0272,$$

or 2.72 percent. The actual change was 2.26 percent. Without the futures position, the duration still would have been 7.83. Plugging into the formula gives a predicted percentage change in the bond price of

$$\frac{\Delta B}{B} \approx -7.83\left(\frac{.0076}{1.1174}\right) = -.0533,$$

or a loss of 5.33 percent. The actual change without the hedge would have been $-\$53,125/\$1,010,000 = -.0526$, or a 5.26 percent loss.

This completes our discussion of Treasury note and bond futures transactions. We now turn to stock index futures.

Stock Index Futures Strategies

Stock index futures contracts offer several interesting applications. We shall look at three: stock index arbitrage, speculating on unsystematic risk, and market timing.

Stock Index Arbitrage

We discussed cash-and-carry arbitrage with Treasury bill and bond futures. The concept is equally applicable to stock index futures. In fact, this type of transaction is one of the most widely used in the futures markets. It is called **stock index arbitrage.**

Recall that the model for the stock index futures price is

$$f = Se^{(r_c - \delta)T},$$

where r_c is the continuously compounded risk-free rate and δ is the continuously compounded dividend yield. Consider the following example of a futures contract that has 40 days to go until expiration. The S&P 500 index is at 652.50, the risk-free rate is 5.2 percent, and the dividend yield is 3 percent. The time to expiration will be $40/365 = .1096$. Thus, the futures should be priced at

$$f = 652.50e^{(.052 - .03)(.1096)} = 654.08.$$

Now suppose the actual futures price is 654.83. Thus, the futures is slightly overpriced. We would sell the futures and buy the stocks in the S&P 500 index in the same proportions as in the index. At expiration, the futures price would equal the spot price of the S&P 500 index. We then would sell the stocks. The transaction is theoretically riskless and would earn a return in excess of the risk-free rate.

Now suppose at expiration the index closes at 650.15. The profit on the futures contract is $654.83 - 650.15 = 4.68$. We bought the stocks for 652.50; however, over the life of the futures this investment lost interest at a rate of 5.2 percent and accumulated dividends at a rate of 3 percent. Thus, the effective cost of the stock was $652.50e^{(.052 - .03)(.1096)} = 654.08$, which by no coincidence is the theoretical futures price. The stock is sold at 650.15 for a profit of $650.15 - 654.08 = -3.93$. Thus, the overall profit is $4.68 - 3.93 = 0.75$. This is the difference between the theoretical futures price and the actual futures price. Since the actual futures price was higher than the theoretical price we were able to execute an arbitrage involving the purchase of stocks and sale of futures to capture the 0.75 differential. Had the actual futures price been less than the theoretical price, then we would have executed a reverse arbitrage involving the purchase of futures and short sale of stock, which would have created a synthetic loan that would have cost less than the risk-free rate.

An alternative way to look at index arbitrage is in terms of the implied repo rate. If the actual futures price is higher than the theoretical futures price, the implied repo rate on this transaction will exceed the risk-free rate. As we noted with our T-bill and T-bond examples, this implies that a long cash-and-carry arbitrage is worthwhile.

Stock index arbitrage has proven to be particularly popular. It turns out, however, that there are a number of serious practical considerations that can limit its profitability.

SOME PRACTICAL CONSIDERATIONS   There are several problems in implementing stock index arbitrage. We referred to the arbitrageur as buying the stock index at 652.50. In reality, the arbitrageur would have to purchase all 500 stocks in the appropriate proportions as the index and immediately execute all of the trades. The New York Stock Exchange has established a computerized order processing system, called the Designated Order Turnaround, or DOT, that expedites trades. Nonetheless, it is still difficult to get all the trades in before the price of any single stock changes. Thus, most arbitrageurs do not duplicate the index but use a smaller subset of the stocks. Of course, this introduces some risk into what is supposed to be a riskless transaction.

Let us assume, however, that the trades can be executed simultaneously. Let the index be 652.50. Now assume an arbitrageur has $20 million to use. Then the arbitrageur will buy the appropriately weighted 500 stocks with that amount. Because of the $500 multiplier on the futures, the S&P 500 is actually priced at $652.50(\$500) = \$326,250$, so the arbitrageur will need to buy $\$20,000,000/\$326,250 = 61.30$ futures contracts. Because one cannot buy fractional contracts, the transaction will not be weighted precisely.

Stock index arbitrage is the purchase or sale of a portfolio of stock that replicates a stock index and the sale or purchase of a futures contract on the index. Stock index arbitrage occurs when the futures price does not conform to the cost of carry model and, if properly executed, will earn, at no risk, the difference between the futures price and the theoretical futures price.

In addition, there are transaction costs, estimated by Stoll and Whaley (1987) at about .006125 of the market value of the stocks. Would this consume the profit in this example? If the index is 652.50 and the net profit is .75, the profit is .0011 of the index and clearly would be absorbed by the transaction costs.

In addition, there are problems involved in simultaneously selling all of the stocks in the index at expiration. These transactions must be executed such that the portfolio will be liquidated at the closing values of each stock. This is very difficult to do and frequently causes unusual stock price movements at expiration.

Program trading is the execution on a stock market of a large number of simultaneous buy or sell orders. It is normally triggered by a computer program that detects an arbitrage opportunity or suggests some other reason for quickly establishing a large portfolio of stock.

Nonetheless, many large financial institutions execute this type of arbitrage transaction. Every day billions of dollars trade on the basis of this futures pricing model. This trading of large blocks of stock simultaneously is called **program trading**.[4] The New York Stock Exchange defines a program trade as the simultaneous or near simultaneous purchase or sale of at least 15 stocks with a total market value of at least $1 million. The NYSE requires that these program trades be reported to it and all index arbitrage trades must be reported. Figure 11.1 shows a weekly report on program trading that is published in *The Wall Street Journal* each Friday. Note that during this five-day period, there were almost 410 million shares involved in program trading, of which more than 90 million shares were associated with index arbitrage.

In this type of trading, the model is programmed into a computer, which continuously monitors the futures price and the individual stock prices. When the computer identifies a deviation from the model, it sends a signal to the user. Many large institutions have established procedures for immediately executing the many simultaneous transactions, usually sending the orders through the DOT system. Table 11.6 illustrates a successful index arbitrage trade using the same example as before, but with a more significantly overpriced futures.

Are stock index futures contracts correctly priced? Is it truly possible to profit from index arbitrage? This question has been studied at great length. In the early days of stock index futures trading, there was considerable evidence that stock index futures prices were too low (Figlewski, 1984). In time, prices began to conform more closely to the model, as shown by Cornell (1985). However, deviations from the model remain, and some can be exploited by traders with sufficiently low transaction costs. MacKinlay and Ramaswamy (1988) revealed that (1) mispricing is more common the longer the remaining time to expiration and (2) when

---

[4]Index arbitrage is but one form of program trading. Another is portfolio insurance, which is covered in Chapter 15. See Hill and Jones (1988) for a discussion of the different forms of program trading.

FIGURE 11.1   **Weekly Program Trading as Reported in** *The Wall Street Journal*

PROGRAM TRADING

NEW YORK—Program trading in the week ended July 25 accounted for 14.9%, or an average 82 million daily shares, of New York Stock Exchange volume.

Brokerage firms executed an additional 26 million daily shares of program trading away from the Big Board, mostly on foreign markets. Program trading is the simultaneous purchase or sale of at least 15 different stocks with a total value of $1 million or more.

Of the program total on the Big Board, 22% involved stock index arbitrage, down from 24.5% the prior week. In this strategy, traders dart between stocks and stock-index options and futures to capture fleeting price differences.

Some 76.2% of program trading was executed by firms for their customers, while 21.9% was done for their own accounts, or principal trading. An additional 1.9% was designated as customer facilitation, in which firms use principal positions to facilitate customer trades.

The report includes a special profile of trading whenever the Dow Jones Industrial Average moves more than 50 points in a single direction during any one-hour period. There were eight such periods in the past week.

The first two periods occurred Monday. The following firms reported making program trades during 9:30-10:30 a.m. when the industrial average moved down more than 50 points: BNP Securities (buying and selling), Interactive Brokers (selling), Natwest (mostly selling), Goldman Sachs (selling), and Bear Stearns (buying and selling).

The following firms reported making program trades during 2:30-3:30 p.m. when the industrials moved up more than 50 points: BNP Securities (buying and selling), Natwest (buying and selling), Salomon Brothers (mostly buying), SBC Warburg (selling), and Morgan Stanley (buying and selling).

The third and fourth periods occurred Tuesday when the industrials moved up more than 50 points in each instance. The following firms reported making program trades during 10-11 a.m.: BNP Securities (buying and selling), Lawrence Helfant (mostly buying), W&D Securities (buying and selling), Morgan Stanley (buying and selling), and Donaldson Lufkin & Jenrette (buying).

The following firms reported making program trades during 2-3 p.m.: BNP Securities (mostly buying), Nomura Securities (mostly buying), First Boston (buying), Lehman Brothers (mostly buying) and Susquehanna Brokerage Services (buying).

The fifth period occurred Wednesday when the industrial average moved down more than 50 points. The following firms reported making program trades during 9:30-10:45 a.m.: Interactive Brokers (buying and selling), BNP Securities (buying and selling), Susquehanna Brokerage Services (buying and selling), Morgan Stanley (buying and selling), and Natwest (buying and selling).

The sixth and seventh periods both occurred Thursday. The following firms reported making program trades during 9:45-11 a.m. when the average moved down more than 50 points: BNP Securities (mostly selling), Natwest (mostly selling), Susquehanna Brokerage Services (mostly selling), Lehman Brothers (mostly selling) and Morgan Stanley (buying and selling).

The following firms reported making trades during 1:30-2:45 p.m. when the industrials moved up more than 50 points: BNP Securities (buying and selling), Natwest (mostly buying), Nomura Securities (mostly buying), WG Trading (buying), and Salomon Brothers (buying and selling).

The final period occurred Friday when the industrial average moved down more than 50 points. The following firms reported making program trades during 10:30-11:30 a.m.: BNP Securities (buying and selling), Morgan Stanley (mostly selling), Nomura Securities (mostly buying), Lawrence Heifant (buying and selling) and Societe Generale (buying and selling).

Of the five member firms reporting the most program activity, BNP Securities, Natwest, Interactive Brokers and Susquehanna Brokerage Services executed all or most of their program activity for customers as agent, while Morgan Stanley split its program trading between its own accounts and those of its customers.

NYSE PROGRAM TRADING
Volume (in millions of shares) for the week ended July 25, 1997

Top 15 Firms	Index Arbitrage	Derivative-Related*	Other Strategies	Total
BNP Securities	...	....	124.6	124.6
NatWest	18.5	0.3	16.4	35.2
Morgan Stanley	5.4	0.3	24.0	29.7
Interactive Brokers	...	....	28.7	28.7
Susquehanna Bkrg. Srvs.	6.9	....	10.9	17.8
Salomon Brothers	...	0.1	16.2	16.3
First Boston	7.4	....	8.0	15.4
W&D Securities	...	....	13.3	13.3
Nomura Securities	7.7	....	4.4	12.1
Lehman Brothers	4.2	....	5.3	9.5
Lawrence Helfant Inc.	...	....	9.0	9.0
Societe Generale	...	....	7.8	7.8
Thomas Williams	3.0	....	4.7	7.7
Goldman Sachs	...	....	7.5	7.5
WG Trading	6.4	....	....	6.4
OVERALL TOTAL	90.3	2.8	316.7	409.8

*Other derivative-related strategies besides index arbitrage
Source: New York Stock Exchange

Source: *The Wall Street Journal*, August 1, 1997

a contract becomes overpriced or underpriced, it tends to stay overpriced or underpriced rather than reversing from overpriced to underpriced or vice versa. Sofianos (1993) found that it was very difficult to profit from index arbitrage after accounting for the problem of simultaneously executing all trades.

TABLE 11.6	**Stock Index Arbitrage**

Scenario: On November 8, the S&P 500 index is at 652.50, the dividend yield is 3 percent, and the risk-free rate is 5.2 percent. The December futures contract, which expires in 40 days, is priced at 658.15. Its theoretical price is

$$f = 652.50e^{(.052 - .03)(.1096)} = 654.08,$$

where $T = 40/365 = .1096$. Thus, the contract is overpriced. An arbitrage will be executed using $20 million. Transaction costs are .6125 percent of the dollars invested.

Date	Spot Market	Futures Market
November 8	The S&P 500 is at 652.50. The stocks have a dividend yield of 3 percent. The risk-free interest rate is 5.2 percent.	The S&P 500 futures, expiring on December 18, is at 658.15. The appropriate number of futures is $20 million/[(652.50)(500)] = 61.30.*
December 18	**Buy $20 million of stock in the same proportions as make up the S&P 500.** The S&P 500 is at 650.18. The stocks will be worth (650.18/652.50) ($20 million) = $19.928889 million. The $20 million invested in the stocks effectively costs ($20 million) $e^{(.052 - .03)(.1096)}$ = $20.048282 million. Transaction costs are $20 million (.006125) = $122,500 (includes futures costs). **Sell stocks**	**Sell 61 contracts** Futures expires at the S&P 500 price of 650.18. **Close out futures at expiration**

Analysis:
Profit on stocks:

$19,928,889 (received from sale of stocks)
−$20,048,282 (invested in stocks)
─────────
−$119,393

Profit on futures:

61(500)(658.15) (sale price of futures)
−61(500)(650.18) (purchase price of futures)
─────────
$243,085

Overall profit:

$243,085 (from futures)
−$119,393 (from stock)
−$122,500 (transaction costs)
─────────
$1,192

---

*The appropriate number of futures contracts to match $20 million of stock is $20 million divided by the index price, *not the futures price*, times the multiplier. Even though the $20 million is allocated across 500 different stocks, it is equivalent to buying $20 million/652.50 = 30,651 "shares" of the S&P 500. The appropriate number of futures is one for each equivalent "share" of the S&P 500. Each futures, of course, has a $500 multiplier.

One consequence of program trading is that large stock price movements often occur quickly and without an apparent flow of new information. For example, when the index or futures price becomes out of line with the cost of carry model, many investors recognize this event simultaneously and react by buying and selling large quantities of stock and futures. Such actions have attracted considerable attention from the media. Critics have charged that program trading has led to increased volatility in the spot markets. Regulators and legislators have called for restrictions on such trading in the form of circuit breakers and reduced access to the DOT system for rapidly executing orders. Others have argued for imposing higher margins on futures trading. These issues continue to generate a lot of debate.

Speculating on Unsystematic Risk

In Chapter 8, we saw how stock returns contain both systematic and unsystematic risk. We already have seen that the systematic risk of a diversified portfolio can be hedged by using stock index futures. Because the portfolio is diversified, there is no unsystematic risk and therefore the portfolio is riskless. With some undiversified portfolios, an investor might wish to hedge the systematic risk and retain the unsystematic risk.

In an efficient market, investors cannot expect to earn returns by assuming unsystematic risk. However, professional financial analysts do not believe this is true. Thousands of analysts devote all of their time to identifying over- and underpriced stocks. An analyst who thinks a stock is underpriced normally recommends it for purchase. If the stock is purchased and the market goes down, the stock's overall performance may be hurt. For example, a drug firm may announce an important new drug that can help cure diabetes. If that announcement occurs during a strong bear market, the stock may be pulled down by the market effect. The extent of the stock's movement with the market is measured by its beta.

We will use the following notation:

$$S = \text{stock price}$$
$$M = \text{value of market portfolio of all risky assets}$$
$$r_S = \Delta S/S = \text{return on stock}$$
$$r_M = \Delta M/M = \text{return on market}$$
$$\beta = \text{beta of the stock}$$

The stock's return consists of its systematic return, βr_M, and its unsystematic return, which we shall call μ_S. Thus,

$$r_S = \beta r_M + \mu_S.$$

If we multiply both sides of the equation by S, we have

$$Sr_S = S\beta r_M + S\mu_S,$$

which is equivalent to

$$\Delta S = S\beta(\Delta M/M) + S\mu_S.$$

This is the return on the stock expressed in dollars. The objective of the transaction is to capture a profit equal to the unsystematic return, $S\mu_S$.

The profit from a transaction consisting of the stock and N_f futures contracts is

$$\Pi = \Delta S + N_f\Delta f.$$

Recall from Chapter 10 that the formula for N_f in an ordinary stock index futures hedge is $-\beta(S/f)$. Let us substitute this for N_f

$$\Pi = \Delta S - \beta(S/f)\Delta f.$$

Now we need to substitute $S\beta(\Delta M/M) + S\mu_S$ for ΔS and assume the futures price change will match the index price change. In that case, $\Delta M/M = \Delta f/f$. Making these substitutions gives

$$\Pi = S\mu_S.$$

Thus, if we use N_f futures contracts where N_f is the ordinary hedge ratio for stock index futures, we will eliminate systematic risk and the profit will be the unsystematic risk.

AN EXAMPLE   Table 11.7 illustrates an application of this result. In this example, you have identified what you believe to be an underpriced stock. You are worried, however, that the market as a whole will decline and drag the stock down. So to hedge the market effect, you sell stock index futures.

This transaction should not be considered riskless. As the title of this section indicates, it involves speculating on unsystematic risk. Suppose your analysis is incorrect and the company announces some bad news during a bull market. Selling the futures contract would eliminate the effect of the bull market while retaining the effect of the bad news announcement. Moreover, this type of trade depends not only on the correctness of the analysis but on the beta's stability.

Stock Market Timing with Futures

Recall that in Chapter 10, we looked at an example in which a portfolio manager sold stock index futures to eliminate the systematic risk. At a later date, the futures contracts were repurchased and the portfolio was

TABLE 11.7	Speculating on Unsystematic Risk

Scenario: On July 1, you are following the stock of Helene Curtis, which has a price of 17 3/8 and a beta of 1.10. Barring any change in the general level of stock prices, you expect the stock to appreciate by about 10 percent by the end of September. However, your analysis of the market as a whole calls for about an 8 percent decline in stock prices in general over the same time period. Since the stock has a beta of 1.10, this would bring the stock down by $1.10(.08) = .088$, or 8.8 percent, which will almost completely offset the expected 10 percent unsystematic increase in the stock price. You decide to hedge the market effect by selling stock index futures.

Date	Spot Market	Futures Market
July 1	Own 150,000 shares of Helene Curtis stock at 17.375. Value of stock: 150,000($17.375) = $2,606,250.	December stock index futures price is 444.60. Price of one contract: 444.60($500) = $222,300. Appropriate number of contracts: $$N_f = -1.10\left(\frac{\$2,606,250}{\$222,300}\right) = -12.90.$$ **Sell 13 contracts**
September 30	Stock price is 17.75. Value of stock: 150,000($17.75) = $2,662,500.	December stock index futures price is 411.30. Price of one contract: 411.30($500) = $205,650. **Buy 13 contracts**

Analysis:
Profit on stock:

$$\begin{array}{r} \$2,662,500 \\ -\$2,606,250 \\ \hline \$56,250 \end{array}$$

Profit on futures:

$$\begin{array}{r} 13(\$222,300) \\ -13(\$205,650) \\ \hline \$216,450 \end{array}$$

Overall profit:

$$\begin{array}{r} \$56,250 \\ +\,\$216,450 \\ \hline \$272,700 \end{array}$$

Overall rate of return:

$$\frac{\$272,700}{\$2,606,250} = .1046$$

returned to its previous level of systematic risk. The number of futures contracts was given by the formula

$$N_f = -\beta(S/f).$$

In some cases, a portfolio manager may wish to change the systematic risk but not eliminate it altogether. For example, if a portfolio manager believes the market is highly volatile, the portfolio beta could be lowered but not reduced to zero. This would enable the portfolio to profit if the market did move upward but would produce a smaller loss if the market moved down. At more optimistic times, the portfolio beta could be increased. In the absence of stock index futures (or options), changing the portfolio beta would require costly transactions in the individual stocks.

Assume we have a portfolio containing stock valued at S and N_f futures contracts. The return on the portfolio is given as r_{Sf}, where

$$r_{Sf} = \frac{\Delta S + N_f\Delta f}{S}.$$

The first term in the numerator, ΔS, is the change in the price of the stock. The second term, $N_f\Delta f$, is the number of contracts times the change in the price of the futures contract. The denominator, S, is the amount of money invested in the stock. The expected return on the portfolio, $E(r_{Sf})$, is

$$E(r_{Sf}) = \frac{E(\Delta S)}{S} + N_f \frac{E(\Delta f)}{S} = E(r_S) + \frac{N_f}{S} E(\Delta f),$$

where $E(r_S)$ is the expected return on the stock defined as $E(\Delta S)/S$ and $E(\Delta f)$ is the expected change in the price of the futures contract.

Recall from Chapter 8 that the Capital Asset Pricing Model gives the expected return on a stock as $r + [E(r_M) - r] \beta$. If the market is efficient, the investor's required return will equal the expected return. If the CAPM holds for stocks, it should also hold for stock index futures; however, it would be written as

$$\frac{E(\Delta f)}{f} = [E(r_M) - r]\beta_f = E(r_M) - r,$$

where β_f is the beta of the futures contract, assumed to be 1. Although in reality β_f will not be precisely equal to 1, it is sufficiently close that we shall assume it to keep the example simple. Note that this CAPM equation seems to be missing the term r from the right-hand side. The risk-free rate reflects the opportunity cost of money invested in the asset. Because the futures contract requires no initial outlay, there is no opportunity cost; thus, the r term is omitted.

The objective is to adjust the portfolio beta, β_S, and expected return, $E(r_{Sf})$, to a more preferred level. Since the CAPM holds for the portfolio, we can write the relationship between expected return and beta as

$$E(r_{Sf}) = r + [E(r_M) - r]\beta_T,$$

where β_T is the **target beta,** the desired risk level. Now we substitute for $E(r_S)$ and $E(\Delta f)$ and get

$$E(r_{Sf}) = r + [E(r_M) - r]\beta_S + N_f(f/S)[E(r_M) - r].$$

Setting this equal to $r + [E(r_M) - r]\beta_T$ and solving for N_f gives

$$N_f = (\beta_T - \beta_S)\left(\frac{S}{f}\right).$$

This formula differs only slightly from the previous formula for N_f. In fact, that formula is but a special case of this one. For example, if the target beta is zero, the above formula reduces to $-\beta_S\left(\frac{S}{f}\right)$, where the negative sign means that you would sell N_f futures. This is the same formula we used in Chapter 10 to eliminate systematic risk.

Buying or selling futures provides a simple way of increasing or decreasing a stock portfolio's beta.

When the manager wants to increase the beta, β_T will be greater than β_S and N_f will be positive. In that case, the manager will buy futures contracts. That makes sense, since the risk will increase. When the beta needs to be reduced, β_T will be less than β_S, and the manager should sell futures to reduce the risk.

An Example   Table 11.8 presents an example in which a portfolio manager, whose beta is 0.95, would like to temporarily increase it to 1.25. The manager buys stock index futures, which results in an overall gain of almost 12 percent when the stocks themselves gained only 10 percent.

Arbitraging Stock Index Futures with Stock Index Options

Recall from Chapter 3 that we examined put-call parity: the relationship between put and call prices and the price of the underlying stock, the exercise price, the risk-free rate, and the time to expiration. We derived the equation by constructing a risk-free portfolio. Now we shall examine **put-call-futures parity** with puts, calls, and futures contracts. To keep things as simple as possible, we shall assume the risk-free rate is constant. This allows us to ignore marking to market and treat futures contracts as forward contracts. We assume the options are European.

The first step in constructing a risk-free portfolio is to recognize that a combination of a long call and a short put is equivalent to a (long)

TABLE 11.8	**Stock Market Timing with Futures**

Scenario: On August 29, a portfolio manager is holding a portfolio of stocks worth $3,783,225. The portfolio beta is 0.95. The manager expects the stock market as a whole to appreciate substantially over the next three months and wants to increase the portfolio beta to 1.25. The manager could buy and sell shares in the portfolio, but this would incur high transaction costs and later the portfolio beta would have to be adjusted back to 0.95. The manager decides to buy stock index futures to temporarily increase the portfolio's systematic risk. The prices, number of shares, and betas are given below. The target date for evaluating the portfolio is November 29.

Stock	Price (8/29)	Number of Shares	Market Value	Weight	Beta
Beneficial Corp.	40.500	11,350	$459,675	.122	0.95
Cummins Engine	64.500	10,950	706,275	.187	1.10
Gillette	62.000	12,400	768,800	.203	0.85
Kmart	33.000	5,500	181,500	.048	1.15
Boeing	49.000	4,600	225,400	.059	1.15
W. R. Grace	42.625	6,750	287,719	.076	1.00
Eli Lilly	87.375	11,400	996,075	.263	0.85
Parker Pen	20.625	7,650	157,781	.042	0.75
			$3,783,225		

Portfolio beta:

$$.122(0.95) + .187(1.10) + .203(0.85) + .048(1.15) + .059(1.15)$$
$$+ .076(1.00) + .263(0.85) + .042(0.75) = 0.95.$$

December stock index futures contract:

Price on August 29: 379.80
Multiplier: $500
Price of one contract: $500(379.80) = $189,900

Required number of futures contracts:

$$N_f = (1.25 - 0.95)\left(\frac{3,783,225}{189,900}\right) = 5.98.$$

---

futures contract. In fact, a long-call/short-put combination is called a **synthetic futures contract.** A risk-free portfolio would consist of a long futures contract and a short synthetic futures contract. Selling the synthetic futures contract requires selling a call and buying a put.

Consider the portfolios illustrated in Table 11.9. We construct two portfolios, A and B. Examining the payoffs at expiration reveals that a long futures and a long put is equivalent to a long call and long risk-free bonds with a face value of the difference between the exercise price (E) and the futures price (f). If f is greater than E, as it could easily be, then instead of long bonds, you will take out a loan for the present value

TABLE 11.8	*(continued)*

Buy 6 contracts

Results: The values of the stocks on November 29 are shown below:

Stock	Price (11/29)	Market Value
Beneficial Corp.	45.125	$512,168
Cummins Engine	66.750	730,913
Gillette	69.875	866,450
Kmart	35.125	193,188
Boeing	49.125	225,975
W. R. Grace	40.750	275,062
Eli Lilly	103.750	1,182,750
Parker Pen	22.875	174,994
		$4,161,500

December stock index futures contract:

Price on November 29: 404.80
Multiplier: $500
Price of one contract: $500(404.80) = $202,400

Sell 6 contracts

Analysis:

The market value of the stocks increased by $4,161,500 − $3,783,225 = $378,275, a gain of about 10 percent.

The futures profit was

$$
\begin{array}{ll}
6(\$202,400) & \text{(sale price of futures)} \\
- 6(\$189,900) & \text{(purchase price of futures)} \\
\hline
\$75,000 & \text{(profit on futures).}
\end{array}
$$

Thus, the overall gain on the portfolio was effectively increased to $378,275 + $75,000 = $453,275, a return of about 12 percent.

of $f - E$, promising to pay back $f - E$ when the loan matures at the options' expiration. With equivalent payoffs, the value of portfolio A today must equal the value of portfolio B today. Thus,

$$P_e(S,T,E) = C_e(S,T,E) + (E - f)(1 + r)^{-T}.$$

We can, of course, write this several other ways, such as

$$C_e(S,T,E) - P_e(S,T,E) = (f - E)(1 + r)^{-T}.$$

		TABLE 11.9	**Put-Call-Futures Parity**		

				Payoffs from Portfolio Given Stock Price at Expiration	
Payoff from			**Current Value**	$S_T \leq E$	$S_T > E$
A.	Futures		0	$S_T - f$	$S_T - f$
	Put		$P_e(S,T,E)$	$E - S_T$	0
				$\overline{E - f}$	$\overline{S_T - f}$
B.	Call		$C_e(S,T,E)$	0	$S_T - E$
	Bonds		$(E - f)(1 + r)^{-T}$	$E - f$	$E - f$
				$\overline{E - f}$	$\overline{S_T - f}$

Put-call-futures parity is the relationship between the prices of puts, calls, and futures on an asset. With minimal assumptions, futures can be replaced by forwards.

Notice that whether the put price exceeds the call price depends on whether the exercise price exceeds the futures price. If the parity is violated, it may be possible to earn an arbitrage profit. Of course, futures can be replaced with forwards under our assumptions.

A good instrument for examining put-call-futures parity is the S&P 500 index options and futures. The options are European and trade on the CBOE, while the futures trade on the Chicago Mercantile Exchange. On September 12 of a particular year, the S&P 500 index was 671.15 and the December futures was at 678.10. The December 670 call was at 24.75, and the put was at 16.875. The expiration date was December 20, and the risk-free rate was 5.38 percent.

Since there are 99 days between September 12 and December 20, the time to expiration is $99/365 = .2712$. The left-hand side of the first put-call-futures parity equation is

$$P_e(S,T,E) = 16.875.$$

The right-hand side is

$$\begin{aligned} &C_e(S,T,E) + (E - f)(1 + r)^{-T} \\ &= 24.75 + (670 - 678.10)(1.0538)^{-.2712} \\ &= 16.76. \end{aligned}$$

Thus, if you bought the call and the bond, paying 16.76, and sold the futures and the put, receiving 16.875, the two portfolios will offset at expiration. So there is no risk and yet you earn a net gain of $16.875 - 16.76 = .115$. Of course transaction costs would almost surely consume the difference. Put-call-futures parity holds very closely here.

Summary

This chapter examined the application of some advanced futures trading strategies. It looked at how T-bill, Eurodollar, Treasury bond, and stock index futures can be used in arbitrage transactions. It also examined some spread strategies and the important concept of the implied repo rate. It examined speculative strategies and techniques for using stock index and bond futures in market timing.

In the final section of the chapter we discovered a parity relationship between the options on an asset and the forward or futures on the asset. This relationship, which we called put-call-futures (or forward) parity, further establishes important linkages between spot assets and their derivatives. Following the approach in previous chapters, we illustrate those linkages, using a stock as the underlying asset, in Figure 11.2, an expanded version of Figures 3.11, 4.13, and 9.9. Note that now the figure introduces put-call-forward/futures parity as linking the call, put, forward or futures, and risk-free bond while the remaining linkages, established by put-call-parity, the Black-Scholes put and call option pricing models, and the cost of carry model, are indicated. In Chapter 12, we shall study a new derivative, the option on a futures, and introduce it into the diagram.

Key Terms

Before continuing to Chapter 12, you should be able to give brief definitions of the following terms.

- futures spread
- cash-and-carry
- repurchase agreement/repo
- implied repo rate

FIGURE 11.2   **The Linkage between Forwards/Futures, Stock, Bonds, and Options**

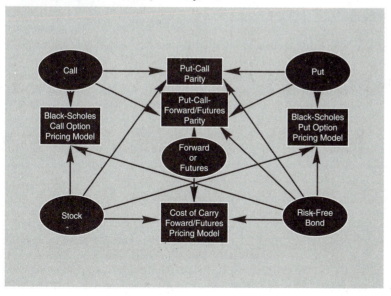

- cheapest to deliver (CTD)
- delivery option
- wild card option
- quality option
- end-of-the-month option
- timing option

- intermarket spread
- target duration
- stock index arbitrage
- program trading
- synthetic futures contract
- put-call-futures parity

Questions and Problems

1. Explain how the repurchase agreement plays a role in the pricing of futures contracts. What is the implied repo rate?

2. On November 1, the T-bill futures contract expiring on December 19 was priced at 93 (IMM Index). The T-bill maturing at that time was priced at a discount of 7.10 and the T-bill maturing on March 20 at a discount of 7.17. Determine the implied repo rate.

3. On November 1, the March T-bill futures price was 92.85. The T-bill maturing at around the futures expiration was selling at a discount of 7.17. You are interested in using the spot T-bill and the March futures contract to construct a synthetic T-bill maturing on June 20. The March contract expires on March 21.
   a. Determine the return on this T-bill.
   b. There is no actual T-bill maturing on June 20, but based on the discounts on bills maturing around that time, such a bill probably would have a discount of 7.31. Compare your result in part a with the return on the hypothetical T-bill maturing on June 20.

4. Why is it difficult to identify the spot instrument that the Treasury bond futures contract is following? How do futures traders determine the bond that the contract is most likely following?

5. On September 26 of a particular year, the March Treasury bond futures contract settlement price was 94-22. Compare the following two bonds and determine which is the cheaper bond to deliver. Assume delivery will be made on March 1. Use 5.3 percent as the repo rate.
   a. Bond A: A 12 3/4 percent bond callable in about 19 years and maturing in about 24 years with a price of 148 9/32 and a CF of 1.4433. Coupons are paid on November 15 and May 15. The accrued interest is 4.64 on September 26 and 3.73 on March 1.
   b. Bond B: A 13 7/8 percent bond callable in about 20 years and maturing in about 25 years with a price of 159 27/32 and a CF of 1.5689. Coupons are paid on November 15 and May 15. The accrued interest is 5.05 on September 26 and 4.06 on March 1.

6. It is August 20, and you are trying to determine which of two bonds is the cheaper bond to deliver on the December Treasury bond futures contract. The futures price is 89 12/32. Assume delivery will be made on December 14, and use 7.9 percent as the repo rate. Find the cheaper bond to deliver.
   a. Bond X: A 9 percent noncallable bond maturing in about 28 years with a price of 100 14/32 and a CF of 1.1106. Coupons are paid on November 15 and May 15. The accrued interest is 2.37 on August 20 and 0.72 on December 14.

b. Bond Z: An 11 1/4 percent noncallable bond maturing in about 25 years with a price of 121 14/32 and a CF of 1.3444. Coupons are paid February 15 and August 15. The accrued interest is 0.15 on August 20 and 3.7 on December 14.

7. Assume that on March 16, the cheapest bond to deliver on the June T-bond futures contract is the 14s callable in about 19 years and maturing in about 24 years. Coupons are paid on November 15 and May 15. The price of the bond is 161 23/32, and the CF is 1.584. The June futures price is 100 17/32. Assume a 5.5 percent reinvestment rate. Determine the implied repo rate on the contract. Interpret your result. Note that you will need to determine the accrued interest. Assume delivery on June 1.

8. During the first six months of the year, yields on long-term government debt have fallen about 100 basis points. You believe the decline in rates is over, and you are interested in speculating on a rise in rates. You are, however, unwilling to assume much risk, so you decide to do a spread. Use the following information to construct a T-bond futures spread on July 15, and determine the profit when the position is closed on November 15.

July 15
December futures price: 76 9/32
March futures price: 75 9/32

November 15
December futures price: 79 13/32
March futures price: 78 9/32

9. Explain how the implied repo rate on a spread transaction differs from that on a nearby futures contract.

10. Explain what a turtle trade is, and give an example.

11. On March 16, the June T-bond futures contract was priced at 100 17/32 and the September contract was at 99 17/32. Determine the implied repo rates on the spread. Assume the cheapest bond to deliver on both contracts is the 11 1/4 maturing in 28 years and currently priced at 140 21/32. The CF for delivery in June was 1.3593, and the CF for delivery in September was 1.3581. Delivery is on the first of the month, and the coupons are on 2/15 and 8/15. The accrued interest is 3.29 on June 1 and 6.16 on September 1.

12. On July 5, a stock index futures contract was at 394.85. The index was at 392.54, the risk-free rate was 2.83 percent, the dividend yield was 2.08 percent, and the contract expired on September 20. Determine if an arbitrage opportunity was available, and explain what transactions were executed.

13. Rework problem 12 assuming that the index was at 388.14 at expiration. Determine the profit from the arbitrage trade, and express it in terms of the profit from the spot and futures sides of the transaction. How does your answer relate to that in problem 12?

14. On August 20 a stock index futures, which expires on September 20, was priced at 429.70. The index was at 428.51. The dividend yield was 2.7 percent. Discuss the concept of the implied repo rate on an index arbitrage trade. Determine the implied repo rate on this trade, and explain how you would evaluate it.

15. Identify and explain some factors that make the execution of stock index futures arbitrage difficult in practice.

16. What is program trading? Why is it so controversial?

17. On November 1, an analyst who has been studying a firm called Computer Sciences believes the company will make a major new announcement before the end of the year. Computer Sciences currently is priced at 27 5/8 and has a beta of .95. The analyst believes the stock can advance about 10 percent if the market does not move. However, the analyst thinks the market might decline by as much as 5 percent, leaving the stock with a return of .10 + (−.05)(.95) = .0525. To capture the full 10 percent unsystematic return, the analyst recommends the sale of stock index futures. The March contract currently is priced at 393. Assume the investor owns 100,000 shares of the stock. Set up a transaction by determining the appropriate number of futures contracts. Then determine the effective return on the stock if, on December 31, the stock is sold at 28 7/8 and the futures contract is at 432.30. Explain your results.

18. You are the manager of a bond portfolio of $10 million of face value of bonds worth $9,448,456. The portfolio has a yield of 12.25 percent and a duration of 8.33. You plan to liquidate the portfolio in six months and are concerned about an increase in interest rates that would produce a loss on the portfolio. You would like to lower its duration to 5 years. A T-bond futures contract with the appropriate expiration is priced at 72 3/32 with a face value of $100,000, an implied yield of 12 percent, and an implied duration of 8.43 years.
     a. Should you buy or sell futures? How many contracts should you use?
     b. In six months, the portfolio has fallen in value to $8,952,597. The futures price is 68 16/32. Determine the profit from the transaction.

19. You are the manager of a stock portfolio worth $10,500,000. It has a beta of 1.15. During the next three months, you expect a correction in the market that will take the market down about 5 percent; thus, your portfolio is expected to fall about 5.75 percent (5 percent times a beta of 1.15). You wish to lower the beta to 1. A stock index futures contract with the appropriate expiration is priced at 425.75 with a multiplier of $500.
     a. Should you buy or sell futures? How many contracts should you use?
     b. In three months, the portfolio has fallen in value to $9,870,000. The futures has fallen to 402.35. Determine the profit and portfolio return over the quarter. How close did you come to the desired result?

20. On March 16, the March T-bond futures settlement price was 101 21/32. Assume the 12 1/2 percent bond maturing in about 22 years is the cheapest bond to deliver. The CF is 1.4639. Assume that the price at 3:00 P.M. was 150 15/32. Determine the price at 5:00 P.M. that would be necessary to justify delivery.

21. On September 12, a stock index futures was at 423.70. The December 400 call was at 26.25, and the put was at 3.25. The index was at 420.55. The futures and options expire on December 21. The discrete risk-free rate was 2.75 percent. Determine if the futures and options are priced correctly in re-

lation to each other. If they are not, construct a risk-free portfolio and show how it will earn a rate better than the risk-free rate.

22. (Concept Problem) Recall from the chapters on options that we learned about bull and bear spreads. Intramarket futures spreads also are considered bull and bear spreads. Describe what you think might be a bull spread with T-bond futures. Of course, be sure to explain your reasoning.

23. (Concept Problem) Referring to problem 12, suppose transaction costs amounted to .5 percent of the value of the spot index. Explain how these costs would affect the profitability and the incidence of index arbitrage. Then calculate the range of possible futures prices within which no arbitrage would take place.

APPENDIX 11A
Derivation of the Hedge Ratio for Adjusting Duration with Treasury Bond Futures*

The value of the position can be specified as

$$V = S + V^f N_f,$$

where V^f is the value of the futures contract. Now we wish to find the effect of a change in r on V. Since $\partial V^f / \partial r = \partial f / \partial r$, we have

$$\frac{\partial V}{\partial r} = \left(\frac{\partial S}{\partial r}\right) + \left(\frac{\partial f}{\partial r}\right) N_f.$$

The overall portfolio of bonds and futures has a yield, y_V, and a target duration, DUR_T. We can use the chain rule to rewrite the above equation as

$$\frac{\partial V / \partial y_v}{\partial r / \partial y_v} = \left(\frac{\partial S / \partial y_S}{\partial y_S / \partial r}\right) + \left(\frac{\partial f / \partial y_f}{\partial y_f / \partial r}\right) N_f.$$

From the material on duration in Chapter 8, we know that by definition $\partial S / \partial y_S = -DUR_S S / (1 + y_S)$, $\partial f / \partial y_f = -DUR_f f / (1 + y_f)$, and $\partial V / \partial y_V = -DUR_V V / (1 + y_V)$. We make the assumption that the spot and futures yields change one for one with the yield on the overall portfolio. Thus, $\partial y_S / \partial y_V = 1$ and $\partial y_f / \partial y_V = 1$. Using this result, setting DUR_V to DUR_T the target duration, and making some algebraic rearrangements enables us to solve for the number of futures contracts:

$$N_f = -\left(\frac{DUR_S - DUR_T}{DUR_f}\right)\left(\frac{S}{f}\right)\left(\frac{1 + y_f}{1 + y_S}\right).$$

*This appendix requires the use of calculus.

CHAPTER 12

Options on Futures

There are no fundamentally new or different risks in derivative products, rather . . . familiar kinds of risks are presented and combined in novel ways.

BRIAN QUINN

Derivatives: Report of an Internal Working Group, Bank of England, 1993

One of the distinguishing features of U.S. financial markets is their ability to innovate. In this chapter, we shall examine one of the most successful innovations in the financial markets: **options on futures.** These instruments combine many of the most attractive features of both options and futures. As a result, they give us an opportunity to extend the principles we learned in our study of options and futures in the preceding chapters. In the latter part of the chapter we shall look at why these instruments exist in many cases alongside options on the underlying spot instrument, which are almost economically equivalent.

Options on futures are not really new instruments. They existed many years ago. However, as a result of several scandals, they were banned in 1936. They were reauthorized in 1982, when the CFTC began a pilot program allowing each exchange to offer one option on futures contract. The program was so successful that in January 1987, options on futures were authorized permanently.

Options on futures are sometimes called **commodity options,** but that term is somewhat misleading. These are not options on commodities but options on futures contracts. Though there are many options on futures contracts in which the futures is an agricultural commodity futures, the most successful have been the options on financial futures.

Options on futures are also referred to as **futures options.** In this book, however, we shall use the term *options on futures.*

Characteristics of Options on Futures

An option on a futures is a contract that grants the holder the right, but not the obligation, to buy or sell a futures contract at a fixed price—the exercise price—up to a specified expiration date. An option to buy a futures is a call, and an option to sell a futures is a put. Although an option on a futures is very similar, in fact in some cases identical, to an option on a spot, there are a number of important differences that will become apparent as we examine how they are priced.

An option on a futures contract differs from an option on the spot instrument in that upon exercise, the option holder establishes a position in the futures contract. For example, on August 8, 1997, a call option on a Treasury bond futures contract was trading at the Chicago Board of Trade with an exercise price of 110. The underlying futures is the December Treasury bond futures. The Treasury bond option on futures is an American option, meaning that it can be exercised on any day prior to and including the option expiration day.

The expiration dates of options on futures can be confusing. This is because the underlying is a futures, which itself has an expiration. Let us take a look at the two primary contracts of our interest, the Chicago Board of Trade's Treasury bond option on futures and the Chicago Mercantile Exchange's S&P 500 option on futures. The Treasury bond option on futures expires in the month prior to the month that identifies the contract. For example, a September contract expires in August. The underlying futures is the next expiring futures. The S&P 500 option on futures expires in the month in which it is identified. In other words, an October option expires in October and is exercisable into the next expiring futures, which is the December. A September option expires in September and is exercisable into the September futures.

Our t-bond option permits the purchase of the December T-bond futures at a price of 110. The option price on that day was 3 22/64, or 3.34375. The option is on one underlying futures, which, as we already learned, has a face value of $100,000. Thus, the option price per contract is $3,343.75. As with options on a spot instrument, the buyer of the option is bullish, in this case on the price of the underlying instrument, the futures.

Suppose that at expiration the futures price was at 113. Then the call holder exercises the option. This establishes for the call holder a long position in the T-bond futures contract at a price of 110. Remember that these prices are in terms of a par value of $100,000 of Treasury bonds. The futures is immediately marked to market, and the buyer thus receives a cash credit of $3,000 based on the difference between the current price, 113—actually $113,000—and the price at which the contract was established, 110—actually $110,000. The investor must either deposit sufficient

funds to meet the futures' initial margin requirement or liquidate the futures. Upon exercise, a short position in the futures at a price of 110, or $110,000, is established for the writer. The writer's account is immediately marked to market for a $3,000 loss and must be supplied with sufficient margin or liquidated. If at expiration the futures price is less than the exercise price, the call simply expires unexercised and the writer retains the premium paid by the buyer.

The December 110 put traded at a price of 1 4/32, or $1,125. Upon exercise, a short position in the futures at a price of 110, or $110,000, is established for the put holder. The position is marked to market, and sufficient margin funds must be deposited or the futures bought back. A long position in the futures at a price of 110, or $110,000, is established for the put writer. The position is marked to market, and sufficient margin funds must be deposited or the futures sold.

Buyers of these options are required to pay the full premium. Writers post margin for their short options in a manner similar to writers of options on spot instruments. In addition, the writers' accounts are marked to market.

Options on futures have been quite popular with investors. Figure 12.1 shows the annual volume from 1983 to 1996. Growth had been quite steady through 1988. Then a decline occurred in 1989. This partially re-

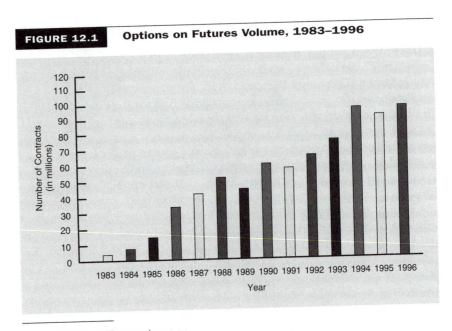

FIGURE 12.1   **Options on Futures Volume, 1983–1996**

Source: CFTC *Annual Report,* various years

flected a decrease in public trading of these options since the market crash of 1987. Another slight decline occurred in 1991. After a large increase in 1994, a decline occurred again in 1995, but volume increased again in 1996.

Figure 12.2 illustrates the composition of the market for options on futures in terms of the type of underlying instrument. As the pie chart indicates, financials compose the largest single group, accounting for about 62 percent of volume. Agriculturals are second at 18.7 percent. Currency and energy futures are tied for third.

Table 12.1 presents the 1996 volume by exchange. Each of the U.S. futures exchanges has options on futures trading. The Chicago Board of Trade, which is first in futures volume, is also first in the volume of options on futures. The Chicago Mercantile Exchange is second and the New York

FIGURE 12.2   Options on Futures Volume by Underlying Instrument, CFTC Fiscal Year 1996

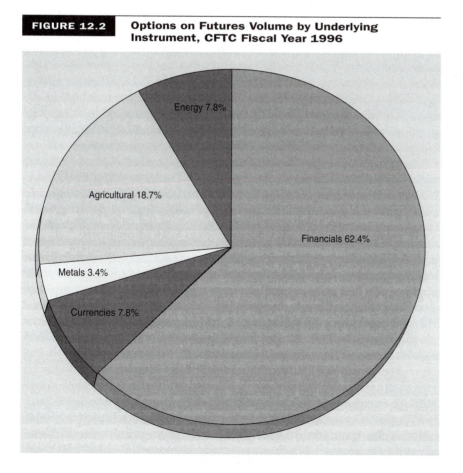

TABLE 12.1	Options on Futures Trading Volume by Exchange, CFTC Fiscal Year 1996

Exchange	Number of Contracts
Chicago Board of Trade	50,755,785
Chicago Mercantile Exchange	34,726,519
New York Mercantile Exchange	7,828,493
Commodity Exchange	3,330,663
Coffee, Sugar and Cocoa Exchange	2,254,762
New York Cotton Exchange	1,302,718
Kansas City Board of Trade	76,335
MidAmerica Commodity Exchange	24,230
Minneapolis Grain Exchange	20,941
	100,320,446

Note: The New York Mercantile Exchange and the Commodity Exchange have since merged.

Source: CFTC *Annual Report 1996*

Mercantile Exchange, with its highly successful energy futures and options, is third.

Figure 12.3 shows *The Wall Street Journal* quotations for some of the options on futures contracts. The tables are virtually the same as those for options on the spot. Beside the contract name and the exchange abbreviation is the contract size and units of quotation. Below the actual price quotations are volume and open interest figures.

Table 12.2 lists all options on futures contracts trading and regularly quoted in *The Wall Street Journal* as of August 8, 1997. Table 12.3 presents the 10 most active options on futures contracts in 1996. The Treasury bond option on futures is the most active, followed by the Chicago Mercantile Exchange's Eurodollar option on futures contract. The list of most active options on futures contracts, in fact, is quite similar to that of the most active futures contracts. This is not surprising, since trading in both the options and the futures occurs side by side. As you might expect, arbitrage between the option and the underlying futures is the basis for pricing these instruments.

Pricing Options on Futures

In this section, we shall look at some principles of pricing options on futures. These principles are closely related to the principles of pricing ordinary options that were established in Chapters 3 and 4. The reader may wish to review those chapters before proceeding. We shall continue to employ the same notation previously used. We will make the assumptions that

FIGURE 12.3 **Options on Futures Quotations in *The Wall Street Journal*, Trading Day of July 23, 1997**

AGRICULTURAL

CORN (CBT)
5,000 bu.; cents per bu.

Strike	Calls-Settle			Puts-Settle		
Price	Sep	Dec	Mar	Sep	Dec	Mar
230	18 5/8	21 7/8	29	1 3/8	4 3/8	4
240	11 1/4	15 5/8	22 3/8	4	8	7
250	6 1/4	10 7/8	16 7/8	9	13	11 3/4
260	3 1/2	7 3/4	12 3/4	16 1/4	19 3/4	17
270	1 7/8	5 1/2	9 3/4	24 1/2	27 3/8	23 1/2
280	1	3 7/8	7 1/4	33 3/4	35 5/8	30 3/4

Est vol 16,000 Tu 9,001 calls 7,014 puts
Op int Tues 194,996 calls 152,359 puts

SOYBEANS (CBT)
5,000 bu.; cents per bu.

Strike	Calls-Settle			Puts-Settle		
Price	Sep	Nov	Jan	Sep	Nov	Jan
600	50 1/4	30 1/4	37 1/4	3	27 1/4	31
625	31 1/4	22	28	9 1/4	43 3/4	46 1/2
650	18 3/4	15 1/2	21	21 1/4	62 1/4	64
675	11 1/4	11	15 1/2	38 1/2	82 1/4	83 1/2
700	6 3/4	8 1/8	12 1/2	59 1/2	103 3/4	104
725	4 1/2	6 1/4	9	82	127 1/4	126

Est vol 13,000 Tu 6,565 calls 3,554 puts
Op int Tues 140,509 calls 72,015 puts

SOYBEAN MEAL (CBT)
100 tons; $ per ton

Strike	Calls-Settle			Puts-Settle		
Price	Sep	Oct	Dec	Sep	Oct	Dec
200	22.10	9.75	8.75	1.00	7.25	13.00
210	13.65	6.00	6.25	2.70	13.40	20.25
220	7.75	3.75	4.25	6.75	21.00	28.25
230	4.50	2.50	3.25	13.50	29.60	37.15
240	2.60	1.75	2.40	21.60	....	....
250	1.50	1.20	2.00	30.50	....	....

Est vol 1,100 Tu 646 calls 1,512 puts
Op int Tues 13,567 calls 12,527 puts

SOYBEAN OIL (CBT)
60,000 lbs.; cents per lb.

Strike	Calls-Settle			Puts-Settle		
Price	Sep	Oct	Dec	Sep	Oct	Dec
2100	....	....	....	....	.400	....
2150	.700	....	....	.400	....	.700
2200	.500	....	1.060	.700	.900	.970
2250	.350	....	.850	1.050	1.230	1.260
2300	.250	.460	.700	1.450	....	1.570
2350	.180	.380	.600	1.880	1.990	1.980

Est vol 500 Tu 291 calls 429 puts
Op int Tues 16,917 calls 6,409 puts

WHEAT (CBT)
5,000 bu.; cents per bu.

Strike	Calls-Settle			Puts-Settle		
Price	Sep	Dec	Mar	Sep	Dec	Mar
340	20 3/4	38 1/4	51	4 1/2	8 3/4	12
350	14 1/4	31 3/4	44 1/2	8	12	15 1/4
360	9 1/2	26	38 1/2	12 3/4	16	19
370	6 1/4	21	33 1/4	19 1/4	20 3/4	....
380	3 1/2	17 1/4	28 3/4	26 1/2	26 1/2	....
390	2 1/8	14	24 1/2	35 1/4	33 1/4	....

Est vol 12,000 Tu 5,656 calls 3,651 puts
Op int Tues 63,838 calls 39,455 puts

COTTON (CTN)
50,000 lbs.; cents per lb.

Strike	Calls-Settle			Puts-Settle		
Price	Oct	Dec	Mar	Oct	Dec	Mar
73	2.59	3.37	....	1.04	1.81	2.20
74	2.01	2.84	4.34	1.45	2.24	2.61
75	1.50	2.36	....	1.95	2.74	3.04
76	1.19	1.94	3.34	2.58	3.30	3.54
77	.83	1.59	2.93	3.27	3.92	4.08
78	.61	1.28	2.55	4.02	4.60	4.67

Est vol 2,150 Tu 1,620 calls 495 puts
Op int Tues 37,446 calls 31,603 puts

OIL

CRUDE OIL (NYM)
1,000 bbls.; $ per bbl.

Strike	Calls-Settle			Puts-Settle		
Price	Sep	Oct	Nov	Sep	Oct	Nov
1850	1.31	....	....	.18	.37	.48
1900	.94	1.24	1.39	.31	.54	.65
1950	.62	.95	1.12	.51	.75	.87
2000	.42	.72	.89	.79	1.02	1.14
2050	.25	.54	.70	1.12	1.34	....
2100	.16	.39	.54	1.53	1.68	1.78

Est vol 16,426 Tu 8955 calls 9,517 puts
Op int Tues 232,987 calls 153,059 puts

HEATING OIL No.2 (NYM)
42,000 gal.; $ per gal.

Strike	Calls-Settle			Puts-Settle		
Price	Aug	Sep	Oct	Aug	Sep	Oct
51	.0240	.0342	.0437	.0012	.0060	....
52	.0146	.0272	.0371	.0018	.0090	.0125
53	.0085	.0211	.0302	.0057	.0128	.0155
54	.0042	.0156	.0256	.0114	.0173	.0208
55	.0018	.0118	.0210	.0190	.0235	....
56	.0008	.0090	.0175	.0280	.0306	.0326

Est vol 4,153 Tu 2,642 calls 512 puts
Op int Tues 82,600 calls 31,967 puts

GASOLINE-Unlead (NYM)
42,000 gal.; $ per gal.

Strike	Calls-Settle			Puts-Settle		
Price	Aug	Sep	Oct	Aug	Sep	Oct
59	.0227	.0268	....	.0015	.0105	....
60	.0147	.0212	.0110	.0035	.0148	....
61	.0087	.0153	.0086	.0075	.0189	....
62	.0045	.0112	.0068	.0133	.0248	....
63	.0021	.0080	....	.0209	....	....
64	.0010	.0060	.0041	.0298	.0395	....

Est vol 4,668 Tu 1,327 calls 258 puts
Op int Tues 40,670 calls 25,670 puts

NATURAL GAS (NYM)
10,000 MMBtu.; $ per MMBtu.

Strike	Calls-Settle			Puts-Settle		
Price	Aug	Sep	Oct	Aug	Sep	Oct
205	.015	.117	.165	.007	.074	.107
210	.068	.092	.138	.020	.098	.132
215	.040	.071	.116	.040	.128	.158
220	.019	.054	.096	.071	.161	.187
225	.008	.040	.079	.110	.196	.220
230	.004	.031	.064	.156	.237	.255

Est vol 9,576 Tu 7,221 calls 7,954 puts
Op int Tues 114,743 calls 93,293 puts

INDEX

S&P 500 STOCK INDEX (CME)
$500 times premium

Strike	Calls-Settle			Puts-Settle		
Price	Aug	Sep	Oct	Aug	Sep	Oct
930	25.35	36.20	60.05	14.15	25.05	39.10
935	22.35	33.35	57.15	16.10	27.15	41.10
940	19.50	30.65	54.35	18.25	29.40	43.20
945	16.85	28.05	51.65	20.60	31.75	45.40
950	14.50	25.60	49.05	23.20	34.25	47.70
955	12.30	23.30	....	26.00	....	....

Est vol Tu30,192 calls 10,097 puts
Op int Tues 48,593 calls 119,146 puts

INTEREST RATE

T-BONDS (CBT)
$100,000; points and 64ths of 100%

Strike	Calls-Settle			Puts-Settle		
Price	Sep	Dec	Mar	Sep	Dec	Mar
113	2-40	....	....	0-17	....	....
114	1-55	2-42	3-16	0-32	1-43	2-35
115	1-15	....	....	0-55	....	....
116	0-48	1-43	2-20	1-23	2-42	....
117	0-26	....	....	2-01	....	....
118	0-12	0-63	1-38	2-51	3-60	....

Est. vol. 100,000;
Tu vol. 70,815 calls; 51,474 puts
Op. int. Tues 373,105 calls; 351,684 puts

T-NOTES (CBT)
$100,000; points and 64ths of 100%

Strike	Calls-Settle			Puts-Settle		
Price	Sep	Dec	Mar	Sep	Dec	Mar
108	2-13	2-23	....	0-04	0-35	1-04
109	1-23	1-45	....	0-13	0-56	....
110	0-44	1-11	....	0-33	1-21	....
111	0-18	0-50	....	....	....	....
112	0-06	0-31	0-51	1-59	....	....
113	0-02	0-19	0-35	....	....	....

Est vol 25,000 Tu 4,382 calls 8,580 puts
Op int Tues 192,949 calls 137,527 puts

5 YR TREAS NOTES (CBT)
$100,000; points and 64ths of 100%

Strike	Calls-Settle			Puts-Settle		
Price	Sep	Dec	Mar	Sep	Dec	Mar
10650	1-00	1-13	....	0-08	0-37	....
10700	0-41	0-58	....	0-16	0-49	....
10750	0-22	0-43	....	0-30	....	....
10800	0-11	....	....	0-50	....	....
10850	0-05	....	....	....	....	....

Est vol 4,800 Tu 3,170 calls 3,727 puts
Op int Tues 30,690 calls 58,557 puts

MUNI BOND INDEX (CBT)
$1,000; times Bond Buyer MBI

Strike	Calls-Settle			Puts-Settle		
Price	Aug	Sep	Oct	Aug	Sep	Oct
119	....	....	....	....	....	....
120	1-46	2-04	....	....	0-01	....
121	....	....	....	....	....	....
122	....	1-02	....	....	....	....
124	....	0-25	....	....	....	....

Est vol 2,125 Tu 4,600 calls 2,900 puts
Op int Tues 15,161 calls 22,918 puts

EURODOLLAR (CME)
$ million; pts. of 100%

Strike	Calls-Settle			Puts-Settle		
Price	Aug	Sep	Oct	Aug	Sep	Oct
9400	2.80	2.80	1.80	.05	.05	.45
9425	.35	.50	.40	.10	.25	1.55
9450	....	....	....	....	2.25	....
9475	....	....	....	....	4.75	....
9500	....	....	....	....	7.25	....
9525	....	....	....	....	9.75	....

Est. vol. 109,484;
Tu vol. 23,610 calls; 10,949 puts
Op. int. Tues 1,135,543 calls; 1,071,968 puts

Source: *The Wall Street Journal*, July 24, 1997

TABLE 12.2	Listed Options on Futures Contracts on U.S. Futures Exchanges Covered in *The Wall Street Journal* (as of August 8, 1997)

Contract	Exchange	Contract Size
Interest Rates		
Treasury bonds	CBOT	$100,000
6 1/2–10-year Treasury notes	CBOT	$100,000
5-year Treasury notes	CBOT	$100,000
Municipal bond index	CBOT	$1,000 × premium
Eurodollars	IMM	$1,000,000
1-year Mid-Curve Eurodollar	IMM	$1,000,000
2-year Mid-Curve Eurodollar	IMM	$1,000,000
Indices and Insurance		
S&P 500 Index	IOM	$500 × premium
NYSE Composite Index	NYFE	$500 × premium
NASDAQ 100 Index	IOM	$100 × premium
Eastern Small Cap 12-month insurance	CBOT	$\frac{1}{10}$ of index point
Midwestern Small Cap 12-month insurance	CBOT	$\frac{1}{10}$ of index point
Commodity Futures		
Corn	CBOT	5,000 bu.
Soybeans	CBOT	5,000 bu.
Soybean meal	CBOT	100 tons
Soybean oil	CBOT	60,000 lbs.
Soybeans	MCE	1,000 bu.
Wheat	MPLS	5,000 bu.
Wheat	CBOT	5,000 bu.
Wheat	KCBT	5,000 bu.
Oats	CBOT	5,000 bu.
Rice	CBOT	2,000 cwt.
Cotton	CTN	50,000 lbs.
Orange juice	CTN	15,000 lbs.
Coffee	CSCE	37,500 lbs.
Sugar—world	CSCE	112,000 lbs.
Cocoa	CSCE	10 metric tons
Crude oil	NYMEX	1,000 bbls.
Heating oil no. 2	NYMEX	42,000 gals.
Gasoline—unleaded	NYMEX	42,000 gals.
Natural gas	NYMEX	10,000 MM Btu.
Feeder cattle	CME	50,000 lbs.
Live cattle	CME	40,000 lbs.
Lean hogs	CME	40,000 lbs.
Copper	COMEX	25,000 lbs.
Gold	COMEX	100 troy ozs.
Platinum	NYMEX	50 troy ozs.
Silver	COMEX	5,000 troy ozs.
Lumber	CME	80,000 bd. ft.
Foreign Currencies		
Japanese yen	IMM	12,500,000 yen
German mark	IMM	125,000 marks
Canadian dollar	IMM	100,000 Canadian dollars
British pound	IMM	62,500 pounds
Swiss franc	IMM	125,000 francs
Brazilian real	CME	100,000 reals
U.S. dollar Index	FINEX	$100 × Index

TABLE 12.3	Most Active Options on Futures Contracts, CFTC Fiscal Year 1996	
Contract	Exchange	Number of Contracts
Treasury bonds	CBOT	25,446,914
Eurodollars	CME	21,133,713
Treasury notes	CBOT	11,056,514
Corn	CBOT	6,520,069
Soybeans	CBOT	4,907,971
Crude oil	NYMEX	4,901,718
S&P 500	CME	4,827,376
British pound	CME	3,276,605
Gold	COMEX	2,216,367
Wheat	CBOT	1,880,246

Source: CFTC *Annual Report 1996*

the options and the futures contracts expire simultaneously and the futures price equals the forward price.

The Intrinsic Value of an American Option on Futures

The minimum value of an American call on a futures is its intrinsic value. We can formally state this as

$$C_a(f,T,E) \geq Max(0, f - E),$$

where $Max(0, f - E)$ is the intrinsic value. It is easy to see that this statement must hold for options on futures in the same way as for options on the spot. If the call price is less than the intrinsic value, the call can be bought and exercised. This establishes a long position in a futures contract at the price of E. The futures is immediately sold at the price of f, and a risk-free profit is made.

Consider a November 685 S&P 500 option on futures on September 13. The underlying futures price is 688.85. The intrinsic value is $Max(0, 688.85 - 685) = 3.85$. The call is actually worth 17.70. The difference of $17.70 - 3.85 = 13.85$ is the time value. Like the time value on an option on the spot, the time value here decreases as expiration approaches. At expiration, the call must sell for its intrinsic value.

The intrinsic value of an American put option on futures establishes its minimum value. This is stated as

$$P_a(f,T,E) \geq Max(0, E - f),$$

The intrinsic value of an American call option on a futures is the greater of zero or the difference between the futures price and the exercise price.

The intrinsic value of an American put option on a futures is the greater of zero or the difference between the exercise price and the futures price.

where $\text{Max}(0, E - f)$ is the intrinsic value. Again, if this is not true, the arbitrageur can purchase the futures contract and the put, immediately exercise the put, and earn a risk-free profit.

The October 695 S&P 500 put option on futures was priced at 13.95 on September 13. The futures price was 688.85. The minimum value is $\text{Max}(0, 695 - 688.85) = 6.15$.

The difference between the put price, 13.95, and the intrinsic value, 6.15, is the time value, 7.80. The time value, of course, erodes as expiration approaches. At expiration, the put is worth the intrinsic value.

The Lower Bound of a European Option on Futures

The intrinsic values apply only to American options on futures. This is because early exercise is necessary to execute the arbitrage. As you should recall from our study of options on stocks, we can establish a lower bound for a European option.

Let us first look at the call option on futures. We construct two portfolios, A and B. Portfolio A consists of a single long position in a European call. Portfolio B consists of a long position in the futures contract and a long position in risk-free bonds with a face value of $f - E$. Note that if E is greater than f, this is actually a short position in bonds and thus constitutes a loan in which we pay back $E - f$ at expiration. We do not really care whether we are borrowing or lending. As long as we keep the signs correct, we will obtain the desired result in either case. Table 12.4 presents the outcomes of these portfolios.

If $f_T \leq E$, the call expires worthless. The futures contract is worth $f_T - f$, and the bonds are worth $f - E$; thus, portfolio B is worth $f_T - E$. If $f_T > E$, the call is worth $f_T - E$, the intrinsic value, and portfolio B is still worth $f_T - E$. As you can see, portfolio A does at least as well as portfolio

---

TABLE 12.4   **The Lower Bound of a European Call Option on Futures: Payoffs at Expiration of Portfolios A and B**

Portfolio	Instrument	Current Value	Payoffs from Portfolio Given Futures Price at Expiration $f_T \leq E$	$f_T > E$
A	Long call	$C_e(f,T,E)$	0	$f_T - E$
B	Long futures	0	$f_T - f$	$f_T - f$
	Bond	$(f - E)(1 + r)^{-T}$	$\dfrac{+ (f - E)}{f_T - E}$	$\dfrac{+ (f - E)}{f_T - E}$

B in all cases. Therefore, its current value should be at least as high as portfolio B's. We can state this as

$$C_e(f,T,E) \geq (f - E)(1 + r)^{-T}.$$

Because an option cannot have negative value,

$$C_e(f,T,E) \geq Max[0, (f - E)(1 + r)^{-T}].$$

Note that we used an important result from Chapter 9: The value of a futures contract when initially established is zero. Thus, portfolio B's value is simply the value of the risk-free bonds.

The price of a European call option on a futures must at least equal the greater of zero or the present value of the difference between the futures price and the exercise price.

This result establishes the lower bound for a European call on the futures. Remember that a European call on the spot has a lower bound of

$$C_e(S,T,E) \geq S - E(1 + r)^{-T}.$$

As we saw in Chapter 9, in the absence of dividends on the spot instrument, the futures price is

$$f = S(1 + r)^T.$$

Making this substitution for f, we see that these two lower bounds are equivalent. In fact, if the option and futures expire simultaneously, a European call on a futures is equivalent to a European call on the spot. This is because a European call can be exercised only at expiration, at which time the futures and spot prices are equivalent.

As an example of the lower bound, let us look at the October 685 S&P 500 call option on futures on September 13. The option expires on October 18; thus, there are 35 days remaining and T = 35/365 = .0959. The risk-free rate is 5.13 percent. The lower bound is

$$C_e(f,T,E) \geq Max[0, (688.85 - 685)(1.0513)^{-.0959}] = 3.83.$$

The actual call price is 13.30.

Note, however, that the lower bound established here is slightly less than the intrinsic value of 3.85. This should seem unusual. For ordinary equity options, the lower bound of $Max[0, S - E(1 + r)^{-T}]$ exceeds the intrinsic value of $Max(0, S - E)$. For options on futures, however, this is not necessarily so. As we shall see in a later section, this explains why some American call (and put) options on futures are exercised early.

Now let us look at the lower bound for a European put option on a futures. Again we shall establish two portfolios, A and B. Portfolio A consists of a long position in the put. Portfolio B consists of a short position in the

| TABLE 12.5 | The Lower Bound of a European Put Option on Futures: Payoffs at Expiration of Portfolios A and B |

| | | | *Payoffs from Portfolio Given Futures Price at Expiration* | |
Portfolio	Instrument	Current Value	$f_T < E$	$f_T \geq E$
A	Long put	$P_e(f,T,E)$	$E - f_T$	0
B	Short futures	0	$-(f_T - f)$	$-(f_T - f)$
	Bond	$+ (E - f)(1 + r)^{-T}$	$+ E - f$	$+ E - f$
			$E - f_T$	$E - f_T$

futures contract and a long position in risk-free bonds with a face value of $E - f$. Again, if f is greater than E, this is actually a short position in bonds, or taking out a loan. Table 12.5 illustrates the outcomes.

By now you should be able to explain each outcome. If $f_T < E$, the put is exercised, so portfolio A is worth $E - f_T$. If $f_T \geq E$, the put expires worthless. In both cases, the futures contract in portfolio B is worth $-(f_T - f)$ and the bonds are worth $E - f$, for a total of $E - f_T$. Portfolio A does at least as well as portfolio B in both outcomes. Therefore, the current value of A should be at least as great as the current value of B,

$$P_e(f,T,E) \geq (E - f)(1 + r)^{-T}.$$

Because the option cannot have a negative value,

$$P_e(f,T,E) \geq Max[0,(E - f)(1 + r)^{-T}].$$

The price of a European put option on a futures must at least equal the greater of zero or the present value of the difference between the exercise price and the futures price.

As we saw with calls, we can substitute S for $f(1 + r)^{-T}$ and see that the lower bound for a put option on a futures is the same as that for a put option on the spot. As is true for calls, European put options on futures in which the put and the futures expire simultaneously are equivalent to options on the spot.

As an example, let us look at the October 690 S&P 500 put option on futures on September 13 of a particular year. The futures price is 688.85, the time to expiration is .0959, and the risk-free rate is 5.13 percent. The lower bound is

$$P_e(S,T,E) \geq Max[0,(690 - 688.85)(1.0513)^{-.0959}] = 1.14.$$

The actual price of the put is 11.50. As we saw for equity puts, the European lower bound will be less than the American intrinsic value. Thus, the

actual minimum price of this American put is its intrinsic value of 690 − 688.85 = 1.15.

Put-Call Parity of Options on Futures

We have looked at put-call parity for options on stocks. We can also establish a put-call parity rule for options on futures.

First let us construct two portfolios, A and B. Portfolio A will consist of a long futures and a long put on the futures. This can be thought of as a protective put. Portfolio B will consist of a long call and a long bond with a face value of the exercise price minus the futures price. If E is greater than F, this is indeed a long position in a bond. If f is greater than E, then we are simply issuing bonds with a face value of f − E. In either case, the cash flow of the bond will be E − f when it matures on the option expiration day. The payoffs are illustrated in Table 12.6.

As we can see, the two portfolios produce the same result. If the futures price ends up less than the exercise price, both portfolios end up worth E − f. If the futures price ends up greater than the exercise price, both portfolios end up worth $f_T − f$. Thus, portfolio B is also like a protective put and its current value must equal the current value of portfolio A. Since the value of the long futures in portfolio A is zero, we conclude that

$$P_e(f,T,E) = C_e(f,T,E) + (E − f)(1 + r)^{-T}.$$

As with put-call parity for options on spot assets, we can write this several different ways, isolating the various terms. Note the similarity between put-call parity for options on futures and put-call parity for options on the spot:

$$P_e(S,T,E) = C_e(S,T,E) − S + E(1 + r)^{-T}.$$

Put-call parity of options on futures is the relationship among the call price, the put price, the futures price, the exercise price, the risk-free rate, and the time to expiration.

TABLE 12.6   Put-Call Parity of Options on Futures

Portfolio	Instrument	Current Value	Payoffs from Portfolio Given Futures Price at Expiration	
			$f_T \leq E$	$f_T > E$
A	Long Futures	0	$f_T − f$	$f_T − f$
	Long Put	$P_e(f,T,E)$	$E − f_T$	0
			$E − f$	$f_T − f$
B	Long Call	$C_e(f,T,E)$	0	$f_T − E$
	Bonds	$(E − f)(1 + r)^{-T}$	$E − f$	$E − f$
			$E − f$	$f_T − f$

Because the futures price must equal $S(1 + r)^T$, these two versions of put-call parity are equivalent. As we stated earlier, in many ways the options themselves are equivalent.

Let us look at the October 685 puts and calls on the S&P 500 futures on September 13. As we saw in Chapter 3, we can calculate the put price and compare it to the actual market price or calculate the call price and compare it to the actual market price. Here we shall calculate the put price. The call price is $13.30. The other input values given earlier are f = 688.85, r = .0513, and T = .0959. The put price should be

$$P_e \ (f,T,E) = 13.30 + (685 - 688.85)(1.0513)^{-.0959} = 9.47.$$

The actual put price was 9.45. This is very close, but we should expect a difference because these are American options and the formula is for European options. The formula price should be less than the market price, but in this case it is not. However, the effect of transaction costs might explain the difference.

Early Exercise of Call and Put Options on Futures

Recall that in the absence of dividends on a stock, a call option on the stock would not be exercised early; however, a put option might be. With an option on a futures contract, either a call or a put might be exercised early. Let us look at the call.

Consider a deep-in-the-money American call. If the call is on the spot instrument, it may have some time value remaining. If it is sufficiently deep-in-the-money, it will have little time value. However, that does not mean it should be exercised early. Disregarding transaction costs, early exercise would be equivalent to selling the call. If the call is on the futures, however, early exercise may be the better choice. The logic behind this is that a deep-in-the-money call behaves almost identically to the underlying instrument. If the call is on the spot instrument, it will move one for one with the spot price. If the call is on the futures, it will move nearly one for one with the futures price. Thus, the call on the futures will act almost exactly like a long position in a futures contract. However, the investor has money tied up in the call but because the margin can be met by depositing interest-earning T-bills, there is no money tied up in the futures. By exercising the call and replacing it with a long position in the futures, the investor obtains the same opportunity to profit but frees up the funds tied up in the call. If the call were on the spot instrument, we could not make the same argument. The call may behave in virtually the same manner as the spot instrument, but the latter also requires the commitment of funds.

From an algebraic standpoint, the early-exercise problem is seen by noting that the minimum value of an in-the-money European call, $(f - E)$

$(1 + r)^{-T}$, is less than the value of the call if it could be exercised, $f - E$. The European call cannot be exercised, but if it were an American call, it could be.

These points are illustrated in panel a of Figure 12.4. The European call option on futures approaches its lower bound of $(f - E)(1 + r)^{-T}$. The American call option on futures approaches its minimum value, its intrinsic value of $f - E$, which is greater than the European lower bound. There is a futures price, $f_a^{\ddagger}$, at which the American call will equal its intrinsic value.

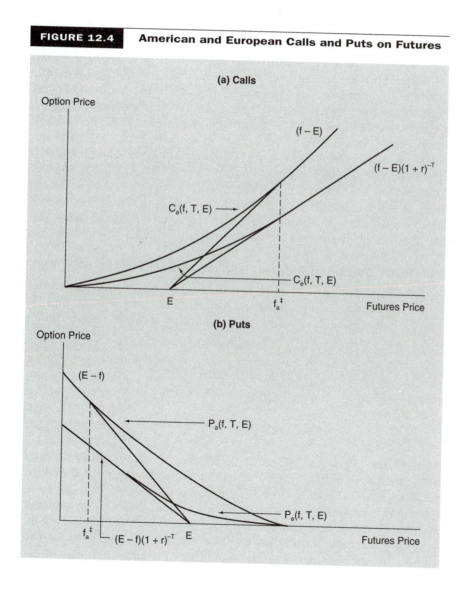

FIGURE 12.4   **American and European Calls and Puts on Futures**

It may be optimal to exercise early either an American call on a futures or an American put on a futures.

Above that price, the American call will be exercised early. Recall that for calls on spot instruments, the European lower bound was higher than the intrinsic value. Thus, there was no early exercise premium—provided, of course, that the underlying asset paid no dividends.

For put options on futures, the intuitive and algebraic arguments work similarly. Deep-in-the-money American puts on futures tend to be exercised early. Panel b of Figure 12.4 illustrates the case for puts. The price of European put options on futures approaches its lower bound of $(E - f)(1 + r)^{-T}$, while the price of the American put option on futures approaches its intrinsic value of $E - f$. The American intrinsic value is greater than the European lower bound. There is a price, $f_a^{\ddagger}$, at which the American put option on futures would equal its intrinsic value. Below this price, the American put would be exercised early.

Although these instruments are options on futures, it is conceivable that one would be interested in an option on a forward contract. Interestingly, these options would not be exercised early. This is because when exercised, a forward contract is established at the price of E. However, a forward contract is not marked to market, so the holder of a call does not receive an immediate cash flow of $F - E$. Instead, that person receives only a position with a value, as we learned in Chapter 9, of $(F - E)(1 + r)^{-T}$. This amount, however, is the lower bound of a European call on a forward contract. Early exercise cannot capture a gain over the European call value; thus, it offers no advantage. Similar arguments hold for early exercise of a European put on a forward contract.

The Black Option on Futures Pricing Model

Fischer Black (1976) developed a variation of his own Black-Scholes model for pricing European options on futures. Using the assumption that the option and the futures expire simultaneously, the **Black model** gives the option price as follows:

$$C = e^{-r_c T}\,[fN(d_1) - EN(d_2)],$$
where
$$d_1 = \frac{\ln(f/E) + (\sigma^2/2)T}{\sigma\sqrt{T}}$$
$$d_2 = d_1 - \sigma\sqrt{T}$$

The Black call option on futures pricing model gives the call price in terms of the futures price, exercise price, risk-free rate, time to expiration, and volatility of the futures.

Here σ is the volatility of the futures. Note that the expression for d_1 does not contain the continuously compounded risk-free rate, r_c, as it does in the Black-Scholes model. That is because the risk-free rate captures the opportunity cost of funds tied up in the stock. If the option is on a futures contract, no funds are invested in the futures and therefore there is no opportunity cost. However, the price of the call on the futures will be the same as the price of the call on the spot. This is because when the call on

the futures expires, it is exercisable into a futures position, which is immediately expiring. Thus, the call on the futures, when exercised, establishes a long position in the spot asset.

To prove that the Black option on futures pricing model gives the same price as the Black-Scholes model for an option on the spot, notice that in the Black model $N(d_1)$ is multiplied by fe^{-rcT}, while in the Black-Scholes model it is multiplied by S. However, we learned in Chapter 9 that with no dividends on the underlying asset, the futures price will equal Se^{rcT}. Thus, if we substitute Se^{rcT} for f in the Black model, the formula will be the same as the Black-Scholes formula.[1]

We know that in the presence of dividends, the futures price is given by the formula $f = Se^{(rc - \delta)T}$. Thus, $S = fe^{-(rc - \delta)T}$. If we substitute this expression for S into the Black-Scholes model, we obtain the Black option on futures pricing model if the underlying spot asset—in this case, a stock—pays dividends. However, the dividends do not show up in the Black model, so we need not distinguish the Black model with and without dividends. Dividends do affect the call price, but only indirectly, as the futures price captures all the effects of the dividends.

Another useful comparison of the Black and Black-Scholes models is to consider how the Black-Scholes model might be used as a substitute for the Black model. Suppose we have available only a computer program for the Black-Scholes model, but we want to price an option on a futures contract. We can do this easily by using the version of the Black-Scholes model in Chapter 4 that had a continuous dividend yield, and inserting the risk-free rate for the dividend yield and the futures price for the spot price. The risk-free rate minus the dividend yield is the cost of carry, so it will equal zero. The Black-Scholes formula will then be pricing an option on an instrument that has a price of f and a cost of carry of zero. This is precisely what the Black model prices: an option on an instrument—in this case, a futures contract—with a price of f and a cost of carry of zero. Remember that the futures price reflects the cost of carry on the underlying

---

[1]This may not be obvious in the formula for d_1. However, if we substitute Se^{rcT} for f in the above formula for d_1, we obtain

$$d_1 = \frac{\ln(Se^{rcT}/E) + (\sigma^2/2)T}{\sigma\sqrt{T}}.$$

The expression $\ln(Se^{rcT}/E)$ is equivalent to $\ln S + \ln e^{rcT} - \ln E$. Now $\ln e^{rcT} = r_cT$, so d_1 becomes

$$d_1 = \frac{\ln(S/E) + (r_c + \sigma^2/2)T}{\sigma\sqrt{T}},$$

which is d_1 from the Black-Scholes formula.

spot asset, but the futures itself does not have a cost of carry because there are no funds tied up and no storage costs.

Let us now use the Black model to price the October 685 call option on the S&P 500 futures. Recall that the futures price is 688.85, the exercise price is 685, the time to expiration is .0959, and the risk-free rate is $\ln(1.0513) = .05$. We now need only the standard deviation of the continuously compounded percentage change in the futures price. For illustrative purposes, we shall use .12 as the standard deviation. Table 12.7 presents the calculations.

The actual value of the call is 13.30. Thus, the call would appear to be overpriced. As we showed in Chapter 4, an arbitrageur could create a risk-free portfolio by buying the underlying instrument, the futures contract, and selling the call. The hedge ratio would be $e^{-r_c T}N(d_1)$ futures contracts for each call. However, remember that the model gives the European option price, so we expect it to be less than the actual American option price.

Your software, bsbin1.xls and bsbwin2.exe, introduced in Chapter 4, can be used to obtain prices of options on futures for the Black model. Simply insert the value you used for the risk-free rate for the continuously compounded dividend yield and insert the futures price for the underlying asset price.

In Chapter 4 when we studied the Black-Scholes model, we carefully examined how the model changes when any of the five underlying variables changes. Many of these effects were referred to with Greek names like delta, gamma, theta, vega, and rho. Since the Black model produces the same price as the Black-Scholes model, we will get the same effects here. The only difference is that with the Black model we express these results in terms of the futures price, rather than the spot or stock price. For

---

TABLE 12.7   Calculating the Black Option on Futures Price

$f = 688.85$ $E = 685$ $r_c = .05$ $\sigma^2 = .0144$ $T = .0959$

1. Compute d_1.

$$d_1 = \frac{\ln(688.85/685) + (.0144/2).0959}{.12\sqrt{.0959}} = .1694$$

2. Compute d_2.

$$d_2 = .1694 - .12\sqrt{.0959} = .1322$$

3. Look up $N(d_1)$.

$$N(.17) = .5675$$

4. Look up $N(d_2)$.

$$N(.13) = .5517$$

5. Plug into formula for C.

$$C = e^{-(.05)(.0959)}[688.85(.5675) - 685(.5517)] = 12.94$$

any of the answers in which S appears, such as the gamma, vega, and theta, we simply replace S with fe^{-r_cT}. In the case of the delta, we must redefine delta as the change in the call price for a change in the futures price. For an option on a stock, we saw that the delta is $N(d_1)$. For an option on a futures, the delta is $e^{-r_cT}N(d_1)$.

We can easily develop a pricing model for European put options on futures from the Black model and put-call parity. Using the continuously compounded version, put-call parity is expressed as $C - P = (f - E)e^{-r_cT}$. Rearranging this expression to isolate the put price gives

$$P = C - (f - E)e^{-r_cT}.$$

The Black call option on futures pricing model can be turned into a put option on futures pricing model by using put-call parity for options on futures.

Now we can substitute the Black European call option on futures pricing model for C in put-call parity and rearrange the terms to obtain the Black European put option on futures pricing model,

$$P = Ee^{-r_cT}[1 - N(d_2)] - fe^{-r_cT}[1 - N(d_1)].$$

Some end-of-chapter problems will allow us to use this model and examine it further.

Earlier we noted that even in the absence of dividends, American calls on futures might be exercised early. Like options on the spot, American puts on futures might be exercised early. The Black model does not price American options, and we cannot appeal to the absence of dividends, as we could for some stocks, to allow us to use the European model to price an American option. Unfortunately, American option on futures pricing models are fairly complex for this book. However, it is possible to price American options on futures using the binomial model.

Recall from Chapter 4 that we developed the binomial model for options on a stock. In the example we used, which you may wish to review, we had a stock that could go up by 15 percent or down by 20 percent. The risk-free rate was 10 percent. The stock was initially priced at 60. We looked at a call option that had an exercise price of 50. Let us assume that the option and the futures will expire after two periods. Figure 12.5 illustrates the binomial trees for the stock (panel a) and the futures (panel b). The futures tree is obtained by noting that at any node of the tree, the futures price would be the stock price compounded at the 10 percent interest rate for the number of periods until it expires. This is our simple futures pricing model, covered in Chapter 9, when there are no dividends. Note that at expiration the futures prices all equal the corresponding stock prices. The current futures price of 72.60 is the current stock price compounded at 10 percent for two periods.

Recall that the price of a call on the stock, at any node, is a weighted average of the next two possible call prices, discounted at the risk-free

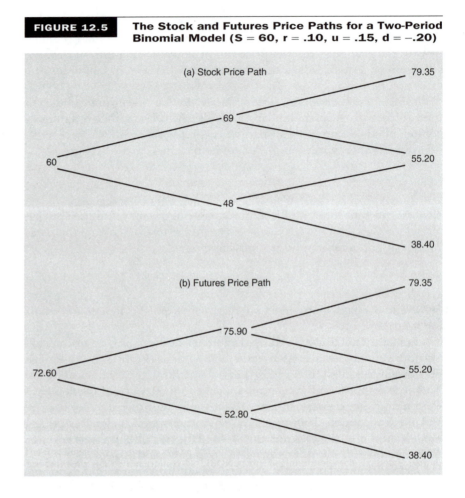

FIGURE 12.5   **The Stock and Futures Price Paths for a Two-Period Binomial Model (S = 60, r = .10, u = .15, d = −.20)**

(a) Stock Price Path

(b) Futures Price Path

rate. The weights are the values, p = (r − d)/(u − d) and 1 − p. Here p is (.10 − (−.20))/(.15 − (−.20)) = .857. The prices of the calls on the stock at expiration (with the corresponding stock prices in parentheses) are 29.35 (79.35), 5.2 (55.2), and 0 (38.4). Thus, the call price when the stock price is 69 is found as

American options on futures should be priced by a model capable of capturing the impact of early exercise. One such model is the binomial model.

$$\frac{29.35(.857) + 5.2(.143)}{1.10} = 23.54.$$

The other call prices are found in the same manner. For the option on the futures, the call prices at expiration are the same as those for the option on the stock. This is true because the futures expires and its price converges to the stock price. The values of p and 1 − p are the same so we will

get the same price at any node for a European call option on a futures as for a European call option on a stock. Thus, when the stock price is at 69 and the futures price is at 75.90, the European call on the stock and the European call on the futures are both worth 23.54.

Suppose they are American calls. We know that the call on the stock will not be worth any more than its European counterpart because there is no dividend. Note, however, that if the futures price is 75.90, it would be possible to exercise an American call on a futures and obtain a futures contract at a price of 50.

The futures could be sold immediately for a gain of 25.90. This is more than the 23.54 it is worth unexercised. Thus, we replace the 23.54 with 25.90. When the stock is at 48 and the futures is at 52.80, the option on the futures is worth 4.05 unexercised but only 2.80 if exercised so we would not exercise it. The price of the option on the futures today would, thus, be

$$\frac{25.90(.857) + 4.05(.143)}{1.10} = 20.70.$$

At this point, we should still check and see if it should be exercised. Since the futures price is 72.60, it is 22.60 points in-the-money so it would be worth exercising. Thus, our American call on the futures is worth 22.60, while its European counterpart, which is also the value of the American call on the spot is worth only 18.87.

In addition to the problem of using a European option pricing model to price American options, the Black model has difficulty pricing the most actively traded options on futures, Treasury bond options on futures. That problem is related to the interest rate component. The Black model, like the Black-Scholes model, makes the assumption of a constant interest rate. This generally is considered an acceptable assumption for pricing options on commodities and sometimes even stock indices. It is far less palatable for pricing options on bonds. There is a fundamental inconsistency in assuming a constant interest rate while attempting to price an option on a futures that is on an underlying Treasury bond, whose price changes because of changing interest rates. More appropriate models are available and we explore one in Chapter 14.

Trading Strategies for Options on Futures

Virtually any strategy that can be done with options on the spot can be done with options on futures. Chapters 5 and 6 discussed many of the popular option strategies and you may wish to review them first. There is little need for much repetition here, as most of those results transfer directly to options on futures. However, it will be helpful to briefly examine

three basic option on futures strategies: buying a call, buying a put, and writing a covered call.

Buy a Call Option on Futures

The profit from a call option on futures that is held to expiration is given by the equation

$$\Pi = \text{Max}(0, f_T - E) - C.$$

Buying a call option on a futures, like buying a call option on the asset, is a bullish strategy that has a limited loss, the call premium, and an unlimited gain.

The two outcomes are

$$\Pi = -C \qquad \text{if } f_T \le E$$
$$\Pi = f_T - E - C \qquad \text{if } f_T > E.$$

The breakeven futures price at expiration is $E + C$. The outcome of this strategy is the same as it is for an option on the spot, provided, of course, that the futures and the option expire simultaneously.

As an example, let us buy the December 110 Treasury bond call option on futures. The price of the call is \$1.234375. Because the contract is based on a \$100,000 par futures contract, the actual premium is $1,000(\$1.234375) = \$1,234.375$.[2] The graph showing the profit for various values of the futures (and spot) price at expiration is presented in Figure 12.6.

Suppose the futures price ends up at 116. Then the call is exercised, which means the futures is purchased at the exercise price of 110 and immediately sold at 116. Subtracting the cost of the call of 1.234375 gives a profit of $116 - 110 - 1.234375 = 4.765625$. The overall profit is $1,000(4.765625) = \$4,765.625$. If the futures price ends up below 110, the option expires worthless and the option holder loses the premium, \$1,234.375. The breakeven futures price is $110 + 1.234375 = 111.23$. The maximum gain is unlimited.

We shall not illustrate the comparison of different exercise prices and different holding periods. The issues are the same as they are for options on the spot. The lower-exercise-price call is more expensive, but it offers greater profit potential. The shorter holding period produces a higher profit for a given futures price but allows less time for the futures price to move.

---

[2]Since the exercise price is quoted in hundreds, the total exercise price is $110(1,000) = \$110,000$. Thus, the total premium is obtained by multiplying by 1,000.

FIGURE 12.6   **Buy Call Option on Futures**

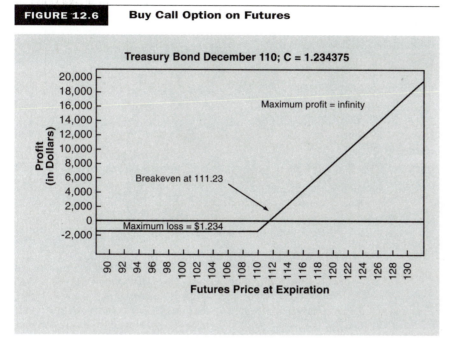

Treasury Bond December 110; C = 1.234375

Maximum profit = infinity

Breakeven at 111.23

Maximum loss = $1.234

Profit (in Dollars) — Futures Price at Expiration

Buy a Put Option on Futures

The profit for a put option on a futures contract held to expiration is given by the equation.

$$\Pi = \text{Max}(0, E - f_T) - P.$$

The two possible outcomes are

$$\Pi = E - f_T - P \qquad \text{if } f_T < E$$
$$\Pi = -P \qquad \text{if } f_T \geq E.$$

Buying a put option on a futures, like buying a put option on an asset, is a bearish strategy that has a limited loss, the put premium, and a large but limited potential gain.

The breakeven futures price at expiration is $E - P$. The is the same as that for a put option on the spot, provided that the two puts expire simultaneously.

As an example, consider the Treasury bond December 110 put option on futures. The cost of the put is $2.515625. Because the multiplier is 1,000, the total premium is $2,515.625. Figure 12.7 illustrates the profit for various futures prices at expiration.

Suppose the futures price at expiration is 102. Then the investor buys the futures at 102 and exercises the put, selling the futures at 110. The

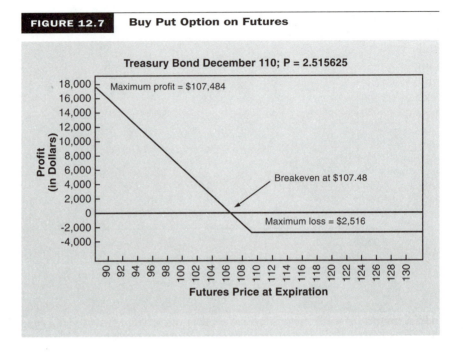

FIGURE 12.7   **Buy Put Option on Futures**

Treasury Bond December 110; P = 2.515625

Maximum profit = $107,484

Breakeven at $107.48

Maximum loss = $2,516

Profit (in Dollars)

Futures Price at Expiration

profit is $110 - 102 - 2.515625$ (the cost of the put) $= 5.484375$ times the multiplier (1,000), or $5,484.375 (1,000) = $5,484.375$. If the futures price at expiration is above 110, the put expires worthless and the investor loses the put premium of $2,515.625. The breakeven futures price is $110 - 2.515625 = 107.484375$. The maximum profit occurs if the futures price goes to zero. The profit would then be $1,000 (110 - 2.515625) = $107,484.375.

The investor should also consider the effect of different exercise prices and different holding periods. These issues are the same as for options on the spot.

Write a Covered Call Option on Futures

Recall from Chapter 5 that a covered call is a strategy in which the investor purchases the underlying instrument and writes a call. When the underlying instrument is a stock, the covered call protects the investor against a substantial decrease in the stock price. If that happens, the call will expire worthless and the investor will retain the premium. If the stock price rises above the exercise price at expiration, the call will be exercised and the investor will have effectively sold the stock for the exercise price.

The covered call option on futures is similar. A long position in a futures contract can be protected by selling a call option. If the futures price falls and the call ends up out-of-the-money, the investor retains the premium, which cushions the loss on the futures. If the futures price rises and the call is exercised, the investor effectively sells the futures contract at the exercise price.

The profit from a single long futures contract is

$$\Pi = f_T - f.$$

A covered call on a futures, like a covered call on an asset, reduces downside losses at the expense of upside gains.

The profit from a short call option on the futures is

$$\Pi = -\text{Max}(0, f_T - E) + C.$$

Combining these into the covered call strategy gives a profit of

$$\Pi = f_T - f - \text{Max}(0, f_T - E) + C.$$

The profit at expiration for the two cases is

$$\Pi = f_T - f - f_T + E + C = E - f + C \qquad \text{if } f_T > E$$
$$\Pi = f_T - f + C \qquad\qquad\qquad\qquad\quad \text{if } f_T \leq E.$$

The breakeven futures price at expiration is $f - C$.

Figure 12.8 illustrates the possible outcomes for the covered call using the Treasury bond December 110 call. The dashed line shows the profit if only the futures position is taken. The call price is 1.234375, and the futures price is 108.71875. Suppose the futures price at expiration is 114. Then the call is exercised. The covered call writer is assigned a short futures contract at 110, which offsets the long futures position established at 108.71875. This leaves a profit of $110 - 108.71875 + 1.234375 = 2.515625$. Multiplying this by 1,000 gives the overall profit of $1,000(\$2.515625) = \$2,515.625$. If the futures price ends up at 100, the futures contract produces a loss of $108.71875 - 100 = 8.71875$. This is partially offset by the call premium of 1.234375, leaving a net loss of 7.484375. Multiplying by 1,000 gives a loss of $1,000(7.484375) = \$7,484.375$. The breakeven futures price is $108.71875 - 1.234375 = 107.48$. The maximum loss occurs when the futures price goes to zero. The loss is $\$1,000(108.71875 - 1.234375) = \$107,484$.

Any strategy that can be executed with options on the spot can also be executed with options on futures. Some end-of-chapter problems ask you to apply options on futures to strategies that are not covered in this chapter but are covered under options on the spot.

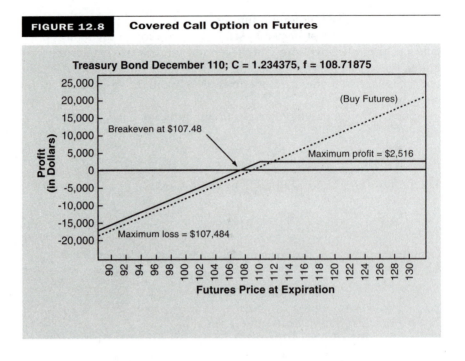

FIGURE 12.8   **Covered Call Option on Futures**

Options on Futures versus Options on the Spot

So far, we have seen that options on futures are equivalent to options on the spot when the options are European and the futures and options expire simultaneously. In this section, we shall introduce some real-world factors that make options on futures unique.

Consider an American call option on the spot and one on the futures. Assume the spot instrument does not pay a dividend. As we already know, the call on the spot will not be exercised early. The call on the futures may be exercised early if it is sufficiently in-the-money. We know that the futures price is given by the formula

$$f = S(1 + r)^T.$$

From the formula, it is apparent that prior to expiration the futures price is always higher than the spot price. Thus, an option on the futures is an option on a higher-priced instrument than is an option on the spot. Accordingly, its price should be higher. This is true, however, only because of the early exercise possibility. If the option could not or would not be exercised early, it would be equivalent to an option on the spot. We observed

this point in our treatment of the binomial model for pricing options on futures.

A similar line of reasoning holds for puts. A put option on a futures is an option to sell a higher-priced instrument—the futures. Because of the possibility of early exercise, the put will be priced lower than the put on the spot instrument itself.

If we add dividends to the picture, things can get very complicated. Dividends lower the spread between the futures and spot prices and, if high enough, can make the futures price be less than the spot price, thus complicating the relationship further.

If the option on the futures expires before the option on the spot, it should be obvious that even European options on the spot and those on the futures are not equivalent. However, even if they expire simultaneously and are European, there are other reasons why these instruments have their own unique properties.

The option on the futures may be more attractive because the underlying futures contract is more liquid, or easier to transact in, than the underlying spot instrument. As an example, options on Treasury bond futures at the Chicago Board of Trade are far more popular than options on Treasury bonds at the Chicago Board Options Exchange. One reason is that the T-bond futures market is much more liquid than the T-bond spot market. Because exercise may require establishing a position in the underlying instrument, the underlying instrument's liquidity is important to the option trader. Even if the option is not exercised, pricing the option off of the more liquid futures market is better than pricing it off of the spot market.[3] This is particularly true in agricultural markets where the spot market is highly decentralized, which is one reason why there are no options on agricultural commodities.

Suppose an investor wishes to construct a hedge, covered call, or protective put using the S&P 500. The option on the spot would require the investor to simultaneously purchase the S&P 500 stocks in the appropriate proportions. The same strategy with the option on the futures would require only a position in the futures and the option. Obviously it would be easier to transact in the futures market than in the spot market.

Exercise of an option on the spot requires delivery of the underlying instrument. Although the possibility is somewhat remote, there is at least some likelihood that there would be a shortage of the deliverable instrument. This is more likely to occur with agricultural commodities, but it could happen with a Treasury bond or note. If using the option on the futures, one need not be concerned about obtaining the underlying

---

[3]The futures market still must price the futures contract off of the spot market.

commodity. Futures contracts can be created in virtually unlimited quantities. However, if a European option and the futures expire simultaneously, the option holder or writer must immediately execute an opposite transaction in the futures market to avoid having to make or take delivery on the futures contract, unless the futures is cash settled.

Finally, we come to what may well be the key attraction of options on futures. Options on spot instruments have traded on the CBOE and several stock exchanges for many years. Individuals who held memberships in the futures exchanges could not easily trade options on the other exchanges. If they wished to trade options, they had to place orders through brokers, who would execute the trades on the CBOE and the stock exchanges. When options on futures were introduced, they gave futures traders the opportunity to trade both futures and options. For most contracts, the trading pits for the options and the underlying futures are adjacent. This greatly facilitated simultaneous trading of the option and the underlying futures. Because options on stocks do not trade side by side with the underlying stocks, futures traders have an advantage over members of the stock and option exchanges. Thus, much of the success of options on futures has come from local traders. That is not meant to imply, however, that the public has not traded these instruments. As noted earlier in this section, options on futures have many attractive features not offered by options on the spot, but neither instrument has a clear advantage over the other. Each is unique and fills the needs of a given clientele of investors and traders.

Summary

This chapter examined options on futures. These contracts are very similar to options on the spot instrument. Most of the basic rules for pricing these two types of options are similar. In particular, if the futures price equals the spot price compounded at the risk-free rate and the options expire simultaneously, a European option on the spot and a European option on the futures are equivalent. The lower bounds, put-call parity, and the Black option on futures pricing model are equivalent to their counterparts in equity options. The performance of trading strategies is also identical.

The chapter discussed several important differences between these two types of options. Prices of American options on the spot differ from those of American options on futures. In addition, options on futures may have more liquidity in the underlying instruments, the futures. Moreover, the options and the underlying futures trade side by side, which offers advantages to floor traders who must execute arbitrage transactions quickly.

Throughout this book we have examined linkages between spot and derivative markets. We saw that put-call parity, put-call-forward/futures parity, the cost of carry forward/futures pricing model, and the Black-Scholes model provide the linkages between these markets. We illustrated those relationships for derivatives

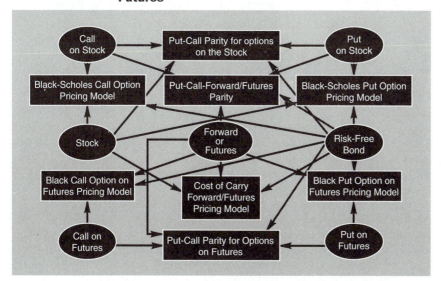

FIGURE 12.9 The Linkage between Forwards/Futures, Stock, Bonds, Options on the Stock, and Options on the Futures

on a stock in Figures 3.11, 4.13, 9.9, and 11.2, with each figure building on the previous one. Figure 12.9 introduces options on futures. Although the figure is now quite crowded with lines, it still provides an organized picture of the relationships between these markets. Note the important role that the risk-free bond plays in virtually all the relationships. Also remember that while the Black-Scholes call (or put) option pricing model is equivalent to the Black call (or put) option pricing model, under the usual assumptions, they are illustrated separately here. In addition, put-call forward/futures parity and put-call parity are equivalent, as a result of the cost of carry relationship between the spot and forward/futures prices. Thus, in general, these markets are all highly related by the readiness of all investors to execute the arbitrage transactions that generate risk-free profits and quickly force prices back in line.

In the next chapter, we shall examine some more widely traded but different instruments: derivatives on foreign currencies.

Key Terms

Before continuing to Chapter 13, you should be able to give brief definitions of the following terms.

- options on futures/
  commodity options/
  futures options

- Black model

Questions and Problems

1. Use the following data from January 31 of a particular year for a group of March 480 options on futures contract to answer parts a through g.

    Futures price: 483.10
    Expiration: March 18
    Risk-free rate: .0284 percent (simple)
    Call price: 6.95
    Put price: 5.25
    ---

    a. Determine the intrinsic value of the call.
    b. Determine the time value of the call.
    c. Determine the lower bound of the call.
    d. Determine the intrinsic value of the put.
    e. Determine the time value of the put.
    f. Determine the lower bound of the put.
    g. Determine whether put-call parity holds.

2. The put-call parity rule can be expressed as $C - P = (f - E)(1 + r)^{-T}$. Consider the following data: $f = 102$, $E = 100$, $r = .1$, $T = .25$, $C = 4$, and $P = 1.75$. A few calculations will show that the prices do not conform to the rule. Suggest an arbitrage strategy and show how it can be used to capture a risk-free profit. Assume no transaction costs. Be sure your answer shows the payoffs at expiration and proves these payoffs are riskless.

3. Explain why American call options on futures could be exercised early when call options on the spot are not. Assume no dividends.

4. Assume a standard deviation of .08, and use the Black model to determine if the call option in problem 1 is correctly priced. If not, suggest a riskless hedge strategy.

5. Describe two problems in using the Black option on futures pricing model for pricing options on Eurodollar futures.

6. Using the information in problem 4, calculate the price of the put described in problem 1 using the Black model for pricing puts.

7. Explain why the futures option pricing model is simply a pricing model for options on instruments with a zero cost of carry.

8. In Chapter 4, we examined the sensitivity of a call's price to different risk-free rates and volatilities. Compute the Black option on futures price using the data for the call given in problems 1 and 4 for the following risk-free rates and standard deviations. Use either the Excel spreadsheet bsbin1.xls or the Windows program bsbwin2.exe.
    a. Use risk-free rates of 1 through 10 percent in increments of 100 basis points. We know that the call price should increase as we increase r. What do you notice about the results? Try to explain. (Hint: Remember that $f = Se^{r_c T}$.)
    b. Use standard deviations of .05 through .50 in increments of .05. Comment on what you find.

9. An asset worth 100 can go up by 10 percent or down by 7 percent. The risk-free rate is 4 percent. There are options with an exercise price of 100. There

are no dividends. Find the values of the following options. Assume two periods until expiration.

a.   A European call on the asset
b.   An American call on the asset
c.   A European call on the futures
d.   An American call on the futures

10.   Find the implied volatility, to three decimal places, of the call in problem 4 if the call is worth 7.25. Use either the Excel spreadsheet bsbin1.xls or the Windows program bsbwin2.exe.

11.   Evaluate the following statement: "Dividends are relevant to the pricing of European call options but not to the pricing of European call options on futures. Amazingly enough, this is true even though the two calls will have the same price."

Problems 12 through 15 and 17 use some options on futures prices on January 31 of a particular year. Determine the profit from the strategy for each of the following futures prices at expiration: 470, 475, 480, 485, 490, 495. Graph the results. Determine the breakeven futures price at expiration. Use a multiplier of 500.

12.   The March 485 call price is 4.875. Construct a simple long call position.

13.   The March 485 put price is 6.75. Construct a simple long put position.

14.   The March futures price is 483.10. Using the March call data from problem 12, construct a covered call position.

15.   Using the information in problems 13 and 14, construct a protective put with the March 485 put.

16.   Discuss why options on futures have advantages not offered by options on the spot.

17.   (Concept Problem) Redo problem 12, but close the position on March 1. The calls expire March 18. Let $\sigma = .08$ and $r_c = .028$. You may wish to use the Excel spreadsheet bsbin1.xls or the Windows program bsbwin2.exe to save time making these calculations.

18.   (Concept Problem) Use the following information to calculate the call option price using the Black model: $f = 30$, $E = 25$, $r_c = .08$, $\sigma = .35$, and $T = .125$. Determine the option's delta. Then recommend a risk-free hedge position, and show why the position is risk free by evaluating its performance if the futures price decreases by $1. Use the Excel spreadsheet bsbin1.xls or the Windows program bsbwin2.exe.

APPENDIX 12A

Selected Options on Futures Contract Specifications

This table includes only certain information for the 10 most active options on futures contracts. Other information can be obtained from the source of the table.

Contract	Size	Expirations Available	Exercise Price Increments	Minimum Price Change
Treasury Bonds (CBOT)	One $100,000 futures contract	First month of current cycle and next three contracts of quarterly cycle	1 point for a band of four surrounding at-the-money and 2 points for outside this band	1/64 = $15.625
Eurodollars (CME)	One $1,000,000 futures contract	Each month of current cycle	25 points	1 point = $25
10-year Treasury Notes (CBOT)	One $100,000 futures contract	First month of current cycle and next three contracts of quarterly cycle	1 point for a band of four surrounding at-the-money and 2 points for outside this band	1/64 = $15.625
S&P 500 (CME)	One $500 × index futures contract	Each month of current cycle	5 points	0.05 point = $25
German Mark (CME)	One DM125,000 futures contract	Jan, Mar, Apr, Jun, Jul, Sep, Oct, Dec	$0.005	$0.0001/DM = $12.50
Corn (CBOT)	One 5,000-bushel futures contract	Mar, May, Jul, Sep, Dec	$0.10	1/8¢/bu. = $6.25
Soybeans (CBOT)	One 5,000-bushel futures contract	Mar, May, Jul, Sep, Dec	$0.25	1/8¢/bu. = $6.25
Wheat (CBOT)	One 5,000-bushel futures contract	Mar, May, Jul, Sep, Dec	$0.10	1/8¢/bu. = $6.25
Gold (COMEX)	One 100-troy-oz. futures contract	Each month of current cycle	$10	10¢/oz. = $10
British Pound (CME)	One £62,500 futures contract	Jan, Mar, Apr, Jun, Jul, Sep, Oct, Dec	$0.01	$0.0002/£ = $12.50

Source: *The Wall Street Journal* and *Futures 1997 Source Book*, published by *Futures* magazine. This information is believed to be correct as of April 1997, but contract specifications sometimes change. Also, there are a few exceptions to the above rules for certain options. Consult the exchanges for more details.

CHAPTER 13

Foreign Currency Derivatives

People in countries with a weak currency learn fast about options.

BRIAN THOMAS, Bank of America
Asia Risk, November 1995

This chapter introduces the world of international finance and the exciting markets for currency derivatives. As in Chapter 12, it breaks away from the approach used previously, which has focused on concepts rather than on specific types of contracts. In the case of currency derivatives, a slightly different approach is necessary. Foreign currencies often are seen as exotic and confusing. While indeed some discipline is needed to organize one's thinking, in the end analyzing foreign currencies actually differs very little from analyzing ordinary stocks and bonds.

Characteristics of Foreign Currencies and Markets

The Nature of Exchange Rates

Each country has a designated currency. In the United States, of course, it is the dollar. In the United Kingdom it is the British pound (sometimes called the sterling), in Germany the deutsche mark (pronounced "doychmark"), in Switzerland the Swiss franc, in Japan the Japanese yen, and in Canada the Canadian dollar. To settle transactions among individuals, corporations, and governments in different countries, there is a rate at which the currency of one country can be converted into the currency of another. That rate is called the **exchange rate.**

For example, suppose you wish to convert U.S. dollars into British pounds. The exchange rate is $1.40 per pound. We denote this as $1.40/£, where £ is the symbol for pounds. Each pound is convertible into $1.40. Conversely, each dollar can be converted into 1/$1.40, or .7143 pounds.

Chapter Objectives

■ To describe the structure of international financial markets

■ To illustrate how to read foreign currency spot, forward, futures, and options price quotations in *The Wall Street Journal*

■ To present the principles of pricing foreign currency forwards and futures, including the cross-rate relationship and interest rate parity

■ To present the principles of pricing foreign currency options, including the intrinsic value, lower bound, and put-call parity

■ To present the Garman-Kohlhagen foreign currency option pricing model

■ To illustrate several foreign currency forward, futures, and options trading strategies

■ To illustrate the execution of a currency swap and the valuation of a currency swap during its life

A foreign currency is simply another asset. The exchange rate is the price at which the asset can be bought.

We can express the exchange rate as the dollar cost of pounds, $1.40, or the pound cost of dollars, £.7143.

This line of thinking often causes some confusion. An easy way to understand the exchange rate is to always think in terms of a single currency—normally your domestic currency—and treat the foreign currency as if it were an asset, which it is. Just as you can buy stocks, bonds, wheat, or gold, so can you buy a foreign currency. When you convert dollars into pounds, you are simply buying an asset that happens to be pounds. When you convert back into dollars, you are selling the asset (pounds). The difference in the dollar price at which you buy the pounds and the dollar price at which you sell them generates a profit or loss that results from changes in the exchange rate.

The illustrations in this chapter primarily use the dollar–pound relationship. However, before we begin examining the foreign currency instruments, let us look at the history of foreign currency markets.

A Brief History of Foreign Currency Markets

From the early nineteenth to the mid-twentieth century, gold was the standard to which most countries fixed their currencies. International transactions were settled in gold, and most currency rates were expressed as a fixed ratio to the price of gold. In 1944, a group of Allied nations met in Bretton Woods, New Hampshire, and established the International Monetary Fund. As part of the agreement, each nation fixed its currency in relation to the gold content of the dollar. Currency rates were allowed to fluctuate within a very narrow range, but foreign governments were obligated to execute the necessary buying and selling of their currencies and the dollar to keep the exchange rate relatively stable. For the most part, exchange rates were fixed.

The system worked well as long as there was confidence that the fixed exchange rate accurately reflected the value of a given currency. When it did not, there was significant buying and selling of that currency. For example, if investors thought, as they did in the late 1940s, that the British pound was overvalued, they would sell pounds. With the price of pounds fixed, no one wanted to hold pounds. The British government was forced to devalue the pound, which meant lowering its official exchange rate.

By the late 1960s, the United States was running a record balance-of-payments deficit. This meant the United States was paying out more dollars than it was taking in. As foreigners were accumulating large quantities of dollars that were quickly losing value in light of record U.S. inflation levels, the dollar came under pressure and finally was devalued by the U.S. government in 1971. At the same time, the dollar's convertibility to gold was suspended. The Bretton Woods system had failed.

An interim system that developed in 1972, called the Smithsonian Agreement, allowed a wider range in which currencies could fluctuate,

but it all too quickly proved inadequate. In 1973, the exchange rates of several countries began to fluctuate freely. Ultimately all exchange rates of free countries fluctuated with market conditions.

Over the years the major countries of Europe have attempted, without much success, to coordinate their monetary policies, with the ultimate goal being a unified Europe with a single currency. In 1979 the Federal Republic of Germany proposed a system in which the European countries attempted to keep their currencies in line with each other. Not all countries participated, however, and the weaker participating currencies came under pressure as their values were held artificially to a narrow range with respect to the stronger currencies. This system was called the European Monetary System (EMS). West Germany was the strongest currency, a result of a tight monetary policy that limited inflation to less than 2 percent. Other countries were forced to align their monetary policies with that of Germany. In 1990 the unification of the two Germanys placed further pressure on the system. Germany's budget deficit grew along with its inflation and interest rates. Other countries were forced to follow similar economic policies. A massive recession hit Europe at the same time that it was attempting to move toward the goal of economic integration by 1992 and a single currency. Other countries wanted to enact policies that would stimulate economic growth while Germany held the line toward tight economic policies to keep its own inflation under control. Several countries began to oppose the single currency concept. In September 1992, Great Britain and Italy, which had two of the weaker currencies, withdrew from the EMS, meaning that they would no longer support their currencies by buying them in the international markets. These currencies fell and interest rates declined. The EMS fell apart and for a few days the currency markets went into turmoil.

Since that time things have stabilized and the major economic powers of Europe have remained committed to European economic and monetary union, though there is considerable disagreement about how and when this should happen. Current plans specify that the participating countries would unify their economies, coordinate their monetary and fiscal policies, and move to a single currency—the European Monetary Unit or EMU. The specific plans are to be finalized in 1998 and a three-year phased-in conversion would begin in 1999. The countries involved have not been finalized but are likely to include Germany, France, Belgium, the Netherlands, and Luxembourg. A few other countries have not yet decided. Everything is subject to change, however, because getting so many different countries to agree is not easy.

What does all of this mean for the U.S. dollar? Figure 13.1 is a graph of the monthly exchange rates from 1975 to mid-1997 of the German mark and Japanese yen, the currencies of our two leading trading partners off the North American continent. The graph shows the price in dollars of one unit of each currency. These currencies depreciated relative to the

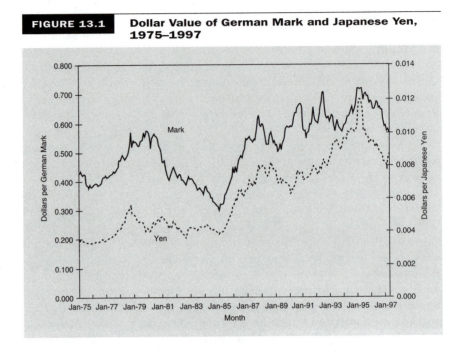

FIGURE 13.1   **Dollar Value of German Mark and Japanese Yen, 1975–1997**

dollar in the early 1980s. This was due primarily to the very low U.S. interest and inflation rates, which led to improved confidence in the U.S. economy. Despite record U.S. fiscal and trade deficits, confidence in and demand for dollars by foreign investors was increasing. However, by 1985 the growing trade deficit and a weakening U.S. economy led to the dollar's decline, which continued through the early 1990s. This weakening of the dollar reflects the growing economic power and more stable monetary policies of Germany and Japan. In early 1996, the dollar began a rebound as the U.S. economy strengthened and the budget deficit decreased.

For our purposes in understanding the currency derivatives markets, the volatility of exchanges rates should be viewed as a source of risk for companies doing business in more than one country. What causes these currency fluctuations? One major factor is a nation's balance of payments. As a country exports more than it imports, the demand for its currency increases. At some point, however, the currency becomes so expensive that the country's goods become prohibitively costly. This leads to a decrease in exports and a lower demand for the currency. A nation running a trade deficit finds the demand for its currency weakening. This lowers its currency's value and ultimately makes its currency, and hence its goods, cheap. This reverses the cycle and turns it into a trade surplus. Unfortunately, there are so many other factors involved that the system never quite works as the theory says it should.

For example, exchange rates are clearly influenced by economic conditions in a country, such as inflation and interest rates. If inflation is high, there is little confidence in the currency, and this weakens the demand for it. High interest rates attract foreigners to the currency; however, if interest rates are high because of high inflation, the effect may be offset. Government policies and political instability are still other factors that influence currency values.

Foreign Currency Spot and Forward Markets

The market for the exchange of foreign currency is large and sophisticated. Major financial institutions and central banks in the various countries are linked through computers and telecommunication systems. Transactions are executed quickly and efficiently.

The spot market is the market for immediate delivery of the foreign currency. This is done by book entry, which is made possible by the fact that the major banks in a given country have accounts with their counterparts in other countries. There is also a large forward market for foreign currency. Like the spot market, there is no central marketplace; it operates through telecommunication systems linking the major financial institutions. For example, if a corporation will need £1 million in 90 days, it can call a major money center bank, which will enter into a forward contract to deliver the pounds at that time. Recall that in a forward contract the price, which is the exchange rate, is agreed upon at the time the transaction is initiated. No money initially changes hands, but the bank may require a small margin deposit. Ninety days later, the corporation acquires the pounds at the forward price. As in the other forward contracts we have covered, each party assumes the credit risk of the other. This market for trading currencies by banks is called the **interbank market.**

A currency forward contract is an agreement between two parties in which one party agrees to buy the currency from the other party at a later date at an exchange rate agreed upon today.

The foreign currency interbank market is extremely large with turnover estimated at over 400 billion dollars per day. That such a market had developed and operated so efficiently for many years is one reason why the over-the-counter derivatives markets developed so well in the 1980s. They were a natural extension of the interbank market. Today, these markets have ultimately become one large, active, and efficient market for global financial transactions.

Figure 13.2 illustrates a sample of foreign currency spot rates from *The Wall Street Journal* for the trading day of July 23, 1997. For many of the major countries, there are also 1-month, 3-month, and 6-month forward quotes. The rates are quoted in both U.S. dollars and foreign currency units per U.S. dollar.

Look at the British pound quotes. The spot rate for pounds is $1.6795, while the spot rate for dollars per pound is 1/$1.6795, or £0.5954. The 1-month forward rate per pound is $1.6778 and per dollar is £0.5960. Because the forward rates per pound decrease the longer the horizon, the

---

FIGURE 13.2   **Foreign Currency Spot and Forward Quotations in** *The Wall Street Journal*, **Trading Day, July 23, 1997**

Wednesday, July 23, 1997

EXCHANGE RATES

The New York foreign exchange selling rates below apply to trading among banks in amounts of $1 million and more, as quoted at 4 p.m. Eastern time by Dow Jones and other sources. Retail transactions provide fewer units of foreign currency per dollar.

Country	U.S. $ equiv. Wed	U.S. $ equiv. Tue	Currency per U.S. $ Wed	Currency per U.S. $ Tue
Argentina (Peso)	1.0014	1.0014	.9986	.9986
Australia (Dollar)	.7362	.7403	1.3583	1.3508
Austria (Schilling)	.07785	.07792	12.846	12.833
Bahrain (Dinar)	2.6525	2.6525	.3770	.3770
Belgium (Franc)	.02653	.02663	37.695	37.550
Brazil (Real)	.9243	.9248	1.0819	1.0813
Britain (Pound)	1.6795	1.6805	.5954	.5951
1-month forward	1.6778	1.6787	.5960	.5957
3-months forward	1.6740	1.6750	.5974	.5970
6-months forward	1.6684	1.6692	.5994	.5991
Canada (Dollar)	.7234	.7253	1.3823	1.3788
1-month forward	.7248	.7267	1.3797	1.3761
3-months forward	.7272	.7290	1.3752	1.3717
6-months forward	.7304	.7322	1.3692	1.3657
Chile (Peso)	.002399	.002397	416.85	417.15
China (Renminbi)	.1202	.1202	8.3209	8.3209
Colombia (Peso)	.0009028	.0008995	1107.70	1111.75
Czech. Rep. (Koruna)				
Commercial rate	.02897	.02896	34.516	34.535
Denmark (Krone)	.1439	.1446	6.9495	6.9175
Ecuador (Sucre)				
Floating rate	.0002515	.0002517	3975.50	3972.50
Finland (Markka)	.1860	.1865	5.3750	5.3620
France (Franc)	.1625	.1628	6.1525	6.1420
1-month forward	.1629	.1631	6.1405	6.1295
3-months forward	.1635	.1638	6.1160	6.1060
6-months forward	.1644	.1648	6.0809	6.0688
Germany (Mark)	.5477	.5481	1.8259	1.8245
1-month forward	.5488	.5493	1.8221	1.8205
3-months forward	.5511	.5515	1.8145	1.8131
6-months forward	.5545	.5551	1.8033	1.8016
Greece (Drachma)	.003508	.003506	285.05	285.22
Hong Kong (Dollar)	.1291	.1291	7.7473	7.7463
Hungary (Forint)	.005126	.005171	195.07	193.38
India (Rupee)	.02802	.02802	35.695	35.690
Indonesia (Rupiah)	.0003861	.0003865	2590.00	2587.50
Ireland (Punt)	1.4819	1.4780	.6748	.6766
Israel (Shekel)	.2846	.2840	3.5136	3.5207
Italy (Lira)	.0005634	.0005643	1775.00	1772.00
Japan (Yen)	.008645	.008699	115.67	114.95
1-month forward	.008683	.008737	115.17	114.45

Country	U.S. $ equiv. Wed	U.S. $ equiv. Tue	Currency per U.S. $ Wed	Currency per U.S. $ Tue
3-months forward	.008758	.008813	114.18	113.46
6-months forward	.008873	.008932	112.70	111.96
Jordan (Dinar)	1.4075	1.4075	.7105	.7105
Kuwait (Dinar)	3.3036	3.2971	.3027	.3033
Lebanon (Pound)	.0006502	.0006501	1538.00	1538.25
Malaysia (Ringgit)	.3788	.3796	2.6400	2.6345
Malta (Lira)	2.5478	2.5543	.3925	.3915
Mexico (Peso)				
Floating rate	.1277	.1276	7.8280	7.8380
Netherland (Guilder)	.4863	.4872	2.0562	2.0526
New Zealand (Dollar)	.6483	.6492	1.5425	1.5404
Norway (Krone)	.1335	.1335	7.4898	7.4933
Pakistan (Rupee)	.02496	.02496	40.070	40.070
Peru (new Sol)	.3797	.3795	2.6338	2.6348
Philippines (Peso)	.03533	.03509	28.305	28.500
Poland (Zloty)	.2909	.2896	3.4378	3.4533
Portugal (Escudo)	.005424	.005431	184.35	184.14
Russia (Ruble) (a)	.0001727	.0001727	5790.00	5791.50
Saudi Arabia (Riyal)	.2666	.2666	3.7505	3.7505
Singapore (Dollar)	.6811	.6841	1.4683	1.4617
Slovak Rep. (Koruna)	.02906	.02894	34.412	34.558
South Africa (Rand)	.2191	.2186	4.5640	4.5745
South Korea (Won)	.001119	.001118	893.50	894.45
Spain (Peseta)	.006503	.006513	153.77	153.54
Sweden (Krona)	.1278	.1280	7.8225	7.8144
Switzerland (Franc)	.6736	.6743	1.4845	1.4830
1-month forward	.6759	.6767	1.4794	1.4777
3-months forward	.6809	.6814	1.4687	1.4676
6-months forward	.6880	.6888	1.4535	1.4517
Taiwan (Dollar)	.03578	.03580	27.948	27.934
Thailand (Baht)	.03200	.03247	31.250	30.800
Turkey (Lira)	.00000637	.00000641	156970.00	155985.00
United Arab (Dirham)	.2723	.2723	3.6730	3.6730
Uruguay (New Peso)				
Financial	.1058	.1058	9.4550	9.4550
Venezuela (Bolivar)	.002027	.002030	493.37	492.70
SDR	1.3699	1.3710	.7300	.7294
ECU	1.0852	1.0851		

Special Drawing Rights (SDR) are based on exchange rates for the U.S., German, British, French, and Japanese currencies. Source: International Monetary Fund.

European Currency Unit (ECU) is based on a basket of community currencies.

a-fixing, Moscow Interbank Currency Exchange.

The Wall Street Journal daily foreign exchange data for 1996 and 1997 may be purchased through the Readers' Reference Service (413) 592-3600.

Source: *The Wall Street Journal,* July 24, 1997

---

pound is said to be selling at a **forward discount** and the dollar at a **forward premium.**

Foreign Currency Futures Markets

During the transition to freely floating exchange rates in 1972, the Chicago Mercantile Exchange established the International Monetary Market for the trading of futures contracts in foreign currencies. We already are familiar with the IMM's T-bill and Eurodollar contracts. However, the foreign currency contracts actually were the first financial futures contracts.

The foreign currency futures contracts call for delivery of a specified number of units of the foreign currency. Prices are always quoted in dollars per unit of that currency. Let us take the British pound contract as an example.

The pound contract calls for delivery of 62,500 pounds. The price is quoted in dollars per pound. For example, if the contract price is $1.5612, the actual price is $1.5612(62,500) = $97,575. The expiration months are March, June, September, and December. The contract expires on the second business day before the third Wednesday of the month. Contract specifications for the major IMM foreign currency contracts are provided in Appendix 13A.

Figure 13.3 presents the historical volume of trading in foreign currency futures contracts broken down by individual currency. The German mark is the most actively traded currency futures, followed by the Japanese yen and the Swiss franc. The solid growth of the early years began to level off around 1990, during which about 28 million contracts traded. In 1993 the volume was still only 28 million and it peaked in 1994 at 30 million. In 1995 volume fell off to 24 million and fell further in 1996. Later we shall look at some reasons for this trend, but first let us look at how to read and interpret currency futures price quotations in *The Wall Street Journal*.

Figure 13.4 illustrates the foreign currency futures quotations in *The Wall Street Journal*. In the quotes for the deutsche mark, the first line indicates that the contract is at the CME (Chicago Mercantile Exchange), it covers 125,000 marks, and the quote is in dollars per mark. The first four columns are the open, high, low, and settlement prices. Thus, the December contract opened at $0.5524, reached a high of $0.5541, reached a low of $0.5517, and had a settlement price of $0.5528. The next column gives the change in the settlement price, which in this case was −.0009. The next two columns give the high and low over the contract's life, and the final column gives the open interest. The last line is a summary of the volume and open interest for all contracts.

Foreign Currency Options Markets

Foreign currency options were first introduced in 1982 at the Philadelphia Stock Exchange. The Chicago Mercantile Exchange briefly offered them from 1985 to 1987. Figure 13.5 illustrates the volume of exchange-traded foreign currency options starting in 1984. Growth was quite rapid in the first few years but, like foreign currency futures, it began to level off. Since 1993 volume has fallen steadily.

The Philadelphia Stock Exchange's options expire in the next two months and in March, June, September, and December. They trade nearly round-the-clock. The contract sizes are one-half the sizes of the corresponding CME futures contracts. The expiration date is the Saturday before the third Wednesday of the month, though some contracts expire at the end of the month. In addition there are some long-term options with

A currency futures contract is an agreement between two parties in which one party agrees to buy the currency from the other party at a later date at an exchange rate agreed upon today. It trades on a futures exchange and works essentially the same as any other type of futures contract.

A currency option is an agreement between two parties in which one party pays a premium and receives the right to buy or sell a currency at a later date at an exchange rate agreed upon today.

FIGURE 13.3   **Foreign Currency Futures Volume, 1981–1996 Five Major Currencies**

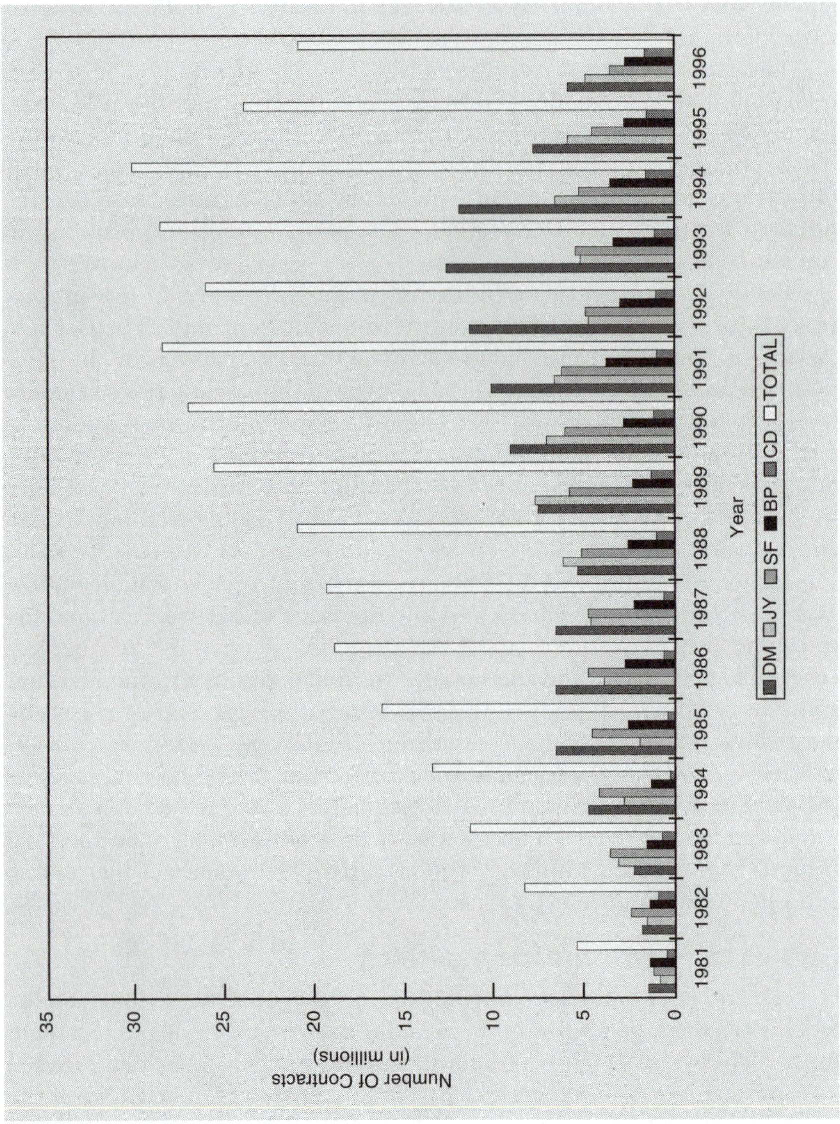

Note: Futures contracts were also traded on several other currencies and various cross-rates.

Source: CFTC *Annual Reports*

FIGURE 13.4   **Foreign Currency Futures Quotations in *The Wall Street Journal*, Trading Day, July 23, 1997**

CURRENCY

JAPAN YEN (CME)-12.5 million yen; $ per yen (.00)

Sept	.8767	.8775	.8688	.8713	—	.0028	.9790	.7946	56,267
Dec	.8840	.8860	.8802	.8825	—	.0028	.9320	.8135	1,706
Mr98	.8916	.8925	.8916	.8939	—	.0028	.9375	.8269	222

Est vol 15,936; vol Tu 8,581; open int 58,195, −544.

DEUTSCHEMARK (CME)-125,000 marks; $ per mark

Sept	.5504	.5520	.5476	.5494	—	.0008	.6635	.5476	114,557
Dec	.5524	.5541	.5517	.5528	—	.0009	.6610	.5517	1,219
Mr98	....	....	....	.5562	—	.0009	.6160	.5636	513
June	.5585	.5600	.5585	.5596	—	.0009	.5995	.5585	104

Est vol 21,514; vol Tu 8,581; open int 58,195, −544.

CANADIAN DOLLAR (CME)-100,000 dlrs.; $ per Can $

Sept	.7283	.7293	.7250	.7263	—	.0023	.7662	.7196	39,779
Dec	.73209	.7328	.7286	.7296	—	.0023	.7685	.7227	2,751
Mr98	.7353	.7353	.7323	.7323	—	.0023	.7670	.7270	575
June	....	....	....	.7347	—	.0023	.7470	.7300	174

Est vol 9,624; vol Tu 3,942; open int 43,314, +626.

BRITISH POUND (CME)-62,500 pds.; $ per pound

Sept	1.6788	1.6832	1.6670	1.6754	—	.0004	1.6960	1.5790	61,535
Dec	1.6740	1.6744	1.6650	1.6696	—	.0004	1.6970	1.5800	879
Mr98	....	....	1.6636	—	.0004	1.6840	1.6200		198

Est vol 9,013; vol Tu 3,506; open int 62,612, −589.

SWISS FRANC (CME)-125,000 francs; $ per franc

Sept	.6796	.6796	.6746	.6771	—	.0017	.8082	.6746	53,002
Dec	.6852	.6852	.6823	.6841	—	.0017	.7740	.6853	1,392
Mr98	.6895	.6920	.6895	.6913	—	.0018	.7450	.6895	953
June	....	....	....	.6986	—	.0018	.7135	.7085	100

Est vol 10,915; vol Tu 8,542; open int 55,447, +901.

AUSTRALIAN DOLLAR (CME)-100,000 dlrs.; $ per A.$

Sept	.7408	.7408	.7358	.7372	—	.0028	.7890	.7322	19,177
Dec	.7380	.7380	.7380	.7384	—	.0028	.7860	.7380	202

Est vol 763; vol Tu 661; open int 19,382, −374.

MEXICAN PESO (CME)-500,000 new Mex. peso, $ per MP

Sept	.12500	.12530	.12479	.12500	+	.0005	.12530	.10250	17,831
Dec	.12085	.12095	.12050	.12067	+	.0005	.12095	.0985	11,973
Mr98	.11690	.11705	.11670	.11685		....	.11705	.10400	4,251
June	.11330	.11340	.11330	.11340		....	.11340	.10050	1,670
Sept	....	....	....	.11020	—	00010	.11020	.10575	143

Est vol 9,821; vol Tu 3,328; open int 35,868, −15.

Source: *The Wall Street Journal,* July 24, 1997

---

expirations of several years. Each option has a European and an American contract. The Philadelphia Exchange also allows trading on both physical delivery and cash-settled options. Appendix 13B gives the contract specifications.

Figure 13.6 illustrates *The Wall Street Journal*'s foreign currency options quotations. As you can see, the system is similar to that used for ordinary stock options. It is important, however, to pay close attention to the contract size and the unit of quotation. For example, consider the European style Swiss franc contract, which is in the third column. It is for 62,500 Swiss francs and is quoted in cents per unit. Thus, the exercise price of 66 is $0.66 per Swiss franc and the price of the September 66 call is 2.18 cents per Swiss franc. As noted in the previous paragraph, some contracts expire at the end of the month. These are denoted with the symbol "EOM." European-style options are also indicated in Figure 13.6.

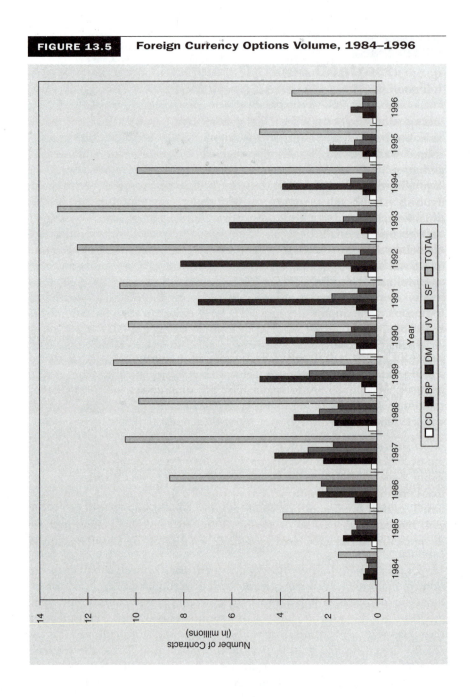

FIGURE 13.5   **Foreign Currency Options Volume, 1984–1996**

FIGURE 13.6 **Foreign Currency Options Quotations in *The Wall Street Journal*, Trading Day, July 23, 1997**

OPTIONS
PHILADELPHIA EXCHANGE

		Calls Vol.	Calls Last	Puts Vol.	Puts Last
FFranc					**162.33**
250,000 French Franc EOM-European style.					
16¾	Aug	16	0.72	...	...
CDollr					**72.36**
50,000 Canadian Dollar EOM-European style					
73	Jul	...	...	20	0.60
Australian Dollar					**73.71**
50,000 Australian Dollars-cents per unit.					
74½	Sep	70	0.47	...	...
50,000 Australian Dollars-cents per unit.					
73	Sep	...	...	5	0.53
British Pound					**167.51**
31,250 Brit. Pound EOM-cents per unit.					
167	Jul	...	...	200	0.12
31,250 Brit. Pounds-cents per unit.					
168	Sep	...	...	4	2.80
British Pound-GMark					**306.03**
31,250 British Pound-German Mark cross.					
286	Jul	70	20.16	...	...
296	Jul	25	10.10	...	...
296	Aug	25	10.00	...	...
31,250 British Pound-German Mark cross.					
284	Sep	2	21.60	...	...
Canadian Dollar					**72.36**
50,000 Canadian Dollars-cents per unit.					
72	Aug	331	0.73	50	0.18
73½	Dec	10	0.59	...	...
French Franc					**162.33**
250,000 French Francs-10ths of a cent per					
16½	Dec	...	...	25	4.84
250,000 French Francs-European Style					
16¼	Aug	20	1.74	...	...
16¾	Aug	36	0.30	...	...
German Mark					**54.74**
62,500 German Marks EOM-European style.					
57½	Jul	...	...	15	2.79
62,500 German Marks EOM-cents per unit.					
54½	Jul	8	0.38	...	...
55½	Jul	1200	0.04	...	...
62,500 German Marks-European Style.					
51½	Sep	...	...	200	0.13
53	Sep	...	...	400	0.30
54	Dec	...	...	25	0.94
54½	Sep	...	...	207	0.75
55½	Aug	...	...	20	0.94
56	Aug	40	0.19	...	...
56½	Aug	50	0.12	...	...
57	Sep	10	0.24	...	...
62,500 German Marks-cents per unit.					
52	Dec	...	...	7	0.42
53	Sep	...	...	2	0.34
53	Dec	...	...	72	0.67
54	Aug	1	1.09	...	...
54	Sep	...	...	4	0.56
54½	Aug	3	0.79	15	0.48
54½	Sep	...	...	2	0.63
55	Aug	30	0.55	15	0.75
55	Sep	...	...	194	0.94
56	Sep	170	0.43	20	1.39
56½	Aug	...	...	5	1.70
57	Sep	...	...	51	2.13
57	Dec	...	...	40	2.48
58	Dec	...	...	1	3.30
59	Dec	...	...	1	4.30
60	Dec	...	...	2	5.22
Japanese Yen					**86.47**
6,250,000J.Yen-100ths of a cent per unit.					
90	Sep	4	0.50	...	...
Swiss Franc					**67.27**
62,500 Swiss Francs EOM-cents per unit.					
68	Jul	...	...	3	0.82
62,500 Swiss Francs EOM.					
67½	Jul	200	0.20	...	...
62,500 Swiss Francs-European Style.					
66	Aug	...	...	90	0.25
66	Sep	43	2.18	33	0.50
66½	Aug	...	...	300	0.39
66½	Sep	9	1.84	9	0.64
67	Aug	20	1.10	45	0.57
67½	Sep	10	1.25	...	...
68	Aug	30	0.53	5	1.12
68	Sep	10	1.02	...	...
69	Aug	...	...	13	1.80
69	Sep	10	0.63	...	...
70	Aug	...	...	12	2.70
71	Aug	...	...	10	3.70
72	Aug	...	...	10	4.64
62,500 Swiss Francs-cents per unit.					
65	Sep	...	...	600	0.29
66	Dec	...	...	5	1.05
66½	Aug	1	1.38	...	...
67½	Aug	...	...	3	0.81
68	Sep	...	...	10	1.45
69	Sep	...	...	40	2.08
70	Sep	223	0.47	...	...
71	Dec	30	1.04	...	...
72	Dec	14	0.78	...	...
Call Vol 8,663		**Open Int ... 163,215**			
Put Vol 9,189		**Open Int ... 147,151**			

Source: *The Wall Street Journal,* July 24, 1997

Exchange-traded currency options also exist in the form of currency warrants, which trade on the American Stock Exchange. These warrants are long-term options, and are usually offered at-the-money when they first begin trading, though there may be several issues offered at different times with different exercise prices.

The over-the-counter currency options market is much larger than the exchange-listed currency options market. Indeed the entire over-the-counter derivatives market is much larger than the exchange-listed derivatives market. The recent decline in volume has reflected a combination of a leveling off of growth in the use of currency derivatives in general and a preference for the more customized over-the-counter products. The reduction in growth of currency derivatives in general does not reflect anything undesirable about them. Rather currency derivatives, particularly currency swaps, which we shall cover later in this chapter, have been widely embraced by corporate financial managers and investment managers. They are so commonly used today that their rapid growth was bound to level off eventually. At this time the Chicago Mercantile Exchange and

the Philadelphia Stock Exchange are working very hard to generate volume, but it is not clear if their efforts will succeed.

Pricing Foreign Currency Derivatives

Foreign currency derivatives are priced according to the same arbitrage principles we have used throughout this book. However, applying these rules is less straightforward than it is for ordinary derivatives. In this section, we shall look at some basic principles of pricing foreign currency derivatives.

Cross-Rate Relationships

Any three currencies are related to each other by the cross-rate relationship.

One of the most elementary principles is the **cross-rate** relationship among foreign currencies. Let us consider three currencies: the U.S. dollar, the British pound, and the deutsche mark. We express the dollar/pound exchange rate as \$/£, the mark/dollar exchange rate as DM/\$, and the pound/mark exchange rate as £/DM. Notice what we get when we multiply these three rates:

$$\left(\frac{\$}{£}\right)\left(\frac{DM}{\$}\right)\left(\frac{£}{DM}\right) = 1.$$

If this relationship does not hold, an arbitrageur can make a riskless profit. For example, consider the spot rates for pounds and marks in terms of dollars on September 26 of a particular year. The rates are \$1.437/£ and DM2.0465/\$. These rates imply that the price of deutsche marks in pounds should be £.34/DM, since (\$1.437)(2.0465)(.34) = 1. Now suppose the price of deutsche marks in pounds is £.36/DM. This means the deutsche mark is overvalued relative to the pound. An arbitrageur will want to convert marks to pounds. Here is how the transaction would be done.

Take 1 dollar and convert it to DM2.0465. Then arrange for a currency dealer to convert the 2.0465 marks to 2.0465(.36) = .7367 pounds. Then convert the .7367 pounds to .7367(1.4367) = 1.0585 dollars. This transaction is riskless and immediately earns a profit of 5.85 cents on a 1-dollar investment. The 5.85 percent return is the amount by which the mark is overvalued relative to the pound. In the real world, there would be a dealer bid-ask spread to cover and some modest transaction costs; however, we shall ignore these for this analysis.

The combined effects of numerous arbitrageurs would drive the exchange rate of marks for pounds down to £.34/DM. This is the cross-rate relationship among any three currencies. Any two rates imply the third rate. The transaction that upholds this relationship is sometimes called **tri-**

angular arbitrage. These relationships will hold for spot, forward, and futures exchange rates.

Interest Rate Parity

Interest rate parity is an important fundamental relationship between the spot and forward exchange rates and the interest rates in two countries. It is the foreign currency market's version of the cost-of-carry forward and futures pricing model that we discussed in Chapter 9. A helpful way to understand interest rate parity is to consider the position of someone who believes that a higher risk-free return can be earned by converting to a currency that pays a higher interest rate. For example, suppose an American corporate treasurer wants to earn more than the 5.46 percent U.S. interest rate and believes that he can convert dollars to pounds and earn the British rate of 9.96 percent. If the treasurer does so but fails to arrange a forward or futures contract to guarantee the rate at which the pounds will be converted back to dollars, he runs the risk, not only of not earning the British rate, but of earning less than the U.S. rate. If the pound weakens while he is holding pounds, the conversion back to dollars will be costly. This type of transaction can be viewed like going to a foreign country but not buying your ticket home until after you have been there for awhile and then decide to come back. You are subject to whatever rates and conditions exist at the time the return ticket is purchased. Buying a round-trip ticket locks in the return price and conditions. Hence the corporate treasurer might wish to lock in the rate at which the pounds can be converted back to dollars by selling a forward or futures contract on the pound. But forward and futures prices will adjust so that the overall transaction will earn no more in U.S. dollars than the U.S. interest rate. The cost of the return ticket will offset any interest rate gains while in the foreign currency. Consider the following situation involving U.S. dollars and British pounds.

The spot exchange rate is S. This quote is in dollars per £. The British risk-free interest rate is ρ, and the holding period is T. You take $S(1 + \rho)^{-T}$ dollars and buy $(1 + \rho)^{-T}$ pounds. Simultaneously, you sell one forward contract expiring at time T. The forward exchange rate is F, which is also in dollars per pound. You take your $(1 + \rho)^{-T}$ pounds and invest them in British T-bills that have a return of ρ.

When the forward contract expires, you will have 1 pound. This is because your $(1 + \rho)^{-T}$ pounds will have grown by the factor $(1 + \rho)^{T}$, so $(1 + \rho)^{-T}(1 + \rho)^{T} = 1$. Your forward contract obligates you to deliver the pound, for which you receive F dollars. In effect, you have invested $S(1 + \rho)^{-T}$ dollars and received F dollars. Since the transaction is riskless, your return should be the U.S. risk-free rate, r; that is,

$$F = S(1 + r)^{T}(1 + \rho)^{-T}.$$

Interest rate parity, the relationship between futures or forward and spot exchange rates, is determined by the relationship between the risk-free interest rates in the two countries.

This relationship is called interest rate parity.[1] It is sometimes expressed as

$$\frac{F}{S} = (1 + r)^T (1 + \rho)^{-T}.$$

Consider the following example. On September 26 of a particular year, the spot rate for pounds was $1.437 and the 90-day forward rate was $1.421. The U.S. interest rate was 5.46 percent, while the British interest rate was 9.96 percent. The time to expiration was $90/365 = .2466$. Thus, we have

$$\frac{F}{S} = \frac{\$1.421}{\$1.437} = .9889,$$

and

$$(1 + r)^T (1 + \rho)^{-T} = (1.0546)^{.2466}(1.0996)^{-.2466} = .9897.$$

The difference is very small, as we would expect in an efficient market.

Suppose, however, that prices do not completely adjust. Then an arbitrage opportunity is available. To illustrate an arbitrage transaction, assume the spot rate is correct but the forward rate is $1.43. An arbitrageur buys $(1.0996)^{-.2466} = .9769$ pounds for $1.437(.9769) = \$1.4037$ and sells one forward contract at a forward rate of $1.43. The .9769 pounds are invested at the British risk-free rate. When the contract expires, the arbitrageur will have 1 pound, which is delivered on the forward contract and for which $1.43 is received. Thus, the arbitrageur has invested $1.4037 and received $1.43 in 90 days. The annualized return is

$$\left(\frac{1.43}{1.4037}\right)^{1/.2466} - 1 = .0782,$$

which exceeds the domestic risk-free rate of 5.46 percent. The combined effects of numerous arbitrageurs would push the spot rate up and/or the forward rate down until the spot and forward rates were properly aligned with the relative interest rates in the two countries.[2] Of course, some transaction costs and the dealer bid-ask spread would prevent the relationship from holding precisely.

Interest rate parity can be confusing to some people because of the difference in the way the rates can be quoted. Many times you may see interest rate parity stated as $F = S(1 + \rho)^T (1 + r)^{-T}$. This is correct if the spot

---

[1] Be alert to the obviously equivalent formula, $F = S(1 + r)^T/(1 + \rho)^T$, which you will see sometimes in other books and articles.

[2] Arbitrage could also put pressure on interest rates in the two countries. The British rate would decrease, while the U.S. rate would increase.

rate is quoted in units of the foreign currency. In our British pound example, we could have stated the spot rate as $1/\$1.437 = 0.6959$ pounds per dollar. In that case the forward rate would be stated in pounds per dollar and the formula would be correctly given as $F = S(1 + \rho)^{T}(1 + r)^{-T}$. As you continue your education and in the financial world, you are likely to encounter it done both ways. An easy way to remember is that the factor for the interest rate for a given country multiplies by the spot quote stated in that country's currency. The other interest rate factor then appears with the $-T$ in the exponent or simply in the denominator to the power T.

As we noted earlier in the chapter, when a forward rate is quoted in units of the domestic currency, e.g., the pound quoted in dollars, a higher forward than spot rate is said to be at a premium. Since the word "premium" tends to imply something higher, we have another reason to quote the currency in terms of your domestic currency. Had we quoted it the other way, a higher forward rate would imply a discount.

It has become common in discussions of international finance to interpret a forward premium (discount) as implying that the currency is expected to strengthen (weaken). As we discussed in Chapter 8, this arises from a belief in the expectations theory. Unfortunately this is a mistaken belief. The expectations theory need not hold here at all. The principle of arbitrage is what gives rise to a forward premium or discount. If a person could convert his or her domestic currency to a foreign currency, lock in a higher risk-free return, and convert back with the currency risk hedged, everyone would do this, which would erase any possibility of being able to earn a return better than the domestic risk-free rate. Any forward premium or discount is strictly caused by a difference in the interest rates of the two countries. If the domestic rate is lower and one forgoes the domestic risk-free return to earn the higher foreign risk-free return, the currency must sell at a forward rate proportional to the relative interest earned and given up. This has nothing to do with what people expect the spot rate to do in the future. People may have quite different beliefs about what might happen to spot rates, but we know they would agree that the forward rate must align with the spot rate by the proportional interest factors, or, in other words, by interest rate parity.

Interest rate parity is a powerful relationship and is used by all international currency traders. It is analogous to the cost of carry model for pricing other types of futures. The only difference is that the cost of carry in the two countries must be considered. For example, when funds are tied up in a foreign currency, the investor forgoes interest at the U.S. rate but earns interest at the foreign rate. The difference between the U.S. rate and the foreign rate is the cost of carry. The foreign interest rate thus is analogous to the dividend yield in the stock index futures pricing model.

As we saw in previous chapters, futures prices are not necessarily equal to forward prices. However, the differences observed in real data are

extremely small. Thus, as we have done previously, we shall usually assume forward exchange rates and futures exchange rates are equivalent.

The Intrinsic Value of an American Foreign Currency Option

Most of the principles of option pricing we previously covered are equally applicable to foreign currency option pricing. Thus, we shall limit our discussion to the most important principles and those that differ slightly from ordinary options. We shall use the same notation as in the option chapters. $C(S,T,E)$ and $P(S,T,E)$ are the call and put prices, with subscripts a and e used when necessary to distinguish American from European options. S_T is the spot rate at expiration. The risk-free rates and time to expiration are r, ρ, and T, as in the preceding section.

The minimum value of an American foreign currency call is

$$C_a(S,T,E) \geq \text{Max}(0, S - E),$$

The intrinsic values of American currency options are the same as those of options on stock with the exchange rate used instead of the stock price.

which is the same as for an equity call. The term $\text{Max}(0, S - E)$ is the intrinsic value. As an example, take the December 140 British pound call on September 26 of a particular year. The spot rate is 143.53 cents. Thus, the intrinsic value is $\text{Max}(0, 143.53 - 140) = 3.53$. The call price is 5.10 cents. The difference, $5.10 - 3.53 = 1.57$, is the time value.

The minimum value of an American foreign currency put is

$$P_a(S,T,E) \geq \text{Max}(0, E - S),$$

where $\text{Max}(0, E - S)$ is the intrinsic value. For example, on September 26, the December 145 British pound put has an intrinsic value of $\text{Max}(0, 145 - 143.53) = 1.47$. The put price is 4.90. The difference of $4.90 - 1.47 = 3.43$ is the time value.

As the options move closer to expiration, their time values erode, and at expiration the options are worth only their intrinsic values. These principles are exactly like those for their equity option counterparts. Now, however, we shall establish lower bounds for European options that differ somewhat from those we did for equity options.

The Lower Bound of European Foreign Currency Options

Consider two portfolios, A and B. Portfolio A consists of a foreign currency call priced at $C_e(S,T,E)$ and a risk-free bond with a face value of E and a present value of $E(1 + r)^{-T}$. Portfolio B is constructed by taking $S(1 + \rho)^{-T}$ dollars, converting it to the foreign currency, and investing it in a foreign pure discount bond with a face value equal to one unit of the foreign currency. The present value of that bond is $S(1 + \rho)^{-T}$ dollars. When the bond matures, it pays one unit of the foreign currency, which is converted back into S_T dollars.

			Payoffs from Portfolio Given Spot Rate at Expiration	
TABLE 13.1	**The Lower Bound of a European Foreign Currency Call: Payoffs at Expiration of Portfolios A and B**			
Portfolio	Instrument	Current Value	$S_T \leq E$	$S_T > E$
A	Long call	$C_e(S,T,E)$	0	$S_T - E$
	Domestic bond	$E(1 + r)^{-T}$	$\underline{E}$	$\underline{E}$
			E	S_T
B	Foreign bond	$S(1 + \rho)^{-T}$	S_T	S_T

Table 13.1 illustrates the payoffs from those portfolios. For portfolio A, if the spot rate at expiration does not exceed the exercise price, the call expires worthless but the bonds are worth E dollars. If the spot rate at expiration is greater than E, the call is worth $S_T - E$ and the bonds are worth E for a total of S_T. Thus, portfolio A is worth the greater of E and S_T. Portfolio B is worth S_T in either case. This is because the British bonds mature and are worth 1 pound in either case, and that pound is converted back into S_T dollars.

The outcome of portfolio A equals or exceeds that of portfolio B in both cases. Thus, portfolio A must sell for at least as much as portfolio B.[3] The current value for portfolio B is $S(1 + \rho)^{-T}$, while the current value for portfolio A is $C_e(S,T,E) + E(1 + r)^{-T}$. We state this inequality as

$$C_e(S,T,E) + E(1 + r)^{-T} \geq S(1 + \rho)^{-T}.$$

This is frequently written as

$$C_e(S,T,E) \geq S(1 + \rho)^{-T} - E(1 + r)^{-T}.$$

Because an option cannot have a negative value, we can state this as

$$C_e(S,T,E) \geq Max[0, S(1 + \rho)^{-T} - E(1 + r)^{-T}].$$

The call price is greater than or equal to the spot rate discounted at the foreign interest rate minus the present value of the exercise price. This is

The lower bound of a European currency call is the same as that of a European call on a stock except that the spot exchange rate is discounted by the foreign interest rate and appears instead of the stock price.

---

[3]Recall from Chapter 3 why this is true. If portfolio B sold for more than portfolio A, British investors would have an arbitrage opportunity. They could go short in portfolio B by selling their own currency. Then they would use the funds to construct portfolio A. This would enable them to earn a nonnegative profit and have cash left over up front.

similar to the lower bound of an equity call, which is the spot price minus the present value of the exercise price. In fact, if there were a dividend on the stock, these two boundaries would be equivalent. The dividend yield would replace the foreign risk-free interest rate.

Converting dollars into a foreign currency is similar to buying a stock with a known dividend. Suppose the dividend yield is equivalent to ρ. You buy the stock, hold it, and collect the dividend; then you sell the stock at S_T. In the case of a foreign currency, you buy the currency, hold it, and collect the interest; then you sell (convert) it.

Let us test the lower bound rule on a European option, the November 145 British pound European call on September 26. The spot rate was 143.53, the domestic interest rate was 5.46 percent, the British interest rate was 9.96 percent, and the option expired on November 14, 49 days later. Thus, T = 49/365 = .1342. The lower bound is

$$143.53(1.0996)^{-.1342} - 145(1.0546)^{-.1342} = -2.25.$$

Thus, the lower bound is zero. The actual price of the call is 1.80, and it obviously exceeds the lower bound.

The lower bound for a European put is derived similarly. Portfolio A consists of a European put plus an investment of $S(1 + \rho)^{-T}$ dollars in a foreign pure discount bond worth one unit of the foreign currency at expiration. Portfolio B consists of a domestic pure discount bond worth E dollars at expiration. Table 13.2 illustrates the payoffs.

Portfolio A performs at least as well as portfolio B and therefore should be priced at least as high. We state this as

$$P_e(S,T,E) + S(1 + \rho)^{-T} \geq E(1 + r)^{-T}.$$

The lower bound of a European currency put is the same as that of a European put on a stock except that the spot exchange rate is discounted by the foreign interest rate and appears instead of the stock price.

| **TABLE 13.2** | **The Lower Bound of a European Foreign Currency Put: Payoffs at Expiration of Portfolios A and B** |

Portfolio	Instrument	Current Value	*Payoffs from Portfolio Given Spot Rate at Expiration*	
			$S_T \leq E$	$S_T > E$
A	Long put	$P_e(S,T,E)$	$(E - S_T)$	0
	Foreign bond	$S(1 + \rho)^{-T}$	$\dfrac{S_T}{E}$	$\dfrac{S_T}{S_T}$
B	Domestic bond	$E(1 + r)^{-T}$	E	E

This is usually written as

$$P_e(S,T,E) \geq E(1 + r)^{-T} - S(1 + \rho)^{-T}.$$

Because an option cannot have a negative value,

$$P_e(S,T,E) \geq \text{Max } [0,\, E(1 + r)^{-T} - S(1 + \rho)^{-T}].$$

The put price must equal or exceed the present value of the exercise price minus the spot rate discounted at the foreign interest rate. This too is identical to the lower bound of a European put option on a dividend-paying stock when the dividend yield is equivalent to ρ.

As an example, consider the December 150 British pound European put on September 26 of a recent year. The lower bound is

$$150(1.0546)^{-.2192} - 143.53(1.0996)^{-.2192} = 7.69.$$

The actual put price is 8.50; therefore, the put conforms to the boundary condition.

As was the case with equity options, these lower bounds establish the lowest possible price for European calls and puts. For American calls and puts, the lowest possible price is the intrinsic value.

Put-Call Parity

Suppose we construct the following portfolio, called portfolio A. Take $S(1 + \rho)^{-T}$ dollars, convert to the foreign currency, buy a foreign bond that pays interest at the rate ρ, and buy a European put on the currency with an exercise price of E. Now consider portfolio B, consisting of a call on the currency and a position in domestic (U.S. dollar) bonds with a face value of E, which pay the U.S. interest rate of r. The payoffs from these portfolios are illustrated in Table 13.3. If the spot exchange rate ends up above the exercise price, both portfolios pay off the spot exchange rate. Portfolio A achieves this result because it contains a position in the $(1 + \rho)^{-T}$ units of the currency, which grow to a value of one unit of the currency worth S_T. The put ends up out-of-the-money. Portfolio B achieves this result by exercising the call to acquire the currency. The maturing dollar-denominated bond generates the E dollars used to pay the exercise price when exercising the call. In effect, both portfolios result in the establishment of a long position in the currency. If the spot exchange rate ends up below the exercise price, both portfolios are worth the exchange rate. Portfolio A achieves this result by selling the currency at the rate E while portfolio B results in the receipt of the face value, E, of the maturing dollar-denominated bond.

Put-call parity of European currency options is the same as for European stock options except that the spot exchange rate is discounted by the foreign interest rate and appears instead of the stock price.

			Payoffs from Portfolio Given Spot Rate at Expiration	
Portfolio	**Instrument**	**Current Value**	$S_T \leq E$	$S_T > E$
A	Foreign bond	$S(1 + \rho)^{-T}$	S_T	S_T
	Long put	$P_e(S,T,E)$	$\dfrac{E - S_T}{E}$	$\dfrac{0}{S_T}$
B	Long call	$C_e(S,T,E)$	0	$S_T - E$
	Domestic bond	$E(1 + r)^{-T}$	$\dfrac{E}{E}$	$\dfrac{E}{S_T}$

TABLE 13.3   Put-Call Parity of Foreign Currency Options

Because these two portfolios produce the same results at expiration, they should have the same initial values. Thus, we obtain the put-call parity relationship for foreign currency options:

$$S(1 + \rho)^{-T} + P_e(S,T,E) = C_e(S,T,E) + E(1 + r)^{-T}.$$

Stated alternatively,

$$P_e(S,T,E) = C_e(S,T,E) - S(1 + \rho)^{-T} + E(1 + r)^{-T},$$

or

$$C_e(S,T,E) = P_e(S,T,E) + S(1 + \rho)^{-T} - E(1 + r)^{-T}.$$

The only difference between this put-call parity and put-call parity for stock options is the presence of the foreign discount factor times the spot rate. Once again, however, this is equivalent to a dividend on a stock. Put-call parity for dividend-paying stocks thus would be identical to the above statement if the dividend were paid at the rate ρ.

Consider the December 150 European put and call on September 26. The call price is $1. According to the formula, the put should be worth

$$1 - 143.53(1.0996)^{-.2192} + 150(1.0546)^{-.2192} = 8.69.$$

The actual put price is 8.50, so the put appears to be slightly underpriced. However, transaction costs could account for the difference.

American put-call parity would be analogous to American put-call parity for options on a dividend-paying stock, which we covered in Chapter 4.

Put-call parity gives the relationship between puts and calls denominated in one currency but exercisable into another. To fully understand

foreign currency options, it is important to recognize another type of put-call parity: A call to buy currency A denominated in currency B with an exercise price of E is equivalent to a put to sell E units of currency B denominated in currency A with an exercise price of 1/E. For example, consider the December 140 British pound call. This is a call to buy 1 British pound at $1.40. It is equivalent to a put to sell 1.40 dollars at 1/1.40 = £.71. Let us see why this is so by considering the payoffs at expiration from these two options. If we buy the call to buy a British pound at $1.40, we shall receive the following payoffs:

$$S_T - \$1.40 \quad \text{if } S_T \geq \$1.40$$
$$0 \qquad \qquad \text{if } S_T < \$1.40.$$

If we buy the put to sell 1.40 dollars at £.71, we shall receive the following payoffs:

$$0 \qquad \qquad \text{if } 1/S_T \geq £.71$$
$$(1.40)[£.71 - (1/S_T)] \quad \text{if } 1/S_T < £.71.$$

The expression $1/S_T$ is simply the £/$ exchange rate at expiration expressed in terms of pounds. The put pays off when $1/S_T < £.71$. Recall that the exercise price of £.71 was simply the inverse of $1.40. Thus, the put pays off when $1/S_T < 1/\$1.40$, which is equivalent to $S_T > \$1.40$. The put payoff when this occurs is $1.40(£.71 - 1/S_T) = £1 - 1.40/S_T$. This amount is in pounds, so we convert it to dollars by multiplying by $\$S_T$, giving us $S_T - \$1.40$. Looking back at the call payoffs, we see that when the put pays off, the call also pays off, and they both pay off the same amount in dollars. It follows that when the call is out-of-the-money, the put is also out-of-the-money, and neither pays off anything. Thus, the call and the put are equivalent.

The Garman-Kohlhagen Foreign Currency Option Pricing Model

Garman and Kohlhagen (1983) derived an option pricing model for foreign currency options. Their model is a simple extension of the Black-Scholes model. The formula is

$$C = Se^{-p_cT}N(d_1) - Ee^{-r_cT}N(d_2),$$

where

$$d_1 = \frac{\ln(Se^{-p_cT}/E) + [r_c + (\sigma^2/2)]T}{\sigma\sqrt{T}}$$

$$d_2 = d_1 - \sigma\sqrt{T}.$$

The Garman-Kohlhagen foreign currency option pricing model is equivalent to the Black-Scholes model except that the spot exchange rate is discounted by the foreign interest rate and appears instead of the stock price.

Table 13.4 illustrates the calculation of the Garman-Kohlhagen foreign currency option price for the British pound November 145 European

---

TABLE 13.4	**Calculating the Garman-Kohlhagen Foreign Currency Option Price**

$S = 143.53$　　$E = 145$　　$r_c = .0532$　　$\rho_c = .0949$
$\sigma^2 = .0225$　　$T = .1342$

1. Compute d_1.

$$d_1 = \frac{\ln(143.53e^{-(.0949)(.1342)}/145) + (.0532 + (.0225)/2).1342}{.15\sqrt{.1342}} = -0.26$$

2. Compute d_2.

$$d_2 = -0.26 - .15\sqrt{.1342} = -0.31$$

3. Look up $N(d_1)$.

$$N(-0.26) = 1 - .6026 = .3974$$

4. Look up $N(d_2)$.

$$N(-0.31) = 1 - .6217 = .3783$$

5. Plug into formula for C.

$$C = 143.53e^{-(.0949)(.1342)}(.3974) - 145e^{-(.0532)(.1342)}(.3783) = 1.85$$

call. Recall from Chapters 4 and 12 that the Black-Scholes and Black models require the calculation of d_1, d_2, and the normal probabilities associated with these values. Then these normal probabilities are inserted into an overall formula. The Garman-Kohlhagen model works similarly. Everywhere we would use the exchange rate S, we simply use S discounted at the continuously compounded foreign interest rate, ρ_c. Of course, as in the Black-Scholes and Black models, we also use the continuously compounded U.S. risk-free rate. The standard deviation in this model is the standard deviation of the log of one plus the percentage change in the exchange rate, expressed in dollars per unit of the foreign currency. In this problem, σ is .15 and σ^2 is .0225.

Put options can also be priced by substituting the Garman-Kohlhagen formula for the call price into the put-call parity formula. Remember, of course, that the Garman-Kohlhagen model, like Black-Scholes, is a European option pricing model. American options would have higher prices and would tend to be underpriced by the model. Thus, to accurately price an American foreign currency option would require an American option pricing model. As we have noted previously, most of the American models

are beyond the scope of this book; however, American currency options can be priced by the binomial model, which we have covered in great detail in earlier chapters.

As you might have expected, the Garman-Kohlhagen and binomial models can be calculated using your Excel spreadsheet bsbin1.xls or your Windows program bsbwin2.exe.

This concludes our discussion of pricing foreign currency derivatives. In the next section, we shall briefly review several strategies using these instruments.

Trading Strategies in Foreign Currency Futures/Forwards and Options

In this section, we shall look at five applications of foreign currency instruments. The first two are long and short hedges using futures/forwards. The next two are simple speculative call and put strategies. The last is a foreign currency hedge using options.

A Long Hedge with Foreign Currency Futures

Recall that a long hedge with futures involves the purchase of a futures contract. In the case of foreign currencies, a long hedger is concerned that the value of the foreign currency will rise. An example is presented in Table 13.5.

Here an American car dealer plans to buy 20 British sports cars. Each car costs 35,000 pounds, which will have to be paid in the British currency. Based on the current forward rate of the pound, the dealer's current cost is $914,200. However, if the pound increases in value, the cars will end up costing more. The dealer hedges by buying futures on the pound. As the table indicates, this was a good decision because the pound did appreciate; the cars ended up costing $1,009,400, which is $95,200 more, but the futures contracts generated a profit of $109,656.25, which more than covered the increased cost of the cars.

As long as the pound spot and futures rates move in the same direction, the hedge will be successful in reducing some of the loss in the spot market. Had the pound weakened, there would have been a loss in the futures market that would have offset some or all of the gain in the spot market.

This transaction was executed in the futures market. Remember that futures contracts have standardized terms and provide a guarantee against default on the part of the other party. Forward contracts permit the parties to customize the terms of the contract. This transaction, however, would not be large enough to justify a forward contract. In the next example we shall execute the hedge in the forward market.

TABLE 13.5	**A Long Hedge with Foreign Currency Futures**

Scenario: On July 1, an American auto dealer enters into a contract to purchase 20 British sports cars with payment to be made in British pounds on November 1. Each car will cost 35,000 pounds. The dealer is concerned that the pound will strengthen over the next few months, causing the cars to cost more in dollars.

Date	Spot Market	Futures Market
July 1	The current exchange rate is $1.3190 per pound. The forward rate of the pound is $1.3060. Forward cost of 20 cars: 20(35,000)($1.3060) = $914,200.	December pound contract is at $1.278. Price per contract: 62,500($1.278) = $79,875. The appropriate number of contracts is $$\frac{20(35,500)}{62,500} = 11.2.$$ **Buy 11 contracts**
November 1	The spot rate is $1.442. Buy the 700,000 pounds to purchase 20 cars. Cost in dollars: 700,000($1.442) = $1,009,400.	December pound contract is at $1.4375. Price per contract: 62,500($1.4375) = $89,843.75. **Sell 11 contracts**

Analysis:
The cars ended up costing $1,009,400 − $914,200 = $95,200 more.

The profit on the futures transaction is

$$
\begin{array}{ll}
11(\$89,843.75) & \text{(sale price of futures)} \\
\underline{-11(\$79,875)} & \text{(purchase price of futures)} \\
\$109,656.25 & \text{(profit on futures).}
\end{array}
$$

The profit on the futures more than offsets the full cost of the cars, leaving a net gain of $109,656.25 − $95,200 = $14,456.25. The dealer effectively paid $1,009,400 − $109,656.25 = $899,743.75 for the 20 cars.

A Short Hedge with Foreign Currency Forwards

A short hedge is a commitment to sell a currency using futures or forwards and is designed to protect against a decrease in the foreign currency's value. In Table 13.6 we have a situation in which a multinational firm has 10 million pounds that it will convert at a later date. A transaction of this size can often be better executed with a customized forward contract. In addition, when the amount of exposure is large, the basis risk of a futures contract may be a risk not worth bearing. In this example the customer is long pounds and is exposed to the risk of the pound weakening. To protect against this risk, it sells a forward contract on the exact number of pounds it will convert, with the contract expiring on the day of conversion. This allows the firm to convert the pounds to dollars by sim-

TABLE 13.6	A Short Hedge with Foreign Currency Forwards

Scenario: On June 29, a multinational firm with a British subsidary decides it will need to transfer 10 million pounds from an account in London to an account with a New York bank. Transfer will be made on September 28. The firm is concerned that over the next two months the pound will weaken.

Date	Spot Market	Forward Market
June 29	The current exchange rate is $1.362 per pound. The forward rate of the pound is $1.357. Forward value of funds: 10,000,000($1.357) = $13,570,000.	Sell pounds forward for delivery on September 28 at $1.357.
September 28	The spot rate is $1.2375.	Deliver pounds and receive 10,000,000($1.357) = $13,570,000.

Analysis:
The pounds end up worth $13,570,000 − $12,375,000 = $1,195,000 less but are delivered on the forward contract for $13,570,000, thus completely eliminating the risk. Had the transaction not been done, the firm would have converted the pounds at the spot rate of $1.2375.

ply delivering them to the dealer on the opposite side of the forward contract. As the table indicates, the pound did depreciate, which would have caused a loss of $1,195,000. Instead the firm locked in the rate on the day it entered into the forward contract.

Buy a Foreign Currency Call

Following the notation used in Chapters 5 and 6, the profit from a single foreign currency call held to expiration is

$$\Pi = \text{Max}(0, S_T - E) - C.$$

Just as we did in Chapter 5, we will look at the outcomes in both cases, $S_T \leq E$ and $S_T > E$, and the breakeven spot rates at expiration. However, the results are the same as they were for equity calls:

$$\Pi = -C \qquad \text{if } S_T \leq E$$
$$\Pi = S_T - E - C \quad \text{if } S_T > E.$$

The breakeven spot rate at expiration is $E + C$.

Consider the December 140 British pound call on the Philadelphia Stock Exchange on September 26 of a particular year. One contract is for

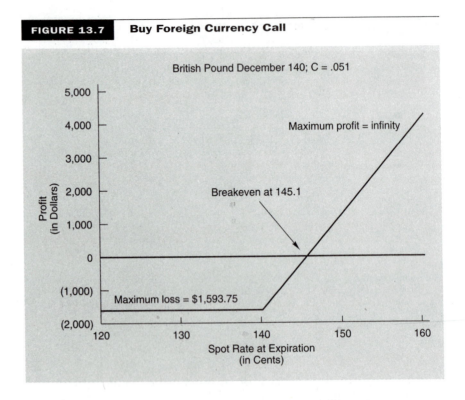

FIGURE 13.7   **Buy Foreign Currency Call**

British Pound December 140; C = .051

Maximum profit = infinity

Breakeven at 145.1

Maximum loss = $1,593.75

Profit (in Dollars)

Spot Rate at Expiration (in Cents)

£31,250. The call costs 5.10 cents per pound. Figure 13.7 illustrates the profit graph with the spot rate shown in cents.

Suppose that at expiration the exchange rate is $1.50. Then the pounds are worth £31,250($1.50 − $1.40) = $3,125. The profit is $3,125 less the cost of the option, £31,250($0.051) = $1,593.75, or $1,531.25. If the spot rate ends up below $1.40, the call will expire worthless and the loss will be the option's cost, $1,593.75. To reach breakeven, the spot rate must be at least $1.40 + $.051 = $1.451. Because there is no upper limit to the spot exchange rate, the maximum profit is infinity. The maximum loss is the call premium of $1,593.75.

When analyzing equity options, we looked at the factors affecting the choice of exercise price and the length of the holding period. We shall not discuss those factors here; the same principles for equity options apply to foreign currency options. In addition, we shall omit a direct discussion of writing foreign currency options, as the principles are similar to those for writing equity options.

Buy a Foreign Currency Put

The profit from the purchase of a single foreign currency put held to expiration is

$$\Pi = \text{Max}(0, E - S_T) - P.$$

This is, of course, the same as the profit for an equity put. The outcomes for the two cases are

$$\Pi = -P \qquad \text{if } S_T \geq E$$
$$\Pi = E - S_T - P \quad \text{if } S_T < E.$$

The breakeven spot rate at expiration is $E - P$.

As an example, consider the December 145 British pound put on the Philadelphia Stock Exchange on September 26 of a particular year. The cost of the put is 2.5 cents. Figure 13.8 illustrates the performance of the strategy.

FIGURE 13.8   **Buy Foreign Currency Put**

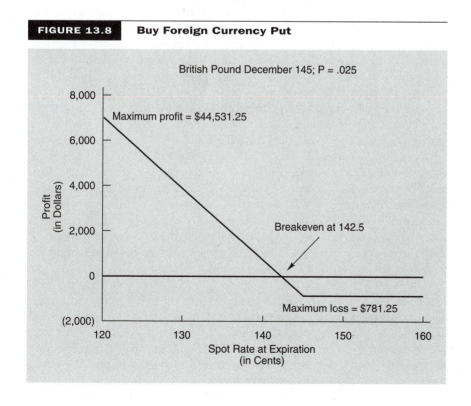

British Pound December 145; P = .025

Maximum profit = $44,531.25

Breakeven at 142.5

Maximum loss = $781.25

Suppose the spot rate at expiration is 138. Then the puts are worth 31,250($1.45 − $1.38) = $2,187.50. You paid 2.5 cents per put, or 31,250($.025) = $781.25. Thus, the net profit is $1,406.25. If the spot rate at expiration exceeds 145, the put will expire worthless and the strategy will lose the premium, $781.25, which is the maximum loss. The breakeven spot rate is 145 − 2.5 = 142.5. The maximum gain occurs if the pound falls to a value of zero. Then the put holder can sell the currency at $1.45 for a profit of 31,250 ($1.45 − $.025) = $44,531.25.

A Foreign Currency Option Hedge

Foreign currency forwards and futures clearly are useful tools for managing exchange rate risk. Lest we leave the impression that foreign currency options are exclusively for speculation, we should look at an interesting hedging application using foreign currency options.

In some situations, a firm does not know for certain whether it will enter into a foreign currency transaction at a future date. For example, suppose an American firm is making a bid on a project. If it wins the bid, the foreign firm or government will pay the American firm in the foreign currency. A forward or futures contract will hedge the risk of a change in the exchange rate. Suppose, however, that the bid is awarded to another firm. This means the American firm will not receive the foreign currency. Had a forward or futures contract been used, the firm either would have a short position in the contract or, if it expired, would have to deliver the currency itself. This means the firm would be exposed to the risk of an increase in the exchange rate. An option can be used to avoid this problem.

For example, suppose an American firm is bidding for a contract to construct a sports complex in London. The bid must be submitted in British pounds. The firm plans to make a bid of £25 million. At the forward exchange rate of $1.437, the bid in dollars is equivalent to £25,000,000($1.437) = $35,925,000. Once the bid is submitted, the firm must be prepared to accept £25 million if the bid is successful. Because it is an American firm, it will convert the pounds into dollars at whatever rate prevails on the date payment is made. If the pound weakens, the firm will effectively receive fewer dollars. To simplify the example somewhat, we shall assume the payment will be made as soon as the decision is made as to which firm is awarded the construction contract.

Table 13.7 summarizes the possible outcomes and compares the general results for a forward or futures hedge with those for an option hedge. The option would be a put, because the firm would need to protect itself against a decline in the pound's value.

If the bid is successful and the pound increases, the firm will receive the pounds, which now are valued at more dollars per pound. However, the forward or futures hedge will reduce this gain, because the hedge will be a short position. If the option is used, the put will expire worthless.

TABLE 13.7	Comparison of a Foreign Currency Forward/Futures Hedge and an Option Hedge		

Assumption: A firm is bidding on a construction project. If the bid is successful, payment will be made in a fixed number of British pounds. The table below indicates the outcome from the forward, futures, or option contract but does not consider the profit from the construction project itself.

Outcome of Bid	No Hedge	Short Forward or Futures Hedge	Option Hedge (Buy Put)
Successful:			
Pound increases	Gain on pound	Gain on pound reduced by hedge Small profit or loss	Put expires Premium lost
Pound decreases	Loss on pound	Loss on pound reduced by hedge Small profit or loss	Loss on pound reduced by exercise of put Small profit or loss
Unsuccessful:			
Pound increases	No effect	Potentially large loss on pound	Put expires Premium lost
Pound decreases	No effect	Potentially large gain on pound	Potentially large gain on pound by exercise of put

If the bid is successful and the pound decreases, the forward or futures hedge will reduce the loss caused by the decline in the pound's value. However, the option will also reduce the loss on the pound.

If the bid is unsuccessful and the pound increases, the forward or futures hedge will result in a potentially large speculative loss. This is because the firm will not receive the pounds if the bid fails but will have a short position in futures. If the option hedge is used, the put will expire worthless. The firm will have lost money—the premium on the put—but the amount lost will be less than it would have been with the futures hedge.

If the bid is unsuccessful and the pound decreases, the forward or futures hedge will result in a potentially large speculative profit, because the firm will be short futures and will not receive the pounds as a result of the failure to win the bid. If the option hedge is used, the put's exercise will also result in a potentially large profit on the put.[4]

Currency options provide flexibility to hedgers who are unsure of whether they will receive or make foreign cash payments.

---

[4]Technically, we have not specified how low the pound goes, but we assume it is lower than the exercise price. There will be a profit only if the spot rate at expiration is less than the exercise price by the amount of the premium.

The option hedge is most beneficial when the bid is unsuccessful. Because the firm does not receive the pounds, the futures or forward position generates a potentially large profit or loss. The option, however, can generate a large profit if the pound declines; if the pound rises, the loss will be limited to the premium. Of course, the option hedge requires payment of the option premium, while the futures hedge requires the initial margin deposit plus the margin calls from marking to market and a forward hedge might require collateral. Neither type of hedge dominates the other, but each has its merits.

Let us now look at some specific outcomes. The firm needs to hedge £25 million. Each option contract is for £31,250, so let the firm use £25,000,000/£31,250 = 800 contracts. The premium for a put with an exercise price of 140 is 2.5 cents per pound. Thus, the price of a contract is 31,250($.025) = $781.25, and the total premium is $781.25(800) = $625,000. Recall that the current forward rate is $1.437, so the bid is effectively $35,925,000.

We shall look at four outcomes: (1) the bid is successful, and the pound increases to $1.48; (2) the bid is successful, and the pound decreases to $1.30; (3) the bid is unsuccessful, and the pound increases to $1.48; and (4) the bid is unsuccessful, and the pound decreases to $1.30.

As a point of comparison, we shall also look at a futures or forward hedge. Let the futures or forward price be $1.424, meaning that one futures contract is priced at £62,500($1.424) = $89,000. Each futures contract is for £62,500, so the firm will sell 400 contracts or do a single forward contract for the full amount of £25 million.[5] We assume the forward or futures expires when the hedge is terminated. Table 13.8 presents the four possible outcomes and compares the two types of hedges along with what happens if the firm does not hedge.

If futures/forwards were used and the firm loses the bid, the potential for a large loss or gain exists. Of course, the firm could choose not to bid, but this is unlikely because bidding on contracts is the nature of the construction business. The firm could choose not to hedge, but it could win the bid and earn a much smaller profit or even a loss if the pound falls significantly. The option hedge provides an alternative that will be attractive to some firms, while the futures hedge will be better for others. The differences in their expectations and willingness to take exchange rate risk will determine whether they use options or futures/forwards.

---

[5]We determined the number of futures contracts by dividing the contract size, in pounds, into the total number of pounds hedged. This commits the firm to deliver the exact number of pounds it expects to receive. A forward contract simply specifies the total number of pounds to be delivered so a single contract of £25 million can be done.

TABLE 13.8	Comparison of Outcomes from Forward/Futures Hedge and Option Hedge		

Outcome	No Hedge	Forward or Futures Hedge	Option Hedge
Bid successful, pound increases to $1.48	Firm converts its pounds to £25,000,000($1.48) = $37,000,000.	Firm converts its pounds to £25,000,000($1.424) = $35,600,000 using its forward or futures contract.	Firm converts its pounds to £25,000,000($1.48) = $37,000,000. Puts expire out-of-the-money. Net gain is $37,000,000 − $625,000 (cost of puts) = $36,375,000.
Bid successful, pound decreases to $1.30	Firm converts its pounds to £25,000,000($1.30) = $32,500,000.	Firm converts its pounds to £25,000,000($1.424) = $35,600,000 using its forward or futures contract.	Firm exercises its puts to convert its pounds to £25,000,000($1.40) = $35,000,000. Net gain is $35,000,000 − $625,000 (cost of puts) = $34,375,000.
Bid unsuccessful, pound increases to $1.48	No cash flow.	Firm must purchase £25,000,000 at $1.48 and deliver on its forward or futures contract for which it receives £25,000,000 ($1.424) = $35,600,000. Net loss is £25,000,000($1.48 − $1.424) = $1,400,000.	Puts expire out-of-the-money. Net loss is $625,000 (cost of puts).
Bid unsuccessful, pound decreases to $1.30	No cash flow.	Firm must purchase £25,000,000 at $1.30 and deliver on its forward or futures contract for which it receives £25,000,000 ($1.424) = $35,600,000. Net profit is £25,000,000 ($1.424 − $1.30) = $3,100,000.	Firm must purchase pounds costing £25,000,000 ($1.30) = $32,500,000 and exercise puts, selling the pounds for £25,000,000 ($1.40) = $35,000,000. Net profit is −$625,000 (cost of puts) + £25,000,000 ($1.40 − $1.30) = $1,875,000.

Other Instruments for Managing Foreign Exchange Risk

As we saw in previous chapters, a variety of techniques can be used to manage risk. In this chapter, we have talked about currency forwards, futures, and options; however, there are a number of other, related ways to manage foreign exchange risk. We shall briefly look at a few here.

Options on Foreign Currency Futures

In Chapter 12, we examined options on futures. There is also an active market for options on foreign currency futures at the Chicago Mercantile Exchange. In fact, as we saw in Chapter 12, some of the options on foreign currency futures are the most active contracts. This is partially due to the fact that extremely active foreign currency futures markets operate side by side with the options.

Currency options on futures are essentially equivalent to any other options on futures.

There really is no need to spend time on the principles of pricing and examples of hedging. Most of these were well covered in Chapter 12 and require little, if any, adaptation to apply them to foreign currency options on futures. The Black model can be used to price these instruments, recognizing that that model prices a European option. The binomial model can be used for American options on foreign currency futures.

Currency Swaps

In Chapter 14, we shall cover interest rate swaps. Here we shall briefly examine a similar arrangement called a **currency swap.** A common business transaction for a multinational firm is to borrow in one currency but need to borrow in another. The firm can go to a swap dealer, which matches it with another firm holding the opposite position. The swap dealer arranges for the two firms to exchange a series of payments. Of course, a particular firm's needs might not always be matched with another firm with exactly the opposite needs; in that case, the swap dealer will attempt to bring in other firms or, if necessary, take an exposed position itself. When it does that, however, it usually will attempt to hedge its own risk in another market.

Let us look at a currency swap example. Alpine Ski Equipment, henceforth called "Alpine," is a Swiss manufacturer of ski equipment. It is a well-known borrower in Switzerland and can easily issue bonds at a favorable interest rate and at low issue costs in Switzerland. It plans a bond issue of SF2.8 million at 7.5 percent interest but actually needs the equivalent amount in dollars, $2 million, for some purchases of American raw materials. If it borrowed the money in the U.S. dollar market, it would pay 9 7/8 percent. Southern Technology, an American firm, specializes in computer circuitry and is a well-known borrower in U.S. bond markets. It plans to issue $2 million in bonds at 10 percent interest in the United States, but it needs SF2.8 million for some purchases of Swiss materials. If it borrowed the money in the Swiss franc market, it would pay 8 1/2 percent. Both firms go to a swap dealer.

The transaction is best understood by observing Figure 13.9. At the onset of the transaction, Alpine issues the bonds and receives SF2.8 million from the bondholders. It pays this to the swap dealer, which passes it on through to Southern. Southern, in turn, issues its bonds and receives

FIGURE 13.9   **Example of a Currency Swap**

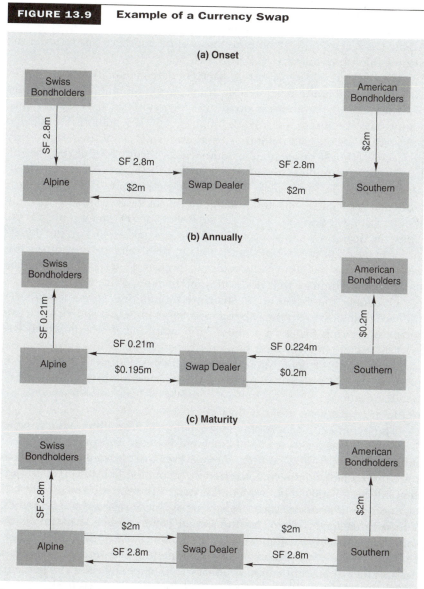

Scenario: Alpine, a Swiss firm, issues SF2.8 million of bonds at 7.5 percent interest and needs $2 million. Southern, an American firm, issues $2 million of bonds at 10 percent interest and needs SF2.8 million. The firms enter into a currency swap with a swap dealer.

A currency swap is an agreement between two parties in which one party agrees to make a series of payments in one currency and the other party agrees to make a series of payments in another currency.

$2 million from its bondholders, which it then sends to the swap dealer, which passes it through to Alpine. The net effect at the onset is that Alpine has received the $2 million it needs and Southern has received the SF2.8 million it requires.

Each year thereafter, interest payments are made. The swap dealer arranges for Alpine to pay interest on the $2 million at 9.75 percent and for Southern to pay interest on the SF2.8 million at 8 percent. Thus, Alpine pays the dealer (.0975)($2 million) = $0.195 million. The dealer, however, passes on $0.2 million to Southern, which then uses that money to pay the interest on its bonds. Southern, in turn, pays (.08)(SF2.8 million) = SF0.224 million to the dealer, which passes on SF0.21 million to Alpine, which uses it to make the interest payments to its bondholders. Note that the dealer nets an annual gain on the Swiss francs of .014 million or SF14,000 and nets a loss on the dollars of .005 million, or $5,000. Thus, the dealer, assuming it operates in dollars, takes a loss on the dollars and is exposed to the risk of fluctuations in the exchange rate at which it will convert the 14,000 in Swiss francs it receives. However, it can reduce and perhaps eliminate that risk with some hedging of its own.

Of course, the dealer might structure the interest payments so that it will face little or no exposure, but it must offer rates that will be attractive to the borrowing firms. In addition, the swap dealer is exposed to the credit risk that either or both of the firms will default.

At the maturity date, Alpine pays $2 million to the swap dealer, which passes on the $2 million to Southern, which uses it to pay off its American bonds. Southern pays SF2.8 million to the swap dealer, which passes it on to Alpine, which uses it to pay off its Swiss bonds.

The net effect is that Alpine converted its SF2.8 million bond issue at 7.5 percent interest to a $2 million bond issue at 9.75 percent interest, thus, saving it 1/8 of a point in interest over what it would pay if it borrowed in dollars. Southern converted its $2 million bond issue at 10 percent interest to a SF2.8 million bond issue at 8 percent interest, saving 1/2 of a point in interest over what it would pay if it borrowed in Swiss francs. The swap dealer profits off of the spread between interest payments received and interest payments made. It pays out Swiss francs at 7 1/2 percent and receives Swiss francs at 8 percent, netting 1/2 percent. It receives dollars at 9 3/4 percent and pays dollars at 10 percent, losing 1/4 percent, for an overall gain of 1/4 percent. It might also have incurred some hedging costs on its exposure to the Swiss francs.

Note that the total gains (1/8 to Alpine, 1/4 to the dealer, and 1/2 to Southern) add up to 7/8, which reflects the 1 percent more that Southern pays in the Swiss market over Alpine minus the 1/8 percent more that Southern pays in the U.S. market over Alpine. In effect, Alpine, the dealer, and Southern have made an arrangement that saves them all money, subject to everyone being paid off as scheduled.

VALUATION OF CURRENCY SWAPS   A currency swap can be viewed as a combination of borrowing in one currency and lending in another. For example, from the perspective of Southern, the swap is equivalent to issuing a Swiss franc-denominated bond and holding a dollar-denominated bond. If the initial exchange of their market values ($2 million vs. SF2.8 million) occurs at the current exchange rate, both bonds have the same current value. In that case, the swap has an initial value of zero and like a forward contract is neither an asset nor a liability at the onset. As the exchange rate changes, however, one bond will gain value at the expense of the other. The swap, like a forward contract, will then have a nonzero value and turn into either an asset or a liability.

For example, suppose the swap is for three years with payments made at the end of each year. Thus, Southern will pay SF0.224 after years one and two and SF0.224 + SF2.8 = SF3.024 at the end of the third year (all figures are in millions). It will receive $.2 after years one and two and $2.2 at the end of the third year. Suppose it is now one year into the swap, the first payment has just been made, and the spot exchange rate is $0.725. The Swiss risk-free rate is 6 percent and the U.S. risk-free rate is 8 percent. We assume a flat term structure.

Recall that to Southern the swap is like issuing a Swiss franc-denominated bond and holding a dollar-denominated bond. How much is the Swiss franc bond worth at this point? We find that value by simply discounting the remaining cash flows at 6 percent. This gives us

$$\text{SF0.224}(1.06)^{-1} + \text{SF3.024}(1.06)^{-2} = \text{SF2.902},$$

meaning that the present value in Swiss francs of the payments Southern must make is 2.902. In dollars, this is $0.725(SF2.902) = $2.104. The value of the dollar bond can be found by discounting the dollar interest payments received at the U.S. risk-free rate

$$\$.2(1.08)^{-1} + \$2.2(1.08)^{-2} = \$2.071.$$

Thus, to Southern the swap represents a liability of $2.104 and an asset of $2.071 for a net value of −$0.033. The Swiss franc strengthened and this hurt Southern. Alpine would, of course, benefit from an increase in the value of the Swiss franc. Recall that the dealer pays out a net of $0.005 ($0.200 − $0.195) and receives SF 0.014 (SF0.224 − SF0.210). With a liability in dollars and an asset in Swiss francs, the dealer gains from a strengthening of the franc.

It is also helpful to recognize that a currency swap is equivalent to a series of forward contracts. Continuing with our example in which we are one year into a three-year swap, Southern has agreed to make payments in Swiss francs and receive payments in dollars. Thus, it is short the Swiss

franc in the forward market on two separate contracts, one expiring in one year and one expiring in two years. It has agreed in one year to make a payment of SF0.224 and receive $.2. This is an exchange rate of $0.893. Thus, we can say that $0.893 is the original forward price. The price of a currency forward contract expiring in one year is (recall from earlier in this chapter) the current spot rate, $0.725, compounded at the domestic interest rate and discounted at the foreign interest rate. This is $0.725(1.08)/(1.06) = $0.739. Thus, Southern has effectively shorted the Swiss franc at a rate of $0.893 and the Swiss franc forward rate has gone to $0.739 so it makes money. Recalling from Chapter 9 that the value of a forward contract is the discounted difference in the original forward price and the new forward price, we have

$$-(\$0.739 - \$0.893)(1.08)^{-1} = \$0.143,$$

with the minus in front signifying the short position. For SF0.224, this amount in dollars is (SF0.224)($0.143) = $0.032. So the value of the first forward contract is positive at $0.032. The second forward contract is an agreement to deliver SF3.024 in two years for which it will receive $2.2, an effective exchange rate of $0.728. The forward rate for contracts in two years is $0.725(1.08)^2/(1.06)^2 = $0.753. Thus, the value of the second forward contract is

$$-(\$0.753 - \$0.728)(1.08)^{-2} = -\$0.0214.$$

For SF3.024, this amount in dollars is (SF3.024)(–$0.0214) = –$0.065. So the second forward contract is a liability. The difference in value between the two contracts is –$0.065 + $0.032 = –$0.033. This is precisely the amount found when we valued the swap as the difference between two bonds.

Of course, as with any over-the-counter transaction, credit risk is important. Each of the three parties has reason to worry about the credit quality of the party on the opposite side of the transaction. We have already discussed some of the credit considerations in over-the-counter instruments and we will return to this issue in Chapter 16.

Other Currency Derivatives

The currency markets have been particularly innovative in creating new derivative contracts for managing foreign exchange risk. As noted earlier in the chapter, the American Stock Exchange has warrants on several foreign currencies, and the Philadelphia Stock Exchange has options written on a nondollar currency but denominated in another nondollar currency. The Chicago Mercantile Exchange has futures on the difference between the German mark and Japanese yen exchange rates. The CME also has a contract that is basically equivalent to a spot position in a currency.

In the over-the-counter currency markets, **basket options** have been particularly popular. A basket option is an option on a portfolio of currencies. For example, suppose a business has revenue coming in from several foreign countries. To protect the conversion of that revenue to dollars, the treasurer could buy puts or sell futures on each currency in the appropriate quantities. Alternatively, the treasurer could recognize that the exchange rates of all of the currencies are not perfectly correlated; thus, they constitute a diversified portfolio of cash flows. A basket option is an option, denominated in dollars, on the overall value of the portfolio. Since the portfolio is less volatile than the average component, the option on the portfolio is less costly than the total cost of options on each component. Basket options are also popular in equity portfolio management.

Another popular type of currency option is called an **alternative currency option.** This is an option that pays off the better or worse of two currencies. For example, consider a Japanese yen–German mark alternative currency option denominated in dollars. The option can be a "better" or "worse" "call" or "put" option. Let us assume it is a call that pays off according to the better performing currency. Now assume that when the option expires, the German mark has gained more (or lost less) than the Japanese yen against the U.S. dollar. Then the option pays off as if it were a standard call option on the German mark. If its payoff were based on the "worse" performing currency, it would pay off as if it were a standard call option on the Japanese yen. Such an option will cost more than a single option on either currency but less than options on both currencies. An example of when such an option might be used is when a corporate treasurer has cash flows coming from two different currencies. He is indifferent about which currency he makes payments in. He could then sell an alternative currency option and collect an option premium that rewards him for the flexibility he has to pay in either currency.

In Chapter 15 we will cover exotic options. Nearly all of the types of exotic options are on currencies as well as other assets. At this point we conclude our discussion of currency derivatives. We gave them only a brief overview, but, as we noted, most of the principles of derivative pricing already covered apply to foreign currency instruments and can easily be adapted to them. Some of the end-of-chapter problems ask you to do some of these applications.

Summary

This chapter examined foreign currency derivatives. We saw that understanding foreign currency derivatives requires an awareness of the special characteristics of foreign currency spot and forward markets. We observed how interest rate parity is the foreign currency forward/futures counterpart of the cost of carry model. We examined several basic principles for pricing foreign currency options and found that they differ only slightly from those for equity options. In particular, we saw

that the Garman-Kohlhagen foreign currency option pricing model is merely a minor modification of the Black-Scholes model.

We saw that foreign currency hedge and speculative strategies are straightforward extensions of previous principles. We also observed an example of the advantage of a foreign currency option hedge. The option can be an effective hedging device when it is uncertain whether the hedger will take a position in the currency at a future date.

In this chapter we also introduced currency swaps, which can be used to convert debt issued in one currency to debt issued in another. In Chapter 14 we examine interest rate swaps. The swaps market is large and still rapidly growing, and is a natural extension of the derivative contracts we have been studying.

Key Terms

Before continuing to Chapter 14, you should be able to give brief definitions of the following terms.

- exchange rate
- interbank market
- forward premium/discount
- cross-rate
- triangular arbitrage

- interest rate parity
- currency swap
- basket option
- alternative currency option

Questions and Problems

1. Explain the difference between the forward and futures markets for foreign currency.

2. Discuss the differences between the use of options and futures (or forward) contracts in hedging foreign exchange risk.

3. On December 10 of a particular year, the German mark exchange rate was $.3937 while the Swiss franc exchange rate was $.4710. The exchange rate for Swiss francs in terms of German marks is 1.21, that is, DM1.21/SF. Explain how an arbitrageur could make a risk-free profit.

4. Suppose you are an analyst with a firm that specializes in following foreign markets and making investment strategy recommendations based on its perception of changing conditions in other countries. You observed the growing Japanese trade surplus with the United States in the 1980s. You believe, however, that during the upcoming six months the trade surplus figures will narrow. Your opinion is contrary to that of most other firms. You would like to recommend a strategy that will be profitable if you are correct. Suggest one option and one futures strategy, and justify your recommendations. Then discuss the risks of your strategies and ways to manage the risks so that your clients will not be wiped out if you are not as prescient as you think.

5. On October 15 of a particular year, the following information was available:
    Spot rate for German marks: $.3746
    December futures rate for German marks: $.3775 (expires on December 16)
    U.S. risk-free rate: 7.57 percent (simple)
    German risk-free rate: 4.21 percent (simple)
    Determine whether interest rate parity holds.

6. On December 9 of a particular year, the Philadelphia Stock Exchange January Swiss franc call option with an exercise price of 46 had a price of 1.63. The January 46 put was at 14. The spot rate was 47.28. All prices are in cents per Swiss franc. The option expired on January 13. The U.S. risk-free rate was 7.1 percent, while the Swiss risk-free rate was 3.6 percent. Answer the following:

   a. Determine the intrinsic value of the call.
   b. Determine the lower bound of the call.
   c. Determine the time value of the call.
   d. Determine the intrinsic value of the put.
   e. Determine the lower bound of the put.
   f. Determine the time value of the put.
   g. Determine whether put-call parity holds.

7. Use the Garman-Kohlhagen model to determine whether the Swiss franc call in problem 6 is correctly priced. Use .145 as the standard deviation of the logarithm of one plus the percentage change in the spot Swiss franc.

8. Differences would be expected in American and European call prices for foreign currency options. How is the relative level of interest rates in the two countries involved likely to affect the spread between European and American call prices?

9. On June 17 of a particular year, an American watch dealer decided to import 100,000 Swiss watches. Each watch costs SF225. The dealer would like to hedge against a change in the dollar/Swiss franc exchange rate. The forward rate was $.3881, and the September futures price was $.3907. Determine the outcome from the hedge if it was closed on August 16, when the spot rate was $.4434 and the futures price was $.4436. What considerations would have been important in deciding whether to use forwards or futures?

10. On January 2 of a particular year, an American firm decided to close out its account at a Canadian bank on February 28. The firm is expected to have 5 million Canadian dollars in the account at the time of the withdrawal. It would convert the funds to U.S. dollars and transfer them to a New York bank. The relevant forward exchange rate was $.7564. The March Canadian dollar futures contract was priced at $.7541. Determine the outcome of the hedge if on February 28 the spot rate was $.7207 and the futures rate was $.7220. All prices are in U.S. dollars per Canadian dollar.

For problems 11, 12, and 13, determine the profit for each of the following spot rates at expiration: 32, 34, 36, 38, 40, and 42. Construct a profit graph. Find the breakeven spot rate at expiration.

11. On December 9 of a particular year, the deutsche mark January 38 call was priced at 1.57 cents per German mark. Construct a simple long position in the call.

12. On December 9 of a particular year, the March 40 put was priced at .72 cents per German mark. Construct a simple long position in the put.

13. Use the information in problem 11 to construct a covered call. Assume the spot rate at the onset is 39.

14.   Suppose it is December 9 and an American firm is bidding on a contract to sell microcomputers to the German government. German officials have stipulated that the bid be made in German marks and the firm receiving the bid be paid in German marks. The decision will be made in January. The firm decides to use German mark options to hedge its position. The current spot rate is $.3945. The firm will bid 11.5 million marks and use the January 39 contract. The call price is $.0079, and the put price is $.0025. Which option, call or put, should the firm use? Why? Assume the day German officials will make their decision is the same day payment will be made. Also on that day, the option expires. Determine the cash flow to the firm under each of the following possible outcomes.
   a.   The firm wins the bid, and the spot rate is 43.
   b.   The firm wins the bid, and the spot rate is 38.
   c.   The firm loses the bid, and the spot rate is 43.
   d.   The firm loses the bid, and the spot rate is 38.

15.   Suppose you are a swap dealer. A French firm arranges to borrow FF10,000,000 from a French bank for 90 days at 12 percent interest. It will make three monthly payments of FF100,000 and then repay the principal with the last interest payment. It wishes to convert the loan to a dollar loan of $2 million based on the prevailing exchange rate of FF5/$. You find an American firm with a $2 million, three-month loan at 9.5 percent that needs the money in French francs. You arrange a swap in which the French firm will pay 11 percent in dollars and the American firm will pay 8.75 percent in French francs.
   a.   Construct the payment schedule for all the payments involved in the swap.
   b.   Determine your exposure.
   c.   From the perspective of the American firm, evaluate the principal repayment as a forward contract. Assume a risk-free interest rate in the United States of 7 percent. Determine the value of the forward contract halfway through the loan if the franc weakens to FF5.2/$.
   d.   From your perspective, find the value of the swap halfway through its life. The exchange rate is now FF5.2/$. The U.S. risk-free rate is 7 percent and the French risk-free rate is 9 percent. The term structure is flat. Explain your result with respect to whether and why you benefitted.

16.   (Concept Problem) Using the information in problem 11, rework the problem under the assumption that the call expires on January 20 and is closed out on December 31. Use .22 as the volatility, .05 as the U.S. interest rate, and .04 as the German interest rate. Use the spreadsheet bsbinl.xls or the Windows program bsbwin2.exe to make these calculations.

17.   (Concept Problem) You plan to buy 1,000 shares of stock of Swissair. The current price is SF950. The current exchange rate is $0.7254/SF. You are interested in speculating on the stock but do not wish to assume any currency risk. You plan to hold the position for six months. The appropriate futures contract currently is trading at $0.7250. Construct a hedge and evaluate how your investment will do if in six months the stock is at SF926.50, the spot exchange rate is $0.7301, and the futures price is $0.7295. The Swiss franc fu-

tures contract size is SF125,000. Determine the overall profit from the transaction. Then break down the profit into the amount earned solely from the performance of the stock, the loss or gain from the currency change while holding the stock, and the loss or gain on the futures transaction.

APPENDIX 13A
Foreign Currency Futures Contract Specifications[*]

These contracts trade on the International Monetary Market of the Chicago Mercantile Exchange. Smaller versions of certain currency contracts trade on the MidAmerica Commodity Exchange and the New York Cotton Exchange. There are also contracts on the cross-rate between certain pairs of currencies, spot contracts, and forward contracts—but volume is small.

- Delivery months: January, March, April, June, July, September, October, December, and spot month
- Last trading day: Second business day before third Wednesday of month
- First delivery day: Third Wednesday of month
- Trading hours: 7:20 A.M. to 2:00 P.M. (local time)

Contract	Contract Size	Minimum Price Change	Margin (Initial/ Maintenance)[a]
Deutsche mark	125,000DM	$0.0001/DM = $12.50	$945/$700
Canadian dollar	100,000CD	$0.0001/CD = $10	$540/$400
Swiss franc	125,000SF	$0.0001/SF = $12.50	$1,823/$1,350
British pound	62,500BP	$0.0002/BP = $12.50	$1,620/$1,200
Japanese yen	12,500,000JY	$0.000001/JY = $12.50	$2,464/$1,825
Australian dollar	100,000AD	$0.0001/AD = $10	$945/$700

[a]Check with the exchange for changes to contract specifications and for spread and hedge margins, which usually are much lower than the speculative margins shown here.

---

[*]Source: www.cme.com. This material is believed to be correct as of August 1997. Contract specifications can change, especially margins and daily price limits. Investors should consult the exchanges for the latest information.

APPENDIX 13B
Foreign Currency Options Contract Specifications[*]

These contracts trade on the Philadelphia Stock Exchange, whose options division is known as the United Currency Option Market, and are available as both American and European options. All contracts have expirations on the March cycle plus the two near-term months. The last trading day is the Friday preceding the third Wednesday of the month. The trading hours are 2:30 A.M. through 2:30 P.M. the next day, Sunday through Thursday, Eastern standard time except for the Canadian dollar, which is 7:00 A.M. through 2:30 P.M. Exercise is by delivery of the currencies. Customized options with nonstandard terms are available and cash-settled options are also traded. In addition, certain options expire on the last day of the month. There are also options on the exchange rate between two nondollar currencies.

Contract	Contract Size	Minimum Price Change
British pound	31,250BP	$0.0001 = $3.125
Canadian dollar	50,000CD	$0.0001 = $5.00
Deutsche mark	62,500DM	$0.0001 = $6.25
Japanese yen	6,250,000JY	$0.000001 = $6.25
Swiss franc	62,500SF	$0.0001 = $6.25
Australian dollar	50,000AD	$0.0001 = $5.00
French franc	250,000FF	$0.00002 = $5.00

---

[*]Source: www.phlx.com/products. This material is believed to be correct as of August 1997. Contract specifications can change. Investors should consult the exchange for the latest information.

CHAPTER 14

Interest Rate Derivatives

Our use of derivatives is just one more step in the evolution of banking.

JOHN B. MCCOY, Chairman and CEO, BankOne Corporation
Journal of Applied Corporate Finance, Fall 1994

In Chapter 13 we discussed two types of over-the-counter derivatives—the currency forward and the currency swap. Partially because of the enormous success of these instruments during the 1970s and early 1980s, the market was ripe for more financial innovation in the form of interest rate derivatives. An **interest rate derivative** is a derivative product that provides a payoff determined by how an interest rate changes. While interest rate options and forward contracts have proven to be quite popular, the most widely used interest rate derivative is the swap. In this chapter we shall take a look at these types of interest rate derivatives. We shall examine forward contracts on interest rates (called forward rate agreements), options on interest rates (commonly packaged as instruments called caps, floors, and collars), as well as interest rate swaps, options on interest rate swaps (called swaptions), and forward contracts on swaps (called forward swaps).

These instruments have grown in popularity for several reasons. Nearly all businesses face some form of interest rate risk. We have already seen several examples, such as a portfolio manager holding bonds or a corporation planning to borrow money. We showed that futures can be used to manage those risks. Since the middle 1980s, however, over-the-counter interest rate derivatives have proven to be the more popular way to manage interest rate risk. These instruments are customized to the needs of the risk manager, and an increasing number of dealer firms have gone into the business of offering these products, leading to a high degree of competition and lower bid-ask spreads.

Chapter Objectives

■ To understand the concept of an interest rate derivative as a derivative for which the underlying is an interest rate, in contrast to derivatives for which the underlying is the price of an asset

■ To learn how forward contracts on interest rates, called forward rate agreements (FRAs), are used in managing interest rate risk

■ To understand the structure of an interest rate swap and how it is used to hedge interest rate risk, how to price an interest rate swap, how interest rate swaps are like combinations of other financial transactions, and how to terminate an interest rate swap

■ To learn how interest rate options pay off, how they are used to hedge interest rate risk, and how interest rate options are combined into caps, floors, and collars

■ To understand how swaptions provide the right to buy or sell an interest rate swap and how forward swaps provide the obligation to enter into an interest rate swap

■ To understand how the binomial model can represent movements in interest rates

■ To learn how the binomial model is used to price forward rate agreements, swaps, interest rate options, and swaptions

An interest rate derivative is a derivative product that provides a payoff determined by how an interest rate changes.

As you should recall from Chapter 8, the prices of bonds are driven by interest rates, which should make interest rate derivatives a lot like derivatives on bonds. That is true to some extent, but derivatives on bonds pay off based on movements in bond prices while interest rate derivatives pay off based on movements in interest rates. Though bond prices are driven largely by interest rates, pricing interest rate derivatives is much more complex than pricing bond derivatives. In fact, pricing interest rate derivatives is one of the most complex subjects in the field of derivatives. In the latter part of this chapter we shall take an initial look at how interest rate derivative prices are driven by the term structure, which itself is a difficult process to capture in a model.

While the current chapter examines the basics of interest rate derivatives, in Chapter 15 we take it one step farther by covering advanced derivatives on stocks, stock indices, and interest rates. Then in Chapter 16 we examine the implications of the growing usage of these derivatives for managing financial risk.

The first interest rate derivative that we examine is a forward contract on an interest rate, called a forward rate agreement.

Forward Rate Agreements

A **forward rate agreement** or **FRA** is similar to any type of forward contract, but the payoff is based on an interest rate, rather than an asset price. For example, suppose a financial manager believed that interest rates were going up and wanted to lock in a specific rate to be paid on a future loan. He could do that by taking a short forward position in a fixed-income security like a Treasury bill or bond. If rates rose, the security price would fall, the forward price would also fall, and the short position would be profitable. If the hedge ratio were properly established, the position could lock in the forward rate at the time the contract was opened. Of course, as demonstrated in Chapter 10, he could also use futures.

In such a transaction, the payoff is determined directly by the price of a fixed-income security, which means that the payoff is determined indirectly by an interest rate. In an FRA the payoff is determined directly by an interest rate. Thus, our financial manager would take a long position in the FRA. The contract would specify a certain amount of notional principal and the terms under which the payment would be made. Typically payoffs are based on LIBOR, the Eurodollar rate. The payment is based on the difference between the resulting value of LIBOR and the contract rate, which was agreed on when the contract was taken out. This difference times the notional principal is prorated according to a specific formula over the length of the period.

The timing of the payoff in a typical FRA is much like that in a forward contract on an asset. At the expiration of the contract, LIBOR is de-

termined and the payoff is made at that time. Surprisingly, however, this is unconventional for interest rate derivatives. As we shall see later, interest rate swaps and options provide for a payoff that occurs a specific number of days after the expiration. Though this appears to be unusual, if not inappropriate, it actually makes more sense in most cases to delay the final payoff. This is because many of these interest rate derivatives are designed to hedge floating rate loans, where the convention is that the interest rate is determined at the beginning of the period but the interest payment is made at the end of the period. This is because borrowers and lenders normally like to know the rate they are paying during a period in which interest is accumulating. Swaps and interest rate options typically follow this convention. In contrast, most FRAs, for reasons no one seems to know, provide for the payoff to occur at the expiration. The difference in the timing of the payoff is really nothing more than a present value adjustment. For illustrative purposes and later to show the similarity between FRAs and swaps, we shall use the more unconventional FRA payoff. That is, the rate will be determined at expiration but the payoff will occur at a later date, corresponding to the date on which the interest is paid on the spot transaction for which the FRA is used to hedge.

The exact manner in which the interest is computed is not always the same. In some cases interest is prorated as if a year has 360 days. In some cases a year is assumed to have 365 days. The number of days over which the interest is paid is sometimes the exact day count and sometimes based on the number of months with the assumption of 30 days in a month. We shall assume a 360-day year, and in most cases, we shall calculate interest over the exact number of days. Thus, six months' interest will be prorated by a factor of 181 to 184 over 360. In a few cases, we shall simply divide the interest rate by 2, effectively using 180 days as six months. This procedure may be confusing, but unfortunately, it is commonplace in the real world. In the examples here and in real-world interest rate agreements, the exact manner in which interest is calculated is stated explicitly.

Table 14.1 presents a typical situation involving an FRA. A corporation wants to lock in a borrowing rate for a loan that will begin in 30 days. The loan is a 90-day loan and its rate will be set at whatever 90-day LIBOR is in 30 days plus one point. Since the corporation is worried about rising rates, it takes a long position in the FRA and agrees on a rate of 10 percent. The terms specify that the FRA will pay off according to 90-day LIBOR 30 days from now. The payoff will be prorated over 90 days, using a 360-day year. In general the holder of a long FRA will have the following cash flow:

$$(\text{Notional principal})(\text{LIBOR} - \text{Agreed-upon rate})\left(\frac{\text{Days}}{360}\right),$$

where Days is the applicable number of days for the underlying interest rate. Here Days = 90 because 90-day LIBOR is used. In this example, the holder of the long FRA will have the following cash flow:

$$\text{(Notional principal)} \, (\text{LIBOR} - .10) \left(\frac{90}{360} \right).$$

So if LIBOR in 30 days exceeds 10 percent, the corporation, being long the FRA, will receive a cash payment. If LIBOR in 30 days is less than 10 percent, the corporation will make a payment. The payment is made at the end of the life of the loan, which is 120 days from now.

Each row in Table 14.1 presents some possible outcomes, based on LIBOR in 30 days. Let us take a look at the case in which LIBOR ends up at 12 percent. Using the above formula, the FRA payoff is

$$(\$20,000,000) \, (.12 - .10) \left(\frac{90}{360} \right) = \$100,000.$$

TABLE 14.1	**Hedging a Planned Loan with a Forward Rate Agreement**

Scenario: A firm plans to borrow at 90-day LIBOR plus a spread of 1 point. The loan will be for $20 million and will be taken out in 30 days. The loan matures 90 days after that and is paid back in one lump sum. The firm would like to lock in the rate it pays on the loan so it establishes a long position in a forward rate agreement based on 90-day LIBOR. The FRA commits the firm to making an interest payment at a 10 percent rate and receiving an interest payment at LIBOR. Interest is computed on 90 days of a 360-day year.

LIBOR in 30 days	Payoff of FRA at Loan Maturity	Interest on Loan at Maturity	Total Effective Interest	Annualized Cost of Loan with FRA	Annualized Cost of Loan without FRA
6.00%	−$200,000	$350,000	$550,000	11.63%	7.29%
6.50	−175,000	375,000	550,000	11.63	7.82
7.00	−150,000	400,000	550,000	11.63	8.36
7.50	−125,000	425,000	550,000	11.63	8.90
8.00	−100,000	450,000	550,000	11.63	9.44
8.50	−75,000	475,000	550,000	11.63	9.99
9.00	−50,000	500,000	550,000	11.63	10.53
9.50	−25,000	525,000	550,000	11.63	11.08
10.00	0	550,000	550,000	11.63	11.63
10.50	25,000	575,000	550,000	11.63	12.18
11.00	50,000	600,000	550,000	11.63	12.74
11.50	75,000	625,000	550,000	11.63	13.29
12.00	100,000	650,000	550,000	11.63	13.85
12.50	125,000	675,000	550,000	11.63	14.41
13.00	150,000	700,000	550,000	11.63	14.97
13.50	175,000	725,000	550,000	11.63	15.54
14.00	200,000	750,000	550,000	11.63	16.10

Since LIBOR is greater than 10 percent, the firm receives a payment from the counterparty. The loan is taken out in 30 days at a rate of 13 percent (LIBOR plus one point), and the firm receives $20,000,000. Ninety days later it pays back the principal plus $20,000,000(.13)(90/360) = $650,000 in interest; however, its FRA payment is received so it has a net payment of $550,000. The annual interest rate for a $20 million loan, paid back 90 days later with $550,000 interest, is

$$\left(\frac{\$20,000,000 + \$550,000}{\$20,000,000}\right)^{365/90} - 1 = .1163.$$

A forward rate agreement is a contract between two parties in which one party agrees to make an interest payment at a future date at an agreed-upon rate, and the other party agrees to make an interest payment at that same date at a floating rate such as LIBOR.

Had the firm not used the FRA, it would have paid back $650,000 in interest. Replacing $550,000 with $650,000 in the above formula gives a rate of 13.85 percent.

Note in the table that regardless of what LIBOR is in 30 days, the cost of the loan with the FRA is always 11.63 percent. Without the FRA the cost varies directly with LIBOR. Thus, the FRA locks in a loan rate, at the expense of the interest savings that would occur if rates fell. Figure 14.1 illustrates this result graphically. The loan plus the FRA is essentially a risk-free transaction. Without the FRA, the loan is susceptible to considerable interest rate risk.

Pricing an FRA is done by determining the fixed rate, which is found as the forward rate embedded in the term structure. We shall look at FRA pricing later in the chapter.

Interest Rate Swaps

An **interest rate swap** is an agreement between two parties in which each party makes a series of interest payments to the other at predetermined dates at different rates. At least one set of rates must be variable, usually called *floating,* in the sense that the rate at which the interest payment will be made is not determined until a later date. Both sets of payments could be variable but our focus in this chapter will be on the **plain vanilla** or **generic swap,** in which one set of payments is fixed and the other is variable. Since each party makes a payment to the other on the same day, the convention is for only one payment, the net owed by one party to the other, to be made. Typical interest rate swap transactions are between a party called the end user and a dealer, which is normally a bank or an investment banking firm that makes a market in swaps and other interest rate derivatives. While some swaps will be conducted between dealers, few are conducted directly between end users. The dealer plays an important role in providing a counterparty with which end users can quickly and easily engage in swaps and other interest rate derivatives. As we shall see in Chapter 16, most dealers hedge the risk they assume from entering into

An interest rate swap is a contract between two parties in which each party agrees to exchange a series of interest payments, where at least one set of payments is determined by a variable interest rate.

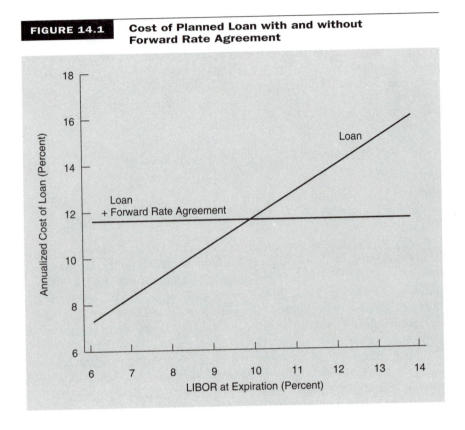

FIGURE 14.1   **Cost of Planned Loan with and without Forward Rate Agreement**

these derivative transactions and earn a profit off of the bid-ask spreads they quote. Let us learn about interest rate swaps by examining a specific transaction.

The Structure of an Interest Rate Swap

Consider a firm called XYZ that is currently borrowing at the floating rate LIBOR but would prefer to borrow at a fixed rate. It contacts a swap dealer called ABSwaps and arranges a swap based on a $50 million notional principal. The current date is December 15. The terms of the swap call for ABSwaps to pay XYZ the 90-day LIBOR on the 15th of March, June, September, and December of the following year. The payment is determined by LIBOR at the beginning of the payment period. For example, LIBOR on March 15 determines the payment on June 15. XYZ agrees to pay ABSwaps a fixed rate of 7.5 percent on each of those payment dates. The terms of this swap also specify that the amount of interest computed for each payment period will be based on the exact number of days in the

period, assuming a 360-day year. The net interest owed will be determined and only one party will make a payment to the other. In general the fixed-rate payer, floating-rate receiver has a cash flow at each interest payment date of

$$(\text{Notional principal})\,(\text{LIBOR} - \text{Fixed rate})\left(\frac{\text{Days}}{360}\right).$$

Thus, from the perspective of XYZ, the cash flow on a payment date will be

$$(\$50,000,000)\,(\text{LIBOR} - .075)\left(\frac{\text{Days}}{360}\right).$$

So if LIBOR exceeds 7.5 percent, XYZ will receive a payment in the above amount from ABSwaps. If LIBOR is less than 7.5 percent, XYZ will make the payment to ABSwaps.

The time pattern of XYZ's payments is illustrated in Figure 14.2. On each payment date XYZ receives a payment based on LIBOR three months prior and makes a payment based on a 7.5 percent rate. XYZ obviously does not know the cash payments it will receive; likewise, ABSwaps does not know the cash payments it will make. Table 14.2 presents an after-the-fact look at the payments on this swap. On December 15, the day the swap is negotiated, LIBOR is 7.68 percent. This determines the first swap payment, which will be made on March 15. There are 90 days from December 15 to March 15. Thus, ABSwaps will owe

$$\$50,000,000(.0768)\left(\frac{90}{360}\right) = \$960,000,$$

while XYZ will owe

$$\$50,000,000(.075)\left(\frac{90}{360}\right) = \$937,500.$$

FIGURE 14.2   Time Pattern of XYZ's Interest Rate Swap

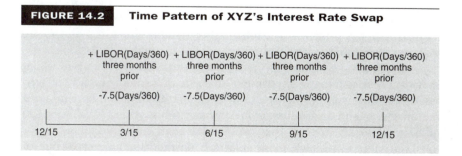

TABLE 14.2	After-the-Fact Payments in Fixed- for Floating-Rate Swap

Notional principal: $50,000,000
Fixed rate: 7.5 percent
Interest based on exact number of days and 360-day year

Date	3-month LIBOR	Days	ABSwaps Owes	XYZ Owes	Net to XYZ
12/15	7.68				
3/15	7.50	90	$960,000	$937,500	$ 22,500
6/15	7.06	92	958,333	958,333	0
9/15	6.06	92	902,111	958,333	−56,222
12/15	—	91	765,917	947,917	−182,000

Note: This is but one of an infinite number of possible outcomes to the swap. It is used only to illustrate how the payments are determined and not their likely amounts.

The net payment will be $22,500 paid by ABSwaps to XYZ. On March 15, LIBOR turns out to be 7.50 percent, meaning that on the next payment date, each party owes the other the same amount. Thus, no payment is made on June 15. The following LIBOR is 7.06, so XYZ makes a payment of $56,222. The final LIBOR is 6.06, making XYZ pay $182,000. Note in Table 14.2 that the number of days in each quarter is slightly different, resulting in the fixed payment being slightly different from quarter to quarter. Except for the different number of days in each quarter, we see that XYZ is now making fixed interest payments while receiving floating interest payments, the latter of which will hedge the floating rate loan it has.

Note that no principal payments are made in an interest rate swap. Thus, the $50 million notional principal is never paid. This contrasts sharply with the currency swap where the notional principal is exchanged.

Transactions Equivalent to Interest Rate Swaps

One consistent observation throughout our treatment of derivatives is that it is possible to construct portfolios of financial instruments with payoffs equivalent to other financial instruments and whose values will be equivalent through the principle of arbitrage. With that in mind, it is easy to see that a swap is equivalent to two other types of financial transactions.

In our previous example, XYZ entered into a one-year swap in which it made a series of quarterly payments at a rate of 7.5 percent and received a series of quarterly payments at a rate set at LIBOR at the beginning of the quarter, with both sets of payments based on a principal value of $50 million. Suppose, instead, that XYZ had issued a $50 million one-year fixed-rate note in which it made quarterly payments at an annual rate of

A fixed- for floating-rate swap is equivalent to issuing either a fixed- or floating-rate note and using the proceeds to buy the other.

7.5 percent and used the $50 million to purchase a $50 million one-year floating-rate note that would pay interest at the end of each quarter at the rate LIBOR at the beginning of the quarter. As long as the interest is computed identically, that is, based on the exact day count in the quarter and 360 days in a year, the transactions are equivalent to XYZ's swap. The $50 million received up front from issuing the fixed-rate loan is used to buy the floating-rate note. When the notes mature, XYZ receives $50 million from the floating-rate note it holds and uses it to pay off the fixed-rate note it issued. The analogy in an interest rate swap is the fact that no principal payments are made either up front or at the termination date. The net interest payments from issuing the fixed-rate note and using the proceeds to buy the floating-rate note are precisely those produced by the pay fixed–receive floating interest rate swap. Likewise, the pay floating–receive fixed side of the swap is equivalent to issuing a floating-rate note and using the proceeds to buy a fixed-rate note.

An interest rate swap is also identical to a spot transaction and a set of FRAs. Recall that in XYZ's swap, initiated on December 15, its first payment, to be made on March 15, is determined by the rate on December 15, which is 7.68 percent. As Table 14.2 shows, the first payment consists of XYZ owing $937,500 and ABSwaps owing $960,000. This is equivalent to a simple spot transaction on December 15 in which ABSwaps simply agrees to give XYZ $22,500 on March 15. Though it may seem a bit perverse for ABSwaps to do this transaction, we cannot view it in isolation. We must remember that XYZ has committed to making ABSwaps a series of fixed payments while ABSwaps is committed to giving XYZ a series of floating payments. The second swap payment is equivalent to an FRA in which XYZ agrees to pay a fixed rate and receive the LIBOR of March 15, with the payment made on June 15. There are also two other FRAs with XYZ committed to making fixed payments and receiving LIBOR. Although we shall discuss this point further later in the chapter, it should be apparent that the terms of the other three FRAs must be sufficiently favorable to ABSwaps to offset the unfavorable spot transaction represented by the first payment. With this point in mind, it is easy to see that the swap is a series of FRAs and one spot transaction at the start representing the first swap payment, which is known when the swap is taken out.

A fixed- for floating-rate swap is equivalent to a spot transaction and a set of forward rate agreements.

Swaps and many other interest rate derivatives can also be shown to be equivalent to other financial transactions, including a strip of Eurodollar futures. In addition, swaps are equivalent to combinations of interest rate options.

Pricing an Interest Rate Swap at the Onset

Pricing an interest rate swap means to determine the fixed rate that is appropriate for the terms of the swap. This is called the **swap rate.** We saw in the previous section that a swap can be viewed as a combination of

fixed- and floating-rate bonds or as a spot transaction and a series of forward rate agreements. Since a swap involves no initial exchange of cash, it should have zero initial value. Thus, to price the swap means to determine the fixed rate that will make the swap have zero initial value.

Let us consider a simple example, which is illustrated in Table 14.3. Quantum Electronics enters into a $20 million notional principal swap in which it agrees to pay fixed and receive LIBOR. Payments will be made every six months with the floating payments based on LIBOR six months

---

TABLE 14.3   **Pricing an Interest Rate Swap at the Onset**

Scenario: Quantum Electronics enters into a $20 million notional principal interest rate swap in which it promises to pay a fixed rate and receive payments at LIBOR. The swap specifies that payments are made every six months with the floating side determined by LIBOR at the beginning of the six-month period. All payments will assume 180 days in each six-month period and 360 days in the year. What fixed rate will give an initial swap value of zero?

The term structure of interest rates, quoted from the LIBOR, is as follows:

Maturity	LIBOR	Effective Compound Rate
6 months	9.00%	9.20% $((1 + .09/2)^2 - 1)$
1 year	9.75	9.99 $((1 + .0975/2)^2 - 1)$
18 months	10.20	10.46 $((1 + .1020/2)^2 - 1)$
2 years	10.50	10.78 $((1 + .1050/2)^2 - 1)$

The effective compound rate is the appropriate rate for discounting cash flows.

The first floating-rate payment will be $20,000,000(.09/2) = \$900,000$. All remaining floating-rate payments will be determined by LIBOR at the beginning of each six-month period. Thus, the floating-rate component of the swap has a current value of $20 million. What is the coupon that will make a fixed-rate bond have a value of $20,000,000?

$$\text{Coupon}(1.092)^{-.5} + \text{Coupon}(1.099)^{-1} + \text{Coupon}(1.1046)^{-1.5} +$$
$$(\text{Coupon} + 20,000,000)(1.1078)^{-2} = 20,000,000$$

Solving for the coupon reveals that

$$1,045,000(1.092)^{-.5} + 1,045,000(1.099)^{-1} + 1,045,000(1.1046)^{-1.5} + 21,045,000(1.1078)^{-2}$$
$$= 20,000,000$$

So a coupon of $1,045,000 will set the bond's value to $20,000,000. This semiannual coupon is equivalent to an annual rate of $2(\$1,045,000/\$20,000,000) = 10.45$ percent.

Thus, if Quantum promises to pay a fixed rate of 10.45 percent and receive a floating rate based on LIBOR at the beginning of the six-month period, the swap will have zero initial value.

prior. For simplicity we shall assume that there are exactly 180 days in each six-month period and, of course, we use 360 days in a year; thus, all annual rates will simply be divided by two to obtain the semiannual rate. What is the appropriate swap rate?

Table 14.3 presents the term structure for six months, one year, 18 months, and two years. The quoted rates are based on LIBOR deposits of the given maturities. However, these are not the effective annual rates. For example, a six-month LIBOR deposit paying 9 percent will actually pay one-half of 9 percent, or 4.5 percent. This is an annual rate of $(1.045)^2 - 1 = .092$. Similar adjustments for the other rates give the third column. Recall from Chapter 8 that the price of a bond is obtained by discounting the coupons at the spot rates for the maturities that correspond to the coupon dates of the bond.

Using the notion that this swap is like issuing a fixed-rate bond and using the proceeds to buy a floating-rate bond means that we need to find the coupon on the fixed-rate bond that would give it an initial value of $20 million, where the coupons are discounted at the spot rates described in the previous paragraph. The floating-rate bond will automatically be worth $20 million. As Table 14.3 shows, a coupon rate of 10.45 percent will make the fixed-rate bond be worth $20 million. You might observe that finding this coupon rate is similar to finding the yield on a bond. In this case, however, it is possible to solve for the coupon directly by factoring it out of the equation. In effect, pricing an interest rate swap at the onset is equivalent to finding the coupon on a par bond.

Thus, an interest rate swap, like we learned with forward contracts, has zero initial value. It is neither an asset nor a liability. During its life, however, it can attain a positive or negative value. We have already seen this occur with currency swaps.

An interest rate swap has zero value at the onset. Pricing the swap means to determine the fixed rate that will give it an initial value of zero.

Pricing an Interest Rate Swap during Its Life

If a party commits to a swap in which it pays a fixed rate and receives a floating rate, it should be apparent that if rates increase, the party will benefit. Its outflows are locked in but its inflows increase. How much will it benefit? To find that answer, we must price the swap during its life.

Consider a firm called Global Resources Inc. (GRI), which enters into a swap in which it pays a fixed rate of 10.67 percent and receives LIBOR. The notional principal is $20 million. Payments are made every six months for two years. For simplicity we assume that the payment dates are exactly 180 days apart so the payments are computed by dividing the appropriate rate by 2 and multiplying by the notional principal. Though this swap was priced at a fixed rate of 10.67 percent at the onset so as to have zero initial value, it is now 1.25 years into the swap and interest rates have changed. On the last payment date, LIBOR was 9.42 percent so GRI's next

receipt will be $20,000,000(.0942)/2 = $942,000. The fixed-rate payments, determined at the onset, were $20,000,000(.1067)/2 = $1,067,000.

The best way to price this swap is to determine the values of the fixed- and floating-rate components of the swap. The fixed-rate component is like a fixed-rate bond that commits GRI to make a payment of $1.067 million in three months (.25 years) and another payment of $21.067 million in nine months (.75 years). Note that since we analyze this as a fixed-rate bond, we must also include the principal payment of $20 million in nine months, even though the swap does not actually require that payment. Based on the last LIBOR, GRI will receive a payment of $0.942 million in three months. The final floating-rate payment it receives in nine months is not yet known. However, viewing the floating side of the swap as a floating-rate bond means that we do not have to try to figure out what that final payment will be. We simply assume that the price of any floating-rate bond will adjust to par on the next payment date.

Figure 14.3 presents the time pattern of GRI's swap 1.25 years into the swap. The asterisk indicates where we are in the life of the swap. Note that the swap has a fixed-rate component equivalent to a fixed-rate bond issued by GRI. The floating-rate components are the upcoming payment of $0.942 million and $20 million, the face value of the floating-rate component. Since the coupon on a floating-rate bond adjusts at each coupon payment date, its price is reset to face value. Thus, we do not have to worry about calculating the final floating payment. By the power of present value, we can assume that the final floating payment plus $20 million face value paid at time 2 has a present value at time 1.5 of $20 million.

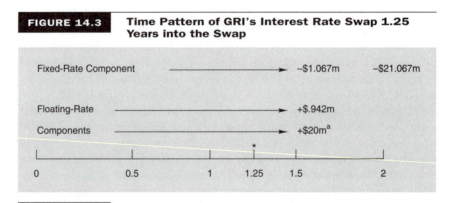

FIGURE 14.3   **Time Pattern of GRI's Interest Rate Swap 1.25 Years into the Swap**

[a]The $20 million indicated at time 1.5 represents the value at time 1.5 of the remaining floating-rate bond component. This value is the present value of the remaining floating-rate payments. At each coupon reset date, a floating-rate bond's price adjusts to par to reflect the present value of all remaining payments.

Thus, we can price the swap by pricing the fixed- and floating-rate bonds that are equivalent to the swap and subtracting the two values. The only thing we need to know is the set of appropriate discount rates. The upcoming payment occurs in .25 years and the final payment occurs in .75 years. Let these discount rates be 9.12 percent and 9.23 percent, respectively. These amounts represent spot rates on Eurodollar deposits of three and nine months, respectively.[1]

The fixed-rate bond that makes up part of the swap is worth

$$\$1,067,000(1.0912)^{-.25} + \$21,067,000(1.0923)^{-.75} = \$20,761,216.$$

The floating-rate bond that makes up part of the swap is worth

$$\$942,000(1.0912)^{-.25} + \$20,000,000(1.0912)^{-.25} = \$20,490,005.$$

The value of an interest rate swap changes from zero to a nonzero value as interest rates change. The swap will have positive value to one side of the contract and negative value to the other. The swap value can be determined by pricing the fixed- and floating-rate bonds that are equivalent to the swap and subtracting the two values.

Since GRI's fixed-rate obligations have a value of $20,761,216 and its floating-rate receipts have a value of $20,490,005, the overall swap has a value of −$271,211. The swap is now a liability of $271,211. Of course, as rates change, it may turn into an asset.

Terminating an Interest Rate Swap

A firm that has entered into a swap may later find that it would like to get out of the swap. There are several ways to terminate a swap. One way is to do a reversal or offset, which simply involves entering into a new swap with the same terms and conditions but structured so that the cash flows on the new swap offset the cash flows on the old. For example, in the previous section, GRI was obligated to pay a fixed rate of 10.67 percent and receive LIBOR. At 1.25 years into the swap, it had two payments remaining, and, as we determined, the swap had a market value of −$271,211. It could offset this swap by finding another party with which it could enter into a swap with identical floating payments. Suppose GRI enters into a new swap obligating it to make floating payments at LIBOR and receive fixed payments at the going market rate. Of course, GRI would not be erasing the liability because its new swap would have zero value while its old swap would still have a value of −$271,211. Its LIBOR payments on the old swap would be offset by LIBOR receipts on the new swap.[2] Its fixed-rate payments would exceed its fixed-rate

---

[1]These rates have been adjusted in the same manner that the rates in Table 14.2 were adjusted.

[2]The upcoming floating payment would not match the $942,000 floating payment it has coming on the old swap, because its first payment on the new swap would be based on a new rate.

receipts. Both swaps would still be in effect so GRI would be exposed to credit risk on both swaps.[3]

Of course, if the swap had a positive value to GRI, it would remain on the books as an asset and the new swap would still have zero value. The LIBOR payments on both swaps would still offset, and its fixed-rate receipts would exceed its fixed-rate payments.

Another way to terminate the swap is by sale or assignment. In this case GRI would find another party who agrees to take over its obligations and accept its receipts on the swap. Since the new party is taking over GRI's negative-value swap, GRI would have to pay it the swap's current market value of $271,211. If the swap had had positive value, GRI could have sold it to the third party and received cash for it. Since the original counterparty to GRI's swap accepted GRI as a counterparty, it would have to agree to allow GRI to replace itself with the new counterparty.

GRI could also buy out of the swap by paying the original counterparty $271,211. This is called a **buy-back** or **close-out.** Of course, the original counterparty would have to agree to accept cash in lieu of continuing the swap.

Finally, had GRI anticipated the need to terminate the swap early, it could have bought an option to terminate the swap. Such an option is like a put. GRI would have paid a premium to a dealer up front and received the right to sell the swap to the dealer. The option would most likely be offered by the original counterparty to the swap. In other words, GRI would have arranged the swap with a counterparty to whom it would have paid a premium for the right to terminate the swap early. That right would have specified a way in which the swap is valued at the option exercise date. In that way, GRI might have found itself owning an option with which it can put the swap back to the dealer and pay less than the $271,211 it is worth. Later in this chapter, we look at these instruments, called swaptions.

Swaps can be terminated by executing an offsetting swap, by finding another party to take over the payments, by paying the market value to the counterparty, or by exercising a previously purchased option to terminate or offset the swap.

Interest Rate Options

Interest Rate Calls and Puts

Interest rate options are like forward rate agreements, but instead of being a firm commitment to receive one interest rate and pay another, they provide the right to receive one interest rate and pay another. An interest rate call pays off if interest rates end up above the agreed-upon rate. The holder pays the agreed-upon rate and receives the market rate, usu-

---

[3]In some cases a firm could enter into an offsetting swap with the same party with which it entered into the original swap. The two parties could then agree to cancel all remaining payments as soon as one party paid the other party the market value, here $271,211, up front.

ally LIBOR. An interest rate put pays off if interest rates end up below the agreed-upon rate. The holder pays the market rate and receives the agreed-upon rate. This agreed-upon rate is also called the **strike rate** or **exercise rate.**

Interest rate options usually are written by dealers and are tailored to the needs of a specific clientele. The options are typically European, meaning they can be exercised only at expiration. The expiration date is chosen, and the strike rate usually is set at the current level of the spot or forward interest rate. As noted, the options pay off on the basis of the difference between an interest rate, usually LIBOR, and an interest rate designated as the exercise or strike rate. Thus, the payoff of an interest rate call is

$$(\text{Notional principal})\,\text{Max}(0, \text{LIBOR} - \text{E})\left(\frac{\text{Days}}{360}\right),$$

where E is the exercise rate. As in interest rate swaps, when exercised, the payment by the writer is made not at the expiration but at a future date that corresponds to the maturity of the underlying spot instrument.

For example, consider a call option written on the 90-day LIBOR at an exercise rate of 10 percent, which is the current LIBOR, for a notional principal of $20 million. This option expires in 30 days. At that time, the buyer determines whether to exercise the option, which depends on whether the 90-day LIBOR is above 10 percent. If the option is exercised, the payment from the writer to the buyer is made 90 days after the exercise, or 120 days from now.

Let us consider an example using this option. A firm decides that in 30 days it will borrow $20 million at LIBOR plus one point. Fearing an increase in LIBOR, it asks a dealer to write it a call option on LIBOR. The option will expire in 30 days and pay off 90 days thereafter. The bank charges a premium of $50,000. The payoff is based on 90 days and a 360-day year.

The payoff of the option is

$$(\$20,000,000)\,\text{Max}(0, \text{LIBOR} - .10)\left(\frac{90}{360}\right)$$

which occurs 90 days after the expiration. If exercised, this amount helps reduce the increased cost of the loan. Table 14.4 illustrates the option payoffs for a range of possible outcomes.

The outcome is determined as follows. Suppose LIBOR at expiration is 6 percent. Since the premium is paid today but the loan is taken out in 30 days, we must compound the premium forward for 30 days at today's spot rate plus the spread of one point. This gives us $50,000[1 + .11(30/360)] = $50,458. Thus, when we take out the loan, we shall

An interest rate call option gives the holder the right to receive an interest payment at a floating rate in exchange for making an interest payment at a fixed rate.

TABLE 14.4	**Hedging a Planned Loan with an Interest Rate Call**

Scenario: A firm plans to borrow at 90-day LIBOR plus a spread of one point. The loan will be for $20 million and will be taken out in 30 days. The loan matures 90 days after that and is paid back in one lump sum. The firm would like to establish a maximum rate it will pay on the loan so it buys an interest rate call based on 90-day LIBOR. The call gives the right to receive an interest payment based on the actual LIBOR in 30 days and has a 10 percent strike rate. The payoff is based on 90 days and a 360-day year. The call premium is $50,000. The current LIBOR is 10 percent.

LIBOR in 30 days	Payoff of Call at Loan Maturity	Interest on Loan at Maturity	Total Effective Interest	Annualized Cost of Loan with Call	Annualized Cost of Loan without Call
6.00 %	$0	$350,000	$350,000	8.39 %	7.29 %
6.50	0	375,000	375,000	8.93	7.82
7.00	0	400,000	400,000	9.48	8.36
7.50	0	425,000	425,000	10.02	8.90
8.00	0	450,000	450,000	10.57	9.44
8.50	0	475,000	475,000	11.12	9.99
9.00	0	500,000	500,000	11.67	10.53
9.50	0	525,000	525,000	12.22	11.08
10.00	0	550,000	550,000	12.78	11.63
10.50	25,000	575,000	550,000	12.78	12.18
11.00	50,000	600,000	550,000	12.78	12.74
11.50	75,000	625,000	550,000	12.78	13.29
12.00	100,000	650,000	550,000	12.78	13.85
12.50	125,000	675,000	550,000	12.78	14.41
13.00	150,000	700,000	550,000	12.78	14.97
13.50	175,000	725,000	550,000	12.78	15.54
14.00	200,000	750,000	550,000	12.78	16.10

effectively receive $20,000,000 − $50,458 = $19,949,542. The interest on the spot loan is based on LIBOR of 6 percent plus one point, so it will be $20,000,000[.07(90/360)] = $350,000. The call is out-of-the-money, so the total interest paid is $350,000. As we have done previously, we should determine the annualized cost of the loan. We paid back $20,350,000 and we received $19,949,542. The rate thus is $(\$20,350,000/\$19,949,542)^{(365/90)} − 1 = .0839$.

If LIBOR ends up at 11 percent, the firm will exercise the option and receive $20,000,000(.11 − .10)(90/360) = $50,000$ at the maturity of the loan. This reduces the amount paid from $600,000 in interest to $550,000. The annualized cost of the loan thus will be $(\$20,550,000)/(\$19,949,542)^{(365/90)} − 1 = .1278$. Therefore, the call caps the interest cost at 12.78 percent. Note that without the call the annualized cost of the loan rises directly with LIBOR. This cost is determined by taking $20 million plus the interest, dividing by $20 million, and annualizing.

Figure 14.4 illustrates the cost of the planned fixed-rate loan with and without the interest rate call. The fixed-rate loan plus the call creates a maximum cost of 12.78 percent, which is reached if LIBOR ends up at 10 percent or above. Note that this payoff graph looks similar to a covered call or short put. However, in our previous option graphs, recall that the payoff was based on an asset price. In this example, the payoff is based on an interest rate.

Table 14.5 illustrates an interest rate put. An interest rate put might be used by a bank that lends at LIBOR plus possibly a spread. It thus is vulnerable to a decline in interest rates. Although declining interest rates generally are considered bullish, a put is appropriate because the payoff is based on LIBOR, and not on the price of a fixed-income security. In general the payoff from an interest rate put is

$$(\text{Notional principal})\text{Max}(0, \text{E} - \text{LIBOR})\left(\frac{\text{Days}}{360}\right).$$

FIGURE 14.4   **Cost of Planned Loan with and without Interest Rate Call**

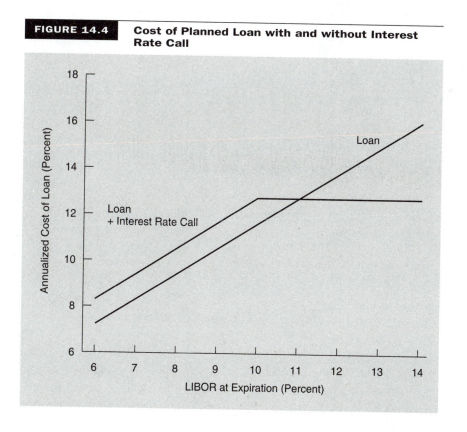

TABLE 14.5	**Hedging a Planned Loan with an Interest Rate Put**

Scenario: A bank plans to lend $10 million in 90 days at 180-day LIBOR plus a spread of 1.5 points. The loan will mature 180 days after that and is paid back in one lump sum. The bank wants to lock in a minimum return on the loan so it buys an interest rate put for $26,500 with a strike rate of 9 percent. The put will pay off to the bank if LIBOR ends up below the strike rate. The payoff is based on 180 days and a 360-day year. The current LIBOR is 9 percent.

LIBOR in 90 days	Payoff of Put at Loan Maturity	Interest on Loan at Maturity	Total Effective Interest	Annualized Return on Loan with Put	Annualized Return on Loan without Put
5.00 %	$200,000	$325,000	$525,000	10.32 %	6.70 %
5.50	175,000	350,000	525,000	10.32	7.22
6.00	150,000	375,000	525,000	10.32	7.75
6.50	125,000	400,000	525,000	10.32	8.28
7.00	100,000	425,000	525,000	10.32	8.81
7.50	75,000	450,000	525,000	10.32	9.34
8.00	50,000	475,000	525,000	10.32	9.87
8.50	25,000	500,000	525,000	10.32	10.40
9.00	0	525,000	525,000	10.32	10.93
9.50	0	550,000	550,000	10.86	11.47
10.00	0	575,000	575,000	11.39	12.00
10.50	0	600,000	600,000	11.92	12.54
11.00	0	625,000	625,000	12.46	13.08
11.50	0	650,000	650,000	13.00	13.62
12.00	0	675,000	675,000	13.54	14.16
12.50	0	700,000	700,000	14.08	14.71
13.00	0	725,000	725,000	14.62	15.25

Like an interest rate call, exercise is determined at expiration, but the payment is made at a later date.

Here the bank plans to lend in 90 days at LIBOR plus a spread of 1.5 points. The amount of the loan will be $10 million, and the loan will be for 180 days and be paid back in one lump sum. The bank finds a writer to sell it a put on LIBOR with a strike of 9, the current LIBOR. The payoff is based on 180 days and a 360-day year. The put premium will be $26,500. Its payoff is

$$(\$10,000,000)\ \text{Max}(0,\ .09 - \text{LIBOR})\left(\frac{180}{360}\right).$$

An interest rate put option gives the holder the right to receive an interest payment at a fixed rate in exchange for making an interest payment at a floating rate.

Let us say that at expiration, LIBOR is 7 percent. Then the put is worth $10,000,000(.09 − .07)(180/360) = $100,000. The put premium was paid up front, so we must compound it at today's LIBOR plus the 1.5 spread. This gives $26,500[1 + .105(90/360)] = $27,196. Thus, we effectively lent

$10,027,196. The interest we receive on the loan will be $10,000,000 [.085(180/360)] = $425,000. With the put payoff the total interest received is effectively $525,000. Thus, it paid out $10,027,196 and received $10,525,000. The annualized return is ($10,525,000/ $10,027,196)$^{(365/180)}$ − 1 = .1032. Note that without the put the annualized return on the loan rises directly with LIBOR. This rate is determined by taking $10 million plus the interest, dividing by $10 million and annualizing.

Figure 14.5 illustrates the return on the planned loan with and without the interest rate put. The payoff looks like what we would have formerly recognized as a call or protective put. In previous examples, these were bullish strategies that paid off if an asset price rose. Here they pay off if an interest rate increases. The floor provides a minimum return of 10.32 percent, which is reached if LIBOR is at 9 percent or below.

PRICING INTEREST RATE OPTIONS   As you recall, we devoted Chapters 3 and 4 to learning how to price options on stocks and stock indices and

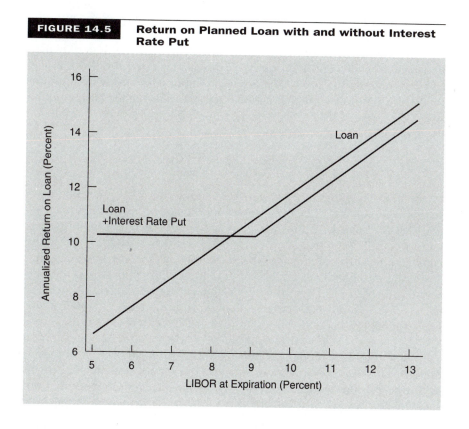

FIGURE 14.5   **Return on Planned Loan with and without Interest Rate Put**

in Chapters 12 and 13 we learned how to price options on futures and currencies. The techniques were quite similar, meaning that the Black-Scholes or Black models generally apply when the options are European. The binomial model is normally required when the options are American. Unfortunately, pricing interest rate options is considerably more complex. In this part of the chapter we look at the simplest way to price interest rate options, which is the Black model that we covered in Chapter 12. Later in the chapter we develop a binomial model of the term structure and use it to price all types of interest rate derivatives.

Recall that the Black model requires the forward price of the underlying asset, the exercise price, the risk-free rate, the time to expiration, and the volatility of the forward price. Here we use the forward rate for the forward price, the strike rate for the exercise price, and the volatility of the forward rate for the volatility of the forward price. The risk-free rate and the time to expiration are the same variables as before. Because of the delay between the option expiration and the day the payoff is actually made, the computed price must be discounted using the forward rate.

For example, consider the interest rate call we examined in Table 14.4. It expires in 30 days and has a strike rate of 10 percent. Suppose the 30-day continuously compounded risk-free rate is 8 percent and the volatility (standard deviation) of the forward LIBOR is .2. Let the 30-day forward LIBOR for 90-day deposits be 11.01 percent. The time to expiration is $30/365 = .0822$. We can insert these values into the Black model and obtain an option price. The actual premium paid for the option must reflect the notional principal and the fact that the option payoff will be based on 90-day LIBOR. Thus, if C is the premium obtained from the Black model, the total cost of the option is

$$(\text{Notional principal})\left(\frac{\text{Days}}{360}\right)C,$$

where "Days" is the number of days in the underlying LIBOR instrument. In this example, Days = 90 because the option pays off according to the 90-day LIBOR. Table 14.6 illustrates the computation of the value of our interest rate call. Note that its price of $49,500 is very close to the price the bank charged. A similar approach can be used to find the value of an interest rate put. First one should compute the call price, going up through Step 5 in Table 14.6. Then using put-call parity for options on futures, $P = C - (f - E)e^{-r_cT}$, one easily obtains the put price. Alternatively, one can use Black's model directly for put options where $P = e^{-r_cT}[E(1 - N(d_2)) - f(1 - N(d_1))]$.

While the Black model is widely used in industry to price interest rate options, it has several limitations. Interest rates are less likely than stocks to conform to the model's assumptions, such as the requirement that the volatility be constant over the life of the option. This can be a particularly

---

TABLE 14.6	Calculating the Black Price for an Interest Rate Call

$f = .1101$ $E = .10$ $r_c = .08$ $\sigma^2 = .04$ $T = .0822$

1. Compute d_1.

$$d_1 = \frac{\ln(.1101/.10) + (.04/2).0822}{.2\sqrt{.0822}} = 1.71$$

2. Compute d_2.

$$d_2 = 1.71 - .2\sqrt{.0822} = 1.65$$

3. Look up $N(d_1)$.

$$N(1.71) = .9564$$

4. Look up $N(d_2)$.

$$N(1.65) = .9505$$

5. Plug into formula for C and discount using the forward rate over the time period between the option expiration and the payoff date.

$$C = (e^{-(.08)(.0822)} [.1101(.9564) - .10(.9505)])e^{-.1101(90/365)}$$
$$= .0099$$

6. Multiply by the notional principal times days over 360.

$$(\$20,000,000)\frac{90}{360}(.0099) = \$49,500$$

---

severe problem for long-term options. In addition, the Black model does not guarantee that all of the fixed income assets and derivatives that a firm may deal in are priced to preclude arbitrage opportunities. More precise and arbitrage-free pricing of interest rate options is based on models that capture the evolution of the term structure as it moves through time. Although such models are complex, we shall take a look at a basic version of these models later in this chapter.

The Black model can be used as a simple method of pricing interest rate options. The forward rate is used for the forward price, the strike rate is used for the exercise price, and the volatility of the forward rate is the appropriate volatility. In this context, however, the model has many limitations.

Interest Rate Caps, Floors, and Collars

Another type of transaction that can be used to protect against rising interest rates is an **interest rate cap,** which is a series of European interest rate calls that pay off at dates corresponding to interest payment dates on a loan. At each interest payment date, the holder of the cap decides

whether to exercise the option based on whether the interest rate has risen above the exercise rate. A price is paid up front for the cap. The price corresponds to the sum of the prices of the series of options that make up the cap. Each option is a separate interest rate call. These individual component options are called **caplets.**

Let us look at an example. On January 2, a firm borrows $25 million over one year. It will make payments on April 2, July 2, October 2, and next January 2. On each date, starting with January 2, LIBOR in effect on that day will be the interest rate paid over the next three months. The current LIBOR is 10 percent. The firm wishes to fix its rate at 10 percent, so it buys a cap for an up-front payment of $70,000. The payoffs are based on the exact number of days and a 360-day year. At each interest payment date, the cap will be worth

$$\$25,000,000\left(\frac{\text{Days}}{360}\right)\text{Max}(0, \text{LIBOR} - .10).$$

An interest rate cap is a series of interest rate calls, designed to limit the cost of a loan with multiple interest payments.

In the formula, LIBOR is the rate that was in effect at the beginning of each quarter. Thus, as with an interest rate option, the decision to exercise is made at the beginning of the quarter but the payoff occurs at the end of the quarter. If LIBOR is greater than 10 percent, the firm will exercise the option and receive a sum as given by this equation. This helps offset the higher interest rate on the loan. Table 14.7 shows the payments associated with this interest rate cap.

For the first quarter, the firm will pay LIBOR of 10 percent in effect on January 2. Thus, on April 2 it will owe $25,000,000(.10)(91/360) = $631,944 based on 91 days from January 2 to April 2.[4] Then, on April 2, LIBOR is 10.68 percent. Because this is greater than 10 percent, the cap will pay off at the next interest payment date and the holder of the cap will receive a payment of

$$\$25,000,000\left(\frac{91}{360}\right)(.1068 - .10) = \$42,972.$$

This will help offset the interest of $674,917, based on a rate of 10.68 percent for 91 days from April 2 to July 2. LIBOR on July 2 is 12.31 percent, so the cap will pay off on October 2. The net effect of these cash flows is seen in column 7 of Table 14.7. On January 2, the firm received $25 million from the lender but paid out $70,000 for the cap for a net cash inflow of $24,930,000. It made periodic payments as shown and, on the next January 2, repaid the principal and made the final interest payment less the cap payoff. Note that because of the cap, the interest payments differ only

---

[4]The first caplet expires out-of-the-money. Since the first loan interest payment is known when the cap is purchased, it need not be hedged so the first caplet is often omitted.

TABLE 14.7   **After-the-Fact Payments for Interest Rate Cap**

Scenario: On January 2, a firm takes out a one-year loan with interest paid quarterly at LIBOR. The face value is $25 million. The firm buys an interest rate cap with a strike of 10 percent for a premium of $70,000. The payoffs are based on the exact number of days and a 360-day year.

Date	Days in Quarter	LIBOR	Interest Due	Cap Payment	Principal Repayment	Net Cash Flow	Net Cash Flow without Cap
1/2	—	10.00%	—	–$70,000	$ 0	$24,930,000	$25,000,000
4/2	91	10.68	$631,944	0	0	–631,944	–631,944
7/2	91	12.31	674,917	42,972	0	–631,944	–674,917
10/2	92	11.56	786,472	147,583	0	–638,889	–786,472
1/2	92	—	738,556	99,667	25,000,000	–25,638,889	–25,738,556

Effective annual rate
  Without cap: 11.7%
  With cap: 10.8%

Note: This is but one of an infinite number of possible outcomes to the cap. It is used only to illustrate how the payments are determined and not their likely amounts.

because of the different number of days during each interest payment period and not because of the rate. The interest rate is capped at LIBOR of 10 percent.

If we wish to know what annualized rate the firm actually paid, we essentially must solve for the internal rate of return. This was discussed in Chapter 8 and, as you may remember, requires a computer or financial calculator. We are solving for the cash flow that equates the present value of the four payouts to the initial receipt:

$$\$24,930,000 = \frac{\$631,944}{(1+y)^1} + \frac{\$631,944}{(1+y)^2} + \frac{\$638,889}{(1+y)^3} + \frac{\$25,638,889}{(1+y)^4}.$$

The solution is $y = .026$. Annualizing this gives a rate of $(1.026)^4 - 1 = .108$. The last column in Table 14.7 shows the cash flows if the cap had not been purchased. Solving for the internal rate of return using those numbers and annualizing the result gives a rate of .117. Thus, the cap saved the firm 90 basis points, because during the life of the loan, interest rates generally were higher than they were at the time the loan was initiated.

Pricing caps proceeds the same as pricing interest rate calls. Each caplet is a separate interest rate call. The total value of the cap is the sum of the values of the individual caplets. The lender in a floating-rate loan may want protection against falling rates. This type of protection can be purchased with an **interest rate floor,** which is a series of interest rate put options expiring at the interest payment dates. Each component put is called a **floorlet.**

At each interest payment date, the payoff of an interest rate floor tied to LIBOR with an exercise rate of, say, 8 percent, payoffs based on the exact number of days and a 360-day year, and a notional principal of $15 million will be

$$(\$15,000,000) \, \text{Max}(0, .08 - \text{LIBOR}) \left(\frac{\text{Days}}{360}\right).$$

As previously, LIBOR is determined at the beginning of the interest payment period.

Suppose a bank makes a one-year, $15 million loan with payments made at LIBOR on March 16, June 16, September 15, and next December 16. Currently, it is December 16, and LIBOR is 7.93 percent. Thus, on March 16 the bank will receive $15,000,000[.0793(90/360)] = $297,375 in interest. The new rate on that day is 7.50 percent. Thus, the floor is in-the-money and will pay off

$$\$15,000,000(.08 - .075)\left(\frac{92}{360}\right) = \$19,167$$

on the next interest payment day. This will add to the interest payment of $287,500, which is lower because of the fall in interest rates. The complete results for the one-year loan are shown in Table 14.8. The floor is in-the-money and thus is exercised on each of the last three interest payment

TABLE 14.8	After-the-Fact Payments for Interest Rate Floor

Scenario: On December 16, a bank makes a one-year loan with interest paid quarterly at LIBOR. The face value is $15 million. The firm buys an interest rate floor with a strike of 8 percent for a premium of $30,000. The payoffs are based on the exact number of days and a 360-day year.

Date	Days in Quarter	LIBOR	Interest Received	Floor Payment	Principal Repayment	Net Cash Flow	Net Cash Flow without Floor
12/16	—	7.93%	—	−$30,000	$ 0	−$15,030,000	−$15,000,000
3/16	90	7.50	$297,375	0	0	297,375	297,375
6/16	92	7.06	287,500	19,167	0	306,667	287,500
9/15	91	6.06	267,692	35,642	0	303,333	267,692
12/16	92	—	232,300	74,367	15,000,000	15,306,667	15,232,300

Effective annual rate
  Without floor: 7.4%
  With floor: 8.1%

Note: This is but one of an infinite number of possible outcomes to the floor. It is used only to illustrate how the payments are determined and not their likely amounts.

dates. This is because in this example, the year was one of interest rates lower than 8 percent.

The lender paid out $15,000,000 up front to the borrower and another $30,000 for the floor. Column 7 in Table 14.8 indicates the periodic cash flows associated with the floored loan. Following the same procedure as in the cap, we can solve for the periodic rate that equates the present value of the inflows to the outflow. This rate turns out to be about 1.97 percent. Annualizing this gives a rate of $(1.0197)^4 - 1 = .081$. The last column shows the cash flows if the floor had not been used. The annualized return associated with these cash flows is 7.4 percent. Thus, the floor boosted the bank's return by 70 basis points. Of course, in a period of rising rates, the bank will gain less from the increase in interest rates.

As with caps, the price of an interest rate floor is found by pricing each of the component floorlets and adding up their prices.

An interest rate floor is a series of interest rate puts, designed to protect the return on a loan with multiple interest payments.

Consider a firm planning to borrow money that decides to purchase an interest rate cap. In so doing, the firm is trying to place a ceiling on the rate it will pay on its loan. If rates fall, it can gain by paying lower rates. However, in some cases a firm will find it more advantageous to give up the right to gain from falling rates in order to lower the cost of the cap. One way to do this is to sell a floor. The combination of a long interest rate cap and short interest rate floor is called an **interest rate collar.** The premium received from selling the floor helps offset the cost of the cap. It is even possible to structure the exercise rates on the collar so that the premium received from the sale of the floor equals the premium paid for the purchase of the cap. This is called a **zero cost collar.** If interest rates fall, the options that comprise the floor will be exercised. The net effect is that the strategy will establish both a floor and a ceiling on the interest cost. The existence of both limited gains and losses should remind you of a money spread with options.

Table 14.9 illustrates a collar in which a firm borrowing $50 million over two years buys a cap for $250,000 with an exercise price of 10 percent and sells a floor for $175,000 with an exercise price of 8 percent. The loan begins on March 15 and will require payments at approximately 91-day intervals at LIBOR.

By now, you should be able to verify the numbers in the table. The interest paid on June 15 is based on LIBOR on March 15 of 10.5 percent and 92 days during the period. The cap pays off on September 14 and December 14 because those are the ends of the periods in which LIBOR at the beginning of the period turned out to be greater than 10 percent. The floor pays off on September 14 of the next year and on March 14 of the following year, the due date on the loan. Note that when the floor pays off, the firm makes, rather than receives, the payment.

Column 8 in Table 14.9 shows the cash flows associated with the collar. Following the procedure previously described to solve for the internal

An interest rate collar is a combination of the purchase of an interest rate cap and the sale of an interest rate floor. It is used to limit the effects of interest rate increases by giving up the benefits of interest rate decreases.

TABLE 14.9	After-the-Fact Payments for Interest Rate Collar

Scenario: On March 15, a firm borrows $50 million with interest paid quarterly at LIBOR. The firm buys an interest rate cap with a strike of 10 percent for $250,000. To help offset the cost of the cap, the firm sells an interest rate floor with a strike of 8 percent for $175,000. The payoffs are based on the exact number of days and a 360-day year.

Date	Days in Quarter	LIBOR	Interest Due	Cap Payment	Floor Payment	Principal Repayment	Net Cash Flow with Collar	Net Cash Flow with Cap Only	Net Cash Flow without Cap or Floor
3/15		10.50%	$ 0	−$250,000	$175,000	$ 0	$49,925,000	$49,750,000	$50,000,000
6/15	92	11.56	1,341,667	0	0	0	−1,341,667	−1,341,667	−1,341,667
9/14	91	11.75	1,461,056	197,167	0	0	−1,263,889	−1,263,889	−1,461,056
12/14	91	9.06	1,485,069	222,181	0	0	−1,263,889	−1,263,889	−1,485,069
3/15	91	9.50	1,145,083	0	0	0	−1,145,083	−1,145,083	−1,145,083
6/14	91	7.62	1,200,694	0	0	0	−1,200,694	−1,200,694	−1,200,694
9/14	92	8.31	973,667	0	−48,556	0	−1,022,222	−973,667	−973,667
12/15	92	7.93	1,061,833	0	0	0	−1,061,833	−1,061,833	−1,061,833
3/14	89	—	980,236	0	−8,653	50,000,000	−50,988,889	−50,980,236	−50,980,236

Effective annual rate
Without cap or floor: 10.08%
With collar: 9.76%
With cap: 9.91%

Note: This is but one of an infinite number of possible outcomes to the collar. It is used only to illustrate how the payments are determined and not their likely amounts.

rate of return gives an annualized rate of 9.76 percent for the collar. Column 9 shows the cash flows had the firm done only the cap. The rate associated with this strategy would have been 9.91 percent. The last column indicates the cash flows had the firm done neither the cap nor the floor. The borrowing rate associated with that strategy would have been 10.08 percent.

The cap by itself would have helped lower the firm's cost of borrowing. By selling the floor and thus creating a collar, the cost of the loan was lowered from 9.91 percent to 9.76 percent.

Interest Rate Swaptions and Forward Swaps

Earlier in this chapter we mentioned that a firm that had entered into a swap could exit the swap before it terminates if the firm had previously purchased an option on the swap. Options on swaps are called **swaptions.** A swaption is an option in which the buyer pays a premium up front and acquires the right to enter into a swap as either a fixed-rate payer, floating-rate receiver or as a floating-rate payer, fixed-rate receiver. The former is called a **payer swaption** while the latter is called a **receiver swaption.**

A swaption can be viewed as a variation of an interest rate option but there are several important differences. Like an interest rate option, a swaption specifies a strike rate stated in terms of an interest rate. A swaption is based on an underlying swap and has a fixed maturity. A swaption can also be American or European style. The parties can agree that exercise is accomplished by either a simple cash settlement or that the parties actually enter into the underlying swap.

Consider the following situation. A company called MPK Resources is considering the possibility that it will need to engage in an interest rate swap two years from now with a notional principal of $10 million. It expects that the swap would be a three-year pay fixed–receive floating swap. The firm is concerned about rising interest rates over the next two years that would force it to pay a higher fixed rate if it enters into the swap at that time. It thus decides to purchase a two-year, European-style payer swaption on a three-year, pay fixed–receive floating swap. Naturally the underlying swap should be identical to the one MPK expects to take out in two years. MPK specifies a strike rate of 11.5 percent and pays the premium in cash up front. To keep the illustration as simple as possible, assume that the underlying swap calls for annual interest payments.

Now let us consider what happens when the swaption expires in two years. Let the following term structure of LIBOR be observed at expiration: one-year rate = .12, two-year rate = .125, three-year rate = .128. Following the procedure in Table 14.3, the price of a three-year swap is found as the solution to

$$\text{Coupon}(1.12)^{-1} + \text{Coupon}(1.125)^{-2} + (\text{Coupon} + \$10,000,000)(1.128)^{-3}$$
$$= \$10,000,000.$$

Solving for the coupon gives Coupon = $1,277,737, which is about 12.77 percent. Thus, at expiration MPK will find that new three-year swaps will have a fixed rate of 12.77 percent. Ignoring the bid-ask spread the dealer would charge, we shall assume that a party can either pay 12.77 percent fixed and receive the floating rate or receive 12.77 percent fixed and pay the floating rate.

MPK, however, holds an expiring swaption that allows it to enter into an identical swap paying only 11.5 percent. If MPK finds that it actually does need to enter into a swap at that time, it can do so by exercising the swaption. This would allow it to enter a swap paying 11.5 percent fixed in a market where it would otherwise have to pay 12.77 percent fixed.

To better understand the payoffs of swaptions, however, let us assume that MPK finds it has no need for the swap but, having an expiring in-the-money swaption, it is worth going ahead and exercising it. Thus, MPK would exercise the swaption, thereby entering into a swap in which it pays a fixed rate of 11.5 percent and receives the floating rate. It goes into the

market and enters into an otherwise identical swap in which it receives 12.77 percent fixed and pays the floating rate. The floating payments on both swaps cancel, leaving MPK with a three-year annuity in which it receives a net interest payment of $12.77 - 11.5 = 1.27$ percent each year. The value of the swaption at expiration is, thus, the present value of a three-year annuity of $.0127(\$10,000,000) = \$127,000$. Using the LIBOR spot rates to discount these cash flows, we obtain

$$\$127,000(1.12)^{-1} + \$127,000(1.125)^{-2} + \$127,000(1.128)^{-3} = \$302,225.$$

An interest rate swaption is an option to enter into a swap where the fixed rate is agreed upon in advance. The right to enter into a swap as a fixed-rate payer, floating-rate receiver is called a payer swaption and the right to enter into a swap as a fixed-rate receiver, floating-rate payer is called a receiver swaption. Exercise of a swaption creates an annuity equal to the difference in the fixed rate on the swaption and the fixed rate on the underlying swap at the time of exercise.

Had the swaption been structured so as to provide a cash settlement instead of the actual execution of a swap, MPK would have simply received $302,225 from the counterparty.

Had the rate on new swaps been less than 11.5 percent at the swaption expiration, the swaption, like any other option, would have expired worthless. It should be apparent that when interest rates end up above the strike rate, payer swaptions are exercised, thus making payer swaptions somewhat like interest rate calls. When interest rates end up below the strike rate, receiver swaptions are exercised, making receiver swaptions like interest rate puts. An important distinction, however, is that swaptions create an annuity or the equivalent value when exercised.

In this example a swaption was used when a firm believed that it might need to enter into a swap at a later date. Swaptions can also be used to speculate on interest rates, specifically the swap rate. Also, as we noted earlier when discussing swaps, a firm that enters into a swap might wish to simultaneously purchase a swaption, which would give it the right to enter into an offsetting swap before the swap life is over. For example, a firm that enters into a pay fixed–receive floating swap might purchase a receiver swaption, which would allow it to enter into a receive fixed–pay floating swap that could be used to offset the original swap before its life is over.

Pricing swaptions is quite complex. We shall address the issue later in the chapter when we look at modeling the term structure.

As you might well imagine, if it is possible to purchase an option to enter into a swap, it is also possible to enter into a forward contract to enter into a swap. This is called a **forward swap.** One party is committed to being the fixed-rate payer on the swap and the other is committed to being the fixed-rate receiver. The fixed-rate payer is long the forward swap and the fixed-rate receiver is short the forward swap.

In our example of MPK, suppose that today the firm is looking at a five-year term structure given as follows: $r(0,1) = .09$, $r(0,2) = .096$, $r(0,3) = .10$, $r(0,4) = .103$, $r(0,5) = .105$. The two-year-ahead forward price of the swap would be found the same way we price a swap executed at the current time except that we move ahead in time and use the implied forward

rates. Thus, in this example to price the forward swap today, we must find the coupon on a three-year par bond using the forward rates r(2,3), r(2,4), and r(2,5) as the new one-, two-, and three-period rates, respectively. Recall that in Chapter 8 we learned how to determine these rates. They are found as follows:

$$r(2,3) = \frac{(1 + r(0,3))^3}{(1 + r(0,2))^2} - 1 = \frac{(1.10)^3}{(1.096)^2} - 1 = .108$$

$$r(2,4) = \sqrt{\frac{(1 + r(0,4))^4}{(1 + r(0,2))^2}} - 1 = \sqrt{\frac{(1.103)^4}{(1.096)^2}} - 1 = .11$$

$$r(2,5) = \sqrt[3]{\frac{(1 + r(0,5))^5}{(1 + r(0,2))^2}} - 1 = \sqrt[3]{\frac{(1.105)^5}{(1.096)^2}} - 1 = .111.$$

The forward price of the swap is then found as the solution to

$$\text{Coupon}(1.108)^{-1} + \text{Coupon}(1.11)^{-2} + (\text{Coupon} + \$10,000,000)(1.111)^{-3} = \$10,000,000.$$

The solution is $1,108,229, which converts to a coupon of about 11.08 percent. Thus, MPK could commit to entering into a three-year swap two years from now by agreeing to pay a fixed rate of 11.08. When the forward swap expires, the difference between the fixed rate on new three-year swaps and 11.08 would determine the value at expiration. Using our previous example, MPK would be the fixed-rate payer. If, at expiration, the new rate on three-year swaps turns out to be 12.77 percent, MPK would lock in a three-year inflow of $(.1277 - .1108)(\$10,000,000) = \$169,000$. The value of the swap at expiration would, thus, be

$$\$169,000(1.12)^{-1} + \$169,000(1.125)^{-2} + \$169,000(1.128)^{-3} = \$402,173.$$

As with any type of forward contract, there may be either a positive or negative value at expiration, but for a swaption, like any option, the holder exercises only if there is positive value at expiration.

A forward swap is a forward contract to enter into a swap in which the fixed rate is agreed upon in advance. One party is committed to paying the fixed rate and receiving the floating rate and the other is committed to receiving the fixed rate and paying the floating rate. At expiration, depending on the direction of rates on the underlying swap, one party receives an annuity paid by the other.

Modeling the Term Structure and Pricing Interest Rate Derivatives

We have noted several times earlier that pricing interest rate derivatives is quite difficult. Interest rates do not evolve in isolation. From our study of how forward and spot rates are related in Chapter 8, we observed that interest rates of various maturities are specified by the term structure of interest rates. To properly model the uncertainty in interest rates, it is

necessary to model the manner in which the term structure changes through time. This means that capturing movements in bonds of many maturities is required. In addition, these movements must be arbitrage-free, meaning that it must not be possible to construct equivalent combinations of interest-paying assets that have different prices. Likewise derivatives on these interest-paying assets and interest rates must have prices consistent with no arbitrage possibilities. A good term structure model would permit arbitrage-free pricing of coupon bonds, zero coupon bonds, all kinds of derivatives on coupon and zero coupon bonds, and derivatives on interest rates. Their prices would be internally consistent. Anyone using the model to determine prices for trading in the market need not fear that a counterparty could execute arbitrage against it.

Building such a model is a difficult task, but there are many models that meet these requirements. A good model combines simplicity with realism in the manner in which it describes movements in interest rates. In this book, we shall not go too deeply into this subject for it can quickly become quite complex. We shall, however, look at one model, the Ho-Lee binomial term structure model, in a simple setting to observe how such models can be used to price interest rate derivatives.

Many interest rate derivatives are based on a short-term interest rate, like the 90-day LIBOR. In our model, we shall examine derivatives based on the shortest possible interest rate, but we leave it unnamed other than to call it the one-period rate. Thus, it might be the one-year LIBOR, but that is not important. It is simply the rate on a one-period zero coupon bond.

Figure 14.6 shows a binomial tree illustrating how the one-period rate evolves. Each node contains four pieces of information. The top piece is the one-period rate. The remaining three pieces are information about the probability that this interest rate will occur. We show how to determine that probability in the next paragraph. We observe that the rate is 10.50 percent today. This means that one could borrow or lend for one year at 10.50 percent today. One year from now, the one-period rate will be either 12 percent or 8.74 percent. This means that one year from now, one can borrow or lend for one year at either 12 percent or 8.74 percent. How these rates were obtained is illustrated in the appendix, but the important point is that the binomial tree specifies the uncertainty in future one-year borrowing and lending rates.

In Chapter 4 when we studied the binomial model for stock prices, we calculated the value of an option as a discounted probability-weighted average of future option payoffs. The probability was not actually the probability of the stock price movement but was related to the risk-free rate and the magnitudes of the up and down movements in the stock price. In our interest rate tree, we let the probability of an up move be .52 and the probability of a down move be .48. Observe on the second line at each node in Figure 14.6 a combination of u's and d's. This is the number of

FIGURE 14.6   **Binomial Model of the One-Period Interest Rate through Four Periods**

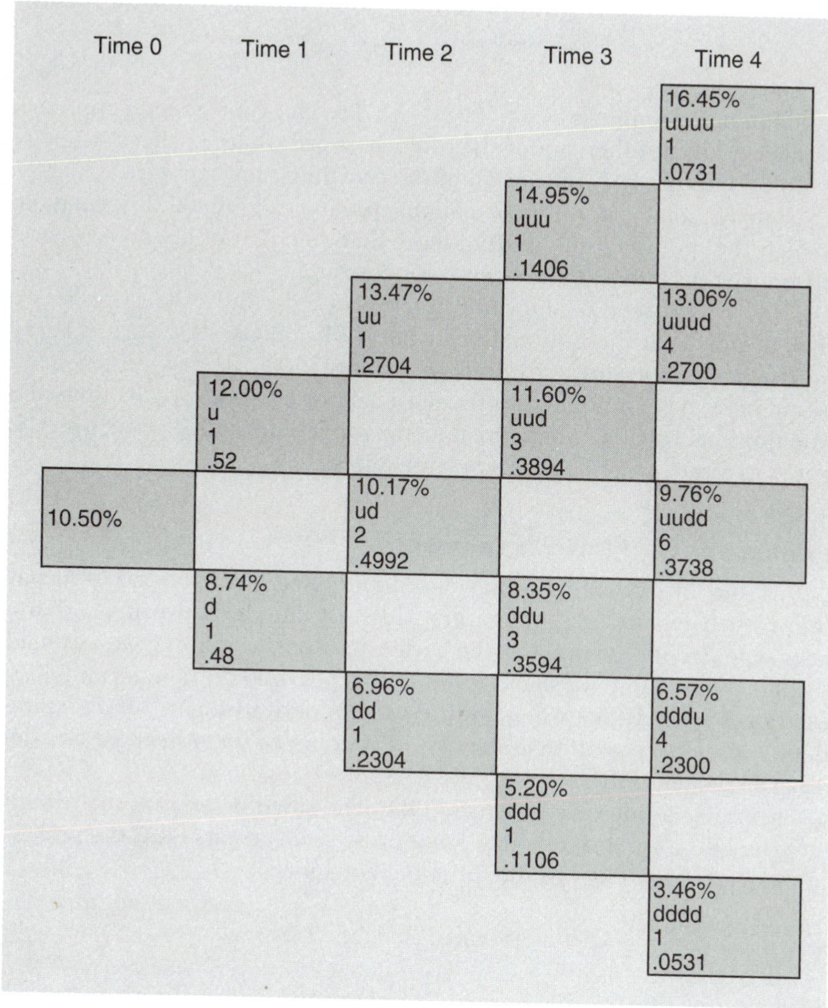

Time 0	Time 1	Time 2	Time 3	Time 4
				16.45% uuuu 1 .0731
			14.95% uuu 1 .1406	
		13.47% uu 1 .2704		13.06% uuud 4 .2700
	12.00% u 1 .52		11.60% uud 3 .3894	
10.50%		10.17% ud 2 .4992		9.76% uudd 6 .3738
	8.74% d 1 .48		8.35% ddu 3 .3594	
		6.96% dd 1 .2304		6.57% dddu 4 .2300
			5.20% ddd 1 .1106	
				3.46% dddd 1 .0531

up and down moves the one-period rate would have to make to reach that node. For example, notice the middle interest rate at time 4 of 9.76 percent. We see the term uudd. This means that to reach 9.76 percent the one-period rate would have to go up twice and down twice though not necessarily in that order. The next row contains the number 6. This is the number of possible ways that the rate could go up twice and down twice. These are (1) up, up, down, down, (2) up, down, up, down, (3) up, down, down, up, (4) down, up, up, down, (5) down, up, down, up, and (6) down, down, up, up. Call this number Q. The final number is the probability of

reaching that node. Let p be the probability of going up and $1 - p$ be the probability of going down. Then the probability of reaching that node is

$$Qp^{(\text{\# of times the rate has gone up})}(1 - p)^{(\text{\# of times the rate has gone down})},$$

which in our example is $6(.52)^2(.48)^2 = .3738$. The same general approach is taken with all other nodes. It would be worthwhile to check a few of them to determine if you can fill in the remaining probabilities.[5]

Finally, some of our calculations require additional information, namely the spot rates on bonds of more than one year of maturity. We will introduce that information when it is necessary.

Now we proceed to show how interest rate derivatives are priced. We shall assume that the notional principal is $1 and the derivative is based on the one-period interest rate. In a real situation, the answer we obtain would have to be multiplied by the notional principal. Also, each time step would probably be less than a year so the quoted derivative price, which is stated as a rate, would need to be annualized.

Pricing Forward Rate Agreements

Let us start by examining a one-period FRA. Recall that typical FRAs pay off on their expirations though most interest rate derivatives pay off at a later date. In our example in the earlier part of the chapter, we assumed the latter case. Here we shall look at both types of FRAs. The terminology used in practice is that when an interest rate derivative pays off at expiration, it is said to pay off **in arrears.** We shall refer to the other case as a **delayed settlement** FRA.

Consider a one-year in-arrears FRA. The price is the rate that would give the FRA a zero value today. For a one-year in-arrears FRA, the price is found as the rate FRA_1 in the following equation:

$$.52(.12 - FRA_1) + .48(.0874 - FRA_1) = 0.$$

Solving gives $FRA_1 = .1044$, which is interpreted as 10.44 percent per $1 of notional principal. Pricing a two-year FRA proceeds along similar lines:

$$.2704(.1347 - FRA_2) + .4992(.1017 - FRA_2) + .2304(.0696 - FRA_2) = 0.$$

---

[5]As an aid to checking yourself, consider the probability of reaching an interest rate of 11.60 percent at time 3. This node represents two up moves and one down move and can be reached three different ways: (1) up, up, down, (2) up, down, up, and (3) down, up, up. Thus, the probability is $3(.52)^2(.48) = .3894$.

Solving for FRA_2 gives .1032 percent. The exact solution is found with the following formula:

$$FRA_t(\text{in arrears}) = \sum_{i=1}^{t+1} p_i r_i,$$

where p_i is the probability of the ith outcome and r_i is the interest rate in the ith outcome. Obviously this is simply the probability-weighted average one-period rate at the FRA expiration.

For the delayed settlement FRA, a slight adjustment is needed. For the one-period FRA, if the rate goes to .12, the FRA pays off $.12 - FRA_1$ but pays it one period later. Thus, its value would be discounted by the one-period rate, which is .12. The payoff discounted from time 2 back to time 1 would be $(.12 - FRA_1)(1.12)^{-1}$. If the one-period rate goes to 8.74, the discounted payoff would be $(.0874 - FRA_1)(1.0874)^{-1}$. Thus, the FRA rate is found as

$$.52(.12 - FRA_1)(1.12)^{-1} + .48(.0874 - FRA_1)(1.0874)^{-1} = 0.$$

Solving for FRA_1 gives .1041. A two-period FRA paying off one period later than the expiration is priced as the solution to

$$.2704(.1347 - FRA_2)(1.1347)^{-1} + .4992(.1017 - FRA_2)(1.1017)^{-1}$$
$$+ .2304(.0696 - FRA_2)(1.0696)^{-1} = 0.$$

The solution is .1027. The general formula for an FRA on the one-period rate of maturity t with delayed settlement is

$$FRA_t(\text{delayed settlement}) = \frac{\displaystyle\sum_{i=1}^{t+1} p_i r_i (1 + r_i)^{-1}}{\displaystyle\sum_{i=1}^{t+1} p_i (1 + r_i)^{-1}}.$$

The remaining rates for FRAs in arrears are .102 (three years) and .1007 (four years) and for FRAs with delayed settlement are .1012 (three years) and .0998 (four years).

Pricing Interest Rate Swaps

Consider a three-period swap with payments made annually based on the one-period rate at the beginning of the period. Let the notional principal be $1. To determine the price of the swap we must solve for the fixed rate that would equate the present value of the fixed payments to the present value of the floating payments. Earlier we saw that this is a simple matter of finding the coupon on a bond that, when discounted at the spot rates for each period up to maturity, will equal the par value of the bond. This

means that in addition to the one-period rate, we would need to know the spot rates on zero coupon bonds of maturities longer than one year. In other words, we need to know the current term structure. Let us say that this information is as follows: $r(0,2) = .1043$ and $r(0,3) = .1041$, and, of course, $r(0,1) = .105$.

Now we can easily price our three-year swap. Again, this amounts to simply finding the coupon on a bond with a present value equal to par. Letting c represent the coupon rate, we have

$$c(1.105)^{-1} + c(1.1043)^{-2} + (c + 1.00)(1.1041)^{-3} = 1.00.$$

Solving for c gives .1041. For the two-year swap, the coupon would be

$$c(1.105)^{-1} + (c + 1.00)(1.1043)^{-2} = 1.00.$$

Solving for c gives .1043.[6]

Pricing Interest Rate Options

Now let us price an interest rate option expiring two years from now. Recall that although this option will expire in two years, the payoff comes three years from now. Let the option have a notional principal of $1 and, of course, be written on the one-period rate. Let the exercise rate be 9 percent and the option be a European call.

Remembering the binomial model in Chapter 4, we price the option by evaluating the discounted probability-weighted value of the option at expiration. In other words, we start at the expiration date and successively discount the probability-weighted value of the option. The values of the option at expiration are not simply the intrinsic values but must also reflect the fact that the payoffs do not occur until one period later. Thus, for example, in the upper state of time 2, where the one-period rate is .1347, the intrinsic value is $\text{Max}(0, .1347 - .09)/1.1347 = .0394$. In the middle state, the intrinsic value is $\text{Max}(0, .1017 - .09)/1.1017 = .0106$, and in the lowest state, the intrinsic value is $\text{Max}(0, .0696 - .09)/1.0696 = 0$. Obviously the discounting does not determine whether the option ends up exercised or not, but it does affect the value of the option when it is exercised. Note that in contrast to the binomial model for stocks in Chapter 4 where we discounted at a constant risk-free rate, here we discount at whatever one-period rate holds at a given time point.

---

[6]At this point you may notice the two-year spot rate being the same as the two-year swap rate and the three-year spot rate being the same as the three-year swap rate. Actually they are not the same but we would require greater precision to notice the difference. The two rates are so close because of a point we made in Chapter 8 regarding the relationship between a bond yield and the zero coupon rate for a bond of equivalent maturity. If the term structure is nearly flat, these rates will be very close.

The exact procedure is illustrated in Figure 14.7. After determining the intrinsic values at expiration at time 2, now step back to time 1 and look at the upper state where the one-period rate is .12. At this point the option will be worth the discounted (at 12 percent) probability-weighted average of .0394 and .0106, the next two possible option values, which is

$$\frac{.52(.0394) + .48(.0106)}{1.12} = .0228.$$

In the lower state at time 1, where the rate is 8.74 percent, the option will be worth the discounted (at 8.74 percent) probability-weighted average of .0106 and zero, which is

$$\frac{.52(.0106) + .48(0)}{1.0874} = .0051.$$

At time 0, the option is worth the discounted (at 10.5 percent) probability-weighted average of .0228 and .0051, which is

$$\frac{.52(.0228) + .48(.0051)}{1.105} = .0129.$$

Thus, for every dollar of notional principal, the call is worth .0129. Had the option been a put, we would have followed the same procedure but

FIGURE 14.7   Binomial Tree Pricing of Interest Rate Call Option, Exercise Rate of 9 Percent, European Style

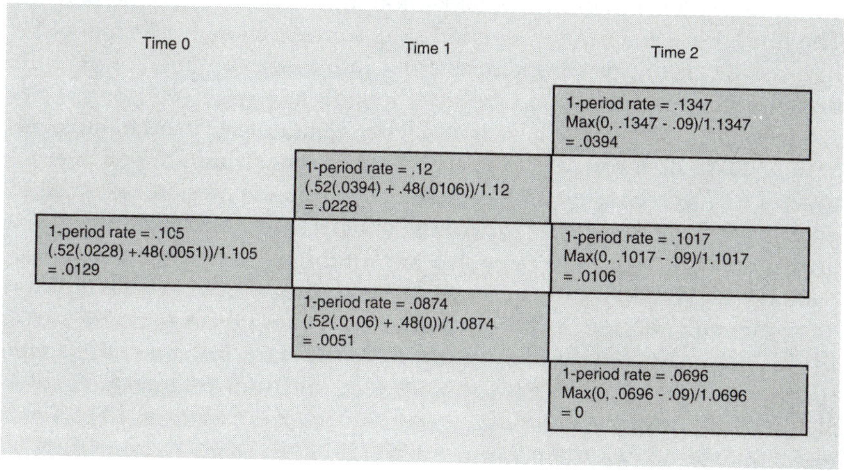

Time 0	Time 1	Time 2
		1-period rate = .1347 Max(0, .1347 - .09)/1.1347 = .0394
	1-period rate = .12 (.52(.0394) + .48(.0106))/1.12 = .0228	
1-period rate = .105 (.52(.0228) +.48(.0051))/1.105 = .0129		1-period rate = .1017 Max(0, .1017 - .09)/1.1017 = .0106
	1-period rate = .0874 (.52(.0106) + .48(0))/1.0874 = .0051	
		1-period rate = .0696 Max(0, .0696 - .09)/1.0696 = 0

the values of the option at expiration would have been zero, zero, and .0191. The resulting answer would be .0036.

To check your understanding of the process, try to determine the values of one-period puts and calls. For an exercise rate of 9 percent, the call will be worth .0126 and the put will be worth .0010. If the options were American, we would follow the same procedure we covered in Chapter 4—meaning that we insert the intrinsic values at any point where the options would be worth exercising early.

Now let us assume the options are caps. For example, consider a two-period cap with 9 percent strike consisting of caplets expiring at times 1 and 2, with payments made at times 2 and 3. We have already determined the prices of the component caplets; they are simply the prices of the one- and two-period calls, or .0126 + .0129 = .0255. A two-period floor would be worth .0010 + .0036 = .0046.

Pricing Swaptions

Recall that a swaption can be set up as either a payer swaption or a receiver swaption. A payer swaption is somewhat like an interest rate call option that when exercised allows the holder to enter into a swap as the fixed-rate payer. A receiver swaption is somewhat like an interest rate put option that when exercised allows the holder to enter into a swaption as the fixed-rate receiver. When exercised, either swaption creates an annuity of fixed payments equal to the difference between the market fixed rate and the strike rate.

The exercise of a swaption depends on whether the rate in the market on the underlying swap is above or below the strike rate. Consequently, determining if a swap is exercised is not simply a matter of looking at the one-period rate. We shall have to determine the rate on swaps for each of the possible outcomes at the swaption expiration.

Consider a two-period payer swaption with a strike rate of 10 percent. The underlying swap is a two-period swap with a notional principal of $1. In other words, this is an option to enter into a swap at time 2, where the swap will begin at time 2 and end two periods later.

Looking at the binomial tree in Figure 14.6, note the three outcomes at time 2. We shall refer to these as the upper state, where the one-period rate is 13.47 percent, the middle state, where the one-period rate is 10.17 percent, and the lower state, where the one-period rate is 6.96 percent. To price the swap, using the same approach we have used several times already, we need to know the one- and two-period spot rates in each of those three outcomes at time 2. The one-period rates are simply the rates 13.47, 10.17, and 6.96. Let us denote these rates as $r(2,3)_{uu}$, $r(2,3)_{ud}$, and $r(2,3)_{dd}$, where the subscripts identify the outcome by indicating how many times rates have gone up and down. Hence, $r(2,3)_{uu} = .1347$. Likewise, $r(2,3)_{ud} = .1017$ and $r(2,3)_{dd} = .0696$. What we need are the values of

$r(2,4)_{uu}$, $r(2,4)_{ud}$, and $r(2,4)_{dd}$. This information cannot be obtained from the information we already have in hand. Since this information is nothing more than the term structure, it would be available at time 2. Let us assume that it is $r(2,4)_{uu} = .1335$, $r(2,4)_{ud} = .1011$, and $r(2,4)_{dd} = .0691$.[7]

Now we can find the swap prices for each of the outcomes at time 2. We denote these as c_{uu}, c_{ud}, and c_{dd}, and they are the solutions to the following equations:

$$c_{uu}(1.1347)^{-1} + (c_{uu} + 1.00)(1.1335)^{-2} = 1.00$$
$$c_{ud}(1.1017)^{-1} + (c_{ud} + 1.00)(1.1011)^{-2} = 1.00$$
$$c_{dd}(1.0696)^{-1} + (c_{dd} + 1.00)(1.0691)^{-2} = 1.00.$$

For any one of the c's, the solution is found as

$$c = \frac{1 - (1 + r(2,4))^{-2}}{(1 + r(2,3))^{-1} + (1 + r(2,4))^{-2}}$$

and the answers are $c_{uu} = .1336$, $c_{ud} = .1011$, and $c_{dd} = .0691$.[8]

Now after all of that work we can begin to price the swaption. Fortunately, it is an easy task, made only slightly more involved by the fact that exercise creates an annuity. For a given outcome, the value of the swaption at expiration is simply $Max(0, c - .10)[(1 + r(0,1))^{-1} + (1 + r(0,2))^{-2}]$, where the bracketed term is simply the present value factor for a two-period annuity. Once these values of the swaption at expiration are determined, the pricing proceeds as in all of our binomial examples. Each period the probability-weighted value of the next two possible swaption prices is then discounted by the appropriate one-period rate. The process is shown in Figure 14.8. Our swaption is worth .0130.

If the swaption were a receiver swaption, then the payoff at expiration would be treated like a put, meaning that the swap rate would need to be less than the strike rate for the swaption to expire in-the-money. If the swaptions were American-style, the intrinsic value would replace the computed value in any state where the former exceeded the latter.

A forward swap would be easily priced by simply pricing the swap as if it were beginning at the forward swap expiration. This means that we would require the spot rates at the forward swap expiration, which is information we have already seen how to obtain.

Now you have seen how a binomial tree is used to price interest rate derivatives. Naturally in practice, the tree must be much larger. Also, it is

---

[7]Although these values were supplied to you, they were not chosen arbitrarily. They are consistent with the absence of arbitrage opportunities.

[8]Again, note that the swap rate would not equal the two-period rate were our calculations done with greater numerical precision.

FIGURE 14.8	**Binomial Tree Pricing of Payer Swaption, Exercise Rate of 10 Percent, European Style, Underlying Swap Has Two-Period Maturity**

Time 0	Time 1	Time 2
		$r(0,1)_{uu} = .1347$ $c_{uu} = .1336$ $Max(0, .1336 - .10)[(1.1347)^{-1} +$ $(1.1335)^{-2}] = .0558$
	$(.52(.0558) + .48(.0019))/1.12 = .0267$	
$(.52(.0267) + .48(.0009))/1.105 = .0130$		$r(0,1)_{ud} = .1011$ $c_{uu} = .1011$ $Max(0, .1011 - .10)[(1.1017)^{-1} +$ $(1.1011)^{-2}] = .0019$
	$(.52(.0019) + .48(0))/1.0874 = .0009$	
		$r(0,1)_{dd} = .0696$ $c_{ud} = .0691$ $Max(0, .0691 - .10)[(1.0696)^{-1} +$ $(1.0691)^{-2}] = 0$

important that the tree be constructed so as to best mimic movements in interest rates, meaning that the volatility of interest rates should be as close as possible to the actual volatility in the market. As we have previously noted, this is an extremely complex subject that you can study in more detail in advanced courses.

Finally, we should note that although we have used the binomial process to price only interest rate derivatives, it can also be used to price any spot or derivative security whose price is determined by the interest rates modeled in the exercise. This would include zero coupon bonds, coupon bonds, and any type of derivative on zero coupon bonds or coupon bonds.

Summary

This chapter examined interest rate derivatives, which are derivatives in which the underlying asset is an interest rate. These derivatives are constructed in the over-the-counter market and are extremely popular among corporations facing interest rate risk.

We first examined the forward rate agreement, or FRA, which is a forward contract on an interest rate. The FRA requires one party to agree to make a future

interest payment at a known rate and to receive a future interest payment at an unknown rate.

We also examined interest rate swaps, which are the most widely used derivative. An interest rate swap is a contract in which one party agrees to make a series of interest payments to the other, while the other makes a series of payments to the first party, with each set of payments at different rates. The standard type of interest rate swap, called the plain vanilla swap, involves one party making payments at a known rate, while the other makes payments at a rate to be determined in the future. Typical swaps have payments based on the rate at one time point, but the actual payment occurs later. This is similar to the way in which floating-rate securities pay interest.

We discovered that interest rate options are similar to options on stocks but the payoff is based on an interest rate. Call options pay off when the interest rate ends up above the exercise rate while put options pay off when the interest rate ends up below the exercise rate. Like swaps, interest rate options make their payoffs a period of time after expiration. When borrowers need to hedge a series of possible interest rate increases, they can combine interest rate calls with different maturities into an overall transaction called a cap. When lenders need to hedge a series of possible interest rate decreases, they can combine interest rate puts with different expirations into an overall transaction called a floor. The purchase of a cap and sale of a floor, called a collar, hedges against interest rate increases by having the user give up some of the gains from falling interest rates. This can reduce or completely eliminate the amount of cash paid up front.

We also examined options on swaps, which are called swaptions. A swaption can be either a payer swaption, which gives the right to enter into a swap as the fixed-rate payer, or a receiver swaption, which gives the right to enter into the swap as a fixed-rate receiver. Exercise of a swaption creates an annuity equal to the difference in the swap rate at expiration and the exercise rate for a period equal to the life of the underlying swap. We also looked at forward swaps, which are forward contracts to enter into swaps.

Finally, we looked at how a binomial process can be used to model the term structure of interest rates, which enables one to obtain accurate, arbitrage-free prices of FRAs, swaps, options, and swaptions.

You have now seen many of the most widely used derivatives, but there are many more products and strategies. We now move on to some advanced topics in derivatives in Chapter 15.

Key Terms

Before continuing to Chapter 15, you should be able to give brief definitions of the following terms.

- interest rate derivative
- forward rate agreement (FRA)
- interest rate swap
- plain vanilla (generic) swap
- swap price/rate
- interest rate option
- interest rate cap
- caplet
- interest rate floor
- floorlet
- interest rate collar
- zero cost collar
- swaption
- payer swaption

- receiver swaption
- forward swap

- in arrears
- delayed settlement

Questions and Problems

1.   Fixed- or floating-rate interest rate swaps can be viewed as equivalent to two other types of financial transactions. Identify these other transactions and explain why they perform the same as the swap.

2.   Compare the use of interest rate options with forward rate agreements. Explain why a financial manager might prefer one type of contract over another.

3.   If you were entering into a swap that you anticipate you might someday wish to terminate early, what features would you want to build into the agreement to give you the flexibility to terminate the swap early?

4.   How are the payment terms of an FRA in practice different from those of most interest rate derivatives?

5.   Explain how a cap is similar to an interest rate call option. How is it different?

6.   Explain how the two types of swaptions are like interest rate options and how they are different.

7.   Explain how a forward swap is different from a swaption.

8.   What is the primary advantage of pricing interest rate derivatives using a binomial term structure model?

9.   What are the advantages and disadvantages of an interest rate collar over an interest rate cap?

10.   Suppose a firm plans to borrow $5 million in 180 days. The loan will be taken out at whatever LIBOR is on the day the loan begins and will be repaid in one lump sum, 90 days later. The firm would like to lock in the rate it pays so it enters into a forward rate agreement with its bank. The bank agrees to lock in a rate of 12 percent. Determine the annualized cost of the loan for each of the following outcomes. Interest is based on 90 days and a 360-day year.
      a.   LIBOR in 180 days is 14 percent.
      b.   LIBOR in 180 days is 8 percent.

11.   Determine the schedule of payments in a swap of floating- for fixed-rate interest payments. The notional principal is $20 million. The fixed-rate payer pays 11 percent. The floating-rate payer pays LIBOR, with the rate determined on the first day of the interest period. Interest payments are based on the exact number of days, which are 90, 180, 270, and 360. The LIBORs that actually result are 10.5 (90 days from now), 10.2 (180 days from now), and 9.6 (270 days from now). The current LIBOR is 11.5.

12.   Jiffy Swaps, Inc. is a large swap dealer. It is in the process of pricing a $25 million fixed- for floating-rate swap. The swap will be for two years and will require semiannual payments. For simplicity assume that the payments are made exactly 180 days apart. The term structure of LIBOR is 12 percent for

six months, 12.25 percent for one year, 12.75 percent for 18 months, and 13.02 percent for two years. These are annual rates. First convert these rates to their effective compound equivalent rates and then verify that a swap rate of 12.967 percent is appropriate.

13. XAC Corporation is currently engaged in a three-year swap with $10 million notional principal. Payments are made every six months. XAC pays a fixed rate of 12 percent and receives a floating rate of LIBOR. The swap is now three-quarters of the way through the second year. The next floating payment will be at 10.25 percent. Determine the value of the swap to XAC and identify it as an asset or a liability. The appropriate discount rates are 9.75 percent (1/4 year), 9.875 percent (3/4 year), and 10 percent (1 1/4 years). The swap payments are calculated as if the six-month period is 180 days of a 360-day year, but do your discounting over the exact number of years.

14. Consider a three-year receiver swaption with a strike rate of 11.75 percent where the underlying swap is a four-year swap. The notional principal is $20,000,000. At expiration, the spot rates on zero coupon bonds of various maturities are: 10 percent (1 year), 10.5 percent (2 years), 10.9 percent (three years), and 11.2 percent (four years). Determine the payoff of the swaption.

15. You are the treasurer of a firm that will need to borrow $10 million at LIBOR plus 2.5 points in 45 days. The loan will have a maturity of 180 days, at which time all the interest and principal will be repaid. The interest will be determined by LIBOR on the day the loan is taken out. To hedge the uncertainty of this future rate, you purchase a call on LIBOR with a strike of 9 percent for a premium of $32,000. Determine the amount you will pay back and the annualized cost of borrowing for LIBORs of 6 percent and 12 percent. Assume the payoff is based on 180 days and a 360-day year. The current LIBOR is 9 percent.

16. A large, multinational bank has committed to lend a firm $25 million in 30 days at LIBOR plus one point. The loan will have a maturity of 90 days, at which time the principal and all interest will be repaid. The bank is concerned about falling interest rates and decides to buy a put on LIBOR with a strike of 9.5 percent and a premium of $60,000. Determine the annualized loan rate for LIBORs of 6.5 percent and 12.5 percent. Assume the payoff is based on 90 days and a 360-day year. The current LIBOR is 9.5 percent.

17. As the assistant treasurer of a large corporation, your job is to look for ways your company can lock in its cost of borrowing in the financial markets. The date is June 28. Your firm is taking out a loan of $20 million, with interest to be paid on September 28, December 31, March 31, and June 29. You will pay the LIBOR in effect at the beginning of the interest payment period. The current LIBOR is 10 percent. You recommend that the firm buy an interest rate cap with a strike of 10 percent and a premium of $70,000. Determine the cash flows over the life of this loan if LIBOR turns out to be 11 percent on September 28, 11.65 percent on December 31, and 12.04 percent on March 31. The payoff is based on the exact number of days and a 360-day year. If you have a financial calculator or a spreadsheet with an IRR function,

solve for the internal rate of return and annualize it to determine the effective cost of borrowing.

18. You are a funds manager for a large bank. On April 15, your bank lends a corporation $35 million, with interest payments to be made on July 16, October 15, January 16, and next April 16. The amount of interest will be determined by LIBOR at the beginning of the interest payment period. Your forecast is for declining interest rates, so you anticipate lower loan interest revenues. You decide to buy an interest rate floor with a strike set at 8 percent and a premium of $60,000. Determine the cash flows associated with the loan if LIBOR turns out to be 7.9 percent on July 16, 7.7 percent on October 15, and 8.1 percent next January 16. The payoff is based on the exact number of days and a 360-day year. If you have a financial calculator or spreadsheet with an IRR function, determine the internal rate of return and annualize it to determine your annualized return on the loan.

19. On January 15, a firm takes out a loan of $30 million, with interest payments to be made on April 16, July 15, October 14, and next January 15, when the principal will be repaid. Interest will be paid at LIBOR based on the rate at the beginning of the interest payment period, using the exact number of days and a 360-day year. The firm wants to buy a cap with a strike of 10 percent and a premium of $150,000. Its bank suggests that the firm sell a floor with a strike of 9 percent and a premium of $115,000. The current LIBOR is 10 percent. Answer the following questions.
    a. What is this transaction called? Why would the firm sell the floor in addition to buying the cap? What is the firm giving up if it adds the short floor to the long cap?
    b. If LIBOR turns out to be 11.35 percent on April 16, 10.2 percent on July 15, and 8.86 percent on October 14, what are the firm's cash flows associated with the loan? If you have a financial calculator or spreadsheet, determine the internal rate of return and annualize it to determine your cost of borrowing.

20. A bank is offering an interest rate call with an expiration of 45 days. The call pays off based on 180-day LIBOR. The volatility of forward rates is .17. The 45-day forward rate for 180-day LIBOR is .1322 and the exercise rate is .12. The risk-free rate for 45 days is .1128. Use the Black model to determine how much the bank should receive for selling this call for every $1 million of notional principal.

21. A firm is interested in purchasing an interest rate cap from a bank. It has received an offer price from the bank but would like to determine if the price is fair. The cap will consist of two caplets, one expiring in 91 days and the other in 182 days. They will both have strikes of 7 percent. The forward rate applicable to the first caplet is 8 percent and the forward rate applicable to the second caplet is 8.2 percent. The 91-day risk-free rate is 7.1 percent and the 182-day risk-free rate is 7.3 percent. The firm's best estimate of the volatility of forward rates is .166. The notional principal is $10 million, and the payoff is based on 90-day LIBOR. Use the Black model to determine a fair price for the cap.

22.   The one-period spot rates in a binomial tree are shown as follows:

At time 0:	6 percent
At time 1:	9.47 percent or 6.28 percent
At time 2:	12.41 percent, 9.13 percent, or 5.95 percent
At time 3:	15.68 percent, 12.31 percent, 9.04 percent, and 5.86 percent
At time 4:	16.86 percent, 13.46 percent, 10.16 percent, 6.95 percent, or 3.83 percent

The probability of an up move is .55. The zero coupon rates are 6 percent (1-year), 7 percent (2-years), 7.8 percent (3-years), and 8.6 percent (4-years). Answer the following questions.

a.   Draw a binomial tree with four time periods. At each node, insert the probability of reaching that node.

Each of the remaining questions asks you to price a derivative using the binomial tree developed in part a. In other words, each derivative is on the one-period rate. Make sure you check your answer to part a before moving on to parts b–g.

b.   Find the price of an in-arrears FRA expiring at time 2. Also find the price of a delayed settlement FRA expiring at time 2.

c.   Find the price of a three-period interest rate swap.

d.   Find the price of a European interest rate put maturing in four periods where the exercise rate is 10 percent.

e.   Find the price of a European interest rate cap with an exercise rate of 9 percent with caplets expiring at times 1, 2, and 3.

f.   Find the price of an interest rate payer swaption expiring in two periods with an exercise rate of 9 percent where the underlying is a two-period swap. The spot rates at expiration on two-year zero coupon bonds in each of the three states are 12.33 percent, 9.08 percent, and 5.79 percent.

g.   Find the price of a two-period forward swap where the underlying is a two-period swap.

23.   (Concept Problem) Use the Black model to determine a fair price for an interest rate put that expires in 74 days. The forward rate is 9.79 percent, and the exercise rate is 10 percent. The appropriate risk-free rate is 8.38 percent. The volatility of forward rates is .1465. The put is based on $22 million notional principal and pays off based on 90-day LIBOR.

24.   (Concept Problem) Using the binomial interest rate tree in problem 22, find the price of an American-style interest rate put expiring at time 4 with an exercise rate of 11 percent. (Hint: You may need to review the procedure for pricing American options on stock using the binomial model in Chapter 4.)

APPENDIX 14A
The Ho-Lee Model of the Term Structure

There are many models that capture movements of interest rates across the term structure. One of the easiest to use is the model of Ho and Lee (1986). Their model is based on a binomial process, which means that it

captures uncertainty by permitting two outcomes to be possible. The Ho-Lee model specifies the entire term structure of zero coupon bonds and allows the term structure to shift either upward or downward. The uncertainty is reflected in shock factors that affect forward rates. In other words, the Ho-Lee model captures the uncertainty in forward rates.

We begin with some notation. Let $r(t,x,y)$ be the rate observed at time t on a bond beginning at time x and maturing at time y. Suppose we start off today with a set of spot rates, $r(0,0,1)$, $r(0,0,2)$, and $r(0,0,3)$, which are the rates today on zero coupon bonds for maturities of one to three periods. Working with the spot rates $r(0,0,1)$ and $r(0,0,2)$, we can find the forward rate $r(0,1,2)$ as $r(0,1,2) = (1+r(0,0,2))^2/(1+r(0,0,1)) - 1$. The forward rate, $r(0,1,3)$, can be found as $r(0,1,3) = \sqrt{(1+r(0,0,3))^3/(1+r(0,0,1))} - 1$.

If there were no uncertainty, then the forward rates would evolve into the future spot rates. In other words, at time 1, the spot rate on one-period bonds, $r(1,1,2)$, would be the same as $r(0,1,2)$. At time 1, the spot rate on two-period bonds, $r(1,1,3)$, would be the same as $r(0,1,3)$. Ho and Lee incorporate uncertainty by permitting these spot rates to deviate from the forward rates by up and down shift factors. Bonds of different maturities have different shift factors. Thus, let us define $u(1)$ and $d(1)$ as the up and down shift factors for bonds with maturity of one year, while $u(2)$ and $d(2)$ are the shift factors for bonds with maturities of two years.

At time 1 the spot rate on a one-period bond can either shift upward,

$$r(1,1,2) = \frac{(1+r(0,0,2))^2}{1+r(0,0,1)}u(1) - 1,$$

or downward,

$$r(1,1,2) = \frac{(1+r(0,0,2))^2}{1+r(0,0,1)}d(1) - 1.$$

At time 1 the spot rate on two-period bonds can either shift upward,

$$r(1,1,3) = \sqrt{\frac{(1+r(0,0,3))^3}{1+r(0,0,1)}u(2)} - 1,$$

or downward,

$$r(1,1,3) = \sqrt{\frac{(1+r(0,0,3))^3}{1+r(0,0,1)}d(2)} - 1.$$

The values of $u(1)$, $d(1)$, $u(2)$, and $d(2)$ are determined by a complex theorem that prevents profitable arbitrage. We omit the details here, but the formulas for the u's and d's are easy to compute, given the required input variables. We need p, the probability of an up move, implying that $1 - p$ is the probability of a down move, and Λ, a factor reflecting the volatility. The values of the probabilities need not be the actual probabili-

ties and, in fact, any set of probabilities can be chosen for a given value of Λ. The value of $d(i)$, where in our example $i = 1$ or 2, is given as

$$d(i) = \frac{p + (1 - p)\Lambda^i}{\Lambda^i},$$

whereas the value of $u(i)$ is

$$u(i) = d(i)\Lambda^i.$$

Ho and Lee show that the choice of Λ is determined by the volatility of the one-period rate according to the formula

$$\sigma = \sqrt{p(1 - p)[\ln(\Lambda)]^2}.$$

In our example, we have $r(0,0,1) = .1050$, $r(0,0,2) = .1043$, and $r(0,0,3) = .1041$. We let $p = .52$ and $1 - p = .48$. We set Λ at 1.03. This gives values of u and d of $d(1) = (.52 + .48(1.03)^1)/(1.03)^1 = .9849$, $u(1) = .9849(1.03)^1 = 1.0144$, $d(2) = (.52 + .48(1.03)^2)/(1.03)^2 = .9701$, and $u(2) = .9701(1.03)^2 = 1.0292$. The arbitrary choice of $p = .52$, $1 - p = .48$, and $\Lambda = 1.03$ implies a standard deviation of the one-period rate of $\sqrt{.52(.48)[\ln(1.03)]^2} = .0148$.

With this information we can find the spot rates at time 1. The one-period spot rate at time 1 can either be

$$r(1,1,2) = \frac{(1.1043)^2}{1.105} \, 1.0144 - 1 = .1195,$$

or

$$r(1,1,2) = \frac{(1.1043)^2}{1.105} \, .9849 - 1 = .0869.$$

The rate on two-period bonds would be

$$r(1,1,3) = \sqrt{\frac{(1.1041)^3}{1.105} \, 1.0292} - 1 = .1196,$$

or

$$r(1,1,3) = \sqrt{\frac{(1.1041)^3}{1.105} \, .9701} - 1 = .0870.$$

These results give us the possible one- and two-period spot rates at time 1. From these we can obtain the implied forward rates at time 1. Applying the up and down factors to the forward rates at time 1 will allow us to extend the tree one step farther. In order to build a tree of n time steps, it is necessary at time 0 to have the spot rates for maturities up to $n + 1$.

Since most derivative contracts are written on the short-term spot rate, which here is the one-period rate, we specified a tree showing the evolution of one-period rates. This was Figure 14.6. The values shown in the tree differ slightly from those computed here because the tree calculations were done on a computer and used a greater degree of precision than we used in this appendix.

CHAPTER 15

Advanced Derivatives and Strategies

The best advice may be this: treat exotic derivatives like powerful medicines, large doses of which can be harmful. Use them in moderation, for a particular purpose (such as risk management) and only after having read the instructions on the bottle.

PHILIPPE JORION
Big Bets Gone Bad, 1995

In this chapter we examine some advanced derivatives and strategies. Though it may seem like we are taking a leap forward, this is not necessarily the case. While some of these derivatives are complex, others are fairly simple and some are constructed by combining derivatives we have already covered.

We shall begin the chapter with a group called equity derivatives. Although these types of derivatives have been written primarily on stocks and stock portfolios, some of them are also written on bonds, interest rates, currencies, and commodities. The second group of derivatives we cover will be strictly derivatives on fixed-income securities and interest rates. Here we shall take a look at some of the variations of the plain vanilla swap as well as structured notes and mortgage derivatives. The third group is called *exotic* options. This is a term used to classify the most advanced types of options. Some of them hardly seem exotic, but they are typically referred to that way.

Advanced Equity Derivatives and Strategies

An **equity derivative** is a derivative on a stock or stock index. While the over-the-counter market is much larger for interest rate derivatives, the

Chapter Objectives

- To build on our previous coverage of the basics of derivatives by examining several new derivatives and strategies, some of which are combinations of previously studied derivatives and others of which are entirely new

- To understand the strategy of portfolio insurance, see how it enables a portfolio to achieve a target minimum return, and illustrate how it can be implemented

- To examine equity forwards, collars, warrants, and equity-linked debt

- To understand and evaluate equity swaps

- To extend the Chapter 14 treatment of interest rate derivatives by examining some popular variations of interest rate swaps

- To examine structured notes so as to understand how they are constructed and to gain an appreciation for their volatility

- To understand mortgage securities, including pass-throughs, IOs, POs, and CMOs, and to gain an understanding of how their values change as interest rates change

- To examine various exotic options, including digital and chooser options, path-dependent options and miscellaneous exotic options, and to use the binomial model to price several of them

over-the-counter equity derivatives market is growing rapidly. Recall that we have already studied at great length exchange-traded equity derivatives such as options on stocks and stock indices and futures on stock indices. While these contracts meet the needs of many investors, the specialization afforded by customized over-the-counter contracts is becoming increasingly worth the cost.

For example, many investors need derivatives that match specific portfolios. Exchange-traded derivatives are based on well-known indices, such as the S&P 500. To use a derivative on the S&P 500 to hedge a position in a portfolio that does not match the index induces some basis risk. While that risk may be acceptable for some investors, others would prefer to avoid it by using derivatives customized to their particular holdings. Such derivatives, called **baskets,** can be constructed by simply showing a derivatives dealer the composition of the portfolio. The dealer then constructs a derivative based on that specific portfolio.

Equity derivatives are especially useful in international investing. Equity derivatives on international stocks or indices allow an investor to capture the gains from investing in foreign securities without actually having to incur the additional transaction cost of acquiring those securities directly. In addition there are often costly foreign regulations to deal with and many countries impose a dividend withholding tax, which requires that some of the dividends be left in the foreign country to cover any future tax liabilities. Equity derivatives are often structured to pay off both capital gains and dividends, but since no money leaves the country, the dividend withholding tax is avoided. While investing directly in foreign securities imposes exchange rate risk, many equity derivatives are structured with a fixed exchange rate, thereby avoiding that risk.

Equity derivatives also permit fast, low-cost realignment of domestic portfolios. For example, an investor holding primarily large cap stocks and wanting to increase the allocation to small cap stocks can do so using derivatives on those two groups of stocks. This is much like our description of adjusting the risk of an equity portfolio in Chapters 10 and 11.

Naturally these features come at a cost that is incurred by the dealer and passed on to the end user. Fortunately the large size and sophisticated operations of most dealers result in efficiency and low costs, which benefit the end user.

While the emphasis in this chapter is on over-the-counter contracts and strategies, we begin with an exchange-listed derivative strategy, portfolio insurance.

Portfolio Insurance

The concept of insurance has been around for hundreds of years. Individuals and business firms routinely insure their lives and property against risk of loss. The concept extends easily to portfolios. In fact, we touched on the subject in Chapter 5 when we covered protective puts.

Suppose we own a portfolio consisting of N_S shares of stock and N_P puts. The stock price is S, and the put price is P. The puts are European, and we assume no dividends on the stock. The value of the portfolio is

$$V = N_S S + N_P P.$$

Letting $N_S = N_P$ and calling this N, we have

$$N = \frac{V}{S + P}.$$

This tells us how many shares of stock and how many puts we can buy. At expiration the portfolio's value is

$$
\begin{aligned}
V_T &= NS_T & \text{if } S_T > E \\
V_T &= NS_T + N(E - S_T) = NE & \text{if } S_T \le E,
\end{aligned}
$$

where S_T is the stock price when the put expires.

The worst possible outcome is that in which $S_T = 0$. Suppose we define V_{min} as the minimum value of V_T, which occurs when $S_T = 0$. Then $V_{min} = NE$ and, since N must also equal $V/(S + P)$,

$$V_{min} = \frac{EV}{S + P}.$$

This establishes the minimum value of the portfolio at expiration.

Let us illustrate how this works. Suppose that on September 26 the market index is at 445.75 and the December 485 put option on the index is priced at \$38.57. The option expires on December 19, which is 84 days away, so the time to expiration is $84/365 = .2301$. The risk-free rate is 3.04 percent, stated as a simple annual rate or 2.99 percent continuously compounded. The standard deviation is .155.

Suppose we hold a diversified portfolio of stocks that replicates the index. The portfolio is worth \$44,575,000, which is equivalent to 100,000 units of the index. In other words we hold a portfolio that is weighted exactly like the index and is worth 100,000 times the index level.

The minimum level of the portfolio is

$$V_{min} = \frac{EV}{S + P} = \frac{(485)(44,575,000)}{445.75 + 38.57} = 44,637,585.$$

Thus, the minimum level at which we can insure the portfolio is \$44,637,585. This means that if we own N shares and N puts, where

$$N = \frac{V}{S + P} = \frac{44,575,000}{445.75 + 38.57} = 92,036,$$

the minimum value of the portfolio on December 19 is \$44,637,585. This is a guaranteed return of .0014 for 84 days, or $(1.0014)^{(365/84)} - 1 = .0061$ per year. This figure must be below the risk-free rate or an arbitrage opportunity would be possible. After all, how could we guarantee a minimum return on a risky portfolio greater than the risk-free rate?

We buy 92,036 shares and 92,036 puts. Suppose that at expiration the index is at 510:

An appropriate combination of stock and puts establishes an insured portfolio.

$$
\begin{aligned}
\text{Value of stock} &= 92{,}036(\$510) = \$46{,}938{,}360 \\
+ \text{Value of puts} &= 92{,}036(\$0) \quad\; = \underline{\hspace{1.2cm} 0} \\
\text{Total} &\qquad\qquad\;\; = \$46{,}938{,}360.
\end{aligned}
$$

This exceeds the minimum value.

If at expiration the index is at 450,

$$\text{Value of stock} = 92{,}036(\$485) = \$44{,}637{,}460 \text{ (by exercising the puts).}$$

While this amount appears to be slightly below the minimum, it is actually the same due to rounding off some of the previously computed values. The error is less than 1/1,000th of 1 percent.

Figure 15.1 shows the value of the insured stock-put portfolio when the put expires. The exact minimum cannot be read from the graph but is mathematically equal to \$44,637,585. The graph should look familiar. It is essentially the same as that of the protective put covered in Chapter 5. In this example, however, we are looking only at the value of the investor's position at expiration and not at the profit. The dotted line shows the value of the portfolio if it were uninsured.

Like any form of insurance, **portfolio insurance** entails a cost. By *cost* we do not necessarily mean commissions, bid-ask spreads, and so on. These certainly are important, but the cost of portfolio insurance is the difference in the return of the insured portfolio and the return of the uninsured portfolio when the market goes up. In other words, it is the return that is given up in bull markets, in which the insurance was not needed. This cost varies with the uninsured value of the portfolio. When the index ended up at 510, the insured portfolio was worth \$46,938,360. Had the portfolio not been insured, it would have consisted of 100,000 shares valued at \$510 each for a total value of \$51,000,000. The cost thus is \$4,061,640, or about 9.1 percent of the portfolio's original value. The difference between 100 percent and the cost of 9.1 percent, or 90.9 percent, is called the **upside capture.** It is the percentage of the uninsured return in a bull market that is earned by the insured portfolio. At low values of the portfolio, the cost of the insurance can be negative, which means that the insurance paid off more than it cost.

Because of put-call parity, an identical result is obtained with calls and Treasury bills, a strategy referred to as a **fiduciary call.** Let B be the price

FIGURE 15.1   **Insured Portfolio: Stock-Put**

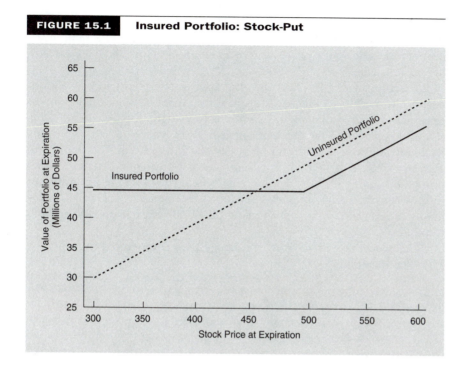

of a Treasury bill and B_T be its face value when it matures. Suppose we own a portfolio of N_C calls and N_B Treasury bills. At expiration, the portfolio will be worth $V_T = N_B B_T$ if $S_T < E$ and $N_C(S_T - E) + N_B B_T$ if $S_T \geq E$. Again, the worst case is S_T going to zero. Call that result V_{min}, which will be the value of the Treasury bills at maturity, i.e., $V_{min} = N_B B_T$. Thus,

$$N_B = \frac{V_{min}}{B_T}.$$

If we buy N_B Treasury bills, we can buy $N_C = (V - N_B B)/C$ calls. The number of calls can be shown to equal the number of shares and puts from the stock-put example. Thus, we also have

$$N_C = \frac{V}{S + P}.$$

Continuing with our numerical example, the call is worth \$2.65 and the bills have a face value of \$100. Thus, we would want \$44,637,585/\$100 = 446,376 Treasury bills and 92,036 calls. At expiration if the index is at 510, the calls will expire \$25 in the money. With 92,036 calls worth \$25 and 446,376 T-bills worth \$100 each, the total portfolio value is \$46,938,500. If

An appropriate combination of calls and Treasury bills establishes an insured portfolio.

the index goes to 450, there will be 92,036 worthless calls and 446,376 T-bills worth $100 each for a total of $44,637,600, which is the same minimum in the stock-put case, subject to a round-off error. The example is illustrated in Figure 15.2.

A European put (or call) with the appropriate terms and conditions would obviously be a means of insuring a portfolio. While such options generally are not available on the options exchanges, it is possible to replicate the behavior of the stock-put or call–T-bill insured portfolio by continuously adjusting a portfolio of stocks and index futures or stocks and Treasury bills. This technique is referred to as **dynamic hedging.** When using stock index futures, dynamic hedging involves selling a number of futures contracts such that the portfolio responds to stock price movements the same way the stock-put or call–T-bill insured portfolio would respond.

The procedure for deriving the hedge ratio is presented in Appendix 15A. The formula is

$$N_f = \left[\left(\frac{V_{min}}{E} \right) N(d_1) - \left(\frac{V}{S} \right) \right] e^{-r_c T}.$$

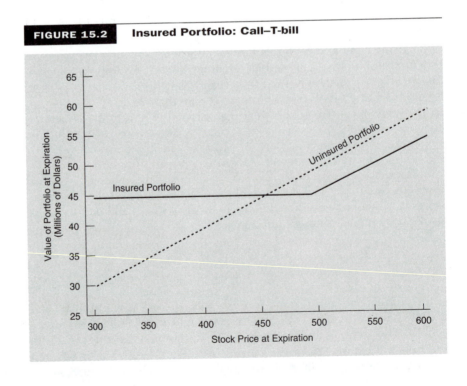

FIGURE 15.2   Insured Portfolio: Call–T-bill

This gives the number of futures contracts. Since most futures contracts have a multiplier, this number should be divided by the multiplier. For example, if using the S&P 500 futures, the contract size is actually 500 times the quoted price. The above formula should then be divided by 500. Since futures require no outlay, the hedger can put all the funds in stock. The hedger must be sure to continuously adjust the number of futures contracts so that it always equals the value of N_f. Since the delta and T will change, this will necessitate frequent revisions.

An alternative approach to the use of futures in dynamic hedging is the use of Treasury bills. It is possible to combine stock and Treasury bills so that the portfolio behaves like the protective put or fiduciary call. The key assumption behind this result is that the Treasury bill price changes only as a result of time. It is not directly influenced by the stock price. This is a fairly reasonable assumption since the long-run correlation between stock returns and Treasury bill returns is nearly zero. Appendix 15A presents the derivation of the appropriate combination of stocks and Treasury bills. The number of Treasury bills is

$$N_B = \frac{V - N_S S}{B}.$$

The number of shares of stock is

$$N_S = \left(\frac{V_{min}}{E}\right) N(d_1).$$

As with the use of futures, these values will change continuously.

Both of these approaches work by equating the deltas of the dynamically hedged portfolios to the delta of the hypothetical portfolio of stock and puts. For example, for the December 485 call, the delta is .1574. This means that the put delta is $.1574 - 1 = -.8426$. A combination of one unit of stock and one put would have a delta of 1 (the stock's delta) plus $-.8426$ (the put's delta), which equals .1574, the call's delta. When using stock index futures for dynamic hedging, the combination of all $44,575,000 in stock along with N_f futures has a delta of .1574, the same delta as would have been obtained if the hedger had owned 92,036 shares and 92,036 puts. When using the combination of stock and Treasury bills, the combination of N_S shares and N_B Treasury bills also has a delta of .1574.

Table 15.1 illustrates the appropriate calculations using stock and futures in a dynamic hedge, stock and T-bills in a dynamic hedge, and the exact hedge that would result if the necessary puts were available.[1] The lower panel

Dynamic hedging is the use of stock and either stock index futures or Treasury bills to achieve portfolio insurance by setting the delta of the stock-futures or stock–T-bill combination to the delta of a combination of stock and puts.

---

[1]The old and new put and futures prices were calculated using the Black-Scholes model, as covered in Chapter 4, and the cost of carry model with continuous compounding, as covered in Chapter 9.

TABLE 15.1	Dynamic Hedge Portfolio Insurance

Basic Information		*Contract Characteristics*	
Current day	September 26	Futures price	448.83
Horizon day	December 19	Futures delta	1.0069
Time to horizon	.2301	Futures multiplier	500
Stock price	445.75	Exercise price	485
Number of shares held	100,000	Put price	38.57
Market value of portfolio	$44,575,000	Call price	2.65
Risk-free rate	2.99%	Call delta	.1574
Volatility of stock	.155	Put delta	−.8426
Price of Treasury bill	99.31		

Minimum portfolio value (V_{min}) $44,637,585

Dynamic Hedge with Futures
Number of contracts needed:

$$N_f = \left[\left(\frac{44,637,585}{485} \right)(.1574) - \left(\frac{44,575,000}{445.75} \right) \right] e^{-(.0299)(.2301)} / 500 \approx -170.$$

Dynamic Hedge with Treasury Bills
Number of shares held:

$$N_S = \left(\frac{44,637,585}{485} \right)(.1574) \approx 14,486.$$

Number of bills needed:

$$N_B = \frac{44,575,000 - 14,486(445.75)}{99.31} \approx 383,827.$$

Effects of a $1 decrease in the stock price

New derivative prices:		
Put	$ 39.42	
Futures	447.82	
Stock plus put:		
Gain on stock	−$92,036	(92,036 shares × −$1)
Gain on put	78,230	(92,036 puts × ($39.42 − $38.57))
Net gain	−$13,806	(0.03% of value of portfolio)
Stock plus futures dynamic hedge:		
Gain on stock	−$100,000	(100,000 shares × −$1)
Gain on futures	85,850	(−170 contracts × (447.82 − 448.83) × 500)
Net gain	−14,150	
Stock plus Treasury bill dynamic hedge:		
Gain on stock	−$14,486	(14,486 shares × −$1)
Gain on T-bills	0	(bill price does not change due to stock price change)
Net gain	−14,486	

shows that the differences in the three methods are very small. These differences can be explained by a combination of round-off error and the fact that a strategy equating deltas is only approximately correct if there is a non-infinitesimal change in the stock price, a point we covered in Chapter 4 and reexamine in Chapter 16. Moreover, dynamic hedging, or any delta-matching strategy, will require that the hedge ratio be adjusted continuously, which obviously cannot be done in the presence of transaction costs.

Portfolio insurance was a widely used strategy in the mid-1980s. Its efficacy depends on the stock market having only small price changes within a short time interval. During the stock market crash of October 1987, however, stock prices experienced enormous jumps over short time intervals. While portfolios that were insured did better than those that were not, they failed to achieve their targets. The massive volume of selling done by portfolio insurers adjusting their hedge ratios was, probably wrongly, blamed for exacerbating the crash. Investors then became disillusioned with portfolio insurance. In response, however, it was not too long afterward that many new, customized equity products began to appear.

Equity Forwards

An **equity forward** contract is simply a forward contract on a stock or portfolio. The principles are the same as those we studied previously in Chapter 9. An investor buying an equity forward simply enters into a contract with a counterparty, the seller, in which the buyer agrees to buy the stock or portfolio from the seller at a future date at a price agreed upon today. In many cases, the equity instrument is a stock index or a basket of stocks. Rather than have the seller deliver stock to the buyer at expiration, the contract frequently specifies that it will be cash settled.

The price agreed upon by the two parties, called the forward price, was covered in Chapter 9. Recall that the price of a forward (or futures) contract on a stock is the current stock price, compounded at the risk-free rate minus the compound future value of the dividends. Since we have covered pricing at great length, we shall not repeat it here, but it may be useful for the reader to review the relevant parts of Chapter 9.

An interesting variation of a forward contract is the break forward. A **break forward** is a combination of spot and derivative positions that replicates the outcome of an ordinary call with one exception—the positions are structured such that the overall position costs nothing up front. This is like a zero-cost call, except that it would be impossible to have an instrument that costs nothing up front and returns either zero or a positive amount, like an ordinary call. The break forward achieves this result by penalizing the investor if the option ends up out-of-the-money. An ordinary call pays off $Max(0, S_T - E)$. A break forward is a call that pays off if it expires in-the-money and incurs a charge if it expires out-of-the-money. However, even the in-the-money payoff can be negative.

An equity forward is simply a forward contract on a stock or stock index. It is an agreement for one party to buy the stock or stock index from another party at a fixed price. It is usually settled in cash.

To illustrate the break forward and to keep the explanation simple, we assume no dividends on the stock. A break forward will pay off $S_T - K$ if $S_T > F$ and $F - K$ if $S_T \leq F$. The value K is the sum of the compound future value of an ordinary call on the stock with exercise price F plus the compound future value of the stock. The latter term, you know, is the forward price. Thus, K will exceed F so when $S_T \leq F$, the payoff, $F - K$, is definitely negative. It is also possible that $S_T - K$ can be negative.

A break forward is similar to an ordinary call in that it has a limited loss and unlimited gain; however, it requires no premium up front. Unlike an ordinary call, its value at expiration can be negative.

A break forward contract is identical to an ordinary long call with an exercise price of F and a loan in which the investor receives the present value of K – F and promises to pay back K – F. Table 15.2 illustrates this result. Recall from Chapters 2–6 that we examined some results for Digital Equipment options. We shall use the same Digital Equipment options for many of the examples in this chapter.[2] The value of the break forward at expiration is illustrated in Figure 15.3.

The example is based on a stock price of 164, a time to expiration of .0959 (35 days/365), a risk-free rate of 5.21 percent continuously compounded, a volatility of .29, and 100 units of the break forward. The forward price of Digital Equipment is $164e^{.0521(.0959)} = 164.82$. This value is the exercise price of the break forward. As noted above, the break forward is equivalent to a loan and a call with exercise price of F so we need the price of a call expiring in 35 days with an exercise price of 164.82. Using the Black-Scholes model, that call price would be 5.878. Next we need to know the value of K. This will equal the forward price plus the compound future value of the call price. This is $164.82 + 5.878e^{.0521(.0959)} = 170.73$. Thus, the break forward will be worth $164.82 - 170.73 = -5.91$ if $S_T \leq 164.82$ and $S_T - 170.73$ if $S_T > 164.82$. In the figure all values are multiplied by $100.

TABLE 15.2   **Payoffs from Break Forward**

Instrument	Current Value	Payoffs from Portfolio Given Stock Price at Expiration	
		$S_T \leq F$	$S_T > F$
Long Call	$C(S,T,F)$	0	$S_T - F$
Loan	$-(K-F)e^{-r_cT}$	$-(K-F)$	$-(K-F)$
	0	$F - K$	$S_T - K$

---

[2]In practice, many of these types of contracts are based on the S&P 500 or a specific portfolio. We use the Digital Equipment examples for convenience and because you should by now be quite familiar with these options.

FIGURE 15.3   **Break Forward**

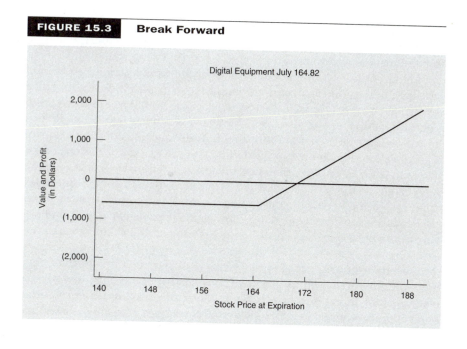

Digital Equipment July 164.82

Since the up-front cost is zero, the value at expiration is also the profit. While this figure looks exactly like a call, it is important to remember that a break forward incurs a payment if it expires out-of-the-money. This is the penalty for having to pay nothing for it up front.

It should be apparent that a break forward is similar to a forward contract and a call option. Like a forward contract, it requires no initial outlay but can have negative value at expiration. Like a call, it has a limited loss. Due to the parity relationships that exist between puts, calls, and forwards, a break forward can also be constructed by entering into a long forward contract at the price F, borrowing the present value of K – F, and buying a put with an exercise price of F. It should also be obvious that there is no reason why break forwards cannot be constructed on interest rates, bonds, commodities, or currencies.

Equity Swaps

In Chapter 14, we examined interest rate swaps. In this chapter we shall examine the **equity swap.** Other than the manner in which the payoffs are calculated, the underlying principles are the same. In equity swaps one counterparty pays according to the performance of a stock index. A typical equity swap would involve one side paying interest according to LIBOR while the other side makes a payment based on the return on the S&P 500 times the notional principal. Such a transaction results in an investor

An equity swap is a transaction in which at least one party agrees to make payments calculated as the return on an equity index times a notional principal. The other party's payments can be calculated by any other agreeable formula.

buying the return on the S&P 500 at a cost of the Eurodollar rate. This can be a useful device for converting interest payments or bond returns to stock returns or vice versa.

Let us consider a simple equity swap of the type described above. On January 2 a portfolio manager enters into a swap with a dealer in which the manager agrees to pay LIBOR and receive the S&P 500 plus a spread. The S&P 500 return is based on Standard & Poor's 500 Total Return Index. This is a slight variation of the S&P 500 and includes the effect of both capital appreciation and dividends. The calculation of the return for this swap is made on the payment date and is based on the exact percentage change in the index since the last payment date. This will be (stock value on payment date − stock value on previous payment date)/stock value on previous payment date. The notional principal is $10 million. Payments will be made on April 2, July 2, October 2, and January 2 of the following year.

An interesting aspect of equity swaps is the fact that it is possible that the equity payment will be negative. In that case, payment must still be made but the direction reverses. Thus, when the stock index goes down, one counterparty receives LIBOR and also receives a payment based on the S&P 500 negative return.

For purposes of this example, let us assume the swap spread is −.10 percent, which is stated as an annualized figure; its quarterly value is −.10 times (days in quarter/360). This means that the net payment will be the return on the S&P 500 minus .10 percent minus the LIBOR payment. Table 15.3 presents a set of after-the-fact payments, based on an assumed series of LIBORs and S&P 500 index values.

The first payment is made on April 2. LIBOR on January 2 was 9 percent. There are 90 days between January 2 and April 2. The first LIBOR payment is, therefore,

$$\$10,000,000(.09)\left(\frac{90}{360}\right) = \$225,000.$$

The S&P 500 was at 662.14 on January 2 and 675.39 on April 2. The first S&P 500 payment will be the return on the S&P 500 times the notional principal:

$$\$10,000,000\left(\frac{675.39 - 662.14}{662.14}\right) = \$200,109.$$

The spread payment of −.1 percent is computed as an interest payment:

$$\$10,000,000(-.0010)\left(\frac{90}{360}\right) = -\$2,500.$$

Thus, the portfolio manager owes $225,000 and is due $200,109 − $2,500 for a net of −$27,391. So the manager pays the swap dealer $27,391.

TABLE 15.3   **After-the-Fact Payments in Equity Swap with LIBOR**

Notional principal: $10,000,000
Swap spread: −.10 percent
Interest and spread based on exact day count and 360-day year
Pay LIBOR, receive S&P 500 Total Return + swap spread

Date	Days	LIBOR (%)	LIBOR Payment	S&P 500 Total Return Index	S&P 500 Total Return (%)	S&P 500 Payment	Spread Payment	Net Payment
1/2		9.00		662.14				
4/2	90	9.15	$225,000	675.39	2.00	$200,109	−$2,500	−$ 27,391
7/2	91	9.35	$231,292	715.24	5.90	590,029	−$2,528	356,210
10/2	92	8.65	$238,944	693.08	−3.10	−309,826	−$2,556	−551,326
1/2	92		$221,056	703.51	1.50	150,488	−$2,556	−73,124

Note: This is but one of an infinite number of possible outcomes to the swap. It is used only to illustrate how the payments are determined and not their likely amounts.

On the next payment date, the manager is owed more than he owes so he receives $356,210. Note, however, that from July 2 to October 2, the S&P 500 went down, so the manager not only owes the LIBOR payment of $238,944 and the spread payment of $2,556 but also *owes* an S&P 500 payment of $309,826 for a net outflow of $551,326.

In spite of the fact that the overall outcome did not turn out well for the manager, the important point is that the manager was able to obtain the S&P 500 total return on a constant investment of $10 million at a cost of LIBOR plus 10 basis points. This is equivalent to one of two possible alternative transactions. If the manager had held a floating rate note paying LIBOR minus 10 basis points, he could have sold that security and used the proceeds to invest in the S&P 500 Total Return portfolio. This would have produced the same outcome. Alternatively, the swap is equivalent to having borrowed at LIBOR plus 10 basis points and using the proceeds to invest in the S&P 500 Total Return portfolio.

There are a couple of slight differences, however, in the actual transactions and the equity swap. In an actual transaction involving S&P 500 stock, the voting rights in the stock would have been acquired. Also, an actual investment in the S&P 500 stock would have earned a return based on a variable notional principal. For example, $10,000,000 invested in the S&P 500 on January 2 would have grown to $10,200,109 on April 2. Then $10,200,109 invested in the S&P 500 on April 2 would have grown to $10,801,945 on July 2, based on the return of 5.9 percent from April 2 to July 2. This is a dollar capital gain of $601,836, which is slightly more than the $590,029 in the swap. The discrepancy results from having the swap

payoff based on a constant notional principal rather than one that changes with movements in the index. This is a simple item to correct, however. The swap could have been structured to pay off based on a notional principal that varies with the index. Many equity swaps are set up that way. If the swap is set up with a fixed notional principal, the transaction is equivalent to a portfolio manager selling floating rate notes or borrowing at LIBOR plus the spread and using the proceeds to invest in the S&P 500 but rebalancing the portfolio by liquidating all gains and replenishing all losses on the equity side of the transaction.

Another interesting and useful application of an equity swap is in international investing. Table 15.4 shows an example in which a U.S. portfolio manager uses an equity swap to convert S&P 500 returns into returns on a French stock market index, the CAC-40. In this $25 million notional principal swap, the manager agrees to pay the S&P 500 Total Return and agrees to receive the return on the CAC-40 plus a spread of .7 percent. The swap is arranged on February 16 and payments will be made on May 17, August 17, November 15, and the next February 15. We shall again use a constant notional principal.

On May 17, the first settlement is made with the S&P 500 having risen from 669.57 to 679.54 and the CAC-40 having fallen from 2229.79 to 2179.40. The first S&P 500 payment is

$$\$25{,}000{,}000\left(\frac{679.54 - 669.57}{669.57}\right) = \$372{,}254,$$

TABLE 15.4	**After-the-Fact Payments in S&P 500/CAC-40 Swap**

Notional principal: $25,000,000
Swap spread: +.70 percent
Interest and spread based on exact day count and 360-day year
Pay S&P 500 return, receive CAC-40 return + swap spread

Date	Days	S&P 500 Total Return Index	S&P 500 Total Return (%)	S&P 500 Payment	CAC-40 Total Return Index	CAC-40 Total Return (%)	CAC-40 Payment	Spread Payment	Net Payment
2/16		669.57			2229.79				
5/17	90	679.54	1.49	$372,254	2179.40	−2.26	−$ 564,963	$43,750	−$ 893,467
8/17	92	699.23	2.90	724,387	2536.24	16.37	4,093,328	44,722	3,413,663
11/15	90	715.62	2.34	586,002	2514.41	−0.86	−215,181	43,750	−757,433
2/15	92	729.15	1.89	472,667	2680.70	6.61	1,653,370	44,722	1,225,425

Note: This is but one of an infinite number of possible outcomes to the swap. It is used only to illustrate how the payments are determined and not their likely amounts.

and the first CAC-40 payment is

$$\$25,000,000\left(\frac{2179.40 - 2229.79}{2229.79}\right) = -\$564,963.$$

The swap spread payment is

$$\$25,000,000(.0070)\left(\frac{90}{360}\right) = \$43,750.$$

The net payment is, therefore, an outflow of $\$564,963 + \$372,254 - \$43,750 = \$893,467$.

The swap easily accomplishes the equivalent of converting $10 million invested in the S&P 500 into $10 million invested in the CAC-40. Moreover, it does so without exchange rate risk, which is borne and probably hedged by the swap dealer, with the costs being passed on in the form of the bid-ask spread.

In these two examples we have illustrated an equity index swapped against LIBOR and one equity index swapped against another. It is also possible to swap an equity index against a fixed rate or against the return on any asset of equivalent value. Remember that a swap has a zero present value at the start. Thus, there is no reason why $10 million of stock could not be swapped against $10 million of oil, Japanese yen, corporate bonds, or any other asset. Naturally a dealer will incur some costs and will deduct those costs against the return paid to one side of the transaction.

Equity swaps are also commonly used by investment managers to convert returns from one asset class to those of another. Suppose a pension fund has its money allocated as 60 percent U.S. stocks, 30 percent foreign stocks, and 10 percent U.S. corporate bonds. It would like to change the allocation to 60-20-20. Instead of selling off foreign stock and investing in corporate bonds, it can execute a swap to pay the rate on a foreign stock index and receive the rate on an index of domestic corporate bonds. This transaction will almost surely incur a lower cost than the actual sale and purchase of the securities.

Equity Collars

In Chapter 14 we examined interest rate collars. Recall that these involve the purchase of a cap and sale of a floor. This establishes minimum and maximum rates on a floating-rate loan. In recent years, the **equity collar** has also become popular. It consists of a position in a stock or portfolio, a long put on the stock or portfolio at one exercise price, and a short call at a higher exercise price. As with interest rate collars, sometimes the exercise prices are set such that the call and put premiums offset so the collar has no cost up front. This transaction is sometimes called a **risk reversal.** Sometimes the transaction involves the borrowing of the present value of F dollars, where F is the forward price of the stock. This combination of

An equity collar, also called a risk reversal or range forward, is the use of a long put and short call along with a position in the stock. It establishes a minimum and maximum terminal value for the stock. It can be structured so that the put and call premiums offset so that it would have no up-front cost.

holding the stock and borrowing F dollars is equivalent to a forward contract, which could be used instead of buying the stock. This gives rise to another name for this transaction, the **range forward,** which describes the fact that it is a forward contract with a range of possible final values.

Table 15.5 illustrates how the equity collar works. We see the payoff from a long put with exercise price of E_1, a short call with exercise price of E_2, and a long position in the stock. Since the exercise prices are not specified here, we cannot say for certain that the put and call prices offset. However, we can easily see that the minimum value at expiration is E_1 and the maximum value is E_2. Figure 15.4 illustrates the strategy with Digital Equipment. The lower exercise price is 160. The value of the put with a 160 exercise price is 3.875. To obtain a call value of 3.875, we would require an exercise price of 169.60.[3] For exchange-traded options, only exercise prices of 160, 165, and 170 are available. This is why a zero-cost collar almost always has to be constructed with over-the-counter options.

Figure 15.4 illustrates the profit from the transaction for a range of stock prices at expiration. All values have been multiplied by $100. The equity collar is the solid line. The profit from a stock-only position is shown as a dashed line. The worst outcome occurs if the stock price ends up below 160, in which case the profit is 160 (E_1) − 164 (the cost of the stock), which is a $4 per share loss. The best outcome occurs when the stock ends up above 169.60, where the profit is 169.60 (E_2) − 164 (the cost of the stock), which is $5.60 per share. Between 160 and 169.60, the profit is the ending stock price minus 164. An equity collar caps the maximum profit and maximum loss. The holder of a stock could, therefore, at no

TABLE 15.5	**Payoffs from Equity Collar (Risk Reversal/Range Forward)**			
		Payoffs from Portfolio Given Stock Price at Expiration		
Payoff from	**Current Value**	$S_T < E_1$	$E_1 \leq S_T \leq E_2$	$S_T > E_2$
Long put	$P(S,T,E_1)$	$E_1 - S_T$	0	0
Short call	$-C(S,T,E_2)$	0	0	$-(S_T - E_2)$
Long stock	S	$\dfrac{S_T}{E_1}$	$\dfrac{S_T}{S_T}$	$\dfrac{S_T}{E_2}$

[3]The only way to determine that a call with an exercise price of 169.60 is needed is to plug exercise prices into the Black-Scholes model until you find the one that produces a call price of 3.875. Like solving for the implied volatility, this is a trial-and-error process.

FIGURE 15.4   **Equity Collar/Risk Reversal/Range Forward**

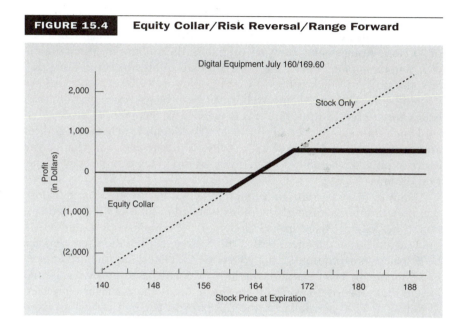

additional up-front cost, impose a maximum and minimum effective stock price. Of course, the put and call prices do not have to offset.

Had we bought a call at the exercise price of E_1 instead of buying the put, and shorted the stock, which would eliminate the long position in the stock, we would have a vertical spread that would pay off like the equity collar. Recall from Chapter 6 that we studied vertical spreads. Note the similarity between this figure and Figure 6.1. Though the exercise prices are different, the strategies are essentially the same. This result holds because of put-call parity.

Equity Warrants

Warrants have been around much longer than exchange-listed options. A warrant is an option written by a firm on its own stock. They are usually offered with a bond issue. Anyone purchasing the bond receives one or more warrants, which give the bondholders the right to buy the stock later. The original life of a warrant is usually 3–10 years. Warrants can be priced similarly to ordinary options except that their exercise dilutes the value of the stock and this must be taken into account. Many warrants trade on stock exchanges.

The warrants that we examine here, however, are not issued by the firm. They are written by one institution, offered for sale to the public, and are typically based on a stock index. The American Stock Exchange

has many of these warrants listed for trading. For example, Hong Kong 30 Index warrants are call and put options based on a value-weighted index of 30 Hong Kong stocks. They pay off half of the amount by which the option is in-the-money. The Hong Kong Index is quoted in Hong Kong dollars, the price of which is fixed in U.S. dollars at $7.729. The options are written by the U.S. firm Paine Webber and can be exercised early. Similar issues are offered by the U.S. firms Bear Stearns, Salomon Brothers, Merrill Lynch, Morgan Stanley, and others. The Merrill Lynch warrants offer an unusual feature: Under some conditions the investor can change the exercise price to the daily average value of the index over a specified period of time.

Many of these warrants on foreign indices offer the interesting feature that even though the underlying index is stated in units of the foreign currency, the payoff is fixed in U.S. dollars. For example, suppose there is a call warrant on the Japanese index, the Nikkei 225. Let the exercise price be ¥19,000. At expiration let the Nikkei be ¥19,950. Thus, the call expires in-the-money by ¥950. Because the index value is based on prices quoted in yen, the call ends up worth ¥950. This figure is automatically converted to dollars at ¥100 per dollar so the call pays off $9.50. This type of fixed exchange rate derivative is called a **quanto.** Quantos are particularly attractive because they permit investors to earn returns in foreign markets without exchange rate risk.[4]

An equity warrant is a long-term option written by an institution with a payoff tied to the performance of a stock or stock index.

Equity-Linked Debt

Equity-linked debt is a combination of a call option and a bond that guarantees a return of principal and either no interest, a small amount of interest, or a guarantee of returning a given fraction of the principal. In addition, it provides an extra payment based on how a stock or stock index performed. Instruments of this sort were first offered in 1987 in the form of certificates of deposit and were available to the general public. These original market-indexed CDs did not prove to be very popular, and they were abandoned. In the last few years they have resurfaced with some alterations.

Suppose a bank or investment banking firm makes the following offer: Purchase a one-year zero coupon bond paying 2 percent interest and receive 50 percent of any upside gain on the S&P 500. Each unit is sold with a principal amount of $10. Currently a one-year zero coupon bond without the S&P feature would pay 5 percent compounded annually. The S&P 500 is at 750, its standard deviation is .11, and its dividend yield is 2.8 percent. Is this a good deal?

---

[4]The equity swap we studied with the S&P 500 swapped against the CAC-40 is also a quanto because the CAC-40 return is applied directly to the dollar amount of notional principal.

If you invest $10, you are guaranteed to receive $10(1.02) = $10.20. Since the opportunity cost is 5 percent, the present value of this amount is $10.20/1.05 = $9.71. This means that you are implicitly paying $10.00 – $9.71 = $0.29 for 50 percent of the S&P 500 upside gain. Obviously the upside gain feature is like a call option. We can easily determine its value.

Since the option payoff cannot be earned early, it is a European call and the Black-Scholes model applies with a slight twist. The payoff is $10(.5)\text{Max}(0, (S_T - 750)/750)$ where S_T is the S&P 500 at expiration. This can be written as $(5/750)\text{Max}(0, S_T - 750)$, making it equivalent to 5/750th of an at-the-money call. The option value will, therefore, be 5/750th of the Black-Scholes value. The inputs to the Black-Scholes calculation are $S = 750$, $E = 750$, $r = \ln(1.05) = .0488$, $T = 1$, $\sigma = .11$, and $\delta = .028$. Plugging into the model gives $C = 39.72$. Thus, the option value to the holder of this security is $(5/750)($39.72$) = 0.265. This is slightly less than the implied cost of the option of $0.29, which is not surprising given that the firm offering the deal must cover its costs and make a profit.

Equity-linked debt offers a guaranteed return of a fraction of the principal, the full principal, or the principal and a below-market interest rate, plus a percentage of the return on a market index.

These equity-linked securities sometimes have other features. Some pay off based on the average price over the last 10 days before expiration. Others pay no interest or even implicitly a negative interest rate by promising to return a given percentage but less than 100 percent of the amount invested. The holder then gets a greater percentage of the gain in the S&P 500. Some of the securities make their minimum interest payments quarterly or semiannually. Others pay off based on any depreciation in the index, which makes the option feature like a put.

The American Stock Exchange has been particularly active in creating these securities but similar instruments have traded at the Chicago Board Options Exchange.

Advanced Interest Rate Derivatives

In Chapter 14 we encountered derivatives on interest rates. These consisted of forward rate agreements, swaps, options, and swaptions. When we covered swaps we discussed only the plain vanilla, fixed-for-floating swap. In this section we shall take a brief look at some variations of interest rate swaps. Later in this section we look at some other widely used interest rate instruments that are not technically derivatives but are generally considered as such.

Variations of Interest Rate Swaps

Although the plain vanilla is the most widely used type of swap, there are numerous variations. Here we shall look at four of them: basis swaps, index amortizing swaps, diff swaps, and constant maturity swaps.

BASIS SWAPS   In the plain vanilla swap, one party pays a fixed rate while the other pays a floating rate. In a **basis swap**, both parties pay a floating rate. Consequently the parties are anticipating a change in the spread between the two rates. A common basis swap would be for one party to pay LIBOR while the other party pays the Treasury bill rate. The difference between LIBOR and the T-bill rate is called the TED spread, for T-bills versus Eurodollars. If you understand the plain vanilla swap, the TED spread swap should not be difficult. From the perspective of the party paying the T-bill rate and receiving LIBOR, the transaction is equivalent to borrowing at the T-bill rate and lending at LIBOR.

A basis swap is a swap in which both parties pay a floating rate.

Since LIBOR is the borrowing rate of London banks and the T-bill rate is the borrowing rate of the U.S. government, LIBOR must always be above the T-bill rate. Consequently this swap could not have a zero value at the start. In other words, the present value of a stream of future, unknown LIBOR interest payments will always exceed the present value of a stream of future, unknown T-bill interest payments. One solution is to have the party paying the T-bill rate and receiving LIBOR make a lump-sum cash payment to the other party up front. More commonly, however, the party receiving LIBOR will receive LIBOR minus a fixed discount.

Table 15.6 illustrates an example of the determination of the basis swap spread. Here we have a one-year swap with semiannual payments. The party pays the T-bill rate and receives LIBOR. Had the party done a plain vanilla swap, paying the T-bill rate and receiving a fixed rate, it would have had a fixed rate of 5.36 percent. Had the party done another plain vanilla swap, receiving LIBOR and paying the fixed rate, it would have paid a fixed rate of 5.58 percent. Combining these two swaps produces a net of paying T-bill, receiving LIBOR, and paying .22 fixed (5.58 − 5.36).

An index amortizing swap is one in which the notional principal is reduced through time. The amortization accelerates as interest rates decrease. This is designed to reflect the prepayments that might occur on a mortgage or other similar loan being hedged with the swap.

INDEX AMORTIZING SWAPS   An **index amortizing swap** is one in which the notional principal is reduced as one moves through time. A typical application of this type of swap would be where the party holds another position in which the notional principal is designed to decline through time. The most common example of this is the mortgage loan. When a homeowner takes out a mortgage, the loan balance reduces through time according to a fixed schedule. Homeowners, however, nearly always have the option to prepay and refinance their mortgages. When interest rates fall, more homeowners exercise their options. The holders of mortgages thus suffer losses by having their income streams reduced to zero and having to reinvest the prepaid principal at lower rates. In an index amortizing swap, the notional principal declines according to a schedule that specifies an acceleration of the amortization rate if interest rates fall. This results in the swap notional principal behaving much like the mortgage notional principal. There are numerous variations of this type of swap.

Securities based on mortgages have become popular instruments and are often classified as derivatives. We discuss them later in this chapter.

TABLE 15.6   **Determination of the Spread on a Basis Swap**

One-year swap with semiannual payments
Pay T-bill, receive LIBOR minus a spread
Payments based on (days/365)

Current Term Structure

Days	T-bill	LIBOR
182	5.05	5.53125
365	5.44	5.65625

Decompose the swap into two plain vanilla swaps:

Plain vanilla swap: pay T-bill, receive fixed
The price of that swap is found using the procedure illustrated in Chapter 14. The swap price is the solution to

$$\text{coupon}/(1 + .0505)^{(182/365)} + (\text{coupon} + 1)/(1 + .0544)^{(365/365)} = 1.00.$$

Solving gives coupon = .0268. Quoted on an annual basis gives .0268(2) = .0536.

Plain vanilla swap: pay fixed, receive LIBOR
Using the same procedure,

$$\text{coupon}/(1 + .0553125)^{(182/365)} + (\text{coupon} + 1)/(1 + .0565625)^{(365/365)} = 1.00.$$

Solving gives coupon = .0279. Quoted on annual basis gives .0279(2) = .0558.

Thus, the overall position can be viewed as the following:

Pay T-bill		Receive LIBOR		Pay T-bill, Receive LIBOR
Receive .0536	+	Pay .0558	=	Pay .0022

In practice, the calculations for the plain vanilla swaps would probably be stated on a 360-day basis, requiring a few slight adjustments. Also, there would be dealer bid-ask spreads that would change the two fixed-rate quotes by a few basis points, which would increase the basis spread.

DIFF SWAPS   A **diff swap** is an interest rate swap based on the interest rates in two countries but where the payments are made in a single currency. For example, a U.S. firm might be concerned that German interest rates will increase relative to U.S. rates. It could hedge this position by purchasing a deutsche mark–denominated floating-rate note and selling a dollar-denominated floating-rate note. This would, however, be assuming unwanted currency risk. Alternatively, it could enter into a diff swap in which it receives the German interest rate and pays the U.S. interest rate, with all payments made in dollars. Thus, if German interest rates rise

A diff swap is a swap in which each party makes an interest payment based on the difference between interest rates in different countries but both payments are made in the same currency. This enables the parties to speculate or hedge on relative interest rate changes of different countries without the currency risk.

relative to U.S. interest rates, the swap will result in a net payment in dollars to the firm. Obviously the dealer in such a swap would incur the currency risk and would probably pass on to the party the cost of hedging that risk, but presumably the dealer could do it much cheaper.

It should be apparent that this swap is simply a currency-hedged basis swap. If the interest rates of one country are consistently higher than those in the other country, there would be a spread similar to that in a basis swap negotiated up front.

CONSTANT MATURITY SWAPS A **constant maturity swap** is similar to a plain vanilla swap or a basis swap. One party pays a floating rate such as LIBOR and the other party pays another floating rate represented by the yield on a security with a maturity longer than the reset period. In other words, if the swap settles every six months, one party pays a rate on a security with longer than six months' maturity. Typically this is the yield on a security with a maturity in the range of two to five years. In dollar-denominated swaps, that rate is often referred to as the Constant Maturity Treasury (CMT) rate. The CMT rate is the yield on a U.S. Treasury note with a maturity closest to the maturity of interest. Naturally there is not always a Treasury note with precisely the desired maturity. In that case, however, the parties agree that the CMT rate will be interpolated from the rates on securities with maturities slightly above and below the desired maturity. Also, the Federal Reserve publishes its own estimate of the CMT rate, which is often used.

As an example, consider a three-year swap with semiannual payments in which one party pays the six-month LIBOR and the other pays the CMT on a five-year U.S. Treasury note. This is just a variation of a basis swap because both rates are floating. Depending on the shape of the term structure, a spread might also be paid by the party paying the lower rate. Constant maturity swaps can also have one party paying a fixed rate, with the other paying the CMT rate. It should be apparent that this is just a variation of a plain vanilla swap where the floating rate has a longer maturity than the standard LIBOR-based plain vanilla swap.

A constant maturity swap is a swap in which one party pays a fixed rate or short-term floating rate and the other pays a floating rate tied to the yield on a treasury security of intermediate-term maturity. This security is usually called the Constant Maturity Treasury. Its maturity is typically longer than the swap settlement period.

This observation gives rise to an important arbitrage relationship. If a party enters into a swap paying LIBOR and receiving the CMT and another swap paying the CMT and receiving the fixed rate, the net result is a plain vanilla swap paying LIBOR and receiving fixed. The fixed rate would reflect the fixed rate on the CMT-versus-fixed swap and the spread on the CMT-versus-LIBOR swap.

The parties to a constant maturity swap are obviously concerned about a change in the shape of the term structure. For example, if a party will be hurt if short-term rates increase more or decrease less than intermediate-term rates, it could engage in a swap to receive LIBOR and pay the CMT.

As LIBOR is widely used as an indicator of short-term interest rates, the CMT rate is also widely used as an indicator of intermediate-term interest rates. Consequently, the CMT rate is found as the underlying rate in many other types of derivatives, including caps and floors.

These examples are designed to give you a basic familiarity with the most popular variations of the plain vanilla swap. The number of variations actually seen in practice is much greater than we can show here. Moreover, many of these variations of interest rate swaps can also be used with commodity, currency, and equity swaps. If you have a good understanding of what we have covered so far, you should be ready to deal with the other types of swaps you may some day encounter.

In the next section we look at a family of instruments that is not always considered a derivative, but has been so widely associated with derivatives that it is necessary to cover it here.

Structured Notes

Corporations routinely issue debt obligations with maturities in the range of 2–10 years. These are usually called notes. Sometimes the notes carry fixed rates. Other times the notes have variable rates, such as those tied to LIBOR. In the early 1990s many corporations began issuing notes with derivative transactions attached so as to change the return pattern from the standard fixed or LIBOR-floating type. These instruments have come to be known as **structured notes.**

Most structured notes are issued by corporations of extremely high credit quality. Consequently, there is very little credit risk. The notes are typically designed with a particular user in mind. The user wants a particular exposure and normally plans to hold the notes until maturity. Thus, these tend to be fairly illiquid instruments.

Some of these notes have coupons indexed to the CMT rate. For example, the coupon could be the CMT rate plus 50 basis points. Some structured notes have leveraged coupons, meaning that, for example, the coupon might be 1.5 times the CMT rate. Let us say the CMT rate was currently 5.5 percent. Then the coupon would be $5.5(1.5) = 8.25$ percent. Suppose that the CMT rate went up 100 basis points to 6.5. Then the structured note coupon would go up to $6.5(1.5) = 9.75$, a 150-basis-point increase.

A structured note is an intermediate-term debt security issued by a corporation with a good credit rating and tailored to a particular investor's needs. The coupon is altered by the use of a derivative transaction to provide an exposure not found in most other securities with similar characteristics.

One interesting type of structured note is the **range floater.** This instrument pays interest only if a specified interest rate, such as LIBOR, stays within a given range. The ranges are sometimes different for each year of the note's life. As an example, consider a two-year note in which the coupon is LIBOR + 3 percent provided that:

For the first year, LIBOR is between 0 and 6 percent, and
For the second year, LIBOR is between 0 and 7 percent.

A range floater is a type of structured note in which a higher coupon is paid but only if a particular interest rate is within a specified range of rates.

An inverse floating-rate note is an intermediate-term security in which the coupon moves opposite to market interest rates.

In other words, if LIBOR is outside the specified range, the coupon is zero. Otherwise, the coupon is LIBOR + 3 percent, which would be considered above normal for a two-year note. You can see that this is a bet on LIBOR staying within a range. To the investor this transaction would be like a standard floating-rate note and the sale of an interest rate cap. If rates rise above a certain threshold, the investor gives up all the interest.

Probably the most widely used and most controversial type of structured note is the **inverse floater,** sometimes called the **reverse floater.** Whereas a standard floating-rate note pays interest at a rate that changes directly with interest rates in the market, an inverse floater pays interest that changes in an opposite manner to rates in the market. In other words, as interest rates go up, the coupon on an inverse floater goes down. This is usually established by setting the coupon at a formula like X – LIBOR, where X is a specified fixed rate. Sometimes it is simply a multiple of the fixed rate on a plain vanilla swap.

Suppose X is 12 percent and LIBOR is currently 5.5 percent. Then the coupon will be 6.5 percent. If LIBOR moves up to 7 percent, the coupon will be 5 percent. If LIBOR moves down to 3 percent, the coupon will be 9 percent. It should be obvious that if LIBOR exceeds 12 percent, the coupon is negative, meaning that the lender rather than the borrower would pay the interest! In practice, however, most inverse floaters specify that the minimum interest rate will be zero or perhaps a very small positive rate.

The issuer of an inverse floater could hedge its position with a plain vanilla swap paying LIBOR and receiving a fixed rate. For the case of LIBOR < 12 percent, the issuer's payment would be 12 minus LIBOR on the structured note and +LIBOR minus the fixed rate on the swap for a total payment of 12 minus the fixed rate. The issuer would have created a synthetic fixed-rate loan at this rate. If LIBOR exceeds 12 percent, the issuer's payment would be the same as a pay floating–receive fixed swap. If the issuer does not want such a position, it might wish to buy a cap with a strike rate of 12, which would pay it LIBOR minus 12 if LIBOR exceeds 12 percent. In that case, for LIBOR of more than 12, the issuer's total payment would be –(LIBOR – 12) from the cap and LIBOR minus the fixed rate on the swap for a total payment of 12 minus the fixed rate. In cases where the inverse floater payment is twice the fixed rate minus LIBOR, the net payment of the issuer after the swap will be twice the fixed rate minus the fixed rate or simply once the fixed rate. In that case, the issuer has offered an inverse floater but effectively pays only the fixed rate.

Some inverse floaters are leveraged with formulas such as three times the fixed rate minus twice LIBOR. Many inverse floaters have caps on the maximum rate. Some are de-levered by using formulas like X – .75LIBOR, where the floating coupon moves less than the movement in LIBOR.

There are many variations found in structured notes. Some have coupons determined by the difference between two interest rates, such as

the TED spread, and others have coupons tied to foreign interest rates but with payments made in the domestic currency. Structured notes have also been based on complex formulas reflecting differences in rates and bond prices at different ends of the term structure.

The success of structured notes is attributed to the fact that they offer return possibilities tailored to specific investors. Unfortunately, structured notes have also been aggressively marketed in some cases to investors who were not well suited for them. Large interest rate changes coupled with high leverage resulted in large losses for investors who were not aware they had so much exposure. Primarily for this reason, original issues of structured notes have declined somewhat in the last few years.

Mortgage-Backed Securities

The fixed-rate home mortgage is the primary means by which individuals purchase houses. Most homeowners pay off their mortgages over a period of 15–30 years with fixed monthly payments, consisting of interest on the remaining balance and a contribution to the principal. Nearly every mortgage also provides the homeowner the right to prepay the mortgage, which will frequently be done if interest rates decline sufficiently to cover the transaction cost of refinancing. A certain number of prepayments occur due to demographic factors, such as a family moving to another city. Mortgage lenders are primarily banks, savings and loan associations, and mortgage companies. These financial institutions that originate mortgage loans are exposed to the risk of interest rate changes. If interest rates increase, the value of a mortgage decreases. If interest rates decrease, the value of a mortgage increases but the increase is limited by the fact that lower interest rates encourage homeowners to refinance. If that happens, the mortgage holder receives the principal early and is forced to reinvest it at a lower rate. This is referred to as **prepayment risk.**

Many mortgages are combined into portfolios and claims on the portfolio are sold to investors in the form of **mortgage-backed securities.** The process of combining loans into portfolios and selling claims on the portfolio is called **securitization.** Not all securitized portfolios are mortgages. Credit card receipts and other types of loans are also securitized, but the mortgage securitization market is one of the largest and most complex. The process of securitization provides depth to the market because lenders know that they can sell the loans they hold and receive immediate cash. This increases the number of willing lenders and provides individual and institutional investors access to investment opportunities in markets that were normally accessible only to financial institutions. Securitized mortgages are nearly always guaranteed against default by the purchase of credit insurance, often from a federal agency such as the Government National Mortgage Association (GNMA).

A mortgage-backed security is a security issued by a party who makes payments based on the payments it receives from a portfolio of underlying mortgages.

Securities that are issued based on mortgage portfolios are generally considered to be derivatives because they derive their values from the values of the underlying mortgages. They are, however, somewhat different from traditional derivatives. Though most mortgages have imbedded prepayment options, mortgage securities are more like mutual funds. They are investments in a security that represents holdings of another security. Nonetheless, we shall cover them here because it is important to know something about them and in practice, nearly everyone, rightly or wrongly, thinks of them as derivatives.

A mortgage pass-through is a mortgage-backed security in which the holder receives the principal and interest payments on a portfolio of mortgages, less a servicing fee.

Interest-only (IO) and principal-only (PO) strips are mortgage-backed securities entitling their holders to the interest and principal payments, respectively, of a portfolio of underlying mortgages.

MORTGAGE PASS-THROUGHS AND STRIPS   Portfolios of mortgages on which claims are sold are called **mortgage pass-throughs.** An investor who purchases a mortgage pass-through receives a monthly check consisting of a proportional share of interest and principal on the portfolio of mortgages, less a servicing fee. Mortgage pass-throughs, however, are still subject to the risk of interest rate changes, which, as we noted above, result in changes to the values of the securities and affect the frequency with which homeowners refinance their mortgages. Consequently, mortgage pass-through values can change dramatically with changes in interest rates.

Some mortgage pass-throughs are decomposed into **mortgage strips,** each consisting of an interest or principal stream, which are sold separately. An investor can purchase either or both strips. The **interest-only strip,** called an **IO,** provides the investor with the interest payments on the portfolio of underlying mortgages. The **principal-only strip,** called a **PO,** provides the investor with the principal payments on the portfolio of underlying mortgages. If interest rates decrease and prepayments accelerate, the holder of an IO will find the value of his position decreasing, perhaps quite dramatically. Thus, it sounds as if the holder of an IO would prefer for interest rates to increase. That will be the case to a limited extent. Beyond a point, however, increases in interest rates will reduce the present value of the interest-only stream.

Understanding the mechanics of mortgage-backed securities is difficult. At this introductory level, our objective is to just grasp the fundamentals. We shall do this by looking at a simple mortgage portfolio, one consisting of but a single mortgage. Let that mortgage be a $100,000 loan at 9.75 percent for 30 years. Although most mortgages have monthly payments, we shall use annual payments in this example. This enables us to show the entire amortization schedule, which is in Table 15.7.

First let us determine the annual payment, a simple problem in the mathematics of compound interest. The payment will equal the loan amount divided by the discount factor for an annuity:

$$\text{Payment} = \frac{\$100,000}{(1 - (1.0975)^{-30})/.0975} = \$10,387.$$

TABLE 15.7	Amortization Schedule for a 30-Year, $100,000 Mortgage at 9.75 Percent

Payment No.	Balance before Payment	Annual Payments Payment	Interest	Principal	Balance after Payment
1	$100,000	$10,387	$9,750	$637	$99,363
2	99,363	$10,387	9,688	699	98,663
3	98,663	$10,387	9,620	768	97,896
4	97,896	$10,387	9,545	843	97,053
5	97,053	$10,387	9,463	925	96,128
6	96,128	$10,387	9,373	1,015	95,113
7	95,113	$10,387	9,274	1,114	94,000
8	94,000	$10,387	9,165	1,222	92,777
9	92,777	$10,387	9,046	1,342	91,436
10	91,436	$10,387	8,915	1,472	89,963
11	89,963	$10,387	8,771	1,616	88,348
12	88,348	$10,387	8,614	1,773	86,574
13	86,574	$10,387	8,441	1,946	84,628
14	84,628	$10,387	8,251	2,136	82,492
15	82,494	$10,387	8,043	2,344	80,147
16	80,147	$10,387	7,814	2,573	77,574
17	77,574	$10,387	7,563	2,824	74,750
18	74,750	$10,387	7,288	3,099	71,651
19	71,651	$10,387	6,986	3,401	68,250
20	68,250	$10,387	6,654	3,733	64,517
21	64,517	$10,387	6,290	4,097	60,420
22	60,420	$10,387	5,891	4,496	55,924
23	55,924	$10,387	5,453	4,935	50,989
24	50,989	$10,387	4,971	5,416	45,573
25	45,573	$10,387	4,443	5,944	39,629
26	39,629	$10,387	3,864	6,524	33,105
27	33,105	$10,387	3,228	7,160	25,946
28	25,946	$10,387	2,530	7,858	18,088
29	18,088	$10,387	1,764	8,624	9,465
30	9,465	$10,387	923	9,465	0

Each payment consists of interest, which is .0975 times the balance owed, plus the contribution to the principal, which is $10,387 minus the interest. For example, the 10th payment of $10,387 consists of interest of $91,436(.0975) = $8,915$ and the contribution to principal of $10,387 − $8,915 = $1,472$, which leaves a balance of $91,436 − $1,472 = $89,964.$[5]

Now let us examine the values of IOs and POs. The value of the IO strip will be the present value of the column of numbers representing the interest. The value of the PO strip will be the present value of the column of numbers representing the principal.

---

[5]The figures in the table reflect more precise calculations so they occasionally differ slightly from manually calculated figures.

To determine these values we need two pieces of information. One is the rate at which to discount the cash flows. Assuming the payments are guaranteed by a federal agency, we can discount these at a rate appropriate for a Treasury security. So at the present, let us assume a rate of 7 percent. We also have to make an assumption about when the loan will be paid off. Although it is a 30-year loan, it has a good chance of being paid off early. We shall assume that it is paid off in its twelfth year, which is considered to be an average payoff date for 30-year mortgages.

At our current interest rate of 7 percent, where we assume the mortgage is prepaid in the twelfth year, the value of the IO strip is found by discounting each of the 12 interest payments at 7 percent. In other words, $9{,}750(1.07)^{-1} + 9{,}688(1.07)^{-2} + \ldots + 8{,}614(1.07)^{-12} = 74{,}254$. The value of the PO strip is found by discounting the 12 principal payments taking into account that the final principal payment will have an extra \$86,574, reflecting the balance paid off after the twelfth payment. That is, the value of the PO strip will be $637(1.07)^{-1} + 699(1.07)^{-2} + \ldots + (1{,}773 + 86{,}574)(1.07)^{-12} = \$46{,}690$. A pass-through would be worth the sum of these two, or \$120,944.

Now suppose the discount rate falls to 6 percent and we assume that this induces the homeowner to prepay two years from now. The value of the IO will be $9{,}750(1.06)^{-1} + 9{,}688(1.06)^{-2} = 17{,}820$. The IO, which was purchased for \$74,254 just two years prior, has lost 76 percent of its value! The PO purchased for \$46,690 is worth $637(1.06)^{-1} + (699 + 98{,}663)(1.06)^{-2} = 89{,}033$. If, instead, interest rates rise immediately to 8 percent and there is no change in the twelfth-year prepayment assumption, the IO value decreases to \$70,532, a loss of 5 percent, and the PO value decreases to \$42,128, a loss of almost 10 percent.

It would appear that IO holders lose either way, but that is not exactly how it works in practice. IO and PO strips represent portfolios of mortgages. Each mortgage will not prepay at the same time. Any increase in interest rates is likely to push the average prepayment date further out. If in our example the interest rate change to 8 percent pushes the prepayment date to year 14, the IO would be worth \$76,445, a gain of about 3 percent. The PO value will go to \$37,276, a loss of about 20 percent. Increases in interest rates beyond a point, however, have little effect on reducing the average prepayment rate. When combined with the discounting effect of higher interest rates, IOs lose with further increases in interest rates.

The combined effects of IOs and POs show up in the value of a mortgage pass-through, the holder of which receives both the interest and principal payments. A mortgage pass-through decreases in value with increases in interest rates. When rates decrease, however, the gains on the pass-through are limited because of the increased prepayment rate. The pass-through is not as volatile as the IO or PO individually but it can

still be fairly volatile and has limited gains because of the prepayment risk.[6]

The main point from this demonstration is that mortgage securities are complex and that POs and IOs can be extremely volatile. Not only are they affected by the discounting effect of interest rates but they are extremely sensitive to the effect that interest rate changes have on prepayments. As you might well imagine, it is difficult to predict prepayments, making it all the more difficult to get a firm grasp on the risk of these securities. This does not mean that investors should avoid them. They are priced fairly for their risk.

COLLATERALIZED MORTGAGE OBLIGATIONS (CMOs)   Another type of mortgage security is the **collateralized mortgage obligation (CMO).** CMOs, like mortgage pass-throughs, are debt securities whose payoffs are based on a portfolio of mortgages. CMOs, however, have risks and rewards that differ substantially from standard pass-throughs or IO and PO strips. In fact, some CMOs have considerably more risk and others have considerably less risk than pass-throughs or strips. This is accomplished by structuring the different types of CMO securities, called **tranches,** to have different priorities on the payments made on the underlying mortgages. In addition, some CMOs serve as equity, providing support to the liabilities and being paid after all other tranches are paid. This is called the residual tranche.

CMOs are extremely complex securities, but we can understand the basics with a few simple examples. In the mortgage pass-through described above, the combined value of the IO and PO is $120,944. Suppose we hold this mortgage and issue debt tranches with a total value of $100,000, leaving a residual or equity tranche of $20,944, which has the lowest priority of claims on the underlying mortgages. There are numerous variations of tranches in CMOs, distinguished by the different coupon rates and prepayment provisions. One type of tranche, called a **planned amortization class** or **PAC,** is characterized by a fixed amortization schedule. In other words, it is designed to not be subject to prepayment risk. If, however, prepayments are dramatically above or below a specified reasonable range, some prepayments may be applied to the PAC tranche. Nonetheless, its substantially reduced prepayment risk results in a lower coupon.

With the PAC tranche protected against prepayment risk, obviously other tranches must bear more of that risk. The other tranches are

---

[6]The limited downside gain is often referred to as the negative convexity. You may recall that we briefly discussed convexity for ordinary bonds in Chapter 8. The concept is the same here except that the convexity is negative, meaning that the value of the pass-through flattens out at low rates.

A collateralized mortgage obligation or CMO is a mortgage-backed security in which different types of CMOs, called tranches, have different risks and returns resulting from different priorities of claims on the payments generated by the underlying mortgages.

arranged in priority according to which bears the greater prepayment risk. The tranches with higher coupons will receive larger percentages of any prepayments. In some cases, the tranche bearing the greatest prepayment risk must be fully paid off before the other tranches begin receiving prepayments. However, all tranches generally accrue interest while higher-priority tranches are being paid off. In that manner the tranches accrue interest and are retired sequentially. Some tranches are called Z-bonds. They accrue interest at a given rate but no principal is paid until all other tranches are paid off.

All tranches tend to gain in value as interest rates decrease but the tranches bearing the greater prepayment risk gain less and the Z-bond gains more. It continues to accrue interest while the other tranches start receiving more prepayments. When interest rates increase, the securities bearing the greater prepayment risk do better because their prepayments are invested at higher rates. Though their values tend to fall, they fall less. The Z-bond value will then fall more.

When all tranches are paid off, there may be value left over, which is paid to the holders of the residual tranche. Any gain in value from the amount paid for the residual tranche will result from unexpected changes in interest rates and their effect on deviations in the prepayment rate from the assumptions built into the original structure.

Collateralized mortgage obligations are some of the most complicated and volatile financial instruments. Like mortgage pass-throughs, they have been aggressively marketed, sometimes to investors who had little understanding of the risks. Unfortunately, considerable misunderstanding occurred because many mortgage-backed securities were referred to as "government guaranteed." Of course, the guarantee is only that if a homeowner defaults, the payments will be made by the government agency, usually GNMA. Thus, this is only a credit guarantee; it does not guarantee against losses arising from interest rate changes and changes in the rate of prepayments. The volatility and illiquidity often seen in the market for mortgage-backed securities suggests that they be used only with caution and then only by investors who fully understand them.

Exotic Options

In recent years, the proliferation of option products has led to a new class of options called **exotic options.** Although it is difficult to identify exactly where ordinary options end and exotic options begin, it is becoming common to refer to almost any option that is not traded on an exchange or not essentially identical to one traded on an exchange as an exotic option. In some cases these options are simple; in other cases, they are quite complex. What distinguishes them from what we have previously covered, however, is the fact that they offer different types of payoffs. What makes them

like what we have previously covered is that their final payoffs are determined by whether a value exceeds or is less than an exercise price.

Digital and Chooser Options

DIGITAL OPTIONS   Digital options, which are sometimes called binary options, are actually very simple options and are of two types. An asset-or-nothing option pays the holder the asset or its equivalent cash value if the asset price at expiration exceeds the exercise price and nothing if the asset price at expiration is less than the exercise price. A cash-or-nothing option pays the holder a fixed amount of cash at expiration if the asset price at expiration exceeds the exercise price and nothing if the asset price at expiration is less than the exercise price. These options can be useful for hedging positions in standard European calls. In fact, there is a simple relationship between digital options and a standard European option.

Table 15.8 illustrates the payoffs to the holder of an asset-or-nothing option who also sells a cash-or-nothing option where E is the amount of cash paid at expiration if $S_T > E$. Notice that the payoffs are $S_T - E$ if $S_T > E$ and zero otherwise. Does this look familiar? It should because it is the payoff of a standard European call. This gives us some insights into how to price digital options. Recall that the Black-Scholes price is $SN(d_1) - Ee^{-r_cT}N(d_2)$. The first term is the price of the asset-or-nothing option. The second term, ignoring the minus, is the price of a cash-or-nothing option that pays off E if it expires in-the-money. In other words, an asset-or-nothing option price is given as

$$O_{aon} = SN(d_1),$$

and a cash-or-nothing option price is given as

$$O_{con} = Ee^{-r_cT}N(d_2).$$

TABLE 15.8	Payoffs to a Position Long an Asset-or-Nothing Option and Short a Cash-or-Nothing Option	
	Payoffs from Portfolio Given Asset Price at Expiration	
Payoff from	$S_T \leq E$	$S_T > E$
Long asset-or-nothing option	0	S_T
Short cash-or-nothing option	0	$-E$
Total	0	$S_T - E$

Two types of digital options are an asset-or-nothing option, which pays the asset value if it expires in the money and nothing otherwise, and a cash-or-nothing option, which pays a fixed cash value if it expires in the money and nothing otherwise.

As an example, consider an asset-or-nothing option written on the S&P 500 Total Return Index, which is at 720. At expiration, the option pays the full cash value of the S&P 500. The exercise price is 720. The risk-free rate is 4.88 percent continuously compounded, the standard deviation is .11, and the option expires in exactly one-half year. Since the option is written on the Total Return Index, which includes the dividends, we need not adjust for dividends when pricing the option. Substituting these values into d_1 for the Black-Scholes model gives $d_1 = .3526$. Using Table 4.2 on p. 136, we have $N(.35) = .6368$. Then the asset-or-nothing option is worth $720(.6368) = 458.50$. If the option had been a cash-or-nothing option paying 720 if it expires in-the-money, we would need d_2, which would be .2748. The $N(.27) = .6064$ and the cash-or-nothing option would be worth $720e^{-.0488(.5)}(.6064) = 426.08$. The difference in these two values, 32.42, is the value of a standard European call.

CHOOSER OPTIONS   A **chooser option** permits the investor to decide at a specific point during the life of the option whether it should be a call or a put. For example, suppose an investor believes the market will make a strong move but does not know which direction it will go. As we studied in Chapter 6, an investor can purchase a straddle, which is a call and a put. A cheaper alternative is to purchase a chooser option. The chooser allows the investor to decide at time t, which is prior to expiration, whether to make it a call or a put. Chooser options are also called **as-you-like-it options.**

Suppose at time t, an investor decides to make it a call. Then at expiration, the call pays off $S_T - E$ if $S_T > E$ and zero otherwise. If the investor had chosen the put, it pays off $E - S_T$ if $S_T \leq E$ and zero otherwise. Note that unless $S_T = E$, a straddle will always pay off through either the call or the put, but it is possible that a chooser will not pay off at all.

A chooser option allows the holder to designate at a specific time prior to expiration whether the option will be a call or a put.

Pricing a chooser option is quite simple. At time t, the investor will make it a call if the value of the call exceeds the value of the put. At t the call price can be expressed as $C(S_t, T - t, E)$ and the put price can be expressed as $P(S_t, T - t, E)$. A little algebra using put-call parity shows that the call would be chosen if $S_t > E(1 + r)^{-(T - t)}$. The chooser can be replicated by simply holding an ordinary call expiring at T with exercise price of E and a put expiring at t with exercise price of $E(1 + r)^{-(T - t)}$. An end-of-chapter problem asks you to verify this statement.

Let us consider a chooser option on the Digital Equipment stock. Recall that the stock price is 164, the exercise price is 165, the risk-free rate is 5.35 percent discrete (5.21 percent continuous), the time to expiration is .0959 (35 days), and the volatility is .29. Let us assume the choice must be made in 20 days. First let us price an ordinary straddle. From Chapter 4, we used the Black-Scholes model and found the call to be worth 5.80 and the put to be worth 5.98. Therefore, the straddle would cost 11.78.

The chooser would be worth the value of an ordinary call (5.80) and the value of a put expiring in 20 days (t = 20/365 = .0548) with an exercise price of $165(1.0535)^{-(.0959 - .0548)} = 164.65$ and a volatility of .29. Plugging into the Black-Scholes model gives a put value of 4.54. Thus, the chooser would cost $5.80 + $4.54 = $10.34. The lower cost of the chooser over the straddle comes from the fact that there is a possibility that the payoff at expiration will be zero.

A chooser option that allows the holder to designate at *any* time before expiration whether it will be a call or a put is called a complex chooser. It is much more difficult to evaluate and we do not cover it here.

Path-Dependent Options

An important distinction among options is whether the path followed by the underlying asset price matters to the price of the option. For standard European options the path taken does not matter. They can be exercised only at expiration so it does not matter how the asset reached a certain price. Standard European options are said to be path-independent. For some options, however, the path taken does matter. American options are a classic case in point. Certain paths lead to early exercise. Though we did not refer to them this way in Chapter 4, we can certainly now call them **path-dependent.**[7]

Path-dependent options are those in which the path followed by the asset during the life of the option has an effect on the option's price. Path-independent options are those in which only the asset price at expiration and not the path followed affects the options' values.

In recent years a family of new options, however, have become better known for their property of path-dependency. Some of these options are based on the average price or the maximum or minimum prices of the underlying asset during the option's life. Others have the property that they can expire worthless before expiration or can expire worthless even if they apparently are in-the-money at expiration. Today when one hears of path-dependent options, the reference is nearly always to these types of options, although these are certainly not all of the path-dependent types.

The binomial model provides a good framework within which to see how path-dependent options work. Table 15.9 presents a simple three-period binomial model where the current asset price is 50 and each period it can go up 25 percent or down 20 percent. The risk-free rate is 5 percent. We shall use an exercise price of 50. The table shows the binomial tree with the asset moving from 50 at time 0 to either 97.66, 62.50, 40, or 25.60 at time 3.

---

[7]The concept of path-independence versus path-dependence is illustrated by considering the following situation encountered in traveling. Suppose you are in Baltimore and need to fly to San Francisco. There are numerous ways to get from Baltimore to San Francisco, including direct flights and many possible connecting flights. If your objective is only to get from Baltimore to San Francisco, it does not matter what route you take. This would be consistent with path independence. If your objective is to get from Baltimore to San Francisco in the least amount of time and/or at the lowest cost, then certain routings, especially direct flights, are preferred. This would be consistent with path dependence.

TABLE 15.9	Path-Dependent Options Information

		Time 0	Time 1	Time 2	Time 3
S_0:	50	S_0	S_1	S_2	S_3
u:	.25				97.66
d	−.20			78.13	
r:	.05		62.50		62.50
E:	50	50.00		50.00	
p:	.556[1]		40.00		40.00
1 − p:	.444			32.00	
					25.60

Path No.	Path	Probability[2]	S_0	S_1	S_2	S_3	Average Price	S_{max}	S_{min}	European Call Payoffs	European Put Payoffs
1	uuu	.171	50.00	62.50	78.13	97.66	72.07	97.66	50.00	47.66	0.00
2	uud	.137	50.00	62.50	78.13	62.50	63.28	78.13	50.00	12.50	0.00
3	udu	.137	50.00	62.50	50.00	62.50	56.25	62.50	50.00	12.50	0.00
4	duu	.137	50.00	40.00	50.00	62.50	50.63	62.50	40.00	12.50	0.00
5	udd	.110	50.00	62.50	50.00	40.00	50.63	62.50	40.00	0.00	10.00
6	dud	.110	50.00	40.00	50.00	40.00	45.00	50.00	40.00	0.00	10.00
7	ddu	.110	50.00	40.00	32.00	40.00	40.50	50.00	32.00	0.00	10.00
8	ddd	.088	50.00	40.00	32.00	25.60	36.90	50.00	25.60	0.00	24.40

[1]Computed as $(r − d)/(u − d)$.
[2]Probability of a given path is $p^{\text{# of times price goes up}}(1 − p)^{\text{# of times price goes down}}$. For example, for path 5 (udd), the probability is $.556^1.444^2 = .110$.

Also shown in the table is a listing of each of the eight paths the asset could take. Notice that it could go up-up-up, up-up-down, or any of six other possible paths. Recalling from our binomial model material in Chapter 4, the probability factor, p, is $(r − d)/(u − d)$, which the table shows is .556. The probability of a given path is $p^{\text{# of times price goes up}}$ $(1 − p)^{\text{# of times price goes down}}$. For example, the probability of going up, down, and then up is $.556^2.444^1 = .137$. Also, keep in mind that this is not the true probability but only the risk neutral probability, as discussed in Chapter 4. It is important not to combine paths, such as the fact that the stock can reach 62.50 at expiration three different ways. Each path can lead to different values of path-dependent options, so we must keep the paths separate.

The table also shows the sequence of asset prices for each path: S_0, S_1, S_2, and S_3. The eighth column shows the average price over the path, counting the original asset price. Thus, for path 1, the average is $(50.00 + 62.50 + 78.13 + 97.66)/4 = 72.07$. The next two columns show the maximum and minimum prices attained over the given path.

The last two columns show the payoffs at expiration for standard European calls. The value for a given path is $Max(0, S_3 − 50)$ for calls and

Max(0, 50 − S_3) for puts, which reflects those options' dependencies on only the final asset price, S_3. To find the price of those options, we simply multiply each option payoff by the probability of that payoff occurring, sum the payoffs, and divide by $(1.05)^3$, which is simply discounting the total to the present. This is the same procedure we used in previous applications of the binomial model in Chapters 4 and 14. The European call price is 11.50 and the European put price is 4.69.[8] We now look at several types of path-dependent options.

ASIAN OPTIONS   An **Asian option** is an option where the payoff is based on the average price attained by the underlying asset during the life of the option. An Asian option can take the form of either a call or a put. The average price can be used in place of either the expiration price of the asset or the exercise price. The former are called **average price options** while the latter are called **average strike options.** For the three-period case, the payoffs at expiration are as follows:

Average price call: Max(0, S_{avg} − E)
Average price put: Max(0, E − S_{avg})
Average strike call: Max(0, S_3 − S_{avg})
Average strike put: Max(0, S_{avg} − S_3).

An Asian option is an option in which either the final asset price or the exercise price is replaced by the average price of the asset over the option's life.

Table 15.10 illustrates how to price an Asian option. Look at the fifth column, which shows the payoffs for the average price call. For path 1, at expiration the average price is 72.07, which makes the option be in-the-money by 22.07. The remaining payoff values are computed similarly using the first formula above. Then the values in the payoff column are multiplied by their respective probabilities (column 3). The sum of these probability-weighted outcomes is then discounted over three periods to the present. We see that both types of Asian options are considerably less valuable than their European counterparts. There are several reasons for this but the most obvious one is that the volatility of an average of a series of numbers is less than the volatility of the series itself.

The lower prices of Asian options relative to European options make them useful for situations in which the user wants to hedge or speculate on the price series but is unwilling to spend the full price required by European options. In some cases a hedge of only an average price is satisfactory. Asian options are also used in markets where prices are unusually volatile and may be susceptible to distortion or manipulation. The averaging process results in the option payoff not being completely dependent on the price at expiration.

---

[8]As an example, the call price is found as (.171(47.66) + .137(12.50) + . . . + .088(0))/$(1.05)^3$ = 11.50.

TABLE 15.10		Pricing an Asian Option					
Path No.	Path	Probability	Average Price (S_{avg})	Average Price Call Payoff[1]	Average Price Put Payoff[2]	Average Strike Call Payoff[3]	Average Strike Put Payoff[4]
1	uuu	.171	72.07	22.07	0.00	25.59	0.00
2	uud	.137	63.28	13.28	0.00	0.00	0.78
3	udu	.137	56.25	6.25	0.00	6.25	0.00
4	duu	.137	50.63	0.63	0.00	11.88	0.00
5	udd	.110	50.63	0.63	0.00	0.00	10.63
6	dud	.110	45.00	0.00	5.00	0.00	5.00
7	ddu	.110	40.50	0.00	9.50	0.00	0.50
8	ddd	.088	36.90	0.00	13.10	0.00	11.30
			Value of Option[5]	5.72	2.37	5.94	2.48

[1] $\text{Max}(0, S_{avg} - 50)$.
[2] $\text{Max}(0, 50 - S_{avg})$.
[3] $\text{Max}(0, S_3 - S_{avg})$.
[4] $\text{Max}(0, S_{avg} - S_3)$.
[5] Value of Option is found as the sum of the product of the payoffs of the option (column 5, 6, 7, or 8) by the respective probability of that payoff (column 3) discounted at the risk-free rate (i.e., divided by 1.05^3).

As we discussed in Chapter 4, the binomial model requires a large number of time steps to give an accurate approximation to the Black-Scholes price for standard European options. Unfortunately there is no formula like the Black-Scholes for Asian options.[9] The binomial model is useful for illustrative purposes, but applying it in practice with a large number of time steps is impractical for Asian options. The computer must keep track of 2^n paths, where n is the number of time periods. For our three-period model, the number of paths is $2^3 = 8$. For a realistic situation, we would require at least 50 time steps, in which case the computer must keep track of 1,125,900,000,000,000 paths! There are some Asian option approximation formulas used in practice, but the most popular method of pricing Asian options is probably by **Monte Carlo simulation.** We illustrate the Monte Carlo procedure in Appendix 15B.

LOOKBACK OPTIONS   Another widely used path-dependent option is the **lookback option.** A lookback option offers the holder the opportunity to buy at the lowest price or sell at the highest price the asset attained during the life of the option. It is said that a lookback option allows you to "buy low, sell high." Since you will never miss in timing the market, the lookback option is also called a **no-regrets option.**

[9]An exception is that if the average is a geometric average, then a formula does exist. Geometric averages are rarely used in practice, however.

For the three-period binomial example, the standard lookback option has payoffs at expiration as follows:

Lookback call: $Max(0, S_3 - S_{min})$
Lookback put: $Max(0, S_{max} - S_3)$.

In other words, the lookback call sets the exercise price at the lowest price the asset attained during the option's life. A lookback put permits the holder to sell the asset at the highest price it attained during the life of the option. In the worst case a lookback option expires at-the-money.

Another class of lookback options, which are sometimes called **modi-fied lookback options,** has the exercise price fixed but replaces the terminal asset price with the maximum price for a call and minimum price for a put. Thus, their payoffs are:

Fixed strike lookback call: $Max(0, S_{max} - E)$
Fixed strike lookback put: $Max(0, E - S_{min})$.

Table 15.11 illustrates the pricing of lookback options. Consider the standard lookback call, whose payoffs are in column 6. If path 1 occurs, the asset ends up at 97.66. The minimum price along that path is 50. Thus, it expires in-the-money worth 47.66. Notice particularly path 7. From Table 15.9, we see that the asset price ended up at 40 but it went as low as 32 so the call ends up worth 8. Similarly, the basic lookback put in

Lookback options base their expiration payoffs on the maximum or minimum price reached by the asset during the option's life. They allow the user to buy at the low price or sell at the high price, thus guaranteeing optimal market timing.

TABLE 15.11   Pricing a Lookback Option

Path No.	Path	Probability	Maximum Price (S_{max})	Minimum Price (S_{min})	Lookback Call Payoff[1]	Lookback Put Payoff[2]	Fixed Strike Lookback Call Payoff[3]	Fixed Strike Lookback Put Payoff[4]
1	uuu	.171	97.66	50.00	47.66	0.00	47.66	0.00
2	uud	.137	78.13	50.00	12.50	15.63	28.13	0.00
3	udu	.137	62.50	50.00	12.50	0.00	12.50	0.00
4	duu	.137	62.50	40.00	22.50	0.00	12.50	10.00
5	udd	.110	62.50	40.00	0.00	22.50	12.50	10.00
6	dud	.110	50.00	40.00	0.00	10.00	0.00	10.00
7	ddu	.110	50.00	32.00	8.00	10.00	0.00	18.00
8	ddd	.088	50.00	25.60	0.00	24.40	0.00	24.40
			Value of Option[5]		13.45	7.73	14.54	6.64

[1]$Max(0, S_3 - S_{min})$.
[2]$Max(0, S_{max} - S_3)$.
[3]$Max(0, S_{max} - 50)$.
[4]$Max(0, 50 - S_{min})$.
[5]Value of Option is found as the sum of the product of the payoffs of the option (column 6, 7, 8, or 9) by the respective probability of that payoff (column 3) discounted at the risk-free rate (i.e., divided by 1.05^3).

path 2 pays off 15.63 because the asset ended up at 62.50 but went as high as 78.13. The remaining payoffs are determined in a similar manner using the appropriate formulas shown above. The value of each option is once again found by multiplying each option payoff by the appropriate probability (column 3), summing these probability-weighted payoffs, and discounting at 5 percent over three periods.

Because lookback options allow their holders to achieve higher payoffs for some outcomes and positive payoffs for some outcomes where European options would have zero payoffs, they are worth substantially more. Is the additional price worth it? That depends on the investor. An investor who experiences anguish over failing to buy when the price is low or sell when the price is high would probably find the extra cost worth it.

Formulas for the prices of most lookback options have been derived. Using these formulas in practice, however, is complicated by the fact that many lookback options do not provide for continuous monitoring of the asset price. Instead they consider only the closing price of the asset in determining the maximum or minimum. Because of the aforementioned large number of paths that must be followed in the binomial model, Monte Carlo methods are often used.

BARRIER OPTIONS   The final type of path-dependent option we examine is the **barrier option.** While lookback options have positive payoffs for more outcomes than do standard European options, barrier options have fewer positive payoffs than European options. This makes them less expensive than standard European options. Investors who want to save a little money and do not want to pay for outcomes they do not believe are likely to occur will be attracted to barrier options.

In one type of barrier option the holder specifies a level of the asset price that, if touched by the asset before the option expires, causes the option to terminate. In the other type of barrier option, the holder specifies a level of the asset price that must be hit by the asset to activate the option. If the asset never hits the barrier during the option's life, the option cannot be exercised even if it expires in-the-money at expiration. Options that can terminate early are called **out-options** and sometimes **knock-out options.** Options that will be unexercisable if they fail to touch the barrier are called **in-options** or sometimes **knock-in options.** Out-options, thus, can expire prematurely with no value if the barrier is hit. In-options must be activated by hitting the barrier. If they are never activated, they automatically expire worthless. If the barrier is set above the current asset price, both in- and out-options are referred to as **up-options.** If the barrier is set below the current asset price, in- and out-options are referred to as **down-options.**

Table 15.12 illustrates the pricing of barrier options. The table shows the payoffs at expiration of all eight types of barrier options. We first look

| TABLE 15.12 | | | **Pricing a Barrier Option** | | | | | | | |

			Down-and-Out and Down-and-In Options (H = barrier)				Up-and-Out and Up-and-In Options (H = barrier)			
Path No.	Path	Probability	Out Call Payoff (H = 45)	In Call Payoff (H = 45)	Out Put Payoff (H = 35)	In Put Payoff (H = 35)	Out Call Payoff (H = 70)	In Call Payoff (H = 70)	Out Put Payoff (H = 55)	In Put Payoff (H = 55)
1	uuu	.171	47.66	*0.00*	0.00	*0.00*	**0.00**	47.66	**0.00**	0.00
2	uud	.137	12.50	*0.00*	0.00	*0.00*	**0.00**	12.50	**0.00**	0.00
3	udu	.137	12.50	*0.00*	0.00	*0.00*	12.50	*0.00*	**0.00**	0.00
4	duu	.137	**0.00**	12.50	0.00	*0.00*	12.50	*0.00*	**0.00**	0.00
5	udd	.110	0.00	0.00	10.00	*0.00*	0.00	*0.00*	**0.00**	10.00
6	dud	.110	**0.00**	0.00	10.00	*0.00*	0.00	*0.00*	10.00	*0.00*
7	ddu	.110	**0.00**	0.00	**0.00**	10.00	0.00	*0.00*	10.00	*0.00*
8	ddd	.088	**0.00**	0.00	**0.00**	24.40	0.00	*0.00*	24.40	*0.00*
	Value of Option[1]		10.02	1.48	1.90	2.80	2.96	8.54	3.75	0.95

[1]Value of Option is found as the sum of the product of the payoffs of the option (columns 4, 5, 6, 7, 8, 9, 10, or 11) by the respective probability of that payoff (column 3) discounted at the risk-free rate (i.e., divided by 1.05^3).

Note: Bold values for out options are outcomes in which the option hit the barrier and, thus, was knocked out. Italicized values for in-options are outcomes in which the option failed to hit the barrier and, thus, was not exercisable at expiration.

at down-and-out and down-and-in options. The bold zero values are outcomes in which out-options hit the barrier and, thus, were knocked out with no value. The italicized values are outcomes in which in-options failed to hit the barrier and, thus, were never activated.

Consider the down-and-out call illustrated in column 4 where the barrier is set at 45. This means that if the asset ever hits 45, the option terminates with no value. This will occur in paths 4, 6, 7, and 8 where in each path the asset hit 40 at time 1. In path 5 the option hits the barrier but expires worthless anyway. Now move one column over to the down-and-in call. This option will never activate if the asset does not fall to 45 during the option's life. This occurs in paths 1, 2, and 3.

The values of the options are shown in the bottom row of the table and are computed the same way as in our previous examples. Notice a very interesting result. If one combines the payoffs from the down-and-out call with those of the down-and-in call, one obtains the same payoffs of a standard European call. This should make sense. When one holds both options, if the out-option knocks out, the in-option immediately knocks in. Thus, the value of the two options combined is 10.02 + 1.48 = 11.50, which is the price we previously obtained for the standard European call. Likewise the down-and-out put and down-and-in put add up in value to the value of the standard European put, subject to a round-off error. Similar results hold for the up-options.

Some barrier options have an additional feature called a rebate. If a knock-out barrier option provides for a rebate, the holder is paid a fixed

Barrier options are options that either terminate early without value if the asset price hits a prespecified barrier or must be activated by the asset price hitting a prespecified barrier. The former are called out-options and the latter are called in-options.

Financial Engineering

Financial engineering is a new and exciting field that focuses on the development of innovative financial instruments and their application to a variety of risk management problems. In the early 1980s Wall Street began hiring a few well-known academics like Fischer Black from MIT and Richard Roll from UCLA to help them develop and market financial products. As the products became more sophisticated, more and more academics were hired. Many of these academics held advanced degrees in the sciences. The term "rocket scientist," or sometimes "quant jock," was used to describe these individuals. However, that term soon began to be used in a pejorative sense to imply that Wall Street was trying to fool the world with mathematical but useless creations. Given the efficiency of the market, deception was not possible over the long run and most of the innovations proved to be popular. In the mid-1980s, the process took on the more palatable name of "financial engineering."

Several factors have contributed to the growth of financial engineering. While risk has always been present, the volatility of interest rates and currencies has increased in recent years. In addition, the markets have grown more efficient, making it more difficult for tradi-

tional investment and financial management strategies to squeeze out acceptable profits. Taxes and regulations have created complex problems. The fact that more small businesses are now marketing their products in foreign countries creates a need for innovative financial risk management products. World financial markets are becoming increasingly integrated, meaning that financial transactions now easily cross borders. On the academic front, innovations in financial theory have proven to be extremely applicable to real-world problems. Indeed Wall Street has benefited greatly from the research conducted in academic institutions. Last, but certainly not least, the development of the personal computer has probably done as much as anything to advance the field of financial engineering. The enormous computing power available on a desktop machine has made it possible for financial engineers to inexpensively develop and price their products.

While the evolution of derivative instruments from exchange-listed options to the exotic and complex derivatives has required a fairly high degree of quantitative ability, not all financial engineers possess the advanced technical skills of a true scientist. Indeed financial engineering is a team concept, requiring the skills of many people with different orientations.

---

sum of cash whenever the option knocks out. If a knock-in option provides for a rebate, the holder is paid a fixed sum of cash at expiration if the option never crosses the barrier. When a barrier option has a rebate, the values of the complementary out- and in-options will add up to more than the standard European option price.

As noted above, barrier options allow investors to avoid paying a price for states they do not believe will occur. As an example of the use of a barrier option, consider a protective put. A standard European put would cost 4.69. To save a little money, an investor might purchase an up-and-out protective put with a barrier of 55 for 3.75. This option would knock out if the asset goes to 55. The holder would in effect be saying that if the asset price rises quickly, he does not expect to need the insurance. Thus, his willingness to terminate the insurance early allows him to save money. Note, however, that this does not guarantee a better result. It simply elimi-

For example, some financial engineers have to be marketing-oriented. They find out what types of risk management problems their clients are facing. They then go back to the drawing board and design products and strategies that will help their clients deal with the risk. In some cases, these strategies are simply applications of existing products. In other cases, entirely new derivatives must be developed. In some cases the complexity of a new derivative necessitates the use of sophisticated mathematical skills to arrive at an appropriate price. In that case, it may be necessary to call on the talents of individuals who hold Ph.D.'s in physics, mathematics, engineering, or computer science. Financial engineering also requires communication skills and the ability to grasp the overall picture of a business. A global awareness and an understanding of accounting, regulatory, and taxation concerns are also important. All the members of a financial engineering team have one thing in common—a willingness to work extremely hard to earn profits or save money for their shareholders.

While financial engineers generally are found working in financial institutions, the practice of financial engineering is not one-sided. A financial institution may develop a new product, but it must sell it to customers, who are generally corporations, investment funds, and governments. For the customer to properly evaluate whether it should engage in one of these transactions, it must also possess individuals with financial engineering skills. For most customers, the financial engineering skills necessary to evaluate these products have not yet been fully developed. This is the area where growth and job opportunities are most likely. Financial engineering should someday become a major part of the knowledge base of financial and investment managers.

You can learn more about financial engineering from the books *The Handbook of Financial Engineering*, by Clifford W. Smith, Jr., and Charles W. Smithson (New York: Harper Business, 1990) and *Financial Engineering*, 2d ed., by John F. Marshall and Vipul K. Bansal (Miami: Kolb Publishing, 1993). *Risk* magazine (see Appendix 1A) gives an excellent feel for the world of financial engineering. The International Association of Financial Engineers' address is 646-16 Main Street, Port Jefferson, NY 11777–2230; 516–331–8069; 516–331–8044 (fax); main@iafe.org. Also you can visit its website at www.iafe.org. The IAFE publishes the *Journal of Financial Engineering*.

nates the payoff in path 5. The knocked-out put will not pay off if the asset goes up, down, and then down because it knocked out at time 1, even though at expiration the asset price is below the exercise price. Similarly an investor interested in holding a call might consider purchasing a down-and-out call. The standard call will cost 11.50 while the down-and-out with the barrier at 45 will cost 10.02. The barrier option will not pay off in path 4 where the asset goes down, up, and up whereas the standard call would pay off if that occurred.

There are many variations of path-dependent options, including some that are American-style, i.e., with early exercise. Barrier options in particular can have many types of twists, including barriers both above and below the current price and requirements that the barrier be hit more than once. Another type of barrier option allows the holder to reset the exercise price if the barrier is hit. A more common and somewhat complicating

factor is that often only the closing price is considered when determining whether the barrier was touched. This necessitates the use of the binomial model with a large number of time steps and special care to position the barrier on the nodes. Monte Carlo methods, as described in Appendix 15B, are also required.

Other Exotic Options

Most of the exotic options described above are reasonably simple to understand. There are many others that are quite complex and we will not attempt to tackle the pricing of these instruments. Because they are so popular, however, it is useful to examine the basic characteristics of these instruments so that you will be aware of them and perhaps recognize them when you encounter them in the future.

Compound options are options on options. For example, you can buy a call option that gives you the right to buy another call option. This is a call on a call. Likewise there are calls on puts, puts on calls, and puts on puts. The latter two give you the right to sell a call or a put. Compound options would be useful if an investor thought he might need an option later and wanted to establish a price at which the option could be bought or sold. A variation of the compound option is the **installment option,** which permits the premium to be paid in equal installments over the life of the option. At each payment date, the holder of the option decides whether it is worth paying the next installment. This is equivalent to deciding whether it is worth exercising the compound option to acquire another option.

Multi-asset options consist of a family of options whose payoffs depend on the prices of more than one asset. A simple type of multi-asset option is the **exchange option.** This option allows the holder to acquire one asset by giving up another. This kind of option is actually a special case of an ordinary European call. In a European call, the call holder has the right to give up one asset, cash, and acquire another asset, the stock. Exchange options are not commonly traded in the over-the-counter market, but they have proven to be useful in valuing many other types of options, such as the quality option in the Treasury bond futures contract that we covered in Chapter 11.

Another type of multi-asset option is the **min-max option.** This is an option that pays off according to the better or worse performing of two assets. For example, consider a min-max call on two assets, stocks X and Y. At expiration, we simply determine which asset has the higher price and then calculate the payoff based on that asset. This is an option on the maximum of two assets. In an option on the minimum of two assets, the payoff is calculated based on the asset with the lower price at expiration. These options can be puts or calls and they are sometimes called **rainbow options.** A slight and more common variation determines the better or worse

performing asset, not on the basis of how high or low its stock price is, but according to the rate of return on the asset during the option's life. This is also called an **alternative option.** Another variation of this is the **outperformance option,** whose payoff is determined by the difference in the prices or rates of return on two assets or indexes relative to an exercise price or rate.

Shout options permit the holder at any time during the life of the option to establish a minimum payoff that will occur at expiration. For example, suppose the stock price is very high relative to the exercise price. The investor, holding such an option and fearing that the stock price will fall, can establish the minimum payoff as the amount by which it is currently in-the-money. A slight variation of this is a **cliquet option,** in which the exercise price can periodically increase as the stock price rises. Still another variation, the **lock-in option,** permits establishment of the exact payoff, as opposed to just the minimum, prior to expiration.

A **contingent premium option** permits the investor to establish an ordinary call or put option without paying a premium. The investor then pays the premium at expiration, but only if the option is in-the-money at expiration. A **pay-later option** allows the investor to pay the premium at expiration. Unlike a contingent premium option, however, the premium must still be paid regardless of whether the option ends up in-the-money. A **deferred strike option** is one in which the exercise price is not set until a specific date prior to expiration.

Forward-start options are options whose lives do not begin until a later date. The premium is paid up front and the purchaser specifies a desired degree of moneyness, such as at-the-money, 5 percent out-of-the-money, etc. Once the option begins, it is like an ordinary option. This type of option is similar to the types of executive and employee stock option plans used by firms. The firm makes a commitment that will result in its awarding options at various future dates. When the options are structured so that as one expires another begins, the combination is called a **tandem option.**

The exotic options described here are the primary ones that are used in today's markets, but there are many more. A few years ago, most of these options did not exist. The pace of creativity is quite rapid. As your career in the financial world evolves, you will likely encounter new ones quite often.

Summary

This chapter carried our treatment of derivatives one step further by examining some advanced derivatives and strategies. We learned how portfolio insurance works and saw several different ways of implementing it. We also examined various equity derivatives that trade in the over-the-counter market, including forwards, break forwards, swaps, collars, and equity-linked debt.

Picking up where we left off with our treatment of interest rate derivatives in the previous chapter, we then looked at several variations of the plain vanilla swap, including basis swaps, index amortizing swaps, diff swaps, and constant maturity swaps. We also examined two other types of interest-sensitive instruments, structured notes and mortgage-backed securities, that are not strictly derivatives but, for better or for worse, are usually viewed as such. We saw that these instruments can have extremely volatile prices and require careful analysis.

We also looked at several types of exotic options, including digital options, chooser options, and path-dependent options. In the latter category, we examined Asian options, lookback options, and barrier options, and observed how their prices are derived in a binomial framework. All of the options classified as exotics have payoffs structured quite differently from standard European and American options.

Nearly all of these instruments are used with slight modifications in equity, currency, commodity, and interest rate markets. In particular, swaps and forwards are becoming increasingly popular in controlling the risk of price changes in raw materials. Firms with significant exposures to oil price risk are major users of derivatives. Indeed derivatives are applicable to risk management problems throughout an organization. In fact, the widespread use of derivatives has spawned the birth of a new profession, risk management.

In the first 15 chapters of this book you have gained exposure to a broad range of derivative contracts. While the coverage here is only introductory, it sets the stage for further study and eventual application of these instruments to solving risk management problems. Accordingly, we devote the next and final chapter to gaining an understanding of the process of risk management, the problems that risk managers must address, some techniques used by risk managers, and the consequences of good and bad risk management.

Key Terms

Before continuing to Chapter 16, you should be able to give brief definitions of the following terms.

- equity derivative
- portfolio insurance
- upside capture
- dynamic hedging
- break forward
- equity swap
- equity collar
- warrant
- quanto
- basis swap
- index amortizing swap
- diff swap
- constant maturity swap
- structured note
- range floater
- inverse floater
- prepayment risk
- mortgage-backed security
- securitization
- mortgage pass-through
- interest-only strip (IO)
- principal-only strip (PO)
- collateralized mortgage obligation (CMO)
- digital/binary option
- asset-or-nothing option
- cash-or-nothing option
- chooser option
- path-dependent (independent) option
- Asian option
- lookback option
- Monte Carlo simulation
- barrier option

Questions and Problems

1. Explain the key differences between an equity swap and an interest rate swap.

2. Explain how a portfolio manager might justify the purchase of an inverse floating-rate note.

3. Demonstrate that the payoffs of a chooser option with an exercise price of E and a time to expiration of T, and which permits the user to designate it as a call or a put at t, can be replicated by buying a call with an exercise price E and a time to expiration of T and a put with an exercise price equal to $E(1 + r)^{-(T - t)}$ and a time to expiration of t. This proof will require that you consider two possible outcomes at t (user designates it as a call or user designates it as a put according to the rule given in the chapter) and, for each outcome at t, there are two possible outcomes at T, which are $S_T \geq E$ or $S_T < E$. Then explain why a chooser option is less expensive than a straddle.

4. Explain why an interest-only (IO) mortgage strip has a value that is extremely volatile with respect to interest rates. What two factors determine its value?

5. Explain the difference between path-dependent options and path-independent options and give examples of each.

6. Give an example of a situation in which someone might wish to use a barrier option.

7. Construct a scenario in which a financial manager or investment manager might wish to enter into a basis swap.

8. On July 5, a market index is at 492.54. You hold a portfolio that duplicates the index and is worth 20,500 times the index. You wish to insure the portfolio at a particular value over the period until September 20. You can buy T-bills maturing on September 20 with a face value of $100 for $98.78.
   a. You plan to use puts, which are selling for $23.72 and have an exercise price of 510. Determine the appropriate number of puts and shares to hold. What is the insured value of the portfolio?
   b. Determine the value of the portfolio if the index on September 20 is at 507.35.
   c. Determine the value of the portfolio if the index on September 20 is at 515.75. Compute the upside capture and the cost of the insurance.

9. Use the information in problem 8 to set up a dynamic hedge using stock index futures. Assume a multiplier of 500. The futures price is 496.29. The volatility is .175. The continuously compounded risk-free rate is 3.6 percent, and the call delta is .3826. Let the stock price increase by $1, and show that the change in the portfolio value is almost the same as it would have been had a put been used.

For the next three problems, use a two-period binomial model on a stock worth 100 that can go up 20 percent or down 15 percent. The risk-free rate is 6 percent each period.

10. Determine the price of an average price Asian call option. Use an exercise price of 95. Count the current price in determining the average. Comment on

whether you would expect a standard European call to have a lower or higher price.

11. Determine the prices of lookback and modified lookback calls and puts. For the modified lookbacks, use an exercise price of 95.

12. Determine the prices of the following barrier options.
    a. A down-and-out call with the barrier at 90 and the exercise price at 95
    b. An up-and-out put with the barrier at 110 and the exercise price at 105
    c. Select any other barrier option but base your selection on the following instructions: Calculate the value of your selected barrier option and use it with the results you obtained in part a or b to determine the price of a standard European call or put. Then calculate the actual value of the European call or put and compare that answer with your answer obtained from the barrier options. Explain why this result is obtained.

13. A portfolio manager is interested in purchasing an instrument with a call option-like payoff but does not want to have to pay money up front. The manager learns from a banker that one can do this by entering into a break forward contract. The manager wants to learn if the banker is quoting a fair price. The stock price is 437.55. The contract expires in 270 days. The volatility is .18 and the continuously compounded risk-free rate is .0375. The exercise price will be set at the forward price of the stock.
    a. Determine the exercise price.
    b. The loan implicit in the break forward contract will have a face value of 40.19. Determine if this is a fair amount by using your answer in a and computing the value of K.
    c. Regardless of whether the break forward is found to be fairly priced, determine the value of the position if the stock price ends up at 465 and at 425.

14. An investment manager enters into an equity swap promising to pay LIBOR on the exact number of days using a 360-day year and receive the stock index return minus .2 percent. The notional principal is $100 million. The current day is January 15. The payments will be made on each July 15 and January 15 for two years. The current LIBOR is 6.25. LIBOR turns out to be 5.97 on July 15, 5.79 on the next January 15, and 6.12 on the next July 15. The current index is at 412.15 and turns out to be 409.45 on July 15, 414.18 on the next January 15, 422.75 on the next July 15, and 418.61 on the next January 15. Find the payments on the swap.

15. An investment manager holds a portfolio worth $4,351,700, which can be thought of as 10,000 shares of a single stock worth 435.17. His performance will be evaluated in 78 days and he would like to establish a maximum and minimum profit over the remaining period until the evaluation is made. He finds that a zero-cost equity collar can be constructed by buying a put with an exercise price of 430 and selling a call with an exercise price of 448.75. The continuously compounded risk-free rate is 4.14 percent and the volatility of the stock is .15.
    a. Determine if the collar is fairly priced at a zero premium.
    b. Assume the manager enters into the transaction. Determine the profit if the stock price at expiration ends up at 460, at 435, and at 415.

16.   A stock is priced at 125.37, the continuously compounded risk-free rate is 4.4 percent, and the volatility is .21. There are no dividends. Answer the following questions.

   a.   Determine a fair price for a two-year asset-or-nothing option with exercise price of 120.

   b.   Assuming you purchased the asset-or-nothing option at the price you determined in a, calculate your profit if the asset price at expiration is (1) 138 and (2) 114.

   c.   Determine a fair price for a two-year cash-or-nothing option with exercise price of 120 that pays 120 if it expires in-the-money.

   d.   Assuming you purchased the cash-or-nothing option at the price you determined in c, calculate your profit if the asset price at expiration is (1) 138 or (2) 114.

17.   Consider a 10-year, fixed-rate mortgage of $500,000 that has an interest rate of 12 percent. For simplification assume that payments are made annually.

   a.   Determine the amortization schedule.

   b.   Using your answer in a, determine the value of both IO and PO strips with a discount rate of 10 percent under the assumption that the mortgage will not be prepaid.

   c.   Now recompute the values of the IO and PO under the assumption that interest rates immediately fall to 8 percent and the mortgage is prepaid in year 6.

   d.   Explain the risk characteristics of IO and PO strips.

18.   An investment manager expects a stock to be quite volatile and is considering the purchase of either a straddle or a chooser option. The stock is priced at 44, the exercise price is 40, the continuously compounded risk-free rate is 5.2 percent, and the volatility is .51. The options expire in 194 days. The chooser option must be declared a call or a put exactly 90 days before expiration.

   a.   Determine the prices of the straddle and the chooser.

   b.   Suppose at 90 days before expiration, the stock is at 28. Find the value of the chooser option at expiration if the stock price ends up at 50 and at 30.

   c.   Suppose at 90 days before expiration, the stock is at 60. Find the value of the chooser option at expiration if the stock price ends up at 50 and at 30.

   d.   Compare your answers in c and d to the performance of the straddle.

19.   Consider a basis swap with a maturity of 90 days in which one side will pay the rate on CDs and the other will pay LIBOR. The term structures are given as follows:

	CDs	LIBOR
30 days	4.78%	5.375%
60 days	4.84%	5.45 %
90 days	4.92%	5.5 %

The swap will have three payments, each 30 days apart with the first occurring 30 days from now. When discounting, convert all rates to the money market equivalent, meaning to multiply the rate by (days/360) rather than raise one plus the rate to the power (days/365). (This is sometimes done in practice.) Work out the following:

a. Determine the fixed rate on two plain vanilla swaps with the CD rate as the floating rate on one and LIBOR as the floating rate on the other. Convert your answer to an annual rate by multiplying by 12.

b. Using your answer in a, determine the spread on the basis swap of CDs against LIBOR. Be sure to make it clear which party pays the spread.

20. (Concept Problem) Suppose you are asked to assist in the design of an equity-linked security. The instrument is a five-year zero coupon bond with a guaranteed return of 1 percent, compounded annually. At the end of five years the bond will pay an additional return based on any appreciation of the Nikkei 300 stock index, a measure of the performance of 300 Japanese stocks. The risk-free rate is 5.5 percent, compounded annually, and the volatility of the index is .15. In addition the index pays a dividend of 1.7 percent continuously compounded. Presently the index is at 315.55 and the additional return is based on appreciation above the current level of the index. You expect to sell these bonds in minimum increments of $100. Overall you expect to sell $10 million of these securities. Your firm has determined that it needs a margin of $175,000 in cash today to cover costs and earn a reasonable profit. Determine the percentage of the Nikkei return that your firm should offer to cover its costs. Your firm would then set the percentage offered at less than this. If your firm sells this security, comment on the risk it creates for itself and suggest how it might deal with that risk.

21. (Concept Problem) The formula we found for the minimum value of an insured portfolio of stock and puts is

$$V_{min} = \frac{EV}{S + P}.$$

In the problem used in the chapter, we established a minimum value of the portfolio of $44,637,585. Recall that E = 485, V = $44,575,000, S = 445.75, and P = $38.57. In that problem, we simply used the 485 put and derived the minimum value we could obtain with this put. However, a portfolio manager might want to choose the minimum value. This would require finding a put that would insure the portfolio at this minimum. Suppose that in this same example, the portfolio manager is willing to tolerate a 1 percent loss. Find the number of shares and puts that would be required. (Hint: The above equation for V_{min} must hold, but you must find a put with a different exercise price, which will result in a different put price, that will make the equation hold. You should probably use the spreadsheet bsbin1.xls or the Windows program bsbwin2.exe to do the repetitive calculations involved in the Black-Scholes model.)

APPENDIX 15A
Derivation of the Dynamic Hedge Ratio for Portfolio Insurance*

Stock-Futures Dynamic Hedge

The stock-put portfolio of N shares and N puts initially is worth

$$V = N(S + P).$$

By this definition, N must equal $V/(S + P)$. The change in the portfolio's value for a small stock price change is given by the derivative of V with respect to S,

$$\frac{\partial V}{\partial S} = N\left(1 + \frac{\partial P}{\partial S}\right) = \left(\frac{V}{S + P}\right)\left(1 + \frac{\partial P}{\partial S}\right).$$

We assume the put is not available, so we shall replicate the position with a portfolio of N_S shares of stock and N_f futures contracts. The value of the portfolio is

$$V = N_S S + N_f V^f,$$

where V^f is the value of the futures contract. Remember that the initial value of a futures contract is zero, so $V^f = 0$. The number of shares then will be $N_S = V/S$. The change in the portfolio's value for a small change in S is the derivative of V with respect to S,

$$\frac{\partial V}{\partial S} = N_S + N_f\left(\frac{\partial f}{\partial S}\right).$$

Note that we must include $N_f(\partial f/\partial S)$ because $\partial V^f/\partial S = \partial f/\partial S$. Assuming no dividends, the futures price is

$$f = Se^{r_c T}.$$

Thus,

$$\frac{\partial f}{\partial S} = e^{r_c T}.$$

---

*This appendix requires the use of calculus.

We can substitute V/S for N_S and $e^{r_c T}$ for $\partial f / \partial S$, giving

$$\frac{\partial V}{\partial S} = \left(\frac{V}{S}\right) + N_f e^{r_c T}.$$

The objective is to make the stock-futures portfolio respond to a stock price change in the same way a stock-put portfolio would. Thus, we should set these two derivatives equal to each other:

$$\left(\frac{V}{S + P}\right)\left(1 + \frac{\partial P}{\partial S}\right) = \left(\frac{V}{S}\right) + N_f e^{r_c T}.$$

Then we solve for N_f:

$$N_f = \left[\left(\frac{V}{S + P}\right)\left(1 + \frac{\partial P}{\partial S}\right) - \left(\frac{V}{S}\right)\right] e^{-r_c T}.$$

This formula might look somewhat simpler if we recognize that $V/(S + P)$ is simply V_{min}/E and that $1 + \partial P / \partial S = \partial C / \partial S$. Thus,

$$N_f = \left[\left(\frac{V_{min}}{E}\right)\left(\frac{\partial C}{\partial S}\right) - \left(\frac{V}{S}\right)\right] e^{-r_c T}.$$

Of course, $\partial C / \partial S = N(d_1)$ from the Black-Scholes model.

Stock–T-Bill Dynamic Hedge

In the preceding section, we derived the sensitivity of a portfolio of N shares of stock and N puts. This value was shown to be

$$\frac{\partial V}{\partial S} = \left(\frac{V}{S + P}\right)\left(1 + \frac{\partial P}{\partial S}\right) = \left(\frac{V_{min}}{E}\right)\left(\frac{\partial C}{\partial S}\right).$$

A portfolio of stock and T-bills is worth

$$V = N_S S + N_B B.$$

Its sensitivity to a change in S is

$$\frac{\partial V}{\partial S} = N_S.$$

Note that the T-bill price does not change with a change in S. Setting this equal to the sensitivity of the stock-put portfolio and solving for N_S gives

$$N_S = \left(\frac{V_{min}}{E}\right)\left(\frac{\partial C}{\partial S}\right)$$

and $\partial C / \partial S = N(d_1)$.

APPENDIX 15B
Monte Carlo Simulation

Simulation is a procedure in which random numbers are generated according to probabilities assumed to be associated with a source of uncertainty, such as a new product's sales or, more appropriately for our purposes, stock prices, interest rates, exchange rates, or commodity prices. Outcomes associated with these random drawings are then analyzed to determine the likely results and the associated risk. Oftentimes this technique is called **Monte Carlo simulation,** being named for the city of Monte Carlo, which is noted for its casinos.

The gambling analogy notwithstanding, Monte Carlo simulation is a legitimate and widely used technique for dealing with uncertainty in many aspects of business operations. For our purposes, it has been shown to be an accurate method of pricing options and particularly useful for path-dependent options and others for which no known formula exists.

To facilitate an understanding of the technique, we shall look at how Monte Carlo simulation has been used to price standard European options. Of course, we know that the Black-Scholes model is the correct method of pricing these options so Monte Carlo simulation is not really needed. It is useful, however, to conduct this experiment because it demonstrates the accuracy of the technique for a simple option of which the exact price is easily obtained from a known formula.

The assumptions of the Black-Scholes model imply that for a given stock price at time t, simulated changes in the stock price at a future time t + Δt can be generated by the following formula:

$$\Delta S = S r_c \Delta t + S \sigma \varepsilon \sqrt{\Delta t},$$

where S is the current stock price, ΔS is the change in the stock price, r_c is the continuously compounded risk-free rate, σ is the volatility of the stock, and Δt is the length of the time interval over which the stock price change occurs. The variable ε is a random number generated from a standard normal probability distribution. Remember from Chapter 4 that the standard normal random variable has a mean of zero and a standard deviation of 1.0, and occurs with a frequency corresponding to that associated with the famous bell-shaped curve.

Generating future stock prices according to the above formula is actually quite easy. A standard normal random variable can be approximated with a slight adjustment to Excel's Rand() function. The Rand() function produces a uniform random number between 0 and 1, meaning that it generates numbers between 0 and 1 with equal probability. A good approximation for a standard normal variable is obtained by the Excel

formula "= Rand() + Rand() + Rand() + Rand() + Rand() + Rand() + Rand() + Rand() + Rand() + Rand() + Rand() + Rand() − 6.0," or simply 12 uniform random numbers minus 6.0.[*] Alternatively, a normal random number generator is available in Excel's Data Analysis tool pack.

After generating one standard normal random variable, you then simply insert it into the right-hand side of the above formula for ΔS. This gives the price change over the life of the option, which is then added to the current price to obtain the price of the asset at expiration. You then compute the price of the option at expiration according to the standard formulas, $Max(0, S_T − E)$ for a call or $Max(0, E − S_T)$ for a put. This produces one possible option value at expiration. You then repeat this procedure many thousands of times, take the average value of the option at expiration, and discount that value at the risk-free rate. Some users compute the standard deviation of the call prices in order to obtain a feel for the possible error in estimating the price.

Let us price the Digital Equipment July 165 call that we first encountered in Chapter 3. The Digital Equipment stock price is 164, the exercise price is 165, the risk-free rate is .0521, the volatility is .29, and the time to expiration is .0959. Inserting the above approximation formula for a standard normal random variable in any cell in an Excel spreadsheet produces a random number. Suppose that number is .733449. Inserting into the formula for ΔS gives $164(.0521)(.0959) + 164(.29)(.733449) \sqrt{.0959} = 11.62$. Thus, the simulated value of the stock at expiration is $164 + 11.62 = 175.62$. At that price, the option will be worth $Max(0, 175.62 − 165) = 10.62$ at expiration. We then draw another random number. Suppose we get −.18985. Inserting into the formula for ΔS, we obtain $164(.0521)(.0959) + 164(.29)(−.18985) \sqrt{.0959} = −1.98$, which gives us a stock price at expiration of $164 − 1.98 = 162.02$, leading to an option price of $Max(0, 162.02 − 165) = 0$. We repeat this procedure several thousand times, after which we take an average of the simulated option prices and then discount that average to the present using the present value formula $e^{−.0521(.0959)}$.

Naturally every simulation is different because each set of random numbers is different. A Monte Carlo procedure written in Excel's Visual Basic produced the following values for this call, whose actual Black-Scholes price is 5.79:

---

[*]This approximation is based on the fact that the distribution of the sum of 12 uniformly distributed random numbers between 0 and 1 will have a mean of six and a standard deviation of 1. By subtracting 6.0, we adjust the mean to zero without changing the standard deviation. What we obtain is technically not normally distributed but is symmetric with mean zero and standard deviation of 1.0, which are three properties associated with the normal distribution. The procedure is widely accepted as a quick and reasonable approximation but would not pass the most demanding tests for normality.

Number of Random Drawings	Call Price
1,000	5.58
10,000	5.51
50,000	5.83
100,000	5.75

It would appear that at least 50,000 random drawings are required for the simplest case of a standard European option.

Applying the Monte Carlo technique to more complicated options such as path-dependent options requires a partitioning of the option's life into time periods, as in the binomial model. For example, suppose you wanted to price an Asian call option in which the average price would be computed by collecting the daily closing price over the life of the option. Ignoring holidays and weekends, let us say that the option has a 90-day life. Then a run would consist of 90 random drawings, each used to simulate the stock price at the end of each of the 90 days. The formula for each ΔS would be based on the previous day's closing price. The value of Δt would be 1/365. Then the average of the 90 stock prices would determine the call payoff at expiration as described in this chapter. You would then need to repeat the procedure at least 50,000 times. The more complex options, however, would probably require at least 100,000 runs.

This may seem like a formidable task but that is what computers are for. More than likely computations such as these would be written in a fast and efficient language like C++. In addition there is a considerable amount of research going on for ways to make Monte Carlo simulations run more efficiently.

For your purposes here, the important thing is to gain an understanding of the principles of option pricing with Monte Carlo simulation, which can be seen with simple European options. Each run generates a possible outcome. Provided enough runs are made, the outcomes will occur with the same relative frequency implied by the probabilities assumed by the Black-Scholes model. The option price will then become what we have so often described throughout this book—a probability-weighted average of the expiration values of the option, discounted at the risk-free rate. More complex options will naturally require modifications to the procedure.

CHAPTER 16

Financial Risk Management

Measuring risk is essentially a passive activity. Managing risk is a proactive process, where, in dynamic markets, people are actively seeking to change their positions so that their institution has the risk profile they want it to have.

PATRICK BRAZEL, Managing Director, Sun Guard Capital Markets
Risk, January 1996

In the first 15 chapters we have studied the use of many different types of derivatives in a variety of situations. In the financial markets of the late 1990s, derivatives are playing a major part in the decision-making process of corporations, financial institutions, and investment funds. Derivatives have been embraced not only as tools for hedging but as means of controlling risk, meaning to reduce risk when one wants to reduce risk and increase risk when one wants to increase it. The low transaction costs and ease of use of derivatives have given firms a flexibility to make adjustments to the risk of a firm or portfolio. Corporations have been particularly avid users of derivatives to manage interest rate and foreign exchange risks.

We presented charts showing volume in the exchange-listed derivatives markets in Chapters 2, 7, 12, and 13. Figure 16.1 shows the volume and levels of interest rate swaps, currency swaps, and interest rate options from 1987 to 1995. The variable called *activity* is the notional principal of swaps created during the given year while *outstanding* is the notional principal of contracts open at year-end. Notional principal overstates the sizes of these contracts because it does not reflect the amount of money transferred. Rather it indicates the value of spot transactions on which derivatives were based. The most important point from this graph, however, is the growth in the market, which has occurred at an exponential pace.

As we have seen throughout this book derivatives generally carry a high degree of leverage. When used improperly they can increase the risk

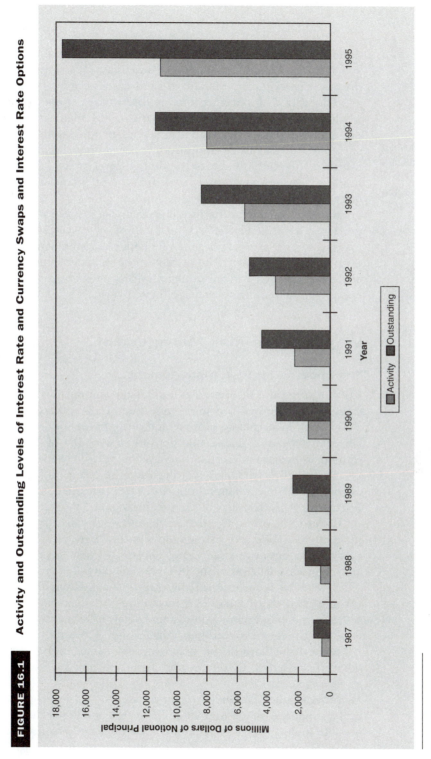

FIGURE 16.1 Activity and Outstanding Levels of Interest Rate and Currency Swaps and Interest Rate Options

Source: International Swaps and Derivatives Association surveys posted at www.isda.org

Risk management is the practice of defining the risk level a firm desires, identifying the risk level it currently has, and using derivative or other financial instruments to adjust the actual risk level to the desired risk level.

dramatically, sometimes putting the survival of a firm in jeopardy. As we conclude this chapter, we shall take a look at a few stories of how derivatives were used improperly, and in some cases were fatal.

The critical importance of using derivatives properly has created a whole new activity called **risk management.** Risk management is the practice of defining the risk level a firm desires, identifying the risk level a firm currently has, and using derivatives or other financial instruments to adjust the actual level of risk to the desired level of risk. Risk management has also spawned an entirely new industry of financial institutions that offer to take positions in derivatives opposite the end users, which are corporations or investment funds. These financial institutions, which we have previously identified as dealers, profit off of the spread between their buying and selling prices and generally hedge the underlying risks of their portfolios of derivatives. The revolution in risk management has also created a large industry in consulting services and software firms devoted exclusively to helping firms manage their risks.

Why Practice Risk Management?

The Impetus for Risk Management

Growth in the use of derivatives to manage risk did not occur simply because people became enamored with them. In fact, there has always been a great deal of suspicion, distrust, and outright fear of derivatives. Eventually, firms began to realize that derivatives were the best tool for coping with markets that had become increasingly volatile over the years.

Figures 16.2, 16.3, and 16.4 illustrate the historical behavior of interest rates, foreign exchange rates, and stock prices. Interest rates are represented by U.S. Treasury bills, foreign exchange rates are represented by the dollar value of the German mark, and stock prices are represented by the S&P 500. Each series shows the monthly high and low along with either the closing or average value. The spread between the high and low gives a good indication of the intrayear volatility.

As can be seen, each of these series has exhibited unusually large volatility at certain times. This increasing and unstable volatility has resulted in more and more firms using derivatives to manage the effects that these fluctuations have on their values.

Some firms have begun practicing risk management because certain other firms failed to do so and incurred painful and embarrassing losses.

Several other factors have contributed to the growing use of derivatives to manage risk. The explosion in information technology made it possible to do the numerous and complex calculations necessary to price

FIGURE 16.2   **High, Low, and Average Three-Month Treasury Bill Auction Rates**

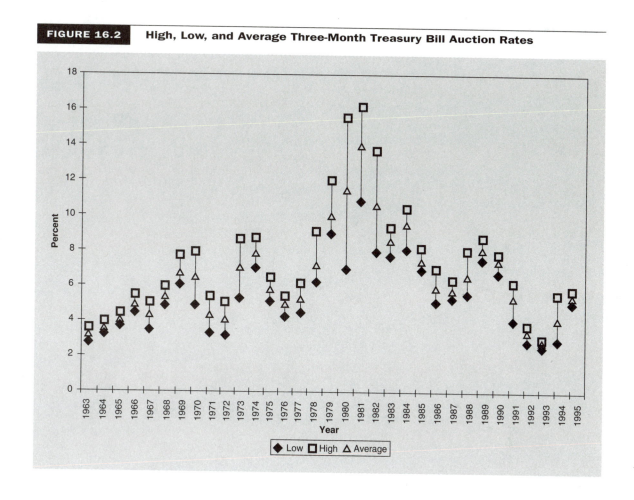

derivatives quickly and at low cost and to keep track of positions taken.[1] Another factor was the favorable regulatory environment. The CFTC adopted a pro-market position in the early 1980s, which paved the way for an increasing number of innovative futures contracts, such as Eurodollars and stock index futures. These contracts established a momentum that led to more innovation in the exchange-listed and over-the-counter markets.

We should note that the industry has gone through a significant evolution in what it calls itself. In its early stages, it was known as *commodities*.

---

[1]In fact, one could argue that the development of the personal computer was one of the single most important events for derivatives.

FIGURE 16.3   High, Low, and Average Price of German Mark

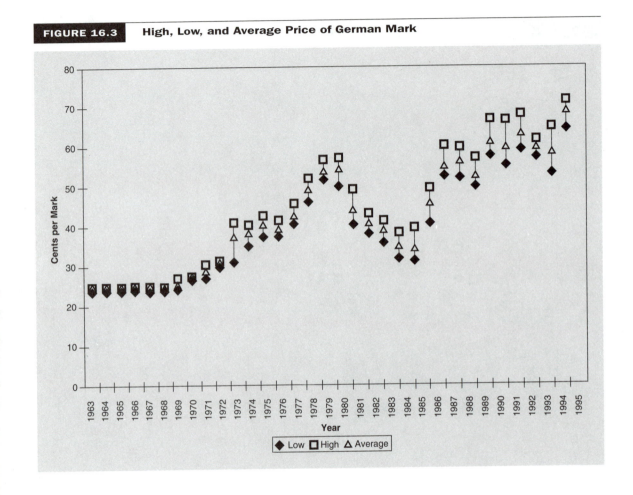

As exchange-listed options and financial futures were created, it began to call itself *futures and options*. When over-the-counter products like swaps and forwards were added, it began to be known as *derivatives*. Now the focus has shifted away from the instruments and toward the process, leaving us with the term *risk management* and sometimes **financial risk management**.

The Benefits of Risk Management

In Chapter 10, we identified several reasons why firms hedge. At this point, however, we are focusing not on the simple process of hedging, but on the more general process of managing risk. Let us restate our Chapter 10 reasons for hedging in the context of risk management.

FIGURE 16.4   High, Low, and Closing S&P 500

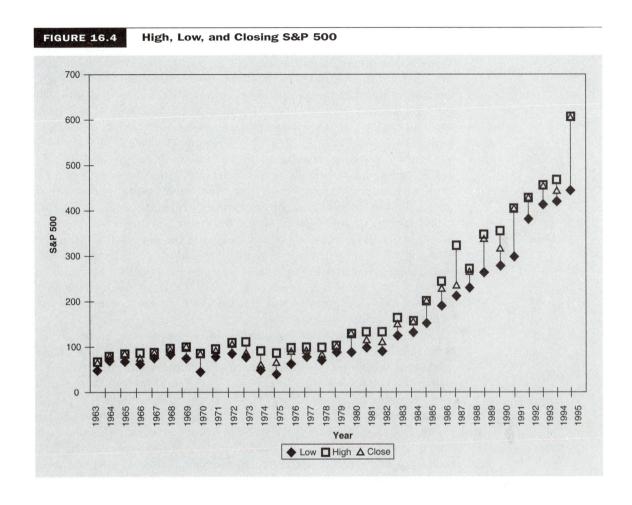

In the Modigliani-Miller world in which there are no taxes or transaction costs and information is costless and available to everyone, financial decisions have no relevance for shareholders. Financial decisions, such as how much debt a firm issues, how large a dividend it pays, or how much risk it takes, merely determine how the pie is sliced. The size of the pie, as determined by the quality of a firm's investments in its assets, is what determines shareholder value. Modigliani-Miller argue that shareholders can do these financial transactions just as well by buying and selling stocks and bonds in their personal portfolios. Thus, risk management can be practiced by shareholders by adjusting their personal portfolios; consequently, there is no need for firms to practice risk management.

This argument ignores the fact that most firms can practice risk management more effectively and at lower cost than shareholders. Their size

and investment in information systems give firms an advantage over their shareholders. Firms can also gain from managing risk if their income fluctuates across numerous tax brackets. With a progressive tax system, they will end up with lower taxes by stabilizing their income. Risk management can also reduce the probability of bankruptcy, a costly process in which the legal system becomes a partial claimant on the firm's value. Risk management can also be done because managers, whose wealth is heavily tied to the firm's performance, are simply managing their own risk.

Firms that are in a near-bankrupt state will find that they have little incentive to invest in seemingly attractive projects that will merely help their creditors by increasing the chance that the firm will be able to pay off its debts. This is called the underinvestment problem and is more thoroughly explored in corporate finance books. Managing risk helps avoid getting into situations like that and, as such, increases the chance that firms will always invest in attractive projects, which is good for society as a whole. Risk management also allows firms to generate the cash flow necessary to carry out their investment projects. If internal funds are insufficient, they may have to look toward external funds. Some firms would cut investment rather than raise new capital.

When a firm goes into a particular line of business, it knowingly accepts risks. Airlines, for example, accept the risks of competition in the market for transporting people from one place to another. The risk associated with volatile oil prices is an entirely different type of risk, one that they often prefer to get rid of. Hence many airlines hedge oil prices, which allows them to concentrate on their main line of business. On occasion, however, they may feel that oil prices are heading downward, suggesting that they lift their hedges. Thus, they are not just hedging but rather practicing risk management by setting the current level of risk to the desired level of risk.

Some firms use risk management as an excuse to speculate in areas where they have less expertise than they think. As we shall see later in the chapter, when a consumer products company speculates on foreign interest rates, it is no longer just a consumer products company. It becomes a financial trading company and it must be prepared to suffer the consequences if its forecasts are wrong. Some firms practice risk management because they truly believe that they can time movements in the underlying source of a risk. When that source of risk is unrelated to the firm's basic line of business, the consequences of bad forecasting combined with highly leveraged derivatives can be dire.

Other firms manage risk because they believe that arbitrage opportunities are possible. For example, suppose a firm could borrow at a floating rate of LIBOR plus 110 basis points or fixed at a rate of 10.5 percent. It can enter into a swap paying a fixed rate of 9.25 percent and receiving LIBOR. Simple arithmetic shows that it would get a lower rate by issuing

floating-rate debt and entering into a pay fixed–receive floating swap. The net effect is to pay LIBOR plus 110 on the floating-rate debt, receive LIBOR, and pay 9.25 on the swap, which adds up to a fixed rate of 9.25 + 1.10 = 10.35, or 15 basis points cheaper than straight fixed-rate debt. Yet if the firm had simply issued fixed-rate debt at 10.5 percent, it would have assumed no credit risk. Now it assumes the credit risk of the swap counterparty and is compensated to the tune of a 15-basis-point reduction in the interest rate. Is this worth it? In the early days of the market, the savings were probably large enough to be worth it, but as the market has become more efficient, the savings decreased and were likely just fair compensation for the assumption of credit risk.

It is important to emphasize that reducing risk is not in and of itself a sufficient reason to hedge or manage risk. Firms that accept lower risks will in the long run earn lower returns. Moreover, if their shareholders truly wanted lower risks, they could easily realign their portfolios, substituting lower risk securities for higher risk securities. Managing risk must create value for shareholders, giving them something they cannot get themselves. To the extent that risk management reduces the costly process of bankruptcy, saves taxes, and makes it easier for firms to take on profitable investment projects, value is clearly created.

The Structure of the Risk Management Industry

The risk management industry is made up of **end users, dealers,** and other firms, including consultants and specialized software companies.

End Users

End users are generally thought of as firms that wish to engage in derivatives transactions to manage their risk. Needing to execute a derivatives transaction, end users contact derivatives dealers, whom we shall discuss in the next section. The end user could be thought of as the party who is purchasing a service while the dealer is the supplier of the service.

The end user community primarily consists of nonfinancial corporations. Other end users include investment funds, which include pension plans and mutual funds. In addition, some financial institutions that are not in the business of being derivatives dealers will still use derivatives to manage their risks. At times even a dealer, managing its own risk, will take the position of an end user opposite another dealer. Many foreign governments use derivatives. In the United States, state and local governments use derivatives, though somewhat less than corporations. However, with the exception of certain agencies, such as the Postal Service, the U.S. federal government does not use derivatives. Many private organizations, such as charities, endowments, and universities, use derivatives.

An end user is a corporation, investment fund, financial institution, government, or private organization that engages in derivatives transactions with a derivatives dealer.

Obviously there are minimum firm sizes necessary to justify certain derivatives activities, but risks of as little as a few million dollars can justify over-the-counter derivatives and even smaller sizes can be managed with exchange-traded derivatives. As one might expect, larger firms use derivatives more and have more organized and sophisticated risk management operations.

In a typical corporation the treasury department has responsibility for managing the firm's cash. It operates in the financial markets on a regular basis, borrowing cash, repaying loans, and wiring funds to and from domestic and foreign offices. If the firm engages in derivatives transactions to manage financial risk, these transactions are typically executed and managed by the treasury department. Normally a treasury department is a cost center and not a profit center, meaning that its job is to perform a function at the lowest possible cost and not to try to earn a profit. In recent years, however, many corporate treasurers, sometimes responding to pressure placed on them by senior management, have begun using derivatives to speculate and turn a profit. Unfortunately, this is what has led some companies to speculate in markets they know little about.

Some derivatives activities are conducted outside of the treasury. For example, a firm might have a commodity purchasing manager who hedges its exposure to commodity prices. Some firms run highly decentralized derivatives activities. They may have numerous subsidiaries, each of which engages in its own hedging. We shall discuss these types of organizational issues later in the chapter.

End users have shown a preference for particular types of derivative instruments for a given type of risk. Forward contracts are preferred for foreign exchange risk with swaps being the primary instrument for managing interest rate risk and futures preferred for commodity price risk. Stock market risk is primarily managed with options, both over-the-counter and exchange-listed.

Dealers

Dealers, as previously noted, are financial institutions making markets in derivatives. These institutions include banks and numerous investment banking/brokerage firms. They quote prices indicating their willingness to take either side of derivatives transactions. These prices are, as we have noted previously, stated in terms of a bid price and an ask price, with the price they are asking higher than the price they are bidding. Dealers will not naturally have offsetting positions. Any risk that remains is usually hedged by taking on new and offsetting derivatives, which may be in the form of exchange-traded or over-the-counter contracts. Thus, the dealer is not exposed to market movements and earns a profit off of the spread between its buying and selling prices.

Most dealer firms have highly sophisticated derivatives operations. They employ individuals with training in finance, economics, mathematics, physics, computer science, and engineering. Many of their technically trained personnel design new derivatives and risk management strategies and determine how to price them. Dealers also employ sales personnel who call on potential end users, examine their risk management needs, and try to convince the end users to engage in transactions with the dealers. Dealers generally make large investments in computer hardware and software for managing their derivatives positions. Derivatives activities have been a tremendous source of profits for many dealers.

Table 16.1 provides a list of dealers cited by the magazine *Institutional Investor* as the best derivatives dealers in 1996. This ranking was a result of a survey of corporations and institutions using derivatives. The survey also ranked the dealers in certain specializations. For example, while J. P. Morgan was the top dealer in interest rate swaps, Citicorp was the top dealer in currency swaps and SBC Warburg was the top dealer in equity swaps. Goldman Sachs was the top dealer in LIBOR-based options while Citicorp was the top dealer in currency options and SBC Warburg was the top dealer in S&P 500 options.

A derivatives dealer is a firm that is in the business of offering to take either side of a derivatives transaction with an end user. The dealer usually hedges its risk and earns a profit off of the difference in the prices it bids and offers.

TABLE 16.1   The Leading Derivatives Dealers

Citicorp
Goldman, Sachs & Co.
J. P. Morgan
SBC Warburg
Merrill Lynch & Co.
Morgan Stanley & Co.
Chase Manhattan Bank
UBS Securities
Deutsche Morgan Grenfell
NatWest
Bankers Trust Co.
BZW
CS First Boston
BankAmerica
Lehman Brothers
Salomon Brothers
Société Général
ABN Amro Bank
Midland Bank
Banque Paribas

Source: *Institutional Investor,* February 1997

Other Participants in the Risk Management Industry

The growth in risk management has created an industry of firms providing consulting and software services. Consulting services include general risk management consulting, legal and accounting/auditing, and personnel search. The specialized knowledge required to program computers, understand the emerging derivatives law, provide proper accounting and auditing functions, and search for specialized technical personnel has led to profitable opportunities for individuals and firms with these skills. Table 16.2 shows a list of the leading firms as compiled from *Risk* magazine.

In previous chapters we have covered topics that have touched on the subject of how risk is managed. Our focus at that time, however, was on understanding the instruments and their uses. Now we turn more directly to the question of how risk is controlled when derivatives are used.

TABLE 16.2   **Risk Management Software, Legal, and Accounting and Consulting Firms**

Software Firms	Law Firms	Accounting and Consulting
AFA Systems	Allen & Overy	Arthur Anderson
Algorithmics	Baker & McKenzie	Coopers & Lybrand
Alphametrics	Blake, Cassels & Graydon	Deloitte & Touche Tohmatsu
Axion Software Laboratories	Brown & Wood	Ernst & Young
BARRA	Cadwalader, Wickersham & Taft	Guildhall Ltd.
Brady	Cleary, Gottlieb, Steen & Hamilton	Moody's Investor Services
C-ATS Software	Clifford Chance	O'Neill Associates
CMG UK	Debevoise & Plimpton	Price Waterhouse
Data Analysis Risk Technology	Fasken Martineau	Standard & Poor's
Datalink International	Field Fisher Waterhouse	Telerate
DBS Financial Systems	Freshfields	TMG Financial Products
Derivative Software	Hebb & Gitlin	Touche Ross
Derivative Trading Systems	Herbert Smith	Reuters
Diagram	Hughes, Hubbard & Reed	
Financial Engineering Associates	Kennedy, Covington, Lobdell & Hickman	
Financial Object Resources	Lavery, de Billy	
Financial Software Systems	Linklaters & Paines	
FNX	Lovell White Durrant	
Front Capital Systems	Mayer, Brown & Platt	
GOVPX	Milbank, Tweed, Hadley & McCloy	
IBM	Mitsui, Yasuda, Wani & Maeda	
Infinity Financial Technology	Norton, Rose	
Integral Development	Richards & O'Neil	
Inventure	Rogers & Wells	
Investment Intelligence Systems Group	Sherman & Sterling	
IRIS Investment Support Systems	Simmons & Simmons	
ITS	Simpson, Thacher & Bartlett	
Kamakura	Skadden, Arps, Slate, Meagher & Flom	
Leading Market Technologies	Slaughter & May	

Although there are many types of risk, the two primary classes are market risk and credit risk. We shall cover these separately and then list and briefly discuss the other types of risk.

Managing Market Risk

Market risk is the uncertainty of a firm's value that is associated with movements in an underlying source of risk. For example, a firm might be concerned about movements in interest rates, foreign exchange rates, stock prices, or commodity prices. Credit risk, which we cover in a later section,

| **TABLE 16.2** | *(continued)* |

Software Firms	Law Firms	Accounting and Consulting
Login	Stikeman, Elliott	
Lombard Risk Systems	Sullivan & Cromwell	
Mamdouh Barakat Risk Management	Tory Tory Deslauries & Binnington	
Management Data	Watson, Farley & Williams	
Marvin Software	Weil Gotshal & Manges	
Mathsoft	Wilde Sapte	
Midas-Kapiti International		
Monis Software		
Multinational Computer Models		
Murex		
Olsen & Associates		
Principia Partners		
Redpoint Software		
Renaissance		
Rolfe & Nolan		
Sailfish Systems		
Saladin		
Savvysoft		
Selkirk Financial Technologies		
Sendero		
Software Options International		
Summit Systems		
Sunguard Capital Markets		
Tech Hackers		
Trema		
Triple Point Technology		
Truerisk		
Visual Numerics International		
Wall Street Systems		
Wilco International		
Wolfram Research		
Zai*net		

Source: Compiled from *The Risk Magazine Guide to ISDA Members,* 1995, and various issues of *Risk* magazine

Market risk is the uncertainty associated with movements in interest rates, foreign exchange rates, stock prices, or commodity prices.

will deal with the possibility of losses resulting from a counterparty's failure to pay when required.

When considering interest rate risk, there is the risk of short-, intermediate-, and long-term interest rates. Within short-term interest rate risk, there is the risk of LIBOR changing, the risk of the Treasury bill rate changing, the risk of the commercial paper rate changing, and numerous other risks associated with specific interest rates. A risk manager responsible for positions in LIBOR-based instruments and instruments tied to the commercial paper rate would have to take into account the extent to which those rates are correlated. A long position in LIBOR and a short position in commercial paper would be a partial hedge since LIBOR is correlated with the commercial paper rate. Thus, the combined effects of all sources of risk must be considered.

The effects of changes in the underlying source of risk will show up in movements in the values of spot and derivative positions. You should recall that in Chapter 4 we introduced the concept of an option's delta, which was the change in the option's price divided by the change in the underlying stock's price. We noted that a delta-hedged option would move perfectly with and be offset by an appropriately weighted position in the stock. A delta-hedged portfolio would be neutral with respect to stock price movements, but only for very small stock price changes. For large stock price changes, the delta may move too quickly. We noted that the risk of delta changing too quickly is captured by the option's gamma. We also saw that if the volatility of the underlying stock changes, the option price can change quite significantly, even without a movement in the stock price. This risk was captured by the option's vega. These risk measures, delta, gamma, and vega, are equally applicable to many instruments other than options and stocks. They are some of the tools used by risk managers to control market risk.

Let us consider a situation in which, to accommodate a customer, a derivatives dealer has taken a position in a $10 million notional principal four-year interest rate swap in which it pays a fixed rate and receives a floating rate. In addition, the dealer has sold a three-year $8 million notional principal interest rate call with an exercise rate of 12 percent. We assume that for both instruments the underlying is LIBOR. To keep things as simple as possible, we shall let the payments on the swap occur once a year. The current term structure of LIBOR and the implied forward rates are shown in Table 16.3.

Let us first price the interest rate swap. Using the procedure described in Chapter 14, we find the price per $1 of notional principal to be 11.85 percent. This is verified with the following calculation, which equates the present value of the payments on a four-year fixed-rate bond to par value, which is the present value of the payments on a four-year floating-rate bond:

$$.1185(1.10)^{-1} + .1185(1.11)^{-2} + .1185(1.116)^{-3} + (1.1185)(1.12)^{-4} = 1.00.$$

TABLE 16.3	Current Term Structure of LIBOR and Forward Rates	
Period	**LIBOR[1]**	**Forward Rate[2]**
1 year	10.00%	12.01%
2 years	11.00	12.81
3 years	11.60	13.21
4 years	12.00	

[1]Spot rate for LIBOR deposit of the maturity indicated.
[2]Forward rate on one-year LIBOR deposit starting 1, 2, and 3 years from today. Computed as follows:

$$.1201 = (1.11)^2/(1.10) - 1$$
$$.1281 = (1.116)^3/(1.11)^2 - 1$$
$$.1321 = (1.12)^4/(1.116)^3 - 1.$$

In Chapter 14 we noted that an interest rate option should be priced by using a binomial term structure model but that as an approximation we could use the Black model that we introduced in Chapter 12 to price options on futures. The inputs to the Black model for a three-year call option with an exercise rate of 12 percent are $F = .1321$ (the forward rate for a one-year Eurodollar in three years), $E = .12$, $r = \ln(1.116) = .1098$, $\sigma = .08$, $T = 3$. Recall that the Black-Scholes software bsbin1.xls or bsbwin2.exe can be used by inserting the forward price as the spot price and setting the dividend yield to the risk-free rate. To obtain the price of an interest rate option, however, the answer must be discounted at the current forward rate to reflect the delay between the expiration and the actual payment. The overall answer is .009215. Thus for each dollar of notional principal, the option costs .009215 or 92.15 basis points.[2] Based on an $8 million notional principal, the price of the option is $8,000,000(.009215) = \$73,722$. Now let us look at how to delta hedge this combination.

Delta Hedging

In order to delta hedge, we must make the portfolio be unaffected by small movements in interest rates. To do this we shall need the delta of the swap and the option. Either can be obtained by taking the mathematical first derivative of the swap or option value with respect to interest rates. In

---

[2]This answer is obtained from the fact that the Black model gives an answer of .0105168. Discounting that answer for one year at 13.21 percent gives .009215.

this example, however, we shall estimate the delta by repricing both instruments when the one-period spot rate and the remaining forward rates move up and down one basis point. Then we shall average the movement in the derivative's price and this will be a good approximation of the delta.[3]

If rates move up one basis point, the new one-period spot rate will be 10.01 percent and the new forward rates will be 12.02 percent, 12.82 percent, and 13.22 percent. This necessitates recalculating the spot rates, which will be 11.01 percent, 11.61 percent, and 12.01 percent.[4] Repricing the swap means to determine the present value of the new floating- and fixed-rate payments. The first floating payment is already set at 10 percent before the interest rate change. The present value of the next three floating payments can be obtained by estimating the present value of the new forward rates. The swap value will be the present value of the difference between the fixed and the floating payments: $10,000,000[(.10 - .1185)(1.1001)^{-1} + (.1202 - .1185)(1.1101)^{-2} + (.1282 - .1185)(1.1161)^{-3} + (.1322 - .1185)(1.1201)^{-4}]$. Using a spreadsheet to obtain more precise values of these calculations gives a new value of $2,130.[5] Table 16.4 shows the results from a one-basis-point increase and decrease in the value of the swap. The delta is then the average change, which is rounded to $2,130.5.

We also need to estimate the delta of the option. Recall that it is an $8 million notional principal call with a strike rate of 12 percent. Although the Black model will give you the delta, we shall recalculate the model price and estimate the delta based on the average change from a one-basis-point move in either direction. Table 16.4 provides this information for the option. The original price was $73,722. The new price if LIBOR moves up one basis point is $74,107, a gain of $385. If LIBOR moves down one basis point, the option is worth $73,338, a loss of $384. The average is $384.5.

Recall that we pay the fixed rate and receive the floating rate on the swap so we are long the swap. That means we have a positive delta of $2,130.5. We are short the option so we have a delta of −$384.5. This makes the overall delta $2,130.5 − $384.5 = $1,746. This means that if rates move up one basis point, we gain $1,746. If rates move down one basis point, we lose $1,746. Because we wish to be hedged, we must find an in-

---

[3]The price change for a one-basis-point move up is slightly different from that for a one-basis-point move down. This is why we take the average price change. This effect results from the convexity of the price curve and plays a role in gamma hedging.

[4]It appears as if the new spot rates are just one basis point above the old spot rates. This is not precisely the case, as would be indicated if we let the forward rates shift by a much larger amount or we carried our results out to more significant digits.

[5]The answer calculating manually is about $2,430. The spreadsheet calculations determine the exact forward and spot rates to a higher degree of precision.

TABLE 16.4   **Estimation of Swap and Option Deltas**

	Derivative Instrument			
	4-Year Swap, Fixed Rate = .1185		3-Year Call Option at Exercise Rate of .12	
LIBOR change	+.0001	−.0001	+.0001	−.0001
New value	$2,130	−$2,131	$74,107	$73,338
Gain or loss*	same as new value		($74,107 − $73,722) = $385	($73,338 − $73,722) = −$384
Estimated delta	[$2,130 − (−$2,131)]/2 = $2,130.5		[$385 − (−384)]/2 = $384.5	

*The original value of the swap is zero. The original value of the option is $73,722. For a swap, the gain or loss is the new value because the old value of the swap was zero.

strument that loses $1,746 if rates move up and gains $1,746 if rates move down.

Naturally we could hedge each derivative with a completely offsetting transaction in the opposite direction. In other words, we could execute a four-year swap, paying floating and receiving fixed, and buy a three-year call with a strike of 12 percent. That is not normally how dealers hedge, however. They would rarely have a customer wanting the exact opposite transaction at that point in time and they would not be willing to take the risk of waiting until their next customer calls. The most typical hedge transaction they would execute is to trade Eurodollar futures. Recall that we studied these instruments in Chapters 7 through 11. They are based on a $1,000,000 Eurodollar deposit and their prices move opposite to interest rates. The delta is −$25, which is based on the calculation −$1,000,000(.0001)(90/360) with .0001 representing a one-basis-point change. Note, however, that if rates move up, a long position loses and if rates move down, a long position gains. In other words, Eurodollar futures are like bonds: Their values move opposite to interest rates. Eurodollar futures are particularly attractive for dealers to hedge with because they are extremely liquid. Also, being futures contracts and not options, they require that no cash be paid up front and their margin requirements are very low.

To offset our risk, we need a position that will gain $1,746 if rates move down and lose that amount if rates move up or, in other words, a delta of −$1,746. This would require a long position in Eurodollar futures.

A delta-hedged position is one in which the combined spot and derivatives positions have a delta of zero. The portfolio would then have no gain or loss in value from a very small change in the underlying source of risk.

The number of contracts would be $-\$1,746/(-\$25) = 69.84$. Since fractional contracts are not allowed, we should probably round up to 70. This would mean our overall delta would be

$$
\begin{aligned}
&+\$2,130.5 \text{ (from the swap)}\\
&-\$384.5 \text{ (from the option)}\\
&70(-\$25) \text{ (from the futures)}\\
&= -\$4.
\end{aligned}
$$

This means that the portfolio value will go down $4 if rates move up one basis point. This is basically a perfect hedge.

In practice, some minor technical problems would make this hedge less than precise. The 90-day LIBOR that the futures is based on and the one-year LIBOR that the swap and option are based on would not both be likely to move exactly one basis point. However, they would almost always move in the same direction at the same time and certainly be highly correlated. A few minor adjustments could take care of any risk in the hedge resulting from differences in the magnitudes of their respective movements.

As we discussed in Chapter 4, a delta hedge takes care of small movements in the underlying. Larger movements, however, can bring about additional risk. This is called gamma risk. To deal with it requires a gamma hedge.

Gamma Hedging

Our estimates of the delta are based on a one-basis-point change. If rates move by a much larger amount, there will be an additional risk caused by the fact that the values of the derivatives do not move equally in both directions. For example, if rates move 50 basis points down, the swap value will change to $-\$107,914$. A 50-basis-point increase will cause the swap value to move to $105,127. Recall that a one-basis-point move caused the swap value to change by virtually the same amount. For the option, a one-basis-point move in either direction caused a virtually equal value change. A 50-basis-point move up would cause the option value to move to $93,793, a loss of $20,071. A 50-basis-point decrease would cause the option value to move to $55,513, a gain of $18,209.[6]

As we learned in Chapter 4, the risk associated with larger price moves in which the delta does not fully capture the risk is called gamma risk. It is the risk of the delta changing. To be fully hedged a dealer would have to be delta hedged at all times. If rates move sharply, the effective delta would not equal the actual delta until the dealer could put on another

---

[6]Recall that we are short the option so gains occur on rate decreases and losses occur on rate increases.

transaction that would reset its delta to the appropriate value. This could be too late. This risk can be hedged, however, by combining transactions so that the delta and gamma are both zero. First, however, we must estimate the gamma. Table 16.5 illustrates the calculation of the gammas of the swap and the option. The gammas are −$12,500 for the swap and $10,000 for the option. This means that as LIBOR increases, the swap delta decreases in value by $12,500(.0001) = $1.25 and the option delta increases in value by $10,000(.0001) = $1. Since we are short the option, its gamma is actually −$10,000. Thus, our overall gamma is −$22,500.

Assuming that we have delta hedged the swap and option with the Eurodollar futures, our gamma will still be −$22,500 because the gamma of the futures is zero. We are delta hedged but not gamma hedged. To become gamma hedged we will need another instrument. Let us assume that the instrument chosen is a four-year call option whose delta is $58 and whose gamma is $10,500, both figures under the assumption of a $1 million notional principal. The problem is to determine the appropriate

---

TABLE 16.5		Estimation of Swap and Option Gammas		
Basis Point Change	Swap Value	Average Change in Swap Value*	Option Value	Average Change in Option Value
−.0002	−$4,263		$72,955	
−.0001	−$2,131	$2,131.50	$73,338	$383.50
.0000	$0	$2,130.50	$73,722	$384.50
+.0001	$2,130	$2,129	$74,107	$385.50
+.0002	$4,258		$74,493	

*Average change in swap value is computed by taking an average of the changes in the swap value around the given point. For example, at a basis point change of .0000, the change in swap value is from 0 to $2,130 and from 0 to −$2,131. This is an average change of $2,130.50. At a basis point change of −.0001, the change in swap value is from −$2,131 to −4,263 and from −$2,131 to $0. This is an average change of $2,131.50. Similar calculations are made for the change in option value.

Swap Gamma Calculation:
The gamma is the average change in the delta divided by .0001. Thus, at a basis point change of .0000 (the current status), the delta of the swap changes from $2,130.5 to $2,131.5 and from $2,130.5 to $2,129. This is an average change of −$1.25. Dividing by .0001, the basis point move, gives a gamma of −$12,500. Although the gamma is quoted as −$12,500, it is understood that the delta moves by −$1.25 for every one-basis-point move in LIBOR.

Option Gamma Calculation:
At a basis point change of .0000 (the current status), the delta of the option changes from $384.50 to $383.50 and from $384.50 to $385.50. This is an average change of $1.00. Dividing by .0001, the basis point move, gives a gamma of $10,000. Although the gamma is quoted as $10,000, it is understood that the delta moves by $1 for every one-basis-point move in LIBOR.

notional principal of this new option so that we will be delta hedged and gamma hedged. This is a simple problem answered by solving simultaneous equations.

Let us assume that we take X_1 Eurodollar futures, which have a delta of –$25 and a gamma of zero, and X_2 of the four-year calls, whose delta is $58 and gamma is $10,500 per $1,000,000 notional principal. Our swap and other option have a delta of $1,746 and a gamma of –$22,500. We eliminate the delta and gamma risk of the portfolio by setting the delta to zero by the equation

$$\$1{,}746 + X_1(-\$25) + X_2(\$58) = \$0,$$

and the gamma to zero by the equation

$$-\$22{,}500 + X_1(\$0) + X_2(\$10{,}500) = \$0.$$

These are simply two equations with two unknowns. The solution is an exercise in basic algebra, but just to make sure you understand, we shall work through the solution. Rewrite the equations as

$$X_1(-\$25) + X_2(\$58) = -\$1{,}746$$
$$X_2(\$10{,}500) = \$22{,}500.$$

A delta and gamma hedge is one in which the combined spot and derivatives positions have a delta of zero and a gamma of zero. The portfolio would then have no gain or loss in value from a small change in the underlying source of risk. In addition, the delta itself would be hedged, which provides protection against larger changes in the source of risk.

Solve the second equation for $X_2 = 2.14$. Insert 2.14 for X_2 in the first equation and then solve for X_1 to get $X_1 = 74.8$. This means we need to go long 74.8 Eurodollar futures. The solution $X_2 = 2.14$ means that we need to go long 2.14 times the notional principal of $1,000,000 on which the new option's delta and gamma were calculated. In other words, we need $2,140,000 notional principal of the four-year option. These transactions combine to set the delta and gamma of the overall position to approximately zero.[7]

Unfortunately the use of options introduces a risk associated with possible changes in volatility. Let us take a look at how that risk arises and how we can hedge it.

Vega Hedging

In Chapter 4 we learned that the change in the option price over the change in its volatility is called its vega. A portfolio of derivatives that is both delta and gamma hedged can incur a gain or loss even when there is no change in the underlying as a result of a change in the volatility. Most

---

[7]As a check, we see that the delta is 1,746 + 74.8(–25) + 2.14(58) = 0.12 and the gamma is –22,500 + 2.14(10,500) = –30. The slightly negative gamma results from rounding off 2.14.

options are highly sensitive to the volatility, which changes often. Consequently it is important to try to hedge vega risk.

Swaps and FRAs do not have vegas because volatility is not a determinant of their prices. In our example, we need consider only the vega of the three-year call option. Although option pricing formulas can often give the vega in its exact mathematical form, we shall estimate the vega by changing LIBOR by one basis point in each direction. Recall that under the initial term structure, the option value is $73,722. If the volatility increases from .08 to .0801, the new option value will be $73,757, a change of $35. If volatility decreases from .08 to .0799, the new option value will be $73,688, a change of −$34. This is an average change of $34.50. Since we are short this option, the vega of our portfolio of the four-year swap and this three-year option is −$34.50.

Now consider the four-year option that we introduced in the last section to use for gamma hedging. It will also have a vega that must be taken into account. Its vega is estimated to be $6.93 for every $1,000,000 notional principal. Our delta- and gamma-hedged portfolio would have $2.14 million face value of this option, making the vega $14.83. That would make our overall portfolio have a vega of $14.83 − $34.50, or −$19.67. Thus, we still have a significant risk that volatility will increase and each .0001 increase in volatility will cost us $19.67.

In order to hedge delta, gamma, and vega we will need three hedging instruments. Because of the vega risk, at least one of the instruments has to be an option. Let us use an option on a Eurodollar futures which trades at the Chicago Mercantile Exchange alongside the Eurodollar futures. The option has a delta of −$12.75, a gamma of −$500, and a vega of $2.50 per $1,000,000 notional principal. This leads to the following set of simultaneous equations:

$$\$1,746 + X_1(-\$25) + X_2(\$58) + X_3(-\$12.75) = 0$$
$$-\$22,500 + X_1(\$0) + X_2(\$10,500) + X_3(-\$500) = 0$$
$$-\$34.50 + X_1(\$0) + X_2(\$6.93) + X_3(\$2.50) = 0.$$

The first equation sets the portfolio delta to zero, the second sets the gamma to zero, and the third sets the vega to zero. The coefficients X_1, X_2, and X_3 represent quantities of $1,000,000 notional principal that should be established with Eurodollar futures, the four-year option, and the option on the Eurodollar futures. To solve these equations, we first note that the second and third equations can be written as

$$X_2(\$10,500) + X_3(-\$500) = \$22,500$$
$$X_2(\$6.93) + X_3(\$2.50) = \$34.50,$$

which is simply two equations with two unknowns. Multiplying the second equation by 200 gives us $\$1,386X_2 + \$500X_3 = \$6,900$. Then adding the

two equations gives $11,886X_2 = $29,400, which gives $X_2 = 2.47$. Inserting 2.47 for X_2 in either of these equations gives $X_3 = 6.95$. Thus, we need $2.47($1,000,000) = $2,470,000$ notional principal of the four-year option and $6.95($1,000,000) = $6,950,000$ notional principal of the Eurodollar futures option. We then insert 2.47 and 6.95 into the first equation for X_2 and X_3, giving us $X_1(-$25) + 2.47($58) + 6.95(-$12.75) = -$1,746$. Solving for X_1 gives a value of 72.02. This means that we would buy 72 Eurodollar futures.[8]

A vega-hedged portfolio is one in which the portfolio value will not change as a result of a change in the volatility of the underlying source of risk.

It should be apparent by now that the dealer should not hedge by setting the delta to zero and then attempting to hedge the gamma and vega risk with other instruments. As these instruments are added to eliminate gamma and vega risk, the delta hedge is destroyed. There are two possible approaches to solving the problem, one being the simultaneous equation approach that we followed here. It is guaranteed to provide the correct solutions. Another approach would be to solve the gamma and vega hedge simultaneously, which will set the gamma and vega to zero, but leave the overall delta nonzero. Then the delta hedge can be set with Eurodollar futures, which have a delta but no gamma or vega. Consequently, adding them to the position at the very end will not change the gamma or vega neutrality.

In spite of a dealer's efforts at achieving a delta-gamma-vega neutral position, it is really impossible to achieve an absolute perfect hedge. The vega hedge is accurate only for extremely small changes in volatility. Large changes would require yet another adjustment. In addition, all deltas, gammas, and vegas are valid only over the next instant in time. Even if there were no changes in LIBOR or the volatility, the position would become unhedged over time if no further adjustments were made. Eventually the portfolio would become significantly unhedged so some adjustments might be made to realign the portfolio to a delta-gamma-vega neutral position, possibly as often as once a day.

It is apt to remember a famous expression: *The only perfect hedge is in a Japanese garden.* Any dealer accepts the fact that a small amount of risk will be assumed. To date, however, no major derivatives dealer who has made the effort to be hedged has suffered a significant loss and most have found market making in derivatives to be a profitable activity with very low risk. This is a testament to the excellent risk management practiced by the major derivatives dealers.

On the other side of the transaction is the end user, the party who approaches the dealer about entering into a derivatives transaction. Most

---

[8]Because of some rounding off, the overall position is not quite perfectly hedged. The delta is $1,746 + 72(-$25) + 2.47($58) + 6.95(-$12.75) = 0.65. The gamma is $-$22,500 + 72($0) + 2.47($10,500) + 6.95(-$500) = -$40$. The vega is $-$34.50 + 2.47(6.93) + 6.95(2.50) = -0.01.

end users are corporations attempting to hedge their interest rate, currency, equity, or commodity price risk. Some will speculate from time to time. Most, however, already have a transaction in place that has a certain amount of risk. They contract with the dealer to lay off that risk. Rarely will the end user engage in the type of dynamic hedging illustrated above. That is because the end user is not typically a financial institution like the dealer. Financial institutions can nearly always execute transactions at lower cost and can generally afford the investment in expensive personnel, equipment, and software necessary to do dynamic hedging. Most end users enter into derivatives transactions that require little or no adjustments. You have, of course, seen many such examples throughout this book. Some end users have, however, suffered losses from being unhedged at the wrong time or from outright speculating. Yet, most end users could have obtained a better understanding about the magnitude of their risk and the potential for large losses had they applied the technique called Value at Risk or VaR.

Value-at-Risk (VaR)

Value-at-Risk or **VaR** is a dollar measure of the minimum loss that would be expected over a period of time with a given probability. For example, a VaR of $1 million for one day at a probability of .05 means that the firm would expect to lose at least $1 million in one day 5 percent of the time. How significant a million dollar loss is depends on the size of the firm and its aversion to risk. But one thing is clear from the probability statement: .05 means that it would be expected to occur once every 20 trading days, which is about once per month.

VaR is widely used by dealers, even though their hedging programs nearly always leave them with little exposure to the market. If dealers feel that it is important to use VaR, that should be a good enough reason for end users to employ it and surveys show that an increasing number of end users are doing so.

The basic idea behind VaR is to determine the probability distribution of the underlying source of risk and to isolate the worst given percentage of outcomes. Using 5 percent as the critical percentage, VaR will determine the 5 percent of outcomes that are the worst. The performance at the 5 percent mark is the VaR.

Table 16.6 provides a simple illustration with a discrete classification of the change in the value of a hypothetical portfolio. Note that each range has a probability and a cumulative probability associated with it. Starting with the class with the worst outcome, VaR is found by examining the cumulative probability until the specified percentage is reached. In this case, VaR for 5 percent is −$3,000,000. This would be interpreted as

Value-at-Risk or VaR is the minimum amount of money that would be lost in a portfolio with a given probability over a specific period of time.

TABLE 16.6	Probability Distribution of Change in Portfolio Value	
Change in Portfolio Value	**Probability**	**Cumulative Probability**
−$3,000,000 and lower	.05	.05
−$2,000,000 to −$2,999,999	.10	.15
−$1,000,000 to −$1,999,999	.15	.30
$0 to −$999,999	.20	.50
$0 to $999,999	.20	.70
$1,000,000 to $1,999,999	.15	.85
$2,000,000 to $2,999,999	.10	.95
$3,000,000 and higher	.05	1.00

follows: There is a 5 percent probability that over the given time period, the portfolio will lose at least $3 million. Of course VaR can be expressed with respect to any chosen probability. Such statements as "There is a 15 percent probability that over the given time period, the portfolio will lose at least $2 million" and "There is a 50 percent probability that over the given time period, the portfolio will incur a loss" are both legitimate statements of the portfolio's VaR.

Figure 16.5 illustrates the principle behind VaR when the distribution of the portfolio change in value is continuous. The familiar normal or bell-shaped curve is widely used though not necessarily appropriate in many cases. Accepting it as legitimate for our purposes, we see where the 5 percent VaR is noted, which is 1.65 standard deviations from the expected change in portfolio value, which in this example is zero. Of course, not all situations have an expected change of zero. In any case the rule for determining VaR when applying normal probability theory is to move 1.65 standard deviations below the expected value. Beyond that point, 5 percent of the population of possible outcomes is found. For a VaR of 1 percent, you would move 2.33 standard deviations below the expected value. A VaR of 10 percent would require a move of 1.28 standard deviations below the expected value.

Calculating VaR in practice is not quite this simple. The basic problem is to determine the probability distribution associated with the portfolio value. This necessitates estimating the expected values, standard deviations, and correlations among the financial instruments. The mechanics of determining the portfolio probability distribution are relatively easy once the appropriate inputs are obtained. The process is the same as the one you might already have encountered when studying investments. We briefly reviewed these concepts in Chapter 8 when we took a look at portfolio theory. Let us take that process a little bit further here.

Assume you have two assets whose expected returns are $E(R_1)$ and $E(R_2)$ and whose standard deviations are σ_1 and σ_2, and where the corre-

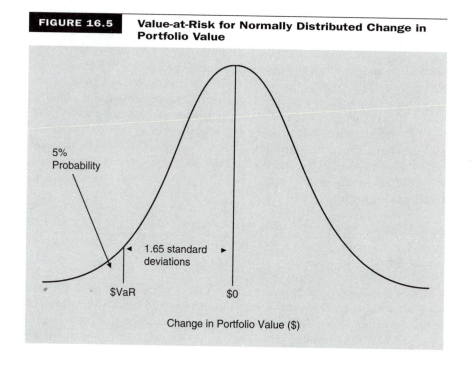

FIGURE 16.5 **Value-at-Risk for Normally Distributed Change in Portfolio Value**

lation between their returns is ρ. The portfolio's expected return is a weighted average of the expected returns of assets 1 and 2,

$$E(R_p) = w_1 E(R_1) + w_2 E(R_2),$$

where w_1 and w_2 are the percentages of the investor's wealth that are allocated to assets 1 and 2, respectively. The portfolio standard deviation is a more complicated weighted average of the variances of assets 1 and 2 and their covariance,

$$\sigma_p = \sqrt{w_1^2 \sigma_1^2 + w_2^2 \sigma_2^2 + 2w_1 w_2 \sigma_1 \sigma_2 \rho},$$

where the expression $\sigma_1 \sigma_2 \rho$ is recognized as the covariance between assets 1 and 2.

There are three methods of estimating VaR.

ANALYTICAL METHOD   The **analytical method** makes use of knowledge of the input values and any necessary pricing models along with an assumption about the type of probability distribution. Typically the normal distribution is assumed but that is not required. The normal distribution,

however, is completely characterized by its expected value and variance, so if normality is not assumed there may be other inputs required.

We illustrate the analytical method with two examples. Suppose a portfolio manager holds two distinct classes of stocks. The first class, worth $20 million, is identical to the S&P 500. It has an expected return of 12 percent and a standard deviation of 15 percent. The second class is identical to the Nikkei 300, an index of Japanese stocks, and is valued at $12 million. We shall assume the currency risk is hedged. The expected return is 10.5 percent and the standard deviation is 18 percent. The correlation between the Nikkei 300 and the S&P 500 is .55. All figures are annualized. With this information we can calculate the portfolio expected return and standard deviation as

$$E(R_p) = (20/32).12 + (12/32).105 = .1144$$
$$\sigma_p = \sqrt{(20/32)^2(.15)^2 + (12/32)^2(.18)^2 + 2(20/32)(12/32)(.15)(.18)(.55)}$$
$$= .1425.$$

Now let us calculate this portfolio's VaR at a 5 percent level for one week. First we must convert the annualized expected return and standard deviation to weekly equivalents. This is done by dividing the expected return by 52 (for the number of weeks in a year) and dividing the standard deviation by the square root of 52, which is 7.21. This gives us .1144/52 = .0022 and .1425/7.21 = .0198. Under the assumption of a normal distribution, the return that is 1.65 standard deviations below the expected return is

$$.0022 - 1.65(.0198) = -.0305.$$

The portfolio would be expected to lose at least 3.05 percent 5 percent of the time. VaR is always expressed in dollars, so the VaR is $32,000,000(.0305) = $976,000. In other words, the portfolio would be expected to lose at least $976,000 in one week 5 percent of the time.

Let us now calculate VaR for a portfolio containing options. In fact, let us make it an extremely risky portfolio, one consisting of a short call on the S&P 500. We assume that the call has one month to go before expiring, the S&P is at 720, the exercise price is 720, the risk-free rate is 5.8 percent, and the volatility of the S&P is 15 percent. We shall ignore dividends. Inserting these figures into the Black-Scholes model tells us that the call should be priced at $14.21. The S&P 500 index option contract at the CBOE has a multiplier of 500, so the total cost is 500($14.21) = $7,105. We shall assume that the investor sells 200 contracts, resulting in the receipt up front of 200($7,105) = $1,421,000. The worst outcome for an uncovered call is for the stock to increase. Let us look at the 5 percent worst outcomes, which occur on the upside. Using the same information on the

S&P 500 from the previous example, we must first convert to monthly data. The expected return on the S&P is .1144/12 = .0095 and .1425/3.46 (the square root of 12) = .0412. On the upside the 5 percent tail of the distribution is .0095 + 1.65(.0412) = .0775. That would leave the S&P at 720(1.0775) = 775.80 or higher. If the option expires with the S&P at 775.80, it will have a value of 775.80 − 720 = 55.80. Thus, our net loss will be 55.80 − 14.21 = 41.59 per option. The total loss will be 200(500)(41.59) = $4,159,000. Thus, the VaR for this short call is $4,159,000 and we can, therefore, say that the portfolio will lose at least $4,159,000 in one month 5 percent of the time. This would be once every 20 months.

The analytical method uses knowledge of the parameters of the probability distribution of the underlying source of risk at the portfolio level. In the case of options or other derivatives, basic pricing principles are applied to determine the portfolio's performance for a given outcome. Obviously certain portfolios will have seemingly diverse sources of risk. For example, suppose a portfolio includes options on the Swiss franc and futures on oil. Then one would need to know the correlation between the Swiss franc and oil as well as their expected changes and volatilities.

The data required to estimate the expected returns and standard deviations can sometimes be purchased. The J. P. Morgan Company publishes much of the data necessary to estimate volatilities and correlations on its World Wide Web home page. This service, called RiskMetrics, can be accessed at www.jpmorgan.com and is free to anyone. Naturally the accuracy of an estimate of VaR will be affected if the correlations and volatilities from the past are poor estimates of future correlations and volatilities.

HISTORICAL METHOD   The **historical method** estimates the distribution of the portfolio's performance by collecting data on the past performance of the portfolio and using it to estimate the future probability distribution. Obviously it assumes that the past distribution is a good estimate of the future distribution.

Figure 16.6 presents an example of the information obtained from a historical sample of daily portfolio returns over approximately one year, 254 trading days in this case. The information is presented in the form of a histogram. The person doing the analysis would arbitrarily choose the intervals. In this case, the 13 worst outcomes, which is about 5.1 percent of the total possible, are shaded. This means that the critical portfolio VaR is at a return of −10 percent. If the portfolio size is $15 million, then the VaR is $15,000,000(−.10) = −$1,500,000. Thus, we can say that the portfolio would be expected to lose at least $1.5 million in one day about 5 percent of the time, which is about once per month.

The accuracy of the historical method depends on whether the portfolio the firm held in the period over which the sampling is done is the same as the one currently held. Since portfolio compositions change

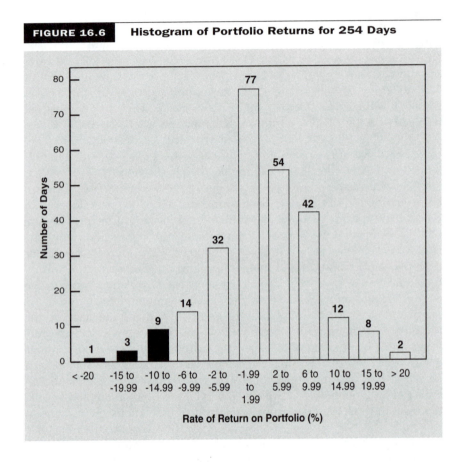

FIGURE 16.6   **Histogram of Portfolio Returns for 254 Days**

often, this method may be very hard to implement. Also, a reasonably large sample is required, which means that the data must be collected over a long time period. This further increases the chance that the portfolio composition during the sample period is quite different from its current composition, for which the VaR is to be estimated. Some adjustments can be made, however, by constructing the historical performance of the current portfolio based on current investment allocations applied to historical data on the returns of various asset classes.

SIMULATION METHOD   The **simulation method** is based on the idea that portfolio returns can be fairly easily simulated. Simulation requires inputs on the expected returns, standard deviations, and correlations for each financial instrument. In an appendix to Chapter 15 we examined one pro-

cedure for simulating stock prices called the Monte Carlo method. Essentially the same procedure is used when calculating VaR except that it is necessary to ensure that the portfolio's returns properly account for the correlations among the financial instruments. This means that one cannot simply independently generate returns for, say, the S&P 500 and Treasury bonds. One set of returns can be generated but the other set of returns must reflect any correlation between the two sets of returns. This is done by making an assumption about the process in which asset returns are generated. Such a process might be something as simple as the market model that we studied in Chapter 8 where the market factor generates returns and other assets have betas that reflect their correlations with the market factor.

The simulation method requires a good understanding of some fairly technical issues along with accurate estimates of the input variables. Again, J. P. Morgan's free RiskMetrics data can serve as a good place to start in obtaining the volatilities and correlations.

VaR is particularly appealing because it expresses risk in terms of money that can be lost along with a probability of losing it. This makes it fairly easy to understand by senior management. Moreover, VaR can be used to reflect the combined risks arising from a variety of diverse sources. One need not provide separate assessments of a firm's oil price risk, interest rate risk, and currency risk. Rather these risks can be consolidated into a single number, provided of course that valid and stable correlations between these markets can be estimated.

The three methods of estimating VaR are the analytical method, the historical method, and the simulation method. Each method is based on specific assumptions and no one method is always better than the others.

With three different methods to chose from in calculating VaR, one might wonder about the consistency of the results. Some studies have shown that the methods can give quite divergent estimates of VaR. Concerns over this problem have led to a great deal of recent criticism of VaR. There is concern that users of VaR will pay too much attention to it and too little attention to other measures.

In addition to estimating VaR, a risk manager will often subject the portfolio to a **stress test,** which determines how badly the portfolio will do under some of the worst and most unusual circumstances. If the portfolio's return in that situation is tolerable, then the portfolio risk is assumed to be acceptable. Stress testing can be quite valuable as a supplement to VaR and other techniques of risk management. Yet, stress testing has its own criticism, including the fact that it places too much emphasis on highly unlikely events.

Stress testing means to estimate how a portfolio will perform if extremely rare events occur.

The important point to remember about VaR and stress testing, as well as any financial statistic, is that these are just estimates and cannot be expected to provide the full picture.

We have now completed our examination of market risk. We next turn to the other major type of risk: credit risk.

Managing Credit Risk

Remember that earlier in the chapter we described a party that could borrow at a fixed rate of 10 1/2 percent or at a floating rate of LIBOR plus 1.1 percent. That party issued floating-rate debt and entered into a swap in which it paid a fixed rate of 9 1/4 percent and received a floating rate of LIBOR, for a net fixed rate of 10.35 percent, a savings of 15 basis points over issuing fixed rate directly.

If the firm had borrowed fixed, it would have assumed no credit risk. A lender cannot default. If it borrows floating and swaps it into a synthetic fixed-rate loan, it faces the risk that the swap dealer will default, leaving it owing the floating rate of LIBOR. Perhaps the 15-basis-point saving is simply compensation for bearing the risk that the dealer will default.

The risk of default is faced by any party that may receive obligatory payments from another party. This risk, called **credit risk** or **default risk,** is faced by any lender. We have mentioned it many times earlier in the book, especially in conjunction with over-the-counter derivatives. Because banks are used to making loans, their derivatives business is not taking on a different kind of risk than one they have already years of experience with. Since the notional principal on a derivative is not at risk, however, the credit risk of derivatives is typically much lower than the credit risk of loans. Nonbank end users typically do not make loans. When they become users of swaps, however, they become creditors.

Earlier in the book we commented on credit risk whenever we discussed over-the-counter instruments. Futures and exchange-listed options are insured against credit risk by the clearinghouse. Since there has never been a default by the clearinghouse, these contracts can be considered credit-risk free. Over-the-counter contracts are subject to credit risk that varies from party to party, from type of contract to type of contract, and from one point in time to another point in time.

In the bond market, credit risk is typically assessed by examining the credit ratings of issuers. Credit ratings are provided by several firms, most notably Standard & Poor's, Moody's, and Fitch's. Although each agency has its own labels, terms like "Triple-A" and "B-double AA" are used, with the more A's the better. Thus, you would see ratings like AAA, AA, A, BAA, BBB, BB, B, and so on down to D. Analysts for these companies base their ratings on a variety of factors, most notably the financial health of the issuer, and also the states of the economy and the issuer's industry.

There are two types of credit risk. **Current credit risk** is the risk to one party that the other party is unable to make payments that are currently

due. Current credit risk is faced by only one party in a derivatives transaction, the party who holds the contract as an asset. In other words, the amount due to that party is positive so it is subject to the possibility that the other party will default. The other party currently owes more than is owed to it, so it faces no current risk of default. **Potential credit risk** is the risk that the counterparty will default in the future.

Both current and potential credit risk of over-the-counter options are faced by the buyer only. Since the buyer pays the premium to the seller and does not have to do anything else, the seller faces no credit risk. The buyer, however, may eventually choose to exercise the option, by which time the seller may be bankrupt. FRAs and swaps have two-way credit risk. Each party is obligated to do something for the other. Holding other things constant, the credit risk of an FRA or interest rate swap is determined by the credit quality of the counterparty, the terms of the contract, and the shape of the term structure. Consider for example a five-year plain vanilla interest rate swap. With an upward-sloping term structure, the implied forward rates are rising. These rates can be equated to the floating rates and will equal the eventual floating rates if there is no shift in interest rates during the life of the swap. When the swap is first established, the party paying the fixed rate and receiving the floating rate will initially pay more than it receives, but later the floating receipts will begin to overtake the fixed payments. At any given time current credit risk is faced by one party only, which is the party to whom the contract has positive value. Potential credit risk will reflect the combined effects of the risk of changes in interest rates and the risk of the counterparty's assets over the remaining life of the contract. Both parties face potential credit risk.

Current credit risk is the risk that the party owing more than the other in a derivatives transaction will default right now. Potential credit risk is the risk that either party will default at any time during the life of the contract.

In the case of swaps, the potential credit risk is largest during the middle of the swap's life. Potential credit risk is low at the beginning of the swap's life because it is assumed that the swap would not be entered into if there were any significant problems on the near horizon. Potential credit risk is high during the middle part of the swap's life because the counterparty has had time to have its financial condition deteriorate. Potential credit risk is low during the latter part of the swap's life because there are fewer payments remaining.

Recall that interest rate swaps do not involve the exchange of principal but currency swaps do. This also keeps the credit risk low at the end of the life of the interest rate swap but raises it somewhat for the currency swap.

The explicit prices of derivative transactions do not necessarily differ according to the credit risk of the transaction. Many derivatives dealers and end users will transact only with customers of a minimum acceptable credit quality. Thus, counterparties who barely pass the hurdle pay the same as counterparties who are essentially risk free. Assessment of a counterparty's credit risk is done much the same way as when extending credit.

Financial statements and ratings are used along with simulations and other statistical techniques. VaR can even be adapted to accommodate credit risk, though it is much more difficult to do. Stress testing is commonly used to assess credit risk by assuming that extreme economic conditions occur and estimating the likelihood of default.

Although qualifying parties pay the same explicit rate on a derivatives transaction, there are some implicit methods of differentiating among parties with different credit risks.

The primary method used to manage credit risk is to limit the amount of exposure to a given party. The higher the credit quality of the counterparty, the greater the amount of business that can be done with it. This is similar to the principal of diversification. A party spreads out its transactions with numerous end users or dealers. An extreme case of this method is to do no business whatsoever with a counterparty whose credit quality is below a minimum level.

Collateral is commonly used in lending and is becoming increasingly used in derivatives transactions. The two parties might agree that each post collateral by depositing cash or securities with a bank or by providing a letter of credit from another bank. The parties may agree that on any settlement date, the party to whom the derivative value is negative will post collateral equal to a given percentage of the notional principal or the value of the contract. Another type of arrangement is for neither party to post collateral but if either party's credit is downgraded by one of the rating agencies, that party will post a specific amount of collateral. Some transactions are structured so that a ratings downgrade gives the other party the right to terminate the contract at that point, meaning that the value of the swap is due and payable at that time.

We discussed marking to market extensively when we studied futures markets. Marking to market is designed to reduce credit risk by forcing losing parties to pay winning parties before losses accumulate to a large amount. Some derivative contracts are structured to have marking to market on a periodic basis. For example, a swap that settles semiannually might stipulate that the contracts are marked to market every two months. When the contract is marked to market, the market value is calculated. The party to whom the value is negative owes that full amount in cash to the other party. The fixed rate is then reset to the current market fixed rate. The actual settlement, meaning the exchange of interest payments, proceeds at the regularly scheduled dates though with a new fixed rate. This procedure forces the party on the losing side to pay up before the accumulated loss is potentially much greater.

One should not always assume that the party with the weaker credit is the dealer. Many dealers are banks whose credit ratings are held down by the possibility of loan losses in their domestic and global banking business. In response to the concerns of some end users, a number of dealers have

set up separate subsidiaries who do exclusively swap and derivatives transactions with end users. These subsidiaries are provided a large capital cushion and are not responsible for the debts of the parent company. Consequently, the subsidiary would have a higher credit rating than the parent company and most of these subsidiaries are rated AAA. These types of firms are called **enhanced derivatives products companies** and sometimes **special purpose vehicles.** When these firms were first created several years ago, they were greeted with much enthusiasm. The amount of business they have generated, however, has been surprisingly little. In fact, many parent companies also maintain derivative groups within the parent company as well as the subsidiary. Most end users were content to do business with the parent company as long as its rating was reasonably high, though not necessarily AAA.

Another recent innovation for managing credit risk is the credit derivative. These are options, forwards, and swaps that pay off contingent on credit downgrades or defaults.

Another procedure widely used to reduce default risk is netting. Because it is used so much and it is so important, we shall devote a special section to it.

Netting

Netting is a term to describe several similar processes that are used to reduce the amount of cash paid from one party to the other by deducting any cash owed by the latter party to the former party. Netting between two parties is called **bilateral netting** while netting across several parties is called **multilateral netting.** Multilateral netting is effectively what happens when there is a clearinghouse, such as the options or futures clearinghouses we discussed in Chapters 2 and 7. At present there are no clearinghouses for over-the-counter derivatives, but the possibilities are being studied.

There are several forms of nettings. We have already seen **payment netting,** in which two parties who owe each other money on a given day agree to simply determine the net amount owed and have one party pay the other. As you should remember, this is a fairly standard procedure in interest rate swaps. If party A owes $1,250,000 to party B who owes $890,000 to party A, then party A simply makes a payment of $360,000 to party B. This eliminates the possibility of party B defaulting, at least on this payment.

In **cross product netting** payments for one type of transaction are netted against payments for another type of transaction. Suppose, for example, that on the date on which party A owes $260,000 to party B, party B also owes A $175,000 as the interest on a loan. If the two parties had agreed to cross product netting, then A would owe B only $260,000 − $175,000 = $85,000. Of course, the two parties might seldom

have transactions with payments due on the same day. Consequently, cross product netting usually comes into play in bankruptcy or in a takeover involving two parties, each owing the other various amounts arising from different transactions.

If the parties agree to **netting by novation,** the net value of their mutual obligations is replaced by a single new transaction. In our example above, if A owes B $85,000, then the transactions that have an aggregate value of $85,000 to B are replaced by a new transaction with a value of $85,000. Netting by novation is used more often in the foreign exchange markets.

Closeout netting is the stipulation that if default occurs, only the net amount is owed. This greatly reduces the credit risk by reducing the amount of cash owed by a defaulting party by the amount owed to it. Consider the following example:

Company XYZ and dealer FinSwaps are engaged in four transactions with each other. From the dealer's perspective, the market values are as follows:

Swap 1	−$1,179,580
Swap 2	+$1,055,662
Option 1	+$1,495,255
FRA 1	−$ 892,530
	+$ 478,807

XYZ defaults with no closeout netting:
Suppose XYZ demands payments on swap 1 and FRA 1 and refuses to pay on swap 2 and option 1. FinSwaps owes XYZ $2,072,110, the sum of the values of swap 1 and FRA 1. This process is commonly called *cherry picking* because the bankrupt party selects the attractive transactions and walks away from the others.
XYZ defaults but closeout netting is used:
XYZ owes FinSwaps $478,807.

Netting is the process of reducing credit risk in which amounts owed from one party to the other are netted against amounts owed from the latter to the former to arrive at an overall amount owed by one party to the other.

Today, there is hardly an issue over the use of closeout netting. It is standard in virtually every swap in most countries and bankruptcy laws of most have been revised to recognize the legitimacy of closeout netting.

In the presence of netting, the credit risk of swaps is clearly limited to the net payments, which is less than the present value of the interest payments on a loan of equivalent notional principal. Because of this and the fact that the over-the-counter derivatives market has imposed strict requirements to reduce the credit risk, its record in the matter of defaults is excellent. The default of the London borough Hammersmith and Fulham in 1988, the result of a legal ruling that permitted it to walk away from losing transactions, accounted for about half of all defaults in the over-the-counter market until that time. The record since that time has been quite good as well. In fact, the swaps market has established a much better record on the matter of default than has the commercial loan market. Clearly the concerns expressed by some over the large size of the market as exemplified by the notional principal outstanding overstate the real risk.

Other Types of Risks

Although market risk and credit risk comprise the two primary risks, they are by no means exhaustive. The unforeseen circumstances that can occur touch on almost all aspects of running a business.

Operational risk is the risk of a breakdown in the operations of the derivatives program or risk management system. This could include such events as power failures, computer problems such as viruses and software bugs, the failure of staff personnel to monitor and record transactions properly, the failure of staff personnel to have the necessary knowledge of potentially complex transactions, the failure to have proper documentation, and fraud perpetrated by traders or staff personnel. These risks are present in virtually any type of business operation but because derivatives transactions are generally somewhat complex and usually involve large amounts of money, the need to avoid these problems is critical.

Perhaps the most important part of operational risk is the effectiveness of proper controls. For example, if certain persons are authorized to engage in derivatives transactions, then it is imperative that their activities be monitored by personnel who report to persons higher in the organization. Anyone authorized to trade must be restricted in what contracts and how much that person can trade. Controls must be in place to make sure that these policies are followed. As obvious as that seems, some firms have not done a good job of ensuring that well-established policies and procedures are actually followed.

Model risk is the risk that in pricing the derivative the firm will use an inappropriate model, use a model containing errors, or use incorrect inputs in a good model. This is certainly critical for dealers because offering derivatives at attractive prices is their business. It can also be critical for end users because they are less likely to have the personnel and knowledge to properly price the instruments.

Liquidity risk is the risk that a firm will need to enter into a derivatives transaction and find that the market for that transaction is so thin that the price is unattractive. This would be evidenced by wide bid-ask spreads and by few dealers willing to make a market. The more complex and exotic the transaction, the greater the degree of liquidity risk. Most plain vanilla swaps, options, and FRAs, however, would have little liquidity risk.

Accounting risk is the uncertainty over the proper accounting treatment. If a firm has relied on certain transactions, it may find later that the method it has used to account for them has been ruled unacceptable by the Financial Accounting Standards Board and/or the Securities and Exchange Commission. This could result in the firm having to restate past performance and/or being subject to sanctions. Many firms have indicated a reluctance to use derivatives if it is not clear how to properly account for them.

Legal risk is the risk that the legal system will fail to enforce a contract. For example, suppose a dealer enters into a swap with a counterparty who, upon incurring a loss, then refuses to pay the dealer, arguing that the dealer misled it or that the counterparty had no legal authority to enter into the swap. These arguments have been successfully used in the legal system, particularly by local governments. The risk of contracts not being enforced is a serious one for dealers.[9] This risk can effectively turn a swap or FRA into an option because the counterparty simply walks away without paying if the market moves against it. Not too surprisingly, no counterparty has ever claimed that it was misled or had no authority to do derivatives after making money on them. We shall see this issue again when we look at the bankruptcy of Orange County, California.

Tax risk is the risk that taxes or the interpretation of tax laws will change unexpectedly. A good example of this was described in Appendix 10B where the tax status of hedging, which had been established almost a half century prior, was called into question. For a period of time, the possibility existed that certain hedging transactions would be taxed in a different manner, rendering them much less attractive. Moreover, the threat that completed transactions will have to be re-taxed always looms. Tax risk has managed to completely eliminate the use of certain transactions, such as the American Stock Exchange's PRIMES and SCORES, which were precursors to the equity-linked debt we covered in Chapter 15. As another example of tax risk, Congress has been considering for many years levying a tax on each futures transaction to pay the cost of regulating the futures markets.

Regulatory risk is the risk that regulations or the regulatory style will change unexpectedly. For example, the Commodity Futures Trading Commission was once chaired by an individual who pursued a free-market, loose-knit style of regulation that encouraged innovation and competition. When a new administration took over the White House, a new chairman was appointed. The philosophy of the agency changed overnight to a much tighter regulatory approach. Obviously, regulatory risk means that certain existing or contemplated transactions can become illegal.

Settlement risk is commonly faced in international transactions. Let us say that a bank in country A engages in a financial transaction with a corporation in country B in which both the bank and the corporation will be required to pay each other rather than net their payments.[10] The bank and the corporation are 12 hours apart with the bank's day begin-

In addition to market and credit risks, risk managers must consider operational risk, model risk, liquidity risk, accounting risk, legal risk, tax risk, regulatory risk, and settlement risk.

---

[9]The aforementioned Hammersmith and Fulham case illustrates the dangers of legal risk to the dealer. The case was supported on the doctrine of *ultra vires,* which means to have no legal authority.

[10]For example, a currency swap is usually done without netting because the payments are occurring in two different currencies.

ning first. On settlement day the bank wires its funds to the corporation under the assumption that when the markets open the corporation will wire its funds to the bank. When the corporation's markets open, however, the corporation announces that it is bankrupt and will suspend all payments. Thus, the bank will be out the money and will have to get in line with the corporation's other creditors. This risk is sometimes called **Herstatt risk,** named for the German bank that in 1974 failed under similar circumstances. Settlement risk can arise out of bankruptcy, insolvency, or fraud.

This enumeration of risks does not necessarily cover every possible contingency. Foreign currency transactions, for example, are subject to political risk, meaning that the government of a country may take over the financial system and declare certain transactions null and void or refuse to allow currency to leave the country. The Chicago Board of Trade was forced to suspend operations one day due to a flood in downtown Chicago. Risk managers needing to trade CBOT products had to look for substitutes in other markets. It would be impossible to have every contingency covered, but risk managers need to be aware of as many problems as possible that could occur.

Systemic risk is the risk that failure of one or more financial institutions will trigger more failures, ultimately leading to a breakdown of the financial system.

There is one final source of risk that is of considerable concern to many people, especially regulators. There is a belief that when one company defaults, it could trigger the default of one of its creditors, which could trigger further defaults. These effects could ripple through the entire financial system, leading to widespread panic and a meltdown of the whole system. This is called **systemic risk.** In modern times, the closest the world's economy has come to such a breakdown was during the stock market crash of October 1987. As it turned out, while there was a great deal of panic and enormous losses, no party that should have been paid failed to be paid, and in fact, the markets did not even come close to a total breakdown. Regulators worry, however, that the volume of derivatives transactions, particularly over-the-counter derivatives, is much greater now. While this might be a legitimate concern in an economy in which most financial institutions do not practice risk management, there is little cause for concern today. Nearly every major financial institution in the world practices risk management and most maintain a relatively hedged position in derivatives. There have been numerous shocks to the financial system in the 1990s but none has come remotely close to causing a systemic breakdown.

Organizational Issues in Risk Management

Most of this book has been focused on various technical issues associated with the use of derivatives. At this point, we turn to a look at the

organizational issues that confront any firm that engages in derivatives transactions. As we noted previously, operational risk can be quite critical. Such risks can be avoided or at least better managed if proper attention is paid to setting up an effective organizational structure to manage risk.

The quality of an organization always starts at the top. This means that senior management and the board of directors must take the initiative for being knowledgeable and aware of the derivatives activities the firm engages in. This does not mean that they must be experts in derivatives, but they should be able to define each of the instruments used by the firm and should know why the firm uses them. Most importantly, they must establish written policies and procedures governing the use of derivatives. These policies must establish a rationale for the use of derivatives, define the circumstances under which derivatives can be used, authorize the appropriate personnel to execute transactions, define trading limits, establish control procedures to ensure that all policies are followed, and address the issue of how the performance of a derivatives/risk management operation will be evaluated.

Senior management is particularly responsible for ensuring that competent personnel with sufficient technical knowledge are employed by the firm when such skills are needed. They must also authorize the expenditure of funds for the necessary hardware and software.

A dealer organization, which is in the derivatives business to earn a profit, will engage in numerous transactions and naturally should practice risk management at the centralized firmwide level. If there are relationships between movements in interest rates, stock prices, and foreign exchange rates, and there nearly always are, it would be unwise to have separate risk managers monitoring the performance of the bond department, the equities department, and the various international operations. Rather, most dealers have opted for a single risk manager, who often reports to the chief executive officer. The risk manager should have access to all of the necessary financial and statistical information and should have the authority to stop traders from trading and/or force them to unwind positions. It should not be possible for traders or derivatives sales personnel to influence the risk manager. Some dealers use a risk management committee, but in either case, the risk manager's or the committee's responsibility is usually to senior management. In any case, independent risk management is probably the most important requirement for an effective risk management system.

A corporate risk management function may be surprisingly decentralized. Some firms may have purchasing departments that hedge purchases of raw materials. Many firms will have foreign subsidiaries who hedge their subsidiary operations. Most corporations delegate domestic interest rate hedging to the treasury department. The treasury's normal responsibility is managing cash and bank loans. In recent years, many corporations have

One of the most important organizational considerations in risk management is to have an independent risk management function, meaning that the risk manager has access to necessary information, the authority to take corrective action, and immunity from the influence of traders and sales personnel.

begun to centralize their risk management activities, focusing on risk management of the firm as a whole. This enables the firm to allow certain natural hedges to work. For example, a firm might be exposed long to German interest rates in one division and short in another. If each division hedges separately, unnecessary transactions are done. A centralized risk management function would determine that the risks of two divisions are at least partially offsetting.

Many corporations unfortunately do not provide for an independent risk management function. To make things worse, they sometimes operate their treasury department as a profit center. Instead of attempting to simply manage the firm's cash and bank loans efficiently, treasurers sometimes start trading in the derivatives markets with the objective of earning a profit. It is not reasonable to expect that they can do this effectively over the long run and, unfortunately, for some firms, the long run came early in the form of large derivatives losses.

Derivatives dealers have two distinct groups of derivatives specialists. One group is the sales personnel, who call on clients, analyze the clients' risks, and offer the dealer's products and services for the purpose of managing the clients' risks. The other group is made up of traders who execute derivatives transactions for the dealer. Most dealers also have research departments, normally made up of technically trained personnel who conduct research, design and price new products, and provide support for sales personnel and traders. Most corporations do not have research departments but may have a few individuals on the staff with trading experience and a high degree of technical expertise.

The derivatives operations of dealers are typically segregated into what are called the **front office** and **back office.** Some firms have an additional layer in between the front office and back office, which is naturally called the middle office. The front office consists of the traders and their assistants. The back office personnel are the clerks and operations officers whose job is to process the paperwork and generate the necessary reports. It is considered critical by nearly every dealer that these two functions be separate. If they are not, as we shall see when we read about the failure of Barings Bank, the proverbial "fox is guarding the chicken coop." In some firms, the back office may be the only control mechanism. While this is not the optimal structure, at the very least the back office should not have to report to the front office or feel any pressure from it.

A typical dealership operation is divided into two groups: the front office, meaning the trading function, and the back office, meaning the clerical, record-keeping function. Effective risk management requires that these two functions be separated.

All firms should also have a legal department or have access to external legal counsel. The attorneys are responsible for ensuring that all contracts are properly documented and conform to appropriate laws.

The accounting function is an important one in all firms. We have already mentioned the complexities of derivatives accounting. Although an accounting system is not the same as a risk management system, the two must not be inconsistent. An accounting system also provides for periodic

Derivatives in Action

Risk Management at Coca-Cola

Although accounting and regulatory rules may some day require that corporations fully disclose their risk management activities, many have been doing so voluntarily. The following excerpt is footnote 8 of the 1996 Annual Report of the Coca-Cola Company. We see that Coke uses swaps, forwards, and options/caps to hedge some of its interest rate and currency exposure. It also pays a great deal of attention to the credit risk associated with these transactions.

8. Hedging Transactions and Derivative Financial Instruments

Our Company employs derivative financial instruments primarily to reduce our exposure to adverse fluctuations in interest rates, foreign exchange rates, commodity prices and other market risks. These financial instruments, when entered into, are designated as hedges of underlying exposures. Because of the high correlation between the hedging instrument and the underlying exposure being hedged, fluctuations in the value of the instruments are generally offset by changes in the value of the underlying exposures. We effectively monitor the use of these derivative financial instruments through the use of objective measurement systems, well-defined market and credit risk limits and timely reports to senior management according to prescribed guidelines. Virtually all of our derivatives are "over-the-counter" instruments.

The estimated fair values of derivatives used to hedge or modify our risks fluctuate over time. These fair value amounts should not be viewed in isolation, but rather in relation to the fair values of the underlying hedged transactions and investments, and the overall reduction in our exposure to adverse fluctuations in interest rates, foreign exchange rates, commodity prices and other market risks.

The notional amounts of the derivative financial instruments do not necessarily represent amounts exchanged by the parties and, therefore, are not a direct measure of our exposure through our use of derivatives. The amounts exchanged are calculated by reference to the notional amounts and by other terms of the derivatives, such as interest rates, exchange rates or other financial indices.

Notes to Consolidated Financial Statements

We have established strict counterparty credit guidelines and only enter into transactions with financial institutions of investment grade or better. Counterparty exposures are monitored daily and any down-grade in credit rating receives immediate review. If a downgrade in the credit rating of a counterparty were to occur, we have provisions requiring collateral in the form of U.S. government securities for transactions with maturities in excess of three years. To mitigate pre-settlement risk, minimum credit standards become more stringent as the duration of the derivative financial instrument increases. To minimize the concentration of credit risk, we enter into derivative transactions with a portfolio of financial institutions. As a result, we consider the risk of counterparty default to be minimal.

Interest Rate Management

Our management has implemented a policy to maintain our percentage of fixed and variable rate debt within certain parameters. We enter into interest rate swap agreements that maintain the fixed/variable mix within these defined parameters. These contracts had maturities ranging from one to seven years on December 31, 1996. Variable rates are predominantly linked to LIBOR (London Interbank Offered Rate). Any differences paid or received on interest rate swap agreements are recognized as adjustments to interest expense over the life of each swap, thereby adjusting the effective interest rate on the underlying obligation.

Additionally, our Company enters into interest rate cap agreements that entitle us to receive from a financial institution the amount, if any, by which our interest payments on our variable rate debt exceed prespecified interest rates through 1997. Premiums paid for interest rate cap agreements are included in prepaid expenses and other assets and are amortized to interest expense over the terms of the respective agreements. Payments received pursuant to the inter-

est rate cap agreements, if any, are recognized as an adjustment to the interest expense on the underlying debt instruments.

Foreign Currency Management

The purpose of our foreign currency hedging activities is to reduce the risk that our eventual dollar net cash inflows resulting from sales outside the United States will be adversely affected by changes in exchange rates.

We enter into forward exchange contracts and purchase currency options (principally European currencies and Japanese yen) to hedge firm sale commitments denominated in foreign currencies. We also purchase currency options (principally European currencies and Japanese yen) to hedge certain anticipated sales. Premiums paid and realized gains and losses, including those on terminated contracts, if any, are included in prepaid expenses and other assets. These are recognized in income along with unrealized gains and losses, in the same period the hedged transactions are realized. Approximately $17 million and $27 million of realized losses on settled contracts entered into as hedges of firmly committed transactions that have not yet occurred were deferred on December 31, 1996 and 1995, respectively. Deferred gains/losses from hedging anticipated transactions were not material on December 31, 1996 or 1995. In the unlikely event that the underlying transaction terminates or becomes improbable, the deferred gains or losses on the associated derivative will be recorded in our income statement.

Gains and losses on derivative financial instruments that are designated and effective as hedges of net investments in international operations are included in share-owners' equity as a foreign currency translation adjustment.

The following table presents the aggregate notional principal amounts, carrying values, fair values and maturities of our derivative financial instruments outstanding on December 31, 1996 and 1995 (in millions):

December 31,	Notional Principal Amounts	Carrying Values	Fair Values	Maturity
1996				
Interest rate management				
Swap agreements				
Assets	$893	$5	$13	1997–2003
Liabilities	25	—	1	2002
Interest rate caps				
Assets	400	1	—	1997
Foreign currency management				
Forward contracts				
Assets	5	1	(2)	1997
Liabilities	2,541	(53)	(42)	1997–1998
Swap agreements				
Assets	398	18	12	1997–1998
Liabilities	1,086	(12)	(114)	1997–2002
Purchased options				
Assets	1,873	42	89	1997
Other				
Assets	537	67	33	1997
	$7,758	$69	$(10)	

December 31,	Notional Principal Amounts	Carrying Values	Fair Values	Maturity
1995				
Interest rate management				
Swap agreements				
Assets	$705	$4	$30	1997–2003
Liabilities	62	—	(2)	2000–2002
Interest rate caps				
Assets	400	2	—	1997
Foreign currency management				
Forward contracts				
Assets	1,927	25	36	1996
Liabilities	554	(17)	(15)	1996–1997
Swap agreements				
Assets	390	17	11	1996–2000
Liabilities	1,686	(46)	(262)	1996–2002
Purchased options				
Assets	1,823	62	90	1996
Other				
Assets	327	7	5	1996
	$7,874	$54	$(107)	

Maturities of derivative financial instruments held on December 31, 1996, are as follows (in millions):

1997	1998	1999	2000–2003
$6,037	$622	$204	$895

auditing, but does not substitute for risk management. Auditing simply determines whether the financial records have been kept in conformance with the policies established by the accounting profession. Auditing is a periodic process. Risk management is a continuous process.

Any firm that engages in derivatives and risk management activities should provide for regular evaluation of its performance. It should define its objectives and establish a system that will provide timely and unbiased assessments of the quality of its activities. This is not a simple task since objective performance evaluation is quite difficult to do but this issue must be addressed, nonetheless.

Although there are many effective variations, Figures 16.7 and 16.8 illustrate examples of a derivatives/risk management operation for a dealer and for a corporate end user. The dealer operation is centralized with an independent risk manager reporting to the chief executive officer. The corporate structure shown here is a little less centralized with derivatives activities undertaken by both a purchasing officer and the treasury. This firm has established a risk management function that reports to the treasury. It is unlikely, however, that the risk manager has sufficient information to monitor the purchasing officer's hedging transactions or the authority to do much about it if policies are not followed or problems occur.

FIGURE 16.7   **Example of a Dealer Derivatives/Risk Management Operation**

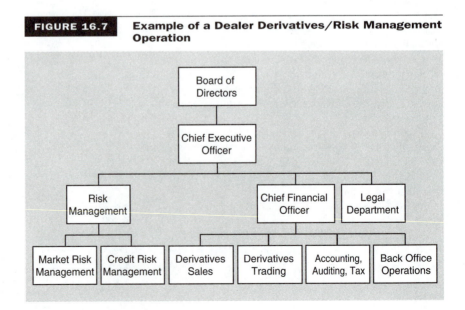

FIGURE 16.8 Example of a Corporate Derivatives/Risk Management Operation

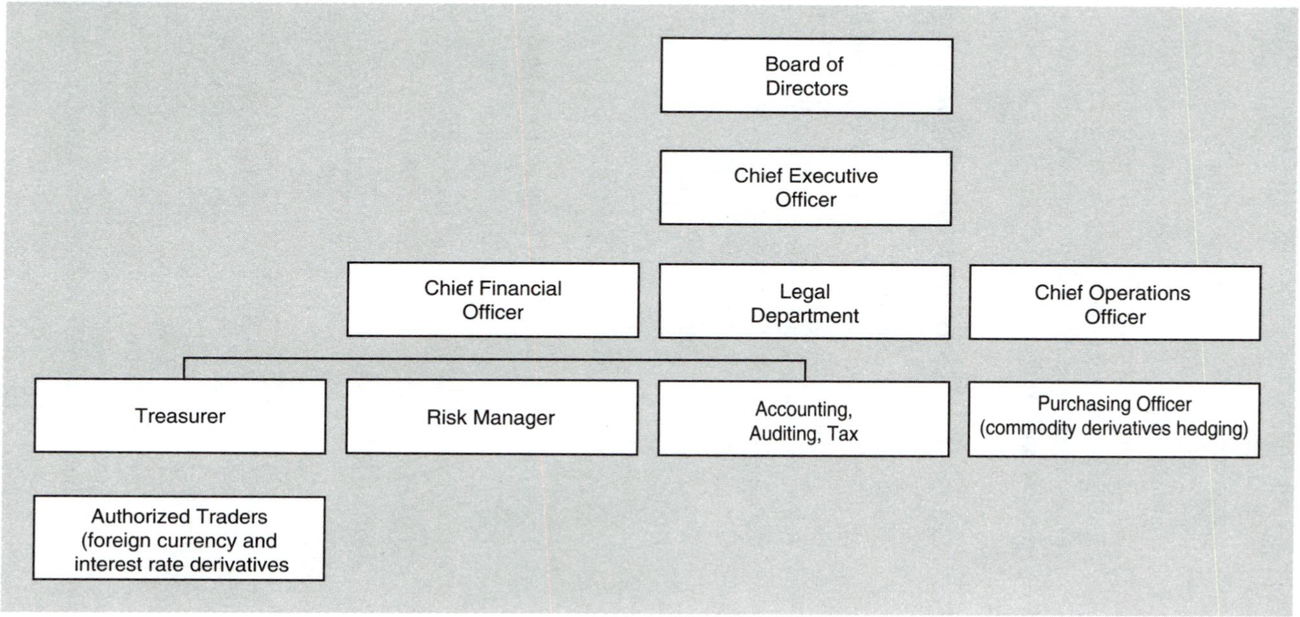

Board of Directors

Chief Executive Officer

Legal Department

Accounting, Auditing, Tax

Chief Operations Officer

Purchasing Officer (commodity derivatives hedging)

Chief Financial Officer

Risk Manager

Treasurer

Authorized Traders (foreign currency and interest rate derivatives)

The G-30 Report is a widely accepted set of standards of practice for effective risk management.

There are certainly many variations in what constitutes effective practices in risk management. A widely accepted set of effective risk management practices is presented in the **G-30 Report.** The G-30, which stands for Group of 30, is a private international organization of economic and financial experts who study and evaluate various issues facing the international economic community. In 1993, the G-30 issued a report on derivatives practices. Table 16.7 presents a condensed version of the G-30 recommendations. The report emphasizes the importance of senior management's involvement in the process and the necessity for having an effective and independent risk management system in place. Note also the importance of such concepts as VaR, delta, gamma, and vega, the need for market *and* credit risk management, and the emphasis on netting.

Some Lessons in Risk Management

Throughout this chapter we have learned about methods for practicing good risk management. Unfortunately, not all firms have followed the best risk management practices. In fact, some of them have hardly practiced risk management at all. During the first few years of the 1990s, an increasing number of firms announced large losses from trading derivatives. Some of the losses were barely large enough to merit an article in *The Wall Street Journal.* In two cases, however, the losses were large enough to bankrupt the organizations. Because learning what not to do is as valuable as learning what to do, we shall take a look at four of the most significant instances where risk management left much to be desired.

Metallgesellschaft: To Hedge or Not to Hedge?

Our proposed risk management program, not only protects the pump profit margins with a minimum amount of risk from the spot market, but also offers us an opportunity for extraordinary upside profit with no additional risk.

METALLGESELLSCHAFT'S BUSINESS PLAN
Quoted in Antonio S. Mello and John E. Parsons
"Maturity Structure of a Hedge Matters:
Lessons from the Metallgesellschaft Debacle"
Working Paper, February 1995, Columbia University

The industrial firm Metallgesellschaft A.G. (MG) was the fourteenth largest corporation in Germany in 1993. Founded in 1883, it employed 58,000 people, had 251 subsidiaries worldwide, and was engaged in a variety of businesses primarily related to mining, metals, and energy products. In late 1993 and early 1994, it incurred losses in futures trading totaling about $1.3

TABLE 16.7   The Group of 30 Recommendations on Derivatives and Risk Management Practices

GENERAL POLICIES

Recommendation 1: The Role of Senior Management
Dealers and end users should use derivatives in a manner consistent with the overall risk management and capital policies approved by their boards of directors. These policies should be reviewed as business and market circumstances change. Policies governing derivatives use should be clearly defined, including the purposes for which these transactions are to be undertaken. Senior management should approve procedures and controls to implement these policies, and management at all levels should enforce them.

VALUATION AND MARKET-RISK MANAGEMENT

Recommendation 2: Marking to Market
Dealers should mark their derivatives positions to market, on at least a daily basis, for risk management purposes.

Recommendation 3: Market Valuation Methods
Derivatives portfolios of dealers should be valued based on mid-market levels less specific adjustments, or on appropriate bid or offer levels. Mid-market valuation adjustments should allow for expected future costs, such as unearned credit spread, closeout costs, investing and funding costs, and administrative costs.

Recommendation 4: Identifying Revenue Sources
Dealers should measure the components of revenue regularly and in sufficient detail to understand the sources of risk.

Recommendation 5: Measuring Market Risk
Dealers should use a consistent measure to calculate daily the market risk of their derivatives positions and compare it to market risk limits.

- Market risk is best measured as "value at risk" using probability analysis based upon a common confidence interval (e.g., two standard deviations) and time horizon (e.g., one-day exposure).
- Components of market risk that should be considered across the term structure include: absolute price or rate change (delta); convexity (gamma); volatility (vega); time decay (theta); basis or correlation; and discount rate (rho).

Recommendation 6: Stress Simulation
Dealers should periodically perform simulations to determine how their portfolios would perform under stress conditions.

Recommendation 7: Investing and Funding Forecasts
Dealers should periodically forecast the cash investing and funding requirements arising from their derivatives portfolios.

Recommendation 8: Independent Market-Risk Management
Dealers should have a market-risk management function, with clear independence and authority, to ensure that the following responsibilities are carried out:

- The development of risk limit policies and the monitoring of transactions and positions for adherence to these policies. (See Recommendation 5.)
- The design of stress scenarios to measure the impact of market conditions, however improbable, that might cause market gaps, volatility swings, or disruptions of major relationships, or might reduce liquidity in the face of unfavorable market linkages, concentrated market making, or credit exhaustion. (See Recommendation 6.)
- The design of revenue reports quantifying the contribution of various risk components, and of market-risk measures such as value at risk. (See Recommendations 4 and 5.)
- The monitoring of variance between the actual volatility of portfolio value and that predicted by the measure of market risk.
- The review and approval of pricing models and valuation systems used by front- and back-office personnel, and the development of reconciliation procedures if different systems are used.

(continued)

TABLE 16.7   *(continued)*

Recommendation 9: Practices by End Users
As appropriate to the nature, size, and complexity of their derivatives activities, end users should adopt the same valuation and market-risk management practices that are recommended for dealers. Specifically they should consider regularly marking to market their derivatives transactions for risk-management purposes; periodically forecasting the cash investing and funding requirements arising from their derivatives transactions; and establishing a clearly independent and authoritative function to design and assure adherence to prudent risk limits.

CREDIT RISK MEASUREMENT AND MANAGEMENT

Recommendation 10: Measuring Credit Exposure
Dealers and end users should measure credit exposure on derivatives in two ways:

- Current exposure, which is the replacement cost of derivative transactions, that is, their market value, and
- Potential exposure, which is an estimate of the future replacement cost of derivatives transactions. It should be calculated using probability analysis based upon broad confidence intervals (e.g., two standard deviations) over the remaining terms of the transactions.

Recommendation 11: Aggregating Credit Exposures
Credit exposures on derivatives, and all other credit exposures to a counterparty, should be aggregated taking into consideration enforceable netting arrangements. Credit exposures should be calculated regularly and compared to credit limits.

Recommendation 12: Independent Credit Risk Management
Dealers and end users should have a credit risk management function with clear independence and authority, and with analytical capabilities in derivatives, responsible for

- Approving credit exposure measurement demands.
- Setting credit limits and monitoring their use.
- Reviewing credits and concentrations of credit risk.
- Reviewing and monitoring risk-reduction arrangements.

Recommendation 13: Master Agreements
Dealers and end users are encouraged to use one master agreement as widely as possible with each counterparty to document existing and future derivatives transactions, including foreign-exchange forwards and options. Master agreements should provide for payments netting and close-out netting, using a full two-way payments approach.

Recommendation 14: Credit Enhancement
Dealers and end users should assess both the benefits and costs of credit enhancement and risk-reduction arrangements. Where it is proposed that credit downgrades would trigger early termination or collateral requirements, participants should carefully consider their own capacity and that of their counterparties to meet the potentially substantial funding needs that might result.

ENFORCEABILITY

Recommendation 15: Promoting Enforceability
Dealers and end users should work together on a continuing basis to identify and recommend solutions for issues of legal enforceability, both within and across jurisdictions, as activities evolve and new types of securities are developed.

TABLE 16.7	*(continued)*

SYSTEMS, OPERATIONS, AND CONTROLS

Recommendation 16: Professional Expertise

Dealers and end users must ensure that their derivatives activities are undertaken by professionals in sufficient number and with the appropriate experience, skill levels, and degrees of specialization. These professionals include specialists who transact and manage the risks involved, their supervisors, and those responsible for processing, reporting, controlling, and auditing the activities.

Recommendation 17: Systems

Dealers and end users must ensure that adequate systems for data capture, processing, settlement, and management reporting are in place so that derivatives transactions are conducted in an orderly and efficient manner in compliance with management policies. Dealers should have risk-management systems that measure the risks incurred in their derivatives activities including market and credit risks. End users should have risk-management systems that measure the risks incurred in their derivatives activities based upon their nature, size, and complexity.

Recommendation 18: Authority

Management of dealers and end users should delegate who is authorized to commit their institutions to derivatives transactions.

ACCOUNTING AND DISCLOSURE

Recommendation 19: Accounting Policies

International harmonization of accounting standards for derivatives is desirable. Pending the adoption of harmonized standards, the following accounting practices are recommended:

- Dealers should account for derivatives transactions by marking them to market, taking changes in value to income each period.
- End users should account for derivatives used to manage risks so as to achieve a consistency of income recognition treatment between those instruments and the risks being managed. Thus, if the risk being managed is accounted for at cost (or, in the case of an anticipatory hedged, not yet recognized), changes in the value of a qualifying risk-management instrument should be deferred until a gain or loss is recognized on the risk being managed. Or, if the risk being managed is marked to market with changes in value being taken to income, a qualifying risk-management instrument should be treated in a comparable fashion.
- End users should account for derivatives not qualifying for risk-management treatment on a mark-to-market basis.
- Amounts due to and from counterparties should only be offset when there is a legal right to set off or when enforceable netting arrangements are in place.
- Where local regulations prevent adoption of these practices, disclosure along these lines is nevertheless recommended.

Recommendation 20: Disclosures

Financial statements of dealers and end users should contain sufficient information about their use of derivatives to provide an understanding of the purposes for which transactions are undertaken, the extent of the transactions, the degree of risk involved, and how the transactions have been accounted for. Pending the adoption of harmonized accounting standards, the following disclosures are recommended:

- Information about management's attitude to financial risk, how instruments are used, and how risks are monitored and controlled.
- Accounting policies.
- Analysis of positions at the balance-sheet date.
- Analysis of the credit risk inherent in those positions.
- For dealers only, additional information about the extent of their activities in financial instruments.

(continued)

TABLE 16.7　　*(continued)*

RECOMMENDATIONS FOR LEGISLATORS, REGULATORS, AND SUPERVISORS

Recommendation 21: Recognizing Netting
Regulators and supervisors should recognize the benefits of netting arrangements where and to the full extent that they are enforceable, and encourage their use by reflecting these arrangements in capital adequacy standards. Specifically, they should promptly implement the recognition of the effectiveness of bilateral close-out netting in bank capital regulations.

Recommendation 22: Legal and Regulatory Uncertainties
Legislators, regulators, and supervisors, including central banks, should work in concert with dealers and end users to identify and remove any remaining legal and regulatory uncertainties with respect to:

- The form of documentation required to create legally enforceable agreements (statute of frauds).
- The capacity of parties, such as governmental entities, insurance companies, pension funds, and building societies, to enter into transactions (ultra vires).
- The enforceability of bilateral close-out netting and collateral arrangements in bankruptcy.
- The enforceability of multibranch netting arrangements in bankruptcy.
- The legality/enforceability of derivatives transactions.

Recommendation 23: Tax Treatment
Legislators and tax authorities are encouraged to review and, where appropriate, amend tax laws and regulations that disadvantage the use of derivatives in risk-management strategies. Tax impediments include the inconsistent or uncertain tax treatment of gains and losses on the derivatives, in comparison with the gains and losses that arise from the risks being managed.

Recommendation 24: Accounting Standards
Accounting standards-setting bodies in each country should, as a matter of priority, provide comprehensive guidance on accounting and reporting of transactions in financial instruments, including derivatives, and should work toward harmonization of standards on this subject. Also, the International Accounting Standards Committee should finalize its accounting standard on financial instruments.

Source: The Group of Thirty, *Derivatives: Practices and Principles* (1993)

billion, which was approximately one-half of its capital at that time. The losses were all the more remarkable for the fact that MG was a firm that had traded futures successfully for many years. Although the firm was saved by a $1.9 billion bailout by a consortium of banks, the affair has raised concerns on several counts. If an extremely experienced firm can be nearly bankrupted trading derivatives, how can less experienced firms expect to use them successfully? And, if losses of that size can be generated trading on the highly regulated exchange-listed futures markets, how dangerous can the unregulated over-the-counter markets be? MG's loss was all the more remarkable for the fact that *it was designed to be a hedge*. Or was it?

The troubles were caused by a U.S. subsidiary of MG called MG Refining and Marketing (MGRM). In 1992, MGRM developed a marketing

strategy whereby it would offer to U.S. firms long-term fixed-price purchase contracts on gasoline, heating oil, and diesel fuel. MGRM's customers were able to lock in their purchase prices for up to 10 years provided they agreed to buy from MGRM. These transactions were forward
contracts at prices $3 to $5 per barrel lower than the spot prices at that
time. Since MGRM was committed to delivering the products at expiration, it was short in the forward markets for these various energy products.

To hedge its risk MGRM entered into long futures contracts on the
New York Mercantile Exchange. Its futures hedges accounted for about 40
percent of its commitment while over-the-counter derivatives contracts
covered about 60 percent. Recognizing the illiquidity of all but the shortest futures contracts, MGRM hedged its position primarily in the shortest-
term futures contracts for unleaded gasoline, heating oil, and crude oil.
Its over-the-counter contracts were also short-term. MGRM also entered
into a contract with a partially owned U.S. firm, Castle Energy, to purchase
all of Castle's output at fixed margins for up to 10 years.

By late 1993, MGRM was long futures contracts for 55 million barrels of
various energy products and had swaps in place to purchase at least another
100 million barrels. These quantities were almost precisely the amount of
its forward commitments to its customers. In other words, MGRM used
what we described in Chapter 10 as "a naive hedge ratio" of one-to-one.

As we learned, however, a one-to-one hedge ratio is rarely appropriate.
If the hedged instrument moves more or less than the hedging instrument, the position may be underhedged or overhedged. Also since the
hedging instruments, futures, had a short maturity, they had to be rolled
over as each contract expired. MGRM simply settled up expiring contracts
and purchased the next shortest maturity contract. This strategy, called a
stack hedge or stack-and-roll hedge, works successfully provided that the
markets were in backwardation, meaning, as we covered in Chapter 9, the
more distant futures price was lower than the spot or nearby futures price.
Energy markets are often in backwardation, a result of the convenience
yield, a concept we also previously covered. We emphasize that while energy markets are *often* in backwardation, they can convert to contango
without much notice and that is precisely what they did.

In late 1993, energy prices began falling and over the course of that
year fell by almost a third. MGRM's long futures positions began incurring
losses, resulting in large margin calls. While the firm was theoretically
gaining on its fixed supply contracts, those gains would not be realized
until the oil was delivered. As we noted, the delivery commitments were
spread out up to 10 years in the future. The company's realized losses
drained its cash and its paper gains produced no cash to offset. Soon the
company was staggering under the weight of these huge losses. The parent
company had to make a decision about unwinding its position or continuing to fund the account. It chose to unwind. In retrospect that was the

worst thing it could have done. In less than six months energy prices recovered all of their lost ground, meaning that MGRM's now unhedged short forward delivery contracts incurred further losses.

As we noted in the first paragraph of this story, the parent company was bailed out by a consortium of banks, some of which were on its own board of directors. The chairman of MG and the head of MGRM's U.S. oil trading operation were both fired and filed suits for conspiracy and defamation against their former employers. MG ultimately reported a loss of over $1.7 billion for its fiscal year ending September 30, 1994.

It is not clear exactly why MGRM's hedge was so poorly balanced. Some experts suggest that MGRM was speculating and knew exactly what it was doing. Others say that MGRM had an effective hedge in place and could have produced the cash to meet its margin calls without liquidating its futures contracts, which, in hindsight, would have recouped their losses less than a year later. The CFTC, exercising a rarely used and somewhat controversial authority, fined MGRM $2.2 million for failing to exercise adequate internal controls and ordered it to demonstrate in the future that such controls were in place.

Orange County, California: Playing the Odds

I am one of the largest investors in America. I know these things.

ROBERT CITRON
Quoted in Philippe Jorion
Big Bets Gone Bad
(Academic Press, 1996)

Due to my inexperience, I placed a great deal of reliance on the advice of market professionals . . . I wish I had more training in complex government securities.

ROBERT CITRON
Testimony before Senate Special Committee
on Local Government Investments, January 17, 1995
Quoted in *RISK*, March 1995

Orange County, California, is one of the wealthiest communities in the United States. Home to Disneyland, the California Angels, and the John Wayne airport, it reported a loss of $1.6 billion in its investment account in 1994 and declared the largest municipal bankruptcy in U.S. history. How this could have happened is not at all a mystery. Orange County's treasurer, Robert Citron, was engaged in a clever investment scheme that turned a low-risk essentially money market fund into a turbo-charged investment account.

The 69-year-old Citron, with 24 years' experience as the county treasurer, operated a fund that invested in short-term, fixed-income securities. The fund not only invested Orange County funds but also accepted the funds of almost 200 other municipal governments in California. How it did this is not surprising. The Orange County fund had been earning 300 to 400 basis points above the returns earned on a similar fund operated by the state of California. The Orange County fund's market value was almost $7.5 billion. In June 1994, Citron was reelected county treasurer in spite of warnings by his opponent that the portfolio was excessively leveraged.

By late 1994, a series of sharp increases in interest rates, triggered by the Federal Reserve's efforts to control inflation, brought the value of the fund down by a staggering $2 billion. Orange County was forced to declare bankruptcy. Citron and his chief investment officer were arrested. Citron declared that he had been tricked by his brokerage firm, Merrill Lynch, into making these investments, about which he now stated that he knew little. Orange County went into reorganization, cut services drastically, laid off employees, and filed a $3 billion lawsuit against Merrill Lynch.

It did not take long to determine what had gone wrong. Citron had used leverage to purchase additional government securities through reverse repurchase agreements. Recall from Chapter 9 that we introduced the concept of a repurchase agreement. Let us say that another municipality gives Mr. Citron $100 million to invest. Citron purchases intermediate-term U.S. Treasury notes, which have an average maturity of about 4 years and a duration of about 3.5 years. Citron then executes a reverse repurchase agreement with a securities dealer or bank, pledging the $100 million of securities for a loan of almost $100 million, let us say $90 million. He then uses the $90 million to purchase additional similar securities. This can be done several times with the same money. Ultimately Citron had leveraged the county about threefold, bringing its total invested funds to about $20 billion while its total equity was only about $7 billion. This tripled its duration. Thus, what should have been a fairly low-risk, short- to intermediate-term fund had the risk of a fund of long-term bonds. When bankruptcy was declared and Citron's strategy was revealed, it should have come as no surprise. *The Wall Street Journal* had reported as early as April 1994 that Citron had leveraged the portfolio almost threefold. It was noted that one municipality withdrew about $4 million at that time because it considered the fund too risky. This probably proved to be the best decision of that treasurer's career.

As in any leveraged bond investment, the results are quite good when interest rates are falling. When the 1994 interest rate increases caused the fund to have a series of huge margin calls from their broker, Orange County began dipping into its cash reserves. When it could no longer generate enough cash to meet its margin calls, its lenders began selling the

collateral, which amounted to about $10 billion. This sent shock waves into the bond market and prices tumbled.

It should be noted that the word *derivatives* has not been mentioned in conjunction with this Orange County story. Although there were some derivatives in the portfolio, mostly in the form of structured notes, the damage had little to do with derivatives. Citron had simply used U.S. government intermediate-term notes, combined with the leveraging power of repurchase agreements, to destroy almost 20 percent of the fund's value.

To say that Orange County invested unwisely and did not practice risk management is probably an understatement. There was no risk management whatsoever. Citron was supposed to be monitored by the elected county board but little monitoring was done. The board trusted the veteran treasurer and let him do what he wanted.

Orange County offered to repay the municipalities and other agencies whose funds it had invested about three-fourths of their money, plus other securities that would be repayable over a long period of time, but most of the payments were contingent on winning the lawsuit against Merrill Lynch. Almost 2,000 of the 15,000 county employees lost their jobs. The county sold nearly $100 million of its assets and proposed a sales tax increase but the voters overwhelmingly turned it down. The county even tried to sell the John Wayne airport but found that it was not permitted by federal law. Citron pled guilty to six felony counts and was sentenced to a year in jail and fined $100,000 in 1996. Orange County was able to issue new debt, deferred repayment of old debt, and by mid-1996 had emerged from bankruptcy though its lawsuit with Merrill Lynch had still not gone to trial and investors were holding promises that they would be paid out of the proceeds of any settlement.

Barings PLC: How One Man Blew Up a Bank

There is little argument about who was the derivatives technology salesman of 1995. Most people will agree that Nick Leeson did more than anyone to raise the awareness of the need for firm-wide risk management.

CLIVE DAVIDSON
"Profiting from Doom"
Risk, January 1996

Barings PLC was a British investment bank that had been founded in 1763. It had played a major role in British history, financing the Napoleonic Wars, and included Queen Elizabeth II among its many well-heeled clients. One weekend in February 1995 Barings was forced to declare bankruptcy,

a result of losses of about $1.2 billion or nearly twice its capital. The losses were attributed to futures trading in its Singapore office by a 28-year-old former clerk named Nick Leeson. Barings was rescued by the Dutch banking concern Internationale Nederlanden Groep (ING), which purchased its assets (approximately $900 million) and assumed most of its liabilities for about $1.61.[11] ING immediately injected about $1 billion in capital. However, some of Barings' liabilities were not assumed and those bondholders suffered big losses.

Leeson had joined the bank in July 1989, having previously worked in London for the American bank Morgan Stanley. As a clerk handling the settling of transactions, he proved to be exceptionally well organized and his work in Barings' back office impressed his superiors. In March 1992 he requested and received a transfer to the Singapore office, which was actively involved in futures trading in Tokyo and Osaka, Japan, and at the Singapore International Monetary Exchange (SIMEX). Again Leeson proved to be excellent at organizing the back office. All the while, Leeson was learning the ropes of trading futures. Soon he was executing arbitrage transactions, buying Japanese stock index futures in Singapore and simultaneously selling the same contract in Osaka, capturing differences in the prices of the same contract on the two exchanges.

Transactions of this sort should be low risk. One position will gain and the other will lose a similar amount. The net should be a small profit resulting from slight differences in the prices of the contract on the two exchanges. As Leeson relates the story in his book, *Rogue Trader*, in 1992 he began hiding his losses in a special account. Soon it began appearing that Leeson was generating huge profits. Because Leeson was responsible for the back office and his employees were loyal to him, he was able to keep the losses tucked safely away whenever reports were required or auditors showed up. In 1994, he reported profits of about £28 million but had hidden losses of £180 million. From January 1, 1995, to February 24, Barings' last day, Leeson produced profits of almost £19 million and losses of over £600 million and it was getting increasingly difficult to cover his trail.

Recall from Chapter 4 that we discussed the straddle, a strategy involving long positions in puts and calls with the same exercise price. Leeson was generating more funds by entering into short straddles, a total of almost 20,000 contracts. This meant that Leeson profited as long as the market stayed fairly stable. With high volatility he would lose big. In late January 1995, Leeson held over 3,000 contracts long of the Japanese Nikkei 225 stock index futures at the Osaka exchange. On January 17, an earthquake struck the Japanese city of Kobe and the index fell about 13

---

[11]Yes, that is one dollar and 61 cents, which at that time was equivalent to approximately one British pound.

percent over the next five weeks. Leeson was generating large losses but increased his bets that the market would turn around. Ultimately Leeson held a $7 billion position that would gain if the market moved up and lose if it moved down. He held about 17,000 contracts in Osaka and over 40,000 in Singapore. He also held huge positions in Japanese government bonds and Euroyen.

The evidence suggests that Barings' executives in London had been warned about Leeson's trading as early as 1992. In 1994, an audit concluded that while Leeson had done nothing wrong, though in fact he had, the potential for wrongdoing was there. It noted that Leeson was running both the front office and back office, though generating large profits with little risk.

Thursday, February 23 was Leeson's last day of work at Barings' Singapore office. He and his wife secretly fled Singapore the next day. They went to several Asian countries before eventually flying to Frankfurt, Germany, where he was arrested by German police a week after fleeing Singapore. Singapore sought extradition while Leeson's British lawyers worked toward having him charged and extradited by England. British authorities were unable to determine that he had violated any of their laws and in October 1995 a German court agreed to turn him over to Singapore. Leeson returned to Singapore and plea bargained a potential 14-year prison sentence down to 6 1/2 years for fraud.

The Barings story shocked the financial world. There were concerns that the SIMEX clearinghouse might fail or use customer funds to cover its losses. The Bank of England, which had rescued Barings once in 1890, considered doing so again, but it quickly became apparent that only investors and not customers would lose money over the Barings failure. While the financial system suffered a shock, it showed no threat of widespread failure, the systemic risk that we previously mentioned. When ING purchased Barings about a week after the failure, the market settled down quickly and no further shocks were felt.

Barings is a classic story in bad risk management. It violates virtually every rule. Leeson was in control of both the back and front offices and, hence, had the ability to hide losses for an extremely long time. Barings' risk management system was nothing more than auditing and regular reports from Leeson showing his positions and performance. The reports were falsified and the auditors' examinations were not sufficient to identify the problem, though they did warn of the potential for fraud. It hardly mattered because they were ignored. The London office was under the impression that this 28-year-old clerk with no college degree was earning large profits arbitraging price differences in two markets. It never questioned how unlikely these profits really were.

Barings was a wake-up call to the rest of the financial world. Risk management became of paramount importance.

Procter & Gamble: Going Up in Suds

I've seen things in the market where I scratch my head and can't imagine why people did it. For example, when P&G lost all that money, I couldn't fathom what anyone at that company was thinking when they looked at that formula of the swap and said, "Yes, that's exactly what I want to put on."

ANONYMOUS
"Confessions of a Structured Note Salesman"
Derivatives Strategy, November 11, 1995

The Procter & Gamble Corporation (P&G) is one of America's best-known companies. It is also a large multinational corporation with extensive foreign operations and significant interest rate and foreign exchange risk. In late October 1993, P&G entered into an exotic swap with its dealer, Banker's Trust (BT). The payment on the swap was determined by a complex formula relating short-term interest rates to long-term interest rates. In early 1994, P&G entered into another exotic swap, this one linked to the exchange rate on the German mark. This transaction was similar to the range floaters that we discussed in Chapter 14. Both parties paid floating rates tied to German interest rates. P&G was betting on deutsche mark swap rates staying between 4.05 percent and 6.10 percent. Both of its positions were essentially bets that U.S. and German interest rates would not increase significantly. If P&G were correct, it would be locking in an attractive below-market borrowing rate of 40 basis points below the commercial paper rate. If it were wrong, P&G would suffer large losses by being forced to borrow at substantially above market rates. The transactions also contained option features that allowed P&G to lock in a cumulative gain or loss.

In April 1994, P&G disclosed that it had taken a $157 million pretax charge as a result of those transactions. Effectively P&G ended up borrowing at 1,412 basis points more than the commercial paper rate. Though the amount lowered its earnings per share only 15 cents, it became a public relations nightmare. P&G's treasurer Norman Mains was reassigned. Later in 1994, P&G filed suit against BT for $130 million under four counts: fraud, negligent misrepresentation, breach of fiduciary duties, and negligence. P&G also pursued charges against BT under the federal RICO (Racketeering Influenced and Corrupt Organizations) Act, a law designed to punish organized crime. The RICO Act had been applied successfully in cases not involving organized crime and it permitted punishment of up to treble damages.

BT argued that P&G ran a sophisticated derivatives operation and was highly experienced in currency and interest rate derivatives. On that

point, BT was certainly correct. P&G had many years of successful experience with these types of instruments, some of them being quite leveraged and exotic. So what was P&G's basis for arguing that BT had defrauded it? BT routinely tape recorded all of its conversations with its derivatives clients. P&G got a court order to obtain the tapes and found that BT derivatives personnel had made statements to the effect that P&G had no idea it was being taken advantage of. P&G argued that BT was its advisor and that it had, therefore, relied on BT's advice and that it was fraudulent for BT to have led it into these transactions.

In the summer of 1996, BT's newly appointed chairman, though confident of a victory in court, elected to put the matter behind them by settling with P&G. BT ended up paying about $80 million to P&G. BT had also settled a number of other cases out of court. Regulators fined it and forced it to agree to take various actions to change its derivatives sales and operating procedures.

In response, a number of leading derivatives dealers organized an informal working group to develop self-regulatory procedures. Though these procedures are nonbinding, they represent an effort by the industry to develop standards of practice in derivatives sales and trading. Of particular note was the fact that, unless made specific, all transactions are at arm's length, meaning that the dealer is not an advisor to the end user.

These four stories were not the only ones that made news. Table 16.8 is a list of other organizations that reported large losses in recent years. Some very familiar names are on the list. Were these firms victims of high-pressure sales tactics of dealers or did they know exactly what they were doing? It seems obvious that one way or the other, they were examples of bad risk management. Whether a firm hedges or speculates, it should know at all times what its exposure is. These casualties of recent years past have, by showing what can go wrong, sent a wake-up call to all users of these highly leveraged instruments: Practice risk management. The message seems to be getting across, because the incidence of organizations incurring large, unexpected losses has dwindled in the last few years.

Summary

In this concluding chapter we have looked at the concept of risk management, meaning to determine the appropriate level of risk, to determine the level of risk a firm currently has, and to take action to ensure that the former is equal to the latter. We examined the risk management industry and noted the differences between how end users and dealers approach risk management.

We looked at some techniques for managing market risk, including delta, gamma, and vega hedging. We also examined the concept of Value at Risk, which measures the minimum loss expected over a period of time with a given probabil-

TABLE 16.8	Organizations Reporting Derivatives Losses		

Time	Organization	Size of Losses	Transactions
1988	Hammersmith and Fulham	£500 million	swaps
March 1991	Allied Lyons	£150 million	currency options
November 1992	Dell Computer	$8 million	currency options and forwards
February 1993	Showa Shell Shekiyu	¥165 billion	currency options and forwards
December 1993	Metallgesellschaft	$1.3 billion	energy futures
January 1994	Codelco	$207 million	copper futures
March 1994	Cargill (Minnetonka Fund)	$100 million	mortgage derivatives
March 1994	Gibson Greetings	$20 million	leveraged interest rate swaps
April 1994	Kashima Oil	$1.5 billion	currency derivatives
April 1994	Mead	$12.1 million	leveraged interest rate swap
April 1994	Procter & Gamble	$157 million	leveraged interest rate and currency swaps
April 1994	Askin Capital Management	$600 million	repurchase agreements and mortgage derivatives
May 1994	Air Products and Chemicals	$113 million	leveraged interest rate and currency swaps
May 1994	Sandoz	$78.5 million	misc. derivatives
May 1994	Dell Computer	$34.6 million	options and leveraged swaps
May 1994	Arco Money Market Plus Fund	$22 million	misc. derivatives
June 1994	International Family Entertainment	$2 million	misc. derivatives
June 1994	Paine Webber Bond Mutual Fund	$33 million	mortgage derivatives
June 1994	Investors Equity Life Insurance Co. of Hawaii	$90 million	bond futures
June 1994	Bank of Montreal's Harris Trust and Savings Bank	$51.3 million	mortgage derivatives
July 1994	CS First Boston Investment Management	$40 million	misc. derivatives
July 1994	Glaxo	£115 million	mortgage derivatives
July 1994	Federal Paper	$19 million	currency derivatives

(continued)

ity. Value at Risk is becoming widely used in the financial world today. We also looked at credit risk, noting how current risk differs from potential risk, and we examined some procedures for reducing credit risk, including the netting of payments owed by parties to each other. We looked at various other types of risks, including operational risk, model risk, liquidity risk, accounting risk, legal risk, tax risk, regulatory risk, and settlement risk. From a broader perspective, we discussed systemic risk, which is the risk of a meltdown of the entire financial system. We looked at procedures and practices for ensuring that an organizational structure is conducive to effective risk management. We looked at the recommendations of the Group of 30 Report on best practices for risk management.

Finally we examined some well-publicized cases of bad risk management. We noted that although many organizations have reported derivatives losses, others have woken up to the practice of risk management.

| TABLE 16.8 | *(continued)* |

Time	Organization	Size of Losses	Transactions
August 1994	Caterpillar Financial	$13.2 million	interest rate caps and swaptions
August 1994	Piper Jaffray Cos.	$700 million	mortgage derivatives
September 1994	Odessa College	$11 million	mortgage derivatives
September 1994	Shoshone Indian Tribe	$5 million	mortgage derivatives
September 1994	Investors Equity Life	$90 million	futures
September 1994	Sears	$237 million	swaps
October 1994	Portage County, Ohio	$8 million	mortgage derivatives and structured notes
October 1994	Community A Management	$44 million	structured notes
November 1994	Three Farm Credit System Banks	$23 million	structured notes
December 1994	Chemical Bank	$70 million	currency derivatives
December 1994	Orange County, California	$1.6 billion	leveraged repurchase agreements
February 1995	Capital Corporate Federal Credit Union	$126 million	mortgage derivatives
February 1995	Barings PLC	£900 million	stock index futures and options
March 1995	Connecticut Pension Fund	$25 million	misc. derivatives
March 1995	Escambia County, Florida	$19 million	mortgage derivatives
March 1995	MCN Corporation	$10 million	forwards
March 1995	State of Wisconsin Investment Board	$95 million	currency and interest rate swaps
May 1995	Five clients of Morgan Stanley	$28 million	forwards, options, repurchase agreements
June 1995	Sumitomo Bank	$1.8 billion	copper futures
July 1995	The Common Fund	$137.6 billion	stock index futures
July 1995	Westchester Jewish Center	$630,000	mortgage derivatives
July 1995	First Capital Strategists	$128 million	stock index futures
August 1995	Postipankki	$110 million	mortgage derivatives and structured notes
July 1996	BZW	£11.5 million	currency derivatives
August 1996	Seita	$29.8 million	currency swaps
February 1997	NatWest	£90 million	interest rate options

Sources: Information taken from a variety of sources, including various issues of *The Wall Street Journal;* Charles W. Smithson, *Managing Financial Risk: 1995 and 1996 Yearbooks* (Chase Manhattan Bank and CIBC Wood Gundy); *Euromoney,* August 1994; *Futures,* October 1995

This book has brought you on a tour of the world of derivatives. As you no doubt feel, the subject is a complex one, but you now have the tools to move on to further study of this fascinating subject. When the time comes that you execute your first derivatives trade, it is hoped that you will ask yourself one simple question: Am I practicing risk management?

Key Terms
You should be able to give brief definitions of the following terms.
- risk management/financial risk management
- multilateral netting
- payment netting

- end user
- dealer
- market risk
- Value at Risk (VaR)
- analytical method
- historical method
- simulation method
- stress test
- credit risk
- current credit risk
- potential credit risk
- enhanced derivatives product company
- netting
- bilateral netting

- netting by novation
- closeout netting
- operational risk
- model risk
- liquidity risk
- accounting risk
- legal risk
- tax risk
- regulatory risk
- settlement/Herstatt risk
- systemic risk
- front office
- back office
- G-30 Report

Questions and Problems

1. How is the practice of risk management similar to hedging and how is it different?

2. Give three reasons why derivatives have become increasingly employed in managing risk.

3. Explain how the function of risk management in an end user differs from risk management in a dealer.

4. Explain the difference between market risk and credit risk. Are techniques for managing market risk appropriate for managing credit risk?

5. If a portfolio of derivatives is delta hedged by adding a position in Eurodollar futures, what other forms of market risk might remain? How can these risks be eliminated?

6. Interpret the following statements about Value at Risk so that they would be easily understood by a nontechnical corporate executive.

   a. VaR of $1.5 million, one week, probability = .01

   b. VaR of $3.75 million, one year, probability = .05

7. Under what conditions would the VaR estimated using the simulation method equal the VaR estimated using the historical method?

8. Comment on the current credit risk you have for each of the following positions. Treat them separately, that is, not combined with anything else.

   a. You are short an out-of-the-money interest rate call option.

   b. You entered into a pay fixed–receive floating interest rate swap a year ago. Since that time, interest rates have increased.

   c. You are long an in-the-money currency put option.

   d. You are long a forward contract. During the life of the contract the price of the underlying asset has decreased below the contract price.

9. Explain how closeout netting reduces the credit risk for two firms engaged in several derivatives contracts.

10. How does the legal system impose risk on a derivatives dealer?

11. What is the most important part of an effective risk management system?

12. Explain why it is critical that the back office not be responsible to the front office in a risk management system.

13. What role should senior management play in a risk management system?

14. If you were the risk manager of a corporation and decided to engage in a derivatives transaction with a dealer, to what extent would you expect the dealer to serve you as an advisor on the transaction?

15. What is Herstatt risk?

16. Suppose your firm is a derivatives dealer and has recently created a new product. In addition to market and credit risk, what additional risks does it face that are associated more with new products?

17. Explain how a firm that does not practice risk management can get into financial difficulties by trading nonderivative financial instruments.

18. Explain why potential credit risk is faced by both parties to a swap while current credit risk is faced by only one party.

19. Consider a portfolio consisting of $10 million invested in the S&P 500 and $7.5 million invested in U.S. Treasury bonds. The S&P 500 has an expected return of 14 percent and a standard deviation of 16 percent. The Treasury bonds have an expected return of 9 percent and a standard deviation of 8 percent. The correlation between the S&P 500 and the bonds is .35. All figures are stated on an annual basis.

   a. Find the VaR for one year at a probability of .05. Identify and use the most appropriate method given the information you have.

   b. Using the information you obtained in part a, find the VaR for one day.

20. Consider two firms, Acme and Nadir. Acme is a dealer and has a better credit rating so it can borrow cheaper than Nadir in both fixed- and floating-rate markets. Specifically, Acme pays 7 1/2 percent fixed and LIBOR plus 3/4 percent floating. Nadir pays 8 7/8 percent fixed and LIBOR plus 1 3/8 percent floating.

   a. Determine the interest rate savings in basis points if Nadir takes out a floating-rate loan and engages in a swap with Acme in which it pays Acme a fixed rate of 7 percent and receives LIBOR.

   b. Explain why Nadir is able to save money by creating the synthetic fixed-rate loan in part a in light of the assumption of efficient markets, wherein everything is priced correctly.

21. The following table lists three financial instruments with their deltas, gammas, and vegas for each $1 million notional principal under the assumption of a long position. (Long in a swap or FRA means to pay fixed and receive floating.) Assume that you hold a $12 million notional principal long position in the three-year call option, an $8 million notional principal short position in the three-year swap, and an $11 million notional principal long position in the FRA. Each derivative is based on the 90-day LIBOR.

Instrument	Delta	Gamma	Vega
3-year call option with exercise rate of .12	$40	$1,343	$5.02
3-year swap with fixed rate of .1125	$152	–$678	$0
2-year FRA with fixed rate of .11	$72	–$390	$0

a. As described above, you have three instruments currently in your portfolio. Determine your current portfolio delta, gamma, and vega. Describe in words the risk properties of your portfolio based on your calculations.

b. Assume that you have to maintain your current position in the call option but are free to increase or decrease your positions in the swap and FRA and you can add a position in a one-year call with delta of $62, gamma of $2,680, and vega of $2.41. Find the combination of notional principals that would make your overall position be delta-, gamma-, and vega-hedged.

22. (Concept Problem) Suppose you enter into a bet with someone in which you pay $5 up front and are allowed to throw a pair of dice. You receive a payoff equal to the total in dollars of the numbers on the two dice. In other words, if you roll a 1 and a 2, your payoff is $3 and your profit is $3 – $5 = –$2. Determine the probability associated with a Value at Risk of $0.

The game isn't over yet. Derivatives haven't established their full role in the world.

DONALD LAYTON, Vice President, Chase Manhattan Bank

Risk, July 1996

LIST OF SYMBOLS

AI, AI_t, AI_T = accrued interest today, at time t, and at time T

b, b_t, b_T = basis today, at time t, and at expiration, T

B, B_T = price of bond or T-bill today, and at maturity, T

β, β_S, β_f, β_p = beta, beta of spot asset, beta of futures, beta of portfolio

β_T = target beta

C = (abbreviated) price of call

$C(S,T,E)$ = price of either European or American call on asset with price S, expiration T, and exercise price E

$C_e(S,T,E)$ = price of European call on asset with price S, expiration T, and exercise price E

$C_a(S,T,E)$ = price of American call on asset with price S, expiration T, and exercise price E

$C(f,T,E)$ = price of either European or American call on futures with price f, expiration T, and exercise price E

C_{asian} = price of asian call option

$C_e(f,T,E)$ = price of European call on futures with price f, expiration T, and exercise price E

$C_a(f,T,E)$ = price of American call on futures with price f, expiration T, and exercise price E

C_u, C_d, C_{u^2}, C_{ud}, C_{d^2} = call price sequence in binomial model

χ = convenience yield

CI_t = coupon interest paid at time t

CP_t = cash payment (principal or interest) on bond at time t

CF = conversion factor on CBOT T-bond contract

CF^t, CF^T = conversion factor on CBOT T-bond contracts deliverable at times t and T

c = coupon rate

Δ = delta of an option

ΔS, Δf = change in spot price, change in futures price

δ = dividend yield

d = (without subscript) downward return on stock in binomial model

d_1, d_2 = variables in Black-Scholes model

D_j = dividend paid at time j

D_T = compound future value of reinvested dividends

DUR, DUR_S, DUR_f = duration, duration of spot, implied duration of futures

ε = standard normal random variable in Monte Carlo simulation

E, E_1, E_2 = exercise price

$E(x)$ = expected value of the argument x

e^* = measure of hedging effectiveness

f, f_t, f_T = futures price or futures exchange rate today, at time t, and at expiration T

f^t, f^T = futures price today of contracts expiring at t and T

$f_a^{\ddagger}$ = critical futures price for early exercise of American option on futures

F, F_t, F_T = forward price or forward exchange rate today, at time t, and at expiration T

FV = face value of bond

h, h_u, h_d = hedge ratios in binomial model

i = interest lost on storing a good

J = number of observations in sample

j = counter in summation procedure

K = parameter in break forward contract

k = discount rate (required rate) on stock

Λ_i = volatility in Ho-Lee model

LIBOR = London Interbank Offer Rate, a Eurodollar rate

MOS = number of months in computing CBOT conversion factor

MOS^* = number of months in computing CBOT conversion factor rounded down to nearest quarter

μ_s = unsystematic return on stock

$N(d_1)$, $N(d_2)$ = cumulative normal probabilities in Black-Scholes model

NPV = net present value of box spread

N_C, N_P, N_S, N_f, N_B = number of calls, puts, shares of stock, futures, and T-bills held in a position

n = number of time periods in n-period binomial model

O_{aon} = value of asset-or-nothing option

O_{con} = value of cash-or-nothing option

Π = profit from strategy

P = (abbreviated) price of put

$P(S,T,E)$ = price of either European or American put on asset with price S, expiration T, and exercise price E

$P_e(S,T,E)$ = price of European put on asset with price S, expiration T, and exercise price E

$P_a(S,T,E)$ = price of American put on asset with price S, expiration T, and exercise price E

$P(f,T,E)$ = price of either European or American put on futures with price f, expiration T, and exercise price E

$P_e(f,T,E)$ = price of European put on futures with price f, expiration T, and exercise price E

$P_a(f,T,E)$ = price of American put on futures with price f, expiration T, and exercise price E

p = variable in binomial model

$PVBP_S, PVBP_f$ = present value of basis point change for spot, futures

$E(\phi)$ = expected risk premium

Q = number of ways to reach a cell in Ho-Lee model

Q_1, Q_2 = quantity of good supplied at times 1 and 2

r = discrete risk-free rate

$r(a,b)$ = interest rate over time interval (a,b) or swap rate between parties a and b

$\hat{r}$ = implied repo rate

r_h = return on hedged portfolio

r_c = continuously compounded risk-free rate

r_f = percentage change in futures price

r_S = return on stock or spot position

r_{St} = return on stock at time t

r_{Sf} = return on portfolio of stock and futures

r_M = return on market

r_{Mt} = return on market at time t

r^c = continuously compounded return

r_t^C = continuously compounded return at time t

$\bar{r}^c$ = mean continuously compounded return

ρ = foreign risk-free rate

s = storage costs

S' = stock price minus present value of dividends

S_{avg} = average stock price during life of option

S_{max} = maximum stock price during life of option

S_{min} = minimum stock price during life of option

$$S, S_t, S_T = \text{stock price (or spot price or spot exchange rate) today, at time t, and at time T}$$

$$S_u, S_{u^2}, S_{ud}, S_d, S_{d^2} = \text{stock price sequence in binomial model}$$

$$S_T^* = \text{breakeven stock price at expiration}$$

$$\sigma = \text{standard deviation or volatility } (\sigma^2 = \text{variance})$$

$$\sigma_{xz} = \text{covariance between x and z}$$

$$\sigma_x^2 = \text{variance of x}$$

$$T, T_1, T_2 = \text{expiration or time to expiration from the current time}$$

$$t = \text{future point in time or time until a particular future date}$$

$$\theta = \text{cost of carry}$$

$$u = \text{upward return on stock in binomial model}$$

$$v, v_t, v_T = \text{value of futures contract today, at time t, and at time T}$$

$$v^f = \text{value of futures contract in hedged portfolio}$$

$$V, V_t, V_T = \text{value of a portfolio, asset, or contract today, at time t, and at time T}$$

$$V_{min} = \text{minimum or insured value of portfolio}$$

$$V_u, V_d, V_{ud} = \text{sequence of values of portfolio in binomial model}$$

$$YRS = \text{number of years in computation of CBOT conversion factor}$$

$$y, y_s, y_v = \text{bond yield, yield on spot bond, yield on portfolio worth V}$$

$$y_f = \text{implied yield on futures}$$

Appendix B

LIST OF FORMULAS

Intrinsic Value of American Call

$$C_a(S,T,E) \geq Max(0, S - E)$$

Maximum Spread of European Calls

$$(E_2 - E_1)(1 + r)^{-T} \geq C_e(S,T,E_1) - C_e(S,T,E_2)$$

Maximum Spread of American Calls

$$(E_2 - E_1) \geq C_a(S,T,E_1) - C_a(S,T,E_2)$$

Lower Bound of European Call

$$C_e(S,T,E) \geq Max[0, S - E(1 + r)^{-T}]$$

Intrinsic Value of American Put

$$P_a(S,T,E) \geq Max(0, E - S)$$

Maximum Spread of European Puts

$$(E_2 - E_1)(1 + r)^{-T} \geq P_e(S,T,E_2) - P_e(S,T,E_1)$$

Maximum Spread of American Puts

$$(E_2 - E_1) \geq P_a(S,T,E_2) - P_a(S,T,E_1)$$

Lower Bound of European Put

$$P_e(S,T,E) \geq Max[0, E(1 + r)^{-T} - S]$$

Put-Call Parity for American Options

$$C_a(S',T,E) + E + \sum_{j=1}^{n} D_j (1 + r)^{-t_j} \geq S + P_a(S',T,E) \geq C_a(S',T,E) + E(1 + r)^{-T}$$

Put-Call Parity for European Options

$$S + P_e(S,T,E) = C_e(S,T,E) + E(1 + r)^{-T}$$

Stock Prices in Binomial Model

$$S_u = S(1 + u)$$
$$S_d = S(1 + d)$$
$$S_{u^2} = S(1 + u)^2$$
$$S_{d^2} = S(1 + d)^2$$
$$S_{ud} = S(1 + u)(1 + d)$$

Call Prices in One-Period Binomial Model

$$C_u = Max[0, S(1 + u) - E]$$
$$C_d = Max[0, S(1 + d) - E]$$
$$C = \frac{pC_u + (1 - p)C_d}{1 + r}$$

Call Prices in Two-Period Binomial Model

$$C_{u^2} = Max[0, S(1 + u)^2 - E]$$

$$C_{d^2} = Max[0, S(1 + d)^2 - E]$$

$$C_{ud} = Max[0, S(1 + u)(1 + d) - E]$$

$$C_u = \frac{pC_{u^2} + (1 - p)C_{ud}}{1 + r}$$

$$C_d = \frac{pC_{ud} + (1 - p)C_{d^2}}{1 + r}$$

$$C = \frac{pC_u + (1 - p)C_d}{1 + r}$$

Value of p in Binomial Model

$$p = \frac{r - d}{u - d}$$

Hedge Ratios in Binomial Model

$$h = \frac{C_u - C_d}{S_u - S_d}$$

$$h_u = \frac{C_{u^2} - C_{ud}}{S_{u^2} - S_{ud}}$$

$$h_d = \frac{C_{ud} - C_{d^2}}{S_{ud} - S_{d^2}}$$

Sequence of Hedge Portfolio Values in Binomial Model

$$V = hS - C$$

$$V_u = hS(1 + u) - C_u$$

$$V_d = hS(1 + d) - C_d$$

Black-Scholes Call Option Pricing Model

$$C = SN(d_1) - Ee^{-r_cT}N(d_2)$$

$$d_1 = \frac{\ln(S/E) + [r_c + \sigma^2/2]T}{\sigma\sqrt{T}}$$

$$d_2 = d_1 - \sigma\sqrt{T}$$

Black-Scholes Put Option Pricing Model

$$P = Ee^{-r_cT}[1 - N(d_2)] - S[1 - N(d_1)]$$

Call Delta

$$Call\ Delta = N(d_1)$$

Call Gamma

$$Call\ Gamma = \frac{e^{-d_1^2/2}}{S\sigma\sqrt{2\pi T}}$$

Call Rho

$$Call\ Rho = TEe^{-r_cT}N(d_2)$$

Call Vega

$$\text{Call Vega} = \frac{S\sqrt{T}e^{-d_1^2/2}}{\sqrt{2\pi}}$$

Call Theta

$$\text{Call Theta} = -\frac{S\sigma e^{-d_1^2/2}}{2\sqrt{2\pi T}} - r_c E e^{-r_c T} N(d_2)$$

Put Delta

$$\text{Put Delta} = N(d_1) - 1$$

Put Gamma

$$\text{Put Gamma} = \frac{e^{-d_1^2/2}}{S\sigma\sqrt{2\pi T}}$$

Put Rho

$$\text{Put Rho} = -TEe^{-r_c T}[1 - N(d_2)]$$

Put Vega

$$\text{Put Vega} = \frac{S\sqrt{T}e^{-d_1^2/2}}{\sqrt{2\pi}}$$

Put Theta

$$\text{Put Theta} = -\frac{S\sigma e^{-d_1^2/2}}{2\sqrt{2\pi T}} + r_c E e^{-r_c T}(1 - N(d_2))$$

Present Value of a Series of Discrete Dividends

$$\sum_{j=1}^{T} D_j(1+r)^{-t_j}$$

Stock Price Minus Present Value of Dividends

$$S' = S - D_t e^{-r_c T} \text{ (one dividend)}$$
$$S' = Se^{-\delta T} \text{ (continuous dividends)}$$

Sample Estimate of Mean of Continuously Compounded Return

$$\bar{r}^c = \sum_{t=1}^{J} r_t^c / J$$

Sample Estimate of Variance of Continuously Compounded Return

$$\sigma^2 = \frac{\sum_{t=1}^{J}(r_t^c - \bar{r}^c)^2}{(J-1)} = \frac{\sum_{t=1}^{J}(r_t^c)^2 - \left(\sum_{t=1}^{J} r_t^c\right)^2/J}{(J-1)}$$

Implied Volatility of At-the-Money Call

$$\sigma \approx \frac{C}{(0.398)S\sqrt{T}}$$

Profit from Call Transaction Held to Expiration

$$\Pi = N_C[\text{Max}(0, S_T - E) - C]$$

Profit from Call Transaction Terminated at T_1
$$\Pi = N_C[C(S_{T_1}, T - T_1, E) - C]$$
Profit from Put Transaction Held to Expiration
$$\Pi = N_p[\text{Max}(0, E - S_T) - P]$$
Profit from Put Transaction Terminated at T_1
$$\Pi = N_p[P(S_{T_1}, T - T_1, E) - P]$$
Profit from Stock Transaction
$$\Pi = N_S(S_T - S)$$
Ratio of Calls in Riskless Spread
$$\frac{N_1}{N_2} = -\frac{\Delta_2}{\Delta_1}$$
Conversion of IMM Index to Futures Price per \$100
$$f = 100 - (100 - \text{IMM Index})(90/360)$$
Conversion Factors for CBOT T-Bond Contract
$$CF_0 = (c/2)\left(\frac{1 - (1.04)^{-2*\text{YRS}}}{.04}\right) + (1.04)^{(-2*\text{YRS})}$$
$$CF_3 = (CF_0 + c/2)(1.04)^{-.5} - c/4$$
$$CF_6 = (c/2)\left(\frac{1 - (1.04)^{-2*\text{YRS}+1}}{.04}\right) + (1.04)^{(-2*\text{YRS}+1)}$$
$$CF_9 = (CF_6 + c/2)(1.04)^{-.5} - c/4$$
Bond Price Using Term Structure
$$B = \sum_{t=1}^{T} CI_t[1 + r(0,t)]^{-t} + FV[1 + r(0, T)]^{-T}$$
Bond Price Using Yield
$$B = \sum_{t=1}^{T} CP_t(1 + y)^{-t}$$
$$= CI\left[\frac{1 - (1 + y)^{-T}}{y}\right] + FV(1 + y)^{-T}$$
Duration
$$DUR = \frac{\sum_{t=1}^{T} tCP_t(1 + y)^{-t}}{B} = \frac{CI(1 + y)\left[(1 + y)^T - 1\right] + Ty(FVy - CI)}{CIy\left[(1 + y)^T - 1\right] + FVy^2}$$
Bond Price Percentage Change
$$\frac{\Delta B}{B} \approx -DUR\frac{\Delta y}{(1 + y)}$$
Capital Asset Pricing Model
$$E(r_S) = r + [E(r_M) - r]\beta$$

Beta

$$\beta = \frac{\sigma_{SM}}{\sigma_M^2}$$

Sample Estimate of Covariance between Returns on Stock and Market

$$\sigma_{SM} = \frac{\sum\limits_{t=1}^{J} r_{St}r_{Mt} - \left(\sum\limits_{t=1}^{J} r_{St} \sum\limits_{t=1}^{J} r_{Mt}\right)/J}{J-1}$$

Sample Estimate of Variance of Return on Market

$$\sigma_M^2 = \frac{\sum\limits_{t=1}^{J} r_{Mt}^2 - \left(\sum\limits_{t=1}^{J} r_{Mt}\right)^2/J}{J-1}$$

Spot Price under Uncertainty and Risk Neutrality

$$S = E(S_T) - s - i$$

Spot Price under Uncertainty and Risk Aversion

$$S = E(S_T) - s - i - E(\phi)$$

Value of a Forward Contract at Time t Prior to Expiration

$$V_t = (F_t - F)(1 + r)^{-(T-t)}$$

Cost of Carry Futures Pricing Model

$$f = S + \theta$$

Cost of Carry Futures Pricing Model with Convenience Yield

$$f = S + \theta - \chi$$

Stock Index Futures Pricing Model

$$f = Se^{(r_c - \delta)T}$$

Stock Index Futures Pricing Model with Discrete Dividends

$$f = S(1 + r)^T - \sum_{j=1}^{T} D_j(1 + r)^{T-t_j}$$

Futures Spread Pricing Model

$$f_2 - f_1 = \theta_2 - \theta_1$$

Basis Today

$$b = S - f$$

Basis at Time t

$$b_t = S_t - f_t$$

Profit from a Short Hedge

$$\Pi = b_t - b$$

Variance of Profit from Hedge

$$\sigma_\Pi^2 = \sigma_{\Delta S}^2 + \sigma_{\Delta f}^2 N_f^2 + 2\sigma_{\Delta s \Delta f}N_f$$

Duration of Futures

$$DUR_f \approx -\left(\frac{\Delta f}{f}\right)\left(\frac{1 + y_f}{\Delta y_f}\right)$$

Minimum Variance Hedge Ratio

$$N_f = -\frac{\sigma_{\Delta s \Delta f}}{\sigma_{\Delta f}^2}$$

Price Sensitivity Hedge Ratio

$$N_f = -\left(\frac{DUR_S}{DUR_f}\right)\left(\frac{S}{f}\right)\left(\frac{1 + y_f}{1 + y_S}\right)$$

Stock Index Futures Hedge Ratio

$$N_f = -\beta_S\left(\frac{S}{f}\right)$$

Hedging Effectiveness

$$e^* = \frac{\sigma_{\Delta s}^2 - \sigma_{\Pi}^2}{\sigma_{\Delta s}^2}$$

Implied Repo on T-Bill or Eurodollar Cash and Carry

$$\hat{r} = \left(\frac{f}{S}\right)^{(1/t)} - 1$$

Spot Price for Justifying Exercise of Wild Card Option

$$S_5 < f_3(CF)$$

Implied Repo on T-Bond or T-Note Cash and Carry

$$\hat{r} = \left[\frac{f(CF) + AI_T}{S + AI}\right]^{(1/T)} - 1$$

Implied Repo Rate on T-Bond or T-Note Spread

$$\hat{r} = \left[\frac{f^T(CF^T) + AI_T}{f^t(CF^t) + AI_t}\right]^{1/(T-1)} - 1$$

Put-Call-Future Parity

$$P_e(S,T,E) = C_e(S,T,E) + (E - f)(1 + r)^{-T}$$

Futures Contracts Required to Achieve Target Duration

$$N_f = -\left(\frac{DUR_S - DUR_T}{DUR_f}\right)\left(\frac{S}{f}\right)\left(\frac{1 + y_f}{1 + y_S}\right)$$

Futures Contracts Required to Achieve Target Beta

$$N_f = (\beta_T - \beta_S)\left(\frac{S}{f}\right)$$

Intrinsic Value of American Call Option on Futures

$$C_a(f,T,E) \geq Max(0, f - E)$$

Intrinsic Value of American Put Option on Futures

$$P_a(f,T,E) \geq Max(0, E - f)$$

Lower Bound of European Call Option on Futures

$$C_e(f,T,E) \geq Max[0, (f - E)(1 + r)^{-T}]$$

Lower Bound of European Put Option on Futures

$$P_e(f,T,E) \geq Max[0, (E - f)(1 + r)^{-T}]$$

Put-Call Parity of Options on Futures

$$P_e(f,T,E) = C_e(f,T,E) + (E - f)(1 + r)^{-T}$$

Black Call Option on Futures Pricing Model

$$C = e^{-r_cT}[fN(d_1) - EN(d_2)]$$

$$d_1 = \frac{\ln(f/E) + (\sigma^2/2)T}{\sigma\sqrt{T}}$$

$$d_2 = d_1 - \sigma\sqrt{T}$$

Black Put Options on Futures Pricing Model

$$P = Ee^{-r_cT}[1 - N(d_2)] - fe^{-r_cT}[1 - N(d_1)]$$

Interest Rate Parity

$$\frac{F}{S} = (1 + r)^T(1 + \rho)^{-T}$$

Lower Bound of European Foreign Currency Call

$$C_e(S,T,E) \geq Max[0, S(1 + \rho)^{-T} - E(1 + r)^{-T}]$$

Lower Bound of European Foreign Currency Put

$$P_e(S,T,E) \geq Max[0, E(1 + r)^{-T} - S(1 + \rho)^{-T}]$$

Put-Call Parity of Foreign Currency Options

$$C_e(S,T,E) = P_e(S,T,E) + S(1 + \rho)^{-T} - E(1 + r)^{-T}$$

Garman-Kohlhagen Foreign Currency Call Option Pricing Model

$$C = Se^{-\rho_cT}N(d_1) - Ee^{-r_cT}N(d_2)$$

$$d_1 = \frac{\ln(Se^{-\rho_cT}/E) + [r_c + (\sigma^2/2)]T}{\sigma\sqrt{T}}$$

$$d_2 = d_1 - \sigma\sqrt{T}$$

Payoff to Holder of Long FRA

$$(\text{Notional principal})(\text{LIBOR} - \text{Agreed upon rate})\left(\frac{\text{Days}}{360}\right)$$

Cash Flow to Floating Rate Receiver in Plain Vanilla Swap

$$(\text{Notional principal})(\text{LIBOR} - \text{Fixed rate})\left(\frac{\text{Days}}{360}\right)$$

Payoff from Interest Rate Call

$$(\text{Notional principal})\text{Max}(0, \text{LIBOR} - E)\left(\frac{\text{Days}}{360}\right)$$

Payoff from Interest Rate Put

$$(\text{Notional principal})\,\text{Max}(0,\, E - \text{LIBOR})\left(\frac{\text{Days}}{360}\right)$$

Number of Shares and Puts to Insure Portfolio

$$N = \frac{V}{S + P}$$

Minimum Value of Insured Portfolio

$$V_{min} = \frac{EV}{S + P}$$

Number of Treasury Bills to Insure Portfolio with Calls and Treasury Bills

$$N_B = \frac{V_{min}}{B_T}$$

Number of Calls to Insure Portfolio with Calls and Treasury Bills

$$N_C = \frac{(V - N_B B)}{C} = \frac{V}{S + P}$$

Number of Futures in Dynamic Hedge with Stock Index Futures

$$N_f = \left[\left(\frac{V_{min}}{E}\right)N(d_1) - \left(\frac{V}{S}\right)\right]e^{-r_c T}$$

Number of Treasury Bills in Dynamic Hedge

$$N_B = \frac{V - N_S S}{B}$$

Number of Shares of Stock in Dynamic Hedge with Treasury Bills

$$N_S = \left(\frac{V_{min}}{E}\right)N(d_1)$$

Value of Asset-or-Nothing Option

$$O_{aon} = SN(d_1)$$

Value of Cash-or-Nothing Option

$$O_{con} = Ee^{-r_c T}N(d_2)$$

Payoff of Average Price Call

$$\text{Max}(0,\, S_{avg} - E)$$

Payoff of Average Price Put

$$\text{Max}(0,\, E - S_{avg})$$

Payoff of 3-Period Average Strike Call

$$\text{Max}(0,\, S_3 - S_{avg})$$

Payoff of 3-Period Average Strike Put

$$\text{Max}(0,\, S_{avg} - S_3)$$

Payoff of 3-Period Lookback Call

$$\text{Max}(0, S_3 - S_{min})$$

Payoff of 3-Period Lookback Put

$$\text{Max}(0, S_{max} - S_3)$$

Payoff of 3-Period Fixed-Strike Lookback Call

$$\text{Max}(0, S_{max} - E)$$

Payoff of 3-Period Fixed-Strike Lookback Put

$$\text{Max}(0, E - S_{min})$$

Appendix C

REFERENCES

This compilation of books, articles, and monographs includes items referenced in this book as well as classic references and other useful articles dealing with topics covered in this book. It is not intended as a comprehensive bibliography of derivatives.

Abken, Peter. "Interest Rate Caps, Collars, and Floors." *Federal Reserve Bank of Atlanta Economic Review* 72 (November–December 1989): 2–24

Abken, Peter A. "Valuation of Default-Risky Interest-Rate Swaps." *Advances in Futures and Options Research* 6 (1993): 93–116.

Arak, Marcelle, Philip Fischer, Laurie Goodman, and Raj Daryanani. "The Municipal-Treasury Futures Spread." *The Journal of Futures Markets* 7 (1987): 355–371.

Arak, Marcelle, Laurie Goodman, and Susan Ross. "The Cheapest to Deliver Bond on the Treasury Bond Futures Contract." *Advances in Futures and Options Research* 1, part B (1986): 49–74.

Arditti, Fred D. *Derivatives: A Comprehensive Resource for Options, Futures, Interest Rate Swaps, and Mortgage Securities.* Boston: Harvard Business School Press, 1996.

Austin, Michael. "Index Option Overwriting: Strategies and Results." *Derivatives Quarterly* 1 (Summer 1995): 77–84.

Baer, Herbert L., Virginia Grace France, and James T. Moser. "What Does a Clearinghouse Do?" *Derivatives Quarterly* 1 (Spring 1995): 39–46.

Barone-Adesi, Giovanni, and Robert E. Whaley. "Efficient Analytic Approximation of American Option Values." *The Journal of Finance* 42 (June 1987): 301–320.

Beckers, Stan. "Standard Deviations Implied in Option Prices as Predictors of Future Stock Price Variability." *Journal of Banking and Finance* 5 (September 1981): 363–382.

Beder, Tanya Styblo. "Equity Derivatives for Investors." *The Journal of Financial Engineering* 1 (September 1992): 174–195.

Behof, John P. "Reducing Credit Risk in Over-the-Counter Derivatives." *Federal Reserve Bank of Chicago Economic Perspectives* 17 (January-February 1993): 21–31.

Bernstein, Peter L. *Capital Ideas: The Improbable Origins of Modern Wall Street.* New York: The Free Press, 1992.

Bessembinder, Hendrik. "An Empirical Analysis of Risk Premia in Futures Markets." *The Journal of Futures Markets* 13 (September 1993): 611–630.

Bhansali, Javesh D. "Managing Interest Rate Risk through Caps." *Derivatives Quarterly* 3 (Spring 1997): 39–45.

Bhattacharya, Mihir. "Transaction Data Tests of Efficiency of the Chicago Board Options Exchange." *Journal of Financial Economics* 12 (1983): 161–185.

Bicksler, James, and Andrew Chen. "An Economic Analysis of Interest Rate Swaps." *The Journal of Finance* 41 (July 1876): 645–656.

Billingsley, Randall S., and Don M. Chance. "Options Market Efficiency and the Box Spread Strategy." *The Financial Review* 20 (November 1985): 287–301.

Black, Fischer. "Fact and Fantasy in the Use of Options." *Financial Analysts Journal* 31 (July-August 1975): 36–41, 61–72.

Black, Fischer. "The Pricing of Commodity Contracts." *Journal of Financial Economics* 3 (January-February 1976): 167–179.

Black, Fischer. "How to Use the Holes in Black-Scholes." *Journal of Applied Corporate Finance* 1 (Winter 1989): 67–73.

Black, Fischer. "How We Came Up with the Option Formula." *Journal of Portfolio Management* 15 (Winter 1989): 4–8.

Black, Fischer, and Myron Scholes. "The Valuation of Option Contracts and a Test of Market Efficiency." *The Journal of Finance* 27 (May 1972): 399–418.

Black, Fischer, and Myron Scholes. "The Pricing of Options and Corporate Liabilities." *Journal of Political Economy* 81 (May-June 1973): 637–659.

Blomeyer, Edward C., and James C. Boyd. "Empirical Tests of Boundary Conditions for Options on Treasury Bond Futures." *The Journal of Futures Markets* 4 (1988): 185–198.

Blomeyer, Edward C., and Robert C. Klemkosky. "Tests of Market Efficiency of American Call Options." In *Option Pricing,* edited by Menachem Brenner. Lexington, Massachusetts: Heath, 1983.

Bodurtha, James N., and Georges R. Courtadon. "Efficiency Tests of the Foreign Currency Options Market." *The Journal of Finance* 13 (March 1986): 151–162.

Bookstaber, Richard M. *Option Pricing and Investment Strategies.* Chicago: Probus Publishing, 1989.

Brennan, Michael J., and Eduardo S. Schwartz. "The Valuation of American Put Options." *The Journal of Finance* 32 (May 1977): 449–462.

Brenner, Menachem, and Marti G. Subrahmanyam. "A Simple Formula to Compute the Implied Volatility." *Financial Analysts Journal* 45 (September-October 1988): 80–83.

Brooks, Robert, and Miles Livingston. "A Closed-Form Equation for Bond Convexity." *Financial Analysts Journal* 45 (November-December 1989): 78–79.

Brown, Keith C., ed. *Derivative Strategies for Managing Portfolio Risk.* Charlottesville, Virginia: Institute for Chartered Financial Analysts, 1993.

Brown, Keith C., and Donald J. Smith. "Default Risk and Innovations in the Design of Interest Rate Swaps." *Financial Management* 22 (Summer 1993): 94–105.

Brown, Keith C., and Donald J. Smith. *Interest Rate and Currency Swaps: A Tutorial.* Charlottesville, Virginia: The Research Foundation of the Institute of Chartered Financial Analysts, 1995.

Burghardt, Galen, and Morton Lane. "How to Tell If Options Are Cheap." *Journal of Portfolio Management* 16 (Winter 1990): 72–78.

Caks, John, William R. Lane, Robert W. Greenleaf, and Reginald G. Joules. "A Simple Formula for Duration." *The Journal of Financial Research* 8 (Fall 1985): 245–249.

Campbell, Tim S., and William A. Kracaw. *Financial Risk Management: Fixed Income and Foreign Exchange.* New York: Harper Collins, 1993.

Carpenter, Jennifer N. "Current Issues in Accounting for Derivatives." *The Journal of Derivatives* 3 (Spring 1996): 65–71.

Castelino, Mark G. "Minimum-Variance Hedging with Futures Revisited." *Journal of Portfolio Management* 16 (Spring 1990): 74–80.

Celebuski, Matthew J., Joanne M. Hill, and John J. Kilgannon. "Managing Currency Exposures in International Portfolios." *Financial Analysts Journal* 46 (January-February 1990): 16–23.

Chance, Don M. *Managed Futures and Their Role in Investment Portfolios.* Charlottesville, Virginia: Research Foundation of the Institute of Chartered Financial Analysts, 1994.

Chance, Don M. "Translating the Greek: The Real Meaning of Call Option Derivatives." *Financial Analysts Journal* 50 (July-August 1994): 43–49.

Chance, Don M. "A Chronology of Derivatives." *Derivatives Quarterly* 2 (Winter 1995): 53–60.

Chance, Don M., and Stephen P. Ferris. "The CBOE Call Option Index: A Historical Record." *The Journal of Portfolio Management* 12 (Fall 1985): 75–83.

Chance, Don M., and Michael L. Hemler. "The Impact of Delivery Options on Futures Prices: A Survey." *The Journal of Futures Markets* 13 (April 1993): 127–155.

Chang, Carolyn W., and Jack S. K. Chang. "Forward and Futures Prices: Evidence from the Foreign Exchange Markets." *The Journal of Finance* 4 (September 1990): 1333–1336.

Chang, Eric C. "Returns to Speculators and the Theory of Normal Backwardation." *The Journal of Finance* 40 (March 1985): 193–208.

Chang, Jack S. K., and Latha Shanker. "Hedging Effectiveness of Options and Currency Futures." *The Journal of Futures Markets* 6 (Summer 1986): 289–305.

Chen, Andrew H., Marcia Millon Cornett, and Prafulla G. Nabar. "An Empirical Examination of Interest-Rate Futures Prices." *The Journal of Futures Markets* 13 (October 1993): 781–797.

Chen, K. C., and R. Stephen Sears. "Pricing the SPIN." *Financial Management* 19 (Summer 1990): 36–47.

Chicago Board Options Exchange. *Market Statistics 1996.* Chicago: Chicago Board Options Exchange, 1996.

Chiras, Donald P., and Steven Manaster. "The Information Content of Option Prices and a Test of Market Efficiency." *Journal of Financial Economics* 6 (June-September 1978): 213–234.

Chriss, Neil A. *Black-Scholes and Beyond.* Chicago: Irwin Professional, 1997.

Chua, Jess H. "A Closed-Form Formula for Calculating Bond Duration." *Financial Analysts Journal* 40 (May-June 1984): 76–78.

Clarke, Roger G. *Options and Futures: A Tutorial.* Charlottesville, Virginia: The Research Foundation of the Institute of Chartered Financial Analysts, 1992.

Clarke, Roger G., and Robert D. Arnott. "The Cost of Portfolio Insurance: Tradeoffs and Choices." *Financial Analysts Journal* 43 (November-December 1987): 35–47.

Commodity Futures Trading Commission. *Annual Report,* 1996.

Conine, Thomas E., and Maurry Tamarkin. "A Pedagogic Note on the Derivation of the Comparative Statics of the Option Pricing Model." *Financial Review* 19 (November 1984): 397–400.

Corcoran, Andrea M. "Developing a Risk Management Plan: A System Checklist for Derivatives." *Derivatives Quarterly* 1 (Winter 1994): 10–15.

Cornell, Bradford. "Spot Rates, Forward Rates and Exchange Market Efficiency." *Journal of Financial Economics* 5 (August 1977): 55–65.

Cornell, Bradford, and Mark Reinganum. "Forward and Futures Prices: Evidence from the Foreign Exchange Market." *The Journal of Finance* 36 (December 1981): 1035–1045.

Cox, John C., Jonathan E. Ingersoll, Jr., and Stephen A. Ross. "The Relation between Forward Prices and Futures Prices." *Journal of Financial Economics* 9 (December 1981): 321–346.

Cox, John C., Stephen A. Ross, and Mark Rubinstein. "Option Pricing: A Simplified Approach." *Journal of Financial Economics* 7 (September 1979): 229–263.

Cox, John C., and Mark Rubinstein. "A Survey of Alternative Option Pricing Models." In *Option Pricing,* edited by Menachem Brenner. Lexington, Massachusetts: Heath, 1983.

Cox, John C., and Mark Rubinstein. *Options Markets.* Englewood Cliffs, New Jersey: Prentice-Hall, 1985.

Crowley, Paul. "Why and How Fundamental Managers Should Use Options: Part I." *Derivatives Quarterly* 2 (Spring 1996): 52–66.

Crowley, Paul. "Why and How Fundamental Managers Should Use Options: Part II." *Derivatives Quarterly* 2 (Summer 1996): 40–55.

Daigler, Robert T. *Financial Futures Markets: Concepts, Evidence, and Applications.* New York: Harper Collins, 1993.

Daigler, Robert T. *Financial Futures & Options Markets: Concepts and Strategies.* New York: Harper Collins, 1994.

Dawson, Frederic S. "Risks and Returns in Continuous Option Writing." *The Journal of Portfolio Management* 5 (Winter 1979): 58–63.

Dawson, Paul. "Comparative Pricing of American and European Index Options: An Empirical Analysis." *The Journal of Futures Markets* 14 (May 1994): 363–378.

Derman, Emanuel, and Iraj Kani. "Riding on a Smile." *Risk* 7 (January 1994): 32–39.

Derman, Emanuel, and Iraj Kani. "The Ins and Outs of Barrier Options: Part I." *Derivatives Quarterly* 3 (Winter 1996): 55–67.

Derman, Emanuel, and Iraj Kani. "The Ins and Outs of Barrier Options: Part II." *Derivatives Quarterly* 3 (Spring 1997): 73–80.

DiMartino, Dawn, Linda Ward, Janet Stevens, and Winn Sargisson. "Procter & Gamble's Derivatives Loss: Isolated Incident or Wake-Up Call?" *Derivatives Quarterly* 2 (Spring 1996): 10–21.

Drennan, Ann S. "Keys to Successful Risk Management: Part 1." *Derivatives Quarterly* 1 (Summer 1995): 54–58.

Drennan, Ann S. "Keys to Successful Risk Management: Part 2." *Derivatives Quarterly* 2 (Winter 1995): 46–51.

Drennan, Ann S. "Keys to Successful Risk Management: Part 3." *Derivatives Quarterly* 2 (Spring 1996): 47–51.

Dubofsky, David A. *Options and Financial Futures: Valuation and Uses*. New York: McGraw-Hill, 1992.

Duffie, Darrell. *Futures Markets*. Englewood Cliffs, New Jersey: Prentice-Hall, 1989.

Duffie, Darrell. "Corporate Risk Management 101: Why Hedge?" *Corporate Risk Management* 3 (May 1991): 22–25.

Dupire, Bruno. "Pricing with a Smile." *Risk* 7 (January 1994): 18–20.

Dusak, Katherine. "Futures Trading and Investor Returns: An Investigation of Commodity Risk Premiums." *Journal of Political Economy* 81 (December 1973): 1387–1406.

Eaker, Mark R., and Dwight M. Grant. "Currency Hedging Strategies for International Diversified Equity Portfolios." *Journal of Portfolio Management* 17 (Fall 1990): 30–32.

Eckerdt, Walter L., Jr., and Stephen L. Williams. "The Complete Options Indexes." *Financial Analysts Journal* 40 (July-August 1984): 48–57.

Ederington, Louis H. "The Hedging Performance of the New Futures Market." *The Journal of Finance* 34 (March 1979): 157–170.

Edwards, Franklin R., and Cindy W. Ma. *Futures and Options*. New York: McGraw-Hill, 1992.

Einzig, Robert, and Bruce Lange. "Swaps at Transamerica: Applications and Analyses." *Journal of Applied Corporate Finance* 2 (Winter 1990): 48–58.

Evans, John, and Stephen H. Archer. "Diversification and the Reduction of Dispersion: An Empirical Analysis." *The Journal of Finance* 23 (December 1968): 761–767.

Fabozzi, Frank. *The Handbook of Fixed Income Securities*, 4th ed. Homewood, Illinois: Business One Irwin, 1994.

Ferguson, Robert. "Some Formulas for Evaluating Two Popular Option Strategies." *Financial Analysts Journal* 49 (September-October 1993): 71–76.

Figlewski, Stephen. "Explaining the Early Discounts on Stock Index Futures: The Case for Disequilibrium." *Financial Analysts Journal* 40 (1984): 43–47, 67.

Figlewski, Stephen. "Hedging Performance and Basis Risk in Stock Index Futures." *The Journal of Finance* 39 (July 1984): 657–669.

Figlewski, Stephen. "Hedging with Stock Index Futures: Theory and Application in a New Market." *The Journal of Futures Markets* 5 (Summer 1985): 183–199.

Figlewski, Stephen. "What Does an Option Pricing Model Tell Us about Option Prices?" *Financial Analysts Journal* 45 (September-October 1989): 12–15.

Figlewski, Stephen. "The Birth of the AAA Derivatives Subsidiary." *The Journal of Derivatives* 1 (Summer 1994): 80–84.

Figlewski, Stephen. "How to Lose Money in Derivatives." *The Journal of Derivatives* 2 (Winter 1994): 75–82.

Figlewski, Stephen, William L. Silber, and Marti G. Subrahmanyam. *Financial Options: From Theory to Practice*. Homewood, Illinois: Business One Irwin, 1990.

Financial Derivatives: New Instruments and Their Uses. Atlanta: Federal Reserve Bank of Atlanta, 1993.

Finnerty, John D. "Financial Engineering in Corporate Finance: An Overview." *Financial Management* 17 (Winter 1988): 14–33.

Finnerty, John D. "The Time Warner Rights Offering: A Case Study in Financial Engineering." *The Journal of Financial Engineering* 1 (June 1992): 38–61.

Francis, Jack Clark, and Avner Wolf. *The Handbook of Interest Rate Risk Management*. Burr Ridge, Illinois: Irwin Professional Publishing, 1994.

Franckle, Charles T. "The Hedging Performance of the New Futures Market: Comment." *The Journal of Finance* 35 (December 1980): 1273–1279.

From Black-Scholes to Black Holes. London: Risk/FINEX, 1992.

Furbush, Dean. "Program Trading and Price Movements: Evidence from the October 1987 Market Crash." *Financial Management* 18 (Autumn 1989): 68–83.

Gadkari, Vilas. "Relative Pricing of Currency Options: A Tutorial." *Advances in Futures and Options Research* 1, part A (1986): 227–245.

Galai, Dan. "Test of Market Efficiency of the Chicago Board Options Exchange." *The Journal of Business* 50 (April 1977): 167–197.

Galai, Dan. "Characterization of Options." *Journal of Banking and Finance* 1 (December 1977): 373–385.

Galai, Dan. "Empirical Tests of Boundary Conditions for CBOE Options." *Journal of Financial Economics* 6 (1978): 187–211.

Galai, Dan. "A Convexity Test for Traded Options." *Quarterly Review of Economics and Business* 19 (Summer 1979): 83–90.

Garcia, C. B., and F. J. Gould. "An Empirical Study of Portfolio Insurance." *Financial Analysts Journal* 43 (July-August 1987): 44–54.

Garman, Mark B., and Steven W. Kohlhagen. "Foreign Currency Option Values." *Journal of International Money and Finance* 2 (1983): 231–237.

Gastineau, Gary L. "An Index of Listed Options Premiums." *Financial Analysts Journal* 33 (May-June 1977): 70–75.

Gastineau, Gary. *The Options Manual,* 3d ed. New York: McGraw-Hill, 1988.

Gastineau, Gary. "An Introduction to Special Purpose Derivatives: Options with a Payout Depending on More Than One Variable." *The Journal of Derivatives* 1 (Fall 1993): 98–104.

Gastineau, Gary L. "An Introduction to Special Purpose Derivatives: Path-Dependent Options." *The Journal of Derivatives* 1 (Winter 1993): 78–86.

Gastineau, Gary L., and Mark P. Kritzman. *Dictionary of Financial Risk Management.* New York: Frank J. Fabozzi Associates, 1996.

Gastineau, Gary L., and Albert Madansky. "Some Comments on the Chicago Board Options Exchange Call Option Index." *Financial Analysts Journal* 40 (July-August 1984): 58–67.

Gay, Gerald D., and Robert W. Kolb. "Immunizing Bond Portfolios with Interest Rate Futures." *Financial Management* 11 (Summer 1982): 81–89.

Gay, Gerald D., Robert W. Kolb, and Raymond Chiang. "Interest Rate Hedging: An Empirical Test of Alternative Strategies." *The Journal of Financial Research* 6 (Fall 1983): 1–13.

Gemmill, Gordon. *Options Pricing: An International Perspective.* London: McGraw-Hill, 1993.

George, Thomas J., and Francis A. Longstaff. "Bid-Ask Spreads and Trading Activity in the S&P 100 Index Options Market." *Journal of Financial and Quantitative Analysis* 28 (September 1993): 381–397.

Geske, Robert. "The Valuation of Compound Options." *Journal of Financial Economics* 7 (March 1979): 63–81.

Geske, Robert. "A Note on an Analytic Formula for Unprotected American Call Options on Stocks with Known Dividends." *Journal of Financial Economics* 7 (December 1979): 375–380.

Geske, Robert, and H. E. Johnson. "The American Put Option Valued Analytically." *The Journal of Finance* 39 (December 1984): 1511–1524.

Gibson, Rajna. *Option Valuation.* New York: McGraw-Hill, 1991.

Gombola, Michael J., Rodney L. Roenfeldt, and Philip L. Cooley. "Spreading Strategies in CBOE Options: Evidence on Market Performance." *The Journal of Financial Research* 1 (Winter 1978): 35–44.

Goodman, Laurie S. "The Use of Interest Rate Swaps in Managing Corporate Liabilities." *Journal of Applied Corporate Finance* 2 (1990): 35–47.

Gould, John P., and Dan Galai. "Transactions Costs and the Relationship between Put and Call Prices." *Journal of Financial Economics* 1 (1974): 105–129.

Grabbe, J. Orlin. "The Pricing of Call and Put Options on Foreign Exchange." *Journal of International Money and Finance* 2 (1983): 239–253.

Gramm, Wendy L., and Gerald D. Gay. "Scams, Scoundrels, and Scapegoats: A Taxonomy of CEA Regulation over Derivative Instruments." *The Journal of Derivatives* 1 (Spring 1994): 6–24.

Gray, Roger W. "The Search for a Risk Premium." *Journal of Political Economy* 64 (June 1961): 250–260.

Group of Thirty. *Derivatives: Practices and Principles.* Washington, D.C.: Group of Thirty, 1993.

Grube, R. Corwin, Don B. Panton, and J. Michael Terrell. "Risks and Rewards in Covered Call Positions." *The Journal of Portfolio Management* 5 (Winter 1979): 64–68.

Hart, James F. "The Riskless Option Hedge: An Incomplete Guide." *The Journal of Portfolio Management* 4 (Winter 1978): 58–63.

Heath, David, Robert Jarrow, and Andrew Morton. "Bond Pricing and the Term Structure of Interest Rates." *Econometrica* 60 (January 1992): 77–105.

Hentschel, Ludger, and Clifford W. Smith, Jr. "Controllings Risks in Derivatives Markets." *The Journal of Financial Engineering* 4 (June 1995): 101–125.

Herbst, A. F., D. D. Kare, and S. C. Caples. "Hedging Effectiveness and Minimum Risk Hedge Ratios in the Presence of Autocorrelation: Foreign Currency Futures." *The Journal of Futures Markets* 3 (1989): 185–197.

Hicks, J. R. *Value and Capital,* 2d ed. Oxford: Clarendon Press, 1939.

Hieronymous, Thomas A. *The Economics of Futures Trading.* New York: Commodity Research Bureau, 1977.

Hill, Joanne, and Frank J. Jones. "Equity Trading, Program Trading, Portfolio Insurance, Computer Trading and All That." *Financial Analysts Journal* 44 (July-August 1988): 29–38.

Hill, Joanne, and Thomas Schneeweis. "The Hedging Effectiveness of Foreign Currency Futures." *The Journal of Financial Research* 5 (Spring 1982): 95–104.

Ho, Thomas S. Y., and Sang-Bin Lee. "Term Structure Movements and Pricing Interest Rate Contingent Claims." *The Journal of Finance* 41 (December 1986): 1011–1030.

Houthakker, H. S. "Can Speculators Forecast Prices?" *Review of Economics and Statistics* 39 (1957): 143–151.

Howard, Charles T., and Louis J. D'Antonio. "The Cost of Hedging and the Optimal Hedge Ratio." *The Journal of Futures Markets* 14 (April 1994): 237–258.

Hsieh, David A., and Merton H. Miller. "Margin Regulation and Stock Market Volatility." *The Journal of Finance* 45 (March 1990): 3–29.

Hull, John. *Introduction to Options and Futures Markets,* 2nd ed. Englewood Cliffs, New Jersey: Prentice-Hall, 1995.

Hull, John. *Options, Futures and Other Derivative Securities,* 3rd ed. Upper Saddle River, New Jersey: Prentice-Hall, 1997.

Jarrow, Robert A. *Modelling Fixed Income Securities and Interest Rate Options.* New York: McGraw-Hill, 1996.

Jarrow, Robert, ed. *Over the Rainbow: Developments in Exotic Options and Complex Swaps.* London: Financial Engineering Ltd., 1995.

Jarrow, Robert, and Andrew Rudd. *Option Pricing.* Homewood, Illinois: Irwin, 1983.

Jarrow, Robert, and Stuart Turnbull. *Derivative Securities.* Cincinnati: South-Western, 1996.

Johnson, L. L. "The Theory of Hedging and Speculation in Commodity Futures Markets." *Review of Economic Studies* 27 (October 1960): 139–151.

Jones, Frank J. "Spreads: Tails, Turtles, and All That." *The Journal of Futures Markets* 2 (Spring 1981): 63–82.

Jorion, Philippe. *Big Bets Gone Bad, Derivatives and Bankruptcy in Orange County: The Largest Municipal Failure in U.S. History.* San Diego: Academic Press, 1995.

Jorion, Philippe. *Value at Risk.* Chicago: Irwin Professional, 1997.

Jorion, Philippe, and Sarkis Joseph Khoury. *Financial Risk Management: Domestic and International Dimensions.* Cambridge, Massachusetts: Blackwell, 1996.

Kamara, Avraham. "Issues in Futures Markets: A Survey." *The Journal of Futures Markets* 2 (Fall 1982): 261–294.

Kamara, Avraham. "The Behavior of Futures Prices: A Review of Theory and Evidence." *Financial Analysts Journal* 40 (July-August 1984): 68–75.

Kat, Harry M. "Portfolio Insurance: A Comparison of Alternative Strategies." *The Journal of Financial Engineering* 2 (December 1993): 415–442.

Kawaller, Ira G. "A Note: Debunking the Myth of the Risk-Free Return." *The Journal of Futures Markets* 7 (1987): 327–331.

Kawaller, Ira G. "Interest Rate Swaps versus Eurodollar Strips." *Financial Analysts Journal* 45 (September-October 1989): 55–61.

Kawaller, Ira G. "Choosing the Best Interest Rate Hedge Ratio." *Financial Analysts Journal* 48 (September-October 1992): 74–77.

Kawaller, Ira G. "Foreign Exchange Hedge Management Tools: A Way to Enhance Performance." *Financial Analysts Journal* 49 (September-October 1993): 79–80.

Kawaller, Ira G. "Comparing Eurodollar Strips to Interest Rate Swaps." *The Journal of Derivatives* 2 (Fall 1994): 67–79.

Kawaller, Ira G. "Understanding Structured Notes." *Derivatives Quarterly* 1 (Spring 1995): 29–32.

Kawaller, Ira G. "Trading and Hedging with Option Calendar Spreads." *Derivatives Quarterly* 1 (Summer 1995): 73–76.

Kawaller, Ira G. "Short-Term Interest Rate Hedging: Hedge Ratios Revisited." *The Journal of Financial Engineering* 3 (September 1996): 267–277.

Kawaller, Ira G. "The TED Spread." *Derivatives Quarterly* 3 (Spring 1997): 46–54.

Keynes, John Maynard. *A Treatise on Money*. London: Macmillan, 1930.

Klein, Robert A., and Jess Lederman, eds. *Derivatives Risk and Responsibility*. Chicago: Irwin Professional, 1996.

Klemkosky, Robert C., and Bruce G. Resnick. "Put-Call Parity and Market Efficiency." *The Journal of Finance* 34 (December 1979): 1141–1155.

Klemkosky, Robert C., and Bruce G. Resnick. "An Ex-Ante Analysis of Put-Call Parity." *Journal of Financial Economics* 8 (1980): 363–378.

Kolb, Robert W. *Options: An Introduction*. Miami: Kolb Publishing, 1991.

Kolb, Robert W. *Understanding Futures Markets*, 3rd. ed. Miami: Kolb Publishing, 1991.

Kolb, Robert W. *The Financial Derivatives Reader*. Miami: Kolb Publishing, 1992.

Kolb, Robert W. *Futures, Options and Swaps*. Miami: Kolb Publishing, 1994.

Kolb, Robert W. *Financial Derivatives*, 2nd ed. Cambridge, Massachusetts: Blackwell, 1996.

Kolb, Robert W., and Raymond Chiang. "Improving Hedging Performance Using Interest Rate Futures." *Financial Management* 10 (Autumn 1981): 72–79.

Kolb, Robert W., Gerald D. Gay, and William C. Hunter. "Liquidity Requirements for Financial Futures Hedges." *Financial Analysts Journal* 41 (May-June 1985): 60–68.

Kritzman, Mark. "What Practitioners Need to Know About Option Replication." *Financial Analysts Journal* 48 (January-February 1992): 21–23.

Kritzman, Mark. "The Minimum-Risk Currency Hedge Ratio and Foreign Asset Exposure." *Financial Analysts Journal* 49 (September-October 1993): 77–78.

Kuserk, Gregory J., and Peter R. Locke. "Scalper Behavior in Futures Markets: An Empirical Examination." *The Journal of Futures Markets* 13 (June 1993): 409–431.

Latané, Henry A., and Richard J. Rendleman, Jr. "Standard Deviations of Stock Price Ratios Implied in Option Prices." *The Journal of Finance* 31 (May 1976): 369–382.

Leeson, Nick, and Edward Whitley. *Rogue Trader: How I Brought Down Barings Bank and Shook the Financial World*. Boston: Little, Brown, 1996.

Leuthold, Raymond M., Joan C. Junkus, and Jean E. Cordier. *The Theory and Practice of Futures Markets*. Englewood Cliffs, New Jersey: Prentice-Hall, 1989.

Lewent, Judy C., and A. John Kearney. "Identifying, Measuring, and Hedging Currency Risk at Merck." *Journal of Applied Corporate Finance* 2 (Winter 1990): 19–28.

Lintner, John. "The Valuation of Risk Assets and the Selection of Risky Investments in Stock Portfolios and Capital Budgets." *Review of Economics and Statistics* 47 (February 1965): 13–37.

Litzenberger, Robert H. "Swaps: Plain and Fanciful." *The Journal of Finance* 47 (July 1992): 831–850.

Macbeth, James D., and Larry J. Merville. "An Empirical Examination of the Black-Scholes Call Option Pricing Model." *The Journal of Finance* 34 (December 1979): 1173–1186.

Macbeth, James D., and Larry J. Merville. "Tests of the Black-Scholes and Cox Call Option Valuation Models." *The Journal of Finance* 35 (May 1980): 285–300.

Mackay, Robert J. "Removing the Major Tax Impediment to Business Hedging." *The Journal of Financial Engineering* 2 (March 1993): 19–26.

MacKinlay, A. Craig, and Krishna Ramaswamy. "Index-Futures Arbitrage and the Behavior of Stock Index Futures Prices." *The Review of Financial Studies* 1 (1988): 137–158.

Malkiel, Burton G., and Richard E. Quandt. *Strategies and Rational Decisions in the Securities Options Market*. Cambridge, Massachusetts: M.I.T. Press, 1969.

Manaster, Steven, and Gary Koehler. "The Calculation of Implied Variances from the Black-Scholes Model: A Note." *The Journal of Finance* 37 (March 1982): 227–230.

Mann, Steven V. "Calls Are Like Air Conditioners; Puts Are Like Heaters." *Journal of Financial Education* 22 (Spring 1996): 61–64.

Margrabe, William. "The Value of an Option to Exchange One Asset for Another." *The Journal of Finance* 33 (March 1978): 177–186.

Marshall, John F., and Vipul K. Bansal. *Financial Engineering*, 2nd. ed. Miami: Kolb Publishing, 1993.

Marshall, John F., and Kenneth R. Kapner. *The Swaps Market*, 2nd. ed. Miami: Kolb Publishing, 1993.

Mason, Scott, Robert Merton, André Perold, and Peter Tufano. *Cases in Financial Engineering: Applied Studies of Financial Innovation.* Englewood Cliffs, New Jersey: Prentice-Hall, 1995.

McCabe, George M., and Charles T. Franckle. "The Effectiveness of Rolling the Hedge Forward in the Treasury Bill Futures Market." *Financial Management* 12 (Summer 1983): 21–29.

McCabe, George M., and Donald P. Solberg. "Hedging in the Treasury Bill Futures Market When the Hedged Instrument and the Delivered Instrument Are Not Matched." *The Journal of Futures Markets* 9 (December 1989): 529–537.

McMillan, Lawrence G. *Options as a Strategic Investment*, 2nd ed. New York: New York Institute of Finance, 1986.

McMillan, Lawrence G. *McMillan on Options.* New York: John Wiley, 1996.

Merton, Robert C. "The Relationship between Put and Call Option Prices: Comment." *The Journal of Finance* 28 (March 1973): 183–184.

Merton, Robert C. "Theory of Rational Option Pricing." *Bell Journal of Economics and Management Science* 4 (Spring 1973): 141–183.

Meulbroek, Lisa. "A Comparison of Forward and Futures Prices of an Interest Rate–Sensitive Financial Asset." *The Journal of Finance* 47 (March 1992): 381–396.

Midanek, Deborah Hicks, and James I. Midanek. "Understanding Mortgage-Backed Securities." *Derivatives Quarterly* 2 (Spring 1996): 39–46.

Miller, Merton H. "Financial Innovation: Achievements and Prospects." *The Journal of Financial Engineering* 1 (June 1992): 1–13.

Miller, Merton H. "Index Arbitrage: Villain or Scapegoat?" *The Journal of Financial Engineering* 1 (December 1992): 319–324.

Modest, David M., and Mahedevan Sundaresan. "The Relationship between Spot and Futures Prices in Stock Index Futures Markets: Some Preliminary Evidence." *The Journal of Futures Markets* 3 (1983): 15–41.

Mossin, Jan. "Equilibrium in a Capital Asset Market." *Econometrica* 34 (October 1966): 768–783.

Mueller, Paul A. "Covered Call Options: An Alternative Investment Strategy." *Financial Management* 10 (Winter 1981): 64–71.

Nance, Deana R., Clifford W. Smith, Jr., and Charles W. Smithson. "On the Determinants of Corporate Hedging." *The Journal of Finance* 48 (March 1993): 267–284.

Neftci, Salih N. *An Introduction to the Mathematics of Financial Derivatives.* San Diego: Academic Press, 1996.

Nelken, Israel. *The Handbook of Exotic Options: Instruments, Analysis and Applications.* Chicago: Irwin Professional, 1996.

O'Brien, Thomas J. "The Mechanics of Portfolio Insurance." *The Journal of Portfolio Management* 14 (Spring 1985): 40–47.

Parkinson, Michael. "Option Pricing: The American Put." *The Journal of Business* 50 (January 1977): 21–36.

Petzel, Todd E. "How Expensive Is It to Insure Your U.S. Equity Portfolio?" *Derivatives Quarterly* 3 (Spring 1997): 81–83.

Phillips, Susan M., and Clifford W. Smith, Jr. "Trading Costs for Listed Options: The Implications for Market Efficiency." *Journal of Financial Economics* 8 (1980): 179–201.

Pounds, Henry M. "Covered Call Option Writing: Strategies and Results." *The Journal of Portfolio Management* 5 (Winter 1978): 31–42.

Pozen, Robert. "The Purchase of Protective Puts by Financial Institutions." *Financial Analysts Journal* 34 (July-August 1978): 47–60.

Rao, Ramesh K. S. "Modern Option Pricing Models: A Dichotomous Classification." *The Journal of Financial Research* 4 (Spring 1981): 33–44.

Rendleman, Richard J., Jr. "A Reconciliation of Potentially Conflicting Approaches to Hedging with Futures." *Advances in Futures and Options Research* 6 (1993): 81–92.

Rendleman, Richard J., Jr., and Brit J. Barter. "Two-State Option Pricing." *The Journal of Finance* 34 (December 1979): 1093–1110.

Rendleman, Richard J., Jr., and Christopher Carabini. "The Efficiency of the Treasury Bill Futures Market." *The Journal of Finance* 44 (September 1979): 895–914.

Rendleman, Richard J., Jr., and Richard W. McEnally. "Assessing the Cost of Portfolio Insurance." *Financial Analysts Journal* 43 (May-June 1987): 27–37.

Rentzler, Joel C. "Trading Treasury Bond Spreads against Treasury Bill Futures: A Model and Empirical Tests of the Turtle Trade." *The Journal of Futures Markets* 6 (1986): 41–61.

Resnick, Bruce G. "The Relationship between Futures Prices for U.S. Treasury Bonds." *Review of Research in Futures Markets* 3 (1984): 88–104.

Resnick, Bruce G., and Elizabeth Hennigar. "The Relationship between Futures and Cash Prices for U.S. Treasury Bonds." *Review of Research in Futures Markets* 2 (1983): 282–298.

Ritchken, Peter. *Options: Theory, Strategy, and Applications.* Glenview, Illinois: Scott, Foresman, 1987.

Ritchken, Peter. *Derivative Markets: Theory, Strategy and Applications.* New York: HarperCollins, 1996.

Ritchken, Peter H., and Harvey M. Salkin. "Safety First Selection Techniques for Option Spreads." *The Journal of Portfolio Management* 9 (1981): 61–67.

Ritter, Jay R. "How I Helped Make Fischer Black Wealthier." *Financial Management* 25 (Winter 1996): 104–107.

Roll, Richard. "An Analytic Valuation Formula for Unprotected American Call Options on Stocks with Known Dividends." *Journal of Financial Economics* 5 (November 1977): 251–258.

Roll, Richard, and Stephen A. Ross. "The Arbitrage Pricing Theory Approach to Strategic Portfolio Planning." *Financial Analysts Journal* 40 (May-June 1984): 14–26.

Ronn, Aimee Gerbarg, and Ehud I. Ronn. "The Box Spread Arbitrage Conditions: Theory, Tests, and Investment Strategies." *The Review of Financial Studies* 2 (1989): 91–108.

Rubinstein, Mark. "Nonparametric Tests of Alternative Option Pricing Models Using All Reported Trades and Quotes on the 30 Most Active CBOE Option Classes from August 23, 1976, through August 31, 1978." *The Journal of Finance* 40 (June 1985): 455–480.

Rubinstein, Mark. "Alternative Paths to Portfolio Insurance." *Financial Analysts Journal* 41 (July-August 1985): 42–52.

Rubinstein, Mark. "Derivative Assets Analysis." *The Journal of Economic Perspectives* 1 (Fall 1987): 73–93.

Rubinstein, Mark. "Portfolio Insurance and the Market Crash." *Financial Analysts Journal* 44 (January-February 1988): 38–47.

Rubinstein, Mark. "Implied Binomial Trees." *The Journal of Finance* 49 (July 1994): 771–818.

Rubinstein, Mark, and Hayne E. Leland. "Replicating Options with Positions in Stock and Cash." *Financial Analysts Journal* 37 (July-August 1981): 63–72.

Rubinstein, Mark, and Eric Reiner. "Breaking Down the Barriers." *Risk* 4 (September 1991): 28–35.

Santoni, G. J., and Tung Liu. "Circuit Breakers and Stock Market Volatility." *The Journal of Futures Markets* 13 (May 1993): 261–277.

Schachter, Barry. "Swap Pricing and Swap Mispricing." *Derivatives Quarterly* 2 (Summer 1996): 59–64.

Senchak, Andrew J., and John C. Easterwood. "Cross Hedging CD's with Treasury Bill Futures." *The Journal of Futures Markets* 3 (1983): 429–438.

Shafer, Carl E. "Hedge Ratios and Basis Behavior: An Intuitive Insight?" *The Journal of Futures Markets* 13 (December 1993): 837–847.

Sharpe, William F. "Capital Asset Prices: A Theory of Market Equilibrium under Conditions of Risk." *The Journal of Finance* 19 (September 1964): 425–442.

Shastri, Kuldeep, and Kishore Tandon. "Arbitrage Tests of the Efficiency of the Foreign Currency Options Markets." *Journal of International Money and Finance* 4 (December 1985): 455–468.

Shastri, Kuldeep, and Kishore Tandon. "On the Use of European Models to Price American Options on Foreign Currency." *The Journal of Futures Markets* 6 (Spring 1986): 93–108.

Shastri, Kuldeep, and Kishore Tandon. "Options on Futures Contracts: A Comparison of European and American Pricing Models." *The Journal of Futures Markets* 6 (Winter 1986): 593–618.

Sheikh, Aamir M. "Transaction Data Tests of S&P 100 Call Option Pricing." *Journal of Financial and Quantitative Analysis* 26 (December 1991): 459–475.

Shimko, David C. *Finance in Continuous Time*. Miami: Kolb Publishing, 1992.

Siegel, Daniel R., and Diane F. Siegel. *Futures Markets*. Hinsdale, Illinois: Dryden Press, 1990.

Siems, Thomas F. "Risk Management: Turning Volatility into Profitability." *Derivatives Quarterly* 2 (Spring 1996): 22–31.

Silber, William L. "Marketmaker Behavior in an Auction Market: An Analysis of Scalpers in Futures Markets." *The Journal of Finance* 39 (September 1984): 937–953.

Silber, William L. "Technical Trading: When It Works and When It Doesn't." *The Journal of Derivatives* 1 (Spring 1994): 39–44.

Singleton, J. Clay, and Robin Grieves. "Synthetic Puts and Portfolio Insurance Strategies." *The Journal of Portfolio Management* 10 (Spring 1984): 63–69.

Slivka, Ronald T. "Risk and Return for Option Investment Strategies." *Financial Analysts Journal* 36 (September-October 1980): 67–73.

Slivka, Ronald T. "Call Option Spreading." *The Journal of Portfolio Management* 7 (Spring 1981): 71–76.

Smith, Clifford W., Jr. "Option Pricing: A Review." *Journal of Financial Economics* 3 (January-March 1976): 3–51.

Smith, Clifford W., Jr. "Corporate Risk Management: Theory and Practice." *The Journal of Derivatives* 2 (Summer 1995): 21–30.

Smith, Clifford W., Jr., and Charles W. Smithson. *The Handbook of Financial Engineering: New Financial Product Innovations, Applications, and Analyses*. New York: Harper Business, 1990.

Smith, Clifford W., Jr., Charles W. Smithson, and Lee Macdonald Wakeman. "The Evolving Market for Swaps." *Midland Corporate Financial Journal* 3 (Winter 1986): 20–32.

Smith, Clifford W., Jr., and R. M. Stulz. "The Determinants of Firms' Hedging Policies." *Journal of Financial and Quantitative Analysis* 20 (1985): 391–405.

Smith, Donald J. "The Arithmetic of Financial Engineering." *Journal of Applied Corporate Finance* 1 (1989): 49–58.

Smithson, Charles W., Clifford W. Smith, Jr., and D. Sykes Wilford. *Managing Financial Risk: A Guide to Derivative Products, Financial Engineering and Value Maximization*. Burr Ridge, Illinois: Irwin Professional, 1995.

Sofianos, George. "Index Arbitrage Profitability." *The Journal of Derivatives* 1 (Fall 1993): 6–20.

Stein, Jerome L. "The Simultaneous Determination of Spot and Futures Prices." *The American Economic Review* 51 (December 1961): 1012–1025.

Stoll, Hans R. "The Relationship between Put and Call Option Prices." *The Journal of Finance* 31 (May 1969): 319–332.

Stoll, Hans R. "Principles of Inter-Market Regulation." *The Journal of Financial Engineering* 2 (March 1993): 65–71.

Stoll, Hans R. "Lost Barings: A Tale in Three Parts Concluding with a Lesson." *The Journal of Derivatives* 3 (Fall 1995): 109–115.

Stoll, Hans R., and Robert E. Whaley. "Futures and Options on Stock Indexes: Economic Purpose, Arbitrage, and Market Structure." *The Review of Futures Markets* 7 (1988): 224–229.

Stoll, Hans R., and Robert E. Whaley. *Futures and Options: Theory and Applications*. Cincinnati: South-Western, 1993.

Strong, Robert A. *Speculative Markets,* 2nd. ed. New York: Harper Collins, 1994.

Stulz, René M. "Options on the Minimum or the Maximum of Two Risky Assets: Analysis and Applications." *Journal of Financial Economics* 10 (July 1982): 161–185.

Sundaresan, Suresh. "Futures Prices on Yields, Forward Prices, and Implied Forward Prices from Term Structure." *Journal of Financial and Quantitative Analysis* 26 (September 1991): 409–424.

Sundaresan, Suresh. *Fixed Income Markets and Their Derivatives*. Cincinnati: South-Western, 1997.

Telser, Lester G. "Futures Trading and the Storage of Cotton and Wheat." *Journal of Political Economy* 66 (June 1958): 233–255.

Toevs, Alden L., and David P. Jacob. "Futures and Alternative Hedge Ratio Methodologies." *Journal of Portfolio Management* 12 (Spring 1986): 60–70.

Tosini, Paula A. "Stock Index Futures and Stock Market Activity in October 1987." *Financial Analysts Journal* 44 (January-February 1988): 28–37.

Trennepohl, Gary. "A Comparison of Listed Option Premiums and Black-Scholes Model Prices: 1973–1979." *The Journal of Financial Research* 4 (Spring 1981): 11–20.

Trennepohl, Gary L., and William P. Dukes. "Return and Risk from Listed Option Investments." *The Journal of Financial Research* 2 (Spring 1979): 37–49.

Trippi, Robert R. "A Test of Option Market Efficiency Using a Random-Walk Valuation Model." *Journal of Economics and Business* 29 (Winter 1977): 93–98.

Tucker, Alan L. "Empirical Tests of the Efficiency of the Currency Option Market." *The Journal of Financial Research* 8 (Winter 1985): 275–285.

Tucker, Alan L. *Financial Futures, Options, and Swaps*. St. Paul: West Publishing, 1991.

Turnbull, Stuart M. "Swaps: A Zero Sum Game?" *Financial Management* 16 (Spring 1987): 15–21.

Veit, W. Theodore, and Wallace W. Reiff. "Commercial Banks and Interest Rate Futures: A Hedging Survey." *The Journal of Futures Markets* 3 (1983): 283–293.

Vignola, Anthony, and Charles Dale. "The Efficiency of the Treasury Bill Futures Market: An Analysis of Alternative Specifications." *The Journal of Financial Research* 3 (1980): 169–188.

Wagner, Wayne, and Sheila Lau. "The Effect of Diversification on Risk." *Financial Analysts Journal* 27 (November-December 1971): 48–53.

Wall, Larry D., and John J. Pringle. "Interest Rate Swaps: A Review of the Issues." *Federal Reserve Bank of Atlanta Economic Review* (November-December 1988): 22–40.

Welch, Robert L., and Louis Culumovic. "A Profitable Call Spreading Strategy on the CBOE." *The Journal of Derivatives* 2 (Spring 1995): 24–44.

Whaley, Robert E. "On the Valuation of American Call Options on Stocks with Known Dividends." *Journal of Financial Economics* 9 (June 1981): 207–212.

Whaley, Robert E. "Valuation of American Call Options on Dividend Paying Stocks: Empirical Tests." *Journal of Financial Economics* 19 (March 1982): 29–58.

Whaley, Robert E. "On Valuing American Futures Options." *Financial Analysts Journal* 42 (May-June 1986): 49–59.

Wilmott, Paul, Sam Howison, and Jeff DeWynne. *The Mathematics of Financial Derivatives*. Cambridge, U.K.: Press Syndicate of the University of Cambridge, 1995.

Yadav, Pradeep K., and Peter F. Pope. "Stock Index Futures Arbitrage: International Evidence." *The Journal of Futures Markets* 9 (December 1990): 573–604.

Yaksick, Rudy. "Swaps, Caps, and Floors: Some Parity and Price Identities." *The Journal of Financial Engineering* 1 (June 1992): 105–115.

Yates, James W., Jr., and Robert W. Kopprasch, Jr. "Writing Covered Call Options: Profits and Risks." *The Journal of Portfolio Management* 6 (Fall 1980): 74–80.

Zivney, Terry L. "The Value of Early Exercise in Option Prices: An Empirical Investigation." *Journal of Financial and Quantitative Analysis* 26 (March 1991): 129–138.

Accounting risk   The risk associated with improper accounting treatment for a transaction, which may arise when accounting procedures and rulings change or have not yet been established.

Accreting swap   A swap in which the notional principal increases through time. *See also* Index amortizing swap.

Accrued interest   The amount of interest accumulated on a bond since its last coupon payment date.

Against actuals   *See* Exchange for physicals.

All or none order   An order to purchase or sell a security or derivative in which the broker is instructed to fill the entire order or not fill any of the order.

All or none, same price order   An order to purchase or sell a security or derivative in which the broker is instructed to fill the entire order at the same price or not fill any of the order.

Alternative currency option   An option in which the payoff is a function of the performance of two or more currencies. The holder has the right to decide which currency will be compared with the exercise price to determine the payoff.

Alternative option   An option involving more than one underlying asset whose payoff is determined by either the better performing (max) of the two assets or the worse performing (min) of the two assets. The rate of return of the better or worse performing of the two assets is compared to the exercise rate.

American option   An option that can be exercised on any day during its life.

Amortizing swap   *See* Index amortizing swap.

Analytical method   A method for estimating the Value-at-Risk in which knowledge of the input values and a pricing model are used with an assumption about the type of probability distribution associated with the risk.

Anticipatory hedge   A transaction in which a hedger expects to make a transaction in the spot market at a future date and is attempting to protect against a change in the spot price by trading a derivative.

Arbitrage   A transaction based on the observation of the same asset or derivative selling at two different prices. The transaction involves buying the asset or derivative at the lower price and selling it at the higher price.

Arbitrage pricing theory   A theory of asset pricing in which the expected return is a function of the asset's sensitivity to one or more underlying economic factors.

Arbitrageur   An individual who engages in an arbitrage transaction.

Arrears swap   A fixed-for-floating rate swap in which the payment is made on the same day that the floating interest rate is determined. *See also* Delayed settlement swap.

Asian option   An option in which the final payoff is determined by the average price of the asset during the option's life. *See also* Average price option *and* Average strike option.

Ask price   The price at which a market maker offers to sell a security or derivative.

Asset-backed security   A security providing the holder returns

based on the payments from a portfolio of underlying securities.

Asset-or-nothing option   An option, which if it expires in-the-money, pays the holder the underlying asset while the holder does not have to pay the exercise price.

Asset pricing theory   The study of the economic processes through which prices and expected returns on securities are formulated.

Assignment   The procedure in which the holder of a short position in an option is instructed to buy or sell the underlying asset or futures from or to the holder of the long position.

Associated person   An individual affiliated with a firm engaged in any line of futures-related business but excluding individuals who execute trades, manage portfolios or pools, give advice, or perform clerical duties.

At-the-money   An option in which the price of the underlying stock or futures equals the exercise price.

Average price option   An Asian option in which the average price of the asset over the life of the option replaces the price of the asset at expiration in determining the option's payoff.

Average strike option   An Asian option in which the average price

of the asset over the life of the option replaces the exercise price at expiration in determining the option's payoff.

Back office   The clerical, record-keeping function in a derivatives/risk management system.

Backwardation   A condition in financial markets in which the forward or futures price is less than the spot price.

Barrier option   An option that either does not begin or terminates early if the underlying asset price hits a certain level called the barrier. If the option does not begin or terminates early, the holder might be paid a rebate. *See also* In-option *and* Out-option.

Basis   The difference between the spot price and the futures or forward price or the difference between a nearby futures or forward price and a deferred futures or forward price.

Basis point   A measure commonly applied to interest rates or yields equal to one 1/100 of 1 percent.

Basis swap   A swap in which both parties make payments at different floating rates.

Basket options   A single option written on a prespecified combination of securities or currencies.

Bear   A person who expects the market to go down. Sometimes referred to as *bearish*.

Bear market   A market in which prices are falling.

Bear spread   An option spread designed to profit in a bear market. Also known as a *bearish spread*.

Beta   A measure of the responsiveness of a security or portfolio to the market as a whole.

Biased expectations   A condition in which investors' expectations of a rate, a security price, or a return systematically differ from the subsequent long-run average rate, price, or return.

Bid price   The price at which a market maker offers to buy a security or derivative.

Bid-ask spread   The difference between the ask price or rate and the bid price or rate.

Bilateral netting   Netting between two parties. *See also* Netting *and* Multilateral netting.

Binary option   *See* Asset-or-nothing option *and* Cash-or-nothing option.

Binomial model   An option pricing model based on the assumption that at any point in time the price of the underlying can change to one of only two possible values.

Black model   A pricing model for an option on a forward or futures contract.

Black-Scholes model   A widely used pricing model for an option on an asset.

Block trade   The sale of at least 10,000 shares of stock normally conducted with considerable care so as to minimize the impact on the stock price.

Board broker   *See* Order book official.

Bond option   An option to buy or sell a bond.

Boundary condition   A statement specifying the maximum or minimum price or some other limitation on the price of an option.

Box spread   A risk-free combination of a call money spread and a put money spread.

Breakeven stock price   The stock price at which a derivative or stock strategy has a zero profit.

Break forward   A forward contract with an upside payoff like a call, but which has a possible negative value at expiration so as to compensate for the fact that it has no initial value.

Broker   A person who arranges a financial transaction by bringing a buyer and seller together and usually earns a commission.

Bull   A person who expects the market to go up. Sometimes referred to as *bullish*.

Bull market   A market in which prices are rising.

Bull spread   An option spread designed to profit in a bull market. Also known as a *bullish spread*.

Butterfly spread   An option transaction consisting of one long call at a particular exercise price, another otherwise identical long call at a different exercise price, and two otherwise identical short calls at an exercise price between the other two.

Buy-back   A method of terminating a swap in which a party makes or receives a cash payment to or from the counterparty in the amount of the value of the swap. Also called a *close-out*.

Calendar spread   An option transaction consisting of the purchase of an option with a given expiration and the sale of an otherwise identical option with a different expiration.

Call   An option to buy an asset, currency, or futures. Also refers to the early retirement of a bond.

Call date   The earliest date at which a bond can be called.

Callability   A feature associated with many bonds in which the issuer is permitted to pay off the

bond prior to its scheduled maturity date.

Callable bond   A bond that the issuer can retire prior to its maturity date.

Cap   An option transaction in which a party borrowing at a floating rate pays a premium to another party, which reimburses the borrower in the event that the borrower's interest costs exceed a certain level, thus making the effective interest paid on a floating rate loan have a cap or maximum amount. Can also be used in other cases where the underlying is an asset price, commodity price, or exchange rate.

Capital Asset Pricing Model   A model that gives the equilibrium expected return on an asset as a function of the risk-free rate, the expected return on the market, and the asset's beta or systematic risk.

Capital market   The financial market in which long-term securities such as stocks and long-term bonds are traded.

Caplet   One of the component options of a cap.

Carry   The difference between the cash received from holding an asset and the interest forgone or other costs associated with holding it.

Cash and carry   A theoretically riskless transaction consisting of a

long position in the spot asset and a short position in the futures contract.

Cash market   *See* Spot market.

Cash-or-nothing option   An option, which if it expires in-the-money, pays the holder the exercise price.

Cash settlement   The feature of certain derivatives that allows delivery or exercise to be conducted with an exchange of cash rather than the physical transfer of assets.

Cheapest bond to deliver   The bond that if delivered on the Chicago Board of Trade's Treasury bond or note contract provides the largest difference between the invoice price and the cost of the bond.

Chooser option   An option in which the holder decides at a specific time during the option's life whether it will be a put or a call. Sometimes called an *as-you-like-it option*.

Circuit breaker   *See* Trading halt.

Class   All of the options of a particular type (call or put) on a given stock, index, currency, or futures commodity.

Clearing firm   A company that is a member of a futures or options clearinghouse.

Clearinghouse   A corporation associated with an options or

futures exchange that guarantees the performance of both parties to the contract, collects margins, and maintains records of the parties to all transactions.

Cliquet option   An option that allows an upward resetting of the exercise price as the asset price crosses a series of thresholds.

Closeout netting   Netting in which at the termination of a transaction only the net amount is owed.

CMO   *See* Collateralized mortgage obligation.

Collar   A combination of a cap and a floor in which the purchaser of the cap also sells a floor or the purchaser of a floor also sells a cap. The sale of the cap or floor reduces the cost of the protection and forgoes gains if interest rates move in that party's favor. Can also be used in other cases where the payoff is tied to an asset price, commodity price, or exchange rate.

Collateral   Any type of cash or security set aside as protection for the lender in a loan. Also, used as a credit enhancement in a swap.

Collateralized mortgage obligation   A type of mortgage-backed security in which mortgage payments are divided into tranches with different payment characteristics, different priorities, and different risks and are passed through, less a service fee, to holders.

Combination   An option strategy involving positions in a put and a call. Sometimes used to refer to any option strategy involving more than one option.

Commercial paper   A short-term promissory note issued by a large, creditworthy corporation.

Commission   A fee paid by the parties in a transaction to a broker for arranging the transaction.

Commission broker   A trader on the floor of a futures exchange who executes transactions for off-the-floor customers.

Commodity   Any asset, but more frequently used to refer to an agricultural product or sometimes a metal or natural resource.

Commodity fund   *See* Futures fund.

Commodity futures   Any futures contract, but primarily a futures on an agricultural product or sometimes a metal or natural resource.

Commodity Futures Trading Commission   The federal agency that regulates the futures markets.

Commodity option   An option on a commodity, but more often an option on a futures contract.

Commodity pool   A private investment arrangement in which individuals combine their

funds and the total amount of funds is used to trade futures contracts, with a cash reserve set aside to meet margin calls.

Commodity pool operator   The organizer or manager of a commodity pool.

Commodity swap   A swap in which two parties agree to make payments to each other with at least one party's payments calculated according to the price of a commodity. The other party's payments can be calculated according to any formula.

Commodity trading advisor   An individual who specializes in offering advice regarding the trading of futures contracts.

Comparative statics   An examination of the effects on a model of changes in the variables that influence the model.

Compound option   An option to buy or sell another option.

Constant maturity swap   A swap where one side pays a rate associated with an instrument of constant maturity, which is usually greater than the settlement period of the swap.

Contango   A condition in financial markets in which the forward or futures price is greater than the spot price.

Contingent premium option   An option in which the premium is

paid at expiration and only if the option is in-the-money. *See also* Pay-later option.

Continuously compounded rate   A rate of return in which the asset value grows continuously.

Convenience yield   A premium imbedded in the spot price that provides an extra return for those holding the commodity and is usually observed during shortages of the commodity.

Conversion   An arbitrage transaction consisting of the sale of a call and the purchase of a synthetic call.

Conversion factor   An adjustment factor applied to the settlement price of the Chicago Board of Trade's Treasury bond and note contracts that gives the holder of the short position a choice of several different bonds or notes to deliver.

Convertible bond   A bond in which the holder can convert into a specified number of shares of stock.

Convexity   A mathematical relationship between the change in a bond price and the change in its yield, beyond that explained by its duration. Knowledge and use of convexity is helpful in obtaining better hedge results.

Cost of carry   The cost involved in holding or storing an asset that consists of storage costs and interest lost on funds tied up.

Coupon   The interest paid on a bond.

Covariance   A measure of the association between two random variables.

Covered call   A combination of a long position in an asset, futures, or currency and a short position in a call on the same.

Credit enhancements   Any of several means used to reduce the credit risk on a swap or other derivative transaction.

Credit risk   The risk that a party to an over-the-counter derivative contract will not pay off as required. Also known as *default risk.*

Credit spread   An option spread in which the amount paid for the purchased option is less than the amount received from the sold option.

Cross product netting   Netting in which payments owed for one transaction are netted against payments owed for another type of transaction. Thus, parties could net one type of derivative against another, as well as against loans.

Cross-rate relationship   The association among the exchange rates of three currencies.

Currency swap   A transaction in which two parties agree to make payments to each other in different currencies.

Currency warrants   Options on various foreign currencies underwritten by investment banking firms and trading on the American Stock Exchange.

Current credit risk   The risk that a party to a transaction will be unable to make payments that are currently due.

Daily price limits   The maximum and minimum prices at which a futures contract can trade. These are established by the clearinghouse and are expressed in relation to the previous day's settlement price.

Daily settlement   The process in a futures market in which the daily price changes are paid by the parties incurring losses to the parties making profits. Also known as *marking to market*.

Day order   An order to purchase or sell a security or derivative that is canceled if unfilled by the end of the day.

Day trader   A derivatives trader who closes out all positions by the end of the trading session.

Dealer   A person or firm engaged in the business of buying and selling securities or derivatives for profit. A dealer stands ready to buy or sell at any time.

Debit spread   An option spread in which the amount paid for the purchased option exceeds the amount received from the sold option.

Deductible   A concept in insurance representing the amount by which an insurance payoff is reduced as a result of the insured assuming some of the risk.

Deep in-the-money   An option that is in-the-money by a significant, though unspecific, amount.

Deep out-of-the-money   An option that is out-of-the-money by a significant, though unspecific, amount.

Deferred strike option   An option in which the exercise price is not set until a later time during the option's life but prior to expiration.

Delayed settlement swap   The standard procedure in an interest rate swap in which the floating interest rate is observed at the beginning of the settlement period and the interest is paid at the end. *See also* Arrears swap.

Delivery   The process in which a futures or forward contract can be terminated at expiration through the sale of the asset by the short to the long.

Delivery day   The day on which an asset is delivered to terminate a futures or forward contract.

Delivery option   Any special right or option inherent in a futures contract, held by the holder of the short position and granting flexibility with regard to

the item delivered or the timing of delivery. *See also* Timing option, Quality option, End-of-month option, Switching option.

Delta   The ratio of the change in an option's price to a given change in the price of the underlying asset or futures.

Delta hedge   A transaction in which an asset or derivative is hedged with another asset or derivative in such a manner that the hedge is adjusted so that the effect of small changes in the underlying is removed and the hedge provides a risk-free return.

Delta neutral   The condition in which an investor's portfolio is delta hedged and, therefore, unaffected by small changes in the value of the underlying.

Derivative   A contract between two parties providing for a payoff from one party to the other determined by the price of an asset, an exchange rate, a commodity price, or an interest rate.

Diagonal spread   An option spread in which the options differ by both time to expiration and exercise price.

Diff swap   A swap in which one party's interest payments are denominated in one currency while the notional principal is stated in another currency.

Diffs   Futures contracts based on the difference between two

prices, exchange rates, or interest rates.

Digital option   *See* Asset-or-nothing option *and* Cash-or-nothing option. Same as Binary option.

Diversification   An investment strategy in which funds are allocated across numerous different assets.

Dividend protection   A feature associated with the original over-the-counter options market in which the exercise price was adjusted by the amount of any dividend paid on the underlying stock.

Dividend yield   The ratio of the dividend to the stock price.

DOT   An acronym for Designated Order Turnaround, the New York Stock Exchange's system for expediting stock transactions that is used frequently in program trading.

Down-and-in option   An in barrier option in which the premium is paid but the option does not actually begin unless the asset price falls to a specified barrier.

Down-and-out option   An out barrier option in which the premium is paid but the option terminates early if the asset price falls to a specified barrier.

Down-option   A type of barrier option in which the barrier is below the current level of the underlying.

Dual trading   The practice of a floor trader on a derivatives exchange trading for his or her own account as well as for a customer.

Duration   A measure of the size and timing of a bond's cash flows. It also reflects the weighted average maturity of the bond and indicates the sensitivity of the bond's price to a change in its yield.

Dynamic hedge   An investment strategy, often associated with portfolio insurance, in which a stock is hedged by selling futures or buying Treasury bills in such a manner that the position is adjusted frequently and simulates a protective put.

Early exercise   Exercise of an American option before its expiration date.

EDPC   *See* Enhanced derivatives products company.

Efficient market   A market in which the price of an asset reflects its true economic value.

Empirical test   A procedure in which data are subjected to various statistical measures to determine if a theory, model, or hypothesis is correct.

End-of-month option   Either the right to defer delivery on the Chicago Board of Trade's

Treasury bond futures contract until the final business days of the month during which the contract does not trade or any similar right inherent in a futures contract. Can also refer to exchange-listed options whose expirations are on the last business day of the month.

End user   A firm that enters into derivative transactions with a dealer for the purpose of managing its risk.

Enhanced derivatives products company   A subsidiary established by a bank or swap dealer for the execution of swaps and designed so as to have a higher credit rating than the parent company itself.

Equity basket   A combination of equity securities, otherwise known as a portfolio, but upon which a derivative contract is created.

Equity collar   A collar, consisting of a long put and a short call, and in which the payoff is determined by the performance of a stock or stock index. Sometimes structured so that the put and call premiums offset and called a *risk reversal*.

Equity derivative   Any type of derivative contract in which the payoff is based on a stock or stock index.

Equity forward   A forward contract in which the payoff is based on a stock or stock index.

Equity-linked debt   A security that promises a minimum return plus a given percentage of any change in the market above a certain level.

Equity option   An option on a common stock.

Equity swap   A swap in which two parties agree to make payments to each other with at least one party's payments calculated according to the performance of a stock or index. The other party's payments can be calculated according to any formula.

Eurodollar   A dollar deposited in a European bank or a European branch of an American bank.

European Monetary Unit   The single unit of currency planned to replace all currencies of participating countries upon completion of the European unification.

European option   An option that can be exercised only when it expires.

Exchange for physicals   A method of delivery on a futures contract in which the long and short agree to delivery terms different from those specified in the futures contract.

Exchange-listed derivative   An option or futures that trades on an exchange.

Exchange option   An option granting the right to acquire one asset by giving up another asset.

Exchange rate   The rate at which a given amount of one currency converts to another currency.

Ex-dividend date   A day designated four business days prior to the holder-of-record date after which an investor purchasing a stock does not receive the upcoming dividend.

Exercise   The process by which a call option is used to purchase or a put option is used to sell the underlying security, futures, or currency or convert to its cash value.

Exercise limit   The maximum number of option contracts that any one investor can exercise over a specific time period.

Exercise price   The price at which an option permits its owner to buy or sell the underlying security, futures, or currency.

Exercise rate   The fixed rate in an interest rate option, cap, or floor.

Exercise value   See Intrinsic value.

Exotic options   A family of options with payoff features different from those of standard European and American options.

Expectations theory   An explanation for the shape of the term structure in which forward or futures rates are considered to be the market's expectation of future spot rates.

Expiration   The date after which a derivative contract no longer exists.

Expiration date   See Expiration.

Extendible bond   A bond in which the holder can choose prior to or at maturity to extend the maturity date.

Face value   The principal amount borrowed on a loan.

Fiduciary call   A form of portfolio insurance in which funds are allocated to calls and Treasury bills such that the transaction is equivalent to a protective put.

Financial asset   An asset representing a claim of one party on another.

Financial engineering   The process of developing, designing, and implementing creative financial contracts, frequently involving derivatives, for the purpose of solving specific risk management problems.

Financial futures   Futures on securities, sometimes including futures on foreign currencies.

Fixed-for-floating rate swap   An interest rate swap involving the

exchange of fixed interest payments for floating interest payments.

FLEX options Options traded at the Chicago Board Options Exchange that allow the user to specify the strike price, expiration date, and other contract terms in contrast to ordinary CBOE options in which the terms are standardized.

Floating-floating swap *See* Basis swap.

Floating rate bond A bond in which the interest payments are adjusted periodically to be consistent with current market interest rates. Also in the form of a loan or note.

Floor An option transaction in which a party lending at a floating rate pays a premium to another party, which reimburses the lender in the event that the lender's interest revenues are below a certain level, thus making the interest received on a floating rate loan have a floor or minimum value. It can also be used in other cases where the payoff is tied to an asset price, commodity price, or exchange rate.

Floor broker A trader on the floor of the options exchange who executes trades for others who are off the floor.

Floorlet One of the component options of a floor.

Foreign currency futures A futures contract providing for the purchase of a foreign currency.

Foreign currency option An option providing for the purchase or sale of a foreign currency.

Forward commitment *See* Forward contract.

Forward contract An agreement between two parties, a buyer and a seller, to buy an asset or currency at a later date at a fixed price.

Forward discount The relationship between the spot and forward exchange rates of a foreign currency in which the forward rate of a currency is less than the spot rate.

Forward market A market in which forward contracts are constructed.

Forward premium The relationship between the spot and forward exchange rates of a foreign currency in which the forward rate of a currency is greater than the spot rate.

Forward rate The rate agreed upon in a forward contract for a loan or implied by the relationship between short- and long-term interest rates.

Forward rate agreement A transaction, similar to a forward contract, in which one party agrees to make a future interest payment based on an agreed-upon fixed rate of interest and receives a future interest payment based on a floating rate, such as LIBOR. Also called *FRA*.

Forward start option An option in which the premium is paid today but the option's life does not begin until later.

Forward swap A forward contract obligating the two parties to enter into a swap at a future date.

FRA *See* Forward rate agreement.

Free market A market characterized by a high degree of efficiency and little or no regulatory influence.

Front office The trading function in a derivatives/risk management system.

Full carry A condition associated with a futures contract in which the futures price exceeds the spot price by no less than the cost of carry.

Futures commission merchant A firm in the business of executing futures transactions for the public.

Futures contract An agreement between two parties, a buyer and a seller, to purchase an asset or currency at a later date at a fixed price and that trades on a futures exchange and is subject to a daily settlement procedure.

Futures fund   A mutual fund that specializes in trading futures contracts.

Futures option   An option on a futures contract.

Gamma   The rate of change of an option's delta with respect to a change in the price of the underlying asset or futures.

Gamma hedge   A hedged position, usually combined with a delta hedge, in which changes in the delta will be unaffected by large movements in the underlying.

Garman-Kohlhagen model   A model for pricing European foreign currency options.

Generic swap   *See* Fixed-for-floating rate swap.

GLOBEX   A system of automated trading operated by the Chicago Mercantile Exchange in which bids and offers are entered into a computer and executed electronically.

Good-till-canceled order   An order that is in effect until canceled and is used most often with stop orders and limit orders that may take some time to execute.

Grade   A measure of a commodity's relative quality.

Group of Thirty   An organization of bankers and economists who conduct studies on various issues important to the efficient operation of international financial markets and systems.

Hedge   A transaction in which an investor seeks to protect a position or anticipated position in the spot market by using an opposite position in derivatives.

Hedge accounting   An accounting method in which the profit from a derivatives transaction is added to the profit from the asset it is used to hedge. The profit of the overall hedged position is then reported as one transaction.

Hedge portfolio   A portfolio being hedged, often used in the context of a long stock–short call or long stock–long put in which the hedge ratio is continuously adjusted to produce a risk-free portfolio.

Hedge ratio   The ratio of derivatives to a spot position (or vice versa) that achieves an objective such as minimizing or eliminating risk.

Hedger   An investor who executes a hedge transaction.

Herstatt risk   *See* Settlement risk.

Historical method   A method for estimating Value-at-Risk that uses historical information on the portfolio's recent performance to estimate its future probability distribution.

Historical volatility   The standard deviation of a security, futures, or currency obtained by estimating it from historical data over a recent time period.

Holder-of-record date   The day on which all current shareholders are entitled to receive the upcoming dividend.

Holding period   The time period over which an investment is held.

Horizontal spread   *See* Calendar spread.

Hybrid   An instrument or contract that possesses some of the characteristics of a derivative.

IMM Index   The method of quoting the price of a Treasury bill or Eurodollar futures contract on the International Monetary Market in which the price is stated in terms of a discount from par of 100.

Immunization   A bond portfolio strategy in which the return is protected against changes in interest rates and is obtained when the duration equals the holding period.

Implied duration   The duration of the bond underlying a futures contract that is implied by using the futures price as though it were the price of the bond.

Implied repo rate   The cost of financing a cash-and-carry transaction that is implied by the

relationship between the spot and futures price.

Implied volatility The standard deviation obtained when the market price of an option equals the price given by a particular option pricing model.

Implied yield The yield on the bond underlying a futures contract that is implied by using the futures price as though it were the price of the bond.

In-arrears swap *See* Arrears swap.

Index amortizing swap A swap in which the notional principal is reduced according to a schedule that may call for an accelerated reduction the lower interest rates fall.

Index arbitrage The purchase (sale) of a portfolio of stocks representing an index and the sale (purchase) of the corresponding futures contract. The trade is designed to profit from mispricing in the relationship between the spot and futures prices.

Index option An option on an index of securities.

Index participations Securities that pay off as if the holder had owned an index of securities. They represent a claim on the portfolio of securities that compose an index.

Index swap A swap in which one party's payments are based on an index, such as an equity index. *See also* Equity swap.

Indication pricing schedule A schedule of the fixed rates that a swap dealer will pay or receive for taking a position in a swap.

Initial margin The minimum amount of money that must be in an investment account on the day of a transaction. On futures accounts, the initial margin must be met on any day in which the opening balance starts off below the maintenance margin requirement.

In-option A type of barrier option in which the premium is paid but the option does not actually begin unless the asset price crosses a specified barrier. *See also* Down-and-in option *and* Up-and-in option.

Installment option An option in which the premium is paid in equal installments. At each payment date, the holder decides whether to continue paying the premium or let the option expire.

Institutional investor A term used to refer to a firm as an investor as opposed to an individual investor.

Interbank market An informal organization of banks that execute spot and forward transactions in foreign currency.

Intercommodity spread A futures transaction involving a long position in a futures on one commodity and a short position in a futures on another commodity.

Interest-only strip A type of mortgage-backed security in which mortgage interest payments are passed through, less a service fee, to holders. *See also* Principal-only strip.

Interest rate cap A cap in which the payoff is determined by a floating interest rate.

Interest rate collar A collar in which the payoff is determined by a floating interest rate.

Interest rate derivative An option, forward, futures, swap, or other derivative instrument in which the underlying instrument is an interest rate. In some uses, the underlying instrument can be a bond.

Interest rate floor A floor in which the payoff is determined by a floating interest rate.

Interest rate futures A futures contract on a fixed-income security.

Interest rate option An option on an interest rate rather than on a security, commodity, or futures price. Exercise is determined by whether the interest rate is above or below the strike.

Interest rate parity The relationship between the spot and forward exchange rates and

the interest rates in two countries.

Interest rate swap   A transaction between two parties who agree to make interest payments to each other according to different formulas.

Internal rate of return   The discount rate on an investment that equates the present value of the future cash flows with the price.

International market integration Condition in which financial markets of different countries are aligned such that prices in one country are aligned with prices in another, no arbitrage is possible across countries, and information is transmitted quickly from one country's markets to another's.

International Swaps and Derivatives Association   An organization of swap dealers, a major activity of which is the simplification and promotion of standardized low cost swap procedures.

In-the-money   A call (put) option in which the price of the asset or futures or the currency exchange rate exceeds (is less than) the exercise price.

Intracommodity spread   A futures transaction consisting of a long position in a futures expiring in one month and a short position in an otherwise identical futures expiring in another month.

Intrinsic value   For a call (put) option, the greater of zero or the difference between the stock (exercise) price and the exercise (stock) price. Also referred to as *parity value*.

Introducing broker   A broker who arranges futures transactions for customers but contracts with another firm or individual for the execution of the trade.

Inverse floater   A type of floating rate structured note that pays more interest as interest rates fall and less as interest rates rise.

IO   *See* Interest-only strip.

ISDA   *See* International Swaps and Derivatives Association.

Johnson-Shad Agreement   The 1982 agreement between CFTC chairman Phillip McBryde Johnson and SEC chairman John Shad that established the lines of regulatory authority over options.

Kappa   *See* Vega.

Knock-in option   *See* In-option.

Knock-out option   *See* Out-option.

Lambda   *See* Vega.

Law of One Price   The principle that two identical assets or portfolios cannot sell for different prices.

LEAPS   Long-term Equity Anticipation Securities. Options

on individual stocks with expirations of more than one year.

Legal risk   The risk that the legal system will fail to enforce a contract. Legal risk is primarily faced by dealers and may arise when an end user loses money in a transaction and claims that the dealer mislead it or that the end user had no legal authority to enter into the transaction and the dealer should have informed it of such.

Leverage   The use of debt to magnify investment returns.

Limit down   An occurrence in which the futures price moves down to the lower daily price limit.

Limit move   An occurrence in which a futures price hits the upper or lower daily price limit.

Limit order   A request to purchase or sell a security or derivative that specifies the maximum price to pay or minimum price to accept.

Limit up   An occurrence in which the futures price moves up to the upper daily price limit.

Liquidity   A feature of a market in which transactions can be quickly executed with little impact on prices.

Liquidity preference theory   An explanation for the shape of the term structure that assumes that

long-term rates exceed short-term rates because of lenders' reluctance to make long-term loans.

Liquidity risk   The risk associated with a thin market for a transaction, as manifested by few dealers and wide bid-ask spreads.

Listing   The offering of a security, option, or futures for public trading on an exchange.

Local   A trader on the floor of the futures exchange who executes trades for his or her personal account.

Local expectations theory   A theory of the term structure of interest rates in which no arbitrage opportunities exist and one-period ahead forward rates equal expected future spot rates under risk neutral probabilities.

Lock-in option   An option which, when the underlying asset reaches a certain level, allows the holder to set the final payout as the current intrinsic value.

Lognormal   A distribution of stock returns that is often used to develop option pricing models.

London Interbank Offer Rate (LIBOR)   The interest rate on certain Eurodollar deposits involving London banks.

Long   A position involving the purchase of a security or derivative. It also refers to the

person holding the long position.

Long hedge   A hedge involving a short position in the spot market and a long position in the futures market.

Lookback option   An option granting the right to either buy the underlying asset at its lowest price during the option's life or sell the asset at its highest price during the option's life. Also called a *no-regrets option*.

Lower bound   A value established as the lowest possible price of an option.

Lower of cost or market   An accounting method, sometimes used for derivatives, in which the derivative is valued at its original value unless the market value decreases, in which case the market value is used as the current value.

Maintenance margin   The minimum amount of money that must be kept in a margin account on any day other than the day of a transaction.

Managed futures   An arrangement in which commodity trading advisors are allocated funds for the purpose of trading futures contracts for a client. Structured as private arrangements, futures funds, and commodity pools.

Margin   Funds kept in a margin account for the purpose of covering losses.

Market efficiency   A concept referring to a market in which prices reflect the true economic values of the underlying assets.

Market maker   A trader in a market who is responsible for buying and selling to the public.

Market-on-close order   An order to purchase or sell securities or derivatives that requests the broker to execute the transaction at a price as close as possible to the closing price.

Market order   A request to purchase or sell a security or derivative in which the broker is instructed to execute the transaction at the current market price.

Market portfolio   The portfolio consisting of all assets in the market.

Market risk   The risk that a firm's value or cash flows will be affected by movements in interest rates, exchange rates, stock prices, or commodity prices.

Market segmentation theory   An explanation of the shape of the term structure of interest rates in which long-term and short-term rates are determined by supply and demand in long-term and short-term markets.

Market timing   An investment strategy in which the investor attempts to profit by predicting the direction of the market.

Mark-to-market   *See* Daily settlement.

Mark-to-market accounting   An accounting method in which the actual current value of any asset or derivative is recorded on the balance sheet.

Master swap agreement   A contract form developed by ISDA for simplifying and standardizing swap transactions.

Middle office   A component function of a derivatives/risk management system between the front and back office.

Minimum variance hedge ratio   The ratio of futures contracts for a given spot position that minimizes the variance of the profit from the hedge.

Min-max option   An option involving more than one underlying asset whose payoff is determined by either the higher value (max) of the two assets or the lower value (min) of the two assets. The value of the better or worse performing of the two assets is compared to the exercise price. Also called a *rainbow option*.

Model risk   The risk associated with the use of an inappropriate model, or a model containing errors or incorrect inputs.

Modified lookback option   A lookback option in which the payoff is determined by replacing the exercise price by either the high or low price reached by the asset during the option's life.

Money market   The market for short-term securities.

Money spread   An option transaction that involves a long position in one option and a short position in an otherwise identical option with a different exercise price.

Monte Carlo simulation   A procedure for pricing derivatives that involves the generation of random numbers representing prices of the underlying and calculating the derivative value as an average of the possible derivative values obtained from the simulations.

Mortgage-backed security   A security providing the holder returns based on the payments from a portfolio of underlying mortgages.

Mortgage-pass through   A type of mortgage-backed security in which mortgage principal and interest payments are passed through, less a service fee, to holders of the security.

Mortgage strip   *See* Interest-only strip *and* Principal-only strip.

Multi-asset option   An option whose payoff is based on the performance of more than one underlying asset. *See also* Exchange option *and* Min-max option.

Multilateral netting   Netting between more than two parties, which is essentially equivalent to a clearinghouse.

Multiple listing   The listing of identical options on more than one exchange.

Mutual fund   A company whose shareholders' money is pooled and used to purchase securities.

Naked call   *See* Uncovered call.

National Association of Securities Dealers   An organization of firms that serve as market makers for stocks traded over-the-counter.

National Futures Association   An organization of firms engaged in the futures business that serves as the industry's self-regulatory body.

Net present value   The present value of an investment's cash flows minus the initial cost of the investment.

Netting   The practice of aggregating all swaps between two parties and determining the net amount owed from one party to the other.

Netting by novation   Netting in which the net value of a combination of transactions is replaced by a single transaction.

Normal backwardation   A condition in which the forward or futures price is less than the expected future spot price at expiration.

Normal contango   A condition in which the forward or futures

price is greater than the expected future spot price at expiration.

Normal probability The probability that a normally distributed random variable will be less than or equal to a given value.

Notice of intention day The second day in the three-day sequence leading to delivery in which the clearinghouse notifies the holder of the long position that delivery will be made the next business day.

Notional principal A measure of the size of a swap, stated in units of a currency, on which the payments are calculated.

Offset A method of terminating a swap in which a party enters into a new swap with payments occurring on the same dates as the old swap. Both swaps remain in effect. *See also* Offsetting order.

Offsetting order A derivative transaction that is the exact opposite of a previously established long or short position.

Open interest The number of futures or options contracts that have been established and not yet been offset or exercised.

Open outcry The process that occurs in a trading arena in which bids and offers are indicated by shouting.

Operational risk The risk of a breakdown in the operations of a derivatives program or risk management system.

Option A contract granting the right to buy or sell an asset, currency, or futures at a fixed price for a specific time period.

Option on futures An option to buy or sell a futures contract.

Option pricing model A mathematical equation or procedure that produces the theoretical fair value of an option.

Options Clearing Corporation The firm that operates as a clearinghouse for the various exchanges that trade options on stocks and indices.

Order book official An employee of the Chicago Board Options Exchange who keeps public limit orders and attempts to fill them at the best available price.

Out-of-the-money A call (put) in which the price of the asset, currency, or futures is less (greater) than the exercise price.

Out-option A type of barrier option in which the premium is paid but the option terminates early if the asset price crosses a specified barrier. *See also* Down-and-out option *and* Up-and-out option.

Outperformance option An option involving two underlying assets in which the final payout is based on the difference between the values or relative performances of the two assets.

Overnight repo A repurchase agreement with a maturity of one night. *See also* Term repo.

Overpriced A condition in which a security or derivative is trading at more than its value.

Over-the-counter derivative A derivative created in an over-the-counter market and in which there is no active secondary market.

Over-the-counter market A market for securities or derivatives in which the transactions are conducted among dealers, brokers, and the public off of an organized exchange.

Parity *See* Intrinsic value.

Path-dependent option An option whose payoff depends on the path taken by the underlying asset as it moves toward the option's expiration.

Path-independent option An option whose payoff does not depend on the path taken by the underlying as it moves toward the option's expiration. Only the possible values of the underlying at expiration are important and not how those values were reached.

Payer swaption A swaption in which the party holding the

option has the right to enter into a swap and pay the fixed rate.

Pay-later option   An option in which the premium is paid at expiration.

Payment netting   Netting in which two parties to a transaction settle the amounts simultaneously owed by having one party pay the other the net amount.

Payoff   The amount of money received from a transaction at the end of the holding period.

PERCS (Preference Equity Redemption Cumulative Stock)   Convertible preferred stock with a maximum payoff, which makes it similar to a covered call.

Perfect hedge   A hedge in which the gain on one side of the transaction exactly offsets the loss on the other under all possible outcomes. Rarely exists in the real world.

Performance bond   A preferred name for the margin deposit required in futures markets. Makes a distinction between stock market margin, which reflects the borrowing of funds, and futures market margin, which is simply a good-faith deposit.

Pit   An octagonally or hexagonally shaped, multi-tiered area on the trading floor of a derivatives exchange within which a group of contracts trades.

Plain vanilla swap   *See* Fixed-for-floating rate swap.

Planned amortization class bonds   One component tranche of a collateralized mortgage obligation in which an assumed rate of prepayments is embedded into the contract terms. Also called PAC bond.

PO   *See* Principal-only strip.

Portfolio insurance   An investment strategy employing combinations of securities, Treasury bills, or derivatives that is designed to provide a minimum or floor value of the portfolio at a future date.

Portfolio theory   The study of the economic processes through which investors' portfolio decisions are made.

Position day   The first day in the three-day sequence leading to delivery in which the holder of the short position notifies the clearinghouse of the intention to make delivery two business days later.

Position limit   The maximum number of options or futures contracts that any one investor can hold.

Position trader   A futures trader who normally holds open positions for a period longer than a day.

Potential credit risk   The risk that a party to a transaction will

be unable to make payments due in the future.

Preferred habitat theory   *See* Market segmentation theory.

Prepayment risk   In mortgage- or asset-backed securities, the risk to the holder that the underlying mortgage or other underlying securities will be paid off early due to falling interest rates.

Price sensitivity hedge ratio   The number of futures contracts used in a hedge that leaves the value of a portfolio unaffected by a change in an underlying variable, such as an interest rate.

Primary market   The market for securities originally issued and not previously traded among the public.

Principal-only strip   A type of mortgage-backed security in which mortgage principal payments are passed through, less a service fee, to holders. *See also* Interest-only strip.

Program trading   The trading of large blocks of stock as part of a program of index arbitrage or portfolio insurance.

Protective put   An investment strategy involving the use of a long position in a put and a stock to provide a minimum selling price for the stock.

Pure discount bond   A bond, such as a Treasury bill, that pays no coupon but sells for a discount from par value.

Put An option to sell an asset, currency, or futures.

Put-call-futures parity The relationship among the prices of puts, calls, and futures on a security, commodity, or currency. Can also be referred to as put-call-forward parity.

Put-call parity The relationship between the prices of puts, calls, and the underlying security, commodity, or currency.

Quality option The right to deliver any one from a set of eligible bonds on the Chicago Board of Trade's Treasury Bond futures contract or a similar right inherent in any other futures contract.

Quantity risk The risk involved in a hedge in which the hedger does not know how many units of the spot asset he or she will own or sell.

Quanto A derivative in which a foreign currency price or rate is converted to another currency at a fixed rate.

Quanto swap *See* Diff swap.

Quasi arbitrage An arbitrage transaction in which the holder of an asset sells the asset, replaces it with a futures contract, and then reverses the transaction later when the price converges to the cost of carry price.

Range floater A type of floating rate structured note in which the interest payments can change depending on whether a reference interest rate remains in a particular range.

Range forward A forward contract with a limited gain and loss. Also known as a *risk reversal* and virtually identical to an *equity collar.*

Ratio spread A spread transaction in which the number of contracts is weighted to produce a risk-free position.

Real asset A tangible asset such as real estate or equipment.

Receiver swaption A swaption in which the party holding the option has the right to enter into a swap and receive the fixed rate.

Registered option trader An options trader on the floor of the American Stock Exchange who trades options for his or her personal account.

Regulatory risk The risk that regulations or the current regulatory style will change, with adverse consequences for a firm. Regulatory risk may render certain existing or contemplated transactions illegal or hinder the development of new products and solutions.

Repo *See* Repurchase agreement.

Reportable position The number of contracts that if held by a futures trader must by law be reported to the regulatory authorities.

Repurchase agreement A securities transaction in which an investor sells a security and promises to repurchase it a specified number of days later at a higher price reflecting the prevailing interest rate.

Reset option An option that permits the holder to change the exercise price if the stock price hits a certain level.

Residual tranche One component tranche of a collateralized mortgage obligation entitling the holder to whatever cash remains after all other tranches have been repaid.

Retractable bond A bond in which the holder can choose to redeem prior to maturity.

Return A measure of the increase in wealth from an investment.

Reversal *See* Offset.

Reverse conversion An arbitrage transaction consisting of the sale of a put and the purchase of a synthetic put.

Reverse floater *See* Inverse floater.

Rho The rate of change of an option's price with respect to the risk-free interest rate.

Risk A measure of the variability or uncertainty of an investment.

Risk aversion   The characteristic referring to an investor who dislikes risk and will not assume more risk without an additional return.

Risk-free rate   The return offered by an investment in an asset with no risk.

Risk management   The practice of identifying the risk level a firm desires, identifying the risk level it currently has, and using derivative or other financial instruments to adjust the actual risk level to the desired risk level.

Risk neutrality   The characteristic referring to an investor who is indifferent toward risk.

Risk preferences   An investor's feelings toward risk.

Risk premium   The additional return risk-averse investors expect for assuming risk.

Risk-return trade-off   The concept in which additional risk must be accepted to increase the expected return.

Risk reversal   *See* Range forward.

Rolling strip hedge   A strip hedge with a relatively long hedge horizon in which the longer maturity futures are added as nearby futures expire.

Rolling up   A covered call strategy using an out-of-the-money call in which an investor buys back the call when the stock price rises to near the exercise price and sells another out-of-the-money call.

Sale or assignment   A method of terminating a swap in which a party makes or receives a cash payment and passes on its swap payment obligations to another party.

Scalper   A trader on the floor of a derivatives exchange whose trading style involves short holding periods and small profits based on small price changes.

Scratch trade   A trade primarily executed to adjust a dealer's inventory and in which no profit or loss is made.

Seat   A term used to refer to a membership on a derivatives or stock exchange.

Secondary market   The market for assets that were issued previously and are now trading among investors.

Securities and Exchange Commission   The federal agency responsible for regulating the securities and listed options markets.

Securities Investor Protection Corporation   A federal agency that provides investors with insurance against failure of a brokerage firm.

Securitization   The process of creating asset-backed securities.

Series   All of the options of a given class with the same exercise price and expiration.

Settlement price   The official price established by the clearinghouse at the end of each day for use in the daily settlement.

Settlement risk   The risk often faced in international transactions in which a firm exchanges payments with a party elsewhere in the world and is subject to the risk that its payments may be sent before receipt of the other party's payments, which may not be sent due to bankruptcy, insolvency, or fraud.

Short   A term used to refer to holding a short position or to the party holding the short position.

Short hedge   A hedge transaction involving a long position in the spot market and a short position in the futures market.

Short sale   An investment transaction in which securities are borrowed from a broker and sold to a buyer and, at a later time, repurchased and paid back to the broker.

Short selling   *See* Short sale.

Shout option   An option which, when the underlying asset reaches a certain level, allows the holder to set the minimum value of the final payout as the current intrinsic value.

Simple return A rate of return that is not compounded.

Simulation method A method for estimating Value-at-Risk that uses inputs on the expected returns, standard deviations, and correlations of the component assets of the portfolio to generate random outcomes from which the Value-at-Risk is estimated.

SPDV (Special purpose derivatives vehicle) *See* Enhanced derivatives products company.

Specialist A trader on the floor of an exchange who is responsible for making a market in certain securities or derivatives.

Speculation Investments characterized by a high degree of risk and usually short holding periods.

Speculative value *See* Time value.

Speculator One who engages in speculative transactions.

Spot market The market for assets that involves the immediate sale and delivery of the asset.

Spot price The price of an asset on the spot market.

Spot rate An interest rate on a loan or bond created in the spot market.

Spread A derivatives transaction consisting of a long position in

one contract and a short position in another, similar contract.

Spreader A person or institution that engages in a spread transaction.

Stack hedge A hedge in which the hedge horizon is longer than the expiration of the shortest-lived futures contract but due to lower liquidity of longer maturity futures, extra contracts of shorter maturity futures are used. Sometimes called a *stack*.

Standard deviation A measure of the dispersion of a random variable around its mean, equal to the square root of the variance.

Stock index A combination of stock prices designed to measure the performance of the stocks as a whole.

Stock index futures A futures contract on an underlying stock index.

Stock option *See* Equity option.

Stop order An order to purchase or sell securities or derivatives that is not executed until the price reaches a certain level.

Storage The process in which an asset is held for a certain time period.

Storage cost The cost of holding an asset, including the physical costs of storage and the interest lost on funds tied up.

Straddle An option transaction that involves a long position in a put and a call with the same exercise price and expiration.

Strangle A long put at one exercise price and a long call at a higher exercise price.

Strap An option transaction that involves a long position in two calls and one put, or two calls for every put, with the same exercise price and expiration.

Stress test A method of testing a risk management system in which a portfolio's performance under extremely large changes in the underlying is examined.

Strike price *See* Exercise price.

Strike rate *See* Exercise rate.

Strike spread *See* Money spread.

Striking price *See* Exercise price.

Strip An option transaction that involves a long position in two puts and one call, or two puts for every call, with the same exercise price and expiration. *See also* Strip hedge.

Strip hedge A hedge in which a series of futures contracts of successively longer expirations are used to cover a hedge horizon longer than the expiration of the shortest-lived futures contract. Sometimes called a *strip*.

Stripped treasuries   Securities that represent claims on coupons and principal of Treasury bonds. The Treasury bond is purchased and stripped treasuries are sold against the coupons and principal on the Treasury bond.

Structured note   A promissory note, usually with floating rate, in which the coupon has been enhanced by a derivative to provide for accelerated or decelerated payments or payments contingent on an event.

Swap   A derivative transaction in which two parties agree to exchange cash flows calculated according to different formulas. *See also* Interest rate swap, Currency swap, Commodity swap, Equity swap.

Swap book   A swap dealer's inventory of swaps.

Swap dealer   A firm that arranges an interest rate or currency swap between two other parties.

Swap option   *See* Swaption.

Swap rate   The fixed rate that a swap dealer will pay or receive on a swap.

Swap spread   The difference between the fixed rate that a swap dealer will pay or receive and the rate on the U.S. Treasury note of equivalent maturity.

Swaption   An option granting the right to enter into a swap.

Switching option   Sometimes defined as the right to switch bonds in a cash-and-carry transaction using Treasury Bond futures although this right is a result of the quality option. *See also* Quality option.

Synthetic call   A combination of a long put and long asset, futures, or currency that replicates the behavior of a call. It may sometimes include a short position in risk-free bonds.

Synthetic futures   A combination of a long call and a short put that replicates the behavior of a long futures contract. It may sometimes include a long or short position in risk-free bonds.

Synthetic put   A combination of a long call and short asset, currency, or futures that replicates the behavior of a put. It may sometimes include a long position in risk-free bonds.

Systematic risk   The risk associated with the market or economy as a whole.

Systemic risk   The risk that failure of one or more financial institutions will trigger more failures, ultimately leading to a breakdown of the financial system.

Tail   The number of additional futures contracts purchased or sold to complete a wild card or quality option delivery.

Tailing the hedge   Adjusting the hedge ratio so that the effects of the interest earned or paid from the daily settlement are taken into account.

Tandem option   An option that actually represents a sequence of options, with a new option automatically beginning as soon as a given option expires.

Target beta   The desired beta of a stock portfolio.

Target duration   The desired duration of a bond portfolio.

Tax risk   The risk that tax laws or the interpretation of tax laws will change, with adverse consequences for a firm.

TED spread   A transaction in which one takes a long position in either a Treasury bill or Treasury bill futures and a short position in a Eurodollar or Eurodollar futures or vice versa. Alternatively, the difference between Treasury bill spot or futures and Eurodollar spot or futures rates.

Term repo   A repurchase agreement with a maturity of more than one day. *See also* Overnight repo.

Term structure of interest rates   The relationship between interest rates and maturities of zero coupon bonds.

Theoretical fair price   The price of a derivative that permits no arbitrage opportunities.

Theoretical fair value The true or appropriate worth of an asset or derivative, which is obtained from a model based on rational investor behavior.

Theta The rate of change of an option's price with respect to time.

Tick The minimum permissable price fluctuation.

Time spread *See* Calendar spread.

Time value The difference between an option's price and its intrinsic value.

Time value decay The erosion of an option's time value as expiration approaches.

Timing option Either the right to defer delivery until any acceptable delivery date on the Chicago Board of Trade's Treasury bond futures contracts or any similar right inherent in a futures contract.

Trading halt A rule associated with futures or stock trading in which trading will temporarily cease if prices move by a specified amount during a specified period of time.

Tranche One component of a collateralized mortgage obligation entitling the holder to a specific stream of payments that may differ in characteristics, priority, and risk from another tranche.

Treasury bill A short-term pure-discount bond issued by the U.S. government with original maturities of 91, 182, and 365 days.

Treasury bond A coupon-bearing bond issued by the U.S. government with an original maturity of at least 10 years.

Treasury note A coupon-bearing bond issued by the U.S. government with an original maturity of one to ten years.

Triangular arbitrage The foreign currency arbitrage transaction that forces the cross-rate relationship to hold.

Triggering event A designated event such as a credit downgrade, which if it occurs, will necessitate further action, such as additional collateral, to enhance the credit of a party.

Turtle trade An arbitrage spread transaction in which a forward borrowing (or lending) rate is locked in on the Treasury bond or note futures market and a forward lending (or borrowing) rate is locked in on the Treasury bill futures market.

Two-state model *See* Binomial model.

Unbiased A characteristic of a forecast in which the prediction equals the actual outcome on average over a large number of predictions.

Unbiased expectations theory *See* Expectations theory.

Uncovered call An option strategy in which an investor writes a call on a stock not owned.

Underlying The asset or instrument on which a derivative's payoff is based.

Underpriced A condition in which a security or derivative is trading at less than its value.

Unsystematic return The portion of a security's return that is related to factors associated with the individual security and not to the market as a whole.

Unsystematic risk The risk of a security related to factors specific to it and not to the market as a whole.

Up-and-in option An in barrier option in which the premium is paid but the option does not actually begin unless the asset price rises to a specified barrier.

Up-and-out option An out barrier option in which the premium is paid but the option terminates early if the asset price rises to a specified barrier.

Up-option A type of barrier option in which the barrier is above the current level of the underlying.

Upside capture The percentage of the market value of an uninsured portfolio earned by an insured portfolio in a bull market.

Uptick   An increase in the price of a security or contract equal to one tick.

Utility   A measure of satisfaction usually obtained from money or wealth.

Value   A monetary measure of the worth of an investment or contract that reflects its contribution to the investor's wealth.

Value-at-Risk   A dollar measure of the minimum loss that would be expected over a period of time with a given probability. Also known as VaR or VAR.

Variance   A measure of the dispersion of a random variable around its mean, equal to the square of the standard deviation.

Variation margin   Money added to or subtracted from a futures account that reflects profits or losses accruing from the daily settlement.

Vega   The rate of change of an option's price with respect to the volatility of the underlying asset or futures.

Vega hedge   A hedged position, usually combined with a delta hedge and a gamma hedge, in which changes in the value of the position are unaffected by

changes in the volatility of the underlying.

Vertical spread   *See* Money spread.

Volatility   The characteristic of fluctuations in price.

Volatility strategy   An option strategy designed to profit from unusually high or low volatility of the underlying asset.

Warehousing   The practice in which a dealer holds positions in various swaps in an inventory.

Warrant   An option issued by a corporation to buy or sell its stock. Usually has a life of several years when originally issued.

Wash sale   A transaction in which a stock is sold at a loss and an essentially identical stock, or a call option on the stock, is purchased within a 61-day period surrounding the sale. Tax laws prohibit deducting the loss on the sale.

Wild card option   The right to deliver on the Chicago Board of Trade's Treasury bond futures contract after the close of trading in the futures market or a similar right inherent in any other futures contract.

Writer   A person or institution that sells an option.

Yield   The discount rate on a bond that equates the present value of the coupons and principal to the price.

Yield beta   The slope coefficient from a regression of the yield on a spot bond on the yield implied by the futures contract. Measures the relationship between the spot yield and the yield implied by the futures price.

Yield curve   The relationship between yields on bonds and their maturities.

Yield to maturity   *See* Yield.

Z-bond   One component tranche of a collateralized mortgage obligation in which interest accrues but no principal or interest is paid until higher priority tranches are repaid.

Zero cost collar   A collar in which the premiums on the long cap and short floor offset so that there is no premium paid up front.

Zero coupon bond   *See* Pure discount bond.

Zero-plus tick   A situation in a financial market in which a trade takes place at the same price as the last trade but the last time a price changed, it increased.

Index